America in the World, 1776 to the Present

America in the World, 1776 to the Present

A Supplement to the Dictionary of American History

VOLUME 2

M–Z, Index

Edward J. Blum

EDITOR IN CHIEF

CHARLES SCRIBNER'S SONS
A part of Gale, Cengage Learning

GALE
CENGAGE Learning

Farmington Hills, Mich • San Francisco • New York • Waterville, Maine
Meriden, Conn • Mason, Ohio • Chicago

America in the World, 1776 to the Present: A Supplement to the Dictionary of American History

Edward J. Blum, *Editor in Chief*

Associate Publisher: Hélène G. Potter

Project Editor: Alan Hedblad

Manuscript Editors: Judith Culligan, Jessica Hornik Evans, Michael J. O'Neal

Proofreaders: Deborah J. Baker, Judith Clinebell, Amy L. Unterburger

Editorial Assistant: Dolores Perales

Rights Acquisition and Management: Moriam Aigoro, Ashley M. Maynard

Composition: Evi Abou-El-Seoud

Manufacturing: Rita R. Wimberley

Imaging: John Watkins

Product Design: Kristine Julien

Indexing: Andriot Indexing LLC

For product information and technology assistance, contact us at **Gale Customer Support, 1-800-877-4253.**
For permission to use material from this text or product, submit all requests online at **www.cengage.com/permissions.**
Further permissions questions can be emailed to **permissionrequest@cengage.com**

While every effort has been made to ensure the reliability of the information presented in this publication, Gale, a part of Cengage Learning, does not guarantee the accuracy of the data contained herein. Gale accepts no payment for listing; and inclusion in the publication of any organization, agency, institution, publication, service, or individual does not imply endorsement of the editors or publisher. Errors brought to the attention of the publisher and verified to the satisfaction of the publisher will be corrected in future editions.

LIBRARY OF CONGRESS CATALOGING-IN-PUBLICATION DATA

America in the world, 1776 to the present : a supplement to the Dictionary of American history / Edward J. Blum, Editor in Chief.
    pages cm
  Includes bibliographical references and index.
  ISBN 978-0-684-32502-6 (set : alk. paper) — ISBN 978-0-684-32503-3 (vol. 1 : alk. paper) — ISBN 978-0-684-32504-0 (vol. 2 : alk. paper)
  1. United States—Foreign relations. I. Blum, Edward J., editor.

E183.7.A53 2016
327.73—dc23   2015029101

Gale, a part of Cengage Learning
27500 Drake Rd.
Farmington Hills, MI 48331-3535

ISBN-13: 978-0-684-32502-6 (set)
ISBN-13: 978-0-684-32503-3 (vol. 1)
ISBN-13: 978-0-684-32504-0 (vol. 2)

This title is also available as an e-book.
ISBN-13: 978-0-684-32505-7
Contact your Gale, a part of Cengage Learning, sales representative for ordering information.

Printed in Mexico
1 2 3 4 5 6 7 20 19 18 17 16

Editorial Board

Contents

M

MACARTHUR, DOUGLAS
1880–1964

Douglas MacArthur was the military commander of US forces in the Pacific during World War II and of United Nations forces during the Korean War (beginning in 1950), the head of the postwar Allied occupation of Japan, and a visible and contentious figure who shaped US military and political relations with East Asia in the twentieth century.

Born in 1880 in Little Rock, Arkansas, MacArthur grew up in a military family. His father, Arthur MacArthur (1845–1912), was a Civil War (1861–1865) veteran and a US Army officer during the Philippine-American War (1899–1902). After graduating from the United States Military Academy (USMA) at West Point in 1903, Douglas MacArthur served in several postings in the newly acquired US territories before taking a position with the War Department's General Staff in Washington, DC. During World War I (1914–1918), MacArthur's distinguished service with the Forty-Second Infantry Division in France—together with a savvy sense of Army politics—won him press attention, rapid promotion to the rank of brigadier general, and appointments as superintendent of the USMA and, from 1930 to 1935, as chief of staff of the US Army. Soon after World War I, he married Louise Cromwell Brooks (1890–1965), whom he later divorced. In 1937, he married Jean Faircloth (1898–2000), and the couple had one son.

After 1935, in anticipation of the announced independence of the Philippines as a US colony, MacArthur worked to organize a Philippine Army that could defend the country from outside invasion. In July 1941, President Franklin D. Roosevelt (1882–1945) appointed MacArthur head of the newly formed US Army Forces in the Far East (USAFFE). Japanese attacks on the Philippines in December 1941 prompted a hasty retreat of US and Philippine forces to Bataan and Corregidor in early 1942. At Roosevelt's command, MacArthur departed for Australia on March 17, 1942, vowing that "I shall return." From Australia, MacArthur, now a full general (later promoted again to five-star general in December 1944) and head of the Southwest Pacific Area Theater (SWPA), planned and executed the slow march westward across the Pacific in anticipation of an invasion of Japan. MacArthur vocally criticized the focus of military planners and the Roosevelt administration on the European theater. He fought to convince Roosevelt and other advocates of bypassing the Philippines that reinvasion was a moral obligation and would deal a knockout blow to the Japanese. The Philippine campaign, launched in October 1944, dragged on until the summer of 1945.

MacArthur accepted the surrender of the Japanese forces on the battleship USS *Missouri* on September 2, 1945, by which point he had already taken charge of the Allied occupation of Japan as the Supreme Commander for the Allied Powers (SCAP). President Harry S. Truman (1884–1972) gave MacArthur a free hand in Japanese occupation policy, which installed a liberal-leaning constitution in 1947, even as it allowed many powerful figures from Japan's wartime era to reclaim their political and economic positions.

By the late 1940s, MacArthur had emerged in American public life as a leading spokesman on Asian and Pacific affairs due to his military victories, his authoritative pronouncements explaining the "Oriental mind," and his genuinely close connections to Asian political and military figures, especially anticommunists such as Jiang Jieshi (Chiang Kai-shek, 1887–1975), whose regime in mainland China and after 1949 on Taiwan MacArthur supported vocally.

Following the North Korean invasion of South Korea on June 25, 1950, MacArthur commanded United Nations forces during the institution's first military engagement. He executed a daring invasion at Inchon on September 15, 1950, and pressed North Korean forces far above the prewar thirty-eighth parallel, a campaign that triggered the deployment of communist Chinese troops to aid the North Koreans. In March 1951, as Truman prepared to announce a ceasefire proposal, MacArthur attacked the plan. Truman, who had ordered MacArthur not to make public policy statements without administration approval, relieved MacArthur of his command on April 11, 1951, exposing tensions within US policy over Cold War military strategy in Asia. Returning to the United States after nearly two decades in Asia, MacArthur hoped to win the 1952 Republican nomination for president, but after that position went to his former subordinate and longtime rival Dwight D. Eisenhower (1890–1969), MacArthur retired from public life. He died in 1964.

As a pivotal figure in the military and political histories of China, Japan, Korea, and the Philippines, Douglas MacArthur embodied for many Americans the country's relationship with twentieth-century East Asia.

SEE ALSO *Cold War; Department of Defense, US; Japan; Korean War; Truman, Harry S.; World War II*

BIBLIOGRAPHY

James, D. Clayton. *The Years of MacArthur.* 3 vols. Boston: Houghton Mifflin, 1970–1985.

MacArthur, Douglas. *Reminiscences.* New York: McGraw-Hill, 1964.

Manchester, William. *American Caesar: Douglas MacArthur, 1880–1964.* Boston: Little, Brown, 1978.

Schaller, Michael. *Douglas MacArthur: The Far Eastern General.* New York: Oxford University Press, 1989.

Christopher Capozzola
Associate Professor of History
Massachusetts Institute of Technology

MACON'S BILL NO. 2 (1810)

Macon's Bill No. 2 marked the end of the United States' efforts to use economic coercion against British and French interdiction of American shipping during the Napoleonic Wars. Its failure provoked the War of 1812.

By 1810, the experiment in economic coercion, which had begun with the Embargo of 1807 and continued with the Nonimportation Act of 1809, was widely perceived as a failure. Macon's Bill No. 1, which was drafted by Treasury secretary Albert Gallatin (1761–1849) rather than the eponymous North Carolina congressman, Nathaniel Macon (1757–1837), who introduced it, appears to have been intended as a graceful way for Democratic-Republicans to back out of their failed policy. Essentially repealing nonimportation until France and England recognized American rights, Macon's Bill No. 1 would have allowed trade with France and England at home and abroad by American vessels only. The measure was to close American ports to English and French vessels unless one or the other power would rescind its restrictions against American ships, in which case the United States would trade only with the obliging power. The bill went down to defeat, but out of its ashes came Macon's Bill No. 2.

Nathaniel Macon had nothing whatsoever to do with the drafting of Macon's Bill No. 2, which was proposed by John Taylor (1770–1832) of South Carolina and ratified on May 1, 1810. Macon's Bill No. 2 removed all restrictions on French and British commerce and threatened that, should one or the other nation lift its anti-American restrictions, the United States would resume nonimportation measures against the country that kept its restrictions in place. Contemporaries, like nearly all modern historians, viewed the measure as a surrender to the European powers. Henry Clay (1777–1852) said it placed the United States into "the tranquil putrescent pool of ignominious peace" (Remini 1991, 60). Faced with a very weak hand after the failure of nonimportation, President James Madison (1751–1836) held out hope that it might entice the French into softening their restrictions and thereby also create leverage against Britain.

After initially ignoring Macon's Bill, Napoléon Bonaparte (1769–1821) did eventually signal his willingness to accept it and repeal French restrictions. On August 5, 1810, under the emperor's personal direction, the French foreign minister, the Duc de Cadore (1756–1834), sent an ambiguously worded letter to the American minister in Paris. The so-called Cadore letter suggested Napoléon was prepared to repeal French restrictions nominally, although they would be replaced with tighter customs regulations that would discriminate against American products.

President Madison took the bait, declaring on November 2 that France was no longer in violation of American neutrality. On March 2 of the following year, Congress voted to resume nonimportation against Britain under the terms of Macon's Bill. Madison's reasons for acting so quickly are not entirely clear, since it would have been easy to argue that the ambiguous Cadore letter did not meet the requirements of Macon's Bill. Most likely, the president hoped that by seizing the initiative and interpreting the Cadore letter in America's favor, he would trap Napoléon into respecting American ships. At the time, Madison wrote that acceptance of the Cadore letter "promises us at least an extrication from the dilemma of a mortifying peace, or a war with both the great belligerents" (Perkins 1961, 251). In this regard, Madison was correct, as acceptance of Napoléon's overtures and resumption of nonimportation led directly to war with Britain.

SEE ALSO *Embargo Act (1807); Impressment; Neutrality Act of 1794; Non-Intercourse Act (1809); War of 1812*

BIBLIOGRAPHY

Perkins, Bradford. *Prologue to War: England and the United States, 1805–1812.* Berkeley: University of California Press, 1961.

Remini, Robert V. *Henry Clay: Statesman for the Union.* New York: Norton, 1991.

Stagg, J. C. A. *The War of 1812: Conflict for a Continent.* New York: Cambridge University Press, 2012.

Lawrence A. Peskin
Professor of History
Morgan State University

MADEIRA

The Portuguese island of Madeira was situated at an important Atlantic crossroads in the Age of Sail, near the confluence of the northeasterly trade winds and the Rennell and Canary currents. Given its central location, temperate weather, constant wind, freedom from fog and ice, and bountiful supply of water and wood, Madeira became a preferred stop on the outbound route to America.

MADEIRA AND WINE EXPORTS

Wine became Madeirans' principal export in the first third of the seventeenth century, when Englishmen began permanently settling in America. Always threatened by the prospect of empty holds on outbound transatlantic voyages, English shippers found in wine a profitable solution. At the same time, English settlers in America, accustomed to drinking wine back home and finding themselves unable to produce it in palatable and profitable quantities until the early 1800s, took to Madeira with gusto, especially after England's Staple Act of 1663

exempted Madeira wine from the requirement that all European commodities first land in England before going to America and from any Crown import duty.

Wine exports from Madeira to the English-speaking colonies soared, from roughly twelve hundred pipes in 1600 (a pipe being the principal container of Portuguese wine, containing 110 gallons) to about ten thousand pipes around 1703; from 1750 to 1815, exports fluctuated between fifteen thousand and twenty-two thousand pipes. Within this overall rise, wine imports varied from year to year, depending on climatic conditions, the openness of shipping channels, and consumer demand. Yet, between the 1640s and the 1770s, Madeira constituted the bulk of the wine that Britain's colonists drank. From 1700 to 1775, wines from the Wine Islands dominated their markets: 76 percent came from Madeira, 6 percent from the Azores, and 6 percent from the Canaries.

THE WINE TRADE

Madeira's dominance arose from fundamental changes in ways that Europeans and Americans conducted business. Among these changes were increases in the density and complexity of arrangements for buying, marketing, selling, and transporting goods around the Atlantic basin. As the scale of commerce increased—in the volumes shipped, the frequency and regularity of shipping, and the spread of markets—so too did the organization and function of the wine enterprise and the culture of consuming the product.

On the one hand, island exporters accumulated savings from past labors and invested them in the trade. They took risks, with the expectation of reaping profits. They engaged in trade that was "roundabout," in the sense that the late eighteenth-century manufactured product required labor and other inputs to the processes of heating, agitating, and fortifying, plus those required to barrel and ship. But the change that really mattered involved their management of business as their investment grew. They organized suppliers and employees. They elaborated consumer networks to reach out to customers who were no longer individuals but were themselves distributors. Their relations with customers and suppliers were developed and cemented by multiple layers of interest and by global infrastructures of partners and agents. They organized their own community, too, to provide mutual aid and to restrict undue competition.

AMERICA AND THE MADEIRA WINE TRADE

Simultaneously, a group of importers and wholesalers arose in America and increased their connective capacities by building networks of customers, suppliers, and competitors on the basis of "weak" connection. Unlike Madeirans, Americans had an advantage in that they could usually meet customers in person and so construct specialized spaces for displaying their wares and meeting and courting customers. Their networks had a particular geometry, characterized by one major link across the Atlantic for each product they imported, and a multitude of links to customers, most of whom lived nearby. Until late in the eighteenth century, American merchants usually maintained relationships with one Madeira house at a time, using them to sell American grain, fish, and furs to Europe and to supply them with wine for resale in the New World. (They dealt with other houses in other places for other wines and liquors.) Such exclusivity in relationships arose from trust and a lack of competition among Europe's wine exporters. At home in America, the importers and wholesalers also cultivated a range of customers. They particularly sought out tavern keepers and storekeepers who bought larger quantities, although most continued to retail to individuals as well.

What did American consumers do with and make of Madeira? Drinking wine was part of their everyday routine and ritual observance at home and in government buildings, mercantile chambers, and counting houses, as well as in the public and club rooms of taverns, inns, and hotels. All people drank it: friends and strangers; men and women; whites, reds, and blacks; elite and middling people. They drank to conduct business, as well as to lubricate party chitchat. They attributed meanings of health, wealth, and refinement to the core acts of quenching thirst, providing hospitality, and getting drunk with wine. As the availability of imported wines expanded, people came to view them less as extraordinary and more as staple "articles of nourishment" necessary for good "domestic management." Wine sustained not only cooking, dining, and hospitality but also housekeeping and doctoring.

The principal locus for drinking in America was the home. Women were principals in managing, storing, and dispensing wine and other drinks. Because it was home based, drinking figured prominently in the homely arts and virtues—feeding the hungry, ministering to the sick and infirm, and providing hospitality to the displaced. Alcohol was a principal ingredient of most people's diets, so people away from home were provided it or provided it for themselves as a way to be "at home." It was an important part of religious, military, and civic rituals and performances. Its homelike character permeated many nonhome venues, especially when hospitality was offered.

WINE AND SOCIAL CLASS

At the same time, just as the consumer revolution was making goods like wine available to more Americans, elite consumers were eager to highlight that both the

wines and the ways they drank them were special—economically, socially, culturally, and politically. Spanish and French wines that had been handicapped by British mercantile regulation before 1776 became competitive with Portuguese wines after that date. The prohibition of Madeira's import during the Revolutionary War and the emergence of competition during and after it led to a marked, permanent reduction in the volume being shipped to North America for the first time since the middle decades of the seventeenth century, as well as to a dramatic increase in its price. Even so, despite the greater variety of wines being sold in the now independent marketplace and the stiff competition there raised by Spanish sherry, the island of Madeira still supplied "America's wine." More than any other drink there, Madeira connoted luxury and refinement. Given its high price—highest of all wines—its value and its reputation for sumptuousness remained unmatched. That was not surprising, of course, for American drinkers set themselves apart as a distinct group by deploying wine, which was expensive relative to other drinks, as well as by the gendered, racialized, and economically stratified circumstances in which they drank it. Some drinks like cider, whiskey, and rum remained "common"; other drinks like Madeira became luxuries, linked to persons, places, and events that signified exotic or extraordinary refinement and wealth. Furthermore, in the new Republic, those who sought to refine wine's use, taste, and status singled out certain types of wine like Madeira as praiseworthy, created "wine" as a subject of discourse, established an etiquette of wine display and consumption (through the creation of specially designed and inscribed Madeira decanters, labels, and glasses), and created rituals around its use (such as retrieving it from the heated cellar). Madeira paraphernalia such as labels and glassware produced in Europe—like the wine itself—projected a cosmopolitan style showing off the foreign origin of the drink. They distinguished their possessors and users from those who drank whatever came to hand in whatever object and fashion was available or known and who might not even know the difference. Madeira's rituals helped its consumers construct an image—and reality—of men and women of "true luxury" and "knowing discernment" at a time when the politics of the day were questioning long-held norms and values.

SEE ALSO *Economics*

BIBLIOGRAPHY

Beechert, Edward. "The Wine Trade of the Thirteen Colonies." MA thesis, University of California, Berkeley, 1949.

Cossart, Noël. *Madeira: The Island Vineyard*. London: Christie's Wine Publications, 1984.

Hancock, David. *Oceans of Wine: Madeira and the Emergence of American Trade and Taste.* New Haven, CT: Yale University Press, 2009.

Pinney, Thomas. *A History of Wine in America: From the Beginnings to Prohibition.* Berkeley: University of California Press, 1989.

David Hancock
Professor of History
University of Michigan

MADISON, JAMES
1751–1836

James Madison, during his lengthy career in federal service (1780–1817), significantly shaped the United States' engagement with the world. Two broad concerns, expansion into the western territories and foreign trade, consistently molded his understandings of the role of the United States in foreign affairs. Madison connected these subjects to his concerns about republican government at home.

Madison recognized that while the West offered possibilities for Thomas Jefferson's "empire of liberty," it bordered the possessions of other European powers who, because of their proximity, could threaten American peace. For example, Madison long considered the problem posed by the Mississippi River. In Congress during the 1780s, Madison tried unsuccessfully to secure navigation rights to the river after Spain closed New Orleans to American shipping in 1784. He realized that American farmers west of the Appalachians needed access to the port of New Orleans to engage profitably in foreign trade. Spain's reluctance to open the port created sectional tensions during the Jay-Gardoqui negotiations (1785–1786), seriously worrying Madison. Two decades later, as secretary of state under Jefferson, Madison supported the Louisiana Purchase, which would prevent foreign nations from again halting westward expansion by bottling up the mouth of the Mississippi.

Madison also worked to undermine Spanish rule in Florida and secure the Gulf Coast for the United States. By annexing part of West Florida in 1810, dubiously claiming Mobile as part of the Louisiana Purchase, and supporting the filibustering activities of George Mathews in East Florida in 1811 to 1812, President Madison sought to remove Spanish influence from the Southeast and allow American farmers to navigate southern rivers to the Gulf of Mexico.

Madison expressed similar attitudes in relation to Native Americans, harping on supposed British encouragement of Tecumseh and Indian resistance in the West as one cause of the War of 1812. The administration's vigorous response to the Creek War (1813–1814) in the Southeast won for the United States millions of acres of Indian land.

Madison believed western expansion could perpetuate an agricultural society friendly to republican virtue and independence, as well as providing security for the country by minimizing the opportunities for foreign conflict.

After the Revolution, Madison hoped American farmers would trade their goods freely with other nations on equal footing. But the nation with the most powerful navy of the age, Great Britain, closed its Caribbean colonies to American merchants and restricted American trade. Madison struggled with Britain throughout his political career. Believing that war should be the last recourse, Madison supported a system of commercial discrimination against Britain in order to gain concessions. While a state legislator in Virginia in 1784, he supported a port bill that would restrict British merchants to a few towns in the state. While a federal congressman in the 1790s, he opposed Alexander Hamilton's system, in part because it yoked the country's economy tightly to Great Britain, thereby threatening its autonomy and constitutional structure.

As secretary of state, Madison supported Jefferson's embargo in 1807 to 1808 to force Britain to acknowledge the rights of the United States—as a neutral power during the Napoleonic Wars (1803–1815)—to trade freely. President Madison failed to influence British trade policy and ultimately asked Congress to declare war on Britain in 1812 to compel respect for the country's independence. Madison applied his principles to the case of the Barbary pirates, who, with Britain's blessing, preyed on American merchants in the Mediterranean. As secretary of state, he supported Jefferson's Tripolitan War (1801–1805) against the pirates in lieu of making tribute payments to the North African kingdoms. In 1815, he sent two naval fleets to the Mediterranean to demand treaties from the Barbary pirates, again refusing to pay tribute. His show of force settled the long-standing conflict between American merchants and the pirates. Madison defended American trade throughout his career.

Madison's views of westward expansion and trade influenced his appreciation of the Union and his constitutionalism. By minimizing conflicts with and the influences of foreign nations on the border of the country, Madison hoped westward expansion would reduce conflicts among the states. Madison worried consistently about threats to the Union and believed that Britain and Spain could divide the states and threaten American liberty. His advocacy for constitutional reform in the 1780s rested in part on his desire, expressed in *Federalist* No. 42, that "if we are to be one nation in any respect, it clearly ought to be in respect to other nations" (Madison 2001, 215). Madison sought a federal government that could protect American interests in the world. As president, he supported stronger military and financial institutions, such as the Bank of the United States, to confront foreign threats. Madison opposed both those who would weaken the ability of the federal government to defend the country's interest and those who would consolidate too much power in the center and compromise self-government in the states. Madison linked, therefore, his foreign and domestic concerns under his broader republican vision.

SEE ALSO *Jefferson, Thomas*

BIBLIOGRAPHY

Banning, Lance. *The Sacred Fire of Liberty: James Madison and the Founding of the Federal Republic.* Ithaca, NY: Cornell University Press, 1995.

Broadwater, Jeff. *James Madison: A Son of Virginia and a Founder of the Nation.* Chapel Hill: University of North Carolina Press, 2012.

Hackett, Mary. "James Madison's Secretary of State Years, 1801–1809: Successes and Failures in Foreign Relations." In *A Companion to James Madison and James Monroe*, edited by Stuart Leibiger, 176–191. Malden, MA: Wiley-Blackwell, 2013.

Ketcham, Ralph. *James Madison: A Biography.* Charlottesville: University of Virginia Press, 1990. Originally published by Macmillan in 1971.

Lambert, Frank. *The Barbary Wars: American Independence in the Atlantic World.* New York: Hill and Wang, 2005.

Lewis, James E., Jr. *The American Union and the Problem of Neighborhood: The United States and the Collapse of the Spanish Empire, 1783–1829.* Chapel Hill: University of North Carolina Press, 1998.

Madison, James. *Federalist* No. 42: "The Powers Conferred by the Constitution Further Considered" (1788). In *The Federalist*, edited by George W. Carey and James McClellan. Indianapolis, IN: Liberty Fund, 2001.

McCoy, Drew. *The Elusive Republic: Political Economy in Jeffersonian America.* Chapel Hill: University of North Carolina Press, 1980.

Owsley, Frank Lawrence, Jr., and Gene A. Smith. *Filibusters and Expansionists: Jeffersonian Manifest Destiny, 1800–1821.* Tuscaloosa: University of Alabama Press, 1997.

Siemers, David J. "President James Madison and Foreign Affairs, 1809–1817: Years of Principle and Peril." In *A Companion to James Madison and James Monroe*, edited by Stuart Leibiger, 207–223. Malden, MA: Wiley-Blackwell, 2013.

Stagg, J. C. A. *Mr. Madison's War: Politics, Diplomacy, and Warfare in the Early American Republic, 1783–1830.* Princeton, NJ: Princeton University Press, 1983.

Adam Tate
Professor of History
Clayton State University

MAHAN, ALFRED THAYER

SEE *The Influence of Sea Power upon History (Alfred Thayer Mahan, 1890).*

MALCOLM X
1925–1965

Born Malcolm Little in 1925, Malcolm X was shaped by the early political influence of his parents' participation in Marcus Garvey's Universal Negro Improvement Association (UNIA), a black nationalist and Pan-African organization of the early twentieth century. In 1952, after years of drug addiction, criminal activity, and imprisonment, Malcolm X became a member of the Nation of Islam (NOI), an organization founded in the early 1930s by Wallace Fard Muhammad, who in 1933 designated Elijah Muhammad as its leader. The NOI transformed itself in the 1950s from an obscure religious group into an important spiritual and political voice among African Americans nationwide, due in part to Malcolm X's work as the national spokesperson.

From his release from prison until 1964, the year he left the NOI, Malcolm X was Elijah Muhammad's most ardent student. During this period he traveled throughout the United States organizing mosques, ministered to members of the Nation of Islam mosque in Harlem, New York, appeared on television, and wrote editorials for African American newspapers throughout the country. He left the NOI in March 1964 and organized Muslim Mosque Incorporated and the Organization of Afro-American Unity (OAAU).

The year 1964 was marked by profound religious and political transformations for Malcolm X. He traveled extensively for twenty-four weeks to immerse himself in world cultures. In April he made a pilgrimage to Mecca, Islam's holiest city, in Saudi Arabia. There he discovered that Elijah Muhammad's teachings were out of line with the majority of the Muslim world. He converted to Sunni Islam and changed his name to El Hajj Malik el Shabazz. From early July to late November, Malcolm X extensively toured Africa, the Middle East, and Europe. In Cairo he attended a conference of the Organization of African Unity (OAU) as an observer. In Ghana he met with the country's president, Kwame Nkrumah, and expatriated African Americans. In Kenya he dined with president Jomo Kenyatta and addressed the Kenyan parliament. His travels in Europe took him to Paris, where he addressed the Maison de la Mutualité, and to London, where he delivered a public lecture at Oxford University. Throughout his journeys he met with people from a variety of political persuasions and racial backgrounds and discussed the American racial dilemma. His sojourn ultimately changed his perspective about race and civil rights.

His 1964 speech "The Ballot or the Bullet" is considered to be his most profound contribution to the black freedom struggle of the 1960s. In it he offered a black nationalist and Pan-African perspective to connect black Americans' struggle with anticolonial struggles and antiracist movements by people of color throughout the world. Additionally, he provided his definition of black nationalism and called for a united African American political front comprised of black political organizations across the political continuum. Finally, he posited the notion that political and social life segregated African Americans in predominantly black communities, and because blacks were not likely to leave them, they should control these communities' political, educational, and economic tools. What is most interesting about his speech is his ability to connect African American civil rights to international human rights struggles. "When you expand the civil rights struggle to the level of human rights," he said when delivering the speech, "you can then take the case of the black man in this country before the nations in the UN. You can take it before the General Assembly."

Malcolm X was assassinated on February 21, 1965, before his ideas came to fruition, but his influence outlived him. (Three Nation of Islam members were tried and convicted for the murder.) Black-power activists of the late 1960s and early 1970s saw Malcolm X as their ideological father, and organizations like the Black Panther Party, the Student Nonviolent Coordinating Committee, and the Congress of Racial Equality incorporated his teachings into their political philosophies. In the 1990s there was a renewed interest in his life and work as seen in Spike Lee's movie *Malcolm X* (1992) and the work of hip-hop groups like Public Enemy. *The Autobiography of Malcolm X,* published posthumously in 1965, politicized and continues to inspire generations of activists and thinkers.

SEE ALSO *Black Power Movement; Cold War: Race and the Cold War; Decolonization; Human Rights; Islam; Pan-Africanism; Student Nonviolent Coordinating Committee (SNCC)*

BIBLIOGRAPHY

Malcolm X. "The Ballot or the Bullet." April 12, 1964. Audio recording and written text available at American Public Media, American RadioWorks. http://americanradioworks.publicradio.org/features/blackspeech/mx.html

Malcolm X, with Alex Haley. *Autobiography of Malcolm X.* New York: Ballantine, 1965.

Marable, Manning. *Malcolm X: A Life of Reinvention.* New York: Viking, 2011.

Wilson, Jamie J. "'Come Down off the Cross and Get Under the Crescent': The Newspaper Columns of Elijah Muhammad and Malcolm X." *Biography* 36, 3 (2013): 494–506.

Jamie J. Wilson
Professor, African American and Modern United States History
Salem State University

MANCHURIA

In the late nineteenth century, the imperialist powers were in the midst of a scramble for empire, and one of the great prizes was China's northeastern provinces, Manchuria. As Russia and Japan used railroad expansion and economic interests to further national policy, the United States, through the so-called Open Door Notes, sought to preserve Manchuria's territorial integrity, and thus to secure raw materials and areas to market excess American production.

EARLY-TWENTIETH-CENTURY DEVELOPMENTS

Competition for Manchuria led to the Russo-Japanese War of 1904–05 and President Theodore Roosevelt's (1858–1919) subsequent efforts for peace, the Treaty of Portsmouth. Roosevelt wanted to make the United States a major player on the world stage and wanted diplomacy to complement the "blue water" navy he favored. But American efforts to preserve the integrity of China's northeast failed before Russian expansion of the Chinese Eastern Railway across the north and Japanese expansion of the South Manchurian Railway (SMR) running up from Port Arthur and Dairen.

Japan tried to take advantage of the First World War by presenting the Chinese government with its Twenty-One Demands in January 1915. Had Beijing conceded, Manchuria would have become a virtual Japanese protectorate, but the Chinese, with American backing, stalled. After the war, and after the Washington Four-, Five-, and Nine-Power Treaties of 1921–22, there was a vacuum of power in northeast Asia and Manchuria. Historian Akira Iriye, in *After Imperialism: The Search for a New Order in the Far East* (1965), has titled the 1920s "the search for order" and charged the United States with leaving a vacuum in this critical region for competing nationalist dreams of China and Japan to fill.

The Great Depression affected the entire industrialized world, and in Japan a flawed constitution and a weak civilian government left Japanese army forces in Korea and Manchuria virtually independent of civilian and military authorities in Tokyo. On September 18, 1931, the Kwantung Army in Manchuria manufactured the Mukden Incident, claiming Chinese bandits blew up the main track of the SMR, and over the next year it seized control of this region, which was roughly the size of Texas. President Herbert Hoover (1874–1964) and Secretary of State Henry Stimson (1867–1950) responded with the Stimson Doctrine (1932), in which the United States proclaimed it would not recognize the Japanese takeover of Manchuria, renaming it Manchukuo, and placing the last Qing emperor, Henry Puyi

(1906–1967), on the throne as leader of an "independent" Japanese protectorate. After the League of Nations condemned this Japanese aggression, the Japanese delegation walked out of the assembly, and many scholars believe Japan's action served as encouragement for the expansionist dreams of Benito Mussolini (1883–1945) in Italy and Adolf Hitler (1889–1945) in Germany.

WORLD WAR II, THE CHINESE CIVIL WAR, AND THE KOREAN WAR

The Second World War was a strange, three-sided conflict in China. Japan controlled most of the coast, interior river valleys, and critical railroad lines. Jiang Jieshi's (1887–1975) Nationalist government retreated to Sichuan province to the west, while Mao Zedong's (1893–1976) communists harassed Nationalist and Japanese units alike from hideouts in caves around Yan'an in the near northwest. As the war drew to a close, the Soviet Union, per agreements at Yalta and later Potsdam, invaded Manchuria in Operation August Storm, drove through weakened Japanese forces, and stopped at the 38th parallel in Korea.

The end of World War II led to a resumption of the Chinese Civil War, now nearly twenty years old. Jiang rejected advice from his American advisers and had the United States lift his forces from Sichuan to Manchuria, leapfrogging Japanese troops in North China as well as communist units harassing them. When the Marshall Mission—the effort by America's well-regarded general George C. Marshall (1880–1959)—failed, attention turned to the battle for Manchuria. Communist forces pinned Nationalist formations into the cities, where they relied on American airdrops for supplies of food and ammunition. One by one, the Red Army seized cities and by 1948 had gained control over Manchuria and most of North China on its way to victory in the civil war.

In June 1950 North Korea invaded the South, and President Harry Truman (1884–1972) interpreted this expected attack, a last phase in a Korean civil conflict, as the first hot war of the Cold War. He ordered American intervention to preserve the Republic of [South] Korea (ROK). American and South Korean forces engaged in a holding action most of the summer but on September 15, 1950, launched the brilliant Inchon invasion, whereby North Korean units quickly disintegrated. Truman faced a serious decision—whether to halt United Nations (UN) forces at the 38th parallel; secure a buffer zone; advance to the narrow neck of northern Korea bounded by Anju to the west and Hungnam to the east, leaving a rump communist state; or rush all the way to the Yalu River (on the border between North Korea and China) despite Chinese threats of intervention. In what was really a nondecision, Truman left it to General Douglas MacArthur (1880–1964) to rush to the Yalu by Christmas.

Beijing, however, feared American forces stationed near its sensitive northeast border. It needed Japanese-built industry in Manchuria to help finance China's reconstruction after decades of war and devastation. American and Nationalist overflights from Taiwan to the mainland caused the new People's Republic to doubt American intentions, and Mao responded to Joseph Stalin's (1878–1953) call for ground forces to protect communist North Korea. In November, Chinese troops—supposed volunteers—made their appearance, surprised US and ROK units, and drove them back pell-mell across the 38th parallel and the Han River near Seoul. US Army general Matthew Ridgway (1895–1993) took over the Eighth Army after General Walton Walker's (1889–1950) death in a jeep accident in December 1950 and assumed command of all UN forces after Truman dismissed MacArthur in April 1951. Ridgway understood the primitive logistics underlying the Chinese offensive and taught his men to absorb the shock and then respond. The result was a stabilized front line to this day, a little below the 38th parallel on the west and a little above to the east.

Thereafter, Manchuria became a site of Chinese industrial expansion, some oil exploration and mineral extraction, and population growth, but it retreated from the central role in East Asian diplomacy that it held from the 1850s to the 1950s.

SEE ALSO *Canton; China; Chinese Exclusion Act (1882); Cold War; Interventionism; Japan; Open Door Policy; Orient; Roosevelt, Franklin D.; Roosevelt, Theodore; Russia; Trans-Siberian Railway; United Nations; World War I; World War II*

BIBLIOGRAPHY

Hunt, Michael H. *Frontier Defense and the Open Door: Manchuria in Chinese-American Relations, 1895–1911.* New Haven, CT: Yale University Press, 1973.

Iriye, Akira. *After Imperialism: The Search for a New Order in the Far East, 1921–1931.* Cambridge, MA, Harvard University Press, 1965.

Jukes, Geoffrey. *The Russo-Japanese War: 1904–1905.* Oxford: Osprey, 2002.

Westad, Odd Arne. *Decisive Encounters: The Chinese Civil War, 1946–1950.* Stanford, CA: Stanford University Press, 2003.

Charles M. Dobbs
Professor Emeritus
Iowa State University

MANHATTAN PROJECT

The Manhattan Project is the informal name for the US government's crash program to build an atomic bomb during World War II. Officially named the Manhattan Engineer District, the Manhattan Project coordinated the efforts of more than 150,000 scientists, technicians, and engineers at dozens of sites in the United States, Canada, and the United Kingdom, at a total cost of more than $2 billion. The Manhattan Project's scientists and engineers built the world's first atomic bomb, detonated at Alamogordo, New Mexico, on July 16, 1945, as well as the devices that destroyed the Japanese cities of Hiroshima and Nagasaki in August 1945.

SCIENTIFIC ORIGINS

The Manhattan Project relied on unprecedented levels of cooperation between scientists and military personnel. Indeed, the very idea for atomic weaponry originated with scientists. In August 1939, just a few months after scientists in Europe announced that they had successfully achieved nuclear fission, the physicists Albert Einstein and Leo Szilard sent a letter to US President Franklin Roosevelt describing the possibilities for a dangerous new weapon. Einstein and Szilard, both of whom had fled Hitler's Germany, warned the president that the Germans might have already begun working on such a weapon. In October 1939 Roosevelt established an ad hoc committee of scientists and military personnel to investigate the problem.

At first the American effort lagged. The so-called Uranium Committee accomplished little in its first eighteen months. Meanwhile the British had established a committee of their own, dubbed "MAUD," for Military Application of Uranium Detonation. As a result of the MAUD Committee's findings, British scientists began a program to enrich uranium under the codename Tube Alloys. In the fall of 1941 the British work came to the attention of Vannevar Bush (1890–1974), who had recently been appointed director of the United States' newly created Office of Scientific Research and Development (OSRD). In October 1941 Roosevelt endorsed Bush's recommendation that the United States pursue an atomic weapon, and the do-nothing Uranium Committee was replaced with a new committee, S-1, headed by civilian scientists. As had Szilard and Einstein before them, S-1's members advised that likely German progress on a fission weapon required that the United States also pursue one.

WARTIME ACCELERATION

It was not until the summer of 1942, however, that the Manhattan Project took on its crash character. Both the American and the British scientists agreed that there were multiple paths to building a weapon based on nuclear fission. A gun-type assembly offered a more straightforward approach but would require relatively large quantities of uranium-235, a rare isotope extraordinarily difficult to separate from the more readily available uranium-238. Plutonium would be easier to produce, but for technical reasons a bomb based on plutonium required a much more sophisticated implosion detonation system. Because no one knew whether either of the plutonium or uranium weapons would work, the project's advisors recommended pursuing all possible options at once. In June 1942 President Roosevelt placed the US Army in charge of this audacious (and expensive) plan.

For the uranium separation effort, the Manhattan Project explored several methods: gaseous diffusion, electromagnetic separation, and thermal diffusion. Each process required the construction of enormous production facilities and instant towns to house the scientific and technical personnel involved. The industrial uranium separation activities were conducted at the Clinton Engineer Works in Oak Ridge, Tennessee. On the other

Physicist J. Robert Oppenheimer and Maj. Gen. Leslie R. Groves view the base of the steel tower on which the first atomic bomb hung when tested near Alamogordo, NM, September 1945. *For a brief period after World War II, as Manhattan Project scientists urged American leaders to embrace the international control of atomic energy, the image of the tortured atomic scientist took root in popular culture, with Oppenheimer attaining cult status as a sort of Faustian genius.* **BETTMANN/CORBIS**

side of the country, scientists and engineers from the DuPont Corporation built a sprawling plutonium separation facility in Hanford, Washington. Scientists at the University of Chicago, Columbia University in New York, the University of California in Berkeley, and many other academic campuses devoted their laboratories to working out the scientific problems at the center of the bomb. And at Los Alamos, New Mexico, the most famous of the Manhattan Project sites, scientists under the direction of the theoretical physicist J. Robert Oppenheimer (1904–1967) worked with military personnel to design deliverable weapons.

The sprawling scale of the project, combined with the inherent uncertainty associated with building a new kind of weapon, posed difficult managerial problems. Brigadier General Leslie R. Groves (1896–1970) maintained the army's command over the entire operation, but he assigned civilian scientific leaders to administer specific aspects of uranium, plutonium, and weapons production: the 1934 Nobel Prize laureate in chemistry Harold C. Urey (1893–1981), of Columbia University, for gaseous diffusion; the 1939 Nobel laureate in physics Ernest Lawrence (1901–1958), of the University of California, Berkeley, for electromagnetic separation; the 1927 Nobel laureate in physics Arthur Compton (1892–1962), of the University of Chicago, for nuclear chain reactions; and Oppenheimer, of the University of California, Berkeley, and the California Institute of Technology, for weapons construction. Military and civilian leaders especially clashed over secrecy restrictions. Groves and the military command structure preferred a compartmentalized system in which knowledge was shared on a need-to-know basis, but Oppenheimer insisted on weekly cross-departmental meetings among the scientists. Eventually the two men reached a truce of sorts in which the participating scientists shared information with each other but agreed to other forms of extreme security measures, including aliases and working behind multiple layers of barbed wire.

Security clearances and background checks were mandatory for all scientists involved in the project. This process was made more difficult by the fact that so many of the physicists involved were either refugees from Hitler's Germany or had flirted with radical politics in the 1930s. Although technically allies in World War II, US and Soviet leaders regarded each other with deep distrust, and the military refused to share information on the bomb—or even the fact of its development—with the Soviet Union until the very end of the war. Groves additionally severely restricted the information provided to the British, even after the Manhattan Project absorbed Tube Alloys in 1943. After the war it became clear that the Manhattan Project's cloak of security had not, in fact, been impenetrable. Several of the Soviet Union's spies infiltrated the Manhattan Project, including most famously Klaus Fuchs

(1911–1988), a German-born British physicist who ended up at Los Alamos via Tube Alloys.

TESTING AND USING THE BOMB

The timing of the first atomic test strengthened President Harry S. Truman's hand at the Potsdam Conference, where the Allied leaders had gathered in the summer of 1945 to discuss their strategies for ending the war and governing the peace. Only the plutonium device was tested; the scientists felt that uranium-235 was too precious, and the gun-assembly method too sure, to waste resources on a dry run. Truman received Groves's full report on the successful detonation, dubbed Trinity, on July 21, 1945, and obliquely shared the information with Soviet leader Joseph Stalin (1878–1953) a few days later. Truman did not explain what exactly the Americans had built; he merely indicated that the United States had tested a "new weapon of unusual destructive force." Stalin asked few questions, most likely because he already knew about the bomb from Fuchs's reports. Many historians now believe that the hand Truman played at Potsdam with both postwar Germany and the Soviet Union was owed to the trump card of the US atomic monopoly.

The use of the atomic bombs a month later in Japan would have dispelled any lingering doubts Stalin may have had about the bomb. Over the course of the summer, several Manhattan Project scientists associated with the University of Chicago had urged military leaders to abstain from using the bomb in Japan, arguing that a demonstration would be just as effective in forcing Japanese surrender without the loss of life. Among the project's scientific leadership at Los Alamos, however, the bomb's use in military operations was never really in doubt. Nor, in any case, did the scientists have control over what was ultimately a military and political decision. On August 6, 1945, the *Enola Gay*, a B-29 bomber, dropped the Little Boy, a uranium-based device, over Hiroshima. Three days later, the *Bockscar* dropped the Fat Man, a plutonium-based device, over Nagasaki. Together, the bombs are estimated to have killed over 200,000 people, primarily through burns and radiation sickness. The vast scale of the destruction, combined with the Soviet Union's entry into the war against Japan on August 8, forced Japan to announce its surrender on August 15.

POSTWAR ATOMIC SCIENCE

The Manhattan Engineer District retained control of American atomic research until January 1947, when the newly formed Atomic Energy Commission took over. Several Manhattan Project sites, including Los Alamos, Oak Ridge, Argonne (outside Chicago), and Ernest Lawrence's University of California, Berkeley, laboratory, continued their work in the postwar era as US National Laboratories.

J. ROBERT OPPENHEIMER

American theoretical physicist J. Robert Oppenheimer (1904–1967) spearheaded the scientific and technical development of the world's first atomic bomb. Despite Oppenheimer's singular contributions to the Manhattan Project, the Atomic Energy Commission (AEC) stripped him of his security clearance in 1954. His security hearing made the scientist a symbol of the excesses of McCarthyism and raised scientists' fears about the limits of their political involvement during the Cold War.

Oppenheimer grew up in a wealthy household in New York City. Though nominally Jewish, the secular German American Oppenheimers raised their two children, Robert and Frank, within the Ethical Culture movement. After graduating from Harvard University in 1924, Oppenheimer received his PhD in physics from the University of Göttingen in Germany at age twenty-three. Back in the United States, Oppenheimer settled into dual appointments at the University of California, Berkeley, and the California Institute of Technology.

Oppenheimer's reputation as one of the country's most brilliant physicists made him an obvious choice for the Manhattan Project. His appointment, however, was delayed by questions about his politics. Oppenheimer participated in left-wing politics in the 1930s; several people close to him, including multiple students, his brother, and his wife, were acknowledged members of the Communist Party USA. Brigadier General Leslie R. Groves (1896–1970) nonetheless insisted that Oppenheimer lead the project's weapons laboratory at Los Alamos, New Mexico. By the time that Oppenheimer's clearance finally arrived in 1943, military intelligence and the Federal Bureau of Investigation (FBI) had already begun assembling a massive file on his activities and personal networks.

The successful detonation of the atomic bombs, first in Alamogordo, New Mexico, on July 16, 1945, and then in August over the Japanese cities of Hiroshima and Nagasaki, made Oppenheimer a national hero and a valued scientific adviser to the military. His advocacy on behalf of the international control of atomic energy and his opposition to the development of a hydrogen bomb,

however, earned him political enemies. In 1953, one of these enemies, Lewis Strauss (1896–1974), then chairman of the AEC, convinced President Dwight D. Eisenhower (1890–1969) to bar Oppenheimer from accessing sensitive information. The move was largely symbolic, as by this time Oppenheimer rarely consulted for the AEC, having accepted a position as director of the Institute for Advanced Study in Princeton, New Jersey, in 1947. Oppenheimer nevertheless decided to fight the charges. The resulting security hearing raised enough doubts about Oppenheimer's honesty and judgment that the AEC officially revoked his clearance the following summer.

The AEC's decision shocked many members of the scientific community, who saw Oppenheimer's administrative hearing as a McCarthyist witch hunt. The release of the hearing transcripts in 1954 under the title *In the Matter of J. Robert Oppenheimer* inspired the German playwright Heinar Kipphardt (1922–1982) to write a popular play under the same name in 1964 that portrayed Oppenheimer as a martyr. Oppenheimer's receipt of the prestigious Fermi Prize for public service, presented by President Lyndon B. Johnson (1908–1973) in 1963, officially marked the end of his political exile. Oppenheimer himself later contributed to the notion that he regretted his participation in the Manhattan Project, telling an interviewer in 1965 that he quoted the Bhagavad Gita, a Hindu scripture, upon witnessing the explosion of the first bomb. Oppenheimer is today remembered as a complicated and ambitious, but loyal, scientist who had an outside impact on the image of scientists and scientific authority in the twentieth century.

BIBLIOGRAPHY

Bird, Kai, and Martin Sherwin. *American Prometheus: The Triumph and Tragedy of J. Robert Oppenheimer.* New York: Knopf, 2005.

Monk, Ray. *Robert Oppenheimer: A Life Inside the Center.* New York: Doubleday, 2012.

Thorpe, Charles. *Oppenheimer: The Tragic Intellect.* Chicago: University of Chicago Press, 2006.

Audra J. Wolfe
Philadelphia, Pennsylvania

For a brief period after the war, Manhattan Project scientists attempted to take on the role of the nation's atomic conscience. The so-called atomic scientists' movement urged American foreign policy leadership to embrace the international control of atomic energy, but their efforts failed in the face of growing anti-Communism. Perhaps because of this, the image of the tortured atomic scientist took root in popular culture, with

Oppenheimer, especially, attaining cult status as a sort of Faustian genius. Of course, not all scientists associated with the Manhattan Project regretted their involvement. The physicist Edward Teller (1908–2003) famously embraced ever larger atomic and nuclear weapons, eventually serving as one of the models for the title character in Stanley Kubrick's 1964 film *Dr. Strangelove*.

Sixty years after Trinity, the Manhattan Project continues as an object of public fascination. In 2014 the cable television network WGN America premiered a television series, *Manhattan*, loosely based on life at Los Alamos. That same year the US Congress passed legislation authorizing the creation of a Manhattan Project National Park, based on sites at Los Alamos, Hanford, and Oak Ridge.

SEE ALSO *Atomic Bomb; Bikini Atoll; Einstein, Albert; World War II*

BIBLIOGRAPHY

Alperovitz, Gar, and Kai Bird. "The Centrality of the Bomb." *Foreign Policy* 94, 3 (1993): 3–20.

Rhodes, Richard. *The Making of the Atomic Bomb*. New York: Simon and Schuster, 1986.

Walker, J. Samuel. *Prompt and Utter Destruction: Truman and the Use of the Atomic Bombs against Japan*. Rev. ed. Chapel Hill: University of North Carolina Press, 2004.

Audra J. Wolfe
Philadelphia, Pennsylvania

MANIFEST DESTINY

The wanderings of the British journalist Harriet Martineau (1802–1876) through 1830s America had her convinced of at least one thing: Americans' "pride and delight ... is in their quantity of land." "I do not remember meeting with one to whom it had occurred," she further quipped, "that they had too much." Expansion, in other words, was the country's obsession. "The possession of land is the aim of all action, generally speaking, and the cure for all social evils, among men in the United States." Whether "disappointed in politics or love" or suffering some disgrace or financial setback, or "if a citizen's neighbours rise above him," the solution remained the same: "He goes and buys land" (Greenberg 2012, 73).

Writing almost a decade before the term *manifest destiny* was supposedly coined, Martineau spoke to the many social and political forces that undergirded the republic's overspreading North America and abroad. But at the heart of it all was the firm conviction—one shared by many people during the antebellum era—that national

expansion was a virtue. Such was the essence of manifest destiny. This was an ideology that explained to Americans (and helped them explain to others) why their growth across space was a good thing. An entire matrix of ideas regarding race, religion, history, and political economy were subsumed beneath that expansive phrase. And yet, ultimately, nineteenth-century Americans would not have spanned a continent, a hemisphere, and many oceans without the belief that in doing so they might benefit not only themselves but the world.

ORIGIN OF THE CONCEPT

This faith did not arise overnight. It had a long history preceding even independence from Great Britain, and so the search for any precise "origin" for manifest destiny becomes something of a fruitless quest. The term itself is generally understood to have emerged out of the Democratic press during debate over the addition of Texas to the Union, wherein newspaper publisher and party loyalist John L. O'Sullivan (1813–1895), or perhaps one of his writers, Jane McManus Storm Cazneau (1807–1878), published a proannexation essay citing "our manifest destiny to overspread the continent allotted by Providence for the free development of our yearly multiplying millions" (Hietala 2003, 255). Yet even then, the phrase would not have taken popular flight without an assist from Whig opponents to the Texas question, who recycled the term in political speeches so as to jeer at those who would excuse aggression as divine intervention.

But again, manifest destiny, most directly associated with the 1840s, had a much longer pedigree. Andrew Jackson (1767–1845) had already spoken of national territorial growth as a benevolent process that "extend[ed] the area of freedom" (Adams 2013, 551). John Quincy Adams (1767–1848), meanwhile, insisted in 1822 that the world "become familiarized with the idea of considering our proper dominion to be the continent of North America." "It was," he observed, "as much a law of nature that this should become our pretension as that the Mississippi should flow to the sea" (Kagan 2006, 47). Yet in saying so, he only echoed Thomas Jefferson's (1743–1826) imagined "empire for liberty," the end result of the country's "rapid multiplication" and eventual covering of "the whole northern, if not the southern continent" (Merk 1963, 9).

Revolutionary rhetoric in the run-up to the War for Independence also contained healthy dosages of what would later come to be known as manifest destiny. When the founding generation promised to "begin the world over again," to usher in a *Novus ordo seclorum* of which *Annuit coeptis*, they announced themes of a providentially sanctioned, American-led process of global regeneration that later citizens would come to see evidence of in various international contexts.

Thus manifest destiny is best thought of not as a specific policy but rather as a tangle of themes meant to legitimate several different varieties of national expansion at many different points in American history. And while this web of justifications (or, better yet, obligations to the world) was densely woven, a few prominent strands stand out. These were: a conception of the American people as particularly virtuous; a conviction regarding the special genius of the country's democratic institutions; and a religiously held certainty about the plan of divine providence to see that body of American values and practices spread across as much of the earth's surface as possible.

AN IDEOLOGY OF EXCLUSION AND EXTERMINATION

The seeming universalism of manifest destiny, however, was complicated by the racial specificity of its progenitors' vision. Only a so-called master race of white Anglo-Saxons, the rhetoric went, was sufficiently mentally equipped and physically fit to inhabit North America. If it was the nation's "destiny" to continually expand, it was no less the destiny of "inferior" races and nations to recede before that irresistible march. For many Americans, national expansion played out the supposedly immutable truths of white supremacy. Accordingly, the extermination of native peoples and cultures was met with little cause for apology or even regret by the supporters of manifest destiny. Such was the essence of manifest destiny, an ideology of expansion but also exclusion and extermination.

At least a portion, therefore, of what collectively came to be known as the spirit of manifest destiny was characterized by a heady, confident, exuberant edge. When politician and eventual western territorial governor William Gilpin (1813–1894) spoke of the "*untransacted* destiny of the American people to subdue the continent ... regenerate superannuated nations ... carry the career of mankind to its culminating point ... [and] shed blessings round the world," he did so with a certitude common among his generation (Weeks 2013, 130). Yet lurking beneath such poised pronouncements was a good deal of anxiety, and that unease must also be seen as a crucial motivator influencing the foreign policy of manifest destiny. For people concerned about a swelling population of slaves in America, western land was presented as a means to "diffuse" that population of "degenerate" Africans across space and funnel it further from the nation. Meanwhile, individuals scraping by in an industrializing country, with its growing reliance on low-status, unskilled, wage-based work, saw in new frontiers a way to climb out of poverty. And those troubled by the increasing social prominence of both "effete" middle-class men and civically engaged

evangelical women found the martial rhetoric of territorial expansion reassuring for its reaffirmation of traditionally "masculine" pursuits. Manifest destiny was for all such people a salve, a panacea for the ills of nineteenth-century modernity.

JAMES POLK'S EXPANSIONIST PRESIDENCY

All of these ambitions, hopes, fears, and apprehensions came to a head in the presidential election of 1844. James K. Polk (1795–1849), the Democratic Party dark horse, ran as the candidate of manifest destiny. He promised, if elected, to pursue the annexation of Texas, the maximum northern boundary of Oregon, and California's commercially valuable Pacific ports. Though Polk won the election by a narrow margin (the upstart abolitionist Liberty Party peeled off just enough northern Whig votes to hand the Democrats a victory), he interpreted those results as a popular mandate to pursue his expansionist platform. The exercise of state power and the execution of conscious political design would belie all talk of "fate," "inevitability," and "destiny."

First came Texas, an issue made "easy" for Polk by his predecessor John Tyler (1790–1862), himself an expansionist, and one who also read the results at the polls in 1844 as a call to action. Before Polk even took office in March 1845, the outgoing administration used whispers of Texas's possible absorption into the British Empire, as well as procedural irregularities in Congress (a so-called joint resolution for annexation, rather than a treaty requiring two-thirds approval in the Senate), to restart a conversation first dodged by Andrew Jackson in 1837. Southerners wanted to see another slave state added to the Union, and refused to accept the appearance of an abolitionist British buffer colony—an 1833 act of Parliament had ended slavery within the empire—to their west. Northern Democrats were, on the other hand, sold on a fantasy of slavery's gradual march farther and farther to the southwest, thus draining "inferior" black populations away from their own communities. As a result, annexation squeaked by and Texas joined the Union, though not before the Mexican ambassador, shocked at American theft of what Mexico still considered its sovereign territory, requested his passport and returned home. With diplomatic ties between the two countries now severed, the threat of war with a neighboring republic loomed large in the United States.

Of course, an entirely different war had been Polk's implicit pledge during his campaign for the presidency. By early 1846, Democrats had begun to swear "Fifty-Four Forty or Fight!" in reference to the northernmost line of latitude (54°40′) along which American claims to Oregon extended. Let the boundary be drawn there, or else, let battle begin. That northwestern territory had been subject to joint occupation by the United States and Great Britain for roughly two decades prior to Polk's ascendancy, but manifest destiny seemed to command an abrogation of this arrangement in favor of American maximalism. Northern Democrats were particularly invested in extending total national dominion in the region because, by the terms of the Missouri Compromise (1820), all of Oregon would be open only to free labor. Here in the lush fields and forests of the Pacific Coast, these politicians promised their voters, was the escape route out of the permanent degradation and dependency that city-dwelling wage-laborers craved. Channeling Thomas Jefferson, many northern politicians were convinced that if European history proved one thing, it was that free institutions could not flourish in the absence of widespread property ownership. Oregon, *all* of Oregon, would be a way to circumvent the worst effects of industrialization and its concomitant social ills, namely, class stratification and inequality.

Polk was more than glad to manipulate those fears so as to force a compromise with Great Britain. While encouraging the belligerent bluster of committed "All Oregon" acolytes, Polk presented to British officials a boundary at the forty-ninth parallel as both a reasonable compromise and the expedient manner to avoid an unwanted Anglo-American war. In mid-1846, Queen Victoria's Foreign Office, well aware of a swelling US population in the Pacific Northwest and unwilling to risk war's interrupting the supply of southern cotton to British mills, assented. Manifest destiny, it seemed to some irate over the negotiated solution, had been sacrificed on the altar of power politics and international diplomacy.

Yet one cannot dismiss another restraining factor in the Oregon case: the supposed racial affinity between American and British Anglo-Saxons. Confronted with the possibility of war to the north, the United States and Great Britain, partly from a sense of shared cultural, political, and religious values—a shared sense, in other words, of all that lay beneath the banner of "whiteness"— opted for a peaceful resolution. But for most white Americans at the time, the bonds of "blood kinship" that fair skin made possible did not extend south. And so it was that with Oregon sidelined, one newspaper bellowed, "now we can thrash Mexico into decency at our leisure" (Herring 2011, 192).

WAR WITH MEXICO

The Polk administration pursued a policy of relentless aggression toward Mexico legitimated largely by broad-based contempt for that country's people, a contempt rooted in racial thinking. Yes, Mexico was a "weaker" country, with a smaller population, much "empty" land, an unstable government, and a perennially bankrupt treasury. But all of that, the argument went, was rooted in the "inferior stock" of its citizens. Even Whig opponents of the US-Mexico War, which broke out in May 1846, conceded that the conflict was a "race war" pitting "the Caucasian and Anglo-Saxon, pure white blood, against a mixed and mongrel race, composed of Indians, negroes, and Spaniards, all three degenerated by the admixture of blood and colors" (DeConde 1992, 32).

Racial "degeneracy" was indeed the watchword of most American coverage of the conflict, and had provided Polk with much of the pretext he needed to provoke hostilities in the first place. After all, the argument went, if Mexican "mongrels" were so inept as to be unable to secure their northern border from repeated Comanche and Apache Indian raids (never mind that American gunrunners had supplied most of the materiel for those plundering expeditions), then perhaps some new power, some more capable race, ought to move in, clear the land of its savage inhabitants, and put it to new and "productive" purpose. That process was not imperialistic, war cheerleaders insisted; rather, it was merely one people fulfilling its manifest destiny to overspread the North American continent. To say otherwise, to call into question providential plan, was heresy. And to oppose the war, Polk also implied, was unpatriotic.

But when it came to the limits of manifest destiny, race cut both ways. Some saw the white republic's endless capacity to absorb or eliminate "inferior" peoples, while others balked at what they viewed as the racial pollution of the body politic that expansion would entail. These competing worldviews clashed during midwar public debate over proposals to annex more (if not the entirety) of Mexico. As American armies pushed deeper into enemy territory, capturing the capital of Mexico City by September 1847, manifest destiny's more strident prophets began to clamor for the United States to seize the entire country. This was the so-called "All-Mexico" faction, led by people like Sam Houston (1793–1863). The senator from Texas, in advocating for complete conquest, liked reminding audiences that "from the first moment they landed," American settlers had been busily "cheating Indians out of their land." And so, because "the Mexicans are no better than the Indians, I see no reason why we should not go on in the same course now, and take their land." Fears of racial incompatibility, mean-while, were exaggerated, for as Houston observed, Mexico's "beautiful *senoritas*, or pretty girls, if you should choose to annex them," well, "no doubt the result of this annexation will be a most powerful and delightful evidence of civilization" (Greenberg 2012, 115). American military domination, followed by white male sexual domination, would quickly "cleanse" the country's bloodline. And yet, All-Mexico's opponents ultimately carried the day. Men like John C. Calhoun (1782–1850), who abhorred the idea of sharing his Senate chamber with dark-skinned "mongrel" representatives from some newly created Mexican state—"Ours, sir, is the Government of a white race," he scolded his opponents—proved more persuasive (DeConde 1992, 34).

President Polk, though sympathetic to the All-Mexico movement, opted to terminate the war with the 1848 Treaty of Guadalupe Hidalgo. Better to pounce on a Rio Grande border and the acquisition of Upper California than to watch the American occupation of Mexico devolve into a brutal guerrilla war. In what many Mexicans referred to as "The Dismemberment," the United States almost doubled in size by seizing nearly half of their sister republic to the south.

MARITIME DOMINANCE

A war in which much territory changed hands can lend the impression that land was the singular obsession of those who championed manifest destiny. In fact, Polk wanted California mostly for the port of San Francisco, the great point of departure for trans-Pacific trade and the fabled China market. Projectors expected the Mississippi Valley to become *the* nexus of global commerce, wherein eastern and western commodity flows would meet: "The trade of China and of a large portion of Asia must find its way … to our Pacific shores," enthused one orator, "and thence across to the Atlantic coast, there to meet the trade of Europe" (Stephanson 1995, 58). Indeed, on a long enough timeline, one is tempted to see the US-Mexico War's most lasting impact not in the acreage gained but the strategic advantage America acquired vis-à-vis the Pacific world.

By the mid-twentieth century, the United States was the dominant commercial and military power within and along the world's largest ocean. And that fact had been the fantasy of many Americans from the early nineteenth century onward, among whom it was a popular boast that the nation's "sails whitened every sea." In other words, the country possessed a maritime empire that complemented its territorial breadth. Ships and sailors helped carve out the foreign markets essential to making the republic's agricultural and manufacturing sectors profitable. The nation's massive whaling fleet and merchant marine were heralded as pioneers fulfilling

Manifest Destiny presents Uncle Sam and Columbia, together at the gate of the US Foundling Asylum, with a basket of crying children representing Puerto Rico, Cuba, Hawai'i, and the Philippines. Political cartoon, c. 1898. As the concept of America's greater mission in the world resulted in the annexation of several new US territories, the nation debated the wisdom of further expansion beyond continental boundaries. **NIDAY PICTURE LIBRARY/ALAMY**

America's maritime manifest destiny. Meanwhile, naval commanders like Commodore Matthew Perry (1794–1858)—a man whose writings trafficked in the era's proexpansionist rhetoric—were charged with enlarging national influence abroad. Perry remains famous for "opening" Japan at cannon point in 1853, but his was only one among many federally funded diplomatic and scientific missions sent into the world at the time to broker treaties, facilitate trade, and gather intelligence. Herein lay the truly global dimensions of early American expansionism: a maritime sector that circled the world, showed the flag in almost every global port, built national commercial and consular outposts, exercised extraterritorial legal jurisdiction, and familiarized many foreign nations with the republic.

FILIBUSTERS

As Americans laid claim to what William Seward (1801–1872) called their "ultimate empire of the ocean," however, carving up a continent was proving more contentious (Stephanson 1995, 61). For while the national borders traced across North America after the war with Mexico did, for the most part, reflect the eventual boundaries of the United States, people alive at the time could not know this. Within their lifetimes, the republic had grown immensely, and there was no reason to believe it would not continue to do so. Indeed, ensuring that expansion persisted became the stated aim of a group of individuals (and their mercenary armies) known as *filibusters*. Filibustering—taken from the Dutch for *freebooter*—involved the armed invasion of foreign countries by private American citizens, usually with the aim of securing eventual recognition and annexation by the United States. While Narciso López's (1797–1851) repeated incursions into Cuba and William Walker's (1824–1860) brief Nicaraguan regime are the best-known examples, other attempts were aimed at northern Mexico, Hawai'i, and South America.

Most active during the 1850s, filibusters both considered themselves soldiers of manifest destiny and deluded themselves that "with swelling hearts and suppressed impatience," foreign peoples "await our coming … with joyous shouts of 'Welcome! Welcome!'" (Stephanson 1995, 65). And yet, by then, manifest destiny had assumed a decidedly sectional flavor. These expeditionary forces were largely staged in New Orleans and other southern ports, and had as their stated aim the creation of a tropical empire suited to slavery's expansion. They spoke of white-led racial regeneration amongst the Western Hemisphere's dark-skinned nations, but also of providing slaveholders with the room their institution required in order to grow. For some, filibusters were romantic heroes, but, for others, they

were evidence of the lengths to which a corrupt slave power might go in order to ensure its continued political relevance in the United States. The Republican Party eventually swelled its ranks with citizens disaffected by what seemed like slavery's dishonorable and piratical approach to foreign relations. The South, meanwhile, griped over America's failure to aid "patriots" like López and Walker before their endeavors collapsed in the face of stiff resistance from those they proposed to govern.

THE CIVIL WAR AND BEYOND

By the late 1850s, if not earlier, manifest destiny had been sheared of the buoyant optimism characterizing its earlier iteration. Increasing numbers of people in the North now saw it as a hollow pronouncement that had been used largely to advance the cause of expanding slavery. An equal number of southerners, meanwhile, came to believe that only secession from the Union would allow for the pursuit of a truly independent foreign policy geared toward providing more and more land to the next generation(s) of slaveholders. Hindsight now designates 1848 as manifest destiny's high-water mark, with the remainder of the tale teleologically told as one of looming Civil War.

Yet manifest destiny did not necessarily disappear in the face of what became a war to end the embarrassment of slavery. Rather, the concept of America's greater mission within the world only found more traction in a postbellum period that had seen the nation right its own great wrong, and so, prepared now to carry that same crusading spirit to more and more of the planet's people. When, in 1898, President William McKinley (1843–1901) pressed for the annexation of Pacific archipelagos, he explained in matter-of-fact terms that "we need Hawaii a good deal more than we did California. It is manifest destiny" (Paterson et al. 2010, 218). The concept thus proved durable, even if the contexts in which it continued to appear were constantly evolving.

SEE ALSO *Filibuster; Mexican-American War; Polk, James K.; Texas Republic*

BIBLIOGRAPHY

Adams, Sean Patrick, ed. *A Companion to the Era of Andrew Jackson.* New York: Wiley, 2013.

DeConde, Alexander. *Ethnicity, Race, and American Foreign Policy: A History.* Boston: Northeastern University Press, 1992.

DeLay, Brian. *War of a Thousand Deserts: Indian Raids and the U.S.–Mexican War.* New Haven, CT: Yale University Press, 2008.

Greenberg, Amy S. *Manifest Manhood and the Antebellum American Empire.* Cambridge: Cambridge University Press, 2005.

Greenberg, Amy S. *Manifest Destiny and American Territorial Expansion: A Brief History with Documents.* New York: Bedford/St. Martin's, 2012.

Herring, George C. *From Colony to Superpower: U.S. Foreign Relations Since 1776*. New York: Oxford University Press, 2011.

Hietala, Thomas. *Manifest Design: American Exceptionalism and Empire*. Rev. ed. Ithaca, NY: Cornell University Press, 2003.

Horsman, Reginald. *Race and Manifest Destiny: Origins of American Racial Anglo-Saxonism*. Cambridge, MA: Harvard University Press, 1986.

Kagan, Robert. *Dangerous Nation: America's Place in the World from Its Earliest Days to the Dawn of the Twentieth Century*. New York: Vintage, 2006.

May, Robert E. *Manifest Destiny's Underworld: Filibustering in Antebellum America*. Chapel Hill: University of North Carolina Press, 2002.

Merk, Frederick. *Manifest Destiny and Mission in American History*. New York: Knopf, 1963.

Nugent, Walter. *Habits of Empire: A History of American Expansion*. New York: Vintage, 2008.

Paterson, Thomas G., J. Garry Clifford, Kenneth J. Hagan, Shane J. Maddock, and Deborah Kisatsky. *American Foreign Relations: A History*. 2 vols. 7th ed. Boston: Wadsworth, 2010.

Stephanson, Anders. *Manifest Destiny: American Expansion and the Empire of Right*. New York: Hill and Wang, 1995.

Weeks, William Earl. *The New Cambridge History of American Foreign Relations*, Vol. 1: *Dimensions of the Early American Empire, 1754–1865*. Cambridge: Cambridge University Press, 2013.

Brian Rouleau
Assistant Professor of History
Texas A&M University

MARINE CORPS, US

The United States Marine Corps (USMC) is a branch of the US Armed Forces whose mission is the projection of power through amphibious and rapid-deployment expeditionary operations. Although the USMC is the smallest branch of the four Department of Defense (DoD) armed services, its ability to deploy quickly in crisis situations has given the USMC a central role in the implementation of American foreign policy.

COMPOSITION AND TRAINING

The USMC is part of the Department of the Navy. A commandant at the rank of general leads the Corps. Three mission-related groups make up the Operating Forces of the USMC. First is the Marine Corps Embassy Security Group, which guards US embassies around the world. Second is the Marine Corps Security Force Regiment, an antiterrorism force guarding naval installations, especially those with nuclear weapons. Third are the Marine Corps Forces (MARFOR), which include the I, II, and III

Marine Expeditionary Forces (MEFs), the largest combat unit in the USMC structure. MEFs include a ground combat division, an aviation combat wing, and a logistics group. Components of the MEFs are assigned to each of the DoD's regional unified combatant commands.

As of 2013, the USMC was comprised of 194,000 active duty marines and 40,000 marine reserves. Marines in the lower enlisted ranks E-2 through E-4 were more likely than personnel in other branches to be young and single. However, as of 2013, 98.6 percent of marine recruits had high-school diplomas. Marines were also more likely than personnel in other branches to complete a four-year tour and separate from the service. Marine Corps officers usually attend Officer Candidate School (OCS) and are commissioned after successful completion of the course. Some officers come from the US Naval Academy, while others are commissioned after ROTC training. As of 2013, women comprised 7.11 percent of the Marine Corps, and 79 percent of the USMC was white.

USMC recruits attend a twelve-week basic training, known as "boot camp," which is longer and more challenging than the basic training of other branches. Physical training standards are rigorous; recruits must be able to do pull-ups (flexed arm hang for females), crunches, and a timed run. Since 1996, every USMC basic training class has culminated in a fifty-four-hour exercise known as the Crucible, which tests recruits on teamwork, decision making, and ability to perform under stressful conditions.

Marines consistently have shown the highest levels of morale and loyalty to their branch. During difficult recruiting environments, while other branches have lowered their standards or downplayed the rigors of military service, the USMC has deliberately emphasized its "the few, the proud" identity and the high standards of the Corps. USMC leadership believes that this enables the USMC to attract sufficient numbers of qualified recruits.

HISTORY OF THE CORPS

The Continental Marines were created in 1775. They were disbanded in 1783 and reformed as the US Marine Corps in 1798, but the USMC officially celebrates November 10, 1775, as the birthday of the Corps. The first marines were essentially infantrymen on ships. Their roles were to protect the crew (and protect officers from mutiny), to board enemy ships, and to carry out amphibious landings in preparation for ground fighting.

In the early nineteenth century, the marines played an important role in the Barbary Wars, when US shipping was threatened by piracy. In 1805, a small force of marines and several hundred mercenaries tried to capture

Tripoli in the Battle of Derne. However, the marines generally performed guard duty on ships.

In the first half of the nineteenth century, Archibald Henderson (1783–1859), the fifth commandant of the Corps (1820–1859), fended off government attempts to merge the USMC with the US Army, and he transformed the USMC from a ships' guard corps into an expeditionary force. During the second half of the nineteenth century, the USMC was involved in missions around the world. A force of marines captured Chapultepec Palace ("the Halls of Montezuma") in Mexico City in 1847, and in the decades after the Civil War (1861–1865), the marines were sent to numerous locations in East Asia and Latin America to protect Americans and American property.

During the Spanish-American War (1898), the United States acquired colonies and became more involved in overseas ventures. The Corps played an important role in expanding US power across the globe. In the early twentieth century, the USMC conducted combat, peacekeeping and occupation duties in China, the Philippines, Mexico, Cuba, Haiti, Nicaragua, Santo Domingo, and Panama.

The USMC fought bravely at Belleau Wood in World War I (1914–1918). After the war Commandant John A. Lejeune (1867–1942) spearheaded a further transformation in the USMC mission, moving toward modernized amphibious operations. Realizing that Japan would likely be the adversary in a future conflict, Lejeune and his protégé, Lieutenant Colonel Earl H. Ellis (1880–1923), imagined a role for the Corps as a projector of American power among the island archipelagos held by Japan. They developed a theory of mechanized amphibious assault, using assault craft to land fully integrated combat units that would include infantry, tanks, and artillery. The landings would be protected by naval gunfire and attack aircraft.

It took years for the theory to become reality, but in World War II (1939–1945), the USMC played a vital role in the counteroffensive against Japan. Using Landing Ship Tanks (LSTs), they spearheaded the "island-hopping" campaign that brought US ground, air, and naval forces within attacking distance of the main Japanese islands.

Throughout the Cold War, marines were the force of choice for many peacekeeping, humanitarian, and evacuation missions. They were sent to evacuate Americans from Egypt during the Suez Crisis of 1956, from Cuba during the revolution in 1959 to 1960, from the Dominican Republic in 1965, from Liberia in 1990 and 1996, and from the Central African Republic in 1996. Marines were involved in the abortive attempt to rescue hostages from Iran in 1980. In 1982, marines were part of the Multinational Force of peacekeepers in Lebanon. On October 23, 1983, a USMC barracks in Beirut was bombed, killing 220 marines. More recently, marines have been sent to Indonesia, New Orleans, Haiti, and elsewhere to help with disaster relief.

Marines fought alongside US Army troops in conventional battles in Korea and Vietnam, and were among the first to arrive for Operation Desert Shield/Desert Storm in 1990. Marines participated in the 2003 invasion of Iraq and played an ongoing role in Operation Iraqi Freedom. They endured fierce fighting against Iraqi insurgents in the Battles of Fallujah in 2004.

PUBLIC IMAGE

The demographics of the Marine Corps—young, single, on a first or second enlistment—is appropriate for the rigorous expeditionary tasks performed by the USMC. This demographic profile also shapes the complex public image of the Corps at home and abroad. Marines are seen by many Americans to represent military virtue and American patriotism, but films like Oliver's Stone's *Platoon* (1986) have portrayed the USMC as an institution led by cruel martinets. Moreover, marine bases, particularly those overseas, have brought social problems to their host regions. For example, Marine Corps Base Smedley D. Butler, the huge base complex in Okinawa, has been a decades-long source of conflict between the Japanese and the DoD. Petty crime, public drinking, and prostitution are alleged to accompany the marine community, and many Okinawans have campaigned to close the bases.

Although the USMC has a complex image both at home and abroad, it continues to be vital to the projection of US power overseas. Misbehavior by marines has sparked protest and opposition to US basing, but marines have also assisted victims of natural disasters, protected civilians in war-torn regions, and endured fierce combat in many parts of the world.

SEE ALSO *Air Force, US; Army, US; Department of Defense, US; Department of Homeland Security; Department of State; The Influence of Sea Power upon History (Alfred Thayer Mahan, 1890); Navy, US*

BIBLIOGRAPHY

Axelrod, Alan. *Miracle at Belleau Wood: The Birth of the Modern U.S. Marine Corps.* Guilford, CT: Lyons Press, 2007.

Cohen, Barney. *The Proud: Inside the Marine Corps.* New York: Morrow, 1992.

Cureton, Charles H. *The United States Marine Corps.* London: Greenhill, 1997.

Millett, Allan R. *Semper Fidelis: The History of the United States Marine Corps.* Rev. ed. New York: Free Press, 1991.

Anni Baker
Associate Professor, Department of History
Wheaton College, Norton, Massachusetts

MARLBORO

The Marlboro brand of filtered cigarettes was first released by the tobacco company Philip Morris in 1924. Marlboro was initially a niche product. It was primarily marketed to women and came with a filter, which was seen as a form of health protection. Filtered cigarettes were unusual at that time. In the early 1950s, scientific confirmation of the link between smoking and lung cancer initiated a major shift in tobacco marketing strategies. In particular, there was a massive increase in the production and promotion of filtered cigarettes. In this context, in 1955, Philip Morris employed the Leo Burnett Company of Chicago, led by influential advertising executive Leo Burnett (1891–1971), to rebrand Marlboro and to capture a share of this new market.

Burnett was famous for reimagining the Campbell's soup can. With Marlboro, Burnett eschewed an obvious emphasis on the health benefits of filtered smoke in favor of a more radical strategy. Burnett gave Marlboro a clean and simple red-and-white color scheme and a new flip-top, crush-proof box. Most importantly, Burnett rebranded Marlboro as a symbol of masculinity. Initial Marlboro figures included a diver, a sailor, and a cinematographer. All ads carried the caption: "A lot of man ... a lot of cigarette" (Leo Burnett Company Inc. 1955). These images soon gave way to the single figure of the cowboy. The masculinity of the cowboy associated Marlboro with virility, freedom, independence, and individualism. Supported by the biggest budget in tobacco advertising history, Marlboro went on to capture 40 percent of the US cigarette market. It was especially popular among younger consumers, where it captured nearly 70 percent of the market.

The Marlboro campaign of the 1950s and 1960s paralleled the broader proliferation of cowboys in American film, television, and popular fiction, as well as in advertising. The Marlboro campaign also built upon the emphasis on lifestyle, self-realization, and personal identity that propelled the radical growth of consumer culture during this period. In addition, the Marlboro cowboy suggested an aloofness to risk that was enormously consequential in the context of the debate about smoking and health. Historian Alan Brandt argues that the emphasis on control of the self, on willpower, and on autonomy "helped define dominant social meanings of dependence and risk for generations" (2007, 261–264).

The brand's major push into the international market came in the late 1980s and early 1990s. The key target-markets included the European Union, Eastern Europe, and Asia, especially China. This internationalization program was accompanied by extensive analysis of global trends in the consumption of identity-driven, branded commodities (like Marlboro). A report commissioned by Philip Morris argued: "The crucial need is to identify how Marlboro 'fits' in the minds of Young Adult Smokers" (Research International 1993, 1). Between 1990 and 1994, Philip Morris conducted "lifestyle studies" in at least fifteen countries across Asia, Europe, and the Middle East (Hafez and Ling 2005, 264).

This research identified strong correlations and convergences in lifestyles, attitudes and aspirations. Burnett described "todays young adults" as "the single most homogenous group in history" (Leo Burnett U.S.A. 1989). Common themes broadly reflected an American model of consumer society. They included "establishing own identity/separating from parents," "preparing for financial independence," and "independence and freedom" (Leo Burnett U.S.A. 1989).

These assumptions of a global community led to the development of a standardized global marketing campaign, administered by the Marlboro Worldwide Creative Review Committee. The first worldwide pool of Marlboro advertisements was released in the fall of 1993. This initiative was once again supported by a massive budget. In 1994, Marlboro had the biggest cigarette-advertising strategy in China. Once again, this campaign was extremely successful. By 2007, Marlboro had developed into the tenth most valuable brand (of any product) in the world, worth an estimated $US27 billion.

These global marketing strategies suggested that Burnett's mid-1950s vision of the Marlboro Man as "an almost universal symbol of admired masculinity" (Burnett) now resonated on a global scale. However, it was also the case that Marlboro's global marketing strategies did far more than transparently communicate shared, preexisting assumptions and expectations about lifestyle, gender, and identity. Rather, this centralized approach to global marketing was self-consciously designed to "push [the] Marlboro state of mind" (M-EEC 1993), to "restore the fantasy" (Philip Morris International) and, above all, to "educate" consumers into Marlboro's "core values" (Philip Morris International).

It was clear, in other words, that the international promotion of Marlboro was intrinsically linked not only to the export of cigarettes but also to the export of ideas and values. These values promoted the possibility of self-realization through consumption, but they were not timeless. They reflected a consumer culture that developed in the United States in the 1950s and 1960s. This was the real "Marlboro country."

SEE ALSO *Coca-Cola; Levi Strauss & Co.; Rock 'n' Roll*

BIBLIOGRAPHY

Brandt, Allan M. *The Cigarette Century: The Rise, Fall, and Deadly Persistence of the Product that Defined America.* New York: Basic Books, 2007.

Burnett, Leo. "Letter from Leo Burnett to Roger Greene, Advertising Director, Philip Morris and Co. Ltd., Inc."

January 7, 1955. Legacy Tobacco Documents Library, University of California, San Francisco. http://legacy.library. ucsf.edu/tid/brp93e00

Cohen, Lizabeth. *A Consumers' Republic: The Politics of Mass Consumption in Postwar America.* New York: Vintage, 2004.

Freeman, B., S. Chapman, and M. Rimmer. "Tobacco Control: Reports on Industry Activity from outside UCSF." eScholarship Repository, University of California, 2007.

Hafez, Navid, and Pamela M. Ling. "How Philip Morris Built Marlboro into a Global Brand for Young Adults: Implications for International Tobacco Control." *Tobacco Control* 14, 4 (2005): 262–271.

Kimmel, Michael S. *Manhood in America: A Cultural History.* 3rd ed. New York: Oxford University Press, 2012.

Leo Burnett Company, Inc. Advertising copy. December 12, 1955. Legacy Tobacco Documents Library, University of California, San Francisco. http://legacy.library.ucsf.edu/tid/xav65e00

Leo Burnett U.S.A., Research Department. *Global Generation: Young Adult Smokers around the World.* Prepared for Philip Morris U.S.A. New Product Division. November 20, 1989. Legacy Tobacco Documents Library, University of California, San Francisco. http://legacy.library.ucsf.edu/tid/dwq03e00

National Cancer Institute. *The Role of the Media in Promoting and Reducing Tobacco Use.* Tobacco Control Monograph No. 19. Edited by Ronald M. Davis et al. Bethesda, MD: US Department of Health and Human Services, National Institutes of Health, National Cancer Institute, 2008.

Philip Morris International. *Marlboro for the 90s and Beyond.* Undated. Legacy Tobacco Documents Library, University of California, San Francisco. http://legacy.library.ucsf.edu/tid/wuu32e00

PM-EEC. *Marlboro Creative Development Advertising Update.* Philip Morris. October 1993. Available from Legacy Tobacco Documents Library, University of California, San Francisco. http://legacy.library. ucsf.edu/tid/vzr22e00

Research International. *Philip Morris Asia: Research Discussion Paper, Marlboro Smokers Research.* March 1993. Legacy Tobacco Documents Library, University of California, San Francisco. http://legacy.library.ucsf.edu/tid/rcu19e00

Slotkin, Richard. *Gunfighter Nation: The Myth of the Frontier in Twentieth-Century America.* New York: Atheneum, 1992.

US Department of Health and Human Services. *Women and Smoking: A Report of the Surgeon General.* Rockville, MD: US Department of Health and Human Services, Public Health Service, Office of the Surgeon General, 2001.

Cameron White
Researcher
University of Technology, Sydney

MARSH, GEORGE PERKINS
1801–1882

George Perkins Marsh was the dean of the US diplomatic corps in Italy during the nineteenth century. His work there coincided with the pivotal years of the Risorgimento,

the movement for Italian unification. His success in planting, nurturing, and strengthening ties between Italy and the United States influenced his successors. He was a friend of President Abraham Lincoln and a strong supporter of the antislavery movement in the United States. A man of many talents and interests, he was also a pioneer in the field of ecology.

Marsh was born in Woodstock, Vermont, to a prominent family, and grew up immersed in the intellectual atmosphere of New England. His father, Charles Marsh, a former member of the US House of Representatives, owned a large personal library that helped to nurture his son's early passions for foreign languages and literatures. Despite weak health, Marsh graduated from Dartmouth College (1820) with highest honors,

George Perkins Marsh, US minister to the Kingdom of Italy, 1860s. As the dean of the US diplomatic corps in Italy during the nineteenth century, Marsh supported the movement for Italian unification and successfully nurtured and strengthened ties between Italy and the United States. © **EVERETT HISTORICAL/ SHUTTERSTOCK.COM**

having shown proficiency in twenty different languages. After further studies, he practiced law in Vermont.

With the benefit of personal connections in Washington, in 1843 Marsh was elected to the US Congress and subsequently was appointed a deputy for the Whig Party. During his first years in office, Marsh made important contributions to the founding of the Smithsonian Institution and to the reorganization of the Library of Congress, deftly applying his knowledge of geography, philology, and natural history. His peers took note, and Marsh attained a reputation as an eminent intellectual who could well represent the United States overseas. In 1849 President Zachary Taylor appointed Marsh as the US minister to the Ottoman Empire. On his journey to Constantinople in December, Marsh stopped in the major Italian cities. Later, he was introduced to Italian political figures, notably the Italian general and patriot Giuseppe Garibaldi, with whom he shared republican views. Their friendship kindled Marsh's great, lifelong interest in Italy and its history, and gained Garibaldi a measure of influence in the United States that would later benefit him greatly.

After dedicating his service in Constantinople to the cause of civil and religious toleration, in 1854 Marsh returned to Vermont because of ill health. He published studies on the expansion of fisheries, served as member of the state railway commission, and lectured on the origins of the English language at Columbia University.

In 1861, assenting to Marsh's expressed wish, President Abraham Lincoln appointed him to represent the United States in the newly established Kingdom of Italy. As minister there he observed the last phase of the unification process that had inspired American intellectuals and writers, and presented the importance of Italy's unification such that the United States was the first country to recognize the new nation. Simultaneously, Marsh was pushing Italian politicians to follow America's example in building a free country by keeping the church's role separate from the affairs of state. With the outbreak of the American Civil War, Marsh enlisted support for the Union cause from liberal Italian politicians such as Garibaldi, Italian prime minister Bettino Ricasoli (1809–1880), and King Victor Emmanuel II, who called a halt to trade with Confederate states. In 1861 Marsh persuaded Ricasoli to reject the king's request to serve as a mediator between Great Britain and the United States during the *Trent* Affair, a diplomatic crisis involving a British mail ship carrying two Confederate envoys.

In 1864 Marsh published *Man and Nature*, a pioneering book on ecology, in both the United States and Italy. In 1866 he demanded the extradition of John Surratt, an alleged accomplice in the assassination of Lincoln, who had fled to Italy, but the Italians refused.

In 1868 Marsh had greater success in stipulating important agreements between Italy and the United States on immigration.

Marsh's second wife, Caroline Crane, whom he married in 1839, supported him through difficult passages in his life, including the death of his son the same year as the assassination of Lincoln, as she later reported in her diaries. Marsh died during his first trip to Vallombrosa, near Florence, in 1882 and is buried in the Protestant cemetery of Rome. A keen observer of Italian society and politics, he is remembered for his skills of diplomacy as well as his studies in philology and ecology.

SEE ALSO *Garibaldi, Giuseppe; Lincoln, Abraham; Risorgimento*

BIBLIOGRAPHY

Dolling, Lisa M., ed. *George Perkins Marsh: An American for All Seasons.* Hoboken: Stevens Institute of Technology, College of Arts and Letters, 2013.

Ducci, Lucia, ed. *George P. Marsh Correspondence: Images of Italy, 1861–1881.* Madison, NJ: Fairleigh Dickinson University Press, 2012.

Marraro, Howard R. *American Opinion on the Unification of Italy, 1846–1861.* New York: Columbia University Press, 1932.

Lucia Ducci
Lecturer
University of Massachusetts, Amherst

MARSHALL, GEORGE C.
SEE *Marshall Plan.*

MARSHALL PLAN

As 1947 began, the nations of Europe found themselves struggling with food and fuel shortages along with crippling winter weather. Two years after the end of World War II (1939–1945), America's European allies were feeling anything but triumphant. It was in reaction to this crisis that America launched the Marshall Plan. Named for General George Marshall (1880–1959), President Harry Truman's (1884–1972) secretary of state, who had gained fame in World War II as Army chief of staff, the Marshall Plan eventually cost the United States $13 billion (roughly $579 billion today) and marked the beginning of foreign aid as we now know it.

During and after World War I (1914–1918), America had provided relief to European nations faced with food shortages, but the Marshall Plan was different.

It was not formulated as an act of charity. Its true economic model was the New Deal. The aim of the Marshall Plan was to get Western Europe back on its feet by stimulating employment and production. In 1933 at Fort Screven in Georgia and Fort Moultrie in South Carolina, Marshall had helped run New Deal Civilian Conservation Corps (CCC) camps, and he was impressed with the fresh start the CCC gave out-of-work men during the Great Depression.

The Marshall Plan had its birth in the June 5, 1947, speech that Marshall delivered at Harvard University's commencement. "The rehabilitation of the economic structure of Europe quite evidently will require a much longer time and greater effort than had been foreseen," Marshall told his Harvard audience. "It is logical that the United States should do whatever it is able to do to assist in the return of normal economic health in the world, without which there can be no political stability and no assured peace."

At home, the Marshall Plan relied on bipartisan support from Republicans, who controlled Congress, and in Arthur Vandenberg (1884–1951), the Republican chairman of the Senate Foreign Relations Committee, Marshall found the legislative partner he needed. Abroad, the Marshall Plan also depended on cooperation. Ernest Bevin (1881–1951), Britain's foreign secretary, compared the Marshall Plan to a lifeline to sinking men (Mills 2008). The Marshall planners never, however, treated the nations of Europe as if they were dependents asking for a handout. Western Europe's governments were asked to decide how they wished to allocate American aid, and as Marshall Plan partners, rather than mere beneficiaries, they were instrumental in making the Marshall Plan run efficiently.

Marshall worked hard to get his plan accepted by Congress and to overcome the objections of those who resented America focusing on Europe rather than on its own peacetime economy. Marshall testified on Capitol Hill and travelled the country explaining his plan. His campaigning worked. The Marshall Plan won Senate approval 69 to 17 and House approval 329 to 74.

On April 3, 1948, President Truman signed the legislation making the Marshall Plan law, and eleven days later, the victory ship *John H. Quick* began taking on the grain it would bring to Bordeaux, France. The speed with which the Marshall Plan began would typify its operation in the years to come, and so would the choice of much needed grain as a first shipment. In coming to the aid of Europe, America resisted the temptation to dump unused surpluses abroad. Marshall Plan aid was targeted. During the first fifteen months of the plan, food, feed, and fertilizers constituted 39 percent of American shipments, raw materials and semifinished products 26 percent, and fuel 16 percent. In Norway, fishermen received new nets;

in Holland, construction workers got the steel needed to rebuild docks; in England, factory workers got carbon black, the toughening agent used for making tire treads.

Under its first administrator, Paul Hoffman (1891–1974), a Republican who previously headed the Studebaker Corporation, the Marshall Plan became a model of efficiency, avoiding the waste and corruption that so often accompany aid programs. The Korean War, which began on June 25, 1950, paved the way for the end of the Marshall Plan. America could not afford to rearm itself and pay for the Marshall Plan. Nonetheless, by December 1951, when the Marshall Plan officially concluded, it was an undeniable success. Industrial production in Europe was 64 percent and food production was 24 percent above the 1947 levels.

In 1953, Marshall was awarded the Nobel Peace Prize. It was an international high point for him and the United States. The Marshall Plan had done what the end of World War II could not: laid the groundwork for a stable postwar Western Europe that even had room at its economic center for a changed West Germany, helped by $3 billion in Marshall Plan aid.

The Marshall Plan was crucial to America's success in the Cold War. One of the goals of the Marshall Plan had been to draw the nations of Western Europe into a bloc that could stand up to the Soviet Union, and in short order that transition took place. The formation of the North Atlantic Treaty Organization (NATO) in 1949 was a direct result of the stability and trust the Marshall Plan fostered, and so, too, was the decline of Europe's powerful post–World War II communist parties, which followed the lead of the Soviet Union and opposed Marshall Plan aid. In 1946, the Communist Party won 29 percent of the popular vote in France, and in Italy the Communist Party and Socialist Party won nearly 40 percent of the popular vote, but Marshall Plan aid and the absence of any comparable help from the Soviet Union soon made anti-Americanism politically untenable in Western Europe.

SEE ALSO *Cold War; Truman, Harry S.*

BIBLIOGRAPHY

Behrman, Greg. *The Most Noble Adventure: The Marshall Plan and the Time When America Helped Save Europe.* New York: Free Press, 2007.

Marshall, George C. "The Marshall Plan Speech." June 5, 1947. http://marshallfoundation.org/marshall/the-marshall-plan/marshall-plan-speech/

Mills, Nicolaus. *Winning the Peace: The Marshall Plan and America's Coming of Age as a Superpower.* Hoboken, NJ: Wiley, 2008.

Nicolaus Mills
Professor of American Studies
Sarah Lawrence College

MARX, KARL
1818–1883

In the twentieth century, Karl Marx was the world's most influential philosopher after his ideas became the governing dogma in nations encompassing more than one-quarter of the world's population. First Russia and then other nations in Europe, Asia, Africa, and Latin America fell to revolutionaries or conquerors acting in his name. Rooted in a materialist philosophy and a critique of the abuses of capitalism, Marxism explains politics, society, and culture in economic terms. According to Marx, history progresses through class struggle between the haves, the have-nots, and those who aspire to have more. In Marx's time, the industrial middle class had largely supplanted the older agriculture-based aristocracy as the ruling elite. The working class would eventually overthrow the middle class in Marxist teleology. After the workers owned the means of production, social inequality would dissolve, the state would wither away, and a new society would emerge in which every person would have the opportunity to follow his own desires and use his leisure time creatively.

In that end time, individuality could flourish. However, in the Bolshevik interpretation of Marx that became the basis for communist regimes throughout the world, the collective as shaped by economic relations was the prime mover of human events. The rights of individuals meant nothing if they stood in the way of building a new world.

MARXISM IN LATE NINETEENTH- AND EARLY TWENTIETH-CENTURY AMERICA

Although Marx never visited the United States, and discovered the models for his theories in British, French, and German economic, political, and philosophical history, he found an American audience from early on. In 1848, Charles Anderson Dana (1819–1897), a follower of the utopian socialist Charles Fourier (1772–1837) and an associate of pundit Horace Greeley (1811–1872), met Marx in Cologne, Germany. The encounter led to Marx's role from 1852 to 1862 as the London-based European correspondent for America's most widely circulated newspaper, the *New York Daily Tribune*. Marxists were evident in some of the earliest labor organizations in the United States, including the Communist Club founded in 1857 in New York by a German immigrant, Friedrich Sorge (1828–1906). The Sorge group became affiliated with Marx's International Workingmen's Association, a confederation of left-socialist political parties later known as the First International. As a result of disputes with anarchist members and other dissidents, Marx transferred the First International's grand council from London to New York in 1872 and placed Sorge in charge. The First International continued to be torn by disputes in the United States between Marxists and followers of the German socialist Ferdinand Lassalle (1825–1864), and the group disintegrated by 1876.

Sorge's failure to capitalize on widespread poverty and labor unrest was emblematic of American Marxism, which tended to draw adherents from immigrant groups and engage in protracted sectarian disputes with little effect on social conditions. America's leading Marxist in the late nineteenth and early twentieth centuries, Daniel De Leon (1852–1914), led the Socialist Labor Party from 1890 through 1914 and published exegeses of Marx that paralleled the writings of Russian Bolshevik leader Vladimir Lenin (1870–1924). He was cold-shouldered by the larger Social Democratic Party, whose cofounder, Eugene Debs (1855–1926), drew his ideas from eclectic sources and spoke of socialism with an American accent.

Marxists gained influence over some labor unions but were thwarted by Samuel Gompers (1850–1924), co-founder of the American Federation of Labor. Rejecting revolution, Gompers strove to gain organized labor a seat at the table alongside corporate leaders, and worked within the existing democratic system to elect officials sympathetic to labor. Gompers was a pragmatist. Focused on improving the present through better wages and working conditions, he gave no thought to any future utopias.

The rigorous systems of thought and historical laws proposed by Marxism also ran aground against the distinctively American philosophical movement called pragmatism. The leading early figure in pragmatism, William James (1842–1910), scarcely mentioned Marx in his writings. The pragmatist psychologist and educational reformer John Dewey (1859–1952) eventually became honorary chairman of the Congress for Cultural Freedom, an international organization of anticommunist intellectuals. By defining the good as that which works, and measuring the usefulness of an idea by what it achieves, pragmatism offered American reformers an alternative to Marxism and a rationale for achieving gradual change.

Marxism had greater appeal in societies where the working or lower classes had little faith in social mobility. In the United States, the class system was more fluid, and opportunities for advancement were evident. The frontier remained open for settlement through the end of the nineteenth century, and the frontier mythos, which shaped American popular culture through the twentieth century, was antithetical to Marxist collectivism. At the height of the Great Depression in the 1930s, the chief standard bearer for American Marxism, the Communist Party USA, numbered no more than one hundred thousand members.

THE COLD WAR

As the Cold War began in the late 1940s, the United States and its Western European allies found themselves in conflict for global ascendance with the Bolshevik Marxists of the Soviet Union, its satellites in Eastern Europe, and its Chinese and Asian allies. The Cold War took place on battlefields in Korea, Vietnam, and other developing nations but was also a war of ideas. The political and economic systems built on espoused Marxist principles were antinomical to the democratic and capitalist principles of the West, and the United States based its self-image and reputation throughout the world as the freedom-loving antithesis of Bolshevik Marxism. In the United States, the British philosopher Adam Smith (1723–1790), author of *An Inquiry into the Nature and Causes of the Wealth of Nations* (1776), was regarded as the prophet of free enterprise. Marx, whose magnum opus, *Das Kapital* (1867, 1885, 1894), was often cited but seldom read, was anathema.

Marx's reputation among the American intelligentsia was refurbished in light of the New Left, the upheavals of the 1960s, and the counterculture's quest for alternative ideas of meaning and social organization. Erich Fromm's *Marx's Concept of Man* (1961) was a turning point for exploring the philosopher's concern for the realization of human potential and satisfaction through conscious, self-directed activity. A humanistic Marx was uncovered behind the quasi-scientific dogma of the Bolsheviks. Many intellectuals who came of age in the 1960s embraced the thinking of unconventional Marxists, such as the social philosophers Herbert Marcuse (1898–1979), who stressed the liberating potential of love, and Jürgen Habermas (b. 1929), who critiqued the social construction of science. It was argued that Marx might not have been a good Marxist in the nations that were ruled according to his ideology. After the 1970s, Marxism became a root of structuralism, which studied the facets of culture and society in terms of their relationship to overarching structures.

EARLY TWENTY-FIRST-CENTURY REASSESSMENT

By the 1990s, the collapse of the Soviet bloc, the substitution of state capitalism for communist economics in China, and the rise of a capitalist global economy led most observers to relegate Marxism to the dustbin of history. However, the worldwide Great Recession (2008) and the debt problems faced by many nations, coupled with the shrinking of the American middle class due to loss of industry, corporate consolidation, the outsourcing of jobs, and other structural changes in the economy, have emboldened some to employ Marxism as a tool of social criticism or as a blueprint for an alternative to a future dominated by transnational financial interests.

Marx's appeal remains rooted in the systemic, totalizing nature of his theories. For some, Marxism has afforded an intellectual framework for categorizing social phenomena. Others have embraced it as a surrogate religion. In the twenty-first century, Marx continues to provide an enduring critique of capitalism and consumer culture.

SEE ALSO *AFL-CIO: Labor's Foreign Policy; Anarchism; Exceptionalism; Haymarket Bombing; International Labor Organization; Secularization; Socialism*

BIBLIOGRAPHY

Appelbaum, Richard P. *Karl Marx*. Newberry Park, CA: Sage, 1988.

Bell, Daniel. *Marxian Socialism in the United States*. Ithaca, NY: Cornell University Press, 1996.

Gouldner, Alvin W. *The Two Marxisms: Contradictions and Anomalies in the Development of Theory*. New York: Oxford University Press, 1980.

Glen Jeansonne
Professor of History
University of Wisconsin–Milwaukee

David Luhrssen
Editor
Shepherd Express

MARX BROTHERS

The Marx Brothers were an influential and anarchic comedy and musical act whose performing career covered the 1920s to the 1950s. They moved from vaudeville to Broadway to movies and later, both individually and together, to radio and television. The Marx Brothers found their greatest fame with cinema.

Silent comedies from the United States held great influence in the global cinema market and played a role in major experimental artistic and philosophical movements in Europe in the early twentieth century. Composed of four biological brothers who sported the stage names and personae of Groucho (Julius Marx, 1890–1977), Chico (Leonard Marx, 1887–1961), Harpo (Adolph Marx, 1888–1964), and Zeppo (Herbert Marx, 1901–1979), the Marx Brothers carried this cinematic influence on European thought from silent to sound comedy. They were much loved and admired by the surrealists and the European avant-garde. Antonin Artaud (1896–1948), Luis Buñuel (1900–1983), and other international artists sang their praises in early reviews of their films, recognizing in the brothers kindred spirits who shared their assault on rationality. The Marx Brothers extended to the United States the *fumisme* aesthetic practiced in nineteenth-century France, which influenced the avant-garde (North 2009, 7–9). These sensibilities displayed an almost mechanical negation of artistic and communicative values, opting for maximum noise in the communications message through ridicule and nonsense.

The surrealist painter and filmmaker Salvador Dalí (1904–1989) especially revered the Marx Brothers, writing a screenplay for them titled *Giraffes on Horseback Salad* (1937), drawing pictures of Harpo complete with lobster headgear, and photographing the brothers. Dalí called the Marx Brothers films "the summit of the evolution of comic cinema," because their "entertaining schizophrenias" led to a "true and palpable lyrical amazement" (Dalí 2007, 77). Surrealism in Europe was revolutionary; in the United States, in contrast, it was largely domesticated in and through popular culture. The Marx Brothers revealed a chaotic, antiauthoritarian stance much in the spirit of European surrealism and dadaism, neatly summed up in the refrain to a song Groucho performs in the film *Horse Feathers* (1932): "Whatever it is, I'm against it."

The Marx Brothers' engagement with surrealism was as much linguistic as it was visual. It is in this way that they most align with the political and social agendas of European surrealists. Their characters staged explicit relationships with issues of class, race, and ethnicity as barriers within the United States, relationships often marked through language. The Marx Brothers place themselves in an anarchic relationship to the dominant language of the United States, and each brother provides a position along a continuum of undermining English and taking advantage of the elasticity of language generally. Each stakes out a position within the immigrant's relation to the linguistic conformity that all immigrants must endure (Beach 2002, 23–46). Groucho exemplifies the overachieving and rapid-fire mastery of the language, Chico the inadvertently punning creole of mock Italian-English, and Harpo the extreme position of silence, using gestures, noises, and objects to communicate. Zeppo, who left the group after the earliest films, often stood as the paradigm of mainstream white Anglo-Saxon Protestant culture, and thus played the "straight" (nonfunny) brother. Zeppo became the foil of normalcy around which the other three brothers could perform their deviation. All meaning is undermined at every turn. Facile and eloquent as Groucho is, he generates non sequiturs and discursive leaps that make a mockery of mastery, and he is easily overrun by the rampant chaos of the other two, showing how primal forces trump those of polite society.

In the latter part of the nineteenth and early twentieth centuries, the United States experienced the large-scale arrivals of newer immigrant groups. The US Census Bureau employed rather slippery taxonomies for these new groups, which made fitting into the melting pot a matter of survival. Alongside this, a literature and aesthetic of "passing" (as white and Christian, along with gender preference) emerged. The Marx Brothers, in their standard character personae playing different roles in films (e.g., Julius Marx playing Groucho playing Rufus T. Firefly in *Duck Soup* [1933]), performed the malleability of identity in a staggeringly complex manner. The performativity of filling social slots exploded in their combustive films.

The Marx Brothers' effect on intellectual and artistic, as well as political, thought was evident at the time. After Dalí gave Harpo a harp made with barbed-wire strings and tuned with cutlery, Harpo sent Dalí a photo of himself dressed in character, with bandages on his fingers. The Italian premier Benito Mussolini (1883–1945) banned *Duck Soup* for its antimilitary, antiwar, antination message. And the brothers' influence continued throughout the twentieth century and into the twenty-first. Frequent allusions to their work can be found in contemporary cinema, ranging from the art-house films of Terry Gilliam to Japanese anime. Every major American comic, from Lucille Ball to Woody Allen to Robin Williams, as well as the UK-based troupe Monty Python, pays homage to them. Every child who has seen a Bugs Bunny cartoon has seen an animated version of Groucho, with a carrot instead of his trademark cigar. Indeed, Groucho's abstracted features (bushy eyebrows, round glasses, greasepaint moustache, and cigar) have become the very icon of US comedy around the world. Most eloquent perhaps is Andy Warhol's 1980 series of prints titled *Ten Portraits of Jews of the Twentieth Century*, which includes a portrait of the brothers along with Franz Kafka and Albert Einstein.

SEE ALSO *Hollywood; Minstrelsy; Whiteness*

BIBLIOGRAPHY

Adamson, Joe. *Groucho, Harpo, Chico, and Sometimes Zeppo: A History of the Marx Brothers and a Satire on the Rest of the World.* New York: Simon and Schuster, 1973.

Beach, Christopher. *Class, Language, and American Film Comedy.* Cambridge, UK, and New York: Cambridge University Press, 2002.

Bishop, Ryan. *Comedy and Cultural Critique in American Film.* Edinburgh, UK: Edinburgh University Press, 2013.

Dalí, Salvador. "Short Critical History of Cinema." In *Dalí and Film*, edited by Matthew Gale, 75–77. London: Tate, 2007.

Mills, Joseph, ed. *A Century of the Marx Brothers.* Newcastle, UK: Cambridge Scholars, 2007.

North, Michael. *Machine-Age Comedy.* Oxford and New York: Oxford University Press, 2009.

Ryan Bishop
Professor of Global Art and Politics
Winchester School of Art, University of Southampton, UK

McCARTHYISM

Against the background of the Cold War and in response to recommendations made by the Presidential Commission on Employee Loyalty, established in November 1946, President Harry S. Truman (1884–1972) issued an executive order in March 1947 calling for an immediate investigation into the loyalty and intentions of every person entering civilian employment in any department or agency of the executive branch of the government. Those already holding positions were to be scrutinized by the Federal Bureau of Investigation (FBI), their fate resting essentially on the decision of their department heads, that is, those who were willing to pledge personal responsibility for their subordinates. Done generally in moderation, the procedure passed over millions of employees, with only a few thousand closely examined. The final effort resulted in several hundred dismissals, mostly based on guilt by association. Of course, the real targets were Communists and Communist sympathizers.

FEAR OF COMMUNISM AND SOVIET ESPIONAGE

To parry accusations that his administration was "soft" on Communism (mainly the repercussion of establishment support for former State Department employee Alger Hiss [1904–1996], who, during two highly publicized trials, was found guilty of perjury in early 1950), Truman went a step further in January 1949 when the nation's leading twelve Communists—later, eleven—were called to trial on charges of violating the Smith Act of 1940, which made it a criminal offence to advocate the forceful overthrow of the government. Convicted, the eleven challenged the constitutionality of the Smith Act. In 1951, in *Dennis et al. v. US*, the Supreme Court upheld the law, with justices Hugo Black (1886–1971) and William Douglas (1898–1980) dissenting. Meanwhile, in September 1950, Congress passed, over the president's veto, the McCarran Act, providing for, among other things, the registration of Communists and Communist-front organizations, as well as for the internment of Communists during national emergencies.

In this atmosphere, it was learned that Dr. Klaus Fuchs (1911–1988), a German-born scientist working for the British and someone who had been deeply involved in the Manhattan Project and postwar atomic research, had provided atomic secrets to the Soviets; furthermore, he implicated a number of Americans, including Julius (1918–1953) and Ethel Rosenberg (1915–1953), who had transmitted classified information to Moscow from 1942 to 1947. This much the public knew, but there was much the public did not know. By virtue of the so-called VENONA transcripts—translations of some three thousand messages sent between Moscow and Soviet intelligence stations in the 1940s—the Truman administration also knew that the Russians had been running a good many spies in the United States in the 1930s and 1940s. In fact, these documents paint a picture of a golden age of Soviet espionage.

The guilt of many Americans had been proved beyond reasonable doubt: atomic spies Julius and Ethel Rosenberg (both of whom were executed in June 1953), State Department officials Alger Hiss and Harry Dexter White (1892–1948), and many others. These events, together with the "loss of China"—the defeat of Jiang Jieshi's pro-Western forces by Mao Zedong's Chinese Communist Party in 1949—and the news just months earlier, in August, that the Soviets had broken the US atomic monopoly, gave extremists their chance.

THE RISE OF JOSEPH McCARTHY

One of these extremists was Joseph R. McCarthy (1908–1957), a Republican senator from Wisconsin. McCarthy declared in a speech at Wheeling, West Virginia, in early 1950 that 205 (later revised to twenty-seven) Communists had infiltrated the State Department. Though McCarthy's accusations gained wide publicity, a special subcommittee of the Senate Foreign Relations Committee found the allegations to be baseless. Despite these findings, the senator's accusations increased, as did the partisan attacks against the Truman administration, in the process taking on some of the most prominent American patriots, such as George C. Marshall (1880–1959). Before McCarthyism would spend itself in 1954, incalculable damage would be done to the careers and lives of many innocent Americans because the loyalty oath overshadowed common sense.

McCarthy, perhaps the most formidable, gifted, and hated American demagogue of the century, proceeded to step up his crusade to purify the American body politic of any and all traces of Communism, real or otherwise. Though few would care to admit it, McCarthy had behind him, at the height of his power, many of the nation's most respected politicians, Republicans as well as some conservative Democrats. The powerful Hearst newspaper network was also solidly behind him. More significantly, according to a Gallup poll of January 15, 1954, 50 percent of the American people had a "favorable opinion" of McCarthy. At the root of McCarthyism lay American disillusionment with the aftermath of World War II, particularly growing evidence of Soviet betrayal of the lofty aims of the war in Eastern Europe and, on a more sinister level, the discovery of evidence of Soviet espionage in the United States.

THE EISENHOWER ADMINISTRATION'S RESPONSE TO McCARTHY

Upon assuming the presidency in 1953, Dwight Eisenhower (1890–1969) showed little inclination publicly to confront the senator, although it is equally clear the president harbored a strong dislike for the man and his methods. In the opening months of the administration, McCarthy attacked the presumably subversive elements in the Voice of America and the Overseas Book Programs, demanding the removal of works even remotely associated with Communists. Without mentioning McCarthy by name, Eisenhower warned against joining the book burners. McCarthy also sought unsuccessfully to stop the nomination of Charles E. Bohlen (1904–1974) as ambassador to the Soviet Union on the grounds of his close connections with the foreign policies of Franklin D. Roosevelt (1882–1945) and Truman. As chairman of the Senate Permanent Investigating Subcommittee of the Government Operations Committee, McCarthy then conducted a series of hearings, lasting to 1954, on the

role of the presumed Communist influence in government and in other areas. Congressional committees simultaneously investigated Communism in the fields of education and entertainment. Again, careers in and out of Washington were ruined as a result of accusation and guilt by association.

In early 1954, the administration finally found itself forced to take a tougher public position against McCarthy. When the army failed to take punitive action against a soldier accused of Communist activities who had been granted an honorable discharge, McCarthy inveighed against the major's commandant as a coddler of Communists and demanded that he be relieved of his command. After some hesitation in the direction of placating the senator, Secretary of the Army Robert T.

Sen. Joseph R. McCarthy, with attorney Roy Cohn to his right, during the McCarthy hearings in the US Senate. *As chairman of a Senate investigations subcommittee, McCarthy conducted a series of hearings, lasting to 1954, on the role of the presumed Communist influence in government and other areas, while other committees investigated the fields of education and entertainment. Careers in and out of Washington were ruined as a result of accusation and guilt by association.* BETTMANN/CORBIS

Stevens (1899–1983) remonstrated that he would "never accede to the abuse of Army personnel … never accede to their brow-beating and humiliation" (Siracusa and Coleman 2002, 144).

THE ARMY-McCARTHY HEARINGS

The stage was now set for the final act in the senator's crusade against Communism. After an investigation of Communist subversion at Fort Monmouth, New Jersey, in late 1953 and early 1954, the Senate Permanent Subcommittee on Investigations, with McCarthy in the role of a witness, convened in April to examine allegations made by the secretary of the army that McCarthy himself and the subcommittee's counsel, Roy M. Cohn (1927–1986), sought by improper means to obtain preferential treatment for a committee consultant, Private G. David Schine (1927–1996). The subcommittee also agreed to look into McCarthy's countercharges that Secretary of the Army Stevens and several of his associates had engaged in a campaign to discourage further investigation of alleged Communist subversion at Forth Monmouth. The proceedings were televised over a period of thirty-five days, lasting from April 22 to June 17; the featured speakers in what soon came to be called the Army-McCarthy hearings were the senator and Special Army Counsel Joseph N. Welch (1890–1960).

In a nation increasingly addicted to television viewing, the Army-McCarthy hearings became compelling drama, the audience at times reaching twenty million people. After thirty-five days of public exposure, the American people had seen enough to be persuaded that McCarthy, sinister-looking with his black, bushy eyebrows and five o'clock shadow, had indeed used improper means in trying to get preferred treatment for Private Schine, despite the subcommittee's majority report exonerating the senator from charges of improper influence. McCarthy's popularity among the American public plunged from 50 percent to 34 percent, according to a June 1954 Gallup poll. Some, including Republican committee member Senator Charles E. Potter (1916–1979) of Michigan, were convinced that the principal accusation of each side was borne out and that perjury had indeed been committed.

CENSURE BY THE SENATE

In August, the Senate established a select committee to investigate McCarthy's own activities in the Senate. On December 2, 1954, McCarthy became only the fourth member of the Senate in the history of the United States to be formally "censured," with a final vote of sixty-two to twenty-two. The resolution of condemnation—the word *censure* was not used in the official language—found that McCarthy's actions were "contrary to senatorial ethics and tended to bring the Senate into dishonor and disrepute, to obstruct the constitutional process of the Senate, and to impair its dignity." His own reputation in tatters, McCarthy's influence rapidly declined until his death in May 1957. The political witch hunt led by McCarthy had finally come to an end.

SEE ALSO *Cold War; Robeson, Paul Leroy; Spies and Espionage*

BIBLIOGRAPHY

Andrew, Christopher, and Vasili Mitrokhin. *The Sword and the Shield: The Mitrokhin Archive and the Secret History of the KGB.* New York: Basic Books, 1999.

Greenstein, Fred. *The Hidden-Hand Presidency: Eisenhower as Leader.* New York: Basic Books, 1982.

Haynes, John Earl, and Harvey Klehr. *Venona: Decoding Soviet Espionage in America.* New Haven, CT: Yale University Press, 1999.

Haynes, John Earl, and Harvey Klehr. *In Denial: Historians, Communism, and Espionage.* San Francisco: Encounter, 2003.

Oshinsky, David M. *A Conspiracy So Immense: The World of Joe McCarthy.* New York: Free Press, 1983.

Schrecker, Ellen. *The Age of McCarthyism: A Brief History with Documents.* 2nd ed. New York: Palgrave, 2002.

Siracusa, Joseph M. and David G. Coleman, *Depression to Cold War: A History of America from Herbert Hoover to Ronald Reagan.* Westport, CT: Praeger, 2002.

US Senate. Senate Resolution 301: Censure of Senator Joseph McCarthy. 1954. http://www.ourdocuments.gov/doc.php?flash=true&doc=86

Weinstein, Allen, and Alexander Vassiliev. *The Haunted Wood: Soviet Espionage in America—the Stalin Era.* New York: Random House, 1999.

West, Nigel. *Venona: The Greatest Secret of the Cold War.* London: HarperCollins, 1999.

Joseph Siracusa
Professor of Human Security and International Diplomacy
Royal Melbourne Institute of Technology University

McDONALD'S

The early history of McDonald's under the McDonald brothers is well known, as is its meteoric growth in the United States after Ray Kroc (1902–1984) took over beginning in the mid-1950s and made it the national and international success that it is today. Its revenues in 2013 were $28.1 billion (greater than the gross domestic product [GDP] of Ecuador), with a net profit of $5.6 billion. McDonald's has well over 35,000 restaurants in 128 countries throughout the world, serving nearly 70 million customers a day.

As late as the mid-1980s, only 25 percent of McDonald's restaurants were outside the United States; today, about 60 percent of McDonald's restaurants are beyond US borders. The majority of the new McDonald's restaurants are being opened overseas. Well over half of McDonald's revenue comes from its overseas operations.

As of 2014, the international leader, by far, was Japan, with 3,096 McDonald's restaurants. There were 1,800 restaurants in China in 2014, and a major expansion is likely to occur there in the future. France, the bastion of fine food, has become the second most profitable market in the world for McDonald's (the United States is first). As of 2013, there were 414 McDonald's in Russia: it is the company's fastest growing market. McDonald's plans to open many more restaurants in the former Soviet Union and in the vast new territory in Eastern Europe that has been laid bare to the invasion of fast-food restaurants. Although there have been recent setbacks for McDonald's in Great Britain, that nation remains the "fast-food capital of Europe."

THE McDONALD'S BUSINESS MODEL

McDonald's created a brilliant business model that has proven highly profitable to both the corporation and those who own its franchises (although McDonald's does own some of its restaurants). In comparison to most of the early (and less successful) franchisers, McDonald's demanded little out-front money from franchisees and relied instead on a percentage of each franchisee's sales. This kept franchisees under the corporation's control and ensured a steady and growing flow of money to the parent company as the franchises grew increasingly successful and the number of franchises exploded. McDonald's retained this approach as the number of restaurants outside the United States grew and spread into many countries worldwide. This allowed McDonald's to retain great control while also according a measure of independence to franchisees throughout the world. While these franchisees operate on the basis of the same principles and offer many of the same products as those sold in the United States, they are able to deviate, at least slightly, to accommodate local cultures and local tastes in food.

The model created by McDonald's (based on those of other industries, such as the automobile assembly line) has proven attractive and successful in not only the United States but much of the world (Ritzer 2015). That model is based on four abstract principles that dominate not only what workers but also customers do in the restaurant. The first is *efficiency*, or finding and using the most direct means to whatever end is desired. Workers cook burgers efficiently, and customers queue up for their food. The second principle is *predictability*, or the fact that settings, products, and service are more or less the same from one time and place to another. Workers do and say (following scripts) what is expected of them, and this makes for a high degree of predictability not only for them, but also for customers who are themselves led to behave in predictable ways in the restaurants. Third, there is a great deal of *calculability*, especially the emphasis on quantity (e.g., the *Big* Mac) rather than quality. Employee performance is tightly measured and customers expect a lot of food for what seems like a small amount of money. Finally, great *control* is exercised over both workers and consumers. Nonhuman technologies, such as largely automatic french-fry machines, control workers, while drive-throughs exert control over customers (e.g., they must take their garbage with them).

This is a highly rational system (Weber 1968), but it has its irrational consequences. The turnover rate is high, as workers tend to leave after only a few months on the job. Customers grow accustomed to mediocre food that has a variety of negative environmental and health consequences (obesity, diabetes, etc.). In spite of the irrationalities, McDonald's has been a huge success both economically and as a model not only for many other restaurants and other types of chains, but also for the organization of everything from universities (Hayes and Wynyard 2002) to churches (Drane 2000).

McDonald's principles meet occidental standards of rationality and, as a result, the chain has been highly successful in the West. However, it has also been successful in many other parts of the world that are not usually considered rational from a Western perspective. McDonald's rational principles, built into an entire system, can be lifted out of the United States and deposited in many different contexts. It has proven to be viable, and has come to be accepted, in societies throughout the world.

FACTORS CONTRIBUTING TO GLOBAL SUCCESS

Looked at from another perspective (Ritzer 2007), McDonald's success, especially globally, is attributable to three factors. First, the McDonald's system, its restaurants, and its products are *centrally conceived* largely at corporate headquarters in Oak Brook, Illinois. While there is some differentiation in various parts of the world, there is great uniformity because of the centralization in the way the system is conceived. Local McDonald's are limited in their ability to alter that conception and forbidden to come up with one of their own.

Second, McDonald's restaurants throughout the world are not simply conceived (and reconceived) centrally. A variety of *centralized controls* are also exercised over local operations everywhere in the world. For example, the regular flow of computerized data to headquarters allows McDonald's to assess business anywhere in the world and, if necessary, to close down restaurants that are not performing

A McDonald's restaurant on Paris's Champs Elysées, near the Arc de Triomphe, 2008. France, the bastion of fine food, is the second most profitable market in the world for McDonald's (after the United States). In 2015, well over half of McDonald's revenue came from its overseas operations. **ALASTAIR MILLER/BLOOMBERG/GETTY IMAGES**

up to standards. Another example is Hamburger University in the United States, with branches elsewhere in the world, which permits managers to be trained in the same way in the same basic principles. Those principles can then be taught to employees anywhere in the world.

Third, McDonald's seeks to offer products that are, as much as possible, *devoid of distinctive content.* That is, they are simple, generic products (hamburgers, french fries, Chicken McNuggets) that can easily be replicated globally. To put it another way, they lack the distinctive content of, say, Indonesian *rijsttafel* or platters of Ethiopian food eaten with one's hands with *injera* (a kind of bread). There is little in any McDonald's meal to startle, let alone offend, most palates. While we think of McDonald's offerings as very American, the fact is that many other cultures have their own variants on hamburgers, fried potatoes, and fried chicken.

GLOBAL PERCEPTION OF McDONALD'S

While McDonald's has succeeded globally because what it offers does not offend the sensibilities of those in many cultures, it has run into strong resistance in some parts of the world. Among the best known are the McLibel group in Great Britain, José Bové and his supporters in France, and, most notably, the Slow Food Movement in Italy. McDonald's has had to adapt to local cultures in various ways, most notably by offering its version of a limited number of local foods. Nevertheless, most of the products offered elsewhere in the world are much the same as those on offer in the United States.

Eating at McDonald's has become a "sign" that, among other things, one is in tune with the contemporary lifestyle. To the degree that America is seen as the center of that lifestyle, eating at McDonald's elsewhere in the world associates people with the modernity that is closely associated with the United States. At the opening of the first McDonald's in Moscow in 1990, one journalist described the franchise as the "ultimate icon of Americana" (Keller 1990). McDonald's has in some ways and to some people become even more important than the United States itself. For example, an Israeli teenager was disappointed when the person officiating at the opening of a new restaurant turned out to be the ambassador from the United States and not a McDonald's official (Friedman 1999).

THE BIG MAC INDEX

A significant indicator of the global success of McDonald's is the annual Big Mac Index, published, tongue in cheek, by *The Economist*. It shows the purchasing power of various currencies around the world based on the local price (in dollars) of a Big Mac. The Big Mac is used because it is a uniform commodity sold in many different nations. In the 2013 survey, a Big Mac in the United States cost an average of $4.20; in China, it was $2.44; and in Switzerland, it cost $6.81. This measure indicates, at least roughly, where the cost of living is high or low, as well as which currencies are undervalued (China) and overvalued (Switzerland). Although *The Economist* is calculating the Big Mac Index only half-seriously, the index demonstrates the ubiquity and importance of McDonald's around the world. Alternatively, *The Economist* measured economic disparity by comparing the labor time required for the average workers in various cities to earn enough to purchase a Big Mac. The least amount of labor time—twelve minutes—was required in Chicago, while workers in Nairobi had to work for nearly 160 minutes to be able to buy a Big Mac.

McDONALD'S IN CONTEMPORARY SOCIETY

McDonald's meshes well with a variety of changes occurring in American society and increasingly in many other parts of the world. For example, the number of single-parent families and the number of women working outside the home have increased greatly. As a result, there is less likely to be anyone with the time to shop for food, prepare it, and clean up afterward. There may not even be time (or money), at least during the workweek, for meals at traditional restaurants. The speed and efficiency of a fast-food meal fits in well with these realities.

McDonald's also thrives in a society that emphasizes mobility, especially by automobile. The most likely devotees of the fast-food restaurant—teenagers and young adults in the United States (and elsewhere)—now have greater access to automobiles. And they need automobiles to frequent most fast-food restaurants, except those found in the hearts of large cities.

The increasing affluence of at least a portion of the population, accompanied by more discretionary funds, is another factor in the success of McDonald's. People who have extra funds can support a fast-food "habit" and eat at such restaurants regularly. At the same time, the fast-food restaurant offers the poor the possibility of an occasional meal out.

The increasing influence of the mass media also contributes to McDonald's global success. Without saturation advertising and the ubiquitous influence of television and other mass media, McDonald's would not have succeeded as well as it has.

No corporation stays on top forever and there were signs in 2014 that McDonald's was slipping in the face of competitors that were doing much of what it does, but doing it better. However, there are so many McDonald's in so many parts of the world, and it is embedded so deeply in the minds and lifestyles of so many people, that it is likely to have a prominent place in both the American and the global landscape well into the future.

SEE ALSO *Coca-Cola; Levi Strauss & Co.*

BIBLIOGRAPHY

Drane, John. *The McDonaldization of the Church: Consumer Culture and the Church's Future.* London: Darton, Longman, and Todd, 2000.

Friedman, Thomas. "A Manifesto for the Fast World." *New York Times Magazine*, March 28, 1999, 40–61.

Hayes, Dennis, and Robin Wynyard, eds. *The McDonaldization of Higher Education.* Westport, CT: Bergin and Garvey, 2002.

Keller, Bill. "Of Famous Arches, Beeg Meks, and Rubles." *New York Times*, January 28, 1990.

Ritzer, George. *The Globalization of Nothing 2.* Thousand Oaks, CA: Sage, 2007.

Ritzer, George. *The McDonaldization of Society.* 8th ed. Thousand Oaks, CA: Sage, 2015.

Weber, Max. *Economy and Society: An Outline of Interpretive Sociology.* Edited by Guenther Roth and Claus Wittich. Translated from the fourth German edition by Ephraim Fischoff et al. 3 vols. Totowa, NJ: Bedminster Press, 1968.

George Ritzer
Distinguished University Professor, Department of Sociology
University of Maryland

McNAMARA, ROBERT S.
1916–2009

The evolution of Robert Strange McNamara's worldview reflected that of many Americans in a tumultuous era of the twentieth century. Having served in uniform during World War II, McNamara joined the Ford Motor Company in 1946 when the power of the United States reigned supreme around the globe. Through brilliant management and determined leadership, McNamara attained the top spot at Ford by 1960, when he was named president of the company. He shared the view held by many Americans that any success was possible in a nation that had mastered atomic energy, strengthened democratic ideals, and become the agricultural breadbasket of the world.

John F. Kennedy (1917–1963) was elected president in 1960 because the youthful, visionary, and energetic senator promised an even brighter future. The United States would show the less-favored peoples of the world how to achieve political maturity, economic prosperity, and security against aggressive nations and corrosive ideologies. Kennedy selected McNamara as his secretary of defense because he believed McNamara possessed the leadership qualities, organizational skills, and dynamism to run a government department that consumed half of the federal budget and whose army, navy, and air force components operated all over the world.

McNamara readily accepted the responsibility, even though he had no significant experience with national security policy, the US armed forces, or America's Cold War global posture. While suggesting to Kennedy that he felt himself "unqualified" for the job, McNamara clearly did not take that deficiency seriously. His subsequent actions displayed a supreme confidence in his ability to face a challenge, dissect the problem based on statistical analyses, and push through a solution.

The new secretary of defense recognized that even though the United States maintained a more capable nuclear arsenal than the Soviet Union, there would be no winners in an all-out nuclear war. Deterring such a conflict came to rest upon his concept of "mutual assured destruction." With resort to nuclear warfare infeasible, McNamara championed the massive buildup of US conventional forces to handle "limited wars" and lesser conflicts.

Like many Americans, McNamara embraced Kennedy's pledge to provide military and economic help to any nation threatened by communist movements. McNamara urged the military to establish "Green Berets," SEALs, and other special forces. With money no object, he supported what came to be called "nation-building" efforts in South Vietnam and elsewhere. He believed that the provision of ample resources, monitored by statistical measures, would bring success against the communists. But he had little understanding of what drove revolutionaries in Asia or of the culture, language, and political imperatives of the Vietnamese people.

Developments with regard to Cuba strongly influenced McNamara throughout his unprecedented seven years in office. He concluded that the Joint Chiefs of Staff (JCS) badly served him and Kennedy in the Bay of Pigs fiasco of April 1961. McNamara also came to believe that his military leaders came close to igniting a nuclear war during the Cuban missile crisis. Conversely, he ascribed the confrontation's successful outcome to his and the president's skillful management. As a result, McNamara

and the next president he served, Lyndon B. Johnson (1908–1973), attempted to direct the Vietnam War almost on a personal basis from Washington, 10,000 miles from the combat theater. Moreover, McNamara relied much more heavily on his subordinate civilians for advice on the conduct of the war than on the JCS.

A prime cause of America's defeat in Vietnam was the failure to understand the enemy. McNamara championed a strategy of "graduated escalation" based on his faulty assessment that North Vietnam had neither the physical capacity nor the will to defy the armed might of the United States. Like many Americans, he ultimately recognized that despite the bombing campaign against North Vietnam, the deployment of 500,000 American troops to South Vietnam, and a defense expenditure of 100 billion dollars, the enemy would not be defeated.

No longer confident in his direction of the war effort, in February 1968 Johnson announced McNamara's resignation as secretary of defense and nomination to head the World Bank. For thirteen years, McNamara guided the international organization. He exuded confidence that the World Bank would solve the economic problems of the "developing countries," global hunger, and poverty. McNamara greatly enlarged his staff, supported revolutionary developmental projects, and raised multibillion-dollar sums from donor governments. Millions of the world's poor benefited from the projects designed and funded by the World Bank. As McNamara and many Americans came to realize during the late Cold War years, however, a massive infusion of resources and innovative approaches does not guarantee success. Despite his fervent efforts, McNamara was unable to rid the world of poverty, hunger, or the continued parlous state of many developing countries.

SEE ALSO *Bay of Pigs; Bundy, McGeorge; Cold War; Cuban Missile Crisis; Johnson, Lyndon Baines; Kennedy, John Fitzgerald; Mutual Assured Destruction (MAD); Vietnam War; World Bank*

BIBLIOGRAPHY

Drea, Edward J. *McNamara, Clifford, and the Burdens of Vietnam, 1965–1969.* Washington, DC: Historical Office, Office of the Secretary of Defense, 2011.

Halberstam, David. *The Best and the Brightest.* New York: Random House, 1972.

Kaplan, Lawrence S., Ronald D. Landa, and Edward J. Drea. *The McNamara Ascendancy, 1961–1965.* Washington, DC: Historical Office, Office of the Secretary of Defense, 2006.

Kinnard, Douglas. *The Secretary of Defense.* Lexington: University Press of Kentucky, 1980.

McMaster, H. R. *Dereliction of Duty: Lyndon Johnson, Robert McNamara, the Joint Chiefs of Staff, and the Lies That Led to Vietnam.* New York: Harper Collins, 1997.

McNamara, Robert S. *The McNamara Years at the World Bank: Major Policy Addresses of Robert S. McNamara, 1968–1981.* Baltimore, MD: Johns Hopkins University Press, 1981.

McNamara, Robert S., with Brian VanDeMark. *In Retrospect: The Tragedy and Lessons of Vietnam.* New York: Times Books/Random House, 1995.

Shapley, Deborah. *Promise and Power: The Life and Times of Robert McNamara.* Boston: Little, Brown, 1993.

Edward J. Marolda
Adjunct Instructor
Georgetown University

MELTING POT

Many Americans and global observers think of the United States as a melting pot, a place where immigrants can easily assimilate and make their culture a part of America. This myth and image, much like "the city on a hill" or "the promised land," is enduring and yet also misleading. This entry will examine the history of the term, how it shapes and connects to other internal and external constructions of American identity, and the groups left out of this conception of what constitutes "America."

THE ROOTS OF THE MELTING POT METAPHOR

The term *melting pot* was formally, though not initially, introduced into American popular culture by British playwright Israel Zangwill (1864–1926) in 1908. Before this, however, the idea of America being a place where different groups (of Europeans) blended or melted together to form a single American identity was often invoked. This type of melted identity and nation-state formation stood in stark contrast to that of Western Europe, where ethnicity and nationality were imagined as one in the same. The very motto for the new US seal and nation-state, *E Pluribus Unum* (one out of many), captured the idea that this new nation would be heterogeneous and yet united. In fact, both normative views—that the United States was a blended, inclusive space and that Western Europe was made up of neat, homogenous nation-states—were severely assumptive, and the reality was much more complicated. Nonetheless, many eighteenth- and nineteenth-century thinkers used the word *melting* to describe American identity.

The first thinker to imagine US identity as melted together was Michel Guillaume Jean de Crèvecoeur (1735–1813). Born in Normandy, France, de Crèvecoeur moved to New France at the age of twenty to serve in the French Colonial Militia during the French and Indian War (1754–1763). In 1759, he moved to New York, where he settled down as a farmer and took the name

John Hector St. John de Crèvecoeur. In 1782, he published *Letters from an American Farmer*, a collection of twelve fictional letters written by an American farmer corresponding with an English gentleman. The letters cover many topics, from the everyday activities of an American farmer to thoughts on slavery, the customs of Nantucket, and perhaps most famously, the question "What is an American?"

This question is answered in de Crèvecoeur's important and widely read third letter. Beyond detailing differences between America and Europe (for example, in the colonies, there are no princes, and there are opportunities to rise above one's "rank"), this letter describes what makes Americans unique. According to de Crèvecoeur, "Here individuals of all nations are melted into a new race of men … once scattered all over Europe; here they are incorporated into one of the finest systems of population which has ever appeared" (de Crèvecoeur [1872] 1904, 55). This melting that de Crèvecoeur describes occurs through marriage, where, for example, a man with an English grandfather, Dutch grandmother, and a French mother has four sons, each of whom marries a woman from a different part of Europe. This mixing/melting through marriage also leads to a type of religious tolerance that does not exist in Europe. De Crèvecoeur observed that "zeal in Europe is confined; here it evaporates in the great distance it has to travel" (de Crèvecoeur [1872] 1904, 66). This essay is aspirational in how it imagines and contrasts American identity in relation to European identity. De Crèvecoeur imagined Europe as fractured and weak, whereas the United States provided an opportunity for unity and strength.

THE CONSTRUCTION OF AMERICAN IDENTITY

During the long nineteenth century, American identity was also imagined to be initially diverse and melted into one as a result of the particularities of the US landscape. In the popular literary magazine *The Galaxy*, Titus Munson Coan (1836–1921) described the process of becoming American in the following way:

> The fusing process goes on as in a blast furnace; one generation, a single year even—transforms the English, the German, the Irish emigrant into an American. Uniform institutions, ideas, language, the influence of the majority, bring us soon to a similar complexion; the individuality of the immigrant, almost even his traits of race and religion, fuse down in the democratic alembic like chips of brass thrown into the melting pot. (Coan 1875, 463)

Born in Hawai'i to missionary parents, Coan was a Civil War physician and prolific writer of poetry, societal observations and water cures. Though he was born in

Hawai'i, Coan was educated on the east coast, and travelled with his father and the army as a doctor. He was thus able to observe the ways in which the American landscape and identity were forming in the antebellum and post–Civil War United States.

While Coan and de Crèvecoeur describe the process of melting occurring only between different European groups, transcendentalist thinker Ralph Waldo Emerson (1803–1882) was more radical in how he imagined the American identity would eventually emerge. In 1845, in his personal journal, Emerson wrote:

> As in the old burning of the Temple at Corinth, by the melting and intermixture of silver and gold and other metals a new compound more precious than any, called Corinthian brass, was formed; so in this continent,—asylum of all nations,—the energy of Irish, Germans, Swedes, Poles, and Cossacks, and all the European tribes,—of the Africans, and of the Polynesians,—will construct a new race, a new religion, a new state, a new literature, which will be as vigorous as the new Europe which came out of the smelting-pot of the Dark Ages. (Quoted in Sherman 1921, xxxiv)

This journal was not published while Emerson was alive. Although his ideas of miscegenation were radical, the metaphor is in line with de Crèvecoeur and Coan. America is a new mix, and one that is better than Europe precisely because it is a mix.

By the end of the nineteenth century, the idea of the United States as non-English and a mix was common. In his seminal work, *The Significance of the Frontier in American History*, the historian Frederick Jackson Turner (1861–1932) observes, "In the crucible of the frontier the immigrants were Americanized, liberated, and fused into a mixed race, English in neither nationality nor characteristics. The process has gone on from the early days to our own" (1921, 23). Turner is describing a historical and contemporary process, one that is continually occurring and defining the ever-changing American frontier, a space where survival and building trumps ethnic identity and enclaves. In many ways, the frontier is much more of a crucible for the formation of American identity, precisely because there are no immigrant-specific spaces or neighborhoods that mimic the domus or landscapes of Europe; rather, the frontier is new and unblemished, and can become whatever the frontiersman would like it to be (once the US empire rids the space of the various indigenous tribes and nations).

Beyond gender and the emerging privilege of whiteness, what connects this diverse group of Euro-American men is the idea of American identity as melting, blending, or fusing together, which is seen as a positive development for the future of the United States. This eschatological and utopian process, in which a new American identity is forged, makes the United States stronger than Europe and holds much promise and hope. Thus, the idea of the melting pot is not only about American identity, but also about possibilities that arise after immigrating to the United States. The better life and future promised through immigration is, at least mythologically, fundamentally tied to how an immigrant becomes American.

Anti-immigration cartoon showing a lone "Yankee" surrounded by a multiethnic crowd. *During the nineteenth century, American identity was seen as comprising diverse backgrounds melted into one, though some believed in the superiority of the Anglo-American. Later, the melting pot was imagined not as a place where everyone becomes the same but a process by which diversity is maintained.* **EVERETT COLLECTION HISTORICAL/ALAMY**

ISRAEL ZANGWILL'S *MELTING POT*

These themes of American promise and identity are fully explored in Zangwill's 1908 play, *The Melting Pot: The Great American Drama*. Zangwill was born in London to Jewish parents from czarist Russia (Zangwill's mother was from what is now Poland, and his father was from what is now Latvia). Although he lived in the United Kingdom,

RANDOLPH BOURNE, "TRANS-NATIONAL AMERICA"

The failure of the melting-pot, far from closing the great American democratic experiment, means that it has only just begun. Whatever American nationalism turns out to be, we see already that it will have color richer and more exciting than our ideal has hitherto encompassed. In a world which has dreamed of internationalism, we find that we have all unawares been building up the first international nation. The voices which have cried for a tight and jealous nationalism of the European pattern are failing. From that ideal, however valiantly and disinterestedly it has been set for us, time and tendency have moved us further and further away. What we have achieved has been rather a cosmopolitan federation of national colonies, of foreign cultures, from whom the sting of devastating competition has been removed. America is already the world-federation in miniature, the continent where for the first time in history has been achieved that miracle of hope, the peaceful living side by side, with character substantially preserved, of the most heterogeneous peoples under the sun. Nowhere else has such contiguity been anything but the breeder of misery. Here, notwithstanding our tragic failures of adjustment, the outlines are already too clear not to give us a new vision and a new-orientation of the American mind in the world.

SOURCE: Bourne, Randolph. "Trans-national America." *Atlantic Monthly* 118 (July 1916): 86–97.
http://www.randolphbourne.columbia.edu/resources.html

his plays were successful beyond the London theater community. *The Melting Pot* opened in the United States in 1909 and was famously attended by Theodore Roosevelt (1858–1919). A few years later, Roosevelt wrote to Zangwill: "That particular play I shall always count among the very strong and real influences upon my thought and my life" (Nahshon 2006, 242). Although the idea of melting as part of the process of American identity formation has a long history in the United States, it was Zangwill's play that widely popularized the term *melting pot*. Interestingly, while de Crèvecoeur, Coan, Emerson, and Jackson were all American citizens, Zangwill was British. In many ways, this play is less about the reality of American life at the beginning of the twentieth century and more about how the United States was imagined by those outside its borders.

The Melting Pot follows a Russian Jew, David Quixano, who lost his family during the 1903 Kishinev pogrom. Quixano sees the United States as a crucible: "America is God's Crucible, the great Melting-Pot where all the races of Europe are melting and reforming ... Germans and Frenchmen, Irishmen and Englishmen, Jews and Russians—into the Crucible with you all! God is making the American" (Zangwill 2006, 288). Zangwill not only uses the metaphor of the melting pot to present the image of the United States as a possible utopia, but he also uses this metaphor to link the United States to a divinity and exceptionalism. The United States is a space where the impossible in Europe is possible. Upon arriving in the United States, Quixano falls in love with Vera, a Russian Orthodox Christian, whose father is responsible for the Kishinev massacre. Unlike Romeo and Juliet, these star-crossed lovers get a happy ending and familial acceptance. Vera's father accepts Quixano and admits guilt, something that, Zangwill hints, could only happen in the United States. Quixano proclaims to his fiancée, "Vera, what is the glory of Rome and Jerusalem where all nations and races come to worship and look back, compared with the glory of America, where all races and nations come to labour and look forward!" (Zangwill 2006, 363). Here Zangwill goes beyond eschatology, linking the melting pot to the idea of the United States as the new promised land, one that carries on and improves upon the ideals of Israel and the Roman Empire.

Perhaps the most unlikely aspect of Zangwill's story is that Quixano and his beloved are able to easily overcome religious differences. Like de Crèvecoeur, Zangwill imagines the United States as a place where ethnic and religious strife and identity can evaporate. In reality, however, immigrants to the United States held on tightly to their ethnic and religious identities. Some observers noted that, over time, religious identities held steadfast, while ethnic identities gave way to a stronger American identity. In his 1955 book, *Protestant-Catholic-Jew: An Essay in American Religious Sociology*, Will Herberg (1901–1977) speculated that there was not one American melting pot, but rather three—a Protestant one, a Catholic one, and a Jewish one. He argued that America is a three-religion country and that "the newcomer is expected to change many things about him as he becomes an American—nationality, language, culture. One thing, however, he is not expected to change—and that is religion" (Herberg 1955, 23). Herberg makes the assumption that not changing one's religion was a matter of choice rather than a product of the rampant anti-Catholicism and anti-Semitism that was entrenched in American culture during the nineteenth and twentieth (and the twenty-first) centuries.

EXCLUDED GROUPS

Thus, beyond reflecting a utopian eschatology that sees the United States as exceptional, superior to Europe, and the new promised land, the idea of the United States as a melting pot also reflects the anti-Semitism, anti-Catholicism, and racism that define a part of American identity. Perhaps even more interesting than imagining the melting pot is examining which groups were considered to be included in this crucible and which groups were and are left out. With the exception of Emerson, the idea of (mainly West) Africans being included in the crucible or melting pot of American identity was not brought up. Given the biological construction of whiteness versus blackness that emerged in the nineteenth century, this is not surprising. In the eighteenth and nineteenth centuries, the United States also had a significant population of Native Americans, Mexicans (Tejanos and Chicanos), and Asians (Chinese, Japanese, and Punjabi Sikhs). None of these groups were ever legally or culturally imagined as a part of the melting pot. It could be argued that the very existence of the "hyphen" as a part of American identity (Asian-American, African-American, etc.) is reflective of exclusion rather than inclusion.

Since the changing of US immigration policy in 1965 (from very closed to being more open to certain types of educated immigrants), there has been an influx of immigrants from Asia, Latin America, and Africa. These immigrants face restrictions in terms of education and quotas. They are largely non-European and thus "unmeltable" in that mixing with them does not present the possibility of maintaining the idea and construction of whiteness that previous immigrants from Europe presented. Yet many of them immigrate for the same reasons that previous generations of immigrants chose to immigrate—the idea that the United States is a place of promise where hard work trumps Old World hierarchies. Thus, while they might not "melt" in a single year or generation as Coan predicted, they buy into the idea of American identity in similar ways. Further, many of these "unmeltable" groups do imagine themselves as part of the American melting pot. The golf player Tiger Woods (b. 1975), for example—famous for defining himself as "cablasian" (to reflect his mixed-race heritage of Caucasian, black, and Asian)—noted in 2001 that "America's a melting pot, all races, cultures, religious choices" (CNN 2001).

CONTEMPORARY RESONANCE

The idea of the United States as a melting pot still resonates today—it is how many Americans and non-Americans imagine the process of creating American identity and culture. It reflects the idea of America as an exceptional nation-state (or empire), backed by providence and full of promise. The term *melting pot* is also now used to describe other diverse places, such as New Delhi, historically and contemporarily. In some ways, the term *melting pot* has become a way to describe any area where blending, trade, and movement are occurring.

In 2011, a *New York Times* article about the ancient city Dura-Europos in modern-day Syria, titled "A Melting Pot at the Intersection of Empires for Five Centuries," asserted that "New Yorkers would have felt at home" in this ancient city because of its diversity and trade (Wilford 2011, D3). In this way, the *melting pot* is not imagined as a place where everything becomes the same; rather, it is a process by which diversity is maintained. Critics of the melting pot metaphor argue that the United States is not a homogenous space, but rather a place where diversity is maintained and thrives. The rhetoric of multiculturalism and other metaphors, such as *mosaic* or *salad*, are sometimes used instead of *melting pot*. However, in many ways, all these metaphors stem from a similar goal: the desire to understand identity, ethnicity, and race in the context of human migration (by choice and forced) and the modern formation of the nation-state as the primary means of international organization.

SEE ALSO *Chinese Exclusion Act (1882); Empire, US; Exceptionalism; Immigration; Immigration Quotas; Indian Citizenship Act (1924)*

BIBLIOGRAPHY

Coan, Titus Munson. "A New Country." *The Galaxy* 19, 4 (1875): 462–472.

CNN. "Tiger Woods Profile: The Remarkable Drive of Tiger Woods." 2001. http://www.cnn.com/CNN/Programs/people/shows/tiger/profile.html

de Crèvecoeur, J. Hector St. John. *Letters from an American Farmer*. New York: Fox, Duffield, 1904. First published in London in 1782.

Herberg, Will. *Protestant-Catholic-Jew: An Essay in American Religious Sociology*. Garden City, NY: Doubleday, 1955.

Nahshon, Edna. "Melting Pot: Introductory Essay." In *From the Ghetto to the Melting Pot: Israel Zangwill's Jewish Plays: Three Playscripts*, edited by Edna Nahshon, 211–264. Detroit, MI: Wayne State University Press, 2006.

Sherman, Stuart P. "Introduction." In *Essays and Poems of Emerson*, vii–xlv. New York: Harcourt, Brace, 1921.

Turner, Frederick Jackson. *The Frontier in American History*. New York: Holt, 1921.

Wilford, John Noble. "A Melting Pot at the Intersection of Empires for Five Centuries." *New York Times*, December 20, 2011, D3.

Zangwill, Israel. *From the Ghetto to the Melting Pot: Israel Zangwill's Jewish Plays: Three Playscripts*, edited by Edna Nahshon. Detroit, MI: Wayne State University Press, 2006.

Shreena Niketa Gandhi
Assistant Professor of Religion
Kalamazoo College

MELVILLE, HERMAN
1819–1891

In early novels such as *Typee* (1846), *Omoo* (1847), *Mardi* (1849), and *Moby-Dick* (1851), Herman Melville placed American characters in the South Pacific and poignantly commented on the dynamic interplay between the United States and the world at the midpoint of the nineteenth century. These works drew on anti-imperialist sentiments opposed to Manifest Destiny and the United States' increasingly aggressive presence on the international stage.

Of course, Melville's complex engagement with US global aggression in his most iconic novel, *Moby-Dick*, stands out as a cornerstone of scholarship devoted to Melville and Empire in the twentieth and early twenty-first centuries (Yothers 150–173). Enthusiastically dramatizing the Nantucket whaling-ship's global-wide and highly destructive pursuit of the white whale, Melville in a sense mirrored the conquest ideologies freighting American attitudes during his time of writing; but throughout, the novel simultaneously enacts a powerful articulation of antebellum counter-imperial impulses. Especially when considered in light of the transcendentally destructive climax of the *Pequod* crew's final, three-chapter battle with the white whale, Melville's enlistment of the hunting motif enacts a poignant reflection of expansionism's negative connotations in the antebellum American mind.

But in fictionalizing his own experience among South Seas islanders—Melville would be known for the remainder of his life as "the man who lived among the cannibals"—*Typee* and *Omoo* (as well as the less autobiographically based *Mardi*) more specifically explore the South Pacific as a staging ground for contact between "civilized" and "savage" humans. At a time when the American West carried explicitly international connotations in antebellum US thought, Melville's texts resonate with debates over westward expansion, which "in these years carried well beyond the West Coast into what was popularly called the Western Ocean" (Fussell 1965, 261). Melville's complex engagement with the United States' international exploits is one of the most dynamic areas of focus in Melville scholarship of the current century (Yothers 2011).

Through much of *Typee* the narrator, Tommo, a sailor on a whaling ship, presents the Typee islanders he encounters in positive terms and favorably contrasts aspects of their culture against his own. Yet the novel ends with a scene in which Anglo-European whalemen lacerate the wrists of a pursuing "savage," and in which a fleeing Tommo nearly kills one of the Typee chieftains. Despite such suggestions of irreconcilable hostility between two worlds, the novel is shot through with anti-imperialist sensibilities. At a crucial moment early in the narrative, Tommo says: "It may be asserted without fear of contradiction, that in all the cases of outrages committed by Polynesians, Europeans have at some time or other been the aggressors, and that the cruel and bloodthirsty disposition of some of the islanders is mainly to be ascribed to the influence of such examples" (Melville 1996, 27). Later on Tommo asserts: "The fiend-like skill we display in the invention of all manner of death-dealing engines; the vindictiveness with which we carry on our wars, and the misery and desolation that follow in their train, are enough of themselves to distinguish the white civilized man as the most ferocious animal on the face of the earth" (Melville 1996, 125).

Melville's condemnation of the violent consequences of imperialism provoked strong responses on both sides of the Atlantic. Indeed, partially in response to some negative reviews in American periodicals, only months after its original publication Melville's American publisher released an edition of *Typee* purged of nearly all its political commentary. This commentary transgressed what Andrew Delbanco terms the United States' "official line" at midcentury: that white American expansion across the continent and then into the Pacific was "a divinely ordained step leading humankind out of darkness and into light" (Delbanco 2005, 47).

Although some critics attacked Melville for criticizing French, British, and American designs on faraway places and their inhabitants—whether in the form of Protestant missionaries or government-sanctioned territorial aggrandizement—most English reviewers enthusiastically praised *Typee* (Anderson 1939). In the United States, many positive reviews specifically embraced *Typee*'s politically charged elements, providing a notable counterbalance to those who critiqued Melville's "unpatriotic" indictments of European and US imperialism. Readers on both sides of the Atlantic fully embraced unexpurgated editions of *Typee*, which brought Melville early commercial success. By the end of the nineteenth century the book had sold more than 20,000 copies. *Typee* lent Melville celebrity status in both nations and earned him a substantial offer from his publisher to write *Omoo*, another tale of seafaring adventure.

The critical and popular reception of *Typee* suggests that Melville's provocative approach to America's role in the world significantly contributed to the novel's commercial success (Lawrence 2009). Melville's early literary fame (which was to evaporate in later decades) reflects his close attunement to the controversies and anxieties bred by the United States' increasingly prominent role on the international stage.

SEE ALSO *Hawai'i; Pacific Islands*

BIBLIOGRAPHY

Anderson, Charles. "Melville's English Debut." *American Literature* 11 (1939): 23–38.

Delbanco, Andrew. *Melville: His World and Work*. New York: Knopf, 2005.

Fussell, Edwin. *Frontier: American Literature and the American West*. Princeton, NJ: Princeton University Press, 1965.

Lawrence, Nicholas. "'[R]eaders who are sick at heart': Melville's *Typee* and the Expansion Controversy." *South Central Review* 26, 3 (2009): 61–71.

Melville, Herman. *Typee: A Peep at Polynesian Life*. Edited by John Bryant. New York: Penguin, 1996.

Yothers, Brian. *Melville's Mirrors: Literary Criticism and America's Most Elusive Author*. Rochester, NY: Camden House, 2011.

Nicholas Lawrence
Assistant Professor of English
University of South Carolina Lancaster

MERCER'S SLAVE TRADE ACT (1819)

SEE *Liberia*.

MEXICAN REVOLUTION

SEE *Mexico*.

MEXICAN-AMERICAN WAR

The US-Mexico War (1846–1848) was the largest conflict ever fought between two nations in the Western Hemisphere. The war had its roots in an aggressive push westward by US leaders in the 1840s. Termed *manifest destiny* by New York newspaperman John L. O'Sullivan (1813–1895), the acquisition of new territory had become a major objective of US foreign policy as the nation began to define its strategic and economic interests in terms that extended beyond its own borders. Southern political leaders sought to protect the interests of the planter class by acquiring the Texas Republic, a slaveholding nation-state that had attained its independence from Mexico nine years earlier. Other Americans were more interested in the pursuit of a maritime empire, and sought access to the harbors of San Francisco and San Diego. Both these goals placed the United States on a collision course with Mexico.

BACKGROUND TO THE CONFLICT

The stage for conflict was set when the US Congress passed a joint resolution in March 1845 offering to annex the Texas Republic as the twenty-eighth state. Since gaining independence in 1836, Texas had continued to spar with its neighbor to the south. In 1842, the Mexican government had twice sent troops to capture San Antonio, reinforcing its claim that Texas was not an independent nation but a province in revolt. In response to the annexation offer, Mexico severed diplomatic relations with the United States and declared that a union between the two Anglo-American republics would constitute an act of war. In one of his first acts as president, James K. Polk (1795–1849), an avowed expansionist, ordered General Zachary Taylor (1784–1850) to march into Texas to protect its southern border with Mexico. In what Mexican leaders regarded as a further act of provocation, Polk instructed Taylor to take up positions below the Nueces River, which had been the southern boundary of Texas under Mexican rule.

While Mexican conservatives clamored for war, moderate president José Joaquín Herrera (1792–1854) sought a diplomatic solution to the crisis, informing Washington that his government might consider a financial settlement for the loss of Texas. Polk promptly dispatched diplomat John Slidell (1793–1871) to Mexico City. Refusing to concede that Mexico still had a valid claim to Texas, the US president was only prepared to compensate Mexico if it would recognize the Rio Grande, not the Nueces, as the legitimate boundary. In return, the United States would assume payment of more than $3 million in long-standing claims that American citizens had filed against the Mexican government. Polk sought to pressure Mexico into making further concessions, however, having received reports that Great Britain wished to acquire Mexican harbors on the Pacific. The US president therefore authorized Slidell to discuss with Mexico's leaders the possibility of selling California and New Mexico.

The news of Slidell's arrival in December caused a public furor in Mexico, with conservatives denouncing as appeasement any negotiation with the United States. Vowing to reassert Mexican sovereignty over Texas, General Mariano Paredes (1797–1849) overthrew the Herrera regime in January 1846. Unable to initiate negotiations, Slidell returned to the United States in March. In Polk's mind, Mexico's rejection of Slidell provided "ample cause of war," and he favored sending Congress a declaration to that effect. In fact, a clash between the two countries had already occurred, the Mexican army having crossed the Rio Grande and attacked a patrol of US dragoons on April 25.

THE WAR

Polk immediately asked Congress for a declaration of war. Ignoring the Mexican claim to the land south of the Nueces, he declared that "American blood" had been spilled on "American soil." The war bill passed both houses by sizable margins, with all but a handful of northern Whigs opposed to the measure. Although New England, a Whig stronghold, never fully supported the conflict, many Americans initially greeted news of the war with a burst of patriotic enthusiasm. By some accounts, more than two hundred thousand men sought to enlist, although the War Department had called for only fifty thousand volunteers to augment the regular army.

In the first US war fought on foreign soil, Americans knew little about the nation they were invading. The years of conflict in Texas had been followed closely in the United States, creating in the American imagination crude racial stereotypes of Mexican males. At the same time, US troops often entertained exotic fantasies of creole Mexican women, casting themselves in the role of rescuers as they marched south into Mexico. American wartime newspaper accounts and popular fiction, such as George Lippard's *Legends of Mexico* (1847), fed these notions, while at the same time encouraging an ideology of Anglo-Saxon superiority.

Early US Victories. The romance of war would soon fade for many volunteers. Following two quick victories in south Texas, Palo Alto and Resaca de la Palma, Taylor took control of several towns along the Rio Grande as he waited for the newly formed regiments to arrive. During the summer of 1846, Taylor's army swelled to more than ten thousand. Poorly trained and lacking in discipline, the volunteers failed to take adequate sanitation precautions. Outbreaks of dysentery and other diseases resulted in the deaths of 12 percent of Taylor's force.

Concerned that Great Britain might intervene on Mexico's behalf to take California, the administration had already ordered Commodore John D. Sloat (1781–1867) to seize Mexican ports on the Pacific in the event of war. Sloat occupied Monterrey and San Francisco in early July, aided by John C. Frémont (1813–1890) and Anglo-American settlers in northern California (the so-called Bear Flag Revolt). Meanwhile, Stephen Watts Kearny (1794–1848) led an expedition from Kansas to Santa Fe, New Mexico. Kearny took the town without resistance in mid-August and established a civil government in New Mexico.

Opposition to the War. Despite these successes, serious opposition to the war quickly materialized, revealing deep divisions in the political fabric of the United States. Some Whigs accused President Polk of partisanship in his appointment of officers to command the army's newly created volunteer regiments; others believed that the president's underlying motive in waging war was to acquire more territory for the expansion of slavery. Many northern Democrats shared Whig concerns that the war would intensify sectional divisions. When the president asked Congress to provide funds for the purchase of New Mexico and California, the request revived the debate about the administration's war aims. Pennsylvania Democrat David Wilmot (1814–1868), formerly a loyal party member, attached a proviso to the bill that would prohibit slavery in any territory acquired from Mexico. Although the bill failed to pass, the Wilmot Proviso highlighted northern Democrats' opposition to the slaveholding agenda.

US Assault from the South. With Taylor in command of the Rio Grande and US forces occupying California and New Mexico, the Polk administration had secured its territorial objectives in the first six months of the war. But Polk was growing frustrated by the Mexican government's unwillingness to sue for peace, and in November decided to open a new front in the south. The War Department ordered General Winfield Scott (1786–1866) to begin preparations to launch a seaborne invasion of Veracruz.

Having recently returned from exile, Mexico's most prominent political leader, Antonio López de Santa Anna (1794–1876), now took charge of the war effort against the United States. Marching north in February 1847, Santa Anna engaged Taylor's army at the Battle of Buena Vista (La Angostura). Although the battle ended in a stalemate, both sides claimed victory. Lacking supplies to continue the offensive, Santa Anna left Taylor's troops in control of northern Mexico and returned to the capital. There he was greeted by rioting by conservatives, angered at the government's decision to confiscate church property to fund the war effort. Brokering a peace with the rebels, Santa Anna hastily organized a new army to meet the imminent US seaborne invasion led by General Scott.

In March 1847, Scott landed an army of ten thousand men near Vera Cruz and laid siege to the town, which surrendered after a heavy bombardment later that month. In mid-April, he routed Santa Anna's army at Cerro Gordo, a mountain pass along the National Road. With the Mexican army in full retreat, the war seemed to be over, but Scott's drive toward the capital stalled unexpectedly when many US volunteers, nearing the end of their twelve-month term of enlistment, declared their intention to go home. Obliged to wait for new volunteer regiments to arrive, Scott's army occupied the town of Puebla, 75 miles (121 kilometers) east of Mexico City, for the next ten weeks.

By the time Scott resumed his march in mid-August, Santa Anna had reorganized his forces once again and taken steps to defend the capital. In some of the heaviest fighting of the war, Scott won battles on the outskirts of the city, then proposed an armistice in an effort to avoid further casualties. Peace talks between Mexican negotiators and US diplomat Nicholas Trist (1800–1874) soon broke down, and two weeks later the final assault on the capital began. After US troops stormed Chapultepec Castle on September 13, Santa Anna evacuated his army from the city and resigned the presidency. Scott entered the capital four days later, where he was greeted by public demonstrations and street violence. Gathering the remnants of his army, Santa Anna continued to attack US troops through October, while sporadic guerilla fighting harassed US troops during the occupation that followed.

Occupation and Peace Negotiations. Back in the United States, growing opposition to the war had enabled the Whigs to win a majority in the House of Representatives when the Thirtieth Congress reconvened in December 1847. Critics of the administration included Abraham Lincoln (1809–1865), a freshman Whig representative from Illinois. In his first speech, Lincoln presented a set of resolutions condemning the war as unnecessary and unconstitutional. The resolutions became known as the "spot" resolutions, because Lincoln demanded to know the exact spot where American blood had been spilled.

By this time, formal military operations between the two countries had come to an end. The conflict remained controversial in the United States, however, with US troops continuing to occupy Mexico while Nicholas Trist and Mexican peace commissioners worked on an agreement to end the war. Some expansionists called for annexing all of Mexico, while Whigs in Congress threatened to cut off military appropriations and bring US forces home immediately. Early in 1848, the peace negotiations finally yielded an agreement by which Mexico ceded Upper California and New Mexico and recognized the US annexation of Texas. In return, Mexico received $15 million, while the United States agreed to assume the $3 million in unpaid American claims. Although Polk now favored acquiring more territory from Mexico, in view of the partisan political climate in Washington, he believed that the Treaty of Guadalupe Hidalgo offered the best option available to him, and he sent the document to the Senate for ratification. The Mexican congress approved the treaty in June, thus bringing the US military occupation of the country to an end.

US TERRITORIAL GAINS

The United States acquired more than 500,000 square miles (1,295,000 square kilometers) as a result of the war with Mexico. In addition, the United States acquired important commercial outlets on the Pacific coast, which would enable it to compete with Great Britain for Asian commerce. An unanticipated benefit to the United States was the conquered region's extraordinary mineral wealth. Less than two weeks before the treaty was signed, settlers in northern California discovered gold; a decade later, prospectors found extensive silver deposits in Nevada. Much of this newfound wealth would be invested in railroads and manufacturing, accelerating the nation's transition from an agricultural economy to an industrial giant.

These spoils of war came at a cost, however. As many had predicted, the conquest of Mexico's northern territories gave a new impetus to the long-standing dispute over the expansion of slavery. Despite its enormous value, California would not be admitted into the Union until 1850, in an elaborate political compromise that revealed how deep the sectional divisions between North and South had become. And while the war established the United States as the indisputable power in the Western Hemisphere, it would leave a legacy of bitterness in Mexico that would help to shape US-Mexico relations in the years that followed.

SEE ALSO *Borderlands; Filibuster; Manifest Destiny; Mexico; North America; Polk, James K.; Texas Republic*

BIBLIOGRAPHY

Greenberg, Amy S. *A Wicked War: Polk, Clay, Lincoln, and the 1846 U.S. Invasion of Mexico.* New York: Knopf, 2012.

Haynes, Sam W. *James K. Polk and the Expansionist Impulse.* New York: Longman, 1997. 3rd ed., 2006.

Henderson, Timothy J. *A Glorious Defeat: Mexico and Its War with the United States.* New York: Hill and Wang, 2007.

Johannsen, Robert W. *To the Halls of the Montezumas: The Mexican War in the American Imagination.* New York: Oxford University Press, 1985.

Pletcher, David M. *The Diplomacy of Annexation: Texas, Oregon, and the Mexican War.* Columbia: University of Missouri Press, 1973.

Streeby, Shelley. *American Sensations: Class, Empire, and the Production of Popular Culture.* Berkeley: University of California Press, 2002.

Sam W. Haynes
Director, Center for Greater Southwestern Studies
University of Texas at Arlington

MEXICO

Mexico and the United States share a long history as neighbors, trade partners, allies, and adversaries. The two nations, both former colonies, developed distinct cultures and political traditions, as the legacies of European imperialism played out differently in Mexico and the United States. Over the past two centuries, the two nations often clashed over territory, trade policy, and immigration, but today their 2,000-mile (3,220-kilometer) border remains a zone of demographic and commercial exchange (US Department of State 2014).

EARLY US RELATIONS WITH NEW SPAIN AND INDEPENDENT MEXICO

When the United States declared independence from Britain in 1776, present-day Mexico remained part of the Spanish colony of New Spain. Although Spain had aided the United States during its Revolutionary War (1775–1783), the two nations soon quarreled over border issues and trade. These disputes increased when the United States purchased the Louisiana territory from France in 1803, bringing the United States into closer contact with New Spain (Fisher 1932, 472). Spain feared US influence in its most lucrative colony, especially as US citizens like Philip Nolan (1771–1801) staged filibustering expeditions in the region in the early 1800s (Fisher 1932, 466).

During this time, many Americans became sympathetic to Spanish American independence, but the US government declined to offer aid to the revolutionaries (Vázquez 1999, 1365). Soon after the Mexican War of Independence (1810–1821) began, Mexican patriots sent agents to Washington to solicit US support, only to realize that the United States, hoping to negotiate with Spain for territorial acquisition, preferred to maintain peace (Vázquez 1999, 1367). The United States waited until 1822 to recognize Mexican independence, when it received José Manuel Zozaya (1778–1853) as Mexican minister to the United States.

The following year, President James Monroe (1758–1831) gave a presidential address in which he declared the Western Hemisphere closed to European intervention, a policy later known as the Monroe Doctrine. Soon after, the United States sent Joel Robert Poinsett (1779–1851) to Mexico as minister plenipotentiary. Poinsett immediately established a precedent for American interventionism in Mexican affairs, as he opposed Mexican tariff policies and pushed Mexico to move its border with the United States north to the Rio Grande (Coatsworth and Williamson 2004, 208). Poinsett also encouraged Mexico to adopt a constitution modeled after the US Constitution (Raat 2010, 238). At the start of the independence movement, Mexican patriots had looked to the US Constitution for political principles to emulate, but had established their own unique form of federalism. Unlike the United States, political power in Mexico was vested in the people and central government, rather than in individual states. Additionally, the central government declared Catholicism the national religion and made slavery illegal (Vázquez 1999, 1362).

THE MEXICAN-AMERICAN WAR AND LATER INTERVENTIONS

The 1830s and 1840s witnessed heightened tensions between the United States and Mexico. American migrants stirred up opposition to Mexican rule in the province of Texas, which became part of Mexico in 1824. Led by Stephen F. Austin (1793–1836), Texans revolted against the centralist policies of dictator Antonio López de Santa Anna (1794–1876) in 1835. While many sought complete independence, others simply wanted greater autonomy within the Mexican republic. Texans suffered a major defeat at the Alamo mission, followed by a victory over Santa Anna's Mexican army. Texans declared independence in 1836, but while the United States recognized its sovereignty, Mexico did not. Despite warnings from the Mexican government that annexation would lead to war, the US Congress made Texas a state in December 1845.

The following year, President James K. Polk (1795–1849) alleged that Mexican troops had invaded US territory and attacked American soldiers; Congress declared war in May 1846. The Mexican-American War (1846–1848), from which the United States emerged victorious, was partly the result of an American ideology known as *manifest destiny*, a term coined by newspaper columnist John L. O'Sullivan (1813–1895) in 1845 to describe the United States' presumed birthright to expand over the North American continent. This ideology would continue to cause problems after the war, as the United States sought additional territory beyond what it acquired in the Treaty of Guadalupe Hidalgo (1848). After several years squabbling over territorial boundaries and Indian raids, the United States paid Mexico $10 million for land that would eventually form part of Arizona and New Mexico. Known as the Gadsen Purchase (1853–1854), this agreement cemented the boundary between Mexico and the United States, even as it failed to end conflicts over border violence or military claims (Jonas 1992).

The 1860s brought new challenges to both nations. When President Benito Juárez (1806–1872) suspended foreign interest payments in 1861, France, backed by Britain and Spain, invaded the country and in 1864 installed Maximilian of Habsburg, Archduke of Austria (1832–1867), as emperor of Mexico. France also threatened to intervene on the side of the Confederacy during the American Civil War (1861–1865). The US government refused to recognize French rule in Mexico and, following the Civil War, provided Juárez with arms and troops to overthrow Maximillian in 1867 (O'Neil 2014, 18). Juárez returned to power and ruled until his death in 1872.

The United States' next intervention occurred when it helped Porfirio Díaz (1830–1915) seize power in 1876. As a result of Díaz's liberal reforms, the United States enjoyed considerable economic influence; in all of Latin America, only in Mexico did it have a stronger economic presence than Britain (Raat 2010, 83). While Díaz enjoyed considerable support in the United States, many of his policies were unpopular for their failure to improve education or the lives of the poor (Davis 1967, 109). An especially strong opposition movement emerged in Texas and northern Mexico, as Díaz's crackdown on antagonist publications in the United States and Mexico engendered comradery among the transborder community (Martinez-Catsam 2009).

THE MEXICAN REVOLUTION

The Mexican Revolution (1910–1920), which ousted Díaz, ended three decades of relative stability and ushered in a new era of US-Mexico relations. President Woodrow Wilson (1856–1924) refused to recognize the new government of Victoriano Huerta (1854–1916) (Henderson 1984), an act of Wilson's brand of "missionary diplomacy." In 1914, Wilson sent marines to the port of Vera Cruz after American sailors were arrested by Mexican officials, contributing to the collapse of Huerta's regime (Skidmore and Smith 2001, 230). Several years later, Wilson sent troops into Mexico in an attempt to halt the movements of revolutionary general Pancho Villa (1878–1923) (Smith 2005, 75).

Fighting continued for several more years, but the United States turned its attention to World War I (1914–1918). Mexico had, in fact, been part of the reason the United States entered the war: the United States declared war on Germany soon after it learned of a German offer of alliance to Mexico if it declared war on the United States. Despite strong anti-American sentiment in Mexico, the government declined Germany's proposal, citing military and diplomatic limitations.

TWENTIETH-CENTURY IMPROVEMENT IN US-MEXICAN RELATIONS

Following the Mexican Revolution and World War I, relations between Mexico and the United States improved. Recognizing that US interventions throughout Latin America generated mistrust and hostility in the region, US president Herbert Hoover (1874–1964) visited Mexico during a goodwill tour of Latin America in 1928 and pledged that the United States would be less imperialistic (Smith 1996, 64). The administration of Franklin Delano Roosevelt (1882–1945) continued this cooperative approach by instituting the Good Neighbor policy, which promised to treat Latin American nations as sovereign entities rather than subordinates (Smith 1996,

65). The 1939 World's Fair in New York provided Mexico the opportunity to present its culture to an international audience and encourage American tourism. The economic policies of both nations, however, continued to breed tension. The United States' highly protective Smoot-Hawley Tariff of 1930 hindered Mexican business, while the nationalization of oil companies in Mexico sparked boycotts in the United States (LaRosa and Mora 2007, 104).

Mexico and the United States were allies during World War II (1939–1945). A diplomatic arrangement known as the bracero program brought Mexican laborers to the United States to fill jobs vacated by the US military draft (Skidmore and Smith 2001, 238). Following the war, however, pro-industrialization policies in Mexico brought new strains to the relationship, as Mexican officials worked to remedy the trade imbalance that had tended to benefit American creditors at the expense of Mexican producers. They promoted domestic manufacturing, much to the dismay of American exporters (Raat 2010, 62). In general, Mexico's refusal to acquiesce to US wishes was part of its increasing assertiveness with its northern neighbor. In 1964, Mexican president Adolfo López Mateos (1910–1969) secured from President Lyndon Johnson (1908–1973) an agreement that gave Mexico sovereignty over a disputed river-bank territory in El Paso. During the Cold War, Mexico supported communist governments and movements in Cuba, Nicaragua, and El Salvador (Skidmore and Smith 2001, 241).

Mexico did, however, implement antileftist measures domestically, as the government waged a "dirty war" from the 1960s to the early 1980s against leftist student and guerrilla groups. The United States opposed these leftist movements, but remained confident that the ruling Partido Revolucionario Institucional (PRI) would remain in control. During this period, too, Mexico and the United States continued to cooperate economically. Following the end of the controversial guest-worker bracero program in 1964, the Mexican government established the Border Industrialization Program to promote factory employment and US investment. Maquiladora plants opened along the border between Mexico and the United States and enabled America companies to import materials without paying duties, to assemble goods with low-cost Mexican labor, and to reexport the goods to the United States (Domínguez and Fernández de Castro 2013, 138). These factories, which generated population growth along the Mexico-US border, increased the extent to which the Mexican North functioned as a distinct region with close ties to the United States (Raat 2010, 187). Maquiladoras, although controversial for their dubious labor practices, coincided with general Mexican economic growth throughout the 1970s.

An economic crises in 1982 left Mexico unable to pay its foreign creditors. Fearing the ramifications of Mexican insolvency, the United States pressured the International Monetary Fund (IMF) to step in with a rescue package. Mexico's economy eventually improved, and under President Carlos Salinas de Gortari (b. 1948), Mexico instituted liberal economic policies favorable to the United States and other foreign investors. In 1994, it signed the North American Free Trade Agreement (NAFTA) with Canada and the United States, generating even greater economic exchange between the two nations. As of the first decades of the twenty-first century, the United States was Mexico's largest trade partner, and Walmart, a US company, was the largest private-sector employer in Mexico.

THE DRUG TRADE

One of the most significant forms of exchange, however, exists outside legal trade agreements. Indeed, the drug trade has been a source of conflict and collaboration between Mexico and the United States. Consumer demand in the United States fuels drug trafficking from Mexico, while the US war on drugs, launched in the 1970s and continued under President Ronald Reagan (1911–2004) and President Bill Clinton (b. 1946), attempts to cut off sources of supply (Skidmore and Smith 2001, 392). When Felipe Calderón (b. 1962) became president of Mexico in 2006, he strengthened Mexico's cooperation with the United States by escalating the crackdown on drug cartels, which have been a major security threat in Mexico and the United States. Despite political cooperation, the war on drugs has largely been a failure and has generated much opposition in both countries.

IMMIGRATION

Whatever the political tensions between Mexico and the United States, immigration has been a mainstay of foreign relations, albeit in ebbs and flows. Large-scale immigration began in the early twentieth century, and since 1980, Mexicans have been the largest immigrant group in the United States. As of 2013, approximately 11.6 million Mexican immigrants resided in the United States (Zong and Batalova 2014). While the majority of immigrants continue to base their cultural and political interests in Mexico, Mexicans do redefine their identities in the United States (Gómez and Zackrison 2003, 80). Mexican Catholics in the United States, for example, may alter their Catholicism by blending US and Mexican culture into their devotional practices, by rejecting Mexican Catholic traditions to assimilate into secular US culture, or by emphasizing their ethnic and religious heritage as a basis for political activism.

Following the financial crisis of 2008, immigration to the United States declined, owing to dwindling economic opportunities and harsher immigration laws. Under President Barack Obama (b. 1961), however, the United States adopted more permissive immigration policies. Americans and Mexicans continue to travel between the two countries for work and vacation, many relocating for good.

In the first decades of the twenty-first century, Obama and Mexican president Enrique Peña Nieto (b. 1966) brought the two nations closer together. A host of bilateral arrangements pertaining to education, economic development, and the environment seems to ensure that the futures of the two nations, like their pasts, will be intertwined. Indeed, Mexico and the United States remain bound by geography and a shared history.

SEE ALSO *Americanization; Borderlands; Confederate States of America; Dollar Diplomacy; Empire, US; Exceptionalism; Internationalism; Interventionism; Isolationism; Mexican-American War; Missionary Diplomacy; Monroe Doctrine (1823); Wilson, Woodrow*

BIBLIOGRAPHY

Coatsworth, John H., and Jeffrey G. Williamson. "Always Protectionist? Latin American Tariffs from Independence to Great Depression." *Journal of Latin American Studies* 36, 2 (2004): 205–232.

Davis, Thomas B. "Porfirio Diaz in the Opinion of His North American Contemporaries." *Revista de Historia de América* 63/64 (1967): 79–116.

Domínguez, Jorge I., and Rafael Fernández de Castro. *The United States and Mexico: Between Partnership and Conflict.* 2nd ed. London: Routledge, 2013.

Espinosa, Gastón, and Mario T. García, eds. *Mexican American Religions: Spirituality, Activism, and Culture.* Durham, NC: Duke University Press, 2008.

Fisher, Lillian E. "American Influence upon the Movement for Mexican Independence." *Mississippi Valley Historical Review* 18, 4 (1932): 463–478.

Garza, Rodolfo O. de la. "Demythologizing Chicano-Mexican Relations." *Proceedings of the Academy of Political Science* 34, 1, Mexico-United States Relations (1981): 88–96.

Gómez, Arturo Santamaría, and James Zackrison. "Politics without Borders or Postmodern Nationality: Mexican Immigration to the United States." *Latin American Perspectives* 30, 2, Citizenship in Latin America (2003): 66–86.

Henderson, Peter V. N. "Woodrow Wilson, Victoriano Huerta, and the Recognition Issue in Mexico." *The Americas* 41, 2 (1984): 151–176.

Jonas, Peter M. "William Parrott, American Claims, and the Mexican War." *Journal of the Early Republic* 12, 2 (1992): 213–240.

LaRosa, Michael J., and Frank O. Mora, eds. *Neighborly Adversaries: Readings in U.S.-Latin American Relations.* 2nd ed. Lanham, MD: Rowman and Littlefield, 2007. 3rd ed., 2015.

Martínez, Anne M. *Catholic Borderlands: Mapping Catholicism onto American Empire, 1905–1935*. Lincoln: University of Nebraska Press, 2014.

Martinez-Catsam, Ana Luisa. "Frontier of Dissent: *El Regidor*, the Regime of Porfirio Díaz, and the Transborder Community." *Southwestern Historical Quarterly* 112, 4 (2009): 388–408.

Matovina, Timothy, and Gary Riebe-Estrella. *Horizons of the Sacred: Mexican Traditions in U.S. Catholicism*. Ithaca, NY: Cornell University Press, 2002.

Nabhan-Warren, Kristy. *The Virgin of El Barrio: Marian Apparitions, Catholic Evangelizing, and Mexican American Activism*. New York: New York University Press, 2005.

O'Neil, Shannon K. *Two Nations Indivisible: Mexico, the United States, and the Road Ahead*. London: Oxford University Press, 2014.

Raat, W. Dirk, and Michael M. Brescia. *Mexico and the United States: Ambivalent Vistas*. Atlanta: University of Georgia Press, 2010.

Skidmore, Thomas E., and Peter H. Smith. *Modern Latin America*. 5th ed. New York: Oxford University Press, 2001.

Smith, Joseph. *The United States and Latin America: A History of American Diplomacy, 1776–2000*. New York: Routledge, 2005.

Smith, Peter H. *Talons of the Eagle: Dynamics of US-Latin American Relations*. New York: Oxford University Press, 1996.

Stephanson, Anders. *Manifest Destiny: American Expansionism and the Empire of Right*. New York: Hill and Wang, 1995.

US Department of State. "U.S. Relations with Mexico." Bureau of Western Hemisphere Affairs, Fact Sheet, September 10, 2014. http://www.state.gov/r/pa/ei/bgn/35749.htm

Vázquez, Josefina Zoraida. "The Mexican Declaration of Independence." *Journal of American History* 85, 4 (1999): 1362–1369.

Weintraub, Sidney. *Unequal Partners: The United States and Mexico*. Pittsburgh, PA: University of Pittsburgh Press, 2010.

Zong, Jie, and Jeanne Batalova. "Mexican Immigrants in the United States." Migration Policy Institute. October 9, 2014. http://www.migrationpolicy.org/article/mexican-immigrants-united-states

Lindsay Schakenbach Regele
Assistant Professor of History
Miami University

MIDDLE EAST

The idea of "the Middle East" is an American invention. US Navy admiral Alfred Thayer Mahan (1840–1914) coined the term in a 1902 article arguing for British domination of the Persian Gulf in order to secure the land and sea routes to "India and the Farther East." The region and peoples subsumed by the term, then as now, was indeterminate and contingent on imperial interests (Khalil 2014). US relations with the Middle East have been shaped by ever-increasing American interventionism in, and Orientalism about, the region. These interventions were first defined in civilizational, religious, and missionary terms; then secularized in the language of humanitarianism, development, oil extraction, and Cold War strategy; and culminated in outright invasion and occupation of key Middle Eastern states and the open-ended "war on terror."

ISLAMIC DESPOTISM, AMERICAN BENEVOLENCE

American representations of "Muslim despotism," "Islamic fanaticism," and a stagnant "Orient" have provided foils from which to define American identity from the late eighteenth century to the present. Already in *Common Sense* (1776), Thomas Paine (1737–1809) contrasted republican government with "popery" and the "superstitious tale" of "Mahomet" (Kidd 2009; Marr 2006). Among the most significant challenges faced by the newly founded United States were the so-called Barbary Wars. Encouraged by the British, French, and Dutch empires, who paid North African principalities to attack their weaker competitors in the Mediterranean, North African pirates challenged American shipping in the Mediterranean from 1785 until the United States defeated Tripoli in 1815. This extended confrontation produced an American fascination with Islam and its alleged despotism, evidenced by the proliferation of lurid captivity narratives and anti-Islamic polemics. "Holy Land" travel narratives were also important in forming a distinctive tradition of American Orientalism.

MISSIONARY MOVEMENTS

The most lasting contributions of nineteenth-century America's Middle Eastern encounter were the Protestant missionary attempts to convert the inhabitants of the region. Arriving on the scene with no indigenous language skills, the American missionary community formed an influential presence encompassing schools, presses, hospitals, churches, commerce, and diplomacy. As William Appleman Williams reminds readers, "Americans founded schools in the Eastern Mediterranean before they did in Montana" (1958, 1). These institutions, especially Robert College in Istanbul (now Boğaziçi University), the Syrian Protestant College (now the American University of Beirut), and the American University in Cairo, have played an important role in the social and cultural history of the region. Missionaries were crucial in shaping both American ideas about the Middle East and local conceptions of Americans and their purposes in the region. Estimations of their contributions range from self-serving and often ethnocentric accounts by the missionaries themselves (Jessup 2002), to the idea that the American missionary presence spurred on an Arabic intellectual revival followed by the Arab nationalist movement (Antonius 1938), to criticism of the missionaries' exceptionalist claims to benevolence and innovation (Tibawi 1966; Makdisi 2008). The classic missionary era was brought to a close by the advent of nationalism and decolonization in the Middle East (Sharkey 2008).

ARAB AMERICAN CIRCUITS OF MIGRATION

In the first wave of Arab American migration, as many as two hundred thousand migrants from Ottoman Mount Lebanon—a third of its population—emigrated during the 1890–1915 period. Predominantly Christian peasants, most of these migrants sailed to the United States with hopes of satisfying their rising expectations. Early interpretations emphasized the relatively quick path "Syrians"—their prevailing designation at the time—took in becoming "assimilated" Americans. However, more recent studies have complicated this picture. Arab Americans founded a number of Arabic-language periodicals that were pivotal in forming early-twentieth-century nationalist ideologies, whether Syrian, Pan-Arab, or Lebanese. Many did not permanently settle, but returned to Mount Lebanon as a new, self-consciously "modern," middle class (Khater 2001). The Syrians that stayed encountered a new guiding principle of social order—race. Immigrants from *bilad al-sham* (present-day Lebanon, Syria, Israel, Palestine, and Jordan) often tried to prove that they were "white" and thus eligible for US citizenship (Gualtieri 2009). To do so, early Syrian Americans marshaled their economic success and Christian religion as arguments for whiteness. Later waves of Arab immigrants faced a tougher challenge maintaining social acceptance, particularly as the proportion of Muslim migrants grew, as Arab American identity was paradoxically developed and stigmatized, and as US intervention in the region increased.

FALL OF THE OTTOMAN EMPIRE, RISE OF WESTERN COLONIALISM

World War I (1914–1918) took a massive toll on the civilian populations of the defeated Ottoman Empire due to wartime violence, famine, ethnic cleansing, conscription, and genocide. The empire itself shattered into a number of nation-states. American missionaries were instrumental in producing the first American humanitarian movement for a foreign population by publicizing the genocide of Ottoman Armenians (Kieser 2010; Watenpaugh 2015). Talaat Bey (1874–1921), the Ottoman minister of interior, emphasized that the Ottomans were dealing with the Armenians as the Americans had done with its indigenous population (Grabill 1971, 63). The humanitarian campaigns during World War I effectively secularized the missionary ideal of converting the region to

Protestant Christianity into an alleged civilizing mission for freedom and democracy.

American solicitude to the Armenians reached a fever pitch, only to be abandoned in the postwar settlement. Prewar British and French imperial designs on the region, embodied by the 1916 Sykes-Picot Agreement, were confirmed by the League of Nations, which granted France "Mandatory" power over Syria and Lebanon, while Britain was given Iraq and Palestine—with the latter declared to be a Jewish national home. On every point, the postwar regime was a refutation of the professed ideals of Wilsonian self-determination and the American-led King-Crane Commission (1919), which consulted the population of Ottoman Syria as to their political future. Their findings were resoundingly clear: the majority wanted a single, independent state; democracy; an end to Zionist colonization of Palestine; and—only if absolutely necessary—an American mandate over Syria as opposed to Britain or France. The report was suppressed.

Despite having no formal League of Nations mandate, American political and economic involvement in the region steadily escalated during the interwar colonial period. American financial missions to Iran backed the shah's centralization programs and consolidation of power with dollar diplomacy. Oil extraction, however, was the most enduring product of this period. The Arabian-American Oil Company (ARAMCO) in the Kingdom of Saudi Arabia claimed to represent generosity and modernization, in contrast to the rapacious colonialism of Britain's Iraq Petroleum Company and the Anglo-Iranian Oil Company (now British Petroleum). Instead, recent scholarship emphasizes ARAMCO's Jim Crow racial hierarchy, fierce antilabor policies, obstruction of political reform, and the numerous American (and other foreign) engineers, scientists, accountants, social scientists, and propagandists who played indispensable roles in forming the Saudi state and the hegemony of the ruling family (Citino 2010; Vitalis 2009; Jones 2010; Mitchell 2013).

COLD WAR: OIL, ISRAEL, AND COUNTERREVOLUTION

Unlike the other major belligerents, the United States emerged from World War II (1939–1945) not only virtually unscathed, but stronger than ever. US policy after the war aimed to maintain, strengthen, and lead the capitalist world order. Despite anticolonial rhetoric, waging the Cold War required the reconstruction of Europe under American hegemony, which necessitated the continued subordination of the resource-rich Middle East. The delivery of Middle East oil to Europe was a key premise of the Marshall Plan, and US military intervention in the Third World also required the availability of

Middle East oil (Painter 2009). Furthermore, the region's position at the southern rim of the Soviet Union compelled the United States to attempt to construct pro-Western military alliances in the 1950s. At the end of World War II, the United States appeared poised to achieve these objectives, as Arab esteem for the United States was high, the British and French were despised, and the Soviet Union's appeal limited.

The establishment of the State of Israel in 1948 was the decisive turning point in both modern Arab history and Arab American relations. The Israelis expelled nearly eight hundred thousand Palestinians, and razed over four hundred villages in what a range of historians now agree was ethnic cleansing (Khalidi 1988, 1992; Pappé 2006; Morris 2004). Both the United States and the Soviet Union quickly recognized the new state of Israel. American policy makers and missionaries on the ground were well aware of Zionist military superiority over the Arabs, as well as the paramount role of violence in imposing a Jewish state in a land whose clear majority had consisted of Arab Muslims and Christians. But US policy was also shaped by decades of Zionist activism in the United States, as well as liberal sympathy for Europe's Jews in the aftermath of the Nazi genocide (Christison 1999; Davidson 2001; Mart 2006). As the Israeli military began to emerge as the clear victors in the 1948 war, US planners were encouraged to incorporate Israeli power into the regional strategy of securing oil and military alliances while denying them to the Soviet Union (Gendzier 2015).

American support for Israel galvanized the antagonistic relationship between the United States and Arabs. Arab nationalist agitation targeted the neocolonial regimes they held culpable in the *nakba* (disaster) of 1948, as well as in the obstruction of modern socioeconomic development and political liberty: Egypt, Syria, Iraq, Jordan, and Lebanon experienced major revolutions, attempted insurrections, or civil wars within a decade of 1948. The most significant of these upheavals was the Egyptian Revolution of 1952 in which nationalist military officers overthrew the pro-British Egyptian monarchy. Egyptian president Gamal Abdel Nasser's (1918–1970) nationalization of the Suez Canal in 1956 prompted a joint Israeli, British, and French invasion of Egypt, which an embarrassed Dwight Eisenhower (1890–1969) administration strongly repudiated. Nasser's success in pushing through nationalization of a strategic resource catapulted him to Pan-Arab and global anti-imperialist leadership.

The Eisenhower Doctrine of 1957 sought to reinforce US backing of pro-US Arab governments and to intimidate those seeking a pro-Soviet, or even neutralist, path (Yaqub 2004). By mid-1958, the attempt to contain Arab nationalism backfired: Egypt and Syria united to form the United Arab Republic; the pro-British Iraqi monarchy was overthrown by nationalist military officers; and Lebanon broke out in its first civil war. In response, the United States sent fifteen thousand marines to Lebanon, while the British sent troops in support of the Hashemite monarchy in Jordan (Gendzier 2006; Louis and Owen 2002).

US concerns about the destabilizing effect of the Palestinian refugee crisis and Arab nationalist agitation waned over the course of the 1960s to 1980s, as Arab nationalism was defeated as a viable alternative by American containment policy, Israeli military power, and the strength of Arab conservatism. US support for the Israeli victories in 1967, 1973, and 1982 reaped dividends, as Soviet allies were consistently defeated and American allies bolstered. From the mid-1970s, Americans have overseen a "peace process" between the Arabs and Israel that has consistently favored Israel (Yaqub 2008). For both liberal and conservative Americans, Israel appeared to fight the Cold War and, later, the war against terrorism more effectively than the United States itself (McAlister 2005). Scholars dispute the nature of the US-Israeli relationship as to whether it is driven by a powerful lobby that sometimes distorts American "national interests" (Mearsheimer and Walt 2007) or by the imperatives of a broader strategy (Chomsky 2006; Plitnick and Toensing 2007).

ISLAM AS THE SOLUTION

Islamists exploited the massive legitimacy crisis facing the Arab governments for their stagnant economies, authoritarianism, and continuous military defeats. This process was aided directly and indirectly by the United States. In the 1950s, Eisenhower promoted Saudi Arabia and pro-Western Islamic movements as counterweights to the secular nationalism and communism then in ascendancy (Jacobs 2011). In Iran, CIA agents helped to depose the democratically elected, secular prime minister Mohammad Mosaddeq (1882–1967) after he nationalized Iranian oil in 1951 (Abrahamian 2013). The coup reconstituted the shah's monarchy, which was overthrown by a popular revolution in 1979 that gave rise to the Islamic Republic.

Following the Soviet invasion of Afghanistan in 1979, which sought to shore up a brittle domestic communist regime, US, Saudi, and Pakistani intelligence assembled jihadists from around the world to fight the Soviets and communism in Afghanistan. This support for the *mujahideen*, including Osama bin Laden (1957–2011), eventually produced the Taliban and al-Qaeda. US support for militant Sunni jihadism began to boomerang in the 1990s, leading to the attacks of September 11, 2001, and the rise of the Islamic State in Iraq and Syria (Mamdani 2005; Atwan 2006; Cockburn 2015).

PAX AMERICANA AND THE WARS ON TERROR

The fall of the USSR in 1991 did not end American ambition to be the final arbiter of world politics. In fact, US intervention in the Middle East only increased at the turn of the twenty-first century. Iraqi president Saddam Hussein's 1990 invasion of Kuwait provided an opportunity to demonstrate the power of the United States in the immediate post–Cold War era. The United States invaded Iraq in Operation Desert Storm in January 1991, quickly repelling Hussein's invasion and defeating his military. The US administration opted to not attempt regime change due to the likelihood of indefinite US occupation. Instead, the United States pushed the United Nations to impose its harshest sanctions regime, estimated to have resulted in the deaths of hundreds of thousands of children (Gordon 2010). Broad Arab official (but certainly not popular) support for the Gulf War announced a new era of American hegemony.

The September 11, 2001, attacks escalated US intervention into the "global war on terror." The US administration of George W. Bush invaded and occupied Afghanistan and Iraq in response. The war on terror legitimized an extensive global surveillance apparatus, torture, assassinations, secret prisons, rendition, and drone strikes that have killed hundreds of civilians. As during the Cold War, undemocratic Arab governments were key partners in this campaign. The US invasion of Iraq in 2003 shattered not only Saddam Hussein's grip on power, but the entire Iraqi state. This sent Iraqi society into a protracted spiral of civil war under occupation, forced displacement, sectarianism, separatism, and foreign intervention. These conditions facilitated the rise of the Islamic State organization, which controlled significant territory in Iraq and Syria by mid-2015. Afghanistan, too, remained at war. The Arab uprisings of 2011, which demanded comprehensive yet largely undefined changes to the US-dominated regional order, have renewed US commitment to the regimes in Egypt, Israel, and the Gulf, and have provoked further interventions in the protracted conflicts in Syria, Libya, and Yemen.

SEE ALSO *Barbary Wars; Cold War; Economics; Foreign Mission Movement; World War I*

BIBLIOGRAPHY

Abrahamian, Ervand. *The Coup: 1953, the CIA, and the Roots of Modern U.S.-Iranian Relations.* New York: New Press, 2013.

Allison, Robert J. *The Crescent Obscured: The United States and the Muslim World, 1776–1815.* Chicago: University of Chicago Press, 1995.

Antonius, George. *The Arab Awakening: The Story of the Arab National Movement.* London: Hamish Hamilton, 1938.

Atwan, Abdel Bari. *The Secret History of Al Qaeda.* Berkeley: University of California Press, 2006.

Chomsky, Noam. "The Israel Lobby?" ZNet. 2006. http://www.chomsky.info/articles/20060328.htm

Christison, Kathleen. *Perceptions of Palestine: Their Influence on U.S. Middle East Policy.* Berkeley: University of California Press, 1999.

Citino, Nathan J. *From Arab Nationalism to OPEC: Eisenhower, King Saʿūd, and the Making of U.S.-Saudi Relations.* 2nd ed. Bloomington: Indiana University Press, 2010.

Cockburn, Patrick. *The Rise of Islamic State: ISIS and the New Sunni Revolution.* London: Verso, 2015.

Davidson, Lawrence. *America's Palestine: Popular and Official Perceptions from Balfour to Israeli Statehood.* Gainesville: University Press of Florida, 2001.

Gendzier, Irene L. *Notes from the Minefield: United States Intervention in Lebanon and the Middle East, 1945–1958.* New York: Columbia University Press, 2006. First published in 1997.

Gendzier, Irene L. *Dying to Forget: Oil, Power, Palestine, and the Foundations of U.S. Policy in the Middle East.* New York: Columbia University Press, 2015.

Gordon, Joy. *Invisible War: The United States and the Iraq Sanctions.* Cambridge, MA: Harvard University Press, 2010.

Grabill, Joseph L. *Protestant Diplomacy and the Near East: Missionary Influence on American Policy, 1810–1927.* Minneapolis: University of Minnesota Press, 1971.

Gualtieri, Sarah M. A. *Between Arab and White: Race and Ethnicity in the Early Syrian American Diaspora.* Berkeley: University of California Press, 2009.

Jacobs, Matthew F. *Imagining the Middle East: The Building of an American Foreign Policy, 1918–1967.* Chapel Hill: University of North Carolina Press, 2011.

Jessup, Henry Harris. *Fifty-Three Years in Syria.* 2 vols. Reading, UK: Garnet, 2002. First published in 1910.

Jones, Toby Craig. *Desert Kingdom: How Oil and Water Forged Modern Saudi Arabia.* Cambridge, MA: Harvard University Press, 2010.

Khalidi, Walid. "Plan Dalet: Master Plan for the Conquest of Palestine." *Journal of Palestine Studies* 18, 1 (1988): 4–33.

Khalidi, Walid. *All That Remains: The Palestinian Villages Occupied and Depopulated by Israel in 1948.* Washington, DC: Institute for Palestine Studies, 1992.

Khalil, Osamah F. "The Crossroads of the World: U.S. and British Foreign Policy Doctrines and the Construct of the Middle East, 1902–2007." *Diplomatic History* 38, 2 (2014): 299–344.

Khater, Akram Fouad. *Inventing Home: Emigration, Gender, and the Middle Class in Lebanon, 1870–1920.* Berkeley: University of California Press, 2001.

Kidd, Thomas S. *American Christians and Islam: Evangelical Culture and Muslims from the Colonial Period to the Age of Terrorism.* Princeton, NJ: Princeton University Press, 2009.

Kieser, Hans-Lukas. *Nearest East: American Millennialism and Mission to the Middle East.* Philadelphia: Temple University Press, 2010.

Louis, William Roger, and Roger Owen. *A Revolutionary Year: The Middle East in 1958.* London: I.B. Tauris, 2002.

Makdisi, Ussama. *Artillery of Heaven: American Missionaries and the Failed Conversion of the Middle East.* Ithaca, NY: Cornell University Press, 2008.

Makdisi, Ussama. *Faith Misplaced: The Broken Promise of U.S.-Arab Relations: 1820–2001.* New York: PublicAffairs, 2010.

Mamdani, Mahmood. *Good Muslim, Bad Muslim: America, the Cold War, and the Roots of Terror.* New York: Doubleday, 2005.

Marr, Timothy. *The Cultural Roots of American Islamicism.* Cambridge: Cambridge University Press, 2006.

Mart, Michelle. *Eye on Israel: How America Came to View the Jewish State as an Ally.* Albany: State University of New York Press, 2006.

McAlister, Melani. *Epic Encounters: Culture, Media, and U.S. Interests in the Middle East since 1945.* Updated ed. Berkeley: University of California Press, 2005.

Mearsheimer, John J., and Stephen M. Walt. *The Israel Lobby and U.S. Foreign Policy.* New York: Farrar, Straus, and Giroux, 2007.

Mitchell, Timothy. *Carbon Democracy: Political Power in the Age of Oil.* London: Verso, 2013.

Morris, Benny. *The Birth of the Palestinian Refugee Problem Revisited.* Cambridge, MA: Cambridge University Press, 2004.

Painter, David S. "The Marshall Plan and Oil." *Cold War History* 9, 2 (2009): 159–175.

Pappé, Ilan. *The Ethnic Cleansing of Palestine.* Oxford, UK: Oneworld, 2006.

Plitnick, Mitchell, and Chris Toensing. "'The Israel Lobby' in Perspective." *Middle East Report* 243 (Summer 2007): 42–47.

Said, Edward W. *Orientalism.* New York: Vintage, 1979.

Schueller, Malini Johar. *U.S. Orientalisms: Race, Nation, and Gender in Literature, 1790–1890.* Ann Arbor: University of Michigan Press, 2001.

Sharkey, Heather J. *American Evangelicals in Egypt: Missionary Encounters in an Age of Empire.* Princeton, NJ: Princeton University Press, 2008.

Sykes-Picot Agreement. 1916. http://avalon.law.yale.edu/20th_century/sykes.asp

Tibawi, A. L. *American Interests in Syria, 1800–1901: A Study of Educational, Literary, and Religious Work.* Oxford, UK: Clarendon Press, 1966.

Vitalis, Robert. *America's Kingdom: Mythmaking on the Saudi Oil Frontier.* London: Verso, 2006.

Watenpaugh, Keith D. *Bread from Stones: The Middle East and the Making of Modern Humanitarianism.* Berkeley: University of California Press, 2015.

Williams, William Appleman. *America and the Middle East: Open Door Imperialism or Enlightened Leadership?* New York: Rinehart, 1958.

Yaqub, Salim. *Containing Arab Nationalism: The Eisenhower Doctrine and the Middle East.* Chapel Hill: University of North Carolina Press, 2004.

Yaqub, Salim. "The Weight of Conquest: Henry Kissinger and the Arab-Israeli Conflict." In *Nixon in the World: American Foreign Relations, 1969–1977,* edited by Fredrik Logevall and Andrew Preston, 227–248. New York: Oxford University Press, 2008.

Nate George
PhD Candidate, Department of History
Rice University

THE MIKADO (ARTHUR SULLIVAN AND W. S. GILBERT, 1885)

The Mikado; or The Town of Titipu, with music by Arthur Sullivan (1842–1900) and libretto by W. S. Gilbert (1836–1911), is one of the most frequently performed comic operas. After its opening on March 14, 1885, at the Savoy Theatre in London, it began to shape British as well as, generally, European, and subsequently American visions of Japan. Until the D'Oyly Carte Opera Company's dissolution in 1982, *The Mikado* was performed every year. Gilbert and Sullivan's most successful collaboration displaced their criticism of British society at the time onto the Asian continent, a make-believe Japan, and, thus, like their contemporary Chinese Canadian novelist and short story writer, Winnifred Eaton (also known as Onoto Watanna, 1875–1954), can be held inadvertently responsible for a romantically inspired understanding of Japan in the Western world and, thus, of a seemingly exotic but also violent Orient.

AMERICAN PERCEPTIONS OF JAPAN

The relationship between the United States and Japan in the late nineteenth century was marked by American imperialism and an increasing Chinese, as well as Japanese, immigration to the United States. Orientalism, *Japonisme,* and exoticism grew in light of American exceptionalism, and led to a gendered discourse about the so-called masculine West and feminine East, clearly visible in the prominent Butterfly myth brought to fame by Giacomo Puccini (1858–1824) in his 1904 opera *Madama Butterfly.*

Although the United States viewed Chinese immigrants as a "yellow peril," interest in anything Japanese was triggered by the travelogues of Matthew Perry (1794–1858) and Bayard Taylor (1825–1878), paintings by James McNeill Whistler (1834–1903), and world exhibitions in Paris (1867, 1878, 1889), Philadelphia (1876), and Chicago (1893). William Elliot Griffis's (1843–1928) two-volume report on his four years in Japan, *The Mikado's Empire* (1876), was, according to Michael Auslin, "the first book on Japan to be published based on serious study of the country's history and culture. Yet it also was a celebration of the growth of Japanese-American relations and the dawning of a new era in world history" (2011, 70). Americans were fascinated by journalist Lafcadio Hearn's (1850–1904) fourteen-year sojourn in Japan, his marriage to a Japanese woman, and his Japanese citizenship, but mostly by his fictional and nonfictional books about a romanticized and idealized Japan. The paradox in the American perception of the Japanese as an inferior human species and yet attractive in art and culture persisted in spite of President Ulysses S. Grant's (1822–1885) visit to Japan in 1877.

After Matthew Perry had initiated trade relations with Japan in 1853, the occasional Japanese immigrant came to the United States but faced nativist rejection. The 1882 Chinese Exclusion Act did not have a Japanese equivalent, but restrictions were established with the 1907 "Gentlemen's Agreement" between the United States and Japan, "by which Japan voluntarily agreed to limit the number of immigrants to the United States" (Auslin 2011, 125). President Theodore Roosevelt (1858–1919) feared Japan's military strength and warned of discrimination against the Japanese, but he also felt the need for restrictive immigration laws because of what he saw as differences between the two races. The political relationship worsened in the first half of the twentieth century and climaxed in the Japanese attack on Pearl Harbor in 1941, followed by the internment of Japanese in the United States and Canada during World War II, and the atomic bombs dropped by the United States on Hiroshima and Nagasaki in 1945. Yet the annual National Cherry Blossom Festival in Washington, DC, celebrates the 1912 gift of three thousand Japanese cherry trees from the mayor of Tokyo to the United States and, most of all, the now respectful relationship between the two nations.

THE OPERA

It has been suggested that Gilbert was inspired to create the Japanese setting of *The Mikado* after a Japanese sword suddenly fell from the wall of his study and after his visit to an exhibition of Japanese culture in London. This origin myth was dramatized in Mike Leigh's *Topsy-Turvy* (1999), a period film about Gilbert and Sullivan's creation of *The Mikado*.

The plot, set in the fictional Japanese town of Titipu, is triggered by a number of mistaken identities and the plight of the star-crossed lovers Nanki-Poo, a wandering minstrel but actually the Mikado's son and heir and claimed by the unwomanly Katisha as her future husband, and Yum-Yum, to be married to Ko-Ko, the Lord High Executioner and former tailor and prisoner. The story ends happily when the lovers are joined, marriages are planned, and the law of execution ridiculed. The title character, the Mikado, is a fictitious Japanese emperor whose name literally means "the honorable gate" of the emperor's palace. While Gilbert strove for authenticity in setting, costumes, and gestures, the names were not authentically Japanese and the white actors performed in "yellowface" (Lee 2010, viii). Both strongly contributed to the comic and satirical effect of the opera. With the exception of the song "Miya Sama," announcing the arrival of the Mikado, the music lacks any Japanese elements, and the text frequently references an unmistakably British context.

THE FIRST AMERICAN PRODUCTION AND LATER ADAPTATIONS

The first authorized American production of *The Mikado* opened in August 1885 at the Fifth Avenue Theatre in New York and ran for 430 performances. Several early unauthorized productions, made possible by less strict American copyright laws, led to court cases. American audiences praised *The Mikado*'s "inconsequential gaiety, an atmosphere of sheer fun that overlays any references to executions, violence, and death" (Williamson 1955, 142).

Numerous adaptations have been produced, including *The Cool Mikado*, a 1963 British film that updated the story to contemporary Japan, and *The Mikado Project*, a 2007 stage play concerning a production of the opera by an Asian American company. Adaptations with black casts—some produced as parodies and others in support of racial uplift—include *The Swing Mikado* (1938), *The Hot Mikado* (1939), and *The Black Mikado* (1975), which testify to the opera's racially critical but ongoing popularity.

IMPACT

The opera's stereotypical representation of the Japanese emperor affirmed the American perception of the Japanese as politically inferior, feminine, and weak, as well as exotically fascinating. The advantage of the Japanese setting clearly lay in the "scope of picturesque treatment, scenes and costumes," as Gilbert himself indicated in an interview with the *Daily News* (Williamson 1955, 141). The "extreme caricature of Japanese bloodthirstiness" (Beckerman 1989, 315) was offensive to the Japanese at the time. Such depictions expressed the Western world's notions of racial difference, as well as Orientalism, which is "a Western style for dominating, restructuring, and having authority over the Orient" (Said 1994, 3). The opera's happy ending, its dissolution of all confusion, its ultimate nonviolence (because all executions are disbanded), and the prevailing of justice contributed to the entertainment of the American audience but also to the assuaging of all possible fears of Theodore Roosevelt's claim of "race suicide" (Roosevelt 1998, 209), to be understood in the context of the American history of "slavery, segregation, and racial formation" (Lee 2010, xiii). *The Mikado* is an opera about East-West relations and a means of coming to terms with the ambivalence inherent in fear of and fascination with the Other.

SEE ALSO *Asia; Foreign Performing Artists; Minstrelsy; World's Fairs*

BIBLIOGRAPHY

Auslin, Michael R. *Pacific Cosmopolitans: A Cultural History of U.S.-Japan Relations.* Cambridge, MA: Harvard University Press, 2011.

Baily, Leslie. *The Gilbert and Sullivan Book.* 4th ed. London: Cassel, 1956.

Beckerman, Michael. "The Sword on the Wall: Japanese Elements and Their Significance in *The Mikado*." *Musical Quarterly* 73, 3 (1989): 303–319.

Berger, Klaus. *Japonismus in der westlichen Malerei, 1860–1920*. Munich: Prestel, 1980.

Birkle, Carmen. "Orientalisms in Fin-de-Siècle America." *Amerikastudien/American Studies* 51, 3 (2006): 323–342.

Chisholm, Lawrence W. *Fenollosa: The Far East and American Culture*. New Haven, CT: Yale University Press, 1963.

Chu, Patricia P. *Assimilating Asians: Gendered Strategies of Authorship in Asian America*. Durham, NC: Duke University Press, 2000.

Cole, Jean Lee. *The Literary Voices of Winnifred Eaton: Redefining Ethnicity and Authenticity*. New Brunswick, NJ: Rutgers University Press, 2002.

Dawson, Carl. *Lafcadio Hearn and the Vision of Japan*. Baltimore, MD: Johns Hopkins University Press, 1992.

Dixon, Wheeler Winston. "Mike Leigh, *Topsy-Turvy*, and the Excavation of Memory." *Senses of Cinema* 37 (2005).

Ferens, Dominika. *Edith and Winnifred Eaton: Chinatown Missions and Japanese Romances*. Urbana: University of Illinois Press, 2002.

Fink, Robert. "Rhythm and Text Setting in *The Mikado*." *Nineteenth-Century Music* 14, 1 (1990): 31–47.

Hein, Patrick. *How the Japanese Became Foreign to Themselves: The Impact of Globalization on the Private and Public Spheres in Japan*. Berlin: Lit, 2009.

Higham, John. *Strangers in the Land: Patterns of American Nativism, 1860–1925*. New Brunswick, NJ: Rutgers University Press, 1994.

Iriye, Akira. *Pacific Estrangement: Japanese and American Expansion, 1897–1911*. Cambridge, MA: Harvard University Press, 1972.

Jackson, Anna. "The Victorian Perception and Acquisition of Japanese Culture." *Journal of Design History* 5, 4 (1992): 245–256.

Kushner, Eve. "Dis-Orientation: Japan from a Western Viewpoint in *Topsy-Turvy* and *The Mikado*." *Bright Lights Film Journal* 30 (2000).

Lee, Josephine. *The Japan of Pure Invention: Gilbert & Sullivan's The Mikado*. Minneapolis: University of Minnesota Press, 2010.

Lee, Rachel C. "Journalistic Representations of Asian Americans and Literary Responses, 1910–1920." In *An Interethnic Companion to Asian American Literature*, edited by King-Kok Cheung, 249–273. Cambridge: Cambridge University Press, 1997.

Long, John Luther. "*Madame Butterfly*." *Century Magazine* (January 1898). In Madame Butterfly *by John Luther Long and* A Japanese Nightingale *by Onoto Watanna (Winnifred Eaton): Two Orientalist Texts*, edited by Maureen Honey und Jean Lee Cole, 25–79. New Brunswick, NJ: Rutgers University Press, 2002.

Lott, Juanita Tamayo. *Asian Americans: From Racial Category to Multiple Identities*. Walnut Creek, CA: AltaMira, 1998.

Lowe, Lisa. *Immigrant Acts: On Asian American Cultural Politics*. Durham, NC: Duke University Press, 1996.

Macfie, A. L., ed. *Orientalism: A Reader*. Cairo, Egypt: American University in Cairo Press, 2000.

MacKenzie, John M. *Orientalism: History, Theory, and the Arts*. Manchester, UK: Manchester University Press, 1995.

McClain, Charles J. "Tortuous Path, Elusive Goal: The Asian Quest for American Citizenship." *Asian Law Journal* (1995): 33–60.

Ostendorf, Berndt. "Einwanderungspolitik der USA: Eine historische Skizze." In *Multikulturelle Gesellschaft: Modell Amerika*, edited by Bernd Ostendorf, 15–31. Munich: Fink, 1994.

Pearson, Hesketh. *Gilbert: His Life and His Strife*. London: Methuen, 1957.

Rapfogel, Jared. "*Topsy-Turvy*." *Film Quarterly* 54, 1 (2000): 39–41.

Roosevelt, Theodore. "Address to the National Congress of Mothers, March 13, 1905." In *Charlotte Perkins Gilman: The Yellow Wallpaper*, edited by Dale M. Bauer, 203–210. London: Macmillan, 1998.

Roosevelt, Theodore. "Letter to Philander Knox, February 8, 1909." Papers of Theodore Roosevelt, Manuscript Division, Library of Congress, 120–126.

Said, Edward. *Orientalism: Western Conceptions of the Orient*. New York: Vintage, 1994. First published in 1978.

Takaki, Ronald. *Strangers from a Different Shore: A History of Asian Americans*. New York: Penguin, 1989.

Takaki, Ronald. *A Different Mirror: A History of Multicultural America*. Boston: Little, Brown, 1993.

Tibbetts, John C. Review of *Topsy-Turvy*, produced by Simon Channing-Williams, written and directed by Mike Leigh, 1999. *American Historical Review* 105, 3 (June 2000): 1061–1062.

Watanna, Onoto. *A Japanese Nightingale* (1901). In Madame Butterfly *by John Luther Long and* A Japanese Nightingale *by Onoto Watanna (Winnifred Eaton): Two Orientalist Texts*, edited by Maureen Honey and Jean Lee Cole, 81–171. New Brunswick, NJ: Rutgers University Press, 2002.

Wichmann, Siegfried. *Japonisme: The Japanese Influence on Western Art in the Nineteenth and Twentieth Centuries*. Translated by Mary Whitall et al. New York: Harmony, 1981.

Williams, Carolyn. "Intimacy and Theatricality: Mike Leigh's *Topsy-Turvy*." *Victorian Literature and Culture* 28, 2 (2000): 471–476.

Williamson, Audrey. *Gilbert and Sullivan Opera: A New Assessment*. 2nd ed. London: Rockliff, 1955.

Yoshihara, Mari. "The Flight of the Japanese Butterfly: Orientalism, Nationalism, and Performances of Japanese Womanhood." *American Quarterly* 56, 4 (2004): 975–1001.

Zanden, James W. Vander. "The Ideology of White Supremacy." In *Race, Class, and Gender in Nineteenth-Century Culture*, edited by Maryanne Cline Horowitz, 90–107. Rochester, NY: University of Rochester Press, 1991.

Carmen Birkle
Professor
Philipps-Universität Marburg, Germany

MILITARY-INDUSTRIAL COMPLEX

"In the councils of government, we must guard against the acquisition of unwarranted influence, whether sought or unsought, by the military-industrial complex." In his 1961 farewell address, President Dwight D. Eisenhower delivered this prescient warning about the risks of a military-industrial complex (MIC)—a powerful network of scientists, engineers, military organizations and corporations that created massive pressures for new weapons. The MIC, he explained, was the result of maintaining both a large military force and a permanent arms industry during peacetime. For Eisenhower, the MIC was necessary so that the United States could respond readily to any communist threat. However, it also threatened democracy and civil society.

The MIC grew out of the World War II mobilization. US industry was unprepared for war when Japan attacked Pearl Harbor in 1941, but it mobilized rapidly under the direction of the War Production Board established in 1942. During the war the United States produced $183 billion of armaments, roughly 40 percent of the world's supply, with the rest of the Allies producing roughly 30 percent and the Axis powers the remaining 30 percent.

Although production dominated Defense Department budgets, research and development (R&D) were crucial to the war. The Office of Scientific Research and Development (OSRD) was directed by scientists and engineers who felt that the armed services were too insular. Thus the OSRD primarily funded wartime R&D through contracts with industrial and academic laboratories. Corporations and universities grew enormously from R&D contracts for radar, the atomic bomb, and other technologies. Many organizations established for wartime R&D continued with Defense Department support after the war. For example, the atomic bomb project continued at the Los Alamos National Laboratory under the management of the University of California, with funding from the new Atomic Energy Commission.

Meanwhile US military enlistments grew to their highest level in US history, totaling more than 8 percent of Americans at the peak of the war. Air power played an important role during World War II—most visibly with the atomic bombing of Hiroshima and Nagasaki—and the air force became a service separate from the army at the end of the war. The US Air Force argued that strategic air power would be decisive in the future and advocated an expanded defense industry. High technology meant prestige and power, and the army and navy also demanded new weapons, with inter-service rivalry increasing demand. Although corporations began converting from wartime to peacetime production after the war ended in 1945, large corporations (which were privileged by wartime contracting) found expanded influence in Washington after the war.

The Soviet detonation of its first atomic bomb in a 1949 test, followed by the eruption of hostilities on the Korea peninsula, triggered a partial remobilization that continued for the duration of the Cold War. Military enlistments began to rise again in 1950, having never completely dropped to prewar levels. Defense R&D also increased throughout the 1950s, with the United States pursuing new technology such as the Semi-Automatic Ground Environment (SAGE) computerized air defense system and the Atlas Intercontinental Ballistic Missile (ICBM). The race for new and better technology only accelerated after the Soviet Union launched the first artificial satellite, Sputnik, in 1957.

Although industry took the lion's share of Department of Defense contract dollars, universities played an important part in the MIC because many academic scientists and engineers depended heavily on Defense funding, maintained ties with industry, and served on military advisory committees. Eisenhower's farewell speech warned of both the potential "domination of the nation's scholars" by federal money and the "equal and opposite danger that public policy could itself become the captive of a scientific-technological elite." Just as intellectual freedom might be stifled by military priorities, policy makers might become unable to critically evaluate the claims of technical committees.

The arms industry employed millions of Americans and was geographically dispersed across the United States, giving Congress strong incentives to support increased spending and making it difficult for the president to refuse military requests. By the time Eisenhower left office, over 71 percent of R&D funding from the Defense Department, Atomic Energy Commission, and NASA was performed by industry, 19 percent by intramural laboratories, and 8 percent by universities. These figures did not change significantly until the 1970s, after the MIC had become a rallying cry for critics of US defense policy.

Concerns about the military-industrial complex persist. For example, the 2005 documentary *Why We Fight* blamed the 2003 invasion of Iraq on the MIC (although many have pointed to other factors). Federal funding for R&D continues to be dominated by military concerns, and the United States vastly outspends the world on national defense. The MIC will remain powerful unless American industry is realigned with new national priorities.

SEE ALSO *Air Force, US; Cold War; Department of Defense, US; Deterrence; Eisenhower, Dwight D.; Intercontinental Ballistic Missiles; International Business*

Machines Corporation (IBM); Navy, US; Nuclear Weapons

BIBLIOGRAPHY

Kevles, Daniel J. *The Physicists: The History of a Scientific Community in Modern America.* 2nd ed. Cambridge, MA: Harvard University Press, 1987.

Koistinen, Paul A. C. *The Military-Industrial Complex: A Historical Perspective.* New York: Praeger, 1980.

Leslie, Stuart W. *The Cold War and American Science: The Military-Industrial-Academic Complex at MIT and Stanford.* New York: Columbia University Press, 1993.

Lowen, Rebecca S. *Creating the Cold War University: The Transformation of Stanford.* Berkeley: University of California Press, 1997.

Pursell, Carroll W., Jr., ed. *The Military-Industrial-Complex.* New York: Harper and Row, 1972.

Rebecca Slayton
Assistant Professor
Cornell University

MINSTRELSY

Minstrelsy was an American entertainment that consisted of songs, skits, dances, and other variety acts performed predominantly by white artists in blackface. Immensely popular during the nineteenth century, minstrelsy broadly influenced American popular culture. Although regarded as a uniquely American art form, early minstrelsy was influenced by a variety of English, French, and Italian musical, dramatic, and literary sources. Early American minstrelsy adopted familiar European texts as a framework for many productions. Early iterations of the minstrel show also fused elements of African American culture with English and Italian stylistic traditions, mixed occasionally with Anglo-American folk materials. At the height of its popularity, minstrel performers and troupes from the United States toured both Britain and Europe.

THOMAS DARTMOUTH RICE AND THE ORIGIN OF JIM CROW

Thomas Dartmouth Rice (1808–1860), an early innovator of minstrelsy, developed a rough-hewn, gyrating blackface caricature that incorporated African American songs and traditions that Rice had encountered during his years as a theatrical performer on the American frontier. This character, subsequently named "Jim Crow," soon became a national sensation, and Rice performed in major entertainment centers, including London. In 1844, Rice performed his version of William Shakespeare's *Othello* in London. He transformed Shakespeare's tragedy into a

musical titled *Othello Travestie*, in which the two main characters, Othello and Desdemona, live happily ever after. In order to appeal to a British audience, Rice would alter the endings to his plays. For American audiences, the character of Jim Crow remained a societal outcast at the end of the performance, despite his victories in revealing middle-class whites as incompetent. For British audiences, for whom class-infused societal tensions predominated, the production's conclusion was changed in favor of a happy ending, whereby Jim Crow found acceptance among the aristocracy.

THE ETHIOPIAN SERENADERS

The enthusiastic reception that Rice encountered in Britain led to tours by other minstrel companies. Preeminent among them were the Ethiopian Serenaders, one of the first professionally organized minstrel troupes. Famous for playing at the White House in 1844, they embarked on a successful tour of Britain in 1846. This group included popular performers Gilbert Pelham (d. 1872), Thomas F. Briggs (d. 1854), and the African American dancer William Henry Lane (c. 1825–1854), also known as Master Juba. Performing in such renowned venues as the St. James Theater in London and Theater Royal in Birmingham, the Ethiopian Serenaders tailored their performances to meet middle-class and aristocratic standards in Britain. No longer performing outrageous musical numbers and dances for a working-class American audience, the Serenaders exchanged their rough costumes for formal wear with bright yellow vests, and they used their well-trained harmonic voices to present a toned-down performance. As a result, their popularity as a minstrel troupe soared in Britain, attracting middle-class audiences with aristocratic pretensions. The Serenaders' private performances for British nobility gave them the genteel respectability that contributed to their success in Britain.

Ironically, the Serenaders' success in Britain never translated into success back in the United States. While touring abroad, one of their competitors, the Christy Minstrels, developed a show that combined refined, sentimental music with the robust comedy, song, and dance expected by American audiences. The elegant and sedate performances of the Serenaders could not compete with the humor of the Christy Minstrels, and their subsequent American tour was financially unsuccessful.

AFRICAN AMERICAN MINSTREL PERFORMERS

After the Civil War (1861–1865), minstrel managers attempted to take advantage of the abilities of African American entertainers by putting them on the commercial stage. One early troupe was a group of fifteen former slaves managed by a white minstrel performer, Sam Hague

686

(1828–1901), who named the company Sam Hague's Slave Troupe of Georgia Minstrels. In June 1866, Hague took the company to England, where it became immensely popular.

The Famous Original Georgia Minstrels, a group of African American performers organized by African American entertainer Charles B. Hicks (1840–1902), also undertook a successful European tour. In January 1870, Hicks left with a small group of minstrels to tour England, Ireland, Austria, Germany, and Wales. Although comprised entirely of African Americans, the Georgia Minstrels continued the inherited minstrelsy practice of portraying African American men through crude and stereotypical images that conformed to the standards of minstrelsy expected by European audiences.

One member of Hicks's troupe, Billy Kersands (1842–1915), became renowned in Europe for his comedic singing and dancing. Kersands rose to fame in the 1870s playing heavily caricatured roles that recreated the slow-witted, slow-moving "Sambo" types that had characterized white minstrelsy since its inception. At the peak of his career, Kersands was among the most highly paid and popular black minstrels in America, and he was noted for entertaining British royalty in a command performance that consisted of him inserting large objects, such as billiard balls and teacups, into his mouth. Despite his talents, his performances never advanced beyond the lazy stereotypes that defined crude minstrelsy.

James A. Bland (1854–1911), one of the first noted African American composers, found popularity in Europe as a singer and composer of minstrel shows. Bland's music and comedy appealed to a more refined European sensibility, making Bland a matinee idol in England and Germany. He became far more popular than Kersands, earning as much as $10,000 a year. Although regarded as an incredibly proficient composer, Bland's popularity in Europe was mostly due to songs that presented a sentimentalized portrait of African Americans and slavery in the American South.

THE RACIAL LEGACY OF MINSTRELSY

While minstrelsy remained popular as a performing art in Britain until the end of the nineteenth century, it never achieved the same level of popularity on the European continent. Nevertheless, minstrel shows presented a view of African Americans as an exotic "other" to British and European audiences. These caricatured images of African Americans were appropriated by British and European audiences, who transformed them into explicitly imperialist and racist concepts of "blackness" that were articulated in various forms in late nineteenth-century European culture and society. The racial legacy of

minstrelsy contributed to the popularity of African villages in numerous European exhibitions and fairs around the turn of the century. These reproductions situated people of color outside of the acceptable boundaries of European modernity and reinforced the virtues of European conquest and colonization.

SEE ALSO *Race*

BIBLIOGRAPHY

Johnson, Stephen. "Death and the Minstrel: Race, Madness, and Art in the Last (W)Rites of Three Early Blackface Performers." In *Burnt Cork: Traditions and Legacies of Blackface Minstrelsy*, edited by Stephen Johnson, 73–105. Amherst: University of Massachusetts Press, 2012.

Lhamon, W. T., Jr. *Jump Jim Crow: Lost Plays, Lyrics, and Street Prose of the First Atlantic Popular Culture*. Cambridge, MA: Harvard University Press, 2003.

Mahar, William J. *Behind the Burnt Cork Mask: Early Blackface Minstrelsy and Antebellum American Popular Culture*. Champaign: University of Illinois Press, 1999.

Pickering, Michael. *Blackface Minstrelsy in Britain*. Aldershot, UK: Ashgate, 2008.

Stuart MacKay
PhD Candidate, Department of History
Carleton University

MISCEGENATION

The term *miscegenation* was first used in the 1860s to describe the mixing of different racial groups through sexual relationships. The historian Peggy Pascoe has argued that the development of the term was the result of two ideas: "white supremacy" and the idea that "interracial marriage is unnatural" (Pascoe 2009, 1).

COLONIAL-ERA VIEWS

Concerns about miscegenation have shaped American interactions with nonwhite people both in the United States and abroad. Fears about interracial marriage initially arose in the seventeenth century, even before the term *miscegenation* had been coined. According to Richard Godbeer, the absence of white women in the colonies did not make white men more enthusiastic about marrying Indian women. While white men sometimes engaged in sexual relationships with Indian women, those who did so risked stigmatization. The reticence to marry Indian women, he argues, partially resulted from a desire to maintain the boundary between white, "civilized" bodies and "savage" ones. (Godbeer 1999, 92–93).

NINETEENTH CENTURY: INCREASING RESTRICTIONS

This desire to maintain racial boundaries affected the Protestant effort to spread the gospel. In 1810, recent graduates from Williams College in Massachusetts founded the American Board of Commissioners for Foreign Missions (ABCFM), which sent missionaries to several fields in the nineteenth century, including Ceylon, British India, the Sandwich Islands (now Hawai'i), western Africa, and Syria. Like the Britain-based London Missionary Society, the ABCFM tried to separate white missionary children from the indigenous people that surrounded them. This was particularly true in the Hawaiian Islands, where missionary children were frequently not allowed to play with Native Hawaiian children (Grimshaw 1989).

Fears about interracial marriage continued throughout the nineteenth century. The Mexican-American War (1846–1848) led the United States to annex large swaths of Mexican territory. Although the Treaty of Guadalupe Hidalgo promised Mexican nationals American citizenship, many Mexican families found themselves excluded from politics. They also found it difficult to retain control of the land and wealth that they had controlled before the war.

Shifting imperial boundaries in the American West had important consequences for non-Mexican families as well. Although many white men and women were suspicious of marriages between white men and indigenous women, it was common for white men living in the American West to marry Native American women. These marriages provided them with access to female labor, indigenous kinship networks, and knowledge about the local community. As a result of changing political dynamics in the American West, white men who had previously cultivated extensive links with indigenous or Mexican communities encouraged their children to develop alliances with American officials in an attempt to protect family assets (Hyde 2011, 279–346). White men also became less likely to marry indigenous women. Sylvia Van Kirk has explored the changes that occurred within Canadian fur trade society over the course of the eighteenth and nineteenth centuries. She argues that the extension of British authority over parts of the American continent led to such marriages becoming less advantageous. Instead, white men sought out white women (Van Kirk 1980). The history of interracial union in what became the United States followed similar contours.

At the same time as American conquest transformed the racial landscape of the American West, the Civil War (1861–1865) further solidified racial boundaries in the southern United States. Although white communities had shown a limited toleration of sexual relationships between black men and white women in the antebellum period, they became less willing to do so after 1865. White communities threatened with violence individuals who considered such relationships, and white women could no longer engage in sexual relationships with black men without being physically intimidated (Hodes 1997). White men, meanwhile, could continue to have sex with black women as long as the relationship was not codified as marriage.

Relationships between white Americans and African Americans were not the only ones to be stigmatized. As Pascoe has pointed out, a variety of states passed or reinstated miscegenation laws in the second half of the nineteenth century, especially after the end of Reconstruction in 1877. These laws forbade marriages between white Americans and a variety of ethnic groups. Antimiscegenation laws did not end sexual relationships between white and nonwhite people. Instead, they tried to make the relationships that did occur invisible by denying them legal standing. Moreover, interracial relationships were generally only illegal when they involved individuals who were considered white. Most white Americans evinced little concern about marriages between Chinese women and Native American men, for example (Pascoe 2009).

The latter point was partially the result of the genesis of fears about miscegenation. Fears about interracial marriage often included a fear that nonwhite immigrants would overwhelm the United States. At the turn of the century, many white Americans were concerned about the number of Chinese immigrants living on the West Coast. According to Yen Le Espiritu, American depictions of Chinese immigrants were often contradictory in that Chinese men were portrayed "as asexual *and* as oversexed." At the same time that Chinese immigrants were seen as overly devoted to their labor, they were described as sexually "voracious" and as threats to the purity of white women (Espiritu 2008, 102). White fears about the presence of Chinese men focused on their dual threat to labor and white women. These fears were exacerbated by restrictive immigration laws, which severely limited the number of Chinese women who could enter the United States. In 1890, there were more than twenty times as many Chinese men as Chinese women in California (Pascoe 1990, 95).

TWENTIETH CENTURY: SHIFTING ATTITUDES

In the twentieth century, understandings of interracial marriage began to shift. The first court case to overturn antimiscegenation laws was *Perez v. Sharp* (1948), in which a Catholic woman named Andrea Perez and an African American man named Sylvester Davis petitioned the California Supreme Court to allow them to marry. As a

Mexican-American woman, Perez could be considered "white" under California law. As a result, the county clerk interpreted the marriage as violating state law, which prohibited marriages between a white woman and a black man. Perez and her husband claimed that the state's unwillingness to allow them to marry violated their civil rights. Since the Catholic Church was willing to countenance the marriage, they argued that the state's prohibition kept her from fully participating in their religion. The California Supreme Court ultimately decided in their favor, ruling that the law violated due process and equal protection of the laws (Pascoe 2009, 206–222).

The US Supreme Court's decision in *Loving v. Virginia* (1967) ended bans on interracial marriage in the United States as a whole. The case involved an African American woman named Mildred Jeter and a white man named Richard Loving who had married in Washington, DC, in 1958 after Mildred became pregnant. The couple resided in Virginia, where they were eventually arrested for violating the state's anti-miscegenation law. They agreed to leave Virginia in 1959 in order to avoid serving a one-year jail sentence. In 1963, the American Civil Liberties Union (ACLU) entered a motion to have the judgment against the Lovings vacated. The Lovings filed a class action suit asking that a court be convened to investigate the constitutionality of Virginia's anti-miscegenation laws a year later. The US Supreme Court ruled in their favor in 1967, handing down a landmark decision which invalidated state anti-miscegenation laws (Pascoe 2009, 271–275).

The pressure to change laws forbidding interracial marriage also came from American GIs who had married Japanese women during or shortly after World War II (1939–1945) and sought to bring their wives to the United States. In 1946, for example, a half-German, half-Japanese woman named Helene Emilie Bouiss tried to enter the United States through the port of Seattle with her white American husband. Although Helene's husband was a former soldier, the racial restrictions contained within US citizenship law at the time prevented her from entering the country as a "war bride" (Villazor 2011, 1363–1365). Although the case was never brought before the Supreme Court, the pressure that such couples placed upon the federal government challenged racial restrictions on marriage and immigration. Amendments to the 1945 War Brides Act temporarily allowed soldiers to bring their Asian wives to the United States (Villazor 2011, 1418–1420).

At the turn of the twentieth century, the United States also became an imperial power with overseas holdings, including Puerto Rico, American Samoa, and Hawai'i. The last would eventually be imagined as a racial paradise, where interactions between different racial groups had none of the tensions that marked such interactions in the continental United States (Desmond 1999, 122–30). That racial paradise, of course, never existed—either in the continental United States or in the Hawaiian Islands.

Throughout the second half of the twentieth century, interracial couples continued to experience discrimination and occasionally violence. Alabama, the last state to legalize interracial marriages, only did so in 2000. Widespread social acceptance of interracial marriages has accompanied formal legalization. According to the 2010 census, nearly one of ten marriages in the United States is between people from different racial backgrounds. It is important to remember, however, that the acceptance of interracial marriage among white Americans is recent. For much of American history, the desire to maintain white supremacy marginalized individuals who tried to legitimize the intimate relationships they had formed with people from different racial groups.

SEE ALSO *Gender; Race*

BIBLIOGRAPHY

Desmond, Jane C. *Staging Tourism: Bodies on Display from Waikiki to Sea World.* Chicago: University of Chicago Press, 1999.

Espiritu, Yen Le. *Asian American Women and Men: Labor, Laws, and Love.* Lanham, MD: Rowman and Littlefield, 2008.

Godbeer, Richard. "Eroticizing the Middle Ground: Indian Sexual Relations along the Eighteenth-Century Frontier." In *Sex, Love, Race: Crossing Boundaries in North American History*, edited by Martha Hodes, 91–111. New York: New York University Press, 1999.

Grimshaw, Patricia. *Paths of Duty: American Missionary Wives in Nineteenth-Century Hawaii.* Honolulu: University of Hawai'i Press, 1989.

Hodes, Martha. *White Women, Black Men: Illicit Sex in the Nineteenth-Century South.* New Haven, CT: Yale University Press, 1997.

Hyde, Anne. *Empires, Nations, and Families: A History of the North American West, 1800–1860.* Lincoln: University of Nebraska Press, 2011.

Pascoe, Peggy. *Relations of Rescue: The Search for Female Moral Authority in the American West, 1874–1939.* New York: Oxford University Press, 1990.

Pascoe, Peggy. *What Comes Naturally: Miscegenation Law and the Making of Race in America.* New York: Oxford University Press, 2009.

Van Kirk, Sylvia. *Many Tender Ties: Women in Fur-Trade Society, 1670–1870.* Norman: University of Oklahoma Press, 1980.

Villazor, Rose Cuison. "The Other *Loving*: Uncovering the Federal Government's Racial Regulation of Marriage." *New York University Law Review* 86 (2011): 1361–2011.

Amanda Hendrix-Komoto
Assistant Professor
Montana State University

MISSIONARY DIPLOMACY

The foreign policies and practices of Woodrow Wilson (1856–1924), the twenty-eighth president of the United States, were often referred to as *missionary* or *moral diplomacy*, or sometimes *Wilsonian idealism*. Wilson was elected in 1912 on a progressive platform to reform national politics. He served two presidential terms from 1913 to 1921.

WOODROW WILSON'S GOVERNMENT PHILOSOPHY

Wilson was a religious man who opposed colonialism but had limited foreign policy experience upon becoming president. Although elected to reform national politics, he spent a great deal of time addressing and responding to various foreign affairs. From the beginning of his first term, Wilson advocated domestic and foreign policies whereby people and nations would adhere to ethical principles that were based on Wilson's own religious and cultural influences (Presbyterian). To Wilson, democracy was the best form of government to promote his progressive and humanitarian objectives. His administration's "New Freedom" policy aimed at restoring free competition and eliminating business practices at home and abroad that he and others perceived to be monopolistic and corrupt. Through missionary diplomacy, the Wilson administration sought to protect and promote democracy, as well as to liberate people living under tyrannical and authoritarian rule around the world. Missionary diplomacy was Wilson's way of proselytizing the moral and ethical benefits of democracy on an international scale.

Missionary diplomacy was essentially an expansion of the Monroe Doctrine (1823), a government philosophy aimed at protecting the Americas from European imperialism. Wilson believed his approach would invoke a reversal of President William McKinley's (1843–1901) expansionism, Theodore Roosevelt's (1858–1919) "big stick" paternalism, and William Taft's (1857–1930) "dollar diplomacy," all of which Wilson viewed as being imperialistic and suitable for achieving short-term business interests but which led to displeasure and even hostility toward the United States. Thus, Wilson put forward an anticolonial, anti-imperialist, anti-expansionist government philosophy designed to limit the United States' foreign involvement while simultaneously promoting democracy in other nations. This shift in the philosophical underpinnings of US policy resulted in considerable opposition from domestic sources, both imperialist and industrialist, who were opposed to status quo changes.

Wilson withdrew support from foreign investors so US companies would return to the United States and reduce their foreign involvement. In reaction to this policy change, US bankers withdrew support for the China-brokered six-nation loan, arranged under the Taft administration, resulting in the loan's collapse. Under missionary diplomacy, the US military could respond unilaterally, based on Wilson's judgment, to foster the development of stable democracies without directly controlling other nations. Those opposed to imperialism were concerned that the missionary-diplomacy approach was so vague that Wilson would be able to intervene under any circumstance. Since Wilson associated "imperialism" with European settler colonialism, he did not view his own interventionist policies as colonial or imperial.

WILSON'S FOREIGN POLICY

Wilson and his secretary of state, William Jennings Bryan (1860–1925), worked together to establish positive relationships with other countries and to promote the democratic ideals of peace, liberty, and the pursuit of happiness in developing nations. Although paternalistic, US intervention was intended to help economically disadvantaged nations and their citizens in their struggle against tyrannical, authoritarian, and corrupt governments and leaders. Advancing democracy and achieving social, economic, and political stability via an ideological and sanctions approach was a considerable task, and Wilson was often compelled to intervene politically and militarily. When Wilson's presidency began, many Caribbean and Latin American nations were impoverished and politically unstable, which was a serious regional concern for the United States. In order to expedite the goals of missionary diplomacy and advance democracy, Wilson sent troops to Mexico (1914), Haiti (1916), the Dominican Republic (1916), Nicaragua (1916), Cuba (1917), Panama (1918), and Russia (1917). The majority of these efforts were viewed as foreign-policy failures, though the deployment of US troops to some Caribbean and Central America countries lasted decades.

The US military was the muscle supporting Wilson's political interventions. The military was used to pressure or even coerce foreign countries to elect prodemocracy leaders, to sign treaties favorable to US interests, and to delegitimize leaders or refuse to recognize nation-states that were opposed to or hostile to US objectives. Wilson viewed these actions as necessary in the face of corrupt, authoritarian, and unstable governments. One of his administration's common foreign-policy practices was to manipulate elections in favor of prodemocracy leaders. From 1914 to 1918, the Wilson administration intervened in elections in Cuba, Haiti, Mexico, and Panama.

Mexico. With US-Mexican relations strained, the Mexican military arrested nine US sailors at Tampico, Tamaulipas, Mexico, on April 9, 1914, an episode known as the Tampico affair. Victoriano Huerta (1850–1916), a general who assumed the Mexican presidency by a military coup, released the sailors the next day and offered a written apology, but he refused to raise the US flag on Mexican soil or provide a twenty-one-gun salute, as the United States requested.

The Wilson administration did not recognize the Huerta regime and learned through US intelligence operatives that Germans were plotting to help Huerta attack the United States by smuggling arms into Mexico onboard the German merchant vessel *Ypiranga*. Without a formal declaration of war, which Congress issued two days later, Wilson ordered twenty-three thousand US troops to the port of Veracruz to prevent the *Ypiranga* from docking. The troops engaged in combat with Huerta's men, resulting in the deaths of 126 Mexicans and nineteen Americans. Wilson explained his intervention as an attempt to defend US interests and protect Mexico from a dictator acting beyond the will of the Mexican people. The mission failed when the German arms were offloaded at a different port, which angered and embarrassed Wilson. US troops remained in Veracruz for six months, while Argentina, Brazil, and Chile (the ABC powers) mediated the withdrawal of US troops from Mexico and prevented war. Intense internal and international pressure forced Huerta to flee to Spain. The following month, José Venustiano Carranza Garza (1859–1920) became president of Mexico.

Even after the issue of the Huerta dictatorship was resolved, US-Mexican relations remained fragile. Wilson distrusted Carranza, as did Pancho Villa (1878–1923), Carranza's former general, who challenged his leadership. Villa felt betrayed by the United States because Wilson supported the Carranza presidency and supplied the Mexican government with arms. In 1916, Villa organized raids near Santa Isabel, Chihuahua, where eighteen Americans were killed, and Columbus, New Mexico, where nineteen Americans died. Wilson sent five thousand troops under the command of Brigadier General John J. Pershing (1860–1948) to capture Villa and his men, known as *Villistas*. General Pershing's troops won several battles against the Villistas, but Pancho Villa eluded capture by hiding in the mountains of northern Mexico, further embarrassing the US military and Wilson. Carranza viewed the presence of US soldiers in the Mexican countryside as an act of war, and the US and Mexican armies clashed in April and June 1916. When the United States amassed one hundred thousand troops at the Texas border in preparation for war, Carranza petitioned for arbitration. An agreement was reached in January 1917, whereby US troops were recalled and the Carranza government was officially recognized. Although war was once again averted, US relations with Mexico challenged the validity of Wilson's missionary diplomacy and its ability to effectively advance democracy.

Nicaragua. The stability of Nicaragua was a concern for the United States due to Nicaragua's proximity to the Panama Canal. Unlike Mexico, Nicaragua had maintained good relations with the United States for several years. In 1911, Nicaragua had requested the help of American bankers and investors in modernizing the country's financial system. The reforms stabilized the economic system, but a revolution that began in 1912 was a threat to the region's stability and the security of the canal. In response, the United States sent 2,500 troops to Nicaragua, where they remained until 1925, although they seldom engaged in combat. Rather, the Wilson administration used the troops to influence the selection of Nicaragua's presidents and to pressure the government to pass the Bryan-Chamorro Treaty of 1914, which authorized the United States to assume Nicaragua's foreign debt and intervene militarily to stabilize the country when necessary.

Haiti and the Dominican Republic. Before Wilson was inaugurated, the United States had sought under the Monroe Doctrine to prevent foreign influence, particularly that of France and Germany, in the Caribbean. Many Caribbean countries, including Haiti, had also been a target of Taft's dollar diplomacy. Wilson ordered a military occupation of Haiti after its president, Jean Vilbrun Guillaume Sam (1859–1915), was killed by a mob in Port-au-Prince and dismembered in the street in July 1915. The US mission was ostensibly to prevent the country from becoming a failed state, but unofficially the troops were sent to protect US citizens and their assets and to thwart a possible German invasion. With the military occupation established, the US manipulated the Haitian legislature to select a pro-US president, Philippe Sudré Dartiguenave (1863–1926). The occupation officially ended with the signing of the Haitian-American Treaty of 1915, according to which the United States was granted authority to appoint the heads of five services (e.g., customs, finance, public safety, pubic works, and public health), although these services remained technically under the control of the Haitian government. The treaty also specified that Haitian property could be transferred only to the United States and not to any other foreign nation. The United States also had the right to enforce the treaty and maintain Haitian independence. US troops remained in Haiti until 1934, supporting US efforts to control Haitian elections and governmental policies. In 1917, Dartiguenave was directed to implement a pro-US constitution—authored by then assistant secretary of the navy Franklin D. Roosevelt (1882–1945)—that allowed foreign land ownership, which had been outlawed since the Haitian Revolution (1790–1804). The United States forced Dartiguenave to dissolve the Haitian legislature after it rejected Roosevelt's constitution and attempted to draft its own anti-US constitution. Haiti's legislature did not reconvene until 1929.

In 1916, Wilson ordered the occupation of the Dominican Republic after President Juan Isidro Jimenes Pereyra (1846–1919) resigned. The United States worked in collaboration with wealthy Dominican landowners to brutally quell the *gavilleros*, a *campesino guerrilla* resistant movement opposed to the US occupation. The occupation lasted until 1924.

The Soviet Union and Cuba. Following the Bolshevik Revolution of 1917, the new Soviet Union withdrew from World War I (1914—1918), compelling the Allied forces to send troops to secure military supplies granted earlier to Russia. Under Wilson's orders, US soldiers chaperoned Czechoslovakian troops as they traveled along the Trans-Siberian Railway. US troops also occupied the ports of Arkhangel'sk (Archangel) and Vladivostok. After several minor skirmishes between Soviet and US troops, most US troops were withdrawn by 1920, although a small force remained until 1922.

Some Cubans, inspired by the Russian Revolution, displayed revolutionary aspirations in 1917. In response, the United States sent troops to Cuba to break labor strikes, protect US citizens and their property, and prevent the establishment of a socialist government. During the occupation, which lasted until 1923, an American governor controlled Cuba's finances under the guidance of representatives from American-owned sugar corporations, who favored pro-US economic policies.

SUCCESSES IN FOREIGN POLICY

Wilson's anti-imperialist policy successes under missionary diplomacy include the repeal of the Panama Canal Tolls Act of 1912, which exempted US ships from paying tolls. This smoothed over an issue with England, which had been upset that the United States received an exemption when the British did not. Wilson also supported China in its border dispute with Japan, which was a reversal from his predecessors. In another example, Wilson signed the Jones Act of 1916, which was an agreement with the Philippines that once a stable government was in place, the Philippines would be granted independence. In actuality, the process took thirty years, and the Philippines did not become independent until 1946. Wilson also signed a treaty with Columbia and offered an official apology and $25 million to pay for the United States having forced Panama from Columbian control.

The US occupations of Haiti and the Dominican Republic created more stable governments and improvements in public safety, as well as better public works and infrastructure. However, the Haitian and Dominican people resented the continued US occupation and control over their countries' governments and policies, leading

critics to charge Wilson with deviating from the principles and intentions that inspired him to promote democracy and humanitarian values.

Such tensions were embedded in missionary diplomacy, which became clear during World War I, when Wilson enthusiastically supported the formation of the League of Nations. He saw the organization as an extension of his mission to promote democracy and humanitarianism on an international scale. Its purpose was to prevent future wars by minimizing conflict and promoting peace between states. Still, critics saw in this community of nations the legacy of settler colonialism and imperialism, perpetuating a hierarchy of nations and people that could incite future conflict.

SEE ALSO *Haiti; Internationalism; Interventionism; League of Nations; Mexico; Paris Peace Conference (1919); Philippines; Preparedness; Wilson, Woodrow; World War I*

BIBLIOGRAPHY

Calhoun, Frederick S. *Power and Principle: Armed Intervention in Wilsonian Foreign Policy.* Kent, OH: Kent State University Press, 1986.

Cooper, John Milton, Jr. "An Irony of Fate: Woodrow Wilson's Pre–World War I Diplomacy." *Diplomatic History* 3, 4 (1979): 425–437.

Haley, P. Edward. *Revolution and Intervention: The Diplomacy of Taft and Wilson with Mexico, 1910–1917.* Cambridge, MA: MIT Press, 1970.

Kant, Immanuel. *Perpetual Peace: A Philosophical Essay.* Translated by M. Campbell Smith. London: Allen and Unwin, 1903. First published in German in 1795.

Levin, Norman Gordon, Jr. *Woodrow Wilson and World Politics: America's Response to War and Revolution.* New York: Oxford University Press, 1968.

Andrew Hund
Assistant Professor
United Arab Emirates University

MODEL T

SEE *Ford, Henry.*

MODEL TREATY OF 1776

The Model Treaty of 1776 was the first state paper that delineated official US foreign policy in the era of the American Revolution. At its core, the Model Treaty embraced principles of free trade and US hegemony over North America, while absenting the US from permanent military alliances with other countries. These principles, embedded in the model plan of treaties, served as a blueprint for American statesmen and diplomats well into the twentieth century and continue to have a lasting influence upon American foreign policy.

John Adams (1735–1826) began work on a draft of "a plan of treaties" during the summer of 1776 at the Continental Congress's behest. Initially intended as a framework for a treaty with France, Adams's plan proposed that the two countries would remove all barriers to trade with the other, including most-favored-nation status for import duties. The plan also addressed such points as the renunciation of the French king's ancient right to claim the property of deceased foreigners within his domain. Should France declare war upon Great Britain, the Model Treaty stipulated that the French would be restrained in their operations through an agreement not to invade former French territory on the North American continent. The United States would be able to make a separate peace with Britain and would not guarantee French claims to captured territory outside the West Indies. Adams believed that the Model Treaty's two pillars of free trade and a nonmilitary alliance were necessary for securing American independence and territorial claims in North America while preventing the United States from getting involved in "future European Wars."

In the fall of 1776, the Continental Congress instructed the American diplomatic mission to France, headed by Benjamin Franklin (1706–1790), to negotiate an agreement based upon Adams's Model Treaty. Negotiations with Charles Gravier, comte de Vergennes (1717–1787), King Louis XVI's foreign minister, resulted in February 1778 with the dual Franco-American Treaty of Amity and Commerce and the Treaty of Alliance. While both treaties were based on the recommendations set forth in Adams's Model Treaty, American negotiators found it difficult to interest the French in accepting a commercial treaty and in becoming involved in a war without the guarantee of a military alliance. Thus, in order to secure French recognition of American independence and most-favored-nation status, Franklin accepted a formal alliance that stipulated mutual military aid and support in future conflicts. In addition to these provisions, the Treaty of Alliance provided that France would renounce all claims to land lost to Britain in North America in the 1763 Treaty of Paris (Canada, Louisiana, and Florida) and specified that both sides would fight until the United States had secured its independence. In order to achieve French recognition of American independence and hegemony over North America, Franklin and the other American negotiators were willing to concede that the United States would not make a separate peace with Britain.

Following the surrender at Yorktown in the fall of 1781, peace negotiations began in Paris between Britain and the allied powers of the United States, France, Spain, and the Netherlands. In discussions with British diplomat Richard Oswald (1705–1784), Franklin suggested that the United States would uphold the original intent of the Model Treaty and negotiate a separate peace if the British would cede Canada. In November 1782, the British delegation agreed to a treaty that secured the American border to the Mississippi River but did not relinquish Canada or Florida.

After the ratification of the 1783 Treaty of Paris, Adams's Model Treaty continued to serve as a functional blueprint for US diplomacy as Americans sought broader commercial relations outside of the British Empire without the corresponding military alliances. During his diplomatic mission to France in the 1780s, Thomas Jefferson (1743–1826) and other American diplomats attempted to negotiate a number of commercial treaties in order to break Britain's commanding influence in the postwar American economy. In order to aid in this endeavor, Jefferson drafted his own model treaty based on the American commercial agreements with France (1778), the Netherlands (1782), and Sweden (1783). The purpose of Jefferson's plan was to offer a systematic and clearly worded treaty that also offered humanitarian concerns for prisoners of war and merchants doing business at the outbreak of hostilities.

Despite several failed attempts by American diplomats to negotiate terms based upon Jefferson's model treaty, including with Denmark, Portugal, and Britain, the model served as a basis for the 1785 Treaty of Amity and Commerce with Prussia, and American diplomats were able to negotiate most-favored-nation status with Morocco in 1786. The principles of the Model Treaty continued to shape American foreign policy during the 1790s and 1800s as George Washington's Farewell Address (1796) warned Americans "to steer clear of permanent alliance with any portion of the foreign world," Jefferson's First Inaugural Address (1801) announced that American policy would be "peace, commerce, and honest friendship with all nations—entangling alliances with none," and the Monroe Doctrine (1823) established in policy, if not in reality, that the Western Hemisphere was the United States' sphere of influence.

SEE ALSO *Adams, John; American Revolution; Franklin, Benjamin; Jay, John; Jefferson, Thomas*

BIBLIOGRAPHY

Adams, John. *Papers of John Adams, The Adams Papers*, Series III: *General Correspondence and Other Papers of the Adams Statesmen*, Vol. 4: *February–August 1776*. Edited by Robert J. Taylor et al. Cambridge, MA: Harvard University Press, 1979.

Gilbert, Felix. *To the Farewell Address: Ideas of Early American Foreign Policy.* Princeton, NJ: Princeton University Press, 1961.

Gould, Eliga H. *Among the Powers of the Earth: The American Revolution and the Making of a New World Empire.* Cambridge, MA: Harvard University Press, 2012.

Hoffman, Ronald, and Peter J. Albert, eds. *Diplomacy and Revolution: The Franco-American Alliance of 1778.* Charlottesville: University Press of Virginia, 1981.

Huston, James H. "Early American Diplomacy: A Reappraisal." In *The American Revolution and "a Candid World,"* edited by Lawrence S. Kaplan. Kent, OH: Kent State University Press, 1977.

Jefferson, Thomas. First Inaugural Address. March 4, 1801. http://avalon.law.yale.edu/19th_century/jefinau1.asp

Perkins, Bradford. *The Creation of a Republican Empire, 1776–1865.* Cambridge, MA: Harvard University Press, 1993.

Washington, George. Farewell Address. September 19, 1796. http://avalon.law.yale.edu/18th_century/washing.asp

Andrew J. B. Fagal
The Papers of Thomas Jefferson
Princeton University

MODERNIZATION THEORY

The 1950s and 1960s were a golden era for development studies. Two important factors contributed to their flourishing. The first was the wave of decolonization that swept the Third World, producing a host of new and independent countries, mostly impoverished and without any viable economic, social, or political infrastructure. The second was the Cold War, during which the United States and the Soviet Union courted these emerging countries and jostled to recruit as many as they could, each to its own sphere. This constellation led American academia and administrations to consider ways of supporting the new states' development while serving American national interests.

ROSTOW'S MODERNIZATION THEORY

Among the development theories, Walt W. Rostow's (1916–2003) modernization theory stands out as academically prominent and politically commanding. The theory is rooted in several academic discourses and intellectual debates, and was influenced by scholars of the transformative processes that turn traditional or underdeveloped societies into modern societies (see, for example, Lipset 1960 and Eisenstadt 1966). Rostow considered modernization from an economic history perspective and put forward a theoretical model to explain the mechanisms of modernization and the causal relations between economic growth, social progress, and democratic consolidation.

These ideas are presented in his numerous writings, especially in two important books, which exemplify the conflation of Rostow the academic and Rostow the practitioner, and no less so the linkage between his theoretical ideas and Cold War strategic concerns.

These two sets of complex associations accompanied Rostow throughout his academic and executive careers, and they are also very conspicuous in the American policies he helped to shape. The first important book was *A Proposal: Key to an Effective Foreign Policy* (1957), which he cowrote with Max F. Millikan. In it, the authors base practical policy recommendations on abstract theory. The book was written with the Dwight Eisenhower administration (1953–1961) in mind and was distributed to members of the US Congress. The second book is *The Stages of Economic Growth* (1961), whose subtitle, *A Non-Communist Manifesto*, shows Rostow's political agenda and strong anticommunist feeling. Though it was academic and theoretical, *The Stages of Economic Growth* arose from Cold War ideological animosity.

Modernization theory proposes the feasibility and potential cooperation between different groups and elites. It argues that social cooperation advances economic growth and thence political development, that is, modernization. Socioeconomic gaps hinder development and modernization in developing countries, and to narrow these gaps social justice parameters are needed that facilitate the emergence of young, new leaderships, encourage social mobility, help in the eradication of gaps between cities and villages, and empower local communities (Millikan and Rostow 1957, 28–34). The culmination of this process is the most modern and positive political institution of them all: democracy. Modernization, with its attendant growth and prosperity, facilitates the emergence of modern democratic societies by enabling education, which leads to social and political awareness (which Rostow termed *Newtonian awareness*) and more modern skills. Thus, modernization creates an active, democratic agency of individuals and communities.

THE FIVE STAGES OF GROWTH

Based on this abstract theory, Rostow constructed a historical model with five stages of growth:

1. Traditional, pre-Newtonian society—unaware of the human ability to manipulate the environment and control fate; limited production capacity.

2. "Preconditions for take-off"—gradual awakening of Newtonian awareness, albeit limited to certain small groups in society.

3. "Take-off"—Newtonian awareness grips society, leading to rapid economic growth.

694

4. Maturity—almost limitless production, optimal utilization of technology, and the development of entrepreneurial capacity.

5. Age of high mass consumption.

Rostow used this theoretical (and normative) framework and historical model to develop his foreign policy recommendations, especially in *A Proposal*. His first argument was that by facilitating modernization, the United States could advance its own national interests and secure and enhance the American way of life. His second contention was that the United States could play a pivotal role in facilitating modernization, but not always or necessarily through direct financial aid. He argued that the United States needed to establish and lead a community of free nations and create an international environment conducive to modernization (Rakove 2013, 43).

WEAKNESSES OF THE THEORY

Rostow's political agency and the administrative posts that he held allowed him to translate his theory into a policy blueprint. But although modernization theory helped shape US policies in the Third World, it also carried several weaknesses that contributed to its demise. First, the theory's sweeping generalizations and Cold War agenda gave little room for the cultural and political particularities of the Third World nations and regions it theorized (Grubbs 2009, 57–59; Rakove 2013, 43). The theory applied an unrealistic, one-size-fits-all socioeconomic model to disparate regions, which acted like a policy straightjacket. This was clear with Africa, which Rostow had little interest in. He left theorizing on African modernization to other colleagues, the keenest of whom was Arnold Rivkin (1968, 1969). Cold War geopolitical calculations also kept the United States from fully engaging with Africa's real problems and needs (or with the needs of other nations and regions). The United States thus settled for general technical assistance rather than targeting specific needs with adequate and tailored financial aid (Grubbs 2009, 60). Unsurprisingly, America's modernization policies in Africa did rather badly.

Southeast Asia suffered a similar fate when it fell victim to the escalation in Vietnam, American fears of a Southeast Asian "domino" (Latham 2000, 163), and Rostow's hawkish anticommunism. Rostow played an active role in the militarized escalation in Vietnam, stressing the importance of the local military elites and American military aid and of harnessing modernization tools to fight communism by diminishing the latter's local attractiveness (Kuklick 2006, 149). The failure to win in Vietnam proved the bankruptcy of modernization theory in Southeast Asia.

LATIN AMERICA AND THE ALLIANCE FOR PROGRESS

Modernization theory had by far the most obvious and dramatic impact in Latin America, and it occurred at a very stormy and sensitive time, when hemispheric relations teetered on the brink of collapse (Ish-Shalom 2006). Despite Franklin D. Roosevelt's Good Neighbor Policy of 1933 to 1945, when America successfully established a positive atmosphere of cooperation with its southern neighbors, relations took a dive during subsequent administrations. America's unwillingness to propose a form of Marshall Plan for Latin America, its all-consuming focus on the Cold War, and its anticommunist agenda led to feelings of ill-treatment among the governments and citizens of Latin America. Furthermore, in January 1959, the Cuban Revolution ousted the American-backed dictator, Fulgencio Batista, and Fidel Castro took over. The US government acknowledged the need for change following this revolution, and Washington responded with several preliminary measures, such as the establishment of the Inter-American Development Bank in 1959 and the Social Progress Trust Fund in 1961.

President John F. Kennedy recognized the deep-seated animosity in Latin America, and, after his inauguration in January 1960, he invested political capital in improving hemispheric relations. Yet he also delivered a blow to these relations with the 1961 Bay of Pigs fiasco. The skepticism of the Latin American republics went back to their former high levels, and Kennedy found himself hard-pressed to rekindle their trust. His efforts to achieve this included establishing the Peace Corps in March 1961, which proved highly effective through the "grassroots" efforts of American volunteers working in remote communities. His next step involved the Alliance for Progress, officially launched in August 1961 at the Punta del Este Conference in Uruguay. The alliance was fashioned along the lines of modernization theory's policy recommendations, which targeted economic growth and greater equity in the distribution of education, health, and so forth, with the establishment of democracies as the ultimate goal. The alliance's aim, as stated in its "Declaration to the Peoples of America," was "to improve and strengthen democratic institutions through application of the principle of self-determination by the people."

The success of the Alliance for Progress was limited however, and it generally failed to achieve most of its goals. This was the result of limited financial resources, the unwillingness of Latin American governments to adopt land and social reforms, and the gradual shift in American attention, especially under President Lyndon B. Johnson, away from the Americas toward the militarized escalation in Vietnam. Throughout the 1960s, a growing number of military coups in Latin America shattered the hopes of modernization and democratization, and the alliance withered away, until it was finally disbanded in 1973 by the Organization of American States. The demise of the Alliance for Progress also marked the demise of Rostowian modernization theory, both academically and politically.

SEE ALSO *Cold War; Rostow, Walt W.; United States Agency for International Development (USAID)*

BIBLIOGRAPHY

Eisenstadt, S. N. *Modernization: Protest and Change*. Englewood Cliffs, NJ: Prentice-Hall, 1966.

Grubbs, Larry. *Secular Missionaries: Americans and African Development in the 1960s*. Amherst: University of Massachusetts Press, 2009.

Ish-Shalom, Piki. "Theory Gets Real, and the Case for a Normative Ethic: Rostow, Modernization Theory, and the Alliance for Progress." *International Studies Quarterly* 50, 2 (2006): 287–311.

Kuklick, Bruce. *Blind Oracles: Intellectuals and War from Kennan to Kissinger*. Princeton, NJ: Princeton University Press, 2006.

Latham, Michael E. *Modernization as Ideology: American Social Science and "Nation Building" in the Kennedy Era*. Chapel Hill: University of North Carolina Press, 2000.

Lipset, Seymour M. *Political Man: The Social Bases of Politics*. Garden City, NY: Doubleday, 1960.

Millikan, Max F., and Walt W. Rostow. *A Proposal: Key to an Effective Foreign Policy*. New York: Harper, 1957.

Rakove, Robert B. *Kennedy, Johnson, and the Nonaligned World*. Cambridge: Cambridge University Press, 2013.

Rivkin, Arnold, ed. *Nations by Design: Institution-Building in Africa*. Garden City, NY: Anchor, 1968.

Rivkin, Arnold. *Nation-Building in Africa: Problems and Prospects*. Edited by John H. Morrow. New Brunswick, NJ: Rutgers University Press, 1969.

Rostow, Walt W. *The Stages of Economic Growth: A Non-Communist Manifesto*. Cambridge: Cambridge University Press, 1961.

Piki Ish-Shalom
Associate Professor, Department of International Relations
The Hebrew University of Jerusalem

MONROE, JAMES
1758–1831

The Monroe Doctrine, a warning to the monarchial powers of Europe to stay away from the Western Hemisphere, was the most famous of James Monroe's accomplishments, as well as the final expression of his career-long dedication to a foreign policy championing American republicanism. Monroe's vision for American foreign policy centered on two primary goals: to preserve republicanism at home and to promote it abroad.

MINISTER TO FRANCE AND ROVING DIPLOMAT

Born in 1758, Monroe joined the Continental Army at the age of sixteen and was wounded at the battle of Trenton on the day after Christmas in 1776. After the war Monroe's political career began under the mentorship of Thomas Jefferson. When Jefferson became secretary of state under George Washington, Monroe was already a key political ally of his. In 1793, because of his relationship with Jefferson and his support of the French Revolution, which had begun in 1789, Monroe was named as the US minister to France. Monroe believed that France was following in the footsteps of the American Revolution and did everything in his power from 1794 to 1797 to persuade the Washington administration to support the movement. He intentionally stressed the similarities of the two "sister-republics" in order to promote the French cause in America. His support was so fervent that he eventually alienated his superiors at home and was recalled from Paris by President Washington. Nevertheless, Monroe's passion for republicanism endured.

When Jefferson became president in 1801, Monroe, as a fellow leader of the Democratic-Republican Party, found himself in a position to help shape foreign policy. During the Napoleonic Wars of the early 1800s the US found itself caught between France and Great Britain. Throughout his eight years in office, Jefferson, along with his secretary of state, James Madison, used Monroe as a kind of roving diplomat throughout Europe. During this period both monarchial Britain and Napoleonic France represented threats to American republicanism. When word reached the United States that France had acquired the Louisiana Territory from Spain in the Treaty of San Ildefonso (1800), the Republicans were alarmed. At the least this acquisition would likely prevent the kind of westward territorial expansion Jefferson envisioned for the country; at worst it might even lead to Napoleon's Grande Armée taking up a position on the US border. In response, Jefferson sent Monroe to France to negotiate the acquisition of New Orleans from Napoleon in 1802, and he eventually concluded a deal to purchase the entire Louisiana Territory.

After his success in Paris, Monroe traveled to London to negotiate a new treaty with Great Britain in 1803. Monroe hoped to avert a looming conflict with Great Britain that, if it led to war, presented a great risk to the still-fragile American republic. The key dividing point between the two countries was the impressment of American sailors. In order to effectively counter the dominant French army, Britain relied on sea power. To man their fleets the royal navy forced American sailors to serve on British vessels. To President Jefferson and his administration this was unacceptable. During the negotiations Monroe quickly discovered that Britain would never make the concessions Jefferson had in mind. As a result, the agreement he concluded with the British, known as the Monroe-Pinkney Treaty (1806), did not deal directly with impressments. When the treaty reached the United States, the administration rejected it out of hand, refusing even to send it to the Senate for confirmation. Monroe, shocked by the rebuff, tried to explain to Jefferson that a settlement on impressments would come in practice if not in the actual wording of the treaty. Jefferson refused to listen, and when news reached London of the treaty's rejection in June 1807 Monroe boarded a ship for home.

SECRETARY OF STATE

In part because of the failure to finalize a treaty, relations between the United States and Britain worsened during James Madison's first term as president, from 1809 to 1813. Monroe's foreign policy experience made him an ideal candidate to replace the ousted secretary of state Robert Smith in April 1811. As secretary of state Monroe faced the same issues that plagued Anglo-US relations during his negotiation of the Monroe-Pinkney Treaty. While fighting a war for survival against Napoleonic France, British leaders paid little attention to how their maritime policies affected the United States. Republicans like Monroe eventually opted for war out of national pride and honor mixed with a heavy dose of lingering hatred for Britain. The British refusal to end impressments represented a slap in the face to the United States for Monroe and Madison. They believed that, though the United States had successfully won political independence during the Revolution, Americans still needed to sever economic, cultural, and even emotional ties to Great Britain. In many ways they wanted to fight a second war of independence in order to preserve American republicanism.

As the War of 1812 began, Monroe acted as Madison's right hand. He served as secretary of state throughout the fighting and even twice spent time as acting secretary of war. Although his record during the war was mixed—Monroe deserves some blame for the fiasco that led to the capture of Washington, DC, in 1814—he and Madison did manage to fight the British to a draw. In fact, after the American victory at the Battle of New Orleans, Americans emerged from the conflict with a renewed sense of nationalism in the years that followed. This helped Monroe emerge as the obvious presidential successor to Madison.

PRESIDENT

After Monroe won the presidency (1817–1825) he continued the same policy of preservation of republicanism at home and promotion abroad. The changing geopolitical situation made this all the more difficult. The monarchists' triumph over Napoleon in 1815 stifled republican government on the European continent. After the Congress of Vienna (1814–1815), the European monarchies worked in concert to prevent the spread of republican revolution. Monroe meanwhile dealt with a crisis at home that nearly led to a clash with the European powers.

During a conflict with the Seminole tribe on the southern US border, General Andrew Jackson seized Pensacola in 1818, effectively giving the United States control over Spanish Florida. This incident provided Monroe and his secretary of state, John Quincy Adams, with an opportunity to promote republicanism across the American continent, but it also represented a potential threat to American security.

On the one hand, Monroe wanted to keep the Florida territory and use the situation to strengthen his negotiating position with the Spanish on the issue of the western border of the United States. He wanted access to the Pacific Ocean and thought that pressuring Spain might help achieve this. On the other hand, Monroe worried that the European monarchs were looking for any excuse to destroy the American republic. A war with Spain might provoke the other European powers. Monroe certainly wanted the United States to acquire Florida, but he did not think the territory was worth a war with Spain or, more importantly, the possible involvement of stronger European nations like Great Britain.

Monroe decided to proceed cautiously. He returned the seized territory immediately to Spain, a move that he believed preserved relations between the two countries and allowed the Spanish to review their relations with the United States. Realizing that they still risked losing Florida for nothing, the Spanish were pressured to come to a quick decision concerning that possession, and over the next few months they negotiated with Adams under the parameters Monroe created. This resulted in the Transcontinental Treaty, signed in February 1819, in which Spain ceded Florida and gave the United States territorial claims to the Pacific Ocean in exchange for the US government's agreement to pay up to five million dollars in American legal claims against the Spanish. The speed with which this occurred owed to Monroe's ability to weigh his competing goals of promotion and preservation of republicanism and shape his policy accordingly.

Before leaving office Monroe took one last opportunity to promote the republican cause. The Spanish American colonies had begun revolting in 1808, and by the end of his presidency many of them had earned some measure of independence and had established working republican governments. Monroe feared that the European alliances might consider reasserting Spanish power in the colonies. These fledgling republics were at risk, and Monroe envisioned Europe's war against revolution spreading to America's doorstep.

Monroe hoped to outline a message to the world that the United States supported these republican movements. The most famous passage of the Monroe Doctrine is steeped in republicanism, and reflects Monroe's attempt to promote it in the New World: "We should consider any attempt on their [Europe's] part to extend their system to any portion of this hemisphere as dangerous to our peace and safety." In other words, should Europe try to reestablish monarchy in place of republicanism in the Western Hemisphere, Americans would see it as an act of aggression against the United States itself. Thus Monroe's most famous act had its origins in his lifelong commitment to championing the republican cause.

SEE ALSO *Adams, John Quincy; Monroe Doctrine (1823)*

BIBLIOGRAPHY

Ammon, Harry. *James Monroe: The Quest for National Identity.* New York: McGraw-Hill, 1971; Charlottesville: University Press of Virginia, 1990.

Bemis, Samuel Flagg. *John Quincy Adams and the Foundations of American Foreign Policy.* New York: Knopf, 1949; Westport, CT: Greenwood, 1981.

Hickey, Donald R. "The Monroe-Pinkney Treaty of 1806: A Reappraisal." *William and Mary Quarterly* 44, 1 (1987): 65–88.

Lewis, James E., Jr. *The American Union and the Problem of Neighborhood: The United States and the Collapse of the Spanish Empire, 1783–1829.* Chapel Hill: University of North Carolina Press, 1998.

Lewis, James E., Jr. *The Louisiana Purchase: Jefferson's Noble Bargain?* Charlottesville, VA: Thomas Jefferson Foundation, 2003.

Owsley, Frank Lawrence, Jr., and Gene A. Smith. *Filibusters and Expansionists: Jeffersonian Manifest Destiny, 1800–1821.* Tuscaloosa: University of Alabama Press, 1997.

Scherr, Arthur. "The Limits of Republican Ideology: James Monroe in Thermidorian Paris, 1794–1796." *Mid-America* 79, 1 (1997): 5–45.

Weeks, William Earl. *John Quincy Adams and American Global Empire.* Lexington: University Press of Kentucky, 1992.

Brook Poston
Assistant Professor of History
Stephen F. Austin State University

MONROE DOCTRINE (1823)

Issued in 1823, the Monroe Doctrine warned European powers to refrain from further intervention in Latin America, while reserving the right of the United States to expand its own influence in the region. In spite of these proscriptions, it stopped short of announcing specific diplomatic policies for the United States.

The open-ended nature of the doctrine was the key to its political utility. Though largely ignored by the European powers at which it was aimed, American statesmen believed President James Monroe's (1758–1831) message embodied the fundamental principles of American foreign policy but adapted its meaning and application as the United States navigated the transition from a group of colonies to a global empire. What began as a statement of the United States' antebellum security requirements, therefore, was transformed into a doctrine supporting US hemispheric hegemony.

US statesmen used the doctrine to shape their interaction with the world's powers and define the changing role of the United States in global affairs. Through the doctrine, Americans' views of their relationship with other peoples, nations, and empires were refined. The chief, and most straightforward, distinction embodied in the Monroe Doctrine was the ideological division of the globe into a presupposed rivalry between New World republics and Old World monarchies. The division of the world into "separate spheres" shaped both the perception of the foreign threats faced by American statesmen and their response. The result was the curious blend of "imperial anticolonialism" identified by the historian William Appleman Williams (1921–1990) in which American statesmen attempted to dismantle European empires in the New World while pursuing imperial policies of their own to consolidate the United States' hemispheric power.

Territorial annexations in Texas and California, protracted warfare against Native Americans, and the century-long struggle for hemispheric ascendancy between the United States and the British Empire all unfolded through the interdependence of American anticolonialism and imperialism. After the Monroe Doctrine's announcement, for instance, some South American leaders hoped the doctrine would provide the basis of inter-American collaboration. However, after proposed defensive treaties of alliance with Colombia and Brazil were rebuffed by the Monroe administration, South American states quickly found that the US had backpedaled from cooperation toward direct intervention. With the rise of racial Anglo-Saxonism and crude Darwinian approaches to international affairs in the late nineteenth century, American statesmen also moved toward a division of the globe between "civilized" and "uncivilized" powers.

Such a cultural division of global affairs underpinned increasing US unilateralism. In one of the most celebrated moments of late nineteenth-century US diplomacy, Secretary of State Richard Olney (1835–1917) used the doctrine as the basis of his "twenty-inch gun," dispatched to convince the British foreign secretary, Lord Salisbury (1830–1903), to submit the Venezuela-Guiana boundary dispute to international arbitration. "Today the United States is practically sovereign on this continent and its fiat is law," Olney warned Britain in June 1895 (Sexton 2011, 203). Hoping to avoid a third Anglo-American war, and overstretched by imperial commitments in Africa, the British Foreign Office ultimately accepted the validity of the Monroe Doctrine in international law for the first time since its announcement.

By 1904, President Theodore Roosevelt (1858–1919) transformed the Monroe Doctrine into an instrument of unilateral intervention. Growing indebtedness of Latin American states, and particularly in the Dominican Republic, where President Carlos Morales (1868–1914) had defaulted on the repayment of European loans, raised the threat of foreign intervention. In response, Roosevelt announced that "the adherence of the United States to the Monroe Doctrine may force the United States, however reluctantly … to the exercise of an international police power" (Sexton 2011, 229). A rising tide of Latin American anti-Americanism and domestic political constraints tempered Roosevelt's inclination to intervene. But in the coming decades, Woodrow Wilson (1856–1924) used the "Roosevelt Corollary" as the ideological rationale for direct intervention in Cuba, Haiti, Mexico, Panama, Honduras, and Nicaragua, where it was entwined with "dollar diplomacy."

Franklin D. Roosevelt's (1882–1945) shift toward the "Good Neighbor Policy" is widely regarded as a partial repudiation of the Monroe Doctrine, yet Roosevelt invoked the doctrine's principle of "separate spheres" to protect the sovereignty of Greenland after Nazi Germany invaded Denmark in April 1940. In the postwar world, the Monroe Doctrine proved an ideological bedfellow for the National Security Council's report NSC-68 (1950), which identified the Soviet Union as the antithesis of American democracy and proposed the policy of "containment" to stifle the expansionist tendencies of the Soviet system. Thereafter, the doctrine indirectly framed US policy toward Latin America as it attempted to counter the threat of Soviet-backed Communism in the region, but was infrequently used as a unilateral doctrine of American foreign policy.

SEE ALSO *Adams, John Quincy; Caribbean; Monroe, James; North America; South America*

BIBLIOGRAPHY

Lewis, James E., Jr. *The American Union and the Problem of Neighborhood: The United States and the Collapse of the Spanish Empire.* Chapel Hill: University of North Carolina Press, 1998.

Ninkovich, Frank. "Theodore Roosevelt: Civilization as Ideology." *Diplomatic History* 10, 3 (1986): 221–245.

Schoultz, Lars. *Beneath the United States: A History of U.S. Policy toward Latin America.* Cambridge, MA: Harvard University Press, 1998.

Sexton, Jay. *The Monroe Doctrine: Empire and Nation in Nineteenth-Century America.* New York: Hill and Wang, 2011.

Stephen Tuffnell
British Academy Postdoctoral Fellow
University of Oxford

MOORISH SCIENCE TEMPLE

The Moorish Science Temple (MST) is an African American religious organization formed in the 1920s in Chicago by Timothy Drew (1886–1929), or Noble Drew Ali, as he was known in the MST. Ali preached a message of racial uplift centered on the organization's religio-racial identity of "Moorish." Moorish was both a racial identity, based in Morocco and the Middle East, and a distinctively Muslim identity. According to the MST, the Moors were descended from the biblical Canaanites and Moabites, but the Moors forgot their true identity and religion when Europeans enslaved them. In reclaiming the Moors' true Islamic heritage, the MST redefined the group's identity as transnational, though its founder and members were born in America.

The MST was one of a number of African American religious sects that developed in early twentieth-century urban environments. Its message of a reconfigured identity had clear appeal in cities like Chicago and Detroit. The MST's claim of a transnational Moorish identity was an attempt to extricate its members from the Jim Crow United States and claim an identity that transcended America's white-over-black racial hierarchy.

Ali pulled from international sources of knowledge when forming the MST's doctrine and when establishing his own prophetic authority. The MST's scriptural text, *The Holy Koran of the Moorish Science Temple of America*, concludes with four chapters written by Ali that describe the historical origin of the Asiatic and Moorish race, the MST's relationship to Christianity, and the MST's prophetic significance. The first forty-four chapters of the MST *Koran* were plagiarized from two esoteric texts, one Theosophical and the other Rosicrucian. The chapters taken from *The Aquarian Gospel*, the Theosophical text, tell of Jesus's experiences in India, Egypt, and Europe. This mobile Jesus discovered ancient knowledge in places beyond the traditional Holy Land. Ali filled an analogous, prophetic role and brought to northern blacks, or Moors, ancient knowledge that affirmed their unique, transnational identity. In addition, Ali proved his status as Allah's prophet when he "mastered the [Egyptian] pyramids" after finding himself lost inside them.

An important facet of this transnational or "ethnic" Moorish identity was its emphasis on respectability. Ali preached that "black," "colored," and "Negro" were false labels for Moorish Americans, given to them through slavery. In pushing off these racial categories, Ali carved out a unique cultural space for MST members outside of America's racial hierarchy. Members were instructed to keep a "neat and clean" appearance and wear fezzes and sashes inspired by the Middle East and Egypt. This way, they would appear more like respectable foreigners than the recent Great Migration arrivals. An additional marker of this transnational Moorish identity was the MST "nationality and identification card" issued to all members. The card identified its carrier as a member of the MST and the Moorish race. Some members used the cards to rebuff northern segregationist practices, and Ali had to instruct members to "stop flashing" their cards to "Europeans," for it was causing "confusion."

The MST frequently referred to white Americans as "Europeans." The MST *Koran* lists not only slavery but also conversions to Christianity as the reasons why MST members forgot their true Moorish identity. Ali wrote how the "nationality of Moors was taken away from them in 1774" through slavery and that they "strayed after the gods of Europe of whom they knew nothing." Although the loss of Moorish identity was due to slavery, the Moors were complicit in this loss by converting to Christianity—a religion that had been prepared for "the European Nations."

Ali and the MST preached a message of racial uplift for American-born Moors and all the "darker" races of the world. For this reason, the FBI began monitoring them during the Great Depression and through World War II. The FBI placed the MST in the category of "Extremist Muslim Groups and Violence." During World War II, the US government considered the MST to be "part of a worldwide organization" to "unite the dark races" and "take over" the United States. FBI agents and informants attended MST meetings and closely observed the organization for pro-Japanese and anti-American teachings. As their rationale for monitoring a local temple, many FBI field briefs cited rumors of pro-Japanese teachings and lectures from Japanese

businessmen or the Japanese Chamber of Commerce. However, most of these field agents found little evidence to support these rumors. Complaints of MST members violating the Selective Service Act as conscientious objectors also fill FBI field reports. Although the agents indicate an initial suspicion of MST members as traitors, most reported that they wanted to obey the law—something Ali always stressed—but they were pacifists. Many indicated that they were happy to serve in a noncombat capacity and frequently purchased war bonds.

Scholars often label the MST as an inauthentic form of Islam. Unlike other forms of Islam, the MST did not emphasize the five pillars or the Qur'an. For members of the MST, Noble Drew Ali and his teachings were vastly more important than the prophet Muhammad. In fact, negative comparisons between the MST and Sunni and Shi'i Islam dominate the MST's small historiography. Whether or not they practiced "orthodox" Islam pales in significance to the contextual importance of Moorish identity and its emphasis on their Moroccan and Muslim heritage.

SEE ALSO *Ali, Muhammad; Black Power Movement; Islam; Malcolm X; Nation of Islam; Orientalism; Ottoman Empire; Universal Negro Improvement Association (UNIA)*

BIBLIOGRAPHY

Clark, Emily Suzanne. "Noble Drew Ali's 'Clean and Pure Nation': The Moorish Science Temple, Identity, and Healing." *Nova Religio: The Journal of Alternative and Emergent Religions* 16, 3 (2013): 31–51.

Curtis, Edward E., IV. "Debating the Origins of the Moorish Science Temple: Toward a New Cultural History." In *The New Black Gods: Arthur Huff Fauset and the Study of African American Religions*, edited by Edward E. Curtis IV and Danielle Brune Sigler, 70–90. Bloomington: University of Indiana Press, 2009.

Gomez, Michael A. "Breaking Away: Noble Drew Ali and the Foundations of Contemporary Islam in African America." In *Black Crescent: The Experience and Legacy of African Muslims in the Americas*, 203–275. New York: Cambridge University Press, 2005.

Johnson, Sylvester. "The Rise of Black Ethnics: African American Religions and the Ethnic Turn, 1916–1945." *Religion and American Culture* 20, 2 (2010): 125–163.

Nance, Susan. "Mystery of the Moorish Science Temple: Southern Blacks and American Alternative Spirituality in 1920s Chicago." *Religion and American Culture* 12, 2 (2002): 623–659.

Nance, Susan. "Respectability and Representation: The Moorish Science Temple, Morocco, and Black Public Culture in 1920s Chicago." *American Quarterly* 54, 4 (2002): 123–166.

Turner, Richard Brent. "The Name Means Everything: Noble Drew Ali and the Moorish Science Temple of America." In *Islam in the African-American Experience*, 71–108. 2nd ed. Bloomington: Indiana University Press, 2003.

Emily Suzanne Clark
Gonzaga University

MORGAN, J. P.
1837–1913

John Pierpont Morgan was one of the most influential businessmen of the Atlantic world in the late nineteenth and early twentieth centuries. As a merchant, banker, and industrial magnate, he had his start in international finance and did much to integrate and manage European and American markets. He traveled widely throughout his life and became a major representative for American business overseas and for foreign business at home in the United States.

CAREER AS AN INTERNATIONAL FINANCIER

Morgan was born in Connecticut, but by age twenty he was accustomed to life abroad. As a teenager, he spent time in Europe both for health reasons and to assist his father, who was partner in the London firm J. M. Beebe, Morgan & Co., with business matters. At age nineteen, Morgan enrolled in university in Germany and soon after was given charge of his father's New York affairs (Strouse 2000, 41–60; Morris 2005, 26). From New York, Morgan corresponded with Beebe, Morgan & Co.'s London office, which provided British financing for American cotton producers (Morris 2005, 26).

Morgan opened his own firm, J. Pierpont Morgan & Co., in 1860 and had his first real experience with international finance during the American Civil War (1861–1865). During the war, Morgan & Co. marketed American securities and US war bonds overseas. Morgan was able to buy low and sell high because he knew the outcome of battles before his English counterparts did. Morgan also engaged in war profiteering by financing a questionable gun sale to the US government and exporting a large amount of gold, making $160,000 in the process (Chernow 2010, 189).

Despite Morgan's predilection for occasional unscrupulous business activities, he was the one American whom overseas financiers trusted (Morris 2005, xiii). Born into a well-to-do family, Morgan was respected almost as European aristocracy. He was, in fact, groomed for international business. His father's company was connected to international banking networks and had invested in the Atlantic Telegraph Company, whose transatlantic cable connected the western shores of the British Isles with eastern points of North America. Morgan's father secured federal subsidies for the operation, which finally succeeded in 1866. This transatlantic cable made possible quick communication, easy trade in foreign currencies, and the sharing of important information, all of which would become increasingly important to Morgan's career (Strouse 2000, 64–65). Although he spent the next several decades amassing his fortune in American railroads, steel, and energy, Morgan remained heavily involved in international finance. His firm lent money to several Latin American countries and did a booming business in Argentinian securities. Despite competing with some British banks for business, Morgan served as an agent for the London-based Rothschild Bank in the United States, and in 1890 he contributed to the Bank of England's rescue package for Barings Bank (Docherty and MacGregor 2013; Chernow 2010, 71).

COOPERATION WITH THE US GOVERNMENT

As Morgan's national and international influence grew, President Grover Cleveland (1837–1908) called on him to help solve the crisis caused by the rapid outflow of gold from US coffers. Morgan & Co. partnered with the London-based Rothschild Bank, with whom it had a long history of collaboration, and in 1895 the two firms worked together to gather gold in exchange for US bonds (Chernow 2010, 75). While to many Americans this business deal seemed to prove an unethical relationship among Washington, Wall Street, and foreign bankers, it revealed Morgan's vast financial power, which he used a decade later to secure foreign lines of credit to rescue the United States from the financial panic of 1907.

In the first years of the twentieth century, Morgan leveraged this power into several major business ventures abroad. In 1899, Morgan & Co.'s debt offering to Mexico made it the first US firm to coordinate a foreign loan package. Several years later, Morgan & Co. arranged fund transfers for the United States to begin construction of the Panama Canal.

INCREASING SCRUTINY OF MORGAN'S FINANCIAL INFLUENCE

Despite these successes, Morgan was not immune to failure. In 1902, he attempted to finance a new subway line in London, but Londoners had grown wary of Morgan's financial influence and he lost the bid to another firm. He also created a shipping trust called the International Mercantile Marine that intended to monopolize North Atlantic maritime traffic. Morgan built up a large Anglo-American fleet and brought

Germany into his trust, but he faced resistance from the British government, which convinced a major British line not to sell out to Morgan. Rate wars with its British competitor and insufficient demand rendered the shipping trust a financial failure (Navin and Sears 1954). By this point, Morgan's reputation was under attack in England, even as London financiers insured his life for $2 million in order to protect their American investments. British cartoons poked fun at Morgan, and many people feared the sway Morgan held over the economy. His reputation took another hit with the 1912 sinking of the *Titanic*, which was owned by one of International Mercantile Marine's subsidiaries (Chernow 2010, 100–104).

The last years of Morgan's life were marked by increased scrutiny of the economic power he had achieved. As Morgan helped shift the center of international finance from England to the United States, his business practices were denounced as greedy and coldhearted, even as Morgan continued to believe that his firm embodied cooperation and private socialism (Chernow 2010, 110–111). He was also the target of antisemitism. Morgan was not Jewish, and he in fact harbored his own antisemitic sentiments, but at the turn of the twentieth century much of the Anglo-American public used antisemitic attacks to express its distrust of the transatlantic banking establishment (Pak 2013). At the same time that he was accused of unjust capitalism practices, he was also actively involved in philanthropy and contributed greatly to the fine arts in the United States. He collected art from all over the globe and helped establish New York's Metropolitan Museum of Art as one of the most impressive museums in the world.

LEGACY

When Morgan died in Italy in 1913, he left a legacy of international financial networks, American banking power, and capitalist greed. He bequeathed his financial empire to his son, J. P. Morgan Jr. (1867–1943), who oversaw J. P. Morgan & Co.'s role as a financier for England, France, and the United States during World War I (1914–1918). Although the firm was sympathetic to the Allied cause in general, it aligned most closely with Britain, and endured a strained relationship with the French government as a result. Morgan & Co. emerged from the conflict as the dominant Wall Street bank, facing accusations that it had facilitated America's entrance in the war in order to rescue its loans. Regardless of public perception, the firm had helped the United States rise from the status of debtor nation to the world's strongest financial power (Horn 2000, 86). Following the war, J. P. Morgan & Co. maintained its

status as one of the most influential financiers of the Western world, but the company increasingly put US interests ahead of international ones, which bred resentment overseas. Its role as a global syndicate also continued to inspire suspicion at home, and during the Great Depression (1929–1939), a federal investigation revealed that it had not paid taxes in several years owing to investment losses (Horn 2005).

Throughout the twentieth century, J. P. Morgan & Co. remained a financial powerhouse: it continued financing foreign governments, moved into Asian markets, and withstood a host of mergers, partnerships, and organizational changes. As of the second decade of the twenty-first century, J. P. Morgan's namesake company has provided financial services for individuals and corporations in more than one hundred countries. Just like its founder, the firm has worked to embody corporate responsibility, while also facing public scrutiny. Despite its controversial history, John Pierpont Morgan's company has survived multiple financial panics and depressions, evolving into one of the most successful multinational banking syndicates in the world.

SEE ALSO *Americanization; Robber Barons*

BIBLIOGRAPHY

Chernow, Ron. *The House of Morgan: An American Banking Dynasty and the Rise of Modern Finance.* New York City: Grove Press, 2010. First published in 1990.

Docherty, Gerry, and James MacGregor. *Hidden History: The Secret Origins of the First World War.* New York: Random House, 2013.

Horn, Martin. "A Private Bank at War: J. P. Morgan & Co. and France, 1914–1918." *Business History Review* 74, 1 (2000): 85–112.

Horn, Martin. "J. P. Morgan & Co., the House of Morgan and Europe 1933–1939." Special issue, "Transnational Communities in European History, 1920–1970." *Contemporary European History* 14, 4, (2005): 519–538.

JP Morgan Chase & Co. https://www.jpmorgan.com/pages/jpmorgan

Morris, Charles R. *The Tycoons: How Andrew Carnegie, John D. Rockefeller, Jay Gould, and J. P. Morgan Invented the American Supereconomy.* New York: Holt, 2005.

Navin, Thomas R., and Marian V. Sears. "A Study in Merger: Formation of the International Mercantile Marine Company." *Business History Review* 28, 4 (1954): 291–328.

Pak, Susie J. *Gentlemen Bankers: The World of J. P. Morgan.* Cambridge, MA: Harvard University Press, 2013.

Strouse, Jean. *Morgan: American Financier.* New York: Harper Collins, 2000.

Lindsay Schakenbach Regele
Assistant Professor
Miami University

MOSSADEGH, MOHAMMAD

Iranian political leader Mohammad Mossadegh was born in Tehran on May 19, 1882. He was raised in an extended family of diplomats and civil servants, and, despite the premature death of his father, he benefited greatly from the education his status afforded him. He accepted an appointment as a tax auditor at age sixteen, and later studied for a year in Paris at the École libres des sciences politiques before illness forced him to return to Iran. Mossadegh suffered from a variety of illnesses throughout most of his life, often crying or fainting during speeches or public appearances. He returned to serious study in Switzerland, where in 1914 he became the first Iranian to earn a European law degree. He then returned to Iran so that he could join the faculty at Tehran's first university.

Mossadegh's political career began in earnest when his uncle, Prime Minister Farman Farma (1859–1939), appointed him as a finance minister in 1917. Working expeditiously, Mossadegh immediately began uncovering corruption, earning a reputation for being intelligent, dogged, and principled. He believed that the tumultuous events of World War I (1914–1918) held great promise for change in Iran, but his work ethic turned to outrage when that promise was thwarted by the Anglo-Persian Agreement of 1919, which granted extensive concessions and power to the British Empire and the Anglo-Iranian Oil Company (AIOC). He was disturbed by the lack of similar outrage from many of his compatriots; civil elites were all too eager to cooperate with the British for their own benefit, fulfilling a standing pattern of corruption. The AIOC was rarely held to even the most lenient provisions in the agreement, leaving Iranian workers with low pay, high unemployment, and poor education across a large portion of the country where the AIOC held independent authority.

Between the world wars, Mossadegh organized a political movement that would become known as the National Front, while Iran endured a series of political crises and twists of fate. Attempting to control Iranian oil potential, the British and some Iranian elites resorted to parliamentary tricks and dynastic manipulations. The British exiled the old shah in 1941, while his son, Shah Mohammed Reza Pahlavi (1919–1980), survived an amateurish but near fatal assassination attempt in 1949. In March of 1951, the issues of oil and nationalization reached a fever pitch. Mossadegh and his National Front were able to pass through parliament the nationalization of Iranian oil. In May, with a surge of popular support, the parliament created the National Iranian Oil Company and made Mossadegh prime minister.

Outraged British officials demanded it all be undone; meanwhile, President Harry Truman's (1884–1972) officials met in Istanbul to discuss this crisis. Concerned that US interests did not align with British oil, they urged the British prime minister, Clement Attlee (1883–1967), to seek reconciliation with Mossadegh through a negotiated compromise. The AIOC would not relinquish what they thought was legally theirs, as it held tremendous value. Iranian petroleum exports accounted for 90 percent of European supply. British agents hatched a plot bribing Iranian officials to have Mossadegh arrested. Mossadegh uncovered the plot and thwarted it, removed British agents and ambassadors from Iran, and the shah fled the country.

In the United States, the administration of recently elected president Dwight Eisenhower (1890–1969) examined more aggressive options in early 1953. CIA director Allen Dulles (1893–1969) pushed hard for a plan to overthrow Mossadegh, on the grounds that he might be a communist. Meanwhile, CIA field agent Kermit Roosevelt Jr. (1916–2000), grandson of Teddy Roosevelt (1858–1919), had already begun in November of 1952 enlisting British spies and accomplices from the previous plot, and thus a plan was already underway when Dulles presented it to the president. Eisenhower was initially dubious and sought instead to use cash to prop up Mossadegh as an American ally in the region. Mossadegh, without precise knowledge of the US plot or internal debates, resorted to a dangerous bluff when he threatened to enlist the Soviet Union as his ally, even though he preferred US support. This turn apparently convinced Eisenhower, already unsure of the intentions of Soviet leadership after the death of Joseph Stalin in March 1953, that a dangerous communist plot was indeed a possibility, and he gave Dulles the go-ahead order for a coup to remove Mossadegh from power.

The coup followed the British pattern of using money to secure influence. The CIA found an ally in the prominent anti-Mossadegh major general Fazlollah Zahedi (1897–1963), who had the imperial guard at his command. The coup unfolded in July and August of 1953, but it was poorly conceived, chaotic, marred by errors, and almost failed. Mossadegh thwarted or ran away from his political enemies, until Zahedi organized a final bloody assault on his home. Casualties on all sides were significant, with hundreds killed. Mossadegh was captured in August, ending his reign as prime minister and head of the National Front. In a court appearance in December, he defended the principle of constitutionalism. He spent three years in jail in solitary confinement, and ten more years under house arrest before his death on March 5, 1967. Shah Mohammed Reza, bolstered by the United States and the CIA, trained new security forces known as SAVAK. His rule returned preferential treatment to the AIOC (later, British Petroleum), and he remained in power until forced into exile by the revolution that began in 1979.

SEE ALSO *Central Intelligence Agency (CIA); Cold War; Covert Wars; Iran*

BIBLIOGRAPHY

Findley, Carter Vaughn, and John Alexander Murray Rothney. *Twentieth-Century World.* 7th ed. Belmont, CA: Wadsworth, 2011.

Fisk, Robert. *The Great War for Civilisation: The Conquest of the Middle East.* New York: Knopf, 2005.

Kinzer, Stephen. *All the Shah's Men: An American Coup and the Roots of Middle East Terror.* Hoboken, NJ: Wiley, 2003.

Weiner, Tim. *Legacy of Ashes: The History of the CIA.* New York: Doubleday, 2007.

Peter A. McCord
Professor of History
State University of New York, Fredonia

MULTICULTURALISM

There has long been a diversity of cultures on American soil. The first settlers, a broad array of Native American peoples, were joined by many different Europeans and Africans. *Multiculturalism* means simply the affirmation of this utterly fundamental fact about the territory of the United States.

STRAINS OF AMERICAN MULTICULTURALISM

While the pluralism of American cultures is very old, fully *affirming* that pluralism is surprisingly new, dating to the middle of the twentieth century. Being quite young, multiculturalism has been a subject of controversy. All multiculturalists agree on the profound pluralism reflected in the national motto "*E pluribus unum*" (one out of many). However, not all agree that the *pluribus* does or should add up to *unum*. Multiculturalists differ, too, in their views on the power relations among groups that make up the American mix.

Moderate multiculturalists hold that the national culture of the United States is vitally enriched by its many "contributing cultures" (in the phrase of historian Lawrence Levine [1933–2006]), all of which merit study and support. Moderates stand against ethnocentrism; they stand for intercultural tolerance and respect.

Since the 1960s, a much more critical strain of multiculturalism has developed among political activists, educators, and artists of color. Arising in the wake of the civil rights movement and reflecting ideas first put forward by black nationalists, these militants protest the denigration and marginalization of black, Indian, Asian American, and Latino cultural traditions. Some militants accuse white Euro-Americans of practicing cultural imperialism. All staunchly oppose assimilationism, the idea that "contributing cultures" ought to dissolve into a universally shared national culture. Militant multiculturalists call for celebrating, promoting, and if necessary restoring their various groups' distinctive values and practices.

WHITE RESISTANCE TO MULTICULTURALISM

To understand why even today multiculturalism remains so contentious, it is necessary to survey the long record of white Americans' resistance to it.

The United States no sooner declared itself a nation than debate about its identity began. "What, then, is the American, this new man?" asked the French-born New York farmer J. Hector St. John de Crèvecoeur (1735–1813) in 1782. Answering his own question, Crèvecoeur linked a key fact of the country's demography with a grand concept of its destiny. "Here individuals of all nations are melted into a new race of men, whose labours and posterity will one day cause great changes in the world" (de Crèvecoeur 2013, 31). Other observers disagreed, considering America's polyglot profile a source of internal disorder and of weakness in its relations with other nations.

Indian peoples had America to themselves until Spaniards, Britons, and Frenchmen planted colonies in the sixteenth and seventeenth centuries. European colonizers imported black Africans to toil as slaves, and Britons in particular permitted other Europeans to come, rendering their colonies more culturally diverse than those of Spain and France. The new United States closed the slave trade in 1808 but left its ports extraordinarily open to European immigration, which exploded with the arrival of millions of Germans, Irish, and Scandinavians. By the middle of the nineteenth century, with its white immigrants from many homelands, black people of many African ancestries, and a plethora of Native peoples, the United States had a population vastly more racially and ethnically diverse than that of any other nation state on earth. "We are not a nation, so much as a world," exulted Herman Melville (1819–1891), whose novels explored his country's unique assortment of peoples and cultures (Melville 1983, 185).

To American political leaders, however, the national miscellaneousness was cause for anxiety. For how could a coherent republic be fashioned out of such different peoples? The founders of the Republic dealt with the problem by hiding their society's bewildering diversity behind universalist principles. They proclaimed American independence on the basis of natural rights that belonged not merely to aggrieved British colonists but to "all men." The new Republic would be a new kind of country, united not by its citizens' common ancestry, religion, or traditions, but rather by their common allegiance to liberty, self-government, and equality under law. Enthralled with this definition of America, Abraham Lincoln (1809–1865) called the Declaration of Independence a beacon the founders erected "to guide their children, and their children's children, and the countless myriads who should inhabit the earth in other ages" (Lincoln 1953a, 546).

But America's novel civic nationalism had to compete with a persisting and very powerful cultural nationalism that defined "American" as white, of European descent, English-speaking, and Protestant in values. The great majority of white Americans took this definition for granted. Much as they wanted their Republic to inspire "all men," they emphatically did not wish "all men" to be eligible for citizenship. The United States remained vastly more open to newcomers than any other nation, to the point that it was sometimes called "a nation of immigrants"—on the understanding that only European immigrants, and especially western Europeans, were wanted.

Even Lincoln saw no contradiction between Americans' Eurocentrism and the universalist principles enshrined in their founding charters. Slavery had to be barred from western territories, he said in 1858, to preserve them "as an outlet for *free white people everywhere*, the world over—in which Hans and Baptiste and Patrick … may find new homes and better their conditions in life" (Lincoln 1953b, 312; emphasis in the original). Lincoln grew more receptive to people of color, but few of his countrymen did. White Americans never imagined accepting the citizenship or celebrating the cultures of people so different from themselves, as rampant legal and social discrimination against black people, the continuing despoliation of Native peoples, and the 1882 ban on Chinese immigration made plain.

Not all European immigrants were welcomed either. In the 1850s, the "Know-Nothing" movement fought to keep out Lincoln's "Patrick," the Catholic Irish. In the 1890s, non-Protestants from eastern and southern Europe were widely regarded as culturally (and often biologically) inferior to native-born whites. Such people should be admitted to the United States, nativists argued, only on the condition that they shed their inherited cultures and wholly Americanize themselves.

THE ETHOS OF ASSIMILATIONISM

But the United States kept its gates open because most native-born Americans assumed European immigrants would assimilate. And they were right: though first-generation immigrants were seldom able to assimilate fully, most of them ardently wished to see their children do so, and the great majority eventually did. Throughout

the nineteenth century and into the early twentieth century, the ethos of *liberal assimilationism* overwhelmingly prevailed in the United States. As long as immigrants learned English and accepted the American civic creed, they could gain naturalization as American citizens. And if they did those things, they could expect at least rough toleration of their religions, their customs, and other nonpolitical elements of their ancestral cultures.

Left completely outside this circle of inclusiveness were people of color. Few Native Americans wanted to assimilate. Most black Americans were avid to do so; following Emancipation their paramount objective was to integrate themselves as equals into American society. They were ruthlessly denied the opportunity. At a time when foreign-born whites were being invited in, people of color descended from ancestors long resident in the United States continued to be shut out.

A 1908 play titled *The Melting Pot* by the Englishman Israel Zangwill (1864–1926) introduced a popular metaphor for American assimilation. Zangwill anticipated everyone's cultural identity, that of natives too, melting together to form a glorious new cosmopolitanism. Native-born Americans thought of putting only immigrants into the melting pot, which would transform them into replicas of native-born Americans. Both versions of the metaphor pictured cultural heterogeneity gradually dissolving into a common national culture. Neither allowed for the assimilation of people of color.

Fifteen million Europeans came to the United States in the 1890–1914 period, straining native-born Americans' confidence in the country's absorptive powers. In 1917, the United States entered World War I (1914–1918), intensifying demands for patriotic unity. Together these events quickly withered toleration for cultural differences. Pressures soared for restricting immigration and for imposing a "100% Americanism" on those who entered.

CULTURAL PLURALISM

In reaction to this illiberal ethos of mandated assimilation, a few progressive reformers and intellectuals developed a philosophy of "cultural pluralism." Social workers like Jane Addams (1860–1935) urged immigrants to treasure their ancestral identities and urged native-born Americans to learn from them. Horace Kallen (1882–1974), a philosopher at the University of Wisconsin, called for making the United States a federation of cultures, "a democracy of nationalities" (Kallen 1998, 116). According to Kallen, true democracy depended on "the perfection and conservation of differences" (53). The radical critic Randolph Bourne (1886–1918) considered the United States to be "already the world-federation in miniature" and foresaw that it would evolve into a new cosmopolitan entity, "not a nationality but a trans-nationality, a weaving back and forth … of many threads of all sizes and colors." People of color, however, would not be among the woven threads. Like other pluralist visionaries of his day, Bourne saw America as "a transplanted Europe" whose evolving "trans-nationality" would remain all white (Bourne 1916).

Nonetheless, Bourne and Kallen are often cited as precursors of today's multiculturalism, and gradually their Eurocentric pluralism made converts. In the 1920s and 1930s, a number of scholars and leaders of immigrant communities endorsed cultural pluralism as a corrective to the coercive Americanization of World War I and to the ending of massive immigration brought about by the National Origins Act of 1924. World War II (1939–1945) and the Cold War generated support for pluralist policies that would distinguish the United States from its authoritarian antagonists. In the 1940s and 1950s, diversity-in-unity became the main motif of government propaganda and a leading motif of American popular culture.

But what was called "cultural pluralism" in the middle decades of the twentieth century typically called for *toleration* of cultural differences rather than *preservation* of differences. Often it really amounted to an enlightened assimilationism, teaching that respect for immigrant cultures was essential to the process of adapting them to American norms. Moreover, the pluralists of sixty years ago remained Eurocentric, paying little attention to black Americans, Native Americans, and other people of color.

THE IMPACT OF THE CIVIL RIGHTS AND BLACK POWER MOVEMENTS

Multiculturalism, affirming the distinctiveness and value of *all* ethnic and racial cultures, did not appear until the civil rights movement finally overturned the long sway of white supremacism in the 1960s. The crusade to establish black citizens' equal rights inspired a parallel crusade to proclaim the integrity and dignity of black culture, with particular emphasis on the creative genius of black people. A related epochal change was a 1965 law that removed racial barrier to immigration, expanding the numbers of Asians and Latin Americans gaining entry to the United States.

Leaders like Ishmael Reed (b. 1938) conceived multiculturalism—a term he coined in 1975—as an instrument of cultural liberation that complemented the achievements of the civil rights movement. But it was Black Power radicalism, rising as civil rights progress stalled, that inspired a militant multiculturalism, joined by other Americans of color, in the 1970s and 1980s. Militants contended that minority cultures, long disparaged or

suppressed, had now to be not only revived and cherished but honored and privileged. Whereas Martin Luther King Jr. (1929–1968) embraced the goal of integration, militant multiculturalists (like proponents of Black Power) went so far as to champion racial separatism. They identified themselves with anticolonial and postcolonial struggles underway in Africa, Asia, Latin America, and the Caribbean.

Multiculturalists were particularly aggressive—their critics would say bellicose—in the realms of art and education. For example, a 1989 report proposing revisions of social studies curricula in New York state alleged that a "systematic bias toward European culture" had inflicted "a terribly damaging effect on the psyche of young people African, Asian, Latino, and Native American descent" (quoted in Schlesinger 1998, 72). Ethnic studies programs proliferated in colleges; artists of color, boldly owning their ancestral roots, gained prominence and support. Surging multiculturalist militancy provoked a backlash by critics like Diane Ravitch (b. 1938) and Arthur Schlesinger Jr. (1917–2007), who charged that the proposed New York curriculum reform would damage the republic by promoting "the division of our people into antagonistic racial groups" (quoted in Glazer 1997, 59). Schlesinger went on to publish an anti-multiculturalist diatribe titled *The Disuniting of America* in 1995.

THE COOLING OF DEBATES OVER MULTICULTURALISM

Since the turn of the twenty-first century, debates over multiculturalism have cooled, in part because multiculturalists have tempered their program, in part because both they and their critics have discovered common ground. Ideologues who preached rebellion against the national culture were never more than a fringe of the movement. Most multiculturalists have continued to subscribe to the liberal assimilationism that has long been the majority American creed—provided assimilation fully and respectfully included people of color. In other words, they have advocated the creation of a dynamic national culture that is *unified* without being *uniform*—a cosmopolitan ideal like Randolph Bourne's "trans-nationality," this time with racial discrimination eliminated.

In a 1997 essay collection titled *MultiAmerica*, Ishmael Reed labeled America's Anglo-Saxon "monoculture" a weapon of white supremacy, but just as ardently he rejected critics' charges of separatism. The movement's ultimate goal, he wrote, was to establish "a new, inclusive definition of the common culture" (Reed 1997 vii). Today, multiculturalists emphasize their commitment to protecting and enhancing both minority cultures and the overarching national culture. They argue that diversity is as vital to healthy cultures as biodiversity is vital to natural ecosystems. In a 1997 book titled *We Are All Multiculturalists Now*, the sociologist

Nathan Glazer (b. 1923) attacked black separatists but concluded that mainstream multiculturalists, far from being divisive, aimed at "a fuller inclusiveness.... They seek inclusion and equality in a common society" (Glazer 1997, 75). An equally apt title for Glazer's book might have been *We Are (At Last) All Assimilationists Now.*

SEE ALSO *Immigration; Immigration and Nationality Act of 1965*

BIBLIOGRAPHY

Bourne, Randolph. "Trans-national America." *Atlantic Monthly* 118, 1 (1916): 86–97. http://www.theatlantic.com/ideastour/idealism/bourne-full.html

Chang, Jeff. *Who We Be: The Colorization of America.* New York: St. Martin's Press, 2014.

de Crèvecoeur, J. Hector St. John. *Letters from an American Farmer and Other Essays.* Edited by Dennis D. Moore. Cambridge, MA: Belknap Press, 2013. First published in 1782.

Glazer, Nathan. *We Are All Multiculturalists Now.* Cambridge, MA: Harvard University Press, 1997.

Gleason, Philip. *Speaking of Diversity: Language and Ethnicity in Twentieth-Century America.* Baltimore, MD: Johns Hopkins University Press, 1992.

Higham, John. *Hanging Together: Unity and Diversity in American Culture.* Edited by Carl J. Guarneri. New Haven, CT: Yale University Press, 2001.

Hollinger, David A. *Postethnic America: Beyond Multiculturalism.* New York: Basic Books, 1995.

Kallen, Horace M. *Culture and Democracy in the United States.* New Brunswick, NJ: Transaction, 1998. Originally published by Boni and Liveright in 1924.

Lincoln, Abraham. "Speech at Lewistown, Illinois." August 17, 1858. In *Collected Works of Abraham Lincoln*, Vol. 2: *1848–1858*, 544–547. Edited by Roy P. Basler, Marion Dolores Pratt, and Lloyd A. Dunlap. New Brunswick, NJ: Rutgers University Press, 1953a.

Lincoln, Abraham. "Seventh and Last Debate with Stephen A. Douglas at Alton, Illinois." October 15, 1858. In *Collected Works of Abraham Lincoln*, Vol. 3: *1858–1860*, 283–325. Edited by Roy P. Basler, Marion Dolores Pratt, and Lloyd A. Dunlap. New Brunswick, NJ: Rutgers University Press, 1953b.

Melville, Herman. *Redburn: His First Voyage.* In *Melville: Redburn, White-Jacket, Moby-Dick*, 1–340. New York: Library of America, 1983. *Redburn* was first published in 1849.

Reed, Ishmael, ed. *MultiAmerica: Essays on Cultural Wars and Cultural Peace.* New York: Viking, 1997.

Schlesinger, Arthur M., Jr. *The Disuniting of America: Reflections on a Multicultural Society.* Rev. and enlarged ed. New York: Norton, 1998.

Eugene E. Leach
Professor of History and American Studies, Emeritus
Trinity College

MULTINATIONAL CORPORATIONS

The earliest manifestations of what today are generally referred to as multinational corporations (MNCs) were present in the ancient world, in the Fertile Crescent, the Mediterranean, India, and Africa. Small and medium-sized enterprises engaged in surprisingly extensive operations, which included resource- and market-seeking behavior, the outsourcing of production, multicultural workforces, and the sophisticated handling of tariff, tax, and currency risk issues.

The next major step in MNCs' evolution came with the founding of colonial trading companies during the period of European imperialism. On behalf of their governments, companies such as the Levante Company, the Hudson Bay Company, the Royal African Company, and the British and Dutch East India Companies increasingly became responsible for a variety of endeavors: conquering and defending new territory by military means (such as fortified trading posts and regular as well as mercenary troops), negotiating local and interregional trade agreements, and securing vital raw materials as well as new export markets. Rapidly, these state-sponsored commercial enterprises—often established as joint-stock companies—shifted from occasional exchange relations with other world regions to a strategic establishment and defense of vital long-distance trade relations that provided raw materials as well as export markets. The existing historical records indicate that their trading volume at this time was greater than has long been supposed. In many ways their mode of organization is also comparable to those of nineteenth-century MNCs, as they relied on 1) professional managers, 2) administrative hierarchies, 3) complex technical and logistical infrastructure as well as 4) financing methods. Nevertheless, the range of goods they produced or traded was mostly limited to raw materials or luxury articles, and their portion of world trade was surely more limited than today. Moreover, the considerable economic and political influence of MNCs was a direct result of colonialism, from which they could practically not be separated.

Whereas MNC activities until the early nineteenth century overwhelmingly concentrated on raw materials, luxury goods, and, in limited ways, on banking and financial services, the industrial revolution required MNCs to integrate and centralize a growing range of activities within the firm. The integrated firm controlled production, sales, distribution, marketing, and research and development. Integration's main goal was the reduction of market insecurity and therefore transaction costs as well as a more efficient overall control of supply and demand. In this context, multinationalization indicated an increasingly geocentric business strategy, which emphasized trade over purely domestic interests. MNCs expanded abroad for various reasons including access to raw materials and other input factors, the development of new markets, exploitation of wage, tax, or regulatory differences between countries, and the circumvention of trade barriers.

Accordingly, foreign direct investment (FDI) rose sharply during the late nineteenth century. It is estimated that on the eve of World War I (1914–1918) 35 percent of all foreign long-term investments represented FDI, mostly concentrated in MNCs' foreign affiliates. In contrast to contemporary MNCs, these affiliates often were not yet part of a fully integrated production chain on a global scale and still experienced considerable autonomy.

The two world wars as well as the turbulent interwar period had a negative impact on MNCs' international business activities because of physical destruction, loss of foreign assets, patents, reparations, and other factors. However, the post–World War II period saw a dramatic resurgence of MNCs. One factor contributing to this resurgence was the incremental liberalization of trade and financial markets through postwar multilateral economic diplomacy. This allowed MNCs such as Levi Strauss & Co., McDonald's, or Coca-Cola to reorganize their business activities on a global and now truly transnational scale. Another vital factor was the emergence of high-tech, large-volume transport technologies such as standardized shipping containers and faster air transportation provided by airplane manufacturers like Boeing and airlines like Pan American World Airways (Pan Am).

Although information and communication technologies like the telegraph, the telephone, and fax machines greatly facilitated the international coordination of production and distribution, parent companies' ability to fully control foreign affiliates' activities remained somewhat limited. Therefore, until the 1970s, MNCs were characterized by centralized management hierarchies, mass production of standardized goods following the Ford Motor Company model, the concentration of certain activities such as research and development (R&D) in the particular MNC's home country, as well as efforts to tighten the direct control of foreign affiliates.

Beginning in the 1970s the digital revolution in information and communication technologies enabled real-time two-way communication, resulting in more efficient modes of coordinating and controlling the global flow of production and distribution. The consequences were a further reduction of transaction costs, improved control over tightly integrated global production chains, and a replacement of vertical organizational hierarchies with flat network structures. New rounds of trade liberalization between countries as well as the removal of capital controls since the 1980s greatly facilitated the continuing growth of global FDI flows.

Consequently, many MNCs no longer display a self-image as a single entity but rather as a collection of discrete surplus-creating entities, situated within a larger and often global value-generating system. This new form of organization is realized in two ways: simple and complex integration. Simple integration means the outsourcing of specific and simple production tasks into world regions with lower production prices while complex production tasks remain close to the headquarter. For example, globally operating car manufacturers often outsource parts of the production process to foreign locations with lower wage levels, such as chassis, car electronics, suspension, and so forth, while design or final assembly remain located in the company's home country. Complex integration means that corporations now apply simple integration to most or all of their global value chains, that is, many elements of the value-adding process are located outside the home country and/or outsourced to third parties. For example, mobile phone manufacturers regularly outsource the production of phones to cheaper and more efficient third parties in order to focus on other core issues like design or software development. The lively information flows between global and regional/local headquarters replaced older and inflexible communication and command hierarchies. Production processes that once were fully integrated within the firm and its foreign affiliates are nowadays often marked by a complex overlap of in-house and outsourced activities, which can still be effectively coordinated and controlled by corporate headquarters with the help of digital information and communication technologies.

SEE ALSO *Boeing Company; Coca-Cola; Levi Strauss & Co.; McDonald's; Pan American World Airways*

BIBLIOGRAPHY

Cohen, Stephen D. *Multinational Corporations and Foreign Direct Investment: Avoiding Simplicity, Embracing Complexity.* Oxford and New York: Oxford University Press, 2007.

Held, David, Anthony McGrew, David Goldblatt, and Anthony Perraton. *Global Transformations: Politics, Economics, and Culture.* Cambridge, UK: Polity Press, 1999.

Moore, Karl, and David Lewis. *The Origins of Globalization.* New York: Routledge, 2009.

Stefan Fritsch
*Assistant Professor of International Relations and
Comparative Government
Bowling Green State University*

MUSICALS

American stage and film musicals of the mid-twentieth century reflected the country's changing role in the world, a result of post–World War II political, social, and historical circumstances. Five musicals provide examples of the United States' new interface with other countries from 1949 to 1959: *South Pacific, The King and I, Lost in the Stars, An American in Paris,* and *The Sound of Music.*

SOUTH PACIFIC

South Pacific, based on James Michener's Pulitzer Prize–winning *Tales of the South Pacific* (1947), opened on April 7, 1949, at New York's Majestic Theatre. The book was adapted by Joshua Logan, who also directed the show, with lyrics by Oscar Hammerstein II and music by Richard Rodgers. Mary Martin and Ezio Pinza starred. The central plot revolves around a US Navy nurse, Ensign Nellie Forbush, who is stationed in the South Pacific during World War II after escaping Little Rock, Arkansas, to see the world. She falls in love with Emile de Becque, an older French plantation owner who has fathered two biracial children with a Polynesian woman. A subplot concerns a Princeton-educated Marine lieutenant, Joe Cable, who falls in love with Liat, a Tonkinese woman. Cable initially rejects the prospect of marriage with Liat because of his racial prejudice. He changes his mind before being killed in an American military mission that also involves de Becque.

The United States had been expanding its presence in the South Pacific as a result of the Cold War policy aimed at securing Asia against further communist control. At the same time, the civil rights movement in the United States was getting underway, and racial issues were drawing increasing attention. *South Pacific* addresses the issue of relations between white Americans and people of other races. The message is clear in the song "You've Got to Be Carefully Taught": prejudice is something passed down but not desirable. Nellie and Joe struggle to overcome their inherited tendency to not accept different traditions and cultures. In the end, Nellie agrees to marry de Becque and become a mother to his biracial children. Cable finally accepts Liat, but he is killed before the marriage can take place. Nellie decides to stay in the South Pacific, with the clear implication that Americans can become a benevolent presence there. She embraces the children and prepares to integrate with her new culture.

A popular and widely seen film version of *South Pacific* was released in 1958. A successful Broadway revival ran from 2008 to 2010 at Lincoln Center's Beaumont Theatre.

THE KING AND I

Rodgers and Hammerstein again focused on Asia in *The King and I,* which opened on March 29, 1951, at New York's St. James Theatre. Jerome Robbins served as the choreographer. The story concerns a young widow, Anna Leonowens, who is employed by King Mongkut of Siam (now Thailand) to teach his numerous children and wives. The musical is based on Margaret Landon's 1944 novel *Anna and the King of Siam,* which is itself based on the writings of the real Anna Leonowens, who worked as a teacher to the children of the king of Siam in the 1860s. Film adaptations were released in 1946 and 1999. A revival of the stage musical opened at Lincoln Center in April 2015.

In the musical, Anna wants to teach members of the Siamese court about Western values like equality and justice without destroying the existing culture. In "The March of the Siamese Children," Anna demonstrates respect for Siamese traditions but aims to change what the children know. A twenty-minute ballet choreographed by Robbins, titled "The Small House of Uncle Thomas," is based on the story in Harriet Beecher Stowe's novel where the slave Eliza and her baby run away from Simon Legree. Narrated by Tuptim, one of the king's concubines, the story is used as a way of declaring that sexual and emotional slavery are no longer appropriate, and Siam and its monarch should consider new values. One of the final numbers, "Shall We Dance," amplifies the idea that Anna can be a force for change as she teaches the King a Western polka. There is a romantic component as Anna proclaims her rights and desires, and the king nearly succumbs to these new ideas of monogamy, romantic love, and women's independence.

After China's turn to communism in 1949, the US government regarded Thailand, which had never been colonized, as an island of stability in Asia. The administrations of Harry Truman and Dwight Eisenhower both gave military, economic, and technical aid to Thailand. However, the musical's portrayal of King Mongkut as autocratic, tradition-bound, and backward did not sit well with the Thai monarchy. Neither did the notion that Anna Leonowens, for them a minor functionary, was responsible for such major changes. The Thai government banned productions of *The King and I,* and when the Thai king and queen visited Australia in 1962, the music was banned from government radio for their eighteen-day stay.

LOST IN THE STARS

Another part of the world came into focus when *Lost in the Stars* opened on October 30, 1949, at New York's Music Box Theatre. American playwright Maxwell Anderson adapted South African writer Alan Paton's *Cry, the Beloved Country* (1948), a tragic story of apartheid, with music by German émigré Kurt Weill. The story concerns Stephen Kumalo, a black South African preacher, and his wife

Grace, who search for their missing son Absalom in Johannesburg, where they find him living in poverty with his pregnant girlfriend. In need of money, Absalom gets involved in a holdup, and he is arrested after killing Arthur Jarvis, a young white man. At the murder trial, Absalom accepts his guilt. Shortly before he is to die, James Jarvis, Arthur's father, arrives at Kumalo's house with a plea that all involved should be forgiven: "I have never had to face what Absalom faced.... Let us forgive each other.... Let us be neighbors. Let us be friends." In the Cold War context, countries with such problems were seen as vulnerable to ideological takeover, and the words "Let us be neighbors. Let us be friends" took on universal meaning.

AN AMERICAN IN PARIS

Paris was a place where American artists, writers, musicians, and people with wealth went to live and tour.

The popular 1951 movie *An American in Paris*, in which an American World War II veteran moves to Paris in his quest to become an artist, presented a different picture. This film conveyed two messages: the United States is not a country that only prizes material success, and the arts have value. The film was directed by Vincente Minnelli, written by Jay Lerner, and based on George Gershwin's music, with lyrics by Ira Gershwin. The story concerns Jerry Mulligan, the American GI played by Gene Kelly, and his compatriot, Adam Cook, a struggling pianist living in Paris. Although a rich heiress, Milo Roberts, wants to support Jerry's art and be his lover, he falls in love with a beautiful French girl, Lise, played by Leslie Caron. Jerry rejects Milo and, initially, her desire to advance his career, sending the message that Americans have integrity and are not ruled by money. In the end, Lise and Jerry are together and life in Paris is good. In

Leslie Caron as Lise and Gene Kelly as Jerry in a dancing scene from **An American in Paris, 1951.** *The popular movie* An American in Paris, *in which an American World War II veteran moves to Paris in his quest to become an artist, conveyed the message that Americans value more than material success: Jerry rejects the advances of an heiress who wants to support his career when he finds true love with Lise.* **MONDADORI/GETTY IMAGES**

March 2015, a new production of *An American in Paris* opened at New York's Palace Theatre, directed and choreographed by Christopher Wheeldon.

THE SOUND OF MUSIC

The Sound of Music opened November 16, 1959, at New York's Lunt-Fontaine Theatre. The musical is based on Maria von Trapp's 1949 memoir *The Story of the Trapp Family Singers*, with music by Rodgers and Hammerstein and book by Howard Lindsey and Russel Crouse. The first Broadway production starred Mary Martin and Theodore Bikel. The plot concerns a young woman named Maria, who comes to the Austrian villa of Captain von Trapp, a widower, to care for his children. The two fall in love, but the dark cloud of the Nazi takeover changes their lives. Von Trapp opposes the Nazis, and although offered a commission in the German Navy, he flees Austria with his family.

Although the plot concerns the Nazis and their murderous agenda, it also serves as a reminder that all oppressive regimes seek control. The musical does not mention Soviet Russia's expansion and totalitarian ideology, but the story implies that freedom and democracy are primary elements of civilization. In the musical, the von Trapp family escapes to Switzerland on foot over the mountains. In actuality, they traveled by train to Italy, then continued to London and finally America. The 1965 film version of *The Sound of Music*, also enormously successful, starred Julie Andrews and Christopher Plummer.

CONCLUSION

These five musicals premiered during the height of the Cold War, when the United States and Soviet Union were vying for dominance with different ideologies and trying to expand their presence and influence around the world. The United States' interface with other countries achieved new dimensions as these uniquely American works were seen by millions, who learned through them about American concerns for freedom and justice.

SEE ALSO *Hollywood; Jazz; Rock 'n' Roll; Television*

BIBLIOGRAPHY

Bordman, Gerald, with updates by Richard Norton. *American Musical Theatre: A Chronicle.* 4th ed. New York: Oxford University Press, 2010.

Green, Stanley. *The World of Musical Comedy: The Story of the American Musical Stage as Told through the Careers of Its Foremost Composers and Lyricists.* 4th ed. San Diego, CA: Barnes, 1980.

Haddow, Robert H. *Pavilions of Plenty: Exhibiting American Culture Abroad in the 1950s.* Washington, DC: Smithsonian Institution Press, 1997.

Klein, Christina. *Cold War Orientalism: Asia in the Middlebrow Imagination, 1945–1961.* Berkeley: University of California Press, 2003.

Prevots, Naima. *Dance for Export: Cultural Diplomacy and the Cold War.* Middletown, CT: Wesleyan University Press, 1998.

Walker, Martin. *The Cold War: A History.* London: Fourth Estate, 1993.

Naima Prevots
Professor Emerita
American University

MUTUAL ASSURED DESTRUCTION (MAD)

Mutual assured destruction, or MAD, was a term developed in the United States in the early 1960s to describe the likely outcome of a major nuclear war. Initially, MAD referred to the numerical reality that both the United States and its Cold War opponent, the Union of Soviet Socialist Republics, had enough nuclear weapons to destroy each other completely should they fully employ their arsenals against each other. Later, MAD came to refer to a strategy of nuclear deterrence, in which the ability to inflict complete destruction on both sides therefore deterred either side from initiating a nuclear attack.

The expression "mutual assured destruction" did not gain common usage until nuclear weapons could be delivered rapidly and unstoppably by long-range intercontinental ballistic missiles (ICBMs). In the early years of the Cold War, US and Soviet nuclear munitions had to be delivered by large bomber aircraft, which were slow and vulnerable to counterattack. Both sides therefore assumed that they could fight a war involving nuclear weapons and yet still survive, because the bombs were relatively small and many would never reach their targets if the aircraft carrying them were destroyed before taking off or shot down in flight.

By 1959, however, the Soviets and Americans began to place their nuclear weapons on ICBMs. These missiles were based in silos underground or in submarines under water, making them difficult to destroy by surprise. This gave each side a *secure second-strike capability*, meaning that both nations would always have enough weapons in reserve to inflict tremendous damage on each other regardless of who attacked first. In the event of war, tens of millions of people, perhaps more, would be killed and injured almost immediately, and major urban areas in North America, Asia, and Europe would be destroyed.

American strategists in civilian and military organizations in the 1960s struggled to make sense of the impact of this new reality. Although they created many scenarios for the use of nuclear weapons in a major war with the Soviet Union, they found that all of them inevitably ended with the complete destruction of both combatants. They therefore referred to this as "assured destruction," and then later amended it to "mutual assured destruction," both to emphasize that the enemy could not escape the same consequences, and because the acronym "MAD" captured the futility of all-out nuclear war.

The United States later accepted MAD not only as a fact but as a strategy. In negotiations with the USSR, the Americans insisted that there could be no point to a nuclear exchange in which both sides would be completely destroyed, and they argued that neither the United States nor the Soviet Union should make plans for fighting such a war. Publicly, Soviet strategists never accepted MAD as a desirable policy, but in practice they behaved in accordance with its realities.

Since the end of the Cold War, the United States and the Russian Federation have reduced their nuclear stockpiles. MAD, however, continues to be an important point of reference for their national security policies, as both sides have long acknowledged their belief that any large-scale use of nuclear weapons would mean the complete destruction of both nations.

SEE ALSO *Cold War; Deterrence; Intercontinental Ballistic Missiles; Nuclear Weapons*

BIBLIOGRAPHY

Freedman, Lawrence. *The Evolution of Nuclear Strategy.* 3rd ed. New York: Palgrave Macmillan, 2003.

Jervis, Robert. *The Meaning of the Nuclear Revolution: Statecraft and the Prospect of Armageddon.* Ithaca, NY: Cornell University Press, 1990.

Nichols, Thomas M. *No Use: Nuclear Weapons and U.S. National Security.* Philadelphia: University of Pennsylvania Press, 2014.

Thomas M. Nichols
Professor
Naval War College

N

NAGASAKI

SEE *Manhattan Project; World War II.*

NAPOLEON BONAPARTE
1769–1821

Napoleon Bonaparte, born Napoleone di Buonaparte on the French island colony of Corsica, rose to global prominence during the wars of the French Revolution. As Napoleon I, he reigned as emperor of France and much of Europe between 1804 and 1814 and again briefly in 1815. Neither friend nor foe of the United States, Napoleon maintained a complex and often contradictory relationship with the American people and government.

FRANCO-AMERICAN RELATIONS DURING THE EARLY NAPOLEONIC ERA

As a young man, Napoleon identified with Corsican struggles for freedom during the period of the American Revolution. He wrote of George Washington (1732–1799): "His cause is that of humanity" (Andrews 1909, 7). Later, after an elite military education, Napoleon supported the French Revolution and accumulated impressive victories as commander of French forces in Italy and Egypt from 1796 to 1799. As he emerged a leading figure of the French Revolution, Napoleon and his fellow revolutionaries no longer upheld the comparatively moderate American Revolution as a model.

In turn, American enthusiasm for the French Revolution waned in the 1790s, especially among members of the Federalist Party. Supporters of the Democratic-Republican Party continued to sympathize with France more than with Britain in the French Revolutionary Wars, but they too soured on the Revolution when Napoleon seized power in France in 1799 and installed himself as first consul. Thomas Jefferson (1743–1826), leader of the Democratic-Republicans, expressed disappointment in the rise of Napoleon and blamed it on the French lacking the "habit of self-government" (Kaplan 1967, 88).

The United States figured prominently in Napoleon's rule as first consul between 1799 and 1804. He responded to Washington's death in December 1799 by ordering ten days of official mourning. Public eulogies drew comparisons between Napoleon and Washington, even though France was still fighting America in the Quasi-War (1798–1800). Napoleon soon supported diplomatic efforts to end the conflict. In early October 1800 France and the United States negotiated a peace known as the Convention of 1800 or the Treaty of Mortefontaine, after the estate in northern France owned by Napoleon's elder brother Joseph (1768–1844), where the treaty was signed. The agreement appeared to inaugurate a new era of goodwill between the two countries after years of mistrust following their successful alliance in the American Revolutionary War.

THE LOUISIANA PURCHASE

Yet Napoleon always placed America's interests after his own. The day after signing the Treaty of Mortefontaine, France acquired Louisiana from Spain in the Treaty of San Ildefonso. Napoleon had designs for an American empire centered on Louisiana and the Caribbean island colony of

Saint-Domingue (now Haiti). The plans clashed with President Jefferson's own ambition to gain control of New Orleans and thereby secure the Mississippi River as a passage for American trade and settlement. France and the United States might have come to blows over New Orleans were it not for the massive slave rebellion in Saint-Domingue, which evolved into the Haitian Revolution. In December 1801 Napoleon sent an army of thirty thousand men to reassert French authority in the colony. Instead, yellow fever and the strong resistance of Haitian revolutionaries led by Toussaint Louverture (1743–1803) combined to destroy Napoleon's army.

By 1803, Napoleon gave up dreams of an American empire. With the prospect of renewed war with Britain following the brief Peace of Amiens, he faced more immediate challenges in Europe. Therefore, in April 1803, France sold Louisiana—a massive area stretching from the Mississippi River to the Rocky Mountains—to the United States for $15 million, or less than four cents an acre. "This accession of territory," Napoleon proclaimed, "strengthens for ever the power of the United States.... I have just given to England a maritime rival, that will sooner or later humble her pride" (DeConde 1976, 173).

MARITIME AND COMMERCIAL CONFLICT

The Louisiana Purchase signified the high point in relations between Napoleon and the United States. After France's naval defeat to Britain in the Battle of Trafalgar in October 1805, Napoleon resorted to commercial warfare to block British trade with Europe. Known in aggregate as the Continental System, Napoleon's measures included the Berlin Decree of 1806 and the Milan Decree of 1807, which targeted neutral ships, including those of the United States, that traded in British ports. The French captured 307 American ships under the Berlin and Milan decrees. The former allies again might have engaged in war, yet America faced even greater maritime depredations by the British from the impressing of sailors and the seizure of ships under the Orders in Council.

The United States struggled to make the warring European powers moderate their commercial policies. Following the disastrous Embargo Act of 1807, Congress passed the Non-Intercourse Act of 1809, which reopened American trade except to French and British ports. In 1810 Macon's Bill No. 2 reinstated trade with Britain and France, but it provided that if either belligerent ended its commercial restrictions against American shipping, the United States would cut off trade with the other. Napoleon responded by announcing a repeal of the Berlin and Milan decrees as they applied to the United States. The British refusal to do the same helped to propel the United States into war with Britain in 1812.

President James Madison (1751–1836) never trusted Napoleon enough to pursue a formal alliance against the British, especially as the emperor's offer to respect American shipping proved disingenuous. Northern Federalists condemned the president for being duped into advancing Napoleon's interests. Daniel Blaisdell (1762–1833), a Federalist congressman from New Hampshire, described Napoleon as a "monster, at whose perfidy and corruption Lucifer blushes and Hell itself stands astonished" (Perkins 1961, 60). Napoleon's former negotiating partners in America spared him no less criticism. In July 1814, after Napoleon's first defeat and exile to the island of Elba, Jefferson exclaimed: "The Attila of the age [is] dethroned, the ruthless destroyer of ten millions of the human race, whose thirst for blood appeared unquenchable, the great oppressor of the rights and liberties of the world, [is] shut up within the circle of a little island in the Mediterranean" (Perkins 1961, 62).

RELATIVES AND ASSOCIATES IN AMERICA

In February 1815, Napoleon returned to France to rule briefly again before his final defeat by the British at Waterloo. Before his permanent banishment to Saint Helena, an island in the South Atlantic, Napoleon hoped to settle in the United States, a plan blocked by the British navy. However, Napoleon's brother Joseph succeeded in fleeing to the United States and ultimately established a large estate in New Jersey. Napoleon's great-nephew, Charles Bonaparte (1851–1921), later became US attorney general and created the Bureau of Investigation, a forerunner of the Federal Bureau of Investigation. Dozens of soldiers from Napoleon's armies also immigrated to America. They settled primarily in Louisiana, where the Napoleonic Code remains the foundation of the state's law to the present day.

SEE ALSO *Embargo Act (1807); France; French Revolution; Impressment; Neutrality Act of 1794; Non-Intercourse Act (1809); War of 1812*

BIBLIOGRAPHY

Andrews, Edward L. *Napoleon and America: An Outline of the Relations of the United States to the Career and Downfall of Napoleon Bonaparte.* New York: Kennerley, 1909.

Blumenthal, Henry. *France and the United States: Their Diplomatic Relations, 1789–1914.* Chapel Hill: University of North Carolina Press, 1970.

Cogliano, Francis D. *Emperor of Liberty: Thomas Jefferson's Foreign Policy.* New Haven, CT: Yale University Press, 2014.

DeConde, Alexander. *This Affair of Louisiana.* New York: Scribner's, 1976.

Egan, Clifford L. *Neither Peace nor War: Franco-American Relations, 1803–1812.* Baton Rouge: Louisiana State University Press, 1983.

Hill, Peter P. *Napoleon's Troublesome Americans: Franco-American Relations, 1804–1815*. Washington, DC: Potomac, 2005.

Kaplan, Lawrence S. *Jefferson and France: An Essay on Politics and Political Ideas*. New Haven, CT: Yale University Press, 1967.

Kukla, Jon. *A Wilderness So Immense: The Louisiana Purchase and the Destiny of America*. New York: Knopf, 2003.

Perkins, Bradford. *Prologue to War: England and the United States, 1805–1812*. Berkeley: University of California Press, 1961.

Denver Brunsman
Associate Professor of History
George Washington University

NAST, THOMAS
1840–1902

Born in Landau, Bavaria, in 1840, Thomas Nast immigrated to the United States six years later, avoiding the Revolutions of 1848. Nast translated his lifelong love of drawing into a career as America's foremost political cartoonist. His work for the illustrated magazine *Harper's Weekly*, in particular, allowed him to engage deeply with American and world events between the 1860s and 1880s. Nast was widely read and admired, and became the most powerful American political cartoonist of his day. The work that produced this fame was both reflective and original. It reflected American sentiments about Catholicism and Irish and Chinese immigration, as well as an ongoing national discussion about the status of Native Americans. As a result, it proved popular not only with nativists but with a wider swath of the public.

Nast absorbed the liberal politics of his father, embracing the values espoused by advocates of greater popular participation in government during the 1840s. Raised in an immigrant enclave in Lower Manhattan, Nast grew to maturity in a world shaped by national origin, religious conviction, and political loyalty—sometimes to an American party like the Democrats or Nativists but as often to the politics of a distant home country. He idolized leaders like Louis Kossuth (1802–1894), the Hungarian revolutionary whose visit to New York Nast witnessed with his father. Those interests and political convictions led him, early in his career, to Italy to sketch the unification efforts of Giuseppe Garibaldi (1807–1882). He returned to New York just as the American Civil War began.

New York shaped Nast's career for the rest of his life, particularly with regard to his view of immigrants. He enjoyed referring to his own immigrant history as an example of the American potential for opportunity, but he also absorbed many of the anti-immigrant ideas so common in the nineteenth century. Anti-Catholicism,

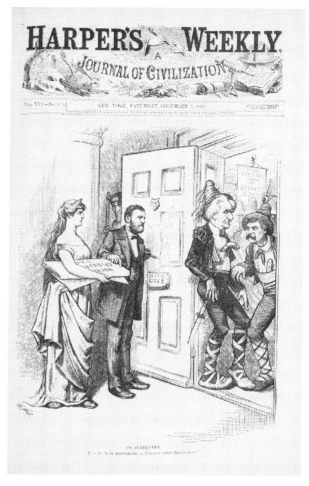

"No Surrender," wood engraving by Thomas Nast, 1872. As America's foremost political cartoonist, featured regularly in the pages of the illustrated magazine Harper's Weekly, *Nast engaged deeply with American and world events between the 1860s and 1880s. Here, he addresses President U. S. Grant's proposals for civil service reform.* THE NEW YORK HISTORICAL SOCIETY/ ARCHIVE PHOTOS/GETTY IMAGES

expressed on its own terms and as anti-Irish sentiment, appeared regularly in his cartoons.

Nast particularly focused on the civic consequences of massive immigration on American political and urban culture. In his cartoons, the Irish (and sometimes the Germans, too) appeared as drunken, violent louts whose commitment to Democratic politics reflected a kind of vestigial clan loyalty rather than the kind of informed citizenship Nast idealized. Repeating stereotypes drawn from English caricature, Nast exaggerated the square jaws of his Irishmen, gave them clubs and pipes, and emphasized their thick, heavy boots. They were, in every way, coarse. In a nation so concerned with refinement and respectability, the Irish represented a serious threat of social decline.

Worst of all, Irish Roman Catholicism appeared in Nast's cartoons as a form of slavish sycophancy or superstition. Among Nast's most famous images are those that portray Catholic bishops threatening American schoolchildren (a critique related to a battle over public school textbooks) and those that show the pope dictating the racial positions of Democratic politics. Nast's anti-Catholicism was typical of his time and of *Harper's Weekly*. Evidence suggests that Nast may have been raised Catholic. If so, his later attacks on it seem even more fraught with meaning: an immigrant Catholic resisting social authority and economic power exerted by other Catholic immigrants.

The origin of Nast's antipathy toward Irish immigrants may lie in his youth. He grew up within blocks of the notorious slum Five Points, aware of its crime, poverty, and machine politics. The New York Draft Riots of 1863 undoubtedly affected his view of his Irish neighbors, though. Shocked by the violence and destruction wrought by the rioters, Nast linked the riots explicitly to Irish resistance to emancipation. The burning of the Colored Orphan Asylum, for example, and the lynching of black New Yorkers, convinced him that New York's Irish population—whom he blamed for the riots—posed a serious threat to urban stability and metropolitan government. For the rest of his career, Nast added the burning asylum and images of lynching to the backgrounds of cartoons attacking white supremacist violence (for example, in his cartoons "Patience on a Monument" and "This Is a White Man's Government").

While Nast's portrayal of the Irish almost always painted a dire picture, his approach to Chinese immigration and sometimes to Native Americans took the opposite path. During Reconstruction, Nast's optimism about the potential for social change led him to portray a multiracial America where Chinese and European immigrants, African Americans, and Native Americans joined in a harmonious community ("Uncle Sam's Thanksgiving Dinner," published in 1869). Later, perhaps because violent attacks on the Chinese during the 1870s sometimes originated with Irish railroad workers, Nast tended to defend Chinese immigrants more actively. In one famous cartoon ("Every Dog [No Distinction of Color] Has His Day"), Nast linked the treatment of Chinese to the experiences of Native Americans and African Americans. In other works, Nast portrayed violence against the Chinese as hypocritical, a case of immigrants pulling up the ladder behind them, or as a Western version of the white supremacist Reconstruction violence he so deplored.

As public opinion among whites in the North moved away from the concerns of Reconstruction and toward the Gilded Age problems of urbanization, labor organization, immigration, and the West, Nast's work generated less

and less applause. His work on the Chinese, therefore, and on the European conflicts of the late 1870s and early 1880s was far less influential than the cartoons of the late 1860s and early 1870s.

SEE ALSO *Chinese Exclusion Act (1882); Garibaldi, Giuseppe; Immigration Quotas; Know-Nothings; Kossuth, Louis; Nativism*

BIBLIOGRAPHY

Choy, Philip P., Lorraine Dong, and Marlon K. Hom. *The Coming Man: Nineteenth-Century American Perceptions of the Chinese*. Seattle: University of Washington Press, 1994.

Curtis, L. Perry, Jr. *Apes and Angels: The Irishman in Victorian Caricature*. Rev. ed. Washington, DC: Smithsonian Institution Press, 1997.

Halloran, Fiona Deans. *Thomas Nast: The Father of Modern Political Cartoons*. Chapel Hill: University of North Carolina Press, 2012.

Levine, Bruce. *The Spirit of 1848: German Immigrants, Labor Conflict, and the Coming of the Civil War*. Urbana: University of Illinois Press, 1992.

Paine, Albert Bigelow. *Thomas Nast: His Period and His Pictures*. New York: Harper and Brothers, 1904.

Fiona Deans Halloran
Rowland Hall-St. Mark's School

NATION OF ISLAM

The Nation of Islam (NOI) is an African American religious tradition that developed in the United States in the twentieth century. The goal of the NOI, as a black nationalist movement that emerged as a religious and political response to American racism, was to improve the lives of African Americans by embracing segregation and supporting spiritual and economic growth within the black community. Members continue to stress the importance of developing stable family lives, preserving traditional gender roles, developing economic security and independence, and maintaining healthy lifestyles through diet and abstaining from alcohol and tobacco use.

The NOI originated in Detroit in the 1930s when W. D. Fard, or Wallace Farad Muhammad, began telling members of the African American community that Islam was the true and natural religion of black people. He was soon joined by Elijah Poole (1897–1975), who threw himself into the movement. By 1934, Poole, who had changed his name to Elijah Muhammad, became the leader of the community after Fard disappeared. Elijah Muhammad became known for teaching, among other things, that Fard had been God incarnate, that white people were naturally evil, and that

Christianity had been corrupted by people of European descent and used to oppress and subjugate people of color. In 1942 Muhammad was arrested for refusing to register for the draft and was charged with sedition for encouraging his followers to do the same. He spent four years in prison, during which time he maintained contact with the community through his wife, Clara Muhammad, and began missionizing to other inmates. Prison missions became an important form of outreach for the NOI, and incarcerated members have been behind various lawsuits calling for religious accommodation for Muslim prisoners.

After being released Muhammad did little to align his teachings with other forms of Islam. He did travel to various Muslim countries and went on a pilgrimage to Mecca, though not during hajj season. Muhammad rose to national attention in the 1950s with his message of black superiority, and he and members of the NOI became known as staunch opponents of the civil rights movement. They rejected the goal of racial integration and an insistence on nonviolence, though members rarely engaged in acts of violence themselves. In 1960 the influence of the NOI continued to spread as the community began producing the newspaper *Muhammad Speaks*. It became one of the most popular publications distributed by an African American organization, with a peak circulation reported at over 600,000 copies per week. The paper focused on providing high-quality news coverage that was deemed relevant to the African American community in addition to providing a medium through which Muhammad could address his community and evangelize to nonmembers.

Although Muhammad led the NOI from 1934 until his death, he was often overshadowed by perhaps the most famous member of the group, Malcolm X (1925–1965). Malcolm X joined the NOI in prison and quickly rose to prominence within the movement after being released. For many years he was the public face of the group and spoke on behalf of the organization, although he eventually left the NOI in 1964. Elijah Muhammad's son, Warith Deen Mohammed (1933–2008), took over leadership of the NOI after his father's death in 1975 and began to move the organization toward the Sunni tradition. He rejected his father's teachings about the divinity of Fard, the supremacy of black people, and the need for racial segregation. He also opened membership to all people regardless of race, took the traditional Muslim title of imam, rather than supreme minister, and eventually renamed the organization the American Society of Muslims.

Approximately three years after W. D. Mohammed initiated this shift, Louis Farrakhan (b. 1933) left the community and reorganized. According to Farrakhan, although he originally accepted Mohammed's leadership as God's will, he felt forced to reject his embrace of Sunni Islam after traveling the world and witnessing racism everywhere he went, including in Muslim nations. After splitting with Mohammed, Farrakhan appropriated the Nation of Islam name for his group and continued to forward many of Elijah Muhammad's teachings about race and politics. In 2015 Farrakhan remained the leader of the reorganized NOI, and although in the 2010s he played down some of Muhammad's more controversial teachings, Farrakhan has remained an outspoken critic of American culture and politics and a polarizing figure.

Although the NOI originated in the United States and the movement developed among people with little knowledge of other Muslim communities and traditions, it cannot be understood in complete isolation from other groups. The NOI emerged much later than other forms of Islam but was nonetheless the entity through which many Americans encountered the Muslim tradition for the first time. American immigration restrictions made it so that there were very few immigrant Muslims in the United States when the NOI first emerged, so the unorthodox teachings of Elijah Muhammad were the first exposure that many Americans had to Islam. This movement provided Americans with a religious alternative to Christianity and opened the door for the spread of more traditional forms of Islam within the United States, especially within the African American community.

When W. D. Mohammed began aligning his message with that of Sunni Muslims, most members of the NOI followed suit and became part of this mainstream tradition. Today the vast majority of African American Muslims identify as Sunnis and understand Islam as an international, interracial religion. Embracing a Muslim identity has also been a way for many adherents to relate to international communities, including Muslims in other parts of the world, and reject conventional American culture, which is predominantly Christian. The NOI has appealed to people who have felt oppressed and exploited by American politics and culture and who have wanted to embrace an African-centered identity.

SEE ALSO *Ali, Muhammad; Black Power Movement; Islam; Malcolm X; Moorish Science Temple; Orientalism; Ottoman Empire; Universal Negro Improvement Association (UNIA)*

BIBLIOGRAPHY

Curtis, Edward E., IV. *Islam in Black America: Identity, Liberation, and Difference in African-American Islamic Thought.* Albany: State University of New York Press, 2002.

Curtis, Edward E., IV. *Black Muslim Religion in the Nation of Islam, 1960–1975.* Chapel Hill: University of North Carolina Press, 2006.

Gardell, Mattias. *In the Name of Elijah Muhammad: Louis Farrakhan and the Nation of Islam.* Durham, NC: Duke University Press, 1996.

Jackson, Sherman A. *Islam and the Blackamerican: Looking toward the Third Resurrection.* Oxford and New York: Oxford University Press, 2005.

Monica C. Reed
Instructor of Religious Studies
Louisiana State University

NATIONAL AERONAUTICS AND SPACE ADMINISTRATION (NASA)

From December 1957 to March 1958, President Dwight Eisenhower (1890–1969) and his advisers debated how best to respond to the Soviet Union's successful launches of *Sputnik 1* and *2* and the positive international reaction to those achievements. Eisenhower, after temporarily giving responsibility for all US space activities to the Department of Defense (DoD), decided by the end of March 1958 that nonmilitary space activities should be the responsibility of a new civilian space organization. The United States could thus carry out a separate, often highly classified, national security–related space program within DoD, while at the same time conducting a "peaceful" space effort that was open to public scrutiny and to potential international participation.

ORIGINS

On April 2, 1958, Eisenhower sent a message to the US Congress proposing the creation of the National Aeronautics and Space Agency (NASA). During its deliberations, Congress changed *Agency* to *Administration*, a bureaucratically higher-level designation. NASA, with its headquarters in Washington, DC, would be built on the foundation of three long-existing research and technology-development centers that were part of the National Advisory Committee on Aeronautics: the Langley Research Center in Hampton, Virginia; the Lewis (now Glenn) Research Center in Cleveland, Ohio; and the Ames Research Center near San Francisco. None of these centers had experience organizing or managing large-scale programs, so a new organization, called the Goddard Space Flight Center, was established in Greenbelt, Maryland, to meet this need. Management of the Jet Propulsion Laboratory, a US Army center operating under the auspices of the California Institute of Technology in Pasadena, was also transferred to the new space agency, which began operations on October 1, 1958. In 1960 a unit within the Army Ballistic Missile Agency in Huntsville, Alabama, that was involved in rocket development and headed by well-known émigré engineer Wernher von Braun (1912–1977) was transferred to NASA and designated the Marshall Space Flight Center. At the end of 1960, NASA thus had a headquarters plus six "field centers," almost sixteen thousand employees, and a budget of $964 million.

THE MERCURY AND APOLLO PROGRAMS

President Eisenhower was not convinced of the political and security significance of civilian space activities and resisted entering into a "space race" with the Soviet Union. Even so, NASA planners, responding to priorities set by the scientific community, defined a series of initial robotic missions. NASA also initiated a human spaceflight effort known as Project Mercury to learn whether an astronaut could survive, and perform useful work, in the space environment. The Jet Propulsion Laboratory, which had been involved since World War II (1939–1945) in rocket development, redefined itself to focus on planetary exploration missions. By mid-1959, NASA had set human missions to the moon as its long-range goal, to be accomplished after 1970. In mid-1960, as an interim step toward that goal, NASA announced that its post-Mercury human spaceflight program would be called Project Apollo. For Apollo, NASA would develop a three-person spacecraft for longer-duration missions in low Earth orbit and possibly for flights around the moon, without landing.

The inauguration of President John F. Kennedy (1917–1963) in January 1961, and his decision a few months later to accept the Soviet space challenge by committing to send Americans to the moon by the end of the 1960s, had a profound impact on NASA. The agency became a key player in the Cold War competition with the Soviet Union. Project Apollo was transformed into a lunar-landing program with the highest national priority. NASA's budget was increased by 89 percent in 1961 and another 105 percent the following year. At the peak of the Apollo buildup, the NASA budget represented more than 4 percent of all federal spending. The NASA staff grew rapidly to more than 33,000 people overseeing a contractor workforce of 400,000 people. The interim Gemini program, based on a two-person spacecraft aimed at gaining experience relevant to Apollo, was begun in early 1962. The Manned Spacecraft Center (now the Johnson Space Center) was established in 1961 in Houston, Texas, to manage the Apollo program. Extensive launch facilities were also constructed at Merritt Island in Florida. After President Kennedy's 1963 assassination, the Merritt Island site was named the Kennedy Space Center.

THE SPACE SHUTTLE AND SPACE STATION PROGRAMS

Kennedy's goal to put a man on the moon was achieved in July 1969 with the successful *Apollo 11* mission. It fell to President Richard M. Nixon (1913–1994) to decide what to do next. Nixon rejected another Apollo-like program to send Americans to Mars in the 1980s, declaring in 1970 that the space program had to compete with other government programs for priority and budget. Nixon treated the space program as primarily a domestic effort, in contrast to Kennedy's use of NASA as a tool of national security and foreign policy.

Nixon's decision set NASA on a path that has persisted since, in which the agency strives to carry out a program of reduced but still substantial ambitions with a budget inadequate to achieve those ambitions. While NASA's 2015 workforce comprised fewer than twenty thousand people and its $18 billion budget was less than 0.5 percent of federal spending, the agency retained the same institutional base as it had during the Apollo era. A rocket-engine testing facility in Mississippi, initially managed by the Marshall Space Flight Center, became the separate Stennis Space Center, and an aeronautical test center in the California high desert, formerly managed by the Ames Research Center, became the Dryden (now Armstrong) Flight Research Center. NASA in 2015 comprises its Washington headquarters and ten other installations scattered across the United States.

In 1972 President Nixon approved the development of a partially reusable space shuttle. In 1984 President Ronald Reagan (1911–2004) approved the development of a space station. Those two programs dominated NASA's human spaceflight activities for more than four decades, with 135 shuttle missions between 1981 and 2011 and the space station scheduled to remain in service until at least 2024. In addition, NASA's continuing program of robotic space and Earth science missions has produced a stream of exciting and valuable discoveries. Two presidents, George H. W. Bush in 1989 and George W. Bush in 2004, proposed that NASA resume human exploration beyond Earth orbit, although neither of those proposals took hold. In 2010 President Barack Obama set as a goal humans reaching Mars in the 2030s. The fate of that initiative is uncertain, although initial steps to develop a launch vehicle and spacecraft for deep space missions are underway.

INTERNATIONAL AND PRIVATE-SECTOR COOPERATION

One of Eisenhower's motivations in 1958 for creating a separate civilian space agency was its ability to cooperate with other countries. In the years since, NASA has entered into more than three thousand agreements with 120 countries and international organizations. Most visible is the fifteen-country partnership aimed at developing and operating the permanently occupied International Space Station.

In recent years, space activities funded and carried out by the US private sector have emerged in parallel with government-funded NASA programs. NASA has begun to work in partnership with these private actors. This combination of NASA and private space programs is likely to characterize the space sector in the twenty-first century. Even in this new environment, NASA remains a widely admired organization with ambitious plans for its future.

SEE ALSO *Apollo Program; Sputnik*

BIBLIOGRAPHY

Advisory Committee on the Future of the U.S. Space Program. *Report of the Advisory Committee on the Future of the U.S. Space Program.* Washington, DC: NASA, December 1990. http://history.nasa.gov/augustine/racfup1.htm

Chaikin, Andrew. *A Man on the Moon: The Voyages of the Apollo Astronauts.* New York: Viking, 1993.

Committee on NASA's Strategic Direction, National Research Council. *NASA's Strategic Direction and the Need for a National Consensus.* Washington, DC: National Academies Press, 2012.

Krige, John, Angela Long Callahan, and Ashok Maharaj. *NASA in the World: Fifty Years of International Collaboration in Space.* New York: Palgrave Macmillan, 2013.

Launius, Roger D. *NASA: A History of the U.S. Civil Space Program.* Malabar, FL: Kreiger, 1994.

Launius, Roger D., and Howard E. McCurdy, eds. *Spaceflight and the Myth of Presidential Leadership.* Urbana: University of Illinois Press, 1997.

Logsdon, John M. *John F. Kennedy and the Race to the Moon.* New York: Palgrave Macmillan, 2010.

Logsdon, John M. *After Apollo? Richard Nixon and the American Space Program.* New York: Palgrave Macmillan, 2015.

Logsdon, John M., et al., eds. *Exploring the Unknown: Selected Documents in the History of the U.S. Civil Space Program.* Vol. 1: *Organizing for Exploration.* NASA SP-4407. Washington: GPO, 1995.

McDougall, Walter A. *The Heavens and the Earth: A Political History of the Space Age.* New York: Basic Books, 1985.

Mieczkowski, Yanek. *Eisenhower's Sputnik Moment: The Race for Space and World Prestige.* Ithaca, NY: Cornell University Press, 2013.

John M. Logsdon
Professor Emeritus, Space Policy Institute
Elliott School of International Affairs
The George Washington University, Washington, DC

NATIONAL ASSOCIATION FOR THE ADVANCEMENT OF COLORED PEOPLE (NAACP)

As the oldest civil rights organization in the United States, the National Association for the Advancement of Colored People (NAACP) has played a seminal role in American politics and culture. It is perhaps most famous for a decades-long fight against legal segregation that culminated in the US Supreme Court's decision in *Brown v. Board of Education of Topeka, Kansas* (1954). With its leadership in social justice reform and its pledge "to ensure the political, educational, social, and economic equality of rights of all persons and to eliminate race-based discrimination" (NAACP 2013, 1), the NAACP has pressed America to live up to its democratic promise of equality before the law.

ROOTS IN ABOLITIONISM AND PROGRESSIVISM

The NAACP is part of a liberal reform tradition rooted in nineteenth-century antebellum abolitionism and postbellum progressivism. Beginning with David Walker's *Appeal* (1829), and William Lloyd Garrison's *Liberator* (c. 1831), militant abolitionism influenced the antislavery politics embodied in the Radical Republican notion of "consent of the governed." By 1870, this notion formed the basis for the Thirteenth, Fourteenth, and Fifteenth Amendments to the US Constitution, through which advocates of egalitarian principles of freedom, equal representation before the law, and voting rights sought the re-creation of American citizenship. In 1908 socialist newspaper editor William English Walling (1877–1936) responded to the antiblack race riots in Springfield, Illinois, by organizing a meeting that led to the NAACP's creation. He invoked these radical abolitionist and republican principles when he proclaimed, "the spirit of the abolitionists, of [Abraham] Lincoln and [Owen] Lovejoy, must be revived and we must come to treat the negro on a plane of absolute political and social equality" (Walling 1908, 534).

In January 1909, Walling hosted an interracial gathering at his New York home to plan a National Negro Conference dedicated to enforcement of the Thirteenth, Fourteenth, and Fifteenth Amendments. Attendees included white progressives, like New York City social worker Mary White Ovington (1865–1951), as well as African American activists who had been fighting against segregation, lynching, and disfranchisement since Reconstruction ended in the 1870s. These African Americans had founded the Afro-American Council and the National Association of Colored Women during the 1880s and 1890s, but racial conservatism and social Darwinism had replaced militant egalitarianism in American politics.

In 1905, a radical group of activists led by Professor W. E. B. Du Bois (1868–1963) and newspaper editor

William Monroe Trotter (1872–1934) founded the Niagara Movement to fight for enforcement of the Reconstruction amendments. Although their efforts provided an additional structural and ideological basis for the NAACP (most members of the black-led Niagara Movement went on to lead local branches of the NAACP), lack of funding and opposition by conservatives of both races limited the Niagara Movement's success. By the time the Springfield race riot erupted in 1908, African Americans across the country were so thoroughly excluded from American political and economic life that one congressman proudly declared in 1903 that "negro suffrage" had been a failure and that the federal government could do nothing to fulfill the Civil War's racial promise.

LEGAL DEFENSE FUND

From its official formation on May 12, 1910 (when the organization adopted its present name), the NAACP dedicated itself to preservation of the Reconstruction amendments and the civil rights that these amendments were designed to protect. Through its first president, white New England attorney Moorfield Storey (1845–1929), the NAACP organized a legal attack on racial inequality by enlisting progressive attorneys to find, prosecute, and argue civil rights cases in state and federal court. A successful appeal on behalf of a black South Carolina sharecropper in 1910 led a wealthy Columbia University literature professor, Joel Spingarn (1875–1939), to create the National Legal Committee, a permanent fixture in the organization that provided free legal counsel from some of the best legal minds of the twentieth century. By 1935, this committee became the Legal Defense Fund (LDF) under Howard University dean Charles H. Houston (1895–1950), who vowed to "use the court as a laboratory" to develop test cases that would gradually chip away at the Supreme Court's "separate but equal" doctrine. Through its assault on segregated graduate schools and its successful attack on segregated public education in 1954, the NAACP LDF has been at the forefront of American civil rights struggles. In 1997, for instance, the LDF supported black farmers in their successful suit against the US Department of Agriculture for years of discriminatory allocation of federal farm loans.

CRISIS

The NAACP's most significant cultural contribution has been its monthly magazine, the *Crisis*, founded and originally edited by Du Bois. As the only African American given an administrative position at the organization's founding, Du Bois transformed the *Crisis* into the most important African American cultural institution in the country between 1910 and the civil rights movement of the 1960s. Although initially designed as the NAACP's official publication, with a broad concern for organizational news and fundraising, Du Bois's subtitle—*A Record of the Darker Races*—placed the magazine at the vanguard of anticolonial struggles and cultural pride across the global African diaspora. As Du Bois stated in the inaugural issue, the *Crisis*'s "editorial page will stand for the rights of men, irrespective of color or race, for the highest ideals of American democracy, and for reasonable but earnest and persistent attempts to gain these rights and realize these ideals" (Du Bois 1910, 10). By 1918, as millions of African Americans continued their migration from the rural, segregated South to the urban, less racially violent North, the *Crisis* reached a monthly circulation of more than 100,000, an audience that peaked during the height of the civil rights movement to nearly 130,000. It was primarily through the *Crisis*, then, that the NAACP influenced African American homes and communities.

In 1915, for instance, when the NAACP launched an attack on D. W. Griffith's racist, pro–Ku Klux Klan film, *The Birth of a Nation*, the *Crisis* reported on black community boycotts from Boston to Detroit while providing readers with monthly updates on organizational efforts to censor the film. In 1917, as America entered World War I and NAACP leader Spingarn successfully lobbied the War Department for an all-black officers' training corps in Des Moines, Iowa, Du Bois published his influential "Close Ranks." The editorial, which urged African Americans to set aside their impatience with American racial policy and support the war effort, prompted thousands of black men, mostly college educated, to enlist. Their treatment during basic training and their restriction to hard labor increased black criticism of the NAACP's predominantly white leadership, yet the *Crisis*'s coverage of black soldiers yielded some of the most iconic images of the Great War. When the celebrated, all-black Harlem Hellfighters marched through the streets of Paris to crowds of cheering white allies, then returned home to a celebratory parade down New York's Fifth Avenue in 1918, the *Crisis* preserved these moments of racial pride in a special edition, complete with photographs depicting black men in uniform, proudly displaying the American flag.

THE NEW NEGRO RENAISSANCE

Perhaps the most significant cultural impact of the NAACP during Du Bois's tenure as editor of the *Crisis* was the New Negro Renaissance, a proliferation of black literature, music, visual art, and criticism that launched the careers of Langston Hughes (1902–1967), Josephine Baker (1906–1975), Jean Toomer (1894–1967), and Claude McKay (1890–1948). With the support of his coeditor, Jessie Redmon Fauset (1882–1961), Du Bois published foundational works of African American literature and art, including Hughes's iconic poem "The Negro Speaks of Rivers" (1921), Aaron Douglas's drawing *Invincible Music: The Spirit of Africa* (1926), and Carter G. Woodson's book *The Mis-education of the Negro* (1933). Through Fauset's *Brownies' Book*, a monthly supplement for children ages six to sixteen, an entire generation of African American children had access, for the first time, to positive images of black history and culture.

TRANSNATIONAL IMPACT

The NAACP's cultural and political impact has also been felt in transnational attacks on racial injustice. Immediately after the war, and into the 1920s, the organization sponsored four Pan-African congresses, designed to unite leaders of color in their fight against European colonialism. The congress' demands for political self-determination and economic independence at the 1919 Versailles Peace Conference attracted fifty-seven delegates from fifteen countries in 1921, 1923, and 1927. During the US occupation of Haiti (1915–1934), James Weldon Johnson (1871–1938), NAACP secretary and former US counsel to Venezuela and Nicaragua, reported on the violence and oppression inflicted by American Marines. His investigations, published in the *Crisis*, launched a decades-long attack on US policy in the region, and helped bolster the organization's leadership during US protests against Italian aggression in Ethiopia in 1935. By the outbreak of World War II, the NAACP's reputation as a global leader in anticolonial and antiracist protest led the United Nations Division on Human Rights to consider citizenship rights for racial minorities in South Africa, Palestine, and Asia. The transnational influence of the NAACP's egalitarian principles can be seen as far back as the 1912 African National Congress—organized to support the black African majority under European colonialism—and as recently as a 2010 initiative that raised over $200,000 for earthquake relief in Haiti. Despite a period of decline following its apex during the civil rights movement, the NAACP has a twenty-first-century membership of over 500,000, distributed across 2,000 branches in all 50 states.

SEE ALSO *Ali, Muhammad; Black Power Movement; King, Martin Luther, Jr.; Malcolm X; Universal Negro Improvement Association (UNIA)*

BIBLIOGRAPHY

Anderson, Carol. *Bourgeois Radicals: The NAACP and the Struggle for Colonial Liberation, 1941–1960*. Cambridge: Cambridge University Press, 2015.

Du Bois, W. E. B. *Crisis* 1, 1 (November 1910): 10.

Russell, Brian Roberts. *Artistic Ambassadors: Literary and International Representation of the New Negro Era.* Charlottesville: University of Virginia Press, 2013.

Sullivan, Patricia. *Lift Every Voice: The NAACP and the Making of the Civil Rights Movement.* New York: New Press, 2009.

Walling, William English. "The Race War in the North." *Independent* 65 (September 3, 1908): 529–534.

"We Shall Not Be Moved: NAACP 2013 Annual Report." National Association for the Advancement of Colored People (NAACP). http://action.naacp.org/page/-/annual%20reports/_NAACP_2013AR_WebFNL.pdf

Kerri K. Greenidge
Lecturer, Department of American Studies
University of Massachusetts Boston

NATIONAL BASKETBALL ASSOCIATION (NBA)

The National Basketball Association (NBA) is the world's premier professional basketball league. Founded in 1949, when the upstart Basketball Association of America and the ten-year-old National Basketball League merged, the NBA has been remarkably successful, growing from seventeen to thirty teams. Indeed, further expansion is a possibility. Former NBA commissioner David Stern once confidently asserted that someday there would be NBA teams in Europe.

A majority of NBA players are African American, but athletes from all over the world play in the league. In 2014 there were a record 101 international players from thirty-seven countries and territories on opening-day team rosters; that is, foreign nationals constituted more than 20 percent of the league's players. Many of them are All-Stars, such as Pau Gasol and Marc Gasol (Spain), Manu Ginobili (Argentina), Dirk Nowitzki (Germany), and Tony Parker (France).

The NBA also has a devoted and global fan base. It includes President Barack Obama, stretches from New York to New Zealand, and is nurtured by NBA offices in more than a dozen markets worldwide. The NBA has television programming in 215 countries and territories in 47 languages, an active social media presence, and merchandise for sale in more than 125,000 stores in 100 countries on six continents. All of this contributes to NBA annual revenues in excess of $5 billion. This is the result of strategic planning, hard work, technological innovations, the power of globalization, and the seemingly universal appeal of putting a ball through a ten-foot-high hoop.

The NBA's rise to worldwide prominence can be traced to the 1980s, specifically 1984, when Stern, the NBA's former general counsel, was hired to be the league's commissioner; the Houston Rockets picked the Nigerian center Hakeem Olajuwon (a future Hall of Famer) with the number one pick in the NBA draft; and the six-foot, six-inch, soon-to-be-global icon Michael Jordan of the University of North Carolina was selected third by the Chicago Bulls.

Years before these seminal developments, however, the Washington Bullets played the NBA's first international exhibition game (in Tel Aviv, Israel) in 1978. A year later, building on the ping-pong diplomacy initiated earlier in the decade, and just months after President Jimmy Carter normalized relations with China, the Bullets were the first US professional sports team to visit China and play exhibition games. These events represent the NBA's nascent internationalism.

Manu Ginobili of the San Antonio Spurs is defended by Marc Gasol of the Memphis Grizzlies in a December 30, 2014, game in Memphis. *In 2014 the NBA's opening-day team rosters had a record 101 foreign nationals from 37 countries and territories, constituting more than 20 percent of the league's players. Many, like Gasol (Spain) and Ginobili (Argentina), were All-Stars.* **STACY REVERE/GETTY IMAGES SPORT/GETTY IMAGES**

Led by the innovative, persistent, and savvy Stern, the NBA worked hard to internationalize itself and basketball by reaching two goals: to find and sign talented players from around the world and to open new markets. Both came to fruition during the late 1980s and the 1990s and continued into the twenty-first century. Considering the NBA draft reveals the league's record in attracting foreign athletes. Over sixty-plus years, only eight non-Americans have been selected with the first pick in the NBA's annual draft, yet five of those picks were chosen in this century: Yao Ming (China) in 2002, Andrew Bogut (Australia) in 2005, Andrea Bargnani (Italy) in 2006, Anthony Bennett (Canada) in 2013, and Andrew Wiggins (Canada) in 2014. With regard to new markets, the NBA and its corporate partners, most obviously Nike with its nearly ubiquitous swooshes, took advantage of new communication technologies, such as elaborate cable networks (ESPN was founded in 1979) and satellite systems, which enabled television to spread the NBA's product and brand. The rapid growth of the Internet only furthered this development.

Of course, the NBA's success must also be attributed to its players, some of whom are among the finest and most well-recognized athletes in the world. Beginning in 1979–1980 the charismatic Earvin "Magic" Johnson of the Los Angeles Lakers and the laconic Larry Bird of the Boston Celtics helped revive interest in the NBA with their sterling play, respectful on-court rivalry, and winning ways. In the 1980s the Lakers won five NBA championships and the Celtics won three. There was more to the Johnson–Bird years, though. As Todd Boyd argues, "Magic and Bird's significance to the game and the culture at large is tied to the way that their presence on the scene could be read as symbolic of the racial and cultural difficulties still circulating through America, especially in the conservative heyday of the Reagan '80s" (2003, 67).

Soon thereafter, in the early 1990s, Michael Jordan was approaching his prime as an athlete and global marketing icon. His acrobatic dunking and overall accomplishments—a 30.1-points-per-game career scoring average, fourteen-time All-Star, five-time NBA most valuable player, six-time NBA champion with the Bulls—are widely celebrated. Talented and hard-working, hyper-competitive yet also affable, Jordan parlayed his basketball success into becoming "the greatest endorser of the 20th century," said Nike founder and chief executive officer Phil Knight (LaFeber 1999, 134). In addition to Nike, Jordan endorsed Coca-Cola, Chevrolet, Gatorade, Hanes, McDonald's, and Wheaties, among other products. Eventually, several years after his third and final retirement in 2003, Jordan became the principal owner and chairman of the NBA's Charlotte Hornets.

On and off the court, Kobe Bryant and LeBron James—transcendently talented basketball players, winners of multiple NBA championships, and successful global

brands—followed in Jordan's impressive footsteps. Their jersey sales are among the top sellers in China, where an estimated 300 million people play the game. According to sports agent Arn Tellem, who represents many NBA players, "more people now play basketball in organized leagues in China than there are people in the United States. And what LeBron and Kobe and Kevin Durant and Derrick Rose mean over there … they are another version of American culture" (Rushin 2014, 86). The NBA, with an assist from the star-studded 1992 US men's basketball team, which dominated the competition to win the gold medal at the Barcelona Olympics, has helped basketball become a global lingua franca and one of the world's most popular sports.

SEE ALSO *Baseball; Olympics*

BIBLIOGRAPHY

Araton, Harvey. *Crashing the Borders: How Basketball Won the World and Lost Its Soul at Home.* New York: Free Press, 2005.

Boyd, Todd. *Young, Black, Rich and Famous: The Rise of the NBA, the Hip Hop Invasion, and the Transformation of American Culture.* New York: Doubleday, 2003.

Farred, Grant. *Phantom Calls: Race and the Globalization of the NBA.* Chicago: Prickly Paradigm Press, 2006.

LaFeber, Walter. *Michael Jordan and the New Global Capitalism.* New York: Norton, 1999.

Riches, Sam. "Basketball and Globalization." *New Yorker,* October 7, 2013. http://www.newyorker.com/business /currency/basketball-and-globalization

Rushin, Steve. "There and Back." *Sports Illustrated* (August 11, 2014): 56–87. http://www.si.com/vault/2014/08/11/ 106623799/there-and-back

Wolff, Alexander. *Big Game, Small World: A Basketball Adventure.* New York: Warner Books, 2002.

Daniel A. Nathan
Professor of American Studies
Skidmore College

NATIONAL CONFERENCE OF CHRISTIANS AND JEWS (NCCJ)

SEE *Federal Council of Churches.*

NATIONAL GEOGRAPHIC (MAGAZINE)

Throughout the twentieth century and into the twenty-first, *National Geographic* magazine has offered its readers "the world and all that is in it" (Bryan 1987, 43) in picture-laden glossy pages depicting nature and cultures from every region on Earth. What began as a somewhat parochial publication had by World War I (1914–1918) firmly established itself in the American national consciousness. Circulation peaked in 1989 at around 10.8 million (Heath 2012). While the magazine has been available on newsstands since 1999, for much of its existence, one needed to join the National Geographic Society (NGS) to receive the magazine, though many encountered it at schools, libraries, and doctors' offices.

FOUNDING AND EARLY YEARS

The NGS was founded in Washington, DC, in 1888. It was one of several new professional and scientific societies based in the nation's capital. With its mission "to increase and diffuse geographic knowledge," the NGS launched its first magazine, sent to members, in October 1888. Many of the NGS's early leaders were highly placed federal government scientists, and many of the magazine's articles were drawn from federal bureau reports.

Events of 1898 changed all that. In January Alexander Graham Bell (1847–1922) became NGS president. Bell envisioned national expansion, reaching for a broader membership beyond Washington, DC, with the magazine as the focus of the organization (Bell 1900, 401). By the end of 1898, in the wake of the Spanish-American War, the United States had achieved its own national expansion, acquiring control over Cuba, Puerto Rico, Guam, the Philippines, and Hawai'i. With the nation's attention turned outward, *National Geographic* shifted its focus as well. Bell's idea was to enhance educational articles about the world with photographs and stories of exploration. In 1899, he hired Gilbert H. Grosvenor (1875–1966) as the first paid editor of the magazine. Grosvenor remained editor for fifty-five years, shaping the magazine into the cultural behemoth it became.

The magazine's editors continued to take full advantage of NGS ties with federal offices, and supported US involvement in overseas territories, pushing illustrated narratives of US-led modernization and progress in Cuba, Puerto Rico, and the Philippines (Rothenberg 2007; Tuason 1999).

National Geographic also courted first-person narratives of travel and exploration. The magazine showcased an American masculinity that matched physical endurance with scientific technology, such as that of Robert Peary, whose 1908–1909 North Pole expedition was the NGS's first sponsorship (Bloom 1993). Articles highlighted automobile and motorbike expeditions across unpaved swaths of Asia and Africa and championed aviation (and the photography such height allowed). Exploits of white women explorers and travelers were also published,

***Member of the Huli wigman tribe, Papua New Guinea, reading** National Geographic.* National Geographic *magazine, founded in the 1880s, became an important source of information for Americans about the rest of the world. The journal became well known for its descriptions of race, region, and culture.* **KEVIN SCHAFER/ALAMY**

however, and the NGS made a point of honoring American aviator Amelia Earhart in 1932.

MAGAZINE CONTENT AND EDITORIAL PRINCIPLES

Grosvenor developed a set of principles, published in 1915, emphasizing positive portrayals of people and places and avoidance of politics. For decades this approach, if imperfectly executed, contributed to an overall picture of a friendly, likable, and usually unthreatening world. A negative side to such positivity included upbeat depictions of countries under oppressive regimes, such as Nazi Germany in the 1930s and apartheid South Africa in the 1960s. And politics—closely aligned with official US policy—lay behind the magazine's heavy coverage of US-allied countries during both world wars, its lack of coverage of the Soviet Union from 1945 to 1959, and the few stories about formerly well-covered Cuba and China from their communist takeovers until well into the 1970s. Coverage of Korea and Vietnam during the US wars featured photos of US military personnel described in captions as helpful or compassionate (Lutz and Collins 1993).

World War I intensified the NGS's cartographic development, and distinctive maps, often included as folded supplements to the magazine, bolstered *National Geographic*'s scientific reputation. By World War II (1939–1945), the US government and military were using NGS maps for strategic purposes (Bryan 1987; Schulten 2001).

Photography became a hallmark of the magazine, from stunning landscapes to portraits of people in their native dress "or lack of it" (Grosvenor 1967, 29). At times, aiming for interest and cultural authenticity, photographers posed subjects in folk costumes more likely to be worn by their parents or grandparents, and the magazine sometimes reprinted photographs taken ten years previously or more, contributing to a sense of timelessness and cultural essence (Lutz and Collins 1993; Rothenberg 2007; Steet 2000).

The first photograph of a bare-breasted woman, a Zulu bride, appeared in 1896. In 1903 Grosvenor and Bell, before running a photograph of two bare-breasted Filipino women working in a field, ruled such photographs objective and scientifically truthful, and therefore acceptable (Bryan 1987). That these were dark-skinned foreign women being shown to a largely white, American, and likely male audience was a given. Some photographs were deliberately sensual portraits, including some with commercial origins. And when a woman's natural skin tone was considered too light, as with a mid-century Polynesian woman, she was "darkened" in the photo lab, thus maintaining the distinction as "other" (Buckley 1970, 23).

The white explorers, travelers, and colonial officials who contributed articles in the first four decades of the twentieth century regularly deemed the natives of places they visited to be "children of nature" (Rothenberg 2007). Even if intended admiringly, the trope reiterated a contrast with modern, white, middle-class America, suggesting an evolutionist ideology, with the white American (usually male) on top, as the natural world leader.

PALEONTOLOGY AND PRIMATES

Into the post–World War II era of decolonization and beyond, however, white explorers faded from the photographs and the social evolutionist approach softened (Lutz and Collins 1993). In the 1960s, the NGS developed a new focus on evolution, sponsoring paleontologist Louis Leakey and his primatologist protégés, Jane Goodall, Dian Fossey, and Biruté Galdikas. For all its coverage of non-Western

places, however, among the magazine's most popular articles were those on Queen Elizabeth's 1953 inauguration and Winston Churchill's 1965 funeral (Poole 2004).

The NGS and its magazine long advocated for conservation and US national parks, but it took a new editorial regime in changing times—grandson Gilbert M. Grosvenor (b. 1931)—to broach global environmental problems in the 1970s. As president of the NGS in 1990, however, Grosvenor pulled back an editorial effort to include social problems, such as refugees and the global drug trade (Trueheart 1990).

NATIONAL GEOGRAPHIC IN THE TWENTY-FIRST CENTURY

In the twenty-first century, animals and science features are as likely to be *National Geographic* cover stories as any specific place. The newsy and the negative may appear amid the celebratory, often within the same article, bolstered by themes of resilience, restoration, and hope, reflecting a mainstream American perspective. In 2006, during the controversial US war in Iraq, *National Geographic* ran a story focusing sympathetically on US medics and returning injured soldiers (Shea 2006). A 2015 article on Laos, however, took the United States to task not only for bombing the country during the Vietnam War, but for spending more money on an embassy than on ordnance removal. Still, the overall positive spin is reflected in the article's title: "Laos Finds New Life after the Bombs" (Allman 2015).

SEE ALSO *Empire, US; Gender; Race*

BIBLIOGRAPHY

Abramson, Howard S. *National Geographic: Behind America's Lens on the World.* New York: Crown, 1987.

Allman, T. D. "Laos Finds New Life after the Bombs." *National Geographic* (August 2015). http://ngm.nationalgeographic.com/2015/08/laos/allman-text

"Announcement." *National Geographic* 1 (October 1888): i.

Bell, Alexander Graham. "Address of the President of the National Geographic Society to the Board of Managers." *National Geographic* 11, 10 (1900): 401–408.

Bloom, Lisa. *Gender on Ice: American Ideologies of Polar Expeditions.* Minneapolis: University of Minnesota Press, 1993.

Bryan, C. D. B. *The National Geographic Society: 100 Years of Adventure and Discovery.* New York: Abrams, 1987.

Buckley, Tom. "With the National Geographic on Its Endless Cloudless Voyage." *New York Times Magazine*, September 6, 1970, 10–23.

Grosvenor, Gilbert H. "The Story of the Geographic." In *National Geographic Index, 1888–1946*, 7–55. Washington, DC: National Geographic Society, 1967.

Hawkins, Stephanie L. *American Iconographic: National Geographic, Global Culture, and the Visual Imagination.* Charlottesville: University of Virginia Press, 2010.

Heath, Thomas. "Gilbert Grosvenor Steps Down as National Geographic Society Chairman after 23 Years." *Washington Post*, October 27, 2010. http://www.washingtonpost.com/wp-dyn/content/article/2010/10/26/AR2010102607056.html

Lutz, Catherine A., and Jane L. Collins. *Reading National Geographic.* Chicago: University of Chicago Press, 1993.

Poole, Robert M. *Explorers House: National Geographic and the World It Made.* New York: Penguin, 2004.

Rothenberg, Tamar Y. "Voyeurs of Imperialism: The *National Geographic* Magazine before World War II." In *Geography and Empire*, edited by Anne Godlewska and Neil Smith, 155–172. Oxford, UK: Blackwell, 1994.

Rothenberg, Tamar Y. *Presenting America's World: Strategies of Innocence in National Geographic Magazine, 1888–1945.* Aldershot, UK: Ashgate, 2007.

Schulten, Susan. *The Geographical Imagination in America, 1880–1950.* Chicago: University of Chicago Press, 2001.

Seelye, Katharine Q. "National Geographic, Known as Old and Venerated, Tries Fast and Hard-Hitting." *New York Times*, September 19, 2005, C6.

Shea, Neil. "The Heroes, The Healing: Military Medicine from the Front Lines to the Home Front." *National Geographic* (December 2006). http://ngm.nationalgeographic.com/2006/12/iraq-medicine/shea-text

Steet, Linda. *Veils and Daggers: A Century of National Geographic's Representation of the Arab World.* Philadelphia: Temple University Press, 2000.

Trueheart, Charles. "Garrett, Grosvenor, and the Great Divide: Behind the Sudden Ouster of the Magazine's Editor." *Washington Post*, May 7, 1990, C1.

Tuason, Julie A. "The Ideology of Empire in *National Geographic* Magazine's Coverage of the Philippines, 1889–1908." *Geographical Review* 89, 1 (1999): 34–53.

Tamar Y. Rothenberg
Associate Professor
Bronx Community College–City University of New York

NATIONAL OCEANIC AND ATMOSPHERIC ADMINISTRATION (NOAA)

The National Oceanic and Atmospheric Administration (NOAA) came into being on October 3, 1970, with the enactment of Reorganization Plan No. 4 for 1970 during the administration of President Richard Nixon (1913–1994). The primary organizations that came together to form NOAA were the Environmental Science Services Administration (originally formed from the Coast and Geodetic Survey, the Weather Bureau, and the Central Radio Propagation Laboratory of the National Bureau of Standards), which resided in the Department of Commerce, and the Bureau of Commercial Fisheries from the Department of the Interior. In addition, the National Oceanographic Data Center, Lake Survey Center, National Sea Grant Program, and other entities were transferred into NOAA from other agencies.

HISTORY

Although NOAA began as a separate administration in 1970, it is also the oldest scientific agency in the US government. The historic core of NOAA began as the Survey of the Coast, which Congress authorized President Thomas Jefferson (1743–1826) to establish in 1807. The Survey of the Coast began as an exercise; after becoming an institution it was renamed the Coast Survey. The Weather Bureau, the oldest environmental monitoring agency in the government, began in 1870 as an arm of the US Army Signals Corps. The Bureau of Commercial Fisheries traces its beginning to the US Commission on Fish and Fisheries, the oldest conservation agency, established in 1871.

The concepts behind NOAA had been evolving since the late 1950s with increasing awareness that the ocean, atmosphere, and resources of the sea all are interrelated and that, to varying degrees, study of each of these requires understanding of the others. Two major studies led to NOAA's creation. The first of these was the National Academy of Sciences report *Oceanography 1960 to 1970* published in 1959, which brought attention to the need for integrated studies of the interactions of ocean and atmosphere and the fact that such programs were spread throughout a large number of uncoordinated agencies in the federal government. The second report, *Our Nation and the Sea*, better known as the Stratton Commission Report, was published in 1969 and led directly to the formation of NOAA. This second report recommended that the many ocean programs residing in the federal government be incorporated into one body that could study the environment as a unified whole from the bottom of the sea to the surface of the sun.

MISSION, ORGANIZATION, AND WORLDWIDE SCOPE OF ACTIVITY

The NOAA of today has the missions of: (1) understanding and predicting changes in climate, weather, oceans, and coasts; (2) sharing that knowledge and information with all interested parties; and (3) conserving and managing coastal and marine ecosystems and resources. To that end, it is organized in distinct line offices: the National Ocean Service; the National Weather Service; the National Marine Fisheries Service; the Office of Oceanic and Atmospheric Research; the Office of Marine and Aviation Operations; and the National Environmental Satellite, Data, and

Information Service, which are complexly interrelated. NOAA operates and maintains a national weather monitoring and prediction network, the national environmental satellite network, and a national network of environmental laboratories that study the ocean, atmosphere, and marine resources. In addition, NOAA operates fleets of research and hydrographic surveying vessels and research aircraft, it manages the network of National Marine Sanctuaries, and it participates in the study and conservation of marine and maritime resources in all American waters and throughout the world.

The scope of NOAA's activities is worldwide, but this is not new, in several senses. First, the agency's scope has also been worldwide from the beginning with regard to fundamental science and the coordinated management of both human systems and natural resources. The Coast Survey was founded using the metric system, and NOAA is still metric. As international scientific bodies and congresses developed in the nineteenth century, NOAA legacy agencies were founding members of most of them, and NOAA remains a member of their present incarnations, including the American Geophysical Union and its many international connections, the International Civil Aviation Organization and many other organizations of the United Nations, the World Meteorological Organization, the General Bathymetric Chart of the Ocean, the Group on Earth Observations, and many other global organizations. As to management of natural resources, as one salient example, all NOAA legacy agencies participated in the research and management work that led to the Northern Fur Seal Protection Convention of 1911, which was the first international treaty that protected anything nonhuman and the model for all related protections of earthly life ever since.

The scope of NOAA's interests in the world and the scope of its legacy agencies have been continually expanding since the early nineteenth century. The original legacy agency of NOAA, the Coast Survey, was and remains a civilian organization, but since the agency began in 1807, every American war has involved it and at times expanded its reach and responsibilities. These expansions include the taking of Florida from Spain in 1821 while also relinquishing American claims to Texas; the joining of the independent republic of Texas to the United States in 1845; the possession of California and expansion to the Pacific coast and the ocean routes to California as a result of the Mexican-American War (1846–1848); the many American islands claimed under the Guano Islands Act of 1856; the purchase of Russian America, or Alaska, in 1867; the "annexation" of the Kingdom of Hawai'i in 1893; the Spanish-American War in 1898, which brought in Puerto Rico and the Philippines as American possessions or dependencies; the purchase of the Danish Virgin

Islands in 1917; the changes in territorial possession after World War I (1914–1918), when, for example, German Samoa became American Samoa; the huge dislocations, invasions, and changes of World War II (1939–1945); and finally the great reconfigurations of territory, strategic bases, and defenses during the Cold War.

In addition, by the 1970s all maritime nations, including the United States, were claiming exclusive economic zones (EEZs) two hundred nautical miles out from their national shorelines. The surface area of the US EEZs is substantially more than the surface area of all the lands the United States possesses or claims. Finally, treaties that the country has signed, and international government bodies that the United States has joined or assists, have enlarged the scope of American interests, and therefore also NOAA's responsibilities, to embrace the planet from beyond the atmosphere to the bottom of the oceans.

SEE ALSO *Atlantic Ocean; Caribbean; Earth Day; Global Warming; Ozone Depletion; Pacific Ocean*

BIBLIOGRAPHY

Dupree, A. Hunter. *Science in the Federal Government: A History of Policies and Activities.* Baltimore, MD: Johns Hopkins University Press, 1986. Originally published by Belknap Press in 1957.

National Research Council, Committee on Oceanography. *Oceanography 1960 to 1970.* Washington, DC: National Academy of Sciences, 1959–.

Shea, Eileen L., comp. *A History of NOAA: Being a Compilation of Facts and Figures regarding the Life and Times of the Original Whole Earth Agency.* Washington, DC: NOAA, 1987. http://www.history.noaa.gov/legacy/noaahistory_1.html

US Commission on Marine Science, Engineering, and Resources. *Our Nation and the Sea: A Plan for National Action.* Washington, DC: US GPO, 1969. http://www.lib.noaa.gov/noaainfo/heritage/stratton/title.html

John Cloud
Historian
NOAA Central Library

NATIONAL SECURITY AGENCY (NSA)

The National Security Agency (NSA) is a US intelligence agency that specializes in the technological acquisition of foreign information. The NSA acts as a key source of military, economic, social, and scientific information and supplies this information to various military, intelligence, and civilian agencies within the US federal government.

The NSA is charged with two broad missions that reflect both its international scope and its technological focus. The agency specializes in signals intelligence (SIGINT), which includes the collection, processing, and distribution of information gleaned from foreign communications. The NSA is also responsible for information assurance, the security of sensitive US government computer systems and the national security information they contain. These missions are reflected in the fact that the director of the NSA is required to be a US military officer and also serves as the commander of the US Cyber Command (USCYBERCOM).

The NSA was founded in 1952 by order of President Harry S. Truman (1884–1972). Unlike the National Security Act of 1947 that established the Central Intelligence Agency (CIA), President Truman's order was not passed by Congress nor formally signed into law. Consequently, the NSA's responsibilities and restrictions were not made publicly available (Bamford 1982, 4). Assessing the historical role played by the NSA in American relations with the rest of the world is difficult due to the classified nature of its operations and management. Certain activities became public after the Church Committee investigated the intelligence gathering practices of the NSA and other defense organizations during US Senate hearings in 1975. One such program was Project SHAMROCK, in which the NSA accessed international telegraph traffic entering and leaving the United States (Bamford 1982, 236).

The mission of the NSA has meant that the agency has long been an important component of US involvement in the world, even if that involvement has been largely secret. The NSA collects information about foreign countries and actors through a variety of technical measures conducted from both US soil and various international locations. Through the Special Collection Service (SCS), an organization run jointly by the NSA and the CIA, the NSA operates collection programs out of American embassies around the world. These programs are often designed to obtain local military, economic, and social information, as well as intelligence relevant to CIA operations (Richelson 2003). Given its technological and analytical prowess, many scholarly estimates rank the NSA as one of the most valuable, and most productive, US intelligence agencies. By one estimate, most of the information in the president's daily intelligence briefing is produced by the NSA (Aid 2006, 980).

For most of its institutional existence, the National Security Agency avoided the same level of popular awareness achieved by its bureaucratic rival, the CIA. This changed abruptly during the early twenty-first century when Edward Snowden leaked a large number of secret NSA documents that testified to the power and reach of the agency in operations around the world. The Pentagon estimated that Snowden took 1.7 million files from government computer systems (Strohm and Wilbur 2014). Competing portrayals of Snowden as a criminal traitor and heroic whistleblower testified to the wide range of reactions directed at the NSA, as well as the complex place of the NSA in American and international culture.

As the scope of the NSA's international spying operations became apparent, the agency drew criticism from around the world. Within the United States, the most criticized programs included those that compelled US telecommunications companies to provide the NSA with information on telephone calls made with their networks. For example, one such order in 2013 required Verizon to provide "location data, call duration, unique identifiers, and the time and duration of all calls," both international and domestic (Greenwald 2013).

The Snowden disclosures also revealed another element of NSA's international involvement, the PRISM program, begun in 2007. Through this program, the NSA eavesdropped on foreign nationals' Internet communication when handled by major US Internet companies, including Google, Yahoo, and Microsoft. The sheer volume of Internet traffic meant that PRISM quickly became a major source of raw intelligence for the NSA.

Information in the leaked documents strained American relations with a number of allies who discovered they were targets of NSA spying. One such example included allegations that the NSA had tapped German chancellor Angela Merkel's mobile phone (Oltermann 2014). The legality and propriety of these actions was widely contested in both the American and international press.

As the NSA continues its operations in the post-Snowden era, it finds itself under renewed scrutiny. The NSA remains a symbol of the extent and involvement of American power in the international community.

SEE ALSO *Central Intelligence Agency (CIA); Department of Defense, US*

BIBLIOGRAPHY

Aid, Matthew. "The National Security Agency and the Cold War." *Intelligence and National Security* 16, 1 (2001): 27–66.

Aid, Matthew. "Prometheus Embattled: A Post-9/11 Report Card on the National Security Agency." *Intelligence and National Security* 21, 6 (2006): 980–998.

Bamford, James. *The Puzzle Palace: A Report on America's Most Secret Agency.* Boston: Houghton Mifflin, 1982.

Bamford, James. *Body of Secrets: Anatomy of the Ultra-Secret National Security Agency from the Cold War through the Dawn of a New Century.* New York: Doubleday, 2001.

Bamford, James. *The Shadow Factory: The Ultra-Secret NSA from 9/11 to the Eavesdropping on America.* New York: Doubleday, 2008.

Greenwald, Glenn. "NSA Collecting Phone Records of Millions of Verizon Customers Daily." *Guardian* (London), June 6, 2013. http://www.theguardian.com/world/2013/jun/06/nsa-phone-records-verizon-court-order

"NSA Slides Explain the PRISM Data-Collection Program." *Washington Post*, June 6, 2013. http://www.washingtonpost.com/wp-srv/special/politics/prism-collection-documents/

Oltermann, Philip. "Germany Opens Inquiry into Claims NSA Tapped Angela Merkel's Phone." *Guardian* (London), June 4, 2014. http://www.theguardian.com/world/2014/jun/04/germany-inquiry-nsa-tapping-angela-merkel-phone

Richelson, Jeffrey. "National Security Agency." In *Dictionary of American History*, edited by Stanley I. Kutler, Vol. 5, 558–559. 3rd ed. New York: Scribner's, 2003.

Strohm, Chris, and Del Quintin Wilber. "Pentagon Says Snowden Took Most U.S. Secrets Ever: Rogers." *Bloomberg*, January 9, 2014. http://www.bloomberg.com/news/articles/2014-01-09/pentagon-finds-snowden-took-1-7-million-files-rogers-says

Michael Graziano
PhD Candidate
Florida State University

NATIONAL SECURITY COUNCIL (NSC)

The National Security Act of 1947, signed into law by President Harry S. Truman, created the National Security Council (NSC) for the purpose of coordinating US foreign policy, defense policy, intelligence, and relevant domestic policy. The NSC replaced the State-War-Navy Coordinating Committee, which had been meeting regularly since World War II. With the growing complexity of the United States' postwar national security policy, however, the integration of national security policy demanded more formal organization.

The NSC's first action was to authorize covert intelligence operations in the Italian elections, and in December 1947 the Truman administration formally gave the NSC authority to commission covert operations. The NSC further expanded its capacity in 1962, after the Bay of Pigs fiasco, when the Kennedy administration created the Situation Room in the White House basement and installed real-time communications with the State and Defense Departments, which allowed the NSC to send out and monitor cable traffic and to centralize national security policy making and crisis management within the NSC.

How presidents use the NSC, what authority they cede to the national security advisor position, and the size and role of the NSC staff depends on their individual management styles. President Dwight D. Eisenhower preferred a formal staff structure and used the NSC to provide regular, fully staffed, interagency reviews of major national security issues. President Lyndon B. Johnson, by contrast, relied heavily on the Tuesday Lunch Group as an informal decision-making body. President Richard M. Nixon centralized the NSC under National Security Advisor Henry Kissinger and increased the size of the NSC staff to over a hundred people. President George H. W. Bush preferred a smaller staff of fifty to sixty professionals but granted considerable authority to General Brent Scowcroft. The NSC staff grew to over two hundred members under President George W. Bush, but in his first term in office the president relied more on other personnel and agencies for setting national security policy than on the national security advisor and the NSC.

The NSC staff expanded to over 350 people under President Barack Obama, yet in his first term in office Obama preferred to rely on personal networks for making national security policy instead of on the formal NSC process. As a general rule, however, all presidents have used the NSC to study issues and present policy options, review existing policies, coordinate interagency relations, manage crises, and issue directives on the content and processes of national security policy making.

Who attends the NSC meetings likewise depends on a president's management style. The NSC's statutory membership, which originally included the president; secretary of state; secretary of defense; secretaries of the army, navy, and air force; and chairman of the National Security Resources Board, was amended in 1949 to eliminate the three service secretaries and add the vice president. Since the Eisenhower administration, the NSC has been led by the assistant to the president for national security affairs (the national security advisor).

The personnel who actually attend an NSC meeting depends on the topic and the administration. The secretary of energy may not attend a meeting unless oil and gas or nuclear energy is implicated, for instance, even though that secretary is now a statutory NSC member. The same holds for the secretary of the Treasury or other cabinet-level officials, whether statutory NSC member or not. Individual presidents may also designate particular cabinet-level officials as NSC members for the purposes of their administration. The NSC under President Obama, for instance, included the secretary of homeland security, US attorney general, and US representative to the United Nations.

Presidents may also establish new organizations that diffuse the power of the NSC. For example, President Bill Clinton created the National Economic Council to integrate foreign policy with respect to the United States' commercial and financial interests, thereby taking international economic policy out of the NSC, and the second President Bush established the Homeland Security Council in October 2001.

SEE ALSO *Central Intelligence Agency (CIA); Cold War; Department of Defense, US; Department of Homeland Security; Department of State; National Security Agency (NSA); Truman, Harry S.; World War II*

BIBLIOGRAPHY

Burke, John P. *Honest Broker? The National Security Advisor and Presidential Decision Making.* College Station: Texas A&M Press, 2010.

Daalder, Ivo, and I. M. Destler. *In the Shadow of the Oval Office: Profiles of National Security Advisers and the Presidents They Served—From JFK to Bush.* New York: Simon and Schuster, 2009.

"History of the National Security Council, 1947–1997." US Department of State, Bureau of Public Affairs, Office of the Historian, 1997. http://fas.org/irp/offdocs /NSChistory.htm

Rodman, Peter W. *Presidential Command: Power, Leadership, and the Making of Foreign Policy from Richard Nixon to George W. Bush.* New York: Knopf, 2009.

Rothkopf, David. *Running the World: The Inside Story of the National Security Council and the Architects of American Power.* New York: PublicAffairs, 2005.

Whittaker, Alan G., Shannon A. Brown, Frederick C. Smith, and Elizabeth McKune. "The National Security Policy Process: The National Security Council and Interagency System." (Research Report, August 15, 2011, Annual Update). Washington, DC: Industrial College of the Armed Forces, National Defense University, US Department of Defense, 2011. http://www.virginia.edu/cnsl/pdf/national-security -policy-process-2011.pdf

Bartholomew Sparrow
Professor of Government
The University of Texas at Austin

NATIVISM

Nativism is a movement based on opposition to immigrants who are perceived to threaten a distinctively American way of life. It encompasses both an attitude of fear and resentment toward foreigners and a set of policies and actions aimed at limiting their impact on society. These have included proposals to curtail the citizenship rights of the foreign-born and efforts to restrict immigration, as well as outbursts of antiforeigner violence. A near-constant presence in the American past, nativism has flared into a major force in periods of social anxiety and political instability.

Though defined by core hostility to foreign influence, nativism has been a complex historical phenomenon. In his landmark work, *Strangers in the Land: Patterns of American Nativism, 1860–1925*, first published in 1955, historian John Higham (1920–2003) identified three distinct though overlapping strains of American nativism: anti-Catholic, antiradical, and racist nativism.

THE EMERGENCE OF ANTI-CATHOLIC NATIVISM AS A POLITICAL FORCE

Anti-Catholic nativism first emerged as a popular and powerful political force in response to the large-scale immigration of Catholics in the 1840s and 1850s. The arrival of several million Irish and German Catholics brought to the fore a central question that animated nativists of all stripes for decades afterward: were these newcomers fit to be citizens in a democratic republic? Nativists argued that Catholics were ill-equipped for the responsibilities of citizenship. Bound to a church and a hierarchy that demanded intellectual and spiritual submission, Catholic immigrants were likely to become political tools. Protestantism, in contrast, was seen to encourage the individual independence and judgment that were the hallmarks of a reliable citizen.

This anxiety about the ability of Catholics to adapt to American institutions, combined with the widespread fear that the Vatican was intent on gaining political power, drove the rise of the Know-Nothings, the first nativist political movement in the United States. Aided by the tumult over slavery extension, the Know-Nothings won a series of elections at the local, state, and national levels in 1854 and 1855, and, under the banner of the American Party, nominated Millard Fillmore (1800–1874) for the 1856 presidential election. The American Party did not propose to ban Catholic immigration. Instead, it sought to inoculate the political system against the influence of Catholic voters by extending the naturalization period from five to twenty-one years, and by barring the foreign-born from holding political office. However, a fracture between the northern and southern wings over the question of slavery led to the party's collapse.

RACIAL AND ANTIRADICAL NATIVISM AFTER THE CIVIL WAR

Nativism, however, was far from extinguished. In the decades after the Civil War (1861–1865), racial nativism attracted adherents from across the political and social spectrum. The first target was the Chinese population in California. Though present in California since the mid-nineteenth-century gold rush, some eighty thousand Chinese arrived between 1870 and 1875, a period that coincided with the 1873 financial panic and a severe economic downturn. Resentful over this competition for work and wages, and drawing on a series of racial stereotypes that depicted the Chinese as unclean, dishonest, and accustomed to living and working in slave-like conditions, labor unions and their supporters mobilized to block further arrivals. Political agitation against Chinese laborers was matched by violence on the ground, with major episodes of anti-Chinese violence breaking out in Los Angeles in 1871, San Francisco in 1877, Denver in 1880, and Seattle in 1886. The result was the 1882 Chinese Exclusion Act, which suspended immigration from China for a decade. Renewed in 1892 and then declared permanent in 1902, the act set the stage for an intense push for other forms of immigration restriction in the ensuing decades.

After 1882, nativist fears turned once again to European arrivals. In the 1871–1914 period, almost 30 million immigrants arrived in the United States, many from southern and eastern Europe. As millions of Italians and Poles settled in American cities, anti-Catholic nativism prospered. Founded in 1887, the American Protective Association drew on similar themes and arguments as the Know-Nothings to combat the threat from political Romanism. But the two other strands identified by Higham, antiradical and racial nativism, were most powerful. Drawing on theories of Anglo-Saxon superiority, an influential group of thinkers and politicians organized the Immigration Restriction League in 1894 to prevent, in their terms, the "racial stock" of the nation from being tarnished by an influx of inferior races. Francis A. Walker (1840–1897), a leading economist and the president of the Massachusetts Institute of Technology, denounced southern and eastern Europeans as lazy, passive, and unintelligent, "beaten men," as he put it, "from beaten races," and as such unfit for citizenship in a republican democracy (Walker 1896).

For other nativists, these European immigrants brought with them a dangerous and radical set of political theories, particularly socialism and anarchism. A key moment in fixing the image of the foreigner as a wild-eyed and dangerous subversive was the Haymarket affair of 1886. When a bomb exploded during a rally for the eight-hour workday at Haymarket Square in Chicago, killing seven policemen, a wave of hostility toward foreign-born anarchists and labor militants ensued. Though there was little evidence of their guilt, six immigrants were subsequently sentenced to death.

IMMIGRANT REACTION

Immigrant communities responded to nativist hostility in various ways. One response was to develop autonomous social and cultural institutions. The Catholic Church reacted to what it perceived as the Protestant bias of the nation's common schools by pouring resources into its parochial school system, as well as developing a network of charities and hospitals. The Chinese community, too, established benevolent associations to help new arrivals find jobs and housing. Many newly arrived immigrants looked to political machines in the nation's cities for much-needed patronage and economic support. However, such strategies also inflamed nativist hostility. Progressive Era reformers blamed foreigners for the corruption and inefficiency associated with machine-style politics. Furthermore, when the Catholic Church sought state funding for its parochial schools, opponents saw a sinister conspiracy to undermine the nation's public schools and indoctrinate children in the beliefs of Rome.

LEGISLATIVE SUCCESS

Despite attracting support from prominent individuals and organizations, nativist legislation made little headway until World War I (1914–1918). From 1882 Congress assumed responsibility for regulating immigration, and a series of piecemeal restrictions were imposed. An 1892 law barred paupers, the insane, those suffering from contagious diseases, and polygamists. That same year, Ellis Island in New York Harbor opened as a screening station for new arrivals. But the number excluded was small, and the major nativist demand, a literacy test for all arrivals, was vetoed by successive presidents. The antiforeigner climate that followed America's entry into World War I gave nativists their chance. In 1917 the literacy test finally became law.

At the same time, the fear of foreign radicals returned with force. The Bolshevik Revolution of 1917, followed by a wave of industrial disputes in 1919, triggered a Red scare that swept up the foreign-born. Attorney General A. Mitchell Palmer (1872–1936) responded to public pressure to act against foreign agitators by arresting and deporting hundreds of Russian-born radicals. A plan to deport thousands more, however, aroused opposition from liberals and conservatives alike, and the Red scare subsided as industrial calm was restored.

Nativists, however, were on the verge of achieving their greatest legislative success. In the early 1920s nativism as a mass movement emerged once again, this time in the form of the Ku Klux Klan. Combining white supremacism with virulent attacks on Jews and Catholics, the Klan reached a membership of more than a million, extending its reach well beyond its base in the southern states to the North and the Midwest. At the same time, constant lobbying and campaigning by proponents of eugenic theories of racial degeneration led to the passage of the 1924 Johnson-Reed Act. That act both cut the level of immigration by more than 50 percent and instituted a complicated quota system, which, because it was based on the 1890 census, discriminated against southern and eastern Europeans while favoring arrivals from northern Europe. An allied bill, the Oriental Exclusion Act, targeted Japanese immigration.

The quota system calmed nativist anxieties. With immigrant numbers declining, the Ku Klux Klan faced increasing opposition from political leaders, as well as the public, and its demise was sealed when its leader in Indiana, David C. Stephenson (1891–1966), was convicted in 1925 of rape and murder. Over the following decades, nativist-inspired laws were gradually unwound. The Chinese Exclusion Act was repealed in 1943, and the 1965 Immigration Act dismantled the national quota system. Anxiety over mass immigration has resurfaced in the decades since, with a notable focus on Mexican arrivals, but organized nativism has never again reached the influence and popularity it attained during the Progressive Era.

SEE ALSO *American Protective Association; Chinese Exclusion Act (1882); Haymarket Bombing; Immigration Quotas; Know-Nothings; Red Scare*

BIBLIOGRAPHY

Bennett, David H. *The Party of Fear: From Nativist Movements to the New Right in American History.* Chapel Hill: University of North Carolina Press, 1988.

Higham, John. *Strangers in the Land: Patterns of American Nativism, 1860–1925.* 2nd ed. New York: Atheneum, 1963.

Jacobson, Mathew Frye. *Barbarian Virtues: The United States Encounters Foreign Peoples at Home and Abroad, 1876–1917.* New York: Hill and Wang, 2001.

Walker, Francis A. "Restriction of Immigration." *Atlantic Monthly* 77, 464 (1896): 822–29. http://www.theatlantic.com/magazine/archive/1896/06/restriction-of-immigration/306011/

Timothy Verhoeven
Senior Lecturer
School of Philosophical,
Historical, and International Studies
Monash University, Australia

NATURALIZATION ACT OF 1790

The First Federal Congress passed the Naturalization Act of 1790 (1 Stat. 103), establishing federal authority over immigration in the United States for the first time. Prior to the ratification of the US Constitution, individual states determined rules for naturalization—the process by which aliens become citizens. The Constitution does not include specific regulations for immigration but grants Congress the power "to establish an uniform Rule of Naturalization" (Art. 1, sec. 8, cl. 4). The 1790 act provided the most generous terms for naturalization in US history, requiring only two years of residence in the country, including at least one year in the state of application for citizenship. Yet the act also limited naturalized citizenship to "free white persons," thereby introducing the tension between equality and racial and ethnic exclusion that has helped to define the US immigration system to the present day.

The Naturalization Act of 1790 built on the liberal principles concerning immigration and citizenship established in the American Revolution. At its founding, the United States departed from common European laws and customs that connected citizenship with religious affiliation. In addition, the United States never created categories of second-class citizenship. By the Constitution, the three routes to becoming a citizen—birth in the United States, having US citizens as parents (even if one is born outside the United States), and naturalization—all result in the same quality of citizenship, with the sole exception that only those who are citizens at birth can be elected president. The 1790 act helped to codify and advance this revolutionary legacy. Aside from the residency requirement, the law only required immigrants to appear before a local judge and prove to be a "person of good character" and take an oath "to support the constitution of the United States." According to the act, "thereupon such person shall be considered as a citizen of the United States."

Some members of Congress viewed even these minimal requirements for naturalization as too stringent. America already enjoyed a wide reputation as an asylum of liberty. In arguing against the proposed two-year residency, Virginia congressman John Page (1743–1808) claimed that Americans would "be inconsistent with ourselves, if, after boasting of having opened an asylum for the oppressed of all nations, and established a Government which is the admiration of the world, we make the terms of admission to the full enjoyment of that asylum so hard as is now proposed" (Kettner 1978, 237–238). Ultimately, the residency requirement passed as a means of ensuring that prospective citizens had sufficient time to embrace America's distinctive republican values. Congress approved the law aware of the possible future dangers of granting citizenship to foreigners. As Michael J. Stone (1747–1812) of Maryland observed, difficulties with immigrants "may allude to the next generation more than this" (Bradburn 2009, 134).

Anxiety over immigration emerged sooner than the framers of the 1790 law could have realized. The radicalization of the French Revolution in 1793, combined with the growing slave rebellion in the French colony of Saint-Domingue (today Haiti), led to fears of violent revolutionaries flooding American shores. In 1795, Congress responded by extending the period of required residence for aliens from two to five years. The Naturalization Act of 1798, considered one of the Alien and Sedition Acts, increased the residence requirement to fourteen years. Passed by a Federalist Congress, the measure aimed to prevent immigrants, who voted predominantly for the rival Democratic-Republican (Jeffersonian) Party, from becoming citizens. In 1802, following the election of President Thomas Jefferson (1743–1826), Congress restored the residence requirement to five years, which it has remained to the present day (three years for aliens married to US citizens).

It is impossible to assess the exact number of immigrants naturalized as US citizens by virtue of the 1790 law. The US government did not keep detailed records on immigration before 1820. By one estimate, net immigration stayed fairly constant during the 1790s, averaging about four thousand annually; the total US population climbed from almost 4 million in 1790 to 5.3 million in 1800 (Carter et al. 2006, 1:30, 1–36). More generally, the 1790 act provided the legal foundation for a massive influx of immigrants into the United States during the nineteenth century. By 1850, nearly 10 percent of all Americans were born abroad, a number that would climb to almost 15 percent in the early twentieth century. During its history, the United States has taken in more immigrants than all other immigrant-recipient nations combined over the same period.

The 1790 law also left a legacy of excluding certain immigrant groups based on race and gender. The provision limiting naturalization to "free white persons" remained in place for most of the nineteenth century. The Naturalization Act of 1870 finally extended naturalization to people of African descent, but groups such as Chinese nationals faced discrimination in the immigration system well into the twentieth century. The 1790 law also treated mothers differently from fathers. Naturalized parents automatically transferred citizenship to their children under the age of twenty-one. But, for children born abroad, citizenship transferred exclusively through the father, who had to be a citizen who had resided in the United States before the child's birth. Congress did not remove this inequity and allow mothers of children born abroad to transfer their citizenship until 1934. The Naturalization Act of 1790 went far in making America a "nation of immigrants," even as it also established important precedents limiting who could qualify for US citizenship.

SEE ALSO *Adams, John; Alien Act (1798); Washington, George*

BIBLIOGRAPHY

Bradburn, Douglas. *The Citizenship Revolution: Politics and the Creation of the American Union, 1774–1804.* Charlottesville: University of Virginia Press, 2009.

Carter, Susan B., Scott Sigmund Gartner, Michael R. Haines, Alan L. Olmstead, Richard Sutch, and Gavin Wright, eds. *Historical Statistics of the United States: Earliest Times to the Present.* Millennial ed. 5 vols. New York: Cambridge University Press, 2006.

Daniels, Roger. *Coming to America: A History of Immigration and Ethnicity in American Life.* 2nd ed. New York: Perennial, 2002.

Kerber, Linda K. "The Meanings of Citizenship." *Journal of American History* 84, 3 (1997): 833–854.

Kerber, Linda K. *No Constitutional Right to Be Ladies: Women and the Obligations of Citizenship.* New York: Hill and Wang, 1998.

Kettner, James H. *The Development of American Citizenship, 1608–1870.* Chapel Hill: University of North Carolina Press, 1978.

LeMay, Michael, and Elliott Robert Barkan. *U.S. Immigration and Naturalization Laws and Issues: A Documentary History.* Westport, CT: Greenwood Press, 1999.

Smith, Rogers M. *Civic Ideals: Conflicting Visions of Citizenship in U.S. History.* New Haven, CT: Yale University Press, 1997.

Denver Brunsman
Associate Professor of History
George Washington University

NAVY, US

In its multiple dimensions, the US Navy is a complex governmental organization that engages and operates within the global maritime environment for the purposes of national security. It is a microcosm and reflection of American society in terms of its governance, organization, foreign relations, culture, social makeup, and educational, professional, scientific, industrial, and technical development.

ESTABLISHMENT AND GROWTH

At the outset of the American Revolutionary War in 1775, the Patriots were clearly aware that they faced the opposition of the world's strongest naval power: Great Britain's Royal Navy. Few in America had any personal experience of naval service. Nevertheless, the years of the American Revolution were a rare moment of relative British naval weakness in the context of the recurring Anglo-French wars of the long eighteenth century. When France entered the war to support the Americans in 1778, it eventually found the opportunity to win temporary local control in North American waters long enough to prevent British naval support for its beleaguered army at Yorktown in 1781, thereby allowing combined Franco-American land forces to defeat the British under General Charles Cornwallis (1738–1805). French, not American, naval power became an essential facilitator for American independence. A few Continental navy ships survived the war, but the government could not sustain or administer them. The last ship was sold in 1785.

The controversies surrounding the ratification of the Constitution in 1787 to 1788 involved a debate over Article I, Section 8, concerning whether or not the US Congress should have the power "to provide and maintain a navy." There were two groups opposing and one supporting a navy. The latter expressed its views fully in *The Federalist Papers*, where Alexander Hamilton (1755–1804), John Jay (1745–1829), and James Madison (1751–1836) were supporters. The new republic had no armed force afloat for five years until August 1790, when Congress created the Revenue Marine to stop smuggling and to enforce tariff collection within territorial waters. The outbreak of the French Revolution gave rise to concerns about the defense of American overseas trade. Portugal's agreement in October 1793 to join the British in the war against revolutionary France involved making peace with Algiers, thereby ending Portugal's restraint on Algerine corsairs attacking neutral trade.

As a result, at the recommendation of President George Washington (1732–1799), Congress passed the Naval Act of March 27, 1794, which authorized the building of six frigates—three with forty-four guns and three with thirty-six guns—and established the initial numbers for officers and men, with details of their pay and rations. The debate over the bill created a North versus South divide, with southerners opposing a navy on economic, political, strategic, diplomatic, and humanitarian grounds. This controversy raised an enduring debate over the purpose of naval power. Navalists saw a navy as an element of national prestige that provided a backbone for diplomacy, as well as for commercial trade and national expansion. Their opponents, the antinavalists, acknowledged the importance of a navy to protect commerce and the coast, but were concerned about the immense expense of building and maintaining a navy, as well as the possibility of provoking a war and becoming entangled in foreign adventures. The War Department oversaw the construction of the first three frigates, launched in 1797. The XYZ affair of 1798 led to the Quasi-War with France, additional naval authorizations, and President John Adams's (1735–1826) establishment of the Navy Department. From that point forward, the naval service grew and developed.

President Madison's determination to force Britain to respect the fledgling country in 1812 nearly resulted in the ruin of the United States, as the overwhelming power of the Royal Navy strangled American trade and eliminated the US Navy, ship by ship. Dramatic American victories in single ship duels in the first six months of the war and in the miniature fleet actions on Lake Erie and Lake Champlain helped make the wartime naval motto of "Free Trade and Sailors' Rights" into a popular reassertion of the nation's founding principles. The exploits of the frigate *Constitution*, fondly named "Old Ironsides," became an enduring popular symbol of the navy's role in national defense.

In the century that followed, the country maintained a small navy that tacitly benefited from the Royal Navy's *Pax Britannica*. The first warships sailed to overseas assignments in the Far East in 1800 and to the Mediterranean in 1801. Gradually, regular cruising stations were established in a pattern of permanent forward deployment to protect American citizens, uses of the sea, and trade in the Mediterranean (1821), the West Indies and the eastern Pacific coast of South America (1821), Brazil (1826), the East Indies (1835), Home (1841), and West Africa (1843). The names changed after 1865, but the areas remained typical of the navy's broader peacetime function and purpose up to 1917. During World War II (1939–1945), fleets were numbered and used for various temporary purposes. After the war, they became associated with specific regions, most prominently the Sixth Fleet in the Mediterranean and the Seventh Fleet in the Western Pacific. From 1995, the Fifth Fleet was associated with the Persian Gulf and the northwestern Indian Ocean.

ASSOCIATION WITH INDUSTRY AND SCIENCE

Throughout its history, the US Navy has had a necessarily close association with industry. Initially, it was dependent on local shipbuilders and suppliers for warship construction, and this connection continued. As industrial establishments, navy yards developed along the coast at Washington, DC (1799), Boston and Portsmouth (1800), Norfolk and New York (1801), and San Francisco (1853), with the first dry docks opening at Boston and Norfolk in 1833. The connection to American industry was critical to the navy in the shift from sail to steam and from wood to steel ships. Naval contracts provided the initial demand for American shipbuilders to acquire the technology from Europe to produce armored steel warships. This relationship was critical for success during all major wars. In more recent times, the connection has expanded to include electronics, computers, and communications.

As a counterpart to the scientific activity that accompanied westward expansion across the continent, the navy looked to the wider world, with expeditions to the South Pacific (1838–1842), the Dead Sea (1847),

Chile (1849–1852), the Amazon (1854), Japan (1853–1854), the La Plata River (1853–1856), and the North Pacific (1853–1856). These naval expeditions gathered information that was used by other governmental agencies that were established to receive and develop it, including the Naval Observatory (1830), the Smithsonian Institution (1846), and the Nautical Almanac Office at Harvard University (1849).

THE DEVELOPMENT OF A NAVAL PROFESSION AND BUREAUCRACY

In the nineteenth century, service in the navy, along with a number of other occupations, developed into a profession. Among the key points of development in this process were the establishment of the Naval Academy in 1845 for educating officers at entry level, the founding of the US Naval Institute in 1873 to provide a forum and journal for advanced professional thought, the organization of a comprehensive naval recruit training system in 1881, and the creation of the Naval War College in 1884 for the highest levels of professional study of warfare. The Naval War College soon became famous for the lectures of Alfred Thayer Mahan (1840–1914), published in 1890 as *The Influence of Sea Power upon History: 1660–1783*; the work of Charles Stockton (1845–1924) in first codifying the law of naval warfare; and William McCarty Little's (1846–1915) development of naval war gaming. The Goldwater-Nichols Act of 1986 fundamentally changed higher service-level professional military education to deal with joint affairs. Naval postgraduate studies began at the Naval Academy in 1909, and in 1945 a separate school was established for advanced academic study in naval-related sciences.

To manage the US Navy, a complex bureaucratic structure slowly developed as a separate department under the civilian control of the cabinet-level secretary of the navy. Its subsequent development parallels the growth of the executive branch of national government and is a significant part of it. In 1947, this department was subsumed under the Department of Defense, and the secretary was no longer a cabinet-level post. A board of naval commissioners managed the professional side from 1815 to 1842. A group of specialized bureaus was in place from 1842 to 1966, when the Department of Defense introduced system commands to replace them. In 1915 the statutory office of Chief of Naval Operations was created for the most senior officer in the navy to be adviser and deputy to the secretary, eventually becoming the equivalent of chief of naval staff. Since 1941, this officer has been a member of the Joint Chiefs of Staff, which exercised joint command authority over US forces until 1986, when this authority was passed to regional unified combatant commanders.

THE NAVAL DIMENSIONS OF SOCIAL ISSUES

Social issues that have arisen in general American society are typically reflected in naval dimensions. In the early Republic, the strong prejudice against entrenched elites, family influence, and political patronage prevented the naval service for more than forty years from developing a professional entry-level academy for officers, as the US Army did at West Point in 1801. Partially influenced by Herman Melville's 1850 novel *White-Jacket*, based on the author's own experience as a seaman on the frigate *United States*, Congress moved during the era of national reform to ban the traditional punishment of seamen by flogging. The decline in the number of African American seamen in the navy by the mid-nineteenth century reflected a general change in society that involved economic trends, as well as the rise of foreign-born seamen and racial prejudice. Similarly, twentieth-century moves toward racial integration, gender equality, and professional opportunity for all, regardless of religion, ethnicity, and gender, are reflected in the navy's changing policies and social makeup.

The first women in the US Navy served as nurses during the Civil War (1861–1865), and a female nurse corps was established in 1908. The first female naval reserve enlisted members were authorized in 1917. In 2014 Michelle Howard (b. 1960) became the US Navy's first female full admiral and in 2015 Nora Tyson became the first female commander of a fleet. In 1961 Samuel L. Gravely Jr. (1922–2004) became the first African American naval officer to command a warship and, in 1971, the first to reach the rank of rear admiral. J. Paul Reason (b. 1941) became the first African American admiral to reach four stars in 1996. Hispanic, Native, and Asian Americans have also reached senior positions in the US Navy.

In other areas, the move for temperance is seen in the abolishment of the rum ration in 1862 and the officers' wine mess in 1914. Continuing reforms through the twentieth and twenty-first centuries in officer selection, promotion, and standards of conduct reflected the evolving changes in professional performance and ethical standards for government employees.

SEE ALSO *Airplanes; Automobiles; Department of Defense, US; Department of Homeland Security; Department of State; The Influence of Sea Power upon History (Alfred Thayer Mahan, 1890); Trains*

BIBLIOGRAPHY

Albion, Robert G. *The Makers of Naval Policy, 1798–1947*. Edited by Rowena Reed. Annapolis, MD: Naval Institute Press, 1980.

Baer, George. *One Hundred Years of Sea Power: The U.S. Navy 1890–1990*. Stanford, CA: Stanford University Press, 1991.

Baugh, Daniel A., and N. A. M. Rodger. "The War for America, 1775–1783." In *Maritime History*, edited by John B.

Hattendorf, Vol. 2: *The Eighteenth Century and the Classic Age of Sail*. Malabar, FL: Krieger, 1997.

Braisted, William R. *The United States Navy in the Pacific, 1897–1909*. Austin: University of Texas Press, 1958.

Braisted, William R. *The United States Navy in the Pacific, 1909–1922*. Austin: University of Texas Press, 1971.

Braisted, William R. *Diplomats in Blue: U.S. Naval Officers in China, 1922–1933*. Gainesville: University Press of Florida, 2009.

Chisholm, Donald. *Waiting for Dead Men's Shoes: Origins and Development of the U.S Navy's Officer Personnel System, 1793–1941*. Stanford, CA: Stanford University Press, 2002.

Crawford, Michael J., and Christine F. Hughes. *The Reestablishment of the Navy, 1787–1801: Historical Overview and Select Bibliography*. Washington, DC: Naval Historical Center, Department of the Navy, 1995.

Dick, Steven J. *Sky and Ocean Joined: The U.S. Naval Observatory, 1830–2000*. New York: Cambridge University Press, 2003.

Dupree, A. Hunter. *Science in the Federal Government: A History of Policies and Activities to 1940*. Cambridge, MA: Harvard University Press, 1957.

Eustace, Nicole. *1812: War and the Passions of Patriotism*. Philadelphia: University of Pennsylvania Press, 2012.

Field, James A., Jr. *America and the Mediterranean World, 1776–1882*. Princeton, NJ: Princeton University Press, 1969.

Gilje, Paul A. *Free Trade and Sailors' Rights in the War of 1812*. Cambridge: Cambridge University Press, 2013.

Godson, Susan H. *Serving Proudly: A History of Women in the U.S. Navy*. Annapolis, MD: Naval Institute Press, 2001.

Hagan, Kenneth J. *This People's Navy: The Making of American Sea Power*. New York: Free Press, 1991.

Hagan, Kenneth J., and Michael T. McMaster, eds. *In Peace and War: Interpretations of American Naval History*. New York: Praeger, 2008.

Hattendorf, John B. "The US Navy and the Freedom of the Seas, 1775–1917." In *Navies in Northern Waters, 1721–2000*, edited by Rolf Hobson and Tom Kristiansen, 151–174. London: Cass, 2004.

Hattendorf, John B. "The Formation and Roles of the Continental Navy, 1775–1785." In *Talking about Naval History: A Collection of Essays*, 185–203. Newport, RI: Naval War College Press, 2011.

Hattendorf, John B. "The U.S. Navy's Nineteenth-Century Forward Stations." In: *Talking about Naval History: A Collection of Essays*, 231–244. Newport, RI: Naval War College Press, 2011.

Hattendorf, John B. "The Third Alan Villiers Memorial Lecture. The Naval War of 1812 in International Perspective." *Mariner's Mirror* 99, 1 (2013): 5–22.

Heinrich, Thomas R. *Ships for the Seven Seas: Philadelphia Shipbuilding in the Age of Industrial Capitalism*. Baltimore, MD: Johns Hopkins University Press, 1997.

Johnson, Robert E. *Thence Round Cape Horn: The Story of United States Naval Forces on Pacific Station, 1818–1923*. Annapolis, MD: US Naval Institute, 1963.

Johnson, Robert E. *Far China Station: The U.S. Navy in Asian Waters, 1800–1898*. Annapolis, MD: Naval Institute Press, 1979.

Langley, Harold D. *Social Reform in the United States Navy, 1798–1862*. Urbana: University of Illinois Press, 1967.

Langley, Harold D. *A History of Medicine in the Early U.S. Navy*. Baltimore, MD: Johns Hopkins University Press, 1995.

Long, David F. *Gold Braid and Foreign Relations: Diplomatic Activities of U.S. Naval Officers, 1798–1883*. Annapolis, MD: Naval Institute Press, 1988.

Magra, Christopher. *The Fisherman's Cause: Atlantic Commerce and the Maritime Dimensions of the American Revolution*. Cambridge: Cambridge University Press, 2009.

McBride, William M. *Technological Change and the United States Navy, 1865–1945*. Baltimore, MD: Johns Hopkins University Press, 2000.

McKee, Christopher. *A Gentlemanly and Honorable Profession: The Creation of the U.S. Naval Officer Corps, 1794–1815*. Annapolis, MD: Naval Institute Press, 1991.

Schneller, Robert J., Jr. *Blue & Gold and Black: Racial Integration of the U.S. Naval Academy*. College Station: Texas A&M University Press, 2008.

Shulman, Mark R. *Navalism and the Emergence of American Sea Power, 1882–1893*. Annapolis, MD: Naval Institute Press, 1995.

Smelser, Marshal. *The Congress Founds the Navy, 1787–1798*. Notre Dame, IN: University of Notre Dame Press, 1959. Reprint, Westport, CT: Greenwood Press, 1973.

Smith, Jason Wirth. "'Twixt the Devil and the Deep Blue Sea: Hydrography, Sea Power, and the Marine Environment, 1898–1901." *Journal of Military History* 78 (April 2014): 575–614.

Still, William N., Jr. *American Sea Power in the Old World: The United States Navy in European and Near Eastern Waters, 1865–1917*. Westport, CT: Greenwood Press, 1980.

Symonds, Craig L. *Navalists and Antinavalists: The Naval Policy Debate in the United States, 1785–1827*. Newark: University of Delaware Press, 1980.

Yerxa, Donald A. *Admirals and Empire: The United States Navy and the Caribbean, 1898–1945*. Columbia: University of South Carolina Press, 1991.

John B. Hattendorf
Ernest J. King Professor of Maritime History
US Naval War College

NAZISM

In the middle of the twentieth century, Germany's Nazi revolution profoundly and unexpectedly shaped the United States, its role in the world, and international perceptions of American character and policies. National Socialism was the totalitarian effort from 1925 to 1945 to create an ironclad, militarized compact out of the German people, whose strength would reside in their alleged racial purity. This union would allow Germany to fulfill its imperial destiny as a world power. Given Germany's robust political reorganization and economic achievements after 1933, the Nazi revolution impressed observers in many developing nations around the world, particularly in South America, but its influence was always limited by the self-absorbed nature of its race doctrine. Even in World War II (1939–1945), the Nazis never sought allies among the people they conquered—the Ukrainians, for example, or even the French. The concentration of German power was always considered paramount in Berlin. If forced to choose, there were Europeans (and Americans in their safe armchairs) who preferred Nazism to communism, but the choice was poor and hardly created genuine attachments to National Socialism. Like other totalitarian regimes, Nazi Germany tried to go it alone without accepting the multilateral give-and-take relationships that are necessary in a globalizing world. In the end, the influence of the Nazis was evident only in the massive destruction and extraordinary loss of innocent civilian life that followed in the wake of Germany's military offensives in Europe and the Soviet Union.

It was Nazi tyranny that pulled the United States into World War II, and it was Nazi tyranny that reflected, like a dark mirror, the more enlightening promises of America's democratic institutions. After 1945, the two great protagonists in the struggle against Adolf Hitler (1889–1945), the United States and the Soviet Union, assumed a global role in international affairs as superpowers. To this day, the United States remains the most important military actor in the world. Although depleted, its fund of goodwill around the world was established with its intervention against the Nazis after 1941 and its lead in constructing global institutions of international order and justice, such as the United Nations.

There was little about Nazi Germany that was attractive to most Americans. Although they admired Germany's unequaled economic recovery from the depths of the Great Depression, in which America in the 1930s remained stuck, they despised its despotic features and especially its persecution of Jews. But the United States had a special place in the worldview of the Nazis. Hitler considered the American conquest of the western frontier and the destruction of indigenous societies to be an excellent example of the imperial rights of a racially superior people. He proposed to follow in America's nineteenth-century footsteps by building a continental empire in eastern Europe and ruthlessly exploiting its populations and resources.

At the same time, the Nazis judged twentieth-century America very differently. In their view, modern America had lost its pioneer virtues to become a weakened, mongrelized society that would ultimately fail to collectively develop its riches. Organized along racial lines, with pioneering masters from the Reich and subject slaves in Poland and Russia, "Greater Germany" would emerge as the world's leading economic and political power. Like the Soviet Union, Nazi Germany wanted to become a better America. Whatever the ideological views of the Nazis, however, American culture and American consumer products always found markets in Nazi Germany: *Gone with the Wind* was a best-selling book at the time Germany invaded Poland in September 1939; Coca-Cola only withdrew licenses to German manufacturers in 1941, who, in turn, reorganized and created Fanta.

Without the immigration of so many, mostly Jewish, refugees from Europe after 1933—tens of thousands of new immigrants, from Albert Einstein (1879–1955) in Princeton to Marlene Dietrich (1901–1992) in Hollywood—the United States would have remained a much more isolated and parochial country. Newly hired German scholars, major scientific mobilizations such as the Manhattan Project during the war, and the GI Bill after 1945 made institutions of world rank out of slumbering American universities. Decades later, Nobel Prizes in the sciences were earned by Americans rather than Germans.

Moreover, the Nazi persecution of Jews and political opponents increasingly disqualified prejudices in the United States. In many ways, Hitler gave anti-Semitism a bad name, and the fight against Nazism in the 1940s fortified the civil rights struggle in the 1950s and 1960s. Because the United States was the principal destination of Jews seeking to emigrate from Europe, both before and after the Holocaust, attentiveness to the persecution of minorities has become interwoven in American civic life. For two generations after World War II, the memory of the "Good War" facilitated a bipartisan political culture that, for better or worse, accepted long-term planning challenges and major military and global responsibilities, such as the Marshall Plan. In turn, peace and economic stability in postwar Europe also allowed developed countries to catch up with America's huge economic lead, but not its military superiority: Nazism was the first of many evils that have shaped the way America's comic-book superheroes, from Superman to Wonder Woman, and its foreign policy experts, from Henry Kissinger to Hillary Clinton, look at and respond to the world. Isolationism was a strong strand in the first half of the twentieth century; interventionism became an even stronger one in the second half. This has raised the question among some Americans about whether the "Good War" against "Nazism" can and should be fought endlessly.

SEE ALSO *Catholicism; Cold War; Exceptionalism; Germany; Interventionism; Isolationism; Judaism; League of Nations; Protestant-Catholic-Jew (Will Herberg, 1955); Protestantism; Religions; United Nations; Universal Declaration of Human Rights; Whiteness; World War I; World War II*

BIBLIOGRAPHY

Dunn, Susan. *1940: FDR, Willkie, Lindbergh, Hitler—The Election amid the Storm.* New Haven. CT: Yale University Press, 2013.

Fritzsche, Peter. *Life and Death in the Third Reich.* Cambridge, MA: Harvard University Press, 2008.

Hoenicke Moore, Michaela. *Know Your Enemy: The American Debate on Nazism, 1933–1945.* New York: Cambridge University Press, 2010.

Novick, Peter. *The Holocaust in American Life.* Boston: Houghton Mifflin, 1999.

Tooze, Adam. *The Wages of Destruction: The Making and Breaking of the Nazi Economy.* New York: Viking, 2007.

Peter Fritzsche
Professor of History
University of Illinois

NEOLIBERALISM

Neoliberalism is a thorny summary label, a catchall phrase that means so many different things that it risks becoming impenetrable for its vagueness. When considering neoliberalism's history in US foreign relations, it may be useful to think of neoliberalism in three distinct yet interrelated ways. First, neoliberalism may be thought of as an ideology of pro-market governance. Second, neoliberalism can be defined as a specific set of domestic and foreign economic policies. Third, it can be discussed as a political project. Developing a satisfactory and brief account of neoliberalism in US foreign relations requires attention to historical tensions within and across these three meanings. Based on that understanding, one can begin to measure the power and limits of neoliberal ideas and policies as driving forces in US foreign relations in the twentieth century.

To understand neoliberalism as an ideology and guiding principle for policy, one must begin with a working definition: a theory of political economic practices that holds that human well-being can best be advanced by liberating individual entrepreneurial freedoms. Above all, neoliberal thinkers and policy makers share a conviction about the benefits of the market and an abhorrence of state power. Markets left unfettered by the state, according to the argument, are efficient: if they

make mistakes, they quickly correct them. Furthermore, the best sort of government is the smallest sort of government. Any regulation impedes innovation.

BELIEF IN THE SELF-REGULATING MARKET

That common belief in the virtuous power of the self-regulating market evolved in the mid-twentieth century to encapsulate a political project of deregulating national economies, liberalizing international trade, and creating a unified global market. Scholars most often describe this politically assisted rise of market rules through the examples of International Monetary Fund and World Bank structural adjustment schemes from the 1980s to the present. But the free-market blueprint of structural adjustment, which was supported by the United States, has a longer history in which neoliberal practices have undergone multiple variations.

A number of historians have described how market-centered ideas and policies have been forcefully advanced as part of US foreign policy at many different moments in the twentieth century. For example, Emily Rosenberg argues in *Spreading the American Dream* (1982) that a vision of "liberal-developmentalism" undergirded American expansion between 1890 and 1945. According to that ideology, the US government assisted American entrepreneurs who sought footholds in overseas markets. From the Open Door Notes (1899–1900) until World War II (1939–1945), Rosenberg argues, the US government used a rhetoric driven by "the right to free and open trade" to promote international economic expansion at the same time that it argued that other nations should follow the example of American development. In another example, Thomas Zeiler writes in *Free Trade, Free World* (1999) that American negotiators pressed for an agenda to open former imperial markets after World War II. The ideal of "free-trade" multilateralism was prevalent in the administrations of Harry Truman (1884–1972) and Dwight D. Eisenhower (1890–1969), and each turned to the 1947 General Agreement on Tariffs and Trade (GATT) to promote trade liberalization.

THE COLD WAR GOAL OF CONTAINMENT

With the dawn and then the entrenchment of the Cold War, the proponents of trade liberalization identified their project with the Cold War goals of containment. The foremost US foreign policy objective in the second half of the twentieth century was to prevent the spread of communism as a political and economic system. The administrations of Eisenhower, John F. Kennedy (1917–1963), and Lyndon B. Johnson (1908–1973) worked assiduously to do so through a number of means, including the promotion of the American claim to prosperity for itself and its allies. That claim often drew on a rhetoric emphasizing the domestic and international benefits of free trade. Domestically, according to the vision, increased trade would benefit the industrial sector of the US economy and improve the national capacity to bear the burdens of international defense. Internationally, a more liberal economy would promote Western unity and prove the superiority of free choice.

US Cold War economic theorists framed capitalism as the economic and moral opposite of state-centered socialism. Yet, throughout the early Cold War, most American elites believed in a mixed economy of social democratic policies and government support for private capital as the best way to further the national well-being. The promotion of "free international trade" also meant a more multilateral economic system. At the same time as American policy makers sought reduced trade barriers to facilitate global growth, they also built in escape clauses that allowed the United States and other nations to maintain protectionist policies. By the late 1960s, the related financial weakness—a combination of rising trade discrepancies with West Germany and Japan, the high-priced and tortuously long Vietnam War, and the costs of Great Society social spending—became unsustainable and ultimately led to a national balance-of-payments crisis that was the most portentous economic legacy of the early Cold War.

THE RISE OF THE WASHINGTON CONSENSUS

As Daniel Sargent argues in *A Superpower Transformed* (2015), the national deficit ultimately led to the rapid breakdown of the Bretton Woods international monetary order and the floating of the US dollar and other major international currencies. These decisions came with shattering suddenness, and the subsequent crisis atmosphere shaped how strategists thought about national and international economic policy. In particular, ideological calls for greater market freedom became more pronounced in both domestic and foreign policy. The causes for that surge are complex, but two are central. First, federal monetary policy was reconstructed in a way that lay great emphasis on the purity of the free market and on the importance of finance capital to US economic well-being. As his monetarist ideas replaced the standard Keynesian principle of economic growth through consumer demand, Milton Friedman (1912–2006) also argued that individual freedom and innovation were central to American economic revival. Second, high oil prices led to a Soviet economic resurgence that seemed to pave the way for a more vigorous ideological stance. When the Soviet army invaded Afghanistan in 1979, the administrations of Jimmy Carter (b. 1924) and Ronald Reagan (1911–2004) depicted the invasion in an ideological context that characterized "Soviet adventurism" as a gauntlet thrown against the free market.

During the 1980s, the Reagan administration harnessed that situation and linked it to conservative probusiness arguments in domestic politics about government regulation to promote a consensus that competitive markets and free trade could reinvigorate American global power. After his election as president in 1992, Bill Clinton (b. 1946) continued to hold that regulation limited innovation and distorted the free market. By the mid-1990s, neoliberalism was considered so powerful by its supporters and detractors that both described it as a "Washington Consensus."

The neoliberal consensus also led to a critical reassessment of development theory, and in the 1970s supporters were forced to reconsider their fundamental values and objectives. Development economists and American officials began to follow the neoliberal line that unrestricted markets would allow citizens to pursue their own interests. That economic freedom, they argued, was "an indispensable means toward the achievement of political freedom" (Friedman 2002, 8). Followers of the antistatist, pro-market doctrine rejected increases in official government aid, national planning, and large-scale development programs as attempts at "social engineering" that would do more harm than good. When a combination of high oil prices, reduced official aid, and increased commercial borrowing led to the "Third World debt crisis" of the early 1980s, the Reagan administration proposed a set of neoliberal solutions. In particular, the United States and other industrialized countries made further assistance on policies of "structural adjustment." In other words, the developing nations would need to privatize state enterprises and open their doors to greater foreign investment.

IMPLICATIONS FOR THE TWENTY-FIRST CENTURY

Because neoliberalism is as much a utopian idea as a set of practices, its execution has always been necessarily flawed and fragmentary. In other words, free-market policies always faced opposition and were thus forced to display a versatility that belied the ruthlessness of their ideology. When one reads the histories described above, the delicate and always-changing balance between ideology and compromise is as important as the totalizing pretension of the ideology. The historians' emphasis on contingency and tension raises a note of caution toward arguments that depict neoliberal globalization as an immovable structural force. Triumphalist neoliberal voices, most famously Francis Fukuyama (b. 1952), saw the collapse of the Soviet Union in 1991 as "the end of history" and the dawn of a new era of global free-market capitalism.

That depiction itself is part of the history of US foreign relations, one that gained influence in the 1990s and continues to be prevalent today. The global financial crisis, the instability of the Eurozone, and the subprime mortgage bubble of the first decade of the twenty-first century all point to a rising sense of confusion to that vision of global neoliberalism. But in his 2009 inaugural address, Barack Obama (b. 1961) argued that the main culprit of those economic woes was not the market itself. The question was not "whether the market is a force for good or ill," he said. "Its power to generate wealth and expand freedom is unmatched." But it is too soon to understand the overarching implications of such a view for the twenty-first century.

SEE ALSO *Bretton Woods; Friedman, Milton; Keynesian Economics; World Bank; World Trade Organization*

BIBLIOGRAPHY

Borstelmann, Thomas. *The 1970s: A New Global History from Civil Rights to Economic Inequality.* Princeton, NJ: Princeton University Press, 2012.

Friedman, Milton, with the assistance of Rose D. Friedman. *Capitalism and Freedom.* 40th anniversary ed. Chicago: University of Chicago Press, 2002. First published in 1962.

Latham, Michael. *The Right Kind of Revolution: Modernization, Development, and U.S. Foreign Policy from the Cold War to the Present.* Ithaca, NY: Cornell University Press, 2011.

Obama, Barack. "Inaugural Address." January 20, 2009. http://millercenter.org/president/obama/speeches/speech-4453

Rosenberg, Emily S. *Spreading the American Dream: American Economic and Cultural Expansion, 1890–1945.* New York: Hill and Wang, 1982.

Sargent, Daniel J. *A Superpower Transformed: The Remaking of American Foreign Relations in the 1970s.* New York: Oxford University Press, 2015.

Zeiler, Thomas W. *Free Trade, Free World: The Advent of GATT.* Chapel Hill: University of North Carolina Press, 1999.

Christopher R. W. Dietrich
Assistant Professor of History
Fordham University

NEUTRALITY

When nation-states go to war, nonbelligerent countries that are caught in the middle frequently declare their intent to remain neutral. Over the centuries, treaties and diplomatic precedent have affected the responsibilities and rights that come with neutrality, but the basic principles have remained the same. In declaring neutrality, countries indicate their intention to stay out of the fray and avoid actions that would assist one belligerent over another. They also expect warring states to respect their territorial boundaries, to honor the rights of their citizens to travel and trade with all nations, and to avoid interference with their merchant and naval vessels at sea. In reality, countries find such obligations and rights difficult to honor and defend.

IDEOLOGY, ECONOMICS, AND THE SAFEGUARDING OF US SOVEREIGNTY

From the 1780s through the 1940s, the United States frequently struggled with the concept of neutrality. Throughout this period, three constants guided America's views of and approach to neutrality: ideology, the defense of US economic interests, and the safeguarding of US sovereignty. Ideologically, most Americans viewed their country as a beacon of light to the world, embracing the idea that it was, in the words of John Winthrop (c. 1587/8–1649), a "city upon a hill." The principles of democracy and free-market capitalism convinced many Americans that the United States was a model for other states to imitate.

Closely tied to their ideological concerns, Americans turned to neutrality to protect their economic interests. US leaders thought that export trade was essential to the country's financial well-being. In the early days of the Republic, the country sold raw materials in foreign markets and purchased finished goods that were necessary to the nation's growth. When the country industrialized in the late 1800s, it remained reliant on overseas trade, exporting manufactured products from steel rails to automobiles. Throughout their history, Americans resisted disruptions to their financial endeavors during wars and sought to trade with nations regardless of their status as a belligerent or neutral.

Finally, Americans embraced neutrality as a means of protecting US sovereignty. They expected declarations of neutrality to deter other states from encroaching on or threatening American citizens, territory, and property at home and abroad.

EARLY US EFFORTS TO AVOID EUROPEAN ENTANGLEMENTS

To safeguard America's ideological, economic, and sovereign interests, the United States sought to avoid political entanglements outside the Western Hemisphere. Americans hoped that doing so would prevent the stronger European powers from influencing the country's future. Efforts to avoid foreign politics occurred as early as John Adams's Model Treaty of 1776 and George Washington's 1796 Farewell Address.

To guide negotiations with France during the American Revolution (1775–1783), John Adams (1735–1826) proposed that the United States not combine its trade and military treaties, separating any accords so that the country could remain politically isolated from the Old

World. He also suggested that the United States needed to establish economic agreements with numerous countries to prevent it from becoming dependent on trade with a single nation. As part of the Model Treaty, Adams included the concept of freedom of the seas. Preparing for a peaceful future, he asserted that neutral ships that did not carry contraband should have the right to sail through war zones without interference. His views were echoed by George Washington (1732–1799) in his Farewell Address. The president asserted that the United States should make every effort to circumvent entanglements with European powers and avoid permanent alliances that could force the country into a foreign war.

When the American Revolution ended, US leaders wanted to remain detached from European affairs in order to focus on internal matters and westward expansion and on increasing America's export trade. America first declared neutrality in 1793 during the French Revolution when France went to war with Great Britain, Spain, and the Netherlands.

France's plan to spread its revolution worried President Washington and his main advisers, Secretary of State Thomas Jefferson (1743–1826) and Secretary of the Treasury Alexander Hamilton (1755–1804). They were concerned that the 1778 Franco-American Treaty of Alliance, which brought France into the American Revolution, could force the United States to take sides in the conflict and thus draw the country into the war. Addressing the quandary, the president announced on April 22, 1793, that the United States would not take sides. He was, nevertheless, cautious and did not initially use the term *neutral* to describe America's position. Instead, Washington announced that the United States would be "friendly and impartial." Considering that the 1778 treaty was defensive in nature and that France initiated the attack on Britain, US leaders ultimately concluded that they were not obligated to support France. Consequently, the United States followed up Washington's announcement with the Neutrality Act of 1794, making the country's stance official.

Despite America's pronouncement, the belligerents frequently violated US neutrality. Great Britain rejected the American idea of freedom of the seas and forced British-born American sailors who worked on US merchant and naval vessels into the service of the Royal Navy. Additionally, the British and French stopped American ships traveling to and from European ports and confiscated their cargos. For nearly twenty years, the United States tried to stop British and French violations of American neutrality. However, with a weak navy, the US government had limited options. The United States sent letters of protest, attempted diplomatic negotiations, participated in the Quasi-War with France (1798–1800), enacted a failed trade embargo, and skirmished

with the Royal Navy at sea, to little avail. Finally, in 1812, feeling forced into the conflict because of the repeated violations of American neutrality, President James Madison (1751–1836) ended American neutrality and called for war against Great Britain.

THE PRESERVATION OF SOVEREIGNTY DURING THE AMERICAN CIVIL WAR

The United States again grappled with neutrality during the American Civil War (1861–1865). However, in 1861, the United States was a belligerent and challenged the neutral rights of foreign countries on the high seas. The status of the Confederacy as a rebellious collection of states would change to that of a recognized belligerent if foreign countries announced that they were neutral. As a belligerent, the Confederacy could legally purchase war material and procure loans from foreign governments. The Confederates would therefore obtain the means to prolong and possibly win the war. Belligerent status could also lead to formal recognition as an independent state, which would make the United States' claim that it was fighting a domestic conflict impossible to support.

Initially, the Union decided to follow the Anaconda Plan devised by General Winfield Scott (1786–1866) and cut off the South's access to foreign trade, but the Union did not establish an official naval blockade. A formal blockade would suggest that a war, rather than an internal rebellion, was taking place between two separate nations. Therefore, on April 19, 1861, President Abraham Lincoln (1809–1865) announced that all southern US ports were closed. Despite Lincoln's careful choice of words, the outcome resulted in controversy because foreign powers struggled with how to respond. In the end, Britain, followed by France, decided to recognize the existence of a Union blockade and officially stated that they would remain neutral.

Once the foreign powers declared neutrality, the United States found itself imposing policies that it had opposed during the French Revolution and Napoleonic Wars. To enforce its cordon of the southern ports, the United States used the doctrine of "continuous voyage," which Britain had used against the United States decades earlier. The doctrine of continuous voyage suggested that ownership of cargo was defined by its port of origin. A merchant vessel could no longer break up a voyage by stopping in a neutral port to change the cargo's ownership before sailing to or from a belligerent port. Under this doctrine, the US Navy detained British ships in the Caribbean and Gulf of Mexico on their way to and from the Confederacy. In 1863 the USS *Vanderbilt* seized the HMS *Peterhoff* after it delivered contraband destined for Texas in the neutral port of Matamoros, Mexico. Earlier, in 1861, the US Navy had removed Confederate diplomats from a British merchant vessel, the HMS *Trent* that was traveling from Havana to St. Thomas, a British port in the West Indies. Although the British did not protest the Union's enforcement of the continuous voyage doctrine, they viewed the *Trent* affair as a matter of national honor. British and US diplomats diffused the crisis after the United States released the Confederate representatives and asserted that the US Navy captain who captured them had acted without orders.

Tension between the United States and the European powers decreased significantly following issuance of Lincoln's Emancipation Proclamation in 1863, because Britain could not in good conscience assist a belligerent that fought to uphold slavery, something it had ended in 1833. With Britain choosing to restrain its actions, France followed suit, ending any possibility that the Europeans would formally recognize the Confederacy as a separate nation.

US DESIRE TO INFLUENCE OUTCOMES OF TWENTIETH-CENTURY CONFLICTS

As the United States entered the twentieth century, the nation again found itself dealing with international conflicts that it could not avoid. America was no longer just a continental power. The country had territorial and economic interests across the globe. Additionally, many of America's leaders sought to spread the country's ideals of democracy and free-market capitalism abroad. Doing so, they hoped, would ensure lasting world peace. Thus, during the two world wars, the United States had a vested interest in the outcome of the conflicts, and the desire to influence the direction of the wars affected its approach to neutrality.

World War I (1914–1918). At the outbreak of World War I in August 1914, President Woodrow Wilson (1856–1924) declared that the United States would remain neutral. Wilson assumed that neutrality would give him the opportunity to be a fair mediator among the belligerents and to mold the postwar world in America's image. Wilson and the majority of his countrymen also intended the declaration of neutrality to protect American economic interests and safeguard US citizens and property overseas. On numerous occasions between August 1914 and the US declaration of war in April 1917, Wilson attempted, without success, to bring the belligerents to the peace table and protested against Britain's and Germany's disruptions of US trade.

Regardless of its efforts to defend its neutral rights, in World War I the United States approached neutrality differently than it had during the early 1800s. As a world power in the early twentieth century, the country had growing international interests and a desire to see Great Britain and France defeat Germany on the battlefield. Ideologically, Wilson and his staff considered German militarism to be the key barrier to mediation and the greatest threat to US sovereignty. This sentiment increased after Germany initiated its U-boat campaign in February 1915. Initially focused on Allied merchant shipping, the Germans warned that American ships and citizens that entered the war zone did so at their own risk. To Wilson, submarine warfare was inhumane compared to Britain's naval blockade, and after the sinking of the HMS *Lusitania* and subsequent deaths of 128 American passengers on May 7, 1915, the president's antipathy toward Germany grew significantly.

Exacerbating the United States' biased stance, the nation developed a strong financial relationship with the Allies. Throughout the period of American neutrality, Great Britain and France borrowed billions of dollars and purchased vast amounts of war material from American banks and manufacturers. The relationship helped the United States shift from a debtor to a creditor nation for the first time in its history. Combined, the US view of Germany and the Allied-American economic bond resulted in America's active support for the Allies and multiple violations of its obligations as a neutral. Wilson's administration tacitly approved loans to the Allies, assisted Britain in its effort to blockade Germany, and initiated clandestine negotiations with Britain that were intended to force Germany to the peace table prior to America's declaration of war.

American experiences in World War I encouraged many people to seek isolation from world politics after 1919. They believed the decisions that US government and business leaders made between 1914 and 1917 led to America's participation in the war. A major concern was the munitions trade with the Allies. To insulate the United States from future wars, lawmakers passed several neutrality acts between 1934 and 1936 that outlawed the sale of munitions to belligerents and barred Americans from traveling on belligerent-owned ships.

World War II (1939–1945). As in the period between 1914 and 1917, the United States wanted to influence the outcome of World War II. US leaders viewed the aggressive territorial expansion of the Axis powers (Japan, Italy, and Germany) as a threat to American security around the world. Consequently, President Franklin Roosevelt (1882–1945) pursued policies that he hoped would thwart Axis imperialism. During the late 1930s and early 1940s, Roosevelt attempted, unsuccessfully, to assist China after it was invaded by the Japanese and to safeguard the US-held Philippines by calling for a trade embargo against Japan. In 1939, following the German attack on Poland, the United States started the cash-and-carry program. The program was an effort by Roosevelt and the US Congress to reopen the arms trade with Britain and its allies. Under cash and carry, the Allies could buy war materials for cash and transport the goods across the Atlantic in their own merchant vessels. The following year, Roosevelt initiated the destroyers-for-bases deal, providing Britain with fifty aging destroyers in exchange for a ninety-nine-year lease on British bases on islands in the Caribbean Sea.

In January 1941, Roosevelt promoted the Lend-Lease program, under which the Allies borrowed or leased US military equipment. Roosevelt also promoted the United States as the "arsenal of democracy," asserting that America must support Britain's war effort. The Congress, agreeing with Roosevelt, approved Lend-Lease in March, ensuring that the United States would provide substantial support for Britain.

By mid-1941, the United States could no longer claim to be neutral because of its active support for the Allies. In addition to its material assistance to Britain and the Soviet Union, US and British military leaders discussed the prospect of America's entrance into the war and developed plans for joint operations. On August 14, the United States and Britain formulated the Atlantic Charter, outlining a vision for the postwar world. The public announcement amounted to an Anglo-American alliance. Through early 1941 America assisted the Allies in the hope that they could defeat the Axis powers before the United States had to intervene. However, as in the 1914–1917 period, US efforts helped set the stage for the country's declaration of war in December 1941.

CONCLUSION

Between the 1780s and the 1940s, ideology, economics, and the defense of US sovereignty remained constant influences on America's view of neutrality. Yet the United States addressed neutrality differently depending on its status as a noncombatant or belligerent and its desire to influence the wars' outcomes. As a young and weak nation in the late 1700s and early 1800s, the United States declared neutrality so it could focus on economic growth and continental expansion, and more importantly avoid being drawn into the French Revolution and subsequent Napoleonic Wars. In the American Civil War, the United States was a belligerent that was attempting to preserve its sovereignty and thus challenged many of the neutral rights that it had defended and gone to war over decades before. Finally, during the world wars of the twentieth century, the United States, which had many global economic and territorial interests, again addressed neutrality differently. Thus, while ideology, economics, and the defense of sovereignty were always factors that influenced America's view and interpretation of neutrality, the US approach

constantly varied to meet the country's changing status and interests.

SEE ALSO *Cash and Carry; Cold War; Department of Defense, US; Department of State; Dollar Diplomacy; Eisenhower, Dwight D.; Embassies, Consulates, and Diplomatic Missions; Empire, US; Exceptionalism; Foreign Service, US; Internationalism; Isolationism; League of Nations; Lend-Lease Act (1941); Missionary Diplomacy; Monroe Doctrine (1823); Navy, US; Reagan, Ronald Wilson; Roosevelt, Franklin D.; Roosevelt, Theodore; Roosevelt Corollary (1904); Taft, William Howard; Truman, Harry S.; United Nations; Vietnam War; Wilson, Woodrow; World War I; World War II*

BIBLIOGRAPHY

Clements, Kendrick A. *The Presidency of Woodrow Wilson.* Lawrence: University Press of Kansas, 1992.

Coogan, John W. *The End of Neutrality: The United States, Britain, and Maritime Rights, 1899–1915.* Ithaca, NY: Cornell University Press, 1981.

Dallek, Robert. *Franklin D. Roosevelt and American Foreign Policy, 1932–1945.* New York: Oxford University Press, 1979.

Divine, Robert A. *The Reluctant Belligerent: American Entry into World War II.* 2nd ed. Austin: University of Texas Press, 1979.

Fleming, Thomas. *The Illusion of Victory: America in World War I.* New York: Basic Books, 2003.

Floyd, M. Ryan. *Abandoning American Neutrality: Woodrow Wilson and the Beginning of the Great War, August 1914–December 1915.* New York: Palgrave Macmillan, 2013.

Jones, Howard. *Blue and Gray Diplomacy: A History of Union and Confederate Foreign Relations.* Chapel Hill: University of North Carolina Press, 2010.

McDonald, Forrest. *The Presidency of George Washington.* Lawrence: University Press of Kansas, 1974.

Tucker, Robert W., and David C. Hendrickson. *Empire of Liberty: The Statecraft of Thomas Jefferson.* New York: Oxford University Press, 1990.

Wills, Garry, *James Madison.* New York: Holt, 2002.

M. Ryan Floyd Sr.
Assistant Professor of History
Social Science Secondary Education Coordinator
Department of History and Philosophy, Lander University

NEUTRALITY ACT OF 1794

The Neutrality Act of 1794 is one of the earliest examples of municipal legislation codifying the obligations of neutrality. The act advanced international law, making noninvolvement in foreign conflicts, not just impartiality, an obligation of neutrality. It influenced Great Britain's

Foreign Enlistment Act of 1819 and other nations' neutrality legislation.

The renewal of war in Europe between revolutionary France and Great Britain in 1793 led President George Washington to issue a neutrality proclamation on April 22, 1793. Washington's proclamation sought to keep the United States out of war and thereby protect American trade from maritime predation. The proclamation effectively annulled the mutual defense commitments of the Treaty of Alliance with France of 1778, and it consequently generated intense constitutional debate, as exemplified in the Pacificus-Helvidius exchanges (pen names for Alexander Hamilton and James Madison, respectively), regarding the relationship of executive and legislative authorities in the conduct of foreign policy. It also sharply divided the nation between pro-French Republicans and pro-British Federalists.

Washington's proclamation, prohibiting Americans from aiding or abetting hostilities against either power, was immediately challenged by the arrival in April 1793 of the new French minister to the United States, Edmond-Charles Genêt (1763–1834). Genêt straightaway began to issue letters of marque to American sailors and to outfit privateers in American ports to attack British commerce. He also recruited Americans to invade Spanish Louisiana and Florida. In the absence of a statutory prohibition, the administration struggled to enforce the proclamation and to punish Americans who had enlisted as French privateers. This imbroglio was finally resolved with the passage of the Neutrality Act on June 5, 1794.

The act prohibited American citizens from accepting foreign commissions as privateers, from arming vessels to be employed against countries at peace with the United States, and from preparing hostile expeditions against friendly nations from American soil. Violators of the act could be found guilty of a misdemeanor and face fines or imprisonment or both. The goal of the act was to prevent the actions of private Americans or foreign nationals living here from drawing the United States into a war and to avoid retaliation by France or Great Britain against American shipping for any perceived American partiality in the current war. The act, however, did not completely succeed, as both France and Great Britain repeatedly seized American vessels and violated the United States' rights as a neutral to trade nonmilitary goods freely with belligerents. These simmering tensions led to the Quasi-War with France (1798–1800) and the War of 1812 with Britain.

Nonetheless, the Neutrality Act of 1794 and revisions of the act in 1797, 1800, 1817, and 1818 enabled the United States to avoid most foreign conflicts and thereby to expand trade. Additionally, the principle of neutrality and of emphasizing neutral rights and obligations in treaties with foreign powers (e.g., the Treaty of Washington in 1871) was

a hallmark of American governmental policy until at least World War I. The act remains part of federal criminal code today (18 US Code § 958–962), though it is rarely used.

ENFORCEMENT IN THE NINETEENTH CENTURY

In the nineteenth century the act was regularly invoked in American courts. The United States was teeming with foreign revolutionaries and American military adventurers (i.e., filibusters), who sought to recruit Americans or foreign nationals living in the United States to man privateers or to join filibuster expeditions setting out from American shores. Filibusters or potential filibusters, such as former Vice President Aaron Burr (1756–1836), were regularly arrested and tried for violating the Neutrality Act of 1794. Enforcement was uneven, though, because many federal officials sympathized with the privateers and filibusters accused of violating the law. Moreover, getting a jury to convict individuals for breach of the Neutrality Act proved difficult. For example, in 1850 Narciso López (1797–1851), the organizer of many filibustering expeditions against Cuba, was arrested and indicted by a New Orleans grand jury for violation of the Neutrality Act of 1818. The government, however, failed to win a conviction, and López was set free.

Even so, the mere existence of the neutrality legislation provided friendly foreign diplomatic agents an important tool to pursue their nations' objectives. This was most notable in the case of privateers. Foreign consuls regularly sought restitution of prizes (i.e., ships captured at sea during wartime) brought into American ports, forcing federal courts to consider whether privateers outfitted in the United States or American sailors serving foreign powers as privateers violated the Neutrality Act of 1794. Such cases became particularly common as decommissioned American privateers from the War of 1812 sought new commissions from the rebellious provinces in Spanish America. By proving in a court of law that a privateer was illegally outfitted in the United States or that its crew consisted of Americans, Spanish consular agents succeeded in restoring many prizes taken from Spaniards (e.g., the *Divina Pastora*, *Santíssima Trinidad*, and *Sereno*) to the original owners. This practice made accepting a commission as a privateer from Latin American revolutionaries a less lucrative venture for American citizens.

Because federal officials often responded half-heartedly to formal diplomatic complaints regarding the outfitting of privateers in the United States, Spain turned to the courts. Judges in prize cases proved less sympathetic to violators of the statute than lower-level officials or jurors in criminal cases. American courts and neutrality legislation became a means for a weaker nation, like Spain, to pursue its foreign policy objectives in the United States through litigation when normal diplomatic channels failed.

CONTEMPORARY RELEVANCE

With the disappearance of privateering and filibustering and the emergence of the United States as a global power in the twentieth century, the international context that led to the passage of the Neutrality Act of 1794 no longer exists. Still, the law remains relevant to American domestic and foreign policy. First, the Neutrality Act prevents the belligerent acts of private individuals from infringing on congressional power to declare war. Second, it maintains the international principle that neutral territory cannot be used to launch hostilities against friendly nations. Finally, though neutrality is now recognized as a congressional prerogative, political debates over the scope of presidential and congressional authority in foreign affairs often refer to the Neutrality Act of 1794.

SEE ALSO *Model Treaty of 1776; Washington, George*

BIBLIOGRAPHY

Carbone, Peter A. "The Neutrality Act of 1794: Is It Being Violated by Private Citizens Who Fund the Contra Rebels in Nicaragua?" *Political Communications and Persuasion* 5, 3 (1988): 191–202.

Fenwick, Charles G. *The Neutrality Laws of the United States.* (1913.) Holmes Beach, FL: Gaunt, 2013.

Hyneman, Charles S. *The First American Neutrality: A Study of the American Understanding of Neutral Obligations during the Years 1792 to 1815.* (1934.) Buffalo, NY: W. S. Hein, 2002.

Lobel, Jules. "The Rise and Decline of the Neutrality Act: Sovereignty and Congressional War Powers in United States Foreign Policy." *Harvard International Law Journal* 24 (Summer 1983): 1–71.

Sean T. Perrone
Professor of History
Saint Anselm College

"THE NEW COLOSSUS" (EMMA LAZARUS, 1883)

Emma Lazarus (1849–1887), a poet who was a member of New York's social elite, was highly regarded on both sides of the Atlantic. She counted the American essayist Ralph Waldo Emerson, the English poet Robert Browning, and other literary luminaries among her friends. Upon her death at the age of thirty-eight the *New York Times* hailed her in her obituary as "an American poet of uncommon talent." A Jewish American of Sephardic descent, Lazarus in her wide-ranging poems took up the cause of Jewish immigrants fleeing pogroms in Russia even as nativism and open anti-Semitism flourished in the United States. "The New Colossus," penned in 1883, became the most famous public lyric in America when its final five lines were engraved on the pedestal of the Statue of Liberty.

Lazarus's work had its origins in the poet's own direct witnessing of the travails of beleaguered and impoverished immigrants. Shortly after the first human cargo of the Jewish migration from Russia arrived in New York in August 1881, Lazarus began to take an activist's interest in the new arrivals. Besides teaching English to immigrant girls and working as a celebrity volunteer in the Hebrew Emigrant Aid Society, Lazarus often visited Ward's Island, where 250 Jewish refugees were held. She was there the day a riot broke out in protest against inadequate food.

Interestingly, certain intimations of "The New Colossus" appeared earlier in a much different mode in her prose poem "Currents":

> From the far Caucasian steppes, from the squalid ghettos of Europe, from Odessa and Bucharest, from Kief, and Ekaterinoslav, Hark to the cry of the exiles of Babylon, the voice of Rachel mourning for her children, of Israel lamenting for Zion. And lo, like a turbid stream, the long-pent flood bursts the dykes of oppression and rushes hitherward. Unto her ample breast, the generous mother of nations welcomes them. (1988, vol. 2, 63)

Lazarus later transformed the immigrant experience of a particular wave of Russian Jews into a representation of America's universal meaning. More significantly, as Diane Lichtenstein argues, the poet's idealistic anthem to America's welcome of its strangers exhibits a sophisticated sense not only of what exile feels like but of the heterogeneous American landscape, "valorizing as it does the status of the alien who finds in America a home, a native ground composed of many alien grounds" (1987, 261).

The sculptor Frédéric Auguste Bartholdi (1834–1904) originally envisioned his "Liberty Enlightening the World," better known as the Statue of Liberty, as a symbol of solidarity between the republican peoples of France and the United States, its torch representing the socially and politically revolutionary spirit of both societies. Lazarus's poem was originally composed to help raise funds in 1883 from a skeptical or indifferent public to fulfill the American commitment to build the pedestal for the statue. It was only in 1902, when Lazarus had already been dead for fifteen years, that the famous final five lines of the poem were engraved on a bronze plaque at the statue's base:

> Give me your tired, your poor,
> Your huddled masses yearning to breathe free,
> The wretched refuse of your teeming shore.
> Send these, the homeless, tempest-tost to me,
> I lift my lamp beside the golden door!

The sonnet achieved a critical ideological shift in terms of the statue's iconic role: whereas Bartholdi had intended to commemorate the endurance of the ideals of the European Enlightenment, Lazarus's words transformed the statue's symbolism into the "Mother of Exiles," welcoming immigrants fleeing economic injustice and religious and ethnic persecution.

In the early decades of the twentieth century, the poem attained an iconic status, often appearing in children's textbooks and popularized in the final song of Irving Berlin's 1949 musical comedy *Miss Berlin*. Ironically and tragically, this was just a few years after many Jews seeking refuge from the Holocaust had been refused entry by the United States. Throughout the 1950s, especially as the Cold War escalated, the song "Give Me Your Tired, Your Poor" was frequently sung at concerts, school assemblies, and patriotic civic ceremonies. Although some have objected to what they interpret as a condescending tone in the poem's final lines, the sonnet has been consistently regarded as one of the nation's cultural treasures. The National Endowment for the Humanities has included it as one of the core texts in its US history curriculum designed for grades 6 through 8. The poem, and the national monument it endowed with new meaning, retains powerful relevance in an increasingly immigrant and multicultural society.

SEE ALSO *Ellis Island; Immigration*

BIBLIOGRAPHY

Higham, John. *Send These to Me: Jews and Other Immigrants in Urban America.* New York: Atheneum, 1975.

Lazarus, Emma. *Poems of Emma Lazarus.* 2 vols. New York: Houghton Mifflin, 1888.

Lichtenstein, Diane. "Words and Worlds: Emma Lazarus's Conflicting Citizenships." *Tulsa Studies in Women's Literature* 6, 2 (1987): 247–263.

Omer-Sherman, Ranen. "'Thy People Are My People': Emma Lazarus, Zion, and Jewish Modernity in the 1880s." In *Diaspora and Zionism in Jewish American Literature: Lazarus, Syrkin, Reznikoff, and Roth.* Hanover, NH: University Press of New England, 2002.

Schor, Esther. *Emma Lazarus.* New York: Schocken, 2006.

Shreiber, Maeera Y. "The End of Exile: Jewish Identity and Its Diasporic Poetics." *PMLA* 113, 2 (1998): 273–287.

Vogel, Dan. *Emma Lazarus.* Boston: Twayne, 1980.

Young, Bette Roth. *Emma Lazarus in Her World: Life and Letters.* Jerusalem: Jewish Publication Society, 1995.

Ranen Omer-Sherman
Jewish Heritage Fund for
Excellence Endowed Chair of Judaic Studies
University of Louisville

NEW LEFT

An international New Left began in the 1950s (the term coined by British ex-communists to signal starting over). It had many sources, from disillusionment with the Marxist tradition represented by communist and socialist parties, to inspiration from new social movements like the American civil rights struggle. Soviet leader Nikita Khrushchev's 1956 speech, admitting Joseph Stalin's crimes, followed by repression of the Hungarian uprising, alienated many radicals, as did the subordination of anticommunist socialists to American Cold War imperatives. The division of the world into two nuclear-armed camps was intolerable to those desiring a "third way" toward a more humanistic radicalism.

The New Left drew on new ways of theorizing contemporary politics, from the rediscovery of feminism to seeing the global system as divided into a "Third World" of colonized peoples independent from both the Western, capitalist "First World" and the Soviet-led "Second World." The Third World emerged from armed struggles for national liberation across Africa, Asia, and Latin America, with the Vietnamese, Algerian, and Cuban revolutions leading the way.

Inside the United States, the catalyst for a New Left was the emergence of a mass movement against racial domination, beginning during World War II (1939–1945), and surging with the Montgomery bus boycott in 1955 to 1956 and the sit-in campaign led by the Student Nonviolent Coordinating Committee (SNCC) in 1960. Over the next decade, this movement revolutionized US politics. For the first time, the majority of African Americans could vote, leading to demands for "Black Power" and inspiring similar movements among Latinos, Asian Americans, and Native Americans. Leaders like Dr. Martin Luther King Jr. consistently linked the struggle for rights at home to the worldwide struggle against colonialism, and Black Power advocates, including Malcolm X and the Black Panthers, called for a Third World revolution inside and outside the United States.

In the later 1960s and 1970s the central cause for the global New Left was the Vietnam War, pitting Ho Chi Minh's nationalist communists against an enormous American military machine. Millions of Vietnamese were killed, but the United States was defeated, in part because the antiwar movement, the "war at home," profoundly disrupted American politics and society. Around the world, solidarity with Vietnam drove a wider Third World internationalism, including campaigns against apartheid in South Africa, Latin America's US-backed military dictatorships, and remaining colonial regimes in Africa and Asia. Young activists in all three worlds were inspired by the Argentine-Cuban revolutionary Ernesto "Che" Guevara's 1966 call for "two, three, many Vietnams." They also shared an eclectic counterculture rooted in popular music (rock, soul, reggae, and much more), alternative ways of constructing social life (communes, festivals, "happenings"), new forms of spirituality, and drugs.

The American New Left expanded steadily in the later 1960s and 1970s as a "movement of movements," including women's liberation, gay liberation, and Brown, Yellow, and Red Power. Paradoxically, lacking strong left-wing parties, the United States often led the way in founding new social movements inside advanced capitalism. But these movements, especially those rooted among peoples of color, faced violent state repression—many activists were killed or jailed, while sixty thousand young men fled to Canada to avoid fighting in Vietnam. Eventually, the American New Left, like similar movements around the world, merged into (or founded) a range of civil society institutions and cultural practices, and the existing left-wing or liberal political parties.

SEE ALSO *Black Power Movement; Feminism, Women's Rights; Military-Industrial Complex; Student Nonviolent Coordinating Committee (SNCC); Students for a Democratic Society (SDS); Third World; Vietnam War*

BIBLIOGRAPHY

Dubinsky, Karen, Catherine Krull, Susan Lord, Sean Mills, and Scott Rutherford, eds. *New World Coming: The Sixties and the Shaping of Global Consciousness.* Toronto, ON: Between the Lines, 2009.

Fraser, Ronald, et al. *1968: A Student Generation in Revolt.* New York: Pantheon, 1988.

Gosse, Van. *Where the Boys Are: Cuba, Cold War America, and the Making of a New Left.* London: Verso, 1993.

Gosse, Van. *Rethinking the New Left: An Interpretive History.* New York: Palgrave Macmillan, 2005.

Hall, Jacquelyn Dowd. "The Long Civil Rights Movement and the Political Uses of the Past." *Journal of American History* 91, 4 (2005): 1233–63.

Marwick, Arthur. *The Sixties: Cultural Revolution in Britain, France, Italy, and the United States, c. 1958–c. 1974.* New York: Oxford University Press, 1998.

Van Gosse
Associate Professor
Franklin and Marshall College

THE NEW REPUBLIC (MAGAZINE)

The New Republic (*TNR*) was founded as a weekly journal of opinion in 1914 and for a century enjoyed a reputation as the flagship of American liberalism. Founded by Herbert Croly (1869–1930), Walter Lippmann (1889–1974), and Walter Weyl (1873–1919), and funded by Willard D. Straight (1880–1918) and his wife, Dorothy Whitney Straight (1887–1968), the magazine aligned itself with the ascendant progressive spirit of the new century. Pragmatic in spirit, it shunned ideological dogma in favor of empiricism and experimentation. For one hundred years, *TNR* would provide a home for a wide range of arguments within the capacious bounds of an evolving American liberalism, usually governed by an aversion to sentimentality and an insistence on high intellectual standards.

THE PROGRESSIVE SPIRIT OF *TNR*'S FIRST DECADES

Initially headquartered in New York, *TNR* in its first decades sought to modify the assumptions of nineteenth-century liberal thought, favoring stronger government in the service of individual liberty and democratic equality—or, as Croly wrote, Hamiltonian means for Jeffersonian ends. Featuring writers such as John Dewey, W. E. B. Du Bois, and Rebecca West, the magazine advocated labor rights, the regulation of business, women's suffrage, a strong presidency, and American leadership on the world stage. Its readers encompassed reformist intellectuals and political insiders, including many in the Woodrow Wilson administration. After supporting American entry into World War I in 1917, *TNR*'s editors broke with Wilson over his wartime clampdown on civil liberties and the postwar settlement, publishing John Maynard Keynes's famous indictment of the 1919 Versailles Treaty.

In the 1920s Bruce Bliven (1889–1977) joined Croly at the magazine, ascending to the editorship when Croly died in 1930. The magazine remained a hub of political argument, lambasting the conservative economics of the era's Republican presidents and launching its long-running Washington column penned by the pseudonymous "T.R.B." (first Frank Kent, later Richard Strout). *TNR* also increased its cultural coverage, showcasing supple critics such as Edmund Wilson, Lewis Mumford, Malcolm Cowley, and Gilbert Seldes.

The Great Depression pushed the magazine, along with many liberals, toward collectivist economics. In their often-fierce debates, writers such as George Soule and Stuart Chase (whose 1932 article first proposed "A New Deal for America") mapped a spectrum of left-liberal opinion—from advocacy of a consumer economy to support for national planning to outright sympathy at times for Soviet communism. Some contributors, such as Felix Frankfurter, became members of Franklin Roosevelt's "Brains Trust," while others faulted the New Deal as insufficiently radical.

Michael Straight (1916–2004), the owners' twenty-five-year-old son, became editor in 1941 and in time moved the magazine's offices to Washington, DC. Having embraced communism at college in Cambridge, Straight remained a covert Soviet informant, and he reasserted the Popular Front liberalism that dueled in *TNR*'s pages with its traditional hard-boiled posture. But as war loomed, Straight also published liberal antifascist writers, such as Max Lerner and Archibald MacLeish, who pointedly challenged the dominant isolationism of the Left—and of many at the magazine. During the war, *TNR* distinguished itself in calling attention to the mass slaughter of European Jewry, and it urged the creation of a Jewish homeland.

MILITANT LIBERALISM OF THE POSTWAR PERIOD

In 1946, Straight named Henry A. Wallace (1888–1965), the recently fired commerce secretary, as editor, a post Wallace held until his 1948 Communist Party–influenced presidential bid. Under his uninspired leadership, *TNR* seemed to squander much of its intellectual vitality. After his departure, however, the magazine returned to the gritty "militant liberalism" it now came to admire in Harry Truman, assailing Soviet communism and McCarthyism with equal fervor. (*TNR* called on the Senate to expel Joseph McCarthy in 1951, three years before his downfall.)

Gilbert Harrison (1915–2008) and his wife, Anne, an heir to the McCormick harvester fortune, bought the magazine in 1953, and Harrison made himself the editor. In his two-decade tenure, *TNR* mainly adhered to what contributor Arthur Schlesinger Jr. dubbed a liberalism of the "vital center." It supported Adlai Stevenson and John F. Kennedy, backed the civil rights movement and the Great Society, and opposed, with growing vehemence, the Vietnam War. Notable contributors in the postwar era included George Orwell (whose 1946 essay "Politics and the English Language" ran in *TNR*), Theodore H. White, Irving Howe, Alfred Kazin, Alexander Bickel, and Murray Kempton. In the late 1960s Harrison's pages increasingly voiced radical opinions on race, foreign policy, and the political system.

REFASHIONING LIBERALISM IN THE WAKE OF THE 1960s

The next chapter in *TNR*'s history opened in 1974, when Harvard professor Martin Peretz (b. 1938) assumed ownership. He hired Michael Kinsley (b. 1951), a young Harvard Law School graduate, as editor in 1979, and Leon Wieseltier (b. 1952), a member of the Harvard Society of Fellows, as literary editor in 1983. Under these men—and Hendrik Hertzberg (b. 1943), a former speechwriter for Jimmy Carter who alternated with Kinsley as editor—*TNR* reigned for roughly two decades as the most important magazine in opinion journalism.

TNR in these years helped to refashion liberalism in the wake of the 1960s and the disastrous George McGovern campaign of 1972, sharply questioning left-wing shibboleths, such as identity politics and the Democratic Party's post-Vietnam neoisolationism (and especially the Left's newfound antipathy to Israel), while vigorously assailing the era's new conservatism. Its political pages offered inside-Washington reportage and wonky policy debates, served up with a witty, irreverent style and contrarian sensibility. Notable writers included Henry Fairlie, Sidney Blumenthal, Michael Lewis, and Jacob Weisberg. Wieseltier's culture section, rivaled only by the *New York Review of Books* as an intellectual forum, published accessible scholarly essays, including by leading academics such as Sean Wilentz, Helen Vendler, and Alan Wolfe and by renowned critics such as Robert Brustein on theater, Stanley Crouch on music, Jed Perl on art, James Wood and Adam Kirsch on literature, and Stanley Kauffmann on film, whose reviews ran from 1958 until his death in 2013.

CHANGES AND CHALLENGES

In the 1990s, under Andrew Sullivan (b. 1963), its first self-proclaimed conservative editor, *TNR* lost key writers, with some joining Kinsley's new online magazine *Slate*. Scandal struck when one young writer, Ruth Shalit, admitted to having plagiarized extensively, and another, Stephen Glass, to having fabricated stories. Like other publications, *TNR*'s readership plummeted with the rise of the Internet, and during the highly polarized George W. Bush years, its contrarian liberalism became increasingly unfashionable. Its advocacy in the 1990s to stop the genocide in Bosnia was hailed as visionary, but its support for the 2003 invasion of Iraq alienated many liberals. Financially burdened, Peretz sold his majority stake in the magazine in 2002, and its ownership structure underwent several changes in the next decade, albeit with Peretz always involved. The magazine's quality oscillated noticeably. But the young editors of these years—Peter Beinart, Richard Just, and Franklin Foer—continued to articulate a hard-headed liberalism that was unafraid to question the prevailing wisdom on the Left or the Right. *TNR* also incubated many of the era's finest young journalists, including Jonathan Chait, David Grann, Hanna Rosin, and Margaret Talbot. In 2014 it celebrated its one hundredth anniversary, winning attention for its storied history of political influence and intellectual contentiousness.

Weeks later, the magazine's new owner, Chris Hughes (b. 1983), a cofounder of Facebook who bought *TNR* in 2012, suddenly fired Foer and slashed the magazine's output to ten times a year amid concern about mounting financial losses. He ceased to identify *TNR* as "liberal" or even a "magazine," preferring the expression "vertically integrated digital media company." Much of the editorial staff quit, creating a furor from which the inexperienced new team did not soon recover. Whether *TNR* will continue for another decade, let alone a second century, seems uncertain, but even if it does, it will take many years to regain its former intellectual and journalistic stature.

SEE ALSO *Cold War; Great Depression; LIFE (Magazine); Lippmann, Walter; Luce, Henry; Red Scare; Vietnam War; World War I; World War II*

BIBLIOGRAPHY

Diggins, John Patrick. "'The New Republic' and Its Times." *The New Republic*, December 10, 1984, 23–73.

Foer, Franklin, ed. *Insurrections of the Mind: 100 Years of Politics and Culture in America.* New York: HarperCollins, 2014.

Luce, Robert B., ed. *The Faces of Five Decades: Selections from Fifty Years of "The New Republic," 1914–1964.* New York: Simon and Schuster, 1964.

The New Republic: Special Anniversary Issue. November 24 and December 8, 2014.

Seideman, David. *"The New Republic": A Voice of Modern Liberalism.* New York: Praeger, 1986.

Wickenden, Dorothy, ed. *The New Republic Reader: Eighty Years of Opinion and Debate.* New York: Basic Books, 1994.

David Greenberg
Professor of History
Rutgers University

NEW WOMAN

The New Woman was both a social reality and a literary and journalistic construction in late nineteenth-century and early twentieth-century America and Britain. For many people, the New Woman embodied the progressive aspirations of an emerging feminist generation, while for others, she represented a degenerating threat to traditional gender norms and cultural institutions.

AN EXPRESSION OF PROFOUND CHANGES IN THE LIVES OF WOMEN

In the summer of 1894, the writers Sarah Grand (1854–1943) and Ouida (1839–1908) took to the pages of the *North American Review* to debate the ambitions and attitudes of young women, who increasingly envisioned bold new social and political perspectives. Grand lauded this "modern girl," who sought to cast off the restraints of her mother's and grandmother's generations and "gradually and involuntarily rais[e] herself" in the world (Grand 1894, 707). "There is no doubt," Grand proclaimed,

"that the modern girl has been caught by the rising tide of progress, and will be borne along bravely…. The modern girl is growing up, and 'more life and fuller' is what she wants" (713). This New Woman was breaking the boundaries between the feminine "private sphere" and the masculine "public sphere" and rejecting the suffocating hold of Victorianism, which had prized domesticity and submission. Ouida tartly responded that these women were merely man-hating creatures, who denied their natural roles, considered themselves "the victim of men," and "entirely ignor[ed] the frequency with which men," in fact, "are the victims of women" (Ouida 1894, 615). Once such women gained further cultural admiration and political power, Ouida feared, the very structure of society would be at risk.

The heated textual conversation between Grand and Ouida was but a sliver of a larger cultural discussion about women's rights and roles in American and British societies at the fin de siècle. Though the label *New Woman* had appeared in print prior to 1894—and though women had pushed aggressively against gender boundaries for more than a decade—the *North American Review* exchange represents arguably the first extended attempt to define the changing attitudes evident in the public lives of many progressive women. The years 1880 to 1920 witnessed profound, formative developments in both the ideological constructions of gender and in the actual lives of women on both sides of the Atlantic as they sought broader spheres of influence in terms of social and financial independence, career opportunities, and political participation. Several cultural and political shifts during this forty-year period—including increased urbanization and industrialization, falling birthrates, larger numbers of coeducational high schools and colleges, and the slow march toward suffrage—provided fertile ground on which progressive ideas about gender could take root, and the New Woman emerged as a shorthand label to describe actual people, as well as a textual and visual construction that frequently veered toward satire.

Newspaper and magazine articles, short stories, novels, and illustrations offered spirited representation of and commentary about the "modern girl," and while she resisted easy categorization, she was most often considered as a progressive, white, middle-class citizen, an ambitious figure who was "independent of spirit, highly competent, and physically strong and fearless" (Matthews 2003, 13). A *Harper's Bazaar* article attempted in 1895 to pin down a description of this "nebulous" woman, envisioning "a woman of liberal education and advanced ideas, a woman prepared to maintain her rights and claim her privileges, and make and keep a fair standing-ground for herself in whatever field she chooses to exploit her convictions or exert her abilities." Rejecting domesticity and child-rearing as the only meaningful feminine paths, she vociferously opposes critics who believe "love and matrimony are cardinal points in the destiny of her sex" ("The New Woman" 1895, 594).

CRITICAL BACKLASH

For as many writers and readers who lauded the New Woman, she was not a figure universally embraced within the pages of journalism and literature. As the 1894 debate between Grand and Ouida suggests, American and British commentators frequently criticized what they saw as "an unattractive, browbeating usurper of traditionally masculine roles" (Patterson 2008, 2). Critics complained that the New Woman represented radical political views, that she stood to disrupt the domesticity that lay as the bedrock of the family, and that she displayed dangerously unnatural sexual mores—that she was "oversexed, undersexed, or same sex identified" (Richardson and Willis 2002, xii). As an 1895 editorial published in the *New York Observer and Chronicle* fretted, this "new woman" was "neither a man or woman but a combination of some of the least desirable qualities of both sexes," an unhealthy model "held up in magazines and books for the imitation of our wives and daughters" ("Editorial: The New Pulpit" 1895, 50).

Even as the artist Charles Dana Gibson (1867–1944) immortalized a generally admiring picture of New Womanhood through his "Gibson Girl" illustrations of the 1890s to 1910s, other artists found in the New Woman irresistible fodder for mocking caricatures. Dozens of magazine cartoons—especially within such periodicals as *Punch*, *Puck*, and *Life*—exaggerated the characteristics of bicycle-riding, mannishly smoking, and bloomer- and trouser-wearing women, eventually turning the New Woman into "a cultural stereotype" (Richardson and Willis 2002, 13). Doggerel verse and satirical quips undermined the image of progressive womanhood even further. One writer for *Puck* magazine, for instance, declared that "the New Woman may be recognized by her preference for creating a sensation rather than a home," while another characterized her as "an old pill with a new coating, which man is expected to swallow." Yet another provided a "recipe" for the New Woman:

> Take equal portions of Faith-Cure, Christian Science and Mind-Cure. Add to these a suitable number of catchy sentiments from a handsome, popular preacher. Sprinkle with vague literary effusions. Boil down with a superficial knowledge of one or two languages. Flavor to taste with a pinch of Political Economy. Put in some totally new ideas on the training of children. Beat well, and serve in Bloomers, on a bicycle. ("The New Woman [A Recipe]" 1895, 3)

Despite steady critical backlash, the New Woman nevertheless symbolized the significant cultural and political transformations at play on both sides of the Atlantic, embodying both the promise and the threat that accompanied first-wave feminism. Though contradictory and amorphous by definition, the New Woman led an actual and ideological charge toward modernizing womanhood and gaining female suffrage in both America and Britain.

SEE ALSO *Gender; Great Depression; LIFE (Magazine); World War I; World War II*

BIBLIOGRAPHY

"Editorial: The New Pulpit." *New York Observer and Chronicle* 73, 16 (1895): 509.

Grand, Sarah. "The Modern Girl." *North American Review* 158, 451 (1894): 706–714.

Heilmann, Ann. *New Woman Fiction: Women Writing First-Wave Feminism.* London: Palgrave Macmillan, 2000.

Marks, Patricia. *Bicycles, Bangs, and Bloomers: The New Woman in the Popular Press.* Lexington: University Press of Kentucky, 1990.

Matthews, Jean V. *The Rise of the New Woman: The Women's Movement in America, 1875–1930.* Chicago: Ivan R. Dee, 2003.

Nelson, Carolyn Christensen, ed. *A New Woman Reader: Fiction, Articles, and Drama of the 1890s.* Peterborough, ON: Broadview Press, 2000.

"The New Woman." *Harper's Bazaar* 28, 30 (1895): 594.

"The New Woman (A Recipe)." *Puck* 37, 948 (1895): 3.

Ouida. "The New Woman." *North American Review* 158, 450 (1894): 610–619.

Patterson, Martha H. *Beyond the Gibson Girl: Reimagining the American New Woman, 1895–1915.* Urbana: University of Illinois Press, 2008.

Rich, Charlotte J. *Transcending the New Woman: Multiethnic Narratives in the Progressive Era.* Columbia: University of Missouri Press, 2009.

Richardson, Angelique, and Chris Willis, eds. *The New Woman in Fiction and Fact: Fin-de-Siècle Feminisms.* London: Palgrave Macmillan, 2002.

Karen Roggenkamp
Professor of English
Texas A&M University–Commerce

NEW WORLD ORDER

President George H. W. Bush (in office 1989–1993) first used the phrase *new world order* in his address to Congress on September 11, 1990. He delivered the speech in the aftermath of Iraq's invasion of Kuwait. Bush asserted that the United States must use its power in conjunction with the United Nations to protect weaker nations from stronger ones. At the time, the Soviet Union was heading for collapse and communism was crumbling in Eastern Europe, changes that would soon leave the United States as the sole world superpower. In this context Bush's use of the phrase had obvious implications, and over time the phrase became associated with the idea of promoting and justifying the ascendancy of the political and economic power of the United States. The winding down of the Cold War signaled a tremendous change in a power structure that had endured for decades.

Initially, Bush's vision of a new world order was focused narrowly on a US military response to Iraq's very recent aggression in Kuwait. In order to secure United Nations Security Council consent for such a response, he engaged diplomatically with the Soviet Union, aided by his favorable relationship with President Mikhail Gorbachev. Critics pointed out that a new world order could not be based on personal relationships and wondered what would happen when new leaders emerged. For this first demonstration of the proper deployment of US power in the post–Cold War era, Bush sought to oust Iraq from Kuwait and restore the Kuwaiti monarchy so as to promote "peace" and "justice," but not democracy. The resulting first Iraq war, executed under the name Operation Desert Storm, lasted only four days in 1991. After the short war, Bush strongly resisted calls from within his party to carry the war from Kuwait all the way to Baghdad with the goal of regime change in Iraq; because of Bush's stance, the Iraqi dictator, Saddam Hussein (1937–2006), emerged as weakened but still in power. This result may have contributed to Bush's failure to win reelection in 1992, and set the stage for the second Iraq war, which began under President George W. Bush (2001–2009) in 2003. Nonetheless, the elder Bush viewed the success of the war to restore Kuwaiti sovereignty as the logical expression of US power under the new world order.

Bush's speech to Congress also laid out a domestic policy agenda that, in contrast to the grandiose nature of a new world order, was not very ambitious. The president emphasized "growth-oriented tax measures" and incentives (a reiteration of Reagan-era supply-side economics, which Bush himself had labeled as "voodoo" economics while campaigning against Ronald Reagan for the Republican nomination in 1980), budget deficit reduction, energy efficiency, and oil security. He asserted that the "world is still dangerous" and that therefore new defense initiatives should address the ongoing risks of "outlaw action." He articulated the US role as the lone remaining superpower, arguing that it was therefore not yet time for a reduction in the size of the defense budget, which might have been a logical outcome of the end of the Cold War. The US economy had suffered from budget deficits, due in part to a large investment in defense technology and weapons systems produced during the 1980s. No longer facing communist foes, the United States would instead release those powerful systems against the Iraqi forces that had invaded and occupied Kuwait.

In the short term, the phrase *new world order* was deployed—perhaps haphazardly as a mere rhetorical flourish—to justify Bush's policy of removing Iraqi forces from Kuwait. In the longer term, considering the larger geopolitical context of the nascent post–Cold War era, the concept of a new world order grew and became associated with a style of global governance that presumed a lasting US position of superiority. Further, many hoped that the emerging global marketplace after 1990 would be dominated by free trade and neoliberal economics, to the benefit of participating nations. Thus free-trade enthusiasts broadened the usage of the idea of a new world order to include an idealistic vision of a global economic system dominated by the United States. On the other hand, critics of Bush, global free trade, or unchecked US power sometimes used the phrase ironically to deride those same policies. In culture the phrase traveled broadly, as when it was adopted by conspiracy theorists to describe an alleged shadow government that covertly controlled the world for some nefarious purpose.

SEE ALSO *Bush, George H. W.; Cold War; Iraq*

BIBLIOGRAPHY

Bush, George H. W. Address before a Joint Session of the Congress on the Persian Gulf Crisis and the Federal Budget Deficit. September 11, 1990. American Presidency Project. http://www.presidency.ucsb.edu/ws/?pid=18820

Gillon, Steven M. *The American Paradox: A History of the United States since 1945.* 3rd ed. Boston: Wadsworth Cengage Learning, 2013.

Hess, Gary R. *Presidential Decisions for War: Korea, Vietnam, the Persian Gulf, and Iraq.* 2nd ed. Baltimore, MD: Johns Hopkins University Press, 2009.

Neack, Laura. *The New Foreign Policy: Complex Interactions, Competing Interests.* 3rd ed. Lanham, MD: Rowman and Littlefield, 2014.

Peter A. McCord
Professor of History
State University of New York, Fredonia

NGUYỄN NGỌC LOAN EXECUTING NGUYỄN VĂN LÉM (EDDIE ADAMS, 1968)

A photograph shot by American photojournalist Eddie Adams (1933–2004) documenting the execution of a Viet Cong prisoner became one of most memorable images of the Vietnam War. At the end of January 1968, to coincide with Tết, the lunar new year, the Communist Viet Cong launched simultaneous attacks on cities along the length and breadth of South Vietnam, an operation known as the Tet Offensive. This coordinated attack by the military force attempting to overthrow the United States' ally, the South Vietnamese government, undermined the optimistic statements about the military situation made by America's political leaders in previous months.

On February 1, Adams, an Associated Press photographer, went to the An Quang Pagoda in Saigon (now Ho Chi Minh City), the scene of fighting between the Communists and government forces. There, he saw the chief of police and head of national security, Brigadier General Nguyễn Ngọc Loan (1930–1998), approach a captured Viet Cong prisoner. Just as Loan raised his pistol to the prisoner's head, Adams raised his camera, and Loan pulled the trigger at the precise moment that Adams tripped the shutter. The photograph shows the instant that the bullet entered the prisoner's skull, its impact forcing his face into a grimace. Adams's photograph, radio-transmitted by the Associated Press, soon appeared on front pages around the world.

The picture cast doubt on the worthiness of the ally America was supporting. The historian Alan Brinkley said

of the shooting, "No single event did more to undermine support in the United States for the war" (Culbert 1988, 257). Millions saw the film footage on television—an estimated 20 million viewers saw the first broadcast by NBC. Yet within a few days it was the photograph rather than the film footage whose impact was said to be decisive. Senator Robert Kennedy (1925–1968) observed: "The photograph of the execution was on front pages all around the world—leading our best and oldest friends to ask … what has happened to America?" (Kennedy 2012, 1004).

The general had the reputation of a homicidal thug who made threatening visits to the South Vietnamese National Assembly during critical votes and, according to the American ambassador, had a habit of playing with a loaded pistol during meetings with government officials (Bunker 1967, 8). *Time* magazine's Wallace Terry (1938–2003) asked a Vietnamese contributor to the magazine who was present at the shooting why he had neglected to mention it. The Vietnamese journalist replied that such an event was not news: "Mr. Terry," he said, "General Loan does that all the time" ("Vietnam: The Camera at War." BBC2, rebroadcast November 7, 1997).

Adams won a Pulitzer Prize for the photograph but always tried to play down its moral significance.

The South Vietnamese chief of police and head of national security executes a Viet Cong prisoner, Saigon, February 1, 1968. *This photograph by American photojournalist Eddie Adams, which appeared on front pages around the world, became one of the most memorable and consequential images of the Vietnam War, as it cast doubt on the worthiness of the ally America was supporting.* **AP IMAGES/EDDIE ADAMS**

In numerous forums, Adams explained that the general told him, "They killed many of my people." Adams asked, "How do you know you wouldn't have pulled the trigger yourself?" ("Eddie Adams Day, Celebrating the Photojournalist" 2012). Once published, though, the photograph assumed a life of its own, independent of the photographer's rationalizations. It experienced an afterlife in the work of the artists James Cannata and Tin Ly, who incorporated it into their paintings. As the scholar H. Bruce Franklin found, its influence continues to be felt in popular-cultural versions of the shooting, which muddle the event by inverting the roles of the Communist side and of the United States' ally.

Loan, who settled in northern Virginia after the war, said later, "My wife gave me hell for not confiscating the film" (Culbert 1988, 257).

SEE ALSO *Vietnam War*

BIBLIOGRAPHY

Braestrup, Peter. *Big Story: How the American Press and Television Reported and Interpreted the Crisis of Tet 1968 in Vietnam and Washington.* Abridged ed. New Haven, CT: Yale University Press, 1983. Originally published in 1977 by Westview.

Bunker, Ellsworth. *Weekly Telegram for the President November 29, 1967.* Virtual Vietnam Archive, Texas Tech University, http://www.virtual.vietnam.ttu.edu/cgi-bin/starfetch.exe?f5S@@N@e2O9bMWWCoMogAZd.kMuGqf7C@9wohYVIpkpHxUi8zp9J1ZjIzexA8LJ.HDCxWdyBqMo@y9hgJ7mwYTUl0Yyc6FIJ5DcKvVxJNZE/0240818006.pdf

Culbert, David. "Television's Vietnam and Historical Revisionism in the United States." *Historical Journal of Film, Radio, and Television* 8, 3 (1988): 253–267.

"Eddie Adams Day, Celebrating the Photojournalist." *Washington Post*, http://www.washingtonpost.com/lifestyle/style/eddie-adams-day-celebrating-the-photojournalist/2012/06/07/gJQAHZb1LV_gallery.html

Hagopian, Patrick. "Vietnam War Photography as a Locus of Memory." In *Locating Memory: Photographic Acts*, edited by Annette Kuhn and Kirsten Emiko McAllister. New York: Berghahn, 2006.

Kennedy, Robert F. "Robert F. Kennedy: Unwinnable War Speech, Chicago, February 8, 1968." In *Encyclopedia of the Kennedys: The People and Events That Shaped America*, edited by Joseph M. Siracusa, Appendix I, 1002–1006. Santa Barbara, CA: ABC-CLIO, 2012.

Moeller, Susan D. *Shooting War: Photography and the American Experience of Combat.* New York: Basic Books, 1990.

"Vietnam: The Camera at War." BBC2, rebroadcast November 7, 1997.

Patrick Hagopian
Senior Lecturer in History and American Studies
Lancaster University, England

NIEBUHR, (KARL PAUL) REINHOLD
1892–1971

Reinhold Niebuhr was one of the most influential theologians of the twentieth century. He developed his vision of the world through the lens of his ethnic heritage, two world wars, and the Cold War. Niebuhr was born, reared, and educated in a German-speaking subculture in the midwestern United States. In 1913 he left the Midwest for Yale, returning two years later as pastor of the German Evangelical Synod's Bethel Evangelical Church in Detroit, Michigan.

World War I shook the synod and Niebuhr's German identity. In an article for the *Atlantic Monthly* in 1916, he attacked pro-German support among his fellow German Americans. Shortly after, synod officials tapped him to head their War Welfare Commission. In this role, Niebuhr ministered to German American soldiers stateside and strengthened ties to other American Protestant organizations. At war's end, he wrote regularly for the German Evangelical Synod's *Evangelical Herald* and spoke at conferences and colleges across the East and Midwest.

These activities impressed Charles Clayton Morrison (1874–1966), editor of the *Christian Century*, and YMCA official Sherwood Eddy (1871–1963). Morrison promised Niebuhr editorial space for the *Century*, and Niebuhr met the invitation with an ecumenical and transatlantic viewpoint. In 1923 Niebuhr joined academics, ministers, and business leaders for one of Eddy's sponsored tours of Europe. During the trip, he visited and recoiled at the French occupation of the Ruhr Valley and traveled to his ancestral homeland for the first time. These experiences provided him with firsthand knowledge of the enmity among nations.

Eddy also proved instrumental to Niebuhr's decision to move to New York City in 1928 by funding positions at Union Theological Seminary and at pacifist *World Tomorrow*. Within three dizzying years there, Niebuhr devoured books of continental theology and philosophy. He traveled to Germany and the Soviet Union. He stood for and lost state and congressional elections on the socialist ticket and studied British socialism and Gandhian nonviolence. He met and married Ursula Keppel-Compton (1907–1997), a British fellow at Union. The German fellow that year was Dietrich Bonhoeffer (1906–1945). Niebuhr benefited from Bonhoeffer's excellent German theological training, while Bonhoeffer engaged Niebuhr's emphasis on Christian action. In 1945, the Nazis executed Bonhoeffer for his resistance to the regime.

Niebuhr had been among the earliest American public figures to warn of the dangers of Nazism and

Japanese fascism. As he confronted these expansionist regimes, he continued to search out a socialist program for world order. Ultimately, the heightened nationalism of the 1930s, his wariness of Stalinism, and his growing skepticism of the "goodness" of human nature frayed his socialist ties, which he began to see as too utopian in a decidedly nonutopian world.

Niebuhr's prominence and perspective distinguished him, next to the Swiss theologian Karl Barth (1886–1968), as a leading Christian theological voice in the world. A marker of that distinction was his selection as the keynote speaker for the 1937 Oxford Conference. This gathering brought together Christian leaders from around the globe to assert a unified Christian response to fascism. Niebuhr stirred the conference with a focus on sin and its role as the underlying source of the present crises. Two years later, Niebuhr focused again on sin in his delivery of the prestigious Gifford Lectures in Edinburgh, Scotland, published later as *The Nature and Destiny of Man* (1941, 1943).

This sin-centered theology anchored his international thought for the remainder of his life and made him a spokesperson for "Christian realism." He favored a chastened but hopeful theology, an outlook that informed his two seminal international relations books: *The Children of Light and the Children of Darkness* (1944) and *The Irony of American History* (1952). In both books, Niebuhr criticized the idealism of Marxists and liberals while eschewing the cynicism of those who governed by power politics alone. Such attitudes accounted for the "ironies" of history, in which actors and governments overestimated or underestimated the human capacity for justice in the world. Rather, Niebuhr argued that only through a balance of Christian pessimism, hope, and finally love could approximations of domestic and international justice be achieved.

Between his writing of these texts, Niebuhr contributed to foreign policy conversations for the US State Department and played a formative role at the inaugural meeting of the World Council of Churches (WCC). In the former case, he offered his analysis on the shape of postwar Europe and Asia, which included an audience with George Kennan's (1904–2005) Policy Planning Staff. The 1948 WCC meeting, an outgrowth of the 1937 Oxford Conference, featured two dominant points of view: Niebuhr's and Barth's. The two thinkers agreed on the primacy of a gospel of sin and grace, but Niebuhr differed with what he understood to be Barth's absolutist gospel, which limited political and social action in history. He found Barth's emphasis on God's ultimate victory over evil irresponsible and insensitive to immediate historical conditions.

Niebuhr grew more frustrated with Barth during the Hungarian uprising of 1956. Barth had clear ties to the Reformed Church of Hungary, so his silence on the brutal Soviet reprisal against the Hungarians dismayed Niebuhr. For Niebuhr, the Hungarian injustice or any injustice required condemnation to the point where use of force, although a last resort, may become necessary. Christians, thought Niebuhr, could not dodge the challenges of history by an appeal to the transcendent. But, as Niebuhr's resistance to Vietnam showed, neither could America excuse its use of force by an appeal to the false god of democratic capitalism.

The Vietnam War was the last major international event to hold his attention. He died June 1, 1971. His death silenced a voice that had shaped the global views of two generations of intellectuals, pastors, and mainline Protestant congregations. Thirty years later, after the terrorist attacks of September 11, 2001, and during the wars in Afghanistan and Iraq, Niebuhr surged back into public consciousness. From the political left and right, intellectuals and presidential candidates—among them Barack Obama—invoked his thought as a guide to the navigation of the ambiguities and ironies of the US role in the world.

SEE ALSO *Cold War; Federal Council of Churches; Protestantism; Realism (International Relations); Secularization; World War II*

BIBLIOGRAPHY

Bacevich, Andrew. *The Limits of Power: The End of American Exceptionalism.* New York: Holt, 2008.

Diggins, John Patrick. *Why Niebuhr Now?* Chicago: University of Chicago Press, 2011.

Finstuen, Andrew. *Original Sin and Everyday Protestants: The Theology of Reinhold Niebuhr, Billy Graham, and Paul Tillich in an Age of Anxiety.* Chapel Hill: University of North Carolina Press, 2009.

Fox, Richard W. *Reinhold Niebuhr: A Biography.* New ed. Ithaca, NY: Cornell University Press, 1996.

Harries, Richard, and Stephen Platten, eds. *Reinhold Niebuhr and Contemporary Politics: God and Power.* Oxford: Oxford University Press, 2010.

Niebuhr, Reinhold. *The Irony of American History.* Reprint, Chicago: University of Chicago Press, 2008. First published in 1952 by Scribner's.

Andrew Finstuen
Dean, Honors College
Boise State University

NIXON, RICHARD MILHOUS
1913–1994

When Richard Nixon became president on January 20, 1969, he assumed the office at a low point in terms of domestic morale and the reputation of the United States around the world. The experience of the 1960s had been searing for the nation: the Vietnam War, the civil rights movement, the 1962 Cuban missile crisis, urban violence, and a breakdown of international order. The postwar period was ending, and some yet unknown new era was beginning. Among modern presidents, few had experienced a more linear path to the Oval Office, with Nixon's service in the US House (1947–1951) and Senate (1951–1953) and eight years as Dwight Eisenhower's apprentice while vice president (1953–1961). The world stage he would appear on as president was one he had glimpsed before, whether unveiling the "Pumpkin Papers" during the House Un-American Activities Committee investigation or squaring off in the 1959 Kitchen Debate with Nikita Khrushchev.

THE NIXON DOCTRINE

Richard Nixon made it an early priority of his presidency to redress the international situation. He was eager to demonstrate that the United States could be a force for peace and constructive activity again and that not all of the nation's creativity and imagination had been sapped by the trauma of Vietnam (an average of two hundred American soldiers died per week in Vietnam during the second half of 1968). Thirty days into his presidency, Nixon made a tour of West European capitals on this basis and planned an American foreign policy that—in the future—would not be based around a war in Southeast Asia.

Nixon had created an outline of these foreign policy plans much earlier. He published his vision of a post-Vietnam world in his influential *Foreign Affairs* article "Asia after Vietnam," published in October 1967, more than a year before he reached the White House and even before he was an official candidate for the nation's highest office. He articulated these views further in Guam on July 25, 1969. In an informal session with reporters dealing with questions mainly about Vietnam and China, Nixon made some important revelations about the way he saw the world and how he intended to govern. These remarks,

US President Richard M. Nixon with President Ferdinand E. Marcos of the Philippines in Manila, July 26, 1969. On a nine-day trip to Guam, the Philippines, Indonesia, and other nations, Nixon made important revelations about the way he saw the world and how he intended to govern. The United States would no longer mobilize forces anywhere to defend against any aggression, and other nations would be expected to take on more responsibility for their own defense, economic affairs, and political development. PAUL SLADE/
PARIS MATCH ARCHIVE/GETTY IMAGES

which became known as the Nixon Doctrine, were not limited to simply the way he saw American Pacific interests.

The Nixon Doctrine represented the first major revision to the Truman Doctrine in nearly a quarter century: the United States was no longer willing to mobilize forces anywhere to defend against any aggression. A harbinger of the détente era, the simplicity in his language suggests that the Nixon Doctrine was indeed meant to have application beyond Vietnam. When Nixon said "we, of course, will keep the treaty commitments that we have," and "we should assist, but we should not dictate," he foreshadowed a new phase in America's engagement with the world in which other nations would be expected to take on more responsibility in the areas of their own defense, monetary and economic affairs, and political development. Future American commitments would be appropriated on a more realistic scale commensurate with a new era of reduced Cold War tensions.

Some have said that Nixon had no real foreign policy strategy and that the Nixon Doctrine was never intended to be applied universally. These same critics say that his remarks at Guam were intended mainly as a vehicle to articulate his new policy of Vietnamization, in which American forces would be replaced by Vietnamese forces. These are obvious conclusions if one limits one's view of Nixon foreign policy to Vietnam and Southeast Asia. In fact, Nixon himself referred to the Nixon Doctrine as having application to many different parts of the world.

CENTRALIZATION AND RESCALING OF FOREIGN POLICY

The structure of foreign policy making that Nixon utilized was overseen by former Harvard professor Henry Kissinger. Newly appointed as Nixon's national security adviser, Kissinger had become famous because of his book *Nuclear Weapons and Foreign Policy* (1957), which led to a role as a national security consultant during the John F. Kennedy and Lyndon Johnson administrations. Working for Nixon, Kissinger centralized the foreign policy–making process to an unprecedented degree in the White House. Relying on increased secrecy and back channels, the Nixon White House reduced the traditional influence over policy making of the Departments of State and Defense.

Due to the long wait before national security records are declassified by the National Archives and made available to researchers and the public, only in recent years has the excavation of the Nixon administration's engagement with the world started to become well documented. This scholarship is currently in its most prolific stage, with recent books focused on US relations with the North Atlantic Treaty Organization (NATO) and Europe, Iran,

and the Middle East, and how the Nixon years would shape America's engagement with the world for the remainder of the decade.

Nixon's interaction with the world occurred at a time of declining American influence over that world. In addition, Nixon and Kissinger had less room to maneuver within the range of influence that remained due to a series of difficulties they had inherited: the Vietnam War, a resurgent Soviet Union, two decades of no contact with the People's Republic of China, a volatile Middle East, and a low point in relations with US allies in Europe. Nixon was also constrained by a declining domestic morale that had been sapped during the 1960s by repeated difficult choices of guns versus butter—that is, Vietnam versus the Great Society—and a political class that did not seem to have answers to the nation's problems.

What Nixon and Kissinger tried to do was to rescale America's commitment with the world in the hopes that reducing the US scope of activity would create an opportunity for creativity with those areas that Nixon and Kissinger concluded were most in the nation's strategic interests. No part of the world consumed more of their time than the relationships between Vietnam, China, and the Soviet Union. However, other issues that also occupied their time included the Middle East, South Asia, anticommunism in the Western Hemisphere, and international finance.

POLICY TOWARD ASIA

During the 1968 presidential campaign, Nixon had pledged that he had a plan to end the Vietnam War. The Nixon tapes—his 3,700 hours of secret White House recordings—demonstrate that there was not so much a plan as a set of preferred outcomes. How could there have been a rigid plan when Nixon spent so much time reacting to events outside of his control, such as casualty reports, politics in North Vietnam, the weather, and the influence of China and the Soviet Union? The best studies, by scholars such as Pierre Asselin and Lien-Hang T. Nguyen, emphasize the international aspects of the conflict and the agency of non-American actors.

In Nixon's thinking, the only people who wanted American GIs out of Southeast Asia more than Americans were the Chinese and the Soviets. Nixon used talk of withdrawal as a bargaining chip with adversaries. Critics are right to point out that it took another four years for the United States to extract itself from Southeast Asia, at a total cost of approximately fifty-eight thousand American dead, not to speak of the wounded or of combined Vietnamese military and civilian casualties. But Nixon believed these losses would be mitigated by long-term gains with China and the Soviet Union.

When Nixon landed in Beijing in February 1972, he was not only the first US president to do so, but he restored relations between the two nations after two decades of no contact. As he foreshadowed in *Foreign Affairs,* Nixon believed that the end of the Vietnam War was close enough in sight that it was necessary to plan a postwar American policy toward Asia. Such a policy could not exclude the world's most populous nation, no matter the past rivalries or differences in Cold War ideology. As Nixon said, his visit was "the week that changed the world." The launch of rapprochement with China was a stunning capstone for a former anticommunist who built his national reputation in the shadow of Senator Joseph McCarthy and the Hiss-Chambers case.

By making peace with China, Nixon put pressure on the Soviet Union. At times rivals and enemies, China and the USSR shared a long border but different types of communist systems. By exposing their differences, Nixon believed he could extract concessions from each. While his original plan was to achieve a summit with the Soviet Union first, when a visit to China materialized that became the more important priority. This quick succession of events meant that Nixon could achieve his three capstone foreign achievements all within a single year, 1972: rapprochement with China, the Strategic Arms Limitations Treaty with the Soviet Union, and a tentative peace in Vietnam. For these efforts, he was crowned with a stunning landslide reelection in November over his Democratic rival, Senator George McGovern.

LEGACY

In addition, during Nixon's presidency, NATO was reorganized, the gold standard was ended, conflict in the Middle East flared up, and Nixon and Kissinger approved of an anticommunist coup in Chile. By 1973, Nixon had become so engulfed in the Watergate scandal that the War Powers Act and other forms of congressional scrutiny seriously hampered his ability to conduct foreign policy. While scholarship of the Nixon presidency continues to evolve as more records become available, thus far Nixon's legacy has been to flex American muscle abroad on a more realistic scale, shifting foreign policy to a Pacific-based strategy, reducing the chance that the Cold War could turn hot, and contributing to factors that made the rise of Ronald Reagan and the Republican right wing—many of whom had been part of Nixon's "silent majority"—possible.

SEE ALSO *China; Détente; Kissinger, Henry; Kitchen Debate; Vietnam War*

BIBLIOGRAPHY

Alvandi, Roham. *Nixon, Kissinger, and the Shah: The United States and Iran in the Cold War.* New York: Oxford University Press, 2014.

Gellman, Irwin F. *The President and the Apprentice: Eisenhower and Nixon, 1952–1961.* New Haven, CT: Yale University Press, 2015.

Logevall, Fredrik, and Andrew Preston, eds. *Nixon in the World: American Foreign Relations, 1969–1977.* New York: Oxford University Press, 2008.

Nichter, Luke A. *Richard Nixon and Europe: The Remaking of the Postwar Atlantic World.* New York: Cambridge University Press, 2015.

Nixon, Richard. "Informal Remarks in Guam with Newsmen." *American Presidency Project.* Edited by Gerhard Peters and John T. Woolley. July 25, 1969. http://www.presidency.ucsb.edu/ws/?pid=2140

Sargent, Daniel. *A Superpower Transformed: The Remaking of American Foreign Relations in the 1970s.* New York: Oxford University Press, 2015.

Small, Melvin, ed. *A Companion to Richard Nixon.* Malden, MA: Wiley-Blackwell, 2011.

Luke A. Nichter
Associate Professor of History
Texas A&M University–Central Texas

NON-ALIGNED MOVEMENT

Long before its formal inception, the Non-Aligned Movement (NAM) represented a fundamental challenge to American conceptions of the Cold War, even as it strove to transcend the global conflict. Emerging by the early 1960s, the NAM united a wide array of states that disavowed alliances with either the West or the Communist bloc. Nonalignment represented a third way in the Cold War world, creating a dynamic middle zone in postwar politics and visibly delineating the limits of American, Soviet, and Chinese influence. It sometimes afforded its adherents considerable leverage in seeking assistance from one or more of the great powers.

The concept of nonalignment preceded the formal establishment of the NAM. Aversion to great-power entanglements constituted one fundamental tenet of nonalignment, but not the only one. Indian prime minister Jawaharlal Nehru (1889–1964) articulated some of the earliest justifications for a nonaligned foreign policy: to offer a moral voice in an increasingly polarized international environment, but also to direct attention toward neglected questions of political and economic self-determination. Nehru and Indonesia's president Sukarno (1901–1970) famously gave voice to principles of nonalignment at the 1955 Asian-African Conference at Bandung, Indonesia.

The states that gathered for the first formal Non-Aligned Conference in Belgrade, Yugoslavia, in 1961 professed concern with the direction of the Cold War but spoke emphatically as well about the urgent battle against imperialism and in favor of equitable social and economic development. They decried the colonialism of the past but also enunciated their fears of its renewal in subtler forms. At the close of the conference, the attendees dispatched envoys to Moscow and Washington to plead for restraint in the ongoing Berlin Crisis.

Embracing this ambitious agenda were twenty-five states, chiefly from Asia and North Africa. Decolonization subsequently bolstered the number of African attendees, while a growing number of Latin American states attended—some as observers, some as outright members. Membership grew to 101 governments by the New Delhi Non-Aligned Conference in 1983, yet the NAM's size worked against it. Its larger states—India, Egypt, and Indonesia among them—moved into de facto alignment with superpowers, while smaller states struggled to surmount economic and geographic divisions within their own ranks.

Yet the emergence of nonalignment indisputably transformed world politics. President Dwight D. Eisenhower (1890–1969) was concerned by the prospect that the Bandung meeting might produce a bloc of uncommitted African and Asian states. Secretary of State John Foster Dulles (1888–1959) went so far as to declare in 1956 that nonalignment was fundamentally "immoral." Privately, Eisenhower and Dulles recognized that nonalignment in the global conflict was often prudent and could conceivably serve as a form of containment, yet, all too often, the demands of grand strategy or alliance solidarity pitted the United States against nonaligned states (Rakove 2012).

President John F. Kennedy (1917–1963) conveyed a broader acceptance of nonalignment in the world. At times hamstrung by a conservative State Department, he nonetheless succeeded in forming meaningful interpersonal bonds and working partnerships with nonaligned states. To the alarm of his European allies, Kennedy pursued a policy of engagement with the nonaligned world, shifting policy on a number of previously divisive colonial conflicts while offering generous economic aid. Tellingly, while the nonaligned world largely condemned his invasion of Cuba in April 1961, it proved more understanding of his policy during the Cuban missile crisis (Rakove 2012).

In the wake of Kennedy's assassination in November 1963, relations foundered again. The nonaligned states balked at President Lyndon Johnson's (1908–1973) war in Vietnam and resented his tendency to make US aid contingent on their explicit support. Growing divisions and conflicts within the nonaligned world served to divide the movement and undermine the rationales for engagement held by US policy makers earlier in the decade. From the late 1960s onward, the United States concerned itself less with the nonaligned world and renewed its commitment to allies in the global South. It clashed visibly and acrimoniously with the NAM in global forums, as the movement turned its attention to lingering territorial issues, Vietnam, the Arab-Israeli conflict, and issues of economic sovereignty (Irwin 2012).

US administrations treated the NAM—stung by its unremitting criticism and declarations of solidarity with North Vietnam—as a hypocritical, intrinsically hostile organization. For its part, the NAM struggled to regain its standing after the passing of its dynamic founding generation and amid the emergence of more coherent regional and economic associations, such as the Organization of the Petroleum Exporting Countries (OPEC) and the Organization of African Unity (now the African Union) (Westad 2005). Of the five most prominent leaders present at Belgrade, only Yugoslavia's president, Josip Broz Tito (1892–1980), lived to attend the September 1970 Lusaka Conference in Zambia; later in the decade, he successfully opposed Cuban efforts to issue a statement of affinity for the Soviet Union.

The NAM survived the Cold War, yet it remains ill-understood by Americans, who treat it as a living anachronism. Yet its endurance attests to the breadth of issues it has addressed—and an enduring sense within the postcolonial world that political and economic justice remains unattained.

SEE ALSO *Bandung Conference (1955); Cold War; Decolonization; India*

BIBLIOGRAPHY

Chamberlin, Paul Thomas. *The Global Offensive: The United States, the Palestine Liberation Organization, and the Making of the Post–Cold War Order.* New York: Oxford University Press, 2012.

Irwin, Ryan M. *Gordian Knot: Apartheid and the Unmaking of the Liberal World Order.* New York: Oxford University Press, 2012.

Prashad, Vijay. *The Darker Nations: A People's History of the Third World.* New York: Norton, 2007.

Rakove, Robert B. *Kennedy, Johnson, and the Nonaligned World.* New York: Cambridge University Press, 2012.

Westad, Odd Arne. *The Global Cold War: Third World Interventions and the Making of Our Times.* New York: Cambridge University Press, 2005.

Robert B. Rakove
Lecturer
Stanford University

NONGOVERNMENTAL ORGANIZATIONS (NGOs)

Nongovernmental organization (NGO), a term coined in the mid-1940s, refers to a group of like-minded individuals, unaffiliated with any government, who seek to affect public policy or provide services to a community. NGOs operate locally, nationally, and internationally, and they address issues that range from human rights and environmental sustainability to disaster relief and economic development. This diversity makes it difficult to generalize their goals and characteristics. Most, but not all, are not-for-profit organizations. Although the vast majority of NGOs are independent of governmental control, some are not, especially in authoritarian countries, and NGOs often receive financial support from governments. Many NGOs supplement this money with private donations or funds from international organizations. Although political parties and guerrilla organizations are not considered NGOs, some NGOs represent people who are not members of a state and therefore operate as quasi-governments.

NGOs existed long before they came to be known as nongovernmental organizations. Since at least the early nineteenth century, NGO-type organizations thrived in the liminal spaces between modern national states, cultivating awareness about the cross-border dimensions of the day's scientific and moral dilemmas. As government policy making grew more bureaucratic in Europe and North America after the Industrial Revolution, nongovernmental advocacy emerged as a cosmopolitan counterweight to nationalism. Focused on the tension between border making and long-distance travel, many NGOs organized their activities around the question: how could the national-state—blessed with new powers yet plagued by self-interest—safeguard humanity in an age of interdependence?

Early NGOs were not reflexive antagonists of government. Quite the contrary, they thrived because of the support they received from the world's great powers. In 1803, for instance, the Royal Jennerian Society advanced a straightforward solution to the smallpox epidemic: society-wide inoculations. Rather than toiling at the margins of political life, the society's scientific expertise led to partnerships with governments around the world, including fourteen European monarchs, the Ottoman sultan, the mughal of India, the pasha of Baghdad, the US president, and the pope.

Even more influential was the antislavery movement, spearheaded by the Quaker-inspired Pennsylvania Society for the Relief of Free Negroes Unlawfully Held in Bondage, which in the late eighteenth century created a network of moral activists that advocated for antislavery legislation on both sides of the Atlantic Ocean. In addition to playing a role in crafting the British Slave Trade Act of 1807, the

movement influenced a series of international conferences that effectively ended the Atlantic slave trade during the mid-nineteenth century.

These nascent efforts blossomed during the late nineteenth century. That era, which saw Europe conquer much of Africa and Asia, witnessed unprecedented efforts to curb the excesses of industrialized warfare. The Red Cross, for instance, formed in Geneva in 1863, married science and morality as it lobbied European governments to let medical personnel care for wounded soldiers on the battlefield. Red Cross organizations proliferated in Europe and North America in subsequent decades, eventually leading to the establishment of an international committee that coordinated medical aid in war zones and petitioned governments to recognize the neutrality of Red Cross workers. The late nineteenth century also saw the establishment of the International Council of Women, the International Federation of Trade Unions, the International Olympic Committee, Rotary International, and the International Socialist Bureau, among many other organizations. These early NGOs shared a common aversion to European nationalism and militarism, and worked to promote humanitarian causes across state borders.

During the twentieth century, international organizations professionalized the activities of NGOs. The League of Nations, created in 1919 to prevent the recrudescence of world war, codified the nation-state's centrality to global life, but it also recognized citizen-based organizations as essential sources of information and technical expertise for league members. By the mid-1920s, letters, telegrams, and resolutions from NGOs were featured regularly in the League of Nations' published reports, and, after 1924, the Secretariat distributed summaries of its correspondence with NGOs to the league's executive body. Some NGOs, such as the International Labour Organization, even participated alongside diplomats in the league's meetings.

After World War II (1939–1945), the United Nations (UN) professionalized nongovernmental activism further. In addition to giving NGOs their name, the UN, which supplanted the League of Nations as the world's preeminent international organization after 1945, invited citizen-based organizations to participate in its Economic and Social Council, which was tasked with identifying cross-border solutions to the world's social, economic, and environmental problems. By the mid-twentieth century, NGOs had carved a niche: they shared technical expertise with governments and cultivated common values among UN members.

Some NGOs challenged this status quo during the late twentieth century. Many stateless actors, for instance, rejected their marginalization from political arenas such as the UN General Assembly and Security Council. During the 1960s, antiapartheid NGOs, casting themselves as the true representatives of South Africa's nonwhite population, successfully established a voice at the UN General Assembly and Secretariat. Since that breakthrough, other organizations—including the Palestine Liberation Organization, Greenpeace, and countless others—have similarly used the UN to legitimize political claims and challenge the nation-state's monopoly over international diplomacy.

In contrast, other NGOs rejected the UN as the natural outlet for nongovernmental activity. During the 1970s, for example, Amnesty International raised awareness about torture by lobbying politicians in Europe and North America and distributing ideas through television and media. Convinced that the Cold War had undermined the UN's effectiveness, and frustrated by the organization's limitations, Amnesty International instead focused energy on public policy in the United States and Western Europe, where power truly resided.

Today's NGOs are somewhat enigmatic. There are more of them than ever, and they continue to thrive in the space between nation-states, engaging in activities that range from sustainable development to human rights. However, despite this continuity with the past, the recent growth of NGOs has prompted questions among activists and scholars: Do NGOs affect change? Why have they proliferated so quickly since the 1970s? Have they advanced or checked European imperialism? Regardless of the answers, NGOs remain as important to the study of international society as national states.

SEE ALSO *Ford Foundation; Gates Foundation; Greenpeace; Rockefeller Foundation; Think Tanks*

BIBLIOGRAPHY

Iriye, Akira. *Global Community: The Role of International Organizations in the Making of the Contemporary World.* Berkeley: University of California Press, 2002.

Iriye, Akira, ed. *Global Interdependence: The World after 1945.* Cambridge, MA: Harvard University Press, 2014.

Moyn, Samuel. *The Last Utopia: Human Rights in History.* Cambridge, MA: Harvard University Press, 2010.

Osterhammel, Jürgen. *The Transformation of the World: A Global History of the Nineteenth Century.* Translated by Patrick Camiller. Princeton, NJ: Princeton University Press, 2104.

Rosenberg, Emily. *A World Connecting: 1870–1945.* Cambridge, MA: Harvard University Press, 2012.

Ryan Irwin
Assistant Professor of History
University at Albany–SUNY

NON-INTERCOURSE ACT (1809)

In the waning days of the presidential administration of Thomas Jefferson (1743–1826), Congress passed the Non-Intercourse Act as a substitute for the Embargo of 1807. The Non-Intercourse Act repealed the embargo and instituted a policy of nonintercourse (no trade) with the warring nations of Great Britain and France. The hope was that the measure would allow the American economy to recover from the dire conditions created by the embargo by opening up commerce with neutrals and providing federal revenue through impost duties. At the same time, passage of the act would continue to pressure both France and Great Britain to repeal regulations (Britain's Orders in Council and France's Berlin and Milan Decrees) that inhibited American neutral commerce. The measure also prohibited French and British warships from entering American ports (unless under duress). The Non-Intercourse Act represented a continued Jeffersonian faith in the power of economic coercion as a tool of foreign policy. The act also included a provision to allow for the resumption of trade with either belligerent if it rescinded its regulations preventing neutral trade with its opponent.

The legislation had several problems. First, since both Great Britain and France were the main US trading partners, opening up commerce to other nations did not radically alter the situation for most merchants: without the option of sailing to either French or British ports, there was little reason for many American ships to leave port. Second, the British and French between them controlled most of Europe and large swaths of territory throughout the globe, either directly or through allies that served as proxies. Indeed, to prevent trade with Great Britain, France had created the Continental System among its allies and subject nations, which left American shipping that stopped in a British port liable to seizure almost everywhere in Europe. Third, any American products sent to a neutral port could be reexported to the belligerents. Finally, once an American ship put out to sea, it could just as easily head to France or Great Britain in disregard of American law.

As convoluted as the law may have been, it almost worked. The British minister to the United States in the spring of 1809 was David M. Erskine (1776–1855), who actually looked upon the Americans favorably. Sidestepping his own instructions, Erskine decided that the Non-Intercourse Act had put Great Britain and France on equal footing and therefore removed the rationale behind the Orders in Council's prevention of American neutral trade. After several meetings with American officials, he signed an accord on April 19, 1809, that promised that Great Britain would remove the Orders in Council and send a special envoy to Washington to negotiate a new commercial treaty if President James Madison (1751–1836) would open trade with Great Britain. Madison did so on June 10, 1809. However, the British foreign minister, George Canning (1770–1827), repudiated the agreement, and Madison resumed nonintercourse with Great Britain on August 9, 1809. As trade continued to languish into 1810, Congress replaced the Non-Intercourse Act with Macon's Bill No. 2.

SEE ALSO *Embargo Act (1807); Neutrality Act of 1794; War of 1812*

BIBLIOGRAPHY

Gilje, Paul A. *Free Trade and Sailors' Rights in the War of 1812.* Cambridge: Cambridge University Press, 2013.

Perkins, Bradford. *Prologue to War: England and the United States, 1805–1812.* Berkeley: University of California Press, 1968.

Paul A. Gilje
George Lynn Cross Research Professor
Department of History, University of Oklahoma

NORTH AMERICA

The American Revolution (1775–1783) fractured the British colonial domination of the eastern half of North America. The new United States extended from what is now Maine south to Georgia and west to the Mississippi River (the west bank of which was controlled by Spain). The province of Quebec and St. John Island (now Prince Edward Island), acquired in the French and Indian War (1754–1763), and the maritime colonies of Nova Scotia and Newfoundland, remained British, but the colony of Florida, also acquired by Britain in 1763, was restored to Spain. Thus the United States remained dominated on three sides by European powers.

SHIFTING BORDERS

Even France, which had assisted the United States during the Revolution, proved unfriendly during what became known as the Quasi-War (1798–1800), but the normalization of relations facilitated the sale of the Louisiana Territory (which France reacquired in 1800) to the United States in 1803. The acquisition of New Orleans and control of the Mississippi River set the path for expansion across the continent and changed the course of American history.

Spain's steady decline during the French Revolution and the Napoleonic Wars left its colonial holdings in North America vulnerable. Cross-border skirmishes in both East and West Florida led to the cession of the colonies to the United States in the Adams-Onís Treaty

of 1819. Spain also lost control of Mexico, which successfully established its independence by 1821. Political stability proved elusive for Mexico, prompting the American settlers who had migrated to Texas in the 1820s and 1830s to rebel and form an independent republic in 1836. However, when Texas sought to join the United States in 1845, this led to the Mexican-American War (1846–1848), at the end of which Mexico gave up in the Treaty of Guadalupe Hidalgo not only Texas but also California and what is now the American Southwest.

US relations with Britain and British North America were more complicated and extended. Ambiguities about the boundary with Canada led to the arbitration of one segment in 1796 to 1798 under the Jay-Grenville Treaty of 1795. Issues of neutral rights and British involvement with Indian tribes south of the Great Lakes led to the War of 1812, but the Treaty of Ghent (1814) that ended the war also created commissions that settled additional parts of the boundary. In that context, naval vessels on the Great Lakes were limited by the Rush-Bagot Agreement of 1817, and the northern extent of the Louisiana Territory was fixed along the forty-ninth parallel of north latitude by the Convention of 1818. However, it was left to the negotiation of the Webster-Ashburton Treaty of 1842 to settle the most difficult sections of the Maine–New Brunswick and Minnesota-Ontario borders. The resolution of the Oregon boundary in 1846, extending the forty-ninth parallel to the Straits of Juan de Fuca, avoided another clash. The American purchase of Alaska from Russia in 1867 created a new boundary problem with Canada, which was finally settled by a tribunal in 1903.

IMPROVING US RELATIONS WITH BRITAIN AND CANADA

With the exception of the period of the American Civil War (1861–1865), US relations with Britain and Canada improved steadily in the late nineteenth century. Later, the crises of World War I (1914–1918), World War II (1939–1945), and the Cold War drew the United States into a close alliance with Britain and Canada in matters of defense and foreign policy, not only through the United Nations but also the North Atlantic Treaty Organization (NATO) and the North American Aerospace Defense Command (NORAD).

ECONOMIC INTEGRATION

North America remained a producer of raw materials throughout the nineteenth century as it had been in the eighteenth. The United States supplied Britain and Europe with tobacco, indigo, rice, flax, and naval stores, to which was added, in increasing importance, cotton for the expanding textile industry. By the 1870s and 1880s, in addition to cotton, wheat, and processed meats, the

United States was producing and exporting increasing volumes of manufactured goods and iron and steel. The two world wars projected the United States into a position of economic and financial dominance, which has only begun to be seriously challenged. In Canada, the export of furs, timber, and fish was gradually superseded in the twentieth century by grain, beef, pulp and paper, and manufactured goods. Indeed, the two world wars helped to stimulate the manufacturing economy in Canada, as did the opening of mining, oil, and gas production. Mexico also produced foodstuff but depended on mineral extraction and, increasingly, oil production.

After several false starts in the nineteenth and early twentieth centuries, the United States and Canada began to integrate key parts of their economies with the Automotive Products (Auto Pact) Agreement in 1965 and the Free Trade Agreement of 1988. The latter was superseded in 1994 by a trilateral treaty, the North American Free Trade Agreement (NAFTA), between the United States, Canada, and Mexico. This treaty, signed by the three parties in 1992, did much to stimulate investment in manufacturing in Mexico and helped bring its economy more in line with those of Canada and the United States.

POLITICAL AND SOCIAL CULTURE

The political and social culture of North America has followed several distinctive paths. The United States was shaped by both the ideas of the Enlightenment and British political tradition. Its basic premise, as articulated in the Declaration of Independence, was that governments derive "their just Powers from the Consent of the Governed," and that it was "self-evident" that the people had "inalienable rights." The new republic faced many contradictions to this ideal, and the United States has struggled to bring the ideal into reality. But with the exception of the Civil War, the United States has enjoyed a remarkably stable political and social history.

Mexico has experienced a much more turbulent political history, with domestic rebellions, claims to monarchies, foreign invasions, authoritarian rule, and extended civil strife. US intervention in 1914 to 1917 could easily have led to a second Mexican-American war, but by the mid-twentieth century, Mexico's relations with the United States had been normalized.

Canada followed the British parliamentary system, and the British worked more skillfully with the Canadians than they had with the Americans in the 1770s. A 1791 constitution provided Upper and Lower Canada with bicameral legislatures, but, in response to the rebellions in 1837, the two provinces were united in 1841, and the legislature was subsequently permitted to form a government responsible to a majority in the elected house. In the 1860s negotiations began to bring the several North American colonies together in confederation, culminating in the North America Act of 1867 that created the Dominion of Canada, which eventually extended across the continent to the Pacific and included all of the British North American colonies.

SOCIAL TENSIONS

All three countries have had to confront serious social tensions. The United States had a large population of African American slaves, who were freed by an amendment to the Constitution in 1865 ratified after the end of the Civil War, although it took another century and Supreme Court decisions to enact effective legislation to guarantee civil rights and voting rights to African Americans. Native Americans were moved from their traditional lands to reservations, often after serious conflicts.

In Canada, tensions between the English and French date back to the eighteenth century and still periodically threaten the integrity of the country. Indians and Métis people have also had difficulties with the Canadian government, with the Métis rising in rebellion in 1869 to 1870 and in 1885, and the Native people struggling to find a place in modern culture. In Mexico, class distinctions based on whether individuals are of Spanish origin, indigenous Indians, or part of the majority community of mestizo have been a historic problem. Vast immigration to North America from Europe and Asia has also complicated the social mix of the three countries, creating a "norm" of assimilation, which in fact has not worked for all immigrant groups and creates a problematic standard for indigenous people.

It may be possible to speak of an emerging North American culture. This is sometimes described as a process of "Americanization," but it is more complicated. McDonald's fast-food restaurants in Mexico may be thought of as distinctly American, but Tex-Mex restaurants are common in both the United States and Canada. American music, motion pictures, and television appear to dominate the North American media, but Canadian and Hispanic musicians, actors, comedians, film directors, and television commentators increasingly shape popular culture in the United States.

Tourism has also contributed to a sense of comfortable familiarity by encouraging movement from one country to another. American sun seekers go to Mexican resorts in Acapulco or Cancún, and Canadian snowbirds spend winter months in Florida or Arizona, while Americans head north on ski trips or fishing expeditions. Relatively free movement across borders has made possible this mixing of cultural talent and pleasure seeking. Of course, Spanish-speaking Nuevomexicanos in Texas and the southwestern states have preserved a distinctive culture since becoming part of the United States, as have the French Canadian communities in New England and across the Great Lakes states. Recognizable border cultures have flourished, with families that have connections in both societies. However, passport controls arising out of security considerations following the terrorist attacks of 9/11, and border restrictions stemming from fears of immigration violations, may infringe on these easy movements and informal borderland cultures.

SEE ALSO *Atlantic Ocean; Borderlands; Canada; Caribbean; Mexican-American War; Mexico; Monroe Doctrine (1823); Pacific Ocean; South America; War of 1812*

BIBLIOGRAPHY

Bumsted, J. M. *A History of the Canadian Peoples.* 4th ed. Don Mills, ON: Oxford University Press, 2011.

Henretta, James A., Rebecca Edwards, and Robert O. Self. *America: A Concise History.* 5th ed. Boston: Bedford/St. Martin, 2012.

LaFeber, Walter. *The American Age: United States Foreign Policy at Home and Abroad since 1750.* 2nd ed. New York: Norton, 1994.

MacLachlan, Colin, and William H. Beezley. *El Gran Pueblo: A History of Greater Mexico.* 3rd ed. Upper Saddle River, NJ: Prentice Hall, 2004.

Ninkovich, Frank. *The Wilsonian Century: U.S. Foreign Policy since 1900.* Chicago: University of Chicago Press, 1999.

Paterson, J. H. *North America: A Geography of the United States and Canada.* 9th ed. New York: Oxford University Press, 1994.

Resnick, Philip. *The Labyrinth of North American Identities.* Toronto, ON: University of Toronto Press, 2012.

Thompson, John Herd, and Stephen J. Randall. *Canada and the United States: Ambivalent Allies.* 4th ed. Montreal: McGill-Queen's University Press, 2008.

Francis M. Carroll
Professor Emeritus
St. John's College, University of Manitoba

NORTH AMERICAN FREE TRADE AGREEMENT (NAFTA)

The North American Free Trade Agreement (NAFTA) created a free-trade area between the United States, Canada, and Mexico. NAFTA took effect on January 1, 1994. It was the first regional economic integration agreement between developed and underdeveloped countries and has since become the world's largest trading bloc.

Ideologically motivated by the principles of neoliberalism, its aims are to facilitate the free movement of capital in North America by eliminating tariff barriers and import and export quotas in a similar way to the World Trade Organization (WTO). However, more controversially, NAFTA's core provisions also grant foreign corporations and investors the right to sue a government over laws and policies that they allege reduce their profits and promote the privatization and deregulation of essential services, such as water, energy, and health care.

Despite significant social and environmental consequences resulting from the agreement's implementation, judged on its own criteria these aims have largely been achieved. In the first few years, tariff and nontariff barriers were removed on 65 percent of goods, although the 1988 Canada-US Free Trade Agreement (CUFTA) had already abolished most tariffs between those two countries. Although some sensitive industries like agriculture, energy, and car production were initially exempted from NAFTA, since 2009 many of these restrictions have been lifted. The value of regional trade has trebled from $341 billion to $1.1 trillion between 1993 and 2013, and inward foreign direct investment flows have increased by five times over the same period and by ten times in Mexico (Wise 2010).

RATIFICATION

Following several years of negotiations, NAFTA was signed by the leaders of the three respective nations on December 17, 1992. Although it then needed to be authorized by each nation's legislative or parliamentary branch, the proposals were strongly opposed by labor unions, environmental groups, and social movements. Opposition was especially strong in the United States and Canada, where following CUFTA, sensitivity to any further transfer of national sovereignty, which would weaken domestic labor or environmental standards, was heightened. The Alliance for Responsible Trade (ART), Common Frontiers, and the Mexican Action Network Against Free Trade (RMALC) are examples of coalitions that emerged in opposition to the agreement in the United States, Canada, and Mexico respectively (Crow and Albo 2005, 12–22). Indeed, many American and Canadian policy makers, businesspeople, and politicians were concerned that corporations would relocate their plants to Mexico, where production costs were cheaper, damaging their own economies and creating unemployment.

In order to prevent this possibility and also to secure enough Democrat votes for NAFTA to obtain congressional assent, incoming US president Bill Clinton added two side agreements: the North American Agreement on Environmental Cooperation (NAAEC) and the North American Agreement on Labor Cooperation (NAALC), which provided a baseline for labor costs by reinforcing a

Mexican farmers block the El Paso, TX, to Ciudad Juárez, Mexico, bridge, in a 20th-anniversary protest against the North American Free Trade Agreement (NAFTA), January 2014. *After implementation of NAFTA, Mexico struggled with declining or barely increasing GDP and wages. Mexican president Carlos Salinas's policies in compliance with NAFTA requirements led to evictions of millions of small farmers from their land.* **AP IMAGES/RAYMUNDO RUIZ**

minimum level of industrial protection for Mexican workers. These were administered by NAFTA's Commission for Labor Cooperation and the Commission for Environmental Cooperation, respectively, and consisted of a council of ministers and a trinational secretariat. Although they did not establish harmonized labor and environmental standards, they did incorporate citizen-participation mechanisms that enable activists, trade unions, legal experts, and civil society groups to mount legal challenges to a third-party adjudicating state's national administrative office in cases where the petitioners believe that domestic labor or environmental laws are being violated.

The NAALC and NAAEC have been dismissed as ineffective tools for achieving labor and environmental protection due to their complicated adjudication processes, which are open to political manipulation (Adams and Singh 1997, 161–181). In the case of the NAALC, the right of assembly, strike, and collective bargaining are not even subject to binding arbitration, and only child labor, minimum wage, and health and safety issues are fully sanctionable. Furthermore, very few cases have been filed under either NAALC or NAAEC since 1994.

However, in contrast, some of the greatest achievements that workers and activists have gained have been through coordinated transnational campaigns that leveraged the side agreements. In view of the initial suspicion and historically protectionist outlooks of the respective national labor confederations—the AFL-CIO, the Canadian Labour Confederation, and the Mexican Workers Confederation, which was tied in to a corporatist relationship with Mexico's pro-agreement governments during the 1990s—these transnational campaigns tended to be spearheaded by individual unions with more internationalist perspectives, such as United Electrical in the United States, the Authentic Workers' Front in Mexico, and the Canadian Steelworkers Union. However, trinational opposition has since expanded as the broader labor movements in each country were hit by job losses and falling wages through vehicles like the Tri-National Solidarity Alliance (Ozarow 2013, 518–520).

IMPACT AND CONTROVERSIES

Most analysts agree that it is difficult to accurately quantify the changes in trade, investment growth, unemployment, and wages that are directly attributable to NAFTA. Since the agreement came into effect, the Organization for Economic Cooperation and Development (OECD) estimates that economic growth in the United States, Canada, and Mexico has increased by two-thirds. However, the US trade gap with Mexico has also risen dramatically since NAFTA took effect—from a $4 billion surplus in 1993 to a deficit of $54 billion in 2012 (Glassman 2013). Although corporate profit margins rose in most industries during that period, NAFTA also generated adverse effects on employment, wages, and bargaining power in all three countries by promoting unrestricted competition between workers.

The agreement's tariff elimination stipulations have facilitated the ability of US and Canadian corporations to shift production and investment to Mexico, a move further encouraged by weak enforcement of environmental regulations and labor costs that are ten times lower in Mexico. Consequently, some 5 million manufacturing jobs in the United States and Canada have been lost to Mexico, although the Economic Policy Institute and the AFL-CIO estimate the number of lost jobs directly attributable to NAFTA to be approximately 700,000.

Mexican workers were also negatively affected. Despite promises from the agreement's architects that foreign investment would bring unprecedented growth, Mexico's per capita gross domestic product (GDP) declined in 1995 and barely increased during the first decade of the twenty-first century. It remained six times lower than that of the United States in 2010. According to the International Labour Organization, real Mexican wages fell by approximately 24 percent between 1995 and 1999, and only returned to pre-NAFTA levels in 2006. Although NAFTA was expected to deliver "convergence effects," Mexican wage levels using purchasing power parity indices have remained several times lower than US equivalents, undermining the bargaining position of Canadian and American labor. Further, when Mexican president Carlos Salinas's neoliberal administration abolished the *ejido* communal land-holding system (previously enshrined in the 1917 constitution) in 1991 as part of pre-NAFTA entry requirements, millions of small farmers were evicted from their land and forced to migrate to Mexico's urban centers. This led to an armed uprising in the Chiapas region by the Zapatista Army of National Liberation against the Mexican state on the day that NAFTA came into force. Import tariffs and subsidies to domestic enterprises were also removed, leading many small and medium-sized firms to go bankrupt.

One of the agreement's main impacts has been the establishment of thousands of maquiladora factories by American and Canadian multinationals along Mexico's border with the United States (MacDonald 2003, 173),

leading to the creation of export-processing zones. These multinationals take advantage of Mexico's lower wage costs, tax advantages, and lax environmental and labor regulation to produce goods on a tariff-free basis in low-skilled plants for assembly, processing, or manufacturing. They then export the products, sometimes back to the country of origin of the raw materials. However, there are major concerns about employment standards in maquiladoras, which mostly employ women.

While it is true that North American governments' environmental policies have sometimes been neglected in the wake of trade liberalization, serious NAFTA-related environmental threats have generally been confined to border areas like Tijuana, where industrialization has been most rapid, and to certain sectors, such as metals, petroleum, and transportation.

As globalization deepens, NAFTA has been used as a model for subsequent bilateral and multilateral free-trade agreements, including the proposed Regional Comprehensive Economic Partnership in Asia and the Transatlantic Trade and Investment Partnership between the United States and the European Union.

SEE ALSO *Clinton, William Jefferson; Globalization; Neoliberalism; World Trade Organization*

BIBLIOGRAPHY

Adams, Roy, and Parbudyal Singh. "Early Experience with NAFTA's Labour Side Accord." *Comparative Labour Law Journal* 18, 2 (1997): 161–181.

Crow, Dan, and Greg Albo. "Neo-liberalism, NAFTA and the State of the North American Labour Movements." *Just Labour* 67 (2005): 12–22.

Glassman, Mark. "Nafta 20 Years After: Neither Miracle nor Disaster." *Bloomberg Business Week*, December 30, 2013.

Graubart, Jonathan. "The Legalization of Transnational Political Opportunity Structures." In *Contentious Politics in North America: National Protest and Transnational Collaboration under Continental Integration*, edited by Jeffrey Ayers and Laura Macdonald, 177–194. Basingstoke, UK: Palgrave Macmillan, 2010.

MacDonald, Ian. "NAFTA and the Emergence of Continental Labor Cooperation." *American Review of Canadian Studies* 33, 2 (2003): 173–176.

Nolan García, Kimberly. "The Evolution of United States–Mexico Labor Cooperation (1994–2009): Achievements and Challenges." *Politics and Policy* 39, 1 (2011): 91–117.

Ozarow, Daniel. "Pitching for Each Others' Team: The North American Free Trade Agreement and Labor Transnationalism." *Labor History* 54, 5 (2013): 512–526.

Wise, Carol. "The North American Free Trade Agreement: A Requiem." *CESifo Forum* 11, 4 (2010): 3–8.

Daniel Ozarow
Middlesex University, London

NORTH ATLANTIC TREATY ORGANIZATION (NATO)

The North Atlantic Treaty Organization (NATO) was created with the signing of the North Atlantic Treaty in Washington on April 4, 1949. The treaty was originally signed by the governments of Belgium, Canada, Denmark, France, Iceland, Italy, Luxembourg, the Netherlands, Norway, Portugal, the United Kingdom, and the United States. The treaty's central purpose was to help these allies deal with the military and ideological threat posed by the Soviet Union.

During the Cold War, Greece and Turkey (1952), West Germany (1955), and Spain (1982) joined the alliance. In the post–Cold War period, the whole of Germany came under the NATO treaty following German unification, then several groups of countries— the Czech Republic, Hungary, Poland (1999); Bulgaria, Estonia, Latvia, Lithuania, Romania, Slovakia, Slovenia (2004); and Albania, Croatia (2009)—were admitted to bring the total membership to twenty-eight. No country has ever given up its membership in the alliance, and the door remains open to new qualified candidates. In 1967 France forced NATO to move its headquarters from Paris to Brussels and withdrew from participation in NATO's Integrated Command Structure. President Charles de Gaulle believed that France would be more independent of US influence outside the command structure. France resumed full participation in 2009.

COLD WAR MISSION

The key commitment made by North Atlantic Treaty signatories has always been the treaty's Article 5, which specifies that all allies will consider an armed attack on one or more of them an attack against them all. And, "if such an armed attack occurs, each of them … will assist the Party or Parties so attacked by taking such action as it deems necessary, including the use of armed force, to restore and maintain the security of the North Atlantic area."

Even though the North Atlantic Treaty was clearly designed to counter Soviet expansion and military power, it was based on common values, specified no enemy, protected the sovereign decision-making rights of all members, and was written in language sufficiently flexible to accommodate changing international circumstances.

In 1955, following West Germany's accession to NATO, the Soviet Union established the opposing Warsaw Pact alliance as a means of solidifying Soviet control over the countries of Eastern and Central Europe (Albania, Bulgaria, Czechoslovakia, East Germany, Hungary, Poland, and Romania) where Moscow-supported communist parties had taken control.

The first major construction on the North Atlantic Treaty's foundation came early on, with a military buildup in Europe and elaboration of an integrated command structure in the early 1950s, which had not been anticipated when the treaty was signed but was judged necessary particularly after North Korea invaded South Korea. The alliance was adapted again following the 1954 failure of the European Defense Community, which was to have organized Europe's contributions to the alliance. In the mid-1960s, in addition to adjusting to France's departure from the Integrated Command Structure, the allies revamped NATO's strategy with the doctrine of a "flexible response" to a possible Warsaw Pact attack. They also approved the *Harmel Report* (1967), giving the alliance the mission of promoting détente as well as sustaining deterrence and defense. In the 1990s, the allies reoriented NATO's goals and activities to take into account the peaceful democratic revolutions in Eastern and Central Europe and the dissolution of the Warsaw Pact and the Soviet Union.

THE POST–COLD WAR PERIOD

In the early years of the twenty-first century, the allies decided to allow NATO to take on tasks beyond Europe to deal with threats to the security of the member states. This cooperation developed increasingly under the terms of Article 4, which specified that the allies would "consult together whenever, in the opinion of any of them, the territorial integrity, political independence or security of any of the Parties is threatened." The commitment to work together to deal with "threats" became a progressively more important aspect of NATO membership in the post–Cold War period, a development confirmed in NATO's 2010 Strategic Concept.

Over the years, NATO established a wide variety of partnership arrangements with European, Middle Eastern, and Asian nations that have, for some countries, facilitated their eventual entry into the alliance and, for others, served as a vehicle for extensive cooperation with the allies and participation in NATO missions.

After Yugoslavia broke up in the early 1990s, NATO eventually led efforts to end ethnic conflict in the Balkans region and, in particular, to block further Serbian aggression against their neighbors. In 2002 the NATO allies agreed to establish a NATO Response Force to be available for security challenges in or beyond Europe. This marked acceptance by all the allies that NATO's security responsibilities are not limited by geography. In 2003 the allies agreed that NATO could take responsibility for the International Security Assistance Force in Afghanistan.

In recent years, NATO and the European Union have worked out ways of ensuring that defense cooperation in the European Union remains consistent with

NATO cooperation. However, attempts to establish a more cohesive European contribution to the alliance fell far short, and European defense efforts fell through the 1990s and into the twenty-first century, exacerbating already-existing burden-sharing tensions between the United States and its allies.

ORGANIZATIONAL STRUCTURE

The North Atlantic Council is NATO's main decision-making body. It meets routinely at the level of "permanent representatives" of the member states, twice a year at the level of foreign ministers, and periodically at the summit. NATO's defense policy decision-making organization, the Defense Planning Committee, is composed of NATO ministers of defense or their representatives. The Military Committee meets regularly at the level of Military Representatives and three times a year at the level of Chiefs of Defense. The Integrated Command Structure, following substantial reform and consolidation over two decades, includes the Allied Command Operations, headed traditionally by an American four-star general (the supreme allied commander Europe, or SACEUR), with a European deputy commander. NATO's civilian organization is run by an International Staff headed by a secretary-general, NATO's top civilian official. That position has always been held by a European.

CURRENT STATUS

NATO remains the "indispensable link" between the United States, Canada, and the European allies and the forum for coordination of defense policies and responses to security challenges. Until 2014 the absence of a unifying threat like that which had been posed by the Soviet Union, the emergence of new challenges beyond NATO's borders, and differences over how best to deal with those threats fed speculation that NATO was dead or dying. NATO's future may now depend on how effectively the United States and its allies respond to expansionist Russian activities in Ukraine and Moscow's threats to the security of other states, particularly NATO member states, on Russia's borders.

SEE ALSO *Cold War; Deterrence; Domino Theory; Iron Curtain; Nuclear Weapons*

BIBLIOGRAPHY

Ducasse, Mark D., ed. *The Transatlantic Bargain.* Rome: NATO Defense College, 2012.

Kaplan, Lawrence S. *NATO before the Korean War: April 1949– June 1950.* Kent, OH: Kent State University Press, 2013.

North Atlantic Treaty Organization (NATO). The North Atlantic Treaty. 1949. http://www.nato.int/cps/en/natolive/official_texts_17120.htm

North Atlantic Treaty Organization (NATO). *Strategic Concept for the Defence and Security of the Members of the North Atlantic Treaty Organisation: Active Engagement, Modern Defence.* Lisbon, Portugal: NATO, 2010. http://www.nato.int/lisbon2010/strategic-concept-2010-eng.pdf

Rynning, Sten. *NATO in Afghanistan: The Liberal Disconnect.* Stanford, CA: Stanford University Press, 2012.

Sloan, Stanley R. *Permanent Alliance? NATO and the Transatlantic Bargain from Truman to Obama.* New York: Continuum, 2010.

Stanley R. Sloan
Visiting Scholar in Political Science
Middlebury College

NORTH KOREA

The United States and the Democratic People's Republic of Korea (hereafter North Korea) have never established formal diplomatic relations. Like the Republic of Korea (hereafter South Korea), North Korea was born out of the joint Soviet-American occupation of the Korean peninsula, which subsequently hardened into a permanent division creating two independent states. Since their founding, both Koreas have claimed to rule the entire peninsula and each has viewed the other's claim as illegitimate. When North Korea attempted to reunify the peninsula by force in 1950, the United States came to the aid of South Korea, becoming a major participant in the Korean War. As part of its response to the North Korean invasion, the United States imposed economic sanctions on North Korea, which have remained in place to varying degrees ever since. As a result, North Korea and the United States have little diplomatic or economic contact. North Korea has occasionally expressed interest in normalizing relations, but the United States has resisted normalization because of North Korea's human rights record, its flouting of international norms, and fears that North Korea would not negotiate in good faith.

NORTH KOREAN–US CONFLICT

The continual American troop presence on the Korean peninsula since 1950 has seen Americans and North Koreans in close proximity and has frequently resulted in conflicts. In 1968 the North Korean navy captured an American spy ship, the USS *Pueblo,* killing one crew member in the process. Both the United States and North Korea still dispute whether the ship had strayed into North Korea's territorial waters. The crew was released after eleven months in captivity, during which some of the ship's officers were tortured. The USS *Pueblo* is still prominently displayed in the Taedong River in Pyongyang, the North Korean capital, as a symbol of American aggression. In 1976 a confrontation over tree trimming in the Joint Security Area of the Demilitarized Zone resulted in the death of two American soldiers in what is commonly known as the "ax murder incident." These incidents occurred in the context of a broader pattern of North Korean aggression, including but not limited to attempts to assassinate South Korean leaders, the bombing of Korean Air Flight 858 in 1987, the kidnapping of Japanese citizens, and the suspicion that the North Korean government is involved in numerous illicit activities including drug smuggling, counterfeiting, and the proliferation of weapons technology. This aggression furthered the perception that North Korea is a pariah state and should be isolated. From 1988 until 2008 North Korea was designated a "State Sponsor of Terrorism" by the US Department of State.

For their part, North Koreans view the continued American military presence in South Korea as an existential threat to their nation. Since the end of the Korean War more than twenty thousand American military personnel have been stationed in South Korea. Annual war games conducted by American and South Korean forces, which the North claims are dress rehearsals for invasion, regularly elevate tensions. North Koreans have frequently used the American presence in South Korea to justify the militarization of their society and their development of a nuclear weapons program.

THE NUCLEAR ARMS ISSUE

North Korea's nuclear program is the most pressing issue in US–North Korean relations. For more than two decades it has been a source of tension and a subject of negotiations. In 1985 North Korea became a party to the Treaty on the Non-Proliferation of Nuclear Weapons (NPT), but then withdrew in 1993 after inspections by the International Atomic Energy Agency found discrepancies in its reporting of weapons-grade materials, suggesting that it might be stockpiling such materials for the development of nuclear weapons. North Korea's withdrawal from the NPT sparked a crisis in US–North Korean relations in which the administration of American president Bill Clinton (b. 1946) considered bombing North Korean nuclear facilities to prevent the development of its program. In 1994 North Korea and the United States reached a nonbinding political agreement called the Agreed Framework in which North Korea agreed to halt its nuclear program and rejoin the NPT in return for the construction of two light-water reactors, 500,000 tons of fuel oil a year until the reactors were operational, a lifting of American sanctions against North Korea, and movement toward a normalization of diplomatic relations with the United States, among other terms.

Although the Agreed Framework offered a comprehensive settlement of the North Korean nuclear issue, the agreement was plagued by mistrust and a lack of political will. Securing international funding for the oil shipments and the light-water reactors proved difficult, causing delays in the delivery of both. This mistrust was aggravated by several North Korean actions, including ballistic missile tests over Japan. In retaliation the Japanese suspended $1 billion in aid to the light-water reactor program, causing further delays. The decision by the administration of George W. Bush (b. 1946) to name North Korea as a part of the "axis of evil" in 2002 exacerbated the problem. When American officials accused Pyongyang of enriching uranium in the fall of 2002, North Korea left the NPT for a second time and the Agreed Framework collapsed. North Korea conducted nuclear weapons tests in 2006, 2009, and 2013.

These tests, coupled with the development of continually more sophisticated missile technology, have made the North Korean nuclear program a cause of ongoing concern. After the collapse of the Agreed Framework, negotiations over the weapons programs broadened to include North Korea's immediate neighbors: China, Russia, South Korea, and Japan. It was hoped that including China and Russia, historically close allies of North Korea, might result in a more durable arrangement. The so-called Six-Party Talks began in 2003 and continued until 2009, when North Korea withdrew after being condemned by the United Nations for continued ballistic missile tests. The issue of North Korea's nuclear weapons program remained unresolved as of 2015.

PERCEPTIONS AND OPENINGS

Given the prevailing view of North Korea as a pariah state, the continued tensions over its nuclear program, its occasional detention of American visitors to North Korea, and its restrictions on North Korean citizens traveling abroad, there is little contact between North Koreans and Americans, and their perceptions of each other are influenced by negative portrayals in their respective media. North Korea is frequently satirized in American film and television, and this satire occasionally rises to the level of an international incident, such as the controversy surrounding Sony Pictures' *The Interview* in 2014. North Koreans are frequently portrayed as brainwashed and their leaders as hedonistic and mentally unstable. These negative views of North Korea are further reinforced by North Korean defectors' writings, which describe in detail the difficult conditions in which most North Koreans live and the repression many suffer. North Korean portrayals of Americans are similarly unflattering. Americans are often portrayed as bloodthirsty, subhuman, and avaricious to the point of violence, as in Han Sorya's novella *Jackals*.

Despite the prevailing difficulties, there have been occasional moments of goodwill between North Koreans and Americans. In 2007 the US Navy came to the aid of a North Korean merchant vessel being attacked by pirates off the coast of Somalia, earning a rare positive mention of the United States in the North Korean press. In 2008 the New York Philharmonic accepted an invitation to play a concert in Pyongyang, marking the first major cultural exchange in the history of the two nations. However, a true breakthrough in bilateral relations has remained elusive.

SEE ALSO *China; Cold War; Kennan, George F.; Korean War; Russia; United Nations*

BIBLIOGRAPHY

Cumings, Bruce. *North Korea: Another Country.* New York: New Press, 2003.

Lankov, Andrei. *The Real North Korea: Life and Politics in the Failed Stalinist Utopia.* Oxford: Oxford University Press, 2013.

Lerner, Mitchell B. *The Pueblo Incident: A Spy Ship and the Failure of American Foreign Policy.* Lawrence: University Press of Kansas, 2002.

Myers, B. R. *The Cleanest Race: How North Koreans See Themselves and Why It Matters.* Brooklyn, NY: Melville House, 2010.

David P. Fields
PhD Candidate, US Diplomatic History
University of Wisconsin–Madison

NORTHWEST ORDINANCE (1787)

During the American Revolution, the new states ceded to the national government most of their claims to unsettled lands in the west. The most important parcel of land, claimed by Virginia as well as some other states, became known as the "Northwest Territory." This consisted of more than 260,000 square miles west of Pennsylvania, east of the Mississippi, between the Great Lakes and the Ohio River. Eventually this area would constitute the states of Ohio (1803), Indiana (1816), Illinois (1818), Michigan (1836), Wisconsin (1848), and part of Minnesota (1858).

BACKGROUND

When the Revolution ended, the national government was effectively bankrupt. Its best potential source for revenue was from selling the land in the Northwest Territory. When an earlier Land Ordinance of 1785 failed to garner sales because it did not provide for the creation of civil governments, the US Congress debated a new law, the Northwest Ordinance, in the spring of 1787. The purpose of the law was to provide a process for creating an orderly civil society in the west, which would encourage

settlement and lead to the sale of land. It also provided the structure by which the United States would expand and incorporate new territory as coequal states.

The structure of the Northwest Ordinance illustrates the needs of settlers and the priorities of many citizens in post-Revolutionary America. The ordinance thus focused on property, government, and the creation of communities. The ordinance was divided into fourteen sections, which dealt with structural issues for governing the territory, and six articles, which were more policy oriented. The ordinance was finally passed by Congress in July 1787. This was before the Constitutional Convention had finished its work, and thus all appointments under the ordinance would be done by Congress. In 1791, after the adoption of the new Constitution, Congress reauthorized the ordinance but gave appointment power to the president.

PROVISIONS

The first substantive provision, Section 2, provided for the distribution of property belonging to people who died without a will (intestate succession). To non-Americans, this might seem like an odd place to begin a statute designed to promote settlement of a remote region. But, in an area where there were few attorneys and where life might be fragile and dangerous, this elaborate discussion of the intergenerational distribution of property made sense. This reflected the deep concern that Americans at this time had for land titles and clear rules. Settlers who cleared land, built houses, and started farms wanted to be guaranteed that the fruits of their hard work would be passed on to their spouses and children. Significantly, this provision also recognized that most of the existing settlers in the region were not of British origin, but in fact had come from France and settled there before the French and Indian War (1754–1763), when this region was owned by France. Thus, the ordinance provided that "the French and Canadian inhabitants, and other settlers of the Kaskaskies, St. Vincents and the neighboring villages" would maintain "their laws and customs now in force among them, relative to the descent and conveyance, of property." This illustrated the complexity of incorporating new people and foreign laws and customs into the new United States.

The next sections, 3 through 11, established procedures for appointing executive officers and judges to govern the territory and to pass laws or borrow them from existing states, as necessary. Reflecting the connection between property and political authority, which was very much part of Revolutionary-era political theory, the ordinance required that officeholders own minimum amounts of land, ranging from 500 acres for the governor to only 50 acres for representatives in the elected assembly.

Sections 12 through 14 contained dramatic innovations in the settlement of the American continent, and reflected the immediate revolutionary past. Section 12 provided that once the territorial legislature was in place it could elect delegates to the US Congress who could participate in debates but not vote on the floor "during this temporary government." Unlike Great Britain, which never allowed the American colonists to send even a nonvoting representative to Parliament, the American colonists in the west would be able to have their voices heard in Congress. Moreover, the status of "territory" was "temporary," and Section 13 authorized the territorial government to write a constitution, while also providing "for the establishment of States, and permanent government therein, and for their admission to a share in the federal councils on an equal footing with the original States, at as early periods as may be consistent with the general interest." In other words, the residents of the eastern states were fully prepared to dilute their own political power by admitting new western states into the American Union, rather than treating them as colonies.

Following these sections were a series of six articles that the ordinance proclaimed were to be "considered as articles of compact between the original States and the people and States in the said territory and forever remain unalterable, unless by common consent." This provision showed that the western territories would not be treated as colonies, to be governed, and perhaps, abused, by the central government. In essence, the ordinance promised to treat the new territories exactly as Great Britain had not treated the American colonies leading up to the Revolution. Article V of the ordinance provided for dividing the territory into between three and five states, and establishing new states when areas of the territory had a population of at least sixty thousand people.

Articles I through IV included provisions that would eventually be found in the American Bill of Rights. Article I guaranteed religious freedom in the territories—something that was not then guaranteed in most of the American states. Article II guaranteed criminal due process, fair trials, jury trials, the right of private property, reasonable bail, and the writ of habeas corpus, while prohibiting the government from interfering in the right of contract or imposing "cruel or unusual punishments." Under this provision, the inhabitants of the territory had greater protections of personal liberty than did most Americans, who were at the mercy of their state constitutions. Article III encouraged the creation of public schools, demanded that the Indians be treated fairly, and that "laws founded in justice and humanity, shall from time to time be made for preventing wrongs being done to them, and for preserving peace and friendship with them." This provision would be flagrantly violated by the settlers in the west, the national government, and the state

governments, but it does illustrate the high hopes of the members of Congress. Article IV regulated taxation and commerce.

Article V provided for subdividing the territory into states that would be then admitted to the Union. The states had to have a written constitution that would provide for an elected legislature and be "in conformity to the principles contained in these articles; and, so far as it can be consistent with the general interest of the confederacy, such admission shall be allowed at an earlier period, and when there may be a less number of free inhabitants in the State than sixty thousand." Significantly, Congress did not envision the territory being kept as a colony by the national government. Furthermore, by providing for new states, the authors of the ordinance understood that they were setting the stage for a reduction in their own political power as more states entered the Union.

Perhaps the most famous provision of the Northwest Ordinance was Article VI, which prohibited slavery in the territory:

> There shall be neither slavery nor involuntary servitude in the said territory, otherwise than in the punishment of crimes whereof the party shall have been duly convicted: *Provided, always*, That any person escaping into the same, from whom labor or service is lawfully claimed in any one of the original States, such fugitive may be lawfully reclaimed and conveyed to the person claiming his or her labor or service as aforesaid.

Significantly, this was the first time in the history of the world that a nation had used a statute to prohibit slavery. This was one of the key moments in creating what would become the great Atlantic antislavery movement of the nineteenth century. Although it was added at the last possible moment, without significant debate or clarification, this provision would set the stage for future debates over the status of slavery in the western territories. The provision was not immediately effective—slaves were held in Indiana until the 1830s and in Illinois until the late 1840s—but the provision did create an assumption that the Northwest Territory would become free soil. At the same time, the provision implied that the Southwest—what became Kentucky, Tennessee, Alabama, and Mississippi—would eventually enter the Union as slave states. Article VI also contained the first national fugitive-slave clause, which would later be copied by the delegates in Philadelphia writing the national constitution.

IMPACT

In the end, the Northwest Ordinance provided a stable process for turning unsettled territories into states. The ordinance would later affect land acquired from France through the Louisiana Purchase (1803) and from Mexico after the Mexican-American War (1846–1848). From Ohio to Oregon—and almost everywhere in between—the model set out in the Northwest Ordinance would be used to allow for an orderly process of settlement, territorial government, and then statehood. This model made the United States quite different from European colonization ventures, such as those in Africa, Australia, and even Canada, where separate territories were created and new settlements were only gradually incorporated into existing colonies or nations. This contrasts, for example, with Canada, where territories had separate governments even after confederation. Newfoundland, for example, did not become a Canadian province until 1949.

The antislavery provisions of Article VI also set the stage for subsequent debates over the place of slavery in the territories. The Missouri Compromise of 1820 was an attempt to replicate the Northwest Ordinance in the West. But, in the end, the issue of slavery was too complicated to be solved by legislation and normal politics. The evolution of the nation, starting with the Northwest Ordinance, guaranteed that many new states would never have slavery, creating what Abraham Lincoln (1809–1865) would call a nation that was "half slave and half free." This contrasts with other New World jurisdictions, such as Brazil and Cuba, where slavery spread with settlement.

SEE ALSO *Empire of Liberty*

BIBLIOGRAPHY

Finkelman, Paul. *Slavery and the Founders: Race and Liberty in the Age of Jefferson.* 3rd ed. New York: Routledge, 2014.

Hunter, Lloyd, ed. *Pathways to the Old Northwest: An Observance of the Bicentennial of the Northwest Ordinance.* Indianapolis: Indiana Historical Society, 1988.

Northwest Ordinance. 1787. http://www.ourdocuments.gov/doc .php?doc=8

Onuf, Peter S. *Statehood and Union: A History of the Northwest Ordinance.* Bloomington: Indiana University Press, 1987.

Taylor, Robert M., Jr., ed. *The Northwest Ordinance, 1787: A Bicentennial Handbook.* Indianapolis: Indiana Historical Society, 1987.

Williams, Frederick D., ed. *The Northwest Ordinance: Essays on Its Formulation, Provisions, and Legacy.* East Lansing: Michigan State University Press, 1989.

Paul Finkelman
Senior Fellow, Penn Program on Democracy, Citizenship, and Constitutionalism, University of Pennsylvania
Scholar-in-Residence
National Constitution Center, Philadelphia, Pennsylvania

NSA

SEE *National Security Agency (NSA).*

NSC-68

US National Security Council Paper 68, or NSC-68—more formally, "United States Objectives and Programs for National Security"—is a Cold War policy recommendation written during the administration of President Harry S. Truman (1884–1972) that called for the United States to engage in a massive military buildup, including development of a hydrogen bomb. It defined the nation's Cold War strategy, and the logic behind that strategy, for much of the Cold War's duration. Although Truman was skeptical of NSC-68's recommendations when he read the paper in March 1950, casting some doubt on the validity of its arguments, the outbreak of the Korean War on June 25, 1950, changed his mind. NSC-68 received official sanction in December 1950 when Truman declared a state of emergency related to the Korean War.

Three events in the summer and fall of 1949 spurred the development of NSC-68: (1) the Soviet Union's acquisition of the atomic bomb; (2) the communist victory in the Chinese civil war; and (3) a severe economic crisis known as the "dollar gap" that threatened to destroy the global economy US officials were determined to create in the postwar era. The ending of the US atomic monopoly saw the Cold War enter an ominous new phase. With the Cold War's primary antagonists—the United States and the Soviet Union—armed with nuclear weapons, an all-out nuclear conflagration seemed possible. Although it came as no surprise, the communist victory in China suggested that communism was on the move. US officials feared that it could spread to other areas of Asia, particularly Vietnam, which partially explains why the United States became involved in that country's civil war. The dollar gap was a systemic global dollar shortage that rendered much of the world, but Western Europe and Japan in particular, incapable of earning, through their own production, the dollars necessary to purchase US goods. To cope with the dollar gap, the United States instituted the European Recovery Program (ERP, also known as the Marshall Plan), a $13 billion grant to Western Europe. However, in the summer of 1949 Great Britain suffered a major dollar crisis, signaling to US officials that the ERP would be insufficient for fixing the dollar gap. If the dollar gap could not be overcome, Western Europe and Japan would have no choice but to pursue some form of autarky that would cut the United States off from those markets and leave it isolated in the Western Hemisphere. NSC-68 was designed to address each of these crises.

NSC-68 was written in the bowels of the State Department by the Policy Planning Staff headed by Paul Nitze (1907–2004) and overseen by Secretary of State Dean Acheson (1893–1971). In this regard the State Department contravened the president's directive of January 31, 1950, which laid the basis for the report and stated that both the State and Defense Departments were to conduct the study. Acheson, however, hijacked the effort and the Defense Department was excluded. This exclusion was significant because the secretary of defense, Louis Johnson (1891–1966), opposed increased military spending, which would be NSC-68's primary recommendation.

NSC-68 describes a grim world rapidly devolving into Cold War. The Soviet Union, its authors argue, is "animated by a new fanatic faith"—communism—and "seeks to impose its absolute authority over the rest of the world." The report rejects compromise with the Soviet Union until it abandons communism, calls for the Soviet Union's ultimate destruction, and, most importantly, argues for the United States to engage in a "rapid build-up of the political, economic, and military strength of the free world" in order to contain Soviet expansionism. This last element of NSC-68 is what makes it such an important document.

Following NSC-68's recommendations, the United States embarked on a monumental expansion of its economic, military, and political power in the world, assuming the role of global superpower from which it has yet to retreat. For this reason, NSC-68 has also been called the US blueprint for global hegemony. Under NSC-68 US military spending jumped sixfold and became a permanent fixture of the US economy, spawning what President Dwight D. Eisenhower (1890–1969) would come to call the "military-industrial complex." US military forces, including four (ultimately six) divisions in Europe, were stationed all over the globe. In addition, US military and economic aid poured into countries around the world, ending the dollar gap and setting the capitalist global economy on the boom path it assumed in the 1950s and 1960s. US covert intervention in foreign countries also began in earnest with the adoption of NSC-68. Perhaps most importantly, under NSC-68's guidelines the decision was made to develop the hydrogen bomb, igniting the nuclear arm's race that is the Cold War's most lasting legacy.

SEE ALSO *Central Intelligence Agency (CIA); Cold War; Department of Defense, US; Nuclear Weapons; Truman, Harry S.*

BIBLIOGRAPHY

Acheson, Dean. *Present at the Creation: My Years in the State Department.* New York: Norton, 1969.

Borden, William S. *The Pacific Alliance: United States Foreign Economic Policy and Japanese Trade Recovery, 1947–1955.* Madison: University of Wisconsin Press, 1984.

Cardwell, Curt. *NSC 68 and the Political Economy of the Early Cold War.* New York: Cambridge University Press, 2011.

Fordham, Benjamin O. *Building the Cold War Consensus: The Political Economy of US National Security Policy, 1949–1951.* Ann Arbor: University of Michigan Press, 1998.

Gaddis, John Lewis. *Strategies of Containment: A Critical Appraisal of American Postwar National Security Policy.* New York: Oxford University Press, 1982.

Hogan, Michael, J. *A Cross of Iron: Harry S. Truman and the Origins of the National Security State, 1945–1954.* Cambridge: Cambridge University Press, 1998.

Leffler, Melvyn. *A Preponderance of Power: National Security, the Truman Administration, and the Cold War.* Stanford, CA: Stanford University Press, 1992.

McCormick, Thomas. *America's Half-Century: United States Foreign Policy in the Cold War and After.* Baltimore, MD: Johns Hopkins University Press, 1995.

US State Department. "United States Objectives and Programs for National Security." US National Security Council Paper 68, Washington, DC, April 14, 1950, http://fas.org/irp/offdocs/nsc-hst/nsc-68.htm

Wells, Samuel F., Jr. "Sounding the Tocsin: NSC 68 and the Soviet Threat." *International Security* 4, 2 (Fall 1979): 116–58.

Curt Cardwell
Associate Professor, Department of History
Drake University

NUCLEAR WEAPONS

The United States tested the first atomic bomb on July 16, 1945, at the Trinity Test Site in Alamogordo, New Mexico, and dropped two more on the Japanese cities of Hiroshima and Nagasaki on August 6 and 9, respectively. Dubbed "Little Boy," the bomb used against Hiroshima, based on the fission of uranium 235, was a design so simple scientists did not even bother to test it. The Nagasaki bomb, dubbed Fat Man, relied on a much more complex implosion process to detonate plutonium, necessitating the Trinity test.

NUCLEAR WEAPONS IN THE POSTWAR ERA

After World War II the United States reconfigured its military strategy around nuclear weapons. Because uranium 235 is much harder to acquire than plutonium, the United States mass-produced Fat Man bombs rather than Little Boys. The air force grew dramatically because of the strategic importance of nuclear weapons, while scientists miniaturized the A-bomb for battlefield use. The United States had clearly won the race to build the

A-bomb, although that ultimately mattered very little, as the Soviet Union tested its own A-bomb in August 1949.

The Soviet A-bomb exacerbated the rampant Red scare paranoia in the United States. By 1950 the United States possessed hundreds of A-bombs and had committed to nuclear deterrence as the basis of national security, but many cold warriors pushed for the Super, a bomb based on thermonuclear fusion and exponentially more powerful than the fission bomb. The design of the Super went almost nowhere until June 1951, when scientists conceived of using the radiation from a fission bomb to ignite and fuse isotopes of hydrogen. Tested as a device in November 1952 and a weapon in March 1954, the hydrogen bomb proved unfathomably large—the 1954 Castle Bravo test measured 15 megatons—and it could be made with cheaper materials to boot. US thermonuclear supremacy lasted only briefly, however, as the Soviet Union tested its first H-bomb in November 1955.

To expand military power and reduce budgets, President Dwight Eisenhower (1890–1969) introduced a policy called the New Look, which replaced conventional weapons with nuclear ones, and massive retaliation, which pledged a nuclear response to conflicts no matter how small. Further feeding the military-industrial complex, a second nuclear weapons laboratory opened in Livermore, California, in 1952, and yet the awesome power of thermonuclear weapons did little to stop the flare-up of Cold War crises in Quemoy and Matsu (Chinese islands in the Taiwan Strait), Indochina, Suez, and elsewhere.

After the H-bomb, nuclear weapons no longer increased substantially in explosive power; the Castle Bravo test remains the largest bomb ever detonated by the United States. Instead, new methods of delivering nuclear weapons came to define the arms race, especially after the 1957 Soviet launch of the *Sputnik* satellite, which spurred the transition from bombs to missiles during the 1960s.

With both superpowers frequently testing thermonuclear weapons, radioactive fallout increasingly worked its way into human bodies, causing birth defects and leukemia. The American public generally supported nuclear deterrence, but a substantial segment of the population mobilized against nuclear testing. Eventually this movement grew so large that Eisenhower and Soviet leader Nikita Khrushchev (1894–1971) suspended testing in late 1958 and attempted—but failed—to work out a permanent test ban.

THE 1960s AND 1970s

By 1960, the United States possessed some ten thousand nuclear weapons, and new technology continued to upset the balance of terror, including multiple independent reentry vehicles—that is, multiple warheads on a single missile—and nuclear-armed submarines. In addition the administration of President John F. Kennedy (1917–1963) built up nuclear and conventional military capabilities, replacing massive retaliation with the doctrine of flexible response. The United States had earlier established missile sites in allied countries near the Soviet Union, most notably Turkey and Italy, but when Khrushchev attempted an identical maneuver by shipping nuclear weapons to Cuba in 1962, the move touched off the Cuban missile crisis.

Sobered by the missile crisis, Kennedy and Khrushchev signed the Limited Test Ban Treaty (LTBT) in 1963, which restricted nuclear testing to below ground. Although this measure reduced fallout almost entirely, the number of nuclear tests actually increased in the following years. Furthermore, hard-liners ousted Khrushchev in the aftermath of the Cuban missile crisis and vowed to surpass the United States in nuclear strength.

Still, the superpowers accepted peace premised on mutually assured destruction, and a series of arms-control agreements in the 1960s and 1970s highlighted the era of détente. The LTBT was followed by the Treaty on the Non-Proliferation of Nuclear Weapons of 1968, which attempted to curb the spread of nuclear weapons, while the 1972 Anti-Ballistic Missile Treaty limited defensive missiles; further agreements regulated testing and peaceful nuclear explosions, and the administration of President Jimmy Carter (b. 1924) pursued the Comprehensive Nuclear-Test-Ban Treaty (CTBT), which the United Nations adopted in 1996 but the US Senate failed to ratify.

Although the Cold War seemed less dangerous in the 1970s, coexistence continued to rely on the threat of annihilation, and when the 1979 Soviet invasion of Afghanistan doomed détente, the arms race again took center stage. President Carter drastically inflated the military budget, a buildup that grew even larger under President Ronald Reagan (1911–2004).

THE 1980s AND BEYOND

In the early 1980s the United States and Soviet Union deployed intermediate-range missiles to their North Atlantic Treaty Organization and Warsaw Pact allies, causing millions of Europeans to take to the streets in protest. Millions of US activists rallied around a nuclear freeze proposal, a call to halt the production of new weapons. Instead, the Reagan administration responded with the Strategic Defense Initiative, allowing Reagan to reconcile his hawkish anticommunism with his genuine dislike of nuclear weapons. Ultimately, Reagan found his Soviet counterpart Mikhail Gorbachev (b. 1931) also personally opposed to nuclear weapons and eager to reallocate defense spending, leading to the removal of the Euromissiles with the Intermediate-Range Nuclear Forces Treaty of 1987.

Nuclear weapons remain the foundation of US national security. The United States abides by the 1996 CTBT, and there have been some reductions in US and Russian stockpiles, but nuclear weapons remain a menacing threat, with nine nations currently controlling roughly 16,300 nuclear weapons. The immense destructive power of nuclear weapons has ultimately done little to enhance national security.

SEE ALSO *Atomic Bomb; Bikini Atoll; Cold War; Cuban Missile Crisis; Deterrence; Intercontinental Ballistic Missiles; Limited Test Ban Treaty; Manhattan Project; Mutual Assured Destruction (MAD); North Atlantic Treaty Organization (NATO); Strategic Arms Limitation Talks (SALT I and SALT II); Strategic Defense Initiative (Star Wars)*

BIBLIOGRAPHY

Kristensen, Hans M., and Robert S. Norris. "Worldwide Deployments of Nuclear Weapons, 2014." *Bulletin of the Atomic Scientists,* August 26, 2014. http://bos.sagepub.com/content/early/2014/08/26/0096340214547619.long

Powaski, Ronald E. *March to Armageddon: The United States and the Nuclear Arms Race, 1939 to the Present.* New York: Oxford University Press, 1987.

Powaski, Ronald E. *Return to Armageddon: The United States and the Nuclear Arms Race, 1981–1999.* New York: Oxford University Press, 2000.

Rhodes, Richard. *Dark Sun: The Making of the Hydrogen Bomb.* New York: Simon and Schuster, 1996.

Seaborg, Glenn T. *Kennedy, Khrushchev, and the Test Ban.* Berkeley: University of California Press, 1981.

Seaborg, Glenn T. *Stemming the Tide: Arms Control in the Johnson Years.* Lexington, MA: Lexington Books, 1987.

Wittner, Lawrence. *Confronting the Bomb: A Short History of the World Nuclear Disarmament Movement.* Stanford, CA: Stanford University Press, 2009.

York, Herbert F. *Race to Oblivion: A Participant's View of the Arms Race.* New York: Simon and Schuster, 1970.

Paul Rubinson
Assistant Professor
Bridgewater State University

O

OBAMA, BARACK HUSSEIN
1961–

Barack Hussein Obama, the forty-fourth president of the United States, was born on August 4, 1961, in Honolulu, Hawaii. As a child, he formed a lasting view of the United States as a country whose destiny was bound up with the wider world. Both of Obama's parents embodied connections between America and the world. His father, a Kenyan economist, lived and studied in the United States before returning to Kenya. His mother, born in Kansas, worked as an anthropologist in Indonesia, where Obama himself spent several formative years. From his parents and the diverse social and cultural environments of Honolulu and Jakarta, Obama developed a cosmopolitan view of the world beyond national borders. As a political leader, that cosmopolitanism would be tested and transformed.

EARLY ENGAGEMENT IN FOREIGN AFFAIRS

Obama's engagement in foreign affairs could be dated to his involvement in the antiapartheid movement during his time as a student at Occidental College in Los Angeles. Obama joined a campaign to convince the Occidental leadership to divest from South African companies. He deepened his knowledge of global politics after transferring to Columbia University in New York, but the focus of his activism shifted to domestic issues. He would remain focused on local problems during his years working in Chicago as a community organizer, as well as during his time in law school at Harvard and as a state senator in Illinois. Despite Obama's local commitments, those formative years left a lasting mark on his approach to foreign affairs. Struggling with the complexities of community development, Obama developed a tendency to seek consensus through pragmatic solutions, a tendency that buttressed his cosmopolitan worldview even as it was tested by the realities of American foreign relations.

VIEWS ON WAR AND PEACE

War proved especially challenging to Obama's worldview. In October 2002, as a candidate for the US Senate, Obama spoke out against President George W. Bush's decision to invade Iraq. When Obama was elected president, he inherited the war he had denounced, along with an equally bloody conflict in Afghanistan. Obama promised to end both wars. In the fall of 2009, he received the Nobel Peace Prize, a testament to the widespread hope that Obama would shift American foreign policy away from war and toward peaceful international collaboration. But Obama's Nobel Peace Prize acceptance speech made clear that he understood military power as a central pillar of American foreign policy, and that he would not hesitate to use that power. "The United States of America has helped underwrite global security for more than six decades," he declared, "with the blood of our citizens and the strength of our arms." After praising Mahatma Gandhi and Martin Luther King Jr., Obama distanced himself from their legacy by asserting that "the instruments of war do have a role to play in preserving the peace." "There will be times," he proclaimed, "when nations—acting individually or in concert—will find the use of force not only necessary but morally justified." Obama's speech was more than a theoretical justification of hypothetical violence. As commander in chief, he was responsible for justifying America's wars, even while he struggled to end them (Obama 2009).

Obama balanced his defense of just wars with a strong commitment to peace. His legacy in Iraq exemplifies that commitment, as well as its limits. In February 2009, soon after assuming the presidency, Obama declared that American combat troops would be withdrawn from Iraq by the end of 2011. As a first step, he outlined plans to reduce the number of troops from 160,000 to 50,000 by the fall of 2010. In August 2010, the only remaining combat brigade partially fulfilled Obama's promise by crossing the border into Kuwait. Some 50,000 American soldiers remained in Iraq to protect American bases, to advise Iraqi soldiers, and to conduct counterterrorism operations. Most of those remaining soldiers were withdrawn by October 2011. In the summer of 2014, Obama authorized the return of several hundred soldiers, as a result of the explosive growth of the Islamic State of Iraq and Syria (ISIS), an organization that Obama deemed "a terrorist organization, pure and simple." Unlike many terrorist organizations, however, ISIS gained control of thousands of square miles, as well as several important cities and oil complexes. The growth of ISIS left in question the long-term stability of Iraq and the wider region, as well as the role that the US military would play in guaranteeing that stability (Hartmann 2014).

As in Iraq, the war in Afghanistan strained Obama's efforts to bring American troops home after he inherited a conflict he promised to end. In Iraq, Obama's predecessor had authorized a "surge" of troops. After extensive lobbying by his military advisers, Obama came to support a similar surge in Afghanistan. Not long after taking office, Obama sent an additional 21,000 troops to Afghanistan, bringing the total number of American soldiers there to approximately 60,000. In December 2009, at the request of General Stanley McChrystal, the commander of US forces in Afghanistan, Obama announced a second surge of some 33,000 troops. Obama promised to begin withdrawing these forces from Afghanistan by July 2011. After General McChrystal's resignation in mid-2010, Obama replaced him with General David Petraeus, who had orchestrated the Iraq surge.

While Obama was criticized by some commentators for sending additional troops, others attacked him for establishing a time limit on the American military presence in Afghanistan. Despite these criticisms, Obama persisted with what he saw as a moderate and pragmatic approach to the conflict. His public approval rating received a boost in May 2011, when a team of Navy SEALs killed Osama bin Laden in a safe house in Pakistan. The following month, Obama announced that 10,000 troops would be withdrawn from Afghanistan by the end of the year and an additional 23,000 troops would leave by the summer of 2012. Those cuts reduced the size of the American force in Afghanistan—roughly 100,000 soldiers—by one-third. Further withdrawals followed. At the end of September 2014, approximately 24,000 US soldiers remained in Afghanistan.

DIPLOMATIC EFFORTS

Obama explained his withdrawal of troops from Iraq and Afghanistan as, in part, a matter of global strategy. He argued that the United States needed to refocus resources in other parts of the world, especially Asia. The growth of China's economy and military led Obama and his first secretary of state, Hillary Rodham Clinton, to seek to strengthen American partnerships in Asia. Obama's first official state visitor was Manmohan Singh, the prime minister of India, who traveled to Washington, DC, in November 2009. In 2012 Obama became the first sitting American president to visit Myanmar, and he worked to strengthen ties with Japan, Indonesia, and other major Asian nations.

In addition to bolstering the American presence in Asia, Obama asked Clinton to encourage a lasting peace accord between Israelis and Palestinians. Obama's second secretary of state, John Kerry, likewise prioritized peace in the Middle East. Neither Clinton nor Kerry proved able to broker any lasting agreements. Meanwhile, a civil war in Syria contributed to the further destabilization of the Middle East.

Obama's diplomats confronted equally stubborn challenges in Africa. In his 1995 autobiography, *Dreams from My Father*, Obama had offered readers an inclusive conception of black identity that reframed his personal history in terms of the larger effort to achieve unity within the global African diaspora. "I can embrace my black brothers and sisters, whether in this country or in Africa," Obama asserted, "and affirm a common destiny without pretending to speak to, or for, all our various struggles" (Obama 1995, xxii). As president, Obama's African initiatives focused on supporting economic development while checking the spread of corruption and violent extremism. In the summer of 2014, Obama told delegates at the US-Africa Leaders Summit in Washington, DC, that he would authorize some $33 billion in new American investments in Africa.

IMMIGRATION AND ENVIRONMENTAL POLICY

As in his relations with Africa, Obama's personal history intersected with his foreign policy when he confronted matters of immigration. During his first campaign for the presidency, Obama declared, "I have brothers, sisters, nieces, nephews, uncles and cousins, of every race and every hue, scattered across three continents, and for as long as I live, I will never forget that in no other country on Earth is my story even possible" (Obama 2008). As he had in regard to American military power, Obama argued that it was precisely American pluralism that defined American exceptionalism. As a candidate for office, Obama had to repel specious claims that he was not born in Hawaii but overseas, or that his name proved that he was a Muslim extremist. Obama's racial identity helped fuel widespread efforts to portray him as an outsider. In response, he used his identity as the child of peripatetic parents to tap into the powerful narrative of the United States as a nation of immigrants. He used the global nature of his childhood to defend his identity as an American. Obama's personal connection to immigration helped inspire him to rethink American immigration policy. In November 2014 Obama declared his intention to use executive orders to transform the American immigration system.

Obama has also used executive orders to defend the environment both within and beyond the borders of the United States. Many threats to environmental sustainability are inherently global and require international collaboration. Obama has argued that no one country can prevent the destruction of the rainforests or the poisoning of the oceans. Global climate change is especially demanding of international attention. In 2008, while campaigning for the presidency, Obama promised to take action against global climate change. "In my administration," he declared, "the rise of the oceans will begin to slow" (McKibben 2013). In 2013 Obama outlined plans to use executive action to reduce greenhouse gases. In November 2014 he signed an accord with China to reduce greenhouse gas emissions.

AMERICA'S PLACE IN THE WIDER WORLD

As his focus on immigration and environmental sustainability make clear, Obama's foreign policy has been informed by his domestic policies. Obama has argued repeatedly that what is best for the world is also best for America and for Americans. Take the importance of tolerance, for example. In the preface to the reissue of his autobiography (2004), Obama connected the struggle against religious fundamentalism on the global stage to the struggle against racism within the United States. He turned to the tragic events of September 11, 2001, to make clear those connections. Obama personalized the linkage between racial division and other forms of global divisiveness by locating his own story in relation to the struggle "between those who embrace our teeming, colliding, irksome diversity, while still insisting on a set of values that binds us together, and those who would seek, under whatever flag or slogan or sacred text, a certainty and simplification that justifies cruelty toward those not like us" (Obama 2004, xiv). In his leadership and his own life,

Obama has struggled to demonstrate that toleration of difference is the only path to lasting harmony—at home or abroad.

Obama has positioned his foreign policy as a middle ground between timid isolationism and bellicose interventionism. Speaking at the US Military Academy at West Point in May 2014, Obama defended his foreign policy and himself against charges that neither sufficiently recognized the "exceptional" role of the United States and its military on the world stage. "I believe in American exceptionalism with every fiber of my being," Obama proclaimed. "But what makes us exceptional," he added, "is not our ability to flout international norms and the rule of law; it is our willingness to affirm them through our actions." Thus, Obama balanced American patriotism with cosmopolitan internationalism by defining internationalism as itself a form of patriotism. He called the United States "the one indispensable nation" and declared, "America must always lead on the world stage" (Obama 2014). But Obama made clear that leadership meant working with other countries—at least whenever possible. He argued that American power increases as a result of participation in international dialogue.

SEE ALSO *Clinton, Hillary Rodham; Exceptionalism; Global Warming; Israel; Middle East; War on Terror*

BIBLIOGRAPHY

Clinton, Hillary Rodham. *Hard Choices*. New York: Simon and Schuster, 2014.

Hartmann, Margaret. "Obama Announces 4-Point Plan to 'Hunt Down' ISIS Terrorists." *New York Magazine*, September 10, 2014. http://nymag.com/daily/intelligencer/2014/09/obama-speech-isis-plan.html

Indyk, Martin S., Michael E. O'Hanlon, and Kenneth G. Lieberthal. *Bending History: Barack Obama's Foreign Policy*. Washington DC: Brookings Institution Press, 2012.

Joseph, Peniel. *Dark Days, Bright Nights: From Black Power to Barack Obama*. New York: Basic Civitas, 2010.

Kloppenberg, James T. *Reading Obama: Dreams, Hope, and the American Political Tradition*. Princeton, NJ: Princeton University Press, 2010.

Mann, James. *The Obamians: The Struggle inside the White House to Redefine American Power*. New York: Penguin, 2012.

McKibben, Bill. "Obama and Climate Change: The Real Story." *Rolling Stone*, December 17, 2013. http://www.rollingstone.com/politics/news/obama-and-climate-change-the-real-story-20131217

Obama, Barack. *Dreams from My Father: A Story of Race and Inheritance*. New York: Times Books, 1995. Reissued by Random House, 2004.

Obama, Barack. *The Audacity of Hope: Thoughts on Reclaiming the American Dream*. New York: Crown, 2006.

Obama, Barack. Transcript: Barack Obama's Speech on Race. March 18, 2008. http://www.nytimes.com/2008/03/18/us/ politics/18text-obama.html?pagewanted=print&_r=0

Obama, Barack. Remarks by the President at the Acceptance of the Nobel Peace Prize. December 10, 2009. http://www .whitehouse.gov/the-press-office/remarks-president- acceptance-nobel-peace-prize

Obama, Barack. Remarks by the President at the United States Military Academy Commencement Ceremony. May 28, 2014. http://www.whitehouse.gov/the-press-office/2014/05/28/ remarks-president-united-states-military-academy-commence ment-ceremony

Sanger, David E. *The Inheritance: The World Obama Confronts and the Challenges to American Power.* New York: Crown, 2009.

Sanger, David E. *Confront and Conceal: Obama's Secret Wars and Surprising Use of American Power.* New York: Crown, 2012.

Sugrue, Thomas J. *Not Even Past: Barack Obama and the Burden of Race.* Princeton, NJ: Princeton University Press, 2010.

Nico Slate
Associate Professor of History
Carnegie Mellon University

OFFICE OF FAITH-BASED COMMUNITY INITIATIVES

SEE *Department of State.*

OFFICE OF THE HISTORIAN

SEE *Department of State.*

OIL EMBARGO

SEE *Organization of the Petroleum Exporting Countries (OPEC).*

OLYMPICS

In the twenty-first century the Olympics rank as the most common shared experience on Earth. More people tune in to televised Olympics coverage than to any other global television program. More than 70 percent of the world's population—or about 5 billion people—watched the 2008 Beijing Olympics and the 2012 London Olympics. In the United States the Olympics rank as the most-watched global event, far outpacing World Cup soccer—a spectacle virtually tied with the Olympics in broadcast ratings around the rest of the globe. The contemporary popularity of the Olympics in the United States has older roots, dating to the origins of the modern games in the 1890s. From the beginning the United States became enmeshed in the Olympics to a greater degree than it did in any international movement. The United States has sometimes resisted cooperative international endeavors and routinely retreated to ideological if not actual isolationism, from refusing to join the League of Nations that US President Woodrow Wilson helped to create after World War I (1914–1918) to a more recent repudiation of the International Criminal Court, but Americans have missed only one Olympics, when the United States boycotted the 1980 Moscow games.

As of 2015 the United States held a commanding lead in the overall medal count, tabulating performances from Athens, Greece, in 1896 to Sochi, Russia, in 2014, with 2,684 gold, silver, and bronze medals, more than double the total won by the Soviet Union (1,204). That lead seems secure given that the now extinct Soviet state will presumably garner no more Olympic medals. The United States has hosted more Olympics than any other nation as well, a total of eight (four summer and four winter games). The next closest rival is France with five (two summer and three winter).

Since the 1890s the Olympics have provided a crucial location for the United States to engage the world. Like the earlier world's fair movement on which much of the Olympic scaffolding is built, these sporting contests create an international space where nations measure themselves against rivals, craft narratives that express national identities, and develop relationships with other nations. At the Olympics the United States has articulated and argued about competing visions of national identity, designed and implemented programs for "Americanizing" the Olympic movement, and collaborated with and confronted other nations as well as the transnational agency that has long governed the movement— the International Olympic Committee (IOC).

AMERICAN EXCEPTIONALISM AND OLYMPIC EXPERIENCES

The modern Olympics emerged at the end of the nineteenth century from a trove of competing schemes for international athletic contests circulating regularly in the world press. The Baron Pierre de Coubertin, a French aristocrat (1863–1937), brought the Olympic movement to life. Inspired in part by the Greek Olympics of antiquity, Coubertin constructed a modern spectacle that embraced international and national dimensions. Like the world's fairs, the Olympics sought to include participants from every corner of the globe and made the nation the fundamental unit of organization, ensuring that the games would serve as measuring sticks of national prowess. Nationalism suffused Coubertin's internationalist venture in another way. Like many of his generation he feared that France was slipping into global insignificance.

In Anglo-American sporting traditions, Coubertin identified an antidote to French decline, seeking to inoculate his own nation against cultural torpor by having it fall in love with competitive sports.

The British routinely ignored Coubertin's Olympics for decades, although imperial dominions, especially Australia and Canada, regularly sent teams. In contrast, the United States played a major role from the beginning.

Flag bearer Lopez Lomong (a Sudanese immigrant distance runner) and other members of Team USA in the Summer Olympics opening ceremony, Beijing, August 2008. Since 1896 the strains of American exceptionalism have dominated narratives of nationhood in Olympic arenas. American teams have embodied an idealized "melting pot" that mixes blacks and whites, immigrants and the native-born, and rich and poor into a world-beating coalition. **BOB ROSATO/GETTY IMAGES**

William Milligan Sloane (1850–1928), who taught French history at Princeton University, served as a founding member of the IOC and organized an American contingent headlined by Princeton athletes to compete in the inaugural 1896 Olympics in Athens. When the Americans dominated the track and field contests, the US media hailed their victories as symbolic of the youthful vitality, democratic institutions, and egalitarian character of the Republic, inaugurating a tradition of defining Olympic triumphs as an element in the folklore of American exceptionalism. As James Connolly (1868–1957), the first US Olympic champion, who later became an international correspondent covering the games, proclaimed, Americans won Olympic victories not because they possessed superior athletes but because they had built a superior society.

Since 1896 the strains of American exceptionalism have dominated narratives of nationhood in Olympic arenas. Early interpreters dubbed US teams "America's athletic missionaries," icons of the Republic who personified the virtues of good citizenship. American teams became avatars of social promise, compromising in popular depictions every social class, ethnic group, and religious affiliation—and, beginning in the 1920s when women gained official entry into Olympic sport, female as well as male "athletic missionaries." In these portraits American teams embodied an idealized "melting pot" that mixed blacks and whites, immigrants and the native-born, and rich and poor into a world-beating coalition. American interpreters have insisted that the nation's Olympic triumphs signify not merely athletic superiority but the preeminence of American culture above the rest of the globe's social constellations.

When, before World War I, the European press condemned American teams as collections of "immigrant mercenaries," its American counterpart replied that US teams were an unbeatable "union of all races." During the 1920s Americans celebrated the ethnic roots of Olympic swimming stars Gertrude Ederle (1905–2003; the daughter of German immigrants) and Johnny Weissmuller (1904–1984; an immigrant from the Austro-Hungarian Empire). At the 2002 Salt Lake City games, melting-pot paeans reappeared in the American media, as African Americans, Asian Americans, and Hispanic Americans earned medals for Team USA in sports previously considered the bastions of mainstream whites. At Beijing in 2008 the American media gushed when Sudanese immigrant distance runner Lopez Lomong (b. 1985) earned the honor of carrying the Stars and Stripes in the opening parade.

The faith in American exceptionalism expressed in these melting-pot narratives emerges in other Olympic tales as well. In the Olympics the United States can magically transform itself from the wealthiest and most powerful nation on Earth into an underdog that overcomes insurmountable odds to conquer rivals. That script resides behind the 1980 "Miracle on Ice" at Lake Placid, when a supposedly ragtag collection of Americans defeated the mighty Soviet ice hockey machine on the way to winning an unexpected gold medal. For more than three decades this Cold War "miracle" has generated an endless supply of "Star-Spangled" books, movies, and other popular culture artifacts that generate powerful visions of American nationhood, although in 1980 the matchup with the Soviets was not even broadcast on live television.

Homages to American exceptionalism also spark alternative Olympic narratives. Other nations point to American affluence as an explanation for US dominance rather than acceding to claims that United States possesses a superior society. Jamaica, Norway, and many other countries have turned to medal counts based on per-capita Olympic victories or triumphs prorated by gross domestic product to celebrate alternative claims of national superiority. The Olympics also provides opportunities for communities within the United States to challenge claims about inclusion and equity. In the early twentieth century Irish American athletes won a host of Olympic medals for the United States, spurring Irish American commentators to challenge stereotypes of Anglo-Saxon superiority. At the 1936 Berlin Olympics, in the face of tremendous racial hostility from the Nazi regime, Jesse Owens (1913–1980) won an unprecedented four gold medals in track and field. His fellow "black auxiliaries," as the German press labeled his African American teammates, added another four gold, three silver, and two bronze medals. Their performances unleashed a torrent of self-congratulatory devotionals proclaiming that black Americans could flourish in the United States A determined cohort of dissenters in both the black and white press replied that while Owens and the black auxiliaries had delivered a blow to Nazi racism in Berlin's Olympic Stadium, in many places in the United States they were not allowed to run, jump, go to school with, or engage in a host of other daily activities with their fellow white citizens.

NATIONAL AND INTERNATIONAL ISSUES

Thirty-two years later, two African American sprinters, Tommie Smith (b. 1944) and John Carlos (b. 1945), dramatically repackaged this racial counternarrative to American exceptionalism when they donned black gloves and gave a Black Power salute on the medal podium after winning gold and bronze medals, respectively, at the 1968 Mexico City Olympics. Their powerful dissent from the traditional Olympic tributes to American exceptionalism represented the culmination of decades of challenges to racial barriers and sparked controversy not only in the United States but around the world. As members of the Olympic Project for Human Rights (OPHR), Smith and Carlos not only campaigned against racism in their own country but also condemned South African apartheid. Australian Peter Norman (1942–2006), who earned a silver medal by finishing between Smith and Carlos, joined in the protest by sporting an OPHR patch on his track suit as well as denouncing his homeland's "White Australia Policy."

National and international issues intersected in many other Olympic incidents. In the early 1900s Irish American Olympians supported the inclusion of their kinsmen on separate Irish teams rather than on Great Britain's squads. In later decades the US government lobbied the IOC to recognize American allies as Olympic "nations," including the US protectorate in the Philippines. In 1972 after Palestinian terrorists attacked Israeli athletes in Munich, West Germany, ultimately killing eleven of them, President Richard Nixon and his advisers pondered declaring a national day of mourning but decided instead to use the murders to press the United Nations to take a more serious stance against global terrorism. During the Cold War, when questions of which of the "two" Germanys, "two" Koreas, and "two" Chinas the IOC should recognize precipitated international diplomatic crises, the United States consistently supported the inclusion of its protectorates—West Germany, South Korea, and the Republic of China (Taiwan)—in the Olympic "family."

The United States also has a long tradition of confronting its rivals and enemies at the Olympics. Great Britain served as the original American Olympic foil. Americans routinely charged the British with anti-American bias, leading even the ardent Anglophile and US president Theodore Roosevelt (1858–1919) to scold Britain from his "bully pulpit" for poor sportsmanship at the 1908 London games. After World War I, as the United States began to surpass Great Britain not only in Olympic medals but in many other measures of national vitality, new enemies appeared. During the 1930s, the American press portrayed the Olympics as surrogate wars against totalitarian powers: Italy, Japan, and Germany. The United States very nearly boycotted the 1936 Olympics in Germany. To register American opposition to the Nazi regime, the American team refused to dip the flag to Adolf Hitler. This 1936 refusal rather than an earlier Irish American challenge to an English king in 1908 in London marked the starting point for the consistent American refusal to lower its national flag at the Olympics.

In spite of the heroics of Owens and his African American teammates, Germany easily bested the United States in the 1936 medal count. Combined with the results that Italy bettered France's total and Japan surpassed Great Britain's mark, the 1936 Olympics was interpreted by many as evidence that the Axis had surpassed the republics of the West. Some American observers offered an alternative explanation. Rather than acquiesce to the arguments that German, Japanese, and Italian victories heralded the superiority of totalitarian societies, they accused their enemies of cheating in various ways and of fielding teams of robotic automatons who subverted the spirit of "true" sport. Such arguments would become stock explanations in the future as new Olympic enemies emerged to challenge American superiority in the games.

THE OLYMPICS AND THE COLD WAR

In the Cold War that followed World War II (1939–1945), the Soviet Union emerged to challenge the United States in Olympic arenas. In the Cold War superpower clashes at summer games, beginning with the Soviet debut in 1952 at Helsinki, the Soviets outpaced the United States in total medals and gold medals at Melbourne in 1956, Rome in 1960, Munich in 1972, and Seoul in 1988. The United States triumphed only at Helsinki in 1952 and Mexico City in 1968. At Tokyo in 1964 the United States won more gold medals but the Soviets won the most total medals. In Montreal in 1976 the United States finished second overall but third behind the Soviets and East Germany in gold medals. In Cold War winter Olympics the Soviets claimed medal count victories in every game from their debut at Cortina d'Ampezzo in 1956 through the 1988 Calgary installment. The United States finished no higher than third and as low as ninth in that era.

When the United States beat the Soviets in Olympic contests, Americans interpreted victory as a signal of social superiority. When the United States lost to the Soviets—a more frequent occurrence—it raised fears of national decline. "Soft Americans" in the parlance of ardent cold warrior president John F. Kennedy (1917–1963) could not compete with their Soviet counterparts. Equally common were explanations that labeled the Soviets as robotic automatons programmed to cheat whenever possible, thus subverting the spirit of "true sport"—a resurrection of the old charges leveled at German, Italian, and Japanese rivals. Routine claims that Olympians from the Soviet bloc won medals with state-sponsored doping programs added a new wrinkle to the charges. In fact, the ingestion of such substances represented a common practice in both the East and the West—with the United States and its allies generally at the cutting edge of the pharmaceutical arms race.

The enmity between the Cold War rivals reached its apogee in the 1980s when the United States boycotted the

1980 Moscow Olympics to protest the Soviet incursion into Afghanistan. The Soviets refused to compete at the 1984 Los Angeles Olympics. A decade later, as the Soviet Empire unraveled and the Cold War evaporated, the Soviet versus US Olympic rivalry dissolved. In the twenty-first century a new superpower emerged to challenge the United States as the People's Republic of China launched an ambitious athletic program to garner Olympic supremacy. At the 2008 Olympics, hosted by Beijing, China won the gold medal race while the United States prevailed in the overall medal count. At the 2012 London Olympics, the United States surged back into the lead in both categories.

DISPUTES WITH THE IOC

Beyond crowing about medal counts and threatening boycotts, the United States has long struggled with the IOC to shape the Olympics. In the early 1900s the head of the American Olympic Committee, James Sullivan (1862–1914), and the head of the IOC, Coubertin, engaged in a protracted struggle for control of the games. In the current era the US Olympic Committee and the IOC quarrel over revenue-sharing agreements. Americans sought to include their national pastimes on the Olympic program, including American football, which was a demonstration sport at Los Angeles in 1932 but has never again been seen at an Olympic venue. Baseball had more success, appearing several times as a demonstration sport before enjoying a short reign as a medal sport from 1992 to 2008 before the IOC dropped it. Basketball has been the most successful at cracking the Olympic lineup, debuting as a medal sport in 1936 at Berlin and remaining on the program ever since.

More recently, American interest groups included US-invented "action sports," including beach volleyball, triathlon, mountain and BMX cycling, snowboarding, and freestyle skiing, on Olympic programs. The inclusion of such sports has not only increased the medal haul for the United States but created new global markets for US corporations to sell products and promote American lifestyles. Entrepreneurs have used the Olympics to market products and ways of life since the 1900s, when America's athletic missionaries won glory and A. G. Spalding and Brothers, an early sporting goods manufacturer, outfitted the team and advertised its wares in Olympic stadiums. A century later Nike and other companies have eclipsed Spalding as Olympian advertisers, but in American corporate and public imaginations the Olympic movement remains the most important international venue for projecting American cultural power around the world.

SEE ALSO *Baseball; National Basketball Association (NBA)*

BIBLIOGRAPHY

Baker, William J. *Jesse Owens: An American Life.* New York: Free Press, 1986.

Barney, Robert Knight, Stephen R. Wenn, and Scott G. Martyn. *Selling the Five Rings: The International Olympic Committee and the Rise of Olympic Commercialism.* Salt Lake City: University of Utah Press, 2002.

Brownell, Susan, ed. *The 1904 Anthropology Days and Olympic Games: Sport, Race, and American Imperialism.* Lincoln: University of Nebraska Press, 2008.

Cayleff, Susan E. *Babe: The Life and Legend of Babe Didrikson Zaharias.* Urbana: University of Illinois Press, 1995.

Dyreson, Mark. *Making the American Team: Sport, Culture, and the Olympic Experience.* Urbana: University of Illinois Press, 1998.

Dyreson, Mark. *Crafting Patriotism for Global Dominance: America at the Olympic Games.* London: Routledge, 2009.

Dyreson, Mark. "The Republic of Consumption at the Olympic Games: Globalization, Americanization, and Californization." *Journal of Global History* 8, 2 (July 2013): 256–278.

Hartmann, Douglas. *Race, Culture, and the Revolt of the Black Athlete: The 1968 Olympic Protests and Their Aftermath.* Chicago: University of Chicago Press, 2003.

Hunt, Thomas M. *Drug Games: The International Olympic Committee and the Politics of Doping, 1960/2008.* Austin: University of Texas Press, 2011.

Katchen, Alan S. *Abel Kiviat, National Champion: Twentieth-Century Track & Field and the Melting Pot.* Syracuse, NY: Syracuse University Press, 2009.

Llewellyn, Matthew P., John Gleaves, and Wayne Wilson, eds. *The 1984 Los Angeles Olympic Games: Assessing the 30-Year Legacy.* London: Routledge, 2015.

Lucas, John A. *The Modern Olympic Games.* South Brunswick, NJ: A. S. Barnes, 1980.

Sarantakes, Nicholas Evan. *Dropping the Torch: Jimmy Carter, the Olympic Boycott, and the Cold War.* New York: Cambridge University Press, 2011.

Smith, Maureen Margaret. *Wilma Rudolph: A Biography.* Westport, CT: Greenwood Press, 2006.

Wenn, Stephen R., Robert Knight Barney, and Scott G. Martyn. *Tarnished Rings: The International Olympic Committee and the Salt Lake City Bid Scandal.* Syracuse, NY: Syracuse University Press, 2011.

Mark Dyreson
Professor of Kinesiology and Affiliate Professor of History
Pennsylvania State University, University Park

Adam Berg
PhD Candidate, History and Philosophy of Sport Program
in the Department of Kinesiology
Pennsylvania State University, University Park

Thomas Rorke
PhD Candidate, History and Philosophy of Sport Program
in the Department of Kinesiology
Pennsylvania State University, University Park

OPEN DOOR POLICY

Open Door is a protean and positive-sounding phrase, but the US government's Open Door Notes of 1899 and 1900 and the Open Door policy resulting from them proved to be much more than a catchy slogan. The policy, calling for international free trade and investment, not only signaled an important turning point in the history of US foreign relations. It also encapsulated many important tenets of the US worldview. In formulating the Open Door policy, US leaders were heavily influenced by British businessman-politician Richard Cobden (1804–1865), who argued that free trade and investment across international borders would lead to an increasingly interdependent, prosperous, peaceful, and stable world. Of course, US leaders also assumed that American businessmen would eventually reap great profits in the China trade, as by the late nineteenth century they were beginning to outcompete their international rivals.

BACKGROUND

US trade with China, although small, stretched back to 1784, and Americans very much coveted China's tea, silks, and furniture. (US traders did not have a great deal the Chinese wanted, with the exception of pelts and furs.) However, the roots of the Open Door policy can be found in the 1839–1842 Opium War, in which the British defeated the Chinese. One important cause of the war was that Chinese leaders, fearing the continued social degeneration of Chinese society due to opium exported from Britain's colony in India, put strict limits on the opium trade. For Britain, opium sales were very important—it was the one lucrative product the Chinese purchased from the British.

Second, after the Opium War, much to the displeasure of the Chinese, the British forced China to give them an indemnity, as well as control of Hong Kong. China also granted extraterritoriality rights to the British—one of the first times such a grant was given to foreigners anywhere. Under extraterritoriality, British citizens in China could be prosecuted under British, rather than Chinese, law.

Third, the British gained control over five Chinese "treaty ports" that had to allow British traders—a significant benefit given the previous restrictiveness of China's trade. The British also required the Chinese to grant them "most-favored-nation" (MFN) status, which meant that if the Chinese extended any trade preference to any foreign nation, that preference would be automatically extended to Britain. The MFN was an effective way for the British to ratchet down trade barriers around the world. The British, as the top industrial nation in the world, needed both inexpensive raw materials from abroad and markets to sell their goods. Free trade, therefore, was a must for them.

Fourth, of special importance, the British experience cleared the way for the United States as it signed similar treaties with China in 1844, 1858, and 1868. These granted the Americans largely the same benefits as the British. The Chinese wanted to keep foreign powers on an equal footing.

From China's perspective, the Opium War was a humiliation that caused antiforeigner movements to spring up in China and a great deal of soul searching on the part of the Chinese. Thus, in the mid-to-late nineteenth century, China put in place the "self-strengthening" movement, which aimed to strengthen China economically and militarily. Despite these efforts, China's humiliation continued, with the further division of China by the late nineteenth century into European and Japanese "spheres of influence" where each imperialist power enjoyed exclusive control. Imperialism was in full swing, as the wealthy nations of the world sought resources as well as political gain in Asia. The fear was that if a nation did not expand its influence in Asia, its competitors would get there first.

US officials looked nervously across the Pacific at these developments. Although the US Navy in the 1890s was one of the fastest-growing navies in the world, the US military did not have the wherewithal to project its power onto the Asia mainland to the extent that the Europeans and Japanese did. Yet, the United States desperately aimed to prevent the imperialists from "carving the Chinese melon," as it was termed in those days, and locking out US businessmen.

By the late nineteenth century, a body of thought was emerging in the United States that the economic ills of the devastating 1890s depression, which had caused a great deal of pain and labor strife in many parts of the United States, could be alleviated by increased foreign trade, facilitated by obtaining access to foreign ports. One key area of interest was Asia. US trade with Asia was small as a percentage of total US trade, but the US-Asian trade was growing briskly. US gunboats "opened" (at the point of a cannon) Japan in 1853. In 1867, Secretary of State William Seward (1801–1872) arranged the purchase of Alaska from Russia largely because of Alaska's excellent ports and proximity to Asia. In 1898, a year before the first Open Door Note was issued, the United States not only "annexed" Hawai'i against the will of many of its inhabitants, but also, by defeating Spain in the 1898 Spanish-American War, obtained key ports in its new colonies of the Philippines and Guam. In addition, the United States obtained from Spain key ports in Cuba and Puerto Rico to bolster trade in Latin America.

POLICY

There were two Open Door Notes, which together constitute the Open Door policy. US Secretary of State

John Hay formally asked France, Germany, Britain, Italy, Japan, and Russia to comply with the Open Door policy. Each one agreed to it in principle. In 1899, the United States issued the first Open Door Note, which aimed to dismantle European and Japanese "spheres of influence" in China. The idea was elegantly simple and reflected deeply held US views. Ideally, all of the outside powers operating in China would agree to an economic "fair field and no favor" policy. US officials were concerned that economic barriers would lead to conflict and war. Thus, if all of the outside nations in Asia agreed to eliminate their spheres of influence, the chances of political or military conflict would disappear over time. Eliminating economic restrictions was key.

US policy makers hoped to globalize the Open Door concept to the world beyond China, which would benefit both the United States and other nations by fostering vibrant, free-market economies everywhere. The Open Door policy worked well for the United States on many levels. The policy allowed the United States to appear to be acting in the best interest of the Chinese while at the same time promoting its own interests, even as the Chinese view proved unimportant to American negotiators. Indeed, Chinese historians have viewed the Open Door policy as one of a series of low points in Chinese history from the late nineteenth to the early twentieth centuries. For their part, US leaders were confident that their businessmen could outcompete others. Thus, a level playing field would most benefit the United States.

But the policy concerned more than economics. Not only did US businessmen dream of investing and selling in China, US Christian missionaries had been operating in China for years before the Open Door policy was introduced. China's population was large, and US missionaries viewed the Chinese as especially open to accepting their religion.

The second Open Door Note, issued in 1900, explicitly called on the outside powers to maintain the "territorial and administrative integrity" of China. The note was issued largely in response to the rise of the antiforeign Boxers in China, who killed a number of foreigners, including missionaries, in Beijing. During the Boxer uprising, many imperialist nations sent troops to Beijing to protect their citizens and their interests. The United States viewed these deployments as potentially dangerous—as the opening shot in a regional war in which China would be carved up by the imperialist powers, as was happening in Africa at the time. Importantly, when President William McKinley (1843–1901) ordered five thousand troops to Beijing in mid-1900 to protect Americans, particularly missionaries, they were the first US troops ever stationed on the Asian mainland. The troops were also expected to monitor the actions of the Europeans and Japanese. In the US worldview, China's territorial integrity was of paramount importance. Given its size and potential, China was a key player in Asia. Only if China could maintain itself as a coherent nation could it pursue the long-term economic growth necessary, it was thought, for political stability.

LEGACY

Why did the European and Japanese imperialists agree to the Open Door policy? From the British perspective, given their need for raw materials and markets, the Open Door policy benefited them more than the spheres-of-influence policy. The other powers agreed to the Open Door policy as a matter of public relations, but simply ignored the policy later when it suited their interests. As such, the spheres of interest were not immediately dismantled. For their part, the Japanese invaded China in 1894 to 1895. After all, there was no enforcement mechanism; in the early twentieth century, the United States did not have the ability to back up the policy with force, even if it wanted to.

The Open Door policy reveals a great deal about US foreign relations. Americans had a strong belief in the ability of vibrant economic activity to create not only stable societies but stable governments. Moreover, US leaders thought that an economically interdependent world, free of interventionism and imperialism, would facilitate the development of stable and eventually pro-US nations. The Open Door policy also represented the roots of Woodrow Wilson's (1856–1924) internationalism and his brainchild, the League of Nations, which had as one of its key goals maintaining the territorial integrity of all nations (i.e., a globalized version of the second Open Door Note). Indeed, one of his famous Fourteen Points called for freedom of the seas, a component of free trade and investment worldwide.

Furthermore, the United States put a lot of stock in noninterventionism in the 1928 Kellogg-Briand Pact, which outlawed war. Although later dismissed as an "international kiss" by many historians, the pact was taken seriously at the time. Eventually signed by sixty-two of the world's more prominent countries, the pact reflected post–World War I shock at the war's senseless slaughter. Like the Open Door policy and Wilson's Fourteen Points, the pact aimed to promote noninterventionism, as well as (especially economic) interdependence, thus supposedly inoculating the world against future wars. But, like the Open Door policy, the Kellogg-Briand Pact had no enforcement mechanism. In 1931, the Japanese defied both the Open Door policy and the Kellogg-Briand Pact in its invasion of Chinese Manchuria, which Japan eventually turned into a Japanese colony.

The Open Door policy marked an important turning point in US policy toward Asia, as well as the rest of the world. Even as US leaders saw the Open Door as indicative of noninterventionism, in the twentieth century the United States would be much more forceful in asserting, and backing up with force, its interests overseas, particularly in Asia. When Japan's early twentieth-century aggression in China and Southeast Asia became so egregious that the United States issued warnings, the result was World War II in the Pacific. The legacy of the Open Door policy continues to have significance for US foreign relations. Current US-China relations in many respects are based on trade and investment, which benefits both countries.

Even though the US leadership in the late nineteenth century viewed the Open Door policy as helping a China in distress, more than a century later, the tables have turned as Chinese economic growth outstrips that of the United States. Further, the Chinese government has purchased a large number of US Treasury securities, allowing the US government to spend beyond its means, perhaps giving the Chinese leverage over US policies. Those who came up with the Open Door policy in the late nineteenth century could never in their wildest dreams have conceived of the deep economic integration that has developed between the two economic giants of the twenty-first century, the United States and China.

SEE ALSO *Britain; China; Internationalism; Interventionism; Japan; Kellogg-Briand Pact; Manchuria; Wilson, Woodrow*

BIBLIOGRAPHY

Cohen, Warren I. *America's Response to China: A History of Sino-American Relations.* 4th ed. New York: Columbia University Press, 2000.

Hu, Shizhang. *Stanley K. Hornbeck and the Open Door Policy, 1919–1937.* Santa Barbara, CA: Praeger, 1995.

Hunt, Michael H. *The Making of a Special Relationship: The United States and China to 1914.* New York: Columbia University Press, 1985.

Wang, Dong. *United States and China: A History from the Eighteenth Century to the Present.* Lanham, MD. Rowman and Littlefield, 2013.

Young, Marilyn B. *The Rhetoric of Empire: American China Policy, 1895–1901.* Cambridge, MA: Harvard University Press, 1968.

Zeiler, Thomas W. "Opening Doors in the World Economy." In *Global Interdependence: The World after 1945*, edited by Akira Iriye, 203–326. Cambridge, MA: Harvard University Press, 2014.

James F. Siekmeier
Associate Professor of History
West Virginia University

OPIUM WAR

The British and the Chinese fought the First Opium War in southern China from 1839 to 1842. A second war, known alternatively as the Second Opium War or the Arrow War, was fought from 1856 to 1860. The First Opium War began as a series of skirmishes over efforts to crack down on the opium traffic into southern China, but underlying causes included the drainage of Chinese silver (and thus currency), concern over opium addiction, conflicting legal and diplomatic norms, and simmering tensions over trade. In the United States, the war inspired headlines and editorializing, largely for its implications for Anglo-American relations. But the war had significant consequences for Americans, both transforming the basis of trade and travel for Americans in China and marking the beginning of formal diplomatic relations between the United States and China.

THE WAR'S BEGINNINGS

The war began with opium. In the 1830s the combined spread of opium addiction and decline in silver elicited concern in Beijing. Opium had a long history in China. Although China produced its own opium, in the latter half of the eighteenth century the trade in Asian opium surged as Portuguese and English merchants exchanged Indian opium for Chinese tea and silks. From 1800 to 1838 opium shipments into China exploded from 4,570 to 40,200 chests annually (Greenberg 1951). Americans also engaged in the trade, with notable exceptions such as Olyphant & Co. Scholars have suggested that by proving that the Chinese market could absorb yet more opium, American competition led the English to increase their own cargoes (Downs 1968; Igler 2004). Exporters often excused the traffic by noting that Chinese officials themselves abetted and profited from opium sales, or even that opium was no worse than alcohol, but critics of the expanded trade in opium could be found in England and America as well as in China.

In October 1838, the Daoguang Emperor (1782–1850) appointed Lin Zexu (1785–1850) to serve as special commissioner to handle the opium problem in southern China. Lin was an experienced reformer. In the 1820s, for example, Lin diffused a rising revolt over flooding along the Song River. By July 1839 Lin's policies led to the confiscation of nearly forty thousand catties of opium, the arrest of approximately sixteen hundred Chinese offenders, and the execution of many others (Chang 1964). But Commissioner Lin faced a greater challenge in handling the foreigners. On March 18, 1839, Lin issued a proclamation calling upon foreign merchants to surrender their opium stocks. Merchants volunteered a mere 1,037 chests, arguing that the drug was not theirs but was held on consignment (Hoe and Roebuck 1999).

Lin moved to arrest the most prominent British opium trader in residence, Lancelot Dent (1799[?]–1853), but he faced further resistance and protests opposing the execution of Dent. Lin responded by blockading the foreigners in Canton. Within six weeks, Lin had received over twenty thousand chests of opium for destruction (Spence 1990).

THE BRITISH RESPONSE

The standoff with Lin sparked outrage in London. Arguments that British honor had been insulted overcame indignation over the opium trade. Such arguments built on irritation over failed missions to press the Chinese to accept British demands for broader, regularized terms of trade and formal diplomatic relations: the 1793 Macartney mission, the 1816 Amherst mission, and, most recently, that of Lord William Napier (1786–1834) in 1834. In April 1840 Parliament narrowly approved taking military action. British fleets blockaded not only Canton but also Ningbo, stopping traffic into the Yangzi delta. Much to the chagrin of British belligerents, Americans continued the trade during the war. Robert Bennet Forbes (1804–1889) reported that the British plenipotentiary had personally entreated the prominent American house of Russell & Co. to withdraw. Forbes quipped, "We Yankees have no Queen to guarantee our losses" (Van 2011, 341). At first, such actions angered British traders, but soon they began trading via American middlemen. Thus, the Canton trade continued during the war.

While it seemed as though the war might end as early as January 1841, the two governments rejected an early settlement between the British plenipotentiary, Charles Elliot (1801–1875), and Lin's replacement, Qishan (1786–1854). In the summer of 1842, the British decisively defeated Chinese forces in the Yangzi delta, leaving the British able largely to dictate their terms.

THE AFTERMATH

The 1842 Treaty of Nanjing and its 1843 addendum, the Treaty of the Bogue, dismantled the existing basis of trade, often referred to as the "Canton system." Chinese officials initially hoped that Anglo-American tensions might allow for a Sino-American relationship to balance British demands. Instead, the American delegation under Caleb Cushing (1800–1879) negotiated what was to be the first of several copycat treaties with Western powers, the 1844 Treaty of Wanghia. These treaties are frequently referred to as the "unequal treaties" for their imposition of new trade and diplomatic relations on China. Western merchants previously traded through a single port in southern China—Canton (now known as Guangzhou). The postwar treaties forced China to open up four new ports to foreign trade and residence, female as well as male: Shanghai, Ningbo, Xiamen (Amoy), and Fuzhou. With Canton, these ports became known as "treaty ports." Further, the Canton system had limited legal trade to a cluster of licensed Chinese merchants belonging to the "Cohong" (a guild of Chinese merchants who operated the import-export monopoly in Canton) in order to regulate and stabilize relations with foreign merchants. The Treaty of Nanjing abolished the Cohong. The center of trade shifted from Canton to Shanghai.

The American treaty also included a provision on extraterritoriality. From 1844 to 1942, the State Department (and starting in 1906, a US district court for China), rather than Chinese courts, exercised legal jurisdiction over Americans in China. The British supplementary treaty included a "most favored nation" clause that stipulated that all privileges extended to other foreigners also applied to British subjects, effectively removing them from Chinese jurisdiction as well. These postwar treaties forced China to adapt to Western norms of statecraft, capitalism, and free trade—which, to Americans of the late nineteenth and early twentieth centuries, came to be known as the Open Door policy. The new "treaty port system" endured from 1842 to 1943.

SEE ALSO *Asia; China*

BIBLIOGRAPHY

Chang, Hsin-pao. *Commissioner Lin and the Opium War.* Cambridge, MA: Harvard University Press, 1964.

Chen, Li. *Chinese Law in the Imperial Eyes: Sovereignty, Justice, and Transcultural Politics, c. 1740s–1840s.* New York: Columbia University Press, 2015.

Downs, Jacques M. "American Merchants and the China Opium Trade, 1800–1840." *Business History Review* 42, 4 (Winter 1968): 418–42.

Downs, Jacques M. *The Golden Ghetto: The American Commercial Community at Canton and the Shaping of American China Policy, 1784–1844.* Bethlehem, PA: Lehigh University Press, 1997.

Fairbank, John K. *Trade and Diplomacy on the China Coast: The Opening of the Treaty Ports, 1842–1854.* Cambridge, MA: Harvard University Press, 1953.

Greenberg, Michael. *British Trade and the Opening of China, 1800–42.* Cambridge: Cambridge University Press, 1951.

Hoe, Susanna, and Derek Roebuck. *The Taking of Hong Kong: Charles and Clara Elliot in China Waters.* Richmond, UK: Curzon Press, 1999.

Igler, David. "Diseased Goods: Global Exchanges in the Eastern Pacific Basin, 1770–1850." *American Historical Review* 109, 3 (June 2004): 693–719.

Lovell, Julia. *The Opium War: Drugs, Dreams, and the Making of Modern China.* New York: Overlook Press, 2014.

Melancon, Glenn. *Britain's China Policy and the Opium Crisis: Balancing Drugs, Violence and National Honor.* Hampshire, UK: Ashgate, 2003.

Norwood, Dael. "Trading in Liberty: The Politics of the American China Trade, c. 1784-1862." PhD diss. Princeton University, 2012.

Scully, Eileen. *Bargaining with the State from Afar: American Citizenship in Treaty Port China, 1844–1942*. New York: Columbia University Press, 2000.

Spence, Jonathan D. *The Search for Modern China*. New York: Norton, 1990.

Van, Rachel Tamar. "Free Trade and Family Values: Kinship Networks and the Culture of Early American Capitalism." PhD diss., Columbia University, 2011.

Wang, Dong. *China's Unequal Treaties: Narrating National History*. Lanham, MD: Lexington Books, 2005.

Wang, Dong. *The United States and China: A History from the Eighteenth Century to the Present*. Lanham, MD: Rowman & Littlefield, 2013.

Rachel Tamar Van
Assistant Professor of History
Cal Poly Pomona

ORDERS IN COUNCIL, THE (1807)

SEE *Impressment.*

ORGANIZATION OF AMERICAN STATES (OAS)

Formed in 1948, the Organization of American States (OAS) was reconstituted from the Pan-American Union, which had been founded in 1890 (as the International Bureau for American Republics) to generate political and economic cooperation among American states. With the formation of the OAS, the Pan-American Union evolved into the new organization's permanent administrative and advisory machinery, with the OAS general secretariat housed in the Pan-American Union building in Washington, DC. The OAS itself was established as a regional agency to coordinate the work of a variety of inter-American departments recognized within the provisions of the United Nations (UN) charter. Its goal is to promote peace, economic cooperation, and social advancement in the Western Hemisphere. Each member state is allotted one representative to the Permanent Council and may send a delegation to the General Assembly, the organization's supreme organ. While most Latin American countries joined in 1948, membership expanded with the end of European imperialism in the Caribbean from the initial twenty-one members to the current thirty-five, with Guyana the last country to join in 1991.

Throughout its history, the OAS has been hampered by historic tensions between Latin American and Caribbean countries and the United States. In 1947, the year prior to the adoption of the OAS charter in Bogotá, the members of the Pan-American Union met in Rio de Janeiro to sign the Inter-American Treaty of Reciprocal Assistance (Rio Pact). Providing for mutual assistance in the event of an armed attack, the Rio Pact was the first permanent collective defense treaty signed by the United States and also the first regional collective security pact formed under the UN charter; the OAS was the first regional organization formed under the same agreement. Together, they form the legal and military structure of US hegemony in the hemisphere. Part of the developing Cold War regional defense architecture built up by the United States alongside the North Atlantic Treaty Organization (1949), Southeast Asia Treaty Organization (1954), and the Central Treaty Organization (1955), the OAS must be seen in the context of containment and Washington's desire to protect its southern flank. Indeed, the OAS is inextricably linked to US power. Thus, the Latin American signatories saw the OAS charter as upholding the principle of nonintervention, the key plank of Franklin Delano Roosevelt's (1882–1945) Good Neighbor Policy, which was codified, along with the equality of states, at the December 1933 Pan-American Conference in Montevideo as the Convention on the Rights and Duties of States. Washington, however, instead emphasized the Rio Pact and the OAS charter's provisions regarding the right of self-defense against external threats to hemispheric security.

Containing communism was made an explicit goal of the OAS in Bogotá in 1948 and, again, with the Caracas Declaration against communist penetration of the hemisphere in March 1954. Months later, a US-sponsored coup overthrew a democratically elected government in Guatemala, beginning a pattern of US Cold War intervention couched in international law based on the three-pronged security regime established in Rio, Bogotá, and Caracas. Thus, provisions for self-defense and anticommunism were invoked to give cover for US operations in the Dominican Republic in 1965, in Nicaragua and El Salvador in the 1980s, and in Panama in 1989, even as the OAS unanimously—except for the lone US vote—condemned the latter operation. However, the most controversial Cold War issue was Cuba, which was excluded from participation in the organization after a contentious vote in January 1962; two years later, OAS members joined in the US economic embargo against the island.

With the end of the Cold War, there was little need for Cuba's exclusion, and Latin American support for US political and economic sanctions—already thin—collapsed. Indeed, with the Soviet Union's implosion, the OAS shifted focus toward the war on drugs and, through the auspices of the Inter-American Court of Human Rights and Inter-American Commission on Human Rights, to dealing with violations of human rights. Pushing for this shift in attention—alongside a major focus on hemispheric free trade—Washington in 1994 also began the Summit of the Americas process, a triennial meeting of the regional heads of government. Beyond trade, drugs, and human rights, the OAS also took renewed interest in democratic development, with member states agreeing, in 2001, to the Inter-American Democratic Charter. Making the practice of democracy an explicit condition of OAS membership, the charter was invoked in 2009 temporarily to expel Honduras following a coup. Washington's questionable conduct during this incident, as well as mounting anger toward neoliberal economic policies, Cuba's continued suspension, and the ineffective drug war, led to major pushback against the United States. Two rival organizations now exist: the Bolivarian Alliance for the Peoples of Our America (2004), a group of ten far-left countries strongly opposed to US hegemony; and the Community of Latin American and Caribbean States (2011), made up of all OAS members, including Cuba, but not the United States or Canada. Whether these organizations will replace the OAS entirely remains to be seen.

SEE ALSO *Good Neighbor Policy; Human Rights; Mexico; South America; War on Drugs*

BIBLIOGRAPHY

Brands, Hal. *Latin America's Cold War.* Cambridge, MA: Harvard University Press, 2010.

Grandin, Greg. *Empire's Workshop: Latin America, the United States, and the Rise of the New Imperialism.* New York: Metropolitan Books, 2006.

Loveman, Brian. *No Higher Law: American Foreign Policy and the Western Hemisphere since 1776.* Chapel Hill: University of North Carolina Press, 2010.

Rabe, Stephen G. *The Killing Zone: The United States Wages Cold War in Latin America.* New York: Oxford University Press, 2012.

Schoultz, Lars. *Beneath the United States: A History of U.S. Policy toward Latin America.* Cambridge, MA: Harvard University Press, 1998.

Asa McKercher
Assistant Professor, Department of History
McMaster University

ORGANIZATION OF THE PETROLEUM EXPORTING COUNTRIES (OPEC)

The Organization of the Petroleum Exporting Countries (OPEC) was formed on September 14, 1960, in Bagdad. Its original membership consisted of Saudi Arabia, Venezuela, Iraq, Iran, and Kuwait (Qatar, Libya, Indonesia, the United Arab Emirates, and Algeria joined in the 1960s). OPEC was designed to challenge the power of the international oil companies that controlled the price, production levels, and distribution of a commodity (oil) upon which their economies depended.

THE CREATION OF OPEC

Until the 1970s, the international trade in oil was dominated by seven Anglo-American companies: Standard Oil of New Jersey (Exxon), Standard Oil of New York (Mobil), Standard Oil of California (Chevron), British Petroleum (BP), Royal Dutch Shell, Texaco Oil Company, and Gulf Oil Company. These companies, known as the majors, produced oil from the Middle East under long-term concession contracts through nation-specific consortiums.

The immediate trigger for the creation of OPEC was Standard Oil of New Jersey's unilateral decision in August 1960, without consulting Saudi Arabia, to reduce the posted price of oil it produced in Saudi Arabia by 7 percent. The other majors quickly followed suit. The posted price was the price that determined the royalties and taxes the majors paid to producing governments. But this was not the first time a major had instituted a price cut that the others quickly adopted. In February 1959 BP initiated a 10 percent price cut. That move inspired the oil-producing countries to convene an Arab Petroleum Conference (with Venezuela in attendance as an observer) in Cairo that April. Jersey's cut in August 1960 led to the Bagdad meeting the following month.

Jersey's decision, like BP's before it, was driven by changing market conditions, for in the middle decades of the twentieth century, the world was awash in oil. Large new discoveries were made in the Middle East in the years after World War II. Relatively poor, these Middle Eastern countries exerted strong pressure on the majors to produce as much oil as quickly as possible so as to maximize their revenue. When President Dwight D. Eisenhower (1890–1969) initiated a mandatory oil import quota for the United States in 1959, he effectively closed off the world's largest oil market to cheaper supplies of Middle Eastern oil. At this very moment, the Soviet Union began exporting sizable quantities of oil for the first time. And smaller, more nimble independent (i.e., nonmajor) American oil companies began exploring and producing oil overseas (which they could not import back into the United States). All of these factors placed a powerful downward pressure on oil prices. As a result, the majors' consortiums found themselves selling oil to their affiliates (related companies) at a discount in order to compete for customers in Europe (where most Middle Eastern oil was marketed in these years). The negotiated posted price no longer bore any relation to the actual price for oil. While world demand was growing rapidly, crude oil production had doubled in the 1950s with reserves skyrocketing.

OPEC was the idea of Juan Pablo Pérez Alfonso (1903–1979), the oil minister of Venezuela. In many ways, he took a page from American oil history. In the early 1930s, when US oil prices crashed, the government developed a system by which supply would be rationed by state authorities (e.g., the Texas Railroad Commission) so as to reduce inefficiency and waste (it was justified as a necessary conservation measure) but also to create an effective price floor. Pérez Alfonso saw that a cartel of major oil producers could also effectively regulate supply, increase prices, and put an end to the wasteful instinct of the oil-producing countries to push for maximum production. It could also become a powerful vehicle that would counter the consortiums and the majors standing behind them, thereby granting the oil-producing countries the power to determine production levels and prices. This desire to recover a basic degree of sovereignty was also inspired by Egyptian president Gamal Abdel Nasser's (1918–1970) belief that the oil-rich Middle Eastern countries needed to use petroleum as a weapon to help all the Arab states.

In the 1960s, OPEC was ignored by Western governments concerned that acknowledging the new organization would only serve to grant it legitimacy. A loose oil market provided OPEC a weak hand by which to negotiate a price increase while foreclosing a strategy of production cuts.

OPEC'S INCREASING CONTROL OVER PRODUCTION AND PRICES

But the United States, the world's largest producer, reached peak oil production in 1970, while the growth of oil demand in the United States and around the world continued to rise, creating a tighter world oil market. The turning point arrived in 1971 when, for the first time, OPEC negotiated collectively with the major Western oil companies, producing the Tehran Agreement, which called for an increase in the posted price and a higher tax rate. Oil producers were also granted a growing percentage of the oil to market on their own. As a result, oil production and prices moved into OPEC's control as the organization subsequently announced additional price increases over the course of the 1970s.

The single biggest price increase occurred during an oil embargo announced on October 17, 1973, by the Organization of Arab Petroleum Exporting Countries (OAPEC). Responding to US support for Israel in the 1973 Yom Kippur War, the Arab members of OPEC embargoed oil shipments to the United States and initiated a 5 percent production cut. On October 29,

OAPEC announced a 25 percent production cut, with the threat of additional 5 percent cuts each month their demands to cease assisting Israel were not met. The major oil companies did their best to lessen the impact of the embargo on the Western nations.

However, the embargo occurred at a time when the resiliency of the domestic US oil market was weakened by price controls and an emergency allocation system designed to promote equitable distribution and to protect independent oil companies. Due to the time it took tankers to deliver oil from the Middle East, the full effects of the embargo were not felt until February 1974, when the United States experienced an 8 percent reduction in oil supplies. Between October and February, prices rose from $3 to $12 a barrel. Americans paid $4 billion for foreign oil imports in 1972 and $25 billion in 1974, despite a 4 percent drop in domestic consumption. Although the embargo was lifted in March 1974, it contributed to an already high rate of inflation and tipped the nation into a balance-of-trade deficit.

US POLICY TOWARD OPEC

The embargo and price spike produced a series of policies designed to reduce domestic oil consumption, including CAFE (corporate average fuel economy) standards for automobiles, right-on-red laws, and speed limits. The embargo also led to policies designed to increase oil production: leasing millions of acres off the Atlantic and Pacific coasts to the oil industry; relaxing price controls on newly discovered oil; and exempting the Alaskan oil pipeline from the National Environmental Policy Act of 1969. The embargo also prodded the US government to create the strategic petroleum reserve, a government-owned stockpile of crude oil totaling (as of 2015) 695 million barrels held in four salt caverns along the Texas and Louisiana coast.

The goal of US foreign policy toward OPEC in the 1970s was to build stability into world oil prices while allowing inflation to blunt their economic impact. This consisted of efforts to strengthen the hand of the price "doves" within OPEC against the price "hawks." Doves, led by Saudi Arabia, argued for lower prices because with large reserves and small populations they had an interest in a more stable oil market. Hawks, led by Iran, consisted of countries with smaller reserves and larger populations; their interest was in maximizing the value of their oil as quickly as possible. The US government also concluded a number of bilateral agreements with important oil producers (most notably Saudi Arabia and Iran) that served to recycle petrodollars while supporting the Nixon Doctrine (both accomplished through arms agreements). At the end of 1978, the real price of oil was 10 percent lower than in 1974.

OPEC'S LONG-TERM IMPACT

High oil prices in the 1970s encouraged fuel substitution and conservation measures among consuming nations. The slow nationalization of the majors' oil concessions and high prices incentivized them to explore for and produce sizable new quantities of oil from the North Sea, the north slope of Alaska, and the Gulf of Mexico. Together, these changes placed downward pressure on oil prices, prompting OPEC for the first time to initiate production cutbacks in 1982. These efforts failed and the price of oil came, for the first time, to be set directly by market forces.

But for a time it appeared that OPEC had pioneered a new model that would reorder the international economy, restructuring the relationship between the Global North and South. This model called for cartels of other resources as part of an effort to make manufactured products and technology transfers cheaper for the Global South. The New International Economic Order was first articulated at the Algiers Conference of Non-Aligned Countries in 1973 and was incorporated into the United Nations Economic Charter in May 1974. However, no additional commodity cartels were successfully established. And lacking the resources to invest in conservation, oil-dependent developing economies suffered balance-of-payment and debt problems that would plague them for the next twenty years.

OPEC successfully engineered, in the 1970s, one of the largest transfers of wealth in world history. The end of the concessionary oil regime reordered the relationship between the Western industrial democracies and the Middle East. But the organization has not served as an economic model for less-developed countries.

SEE ALSO *Carter, James Earl, Jr.; Deindustrialization; Nixon, Richard Milhous*

BIBLIOGRAPHY

Rubino, Anna. *Queen of the Oil Club: The Intrepid Wanda Jablonski and the Power of Information.* Boston: Beacon Press, 2008.

Venn, Fiona. *The Oil Crisis.* London: Pearson, 2002.

Yergin, Daniel. *The Prize: The Epic Quest for Oil, Money, and Power.* New York: Free Press, 1991.

Robert Lifset
Donald Keith Jones Associate Professor of Honors and History
University of Oklahoma

ORIENT

The Orient is a not a specific place but rather a collection of ideas about imagined spaces. These ideas are embedded in US and European colonialism and imperialism.

Although the United States did not have heavy imperial investments in Africa or Asia (with the exception of the Philippines) until the mid-twentieth century, it was connected to European colonial conquests through trade and missionary networks. There were three main groups of Americans through which the Orient was imagined: missionaries, metaphysical seekers, and academics. These groups defined the Orient as the area between and including northern Africa, Palestine, and the Pacific coast—a vast region populated by heathens and characterized by deep spirituality and inferior cultures.

American Protestant missionaries followed their English and Scottish counterparts deep into the British Empire. One American Baptist missionary couple, Justus Vinton (1806–1858) and Calista Vinton (1807–1864), traveled from Connecticut to Burma (now Myanmar) in 1834 to preach the gospels to the Karen people. After their deaths, the Vintons' daughter, Calista Luther (c. 1841–1924) carried on their missionary work and chronicled their adventures in *The Vintons and Karens* (1880). This biography describes the lives of the Karen people, who are referred to as "heathens." After Justus was able to help the Karen people during a famine, Luther observes that "in the excess of their joy and gratitude, he had difficulty in preventing some of the heathen from worshipping him" (109). This book is just one example of a plethora of Protestant missionary books, magazines, and pamphlets that circulated in the United States during the nineteenth century. These interpretations were full of conversion narratives and drawings of "heathens" from the Orient, who were described as scantily clothed, uncivilized "idol" worshippers.

Such printed materials also introduced Americans to sacred texts from India, Persia, and the Middle East, which metaphysical seekers, like the Transcendentalists and Theosophists, absorbed. While missionaries imagined the Orient as the abode of heathens, these seekers romanticized the Orient as exotic, spiritually superior, and harboring ancient secrets. The writings of Theosophy cofounder William Quan Judge (1851–1896) were published under the title *Echoes of the Orient*, demonstrating how Judge and other Theosophists imagined the Orient. The text illustrates how Theosophists constructed the Orient as a place of ancient spiritual wisdom. According to Judge, the West needs "a greater light on the subject of the Hindu religion, and in deepening the effect on the Western mind of ancient philosophy … every day, more and more, the West will look for the treasures of the East, if these are not deliberately hidden away" (Judge 1980, 2:52). For Judge and many other nineteenth-century and present-day metaphysical seekers, the Orient is superior to the West in its spiritual wisdom. However, this type of characterization casts a diverse area in a particular way, and the reality is much different than the stereotype.

Missionaries and metaphysical seekers helped establish centers and departments for studying the imagined Orient in many US colleges and universities. Presbyterian missionary Henry W. Luce (1868–1941) was stationed for many years in China, where he was a professor at Cheeloo University. Luce helped establish a foundation— the Yale Foreign Missionary Society, now called the Yale-China Association—for cultural and scholarly exchange between China and the United States. Sociologist William Isaac Thomas (1863–1947) argued in "The Significance of the Orient for the Occident" (1908) that Japan was ready for change, but that "a jump from savagery to civilization would be like a jump from arithmetic to calculus, and could not be made" (738). Thomas identified areas where the Occident could learn from the Orient, but the exchange is unequal, since the Orient is imagined as an unequal place. In other words, those in the Occident felt that they were culturally, economically and politically superior and could give more to the Orient than they could gain. The Occident's imperialism of the nineteenth and twentieth centuries had led to economic under development, political instability, and cultural commodification in areas of the Orient where these exchanges took place.

The scholar Edward Said (1935–2003) was critical of the ways in which academics have historically constructed the Orient—a process he called orientalism. Said argued that academic inquiries into the Orient were deemed to be nonpolitical, but in reality they were enabled by and embedded in larger American, British, and French colonial and imperial matrixes. In other words, scholars like Thomas might have imagined themselves as objective learners and observers, but they were actually enmeshed in the construction of the subjective Orient.

In the United States, the Orient is seen as a monolithic and foreign place. Immigrants from throughout Asia are thus often lumped together as "Asian American" and are still deemed foreign even after their families have been in the United States for generations. The ways in which missionaries, metaphysical seekers, and academics shaped understanding of the constructed "Orient" as a space that can be consumed but that also needs to be civilized (and Christianized) fuels contemporary imaginings of Asia and Africa.

This East/West binary, with imagined ontological differences between the two regions, was embraced by people in parts of Asia and Africa. Late nineteenth-century yoga "missionary" Swami Vivekananda (1863–1902), for example, co-opted Western ideas of the Orient and Occident, constructing the "East" as wholly and ontologically different from the "West." According to Vivekananda,

"when the Oriental wants to learn about machine making, he should sit at the feet of the Occidental and learn from him. When the Occident wants to learn about the spirit, about God, about the soul, about the meaning and the mystery of the universe, he must sit at the feet of the Orient to learn" (Vivekananda 1992, 4:154). Ideas of the Orient constructed by American and European missionaries, metaphysical seekers, and academics thus looped back to parts of Asia and Africa, influencing how people there imagined their place in the larger world.

SEE ALSO *Buddhism; Chinese Exclusion Act (1882); Hinduism; Immigration; Immigration Quotas; Immigration Restriction League; Islam; Melting Pot; Nativism; Orientalism; Said, Edward; Whiteness*

BIBLIOGRAPHY

Judge, William Quan. *Echoes of the Orient*, Vol. 2. Compiled by Dana Eklund. Pasadena, CA: Theosophical University Press, 1980.

Luther, Calista V. *The Vintons and Karens: Memorials of Rev. Justus H. Vinton and Calista H. Vinton.* Boston: Corthell, 1880.

Said, Edward. *Orientalism.* New York: Vintage, 1979.

Thomas, William Isaac. "The Significance of the Orient for the Occident." *American Journal of Sociology* 13 (1908): 729–742.

Vivekananda, Swami. *The Complete Works of Swami Vivekananda*, Vol. 4. 5th ed. Calcutta, India: Advaita Ashrama, 1992.

Shreena Niketa Gandhi
Assistant Professor of Religion
Kalamazoo College

ORIENT EXPRESS

The Orient Express is Europe's most famous train. For almost a century, this long-distance passenger train was the most popular means of transportation for the wealthy of Europe and abroad. For many people, its name has become synonymous with luxury train travel (providing comfortable beds and gourmet food), as well as mystery and intrigue. The train has been incorporated into movies and novels, such as Bram Stoker's *Dracula* (1897), Graham Greene's *Stamboul Train* (1932), and Ian Fleming's *From Russia, with Love* (1957). It figures most significantly in Agatha Christie's *Murder on the Orient Express* (1934), which features Belgian detective Hercule Poirot, one of her most famous and long-lived characters. Christie, the best-selling novelist of all time, made the Orient Express a household word in the United States.

The Orient Express was created by the Compagnie Internationale des Wagons-Lits (CIWL) in 1883. The founder of CIWL, Belgian Georges Nagelmackers (1845–1905), had

Poster showing the winter 1889–1890 schedule for the Orient Express, which featured luxury rail service from London to Bucharest and Constantinople by way of Paris and Vienna. *For almost a century the* Orient Express, *a long-distance passenger train, was the most popular means of travel for the wealthy of Europe and abroad. The luxury train has been depicted in many movies and novels, most notably in Agatha Christie's* Murder on the Orient Express *(1934), which made it a household word in the United States.* **AKG-IMAGES**

visited the United States and was captivated by the luxury and service offered on rail cars built and operated by the Pullman Palace Car Company. Determined to establish a network of luxury trains across international borders in Europe that would exceed the luxury offered to rail passengers in the United States by George Pullman (1831–1897), Nagelmackers built a network of luxury trains throughout Europe at a time when rail travel was uncomfortable and time-consuming. CIWL became the world's first modern multinational corporation dedicated to transport and travel.

The two cities most often associated with the Orient Express are Paris and Istanbul, the original endpoints of the rail service. Whereas Paris was acknowledged by the elite as an international cultural capital, Istanbul's appeal as a travel destination for Europeans was enhanced by the rise of Orientalism, a literary and artistic movement that became popular during the nineteenth century. As such, the Orient Express's popularity was fueled by the growing interest in all things Oriental, especially Middle Eastern.

The route traveled by the Orient Express changed over the years. The earliest route, which passed through Vienna, required passengers to change trains. It was not until 1889 that the Orient Express offered nonstop train service to Istanbul. Service was suspended during World War I (1914–1918). Beginning in 1919, after the opening of the Simplon Tunnel between Switzerland and Italy, a second (and more popular) route ran from Paris to Istanbul via Venice. Service was interrupted once again during World War II (1939–1945). By 1977, however, service to Istanbul on both routes had been discontinued. The advent of comfortable high-speed trains in Europe, such as France's TGV, heralded the end of the Orient Express, which officially ceased its truncated operations in 2009.

The legacy of the Orient Express, however, lives on. The Venice-Simplon Orient Express (VSOE), a private company established by American James Sherwood (b. 1933) in 1982, offers luxury rail tours from London to Venice and other popular European destinations. VSOE, which uses beautifully restored CIWL sleeping carriages and dining cars from the 1920s and 1930s, is popular with international tourists. In addition to its regular services, the company offers a once-a-year six-day journey from Paris to Istanbul for $10,000. Another company that capitalized on the Orient Express name, the American Orient Express, offered luxury rail tours in the United States from 1989 to 2008 that tried to re-create the splendor and mystique of traveling on the original Orient Express. That company, however, went bankrupt as a result of the recession that began in 2007/2008.

SEE ALSO *Orient; Orientalism; Trains*

BIBLIOGRAPHY

Burton, Anthony. *The Orient Express: The History of the Orient Express Service from 1883 to 1950.* Devon, UK: David and Charles, 2001.

Christie, Agatha. *Murder on the Orient Express.* New York: Harper, 2011. First published by Collins in 1934.

Cookridge, E. H. *Orient Express: The Life and Times of the World's Most Famous Train.* New York: Random House, 1978.

Muhl, Albert, and Jurgen Klein. *125 Years International Sleeping Car Company: Trains de Luxe—History and Posters.* Bonn, Germany: VG-Bild-Kunst, 1998.

Michael R. Hall
Professor of History
Armstrong State University

ORIENTALISM

With the 1978 publication of the book with this very title, Orientalism became an established concept for understanding East-West relations. In *Orientalism*, drawing from Antonio Gramsci's (1891–1937) notion of hegemony and Michel Foucault's (1926–1984) theory of discourse and genealogy, Palestinian American critic Edward W. Said (1935–2003) examined the nature of Western discourse about the "Orient," which is built upon unequal relations between the East and the West and the premise of an essential binary between the two. Covering a broad chronological span but focusing mostly on the era of high imperialism of the nineteenth century, Said theorized the discursive work of Orientalism and its connection to realpolitik.

SAID'S MODEL OF EAST-WEST RELATIONS

In Said's formulation, Orientalism has several key modes of expression. It exoticizes the Orient, finding its value in its essential foreignness from the Western self; it homogenizes the Orient, treating the vast landmass and diverse peoples and cultures as a monolith; and it feminizes the Orient, seeing it as a gendered and sexualized object of Western male protection and penetration. These expressions constitute a discourse, Said argued, through dense intertextuality of intellectual and cultural productions, ranging from philological and historical scholarship to records of colonial bureaucracy and works of art and literature. Examining the intricate and intimate relationship between power—military, political, economic—and knowledge, Said made a provocative assertion that there is no such thing as neutral, objective knowledge about the Orient that exists outside of Orientalist discourse and that, regardless of the subjectivity and intent of individual thinkers, any knowledge about and representations of the Orient are always part of the dominant ideologies underpinning the discourse.

Said's theoretical interest in the book was focused on the relationship between power and knowledge production, and his broader concerns lay with Western understanding of the Arab world. Hence it is not surprising that the bulk of the attention in the book is devoted to the British and French relationship with the Middle East in the era of colonialism, which created a highly productive condition for Orientalist knowledge production. In the book, Said asserts that the United States became a serious player in the field of Orientalism after World War II (1939–1945), when it acquired the status of a global hegemon and became directly involved in world affairs, particularly in the Middle East.

CRITIQUES AND APPLICATIONS OF SAID'S THEORY OF ORIENTALISM

Many scholars have challenged Said's theory and historicization of Orientalism. One criticism has been that Said's binary model falsely constructs Orientalism and its producers as monoliths, not accounting for the diversity of ideologies and identities within the West—religious, racial, ethnic, and gender, for instance—that make for much more complex and varied relationships with the Orient than Said portrays. Some historians have pointed out that, for example, the genealogy and nature of German Orientalism have been distinct from the British and French discourse on which Said focuses. Others have challenged Said's assertion that the United States entered the field of Orientalism only after World War II, pointing out the importance of the Holy Land in the ideology undergirding settler colonialism and westward expansion on the North American continent, as well as the United States' involvement in the Middle and Far East dating long before the twentieth century. Others have also objected to the idea that there is no such thing as neutral, objective knowledge and that there can be no ideas and representations outside of dominant ideology and discourse, arguing that such a claim undermines the very principle of academic inquiry, as well as individual agency and resistance.

Despite such criticisms, *Orientalism* marked Said as one of the founding scholars of the field of postcolonial studies, and his critique of Orientalism has had a tremendous influence on a wide range of fields in the humanities and social sciences. Said's theory has been applied to a diverse array of historical, political, social, and cultural conditions far beyond European relations with the Middle East, which was Said's focus.

ORIENTALISM AND US FOREIGN RELATIONS

Among the many analytical uses of Orientalism, there are several ways in which Orientalism is of particular relevance to the study of the United States' relations to the world.

First is the analysis of the mutually shaping relationship between military, political, and economic power on the one hand and cultural representations on the other. Second is the examination of the ideologies shaping US foreign policy that are often racialized and gendered. Third is the understanding of the dialectical relationship between US foreign relations and domestic social relations.

In the context of US history, the concept of Orientalism has thus been used widely to critically examine the ideology underpinning US foreign policy, race relations, and cultural imaginaries, not only about the Middle East but the non-Western world at large.

In the late eighteenth century, the outrage over the capture and enslavement of American sailors by Algerians produced Orientalist narratives about North African despotism and immorality by such writers as Royall Tyler (1757–1826) and Susanna Rowson (1762–1824). Orientalism has provided a framework to understand the interest in Asian religions among the mid-nineteenth-century Transcendentalists, such as Ralph Waldo Emerson (1803–1882), Henry David Thoreau (1817–1862), and Walt Whitman (1819–1892).

The crew of Commodore Matthew Perry's (1794–1858) Pacific expedition in 1853 to 1854 depicted Asian and Pacific lands, peoples, and cultures in ways typically characterized as Orientalist, and such portrayals provided rhetorical ammunition for a series of unequal treaties favoring US interests in its diplomatic and economic relations with Japan. Orientalism was central to the ideas about the China market driving westward expansion, as well as the assertion of US interests in Secretary of State John Hay's (1838–1905) Open Door policy issued in 1899 to 1900, promoting equal opportunity (for Western powers) for commerce with China.

Orientalist notions of despotic Orientals incapable of self-governance provided ideological support for jingoism undergirding the Spanish-American (1898) and Filipino-American (1899–1903) Wars and subsequent US colonization of the Philippines lasting until 1946. Orientalist cultural representations, such as Bret Harte's (1836–1902) short stories and Thomas Nast's (1840–1902) political cartoons in the nineteenth century, popularized the narratives of the "yellow peril"—the Asian menace presumably embodied in Chinese immigrant labor in the late nineteenth century—and were at the core of advocacy for restrictions on Asian immigration beginning with the 1882 Chinese Exclusion Act. With the rise of Japan's military power, demonstrated by its victory in the Russo-Japanese War (1904–1905), the yellow peril narrative was then applied to racist depictions of Japan and its people during the Pacific War.

After World War II, social scientific studies and journalistic accounts of Asian immigrants' and Asian

Americans' adaptation and assimilation in the United States and the popular narrative of Asian Americans as the "model minority," while ostensibly benign and sympathetic to the subjects, were also undergirded by Orientalist ideas about Asian character, behavior, and family patterns. After the "loss" of China to communism in 1949, Orientalist notions of Asians as the racial "other" were part of Cold War US foreign policy in East and Southeast Asia and cultural representations of the Viet Cong and the Vietnamese people in general during the Vietnam War (1954–1975).

Dominant American accounts of Israel-Palestine conflicts have also been shaped considerably by the Orientalist ideology that racializes both Jews and Arabs and portrays Muslims as fanatic terrorists. Orientalism can be easily identified in the ideas about global political, economic, and ideological conflicts advanced by such figures as political scientists Francis Fukuyama (*The End of History and the Last Man*, 1992) and Samuel Huntington ("The Clash of Civilizations?" 1993) after the end of the Cold War. Orientalism has been a significant factor in American understandings of the causes and meanings of the terrorist attacks of 9/11, as well as the subsequent treatment of the people of Middle Eastern and South Asian origin both within and outside the US borders. In the age of Barack Obama, the rise of China and India as economic giants and the United States' "pivot to Asia"—exemplified by Hillary Clinton's 2011 statement about "America's Pacific Century"—have brought about a resurgence of American Orientalism in the twenty-first century.

VARYING STRAINS OF ORIENTALISM

While it is easy to find various elements of Orientalism in US foreign relations throughout its history, it is also important to understand the significant changes in the nature of American Orientalism in different historical and political contexts. Just as racial ideology changed its form from white supremacy, scientific racism, and "benevolent assimilation" to cultural relativism, pluralism, multiculturalism, and color blindness, Orientalism has also transformed in shape and content. For instance, the Orientalism of American engineers, agriculturalists, scientists, and Japanologists hired by Japan's Meiji (1868–1912) government eager to modernize and Westernize was distinct from Orientalism vis-à-vis Japan during the US occupation under General Douglas MacArthur (1880–1964), when the United States treated Japan as a junior ally to incorporate into its post–World War II global hegemony. It was also different from Orientalism directed at the Japanese nationals, Asian immigrants, and Asian Americans during the period of Japan's economic dominance in the 1970s and 1980s,

which resulted in such tragic incidents as the 1982 murder of Chinese American Vincent Chin in Detroit.

Likewise, the depictions of Chinese immigrants in the American West in the nineteenth century were considerably different from the American portrayals of Chinese fighting Japanese imperialism in the 1930s and 1940s, which differed just as much from the US accounts of Red China during the Cold War. Likewise, American Protestants making religious pilgrimages to the Holy Land in the nineteenth century; US military, economic, and cultural investment in the Middle East during the Cold War; and the discourse of the war on terror in the twenty-first century share common threads yet are also considerably different from each other in their motivations and manifestations. Therefore, while all of the above examples can be understood in terms of Orientalism, to make full use of it as an analytical framework, it is important to carefully consider the historical, political, and economic contexts that shape Orientalism in specific ways.

Although Said's theory of Orientalism relied on a binary model of East and the West, scholars have also shown that Orientalism is not an exclusively Western, white, male discourse. Within the United States, different segments of the population have invested diverse, complex meanings in the Orient, claimed their own connections to it, and deployed those connections toward their own goals. For instance, in the early twentieth century, black internationalists, such as W. E. B. Du Bois (1868–1963) and Marcus Garvey (1887–1940), saw Japan's victory in the Russo-Japanese War as an inspiration for the fight against white domination, embraced the nation as a potential champion of the darker races, and sought to forge an alliance with Japan. From the late nineteenth to the mid-twentieth century, a number of white, middle-class American women—ranging from poet Amy Lowell (1874–1925), writer Pearl Buck (1892–1973), and revolutionary Agnes Smedley (1892–1950), to name a few—looked to the East, in their physical or imaginary travels or cultural embrace, for alternatives to the gendered constraints in their own society.

The culture of Orientalism also provided a stage for professional opportunities and social visibility for a number of Asian and Asian American performers, including actor Sessue Hayakawa (1889–1973) and actress Anna May Wong (1905–1961). In the context of Cold War Orientalism and multiculturalism in post–World War II America, many Asian Americans—ranging from political leaders such as Daniel Inouye (1924–2012) to artists like Isamu Noguchi (1904–1988) and Minoru Yamasaki (1912–1986)—eagerly promoted their ties to their Asian homeland as a means to advance their ethnic community's integration into American society. In the second half of the twentieth century, many African

Americans—most notably Muhammad Ali (b. 1942) and Malcolm X (1925–1965)—were drawn to the Nation of Islam as providing a spiritual alternative to Christianity and a basis for a black nationalist consciousness different from one seeking integration into the white-dominated social society of the United States. During the 1960s, Mao Zedong (1893–1976) issued statements supporting the African American struggle against racial discrimination, and in turn, Maoist thought had a significant influence on African American leftist activists.

Moreover, the worldview and discourse characteristic of Orientalism—whether one chooses to use the term or not—have not been exclusive to the West. There has been a strong tradition within Arabic thought that draws ontological distinctions between East and the West. China's view of itself as the "Middle Kingdom," established through the imperial tributary system from the Ming through the Qing dynasties, was also based on the belief in China's superiority over the rest of the world. In the first half of the twentieth century, Japan's imperial expansion in Asia with the goal of building the "Greater East Asia Co-Prosperity Sphere" was undergirded by a vision of the world divided into the East and the West while objectifying, containing, and controlling China in ways similar to Western Orientalism in the colonial Middle East.

While Orientalism thus has been a highly useful framework for analysis of a wide range of relations, some scholars critique the facile application of the term that undermines the critical force of Said's original theorization. Indeed, Orientalism has become such a common concept that it is often used in reference to any relations between groups of unequal power, without geographical, historical, political, racial, and other specificities. In these applications, Orientalism is not always distinguished from such related concepts as racism, colonialism, exoticism, primitivism, and so forth, and it is sometimes used to discuss any groups or cultures ranging from the Pacific Islands to Africa. Some critics have argued that such a loose application of the term dilutes the analytical power of Orientalism, and they have called for a more precise usage with attentiveness to the particularities of Western relations with the Middle East. In fact, despite Said's pointed critique of Western constructions of the Arabs, Muslims, and particularly the Palestinians, until recent years Orientalism has been used in Americanist scholarship more commonly in reference to US relations with East and Southeast Asia rather than with the Middle East. Particularities of the United States' military, political, economic, and cultural interests in the Middle East and the nation's role in the region, especially the Israel-Palestine conflict, call for a more precise deployment of Orientalism and other analytical frameworks than have often been done.

SEE ALSO *Immigration; Immigration Quotas; Immigration Restriction League; Middle East; Nativism; Said, Edward; Whiteness*

BIBLIOGRAPHY

Ahmad, Aijaz. *In Theory: Classes, Nations, Literature*. London: Verso, 1992.

Berman, Jacob Rama. *American Arabesque: Arabs and Islam in the Nineteenth-Century Imaginary*. New York: New York University Press, 2012.

Fukuyama, Francis. *The End of History and the Last Man*. New York: Free Press, 1992.

Gallicchio, Marc. *The African American Encounter with Japan and China: Black Internationalism in Asia, 1895–1945*. Chapel Hill: University of North Carolina Press, 2000.

Ho, Fred, and Bill V. Mullen, eds. *Afro Asia: Revolutionary Political and Cultural Connections between African Americans and Asian Americans*. Durham, NC: Duke University Press, 2008.

Huntington, Samuel. "The Clash of Civilizations?" *Foreign Affairs* 72, 3 (1993): 22–49.

Iwamura, Jane Naomi. *Virtual Orientalism: Asian Religions and American Popular Culture*. New York: Oxford University Press, 2011.

Leong, Karen J. *The China Mystique: Pearl S. Buck, Anna May Wong, Mayling Soong, and the Transformation of American Orientalism*. Berkeley: University of California Press, 2005.

Lubin, Alex. *Geographies of Liberation: The Making of an Afro-Arab Political Imaginary*. Chapel Hill: University of North Carolina Press, 2014.

McAlister, Melani. *Epic Encounters: Culture, Media, and U.S. Interests in the Middle East since 1945*. Updated ed. Berkeley: University of California Press, 2005.

Miyao, Daisuke. *Sessue Hayakawa: Silent Cinema and Transnational Stardom*. Durham, NC: Duke University Press, 2007.

Mullen, Bill V. *Afro-Orientalism*. Minneapolis: University of Minnesota Press, 2004.

Said, Edward W. *Orientalism*. New York: Vintage, 1978.

Schueller, Malini Johar. *U.S. Orientalisms: Race, Nation, and Gender in Literature, 1790–1890*. Ann Arbor: University of Michigan Press, 1998.

Tanaka, Stefan. *Japan's Orient: Rendering Pasts into History*. Berkeley: University of California Press, 1993.

Wu, Judy Tzu-Chun. *Radicals on the Road: Internationalism, Orientalism, and Feminism during the Vietnam Era*. Ithaca, NY: Cornell University Press, 2013.

Yoshihara, Mari. *Embracing the East: White Women and American Orientalism*. New York: Oxford University Press, 2003.

Mari Yoshihara
Professor of American Studies
University of Hawai'i

OTTOMAN EMPIRE

Established in the thirteenth century by Turkic invaders of Anatolia, the Ottoman or Turkish Empire conquered the Byzantine Empire and had subjugated much of the Islamic world by the end of the fifteenth century. The Ottoman Empire was regarded as an existential threat to Christendom and Western civilization, but with defeats at the sea battle of Lepanto (1571) and at the gates of Vienna (1683), a period of retrenchment began, followed by gradual decline.

EARLY US-OTTOMAN RELATIONS: A BALANCE OF VALUES AND COMMERCE

By the time the United States achieved independence, the Ottoman Empire had lost control of North Africa in all but name. One of America's earliest encounters with Islamic states, the Barbary Wars (1801–1815) was a largely naval campaign against privateers sailing from Ottoman tributaries in Algeria, Tunisia, and Libya. The fight against the "Barbary pirates" preying on US shipping in the Mediterranean Sea triggered the expansion of the US Navy and a projection of military power far from American shores. The conflict is remembered in the "Marine's Hymn" reference to "the shores of Tripoli." Although some have tried to cast the Barbary Wars as the opening salvo in a clash between America and Islam that continues into the present, the conflict had little religious and no ideological significance, but was a struggle over commerce and freedom of the seas. President John Adams (1735–1826) had ensured that this point was made clear in the 1796 treaty with Tripoli, Article 11 of which asserts "the United States of America is not in any sense founded on the Christian Religion" and, as a result, "has in itself no character of enmity against the laws, religion or tranquility" of Islam or Muslims.

By the end of the Barbary Wars, the United States began dispatching Jewish Americans as diplomats in the Ottoman tributaries, a custom that continued with the frequent appointment of Jews as diplomats in the Ottoman capital, Constantinople (now Istanbul), through the end of the empire. Formal relations between the United States and the Ottoman Empire were finally established in a treaty signed in 1830 by Andrew Jackson (1767–1845). With diplomatic relations in place, the United States set a precedent for its relations with present-day Turkey by selling weapons to the Ottoman army and warships to its fleet, dispatching military advisers, and cultivating official trade links. The United States imported dates, figs, and carpets from the empire and sold the Turks manufactured goods of all kinds. *Americano* entered the Turkish language as a word for cotton fabric. For much of the nineteenth century, Ottoman officials tended to favor the United States over European nations; America was far away, had no interest in expanding at the empire's expense, and was seen as largely neutral in the great game of old world politics.

Even before the signing of commercial pacts, adventurous American entrepreneurs made headway in the bribery-ridden Ottoman economy. Through the 1820s the twin poles of US foreign policy, with economic-based realpolitik on one hand and concern for human rights and democratic ideals on the other, played out in America's attitude toward the Ottomans. Most Americans supported the Greeks in their struggle for independence from the Turks. Money was raised for the Greek cause, a frigate was outfitted as the flagship for the Greek fleet, and Americans fought as volunteers on behalf of the ancient birthplace of democracy. As secretary of state, John Quincy Adams (1767–1848) kept the United States out of the war, arguing that such intervention would preclude closer trade relations with the empire. As president, however, Adams issued declarations on behalf of "the suffering Greeks."

After 1830 the US continued to balance values with commerce. America's first ambassador in Constantinople, David Porter (1780–1843), facilitated trade but protested against Ottoman persecution of Jews and other minorities. However, private initiative often took the lead in US-Ottoman relations. American philanthropists were responsible for the inauguration in 1863 of Robert College in Constantinople, which became a conduit of Western ideas and a seedbed of political reform. Similar institutions established in the Ottoman provinces of Lebanon helped to fan the Arab nationalism that would contribute to the empire's demise.

AMERICAN MISSIONARIES IN THE OTTOMAN EMPIRE

Palestine was the Ottoman district that attracted the greatest attention from Americans for its association with the Abrahamic religious tradition and the life of Jesus. Most nineteenth-century Americans had a vivid impression of the Holy Land through their reading of scripture, and while most visitors were disappointed by the reality of the land, and regarded the inhabitants with cultural chauvinism, Palestine became the special, but not the only, focus of effort for American Protestant missionaries. By the 1820s, some of America's largest denominations, including the Methodists, Presbyterians, and Congregationalists, were promoting missions to the Ottoman Empire. They won few converts among Muslims; the penalty for apostasy in Islam is high. The Jews were not interested, and the missionaries were shocked when the US consul to Jerusalem, Warder Cresson (1798–1860), converted to Judaism.

The missionaries had greater success among the empire's Eastern Christians, who were divided under institutions that had crumbled under centuries of Ottoman rule and included congregants who saw conversion as a gateway to greater opportunities in the world beyond the Middle East. The Ottomans sometimes encouraged missionary activities among the Eastern Christians to further divide and weaken the religious minorities, even if they also chafed at the insolence of the evangelists. In the United States, the missionaries had no trouble raising funds and no lack of adherents in high places, including congressmen, cabinet secretaries, and presidents. The US Navy, which maintained a presence in the Mediterranean after the Barbary Wars, was called upon to rescue missionaries threatened with violence by the people they hoped to save.

An important facet of the mission endeavor was the support among many Protestant denominations for establishing a Jewish homeland in Palestine. Some of the impetus came from an appreciation of the historical roots of Christianity in Judaism, yet many evangelical Christians saw a Jewish homeland as the means to their own ends. In their interpretation of end-time prophesy, the return of the Jews to the Holy Land was a necessary prerequisite for the Second Coming of Christ. Such beliefs are still held by some evangelical groups in the twenty-first century. The attitude of the Reverend Henry White Warren (1831–1912) was typical; he made himself at home in Palestine while declaring that the Jews he met there gave him "the greatest temptation toward despising a brother a man ever encountered" (Warren 1874, 284).

THE ARMENIAN CRISIS AND WORLD WAR I

The massacre of 200,000 Armenians by Ottoman troops in 1894, the first in a series of large-scale assaults by the empire against its minorities, drew condemnation from American pundits and politicians. Senator Newton Blanchard (1849–1922) of Louisiana called upon the William McKinley (1843–1901) administration to erase the empire as a "blot upon civilization." The president of Robert College, George Washburn (1833–1915), asked his cousin, Secretary of State John Hay (1838–1905), to intervene. In 1900 the battleship *Kentucky* anchored off Smyrna with threats to shell Ottoman installations unless the violence ceased. More pacific actions were taken by Clara Barton (1821–1912), the founder of the American Red Cross, who traveled to Turkey and personally supervised the distribution of food and medicine to pillaged Armenian districts.

President Theodore Roosevelt (1858–1919) brought the United States close to military intervention in the Ottoman Empire. Responding to rumors that the US consul in Beirut, William Magelssen, had been assassinated, Roosevelt ordered warships to Beirut harbor. Although the assassination report proved false, the threat of force

extracted pledges for the safety of American missionaries, and the squadron remained on patrol off the empire's coastline. Chilly relations continued after the "Young Turks," many of them graduates of Robert College, seized power in a coup in 1908 and initiated another wave of Armenian massacres. The US-based American-Ottoman Company's bid to build railroads was rejected and the contract given to Turkey's new ally, Germany. However, Standard Oil was granted permission to prospect in Ottoman Mesopotamia in 1910, and the network of missionary-based schools and hospitals continued to spread.

In November 1914, the Ottoman Empire entered World War I on Germany's side and struck at their mutual enemy, Russia. Under the guise of military necessity, the Young Turk regime launched a concerted campaign against its Armenian subjects. Accused of complicity with the Russians, Armenians were massacred and deported on death marches that have been categorized as genocide. US consuls in Harput, Aleppo, and elsewhere, along with American missionaries and other foreign observers, issued eyewitness accounts. The American media reacted with front-page coverage, but the Woodrow Wilson (1856–1924) administration hesitated to respond for fear of jeopardizing American lives. The Armenian cause became one of the great human rights campaigns of the era, with large funds raised for the "starving Armenians."

The US ambassador to Turkey, Henry Morgenthau (1856–1946), gave the most influential account of the ethnic cleansing after becoming convinced that the Young Turks were executing a deliberate policy of "race extermination." Morgenthau received no support from the Wilson administration but solicited funds for Armenian relief from Christian and Jewish philanthropists in the United States. Morgenthau's successor as ambassador, Abram Elkus (1867–1947), informed the State Department of the ongoing "unchecked policy of extermination" waged by the Young Turks against Armenians, as well ethnic cleansing of Greeks and Arabs.

The United States entered World War I in April 1917, declaring war on Germany and Austria but not on the Ottoman Empire. Roosevelt, elements of the missionary lobby, and most members of Congress, including Senator Henry Cabot Lodge (1850–1924), demanded war against the Turks for their human rights abuses, as well as their alliance with Germany. Wilson, concerned for the well-being of the many Americans in the empire, remained unmoved. The Young Turks responded by severing diplomatic relations with the United States while attempting to placate the United States by banning anti-American references in Turkish newspapers and tolerating American relief efforts.

US-Ottoman relations were an anomaly for the remainder of the conflict. Wilson's refusal to declare war on the Ottoman Empire left the United States with little influence on the map of the Middle East that took shape in the postwar settlement. Britain and France drew the lines and helped themselves to Palestine, Syria, Lebanon, Jordan, and Iraq, with repercussions still being felt a century later. What the United States may have gained from neutrality was a sense of appreciation from the leaders of the Ottoman Empire's successor state, the Turkish Republic, which laid the foundation for the US-Turkey alliance that continues into the present.

SEE ALSO *Armenian Genocide; Islam; League of Nations; Middle East; Paris Peace Conference (1919); Treaty of Versailles; World War I*

BIBLIOGRAPHY

Balakian, Peter. *Burning Tigris: The Armenian Genocide and America's Response.* New York: HarperCollins, 2003.

Barbary Treaties, 1786–1816: Treaty of Peace and Friendship, Signed at Tripoli November 4, 1796. http://avalon.law.yale.edu/18th_century/bar1796t.asp

Lambert, Frank. *The Barbary Wars: American Independence in the Atlantic World.* New York: Hill and Wang, 2005.

Oren, Michael B. *Power, Faith, and Fantasy: America in the Middle East, 1776 to the Present.* Updated ed. New York: Norton, 2011.

Warren, Henry White. *Sights and Insights, or, Knowledge by Travel.* New York: Nelson and Phillips; Cincinnati: Hitchcock and Walden, 1874.

Glen Jeansonne
Professor of History
University of Wisconsin–Milwaukee

David Luhrssen
Editor
Shepherd Express

OUR COUNTRY (JOSIAH STRONG, 1885)

The book *Our Country*, published in 1885, is the quintessential example of a "Christian civilization" discourse. During the Gilded Age and Progressive Era such discourses influenced the way Americans viewed both the immigrant and the foreigner. The book quickly made its way into the hands of more than half a million people and in the process catapulted its author, the Reverend Josiah Strong, into the ranks of the nation's best-known ministers. Much of Strong's early career had been devoted to Christianizing the American West. In fact, it was the Ohio Home Missionary Society that commissioned him to write *Our Country*. But in the midst of working on the book he was called to the pastorate of the Central Congregational Church in Cincinnati, a move that decisively shifted his focus to the problems of the urbanizing United States.

For Strong and countless American Protestant leaders, the late-nineteenth-century city was a fearsome place because it was an epicenter of demographic and cultural change. He perceived any number of "perils on our national horizon," but none loomed larger than immigration (Strong 1885, 30). As Strong went on to declare: "During the last four years we have suffered a peaceful invasion by an army more than twice as vast as the estimated number of Goths and Vandals that swept over Southern Europe and overwhelmed Rome" (30). These newcomers and their American-born children posed a multipronged threat. Strong harped on their lack of education and inadequate, if not outright "false," religious formation (40); their propensity for intemperance and "continental ideas of the Sabbath" (42); and their unfamiliarity with American political culture and resulting susceptibility to the demagogue. "Immigration complicates our moral and political problems by swelling our dangerous classes," Strong averred (44). Putting an even finer point on the matter, he warned that this tide of immigration might soon destabilize the nation's democratic foundations: "there is a dead-line of ignorance and vice in every republic, and when it is touched by the average citizen, free institutions perish" (44). According to his nativist calculus, it was only by restricting the inflow of foreign peoples and finding ways to "Americanize" those already present that the United States could be saved (45).

Yet if anxieties about the nation's future permeated *Our Country*'s pages, so did a brash confidence about the prospects for "Christian civilization" around the world. The book brimmed with optimism about what the waning years of the nineteenth century might hold, as Strong breathlessly declared: "The world is to be Christianized and civilized. There are about 1,000,000,000 of the world's inhabitants who do not enjoy a Christian civilization. Two hundred millions of these are to be lifted out of savagery" (14). Strong and many other influential American Protestants of the era embraced the view according to which entire races of human beings were understood to advance along a set trajectory from "savagery" to "civilization." Within this framework, the "Anglo-Saxon" was regarded as the pinnacle of human achievement. In Strong's reasoning, "if human progress follows a law of development, if 'Time's noblest offspring is the last,' our civilization should be the noblest" (168). Anglo-Saxons were, in his estimation, distinctive in a variety of ways: they were "the great wealth-creators of the world," the foremost champions of "civil liberty" and "pure *spiritual*

Christianity," and possessed of a clear "genius for colonizing" (115, 159–160, 173). In case the ominous implications of this ideology were not clear enough, Strong went on to make them explicit in this prediction:

> This race of unequaled energy, with all the majesty of numbers and the might of wealth behind it—the representative, let us hope, of the largest liberty, the purest Christianity, the highest civilization—having developed peculiarly aggressive traits calculated to impress its institutions upon mankind, will spread itself over the earth. If I read not amiss, this powerful race will move down upon Mexico, down upon Central and South America, out upon the islands of the sea, over upon Africa and beyond. And can any doubt that the result of this competition of races will be the "survival of the fittest?" (175)

The ideas Strong advanced in *Our Country* seized the imagination of many white Protestant Americans in the decades immediately following its publication. It was during those same decades that the United States acquired its first overseas colonies and passed the most restrictive immigration bill in its history. Assumptions about the merits and prerogatives of the Anglo-Saxon race, and the noble cause of "Christian civilization," propelled the nation's forays into international affairs.

SEE ALSO *Immigration and Naturalization Service; Immigration Quotas; Nativism; Protestantism; Whiteness*

BIBLIOGRAPHY

Boyer, Paul. *Urban Masses and Moral Order in America, 1820–1920.* Cambridge, MA: Harvard University Press, 1978.

Hopkins, C. Howard, and Ronald C. White Jr. *The Social Gospel: Religion and Reform in Changing America.* Philadelphia: Temple University Press, 1976.

Jacobson, Matthew Frye. *Barbarian Virtues: The United States Encounters Foreign Peoples at Home and Abroad.* New York: Hill and Wang, 2000.

Strong, Josiah. *Our Country: Its Possible Future and Its Present Crisis.* New York: Baker and Taylor, 1885.

Heath W. Carter
Assistant Professor of History
Valparaiso University

OZONE DEPLETION

Ozone is a gas consisting of three oxygen atoms (O_3). In the upper atmosphere, known as the stratosphere, ozone occurs naturally when the kind of oxygen animals breathe (O_2) is split in half by sunlight. These single oxygen atoms can then reconnect as O_2, which in turn can join with another single oxygen atom to form O_3. Stratospheric ozone is maintained by a continuous process of oxygen atoms splitting and joining, which forms the planet's ozone layer. This crucial part of the atmosphere blocks most of the sun's ultraviolet radiation, thereby allowing life on Earth.

In the 1970s, American scientists began to note a significant thinning of the ozone layer. This phenomenon was linked to the widespread use of chlorofluorocarbons (CFCs), an industrial compound composed of chlorine, fluorine, and carbon used in refrigerants and aerosols. When CFCs are released into the air, they rise to the stratosphere, become exposed to the sun's ultraviolet rays, and are broken down into their component parts. The major culprit of ozone depletion is chlorine, of which a single atom can destroy 100,000 ozone molecules. The effects of this process have been most severe over Antarctica, where the frigid atmospheric air creates a polar vortex, causing winds to move in a circular motion, thus allowing the most efficient reaction between chlorine atoms and the ozone it destroys. By the end of the 1980s, the Antarctic region's ozone during the spring was observed to have dropped by as much as 95 percent, according to research conducted by the US National Oceanic and Atmospheric Administration. This occurrence became known as the ozone hole.

Scientific and public concern led to international action at the behest of the Ronald Reagan administration (1981–1989). The Montreal Protocol on Substances that Deplete the Ozone Layer, signed under United Nations (UN) auspices, went into force in January 1989. This treaty, widely hailed as the most successful international environmental agreement, was the culmination of twenty years of US-led research on the correlation of CFCs and ozone depletion, and consequently, the urgent need to develop global policies to halt CFC production without undue economic hardship. The Montreal Protocol mandated the phaseout of CFCs by the year 2000, and adopted a "carrot and stick" approach to compliance: trade sanctions would be levied against signatories who failed to meet phase-out quotas, while nonsignatory states were offered generous economic incentives to join the treaty. The protocol has achieved universal acceptance by UN member states; it is the first and only treaty to achieve this distinction. As a result, nearly all CFC production has ended, and the ozone is projected to return to 1970 levels by the mid-twenty-first century.

A major, if tangential, accomplishment of the Montreal Protocol has been its salutary effect on climate change, because CFCs are among the most powerful greenhouse gases. A major technological challenge for the future is therefore to develop replacements for CFCs that do not exacerbate global warming. While the ozone is on the path to recovery, the effects of its damage will be felt for decades to come. Scientists have linked ozone depletion to increasingly violent storms and ocean acidification, among other problems, which undoubtedly would be even more severe had the world community failed to act when it first faced the dire threat of the planet's vanishing ozone layer.

SEE ALSO *Global Warming; National Oceanic and Atmospheric Administration (NOAA)*

BIBLIOGRAPHY

Benedick, Richard Elliot. *Ozone Diplomacy: New Directions in Safeguarding the Planet.* Enlarged ed. Cambridge, MA: Harvard University Press, 1998.

Gillis, Justin. "The Montreal Protocol: A Little Treaty that Could." *New York Times*, December 9, 2013.

Solomon, Susan. "Stratospheric Ozone Depletion: A Review of Concepts and History." *Reviews of Geophysics* 37, 3 (1999): 275–313.

United Nations Environment Programme (UNEP). "Ozone Layer on Track to Recovery: Success Story Should Encourage Action on Climate." UNEP News Centre, September 10, 2014. http://www.unep.org/newscentre/Default.aspx?DocumentID=2796&ArticleID=10978

David Zierler
Office of the Historian
US Department of State

P

PACIFIC ISLANDS

The historical relationship between the United States and the Pacific Islands, identified here as the geographical areas of Melanesia, Micronesia, and Polynesia, is long and deep. Its most immediate origins lie in the area of commerce. Following the US War for Independence, interest in trade with China brought American vessels into the region, beginning with the 1784 voyage of the *Empress of China*. The search for marketable products to use in China led traders from Salem, Massachusetts, and other American traders to exploit the sandalwood forests of Fiji, Hawai'i, and the Marquesas, and the offshore populations of *bêche-de-mer*, or sea cucumber, in other island areas. The fur trade linked the west coast of the North American continent with Asia and the islands. Americans came to control that trade in the period between 1778 and 1830.

EARLY AMERICAN ACTIVITY IN THE PACIFIC

By the early 1790s, Americans were actively engaged in Pacific whaling and sealing, with devastating consequences for those marine mammal populations. Sealing was concentrated in the far northern and southern areas of the Pacific, including New Zealand. By 1820, American whalers dominated the Pacific fishery and focused on the central equatorial grounds; this area extended from Hawai'i and Tahiti to western Polynesia and Micronesia. Islands were used as places to rest, provision, and replace crew members. The consequences of this contact were mixed, and included the introduction of new ideas, technologies, plant and animal species, material goods, deadly disease, and the opportunity for a few islanders to travel.

The Hawaiian Islands proved an early center of American commercial and religious activity in the Pacific Islands region. Congregationalist missionaries sent by the American Board of Commissioners for Foreign Missions reached Hawai'i in 1820, where they and their descendants came to exert strong political and economic as well as religious influence in the islands. American missionary activity later spread south to the Marquesas Islands and to eastern Micronesia, more particularly the Marshall and Caroline Islands. By the 1830s, Hawai'i hosted the largest colony of American residents in the Pacific.

The US government sent its naval vessels to police and protect early American interests in the region. Commander David Porter (1780–1843) engaged in a sea battle with British warships off the Marquesas as part of the War of 1812. Commanded by Charles Wilkes (1798–1877), the United States Exploring Expedition traversed the islands from 1838 to 1842, adding significantly to scientific knowledge of the region and facilitating American trade and navigation there. In 1878 the United States established a naval station at Pago Pago on the island of Tutuila in eastern Samoa. The need for soil fertilizer led the US Congress in 1856 to authorize citizens' claims to guano-rich islands in the equatorial waters of the eastern-central Pacific. While the mining of guano had largely ceased by the mid-1880s, American commercial interests ultimately resulted in the acquisition of several of the Line Islands.

American interests in the region waned in the latter half of the nineteenth century as the whaling industry declined and steam replaced sail as a source of energy, thus allowing American flag vessels to bypass islands previously visited on a more or less regular basis. The Spanish-American War of 1898 reinvigorated America's presence in the region. As a result of the treaty ending the war with Spain, the United States acquired Guam, Wake, and the Philippines. The United States annexed Hawai'i that same year after American residents, with the assistance of the USS *Boston* at anchor in Honolulu Harbor, had overthrown the Hawaiian monarchy in 1893. In 1899 the United States acquired eastern Samoa as a result of the Final Act of the Conference on Samoan Affairs held in Berlin. The US Navy was given administrative authority for both Guam and what was now called American Samoa. Hawai'i had a territorial form of government that included a sizable naval presence based at Pearl Harbor, a site secured by the United States via a lease agreement with the then Hawaiian Kingdom in 1878. Despite the denial of empire that accompanied these acquisitions, the United States had established itself as an imperial power in the region. The deeper history of colonialism in the region resulted in the construction of artificial boundaries. The Philippines are a case in point. While understood as a part of Southeast Asia rather than the Pacific Islands, their colonization by the United States made them very much a part of an American lake, and thus linked to other American possessions in the Pacific Islands. That connection continues.

THE IMPACT OF WAR

Japan became an increasingly prominent power in the region following World War I (1914–1918). Disputes with the United States in the aftermath of that war foreshadowed the larger conflict to come in the form of World War II (1939–1945). Some of the bloodiest battles of the Pacific war were fought on or around Pacific islands; these included the naval engagement between American and Japanese forces at Midway and the land battles on Guadalcanal, Tarawa, Kwajalein, Saipan, Peleliu, and Angaur. The United States also recaptured Guam and the Philippines. In Hawai'i, the outbreak of war brought martial law and the internment of some citizens of Japanese ancestry.

The war's aftermath also found the United States with newly acquired island territory to administer. The Carolines, Marianas, and Marshalls of the Micronesian geographical area, formerly Japan's Mandate Islands, became a United Nations Trusteeship administered by the United States as the Trust Territory of the Pacific Islands. Global security concerns in the postwar and Cold War periods led to American nuclear testing in the Marshalls. Starting with the detonation of a nuclear device code-named Able on Bikini Atoll, the United States conducted sixty-seven nuclear tests in the Marshalls from 1946 to 1958. The United States acquiesced to the demands for self-government in the region, although at

times slowly or reluctantly. Civilian government replaced military administration in Guam, American Samoa, and the Trust Territory of the Pacific Islands. Hawai'i became a state in 1959, while the Organic Act of 1946 made Guam an unincorporated territory under a civilian administration that reported to Washington. American Samoa was granted a similar status. Between 1975 and 1991 the Trust Territory of the Pacific Islands split into four separate entities; Saipan and the Northern Mariana Islands opted for commonwealth status, while the Federated States of Micronesia, the Republic of the Marshall Islands, and the Republic of Palau stand as self-governing entities in free association with the United States. Under the status of free association, these three island governments are self-governing but dependent on the United States for financial assistance and their defense needs. There is considerable debate over how self-governing this arrangement of free association allows the islands to be.

CONTEMPORARY ISSUES

The last decades of the twentieth century found the United States dealing with a host of independent island states over issues involving the law of the sea, multilateral fisheries treaties, and foreign aid. The failure to ratify the three protocols of the South Pacific Nuclear Free Zone Treaty, also known as the Treaty of Rarotonga, put the United States at odds with the independent island nation-states of the Pacific. While the dissolution of the Soviet Union relaxed Cold War tensions in the region, native peoples in some American-held territories insisted on recognition and the redress of grievances. Groups of Native Hawaiians, for example, seek the restoration of their sovereignty, while the Marshallese demand additional compensation for the harm done to their lands, seas, and health by American nuclear testing. At the same time, the visa-free entry of Micronesian peoples into the United States and its territories under the provisions of the Compact of Free Association has increased markedly, creating diasporic communities in Guam, Hawai'i, and several locations across the continental United States. The economic rise of the People's Republic of China and its diplomatic competition with the Taiwan-based Republic of China has led to a "Pacific turn" in American foreign policy that continues to privilege the rim countries and bordering lands at the expense of the islands. America's military presence in the region remains strong.

With the Pacific Islands region being most immediately and dramatically affected by global warming and the subsequent rising of the seas, countries such as Kiribati, the Republic of the Marshall Islands, and the Federated States of Micronesia have pressed the United Sates and other major powers to limit their greenhouse emissions and reduce the reliance of their economies on fossil fuels. The refusal of the United States to sign the Kyoto

Protocol has been a source of frustration. In 2013 the Pacific Islands Forum, comprising sixteen independent island nations in the region, issued the Majuro Declaration, calling for immediate action by the United States and other industrialized nations to combat the threat of climate change.

American political institutions, popular culture, material goods, technology, telecommunications, commercial aviation, and tourism have had a profound effect on the region, especially on the islands of the American-affiliated Pacific. Conversely, the idea of the Pacific as a pristine, idyllic, and sensual paradise has impacted most Americans' understanding of the islands. The literary works of Herman Melville (1819–1891), the early-twentieth-century travel writings of Frederick O'Brien (1869–1932), and the films of Robert J. Flaherty (1884–1951) helped promote this older Pacific imagery, which was deeply rooted in European intellectual history. Later publications and performances sustained the image of the Pacific Islands as exotic, enticing, sexualized, and compliant places. James Michener's (1907–1997) *Tales of the South Pacific* and *Hawaii,* Margaret Mead's (1901–1978) popularized ethnography *Coming of Age in Samoa,* the Broadway musical *South Pacific,* and more recent popular culture forms such as the TV show *Survivor* have reinforced these stereotypes and helped feed a large tourist industry in Hawai'i and elsewhere that is reflective of America's long-standing interests and activities in the region.

SEE ALSO *Hawai'i; Pacific Ocean; Spanish-American War*

BIBLIOGRAPHY

Armitage, David, and Alison Bashford, eds. *Pacific Histories: Ocean, Land, People.* New York: Palgrave Macmillan, 2014.

Dudden, Arthur Power. *The American Pacific: From the Old China Trade to the Present.* New York: Oxford University Press, 1992.

Geiger, Jeffrey. *Facing the Pacific: Polynesia and the U.S. Imperial Imagination.* Honolulu: University of Hawai'i Press, 2007.

Igler, David. *The Great Ocean: Pacific Worlds from Captain Cook to the Gold Rush.* New York: Oxford University Press, 2013.

Lyons, Paul. *American Pacificism: Oceania in the U.S. Imagination.* New York: Routledge, 2006.

Matsuda, Matt K. *Pacific Worlds: A History of Seas, Peoples, and Cultures.* New York: Cambridge University Press, 2012.

McDougall, Walter A. *Let the Sea Make a Noise … : A History of the North Pacific from Magellan to MacArthur.* New York: Basic Books, 1993.

Thomas, Nicholas. *Islanders: The Pacific in the Age of Empire.* New Haven, CT: Yale University Press, 2010.

David Hanlon
Professor and Chair, Department of History
University of Hawai'i at Mānoa

PACIFIC OCEAN

The Pacific Ocean encompasses 63.8 million square miles (165.25 million square kilometers) of water, more than 30 percent of Earth's total surface. It is bounded by the Americas, Australia, and Asia, and extends from the Arctic in the north to the Antarctic in the south (Lavery 2013, 323). Defining what the Pacific Ocean is, however, is not as easy as simply identifying the surface area it covers or naming the landmasses that border it. As Epeli Hau'ofa has argued in "Our Sea of Islands," the emphasis on the immense distances of the Pacific Ocean has meant that the islands that fill its spaces seem insignificant—"much too small, too poorly endowed with resources, and too isolated from the centres of economic growth" (Hau'ofa 1993, 4). Rather than accept this valuation of the Pacific Islands, Hau'ofa suggests a rethinking of the Pacific Ocean as a space that connects rather than divides island nations (9). Doing so creates a Pacific that is connected to the rest of the world rather than isolated from it and that can draw from its oceans for income rather than lament its paucity of terrestrial resources. It also implicitly encourages historians of the United States to reframe the country's interactions with the Pacific. The Pacific Ocean becomes a space filled with people rather than an empty blue expanse.

EARLY AMERICAN ACTIVITY IN THE PACIFIC REGION

When Americans entered the Pacific, they entered a space that was subject to contests between imperial powers, and in fact, it was in the Pacific that the United States became an imperial power. In its conquest, the United States also had to contend with local power structures. Americans' ability to engage in trade depended on their ability to navigate these overlapping, complicated political systems. American engagement with the region only began in earnest in the nineteenth century. In 1791, Yankee whalers first rounded Cape Horn to hunt sperm whales (Ellis 2006, 207). In the years that followed, the Yankee whaling fleet experienced enormous growth. It doubled in the 1820s and again in the 1830s (Kasarda and Lindsay 2011, 327). In 1846 the fleet numbered 735 vessels (Lal and Fortune 2000, 210). American traders also sought sandalwood and a sea cucumber called *bêche-de-mer,* which they traded to China (Campbell 2011, 117–125).

American traders established extensive commercial networks and jockeyed for influence with local governments. Perhaps the most influential Americans to enter the Pacific, however, did so as missionaries. In 1819 the American Board of Commissioners for Foreign Missions (ABCFM) sent several married couples to the Sandwich Islands (present-day Hawai'i) to serve as missionaries.

When the American missionaries arrived in the Sandwich Islands, they rejoiced to discover that the *kapu* system that governed the religious beliefs, politics, and cultural life of Native Hawaiians had been abolished. In 1824 the queen regent, Ka'ahumanu (c. 1768–1832), converted to Christianity and encouraged her subjects to do the same. The historian John Garrett wrote that Ka'ahumanu served as "the great mother" of the Protestant church in Hawai'i (1982, 46). She ensured that the white missionaries had access to political power and land to build churches.

The missionaries aided in the transformation of the Sandwich Islands. Gerrit P. Judd (1803–1873), a white physician who had accompanied the third ABCFM delegation to the islands, helped to orchestrate the division of communal lands into private property (Trask 1999, 6–7). Other missionary children saw their future in Hawaiian sugarcane and helped to create the plantation culture that dominated the islands' economy for much of the nineteenth and twentieth centuries. Some scholars have argued that it was the marriages and business endeavors of the children of white missionaries that eventually led to the illegal annexation of Hawai'i by the United States (Garrett 1982, 58).

THE MILITARIZATION OF THE PACIFIC

American involvement with the Pacific was not limited to the Hawaiian Islands. This was true in the twentieth century as well as the nineteenth. In 1898 the Spanish ceded the Philippines, Guam, and Puerto Rico as part of peace negotiations after the Spanish-American War. A year later, the United States signed a treaty with Germany and the United Kingdom agreeing to divide governance of the Samoan Islands between the US and Germany. The part of the archipelago that the United States controlled became American Samoa. Although the United States controlled key island chains in the Pacific, US control of the area would not be consolidated until World War II (1939–1945). During this period, the Pacific became a theater of war between the United States and Japan. Hostilities included countries along the Pacific Rim, such as China and Thailand, as well as the Pacific Islands. The Battle of Tarawa in Kiribati was one of the most fiercely fought in World War II (Wukovits 2006, 237).

The militarization of the Pacific did not end with World War II. In the postwar period, the United States maintained several military bases in the Pacific, including those in Guam, the Hawaiian Islands, and the Kwajalein Atoll. The United States also used the Pacific Islands as a site for tests on nuclear radiation and its effects. In 1946 the US government asked the population of the Bikini Atoll to allow nuclear testing on their islands. The United States promised to relocate the islanders (Teaiwa 1994). Over twenty nuclear devices were eventually detonated on or near the atoll. On March 1, 1954, for example, the US military detonated a hydrogen bomb on a reef in the atoll. Although it was initially meant to weigh 4 to 8 megatons, it weighed 15 megatons when it was finally dropped due to calculation errors. As of 2014, the islanders were still unable to return to their homelands (Agence France Press 2014). In addition to highlighting the role that the American military has played in the Pacific Islands, the story of the Bikini Atoll also underscores the way that the region has been sexualized. For Native Hawaiians in the early twentieth century, for example, the presence of the American military had ambiguous effects. While the military's presence boosted the economy, it also threatened the safety of Native Hawaiian women. Native Hawaiian surfers in Waikiki sometimes confronted American servicemen who took liberties with local women (Walker 2014, 76–77).

IMMIGRATION, SOVEREIGNTY, AND AMERICANS' VISION OF THE PACIFIC

The United States has become an important site of immigration for Pacific Islanders. In 2010 an estimated 1.2 million Pacific Islanders lived in the United States (Hixson, Hepler, and Kim 2012, 1). In addition to Hawai'i, many were concentrated in California and Utah; the latter was partially driven by conversion to Mormonism. When most Americans think of the Pacific Islands, however, they do not imagine the Pacific diaspora. Instead, they imagine a generalized tropical space that is filled with beguiling young women. Native men are either absent from this vision or are demasculinized (Tengan 2008). Scholars like Haunani-Kay Trask (1999) have argued that the vision of the Pacific that American tourism promotes masks the poverty of Native Hawaiians and other Pacific Islanders and the role that the United States has had in perpetuating that poverty.

Questions about the role of the United States in the Pacific Islands have become especially pointed since the 1960s and the development of a Hawaiian sovereignty movement. The movement has argued that the United States should grant the Hawaiian Islands independence or a form of legal sovereignty in recognition of the illegal overthrow of the Hawaiian monarchy in the nineteenth century (Trask 1999; Silva 2004; Tengan 2008; Goodyear-Ka'ōpua, Hussey, and Wright 2014). Few white Americans are aware of the extent of the country's involvement in the Pacific. Scholars, however, have frequently pointed out the neocolonial relationship between the region and the United States. In the twenty-first century, American relationships with the

Pacific world may have to take into account the voices of Pacific Islanders.

SEE ALSO *Hawai'i; Pacific Islands; Spanish-American War*

BIBLIOGRAPHY

Agence France Press. "Bikini Atoll Nuclear Test: 60 Years Later and the Islands Are Still Unliveable." *Guardian* (London), March 1, 2014. http://www.theguardian.com/world/2014/mar/02/bikini-atoll- nuclear-test-60-years

Campbell, Ian C. *Worlds Apart: A History of the Pacific Islands.* 2nd ed. Christchurch, New Zealand: Canterbury University Press, 2011.

Ellis, Richard. *Monsters of the Sea.* Guilford, CT: Lyons Press, 2006. First published by Knopf in 1994.

Garrett, John. *To Live among the Stars: Christian Origins in Oceania.* Suva, Fiji: Institute of the Pacific Studies; Geneva, Switzerland: World Council of Churches Publications, 1982.

Goodyear-Ka'ōpua, Noelani, Ikaika Hussey, and Erin Kahunawaika'ala Wright. *A Nation Rising: Hawaiian Movements for Life, Land, and Sovereignty.* Durham, NC: Duke University Press, 2014.

Hau'ofa, Epeli. "Our Sea of Islands." In *A New Oceania: Rediscovering our Sea of Islands,* edited by Eric Waddell, Vijay Naidu, and Epeli Hau'ofa, 2–16. Suva, Fiji: School of Social and Economic Development, University of the South Pacific Press in association with Beake House, 1993.

Hixson, Lindsay, Bradford B. Hepler, and Myoung Ouk Kim. *The Native Hawaiian and Other Pacific Islander Population: 2010.* 2010 Census Briefs. Washington, DC: US Census Bureau, 2012. https://www.census.gov/prod/cen2010/briefs/c2010br-12.pdf

Kasarda, John D., and Greg Lindsay. *Aerotropolis: The Way We'll Live Next.* New York: Farrar, Straus and Giroux, 2011.

Lal, Brij V., and Kate Fortune, eds. *The Pacific Islands: An Encyclopedia.* Honolulu: University of Hawai'i Press, 2000.

Lavery, Brian. *The Conquest of the Ocean: The Illustrated History of Seafaring.* London: DK, 2013.

Silva, Noenoe K. *Aloha Betrayed: Native Hawaiian Resistance to American Colonialism.* Durham, NC: Duke University Press, 2004.

Teaiwa, Teresia K. "Bikinis and Other S/Pacific N/Oceans." *Contemporary Pacific* 6, 1 (1994): 87–109.

Tengan, Ty P. Kāwika. *Native Men Remade: Gender and Nation in Contemporary Hawai'i.* Durham, NC: Duke University Press, 2008.

Trask, Haunani-Kay. *From a Native Daughter: Colonialism and Sovereignty in Hawai'i.* Rev. ed. Honolulu: University of Hawai'i Press, 1999.

Walker, Isaiah Helekunihi. *Waves of Resistance: Surfing and History in Twentieth-Century Hawai'i.* Honolulu: University of Hawai'i Press, 2014.

Wukovits, John. *One Square Mile of Hell: The Battle for Tarawa.* New York: New American Library, 2006.

Amanda Hendrix-Komoto
Assistant Professor
Montana State University

PAINE, THOMAS
1737–1809

Born in Thetford, England, in 1737, Thomas Paine was trained as a staymaker but spent many years as an exciseman in Lewes, a town known for its reformist and radical republican ethos. He would come to be a leading figure in the revolutionary era for his writings on these themes. While Paine may have dabbled with writing in Lewes, his literary career began in earnest after he immigrated to Philadelphia in 1774. Armed with a personal letter of recommendation from Benjamin Franklin (1706–1790), Paine quickly settled into the bustle of colonial life as an editor of the *Pennsylvania Magazine*, putting him in the forefront of colonial discontent with Britain.

COMMON SENSE

Paine would become an international figure with the publication in 1776 of the pamphlet *Common Sense*, a runaway best seller that took the colonies by storm. Although scholars question Paine's estimate that 150,000 copies were sold in the colonies alone, none doubt that it was wildly popular and galvanized the resolve of many colonists to forgo reconciliation and to declare independence from Britain. Written in a bold and simple style, *Common Sense* emphasized the stark differences between the Old World and the New, and Paine argued not only that the colonies would be better off on their own, but that the time was ripe for severing ties with Britain. At its heart, *Common Sense* paired a deep hostility to monarchical governments with an unwavering faith in the ability of the people to govern themselves. Paine would reprise these themes throughout his literary career, during and after the American Revolution.

RIGHTS OF MAN AND THE BURKE-PAINE CONTROVERSY

In 1787 Paine returned to England, taking with him a fervent belief that Americans were at the vanguard of great political change and that their republican revolution would be an inspiration to the despot-ridden people of Europe. For Paine, the first rumblings of the French Revolution in 1788 and 1789 were proof that the American republican fever was spreading to the continent, and he hoped a revolution in England would soon be next. British statesman Edmund Burke (1729–1797), however, saw only danger in France and impending disaster for Britain. In 1790, Burke published *Reflections on the Revolution in France* as a warning to British elites that France's revolution was based on dangerously speculative premises that could be twisted for bloody and demagogic purposes. Burke, who advocated gradual reform, criticized the recklessness of the revolutionaries and chastised those who wished to follow the French in their foolhardy republican course. Paine fired back in 1791 with *Rights of Man*, combining a full-voiced defense of the republican principles of the French Revolution with a scathing critique of Burke and the oppressive British political system. The following year, Paine published a second part of *Rights of Man*, continuing his attack on the British monarchy by holding up the United States as the exemplary model of a real and working republican system of government.

The Burke-Paine controversy, as it came to be called, spawned an immense pamphlet war with hundreds of works responding to the positions of both men. *Rights of Man* became a huge sensation in Britain, and Paine gained the reputation as the chief agitator for republican revolution. Radical organizations like the London Corresponding Society were energized by *Rights of Man*, taking its forceful and plainspoken arguments as foundational arguments for democracy, and producing cheap editions of the book that they widely distributed. Not surprisingly, *Rights of Man* stoked the fears of conservatives who worried that it was winding up in the hands of common people and was fomenting revolution among society's lower orders. Conservatives mounted a huge anti-Paine propaganda campaign that included pamphlets, scurrilous biographies, hostile political cartoons, and effigy burnings. The second part of *Rights of Man* brought down on Paine an indictment for seditious libel, causing him to flee to France in September 1792. Two months later, an English court convicted him in absentia, making him a permanent exile from his native land.

Although the reaction to *Rights of Man* in America was not nearly as heated as it was in Britain, it still sold briskly and became a part of the partisan political battles of 1790s over the nature and future of the American polity. Like Paine, a number of radicals were forced to flee Britain, but they took their Paineite republicanism with them. Many of these transatlantic radicals found their way to the United States and became key players in publishing ventures that supported Jeffersonians against Federalists.

SOJOURN IN FRANCE

In France, Paine received a hero's welcome, was granted honorary French citizenship, and was elected representative from Calais to the upcoming National Convention. Despite speaking little French, he took an active part in French politics while trying to remain above the increasingly fractious partisanship of the convention. He assisted in drafting a new French constitution, made an unsuccessful petition to spare the king's life (earning him the enmity of the Jacobins), and turned his hand to writing about religion in *The Age of Reason*, outlining his

deistic beliefs that were highly critical of Christianity. As a polarized French society hurtled toward the Terror, Paine's fortune faltered, and he was thrown into the Luxembourg Prison at the end of 1793. After eleven months under threat of the guillotine, Paine was released after James Monroe (1758–1831), recently appointed American minister to France, intervened on his behalf. Paine hoped to return to the United States, but his departure was delayed by illnesses, a reengagement in French politics, and unsafe seas during France's wars with Britain. He continued writing on social, political, economic, and religious topics, most notably a second part of *The Age of Reason* in 1795 and *Agrarian Justice* in 1796. He applauded the Irish uprising of 1798 and envisioned a republican revolution in Britain that would be supported by a French invasion.

RETURN TO THE UNITED STATES

Disheartened by Napoleon Bonaparte's rise to power, and seeing the Treaty of Amiens as an opportunity for safe passage, Paine finally returned to America in 1802. Instead of being heartily welcomed, however, Paine discovered that his reputation had suffered sorely at the hands of the Federalist press, which used him as a way to score points against Jeffersonians. *Rights of Man* had already become a chip in the larger partisanship roiling the political scene, and *The Age of Reason*'s attacks on Christianity shocked and angered even some of his most ardent supporters. The final straw had come in 1796 when Paine published a scathing letter to his old friend George Washington (1732–1799), whom Paine rebuked for having done nothing to secure his release from the Luxembourg Prison. Paine not only attacked Washington's policies, but characterized him as a duplicitously ambitious politician with aristocratic tendencies. In the increasingly vitriolic political climate of the late 1790s, Federalists took every opportunity to blast Paine, smearing him (and by implication, Jefferson) as a dangerously radical Jacobin and an immoral atheistic blasphemer.

In the final seven years of his life, Paine did not shy away from controversy, and he continued to do what he had done since his first arrival on American shores: write. Despite recurrent illnesses and the physical effects of old age, he waged protracted battles with Federalists, continued to defend his religious beliefs, and wrote articles on domestic and international affairs. Paine died in 1809 in Greenwich Village and was buried at his farm in New Rochelle, New York.

SEE ALSO *American Revolution; French Revolution*

BIBLIOGRAPHY

Claeys, Gregory. *Thomas Paine: Social and Political Thought.* New York: Routledge, 1989.

Cotlar, Seth. *Tom Paine's America: The Rise and Fall of Transatlantic Radicalism in the Early Republic.* Charlottesville: University of Virginia Press, 2011.

Keane, John. *Tom Paine: A Political Life.* Boston: Little, Brown, 1995.

Newman, Simon P., and Peter S. Onuf, eds. *Paine and Jefferson in the Age of Revolutions.* Charlottesville: University of Virginia Press, 2013.

Philp, Mark. "The Role of America in the 'Debate on France' 1791–5: Thomas Paine's Insertion." *Utilitas* 5, 2 (1993): 221–237.

Young, Alfred. "*Common Sense* and the *Rights of Man* in America." In *Science, Mind, and Art: Essays on Science and the Humanistic Understanding in Art, Epistemology, Religion, and Ethics in Honor of Robert S. Cohen*, edited by Kostas Gavroglu, John Stachel, and Marx W. Wartofsky, 423–424. Boston: Kluwer Academic, 1995.

Patrick W. Hughes
University of Pittsburgh

PALESTINE

The term *Palestine* is multivalent and has entailed different references throughout American history. Geographically, *Palestine* derives from the Roman *Palestina*, referring to its administrative region. Although the Ottoman Empire tended to refer to the region administratively as *Syria* from the late medieval period until the twentieth century, the people who lived there continued to call it *Filastin*. After World War I (1914–1918), the British Mandate revived the administrative use of the term *Palestine*. Americans referred to the region as *Palestine* until the mid-twentieth-century establishment of the State of Israel. At that point, the political territory became known as *Israel*, and *Palestine* has increasingly referred to the local nationalist movement as distinct from the Jewish state.

Pan-Arabism and Pan-Muslimism were popular ideologies among some in the Middle East, and binationalism and civil democracy with no ethnic concept of the nation had proponents among some Jews and non-Jews in the Middle East and the United States until the mid-twentieth century. However, most political negotiations in which the United States advocated any kind of rights for Palestinians centered on a two-state model—Jewish Israel and a Palestinian state—especially after the 1960s.

The region of Palestine loomed large in the American imagination as the "Holy Land" from the earliest arrival of colonial-era Christians. Americans imagined themselves as the "New Israel," comparing their providential progress to the failure of the Israelites to keep the covenant in biblical Palestine. During the nineteenth century, when technology permitted an increase in travel to Palestine along with widespread reproduction of representations of Palestine, the region became even more popular. During that time, Palestine was an identifiable region and subject within the Ottoman Empire. Disputes within the Ottoman Empire that led to massacres and oppression of Christians, such as the Greek war for independence and revolts in Bosnia, Herzegovina, and Bulgaria, influenced Christian-American views not only of the empire and Turks but also of Muslims and Arabs. Even as Americans referred to "Palestine" as its own geographic region, they also placed it into the larger category of the "Holy Land," the place of the sacred history of the Old Testament and the life of Jesus, including Syria and portions of Lebanon, plus much of the broader Middle East.

The tendency among Americans of various Jewish and Christian backgrounds to see Palestine as the "Holy Land" remained in tension with a vision of the United States as a "New Israel" or "New Holy Land," although frequently, the two conceptions worked in tandem. The power of the concept of both America and Palestine as "Holy Lands" has been its malleability, the possibility to adapt such a concept to various national, regional, racial, religious, class, and gendered views. The biblical lens also served as the frame of reference for twentieth-century American diplomacy in the Middle East. The question of politics became increasingly important for the United States after Britain formally gained control over the Mandate in 1920. Popular culture and formal politics have represented Palestine in distinct but mutually influential ways, and therefore it is important to understand Palestine from religious, cultural, and political perspectives.

REPRESENTATIONS OF PALESTINE IN AMERICAN CHRISTIANITY

The importance of the Holy Land as the location of the sacred history of the Torah for Jews and of the Old and New Testaments for Christians has influenced the forms and practices by which Americans have engaged Palestine. It has also shaped the voices of political and social power in those representations. Technological advancements in the nineteenth century led to an increase in ever-more luxurious and speedy travel, as well as the availability of photographs, stereographs, and panoramas that seemed to bring Palestine closer to the United States. In these photographs, Palestine merged with the broader Middle East as a visual representation of the Holy Land at large. Prolific photography houses created a recognizable image of the Holy Land. Photographs of the Holy Land frequently accompanied books, pamphlets, and exhibits related to the Bible and the region. The same images were printed and reprinted, shared and reinterpreted by Americans from various backgrounds. Americans viewed images of Palestine through their particular personal and social backgrounds, but they also created a larger national culture and practice of circulating and viewing images of Palestine.

The technology that made travel to the Middle East increasingly possible coincided with the rise of biblical criticism in seminaries and universities. Thus, at a moment when many Christians and Jews perceived an attack on the authority of the Bible, Palestine and academic studies of it became a claim for religious authority. For some Christians, biblical archeology in Palestine became a kind of "fifth gospel," and for some Jews it became historical evidence for the chosenness of Jews as a nation. American views of Palestine were also informed by Orientalism and a sense that Palestine had changed less than the rest of the world, leading many Americans to assume that contemporaneous Palestinian people, lifestyles, and cultures could be taken as evidence of the biblical period.

Americans also constructed models, museums, expositions, plays, films, and political demonstrations that made Palestine come alive in American life. For example, the Chautauqua Institution, founded in 1874 in southwestern New York, built a 400-foot-long (122-meter-long) scaled replica of biblical Palestine and held meetings during which actors dressed up as residents of Palestine and interacted with visitors. At the 1904 Louisiana Purchase Exposition (the St. Louis World's Fair), white Protestants created an almost full-sized replica of Jerusalem as it looked at the turn of the twentieth century. Visitors could "travel to Palestine" without leaving the United States, and depictions of Palestine were linked with American national performance and the goal of appearing as a legitimate political power. Christian exhibits, along with passion plays and other dramas, have continued to appear across America throughout the twentieth and into the twenty-first century.

NEW VOICES AND REPRESENTATIONS OF PALESTINE

Jews were frequently the objects in American Christians' visions of Palestine. In light of this, Jewish Americans sought to create their own representations of themselves and Palestine. Christians have tended to see Jews as living evidence of the Old Testament: once a chosen people, but now superseded by the new covenant through Jesus. If rhetoric about America as a "New Israel" and about Palestine as the "Holy Land" increased the visibility of Jews in Christianity, it also drew attention to the question of Jews in America. Jewish Americans were uncomfortable with the theological and stereotypical nature of this

visibility designed by Christians. Jewish Americans also focused on Palestine as a holy land within their religious practices and in their representations of Palestine, from photographs to world fairs. Jewish participation, however, has included a tension between the shared value of Palestine as a holy land with Christian Americans and Jewish investment in reshaping images of Jews in America and Palestine.

When the Ottoman Empire fell and Palestine became a part of the British Mandate in 1920, competition for authority over Palestine became increasingly complicated. Differing perspectives on Palestine, and who properly represented it, converged at the 1933 Century of Progress World's Fair in Chicago. By that time, the British government was trying to extricate itself from Palestine, and did not wish to promote any representation of Palestine as an autonomous region. Zionists, for their part, held a "Jewish Day" that paralleled official days celebrating other nations at the fair, culminating in a pageant titled *The Romance of a People*, which featured more than three thousand Jewish American performers on a replica of the Temple in Jerusalem at Soldier Field. At the 1939 World's Fair in New York City, Zionists created a Palestine Pavilion that continued to link Jewish nationalist efforts with territory in Palestine.

These performances helped shape and legitimize the idea of a Jewish state in Palestine, even before the State of Israel was founded in 1948. They also helped to legitimize Jewish American identity in the United States. They played on earlier Christian attachments to the land of Palestine, while also revising visions of Palestine and of Jews inside and outside of the Holy Land. Jewish exhibits at the world's fairs thus rejected a view of Jewish Americans or members of a potential Jewish nation-state as Oriental relics, though they also played on certain Orientalist visions of Sephardic and Mizrahi Jews, as well as Arabs and Muslims.

Arabs and Muslims were frequently omitted or poorly represented in Christian and Jewish representations of Palestine. Palestinians have thus critiqued Zionist and biblical understandings of contemporary Palestine, especially those that did not give voice to Palestinians. In the early twentieth century, a Palestine National League was formed to seek political rights for the Palestinian national movement. These efforts received very little attention in America, however, due in part to the small number of Palestinian and Arab Americans.

POLITICS IN PALESTINE AND AMERICAN DIPLOMACY

American diplomacy and policies addressing the region of Palestine before and after the creation of the State of Israel in 1948 have been complex. Following the Balfour

Declaration (1917) and the end of World War I, American Zionists balanced an interest in a Jewish national homeland—if not a state—with careful negotiations and diplomacy with successive US presidents and the US State Department. A practicing Presbyterian, President Woodrow Wilson responded to debates over the mandate through his view that a Jewish return to the Holy Land would fulfill biblical prophecy while balancing American national interests. Thus, while he advocated "self-determination" internationally, he was sympathetic to Zionism in Palestine and did not advocate a Palestinian state. In 1937 the British Peel Commission proposed partition as an end to the Mandate. In 1939 the British government's MacDonald White Paper promised an independent state in Palestine and limited Jewish land purchases and immigration. Many American Zionists considered this a violation of their understanding of the Balfour Declaration and pushed harder for a Jewish state, against both British and Arab visions for Palestine's future.

The US State Department prioritized American political and financial interests. However important the question of Jewish refugees in Europe may have been to Jewish Americans, the State Department did not consider immigration from Europe to Palestine to directly affect US national interests and isolation. Therefore, the State Department avoided involvement with the question of Jewish immigration to Palestine even during World War II (1939–1945). During the war, President Franklin D. Roosevelt tried to appease Arabs and Zionists, though ultimately neither group was pleased with the president's policies toward Palestine. Roosevelt opposed partition of Palestine. President Harry Truman was influenced in large part by the end of the war and its constraints. Truman supported a Jewish state, partially influenced by his Christian reading of the Bible and the problem of Holocaust survivors who languished in European displacement camps even after the end of World War II.

In 1947, Britain passed responsibility for Palestine to the United Nations (UN), at which point American Zionists supported the partition of Palestine. The United Nations approved partition and a Jewish state. In 1948 Britain withdrew from Palestine, but surrounding Arab states joined local Palestinians in a war against the State of Israel. At the end of the war in 1949, Israel had gained 50 percent more territory than offered in the UN partition plan. Although the State of Israel was established at that point, no Palestinian state was created. Instead, the regions of Palestine not integrated into Israel became integrated with surrounding Arab states: Jordan controlled the West Bank, and Gaza came under Egyptian rule. Palestinians refer to the creation of the State of Israel in 1948 as "the Nakba" (the catastrophe).

Throughout the 1950s and 1960s, the US government supported Israel and did not address the idea of Palestinians as a potential nation-state. Presidents Dwight Eisenhower, John F. Kennedy, and Lyndon B. Johnson considered the United States to have a special affinity with Israel, and their administrations offered aid and diplomatic support to Israel. Kennedy announced that the United States had a "special relationship with Israel in the Middle East" and signed the first arms agreement with Israel in 1962. This idea of a special relationship with Israel influenced American diplomacy throughout the twentieth century, especially the US role in negotiations between the State of Israel and the Palestine national movement, which has increasingly defined Arab identity in the region.

In American politics and popular culture, Palestinians have often been represented as attacking the peaceful democratic State of Israel, especially after the 1967 war. While Jews typically refer to the war as the Six-Day War, Palestinians call it the June War, the 1967 Arab-Israeli War, or "The Setback." Israel launched a preemptive strike against Egypt, Syria, and Jordan as those countries prepared for war against Israel. After the war, Israel occupied territory in the Sinai, Golan Heights, Gaza, and the West Bank (along the Jordan River and Dead Sea, including East Jerusalem and the Western Wall). While Israel did not necessarily intend to continue to occupy the territories, negotiations proved difficult. The United States supported Israel, and six Arab states ceased diplomatic relations with the United States in the wake of the war and failed negotiations. The September 1967 Khartoum Conference led to an Arab resolution of "No peace with Israel, no recognition of Israel, no negotiations with Israel" that would influence official policies, though not always practical actions, for decades after.

The Palestine Liberation Organization (PLO) was established in 1964, and the Palestinian National Charter was created in 1968. Yasser Arafat, head of the political party Fatah, became chairman of the PLO in 1969. During the late 1960s, some Palestinians turned toward suicide bombing and other violent means to gain political power. The United States labeled the PLO a terrorist organization, and therefore refused to negotiate with the PLO.

Israel fared much worse during the 1973 Arab-Israeli War. Under Presidents Richard Nixon and Gerald Ford, the United States stepped up negotiations with Syria and Egypt, but not with the PLO. In 1978 the United States (Jimmy Carter), Israel (Menachem Begin), and Egypt (Anwar Sadat) signed the Camp David Accords, which led to a successful treaty between Egypt and Israel and the return of the Sinai to Egypt's governance. President Carter explicitly asserted Palestinians' need for a homeland and called for mutual recognition between Israel and Palestine. However, successful deals over other territories, including the West Bank and Gaza, did not follow.

During Israel's 1982 invasion of Lebanon, Phalangist (right-wing Lebanese Christian) militiamen massacred hundreds of Palestinians in the Sabra and Shatila refugee camps in Beirut while Israeli forces surrounded the camps. US Marines arrived in Beirut as part of a multinational peacekeeping force. Jewish and non-Jewish Americans tended to be critical of attempts by Israel to expand geographic limits and of the massacre of Palestinians in refugee camps, although Israelis were not directly responsible.

In December 1987 the Palestinian Intifada (uprising) began in the West Bank and Gaza. The Islamist political party Hamas was founded during the uprising. Jewish Americans continued to respond to events in Palestine-Israel in a variety of ways, including outspoken support of the State of Israel but also an increasing level of criticism of actions toward Palestinians. But in 1988 Arafat recognized Israel's right to exist, and the United States became willing to negotiate with the PLO. Though President Ronald Reagan had not been interested in negotiating with Palestinians, President George H. W. Bush renewed US involvement. In December 1989, some US activists met with the PLO. About three-quarters of Jewish Americans expressed support for these negotiations, though this increased tension among Jews in the United States and Israel.

In the 1993 Oslo Declaration of Principles, Israel and the PLO agreed to mutual recognition. This paved the way for the September 1995 establishment of the Palestinian National Authority. Two months later, an Israeli who opposed these steps toward Palestinian statehood assassinated Israeli prime minister Yitzhak Rabin. Thereafter, the Jewish American response became more fragmented, as did Israeli and Palestinian responses.

The United States (Bill Clinton), Israel (Ehud Barak), and Palestine (Yasser Arafat) met in 2000 for the second Camp David summit, though the meeting did not lead to a peace agreement. As the peace process stalled, there was an outbreak of suicide bombings by some Palestinians after 2002. Although negotiations have not ended Israel's authority in the occupied territories, Palestinians have gained some governing powers. Fatah, headed by Mahmoud Abbas after Arafat's death in 2004, was elected in the West Bank, and elections in 2007 placed Hamas in power in Gaza. While some Palestinians see Fatah as corrupt or unable to achieve Palestinian national goals through negotiations with Israel, the increase in Hamas's power has prompted the United States and Israel to

negotiate with Fatah. Various peace talks have begun and failed since the beginning of the twenty-first century, a period also punctuated by outbreaks of violence.

SEE ALSO *Islam; Israel; Judaism; League of Nations; Middle East; Treaty of Versailles; United Nations; World War I; Zionism*

BIBLIOGRAPHY

Adler, Jennifer Axsom. "The Other Witness: Nineteenth-Century American Protestantism and the Material Gospel Theology." PhD diss., Vanderbilt University, 2015.

Carr, Jessica. "Palestine in Jewish-American Life, 1901–1948." PhD diss., Indiana University, 2013.

Christison, Kathleen. *Perceptions of Palestine: Their Influence on U.S. Middle East Policy.* Berkeley: University of California Press, 1999.

Cohen, Naomi. *The Americanization of Zionism, 1897–1948.* Hanover, NH: Brandeis University Press, 2003.

Davidson, Lawrence. *America's Palestine: Popular and Official Perceptions from Balfour to Israeli Statehood.* Gainesville: University Press of Florida, 2001.

Davis, John. *The Landscape of Belief: Encountering the Holy Land in Nineteenth-Century American Art and Culture.* Princeton, NJ: Princeton University Press, 1996.

Friedman, Thomas. *From Beirut to Jerusalem.* New York: Macmillan, 2010. First published in 1989.

Gerber, Haim. *Remembering and Imagining Palestine: Identity and Nationalism from the Crusades to the Present.* New York: Palgrave Macmillan, 2008.

Greenspoon, Leonard, and Ronald Simkins, eds. *"A Land Flowing with Milk and Honey": Visions of Israel from Biblical to Modern Times.* Omaha, NE: Creighton University Press, 2001.

Khalidi, Rashid. *Palestinian Identity: The Construction of Modern National Consciousness.* New York: Columbia University Press, 1997.

Khalidi, Walid. *Before Their Diaspora: A Photographic History of the Palestinians, 1876–1948.* Washington, DC: Institute for Palestine Studies, 1984.

Kirshenblatt-Gimblett, Barbara. *Destination Culture: Tourism, Museums, and Heritage.* Berkeley: University of California Press, 1998.

Kirshenblatt-Gimblett, Barbara, and Jonathan Karp, eds. *The Art of Being Jewish in Modern Times.* Philadelphia: University of Pennsylvania Press, 2008.

Long, Burke. *Imagining the Holy Land: Maps, Models, and Fantasy Travels.* Bloomington: Indiana University Press, 2003.

Love, Lauren. "Performing Jewish Nationhood: *The Romance of a People* at the 1933 Chicago World's Fair." *TDR: The Drama Review* 55, 3 (2011): 57–67.

Rosenthal, Steven T. "Long-Distance Nationalism: American Jews, Zionism, and Israel." In *The Cambridge Companion to American Judaism*, edited by Dana Evan Kaplan. Cambridge: Cambridge University Press, 2005.

Said, Edward. *Orientalism.* New York: Random House, 1978.

Sarna, Jonathan. "A Projection of America as It Ought to Be: Zion in the Mind's Eye of American Jews." In *Envisioning Israel: The Changing Ideals and Images of North American Jews*, edited by Allon Gal. Detroit, MI: Wayne State University Press, 1996.

Shandler, Jeffrey, and Beth Wenger, eds. *Encounters with the "Holy Land": Place, Past, and Future in American Jewish Culture.* Hanover, NH: National Museum of American Jewish History, Trustees of the University of Pennsylvania, University Press of New England, 1997.

Sher, Gilead. *The Israeli-Palestinian Peace Negotiations, 1999–2001: Within Reach.* New York: Routledge, 2006.

Jessica Carr
Assistant Professor in Religious Studies
Lafayette College

PALESTINE LIBERATION ORGANIZATION

SEE *Arab-Israeli Conflict; Palestine.*

PALMER, PHOEBE

SEE *Foreign Mission Movement.*

PAN AMERICAN WORLD AIRWAYS

Pan American World Airways, or Pan Am, was the United States' first international airline and the nation's de facto flagship carrier for most of the twentieth century. Although Pan Am is most closely associated with its charismatic longtime president, Juan Terry Trippe (1899–1981), the airline was founded in 1927 by three military officers: Henry "Hap" Arnold and Carl Spaatz of the US Army Air Corps and Jack Jouett of the US Navy. Pan Am's early history illustrates interconnections between military and commercial aviation, and between the United States' strategic and commercial interests. During the mid-1920s, US military leaders had become increasingly concerned about airlines in South America that were financed or managed by German and Austrian émigrés—in particular, the powerful Sociedad Colombo-Alemana de Transportes Aéroes (SCADTA). The prospect of German-run airlines flying in the vicinity of the Panama Canal alarmed US military leaders. To protect the security of the canal—and to uphold the 1823 Monroe Doctrine, which aimed to limit European influence in the Western Hemisphere—

Arnold, Spaatz, and Jouett incorporated Pan American Airways in early 1927 and subsequently received a US Post Office contract for airmail carriage between Miami and Havana.

Later that year, Trippe, a twenty-eight-year-old Yale alumnus and aviation entrepreneur, purchased the start-up airline, using his college connections to secure financial backing from Vanderbilt, Whitney, and Rockefeller scions of fortune. On October 28, 1927, Pan Am inaugurated scheduled airmail flights between Key West and Havana; passenger flights began in January 1928. Nicknamed "the cocktail circuit" because many passengers flew to Cuba to seek relief from Prohibition, this 90-mile (145-kilometer) route was the humble beginning of what would soon become a worldwide aerial empire. When Pan Am purchased fledgling competitor New York, Rio, and Buenos Aires Line (NYRBA) in 1930, it became the United States' exclusive international airline. By 1931, Pan Am's routes encircled the Americas. It inaugurated service across the Pacific in 1935 and across the Atlantic in 1939. Pan Am emerged from World War II (1939–1945) as a truly global airline, connecting the United States to every continent except Antarctica. Even after the Civil Aeronautics Board voted, in late 1945, to dismantle its monopoly on international routes, Pan Am continued for decades to function as the world's most powerful airline.

Some aviation historians have credited Trippe for Pan Am's rapid ascendancy. To be sure, Trippe was a visionary leader; like the railroad barons of the nineteenth century, he was an empire builder who imagined and then created a globe-girdling network of US-operated airways. By hiring expert advisers, such as Charles Lindbergh (1902–1974), investing in the most advanced technologies, and prioritizing passenger service, Trippe made Pan Am into an industry standard-bearer for both safety and luxury in air travel. However, the US government also played an indispensable role in Pan Am's success. Airmail subsidies largely financed its operations during its early decades; State Department assistance secured generous operating concessions from foreign governments. During World War II, Pan Am solidified its close relationship with Washington by serving as a military contractor. In 1940 and 1941 the Franklin D. Roosevelt (1882–1945) administration authorized Pan Am to construct or improve airfields throughout Latin America (in order to increase the security of the Western Hemisphere) and to transport Lend-Lease supplies across Africa and the Middle East. Pan Am continued to serve as a military contractor during the Cold War; its Guided Missiles Range Division, for example, obtained air force contracts to manage a 6,000-mile (9,656-kilometer) chain of missile-testing stations from Florida through the Caribbean.

Pan Am rose to the height of its influence during the 1950s and 1960s, an era nostalgically remembered as the "golden age of air travel." It was the first airline to operate scheduled round-the-world service (1947), the first US airline to introduce jets on transatlantic routes (1958), and the first US airline to offer flights to the Soviet Union (1968). While symbolizing the glamour of the cosmopolitan jet set, Pan Am also made international flights accessible to less wealthy travelers, thanks to tourist-class fares (introduced in 1952) and "Fly Now, Pay Later" installment plans (1954).

Beginning in the late 1960s, however, Pan Am grappled with a series of internal and external crises that ultimately led to its 1991 bankruptcy and subsequent demise. First, Trippe retired in 1968. In the absence of his visionary yet autocratic leadership, Pan Am floundered as a series of CEOs made controversial business decisions and lost employee and customer loyalty. Second, Pan Am suffered financially from Trippe's decision to purchase an expensive fleet of Boeing 747 jumbo jets—which were delivered right before the 1973 oil crisis increased fuel prices and discouraged discretionary travel expenses. Third, the Airline Deregulation Act of 1978 dismantled federal regulation of routes and fares, subjecting Pan Am and other "legacy" carriers to intense competition from low-cost, nonunionized airlines, such as Delta. Finally, the 1988 bombing of Pan Am Flight 103 over Lockerbie, Scotland, caused travelers to lose confidence in the "World's Most Experienced Airline." Lockerbie was, according to one pilot, "the day the heart of Pan American died." After declaring bankruptcy in January 1991, Pan Am operated its last flight, from Barbados to Miami, on December 4, 1991.

Even after going out of business, Pan Am has retained its status as a cultural icon. In 2006 fashion designer Marc Jacobs created a limited-edition line of "Pan Am" travel bags, nearly identical to the original sky-blue bags carried by the airline's flight attendants—except for the presence of the designer's signature opposite Pan Am's logo. The boutique Flight 001, which sells high-end travel accessories, was named after Pan Am's famous around-the-world route. The airline has also featured prominently in such films as *Catch Me If You Can* (2002, dir. Steven Spielberg) and ABC's eponymous period drama, *Pan Am*, which premiered in September 2011. Although the series aired for only one season, it vividly captured the glamour of Pan Am during the 1960s jet age—as well as the airline's enduring cultural allure as a symbol and conduit of US global power during the so-called American Century.

SEE ALSO *Boeing Company; Globalization*

BIBLIOGRAPHY

Bender, Marylin, and Selig Altschul. *The Chosen Instrument: Pan Am, Juan Trippe, the Rise and Fall of an American Entrepreneur.* New York: Simon and Schuster, 1982.

Daley, Robert. *An American Saga: Juan Trippe and His Pan Am Empire.* New York: Random House, 1980.

Gandt, Robert. *Skygods: The Fall of Pan Am.* New York: Morrow, 1995.

Newton, Wesley Phillips. *The Perilous Sky: U.S. Aviation Diplomacy and Latin America, 1919–1931.* Coral Gables, FL: University of Miami Press, 1978.

Van Vleck, Jenifer. *Empire of the Air: Aviation and the American Ascendancy.* Cambridge, MA: Harvard University Press, 2013.

Jenifer Van Vleck
Assistant Professor of History
Yale University

PAN-AFRICANISM

Pan-Africanism encompasses a diverse set of ideologies, political movements, and initiatives that gained currency among a significant number of African American leaders from the nineteenth century through the mid-twentieth century and beyond. At some points, especially in the early nineteenth and early twentieth centuries, Pan-Africanism involved proposals for a mass exodus or emigration back to Africa of African peoples (enslaved or free) living in diaspora. At other points, frequently simultaneously, Pan-Africanism involved a fundamental critique of European colonialism and empire, as well as the systems of racial slavery and unfree labor these regimes imposed on African peoples throughout much of the Atlantic world during the modern era. US-based Pan-Africanists held diverse goals and political and cultural beliefs, and they participated in these broad movements directly at their outset. Pan-Africanism in the United States often united around initiatives for increasing commercial, political, and cultural relations with independence struggles on the African continent itself, while advocating against racial discrimination, especially in America.

BACK-TO-AFRICA AND COLONIAL-REFORM EFFORTS

Black nationalist figures led one arm of the Pan-Africanist appeal and advocated various forms of return migration to parts of West Africa, where countries like Sierra Leone and Liberia later emerged as independent nations. In the United States, nineteenth-century nationalist figures included militant abolitionists (many of whom were born into slavery or who had parents that were), such as Paul

Cuffe (1759–1817), Martin R. Delany (1812–1885), and Henry Highland Garnet (1815–1882). Some of these nationalist figures also shared a Christian missionary spirit that imagined bringing "civilization" or "uplift" to Africa as part of efforts to promote emigration. Others, like Edward Wilmot Blyden (1832–1912) from St. Thomas in the Caribbean, heralded the great civilizations of the African past and sought to redeem the continent through emigration schemes.

During the early twentieth century, the Jamaican-born immigrant Marcus Garvey (1887–1940) headed the Universal Negro Improvement Association (UNIA), which became one of the largest and most prolific black nationalist organizations in the history of the United States. At its height during the late 1910s and early-to-mid 1920s, the UNIA claimed to have over 6 million members worldwide. The UNIA promoted various "back-to-Africa" projects to ensure the continent would be returned to Africans and that blacks around the diaspora were conscious of their ancestral origins. Garvey took an even more critical position on European empires and on racial oppression in the United States than his nineteenth-century nationalist predecessors had, arguing for full and complete independence and freedom for African nations and peoples around the world.

Other figures at the dawn of the twentieth century, like the prolific African American intellectual W. E. B. Du Bois (1868–1963) and other like-minded intellectuals, convened the first of several global congresses for Pan-Africanism. At first, these congresses sought to engage directly with European governments to reform colonial policies. Du Bois and his contemporaries initially promoted political and moral reforms within prevailing colonial systems because the British, French, Germans, Italians, Belgians, and Dutch had gained vast possessions throughout much of Africa over the course of the late nineteenth century and dominated the development of government structures in these colonies. In 1900 Du Bois joined H. Sylvester Williams (1869–1911) of Trinidad and Bishop Alexander Walters (1858–1917) of the African Methodist Episcopal Zion Church from the United States, along with a group of mainly black British intellectuals, in organizing the first of several Pan-African Congresses in London. Later meetings of the Pan-African Congress took place in 1919, 1921, 1927, and 1945.

A SHIFT TOWARD RADICALISM

After the devastations of World War I (1914–1918), which pitted empires against each other and adversely affected people of color as colonial subjects, the Pan-Africanist movement started to move away from colonial-reform efforts and took on more emancipatory goals and radical political views, like immediate appeals for independence and nationhood. Writing in the *Crisis* magazine about the racial policies of the Warren Harding (1865–1923) administration in the United States, Du Bois echoed sentiments expressed by the Pan-African Congress of 1921 for peace, the "uplift of all men," and the "absolute equality of races" (Du Bois 1986, 1192).

This rhetorical shift within the Pan-African Congress movement was at least partly a response to challenges in the consensus of what Pan-Africanism was by the post–World War I period. Nationalist groups like the UNIA, with broader bases of support among African American working classes in the United States, especially criticized Du Bois and the early Pan-African Congresses for their elitism. Such critiques revealed how African American political and intellectual leaders like Du Bois espoused notions of race leadership that were also based on the idea that "talented," educated members of the black diaspora were best positioned to advance both the ideals of African independence and the advocacy needed to combat racial discrimination in the United States.

In light of such debates among black political leaders, especially after World War I, Pan-Africanism became increasingly open to new ideologies and mediums of communicating about the movement as older European empires dissolved. These developments included the rise of an internationalist Left, given the successes of the Bolshevik Revolution (1917) in Russia, the growth of anticolonialism throughout much of the Third World by the mid-twentieth century, and the proliferation of the black international press (which included such US black outlets as the *Chicago Defender*, the *Pittsburgh Courier*, and the Associated Negro Press, who each covered African independence struggles extensively).

These developments meant that Pan-Africanism from the 1920s onward demanded more immediate forms of independence from European empire, as well as varying degrees of radical social reform and revolution. For example, some black Americans, such as the famous singer and civil rights activist Paul Robeson (1898–1976), and even Du Bois later in his life, engaged with Pan-African ideas through US Communist Party front organizations like the Negro Trade Union Committee and the Council on African Affairs through the 1930s and 1940s—offering some of the earliest critiques of Italian fascism in Ethiopia and apartheid in South Africa.

Likewise, US black nationalists of the 1950s and 1960s, such as Malcolm X (1925–1965), missed few chances to critique America's foreign policy exploits in Africa, notably the Central Intelligence Agency's involvement in the assassination of Patrice Lumumba (1925–1961) in the Congo. Such perspectives were buoyed by the fact that from World War I through World War II

(1939–1945) and afterward, European empires had fragmented and given way to a new global order based ostensibly on keeping international peace in an increasingly bipolar world as the United States ascended to its status as the preeminent global industrial and military power. Over this period, black struggles for racial justice in the United States certainly identified with Pan-African identities as they themselves engaged with American power through civil rights movements and related appeals for racial reform. However, by the mid-twentieth century and with some exceptions, black Americans were no longer the leading intellectuals of Pan-Africanism as a movement but rather more often observers and supporters from afar.

SEE ALSO *Africa; Ali, Muhammad; Back-to-Africa Movement; Black Power Movement; Decolonization; Liberia; Malcolm X; Mexico; Monroe Doctrine (1823); Nation of Islam; South America; Universal Negro Improvement Association (UNIA)*

BIBLIOGRAPHY

Du Bois, W. E. B. "President Harding and Social Equality" (1921). In *W. E. B. Du Bois: Writings*, edited by Nathan Huggins. New York: Library of America, 1986.

Gilroy, Paul. *The Black Atlantic: Modernity and Double Consciousness.* Cambridge, MA: Harvard University Press, 1993.

Plummer, Brenda Gayle. *Rising Wind: Black Americans and U.S. Foreign Policy Affairs, 1935–1960.* Chapel Hill: University of North Carolina Press, 1996.

Singh, Nikhil Pal. *Black Is a Country: Race and the Unfinished Struggle for Democracy.* Cambridge, MA: Harvard University Press, 2004.

Von Eschen, Penny M. *Race against Empire: Black Americans and Anticolonialism, 1937–1957.* Ithaca, NY: Cornell University Press, 1997.

Ian Rocksborough-Smith
Visiting Assistant Professor of History
Saint Francis Xavier University

PANAMA CANAL

The United States first expressed interest in building a transoceanic canal across Central America in the late 1700s when Thomas Jefferson (1743–1826) speculated on the utility of such a channel for US and global trade. The Spanish emperor Charles V (1500–1558) had spoken on the subject more than two centuries earlier when Panama's mule road for hauling Peruvian silver from one ocean to another established the region as a major transportation hub for the burgeoning Atlantic economy. But the first step toward a US isthmian canal occurred in

1846, with the signing of the Mallarino-Bidlack Treaty between the United States and New Granada (later called Colombia). This accord granted transit rights to the United States across the Isthmus of Panama, then a province of New Granada, to ensure a shorter route for settlers heading for Oregon after the 1846 US acquisition of that territory. The discovery of gold in California two years later, following the US-Mexican War (1846–1848), sparked the building of a railroad across the isthmus as a precursor for an eventual canal. The demand for a shorter route to the goldfields prompted the beginning of this rail construction in 1850.

On the diplomatic front, US officials negotiated the 1850 Clayton-Bulwer Treaty between the United States and Great Britain. This agreement bound both nations not to "obtain or maintain" unilateral control over any future waterway on the isthmus. The treaty also called for the neutralization of any jointly built Anglo-American canal. Since Great Britain dominated the Caribbean in the mid-nineteenth century, such an accommodation proved essential before Washington could move to build any transportation system there. Five years later, in a great event in the early history of globalization, American investors completed the world's first transcontinental railroad in Panama, a mere 42 miles (68 kilometers) long from Colón on the Atlantic to Panama City on the Pacific. Due to the strong American presence around the line, it soon became known as the "Yankee Strip," a precursor to the later Canal Zone.

THE FRENCH CHALLENGE

The next major event related to US and global interest in a Panamanian canal arrived as a shock in 1879 when Ferdinand de Lesseps (1805–1894), the builder of the Suez Canal, announced his plans to excavate a waterway across Panama as his next great achievement in the positivist expansion of global trade. The Colombian government granted de Lesseps's company a concession, and digging began in 1880. Americans fumed at what they considered a violation of both the Monroe Doctrine and the Mallarino-Bidlack Treaty. But following nine years and thousands of deaths from mudslides, torrential rains, and an epidemic of yellow fever, plus huge cost overruns, the French project collapsed. A key error committed by de Lesseps was his attempt to construct a sea-level canal and not a multileveled lock canal, a mistake that Americans would heed when building the waterway themselves. The New Panama Canal Company emerged from the wreckage of de Lesseps's project. Headed by the old company's chief engineer, Frenchman Philippe Bunau-Varilla (1859–1940), the consortium began lobbying to sell its equipment, completed work, and concession to the United States, the newly emergent hemispheric power.

AN AMERICAN CANAL

The machinations of Bunau-Varilla and his Wall Street lawyer, William Nelson Cromwell (1854–1948), helped eliminate Nicaragua as a competitor to the Panama route and elbowed Great Britain aside as a viable partner in the 1901 Hay-Pauncefote Treaty. Following its victory in the 1898 Spanish-American War, the United States employed its muscle to get what it wanted in the circum-Caribbean region. When the Colombian Senate balked at ratifying the 1903 Hay-Herrán Treaty negotiated between Washington and Bogotá that granted the United States broad powers to build a canal in the Colombian state of Panama, the administration of Theodore Roosevelt (1858–1919) began conspiring with Panamanian secessionists. Together they engineered a separatist revolution that would grant a US concession under more favorable conditions. The result was the November 3, 1903,

Panamanian Revolution, immediately followed by US military intervention and the Hay–Bunau-Varilla Treaty, which accorded Washington the rights to build and maintain a canal across Panama "as if sovereign" for "perpetuity." The driving motivation behind this coup was the United States' strategic desire to move its relatively small navy quickly from one ocean to another to counter any national security threats and to promote US and global trade along a shorter route to Europe, Asia, Africa, and Oceania. After a ten-year construction project, costly in both lives and money, that goal was accomplished.

The opening of the Panama Canal on August 15, 1914, was a monumental event in US, Panamanian, Latin American, and global history. The opening confirmed the ascension of the United States to the rank of world powers. While other European and Latin American

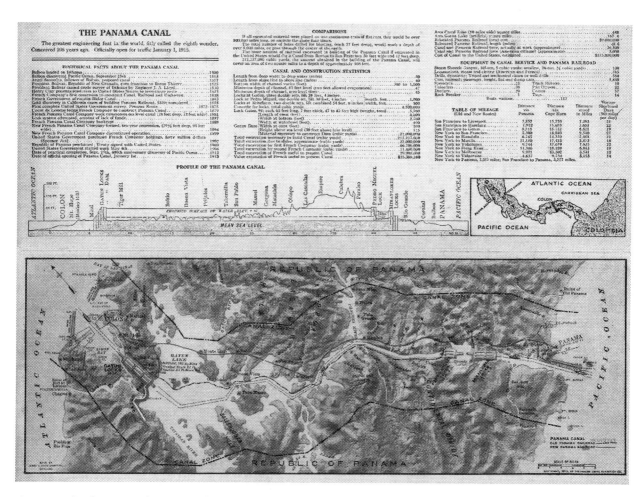

A statistical information sheet, created in 1913, provided detail on the construction of the Panama Canal before its planned opening. The accompanying topographical map offered a visual outline. The opening of the Panama Canal on August 15, 1914, was a monumental event in US, Panamanian, Latin American, and global history, and confirmed the ascension of the United States, which had succeeded in a task at which other nations had failed, to the rank of world power. **TRANSCENDENTAL GRAPHICS/ARCHIVE PHOTOS/GETTY IMAGES**

nations had dreamt of the canal's excavation, and France had failed in its recent attempt, only the United States had succeeded, affirming its technological and moral superiority in the minds of many of its citizens. (Americans were annoyed, though, that the outbreak of World War I overshadowed the story). In global terms, the completion of this strategic waterway made the world a much smaller place, saving cargo and passenger carriers thousands of miles of travel and millions in costs with its shorter route between the Atlantic and Pacific, and ending the need to round the horn of South America to reach one ocean from the other. As such, the canal's opening facilitated the process of interconnecting the entire world in networks of trade and culture, what we now call globalization. The workers, technology, science, and capital from all over the world that helped build the channel in a brutal ten-year struggle (1904–1914) of man versus tropical nature, accentuated the canal's globalized character. The conquest of yellow fever, mudslides, cave-ins, and dynamite explosions during construction took a terrible human toll, especially on the non-US workforce made up mostly of black West Indians, though Spaniards, Italians, Latin Americans, Chinese, and Hindustanis labored there as well.

While the Panama Canal's opening aided Latin American trade, it also had unfortunate consequences for America's southern neighbors by enhancing US dominance of the hemisphere, particularly in the circum-Caribbean region and Central America, where the canal and its adjoining zone's military bases established the United States as a hegemonic power. Numerous US interventions in the area could now be justified to "protect the Panama Canal." These interventions often occurred in the republic of Panama itself, where US troops marched in to "establish order" and "protect US interests" nine times between 1904 and 1925. Indeed, no nation was more intimately affected by the waterway than Panama, a small new country created in part by US efforts to dominate the process of canal building and the strategic environment surrounding the waterway.

The 50-mile long (80-kilometer-long), 10-mile-wide (16-kilometer-wide) zone around the canal created by the 1903 treaty quickly coalesced into a state within a state, with a US government, military bases, police force, law code, prison, and numerous clubhouses and commissaries for US and foreign workers. Within this zone, foreign laborers, the overwhelming number of them West Indians, endured lower wages and segregated facilities on the "silver roll" versus American foremen and workers on the higher-paid "gold roll." West Indians carried out most of the dangerous and arduous work on the canal, with more than four thousand official deaths and perhaps three times more undocumented ones. Their ancestors still lament the West Indians' lack of recognition for these

sacrifices and the racial discrimination they endured. But for optimistic white Americans, the construction heralded a heroic saga of American science and optimism in conquering the decadent tropics. Indeed, the Canal Zone provided a rich tableau for testing some of the new labor theories of Bellamite progressivism that lent the Canal Zone its socialist structure for privileged white workers and administrators.

IMPACT OF THE US PRESENCE ON PANAMA

After construction, the overwhelming US presence in Panama sparked local resistance and complaints about unequal treatment and an unfair sharing of the canal's financial benefits. Racial discrimination in the Canal Zone and the advantaged lifestyles of the US workers and their families compared to impoverished Panamanians provoked frustration. Access to the zone was barred for most Panamanians, and, when crossing from one side of their country to the other, they faced questioning from a foreign police force speaking a foreign language, threatening at times to send them to a foreign prison, Gamboa Penitentiary, in the Canal Zone.

Americanization—that is, the strong influence of US popular culture emanating from the zone—also challenged Panamanian identity, customs, and social mores. A large sex industry that catered to the US garrison and workers wounded local sensibilities. The 1946 US establishment of the School of the Americas in the Canal Zone transformed the enclave into an instrument of political repression throughout the hemisphere in the view of many Panamanians, who saw this institution as a violation of the 1903 treaty that granted US rights for canal defense only.

While the successful construction and maintenance of the canal enhanced US pride and imperial identity, such domination had a debilitating effect on Panamanian efforts at state formation and political sovereignty. Treaty revisions in 1936 and 1955 that granted only modest concession to the locals failed to address this problem. In 1964, pent-up Panamanian anger exploded in an anti-American uprising that took the lives of twenty-one Panamanians and four US soldiers. After a long diplomatic process in 1977, the Jimmy Carter administration negotiated new treaties that called for the end of the Canal Zone and the gradual transfer of the waterway to Panama. This effort culminated on December 31, 1999, with the granting of complete local control over the channel.

The 1964 riots and the canal treaty process that followed emerged as part of the global process of decolonization that began with the British and Dutch withdrawals from India and Indonesia, respectively, in the late 1940s and the US grant of formal independence to the Philippines in 1946. This global shift in relations continued with the liberation from European control of all Asia and Africa—and, in the case of the United States, its loss of hegemony in Cuba. Indeed, Panama's final gain of sovereignty over all of its national territory in 1999 coincided with Hong Kong's and Macao's cutting of colonial ties with Britain (1997) and Portugal (1999), respectively, in one of the final phases of decolonization.

President Carter felt that better relations with Latin America and projecting a positive image of US fair play toward all nations was more important than the privileges of a few thousand American canal workers. He was helped by the fact that the canal had, by the late 1970s, lost much of its strategic importance. Forrestal-class aircraft carriers could not transit its now narrow locks (110 feet; 33.5 meters) and the United States had long possessed a large, two-ocean navy. The Pentagon now relied more on rapid airlift than sealift. Still, a postcolonial relationship endured due to the DeConcini amendment attached to the treaty, which afforded the US government the right to intervene militarily if any outside force (including Panama) interfered with the free flow of traffic through the canal. Indeed, the ratification fight over the treaty provoked an epic battle and a close vote as many conservative Americans identified so strongly with the historical memory of the canal as a symbol of America's youthful vigor and global supremacy. Countenancing its loss amounted to "surrender," a "giveaway," or an acknowledgment of American retreat in the wake of the recent defeat in Vietnam. As a result, voters punished several of the senators who voted for the treaties with electoral defeat in 1978 and 1980.

A POSTCOLONIAL CANAL

The United States' stormy postcolonial relations with Panama over the subject of the canal continued. A military government under left-leaning General Omar Torrijos (1929–1981) had seized power in 1968 and used the leverage of the decolonizing Third World in his contest over the canal with the US government. Torrijos painted the American canal as a shameful relic of gunboat colonialism, which sped the transfer. His successor, General Manuel Noriega, a former US collaborator and Central Intelligence Agency operative, appeared to threaten the canal with his growing belligerence, political tyranny, and large-scale drug trafficking. Anxious to prove his mettle with foreign foes and guarantee the security of the canal, President George H. W. Bush authorized a US invasion of Panama in December 1989, evoking much criticism from Latin Americans who had hoped that with the ending of the Cold War, such US interventions would subside.

Though the Bill Clinton administration tried to negotiate a deal for continued US bases in Panama after the 1999 transfer, the Panamanian National Assembly rejected such offers, and the treaty went into effect as scheduled. In 2007, Panama began construction on a new set of wider locks to enlarge the canal's capacity and make it viable for the larger supertankers and cargo carriers. These new 180-feet-wide (55-meter-wide) locks were scheduled to open in early 2016. Today, Panamanians celebrate the one hundredth anniversary of the canal's opening, and much of the bitterness over their colonial relationship with the United States has faded. Both the old and the new canals have and will amplify global trade and the interconnected nature of our world. Yet other projects threaten the monopoly that the canal once held for over a century. A proposed Chinese-built and financed canal in Nicaragua and the opening of the Northwest Passage due to the melting of the northern polar ice cap may create new avenues to link the Atlantic with the Pacific. For Americans, the idea of a rising new hegemon, the People's Republic of China, outdoing them with their own Central American canal right in America's "backyard" remains unsettling—and harks back to an era when the United States replaced the older dominant power in the region, Great Britain.

SEE ALSO *Bush, George H. W.; Carter, James Earl, Jr.; Roosevelt, Theodore; Spanish-American War; Taft, William Howard; Wilson, Woodrow*

BIBLIOGRAPHY

Conniff, Michael L. *Panama and the United States: The End of the Alliance.* 3rd ed. Athens: University of Georgia Press, 2012.

Donoghue, Michael E. *Borderland on the Isthmus: Race, Culture, and the Struggle for the Canal Zone.* Durham, NC: Duke University Press, 2014.

Greene, Julie. *The Canal Builders: Making America's Empire at the Panama Canal.* New York: Penguin Press, 2009.

LaFeber, Walter. *The Panama Canal: The Crisis in Historical Perspective.* New York: Oxford University Press, 1989.

Lindsay-Poland, John. *Emperors in the Jungle: The Hidden History of the U.S. in Panama.* Durham, NC: Duke University Press, 2003.

Major, John. *Prize Possession: The United States and the Panama Canal, 1903–1979.* New York and London: Cambridge University Press, 1993.

McCullough, David. *The Path between the Seas: The Creation of the Panama Canal, 1879–1914.* New York: Simon and Schuster, 1977.

Missal, Alexander. *Seaway to the Future: American Social Visions and the Construction of the Panama Canal.* Madison: University of Wisconsin Press, 2008.

Sánchez, Peter M. *Panama Lost? U.S. Hegemony, Democracy, and the Canal.* Gainesville: University Press of Florida, 2007.

Michael E. Donoghue
Associate Professor of History
Marquette University

PAN-AMERICANISM

Pan-Americanism was a transnational movement advanced by prominent entrepreneurs, political leaders, and diplomats from throughout the Americas. It was firstly a US-led policy promoting hemispheric economic integration, and secondarily a forum before 1880, then again after 1930, for the criticism of US imperialism by Latin American diplomats. Its legacy persists in institutions like the Pan American Health Organization, the Pan American Institute of Geography and History, and the Pan American Games. Even so, the movement's significance diminished quickly after World War II (1939–1945) with the de facto replacement of the Pan American Union by the Organization of American States (OAS) as the Washington-based, hemisphere-wide cooperative governance body.

THE FACE OF US DOMINANCE IN THE AMERICAS

Pan-Americanism was conceived in the late nineteenth century as a project to organize the republics of the Western Hemisphere into cooperative bodies—the Pan American Union and its affiliates. Though imagined and developed as a multilateral organization, in practice the Pan American Union was financed and dominated by American political leaders and bureaucrats. While cast as a movement for the promotion of international cooperation and cultural exchange, Pan-Americanism was always defined by an American agenda for US-led political, strategic, and particularly commercial and financial stability in the hemisphere. From the 1880s through 1948, Pan-Americanism was the friendly face of US dominance in the Americas and a movement whose first objective was hemispheric economic calm. The latter was to dovetail with new opportunities for US business and financial expansion in the region, facilitated in part by economic stability in the United States after 1895 and by Progressive Era regulations that permitted expanded international roles for American banks.

The Monroe Doctrine and the Congress of Panama (1826) were precursors of Pan-Americanism, as were a series of nineteenth-century meetings of Latin American diplomats. The latter often incorporated an anti-US organizing theme; at the Congress of Santiago (1856), for example, Peru, Chile, and Ecuador signed a defense pact anticipating possible US military action. In 1881 US secretary of state James G. Blaine (1830–1893) began to characterize Pan-Americanism as the facilitation of inter-American trade and cultural cooperation. He proposed the First Conference of American States (1889–1890), whose objectives integrated ambiguous notions of peace and cooperation with more sharply defined goals for the standardization and simplification of inter-American trade terms. The latter would form the

backdrop for Pan-Americanism through World War II. The dichotomy between lofty ideals of peace and a workaday agenda for the elimination of trade and financial barriers caught the eye of Latin American nationalists, including José Martí (1853–1895), who attacked Pan-Americanism as a smoke screen for US imperial expansion.

The First Conference created the Commercial Bureau of American States (later renamed the Pan American Union). Latin American delegates made the Second (1901–1902) and Third (1906) Conferences of American States forums for criticizing US military intervention in the region, but stopped short of any action against Washington. Seeking distance from President William Howard Taft's (1857–1930) dollar diplomacy, the administration of President Woodrow Wilson (1856–1924) revived Blaine's association of benign cultural ties with commercial cooperation in a Pan-American ideal. In the end, though, Pan-Americanism and the US-funded Pan American Union, which oversaw the conferences of American states and other inter-American meetings, including the First Pan American Financial Conference, continued to stress the normalization and stabilization of economic relations in the hemisphere.

LEO STANTON ROWE

From 1920 to 1946, Leo Stanton Rowe (1871–1946), a former US assistant secretary of the treasury, loomed large in shaping Pan-Americanism as director of the Pan American Union. His ideas dovetailed with the growing tendency of the US government to trumpet Pan-American cooperation while stressing a more subtle emphasis on economic cooperation. Rowe found Latin America backward and saw Pan-Americanism as a means to modernize the region. Rowe's vision for the Americas was at once culturally sensitive, ethnocentric, a reflection of US Progressive Era ideals, and a program of US investment in Latin America toward what he believed would be economic development throughout the hemisphere. He had a missionary faith in Pan-Americanism that highlighted a shared commitment to US democratic values.

PEACE AND SECURITY

The Clark Memorandum (1928) and the Good Neighbor Policy made priorities in US foreign relations of the cooperation and peace components of Pan-Americanism values. They helped prompt several key Pan-American achievements in the 1930s, including the nonintervention resolution passed at the Seventh Conference of American States (1933) criticizing the interference of one state in the internal affairs of a second. Anticipating both World War II and the 1947

Inter-American Treaty of Reciprocal Assistance, a bulwark of the US-led Cold War alliance in the Americas, diplomats at the Eighth Conference of American States (1938) declared continental solidarity in the event of war. At the same time, the new emphasis on mutual defence agreements between 1938 and 1945 under the umbrella of Pan-Americanism, along with the 1947–1948 founding of the OAS as a security-based alliance, helped marginalize Pan-Americanism in US foreign policy, which became more concerned with global strategy, warfare, and the purported communist menace.

POST-1950

After 1950, Pan-Americanism survived as a more culturally and socially oriented remnant of Blaine's original ideal, at some distance from the commercial, financial, and political priorities in US foreign relations. The Inter-American Indian Institute was a pioneer in advancing first peoples' rights. The Pan American Health Organization played a crucial role in the control of malaria, Chagas, and other infectious diseases. Perhaps the most important element of late twentieth-century Pan-Americanism was the work of the Inter-American Court of Human Rights and the Inter-American Human Rights Commission. Each reflected the emergence of human rights as a US foreign policy priority after 1975, while remaining outside the influence of US foreign policy makers and breaking new ground in the investigation and prosecution of human rights violators from periods of dictatorial rule. These bodies helped make international pariahs of brutal military officers and offered legal precedent for the prosecution of Latin American human rights violators in US federal courts.

SEE ALSO *Mexico; Monroe Doctrine (1823); South America*

BIBLIOGRAPHY

Berger, Mark T. "'Toward Our Common American Destiny?' Hemispheric History and Pan American Politics in the Twentieth Century." *Journal of Iberian and Latin American Research* 8, 1 (2002): 57–88.

Coates, Benjamin A. "The Pan-American Lobbyist: William Eleroy Curtis and U.S. Empire, 1884–1899." *Diplomatic History* 38, 1 (2014): 22–48.

González, Robert Alexander. *Designing Pan-America: U.S. Architectural Visions for the Western Hemisphere.* Austin: University of Texas Press, 2011.

Sheinin, David M. K., ed. *Beyond the Ideal: Pan Americanism in Inter-American Affairs.* Westport, CT: Praeger, 2000.

Spellacy, Amy. "Mapping the Metaphor of the Good Neighbor: Geography, Globalism, and Pan-Americanism during the 1940s." *American Studies* 47, 2 (2006): 39–66.

Weis, W. Michael. "The Twilight of Pan-Americanism: The Alliance for Progress, Neo-colonialism, and Non-alignment in Brazil, 1961–1964." *International History Review* 23, 2 (2001): 322–344.

David M. K. Sheinin
Professor
Trent University

PARIS PEACE CONFERENCE (1919)

On January 18, 1919, representatives of more than twenty-five nations convened in Paris for a peace conference. Charged with bringing an end to World War I, the conference represented the greatest diplomatic assembly in world history. At the conference, national delegates wrote the treaties that restored peace, most notably the Treaty of Versailles, and for the first time, recognized the entire planet as one interconnected space. In doing so, the Paris Peace Conference set forth many of the themes that would shape world history during the twentieth century.

Although representatives from many countries attended, the conference was dominated by the "Big Four": Great Britain, France, Italy, and the United States. Although all four wanted to create a durable peace while also punishing Germany for starting the war, they did not see eye to eye in all matters. The European powers, and French prime minister Georges Clemenceau (1841–1929) in particular, wanted to deal with Germany harshly. France had suffered two German invasions in the last half-century and wanted to make sure Germany could not threaten France again. The Europeans blamed the war's tremendous devastation, both human and material, on the Germans, arguing that Berlin was obligated to make good the damage it had caused. The European powers also wanted to fulfill diplomatic plans outlined in a series of secret treaties made before and during the war, such as the Sykes-Picot Agreement (1916), which divided the Ottoman Empire between Britain and France.

The Americans, in contrast, tended to take a more idealistic view of the peace. In his "Fourteen Points" speech, President Woodrow Wilson (1856–1924) emphasized peace and reconciliation rather than victory and revenge, and he called for the global application of democratic principles and popular sovereignty. European leaders like David Lloyd George (1863–1945) of Britain, Vittorio Orlando (1860–1952) of Italy, and especially Clemenceau considered Wilson naive, and they fought for concrete gains at Germany's expense. Wilson's message was tremendously popular in Europe and elsewhere in the world, however. Many considered it a clarion call for peace and liberty.

Over the next several months, diplomats hammered out the details of several treaties that ended the war, most notably the Versailles Treaty, signed in June. The peace terms for Germany were harsh. The Germans lost not only their overseas colonies but also territories in the east that went to the new Polish state created by the conference. The Versailles Treaty stripped Germany of most of its military force, reducing its army to no more than 100,000 soldiers. Nothing was more controversial, however, than the treaty's Article 231, which stated that Germany was to blame for starting the war. The Allies used the so-called war guilt clause to justify forcing Germany to pay reparations, ultimately estimated at $32 billion, for war damages. The peace could have been harsher: Germany remained a united nation, and retained full political sovereignty. As many would argue, the peace was too harsh to permit reconciliation yet not harsh enough to significantly weaken Germany. Germany remained, at least potentially, the most powerful nation in Europe, and it was full of resentment against the 1919 terms of peace.

In Paris, the victors also confronted the problem of revolutionary Russia. The Soviets were excluded from the conference, in part because the Bolsheviks had signed a separate peace with Germany early in 1918, but also because Moscow's call for the overthrow of capitalism violently opposed the new world order championed at the conference. The year 1919 was revolutionary, both throughout Europe and around the world, and the Big Four worried that the defeated militaristic Germany would be succeeded by a communist regime in the heart of the continent. While many looked to Wilson as the harbinger of peace, others saw Vladimir Lenin (1870–1924) and the Bolsheviks as the leaders of world revolution. The global conflict between capitalism and communism that would play such a major role in the history of the twentieth century began during the Paris Peace Conference.

The conference also excluded representatives of the colonized world from any significant participation. Many popular Asian and African leaders were heartened by Wilson's calls for democracy and national self-determination, and hoped to see the peace conference recommend independence or greater autonomy for their countries. They were, without exception, bitterly disappointed. In deciding what to do with the colonies of Germany and the Ottoman Empire, the Big Four rejected granting them independence. Instead, they recast them as mandates, arguing that their peoples were not yet ready for self-rule. The mandates, distributed mostly to Britain and France, were in effect colonies under a different guise, making it clear that the victors had no intention of granting self-determination to the colonized. A number of individuals, ranging from W. E. B. Du Bois (1868–1963) to Ho Chi Minh (1890–1969), came to Paris to plead the case of racial minorities and the colonized, but their pleas largely fell on deaf ears. While championing the collapse of empires in Europe, the conference reinforced and extended them overseas. Moreover, the delegates rejected a resolution for racial equality sponsored by the Japanese government. In general, the Paris Peace Conference made it clear that democracy and national self-determination were for whites only.

Many historians have considered the conference a failure. It did establish Wilson's dream of a League of Nations, but the US Senate refused to ratify the league and, in general, it remained powerless. The resentment the conference provoked in Germany contributed to the rise of Adolf Hitler (1889–1945) and a second, even more terrible, world war. The isolation of the Soviet Union led not to its collapse but to the horrors of the Stalinist dictatorship, and the rejection of colonial independence produced a massive wave of decolonization after 1945. The Paris Peace Conference did, nonetheless, solidify the idea that the world was a single diplomatic and political unit. It was, in short, a foundational moment in the history of globalization.

SEE ALSO *Internationalism; Interventionism; Isolationism; League of Nations; Lodge, Henry Cabot; Missionary Diplomacy; Roosevelt, Theodore; Self-Determination; Taft, William Howard; Treaty of Versailles; Wilson, Woodrow; World War I*

BIBLIOGRAPHY

Ambrosius, Lloyd E. *Wilsonianism: Woodrow Wilson and His Legacy in American Foreign Relations.* New York: Palgrave Macmillan, 2002.

Andelman, David A. *A Shattered Peace: Versailles 1919 and the Price We Pay Today.* Hoboken, NJ: Wiley, 2008.

MacMillan, Margaret. *Paris 1919: Six Months That Changed the World.* New York: Random House, 2001.

Manela, Erez. *The Wilsonian Moment: Self-Determination and the International Origins of Anticolonial Nationalism.* Oxford: Oxford University Press, 2007.

Tyler Stovall
Professor of History
University of California, Berkeley

THE PASSING OF THE GREAT RACE (MADISON GRANT, 1916)

Published in 1916, Madison Grant's *The Passing of the Great Race, or, The Racial Basis of European History* stands as a leading example of the early twentieth-century theory of "scientific racism," an idea that influenced both the science of eugenics and the politics of immigration restriction in the United States.

GRANT'S RACIALIST THEORIES

Madison Grant was a patrician New York lawyer born in 1865. Educated at Yale University and Columbia Law School, Grant became one of the leading American conservationists. He helped found the Bronx Zoo, helped create Glacier and Denali National Parks, led the movement to preserve the California redwoods and save the American bison from extinction, and was a longtime board member of the American Museum of Natural History.

However, Grant is best known as the author of *The Passing of the Great Race*. In the book, Grant argues that Europeans can be defined as belonging to one of three races: Nordic, Alpine, and Mediterranean. To Grant, the mostly northern European Nordics were clearly the superior race. Tall with light hair and long heads, Nordics were, according to Grant, "all over the world, a race of soldiers, sailors, adventurers, and explorers, but above all, of rulers, organizers, and aristocrats" (Grant 1916, 198). He surmised that the harsh climate of northern Europe had imposed a "rigid elimination of defectives" (25), leading to a hardier race of peoples. Grant contrasted Nordics with the stocky, round-headed Alpines, who were of "essentially peasant character" (198), and darker, long-headed Mediterraneans, who were largely "inferior in bodily stamina to both the Nordic and the Alpine" (198).

The Passing of the Great Race popularized the scientific theories of genetics and evolution. For Grant, "race" and racial characteristics were immutable and "heredity is the controlling factor in human development" (xvi). He believed that the idea that environmental factors, such as education and upward mobility, could supersede heredity was folly. Throughout the book, Grant is suspicious of Christianity and democracy, both of which he argues led to a sentimental and romantic view of human equality at odds with the racial history presented in his book.

Although *The Passing of the Great Race* spans thousands of years of human history, the driving concern of the book is Grant's fear that the Nordic race was at the time in danger of being overwhelmed by inferior races. He argued that the United States was heading toward a "racial abyss" (228). During the late nineteenth and early twentieth centuries, the United States was experiencing a large influx of immigrants from southern and eastern Europe. For Grant, this large-scale immigration of mostly Alpine and Mediterranean races with higher birthrates threatened the status of Nordic peoples—the descendants of British colonists who settled the country. By not

producing as many children as newer immigrants from "inferior" races, Americans of Nordic background were committing "race suicide" (43). Grant wrote: "If the Melting Pot is allowed to boil without control … the type of native American of Colonial descent will become as extinct as the Athenian of the age of Pericles, and the Viking of the days of Rollo" (228).

RECEPTION AND INFLUENCE

By 1921, Grant had published four editions of *The Passing of the Great Race*. Even so, the book only sold roughly 17,000 copies and never achieved widespread popularity. Its first two editions were published during World War I (1914–1918), when anti-German hysteria was at its peak, and Americans were therefore less receptive to appeals to Nordic strength. The book's antidemocratic, elitist, and anti-Christian overtones also made it unlikely to appeal to a broader audience.

The book did receive largely positive reviews. One exception was from anthropologist Franz Boas (1858–1942), who disagreed with Grant's racialist theories. Boas and his disciples in cultural anthropology argued instead for the greater influence of environment over heredity.

Though it did not have a popular following, *The Passing of the Great Race* had an important impact on elite opinion. Grant had been a longtime member of the Immigration Restriction League, and his book's theories would have a significant impact on American immigration policy. Grant's theories influenced the congressional debates over immigration restriction that led to the Emergency Quota Act of 1921 and the Immigration Act of 1924. Both laws made use of quotas to restrict immigration from southern and eastern Europe, while retaining larger quotas for immigrants from northern Europe. Grant's racialist theories helped frame the congressional debates that led to the immigration quotas.

The influence of *The Passing of the Great Race* can also be seen in the rising influence of eugenics theories in the 1920s. The book endorsed the idea of a "rigid system of selection through the elimination of those who are weak or unfit" (46). Grant himself was deeply active in the eugenics movement. He was elected president of the Eugenics Research Association in 1918 and helped form the American Eugenics Society in 1926, which disseminated eugenics research to influence public opinion and legislation. In the 1920s Grant also worked behind the scenes with state legislators in Virginia to win passage of the Racial Integrity Act in 1924, which legally classified as white only those persons with "no trace of any blood other than Caucasian." The bill also banned marriages between whites and nonwhites.

By the early 1930s, the influence of Grant and *The Passing of the Great Race* had waned in the United States.

Immigration was severely curtailed because of quotas, the Great Depression focused the minds of most Americans on economic matters, and the disciples of Franz Boas began to dominate the field of anthropology and academia in general.

Grant would pass away in 1937. However, his theories remained popular in England and Germany into the 1930s. Leading Nazi scientists were fans of *The Passing of the Great Race* and its racialist theories, although the Nazis would substitute *Aryan* for *Nordic*. Adolf Hitler (1889–1945) even wrote Grant a letter telling him "the book is my Bible." During one of the Nuremburg trials in 1946 to 1947, Nazi doctor Karl Brandt (1904–1948) had excerpts of *The Passing of the Great Race* read into the court records.

Historian John Higham (1920–2003) wrote that Grant was "intellectually the most important nativist in recent American history" and that "all of the trends in race-thinking converged upon him" (1955, 155). Although *The Passing of the Great Race* was not quite as popular a book in its day as is often portrayed, it still stands as a symbol of the racialist, nativist, and eugenic thinking that deeply influenced elite opinion in the United States in the early 1920s.

SEE ALSO *Immigration and Naturalization Service; Immigration Quotas; Nativism; "The White Man's Burden" (Rudyard Kipling, 1899); Whiteness*

BIBLIOGRAPHY

Grant, Madison. *The Passing of the Great Race, or, The Racial Basis of European History.* New York: Scribner's, 1916.

Higham, John. *Strangers in the Land: Patterns of Nativism, 1860–1925.* New Brunswick, NJ: Rutgers University Press, 1955.

Spiro, Jonathan Peter. *Defending the Master Race: Conservation, Eugenics, and the Legacy of Madison Grant.* Burlington: University of Vermont Press, 2009.

Vincent Cannato
Associate Professor of History
University of Massachusetts Boston

PASSPORT

From the inception of the United States, Americans have used passports as basic tools in their relations and dealings with one another, with their governments, and with peoples, states, and empires throughout the world. Beginning early in the Revolutionary War, the Continental Congress, their diplomatic representatives in Europe, and the individual states issued passports for travel to, from, and within the United States as well as abroad.

In 1782, under the newly enacted Articles of Confederation, Congress explicitly granted authority to the Department of Foreign Affairs to issue passports on behalf of the United States. But states and a variety of other authorities, in addition to the federal government, continued to issue their own passports through much of the nineteenth century.

PASSPORTS IN THE EARLY REPUBLIC

From the end of the Revolutionary War, otherwise free Americans could generally travel among the states without passports. Travelers and settlers in the territories, however, faced more hazards and legal uncertainties, and many sought and obtained passports and passes from local, state, and national governments. On the international front, US law did not require a passport to leave or reenter the country in peacetime. But it was commonly understood that the laws of foreign nations often made passports indispensable. Within a decade of the Peace of 1783, the French and Haitian revolutions and the resulting wars had given rise on all sides to new or reinvigorated passport and alien registration requirements meant to prevent the spread of revolution, counterrevolution, or slave revolt. Many European and other foreign powers maintained such requirements following these crises, shaping the essential considerations for US travelers as the nineteenth century progressed. In 1845 the State Department recommended that US citizens going abroad should, before departing, secure a passport. In addition to a US passport, travelers might need passports or visas from those countries they were to visit. It was not until the mid-twentieth century that a more or less standardized international system was established stipulating that travelers bear passports only from the nation or nations of which they were members and acquire prior visas for travel to any others.

The multiplicity of American passports—national, state, and local, each in a variety of forms—fostered confusion and suspicion among American and foreign governments concerning the authority and authenticity of the documents Americans proffered. By the mid-nineteenth century the federal government was warning Americans intending to travel abroad that they should not expect that foreign governments would respect state, local, or other passports not issued by US national authorities. In 1856 Congress reserved to the State Department the sole authority to issue passports in the name of the United States or identifying the bearer as a US citizen, though some states continued to issue their own passports for years thereafter.

PASSPORTS AND CITIZENSHIP

From the Revolution onward, American passports typically identified the bearers as citizens of the United

States or of a particular state. But American authorities also issued such documents to foreigners, varying the language or amending the forms accordingly. There was in any case no guarantee that any attestation of citizenship would be respected by foreign powers, or even by domestic authorities outside the issuing department. In 1835 the Supreme Court ruled that, given neither statute to the contrary nor clear standards for proof of citizenship in granting passports, a US passport identifying the bearer as a citizen was not in itself legal evidence of citizenship. In 1846 the State Department first issued specific instructions regarding the evidence of citizenship to be required of applicants.

In the 1856 passport statute Congress prohibited the issuance of US passports to any but US citizens. An oath of allegiance was added to the passport application requirements during the Civil War and was intermittently required after the war until the 1970s. Yet until the late twentieth century the courts considered passports as at best contributing evidence but not conclusive proof of citizenship. A 1982 congressional statute established that a US passport issued to a US citizen was to have the same "force and effect" as legal proof of citizenship as certificates of citizenship and naturalization. (Since 2012 discrepancies of interpretation among circuit courts have rendered the scope and meaning of this statute less clear than in the first three decades following its passage.)

US passports, well into the twentieth century, were reserved almost exclusively for free (usually white) males of the middle and upper classes. The wife, children, servants, slaves (before the Civil War), and other dependents of any such man might be included as additional parties to his passport, though they were typically not identified by name. Until World War I the United States issued joint passports for married couples that gave the husband's name but included his spouse only in the phrase "accompanied by his wife." During World War I, in part in response to foreign requirements that each adult bear his or her own passport, the United States began to issue married women separate passports, but only under their married names. As late as 1925 a new State Department policy allowing married women to obtain passports in their maiden names stipulated that this was to be followed by "wife of...." In 1937 the department dropped this stipulation.

For a century and a half following independence, the fact that the American people included numerous free persons who were subject to US law but whom US law or government considered inadmissible as citizens prompted a variety of ad hoc accommodations in US passport policy. Early approaches attempted to preserve the link between citizenship and the passport without liberalizing access to citizenship, while later measures decoupled US passports from US citizenship. Thus in 1847 Secretary of State James Buchanan insisted that it had never yet been the custom to grant to "free persons of color, born or resident within the United States," passports "in the ordinary form, recognizing them as citizens," but to issue instead "a certificate suited to the nature of the case" (Moore 1909, 236). During the Civil War, to widen the pool of available conscripts and raise funds, temporary revisions to the law allowed the issuing of passports to noncitizens liable to military service who posted bond before going abroad. In 1902, the United States having recently acquired sizable new colonial possessions (and numerous colonial subjects, or noncitizen nationals) in the Spanish-American War, Congress revised the law again to allow passports to be issued to anyone "owing allegiance to the United States, whether a citizen or not," and to add the governors of insular possessions to the list of those officials who might be authorized to issue them. In 1907 the Department of State was authorized to issue passports to immigrants who had formally declared their intention to become citizens. This authority was revoked in 1920.

PASSPORTS IN MODERN WAR AND PEACE

Briefly during the War of 1812 and then during the years of the Civil War, the United States had imposed wartime passport requirements for those entering and leaving the country, including citizens. World War I brought renewed wartime passport and visa requirements, both at home and abroad. These wartime measures subsequently formed the basis for permanent peacetime passport and visa requirements around the world. The US wartime emergency measures imposed passport and visa requirements for the entry and exit of both aliens and citizens. In 1921 the requirements for citizens were lifted, but those for aliens were maintained. The 1924 immigration act permanently established the requirement that would-be immigrants first acquire visas from US officials abroad. World War II prompted the renewal of wartime emergency passport requirements for citizen entry and exit beginning in 1941 and continuing through 1953. A 1952 statute, meanwhile, authorized the president to continue these regulations as emergency measures as long as necessary for the security of the country. A 1978 amendment to the statute eliminated the stipulation of a presidential proclamation and made permanent the requirement that US citizens have passports to leave and enter the country.

Meanwhile, in the wake of World War I the League of Nations created a system of identification and travel documents (Nansen passports) to help protect and resettle the immense numbers of refugees and stateless persons produced by the war and subsequent crises. These arrangements would be replaced and supplemented following World War II by refugee passports issued by the United Nations and individual states. The United States, never a member of the League of Nations and at its peak of restrictionist immigration sentiment and policy in the interwar period, never recognized the Nansen passports. After World War II the United States likewise declined to be party to a similar intergovernmental arrangement in 1946 or to the 1960 United Nations Convention relating to the Status of Stateless Persons, preferring to maintain autonomy and discretion, and often more limited or restrictive policies, in its provision of passports and other protections for refugees and asylum seekers.

It was during the interwar period, in light of the 1917 Russian Revolution, that the United States began to use its passport policy to oppose the spread of communism, at home and abroad. The United States and the individual states had since the early republic used immigration, naturalization, and travel restrictions to exclude, isolate, or restrain the purported agents of subversion, from slave revolt to anarchism. Now the federal government restricted the immigration of known or suspected communists, and the State Department denied new passports and revoked or refused to renew those previously granted to suspected American communists. Following World War II and the onset of the Cold War, the Internal Security Act of 1950, among many other provisions, prohibited the issuance or renewal of passports or visas to registered communists and other subversives. Challenges in the federal courts led in 1958 to Supreme Court rulings that the State Department lacked the authority to deny passports to communists and others more generally, on a discretionary basis, and affirming that the liberty to travel abroad was a constitutionally protected right that might not be abridged without due process.

Subsequent efforts to pass an overriding passport law failed. General bans and restrictions on travel to and from communist and other proscribed or hostile countries, limiting the ambit of all US passports, remained key foreign policy tools for isolation and coercion of hostile regimes through the Cold War and beyond. In the early twenty-first century such tools found renewed application, in particular, in counterterrorism. Conversely, the easing of travel restrictions or passport and visa requirements was used to ease tensions and initiate the normalization of diplomatic relations. Thus in 1971, as an initial rapprochement and a prelude to his landmark visit, President Richard Nixon lifted certain passport restrictions for travel to China.

INTERNATIONAL AGREEMENTS AND RENEWED DIVISIONS

Following the world wars, allies on either side of the Iron Curtain and other overlapping and subsequent geopolitical divisions moved to consolidate diplomatic ties and economic cooperation, while globalization and the ascent of transnational business and industry accelerated. One consequence was the gradual rise of multiple regional and multilateral passport agreements and free-trade zones that included provisions for the free or more ready travel of labor and workers. Some, including the 1994 North American Free Trade Agreement, to which the United States was party, involved US citizens directly; others of the mid- to late twentieth century, such as the European Economic Community (later the European Union), the Benelux agreements, and the Schengen Accords, in some instances indirectly eased travel for US citizens among groups of countries abroad.

The increased salience of international terrorism in the latter twentieth and early twenty-first centuries, especially following the September 11, 2001, attacks on New York City and Washington, DC, increased government surveillance and scrutiny of travelers in the United States and abroad. In 2004 the United States moved to reverse previous measures to ease travel in the Western Hemisphere and once again established blanket passport requirements (effective as of 2007) for entry and exit by citizens regardless of destination or point of origin.

SEE ALSO *Immigration*

BIBLIOGRAPHY

Benoit, Claire. "Force and Effect: A Look at the Passport in the Context of Citizenship." *Fordham Law Review* 82, 6 (2013–2014): 3307–3340.

Huffman, John M. "Americans on Paper: Identity and Identification in the American Revolution." PhD diss., Harvard University, 2013.

Moore, John Bassett, ed. *The Works of James Buchanan*. Vol. 7. Philadelphia: J. B. Lippincott, 1909.

Ngai, Mae M. *Impossible Subjects: Illegal Aliens and the Making of Modern America*. Princeton, NJ: Princeton University Press, 2004, 2014.

Robertson, Craig. *The Passport in America: The History of a Document*. New York: Oxford University Press, 2010.

Torpey, John. *The Invention of the Passport: Surveillance, Citizenship and the State*. Cambridge and New York: Cambridge University Press, 2000.

US Passport Office. *The United States Passport: Past, Present, Future*. Washington, DC: Government Printing Office, 1976.

John M. Huffman
Assistant Editor, The Papers of Benjamin Franklin
Yale University

PAUL, ALICE STOKES

1885–1977

Alice Stokes Paul devoted her life to promoting equality for women. She was a central figure in gaining the vote for British and American women, as well as earning recognition of the rights of women in the United Nations (UN) Declaration of Human Rights and Title VII of the 1964 Civil Rights Act. Her championing of the Equal Rights Amendment (ERA) connected the success of first-wave feminists who had won suffrage to second-wave feminists who took up her campaign for legal equality. Always working from a global vision, Paul asserted "There will never be a new world order until women are a part of it" (quoted in "Alice Paul, 92" 1977, 42).

Born in Moorestown, New Jersey, Paul came from a prosperous Quaker family. Quaker women had long exercised a greater degree of autonomy than women in the larger society, a value Alice absorbed from her mother, whom she accompanied to woman suffrage meetings. An outstanding student, Paul earned a BA in biology from Swarthmore College, and an MA in sociology and PhD in economics from the University of Pennsylvania. Her dissertation was titled "The Legal Position of Women in Pennsylvania." Paul went on to earn three law degrees.

Upon graduating from Swarthmore in 1905, Paul did settlement-house work, first in the United States and then in England. In England, she met Christabel (1880–1958) and Sylvia Pankhurst (1882–1960), and joined the Women's Social and Political Union (WSPU) that the sisters led with their mother, Emmeline (1858–1928). Paul was arrested seven times and served three sentences in prison, where she undertook hunger strikes and suffered forced feedings.

Paul's experience abroad established her as a seasoned strategist willing to take personal risks for the cause of suffrage. Returning to the United States in 1910, Paul continued her work for suffrage. In 1912 she and her political partner, Lucy Burns (1879–1966), were appointed to the National American Woman Suffrage Association's (NAWSA) Congressional Committee. In 1913 Burns and Paul employed the tactics they had learned abroad to rally support for a suffrage amendment to the US Constitution with a parade to precede the first inauguration of Woodrow Wilson (1856–1924). The artful spectacle involved thousands in a peaceful procession but ended in a fracas when male bystanders attacked the marchers. Emboldened, suffragists willing to risk more confrontational tactics left NAWSA in 1914 to form the Congressional Union.

Paul applied the "hold the party in power responsible" principle she had learned from the Pankhursts to the American situation. Prompted by the enfranchisement of women in some states, the Congressional Union fostered the Woman's Party in 1916. In 1917, the two organizations merged to form the National Woman's Party (NWP), which pledged to withhold support from the existing political parties until women had gained the right to vote. The NWP aimed its creative nonviolent action campaign at President Wilson and Congress, staging picket lines and prison hunger strikes at the highly charged moment when the United States was entering World War I (1914–1918). Paul and the NWP garnered media attention and rallied public support sufficient to pressure Wilson to back a federal suffrage amendment; Wilson then pushed Congress to do the same.

Upon ratification of the Nineteenth Amendment in 1920, Paul turned her attention to attaining full equality for women through research and lobbying. In 1923 she crafted the Equal Rights Amendment (ERA), which was entered as a bill in Congress for the next forty-nine years. Taken up by the National Organization for Women in the 1960s, the ERA was finally passed by Congress in 1972; it remained three states short when the period established for ratification expired in 1982.

In 1928 the NWP helped create the Inter-American Commission of Women to advise the Organization of American States. Paul sought equality measures for women at the League of Nations; to that end, she founded the World Woman's Party in 1938. Paul was instrumental in the incorporation of language regarding women's equality in the UN Charter and in the establishment of a permanent UN Commission on the Status of Women. Paul successfully lobbied for the inclusion of the rights of women in the 1948 UN Declaration of Human Rights. The inclusion of the prohibition of sex discrimination into the 1964 Civil Rights Act resulted from her years of lobbying and building alliances.

Having made equality her vocation, Paul retired after Congress passed the ERA in 1972. At the onset of World War II (1939–1945), Paul had articulated the vision she pursued all her life: "If the women of the world had not been excluded from world affairs, things today might have been different" (Sochen 1973).

SEE ALSO *Feminism, Women's Rights; Suffrage*

BIBLIOGRAPHY

"Alice Paul, 92, Led Early Protests for Equal Rights." *Washington Post*, July 10, 1977, 42.

Alice Paul Institute. Mount Laurel, NJ. http://www.alicepaul.org

Bacon, Margaret Hope. *Mothers of Feminism: The Story of Quaker Women in America.* San Francisco: Harper and Row, 1986.

Cott, Nancy F. *The Grounding of Modern Feminism.* New Haven, CT: Yale University Press, 1987.

DuBois, Ellen Carol. *Woman Suffrage and Women's Rights*. New York: New York University Press, 1998.

Lunardini, Christine A. *Alice Paul: Equality for Women*. Philadelphia: Westview Press, 2013.

Sewall Belmont House and Museum. Washington, DC. http://www.sewallbelmont.org

Sochen, June. *Movers and Shakers; American Women Thinkers and Activists, 1900–1970*. New York: Quadrangle, 1973.

Tetrault, Lisa. *The Myth of Seneca Falls: Memory and the Women's Suffrage Movement, 1848–1898*. Chapel Hill: University of North Carolina Press, 2014.

Walton, Mary. *A Woman's Crusade: Alice Paul and the Battle for the Ballot*. New York: Palgrave Macmillan, 2010.

Zahniser, Jill Diane, and Amelia R. Fry. *Alice Paul: Claiming Power*. New York: Oxford University Press, 2014.

David L. Hostetter
Independent Scholar
La Crescenta, CA

PEACE CORPS

Superpower rivalries in the 1950s and 1960s magnified a larger trend in world and American history: the breakdown of empires and emergence of postcolonial nation-states. Underway since 1776, the trend gained further momentum after World Wars I and II.

The US Peace Corps became the most prominent example of the international volunteer movement that arose in response to decolonization and the Cold War. Volunteers from Australia and Great Britain took up posts in Indonesia and Southeast Asia in 1951 and 1958, respectively. Living on small stipends and trained in native languages, volunteers expressed solidarity with those whom Frantz Fanon (1925–1961) dubbed the "wretched of the earth." In August 1961, young people from the United States and Canada arrived in Ghana to promote economic development and express solidarity across the "color line" described by W. E. B. Du Bois (1868–1963).

None of these volunteer organizations coordinated their activities. Their remarkable similarity thus reveals a worldwide change in political norms and goals. Senator John F. Kennedy (1917–1963) first expressed support for activities to improve relations with people of color in the turbulent Third World in an improvised, late-night campaign speech at the University of Michigan in October 1960. He asked a crowd of thousands of students:

> How many of you who are going to be doctors, are willing to spend your days in Ghana? Technicians or engineers, how many of you are willing to work in the Foreign Service and spend your lives traveling around the world? On your willingness to do that, not merely to serve one year or two years in the service, but on your willingness to contribute part of your life to this country, I think will depend the answer whether a free society can compete.

As president, Kennedy created the Peace Corps by executive order on March 1, 1961. He appointed his brother-in-law, R. Sargent Shriver (1915–2011), to head the agency. Shriver had previously led the fight to integrate Illinois schools as head of the Chicago Board of Education and the Catholic Interracial Council. Under Shriver's directorship, the Peace Corps became a popular symbol of Kennedy's "New Frontier," allowing citizens to respond to the young president's inauguration appeal to "Ask not what your country can do for you—ask what you can do for your country."

Six months later, Shriver obtained authorization for the Peace Corps from the US Congress. The Peace Corps Act of September 22, 1961, established three formal goals: (1) to help people of interested "countries and areas in meeting their needs for trained manpower"; (2) to "help promote a better understanding" of Americans "on the part of the peoples served"; and (3) to help promote "a better understanding of other peoples on the part of Americans."

Other volunteers immediately followed the ones who went to Ghana, taking up two-year assignments in twelve more countries of Asia, Africa, and Latin America. Participants numbered 750 by the end of the first year. At its height in 1965, the Peace Corps fielded 15,000 men and women in dozens of countries. They brought a wide range of professional skills, from agronomy to zoology, but the majority were college graduates with liberal arts degrees. Many went to Africa, where the corps responded to numerous requests for schoolteachers. The corps also offered community development, especially in Latin America. This activity, Kennedy believed, would supplement efforts of the Alliance for Progress to direct regional revolutionary change into peaceful channels and avoid the further spread of communism.

The United States encouraged other Western nations to develop their own programs. Most did. Germany, France, Israel, the Philippines, the Netherlands, Argentina, Japan, and numerous other countries subsequently sent volunteers worldwide—following the trend set by Australia in 1951.

The US Peace Corps declined in the late 1960s, when policies in Southeast Asia disaffected American youth. (Volunteers' average age was twenty-four.) By the end of the Vietnam War, the agency had shrunk 50 percent. The ratio of male to female volunteers became skewed (7:3) as males sought to avoid the draft by joining the Peace

Corps. President Richard Nixon (1913–1994) soured on the program, but resigned in disgrace as a result of the Watergate scandal before he could eliminate it.

The Peace Corps retained bipartisan support in Congress. It continued sending six thousand volunteers abroad annually. By 2015, more than 220,000 Americans had served in 139 countries, building roads, introducing new agricultural techniques, teaching children, advising small businesses, and undertaking hundreds of other tasks as diverse as the volunteers themselves. Long after the Cold War ended, the Peace Corps and its international counterparts maintained robust programs around the planet.

SEE ALSO *Alliance for Progress; Cold War; Decolonization; Kennedy, John Fitzgerald; United States Agency for International Development (USAID)*

BIBLIOGRAPHY

Adams, Michael. *Voluntary Service Overseas: The Story of the First Ten Years.* London: Faber and Faber, 1968.

Brouwer, Ruth Compton. *Canada's Global Villagers: CUSO in Development, 1961–86.* Vancouver: University of British Columbia Press, 2013.

Cobbs Hoffman, Elizabeth. *All You Need Is Love: The Peace Corps and the Spirit of the 1960s.* Cambridge, MA: Harvard University Press, 1998.

Fischer, Fritz. *Making Them Like Us: Peace Corps Volunteers in the 1960s.* Washington, DC: Smithsonian Institution Press, 1998.

Kennedy, John F. "Remarks of Senator John F. Kennedy." University of Michigan Union, October 14, 1960. http://www.peacecorps.gov/about/history/speech/

Peace Corps Act of 1961, Pub. L. No. 87-293, 75 Stat. 612 (1961). http://research.archives.gov/description/299874

Rice, Gerard. *The Bold Experiment: JFK's Peace Corps.* South Bend, IN: University of Notre Dame Press, 1985.

Elizabeth Cobbs
Melbern G. Glasscock Professor
Texas A&M University

PEARL HARBOR

More than seven decades after the surprise Japanese attack in Hawai'i killed 2,390 Americans on December 7, 1941, the phrase "Remember Pearl Harbor" remains well known throughout American society. The devastating loss to Japan is regarded as embodying an important lesson that should never be forgotten—that the United States must always be prepared for unexpected attacks and ready to defend its freedom at all cost. As a result, the Japanese attack on Pearl Harbor has been the subject of numerous historical accounts. Many of these have focused on the political context leading up to December 7, as well as the actual attack, thereby limiting the range of approaches primarily to political, diplomatic, and military histories. The attack on Pearl Harbor, however, should be viewed from other perspectives as well, including, among others, Native Hawaiian history, colonialism in the Pacific, transpacific history, and memorial studies.

PEARL HARBOR BEFORE DECEMBER 1941

First and foremost, it is critical to remember that this area was not always a US Navy site or even called Pearl Harbor. Like the rest of Hawai'i, this was a site of thriving Native Hawaiian life for many generations. Hawaiians referred to the bay as *pu'uloa* and considered it sacred because one of their gods (*'aumakua*) called Ka'ahupahau, or guardian sharks, lived there.

As the United States expanded its sphere of interest in the Pacific and Asia, it became increasingly interested in Hawai'i and particularly in the bay around "Pearl River" as a potential military harbor. As early as 1872, a US military mission was sent to secretly investigate the area for possible military use. The reciprocity treaty between the United States and the Kingdom of Hawai'i, enacted in 1876, further strengthened the American interest. In return for allowing Hawaiian goods, including sugar, to be exported duty-free to the United States, King David Kalakaua (1836–1891) agreed that he would "not lease or otherwise dispose of or create any lien upon any port, harbor, or other territory in his dominions" to other nations. A supplementary treaty of reciprocity, ratified in 1887, granted "the United States the exclusive right to enter Pearl River" and establish a "coaling and repair station for the use of vessels of the United States."

It was thus no surprise that the United States began developing the bay into a naval port after the annexation and colonization of Hawai'i in 1898. By the time of the Japanese attack, Pearl Harbor was a large naval base and home to the powerful US Pacific Fleet. Other large tracts of land in Oahu had also been fortified as military bases. It was no secret that Hawai'i was a key military site for the United States. The Japanese navy had plenty of information about the American military capability in Hawai'i and used the knowledge to prepare carefully for the attack, even simulating Pearl Harbor at a harbor in southern Japan. Thanks to the extensive information they had acquired, the Japanese were able to efficiently destroy not only the many battleships and cruisers moored in the harbor but also in surrounding areas, including Wheeler Army Airfield and Hickam Field, where they knew a number of military aircraft would be parked.

THE JAPANESE ATTACK

Not only did the Japanese military carefully plan the Pearl Harbor attack, but it also executed it in tandem with attacks on other targets in Asia. In fact, about ninety minutes prior to the beginning of the attack on Pearl Harbor, the Japanese army had already landed in Kota Bharu on the Malay Peninsula without declaring war against Great Britain. Shortly after the attack in Hawai'i, the Japanese mounted a wave of attacks on other US colonies, such as Wake Island, Guam, and the Philippines, as well as on the British colonies of Hong Kong and Singapore. The surprise appearance of Japanese planes over the sky of Hawai'i was not so much a simple one-way attack against the United States as it was a part of a multifaceted military strategy pursued by the Japanese to wrest colonial interests in Asia from their Euro-American rivals.

The success of the Japanese attack was reported with great fanfare in the Japanese media. *Yomiuri Shimbun*, one of the national newspapers, boasted in its editorial that "the path of brilliant light has finally opened up before the empire" of Japan. Such belligerent discourse greatly enhanced the morale of the nation, contributing to the tenacity of misguided faith in the power of the Japanese military among the people.

REACTION AND IMPACT

In the United States, the news from Hawai'i was heard with a sense of disbelief and anger, particularly because Japan had failed to deliver its declaration of war ahead of the attack. This failure exacerbated an existing prejudice against the Japanese as cunning and untrustworthy, and contributed to Franklin D. Roosevelt's (1882–1945) decision to forcefully displace all Japanese and Japanese American residents living on the West Coast.

Heavy smoke rolls out of the USS West Virginia *and a small boat rescues a crew member after the Japanese bombing of Pearl Harbor, Hawai'i, December 7, 1941. The success of the Japanese attack was reported with great fanfare in the Japanese media. In the United States, the news from Hawai'i was heard with a sense of disbelief and anger, particularly because Japan had failed to declare war ahead of the attack.* **AP IMAGES**

In Hawai'i, the impact of the Japanese attack was felt way beyond the targeted military facilities. According to the data collected by the National Park Service, of the Americans killed that day, forty-eight were civilians. Some of them lost their lives not in military areas but in the residential and commercial districts of Honolulu, where American antiaircraft gun shells fell.

The civilians most affected by the attack in Hawai'i were the local Japanese residents, who constituted about 40 percent of the island population. Almost immediately after the attack, the local and federal authorities began arresting teachers, priests, and many other residents of Japanese origin who were leaders of the Japanese community. They were initially detained in Sand Island in Honolulu and later sent for longer confinement at interment camps in Honouliuli in Oahu or other camps on the mainland. In the face of this crisis, many second-generation men of Japanese descent in Hawai'i tried to prove their loyalty to the United States by joining the US military and fighting for their nation.

The Japanese were not the only residents affected by the attack. Within hours of the attack, martial law was declared over the territory of Hawai'i. The basic civil rights of all citizens were curtailed or suspended under the pretext of military necessity. Curfews were imposed, all communications were subject to censorship, and other restrictions became common. For much of the duration of the war (until October 1944), Hawai'i, which supposedly served as the forefront of America's effort to fight for freedom in the Pacific theater, became a place of military dictatorship.

PEARL HARBOR'S SIGNIFICANCE

Pearl Harbor remains a site of military significance to this day. Today, the Joint Base Pearl Harbor–Hickam is the second-largest naval base in the United States. The significance of the area, however, goes beyond actual military utility, as the memory of the Japanese attack and America's eventual victory continues to be invoked in American popular culture. The historian Emily Rosenberg has even argued that Pearl Harbor has come to "gain emotive power as an icon" of American culture (2003, 14).

An example of this iconic emotive power is today palpable at the USS *Arizona* Memorial in Pearl Harbor, which attracts approximately a million and a half visitors every year, including a significant number of Asian tourists. That this memorial to the battleship exists in an active military harbor, which used to be a sacred place for Native Hawaiians, and attracts an international audience of visitors shows that multiple layers of the past are embedded in Pearl Harbor, and that, as a result, multidisciplinary and

transnational approaches are required to fully appreciate its tragic history.

SEE ALSO *Four Freedoms; Japan; Navy, US; Roosevelt, Franklin D.; World War II*

BIBLIOGRAPHY

Dower, John W. *Cultures of War: Pearl Harbor, Hiroshima, 9-11, Iraq*. New York: Norton, 2010.

Farber, David, and Beth Bailey. *The First Strange Place: Race and Sex in World War II Hawaii*. Baltimore, MD: Johns Hopkins University Press, 1994.

Gonzalez, Vernadette Vicũna. *Securing Paradise: Tourism and Militarism in Hawai'i and the Philippines*. Durham, NC: Duke University Press, 2013.

Odo, Franklin. *No Sword to Bury: Japanese Americans in Hawai'i during World War II*. Philadelphia: Temple University Press, 2004.

Osorio, Jon Kamakawiwo'ole. "Memorializing Pu'uloa and Remembering Pearl Harbor." In *Militarized Currents: Toward a Decolonized Future in Asia and the Pacific*, edited by Setsu Shigematsu and Keith Camacho, 3–14. Minneapolis: University of Minnesota Press, 2010.

Rosenberg, Emily S. *A Date Which Will Live: Pearl Harbor in American Memory*. Durham, NC: Duke University Press, 2003.

Yaguchi, Yujin. "War Memories across the Pacific: Japanese Visitors at the *Arizona* Memorial." In *The Unpredictability of the Past: Memories of the Asia-Pacific War in U.S.–East Asian Relations*, edited by Marc Gallicchio, 234–252. Durham, NC: Duke University Press, 2007.

Yujin Yaguchi
Professor
The University of Tokyo

PENTAGON
SEE *Department of Defense, US.*

PERSHING, JOHN JOSEPH
1860–1948

The United States emerged from the 1898 Spanish-American War as a world power with forces deployed well beyond North America. Many American leaders, however, associated their country's new global status with a superior morality and viewed with mounting alarm the mass armies, deadly advanced weaponry, and hair-trigger alliances developed by the European powers in the years prior to World War I. Yet the United States would eventually be drawn into this conflict, dispatching an army of some 2 million men to Europe. Its commander, John Joseph Pershing, a man of Alsatian ancestry who had grown up on a farm in south-central Missouri near the tiny town of Laclede, played a central part in defining America's military role.

PRE–WORLD WAR I MILITARY CAREER

A graduate of West Point, Pershing had distinguished himself as a student more for his leadership than for his scholarship. His prewar experiences included the campaign against the Lakota (Sioux) Indians although his unit did not play a role in the infamous Wounded Knee Massacre, combat at San Juan Hill in Cuba during the Spanish-American War, a tour of duty in the Philippines against the rebellious Moros, and service as an observer in Manchuria in northern China during the Russo-Japanese War. In 1916, he led the Punitive Expedition in Mexico against Pancho Villa (1878–1923), a command that involved both military and delicate political questions.

THE AMERICAN EXPEDITIONARY FORCE

After selecting Pershing in 1917 to command the American Expeditionary Force (AEF) in Europe during World War I, President Woodrow Wilson (1856–1924) and Secretary of War Newton D. Baker (1871–1937) instructed him to keep in view that the overseas forces he commanded must preserve a "separate and distinct" identity. They feared that if the AEF's role in checking German expansionism was not clear, then President Wilson's liberal influence over the subsequent peace settlement would be seriously diminished.

Wilson and Baker chose well. Few if any US officers had a more stubborn determination or formidable presence. Although the United States initially had neither the soldiers nor modern weaponry to confront the powerful Germany army, Pershing believed that his expeditionary force, once fully formed, would play a decisive role in bringing Berlin to its knees. When he and his staff arrived in Europe, he was asked if he thought the formidable German trench system could be breached. "Of course the western front can be broken," he responded. "What are we here for?" (Woodward 2014, 101). Pershing thought that his country, composed of immigrants, produced "a type of manhood superior in initiative to that existing abroad, which given approximately equal training and discipline developed a superior soldier to that existing abroad" (Woodward 2014, 317). He also thought in terms of total victory, which was not in sync with Wilson's hope that the Allies might check Germany's expansionist goals without beating the country flat, thereby increasing the prospect of a dictated and vindictive peace.

Major General John J. Pershing after his arrival in France to command the American Expeditionary Force, 1917. *When Pershing and his staff arrived in Europe in the midst of World War I, he was asked if he thought the formidable German trench system could be breached. "Of course the western front can be broken," he responded. "What are we here for?"* **AP IMAGES**

Pershing eventually achieved Washington's goal of forming and commanding an independent army in France, but not without great difficulty and considerable acrimony with Allied leaders, especially after the Germans launched a series of offensives, beginning in March 1918, to defeat the French and British before a great US force could be established on European soil. German success during the first half of 1918 placed tremendous pressure on Pershing to place his soldiers, known as doughboys, into existing Allied units with their battle-tested staffs and well-developed logistical systems. Pershing's unbending opposition to amalgamation, which would have made it difficult if not impossible to form a powerful American force in France, infuriated Allied leaders. One British general did not mince words: "The man's an ass, I think—he doesn't mean business … the God-damned American programme is going to f—k up the whole show" (Woodward 1993, 159). General Jan Christiaan Smuts (1870–1950), the South African leader, even dared to suggest to Prime Minister David Lloyd George (1863–1945) that he himself be designated the "fighting" commander of all American forces, with Pershing relegated to supervising "all organizations in the rear" (Woodward 2014, 190).

The five German offensives from March into July 1918 threatened Paris and prompted the British to make plans to evacuate their troops from the continent. During the last half of July, however, the Allies regained the initiative, while US troops flowed across the Atlantic in increasing numbers. In early August, Pershing began to create an independent US Army, and, on September 12, he launched the first largely American offensive at St. Mihiel in northeastern France. Several weeks later, the AEF launched another offensive in the Meuse-Argonne. This American offensive, along with successful drives by the French and especially the British, soon led to Germany's defeat.

The famous British military historian Captain B. H. Liddell Hart's (1895–1970) title for his chapter on Pershing in his book on World War I generals is "'Black Jack' Pershing, the 100-Percent American" (Liddell Hart 1928). Sensitive to Allied criticisms (some of them valid) of the AEF's performance, Pershing believed that the AEF had played the key role in Germany's defeat and had ultimately proven that its soldiers were superior to either German or Allied soldiers. Many historians question Pershing's contention that the AEF had no equal in Europe and was ultimately responsible for the Second Reich's defeat, but it can be argued that the AEF's commander set the tone for the US Army's interaction with its allies in future wars, declared or otherwise.

POSTWAR CAREER

Following the war, Pershing contemplated a run for the presidency in 1920. In some respects, it would have been surprising if he had not entertained such aspirations. Following every previous major US conflict, a military hero had eventually become president (George Washington, Andrew Jackson, William Henry Harrison, Zachary Taylor, Ulysses S. Grant, and Theodore Roosevelt). But popular support was not forthcoming. From 1921 to 1924, he served as chief of staff in the War Department. As the nation's most prominent soldier, he did not foresee another overseas campaign in Europe and favored a relatively small standing army composed of citizen rather than professional soldiers. On the other hand, he emphatically rejected the idea that World War I had been a "war to end all wars."

SEE ALSO *Mexico; Philippines; Roosevelt, Theodore; Spanish-American War; Wilson, Woodrow; World War I*

BIBLIOGRAPHY

Liddell Hart, B. H. *Reputations: Ten Years After*. London: John Murray, 1928.

Smythe, Donald. *Pershing: General of the Armies*. Bloomington: Indiana University Press, 1986.

Trask, David F. *The AEF and Coalition Warmaking, 1917–1918*. Lawrence: University Press of Kansas, 1993.

Woodward, David R. *Trial by Friendship: Anglo-American Relations, 1917–1918*. Lexington: University Press of Kentucky, 1993.

Woodward, David R. "'Black Jack' Pershing: The American Proconsul in Europe." In *Leadership in Conflict: 1914–1918*, edited by Matthew Hughes and Matthew Seligman. Barnsley, UK: Leo Cooper, 2000.

Woodward, David R. *World War I Almanac*. New York: Facts on File, 2009.

Woodward, David R. *The American Army and the First World War*. Cambridge: Cambridge University Press, 2014.

David R. Woodward
Emeritus Professor
Marshall University

PHAN THỊ KIM PHÚC (NICK UT, 1972)

During the Vietnam War, the mass media played an instrumental role in shaping public opinion and defining how American citizens would come to understand and ultimately remember the war. New media technologies and unprecedented access to battlegrounds produced graphic images of atrocities and death that led to deep divisions in US society as Americans began to rethink the role of the United States in Vietnam. Photojournalism, in particular, galvanized opposition to the war in the United States and around the world. One of the most indelible photographs that continues to dominate American public memory of the war is that of Phan Thị Kim Phúc taken by Huỳnh Công Út (Nick Ut) on June 8, 1972, in the village of Trảng Bàng in the Republic of (South) Vietnam. In this Pulitzer Prize–winning image, captioned "Accidental Napalm" or "The Terror of War," a nine-year-old girl, Kim Phúc, runs down the road toward Ut, arms outstretched, screaming in pain as her naked body—her scorched clothing torn off—burns from napalm dropped on civilians during an air strike. In the events leading up to the photograph that would stir viewers and incite action across the globe, Kim Phúc had been fleeing her village with a group of adults and children, including several family members also captured in the image, when South Vietnamese air forces mistook them for communist soldiers. Plumes of black smoke billowed behind the terrified children as they attempted to escape, but they were caught in the fiery blast of napalm. The photograph was published the following day in the national and international press, further fueling the antiwar movement.

South Vietnamese forces follow after terrified children as they run down Route 1 near Trảng Bàng after an aerial napalm attack on suspected Viet Cong hiding places, June 8, 1972. *The photograph by Huỳnh Công Út (Nick Ut) of nine-year-old Phan Thị Kim Phúc as she runs down the road, arms outstretched, screaming in pain from burns—her scorched clothing torn off—is an indelible image that continues to dominate American public memory of the Vietnam War.* **NICK UT/AP IMAGES**

Ut's image of Kim Phúc has since taken on an iconic status in the pictorial history of the Vietnam War and, more broadly, the history of war photography. Along with a number of other defining images from the war, such as Eddie Adams's photograph of General Nguyễn Ngọc Loan executing Nguyễn Văn Lém in the streets of Saigon (now Ho Chi Minh City) on February 1, 1968, and Ronald Haeberle's photographs of the massacre at Mỹ Lai on March 16, 1968, the image of the "napalm girl" continues to resonate across time and space. The wide circulation of the suffering body of Kim Phúc has raised critical questions about the morality of warfare and its violent impact on the most innocent and vulnerable victims of war: children. In contemporary politics, the image of Kim Phúc has been reappropriated and inserted into new contexts to incite the public to rethink military intervention and the development of advanced technologies of war.

After taking the photograph, Ut transported Kim Phúc to the hospital, where she underwent a series of surgeries over the course of a year. She survived, immigrated to Canada as an adult, and emerged as an international symbol of peace and reconciliation. In 1997, she helped to found a nonprofit organization, the Kim Foundation International, which provides medical assistance to child victims of war and terrorism around the world.

SEE ALSO *Vietnam War*

BIBLIOGRAPHY

Chong, Denise. *The Girl in the Picture: The Story of Kim Phuc, the Photograph, and the Vietnam War.* London: Simon and Schuster, 1999.

Hagopian, Patrick. "Vietnam War Photography as a Locus of Memory." In *Locating Memory: Photographic Acts*, edited by

Annette Kuhn and Kirsten Emiko McAllister, 201–222. New York: Berghahn, 2006.

Hariman, Robert, and John Louis Lucaites. *No Caption Needed: Iconic Photographs, Public Culture, and Liberal Democracy.* Chicago: University of Chicago Press, 2007.

Schwenkel, Christina. *The American War in Contemporary Vietnam: Transnational Remembrance and Representation.* Bloomington: Indiana University Press, 2009.

Christina Schwenkel
Associate Professor of Anthropology
University of California, Riverside

PHILIPPINES

The Republic of the Philippines is an archipelago of more than seven thousand islands in the western Pacific Ocean separated from mainland Asia by the China Sea. Since the end of the nineteenth century, the United States and the Philippines have maintained tight military, economic, social, and cultural ties.

THE SPANISH COLONIAL PERIOD

The Philippines' relationship with the Western world extends back to colonial Spain, when Spanish merchants and traders understood the role the islands could play as a conduit for Chinese goods (especially silk and spices) to be traded in Spain and throughout Europe and the Spanish Empire. After the Spanish formally colonized the islands as part of the Viceroyalty of New Spain in the mid-sixteenth century, naming them after King Philip II (r. 1556–1598), they established a gateway for commerce flowing east to the Mexican port of Acapulco in a series of merchant fleets known as the Manila Galleon. Lasting for nearly three centuries from the 1500s to the early 1800s, the twice-a-year galleon carried European goods and ideas west and Asian goods east.

During this period, resident Filipinos adopted the Roman Catholic religion, the legacy of which is reflected in the Philippines being one of Asia's few predominantly Christian nations. Filipinos also adopted Spanish surnames and aspects of the Spanish language, now mainly apparent in "borrowed words" in Tagalog or Filipino, the official Philippine language but one of dozens of regional languages spoken in the islands. The Filipinos also adopted Western-style dress, customs, economies, and culture. This blend of things Asian and European has created a distinctive Filipino culture.

THE AMERICAN OCCUPATION

Americans arrived into that milieu at the end of the Spanish-American War (sometimes more accurately referred to as the Spanish-American-Cuban-Filipino War) in 1898. In that year, the Treaty of Paris ended the Spanish-Cuban conflict, guaranteeing Cuba its "independence" from Spain (only to become a veritable US protectorate). The United States, as the "victor" in the war, was guaranteed a military base at Guantánamo Bay in Cuba and the new territorial possessions of Puerto Rico, Guam, and the Philippine Islands—quite a spoil of former Spanish colonies, with the US government paying Spain $20 million for the Philippines. Thus, without even having a seat at the treaty negotiations in Paris, the Filipinos, after more than four hundred years of Spanish rule, now found themselves under a new colonial ruler—the United States.

The Filipinos did not take this new development sitting down. There had already been armed uprisings protesting Spanish colonialism in the islands, resulting in a de facto declaration of independence from Spain in 1898. By the end of the nineteenth century, the uprising was redirected toward the Americans, who refused to recognize Philippine independence. The revolution was led by General Emilio Aguinaldo (1869–1964), whose forces had to confront a very powerful US military that did not hesitate to use brutal scorched-earth tactics against the Filipinos, tens of thousands of whom died in the war.

This suppression of Philippine sovereignty occurred during the administration of US president William McKinley (1843–1901), who wanted the United States to take its place on the global stage. McKinley's policies of expansionism and empire building included a stronger grip on the Hawaiian Islands, the annexation of Puerto Rico and Guam as US territories, efforts in Panama for the creation of a US-controlled canal, and the establishment of US control in the Philippines.

Such control meant that the new territory, so far from US shores, needed a strong military presence and the leadership of presidentially appointed governors, one of the first of whom was future US president William Howard Taft (1857–1930). English then replaced Spanish as the new colonial language, although many Filipinos continued to use Spanish in government and business, while Tagalog remained Manila's principal language. But with English now taught in schools as the official language of the territorial government, and with an increasing American business presence, the cultural landscape of the Philippines began to change, reflecting a more American lifestyle. A robust US missionary effort introduced a variety of Protestant denominations, as well as the Church of Jesus Christ of Latter-Day Saints (Mormons), Jehovah's Witnesses, and other churches, into the heavily Catholic Philippines. The country remains around 85 percent Christian in the twenty-first century. In addition, the success of US business ventures in overseas markets like the Philippines demonstrated the "dollar diplomacy" component of US imperialism. Expansionism was good for business, as US overseas territories not only opened doors to new markets for American manufactured goods but also secured sources of raw materials, commodities, and labor.

FILIPINO AMERICANS

Filipino laborers started immigrating to the United States by the tens of thousands in the late nineteenth and early twentieth centuries. They became workers in Hawai'i's sugarcane and pineapple fields, in California's mines and fruit industry, and for other agricultural interests up and down the US West Coast. Significant communities of Filipinos developed in places like Santa Clara, California, where they competed with Mexican and other migrant farmworkers. In the 1930s during the Great Depression, Filipinos also competed with impoverished workers from Oklahoma, Arkansas, and elsewhere in the United States. Their descendants—second-, third-, and fourth-generation Filipino Americans—remain a vital presence in the United States. According to the 2010 census data, there are nearly 11 million Filipino Americans, making them the second-largest group of Asians in the United States after the Chinese, and the largest population of Filipinos outside the Philippines. The largest US concentrations of Filipinos live in California, Hawai'i, New York (particularly New York City), New Jersey, Texas, and Illinois. Census data also reveal that Filipino Americans earn more than the US average household income and achieve a higher level of education than the US national average.

WORLD WAR II

In 1935, the Philippines became a "commonwealth" of the United States (the status that Puerto Rico yet retains), a semi-independent state that the Filipinos saw as a step toward complete independence. Those plans, however, were soon interrupted by the next wave of colonialism, this time by Imperial Japan. The Japanese invaded the Philippines in late 1941 and curried favor with a collaborator faction of Filipinos. Japanese brutality on the islands was intense, as exemplified by the infamous Bataan Death March (1942) and the Manila massacre during the Battle of Manila (1945), with the Japanese coming to control much of the Philippines from 1942 to 1944.

Because the Philippines was a significant part of the Allied Pacific theater during World War II, the United States worked with the Filipino military to end the Japanese occupation and to stem further Japanese overseas adventurism. This effort, which became known as Operation Musketeer and the Battle for the

Philippines (1944–1945), was led by General Douglas MacArthur (1880–1964), the supreme commander of the southwest Pacific theater of operations and field marshal of the Philippine army. By the invitation of Filipino president Manuel Quezon (1878–1944) and with the approval of President Franklin Roosevelt (1882–1945), MacArthur supervised the creation of the Philippine army. The battles of Leyte Gulf (1944), Mindoro (1944), and Luzon (1945) in the Philippines were some of the more horrific of the Pacific war. By the time Allied forces defeated the Japanese in 1945, an estimated 1 million Filipinos had died. The US occupation also ended at the conclusion of World War II, and the Philippines became independent in 1946.

THE ABACA INDUSTRY AND THE PHILIPPINE ECONOMY

The production of abaca (Manila hemp), a fiber made from the bark of *Musa textilis*, a plant in the banana family, became one of the most important industries in the Philippines and commercially connected the islands to the United States before, during, and after the war. Twine was in high demand from the 1870s through the 1950s as grain farmers throughout the world harvested crops with an implement known as a binder (or reaper binder), which cut grain stalks and tied them in bundles with twine to dry and await threshing. Abaca was the best fiber for binder twine, and farmers throughout the wheat belt of the United States and Canada preferred it. Having to import it from across the Pacific, however, made it an expensive cordage commodity. As a result, henequen and sisal producers in Yucatán, Mexico, eventually outcompeted Filipino growers for the binder twine market, although Manila twine remained popular and was often mixed with other fibers to create high-quality blended twines. World War II disrupted the Philippine abaca market as the Japanese threatened commercial seaways across the Pacific. At the same time, demand for naval rope grew during the war, and the Allied powers provided a robust market for abaca and other cordage fibers from around the world.

After the war, the demand for rope and twine dropped. The abaca market slumped further as combine harvesters, which cut and thresh grain without the need to bind sheaves, replaced binders by the 1950s. But by the end of the twentieth century, the abaca industry had learned to diversify. Now the fiber is central to thriving niche markets in the United States and Europe, especially Germany, for the manufacture of coffee filters, cigarette paper, mats and rugs, and fabric for airline and bus seats, among hundreds of other uses. The expanding industry has helped the Philippine economy grow in the twenty-first century. By 2013, the Philippine economy was the second fastest growing in Asia after China's, as indicated by a 7.2 percent growth in gross domestic product. But, with a population of more than 100 million people in a nation about the size of New Mexico, the Philippines is the twelfth-most-populous country in the world. As a result, millions of Filipinos continue to seek work abroad, especially in Hong Kong, Singapore, Dubai, Canada, and the United States.

CONTEMPORARY US-PHILIPPINE RELATIONS

The end of the twentieth century and the beginning of the twenty-first have witnessed a continuation of strong relations between the United States and the Philippines. Militarily, while large US installations in the Philippines such as Clark Air Base and Subic Bay Naval Station were closed in 1991, the United States has continued an active presence. Following the events of September 11, 2001, the Philippines allowed US forces to help in counterterrorism training and security against Muslim militants on the east side of the island of Mindanao. Likewise, the Filipinos have been concerned about China's assertive behavior in disputed areas of the South China Sea, especially when in 2012 Chinese paramilitary forces tried to exert control of rich fishing grounds in the sea. Thus, the United States and the Philippines signed the ten-year Enhanced Defense Cooperation Agreement in April 2014, which allows American forces temporary access to Philippine military facilities to assist and train the Philippine forces. Likewise, commercial relations between the United States and the Philippines also remain strong, with a robust trade between the two countries. And immigration of Filipinos to the United States, for employment opportunities and to connect with family members living abroad, has continued apace into this period. Diplomatic relations remain warm between the two countries, but with the United States understanding that it must respect Philippine sovereignty.

SEE ALSO *Dollar Diplomacy; Empire, US; Exceptionalism; Gender; Internationalism; Interventionism; Isolationism; Missionary Diplomacy; Monroe Doctrine (1823); Open Door Policy; Roosevelt, Theodore; Spanish-American War; Taft, William Howard; Twain, Mark; Wilson, Woodrow*

BIBLIOGRAPHY

Feuer, A. B. *America at War: The Philippines, 1898–1913*. Westport, CT: Praeger, 2002.

Fujita-Rony, Dorothy B. *American Workers, Colonial Power: Philippine Seattle and the Transpacific West, 1919–1941.* Berkeley: University of California Press, 2003.

Knightley, Phillip. *The First Casualty: From the Crimea to Vietnam: The War Correspondent as Hero, Propagandist, and Myth Maker*. New York: Harcourt Brace Jovanovich, 1975.

Kramer, Paul A. *The Blood of Government: Race, Empire, the United States, and the Philippines*. Chapel Hill: University of North Carolina Press, 2006.

Linn, Brian McAllister. *The Philippine War, 1899–1902*. Lawrence: University Press of Kansas, 2000.

McCoy, Alfred W., and Francisco A. Scarano, eds. The *Colonial Crucible: Empire in the Making of the Modern American State*. Madison: University of Wisconsin Press, 2009.

Molina, Antonio M. *The Philippines through the Centuries*. Manila: University of Santo Tomas Cooperative, 1961.

Owen, Norman G. *Prosperity without Progress: Manila Hemp and Material Life in the Colonial Philippines*. Berkeley: University of California Press, 1984.

Sievert, Elizabeth Potter. *The Story of Abaca: Manila Hemp's Transformation from Textile to Marine Cordage and Specialty Paper*. Manila: Ateneo de Manila University Press, 2009.

Tarling, Nicholas. *The Cambridge History of Southeast Asia*, Vol. 4: *From World War II to the Present*. New York: Cambridge University Press, 2000.

Zaide, Sonia M. *The Philippines: A Unique Nation*. 2nd ed. Quezon City, Philippines: All-Nations, 1999.

Sterling Evans
Department of History
University of Oklahoma

PICKERING, TIMOTHY

SEE *Adams, John.*

PINCKNEY'S TREATY (1795)

The Treaty of San Lorenzo, better known as Pinckney's Treaty in honor of Thomas Pinckney (1750–1828), one of the US negotiators, was signed by the United States and Spain on October 27, 1795. It was ratified by the US Senate on March 7, 1796, and by Spain on April 25, 1796. The treaty went into effect on August 2, 1796. The passage of the treaty was the result of more than a decade of negotiations, but ultimately it was Spain's anxieties over the terms of Jay's Treaty (1794), which Spanish officials believed would give Britain undue influence over the United States in the ongoing wars of Revolutionary France, that led to the passage of the treaty.

The treaty settled several long-standing disagreements between the United States and Spain. The first was over the boundary between the two nations, which had been in dispute since the signing of the Treaty of Paris in 1783. Basing its claims on Spanish troops' defeat of the British during the American Revolution, Spain claimed territory stretching from the Gulf of Mexico north along the Mississippi River and east through parts of the modern-day states of Kentucky, Tennessee, Georgia, and North Carolina, along with all of Mississippi and Alabama. Pinckney's Treaty resolved the dispute in the United States' favor, giving the United States title to all territory north of the 31st parallel—the northern border of Florida—which the treaty stipulated would be jointly surveyed by the United States and Spain. The transfer gave the United States title to large portions of territory claimed by the Creek, Cherokee, Chickasaw, and Choctaw Nations and dramatically reduced Spanish holdings in the Southeast.

The treaty also partially reopened the Mississippi River, which had been closed to American merchants since 1784. The treaty gave Americans the "Right of Deposit" at New Orleans—the ability to transship goods through Spanish territory without paying either an import or export tax. The reopening of the Mississippi allowed the Anglo-American settlers of the trans-Appalachian West to export furs, flour, salted meat, and cotton to Atlantic world markets.

Passage of the treaty led to the expansion of American trade at the port of New Orleans and in the Caribbean more broadly, where despite the official neutrality of American shipping during the War of the Second Coalition, French and British privateers regularly attacked American ships. This, coupled with growing American resentment of Spanish interference with the trade of New Orleans, led to agitation for the United States to purchase the mouth of the Mississippi River from Spain. In 1801 Spain secretly retroceded Louisiana to France in the Treaty of Ildefonso, although Spanish officials remained in power in the region. In October 1802 Spanish officials closed the American deposit at New Orleans, setting off outrage throughout the American West and among eastern merchants who traded at New Orleans. This action led President Thomas Jefferson (1743–1826) to dispatch James Monroe (1758–1831) to Paris to negotiate the purchase of the mouth of the river, ultimately leading to the Louisiana Purchase.

SEE ALSO *Empire of Liberty*

BIBLIOGRAPHY

Bemis, Samuel Flagg. *Pinckney's Treaty: A Study of America's Advantage from Europe's Distress, 1783–1800*. Baltimore, MD: Johns Hopkins Press, 1926.

Grant, Ethan. "The Treaty of San Lorenzo and Manifest Destiny." *Gulf Coast Historical Review* 12, 2 (January 1997): 44–57.

Haynes, Robert V. *The Mississippi Territory and the Southwest Frontier, 1795–1817*. Lexington: University Press of Kentucky, 2010.

Kukla, Jon. *A Wilderness So Immense: The Louisiana Purchase and the Destiny of America*. New York: Knopf, 2003.

Weeks, Charles. *Paths to a Middle Ground: The Diplomacy of Natchez, Boukfouka, Nogales, and San Fernando de las Barrancas, 1791–1795*. Tuscaloosa: University of Alabama Press, 2005.

Whitaker, Arthur Preston. *The Mississippi Question, 1795–1803: A Study in Trade, Politics and Diplomacy*. Gloucester, MA: P. Smith, 1962.

Young, Raymond A. "Pinckney's Treaty—A New Perspective." *Hispanic American Historical Review* 43, 4 (November 1963): 526–535.

Susan Gaunt Stearns
Visiting Assistant Professor
Northwestern University

POGROM

The Russian word *pogrom* refers to any mass attack, accompanied by physical violence, murder, rape, looting, and destruction of property, perpetrated on one section of the population by another. Although such outrages have spanned human history, over the course of the twentieth century the term came to be synonymous with the plight of Jews in the Russian Empire. Earlier mass acts of violence against Jews outside of the Czarist lands tend not to be called pogroms, even though some, for example, the so-called Hep Hep riots in Bavaria and other German states in 1819, were very similar to later outbursts—in Yelizavetgrad in 1881 and Kishinev and Odessa in 1903—considered the quintessential pogroms.

Pogroms against Jews in Russia and then the Soviet Union took place in three distinct time clusters. They flared in the early 1880s; in the years from 1903 to 1906; and then in the aftermath of World War I, the 1917 Russian Revolution, and the subsequent civil war. They tended to be concentrated in the regions of the Ukraine and Moldova, but they also cropped up elsewhere in the vast Russian lands. Knowledge of the pogroms as gleaned from newspapers, lectures, and published firsthand accounts spread among the Jews. The memory of the pogroms, and widespread fear that they could happen again at any time, left its mark on the consciousness, culture, and political activities of East European Jewry. The pogroms figured prominently in the rhetoric of Zionists, particularly after the 1897 founding of the World Zionist Congress, where it was argued that the pogroms proved that Jews could not continue to live in Russia or elsewhere in Eastern Europe but needed a land of their own.

The pogrom era, starting in 1881, coincided with the onset of the mass Jewish emigration from Eastern Europe. Nearly one-third of the Jews of the Russian Empire, as well as the Austro-Hungarian Empire, emigrated, 85 percent of them to the United States. Others resettled in Western Europe, Canada, South Africa, Palestine, Australia, Argentina, Cuba, and elsewhere in Latin America.

They arrived in the United States and the other destinations at a time of steeply rising anti-Semitism. In the receiving countries, much of the population began to worry about the negative impact of continued immigration, and some organized themselves into anti-immigration associations, pressuring their governments to restrict the number and type of immigrants who might be admitted. Jewish communal leaders in the United States hoped to lessen anti-Jewish sentiment and stave off immigration restriction by depicting Jewish immigrants as people fleeing for their lives, in contrast to the other immigrants who flooded the country in pursuit of jobs. Well-off and well-connected Jews in the United States, many the children and grandchildren of previous immigrations, emphasized the pogroms as the cause of the large influx of East European, usually designated as "Russian," Jews. Jewish notables organized rallies, pageants, and other public programs to draw public attention to the pogroms. They lobbied their governments to aid the Jews of Russia and produced pamphlets and articles to describe the violence and the Jews' suffering. They had little confidence that Russia would change but rather hoped that the gates to America would remain open.

Yet the pogroms, despite their savagery and the eloquent and moving concerns articulated by American and other Jewish community notables, cannot rightly be seen to have sparked the migration. Jews from Lithuania, in the northwest Russian Empire, outnumbered all other emigrants until 1910, but no pogroms took place there. A large percentage of the Jews of Galicia emigrated, but these citizens of the Austro-Hungarian Empire had not endured pogroms. So too the Jews of Lithuania left in droves but no pogroms had taken place there. On the other hand, Jews in the Ukraine and Moldova, the epicenter of the pogroms, began leaving only with the introduction of the railroad into their regions and changes in steamship routes, which gave them access to transoceanic ports. They did not leave in large numbers with the outbreak of the pogroms but rather, like so many other East European Jews, when the means to emigrate were present.

The migration of the Jews took place in the context of the impoverishment of the Jewish masses in Eastern Europe, their skyrocketing birthrates, and the decline of their economic niche. Jews also responded to beckoning economic prospects in the United States and other lands, with the flowering of the garment industry in New York a

particular draw. Yet historians and Jewish communal sources persist in depicting the Jewish migration to the United States as a by-product of the pogroms.

SEE ALSO *Immigration; Judaism*

BIBLIOGRAPHY

Best, Gary Dean. *To Free a People: American Jewish Leaders and the Jewish Problem in Eastern Europe, 1890–1914*. Westport, CT: Greenwood Press, 1982.

Klier, John D., and Shlomo Lambroza. *Pogroms: Anti-Jewish Violence in Modern Russian History*. Cambridge and New York: Cambridge University Press, 2004.

Hasia R. Diner
Professor
New York University

POINT FOUR

Point Four was the popular name of a US technical assistance program administered by the Technical Cooperation Administration (TCA) under the authorization of the Foreign Economic Assistance Act of 1950. The term *Point Four* came from the program's origins in President Harry S. Truman's 1949 inaugural address. Warning that "the actions resulting from the Communist philosophy are a threat to the efforts of free nations to bring about world recovery and lasting peace," Truman announced that the United States would respond with a "program for peace and freedom" that emphasized "four major courses of action." The United States, he explained, would continue to support the United Nations, continue its global economic recovery plans, provide support to "freedom-loving nations" against the dangers of aggression, and "embark on a bold new program for making the benefits of our scientific advances and industrial progress available for the improvement and growth of underdeveloped areas." The last point—the fourth point—was unexpected.

The US government had been involved in international technical assistance programs in the past, but those had been largely limited to its colonies, such as the Philippines, and to its Latin American neighbors. Truman's fourth point called for something very different: assistance to countries around the globe in order to prevent communism's expansion. The idea came from Benjamin H. Hardy (1906–1951), a speechwriter in the State Department who had previously worked under Nelson Rockefeller (1908–1979) in the Office of the Coordinator of Inter-American Affairs. Hardy's experiences there had convinced him of the utility of a global technical assistance program. When his State Department superiors rejected the idea in November 1948, Hardy went to the White House. Although Truman had been planning to stick to domestic issues in his inaugural address, Hardy's idea helped persuade him to use the speech to announce a more assertive foreign policy for the coming years.

The fourth part of that policy garnered the greatest attention, both at home and abroad. At home, Truman pressured Congress to pass White House–sponsored legislation that would make Point Four a program with an initial $35 million budget. The debate took a year. In the meantime the United Nations General Assembly established the United Nations Expanded Program of Technical Assistance for Economic Development of Underdeveloped Countries. Truman's inaugural address had changed more than US foreign policy; it had popularized the idea that "technical assistance" was the appropriate international response to "underdevelopment," a term that also gained widespread use in the aftermath of the speech. A Point Four pamphlet explained that "the basic problems of the underdeveloped areas are hunger, disease, and ignorance. Point 4 must concentrate on them first"; it would do so through "teaching, training, demonstrating" (Bingham 1953, 28).

Foreign leaders in financially burdened nations largely welcomed the program, which was made available to those not already controlled by a European power. Iran signed the first "Point Four General Agreement" on October 5, 1950. It was followed by Libya, Saudi Arabia, Israel, Jordan, Iraq, Lebanon, Egypt, Ethiopia, Liberia, Bolivia, Brazil, Chile, Colombia, Costa Rica, Cuba, the Dominican Republic, Ecuador, El Salvador, Guatemala, Haiti, Honduras, Mexico, Nicaragua, Panama, Paraguay, Peru, Uruguay, Venezuela, Afghanistan, Burma, India, Indonesia, Nepal, and Pakistan. The initial country agreement "to cooperate with each other in the interchange of technical knowledge and skills" was always followed by a number of specific agreements that dealt with the particulars of defined cooperative programs. These programs, which had to be specifically requested by the recipient nations themselves, generally focused on public health, education, industry, agriculture, living standards, and access to clean water. Point Four funding was initially very modest—it was, the US government insisted, an assistance program, designed to help nations help themselves.

The scope of the program's budget changed in the aftermath of the Mutual Security Act of 1951, which linked technical assistance together with military and economic assistance. The TCA's budget jumped from $35 million to $211 million, but Point Four aid became more tightly tied to US security concerns as it was subsumed within the new Mutual Security Agency. In 1953, in an effort to disassociate the idea of technical assistance from Truman, the Eisenhower administration moved the technical assistance functions of the Mutual Security Agency into the new Foreign Operations Administration (FOA). In 1955 the FOA was renamed the International Cooperation Administration. Despite these changes, Point Four remained a popular term for US technical assistance throughout much of the 1950s.

SEE ALSO *Rockefeller Foundation; Truman, Harry S.; United States Agency for International Development (USAID)*

BIBLIOGRAPHY

Bingham, Jonathan B. *Shirt-Sleeve Diplomacy: Point 4 in Action.* New York: John Day, 1953.

Cullather, Nick. "Development? It's History." *Diplomatic History* 24, 4 (2000): 641–653.

Cullather, Nick. *The Hungry World: America's Cold War Battle against Poverty in Asia.* Cambridge, MA: Harvard University Press, 2010.

Daniels, Walter M. *The Point Four Program.* New York: Wilson, 1951.

Ekbladh, David. *The Great American Mission: Modernization and the Construction of an American World Order.* Princeton, NJ: Princeton University Press, 2010.

Latham, Michael E. *Modernization as Ideology: American Social Science and "Nation Building" in the Kennedy Era.* Chapel Hill: University of North Carolina Press, 2000.

McVety, Amanda Kay. "Pursuing Progress: Point Four in Ethiopia." *Diplomatic History* 32, 3 (2008): 371–403.

McVety, Amanda Kay. *Enlightened Aid: U.S. Development as Foreign Policy in Ethiopia.* New York: Oxford University Press, 2012.

Amanda Kay McVety
Associate Professor of History
Miami University

POLK, JAMES K.
1795–1849

The single term of James Knox Polk as the eleventh president of the United States (1845–1849) saw the increase of US territory by approximately one-third. More a practical politician than a theorist of expansion—he appears never to have written the words *manifest destiny* (Chaffin 2014, 22)—this Democrat, through diplomacy and war, turned his country into a transcontinental nation.

TEXAS AND OREGON

The Republic of Texas, formed in 1836 from the Mexican province of Texas, had long called for annexation to the United States. Polk believed that the United States had acquired it as part of the Louisiana Purchase (1803) but given it up in the Adams-Onís Treaty (1819). His predecessor, John Tyler (1790–1862), interpreted Polk's election in 1844 on a pro-Texas platform as a referendum in favor of annexation. Congress passed and, on March 1, 1845—three days before Polk's inauguration—Tyler signed a joint resolution inviting Texas to apply to join the Union. Polk, in his inaugural address, described annexation as a fait accompli. On December 29, he signed a joint resolution admitting Texas as a state.

The Democratic Party's platform also had called for an undisputed US title to the Oregon Country. This land stretched between the Rocky Mountains and the Pacific Ocean and between the parallels of 42° and 54° 40′. Under treaties of 1818 and 1826, the United States and the United Kingdom held it in "joint occupation." Either nation, under the latter treaty, could demand a settling of the boundary with one year's notice. In the 1840s thousands of Americans traveled to the area on the Oregon Trail, giving urgency to the question of title. Polk, in his inaugural address, quoted the Democratic platform on the United States' "clear and unquestionable" title to Oregon (Richardson 1897, 381). In July 1845, however, his administration offered a compromise, dividing US and UK territory at 49°. After the British rejected the compromise, Polk, in December, called on Congress to give notice ending joint occupation. Congress did so the next April.

The British, in May 1846, proposed setting the boundary at 49° but leaving Vancouver Island to the United Kingdom and permitting the British Hudson's Bay Company to navigate the Columbia River. Polk and his cabinet, deciding that the Columbia provision would expire when the company's charter did in 1859, agreed. The Senate approved the Buchanan-Pakenham Treaty on June 18. Polk signed a law creating Oregon Territory on August 14, 1848.

WAR WITH MEXICO

Meanwhile, Mexico had severed diplomatic relations with the United States the month Polk took office. Mexico never had recognized Texas's independence, and it denied the claim by Texans and Americans that the new state included the area southwest of the Nueces River and northeast of the Rio Grande. Polk hoped both to resolve the disputes diplomatically and to ensure that no European power acquired the Mexican province of Upper California. In September 1845 he sent John Slidell (1793–1871) to buy California and New Mexico

(a Mexican province comprising today's American Southwest), but Mexico refused to negotiate. In January 1846, Polk ordered General Zachary Taylor (1784–1850) into the disputed land beyond the Nueces. On April 25, Mexicans fired on US soldiers there. On May 11, Polk told Congress that "war exists" because Mexico had "shed American blood upon the American soil" (Richardson 1897, 442). Two days later, he signed a declaration of war.

Polk, exceeding the military involvement of his predecessors, directed the Mexican-American War as much as he could from Washington. Twice the president replaced the commanding general when unhappy with his performance: Taylor gave way to Winfield Scott (1786–1866) in November 1846, and Scott to William O. Butler (1791–1880) in January 1848. Taylor and Scott, who became prominent Whigs, concerned Polk as potential political enemies.

Polk encountered opposing views in Congress oven the acquisition of land from Mexico. The Democratic Party's "All Mexico" faction demanded just that. Opponents of slavery's expansion, on the other hand, supported the Wilmot Proviso. Repeatedly amended to bills but never passed, it forswore the expansion of slavery into any land acquired from Mexico. Some believed that stipulation would prevent any acquisitions. Polk, rejecting both extremes, wanted to obtain California, New Mexico, and the Rio Grande boundary of Texas.

After US forces took Mexico City in September 1847, negotiator Nicholas P. Trist (1800–1874) signed the Treaty of Guadalupe Hidalgo on February 2, 1848. The Senate approved it on March 10. The terms of the treaty included the land acquisitions that Polk wanted in exchange for $15 million. Polk described California and New Mexico, in a message to Congress on July 6, as "large enough for a great empire" (Richardson 1897, 588). They continued to be governed by military administrations set up during the war. Neither reached territorial or state status during Polk's presidency.

BEYOND MEXICO

Polk expanded US relations with countries throughout the Western Hemisphere. In September 1845 he sent a commissioner to the Kingdom of Hawaii to negotiate a treaty facilitating peace, trade, and the rights of US citizens on the islands; it was signed in 1849, during Taylor's presidency. In December 1846 negotiators signed the Mallarino-Bidlack Treaty between the United States and New Granada (Colombia), eliminating tariff discrimination against US goods and giving the United States the right of transit across the Isthmus of Panama, a likely site for a canal. In March 1847, Polk signed a joint resolution putting two naval ships into civilian hands to carry privately donated supplies to Ireland and Scotland during the potato famine. In March 1848, he signed a law creating diplomatic missions to Bolivia, Ecuador, and Guatemala.

Not all of Polk's initiatives succeeded. He endorsed the Monroe Doctrine in his annual message to Congress on December 2, 1845, and gave it an early version of its modern name—"Mr. Monroe's doctrine"—in his diary on October 24, 1845 (Quaife 1910, 1:70, 71). Not wanting powerful European nations to acquire any new American land, he applied that doctrine not only to Oregon and California but also to Cuba. In June 1848, concerned that the island might fall into British hands, his administration offered Spain $100 million for it. Spain, however, declined to sell. Nevertheless, Polk had established Washington's dominion over nearly all of today's contiguous United States.

SEE ALSO *Manifest Destiny; Mexican-American War*

BIBLIOGRAPHY

Bergeron, Paul H. *The Presidency of James K. Polk.* Lawrence: University Press of Kansas, 1987.

Borneman, Walter R. *Polk: The Man Who Transformed the Presidency and America.* New York: Random House, 2008.

Chaffin, Tom. *Met His Every Goal? James K. Polk and the Legends of Manifest Destiny.* Knoxville: University of Tennessee Press, 2014.

Cutler, Wayne, Tom Chaffin, and Michael David Cohen, eds. *Correspondence of James K. Polk.* Vols. 7–12. Knoxville: University of Tennessee Press, 1989–2013.

McCormac, Eugene Irving. *James K. Polk: A Political Biography.* Berkeley: University of California Press, 1922.

Pinheiro, John C. *Manifest Ambition: James K. Polk and Civil-Military Relations during the Mexican War.* Westport, CT: Praeger Security International, 2007.

Quaife, Milo Milton, ed. *The Diary of James K. Polk during His Presidency, 1845 to 1849.* 4 vols. Chicago: McClurg, 1910.

Richardson, James D., ed. *A Compilation of the Messages and Papers of the Presidents.* Vol. 4. Washington, DC: GPO, 1897.

Sellers, Charles. *James K. Polk: Continentalist, 1843–1846.* Princeton, NJ: Princeton University Press, 1966.

Michael David Cohen
Research Assistant Professor of History
University of Tennessee, Knoxville

POLYGENISM

SEE *Race.*

PORT HURON STATEMENT

SEE *Students for a Democratic Society (SDS).*

POSTMODERNISM

In the United States, postmodernism is a term that might apply to the collective body of work of seemingly unrelated artists, or diverse movements within various academic disciplines, or a historic period of thought and culture that emerged after 1968. At the core of all things postmodern is the rejection of any grand narrative, sometimes referred to as a meta-narrative. This rejection can in turn be seen as its own grand narrative, which presents a contradiction and raises the question of whether postmodernism is an ideology, a description of the times, a movement, or a methodology. In different circumstances, postmodernism might exhibit each of these characteristics in different ways. Postmodernism can appear to be a form of intellectual extremism when it seems to claim that all things are relative and that science is nothing more than a rhetoric of power. Artists and intellectuals have, however, used postmodernism to explain thought and power relationships in culture within the context of postindustrial society. They do so by identifying important phrases or symbols and analyzing them, looking for coded language, political doublespeak, or perhaps hidden meaning. In so doing, they seek to explain reality in terms that undermine or resist the authoritatively obfuscating language of government or any hegemonic power structure in society.

THE RISE OF POSTMODERNISM

The rise of postmodernism occurred after the politically tumultuous movements of 1968, which questioned the legitimacy of many Western governments. Even so, the seeds of postmodernism were planted in earlier decades with jazz music, the literature of the Harlem Renaissance, the surrealist art of the 1920s and 1930s, and the Beat poetry of the 1950s, to name just a few examples. In the early 1970s, the United States began a transition into a postindustrial service and financial economy, and the rise of the postmodern period replaced the modernism that had characterized the old industrial era. In that light, one influential theorist, David Harvey (1999), has argued that postmodernism might only reflect a superficial view of the complex changes of postindustrial financial capitalism. He argues that the condition of postmodernism is coincident with the neoliberal era, which has brought about changes in the management of the global economy, but might not signal the end of a historical era. Harvey's postmodern condition also contains a critique of right-wing revisionism and information-age politics, which are skewed toward a narrative that privileges the financial elite.

POSTMODERN ARCHITECTURE

Postmodernism can be found in the arts and in music, but perhaps most symbolically it can be found in architecture. Built in the modern era, the Empire State Building defined the New York City skyline with a beautiful form that also served the functional needs of those who sought space within it. In contrast, signaling a turn toward postmodernism, the construction of the World Trade Center towers, completed in 1970 and 1971, revealed a new architectural style where form was subordinated to function to the point that they were indistinguishable from each other—much to the dismay of modernist critics, who found the aesthetic off-putting, cold, and lifeless. Similarly, the Pompidou Centre in Paris, completed in 1977, showed its structural elements on the exterior, as a statement on the importance of laying form bare as an example of its function—to reveal once-hidden things. One architectural theorist, Charles Jencks (1991), suggested an exact start date for the postmodern era (or condition) of 3:32 P.M., July 15, 1972, when failed, unlivable public housing projects were demolished in St. Louis. Old architectural forms, especially ones that were an expression of government policy, were either nonfunctional or romantic, and in modernist ways served a grand narrative of Man rather than the needs of ordinary people.

THEORY AND DEBATE

In academia, one very influential postmodern theorist was Michel Foucault (1926–1984). He focused his research on power and how even seemingly powerless or marginalized people sought power. According to Foucault, the human desire for power will outweigh any moral appeal to reason or egalitarianism. In this construction, any Enlightenment-inspired appeal to reason is itself a form of power and control, and will be resisted. Therefore, a discourse of power exists even in "low" communication forms, such as advertising, popular culture, and pop music. Rejecting the grand narrative of white male history, Foucault showed, in his postmodern way, that language subordinated women, homosexuals, and ethnic minorities into "others" who thereby were prevented from achieving power in society, even while they sought it. He reached these conclusions during a decade where previously marginalized groups were seeking power and changes to the United States, with some political success.

During the 1990s, academic history departments experienced some amount of anguish over the meaning of postmodernism for history, its methods of research, and its reception by students and the public. One very influential work, *Telling the Truth about History* (Appleby, Hunt, and Jacob 1994), raised the question of whether postmodernism presented a crisis, and how it might be resolved. Some critics of postmodernism blamed the perceived excesses of multiculturalism, which in their view led to hopeless relativism, while still others decried the heavy doses of skepticism that postmodern theory seemed to engender. Since then, historians have shown social and cultural history, including feminism and women's history, to be viable alternatives or complementary to state and national histories.

At the same time, another debate emerged among historians over how postmodernism might affect Holocaust studies. Historians Saul Friedlander and Hayden White (1997) clashed over whether postmodernism would adversely affect Holocaust studies and remembrance by contributing a methodology that might serve those who wish to deny the Holocaust ever occurred. However, the deeply disturbing ideas of Holocaust deniers never achieved any momentum, because the historical record so thoroughly contradicted them. In each case, the crisis was more imagined than real. Historians have long been skeptical and concerned with context. Dating back at least to the pragmatism of Charles Beard (1874–1948), historians have assumed the documents they analyze are blurred by the exigencies of the power politics of the day in question.

Postmodernism's rejection of the grand narrative originated in the idea that language constitutes reality rather than describing or representing it. Even among postmodern theorists, there is disagreement over how to interpret language. Outside of the world of theory and art, a great number of people living in the postmodern age either do not believe postmodernism's assertions (indeed it has often been misrepresented or misunderstood) or they are unaware of them. And yet postmodernism contains many powerfully suggestive ideas and reflections on society in recent times. In literature, art, history, and music, postmodernism has remained alluring, most likely because its tools allow people to better understand culture in a complicated era.

BIBLIOGRAPHY

Appleby, Joyce, Lynn Hunt, and Margaret Jacob. *Telling the Truth about History.* New York: Norton, 1994.

Beard, Charles. *An Economic Interpretation of the Constitution of the United States.* New York: Macmillan, 1913.

Best, Steven, and Douglas Kellner. *Postmodern Theory: Critical Interrogations.* New York: Guilford Press, 1991.

Best, Steven, and Douglas Kellner. *The Postmodern Turn.* New York: Guilford Press, 1997.

Butler, Christopher. *Postmodernism: A Very Short Introduction.* New York: Oxford University Press, 2002.

Derrida, Jacques. *Dissemination.* Translated by Barbara Johnson. Chicago: University of Chicago Press, 1981.

Foucault, Michel. *Madness and Civilization: A History of Insanity in the Age of Reason.* Translated by Richard Howard. New York: Random House, 1965.

Friedlander, Saul. "Probing the Limits of Representation." In *The Postmodern History Reader*, edited by Keith Jenkins, 387–391. New York: Routledge, 1997.

Harvey, David. *The Condition of Postmodernity: An Enquiry into the Origins of Cultural Change.* Malden, MA: Blackwell, 1999.

Jencks, Charles. *The Language of Post-modern Architecture.* 6th ed. London: Rizolli, 1991.

Jenkins, Keith, ed. *The Postmodern History Reader.* New York: Routledge, 1997.

White, Hayden. "Historical Emplotment and the Problem of Truth." In *The Postmodern History Reader*, edited by Keith Jenkins, 392–396. New York: Routledge, 1997.

Peter A. McCord
Professor of History
State University of New York, Fredonia

POTSDAM CONFERENCE (1945)

The Potsdam Conference, held in Potsdam, Germany, from July 17 to August 2, 1945, was the last wartime conference of World War II (1939–1945). Its chief participants represented the big three powers: Harry S. Truman (1884–1972), president of the United States; Winston Churchill (1874–1965) and, later, Clement Attlee (1883–1967), prime ministers of Great Britain; and Soviet premier Joseph Stalin (1879–1953).

The leaders met primarily to discuss the occupation of Germany, war reparations, the borders of Poland, and the establishment of new governments in Eastern Europe. The tone and personnel at Potsdam were different from those of the previous wartime conferences. The objective that had brought the three great powers together—the defeat of Germany—had occurred in early May 1945. Franklin D. Roosevelt (1882–1945), whose personal charm and broad vision had guided much of the wartime strategy, had died on April 12, 1945. During the conference, Churchill and his party were defeated in British elections, and he was replaced by Attlee of the Labour Party. Combining this with the fact that all three powers were now looking for advantages in the postwar world, there were greater tension and suspicion at Potsdam than at earlier conferences.

By the time of Potsdam, the Americans had come to believe that a Germany that recovered its former economic prowess under a democratic government would be best for the future. This stand led to resistance from the Soviets, who demanded that Germany be stripped of its industrial base. As negotiations about Germany ensued, Truman endeavored to limit the reparations that the Soviet Union sought by insisting they mainly be found in the Soviet sector.

US secretary of state James F. Byrnes (1882–1972) engaged in hard bargaining with Soviet foreign minister Vyacheslav Molotov (1890–1986) to hammer out a deal. In return for limiting Soviet reparations from non-Soviet sectors, the United States would agree to the transfer of a large portion of German territory to Poland. This moved the western border of Poland several hundred miles west to a boundary set by the Oder and Neisse Rivers. In addition, Byrnes offered diplomatic recognition of the nations of Eastern Europe under Soviet occupation, a situation Stalin had repeatedly compared to the Anglo-American occupation of Italy (but no satisfactory agreement was reached on the makeup of those governments, including Poland). This was combined with a provision limiting the Soviets to 10 to 15 percent of the industrial equipment in the Western zones in exchange for agricultural and a few other products from the Soviet sector because of the great losses suffered by the Soviet Union. Managing this arrangement and the occupation of Germany would be an Allied Control Council, with zone commanders responsible for each Allied sector

While the United States regularly abhorred sphere-of-influence strategies, by insisting that each nation take Allied reparations from its own zone, it is clear that US policy was assisting in the division of Europe into spheres of influence. All sides gave lip service to the future unification of Germany, but as Cold War tensions developed, that was not to be. They did agree to establish a series of meetings and a Council of Foreign Ministers to continue to work out differences.

Just prior to the start of the conference, on July 16, the first atomic bomb was detonated in New Mexico. Historians often point to comments from Churchill and others that Truman behaved with a great deal more assertiveness after news of the successful test. Churchill was overjoyed at having such a weapon in Anglo-American hands. After one of the meetings, Truman casually told Stalin of this new weapon. Stalin responded the he hoped the United States would use it. Truman at the time believed that Stalin did not understand the importance of what he had heard, but in reality Stalin was well informed because of Soviet spies in the Manhattan Project.

During the Yalta Conference in February 1945, while Allied forces were engaged in a bloody battle with Japan in the Marshall Islands, Roosevelt saw it as one of his primary goals to persuade the Soviet Union to become involved in the Pacific War. However, by the time of the Potsdam Conference, it was thought that Soviet help was no longer needed and, in fact, would be an unnecessary complication.

Three-way handshake of the Big Three—UK prime minister Winston Churchill, US president Harry Truman, and Soviet premier Joseph Stalin—at the Potsdam Conference, Germany, July 1945. With all three powers looking for advantages in the postwar world, tension and suspicion at Potsdam were high. The leaders met to discuss the occupation of Germany, war reparations, the borders of Poland, and the establishment of new governments in Eastern Europe. **BETTMANN/ CORBIS**

Truman (along with the United Kingdom and China) released the Potsdam Declaration on July 26, without consulting the Soviets, informing the Japanese that if they did not surrender they would face "prompt and utter destruction." Truman's failure to consult the Soviets has helped feed the debate since the atomic bombing that perhaps the United States was aiming more to intimidate the Soviet Union than to defeat Japan with the use of the weapons.

The Potsdam Conference, with its deeply compromised agreements, frustrated ambitions, and increasing suspicion, marked the end of the wartime alliance and was a harbinger of the dangerous Cold War era to come.

SEE ALSO *Cold War; Germany; Truman, Harry S.; World War II; Yalta Conference (1945)*

BIBLIOGRAPHY

Gaddis, John Lewis. *The United States and the Origins of the Cold War, 1941–1947.* New York: Columbia University Press, 1972.

Leffler, Melvyn. *A Preponderance of Power: National Security, the Truman Administration, and the Cold War.* Stanford, CA: Stanford University Press, 1992.

McCullough, David. *Truman.* New York: Simon and Schuster, 1992.

Mee, Charles L., Jr. *Meeting at Potsdam.* New York: Evans, 1975.

Miscamble, Wilson D. *From Roosevelt to Truman: Potsdam, Hiroshima, and the Cold War.* New York: Cambridge University Press, 2007.

John McNay
Professor of History
University of Cincinnati

POWELL, ADAM CLAYTON, JR.
1908–1971

Adam Clayton Powell Jr. was born to Mattie Powell and Adam Clayton Powell Sr. on November 29, 1908, in New Haven, Connecticut. Educated in the New York City public school system, Powell earned a bachelor's degree from Colgate University (1930), a master's degree in religious studies from Columbia University (1932), and a divinity degree from Shaw University (1934).

In 1937, Powell succeeded his father as the pastor of Abyssinian Baptist Church in Harlem. His pastoral leadership of the African American churches in New York put him at the forefront of civil rights and community activism in the city. Powell continued to serve as pastor of Abyssinian until 1971. He leveraged his position as pastor, along with his newspaper, the *People's Voice*, to galvanize the community to protest unfair employment practices and inadequate housing and to push for effective public assistance programs in Harlem.

Powell's rising popularity led to his election to the New York City Council in 1941; service with the Consumer Division of New York State's Office of Price Administration (1942–1944); and his election to Congress representing Harlem's Twenty-Second Congressional District in 1944. Powell was the first African American congressman to represent New York. Often scrutinized for his unwavering outspokenness and questionable ethics, Powell was denied his seat in the Ninetieth Congress that began in January 1967 because he was under investigation by the Judiciary Committee, and in March 1967 the House voted to expel him. In April 1967 Harlem voters in a special election voted Powell back into Congress. However, Powell did not reassume his seat until January 1968. He continued to serve in Congress until 1971.

During his political career, Powell fought for racial and social equality for all Americans. His most important legislative contributions came while serving as chair of the Committee on Education and Labor during the 1960s, when he successfully petitioned Congress to approve the federal student loan program and increase the minimum wage. He was also instrumental in the creation of school lunch programs and vocational education for individuals with disabilities, and he introduced numerous bills to advance the public good.

Powell was a staunch supporter of civil rights and equity in the United States and abroad. As an attendee at the 1955 Bandung Conference in Indonesia, he pushed for improved relations between the United States and Asian and African countries. During the conference, Powell argued that the failures and successes of race relations in the United States were interconnected with the global plight of people of color and that by embracing democracy they too would be able to eliminate racial and economic divides within their countries.

Following the Bandung Conference, Powell focused on efforts to employ cultural diplomacy during the Cold War to fight communism. One program sent prominent jazz artists, such as Dizzy Gillespie and Louis Armstrong, to represent democracy on the international stage through music.

The charismatic Powell married singer Isabel Washington in 1933, entertainer Hazel Scott in 1945, and Yvette Flores in 1960, with all three marriages ending in divorce. Powell died of cancer in 1971 in Miami, Florida. Described as brash, flamboyant, and unapologetic, Powell fought valiantly against inequality and injustice domestically and internationally. He was one of the most influential politicians of the twentieth century.

SEE ALSO *Bandung Conference (1955); Cold War; Cold War: Race and the Cold War; Human Rights; Jazz*

BIBLIOGRAPHY

Frazier, Robeson Taj P. "Diplomacy as Black Cultural Traffic: Debates over Race in the Asian Travels of Adam Clayton Powell and Carl Rowan." *Journal of History and Culture* 3 (2013): 33–48.

Von Eschen, Penny M. *Satchmo Blows Up the World: Jazz Ambassadors Play the Cold War.* Cambridge, MA: Harvard University Press, 2004.

Felicia W. Mack
Part-Time Faculty
Eastern Kentucky University

POWELL, COLIN
1937–

Few figures of the late twentieth and early twenty-first centuries have played a more prominent role in American foreign policy than Colin Powell. His career was in many ways unique in American history, with senior appointments in the Pentagon, the White House, the US Army, and the Department of State. Over two decades he played a senior role in four administrations, Republican and Democrat, and he was frequently mentioned as a possible nominee for either vice president or president between 1988 and 2000. His public career nonetheless amounted to more than the offices he held. It was a career of paradoxes: astonishing rapid acclaim ending, ultimately, with marginalization and resignation.

Born in New York City's Harlem in 1937 and raised in the Bronx by Jamaican immigrant parents, Powell graduated from the City College of New York in 1958 and served two tours of duty in Vietnam. In his popular 1995 memoir, *My American Journey*, Powell laid out an elaborate critique of the conduct of the war in Vietnam, charging several US administrations with concealing its true costs and consequences from the public. Vietnam was formative for Powell. The lessons he carried away from that war influenced him as an aide to Ronald Reagan's first secretary of defense, Caspar Weinberger (who served from 1981 to 1987), and later during Powell's tenure (1989–1993) as chairman of the Joint Chiefs of Staff, when he articulated the Powell doctrine. Borrowing liberally from the earlier Weinberger doctrine (1984), the Powell doctrine called for the overwhelming use of force backed by widespread public support.

As Reagan's sixth and final national security adviser (1987–1989), Powell worked harmoniously with Secretary of State George P. Shultz (1982–1989) and the new Secretary of Defense Frank Carlucci (1987–1989). Powell became a facilitator of a well-balanced foreign-policy team. Along with Shultz and Carlucci, Powell played an important role in improving US–Soviet relations and became a key player in the administration's response to Soviet leader Mikhail Gorbachev's bold initiatives.

Powell's political connections helped propel him to the rank of four-star general in January 1989 and led to his appointment as chairman of the Joint Chiefs of Staff in the first year of the George H. W. Bush administration (1989–1993). He held the post of chairman for the remaining three years of the Bush administration and into part of the first year of the Bill Clinton administration (1993–2001). He served as chairman during the first Iraq war (1991), successfully applying aspects of the Powell doctrine such as the deployment of overwhelming force, the garnering of public support, and the genuine inclusion of international institutions and allies.

As a result of his high visibility during the 1991 Iraq conflict, Powell was transformed into a national figure, stirring speculation about a possible run for the presidency in 1996. His flirtation with national office was one of the more curious and unconventional presidential trial balloons in American history because Powell had never before held elective office and his views on major political issues remained largely a mystery. He ultimately announced, in late 1995, that he would not be a candidate for any political office in 1996.

With his appointment in January 2001 as secretary of state in the George W. Bush administration (2001–2009) many anticipated that Powell would achieve the kind of state/defense balance he had achieved from 1987 to 1989. Instead, the balance of power between the State Department and the Pentagon broke down entirely. Bush's vice president, Dick Cheney, orchestrated the appointment of an old ally, Donald H. Rumsfeld, as secretary of defense (2001–2006). The vice president did this in part to provide a counterweight to Powell who, Cheney anticipated, would prove to be a vigorous secretary of state. Cheney's extraordinary alliance with Rumsfeld allowed both the vice president's office and the Pentagon to assume unprecedented powers. The Pentagon's assertion of power over many of the State Department's traditional responsibilities created a difficult environment for Powell as he fought to protect his department's prerogatives against the encroachments of the Pentagon.

The launching of the second war with Iraq in 2003 occurred with little input from Powell or the State Department and contrary to the precautionary Powell doctrine. The defense secretary promoted a Rumsfeld doctrine calling for smaller and shorter deployments. As the most compelling and credible figure in the administration, Powell was deployed to make the case for war in a speech before the United Nations Security Council in February 2003. The central premise of his presentation, that Iraq possessed and was concealing weapons of mass destruction, proved to have been based on faulty intelligence. His resignation, following Bush's reelection in November 2004, came as a surprise to few although Powell later claimed he had been fired. In a remarkable turn of events, Powell once again made national headlines in 2008 when he broke with his party and endorsed the 2008 Democratic presidential nominee, Barack Obama.

SEE ALSO *Bush, George H. W.; Bush, George W.; Cheney, Dick; War on Terror*

BIBLIOGRAPHY

DeYoung, Karen. *Soldier: The Life of Colin Powell*. New York: Vintage, 2007.

O'Sullivan, Christopher D. *Colin Powell: American Power and Intervention from Vietnam to Iraq*. Lanham, MD: Rowman and Littlefield, 2009.

Powell, Colin L., with Joseph Persico. *My American Journey*. New York: Random House, 1995.

Christopher D. O'Sullivan
Lecturer in History
University of San Francisco

PREPAREDNESS

Preparedness was a keyword and an agenda in American politics and culture prior to the US entry into World War I in 1917. The term referred to the case for a rapid military buildup and societal militarization in the face of the unfolding world war in Europe. The contest over preparedness surrounded American debates over wartime neutrality and mediation, and it reached deep down into the fabric of American society. Most directly, the plea for preparedness resulted in major pieces of legislation in 1916, including new army, navy, and tax bills. More generally, it created a space for the articulation of conflicting ideas about the size of the military and its form of organization and the nation's proper approach to military geopolitics and international affairs in the present and future. With the US intervention in the war, the push for preparedness lost its salience, and the term ceased to define policy agendas and public debate.

THE CONTEST OVER PREPAREDNESS

Throughout the entire period of US abstention from World War I, the proposition for preparedness was an explosive issue. It sparked acrimonious debate in the nation's halls of political power and cast a long shadow on presidential and congressional politics. Cutting across party lines, the debate over preparedness laid bare profound sectional differences between the industrial Northeast and the agrarian South and Midwest, and it divided the so-called Progressive movement, that loosely knit coalition of diverse reformist agendas, languages, and actors.

The struggle over preparedness also transcended the world of policy making as it played out on the streets and in the realms of popular politics and mass culture. Hundreds of thousands of Americans participated in parades and rallies: 135,000 people marched in New York City in May 1916, for example, in support of preparedness. A variety of new organizations emerged in support of or in opposition to preparedness, reaching tens of thousands of members, volunteers, and sympathizers across most states, and producing reams of print material. The film industry got involved, too, with the two most prominent films of the pro- and anti-preparedness camps, *The Battle Cry of Peace* (1915) and *Civilization* (1916) respectively, achieving considerable commercial success. Furthermore, in the summer of 1916, more than sixteen thousand men of upper- and middle-class background took their belief in preparedness quite personally by volunteering to receive military training in specially created camps, most prominently in Plattsburgh, New York, following the nearly four thousand volunteers who had done so a year earlier.

The contest over preparedness unfolded in several steps. Agitation for preparedness began in the fall of 1914, with former president Theodore Roosevelt (1858–1919), General Leonard Wood (1860–1927), and well-connected Republican congressman Augustus Gardner (1865–1918) taking the lead. In December 1914 members of the New York business and financial elite founded the most important organization of the growing preparedness movement, the National Security League. The movement, driven by military men, northeastern Republican political figures, northeastern leaders of industry, finance, and the press, and other professional elite figures, initially met with little success. The Woodrow Wilson (1856–1924) administration and a Democratic-controlled Congress proved unresponsive.

This changed in the wake of the diplomatic crisis with Imperial Germany over the sinking of the British ocean liner *Lusitania* by a German submarine in May 1915, after which Wilson embraced the cause of what he came to call "reasonable" preparedness and made it central to his legislative agenda for the next year. This shift, in turn, sparked mobilization among a broad yet disparate anti-preparedness coalition, including farmers', workers', and women's right organizations, southern Democrats and midwestern Republicans, pacifist groups (both secular and Christian), northeastern liberal reformers, and social-justice Progressives. The American Union against Militarism, which was originally founded under a different name in New York in 1915, emerged as the most prominent organization of this coalition. In Congress, the core of the anti-preparedness lobby consisted of a group of about sixty Republicans and Democrats in the House, primarily from rural districts in the Midwest and the South.

Though preparedness advocates had been agitating for many months by the time the Wilson administration took up (a moderate version of) their cause, the president's change of position set the stage for the making of preparedness legislation. This body of legislation emerged in a piecemeal and compromise manner in the context of increased domestic political polarization on the one hand, and successive submarine crises with Germany and escalating violence on the border with Mexico on the other. Passed in 1916, several acts enhanced American military power yet fell short of key preparedness demands. The 1916 National Defense Act nearly doubled the size of the regular army, raising it to 175,000 over five years, and expanded the National Guard to 450,000 men. The act also increased federal control over the National Guard, provided federal funding for reserve officer training, and granted the federal government emergency powers over industry in wartime. The Navy Act of 1916 authorized a massive three-year construction program costing more than $500 million and involving sixteen new capital ships (that is, more capital ships than the United States possessed in 1914), as well as a large number of smaller naval craft. The Revenue Act of 1916 underwrote the new army and navy bills by instituting a new estate tax and substantially increasing the top tax rates of the income tax, thus placing the financial burden of the new armaments on the shoulders of the wealthy. These acts were complemented by two other important measures. The Army Appropriation Act created a new institutional framework for industrial-military mobilization by setting up a Council of National Defense and endowing it with business advisory committees. The Merchant Marine Act established a US Shipping Board to help create a vast merchant marine to support the US Navy in wartime.

THE MILITARY, STATE, AND SOCIETY

The debate over preparedness was fought out over the issues of the size of the US military, its organizing principle, and its relationship to state and society. The demand for preparedness was a plea to make the American armed forces more competitive with the big powers of Europe. Proponents demanded a massive expansion of the existing military establishment (army and navy) and the creation of a national army reserve on the basis of a centrally directed system of compulsory military service, at the expense of any reliance on militias and wartime volunteers. This program rested on two pillars: the embrace of the promise of a professional military as part of a powerful central state capable of harnessing societal resources in conjunction with corporate and expert elites; and the acceptance, as a matter of principle, of the idea of a continental European-style mass reserve army and universal military training, and its particular adaptation (through a system of short-term training) to the United States.

But the demand for preparedness also went well beyond considerations of military capability: it aimed at nothing less than the regeneration of the entire nation. Imagining a cohesive nation in an Anglo-Saxon image and rising to the defense of corporate order and elite rule, preparedness advocates touted the beneficial impact of military service as an agent of moral reform, social discipline, nationalist sentiment, and civic education. They explicitly presented common military training as the proper antidote to militant labor politics, the continuing transnational allegiances of immigrant communities, and the gender trouble associated with both materialist civilization and women's rights advances. In short, here was a plea for societal militarization to maintain the right order at home by envisioning mass military training as a rejuvenating school of proper citizenship, manhood, and nation building.

By contrast, opponents of preparedness associated the demand for an increased military and universal military training with "militarism." They presented it as a threat to the sanctity and promise of the United States as a republican nation founded in open opposition to the warmongering and the military machinations of the Old World. Not fearing for the safety of the United States, they cast preparedness as a decisive step toward full US entanglement with a Europe-centered politics of war and empire and as a turn away from what they understood to be the providential, civilizing mission of the United States. They offered a critique of the military by casting it as an antidemocratic institution of domination, viewing compulsory military service in peacetime as inimical to the proper spirit and civil liberties of a republican citizenry, and emphasizing the superiority of the militia and voluntary enlistment in wartime. They argued that the drive for preparedness reflected the pursuit of power, interest, and privilege by self-aggrandizing military and corporate oligarchies. Couched in various languages, from agrarian populist and labor-socialist, to urban-Progressive and radical-democratic, opponents of preparedness placed the entire preparedness movement in the deplorable context of the new corporate economy and the centralization of power in the national state.

After the summer of 1915, when President Wilson embraced the case for a military buildup, he nonetheless shared these critics' apprehension about large militaries as institutions of domination and of militarism as a threat to the republican nation. While going along, by and large, with maximum demands for naval expansion, Wilson carved out a distinctive position in relation to the increase of the army and universal military service, separating him from the preparedness movement proper. He and his administration promoted only a moderate expansion of the regular army; they opposed the idea of universal military training; and they wanted to create a reserve of army-trained soldiers through voluntary service and also severely limit the army's overall size. "Reasonable" preparedness along these lines put an emphasis on a robust albeit numerically limited professional military, yet yoked the idea of a mass reserve to the principle of civic voluntarism in peacetime (and the acceptance of the idea of a new progressive tax schedule to make the wealthy pay for the increased military expenditures).

PREPAREDNESS, STRATEGY, AND FOREIGN POLICY

Divisive as it was as a political-military issue, the case for preparedness was not in itself a transformative strategic proposition, in either its full or Wilsonian iterations. The goal was to prepare the country for an imagined war of continental or hemispheric defense. This was not a brief for intervention into the ongoing world war, or a crash program to ready the United States for a war in the present or a sustained projection of military force to confront big powers across the seas. Its premise was the expectation of big-power confrontation over empire in the Western Hemisphere in some postwar future, with the United States standing alone and facing the winner(s) of the war.

The most sensationalist expression of this expectation was the dire scenario of a foreign invasion by a victorious Germany, a prospect that enjoyed great and consistent popularity among preparedness advocates, regardless of its eventual dismissal as pure fantasy by the army's and navy's main operational agencies. Accordingly, the preparedness legislation of 1916 did little to directly prepare the US military for its wartime pursuits after April 1917. In fact, the core of the naval program passed in 1916 had to be quickly suspended when the United States entered the war in order to make room for the creation of the maritime capabilities actually needed to help secure the Atlantic against German submarines and fight the war on the European continent.

Preparedness was nonetheless also linked to new challenges and departures. Most directly, the ratcheting up of military power was to underwrite new diplomatic roles for the United States as a powerful neutral nation, mediator in the war, and shaper of a postwar order. In the calculus of Wilson and others, the massive increase of the navy served the purpose of dramatically increasing US diplomatic leverage during and after the war and vis-à-vis both the Allies and Germany. The Naval Act of 1916, then, turned into official policy what previously had only been a subject of talk among ardent American navalists: it committed the United States to building the world's leading (battleship) navy and advanced the prospects of future US naval preeminence. In fact, this act received more attention abroad than did other preparedness legislation, as it was taken to signal newly developing US aspirations to global dominance. (By contrast, the new army legislation provoked less interest or concern abroad, among observers well aware that it hardly created an army of a size or fighting power to rival the warring armies in Europe.)

More importantly, the debate over preparedness took place as competing visions of the United States' place in the world came into focus. It was tied to larger debates over power politics, international reform, and the direction of US foreign policy, in which several schools of thought vied for influence among America's political class and intelligentsia. Liberal internationalists, from Wilson to the more conservative elite figures led by former president William Howard Taft (1857–1930), who dominated the newly created League to Enforce Peace, promoted preparedness in the context of an overall investment in the creation of a new system of collective security. Their pleas for some kind of international league of peace were premised on a critique of the inherent instabilities and war-prone nature of power politics, of what Wilson referred to as the "balance of power." In this view, only a combination of national military power and international reform could ensure the security of the United States and prevent it from turning militaristic in order to survive in a (unreformed) hostile world of big-power politics.

By contrast, figures such as Roosevelt, Henry Cabot Lodge (1850–1924), and Elihu Root (1845–1937), as well as most leading members of the National Security League, belonged to a second grouping of voices, the Atlanticists. This camp promoted the virtues of self-sustaining national power and a politics of military threat, deterrence, and balancing, yet they also advocated some sort of security partnership with Britain to protect American interests and keep the centrifugal forces of world politics in check.

Making up a third, rather loosely defined, school of thought were all those who offered a comprehensive critique of power politics and militarism (and empire) as inseparable, while denying the existence of a security threat to the United States in the present and foreseeable future. This critique ultimately opened up to a wide variety of positions. They ranged from a preference for continuous US detachment from any politics of war and empire to demands for a broader transformation of states, societies, and diplomacy, framed, for example, in radical democratic, maternalist pacifist, laborite, outright socialist, or Christian-civilizational terms.

THE END OF PREPAREDNESS

While debates over these visions of the evolving place of the United States in the world stretched into the 1920s and beyond, the notion of preparedness itself, as defined by both its advocates and opponents, proved short-lived. A highly charged issue until the winter of 1916 to 1917, when proponents of universal military training continued to argue their case in public and before Congress, the case for preparedness had run its course with the US entry into the war and then gave way to a new regime of wartime discourse and mobilization. In the interwar years, preparedness did not reemerge as an organizing term that set a specific agenda for US diplomacy and pursuits of military force. In fact, the preparedness movement from 1914 to 1917 was subjected, in the 1930s, to withering retroactive criticism driven in Congress by the so-called Peace Progressives and in the larger public by revisionist writers, such as Walter Millis (1899–1968). These people were all highly critical of the US intervention in World War I and engaged in debates over US foreign policy and armaments in the present. When, in the late 1930s and early 1940s, a new agenda-setting language emerged to define the United States as a dominant global empire and military superpower, the capacious notion of "national security" moved to the fore. While this term had already been used loosely in the 1910s (and had even lent its name to the most important pro-preparedness organization of the era), it gained its traction at midcentury from both its substance and its ability to establish rhetorical distance to past US approaches to national interest and military readiness. Among these approaches now considered inadequate was indeed the case for preparedness, which had, for a brief moment prior to the US entry into World War I, given issues of military capability and national defense a public prominence that they were to attain more permanently a few decades later.

SEE ALSO *Internationalism; Interventionism; Isolationism; Navy, US; Roosevelt, Theodore; Taft, William Howard; Wilson, Woodrow; World War I; World War II*

BIBLIOGRAPHY

Alonso, Harriet Hyman. *Peace as a Women's Issue: A History of the U.S. Movement for World Peace and Women's Rights.* Syracuse, NY: Syracuse University Press, 1993.

Chambers, John Whiteclay, II. *To Raise an Army: The Draft Comes to Modern America.* New York: Free Press, 1987.

Clifford, J. Garry. *The Citizen Soldiers: The Plattsburgh Training Camp Movement, 1913–1920.* Lexington: University Press of Kentucky, 1972.

Doenecke, Justus D. *Nothing Less than War: A New History of America's Entry into World War I.* Lexington: University Press of Kentucky, 2011.

Finnegan, John Patrick. *Against the Specter of a Dragon: The Campaign for American Military Preparedness, 1914–1917.* Westport, CT: Greenwood Press, 1974.

Kennedy, Ross A. *The Will to Believe: Woodrow Wilson, World War I, and America's Strategy for Peace and Security.* Kent, OH: Kent State University Press, 2009.

Pearlmann, Michael D. *To Make Democracy Safe for America: Patricians and Preparedness in the Progressive Era.* Urbana: University of Illinois Press, 1984.

Dirk Bönker
Associate Professor of History
Duke University

PRESLEY, ELVIS AARON
1935–1977

Elvis Presley was an American popular music entertainer associated with the post–World War II rise of rock 'n' roll. His emergence in the mid-1950s sparked in seemingly equal measures both veneration and disdain. This dichotomy would characterize his career and continue long after his death.

Contradiction was no stranger to the Mississippi-born "Hillbilly Cat" who displayed qualities equally rebellious and conventional. Indeed, Presley was defined by his dualisms: A product of the racially segregated South, he loved rhythm and blues. A white man who sounded black, he wanted to be the next Dean Martin (perhaps the quintessential white lounge-singer). A hip-swiveling performer whose on-stage routine resembled burlesque, offstage he appeared to be a shy and withdrawn "mama's boy." Often perceived as the devil incarnate, Presley recorded and performed gospel songs with a sincerity that left listeners in awe. A serious film enthusiast, he became the highest-paid actor in Hollywood while making instantly forgettable B movies. Vehemently opposed to illicit drug use, he succumbed to a heart attack brought on by his abuse of prescription drugs. Ostensibly independent, he is perpetually linked to his manager, Col. Tom Parker. Such discrepancies have astounded fans and foes alike. But they have never seemed to diminish the fascination that Presley inspired from the moment he entered public life. Despite having never performed outside of North America, Presley gained worldwide popularity. According to Gallup, his is the most recognizable recorded voice in the world.

As an anonymous teenage migrant from rural Mississippi, Presley behaved like many of the other working-class white male students who attended L. C. Humes High School in Memphis. A voracious consumer of popular culture, he loved working on and driving cars and motorcycles, playing football, and going to the movies. He also tuned in to the radio and absorbed an eclectic assortment of musical styles: rhythm and blues, country, pop, and both black and white gospel. His exhaustive and all-encompassing absorption of popular music and culture had a purpose. In his quest to establish an identity, and inspired by movie stars and musical performers, he developed a penchant for flashy clothes, slicked-back hair, long sideburns, and hep-cat dialect. Presley would be invisible no more.

In the process of inventing himself, consumption as a way of life came to define Presley's worldview. It lay behind both his work and leisure activities until the day he died. An untrained and amateur musician who later would make choices in the recording studio as if he were a customer in a record store, Presley applied a fan's eclectic and undisciplined approach to making music. This consumerist impulse produced both positive and negative results. Sometimes it generated a creativity that sustained classic vocal performances, stage routines, and television appearances. More often, however, it led to seemingly mindless playing, purchasing, eating, womanizing, and drug use. Presley embraced popular culture so thoroughly that he succeeded in replacing what was real with what was fantasy. And he did it to excess.

Until his untimely death at forty-two, Presley firmly believed that he owed his success to a Christian God that had inexplicably plucked him out of the crowd.

***Fans of Elvis Presley sign a letter praising the star of** Love Me Tender, **Nottingham, England, 1957.** Presley recordings were heard on radio programs around the world, and television shows on which the singer appeared were broadcast overseas, giving rise to an extensive international fan club. When Presley turned to making movies, these networks played a major role in generating interest.* **POPPERFOTO/GETTY IMAGES**

Consequently, despite attaining vast wealth and fame, he remained a perpetual member of the very audience he entertained. He epitomized their aspirations, frustrations, and tastes.

Presley's greatest significance arguably was his blurring of racial boundaries, making him a representational figure for those seeking to comprehend the cultural dynamics of the postwar South. Yet Presley remained moored to a socially shunned region and its people. He was an unashamed son of the South, and neither fans nor detractors separated his image from his unfashionable origins and kin; he remained the exotic and repulsive Other.

The initial wave of rock 'n' roll's popularity that swept him into the mainstream neutralized concerns about his class and regional roots. Those origins, however, would eventually work to cast doubt on everything that he achieved. Once likened to a "jug of corn liquor at a

champagne party," the so-called King of Rock 'n' Roll never obtained the credentials necessary to attain legitimacy and rise above caricature. In the end, Presley's despised working-class southern roots and refusal to abandon them endeared him to a large segment of people who in some way felt marginalized. He used the tools of popular culture and music to create his own world, demonstrating that it was possible for anyone and everyone to succeed on his own terms. And despite the fame, fortune, and trappings that accompanied his rise to celebrity, Presley remained what many perceived to be authentic. In this he embodied a universal message.

Following his start at Sun Records, a regional recording company, Presley signed a contract with RCA, an international corporation that held offices in major cities around the world. From the very beginning, RCA marketed the singer internationally. With its clout, the conglomerate was able to place Presley recordings on radio programs and in retail outlets nearly everywhere. Music publications such as *Melody Maker* and the *New Musical Express* in the United Kingdom (and their counterparts elsewhere) took their cue from the United States and publicized Presley's activities. Television programs on which the singer appeared were eventually broadcast overseas, creating a huge demand for Presley product. Behind the Iron Curtain, unorthodox brokers sold bootleg copies of songs that had been transferred to discarded X-rays. An extensive international fan club network sprang up that continuously kept Presley's music on juke boxes, on radio programs, and in record stores. When Presley turned to making movies, these networks played a major role in generating interest. By the time he appeared in 1973 on a satellite program reportedly beamed to over a billion people around the world, Presley was a transnational enterprise that had been successful for nearly twenty years.

In the Presley phenomenon an exceptional combination of his own talent, charisma, and creativity fused with skillful management, modern marketing, and communication technology. Presley was one of those rare historical figures upon whom observers projected their own fantasies, fears, and anxieties. He was a consumer culture hero from the American South who became an international household name.

SEE ALSO *Dylan, Bob; Hollywood; Rock 'n' Roll*

BIBLIOGRAPHY

Bertrand, Michael T. *Race, Rock, and Elvis*. Urbana: University of Illinois Press, 2004.

Guralnick, Peter. *Last Train to Memphis: The Rise of Elvis Presley*. Boston: Little, Brown, 1994.

Guralnick, Peter. *Careless Love: The Unmaking of Elvis Presley*. Boston: Little, Brown, 1999.

Hopkins, Jerry. *Elvis: A Biography*. New York: Simon and Schuster, 1971.

Marcus, Greil. *Mystery Train: Images of America in Rock 'n' Roll Music*. 6th rev. ed. New York: Plume, 2015.

Marsh, Dave. *Elvis*. New York: Times Books, 1982.

Mason, Bobbie Ann. *Elvis Presley: A Life*. New York: Viking, 2003.

Michael T. Bertrand
Associate Professor of History
Tennessee State University

PRISON REFORM MOVEMENT

SEE *Transatlantic Reform.*

PROHIBITION

SEE *Temperance Movement.*

PROTESTANT-CATHOLIC-JEW (WILL HERBERG, 1955)

First published in 1955, *Protestant-Catholic-Jew*, by Will Herberg (1901–1977), is an examination of religion from a sociological perspective in mid-twentieth-century America. At the time the theologian Reinhold Niebuhr (1892–1971) called it "the most fascinating essay on the religious sociology of America that has appeared in decades" (Niebuhr 1955, 6). Since then, Herberg's book has become a staple of scholarly and popular literature on religion and pluralism in the United States. In his introduction to the 1983 edition, the religion scholar Martin Marty calls *Protestant-Catholic-Jew* "the most honored discussion of American religion in mid-twentieth-century times."

Described by his biographer as "a Protestant by theological inclination, a Catholic by temperament, and a Russian Jew by birth" (Ausmus 1987, 1), Herberg offered a template for thinking about mid-century American identity in strictly religious terms. By 1955 the writer—who dropped out of City College of New York but successfully faked his academic credentials for much of his career—had drifted from Marxism to a Judaism influenced by Niebuhr and Paul Tillich's neo-Orthodox emphasis on transcendence and sin. As one critic has written, "Herberg was a Lancelot in search of the philosophical absolutes and intellectual certitudes that reveal the patterns of history" (Shapiro 2003, 261). *Protestant-Catholic-Jew* demonstrated Herberg's commitment to the concept of the soul, both as a personal allegiance and a significant weapon in America's arsenal as it confronted the Soviet Union in the Cold War.

HERBERG'S ARGUMENT

Protestant-Catholic-Jew was Herberg's most famous and most cited work. He built on the language of the "Judeo-Christian tradition" popularized during World War II to make two interrelated arguments. First, he wrote, the United States was a "triple melting pot" in which being "a Protestant, Catholic, or Jew are today the alternative ways of being an American" (258). In his view, the three religions stood together as equals and equally American. He thus advocated for a theologically limited pluralism, a "stable co-existence of three equi-legitimate religious communities grounded in the common culture-religion of America" (259). Though enamored with the resurgence of religious activity in postwar America, Herberg remained less sanguine about the depth of the religious revival he catalogued. He therefore urged a religious reformation that returned to questions of sin, judgment, and faith rather than one that traded in testaments to positive thinking and feelings.

Second, he asserted the existence of "the American Way of Life" as "the operative faith of the American people" (75). As a creedal system, it unified the American people around the important tenets—democratic idealism, pragmatic individualism, idealistic moralism—and events celebrated by Americans. It existed alongside and in a reciprocal relationship with Protestantism, Catholicism, and Judaism, but was not itself religion. "The American Way of Life," he concluded, "is not avowed as a super-faith above and embracing the historic religions. It operates as a 'common faith' at deeper levels, through its pervasive influence on the patterns of American thought and feeling. It makes no pretensions to override or supplant the recognized religions, to which it assigns a place of great eminence and honor" (88–89). In other words, Herberg acknowledged a resemblance between the American way of life and religion; he refused to call it religion or even civil religion. Concerned with the rise of a therapeutic "cult of faith" that diminished the trio of religions he admired, he resisted the American way of life as too facile, underwhelming, and insufficiently transcendent.

Drawing on the work of several immigration scholars, Herberg constructed explanations for the postwar rise of religious identification, church and synagogue membership rates, Sunday school enrollments, and building campaigns. From a 1908 play by the British writer Israel Zangwill, Herberg borrowed the term *melting pot* but altered its configuration. Whereas earlier scholars viewed the American melting pot as a true mixture of European cultures, Herberg recognized the hegemony of the Anglo-Saxon, or white Protestant, Western European ideal. The "transmuting pot," as he labeled it, described the space and goals of American cultural assimilation. From the historian Oscar Handlin (*The Uprooted*, 1951), he borrowed the argument that the United States was a nation of immigrants. Upon arrival in America, ethnicity—as defined by the combination of national origin, religion, and language—overtook immigration status as the preferred mode of identification. Religious affiliation enabled these European newcomers to simultaneously Americanize and retain in-group ties.

Yet the durability of this transformation was suspect, as the historian Marcus Lee Hansen had demonstrated in a 1938 essay, "The Problem of the Third Generation Immigrant." Herberg turned Hansen's aphorism, "What the son wishes to forget the grandson wishes to remember," into "Hansen's law" in order to mobilize

generational change in support of his analysis of religion and secularism. From the sociologist Ruby Jo Reeves Kennedy's 1952 study of marriage patterns in New Haven, Connecticut, Herberg found religious endogamy central to the "triple melting pot" (a concept he also nabbed from Kennedy's work). By blending Hansen's and Kennedy's ideas, Herberg asserted that the second generation attempted to shed foreign attributes and reject ethnic-religious ties, while the third generation sought to reestablish connections to the past and reinvigorate religious (rather than ethnic) observance as part and parcel of their American identities.

RECEPTION BY READERS AND CRITICS

Although many readers initially accepted Herberg's description of immigrant assimilation, religious recommitment, and a tri-faith American population, critics later highlighted the precarious underbelly of Herberg's sociological claims. Little data supported either strict maintenance of religious endogamy in postwar America (interfaith marriages became more acceptable, as laments by religious leaders indicate) or third-generation religious rejuvenation (notably, despite the presence and growth of evangelical Protestantism, it—like Eastern Orthodoxy, Islam, and Buddhism—plays an insignificant role in Herberg's assessment of religious America). Moreover, the elevation of Catholicism and Judaism alongside Protestantism as the major religious players in American society and politics represented an intentional sleight of hand. Three equal-sized chapters charting the histories of Protestantism, Catholicism, and Judaism in the United States helped make his case. But, though Catholics and Jews together composed about one-quarter of the American population in the 1950s, Herberg resisted any suggestion that they constituted religious minorities. Instead, he positioned them as central components—or even compasses—of American life.

Published in the early years of the Cold War, *Protestant-Catholic-Jew* resonated in a society that valued democracy and theism over communism and atheism. But for Herberg, the instrumentalist use of religion in Cold War politics reflected a nonjudgmental shallowness, a "spiritual anodyne" ill-equipped to censor American idolatry. Indeed, from across the Atlantic, D. W. Brogan's review of *Protestant-Catholic-Jew* underscored Herberg's concern with the absence of divine judgment in American religious life when he identified "the acceptance by 'America' of these three organizations (one can hardly say forms of belief) as really American" (1956, 4) as a major component of the book.

Empirically flimsy, conceptually attractive, and culturally powerful, *Protestant-Catholic-Jew* offered a religious taxonomy that appeared inclusive even as it formalized a rigid tripartite division of American religion. In this way, it distracted its readers from the exclusivity, particularity, and criticism embedded in Herberg's argument and crafted a powerful foundation for a common, if flawed, understanding of American religion as a triad of faiths committed to democracy and capitalism.

SEE ALSO *Immigration and Naturalization Service; Immigration Quotas; Nativism; Whiteness*

BIBLIOGRAPHY

Ausmus, Harry J. *Will Herberg: From Right to Right*. Chapel Hill: University of North Carolina Press, 1987.

Brogan, D. W. "Religion in America." *Manchester Guardian*, January 6, 1956, 4.

Gaston, K. Healan. "The Cold War Romance of Religious Authenticity: Will Herberg, William F. Buckley, Jr., and the Rise of the New Right." *Journal of American History* 99, 4 (2013): 1133–58.

Herberg, Will. *Protestant-Catholic-Jew: An Essay in American Religious Sociology*. Garden City, NY: Doubleday, 1955.

Marty, Martin E. "Introduction." In *Protestant-Catholic-Jew: An Essay in American Religious Sociology*, by Will Herberg. Chicago: University of Chicago Press, 1983.

Niebuhr, Reinhold. "America's Three Melting Pots." Review of *Protestant-Catholic-Jew*, by Will Herberg, 1955. *New York Times*, September 25, 1955, 6.

Shapiro, Edward. "Will Herberg's *Protestant-Catholic-Jew*: A Critique." In *Key Texts in American Jewish Culture*, edited by Jack Kugelmass, 258–274. New Brunswick, NJ: Rutgers University Press, 2003.

Stahl, Ronit Y. "A Jewish America and a Protestant Civil Religion: Will Herberg, Robert Bellah, and Mid-Twentieth Century American Religion." *Religions* 6, 2 (2015): 434–450.

Ronit Y. Stahl
Postdoctoral Research Associate
Washington University in St. Louis

PROTESTANTISM

Protestants, the theological descendants of Martin Luther (1483–1546) and the Protestant Reformation he engendered in 1517, have left an indelible mark on both American culture and the world, from the Puritans of the seventeenth century to the civil rights movements of the twentieth and twenty-first centuries. Along the way, Protestants have shaped everything from music and architecture to social reform and the configuration of religion and politics.

Protestantism is, by its very nature, fissiparous, and nowhere more so than in North America. Luther's assertion of *sola scriptura*, the Bible alone, as the source of authority, removed the Roman Catholic Church as a unifying force. Protestants, increasingly literate so they could read and interpret the Bible for themselves, proceeded to do exactly that, coming away from the text with sometimes wildly divergent interpretations. This led, in turn, to seemingly endless dissent and a multiplication of sects and denominations as each group staked its claims to truth and what was assuredly the correct interpretation of the scriptures.

EARLY PROTESTANT SETTLERS IN NORTH AMERICA

The two earliest groups of Protestants in North America, the Pilgrims and the Puritans, represent two broadly different impulses, separatism and engagement, that have been present among American Protestants ever since. The Pilgrims, who arrived in 1620, had already separated from the Church of England. After a sojourn in the Netherlands, they returned briefly to England before sailing across the Atlantic aboard the *Mayflower*. The Puritans, by contrast, had been pushing for reforms from within the Church of England—they sought to "purify" the church of all vestiges of Roman Catholicism—but political machinations within Anglicanism in the 1620s finally persuaded a small band of Puritans to head to America. Their mission, famously articulated by John Winthrop (1587–1649), was to construct a "city on a hill" in Massachusetts so that all the world, and especially England, would see how to configure church and state, how to build a pure and godly church.

Within a decade, however, the Puritans of New England lost their audience across the Atlantic; English Puritans had taken matters into their own hands, deposing the king and forming a commonwealth. Some of the Puritans in Massachusetts returned to England to be part of the action, and those who remained were, in Perry Miller's haunting phrase, "left alone with America" (1956, 15).

Although the history of Protestantism in America is typically viewed through the prism of New England, other Protestants established a foothold as well. In 1628 Jonas Michaëlius (1577–c. 1638), a Dutch Reformed minister, conducted the first service of worship in New Amsterdam, with a motley, ethnically diverse congregation. Farther south, Swedish Lutherans established a foothold in the Delaware River valley, and Anglicans settled in Virginia and the southern colonies. By the dawn of the eighteenth century, the Atlantic seaboard provided a veritable laboratory of Protestant diversity: Quakers in New England; Scots-Irish Presbyterians in New Jersey; Huguenots (French Protestants) in Massachusetts, New York, and South Carolina; various German groups in Pennsylvania.

The Moravians settled initially in Georgia and South Carolina, but a group migrated from there to Pennsylvania to participate in William Penn's (1644–1718) "Holy Experiment" of religious toleration.

THE FIRST GREAT AWAKENING

By the early decades of the eighteenth century, the Puritan experiment in New England was foundering. The rise of a merchant class, together with difficulties of passing the faith from one generation to the next, signaled a decline in piety. Preachers called for renewal, and reports of revival began appearing as early as the 1690s from Solomon Stoddard (1643–1729) in Northampton, Massachusetts, Guilliam Bertholf (1656–1724) in northern New Jersey, and Lars Tollstadius (d. 1706) in the Delaware River valley. During the winter of 1734 to 1735, Stoddard's grandson, Jonathan Edwards (1703–1758), witnessed an outbreak of piety and religious conversions in Northampton. The fervor ebbed, only to be rekindled by the visit of George Whitefield (1714–1770), an Anglican preacher. Whitefield had been trained in the London theater, and he understood the importance of a stentorian voice, grand gestures, and dramatic pauses. In a society that, at that time, had no dramatic tradition, Whitefield was extraordinarily successful. Contemporaries said that he could bring tears to your eyes simply by saying Mesopotamia.

As Whitefield and other revival preachers circulated throughout the Atlantic colonies, from Georgia north to the Maritimes, contemporaries began talking about a "great and general awakening," one known to historians simply as the Great Awakening. This revival introduced extemporaneous preaching, eroded ethnic barriers, divided communities between those sympathetic to and those opposed to the revival, and established patterns of communication that would abet the Patriot cause and the American Revolution several decades later.

The Great Awakening also introduced a distinctly American form of evangelicalism to North America. The term *evangelical* refers to the first four books of the New Testament—Matthew, Mark, Luke, and John, the evangelists—but it had been appropriated by Luther and the Protestant Reformation. In America, however, it was further defined in the confluence of three streams during the course of the Great Awakening: the vestiges of New England Puritanism, Scots-Irish Presbyterianism, and Pietism from the Continent. To this day, evangelicalism can trace its penchant for spiritual introspection to the Puritans, its doctrinal precisionism to the Presbyterians, and its emphasis on a warmhearted, affective faith to the Pietists.

THE FIRST AMENDMENT AND THE SEPARATION OF CHURCH AND STATE

Amid all of this diversity among Protestants, a Baptist in Rhode Island provided the basis of a formula for ensuring religious freedom, toleration, and stability. Roger Williams (c. 1603–1683), a Puritan minister in seventeenth-century Massachusetts, had been banished from the colony for condemning the conflation of church and state. In time, he warned that the garden of the church would be contaminated by the wilderness of the world if not for a wall of separation between the two. The notion of constructing a society without an established, or state-supported, church was novel, but Williams proceeded to demonstrate in Rhode Island that religious toleration and liberty of conscience would work. Religious pluralism in other places, especially the Middle Colonies, also corroborated his conviction that the state should remain neutral in religious matters.

Following the American Revolution, the founders of the new nation (wittingly or not) appropriated the principle that Williams had articulated more than a century earlier. The First Amendment guaranteed both freedom of religion and government neutrality in religious matters, thereby setting up a free marketplace of religion where all religious groups are free to compete with one another for popular followings. Many clergy feared that the absence of state support would spell the end for religion and even morality. But the result was exactly the opposite. Religion has flourished in America as nowhere else precisely because of the First Amendment and the separation of church and state. No religious group can depend on the largess of the government; all must compete for popular followings on a more-or-less equal footing.

Protestants, and especially evangelicals, have historically fared well in that competition. Largely unconstrained by ecclesiastical hierarchies, creedal standards, or liturgical rubrics, Protestants have crafted their message, and sometimes their theology, to appeal to the masses. More than occasionally, this yields a theology of the lowest common denominator, but it also ensures a populist, salubrious religious culture.

THE SECOND GREAT AWAKENING

If the First Great Awakening introduced a peculiar form of evangelicalism to North America, the Second Great Awakening, which straddled the turn of the nineteenth century, enlarged the geographical and cultural sphere of Protestantism. The Second Awakening convulsed three theaters of the new nation: New England, the Cumberland Valley of Kentucky, and upstate New York. The revival in New England was generally tame, even conservative. Contemporaries at Yale College reported an outbreak of piety among students who, not long before, had been so enamored of Enlightenment rationalism that they addressed one another by the names of the French *philosophes*. As graduates fanned out across New England, communities reported surges in religious sentiment.

The Awakening in the Cumberland Valley, also known as the Great Revival, was by far the most dramatic. The frontier was wild and untamed; alcohol consumption was rampant, and a reported one in three brides was pregnant. James McGready (1763–1817) and other preachers began holding camp meetings, a frontier adaptation of the Scottish practice of "sacramental seasons." The Gaspar River camp meeting in the summer of 1800 drew large crowds; people from widely scattered settlements seized on the rare opportunity to socialize. One of those in attendance was a Presbyterian minister from Cane Ridge, Barton W. Stone (1772–1844), who decided to convene a camp meeting of his own the following August. The Cane Ridge camp meeting drew as many as twenty-five thousand for hymn singing and preaching. Although critics contended that more souls were conceived than converted in camp meetings, the revivals were marked by all sorts of ecstasy as participants were overcome by the Holy Spirit: laughing, falling down, rolling, involuntary contortions known as the *jerks*. Preachers dispensed with the Calvinist language of "particular election," that only the elect were saved, and called on their auditors to exercise their free will and experience spiritual new birth. Among a people who had only recently taken their political destiny into their own hands, revival preachers of the Second Great Awakening assured them that they controlled their spiritual destiny as well.

The third theater of the Second Awakening was upstate New York, an area so frequently singed by the fires of revival that it became known as the Burned-Over District. The construction of the Erie Canal had opened markets to the east and transformed western New York into a boom area. Preachers, notably Charles Grandison Finney (1792–1875), tilled the fertile religious soil. Though less spectacular than the Great Revival, the spiritual awakening in upstate New York arguably had a greater effect on nineteenth-century America. Finney had introduced a series of "new measures" to the revival playbook—protracted meetings, advertising, allowing women to speak, the "anxious bench," where auditors could wrestle with their eternal destiny—but Finney's message that individuals controlled their religious destiny also translated into the larger arena of social reform. Converts not only could choose salvation, they could collectively bring about the millennial kingdom, one thousand years of righteousness predicted in the book of Revelation, by dint of their own efforts.

REFORM INITIATIVES AND MISSIONARY ACTIVITY

This impulse to reform society according to the norms of godliness animated a remarkable array of reform initiatives, from the abolition of slavery and prison reform to public education and equality for women. Lyman Beecher (1775–1863), to cite one example, believed that the practice of dueling was barbaric and not a fixture of the millennial kingdom; he embarked on a campaign to have it outlawed. The aggregate efforts of Protestants, especially in the North, set the social and political agenda for much of the nineteenth century.

Protestants also began to look abroad. The Haystack Prayer Meeting in Williamstown, Massachusetts, in August 1806, led to the formation of the American Board of Commissioners for Foreign Missions. In 1812, the board dispatched its first missionaries to India, and other missionaries followed to China, India, Hawai'i, and Southeast Asia. In addition to their evangelism efforts, missionaries built schools and hospitals and translated the Bible into native languages, a process that often provided the first codification of those languages. Many Protestants were inspired by the life and career of an eighteenth-century missionary, David Brainerd (1718–1747), whose work among the Indians was memorialized by Edwards, whose daughter had been engaged to Brainerd at the time of the missionary's death in 1747.

Missionary activity abroad was part of American Protestants' vision for spreading Christianity throughout the world and ringing in the kingdom of God. The carnage of the Civil War (1861–1865), however, began to dim hopes for a millennial kingdom. American society was changing—and not in ways that suggested the millennium was at hand. Industrialization, urbanization, and the arrival of non-Protestant immigrants, most of whom did not share Protestant scruples about temperance, forced Protestants to reconsider their views of society. Some Protestants protested the influx of Roman Catholics, engaging in ugly attacks, rhetorical and sometimes physical. For many Protestants, teeming, squalid tenements, seething with labor unrest, hardly resembled the precincts of Zion.

By the waning decades of the nineteenth century, more conservative Protestants had adopted a different mode of biblical interpretation that they had imported from Britain, dispensational premillennialism. Dispensationalism divided all of human history into different ages, or dispensations, and asserted that we were now living in the final age just prior to the return of Christ. Jesus, in fact, might return at any moment, which absolved these evangelicals of responsibility for social amelioration. "I look upon this world as a wrecked vessel," evangelist Dwight L. Moody (1837–1899) declared. "God has given me a lifeboat and said to me, 'Moody, save all you can'' (quoted in Marsden 1991, 21).

Although Moody did not entirely forsake social amelioration, his own evangelistic efforts assumed greater importance, not only in North America but abroad. In the summer of 1886, Moody convened a meeting of 251 college students at his conference center in Mount Hermon, Massachusetts. Out of that gathering emerged the Student Volunteer Movement for Foreign Missions, one of the most successful missions organizations in American history, aspiring to send missionaries to every nation in the world.

As conservatives retreated from social reform toward an emphasis on individual regeneration, liberal Protestants embraced the Social Gospel, believing that the Christian faith was capable of redeeming not merely sinful individuals but sinful social institutions as well. Working hand in hand with progressives, Social Gospelers, such as Washington Gladden (1836–1918), Josiah Strong (1847–1916), and Walter Rauschenbusch (1861–1918), advocated the rights of labor to organize, the six-day workweek, and the abolition of child labor. Strong's classic book, *Our Country*, published in 1885, argued that Americans owed a debt to the world to spread Anglo-Saxon Christianity. The United States, he argued, had "the largest liberty, the purest Christianity, the highest civilization," and therefore a responsibility to the world.

In 1893, "the world" came to America. In conjunction with the Columbian Exposition in Chicago, religious leaders from around the world gathered for the World's Parliament of Religions, held in what is now the Art Institute of Chicago. Americans had long been intrigued by the mysterious East, and representatives of Hinduism, Islam, Buddhism, Shinto, and other traditions provided many Americans with their first glimpse of these "exotic" religions. More conservative Protestants generally looked askance at the gathering, and some protested, while Protestants of a more liberal and inclusive ilk were prominent among the organizers of the parliament.

PENTECOSTALISM

Conservatives continued to view the world as a mission field and adherents of these religions as targets for proselytization. Pentecostalism provided a major impetus for missions. On the first day of the new century, January 1, 1901, an outbreak of *glossolalia* (speaking in tongues) occurred among students at Bethel Bible College in Topeka, Kansas. Under the influence of the Holy Spirit, students began speaking in unknown languages, similar to what happened to first-century Christians on the day of Pentecost, according to the New Testament book of Acts. As word spread of this phenomenon, many believers understood this restoration of spiritual gifts as heralding

the end of human history; God was even now pouring out his spirit in these "last days."

The school's founder, Charles Fox Parham (1873–1929), carried word of the Topeka Outpouring, as it came to be known, in his travels throughout Kansas, Oklahoma, and Texas. One particularly keen auditor was William J. Seymour (1870–1922), an African American hotel waiter in Houston. When Seymour headed west to Los Angeles in 1906, he began preaching about Pentecostalism, and soon crowds were gathering outside the home of Richard and Ruth Asberry on Bonnie Brae Street. When *glossolalia* broke out, the informal meetings adjourned to Azusa Street, where reports of speaking in tongues and divine healing became commonplace.

The Azusa Street Revival, which was remarkable both for its interracial character and for the inclusion of women in leadership roles, drew the faithful and the curious from all over North America. The thrice-daily meetings at the Azusa Street Mission were lively and, for many participants, transformative. Those who were baptized by the Holy Spirit fanned out across North America and the world with their Pentecostal fervor. Over the course of the ensuing century, Pentecostalism would establish a foothold around the globe, with particular success in Africa and Latin America, where by the close of the twentieth century it had eclipsed liberation theology as the "theology of the people."

GROWING DIVISION BETWEEN FUNDAMENTALIST AND MODERNIST PROTESTANTS

The Protestant strain of engagement took institutional form with the formation of the Federal Council of Churches in 1908, which promptly issued *The Social Creed of the Churches*, a Social Gospel manifesto. Liberal Protestants understood the value of cooperation in order to achieve their ends. Theological disputes and competition among denominations came to be seen as unnecessary and distracting from the larger project of social reform, and the Federal Council aspired to elide differences in the name of Christian unity.

Conservative, separatist Protestants begged to differ. Theology mattered, they insisted; it mattered very much, especially the doctrine of biblical inspiration. For more than half a century, conservative, literalistic approaches to the Bible had been imperiled by two intellectual strains: Darwinism and the German discipline of higher criticism. Pushed to its logical conclusions, Charles Darwin's *The Origin of Species*, published in 1859, undermined the traditional understandings of creation as set forth in the opening chapters of Genesis. Using sophisticated tools of textual analysis, higher criticism cast doubt on the integrity of the biblical texts—positing, for example, that there were actually three books of Isaiah and that Moses, the putative author of the entire Torah (or Pentateuch) was not the author, that the text as we have it was actually a redaction of several sources. (How, after all, could Moses have recorded his own death in the final chapter of Deuteronomy?)

Conservatives, led by the theologians associated with Princeton Theological Seminary, had responded by asserting the *inerrancy* of the scriptures in the original autographs; any apparent mistakes or contradictions crept in through the agency of copyists. The original manuscripts were no longer extant, of course, but this claim provided a measure of epistemological certainty against the attacks of Protestant liberals, who increasingly viewed the Bible as a collection of human writings, not divine revelation. These liberals, also known as *modernists*, began also to question such orthodox touchstones as the virgin birth, the divinity of Jesus, and his bodily resurrection from the dead.

Conservative Protestants, convinced that orthodoxy was imperiled, responded with a series of pamphlets called *The Fundamentals.* Financed by Milton Stewart (1838–1923) and Lyman Stewart (1840–1923) of Union Oil Company of California and appearing between 1910 and 1915, *The Fundamentals* contained articles written by theologians from the United States, the United Kingdom, New Zealand, and Australia defending the "fundamentals" of the faith: the virgin birth, Christ's divinity, the Resurrection, the inerrancy of the Bible, and the imminent return of Jesus. The Stewart brothers wanted these pamphlets distributed to every pastor, missionary, Sunday school superintendent, and YMCA and YWCA secretary throughout the English-speaking world. Those who subscribed to the doctrines set forth in *The Fundamentals* came to be known as *fundamentalists*, and soon enough a kind of civil war was raging among American Protestants between the fundamentalists and the modernists.

In the short term, the modernists prevailed. In a series of institutional battles played out at Princeton Theological Seminary and in various denominations and missions agencies, the modernists held on to the reins of power—and with it the spoils of buildings, bureaucracies, campuses, and endowments. The fundamentalists, like the Pilgrims of an earlier era, separated away from those institutions in order to maintain their doctrinal purity, but doing so exacted a fearsome cost. They were forced to start anew, to build from scratch. Beginning in the 1920s, conservative Protestants set about constructing their own evangelical subculture, a vast and interlocking network of congregations, denominations, Bible camps, Bible institutes, colleges, seminaries, publishing houses, and missionary societies. Especially after the embarrassment of the Scopes trial of 1925 and the popular opprobrium directed

at fundamentalists, the evangelical subculture provided refuge from the depredations of the larger world.

As evangelicals were ramping up their missionary efforts, liberal Protestants, also known as mainline Protestants, were backing away from what they increasingly regarded as cultural imperialism on the mission field. In 1932 a book appeared called *Re-thinking Missions*, a summation of extensive fieldwork conducted in various mission fields where Protestants were active. This summary, written by William Ernest Hocking (1873–1966), a philosopher at Harvard University, argued that Protestant missionaries should be more sensitive to non-Christian religions and cultures. Rather than seek conversions, they should seek cooperation with indigenous peoples in pursuit of social amelioration. *Re-thinking Missions* was reviewed in the *Christian Century*, the flagship publication of mainline Protestantism, by Pearl S. Buck (1892–1973), acclaimed novelist and former wife of a missionary in China. Buck had remembered the visit of fieldwork researchers several years earlier and was not much impressed at the time, but she applauded the findings and the recommendations contained in what became known as the *Hocking Report.*

BILLY GRAHAM, MARTIN LUTHER KING JR., AND OTHER TWENTIETH-CENTURY PROTESTANT LEADERS

Evangelical institution building arguably reached its apotheosis with the formation of the National Association of Evangelicals (NAE) in 1942. Meant as a counterpart of the Federal Council of Churches, the NAE brought together many like-minded evangelicals, although many of the more separatist fundamentalists refused to join. By midcentury, however, an increasing number of evangelicals were backing away from the strident rhetoric and militancy of the fundamentalists. Billy Graham (b. 1918), for example, made a conscious decision about the time he graduated from Wheaton College to forswear the narrow fundamentalism of his childhood in favor of a more capacious, irenic evangelicalism, also known as neo-evangelicalism. Blessed with extraordinary charisma, Graham soon became a national and then an international figure. He burst onto the national scene with his 1949 revival campaign, or "crusade," in Los Angeles. Newspaper magnate William Randolph Hearst (1863–1951), impressed with the young preacher's anticommunist rhetoric, instructed his papers to "puff Graham." Soon, the evangelist appeared on the cover of *Time* magazine, and in 1954 he took his preaching abroad, first to London, then to Europe and India, and eventually to many nations around the world.

Another Wheaton College alumnus, Jim Elliot (1927–1956), exemplified evangelical commitment to missions. Elliot and four other missionaries decided to take the gospel to the Waorani Indians of Ecuador, where they were martyred for their faith on January 8, 1956. When news of their dedication and bravery reached North America, the Ecuadoran Martyrs, and Elliot especially, became heroes of the faith and an inspiration to succeeding generations, just as Brainerd had been to missionaries in the nineteenth century.

If Graham embodied the values of white, middle-class Protestantism, another American Protestant began to call those values into question. Martin Luther King Jr. (1929–1968) accepted the pastorate of the Dexter Avenue Baptist Church in Montgomery, Alabama, in 1955, shortly after completing his doctorate at Boston University. The ardor of the Social Gospel had begun to wane about the time of the Bolshevik Revolution in 1917, but King had encountered the writings of Walter Rauschenbusch and other Social Gospel theologians in the course of his studies. His career would resuscitate the Social Gospel. Although a newcomer to Montgomery, King accepted the offer of leadership of the Montgomery Improvement Association, formed to organize a bus boycott following the arrest of Rosa Parks (1913–2005) for refusing to obey city ordinances mandating segregated seating.

King, together with other black Protestant ministers and community leaders, masterfully coordinated the year-long boycott, and once the Supreme Court ruled in favor of desegregation, King turned his attentions to the pursuit of civil rights and voting rights throughout the South. Influenced by the writings of Mohandas (Mahatma) Gandhi (1869–1948) and Howard Thurman (1899–1981), King advocated nonviolent resistance and civil disobedience to call attention to racial inequality. Under the aegis of the Southern Christian Leadership Conference and with the cooperation of other black ministers, notably Fred Shuttlesworth (1922–2011) and Ralph David Abernathy (1926–1990), King confronted southern racism as well as white apathy. While sitting in jail following his arrest on Good Friday, 1963, King wrote his manifesto for the civil rights movement, "Letter from a Birmingham Jail," which argued against those, notably white clergy, who had counseled patience and what he would later call "the tranquilizing drug of gradualism."

King's activities helped persuade the president and Congress to pass the Civil Rights Act of 1964 and the Voting Rights Act of 1965. With those successes in hand, King turned his attention to issues of poverty and foreign policy. On April 4, 1967 (a year to the day before his assassination in Memphis), King addressed a gathering of Clergy and Laity Concerned about the War in Vietnam, meeting at Riverside Church in New York City. In so doing, King finally—some said belatedly—added his voice to the growing number of clergy, many of them liberal Protestants, who opposed the Vietnam War.

PROTESTANTISM AND POLITICS

Though not yet organized politically, many evangelical Protestants supported the war as part of America's continuing crusade against the specter of "godless communism." Graham, who courted the favor of a succession of American presidents beginning with Harry Truman (1884–1972), had a particularly close connection with Richard Nixon (1913–1994), nominally a Quaker, who expanded American involvement in Southeast Asia; many evangelicals followed Graham's lead.

Nixon's downfall in the Watergate scandal led to the election of another Protestant, whose religious convictions had significant repercussions on American foreign policy. Jimmy Carter (b. 1924), a Southern Baptist Sunday school teacher, had promised never knowingly to lie to the American people, a tonic after Nixon's endless prevarications. Carter recognized that if the United States was to have any meaningful relationship with the nations of the Third World, especially Latin America, the Panama Canal treaties must be renegotiated. He also sought, with mixed success, to move American foreign policy away from the reflexive dualism of the Cold War and toward an emphasis on human rights. Finally, his painstaking negotiations at Camp David in 1978 provided the framework for peace in the Middle East.

Evangelical Protestants, who had helped propel Carter to the White House in 1976, however, turned dramatically against him four years later. The Religious Right, building on the foundation of institutions they had constructed in the middle decades of the twentieth century, emerged in the late 1970s in defense of racially segregated schools, especially Bob Jones University. But in 1979, the leaders of the Religious Right seized on opposition to abortion to energize evangelical voters at the grassroots. Judging Carter insufficiently "pro-life," they embraced Ronald Reagan (1911–2004) over their fellow evangelical. The Religious Right continued to influence presidential elections for decades thereafter, especially the elections of 2000 and 2004, although its heft began to diminish in the second decade of the twenty-first century.

SUMMARY

Throughout the long sweep of American history, Protestantism has played a formative role, despite the fact that the First Amendment prohibits a religious establishment. All of the presidents of the United States, with the exception of John F. Kennedy (1917–1963), have been Protestants, albeit with varying degrees of commitment or ardor. Protestant theology and sensibility can be seen in everything from the simple lines of church architecture to the tropes of redemption ubiquitous in country music. The town meetings and direct democracy of New England resemble the congregational polity of many Protestant churches. Protestant missionary activity has spread both religious and cultural values throughout the world, sometimes in unflattering and imperialistic ways, although missionaries have also ministered to the sick, the uneducated, and the needy. For much of the twentieth century, American foreign policy was shaped by a kind of Protestant messianism: "making the world safe for democracy" or the "containment" strategy directed against godless communism.

Ever since the Hart-Celler Immigration Act of 1965, Protestants have encountered a changing religious configuration. Hindu temples, Muslim mosques, Buddhist stupas, and Sikh gurdwaras now dot the landscape. Not all Protestants have embraced these changes; the more separatist strain seeks to reassert its sectarian values, even to the point of codifying those values into law. But such a posture defies the protection for minorities written into the nation's charter documents. Protestantism in America now inhabits a more crowded field, but its influence, especially the liberal Protestant values of toleration and inclusiveness, endures.

SEE ALSO *American Board of Commissioners for Foreign Missions; Democracy in America (Alexis de Tocqueville, 1835–1840); Federal Council of Churches; Graham, William (Billy) Franklin, Jr.; King, Martin Luther, Jr.; Niebuhr, (Karl Paul) Reinhold; Our Country (Josiah Strong, 1885); Protestant-Catholic-Jew (Will Herberg, 1955)*

BIBLIOGRAPHY

Balmer, Randall. *Redeemer: The Life of Jimmy Carter.* New York: Basic Books, 2014.

Blum, Edward J. *Reforging the White Republic: Race, Religion, and American Nationalism, 1865–1898.* Baton Rouge: Louisiana State University Press, 2005.

Espinosa, Gastón. *William J. Seymour and the Origins of Global Pentecostalism: A Biography and Documentary History.* Durham, NC: Duke University Press, 2014.

Garrow, David J. *Bearing the Cross: Martin Luther King, Jr., and the Southern Christian Leadership Conference.* New York: Morrow, 1986.

Hatch, Nathan O. *The Democratization of American Christianity.* New Haven, CT: Yale University Press, 1991.

Heyrman, Christine Leigh. *Southern Cross: The Beginnings of the Bible Belt.* New York: Knopf, 1997.

Hollinger, David. *After Cloven Tongues of Fire: Protestant Liberalism in Modern American History.* Princeton, NJ: Princeton University Press, 2013.

King, Martin Luther, Jr. "Letter from a Birmingham Jail." April 16, 1963. https://kinginstitute.stanford.edu/king-papers/documents/letter-birmingham-jail

Marsden, George M. *Understanding Fundamentalism and Evangelicalism.* Grand Rapids, MI: Eerdmans, 1991.

Miller, Perry. *Errand into the Wilderness.* Cambridge, MA: Belknap Press of Harvard University Press, 1956.

Stout, Harry S. *The Divine Dramatist: George Whitefield and the Rise of Modern Evangelicalism.* Grand Rapids, MI: Eerdmans, 1991.

Wacker, Grant. *Heaven Below: Early Pentecostals and American Culture.* Cambridge, MA: Harvard University Press, 2001.

Randall Balmer
John Phillips Professor in Religion
Dartmouth College

PUERTO RICO

The acquisition of Puerto Rico by the United States in 1898 as a result of the Spanish-American-Cuban-Filipino War marked a new phase of American territorial expansion. By virtue of the Treaty of Paris, which put an end to the war, Spain relinquished its sovereignty over Cuba and ceded Puerto Rico, Guam, and the Philippine Islands to the United States. Thus the United States gained strongholds in the Caribbean and Pacific regions.

EVOLVING RELATIONSHIP WITH THE UNITED STATES

From 1898 to 1900, the United States ruled Puerto Rico through a military government. In 1900 the US Congress passed the Foraker Act, establishing a civilian government, which included a popularly elected House of Delegates and a governor appointed by the president of the United States. The conditions imposed by the new sovereign prompted diverse reactions among the population. Realigned political forces began to advocate different solutions for the political future of Puerto Rico. That discussion is still raging today.

The advent of World War I (1914–1918) highlighted the risks that Germany posed to the strategic interests of the United States in the Caribbean (Estades Font 1988). This led to a renewed focus on Puerto Rico on the part of the US government. In 1917 Congress passed the Jones-Shafroth Act, which reorganized the Puerto Rican government and extended US citizenship to persons born in Puerto Rico. With these actions, the US government sought to allay a generalized dissatisfaction among Puerto Ricans regarding what many considered an outright colonial relationship. Congress took no major legal step regarding the political status of Puerto Rico for the next thirty years. Moreover, through a group of decisions known as the Insular Cases, the US Supreme Court reaffirmed its determination that Puerto Rico had to be considered unincorporated territory of the United States, which meant that Puerto Rico belonged to, but was not a part of, the United States (Rivera Ramos 2001, 71–142).

A serious economic crisis struck the island in the 1930s. Social upheaval, especially in the workers' front, began to rattle the island. A militant nationalist movement, headed by Harvard-trained lawyer Pedro Albizu Campos (1891–1965), posed a challenge to American rule. The confrontation led to bloodshed in the nationalist and police ranks. Many nationalist leaders were incarcerated.

World War II (1939–1945) gripped the attention of the United States in the 1940s. Again, strategic concerns, deepened by the internal social and political conflicts in the island, moved the US government to promote political and social reforms in its Caribbean colony (Rodríguez Beruff 2007).

In the mid-1940s, the United States began to strengthen military installations in Puerto Rico and its adjacent islands, resulting in a substantial upgrade in military and civilian infrastructure. In 1947 Congress authorized Puerto Rican voters to elect their own governor. As a result, in 1948 Puerto Rican residents chose Luis Muñoz Marín (1898–1980), the charismatic founder of the recently created Popular Democratic Party, to become their first elected governor. With support from the administration of President Harry S. Truman (1884–1972), Muñoz Marín led Puerto Rico through a series of social and economic reforms that contributed to economic growth, helped alleviate widespread poverty, extended access to public education, improved health services, and modernized governmental operations.

The emergence of a worldwide decolonization movement after World War II raised new questions about the colonial condition of Puerto Rico, which remained subject to US sovereignty. In 1950, at the urging of the Puerto Rican government backed by the Truman administration, Congress enacted Public Law 600, which authorized Puerto Ricans to adopt their own constitution. A constitutional convention drafted a text that was sanctioned by a majority of Puerto Rican voters. Congress approved the proposed constitution, subject to the repeal of several provisions. So amended, the new Puerto Rican constitution was proclaimed by Governor Muñoz Marín on July 25, 1952. The constitution adopted a new official name for Puerto Rico: the Estado Libre Asociado de Puerto Rico, translated into English as the Commonwealth of Puerto Rico. As a result of these developments, in 1954 the United Nations (UN) General Assembly acquiesced to the decision of the US government to cease sending reports about Puerto Rico as required by the UN Charter of all members that had non-self-governing or trust territories under their administration (Ramírez Lavandero 1988, 613–624).

By this time, the Cold War was in full force. A key development would prove to be the Cuban Revolution of 1959. Revolutionary Cuba was seen by the United States as a menace to its interests in Latin America and the Caribbean. The United States responded, in part, by showcasing the largest of its Caribbean colonies, Puerto Rico, as an alternative to the Cuban model, due to the successful social and economic reforms undertaken by Puerto Rico in the 1940s and 1950s.

ROLE IN THE WORLDWIDE POLITICS AND CALLS FOR SELF-DETERMINATION

Hundreds of foreign government officials were invited to Puerto Rico to assess the results of Puerto Rico's economic development program. US presidents drafted Puerto Rican leaders to promote American policies in the region. For example, in 1961, President John F. Kennedy (1917–1963) appointed a Puerto Rican, Teodoro Moscoso (1910–1992), to be the US ambassador to Venezuela and, later, the US coordinator of the Alliance for Progress, an ambitious program launched by the Kennedy administration to promote economic and social development in the American hemisphere. Twenty Latin American countries formally joined the alliance (Moscoso 1963). Cuba was expressly excluded. The program turned into another weapon in the arsenal of the Cold War. The Alliance for Progress eventually faltered for a number of reasons, including the contradictions between its public objectives and the US counterinsurgency and other military strategies deployed against Latin American progressive governments and movements during that period (Offiler 2010, 1–22; Horowitz 1964, 127–145). The latter, more militaristic, policies also found a suitable platform in Puerto Rico, as it became the site of one of the most important US naval bases in the Atlantic Ocean, frequently used to train foreign navies and to launch military interventions in the region.

Puerto Rico also became entangled in the worldwide politics of alignment and nonalignment. Supporters of Puerto Rican independence saw in the recently created Non-Aligned Movement (NAM) another forum from which to obtain support and solidarity. Pro-independence groups were invited to join NAM as observer organizations. NAM has repeatedly passed resolutions reaffirming Puerto Rico's right to self-determination and independence and has supported the intervention of the UN Decolonization Committee urging the United States to provide for an effective process of self-determination for the Puerto Rican people (see Ministers of the Movement of Non-Aligned Countries 2011). Repeatedly, Latin American governments and regional political organizations have called for the United States to recognize Puerto Rico's right to self-determination and to move to resolve Puerto Rico's political status.

The end of the Cold War found Puerto Rico in a modified scenario. Competition from emerging economies, the loss of privileged access to the US market, and the elimination by Congress of tax incentives for US firms established on the island, along with a deep, prolonged recession and serious fiscal difficulties, created a dire situation marked by high unemployment and low labor-participation rates. Puerto Rico could no longer be held as a paradigm for the region, as emerging Latin American and Caribbean economies exhibited a greater capacity for growth. One effect of this crisis has been a new wave of migration to the United States. For the first time in history, there are more persons of Puerto Rican origin living in the United States and its other territories than in Puerto Rico. Politically, there is a growing dissatisfaction among most political sectors in Puerto Rico with the current political arrangement between Puerto Rico and the United States.

SEE ALSO *Americanization; Cold War; Empire, US; Exceptionalism; Insular Possessions; Internationalism; Interventionism; Isolationism; Manifest Destiny; Monroe Doctrine (1823)*

BIBLIOGRAPHY

Estades Font, María Eugenia. *La presencia militar de Estados Unidos en Puerto Rico, 1898–1918.* Río Piedras, PR: Huracán, 1988.

Horowitz, David. "The Alliance for Progress." *The Socialist Register* 1 (1964): 127–145.

Ministers of the Movement of Non-Aligned Countries. *Final Document.* XVI Ministerial Conference and Commemorative Meeting of the Non-Aligned Movement, Bali, Indonesia, May 23–27, 2011. http://www.kemlu.go.id/Documents/GNB%20ke-16/NAMDOC1-Rev1-final%20Document-English-Final.pdf

Moscoso, Teodoro. *The Alliance for Progress: Its Program and Goals.* Washington, DC: Agency for International Development, 1963.

Offiler, Benjamin. "The Alliance for Progress during the Kennedy and Johnson Administrations: Laudable Idea, Poorly Implemented?" *49th Parallel* 24 (Spring 2010): 1–22.

Ramírez Lavandero, Marcos, ed. *Documents on the Constitutional Relationship of Puerto Rico and the United States.* 3rd ed. Washington, DC: Puerto Rico Federal Affairs Administration, 1988.

Rivera Ramos, Efrén. *The Legal Construction of Identity: The Judicial and Social Legacy of American Colonialism in Puerto Rico.* Washington: APA, 2001.

Rodríguez Beruff, Jorge. *Strategy as Politics: Puerto Rico on the Eve of the Second World War.* San Juan, PR: La Editorial Universidad de Puerto Rico, 2007.

Efrén Rivera Ramos
Professor of Law
University of Puerto Rico

Q–R

THE QUIET AMERICAN (GRAHAM GREENE, 1955)

Graham Greene (1904–1991)—distinctly English, privately schooled and publicly Catholic, a depressive, a globetrotter, and, for a while, a spy for MI6—remains one of the most celebrated storytellers in twentieth-century fiction. His reputation for exploring morally ambivalent themes within popular narrative forms marks out *The Quiet American* (1955) as one his quintessential achievements: both a tightly wound, politically layered Cold War novel and an intimate but troubling portrait of an unlikely love triangle.

Set in Saigon somewhere toward the end of the First Indochina War (1946–1954), it tells of how a middle-aged British journalist, Thomas Fowler, and his much younger Vietnamese girlfriend, Phuong, come into the company of a newly arrived American attaché called Alden Pyle. Phuong wants the security of marriage, but Fowler, denied a divorce by his estranged wife back home, cannot reciprocate. The two men—one aging and cynical, the other youthful and idealistic—start to vie for her amorous attention. Pyle has been drawn to Vietnam in the first place by US efforts to establish influence in the region as the old French colonial order begins to crumble; he turns out to be an intelligence operative (Greene infers, but does not name, the Central Intelligence Agency [CIA]) charged with stemming the rising tide of communism and helping to put in place an alternative "Third Way." He sees the enigmatic General Thé as the most likely candidate to further US interests, and works with him to undermine the colonial regime (including supplying explosives for what he assumes will be strikes on military targets). But in the novel's most powerful scene, Fowler and Pyle are present when Thé's real intentions become devastatingly clear: a bomb detonated in a busy public square in central Saigon.

Pyle is unwavering in his ideological commitment—the obliterated women and children have "died for democracy," he claims (Greene [1955] 2001, 179)—but Fowler, roused from his political apathy, now quietly arranges for Pyle to be assassinated. The romantic entanglement violently solved and political tensions escalating all around them, Phuong returns to Fowler and his new promise of marriage. As ever with Greene, though, it is hardly happy-ever-after: Fowler, plagued by personal guilt and a growing sense of ideological cynicism, ends the novel in anguish, wishing "that there existed someone to whom I could say that I was sorry" (Greene [1955] 2001, 189).

To contemporary readers, it might well be the spectacle of two white men tussling over a Vietnamese woman that seems the novel's least edifying aspect, but on its original publication it was Greene's undisguised anti-Americanism that drew most ire. The *New York Times*, reviewing the novel in March 1956, refuted what it saw as the story's "central thesis," that "America is a crassly materialistic and 'innocent' nation with no understanding of other peoples" (Davis 1956). Greene had been an outspoken critic of the United States in his journalism, and clearly uses *The Quiet American* to play out some of the same sentiment in a fictional story. Given our own historical distance from Cold War tetchiness, however, the accusations of political partisanship seem less convincing. The relationships at the heart of the story effectively map out in human terms the wider geopolitical convergence of Europe, the United States, and Southeast Asia—the imperial dynamics and shifting power relations between them in the mid-twentieth century—and in this way lend the novel an air of uncanny prescience. Greene saw early on in the Cold War what we now know to be the period's lasting legacy: that true absolution, just like a simple political fix, is rarely how the story ends.

SEE ALSO *Central Intelligence Agency (CIA); Cold War; Covert Wars; Decolonization; Vietnam War*

BIBLIOGRAPHY

Davis, Robert Gorham. "In Our Time No Man Is a Neutral." *New York Times*, March 11, 1956. http://www.nytimes.com/books/00/02/20/specials/greene-quiet.html

Greene, Graham. *The Quiet American*. London: Vintage, 2001. First published by Heinemann in 1955.

Mark Storey
Assistant Professor of English
University of Warwick

QUTB, SAYYID

1906–1966

Sayyid Qutb was one of the twentieth-century's most prominent Islamist activists, writers, and thinkers. He was born in September 1906 in Musha, a rural farming village in central Egypt of mixed Muslim and Christian population. By the 1950s, Qutb had become a leading figure of the Society of the Muslim Brotherhood, which spoke out against colonialism, secularization, and Western influence in Egyptian culture. After being accused and convicted of attempting to assassinate Egyptian president Gamal Abdel Nasser (1918–1970), Qutb was hanged by the Nasser regime in 1966. His trial and execution were controversial and were questioned by many around the world.

Qutb was a prolific writer, publishing more than twenty books, including *Maalim fi al-Tariq* (Sign posts), from which many of the charges in the case against Qutb were drawn. In this book, which some describe as the manifesto of political Islam, Qutb lays out a plan and calls for creating a new Muslim society. He showed an early enthusiasm for modern public education, as well as other aspects of modern life. At the same time, he expressed contempt for traditional Quranic schools (*kuttab*) and their teachers and for the traditional Muslim way of life. He attended Dar al-ʿUlum, a teaching college designed to modernize Egyptian education. The college espoused a reformist tradition that was highly influential in the development of Qutb's later thinking.

Until 1945 and the end of World War II, Qutb wrote mostly literary criticism, but after becoming disenchanted with the Wadf Party, an influential nationalist liberal political party in Egypt for a period between the two world wars, his writings began to move toward nationalism and politics. In 1948, he was sent to the United States for two years as part of a government-sponsored program to study the American educational system. His journey took him from New York to what was then Wilson Teachers' College in Washington, DC, the Colorado State College of Education in Greeley, and Stanford University in California.

During his stay in the United States, he wrote articles for Egyptian newspapers and magazines that detailed his impressions of American life. It was a tradition among Egyptian intellectuals who studied in the West to write and entertain their countrymen about certain aspects of Western culture, society, and ways of life. Some of these writers, including Rifaa Rafi al-Tahtawi (1801–1873), Taha Hussein (1889–1973), Tafiq al-Hakim (1898–1987), and Louis Awad (1915–1990), became major literary figures. In general, their writings expressed admiration for the West and an intellectual engagement with modernity, both during their time abroad and later when they were back in Egypt.

After World War II (1939–1945), the intellectual debate was defined and to a great degree dominated by a pessimistic spirit initiated earlier by Oswald Spengler's *The Decline of the West* (1918) and T. S. Eliot's poem *The Waste Land* (1922), which described "the terrible dreariness of the great modern city" (Wilson 2004, 89). The nineteenth-century British philosopher of history Arnold Toynbee's idea of the rise of civilizations and religion was an important part of that debate in both the West and Middle East. Intellectuals in the Middle East also considered socialism as an alternative to Western capitalism, all of which added to the anticolonial liberation debate then occurring in the Egyptian, Arab, and Muslim world. But what influenced Qutb's ideas the most was Alexis Carrel's *Man, the Unknown* (1935), in which Carrel, a French scientist who worked for the Rockefeller Institute of Medical Research, argued that Western civilization is based on doubtful assumptions and mistaken ends. What fascinated Qutb the most about Carrel's conclusions is that "modern civilization seems to be incapable of producing people endowed with imagination, intelligence, and carriage" (21).

Qutb's perception of the United States developed during the short time he spent in the different areas of the country. The America he encountered was not like Egypt, nor did it resemble France, which other Egyptian intellectuals admired. To make sense of this advanced industrial country, he looked to the above-mentioned pessimistic writers. Qutb approached his new experience with apprehension, but he tried to make sense of America. He described his immediate impressions in letters sent to friends back in Egypt and in his poetry, which reflected his nostalgia for the Egyptian intellectual environment. After he left the United States, he serialized these impressions in three long articles titled "The America I Have Seen," published in *al-Risala* magazine in 1950.

From the beginning, Qutb was impressed by America's "vast, far-flung world that occupies in the mind's eye more than its reality on this earth" (quoted in Abdel-Malik 2011, 9). Qutb was neither an academic nor a researcher, so the more he learned about America from Arab students in American colleges at that time and his own observations, the more he withdrew to Alexis Carrel's refuge and became anxious to discuss anything concerning music, sports, religion, sex, or even hairstyles and American primitiveness. Hence, according to Qutb, "America's are the virtue of the brain and hand, and not those of taste and sensibility" (quoted in Abdel-Malik 2011, 9).

When Qutb returned to Egypt, to make sense of the world as he saw it, he took his American experience, Carrel's views about the dehumanizing impact of modernity, and the ideas of Abu al-Hassan al-Nadwi, a prominent Indian Islamic scholar (1914–1999), and Abul Ala Maududi (1903–1979), the Indo-Pakistan Islamist and founder of Jamaat-e-Islami, the largest Islamist party in India, Pakistan, and Bangladesh. Accordingly, the central theme of Qutb's *jahiliyya* (ignorance) depiction of the twentieth century was a synthesis of all of his influences. By describing contemporary Western and Islamic societies as *jahili*, he reduces today's societies to the condition of *jahiliyya* resembling the state of ignorance of God before Islam. After Qutb's tragic death, his followers and sympathizers canonized him, and the problem became not America and the world Qutb saw, but the way his admirers idealized and ideologized his legacy and views.

SEE ALSO *Universities*

BIBLIOGRAPHY

Abdel-Malek, Kamal, and Mouna El Kahla, eds. *America in an Arab Mirror: Images of America in Arabic Travel Literature, 1668 to 9/11 and Beyond.* New York: Palgrave Macmillan, 2011. Includes a translation of Qutb's "The America I Have Seen."

Calvert, John. *Sayyid Qutb and the Origins of Radical Islamism.* New York: Columbia University Press, 2010.

Carrel, Alexis. *Man, the Unknown.* New York and London: Harper, 1935.

Qutb, Sayyid. *Al-Islam wa Mushkilat al-Hadara* [Islam and the problems of civilization]. Cairo: al-Baba al-Halabi, 1962.

Qutb, Sayyid. *Fi Zilal al-Quran* [In the shades of the Quran]. Beirut, Lebanon: Dar al-Shuruq, 1974.

Qutb, Sayyid. *America alti Ra'it* [The America I have seen]. Alexandria, Egypt: Dar al-Madien, 1998.

Qutb, Sayyid. *In the Shade of the Quran.* Leicestershire, UK: Islamic Foundation (UK), 2009.

Shepard, William. *Sayyid Qutb and Islamic Activism: A Translation and Critical Analysis of Social Justice in Islam.* Leiden, Netherlands: Brill, 1996.

Wilson, Edmond. *Axel's Castle: A Study of the Imaginative Literature of 1870–1930.* New York: Farrar, Straus and Giroux, 2004.

Abdullahi Gallab
Associate Professor, African and African American/Religious Studies
Arizona State University

RACE

During the late eighteenth century, the people of the newly inaugurated United States of America busied themselves with determining the precise geographic boundaries of their new nation, debating the nature and meaning of their new constitutional government, and integrating the myriad strands of the American economy. In short, having survived the long and arduous war for their independence, Americans now began the even more difficult work of defining exactly what they and their new nation were.

BUILDING AN AMERICAN RACIAL IDENTITY

For a number of Americans, including prominent citizens like Thomas Jefferson (1743–1826) and Benjamin Franklin (1706–1790), one part of that process of definition was taking a quite definite form. Racial notions of what it meant to be American had existed from the time of the earliest colonists, many of whom saw themselves as the most recent incarnation of the westward moving Anglo-Saxons. Clashes with Native Americans and the importation of African slaves helped to sharpen the racial perspective that the white, Anglo-Saxon colonists were superior and therefore destined to take the natives' lands and completely justified in enslaving the black Africans. By the late 1700s, however, the idea that such superiority and justifications were due to the more advanced cultural, political, and economic institutions of the white Americans was undergoing a dramatic evolution. As historian Reginald Horsman explains, "in the nineteenth century the Americans were to share in the discovery that the secret of Saxon success lay not in the institutions but in the blood" (Horsman 1981, 24).

This transformation in racial thinking, which moved from cultural and institutional to biological explanations for white superiority, was instrumental in building an American identity at home and in helping to shape America's relations with the rest of the world. The same understanding of race that shaped Americans' views of themselves as "Anglo-Americans" also served as a powerful ideological undergirding in the formation of US foreign policy during the nineteenth and twentieth centuries. Sometimes used as a justification for US actions abroad, sometimes functioning as a motivating factor in policy decisions, and, particularly in the post–World War II period, serving as an international embarrassment that hindered relations with much of the Third World, American theories of race—and the resulting racism—were constant elements in US diplomacy.

RACE AS THE DRIVING FORCE OF AMERICA'S WESTWARD EXPANSION

In the first half of the 1800s, as more and more Americans rushed westward to claim land and resources, race played an integral role in justifying the removal and slaughter of Native Americans and the war with Mexico (1846–1848) that led to the acquisition of most of present-day western America. Having been judged by Benjamin Franklin in the late 1700s as "savages that delight in war and take pride in murder" (Franklin 1806, 95), Native Americans by the early 1800s were also seen as a decidedly inferior people who occupied valuable land desired by white Americans. As Andrew Jackson (1767–1845) explained, it defied all logic to leave such valuable real estate in the hands of a "few thousand savages," when millions of white Americans could fill those territories with "all the blessings of liberty, civilization, and religion" (Jackson 1830).

Mexicans fared little better in the racial estimations of their American neighbors. White American settlers to the Mexican territory of Texas chafed under the governance of people they routinely referred to as "apes," "barbarians," and racial "mongrels" who were tainted by mixing with black and Native American blood. When the United States declared war on Mexico in 1846 and proceeded to take two-thirds of the Mexican nation as the victor's spoils in 1848, all under the banner of "manifest destiny," race was again invoked as a justification. The results of the conflict, as one American newspaper opined, were simply the natural outcome of "a superior population" attempting to bring civilization to the barbaric West by "exterminating her [Mexico's] weaker blood" ("The Destiny of Our Country" 1847, 239).

The interweaving of race and American foreign policy was nowhere better illustrated than in the institution of slavery. While generally understood as America's most pressing domestic issue of the first half of the nineteenth

century, slavery also served as a driving force in the nation's westward expansion. Historian Adam Rothman argues that, "Slaveowners and their allies successfully harnessed the resources of the new United States to defend and extend plantation slavery in the early national era" (2005, 219). Yet, slavery also created foreign policy problems. Lecture tours by the ex-slave Frederick Douglass (c. 1818–1895) in Great Britain helped to stir anti-American sentiments among British abolitionists. And when the Civil War (1861–1865) threatened to permanently destroy the Union, President Abraham Lincoln (1809–1865) used the Emancipation Proclamation (1863) to simultaneously destabilize the Confederacy and convince England to remain neutral in the conflict.

The Civil War temporarily halted America's quest for territory, but even though the conflict brought an end to slavery it did little to alter the prevailing racial views of most white Americans. Thus, when the United States entered the imperial competition for markets and resources in the late nineteenth century, race again played an important role in justifying America's overseas expansion. As America's burgeoning industrial and agricultural output led to frequent episodes of overproduction, economic downturns, and unrest among laborers and farmers, the United States looked overseas for both consumers of its factory and farm production and producers of raw materials vital to its economy. In both of the areas primarily targeted by the United States—Latin America and the Far East—race helped to define the purpose of American diplomacy.

THE RACIAL JUSTIFICATION FOR COLONIALISM

Race helped the American public understand the necessity for US intervention in foreign lands, despite their initial skepticism about undertaking a program of colonialism. In the case of the Spanish-American War (1898), American newspapers at first cast the Cuban revolutionaries as "bronzed Europeans" seeking independence from the cruel and inept Spanish. When US military forces discovered that large numbers of the Cuban freedom fighters were, in fact, Afro-Cuban, the American press and government changed their tune and invoked traditional racist stereotypes of African Americans to justify US political and economic "tutelage" of the childlike Cubans.

In the Philippines, race provided a useful explanation for the American occupation of the former Spanish colony. Josiah Strong (1847–1916), the pro-imperialist clergyman, took a somewhat apocalyptic viewpoint by declaring that the Anglo-Saxon race was fighting for its very survival against lesser peoples in the struggle for land, food, and other resources. What was occurring was, in fact, "the final competition of races, for which the Anglo-Saxon is being schooled" (Strong and Mulhall 1889, 49).

Other Americans adopted a more paternalistic approach, pointing out that Asians, in particular, were sitting on unimaginable amounts of wealth and resources but, because of their racial deficiencies, were unable to turn that wealth into civilization and progress. It was, therefore, necessary for Americans to take up what the British writer Rudyard Kipling (1865–1936) referred to as the "white man's burden" and lift these benighted peoples up from barbarism and decadence.

In 1904, at the Louisiana Purchase Exposition held in St. Louis, Americans could see the benefits of carrying that "burden" by visiting the "Philippine Reservation." Over one thousand Filipinos were transported to the United States for the fair. On entering the exhibit, American visitors were brought face to face with "primitive" Filipinos in their "traditional" native settings. These represented the state of the Filipino people prior to the American occupation. As the American tourists moved along, however, they came upon the more "civilized" Filipinos, dressed in Western clothing, attending school, and industriously hunched over American sewing machines. The message was clear: only with America's guidance could the savages ever hope to aspire to civilization and prosperity.

THE IDEOLOGICAL UNDERGIRDING OF US FOREIGN POLICY

Throughout the first decades of the twentieth century, race continued to make its presence known in US relations with the world, whether it was Theodore Roosevelt (1858–1919) chastising the "dagoes" of Colombia for refusing to sell him land in Panama for his canal, or Woodrow Wilson (1856–1924) single-handedly vetoing the Japanese proposal to eliminate racism from international relations at the Versailles Peace Conference, or Franklin Roosevelt (1882–1945) paternalistically declaring that his Good Neighbor Policy was motivated by the fact that Latin Americans believed they were as good as their North American neighbors "and many of them are." With the end of World War II (1939–1945), however, the racial context of America's foreign policy changed dramatically due to events in the United States, as well as dynamic changes in the international realm.

The simultaneous calls for civil rights action at home and cries for independence from colonized peoples abroad put the United States in a new and unfamiliar position in regard to race and foreign policy. The desperate pleas from African Americans for an end to segregation and bias drew the attention of a worldwide audience. Racist acts of violence against black Americans were often front-page news. The Soviet Union had a field day with the issue, pointing out the hypocrisy of US calls for free elections in Eastern Europe while millions of African Americans were

denied the vote. Even allies were concerned that racial discrimination within its own borders detracted from US claims to be the leader of the "free world." The impact went even deeper, however, as colonial peoples in Asia and Africa demanded their own freedom from white subjugation. America's racism toward its own African American population concerned people of color around the globe and made it more difficult for the United States to win the battle for "hearts and minds" in the Third World.

RACE AS PART OF THE INTERNATIONAL DYNAMIC

At least initially, US policy makers in the post–World War II period attempted to deny that America had a serious "race problem" and that whatever small issues remained were being addressed. Soviet propaganda was blamed for painting an inaccurate picture of the civil rights situation in the United States. When it became clear that ignoring the problem would not make it go away, American officials turned to token efforts to try to stem the tide of international criticism of the treatment of African Americans. Black jazz musicians, writers, and athletes were sent on government-sponsored trips abroad, full productions of the opera *Porgy and Bess* (1935) became staples of America's cultural diplomacy, and the Harlem Globetrotters were sent on several world tours, all to show to the world that racism was not a problem in the United States.

The crisis at Little Rock Central High School in Arkansas in 1957, however, came as an unpleasant jolt to American diplomacy. The spectacle of black schoolchildren being screamed at, spat upon, physically assaulted, and, finally, blocked from entering a white high school by Arkansas National Guardsmen inflamed world opinion. The Dwight Eisenhower (1890–1969) administration recognized the foreign policy impact of the events in Little Rock, and the president eventually ordered US troops to protect the black children so that they could attend the school.

Just a year later, at the 1958 World's Fair in Brussels, the US government took on the race issue in the "Unfinished Business" exhibit. Admitting that America had a serious civil rights problem, the exhibit explained what the US government was doing to solve the issue and ended with a portrayal of white and black children playing together. European audiences were generally favorably impressed by this show of honest self-appraisal. Southern congressmen vehemently opposed the exhibit, however, and the Eisenhower administration hastily revised "Unfinished Business" to focus instead on public health. Even in the heat of the Cold War, race trumped a propaganda victory against the Soviets.

Asians and Africans, many of them fighting for their independence from colonial masters, were intimately aware of race as part of the new international dynamic. At the 1955 Bandung Conference in Indonesia, twenty-nine "nonaligned" nations (mostly from Asia and Africa) met to discuss their future. Race was a constant theme, and Carlos Romulo (c. 1898–1985), representing the Philippines, declared that racism was an "albatross around the necks" of those who desired a truly free world. Diplomatic representatives from the newly independent nations witnessed American racism firsthand while they were living in Washington, DC: housing in the nation's capital was segregated, and traveling outside of the capital often resulted in humiliating episodes of African and Asian diplomats being denied the use of restrooms or eating facilities in neighboring Maryland and Virginia.

After the passage of landmark civil rights bills of the mid-1960s, many US officials believed that the issue of race as an international concern had been laid to rest. The violent racial clashes in many northern and western urban areas during the next few years, however, rekindled foreign interest. In addition, America's tacit support of the apartheid regime in South Africa resulted in international denunciations and increasing domestic protest. Both the Soviet Union and Red China hammered away at American racism in their propaganda and portrayed black protest as part of a worldwide "people's revolution."

With the end of the Cold War in the late 1980s also came the virtual end of US propaganda efforts concerning race. The US Information Agency was disbanded in 1999. The election of America's first African American president in 2008 encouraged some observers to declare that the United States was entering a "postracial" period of its history. Race, however, has demonstrated a remarkable staying power. In the wake of the 9/11 terrorist attacks, the United States confronted not only racially inspired assaults on Arab Americans at home, but renewed suspicions abroad that America remained an essentially racist nation. When, in 2012, an adviser to presidential candidate Mitt Romney argued for better relations with America's traditional European allies and declared that "We are part of an Anglo-Saxon heritage," it was not difficult to believe that the close connections between race and US foreign policy had come full circle (Blow 2012).

SEE ALSO *Africa; Atlantic Slave Trade; Back-to-Africa Movement; Captivity Narratives; Colonialism; Colonization Movement; Economics; Gender; "The White Man's Burden" (Rudyard Kipling, 1899)*

BIBLIOGRAPHY

Blow, Charles M. "Anglo-Saxon Heritage, Multicultural Future." *Campaign Stops* (*New York Times* blog), July 25, 2012. http://campaignstops.blogs.nytimes.com/2012/07/25/anglo-saxon-heritage-multicultural-future/

Dain, Bruce. *A Hideous Monster of the Mind: American Race Theory in the Early Republic.* Cambridge, MA: Harvard University Press, 2002.

De León, Arnoldo. *They Called Them Greasers: Anglo Attitudes toward Mexicans in Texas, 1821–1900.* Austin: University of Texas Press, 1983.

"The Destiny of Our Country." *American Review* 5, 3 (1847): 231–239. A Whig journal.

Drinnon, Richard. *Facing West: The Metaphysics of Indian-Hating and Empire Building.* Norman: University of Oklahoma Press, 1997. First published by the University of Minnesota Press in 1980.

Dudziak, Mary L. *Cold War Civil Rights: Race and the Image of American Democracy.* Princeton, NJ: Princeton University Press, 2000.

Dyer, Thomas G. *Theodore Roosevelt and the Idea of Race.* Baton Rouge: Louisiana State University Press, 1980.

Franklin, Benjamin. *The Complete Works, in Philosophy, Politics, and Morals, of the Late Dr. Benjamin Franklin, Now First Collected and Arranged: With Memoirs of His Early Life, Written by Himself.* Vol. 3. London: Printed for J. Johnson, and Longman, Hurst, Rees, and Orme, 1806.

Heywood, Linda, Allison Blakely, Charles Stith, and Joshua C. Yesnowitz, eds. *African Americans in U.S. Foreign Policy: From the Era of Frederick Douglass to the Age of Obama.* Champaign: University of Illinois Press, 2015.

Hietala, Thomas R. *Manifest Design: Anxious Aggrandizement in Late Jacksonian America.* Ithaca, NY: Cornell University Press, 1985.

Horsman, Reginald. *Race and Manifest Destiny: The Origins of American Racial Anglo-Saxonism.* Cambridge, MA: Harvard University Press, 1981.

Hunt, Michael H. *Ideology and U.S. Foreign Policy.* New Haven, CT: Yale University Press, 1987.

Jackson, Andrew. "Second Annual Message to Congress." December 6, 1830. http://millercenter.org/president/jackson/speeches/speech-3634

Kramer, Paul A. *The Blood of Government: Race, Empire, the United States, and the Philippines.* Chapel Hill: University of North Carolina Press, 2006.

Krenn, Michael L. *Black Diplomacy: African Americans and the State Department, 1945–1969.* Armonk, NY: Sharpe, 1999.

Krenn, Michael L. *The Color of Empire: Race and American Foreign Relations.* Washington, DC: Potomac, 2006.

Lauren, Paul Gordon. "Human Rights in History: Diplomacy and Racial Equality at the Paris Peace Conference." *Diplomatic History* 2 (1978): 257–78.

Ledwidge, Mark, Kevern Verney, and Inderjeet Parmar, eds. *Barack Obama and the Myth of a Post-Racial America.* New York: Routledge, 2014.

McAlister, Melani. *Epic Encounters: Culture, Media, and U.S. Interests in the Middle East, 1945–2000.* Berkeley: University of California Press, 2001.

Pike, Fredrick B. *The United States and Latin America: Myths and Stereotypes of Civilization and Nature.* Austin: University of Texas Press, 1992.

Plummer, Brenda Gayle. *Rising Wind: Black Americans and U.S. Foreign Affairs, 1935–1960.* Chapel Hill: University of North Carolina Press, 1996.

Rothman, Adam. *Slave Country: American Expansion and the Origins of the Deep South.* Cambridge, MA: Harvard University Press, 2005.

Rydell, Robert W. *All the World's a Fair: Visions of Empire at American International Expositions, 1876–1916.* Chicago: University of Chicago Press, 1984.

Strong, Josiah, and Michael G. Mulhall. *The United States and the Future of the Anglo-Saxon Race, by Rev. Josiah Strong; and The Growth of American Industries and Wealth, by Michael G. Mulhall.* London: Saxon, 1889.

Weston, Rubin Francis. *Racism in U.S. Imperialism: The Influence of Racial Assumptions on American Foreign Policy, 1893–1946.* Columbia: University of South Carolina Press, 1972.

Michael L. Krenn
Professor of History
Appalachian State University

RAND, AYN
1905–1982

Ayn Rand was a novelist and political thinker whose work, as one of her biographers puts it, is America's "ultimate gateway drug to life on the right" (Burns 2009, 4). Born in 1905 under the name Alisa Zinovyevna Rosenbaum in prerevolutionary St. Petersburg, she completed a degree in history and subsequently pursued studies at the State Technicum for Screen Arts. She then applied for a Soviet passport, purportedly only to visit relatives, but with permanent emigration in mind. In 1926 she reached the United States, where she intended to work as a screenwriter. Around that time she adopted her pen name—a Finnish first name and a surname inspired by the typewriter she used at that time.

In Los Angeles Rand met her future husband, the actor Frank O'Connor (1897–1979), and managed to sell a screenplay, *Red Pawn*. Because of her firsthand knowledge of the film industry, she would later be summoned as a witness to the House Un-American Activities Committee to comment on allegedly pro-Soviet movies. Her first major success was a play, the courtroom drama *Night of January 16th* (1934), which is loosely based on the life of the Swedish entrepreneur Ivar Kreuger. Shortly thereafter she published her debut novel, *We the Living* (1936), a book "as near to an autobiography" as she would ever write (2011, xii). It was turned into two award-winning Italian movies, *Noi Vivi* and *Addio Kira* (1942), albeit with neither Rand's knowledge nor consent.

Although Rand's political ideas animate her early works, including the novella *Anthem* (1938), it is in *The Fountainhead* (1943) that they come to fruition. The novel, a word-of-mouth best seller that was turned into a 1949 movie starring Gary Cooper, is notably influenced by the ideas of the German philosopher Friedrich Nietzsche (1844–1900) in its celebration of individualism and its claim that the creative mind does not owe society's "second-handers" anything. This attitude would later echo in *Atlas Shrugged* (1957), namely in the credo of that novel's protagonist John Galt: "I swear … that I will never live for the sake of another man, nor ask another man to live for mine" (2005, 979).

The Fountainhead and *Atlas Shrugged* encapsulate the essence of Rand's philosophy, objectivism. Thanks to her earlier mentor, the writer Isabel M. Paterson (1886–1961), Rand had developed the philosophic frame of reference to systematize her ideas; she also acknowledged Aristotelian influences. She regarded objectivism as an independent set of tenets distinct from libertarianism. Objectivism holds that there is an objective reality that we as humans can perceive through reason. Our actions should be guided by an ethics of rational self-interest, which entails our rejection of altruism. For Rand, altruism demands self-sacrifice and is not to be mistaken for mere—voluntary—acts of kindness. At the same time, however, rational egoism means that we must identify our objectives in life and be self-reliant rather than simply pursue whims. The political system best suited to allow us to achieve happiness is capitalism.

Rand moved to New York in the late 1940s and established a circle of followers there, including the future chairman of the Federal Reserve Alan Greenspan (b. 1926), that would be instrumental in the promotion of objectivism. Although she was shunned by intellectual circles, Rand became a sought-after speaker and commentator, sharing her ideas in campus lectures and a newsletter. Two think tanks maintain Rand's intellectual legacy: the Ayn Rand Institute, established in 1985 by her heir, the philosopher Leonard Peikoff, and the Atlas Society, established in 1990. Many well-known personalities in American business and politics, in particular politicians associated with the tea party movement and libertarianism, are known as admirers and adherents of Rand's philosophy, including Jimmy Wales (b. 1966), the founder of Wikipedia, and John A. Allison IV (b. 1948), former CEO of BB&T Corp. and the president and CEO of the Cato Institute, a libertarian think tank in Washington, DC. Her impact is also reflected in US popular culture. Steve Ditko, the cocreator of the *Spider-Man* comics, describes himself as an objectivist, and the animated TV series *The Simpsons* parodied her twice.

SEE ALSO *Neoliberalism; Think Tanks*

BIBLIOGRAPHY

Britting, Jeff. *Ayn Rand*. Woodstock, NY: Overlook Press, 2004.

Brühwiler, Claudia Franziska. "'A Is A': Spider-Man, Ayn Rand, and What Man Ought to Be." *PS: Political Science & Politics* 47, 1 (2014): 90–93.

Burns, Jennifer. *Goddess of the Market: Ayn Rand and the American Right*. Oxford: Oxford University Press, 2009.

Heller, Anne C. *Ayn Rand and the World She Made*. New York: Nan A. Talese/Doubleday, 2009.

Rand, Ayn. *Night of January 16th: A Play*. (1934.) New York: Signet, 1987.

Rand, Ayn. *We the Living*. (1936.) New York: Signet, 2011.

Rand, Ayn. *Anthem*. (1938.) London: Penguin, 2008.

Rand, Ayn. *The Fountainhead*. (1943.) New York: Signet, 1996.

Rand, Ayn. *Atlas Shrugged*. (1957.) New York: Signet, 2005.

Rand, Ayn. *Answers: The Best of Her Q & A*. Edited by Robert Mayhew. New York: New American Library, 2005.

Claudia Franziska Brühwiler
Lecturer and Postdoctoral Researcher in American Studies
University of St. Gallen, Switzerland

RAND CORPORATION

The Rand Corporation is an American nonprofit research organization headquartered in Santa Monica, California. As of 2015, it had offices in four other cities in the United States, as well as the United Kingdom and Australia. Rand employs some 1,800 staff with expertise in the natural sciences, engineering, and the social sciences. It counted at least 350 clients and grant supporters in 2014, providing revenue of nearly $270 million. While most of the Rand Corporation's 2014 revenue came from US national security agencies, the US Department of Health and Human Services was also a major supporter. Significantly smaller portions of revenue came from other government entities (including non-US), universities, philanthropies and nonprofits, and the private sector.

Rand's origins can be traced to Project Rand, a research effort begun in late 1945 at Douglas Aircraft Company's Santa Monica facilities under the sponsorship of the US Army Air Forces. The project's name was a play on the phrase "research and development"—a slight misnomer given its explicit focus on "research" to the exclusion of actual "development." The project's formal contract of 1946 called for Douglas to investigate intercontinental air warfare and advise the US Army Air Forces concerning the selection and use of relevant equipment. In 1948, the Rand contract was transferred from Douglas to the nonprofit Rand Corporation, which was created to receive it.

As a private nonprofit working under contract with the US Air Force, Rand represented one possible solution to a problem that World War II (1939–1945) had posed: how to structure relations among scientific researchers, the military, and the government. Science was plainly crucial to the development of many key technologies of the war. However, scientists might serve government in many different capacities. They might be uniformed officers; employees at for-profit corporations building weapons to military specifications; government employees and advisers outside military classification; or university professors working under contract with military or civilian agencies. Each arrangement had advantages and disadvantages in terms of its ability to provide independent and relevant advice to policy makers and its attractiveness to technical talent.

Rand thus had both institutional strengths and weaknesses. Although it was not a university, its broad mission, munificence, and liberal publication policies made it attractive to researchers with significant academic credentials. Yet providing truly "independent" advice could be difficult. Lodging the Rand contract in a nonprofit corporation may have separated it from the defense contractors whose products its researchers were evaluating, but prior to the 1960s Rand remained largely dependent on US Air Force patronage. This could be problematic if Rand recommendations clashed with air force institutional objectives, as they did on more than one occasion during the 1950s. Partly as a result, in the 1960s the Rand Corporation began to cultivate clients other than the air force, providing advice to other government agencies on budgeting, program assessment, and logistics, among other things. More recently, Rand has developed expertise in the economics of health care.

Rand's influence on policy can be difficult to assess precisely. The corporation's research was referenced in a number of high-level policy debates during the Cold War era, and in some instances, apparently triggered changes in national security strategy. For example, a famous 1954 study convincingly argued that Air Force air-base selection doctrine had left the United States' nuclear deterrent vulnerable to Soviet surprise attack. In other instances, research done by the corporation's staff entered the political arena in less controlled ways. Thus, in 1971 former Rand analyst Daniel Ellsberg leaked a study of US involvement in the Vietnam War (the so-called Pentagon Papers) that he had helped prepare while at Rand.

Rand's influence has been felt in other ways as well. Throughout the years, the Rand Corporation has spun off operations that subsequently became important entities in their own right, such as the Systems Development Corporation. The corporation's alumni have spread signature Rand ideas like "systems analysis" and defense budgeting far and wide in government and industry. Moreover, ideas developed or refined at Rand—such as linear programming, dynamic programming, and game theory—have also proven influential in university departments of economics, political science, operations research, and business schools. Some twenty-nine Rand research staff members have gone on to win Nobel Prizes, mostly in economics. In popular culture, Rand was satirized by folk singer Pete Seeger's "Rand Hymn," dating to the early 1960s. Rand it was also presumably referenced as "the Bland Corporation" in Stanley Kubrick's 1964 film *Dr. Strangelove*. In short, Rand was—and remains—an iconic institution in American and world intellectual culture.

SEE ALSO *Air Force, US; Think Tanks*

BIBLIOGRAPHY

Abella, Alex. *Soldiers of Reason: The Rand Corporation and the Rise of the American Empire.* Orlando, FL: Harcourt, 2008.

Jardini, David. "Out of the Blue Yonder: The Transfer of Systems Thinking from the Pentagon to the Great Society, 1961–1965." In *Systems, Experts, and Computers: The Systems Approach in Management and Engineering, World War II and After*, edited by Agatha C. Hughes and Thomas P. Hughes, 311–357. Cambridge, MA: MIT Press, 2000.

Kaplan, Fred M. *The Wizards of Armageddon.* New York: Simon and Schuster, 1983.

Rand Corporation. http://www.rand.org

Smith, Bruce L. R. *The Rand Corporation: Case Study of a Nonprofit Advisory Corporation.* Cambridge, MA: Harvard University Press, 1966.

Paul Erickson
History Department
Wesleyan University

RASTAFARI

Rastafari is a relatively new religious movement with origins in Jamaica in the 1930s. An African-centered tradition, it was named for the former emperor of Ethiopia, Haile Selassie I (1892–1975), who was born Tafari Makonnen Woldemikael and whose title of nobility was *ras*. Rastafari developed among descendants of African slaves who understood themselves as exploited and oppressed people in exile. It also drew on Judeo-Christian traditions by claiming that people of African descent were the new Israelites and that as God's chosen people they would be led out of oppression by a divine leader. Many consider Rastafari a resistance movement because participants generally see themselves as struggling against the Christian mainstream and the oppressive forces of poverty and racism.

Rastafari grew out of the teachings of Marcus Garvey (1887–1940), a Jamaican black nationalist known for his Pan-Africanism. Garvey told Jamaicans to look for the crowning of an African king who would be the redeemer of black people, and Rastas believe that Selassie was that king. Leonard P. Howell (1898–1981), also a Jamaican, expanded on Garvey's teachings and articulated some of the founding principles associated with the Rastafari tradition. He insisted that Selassie was the living god and rightful leader of all people of African descent and that he would provide for the return of diasporic Africans to the continent. Howell also taught that black people were chosen by God and superior to whites, that white people were evil and could not be trusted, and that people of African descent would soon rule the world. He also led a group in forming the Pinnacle commune in the Jamaican hills. After repeated raids by the government, Howell and his followers were relocated to Kingston, where the tradition began to develop within an urban setting.

Haile Selassie's visit to Jamaica in the 1960s propelled the Rastafari movement to greater prominence and increased its momentum. It was also around this time that reggae music developed. The international success of Jamaican reggae musicians like Bob Marley (1945–1981) moved the Rastafari tradition into the Jamaican mainstream and increased its visibility outside the country. Since the late twentieth century Rastafari has become more interracial, as many of the early teachings about the natural superiority of black people have been played down or rejected by many contemporary Rastas.

Because there is no organized or centralized system of governance within the Rasta community, nor a set creed, Rastafari is highly diverse. Even so, there are a number of common symbols and practices associated with this tradition. The lion is an important symbol of Selassie, the "Conquering Lion of Judah." The colors red, green, gold, and black are also symbolically significant, with red representing the blood of Jamaican martyrs, green the Jamaican vegetation and the hope of success over the forces of oppression, gold the wealth and promise of Ethiopia, and black the color of people of African descent. Another important and highly visible religious symbol is a Rasta's hair, which is not cut but instead allowed to form dreadlocks. A Rasta's hair represents a lion's mane and is an outward expression of one's affiliation and rejection of the status quo. Among a number of explanations given for this tradition, the most common is based on a biblical command that a man not shave his head nor cut the corners of his beard.

Certain practices are associated with Rastafari, such as eating a plant-based diet and refraining from eating meat and animal products. Smoking cannabis, or marijuana, is considered a religious practice among many Rastas, as it is said to aid in meditation by calming the smoker, to provide a deeper sense of community, and to produce religious visions. Although there are no set times or places of worship within the Rasta community, the gathering of Rastas in meetings is common, especially in Jamaica. Some of these meetings are relatively mundane and are used to discuss business issues, while others concern communal practice. The biggest and most important meeting is the Nyabingi, during which participants from all over Jamaica spend several days praying, dancing, eating, and smoking cannabis.

SEE ALSO *Ali, Muhammad; Black Power Movement; Islam; Malcolm X; Moorish Science Temple; Nation of Islam; Orientalism; Universal Negro Improvement Association (UNIA)*

BIBLIOGRAPHY

Barrett, Leonard E. *The Rastafarians.* Boston: Beacon Press, 1997.

Chevannes, Barry. *Rastafari: Roots and Ideology.* Syracuse, NY: Syracuse University Press, 1994.

Edmonds, Ennis B. *Rastafari: A Very Short Introduction.* Oxford: Oxford University Press, 2012.

Monica C. Reed
Instructor of Religious Studies
Louisiana State University

REAGAN, RONALD WILSON
1911–2004

Ronald Reagan, the fortieth president of the United States, remains something of a chameleon, though changing according to perspective rather than context. Some see him as incompetent, wayward, disengaged, and overly influenced by his wife, Nancy Reagan. Others see him as an effective statesman either because of his pragmatic pursuit of core objectives, or because of an aggressive agenda dictated by his right-wing ideology. Common to all these views are elements of truth distorted by partisanship. Reagan is partly to blame for this. The robustness of his political declarations could be divisive. They were also sometimes misread, and often he spoke somewhat differently to different constituencies.

Soon after Reagan's presidential election victory in 1980, the journalist Hedrick Smith struck a characterization that spoke of "two Reagans," which resonates down the years. Smith wrote of Reagan as a populist rhetorical right-winger bemoaning Soviet advances in the world, warning of the dangerous consequences, and advocating

robust countermeasures, but also as someone who was pragmatic and measured in his actual actions (Smith 1981, 98). How Reagan developed into this rather complex personality has much to do with the richness of experience in his prepresidential career.

PREPRESIDENTIAL CAREER

Reagan was not a born Republican, but like Democratic president Woodrow Wilson (1856–1924), he believed that "liberty has never come from government. The history of liberty is the history of limitation of government's power, not the increase of it" (Reagan 1992, 135). By 1960, he believed that the Democratic Party had moved a long way from that principle, and he thus became Republican. Along the way from being a Democrat to becoming a Republican, he worked as a radio sports commentator, had a successful film acting career beginning in 1937, and transitioned to television in 1954, hosting *General Electric Theater*. Interwoven throughout was a web of public and political activity, informed after 1945 with strong anticommunist beliefs. Reagan served as president of the Screen Actors Guild from 1947 to 1952 and again in 1959. After he began hosting *General Electric Theater*, he also traveled around General Electric factories, delivering talks that stood him in great stead for developing his oratorical skills. By the early 1960s, the call of politics began to take hold.

Reagan emerged as a significant political figure in 1964 when he campaigned for Barry Goldwater (1909–1998), the Republican presidential candidate. In 1967, he succeeded in becoming the governor of California and served for two consecutive terms. This was a hugely important experience for Reagan. At the time, if California had been an independent state, its economy would have ranked seventeenth in size in the world. In 1976, Reagan fought Gerald Ford (1913–2006) for the Republican nomination but failed, and then campaigned on Ford's behalf in his losing battle with Jimmy Carter (b. 1924).

REAGAN'S WORLDVIEW

In 1980, the story was different. Reagan beat Carter in what approached a landslide victory. That victory was largely due to three key views that Reagan sold to the American people and which were dear to his own heart. The first concerned economics. Reagan rejected the need for interference by government and reasserted the free market, limited only by the need to ensure that its operations did not restrict the freedom of anyone. The second was on security, the need to renew America's military strength, contain communism, and reduce the threat of nuclear Armageddon. Thirdly and finally, and perhaps most importantly, America's faith in itself had to be restored. These principles informed all that Reagan did in his two terms as president, but they were sometimes camouflaged by the pragmatism with which he pursued them.

From this emerges a somewhat more nuanced statesman. But before exploring that, it is important to record what is incontestable about Reagan: his sense of purpose to restore American power and prestige; his unwavering belief that the United States was exceptional and God-fearing with its democracy, free market, and rights protected by law; that as a nation-state, the United States was *the* force for good in the world and should confront the spread of communism and support anticommunist freedom fighters everywhere; and that personal relationships count in world politics. After that, things become more difficult.

Reagan's view of the world was painted in broad brushstrokes, but it was not simplistic, nor was he naive. In order to interrogate these claims, what follows will examine in turn Reagan's views on the Middle East, communism, and the importance of personal relationships in diplomacy. The latter discussion will explore his friendship with Soviet leader Mikhail Gorbachev (b. 1931) and his relationship with British prime minister Margaret Thatcher (1925–2013).

THE MIDDLE EAST

The turbulent complexities of the Middle East were exacerbated for Reagan by the triumph of the ayatollahs in Iran and had an impact on four perspectives and interests that he saw as defining the region for the United States. First and foremost of course, the United States had strategic and economic interests in the Middle East, which had to be protected. Secondly, Reagan was committed to ensuring the survival of the State of Israel. Thirdly, he recognized the complexities of ethnic, religious, factional, and geopolitical interests that plagued the region. And finally, he was determined to prevent further Soviet encroachment into the area. This collection of perspectives and interests was often not easy to reconcile.

In many ways, the Middle East was the least successful policy area abroad for Reagan. Little progress was made on reconciling Jews and Arabs, and there was a long and bitter dispute with Israel over the US sale of AWACSs (airborne warning and control systems) to Saudi Arabia despite repeated assurances by Washington that it would not allow Israel's security to be jeopardized. Further difficulties arose when Israel invaded Lebanon in 1982. Israel's actions led directly to an American military presence in Beirut to try to stabilize the situation, but 214 marines then fell victim to terrorist car bombs in October 1983, and the United States rapidly withdrew.

The Middle East also occasioned the biggest scandal of the Reagan era. During Reagan's second term, the United States secretly sold $30 million worth of arms to Iran, but only $12 million appeared in the US government account. The other $18 million had been redirected elsewhere, and at least some of it went illegally to the Nicaraguan Contras courtesy of Colonel Oliver North (b. 1943). Reagan apparently blanched when White House Chief of Staff Donald Regan (1918–2003) informed him of North's activities. In the ensuing furor, including congressional investigations, many thought Reagan was lucky to emerge only somewhat tarnished (Regan 1988, 38).

One area in the Middle East that did provide a more immediate success story was Afghanistan, where the Central Intelligence Agency's Operation Cyclone provided increasing amounts of financing, primarily for the mujahideen. The program started under President Carter, but was vastly expanded under Reagan and reached over $600 million in 1987. Its effect on the Soviet occupation was severe and contributed to the Soviets' eventual withdrawal in 1988 to 1989. However, arming fundamentalist Islamists also proved to have damaging consequences for the United States and its allies in the longer term. The Middle East is a notoriously difficult area for Western powers, and Reagan and the deployment of his principles there only had limited success: elsewhere the story was different.

COMMUNISM AND THE SOVIET UNION

During the 1980 election campaign, Reagan noted: "the Soviets have been racing but with no competition. No one else is racing. And so I think that we'd get a lot farther at the table if they know that as they continue, they're faced with our industrial capacity and all that we can do" (Smith 1981, 98). From that premise followed a series of policies. Reagan aimed to reseize the high ground morally and condemned the evils of communism publicly and repeatedly. He increased defense spending massively and authorized aggressive action by the Central Intelligence Agency (CIA). CIA director William Casey (1913–1987) was conferred with an unprecedented cabinet post, which indicates just how important Reagan thought such actions were. He generally tightened up on strategic exports to the communist bloc and demoted the importance of human rights abroad in favor of engaging with and supporting anticommunist freedom fighters.

What did Reagan actually hope to achieve by these measures? First and foremost, he wanted to renew US strength and the country's sense of self-worth and to regain international respect. To do that, he worked with hard-line advisers and officials, including Casey; William P. Clark (1931–2013), national security adviser; Caspar Weinberger (1917–2006), secretary of defense; Richard Perle (b. 1941), assistant secretary of defense for international security policy; Richard Pipes (b. 1923), initially the main Soviet specialist on the National Security Council (NSC); and Lawrence J. Brady (b. 1939), assistant secretary of commerce for export administration. Like these hard-liners, Reagan's language was often provocative and harsh, but his actions toward the Soviets were consistently more moderate. In 1983, when the administration formulated its main Cold War strategy, there was every intent to wage the Cold War more vigorously. But the policy was also intended for "the long haul … the U.S. must demonstrate credibly that its policy is not a blueprint for an open-ended, sterile confrontation with Moscow, but a serious search for a stable and constructive long-term basis for U.S.-Soviet relations" (National Security Decision, Directive Number 75, "US Relations with the USSR," 1983).

The hard-liners wanted to challenge and exhaust the Soviet system and bring about regime change. Reagan had a different agenda. As the United States renewed its military strength and Reagan won international respect (albeit grudgingly from some), the balance in the administration between the pragmatists and the ideological hard-liners shifted. Pipes left after only two years, and Secretary of State Al Haig's (1924–2010) successor, George Shultz (b. 1920), gradually outmaneuvered the vestiges of the ideological hard-liners in a way Haig had not managed to do.

The year 1983 was a crucible for change. On March 8, Reagan made his most notorious speech on the Soviet Union in front of the National Association of Evangelicals in Florida, condemning the Soviet Union as an "evil empire." Later that month, he announced the Strategic Defense Initiative, or the Star Wars program, as it was widely dubbed. The tone was harsh at the outset of the year, and in the autumn a series of events cast an even deeper pall over US-Soviet relations. On September 1, 1983, the Soviets shot down KAL-007, a Korean civilian airliner. On October 6, much to Soviet embarrassment, Lech Wałesa (b. 1943), the Polish head of the Solidarity union who had led the movement toward democracy before the declaration of martial law in Poland, was awarded the Nobel Peace Prize. In the Caribbean, a US force invaded Grenada to restore order, protect US lives, and overthrow the communist regime there. In early November, the Soviets briefly believed that a North Atlantic Treaty Organization exercise known as Able Archer was real, that is, a preemptive Western strike against the Soviet Union. And finally, in November, the United States started to deploy Pershing II missiles and cruise missiles in Europe, leading the Soviets to walk out of the arms talks in Geneva. It was against this backdrop of rising tensions that Reagan shifted tack.

RELATIONSHIP WITH GORBACHEV

Reagan had renewed American strength and regained America's sense of self-worth. To his mind, he had achieved the position from which he could negotiate effectively. Furthermore, Reagan had a visceral horror of nuclear weapons. The intelligence that the Soviets had thought Able Archer might be an actual attack horrified him. This was another incentive to talk with the Soviets, and his goal was negotiation, not the collapse of or uncontrollable turmoil in the Soviet Union. It was on these objectives that he parted company with the hard-liners in his entourage, and for which he engaged with and befriended Gorbachev in an effort to talk down Cold War tensions and radically reduce nuclear weapon systems. At this point, the personal dimension entered into play.

Reagan was forthright in the United Nations General Assembly in September 1984: "America has repaired its strength…. We are ready for constructive negotiations with the Soviet Union." In December 1984, British prime minister Thatcher met Gorbachev at Chequers, her official country residence. She pronounced him to be a man with whom she could do business. Shortly after, in March 1985, Gorbachev became leader of the Soviet Union, and the world discovered that Reagan also could do business with him.

There was now no more talk of the evil empire. Shultz soon became the key policy maker for US relations with the Soviets, and Reagan gave him the task of exploring new avenues of communication. Back in 1983, the Soviet specialist Jack F. Matlock (b. 1929) was brought into the NSC to craft a negotiating strategy for dealing with the Soviets and to end the arms race. He became a key figure in the development of Reagan's Cold War strategy and directly oversaw the fruits of much of his own planning after becoming US ambassador to the Soviet Union in 1987. By 1985, this forward planning had already begun to pay off, with Reagan pushing forward vigorously for negotiations with Gorbachev and radical disarmament.

In a series of head-to-head meetings, Reagan and Gorbachev began to negotiate down the Cold War. Two aspects of this are startling. First, that the negotiations were so successful. Second, that it was Reagan on the US side who was so insistent on moving forward with the Soviets. He worked closely with Gorbachev because he came to trust and like him. Contrary to much of the advice from the Pentagon and the CIA, Reagan pressed on with his version of détente. Together, Reagan and Gorbachev succeeded. It was not just because of their personal chemistry, but the relationship was important.

RELATIONSHIP WITH THATCHER

Personal chemistry was even more in evidence with Reagan's closest ally, Thatcher. However, that friendship was severely tested in the 1982 Falklands War, because support for Britain compromised Reagan's support for anticommunist forces in Latin America.

From the outset of his presidency, Reagan believed that President Carter's priorities had to be modified, especially in America's backyard—Latin America—in order to turn around what he saw as a rising tide of communism there. Human rights would have to take second place behind the need to support noncommunist regimes, irrespective of their human rights record. The leading articulator of this policy was the US ambassador to the United Nations, Jeane Kirkpatrick (1926–2006), who believed that it was possible and desirable to distinguish between irredeemable communist and redeemable noncommunist authoritarian regimes. Reagan's rhetoric consistently echoed such views, though it was not until February 1985 that they coalesced into the Reagan Doctrine: "We must stand by all our democratic allies. And we must not break faith with those who are risking their lives—on every continent, from Afghanistan to Nicaragua—to defy Soviet-supported aggression and secure rights which have been ours from birth." Squaring these views with support for Prime Minister Thatcher during the Falklands War was not easy. Kirkpatrick in particular was adamant that supporting Britain would alienate US allies and undermine concerted efforts against communism in Latin America. Reagan had a difficult choice to make.

Thatcher and Reagan's mutual affection is indisputable, and when the Falklands crisis erupted, it counted. Later Reagan recalled: "The depth of this special relationship made it impossible for us to remain neutral during Britain's war with Argentina over the Falkland Islands in 1982, although it was a conflict in which I had to walk a fine line" (Reagan 1992, 357).

When Argentina illegally seized the Falklands by military force on the pretext that they were the Argentine Malvinas Islands, walking a fine line was indeed necessary. In addition to endangering US relations with Latin American states that were fighting communists, the Falklands crisis raised concerns related to Britain's latter-day imperialism and interference in the Western Hemisphere by a European power, contrary to the strictures of the Monroe Doctrine. Reagan seemingly confronted an impossible situation, but he acted decisively, cutting to what he saw as the quick of the matter, and overrode the United States' immediate Cold War priorities. He was prepared to discount the adverse repercussions that would inevitably arise among members of the Organization of American States at Britain's military counter-intervention because of affection for Thatcher, loyalty to the Anglo-American special relationship, and the rule of international law. When hostilities began, the United States assisted the British with intelligence, logistics, and weapons to help prosecute the war to a successful conclusion.

CONCLUSION

Reagan was a consummate politician who brought a unique array of talents to the job of reinvigorating US foreign policy. Not everything went smoothly, as the tragedy in Beirut and the Iran-Contra affair demonstrate only too well, but Reagan achieved much. He had clear broad objectives that arose from the way that he saw the world and robustly pursued them. He believed that it was possible to change the strategic landscape of the Cold War and reduce the horror posed by nuclear weapons by renewing US power, both hard and soft. Once that was accomplished, he negotiated from a position of strength, aided and abetted by his ability to establish close personal relationships with other world leaders. The result was a dramatic reduction of the nuclear arsenals of the United States and the Soviet Union. Interestingly, while he was single-minded and determined to halt what he perceived as the progressive expansion of communism, he was not dogmatic. He recognized that reform of the Soviet Union was infinitely better than its collapse and he was prepared to set aside his immediate Cold War priorities during the Falklands War in order to help his personal friend and closest ally. Few presidents have entered the White House with a clearer vision of what they wanted to do; even fewer consummated as much of their vision as Reagan.

SEE ALSO *Cold War; Détente; Exceptionalism; Freedom Fighters; Friedman, Milton; Iran-Contra Scandal; Neoliberalism; Nuclear Weapons; Strategic Defense Initiative (Star Wars); War on Drugs*

BIBLIOGRAPHY

Cannon, Lou. *President Reagan: The Role of a Lifetime.* New York: Simon and Schuster, 1991.

Dobson, Alan P. "The Reagan Administration, Economic Warfare, and the Closing Down of the Cold War." *Diplomatic History* 29, 3 (2005): 531–556.

Fisher, Beth A. *The Reagan Reversal: Foreign Policy and the End of the Cold War.* Colombia: University of Missouri Press, 1997.

Kirkpatrick, Jeane. "Dictatorships and Double Standards." *Commentary Magazine* 68, 5 (1979): 34–45.

Mann, James. *The Rebellion of Ronald Reagan: A History of the End of the Cold War.* New York: Viking, 2009.

Matlock, Jack F., Jr. *Reagan and Gorbachev: How the Cold War Ended.* New York: Random House, 2004.

Reagan, Ronald. National Security Decision, Directive Number 75: "US Relations with the USSR." January 17, 1983. http://www.reagan.utexas.edu/archives/reference/Scanned%20NSDDS/NSDD75.pdf

Reagan, Ronald. "Address to the 39th Session of the United Nations General Assembly in New York, New York." September 24, 1984. http://www.reagan.utexas.edu/archives/speeches/1984/92484a.htm

Reagan, Ronald. "Address before a Joint Session of the Congress on the State of the Union." February 6, 1985. http://www.reagan.utexas.edu/archives/speeches/1985/20685e.htm

Reagan, Ronald. *An American Life*. New York: Pocket Books, 1992. First published in 1990 by Simon and Schuster.

Regan, Donald T. *For the Record: From Wall Street to Washington*. London: Hutchinson, 1988.

Smith, Geoffrey. *Reagan and Thatcher*. London: Bodley Head, 1990.

Smith, Hedrick. "Reagan's World." In *Reagan: The Man, the President*, by Hedrick Smith, Adam Clymer, Leonard Silk, Robert Linsey, and Richard Burt, 95–127. Oxford: Pergamon Press, 1981.

Alan P. Dobson
Professor (Honorary)
Swansea University

REALISM (INTERNATIONAL RELATIONS)

Realism is an intellectual paradigm in the study of international relations. It has long been considered the dominant school of thought for conceptualizing world politics. Realism is based on five core assumptions. First, states are by far the most important actors in world politics, be they ancient Greek or Italian city-states, dynastic-imperial states, or modern nation-states. Individuals, multinational corporations, political parties, and domestic interest groups simply do not matter much to realists, who believe these entities have little influence on world politics compared to that of states.

Second, the international states system is anarchic, with no higher authority (such as a world government) policing states' behavior. Because of anarchy, and third, states must constantly be mindful of their external security above all, as there is no other entity they can appeal to or rely on if their survival is threatened. In an anarchic world, where today's friend could be tomorrow's enemy, states typically define their interests in terms of how much power they have or can get relative to other states around them.

Fourth, realists argue that states typically approach world politics as integrated, single units rationally responding to their external environment, rather than as coalitions of diverse domestic constituencies with competing aims. Because of the weighty effects of anarchy, states' objectives are predominantly conditioned by external rather than internal sources. Realists therefore do not ascribe much importance to domestic and individual factors—culture, regime type, ideology, or particular leaders' personalities, for example—when compared with the influence of international factors.

Finally, most realists agree that the most important external incentive acting upon states, aside from anarchy, is the international distribution of power. Traditionally, most realists have emphasized the importance of a balance of power for checking the influence of aggressive, power-hungry states under anarchy (e.g., Morgenthau 1960; Waltz 1979; Mearsheimer 2001). More recently, however, other realists have posited instead that international peace and stability are best achieved not by balancing power, but by the imbalance or preponderance of power favoring one state standing above all the rest (e.g., Gilpin 1981; Wohlforth 1999). In spite of this divide, realists remain united in attributing great importance to the distribution of power between states for determining the trajectory of world politics.

INTELLECTUAL HISTORY

Realist thought traces its roots to classical and early modern political theorists. For instance, Thucydides's famous account of the Peloponnesian War (fifth century BCE) emphasized the role of shifting distributions of power in provoking the conflict between Athens and Sparta, while also pointing to the prudence of statesmen remaining mindful of the realities and limits of power when conducting statecraft. Niccolò Machiavelli's (1469–1527) most well-known work, *The Prince*, is read today as a handbook for how to gain, command, and exercise power in statecraft. And in *Leviathan*, Thomas Hobbes (1588–1679) articulated the bleak depiction of human nature, particularly under anarchy, that forms the basis of the realist view of world politics (see Viotti and Kauppi 2012, 42–52).

Yet with the emergence of international relations as its own distinct intellectual discipline in the twentieth century, the majority of modern realism's most influential contributors have been Americans. Along with the theologian Reinhold Niebuhr (1892–1971), the German American academic Hans Morgenthau (1904–1980) was responsible for articulating the most comprehensive conception of political realism early in the postwar era. In his famous *Politics among Nations*, Morgenthau argued that the political realist above all "believes that politics … is governed by objective laws that have their roots in human nature," rather than in abstract principle and moralistic thinking (Morgenthau 1960, 4).

Morgenthau's conception remained paramount until American scholar Kenneth Waltz's (1924–2013) seminal 1979 update to realist theory, *Theory of International Politics*. Morgenthau's brand of realism (now typically referred to as classical realism) often emphasized the importance of historical context to explain particular foreign policy decisions, as well as the importance of human nature in accounting for realism's bleak view of world politics. By contrast, Waltz's structural realism (also known as neorealism) exclusively emphasizes the role of international structure—the general condition of anarchy and the particular distribution of power at a given time—for explaining decisions and outcomes in world politics. Notable contemporary realists, including American scholars John Mearsheimer and Stephen Walt, have followed in Waltz's structural realist footsteps, seeking to build a more scientific and testable version of realism than the realists of prior generations (Lebow 2013, 59–76; Mearsheimer 2013, 77–93).

INFLUENCE ON AMERICAN FOREIGN RELATIONS

In spite of American scholars' central role in developing the realist paradigm, realists themselves typically agree that Americans have long been averse to realist ideas and policy prescriptions (Drezner 2008). Some of realism's central tenets—that internally dissimilar states behave similarly and that international politics is more about power than values—directly challenge the idea of American exceptionalism. As one realist famously put it, "realism is at odds with the deep-seated sense of optimism and moralism that pervades much of American society. Liberalism, on the other hand, fits neatly with those values. Not surprisingly, foreign policy discourse in the United States often sounds as if it has been lifted right out of a Liberalism 101 lecture" (Mearsheimer 2001, 23). International relations liberals are more optimistic about cooperation and progress in world politics. They also believe that states' internal characteristics are invaluable in explaining their foreign policy choices and behaviors. In combination, these elements allow liberalism to fit comfortably alongside ideas of American exceptionalism: the United States is a different kind of actor in international relations, and its rise to power has been a significant impetus for positive change in world politics.

Though realists agree that the American public dislikes the rhetoric of realism, they have been more divided on how often US leaders adopt realist policies in practice. Some believe that, for good or for ill, the United States has never really behaved as realists would predict or advise. Lamenting the dominance of "legalist-moralist" thinking in policy making, the prominent Cold War diplomat and scholar George Kennan (1904–2005) famously decried "a curious American tendency to search, at all times, for a single external center of evil, to which all [its] troubles can be attributed" (Kennan 1951, 154). Others have argued that while the United States is rhetorically averse to realist propositions, American leaders have often wholeheartedly embraced realist strategic principles in practice (e.g., Morgenthau 1950; Mearsheimer 2001; Drezner 2008). Still others have posited that the United States often does submit to realist principles,

but by embracing a distinctly "American realism" (Rice 2008) that includes a commitment to liberal principles like democracy promotion and an open economic order between states (Dueck 2006, 33).

INFLUENCE IN AMERICAN FOREIGN RELATIONS

In spite of the contestation over realism's influence in US foreign policy making, some of America's most prominent foreign policy practitioners in the twentieth century have been self-professed realists. This includes Kennan, Richard Nixon, Henry Kissinger, Zbigniew Brzezinski, George H. W. Bush, James Baker, Brent Scowcroft, and Condoleezza Rice. Notable antirealists include Woodrow Wilson, Jimmy Carter, Ronald Reagan, and, more controversially, Bill Clinton and George W. Bush.

America's most prominent grand strategic debates of the twentieth century often involved realist ideas and policy prescriptions. In calling for America and the world to embrace a fundamentally new vision of international relations through the League of Nations, Wilson is often described as the ultimate antirealist (e.g., Kissinger 1994, 29–55). By contrast, Wilson's chief domestic rival on the issue of the League of Nations, Senator Henry Cabot Lodge (1850–1924), offered a much more realist alternative: a traditional security alliance with France meant to restore a balance of power to Europe. In fact, the birth of modern realist thought is often traced back to critiques of Wilson, characterizing his attempt to fundamentally transform world politics as foolish and his ultimate failure as inevitable (e.g., Carr 1964).

The Cold War is typically treated as the heyday of realism's influence on American foreign policy (Mead 2002, 66–77). Kennan became famous for articulating a policy of containment against the Soviet Union (USSR). True to realist prescription, his vision called for the United States to focus on limiting Soviet material power in certain strategic theaters rather than waging a global ideological struggle based on universal moral principles (Gaddis 2005, 24–86). Nixon and Kissinger sought detente—or a relaxation of tensions—with the Russians based on the realist assumption that strategic interests were (or should be) more important than abstract values related to ideology or human rights. Realists Baker, Scowcroft, and Rice occupied key positions in the George H. W. Bush administration and adopted many realist policies as the Cold War ended. This included decisions to not heavily sanction China after the Tiananmen Square massacre in 1989; to avoid excessive triumphalism in the wake of the Berlin Wall collapse and German reunification in 1989 to 1990; to encourage caution as many Eastern European regimes sought to rapidly emancipate from the Soviet Union; and, after Cold War tensions had largely subsided, to nonetheless insist on the continuation of the North Atlantic Treaty Organization as the dominant security institution through which a balance of power could be maintained in Europe (Engel 2010).

In the Cold War's later years, realists battled with liberals and neoconservatives who called for renewed focus on the ideological and moralistic aspects of the conflict with the USSR. The Carter and Reagan administrations each embraced aspects of these positions, rebuking realists. The former elevated the importance of human rights issues while bringing attention to Soviet abuses. The latter sought to reframe the conflict as a moral struggle against an "evil empire" that needed to be defeated rather than contained (Mead 2002, 74–77).

In the grand strategic debates that have taken place since the Cold War's end, realists have been informally divided into two camps. Neo-isolationists (e.g., Gholz, Press, and Sapolsky 1997; Layne 2006) argue that the United States should largely disengage from its Asian and European security commitments and generally return to avoiding foreign entanglements. Other realists have advanced a policy of "offshore balancing" (e.g., Walt 2006; Rosato and Schuessler 2011). This also involves some strategic disengagement, yet is distinct from neo-isolationism in championing the use of American capabilities abroad to maintain a rough equilibrium of power between the regional great powers of Europe and Asia.

Realism has been opposed in the post–Cold War era by two additional camps. Neoconservatives (e.g., Kristol and Kagan 2000; Krauthammer 2002–2003), also called American primacists, argue for a more muscular, assertive, and activist American foreign policy aimed at preserving US military preponderance while deterring or eliminating potential threats to American interests before they gain strength. Liberal internationalists (e.g., Brooks, Ikenberry, and Wohlforth 2012) similarly part ways with realists in advocating for continued American activism and leadership in world affairs, yet they do so through emphasizing a renewed commitment to multilateral institutions and alliances. In general, both camps have been much more supportive than realists of humanitarian and democracy-promotion missions. Realists typically deride such endeavors for being a waste of resources and irrelevant—or even counterproductive—for advancing American interests (Dueck 2006, 115–124).

Conventional wisdom suggests that realism has had less influence on American foreign policy since the fall of the Soviet Union. After George H. W. Bush's defeat in the 1992 presidential election, realists were displaced by liberal internationalists in the Bill Clinton administration. Prominent realists strongly criticized Clinton's foreign policy team for its open-ended humanitarian and nation-building missions in places like Somalia, Haiti, Bosnia,

and Kosovo, which they argued bore little connection to vital strategic interests and were hopelessly unrealistic and naive (e.g., Mandelbaum 1996). George W. Bush echoed these arguments during the 2000 presidential campaign, promising a less activist and interventionist foreign policy that appealed to realists for its seeming rededication to core strategic interests (e.g., Rice 2000). After the terrorist attacks of September 11, 2001, however, the Bush administration swiftly adopted neoconservative/primacist policies, focusing much more on nonstate security threats and emphasizing the importance of democracy promotion and military prevention/preemption of emerging threats in distant theaters (Dueck 2006, 148–162; Chollet and Goldgeier 2010, 280–330). These principles formed the basis of the 2003 invasion of Iraq, a war that prominent American realists strongly and publicly opposed (e.g., Mearsheimer and Walt 2003).

SEE ALSO *Americanization; Anti-imperialism; Cold War; Department of Defense, US; Department of State; Eisenhower, Dwight D.; Embassies, Consulates, and Diplomatic Missions; Exceptionalism; Imperialism; Internationalism; Interventionism; Isolationism; Kissinger, Henry; Korean War; League of Nations; Niebuhr, (Karl Paul) Reinhold; Nixon, Richard Milhous; Paris Peace Conference (1919); Race; Reagan, Ronald Wilson; Roosevelt, Franklin D.; September 11, 2001; Spanish-American War; Truman, Harry S.; United Nations; Vietnam War; War on Terror; Whiteness; Wilson, Woodrow; World War I; World War II*

BIBLIOGRAPHY

Brooks, Stephen G., G. John Ikenberry, and William C. Wohlforth. "Don't Come Home, America: The Case against Retrenchment." *International Security* 37, 3 (2012): 7–51.

Carr, E. H. *The Twenty Years' Crisis, 1919–1939: An Introduction to the Study of International Relations.* 2nd ed. New York: Harper Perennial, 1964. First published in 1946.

Chollet, Derek, and James Goldgeier. *America between the Wars, from 11/9 to 9/11: The Misunderstood Years between the Fall of the Berlin Wall and the Start of the War on Terror.* New York: PublicAffairs, 2008.

Drezner, Daniel W. "The Realist Tradition in American Public Opinion." *Perspectives on Politics* 6, 1 (2008): 51–70.

Dueck, Colin. *Reluctant Crusaders: Power, Culture, and Change in American Grand Strategy.* Princeton, NJ: Princeton University Press, 2006.

Engel, Jeffrey A. "A Better World ... but Don't Get Carried Away: The Foreign Policy of George H. W. Bush Twenty Years On." *Diplomatic History* 34, 1 (2010): 25–46.

Gaddis, John Lewis. *Strategies of Containment: A Critical Appraisal of American National Security Policy during the Cold War.* Rev. ed. New York: Oxford University Press, 2005.

Gholz, Eugene, Daryl Press, and Harvey Sapolsky. "Come Home, America: The Strategy of Restraint in the Face of Temptation." *International Security* 21, 4 (1997): 5–48.

Gilpin, Robert. *War and Change in World Politics*. New York: Cambridge University Press, 1981.

Kennan, George F. *American Diplomacy*. Chicago: University of Chicago Press, 1951.

Kissinger, Henry A. *Diplomacy*. New York: Simon and Schuster, 1994.

Krauthammer, Charles. "The Unipolar Moment Revisited." *National Interest* 70 (Winter 2002–2003): 5–17.

Kristol, William, and Robert Kagan, eds. *Present Dangers: Crisis and Opportunity in American Foreign and Defense Policy*. San Francisco: Encounter, 2000.

Layne, Christopher. *The Peace of Illusions: American Grand Strategy from 1940 to the Present*. Ithaca, NY: Cornell University Press, 2006.

Lebow, Richard Ned. "Classical Realism." In *International Relations Theories: Discipline and Diversity*, edited by Tim Dunne, Milja Kurki and Steve Smith, 59–76. 3rd ed. Oxford: Oxford University Press, 2013.

Mandelbaum, Michael. "Foreign Policy as Social Work." *Foreign Affairs* 75, no. 1 (1996): 16–32.

Mead, Walter Russell. *Special Providence: American Foreign Policy and How It Changed the World*. New York: Routledge, 2002.

Mearsheimer, John J. *The Tragedy of Great Power Politics*. New York: Norton, 2001.

Mearsheimer, John J. "Structural Realism." In *International Relations Theories: Discipline and Diversity*, edited by Tim Dunne, Milja Kurki, and Steve Smith, 77–93. 3rd ed. Oxford: Oxford University Press, 2013.

Mearsheimer, John J., and Stephen M. Walt. "An Unnecessary War." *Foreign Policy* 134 (January/February 2003): 51–59.

Morgenthau, Hans J. "The Mainsprings of American Foreign Policy: The National Interest vs. Moral Abstractions." *American Political Science Review* 44, 4 (1950): 833–854.

Morgenthau, Hans J. *Politics among Nations*. 3rd ed. New York: Knopf, 1960.

Rice, Condoleezza. "Promoting the National Interest." *Foreign Affairs* 79, 1 (2000): 45–62.

Rice, Condoleezza. "Rethinking the National Interest: American Realism for a New World." *Foreign Affairs* 87, 4 (2008): 2–14, 16–26.

Rosato, Sebastian, and John Schuessler. "A Realist Foreign Policy for the United States." *Perspectives on Politics* 9, 4 (2011): 803–819.

Viotti, Paul R., and Mark V. Kauppi. *International Relations Theory*. 5th ed. Boston: Pearson-Longman, 2012.

Walt, Stephen M. *Taming American Power: The Global Response to U.S. Primacy*. New York: Norton, 2006.

Waltz, Kenneth N. *Theory of International Politics*. Reading, MA: Addison-Wesley, 1979.

Wohlforth, William C. "The Stability of a Unipolar World." *International Security* 24, 1 (1999): 5–41.

Kyle M. Lascurettes
Assistant Professor of International Affairs
Lewis & Clark College

RED CROSS

The American Red Cross (ARC) has been engaged in international humanitarian activities since its founding in 1881. The organization, though autonomous and based in Washington, DC, is affiliated with the Geneva, Switzerland–based International Red Cross and Red Crescent Movement. This movement comprises the International Committee of the Red Cross (ICRC) and the International Federation of Red Cross and Red Crescent Societies (IFRC).

ORIGINS AND EARLY HISTORY

The Red Cross originated in an idea by Swiss entrepreneur Henri Dunant (1828–1910). After witnessing an 1859 battle where wounded soldiers were left to languish on the field, Dunant proposed a humanitarian standard for treatment of sick and wounded combatants and the creation of volunteer societies that would provide immediate battlefield assistance. Dunant and four other Geneva citizens formed the ICRC, and in 1864 organized an international conference to draft the Geneva Convention, a treaty codifying humanitarian standards for treatment of combatants, volunteers, and medical personnel. Volunteer aid groups formed by signatories became known as "Red Cross" societies because members wore white armbands marked with a red cross to identify themselves as noncombatants. This symbol was the reverse of the Swiss flag, a recognized symbol of neutrality in Europe. Within two years, nineteen nations had signed the treaty. The ICRC agreed that the Turkish society would be allowed to use a red crescent instead of a red cross as its identifying symbol.

Although US representatives attended the 1864 Geneva conference, the United States did not immediately embrace the convention. It was only when Clara Barton (1821–1912), a famous aid volunteer during the American Civil War (1861–1865), launched a campaign to persuade the United States to sign the convention that President James Garfield (1831–1881) agreed to do so in 1881. Barton, who had learned of the Red Cross while in Switzerland, founded the American Red Cross (ARC) that year to comply with US obligations under the treaty. The organization remained insignificant until the Spanish-American War (1898), when it aided American troops and Cuban civilians with limited success.

In 1900, the ARC obtained a congressional charter, which solidified its status as the organization responsible for carrying out the US obligations under the original Geneva Convention and made it subject to congressional oversight. It also made the organization responsible for conducting disaster relief and aiding military personnel and their families. The charter was revised in 1905, 1947, and 2007 to adjust the ARC's governing structure. The

ARC has also promoted first aid, and since 1948 has been the United States' largest blood supplier. The Geneva Conventions have been amended numerous times, most recently being rewritten in 1949 to encompass civilians as well as armed forces.

DISASTER RELIEF

Disaster relief has been the most significant US contribution to the Red Cross and Red Crescent Movement. Although the ARC was not the only Red Cross society to aid victims of disasters in its early years, it became the first society to make disaster relief its central peacetime activity. Barton increased popular support for the ARC by making it a national vehicle for volunteer efforts to address "the misfortunes of other nations" and for aid in domestic disasters (Barton 1878).

The ARC launched its first international relief effort during the 1891–1892 Russian famine. The organization collected corn, grain, and foodstuffs, and raised funds to hire ships to transport these items to Russia. The famine had mainly passed by the time the American donations arrived, but this effort was regarded in both nations as a demonstration of international friendship. The ARC's largest humanitarian effort during this period, however, was its involvement in China between 1906 and 1930 to aid millions affected by repeated flooding and famine. In 1915 the organization tried to sponsor an engineering project in the Huai River valley to prevent flooding, but Chinese nationalists resisted foreign interference, and the project garnered little financial support from Americans.

World War I (1914–1918) narrowed the scope of the ARC's international relief efforts to the conflict-affected countries but greatly deepened its involvement in humanitarian aid. Between 1914 and 1919, the organization raised more than $400 million to finance its war efforts, and employed over 12,700 paid staff in twenty-five countries (Davison 1919, 8–9, 47, 65). The ARC also served as the official recruiter of nurses for the US military and engaged 8 million female volunteers. These volunteers, together with 11 million schoolchildren from the Junior Red Cross (Davison 1919, 106), produced millions of surgical dressings, supplies, and clothing for military personnel and war refugees. Other women volunteers assisted families of servicemen; brought snacks to servicemen in training camps and mobilization points; and transported servicemen, doctors, and nurses to mobilization depots, bases, or hospitals. Men also volunteered to organize ARC fundraising drives.

PUBLIC RELATIONS

During this era, the ARC became the first US philanthropic organization to launch a modern public relations campaign. It hired magazine illustrators to draw fundraising posters featuring sexualized images of young women in makeup and nurse's caps or depicting the Red Cross nurse as a statuesque mother—"The Greatest Mother in the World"—cradling a wounded soldier on a stretcher. These widely reproduced images embedded the organization in the American psyche as a symbol of American humanitarianism and made the Red Cross nurse a popular icon.

FORMATION OF THE IFRC

In 1919, the ARC's wartime leader, J. P. Morgan partner Henry P. Davison (1867–1922), founded the League of Red Cross Societies in Geneva. Davison created this organization to strengthen Red Cross societies in Europe and foster international cooperation in public health and disaster relief. The ICRC initially regarded the league as a rival body. But eventually the two organizations agreed to work together. The ICRC has monitored nations' adherence to the Geneva Conventions in conflict zones, and the league has fostered international cooperation in humanitarian aid. In 1991, the league changed its name to the International Federation of Red Cross and Red Crescent Societies.

WORLD WAR II AND AFTER

During World War II (1939–1945), the ARC again marshaled an army of volunteers. In addition to sewing garments and making bandages, volunteers collected 13 million pints of donated blood and plasma for use in war hospitals (Jones 2012, 263). This new service was controversial because the ARC initially refused to allow African Americans to donate blood, and then separated the blood by race despite lack of scientific evidence for the necessity of doing so. After the war, ARC personnel helped establish national blood programs in West Germany and Japan and in numerous developing countries.

During the Cold War, the ARC's international relief activities overlapped with US foreign policy. Disaster aid to a country with a strong communist party could bolster a fragile anticommunist regime. The ARC-led relief effort following the 1960 Chile earthquake exemplifies this confluence, although ARC officials denied a political motivation. In Vietnam, the ARC's involvement stretched from 1954 through 1973. The ARC helped the Vietnamese Red Cross (VRC) in the South care for refugees who had fled the communists in the North throughout the conflict, opening refugee centers and recruiting nurses for South Vietnamese hospitals. The ARC's association with the unpopular Vietnam War, along with a general decrease in voluntarism, led the ARC's popularity to decline in the post–Vietnam era.

By the twenty-first century, the increase in the number of large-scale disasters worldwide, such as the

2004 Indian Ocean tsunami, the 2010 Haitian earthquake, and the 2011 Japanese tsunami, prompted global outpourings of philanthropy from the ARC and other Red Cross societies. The ability to raise funds quickly online has enhanced these organizations' capacity to channel the resources of large donor networks to meet global emergencies. The ARC has repeatedly come under criticism for mismanagement of disaster-relief funds in recent years. However, its history, expertise, and infrastructure make it likely to continue as a major vehicle for international humanitarianism in the near future.

SEE ALSO *Salvation Army; World War I; World War II; World's YWCA/YMCA*

BIBLIOGRAPHY

Barton, Clara. *The Red Cross of the Geneva Convention: What It Is.* Washington, DC: Darby, 1878.

Davison, Henry P. *Work of the American Red Cross during the War: A Statement of Finances and Accomplishments for the Period July 1, 1917, to February 28, 1919.* Washington, DC: American Red Cross, 1919.

Hutchinson, John F. *Champions of Charity: War and the Rise of the Red Cross.* Boulder, CO: Westview Press, 1996.

Irwin, Julia F. *Making the World Safe: The American Red Cross and a Nation's Humanitarian Awakening.* New York: Oxford University Press, 2013.

Jones, Marian Moser. *The American Red Cross from Clara Barton to the New Deal.* Baltimore, MD: Johns Hopkins University Press, 2012.

Marian Moser Jones
Assistant Professor
University of Maryland College Park

RED SCARE

The periodic Red scares in twentieth-century America were buoyed by fears of foreign enemies and alien influences, apprehensions that were deeply rooted in American political culture. Such fears owe something to the origins of the Republic and to the conviction that republicanism could easily be subverted.

FEARS OF FOREIGN INFLUENCE

The United States was a favorite refuge for European communists in the mid-nineteenth century, which saw a scattering of communist clubs in the major cities. The *New York Herald* in 1850 inveighed against the "vast importations of foreign socialists," and hunger demonstrations in 1857 were blamed on "the ultra communistic radicals … and other foreigners" (Heale 1990, 15).

Marxism, it was said, with its premise of class conflict, was incompatible with the fraternal ideals of the American Republic. Even before the Civil War, communism was seen as a foreign import, and its imputed atheism further underscored its alien nature. The infamous bombing in Chicago's Haymarket Square in 1886 was attributed to foreign radicals bent on insurrection.

The perceived threat was from the "dangerous classes" below. The wrenching process of industrialization between about 1870 and 1920, made possible by massive European immigration, triggered socialist movements and greatly intensified the conviction that communism was a menace posed by a brutalized and imported working class. It was this economic drive that created the conditions for the notorious Red scare of 1919, but it was the 1917 Russian Revolution, along with the contemporary industrial strife, that triggered its excesses. The Russian Revolution also meant that the communist threat took on a more focused geopolitical form in the shape of the Soviet Union.

Many Americans initially greeted the Russian Revolution as an uprising in their own tradition, but as it fell under Bolshevist control it took on a more alarming aspect, particularly to conservative and wealthy elites. Still, American radicals were enthused by the exciting events in Russia, and by further communist risings in 1918 and 1919 in parts of Europe. Several prominent socialists were arrested under wartime espionage and sedition legislation, including their party's usual presidential candidate, Eugene Debs (1855–1926). Conservative fears that Bolshevism had arrived in the United States seemed vindicated in 1919 when bombs were detonated in American cities and were confirmed by the formation of the Communist Party and the Communist Labor Party in September.

1919–1920 RED SCARE

World War I (1914–1918) had been accompanied in the United States by growing class conflict. Wartime demand was good for the American economy, and many businesses prospered, but the same condition allowed the labor movement to expand and exact concessions. After the return of peace, a strike wave engulfed the country from 1919 to 1921. Many saw a Bolshevik hand behind the strikes, or at least affected to do so.

It was a general strike in Seattle in February 1919 that heralded the Red scare, a strike described by Seattle mayor Ole Hanson (1874–1940) as the work of men who "want to take possession of our American Government and try to duplicate the anarchy of Russia" (Heale 1990, 63). There followed the discovery of several bombs in the mail sent to leading figures, which, like major coal and steel strikes in the autumn, not to mention an unsettling police

Boston police with a haul of what was believed to be subversive literature confiscated during the post–World War I Red scare. Red scare emotions were triggered by the discovery of several bombs sent by mail to leading figures, strikes (including a police strike in Boston), and growing class conflict. Fears of communist subversion led to crackdowns on socialist meetings and raids on radical groups. **TOPICAL PRESS AGENCY/HULTON ARCHIVE/GETTY IMAGES**

strike in Boston, were read as evidence of communist subversion. This was the message of a conservative press, and across the country strikes and socialist meetings were broken up, often brutally, at the hands of officials and vigilantes, sometimes with the loss of life. In November 1919 and January 1920, US attorney general A. Mitchell Palmer (1872–1936) directed raids on radical groups, and many of the six thousand arrested were aliens. Red scare emotions peaked, but actual evidence of revolutionary activity failed to materialize and abuses in the procedures soon became apparent, as the Supreme Court itself acknowledged. The Red scare began to ebb before the end of 1920.

In the longer perspective, fears were eased too by governmental precautions. It was foreigners who were widely assumed to be importing communist ideology, as

the arrest of thousands of aliens indicated, and in keeping with this analysis, state and federal governments in the late 1910s and early 1920s enacted measures to keep America American. A network of state sedition laws was laced across the country, and the federal government erected high immigration barriers against suspect foreigners, particularly against the peoples of eastern and southern Europe. By about 1924, the Republic had been secured against un-American subversion; the Red scare similarly contributed to a foreign policy of isolationism, with its disenchantment with all things European.

THE INTERWAR CAMPAIGN AGAINST COMMUNIST IDEOLOGY

At the same time, the new geopolitical situation had an impact on American perceptions of communism. With foreigners deemed undesirable now kept out of the country, a violent worker uprising seemed less likely, but the very presence in the world of the Soviet Union, dedicated to the international promotion of communism, meant that the threat was more clearly ideological, alien ideas rather than alien bodies. American minds might be vulnerable to seduction. In the 1920s and 1930s, patriots busied themselves with combating socialist ideas in schools and colleges. Leading anticommunist campaigners expressly denounced what they called "isms." This was the title of an influential American Legion exposé in 1936, which spent 265 pages detailing the dangers of communism, before adding seventeen grudging pages on fascism and Nazism. Congressman Martin Dies (1900–1972), the first chair of the House Un-American Activities Committee, defined the key issue as being between "Americanism" and "alienism."

The problem when communism had become an "ism" was that even the highest in the land might be infected. With the growth in government in the 1930s, Washington itself came under suspicion. President Franklin Roosevelt (1882–1945) was said to be spearheading the "Red New Deal with the Soviet Seal." Big business elements attacked Roosevelt in these terms, but so did relatively powerless elements, such as the Dies Committee and local patriots in the so-called little Red scare of the late 1930s. But this scare was cut short during World War II (1939–1945), when the Soviet Union became a major ally.

THE COLD WAR RED SCARE

The course of international affairs, however, soon precipitated a new and intensive scare. The administration of Harry S. Truman (1884–1972) made containing international communism its primary foreign policy objective, and as the Cold War cast the Soviet Union in ever more menacing terms, the old anticommunist constituencies within American society, from veterans associations to democratic socialists, redoubled their warnings. Large numbers of working-class Roman Catholics were deeply disturbed by the expansion of Soviet control over countries from which their families had fled within living memory. The director of the Federal Bureau of Investigation (FBI), J. Edgar Hoover (1895–1972), added his powerful weight to the anticommunist campaign.

Reverses in American foreign policy quickly made communism a party political issue, as Republicans castigated the Truman administration for being "soft on communism" and the Truman administration hastened to establish its own anticommunist credentials, such as by introducing a loyalty program for federal employees and prosecuting leaders of the American Communist Party

under the 1940 Smith Act, which had outlawed conspiracy to overthrow the government. With both major parties proclaiming their intolerance of communists on American soil, Red scare sentiments surfaced across the land. Institutions held to be capable of surreptitiously advancing communist ideas, whether in Hollywood films, school curricula, or library holdings, were subjected to suspicious surveillance, as were elements thought capable of industrial sabotage, such as left-wing trade unions. Many people lost their jobs as public opinion accorded little protection to those deemed sympathetic to socialism or communism. In the nine years from 1947, on one count, nearly nine thousand were dismissed under federal programs alone, and probably much greater numbers in state and local government and private employment.

In January 1950, a former State Department official, Alger Hiss (1904–1996), who had been with President Roosevelt at Yalta (where right-wingers thought the president had sold out to the Soviets), was in effect convicted of espionage, although technically of perjury. A month later, Senator Joseph McCarthy (1908–1957) spectacularly charged the State Department with harboring communists and claimed documentary evidence to prove it. What gave his charges a veneer of plausibility had been the course of the Cold War. China had "fallen" to the communists in 1949, the consequence, Republicans claimed, of incompetent or even outright disloyalty in the State Department. In the same year, the Soviet Union had exploded a nuclear device, several years earlier than expected, prompting suspicions that American secrets had been leaked. Greatly augmenting fears of communist subversion was the outbreak of the Korean War in the summer of 1950, so that American soldiers were soon dying, the victims, it seemed, of Soviet aggression, and possibly of betrayal in American government.

The Korean War made possible the intensive Red scare known as McCarthyism, which might have been more aptly named the Korean War Scare. Following the outbreak of war, Congress passed the Internal Security Act, requiring communists and communist-front organizations to register with the government, which meant that private associations and individuals, not just government employees, were subject to scrutiny. The act lent some legitimacy to the ongoing purges of suspect employees across the public and private sectors. The House Un-American Activities Committee, which had been revived after the war, continued its investigations of alleged communist infiltration, an activity in which it was joined by the Senate Internal Security Subcommittee in 1951. In that year, the Supreme Court upheld the Smith Act convictions of communist leaders, triggering further prosecutions. In 1951 Julius (1918–1953) and Ethel Rosenberg (1915–1953) were tried for espionage, as participants in what the judge called a "diabolical conspiracy to destroy a

God-fearing nation" by giving nuclear secrets to the Soviet Union and thus sharing responsibility for the war in Korea. They were executed in 1953.

The Korean War and Red scare tactics helped the Republicans not only win the presidential election of 1952 but also regain control of both houses of Congress. This allowed McCarthy to assume the chairmanship of an investigative Senate subcommittee, and by the end of 1953 he was even probing the US Army for communist influences. McCarthy and the army exchanged angry charges, which became the subject of the celebrated Army-McCarthy hearings of 1954. The hearings brought the senator his greatest audience but also turned public opinion against him as his reckless accusations were exposed on national television. Detested by the White House and increasingly deserted by his embarrassed fellow Republicans, who had little interest in using Red scare tactics against a Republican administration, McCarthy was humiliated in December when the Senate voted to "condemn" him. He quickly faded into obscurity and died in 1957.

THE END OF THE RED SCARE

McCarthy's power would have weakened anyway because the Korean War ended in the summer of 1953. With American soldiers no longer dying at communist hands, the Cold War increasingly came to be seen as a long-term contest for the goodwill of the peoples of the world. Public figures argued for a more convincing display of the "freedom" and "democracy" of which Americans boasted, including greater respect for civil liberties and civil rights. The Supreme Court curbed anticommunist programs, most decisively in a series of decisions in 1957. Many Americans remained suspicious of communist machinations, but the scare was over.

McCarthyism damaged the international image of the United States. Foreign observers often concluded that the country was susceptible to anticommunist hysteria, and European policy makers worried that the Red scare presaged a return to isolationism. In fact, American fears of the Soviet Union ensured that the United States would long maintain an internationalist foreign policy and vigilant internal security programs; socialism remained deeply suspect. The American Red scare also had repercussions abroad. For decades, citizens of other countries who had been members of communist groups found it difficult to secure visas to visit the United States. Prominent American filmmakers, academics, and others who had fallen foul of the Red hunters sometimes resumed their careers overseas, as did the screenwriter Carl Foreman (1914–1984) and the distinguished classicist Moses Finley (1912–1986). Another example was H. S. Tsien (1911–2009), a Chinese-born scientist who worked on the US space program in the 1940s; after his loyalty was questioned during the McCarthy era, he returned to China, where he spearheaded the Chinese rocket program.

SEE ALSO *Bolshevism; Cold War; Debs, Eugene V.; Great Depression; Hollywood; Marx, Karl; McCarthyism; Nativism; Russia; Socialism; World War I; World War II*

BIBLIOGRAPHY

Bennett, David H. *The Party of Fear: From Nativist Movements to the New Right in American History.* Chapel Hill: University of North Carolina Press, 1988.

Fried, Richard M. *Nightmare in Red: The McCarthy Era in Perspective.* New York: Oxford University Press, 1990.

Griffith, Robert. *The Politics of Fear: Joseph R. McCarthy and the Senate.* 2nd ed. Amherst: University of Massachusetts Press, 1987.

Heale, M. J. *American Anticommunism: Combating the Enemy Within, 1830–1970.* Baltimore, MD: Johns Hopkins University Press, 1990.

Heale, M. J. *McCarthy's Americans: Red Scare Politics in State and Nation, 1935–1965.* Athens: University of Georgia Press, 1998.

Morgan, Ted. *Reds: McCarthyism in Twentieth-Century America.* New York: Random House, 2004.

Murray, Robert K. *Red Scare: A Study in National Hysteria, 1919–1920.* Minneapolis: University of Minnesota Press, 1955.

Powers, Richard Gid. *Not without Honor: The History of American Anticommunism.* New York: Free Press, 1995.

Preston, William, Jr. *Aliens and Dissenters: Federal Suppression of Radicals, 1903–1933.* Cambridge, MA: Harvard University Press, 1963. 2nd ed., Urbana: University of Illinois Press, 1994.

Schrecker, Ellen. *Many Are the Crimes: McCarthyism in America.* Princeton, NJ: Princeton University Press, 1998.

M. J. Heale
Emeritus Professor of American History, Lancaster University
Supernumerary Fellow, Rothermere American Institute, Oxford

REED, JOHN
SEE *Lost Generation.*

RE-EXPORT TRADE
SEE *War of 1812.*

RELIGIONS

The word *religions* does not appear in the Declaration of Independence, although there are references to concepts like the creator, nature's God, and Providence that many would classify as religious. Within the Declaration, the creator invests citizens with unalienable rights. Many Americans have concluded that liberties are granted by God, and that a nation unified in belief in the creator makes freedom possible. The specific identity of the creator is less clear, however. Critics of the Christian-nation ideal have called attention to the views of Thomas Jefferson (1743–1826), the Declaration's author. Jefferson held heterodox religious positions and was a proponent of the separation of church and state. This raises the question of why someone who believed in the separation of religious and civic institutions placed the creator within the founding document of the United States. One possibility is that the singularity of the creator appealed to a generic concept in a way that did not offend eighteenth-century ideas of religious toleration. Thus while the Declaration referenced divinity, it said nothing about religions.

During the Revolutionary era, the American relationship to the world was defined largely by its relationship to England. While advocates for independence rejected monarchical rule, English politics shaped their view of religion and religious freedom. Jefferson's understanding of tolerance was influenced by John Locke's (1632–1704) *Letter concerning Toleration* (1689). Plural religions were not the focus of Locke's treatise. He spoke instead of "the mutual toleration of Christians in their different professions of religion" (Locke 2003, 215). While there were multiple professions of religion, religion was still singular. This is a subtle distinction, but it might have significant effects for how to define religions in the United States. For Locke, religion was a subject matter about which people have different opinions. This subject matter could be roughly divided into beliefs and forms of worship, with beliefs taking priority.

CLASSIFYING RELIGIONS

The focus on belief has been a pervasive feature of the interpretation of constitutional protections of religious freedom. The words *religion* and *religious* do appear in the US Constitution. These references appear to limit entanglements between state and religion. Article Six states that "no religious Test shall ever be required as a Qualification to any Office or Public Trust under the United States." The First Amendment asserts that "Congress shall make no law respecting an establishment of religion or prohibit the free exercise thereof." As with the Declaration of Independence, proponents and critics of a Christian nation read the text of the Constitution to support their own views. Proponents insist that the purpose behind the First Amendment was to protect religion from state encroachment, and that while the state might be barred from promoting a particular denomination, there is nothing in the text that prohibits civic

support for nonsectarian principles of Christian nation-hood. Critics have asserted that there is no such thing as nonsectarian religion, and that a Christian nation inherently supports one religion over another. Much of this debate comes down to whether a singular religion is a unifying force that produces a socially cohesive nation, or whether the purpose of religious freedom is to enable civic equality between members of plural religions.

While there is much disagreement about what the framers meant by religion, it is safe to say that contemporary usages of the word *religions* would have been foreign to them. Instead of diverse opinions about some familiar subject matter, religions are now understood to be discreet things that are imagined as complex wholes. In contemporary American discourse, the word *religion* refers primarily to belief (for this reason, the word *faith* is often used as a synonym for *religion*), but it can also include ritual practices (often understood to perform or represent beliefs), as well as institutions that include organizations with people in authority (often to decide what counts as true belief) and rules for moral behavior. This has expanded the definition of *religion* beyond propositions about Christian divinity to include diverse social phenomena like animal sacrifice, ingestion of intoxicating substances, objections to conventional medical practices, and moral convictions about contraception.

Part of the reason for the expansion of phenomena classified as religious is the changing relationship between America and the world over the past couple centuries. The imagination of the framers was shaped by the Protestantism common among people who shared their mostly English heritage. Catholics and Jews were still relatively small minorities in the eighteenth century. Eighteenth-century Protestants assumed Native Americans had no religion at all, and they would classify Native Americans instead as heathens or savages who could become religious if converted by Christian missionaries. While many of the framers lived in close proximity to people of African descent, slaveholders thought little about Muslim or traditional African practices retained by their slaves or free people.

PLURALISM, RELIGIOUS LIBERTY, AND THE SEPARATION OF CHURCH AND STATE

In the early republic, then, the relationship between religion in America and the world was measured by the contrast between the United States and Europe. In his *Democracy in America* (1835/1840), the French tourist Alexis de Tocqueville (1805–1859) observed that religion was the first among American political institutions. De Tocqueville argued that religion flourished in the United States precisely because it enjoyed no state support. The voluntary quality of religious adherence meant that varieties of Christianity thrived in a way that compared favorably to decadent Europe.

While de Tocqueville was Catholic, not all Catholics shared his impression of the tolerance of American Protestants. Many German and Irish Catholic immigrants in the nineteenth century found themselves the targets of nativist hostility. As Roman Catholicism grew to become the largest single denomination in the United States by the 1840s, some Protestants felt that Catholic loyalty to a foreign ecclesiastical institution threatened the separation of church and state. According to anti-immigrant nativists, a hierarchical church opposed American democratic principles and invited sectarian strife into a nonsectarian Protestant nation. Catholics responded by rejecting nativist arguments that Protestantism was nonsectarian. They insisted instead that the separation of church and state should protect distinct religious groups while favoring none. Catholics, along with groups like the Church of Jesus Christ of Latter-Day Saints, maintained clear differences from the Protestant majority while strenuously defending their American patriotism.

With increased visibility of the contact between United States and the world outside of Western Europe, the scope of what counted as religion at times expanded and at times contracted. The late nineteenth century brought larger numbers of Catholic and Jewish immigrants from southern and eastern Europe. Economic opportunities also drew Asian immigrants, who were in turn met with nativist hostility. While the Chinese exclusion act of 1882 demonstrated that Americans of European descent did not always welcome Asian people, some were drawn to ideas from Asian philosophical systems that they saw as religious. The 1893 World's Parliament of Religions in Chicago marked an increasing interest in "world religions." Representatives of newly classified religions like Buddhism and Hinduism tended to play down practical and institutional matters in favor of complex philosophical concepts and deep spiritual wisdom. To this end, the American encounter with Asian thought expanded the global scope of religion while reinforcing Protestant conceptions that religions were belief systems.

Arguments about the role of plural religions within the nation continued in the twentieth century with debates about a metaphorical melting pot in which "hyphenated" Americans were expected to assimilate to existing social and religious norms. The Jewish writer Horace Kallen (1882–1974) protested that the melting pot was an un-American idea and advocated instead for "cultural pluralism." Kallen's arguments did not enjoy broad political support, and the Johnson-Reed Act of 1924 essentially eliminated Asian immigration and created quotas for new immigrants based on the national origin of Americans in the 1890 census.

In the twentieth century, the world outside the United States promised opportunities for imperial expansion but also posed perceived threats to American security. The 1910s and 1920s witnessed the rise of the Red scare, in which the specter of communism was seen to threaten American capitalism, democracy, and religious freedom. For a period, the United States allied with the Soviet Union against the mutual enemy of fascism. In some ways, fascist ideals of national purity increased support for religious minorities in the United States. For example, in the wake of Nazi persecution of Jehovah's Witnesses, the Supreme Court decision in *West Virginia Board of Education v. Barnett* (1943) reversed a 1940 ruling that refused to give Jehovah's Witnesses a religious exemption from saluting the American flag. American respect for religious liberty was celebrated as a feature of a free nation that rejected both fascism and communism.

With fascism defeated after World War II (1939–1945), an increasingly prosperous United States immersed itself in the Cold War. This was sometimes framed as an existential battle between a religious civilization and godless communism, and 1950s America promoted generic interfaith religiosity. In 1954, as part of the celebration of general religiosity, "under God" was inserted into the Pledge of Allegiance.

Affirming the underlying unity of religion was one response to anxieties about what pluralism was coming to mean. In the 1960s, the attempt to include more world religions within an American consensus came into conflict with Christian-nation ideals in Supreme Court decisions. *Engel v. Vitale* (1962) and *Abington v. Schempp* (1963), for example, classified practices like school prayer as forms of religious establishment instead of religiously neutral civic exercises. Protestant Christianity found itself as a religion among religions.

The 1960s also saw more radical challenges to national consensus. Martin Luther King Jr. (1929–1968) criticized generic religiosity when he lamented the complacency of white moderates who had turned the church into an "irrelevant social club" (King 1963, 17). Malcolm X (1925–1965) rejected the purported tolerance of Christianity and proclaimed that "America's conscience is bankrupt" (Malcolm X 1965, 40). He turned to Islam and called for greater solidarity with global struggles against colonialism in Africa and Asia. The year of Malcolm X's death also marked a change in American relations to the world as the Immigration and Nationality Act of 1965 eliminated the national-origins quota system of the 1920s. Since 1965, immigrants from Asia and Africa have expanded the numbers of Americans who do not identify as Christian and Jewish, with notable growth among Hindus, Buddhists, Sikhs, and Muslims.

WHITE CHRISTIAN CONSERVATISM

Support for a white Christian nation remained vigorous, however. During the 1970s and 1980s, political mobilization occurred among groups convinced that the Supreme Court's banning of school prayer, along with protections for sexual freedom in *Griswold v. Connecticut* (1965) and *Roe v. Wade* (1973), portended decay into moral anarchy. Defending "family values," figures like Phyllis Schlafly (b. 1924), Jerry Falwell (1933–2007), and Pat Robertson (b. 1930) attacked what they labeled "secular humanism." In their view, secular humanism functioned as a religion in its own right, and its pervasiveness in the public schools amounted to a secular religious establishment that used tactics like teaching evolution and sexual education as a means to destroy the Christian faith of students. While the courts have not accepted that secular humanism is a de facto religion, this argument shows the expansiveness and malleability of religious classification.

White Christian conservative activism reached a high-water mark with the apotheosis of Ronald Reagan (1911–2004) in the 1980s. Reagan tied his Christian faith to attacks upon progressive reforms of the previous half-century and a rededication to anticommunism. Using a biblical lens to interpret America's place in world affairs, he characterized the Soviet Union as an "evil empire" and supported "freedom fighters" in Afghanistan. This period also corresponded with a widely reported rise of "fundamentalism" as an apparently global phenomenon. While *fundamentalism* was initially coined to describe resistance to modernism within Protestant denominations in the 1920s, the term was applied to groups from a variety of religions who challenged secular distinctions between religion and politics. Concerns about "religious extremism" peaked after the attacks of September 11, 2001, after which increased levels of American involvement in foreign affairs were justified by the conviction that national security was enhanced by spreading American religious freedom throughout the world.

THE RELIGIOUS FREEDOM RESTORATION ACT

Another lasting influence of the Reagan era has been the increasingly conservative trajectory of the US Supreme Court. One Reagan appointee, Justice Antonin Scalia (b. 1936), penned the unpopular *Oregon Employment Division v. Smith* (1990) decision, in which the court upheld the denial of unemployment benefits to a man fired for using peyote as part of his participation in the Native American Church. Although Scalia rejected Smith's request for a religious exemption from drug laws, he accepted that Native American practices were religious. This meant, however, that the rules for Native American religions might also apply to Christians. To heighten

protections for religious exercise, Congress passed the Religious Freedom Restoration Act (RFRA) in 1993. This act instructed the court to apply strict scrutiny when adjudicating free-exercise cases, essentially expanding the ability of citizens to ask for religious exemptions from federal and state laws.

While many have challenged the constitutionality of RFRA and the Supreme Court banned its use at the state level, it continues to guide the court's interpretation of federal law and played a crucial role in the *Burwell v. Hobby Lobby* (2014) decision. In this case, Hobby Lobby, a nationwide chain of arts-and-crafts stores, claimed that its religious freedom was violated by a government mandate forcing it to provide coverage for contraception in employee health-care plans. Justice Ruth Bader Ginsburg (b. 1933) argued this was not necessarily a religious matter and that corporations could not exercise religious liberty anyway. Her decision returned to narrower views of religion that restricted religious practices to activities like "prayer, worship, and the taking of sacraments." Ginsburg's view did not prevail and religious freedom continues to protect an increasing range of ideas and practices.

In 2015, Christian activists sought to use state RFRAs to protect religiously motivated forms of discrimination on the basis of sexual orientation. While this might be understood as a return to the singular religion of a Christian nation, the preferred rhetorical strategy of Catholics and Protestants in RFRA debates was to identify as minority religions whose freedom was under threat by a secular state. On both the domestic and international fronts, then, many Americans saw religious freedom as under attack. RFRA laws at home were complemented by the State Department's creation of an Office of International Religious Freedom to monitor threats to religious liberty abroad. Whatever the official status of religion might be, then, the defense of religions continue to shape America's sense of its purpose in the world.

SEE ALSO *American Revolution; Americanization; Buddhism; Catholicism; The Civil War; Cold War; Exceptionalism; Federal Council of Churches; Foreign Mission Movement; Hinduism; Internationalism; Interventionism; Islam; Isolationism; Jewish Welfare Board; Judaism; Knights of Columbus; Moorish Science Temple; Nation of Islam; Protestantism; Rastafari; Secularization; Shinto; Spanish-American War; Vietnam War; World War I; World War II; World's Fairs; World's Parliament of Religions (1893); World's YWCA/YMCA*

BIBLIOGRAPHY

Albanese, Catherine L. *America: Religions and Religion*. 5th ed. Boston: Wadsworth Cengage Learning, 2013.

Fessenden, Tracy. *Culture and Redemption: Religion, the Secular, and American Literature*. Princeton, NJ: Princeton University Press, 2007.

Hamburger, Philip. *The Separation of Church and State*. Cambridge, MA: Harvard University Press, 2002.

Hurd, Elizabeth Shakman. *The Politics of Secularism in International Relations*. Princeton, NJ: Princeton University Press, 2008.

King, Martin Luther, Jr. "Letter from a Birmingham Jail." April 16, 1963. https://kinginstitute.stanford.edu/king-papers/documents/letter-birmingham-jail

Locke, John. *Two Treatises of Government and A Letter concerning Toleration*. Edited by Ian Shapiro, with essays by John Dunn, Ruth Grant, and Ian Shapiro. New Haven, CT: Yale University Press, 2003.

Malcolm X. "The Ballot or the Bullet," April 3, 1964, Cleveland. In *Malcolm X Speaks: Selected Speeches and Statements*, edited by George Breitman, 23–44. New York: Merit, 1965.

Smith, Jonathan Z. "Religion, Religions, Religious." In *Critical Terms for Religious Studies*, edited by Mark C. Taylor, 269–284. Chicago: University of Chicago Press, 1998.

Wills, Garry. *Under God: Religion and American Politics*. New York: Simon and Schuster, 1990.

Finbarr Curtis
Assistant Professor of Religious Studies
Georgia Southern University

RESERVATION

According to the Bureau of Indian Affairs (BIA), there were 326 reservations in the United States in 2015. Most reservations were created in the nineteenth century and are located west of the Mississippi River. East of the Mississippi, barely 3 percent of former tribal lands remain in reservation status and half of the states have no reservations at all (Frantz 1999, 41). Some reservations are remnants of a tribe's original homeland, while others are located far from their traditional lands. Many federally recognized tribes do not have a reservation. Although the BIA administers reservations, tribes possess autonomy over their lands (Sutton 1976, 283). The history of reservations is one of contradictions and abrupt policy changes. One constant, however, was the federal government's aspiration to acquire tribal lands in exchange for smaller reservations.

REMOVAL FROM TRIBAL LANDS

The policy of forcing land cessions and removing tribes to reservations began in colonial times, when British officials signed treaties with tribes for their lands. British policy established the first reservations after Bacon's Rebellion of 1676 in Virginia. Following the Revolutionary War, the United States continued the British policy of signing treaties with tribes for their lands and removing tribes to reservations. By 1800, for example, members of the Iroquois Confederation resided on small reservations carved from their traditional northeastern homeland.

During the early nineteenth century, the United States accelerated its removal policy with the goal of removing all eastern tribes to areas west of the Mississippi River. The United States justified this policy in many ways. Most important, Thomas Jefferson (1743–1826) and subsequent presidents argued that Indians were not "civilized"; for example, tribes focused on hunting instead of agriculture (which ignored the role that farming played in many eastern tribes), did not follow Euro-American gender roles, and practiced "savage" religions. Removing tribes to reservations purportedly would encourage the Indians' "civilization."

In May 1830, Congress passed the Indian Removal Act with strong support from President Andrew Jackson (1767–1845). This act authorized the president to sign treaties with Indian tribes living in the east for their removal to areas west of the Mississippi River. By the end of Jackson's second administration, the Senate had ratified numerous treaties with eastern tribes for their removal. Most southeastern tribes, including the Creeks, Seminoles, and Cherokees, were relocated to reservations in "Indian Country," or present-day Oklahoma. Tribes farther north were also moved, both to Oklahoma and to other territories west of the Mississippi. Although some eastern tribes, including the Mississippi Choctaws and the Eastern Band of Cherokees, resisted removal and remained on much-reduced lands in the east, nearly fifty tribes were removed to reservations prior to the Civil War (1861–1865) (Frantz 1999, 14).

The best-known case of the accelerated relocation policy is that of the Cherokees. Jackson argued that removal would help civilize tribes. The Cherokees, however, had already made cultural adaptations, as evidenced by their written language, tribal government, and a newspaper known as the *Cherokee Phoenix*. Furthermore, many practiced plantation agriculture. These adaptations did not save the Cherokees, however, and the state of Georgia, with the support of Jackson, inaugurated a campaign to remove them.

The Cherokees resisted removal by suing the state of Georgia. In 1831, *Cherokee Nation v. Georgia* made its way to the Supreme Court. Chief Justice John Marshall (1755–1835) declined to rule on the case because the Cherokees were not US citizens or an independent nation; rather, they were a "domestic dependent nation," according to the court. A second case, *Worcester v. Georgia* (1832), brought by white missionaries in the Cherokees' name, was more favorable toward the Cherokees. Marshall wrote that the Cherokee Nation was a "distinct community, occupying its own territory," in which "the laws of Georgia have no force." Despite this ruling, the Cherokees were forcibly relocated to Oklahoma and suffered greatly during removal in what has become known as the Trail of Tears (1838–1839).

Throughout the rest of the nineteenth century, the basic framework of the Indian Removal Act of 1830 continued: tribes signed treaties ceding their lands for smaller reservations. Following the Civil War, however, reservations generally were located on reduced areas of a tribe's original territory, rather than in Oklahoma. Although their location changed, reservations continued to be extremely problematic. Many reservations were situated on poor land that was isolated and arid, had little opportunity for economic development, and were mismanaged by corrupt agents. Following frontier wars, many

reservation lands were further reduced or taken away. For example, the Great Sioux Reservation was illegally reduced to six smaller reservations in the 1880s, leading to a land loss of approximately 14,000 square miles (36,260 square kilometers) (Frantz 1999, 15). In 1871, the treaty process ended and reservations were created by agreements, statutes, and presidential executive orders. By these means, the majority of tribes were confined to reservations by the late 1800s (Ficken 2005, 442).

SHIFTING FEDERAL POLICY

In the late nineteenth century, federal reservation policy abruptly changed. Reformers known as "Friends of the Indian" argued that reservations had failed to "civilize" Indians. Because reservations were now seen as impediments to progress, these reformers influenced Congress to

A home on the Pine Ridge Indian Reservation, South Dakota, 1956. Most reservations were created in the nineteenth century and are located west of the Mississippi River. Some are remnants of a tribe's original homeland, but many are located far from traditional tribal lands. **AP IMAGES**

dismantle reservations to "kill the Indian, and save the man." The Dawes Act (1887) broke up reservations by allotting lands to individual Indians so they could become small farmers. After reservations had been allotted, the rest of the "surplus" land was sold. The result was a loss of 100 million acres, or two-thirds of the Indians' land base (Wall 2010, 6). Lands purchased by non-Indians led to the "checkerboarding" of reservations (Indian lands surrounded by non-Indian lands), which continues into the present day.

In the 1920s and 1930s, federal policy once again changed. In 1928, a group of scholars headed by Lewis Meriam (1883–1972) surveyed Indian reservations. The resulting *Meriam Report* was a scathing indictment of conditions on reservations. The report told of dire poverty, inadequate health care, disease, high infant mortality, and poor housing and infrastructure. "Indian reformers," including John Collier (1884–1968), who became the commissioner of Indian Affairs under President Franklin Roosevelt (1882–1945), offered some relief for Native Americans through the Indian Reorganization Act of 1934, which supported tribal culture, religion, government, and sovereignty.

The reforms did not last. In the 1950s federal Indian policy again shifted to assimilationist policies designed to dismantle reservations. First, termination challenged reservations by ending all tribal services and tribes as independent sovereign entities. Second, the policy of relocation attempted to move Indians from reservations to cities. While relocation was voluntary, participants were given incentives (e.g., limited housing support and job training) to move. Relocation accelerated urbanization, which continues into the present day. According to 2013 census data, approximately 70 percent of all Native Americans lived in urban settings rather than on reservations.

CONTEMPORARY CHALLENGES

While many contemporary Native Americans reside in urban areas, issues facing reservations continue to be important. First, many reservations still struggle with economic development, poverty, and health issues. Tribes have opened businesses and debate how, or whether, to develop resources (e.g., oil, gas, coal, and uranium) located on reservation lands. Second, tribes work to regain reservation lands; since the 1940s, tribes have regained approximately 6,000 square miles (15,540 square kilometers) of their original tribal lands (Frantz 1999, 41). Third, tribes defend on- and off-reservation hunting and fishing rights.

Fourth, tribal sovereignty remains an important issue. According to the BIA, tribes possess all powers of self-government: they can form their own governments, make

and enforce laws, and establish and determine tribal membership. Court cases and congressional acts have confirmed a "legal status that encouraged local decision making and nation building" (Wall 2010, 7). Recent acts and court decisions have both acknowledged and undercut tribal sovereignty. For example, the Indian Gaming Regulatory Act of 1988 allowed some tribes to open profitable gaming facilities on reservation land but required tribes to enter into compacts with states before they could open gaming operations (Biolsi 2005, 243).

CANADA AND AUSTRALIA

The United States' policy of removing native peoples from traditional lands was replicated in other nations. In Canada, for example, native peoples were removed to isolated "reserves" where they were expected to become "civilized" by adopting agriculture and Christianity. Today, there are approximately 3,100 reserves across Canada; these lands are held in trust for bands by the British Crown.

Likewise, native Australians lost lands and faced "civilization" programs. In 1992, the Australian government recognized indigenous ownership of land; as a result, there are an increasing number of indigenous reserves across Australia.

CONCLUSION

Throughout American history, as well as the history of other nations, reservations and reserves have been seen by governments as the answer to, and the cause of, all problems with native peoples. Despite the vacillating government policies with regard to native lands, indigenous peoples have survived, and continue to defend their remaining lands, sovereignty, and cultural and religious identities.

SEE ALSO *Cherokee Nation v. Georgia (1831); Civilization Fund; Frontier Wars; General Allotment Act (Dawes Severalty Act, 1877); Indian Removal Act (1830)*

BIBLIOGRAPHY

Biolsi, Thomas. "The Birth of the Reservation: Making the Modern Individual among the Lakota." *American Ethnologist* 22, 1 (1995): 28–53.

Biolsi, Thomas. "Imagined Geographies: Sovereignty, Indigenous Space, and American Indian Struggle." *American Ethnologist* 32, 2 (2005): 239–259.

Bureau of Indian Affairs (BIA). "Frequently Asked Questions." http://www.bia.gov/FAQs/

Ficken, Robert E. "After the Treaties: Administering Pacific Northwest Reservations." *Oregon Historical Quarterly* 106, 3 (2005): 442–461.

Frantz, Klaus. *Indian Reservations in the United States: Territory, Sovereignty, and Socioeconomic Change.* Chicago: University of Chicago Press, 1999. Originally published in German in 1993.

Prucha, Francis Paul. *The Great Father: The United States Government and the American Indians.* Lincoln: University of Nebraska Press, 1984.

Sutton, Imre. "Sovereign States and the Changing Definition of the Indian Reservation." *Geographical Review* 66, 3 (1976): 281–295.

Wall, Stephen. "The State of Indigenous America Series: Federalism, Indian Policy, and the Patterns of History." *Wicazo Sa Review* 25, 1 (2010): 5–16.

Linda Clemmons
Associate Professor of History
Illinois State University

RISORGIMENTO

Risorgimento, an Italian term that means "rebirth," is the geopolitical process that transformed the Italian peninsula from a constellation of small states under foreign control into a unified nation-state controlled by a domestic constitutional monarchy. Its temporal boundaries are conventionally set between 1815 and 1870, the dates of the Congress of Vienna, from which Italy emerged fragmented and directly or indirectly under Austrian control, and the conquest of Rome in 1870 by the army of the Kingdom of Italy, which put an end to the temporal power of the popes and completed the unification of the country. The course of nation formation in Italy sent two different, chronologically staggered, waves of Italian immigrants to the United States, the first one constituted by a small number of political exiles and the second by millions of economic refugees.

The history of Italian nationalism is closely intertwined with involuntary migration, either to escape persecution or as a form of punishment. Given the choice, Italian patriots preferred to stay close to home, in Turin, the only Italian capital not controlled by Austria, or in Paris or London, and the United States only received about 200 of the about 1,900 exiles of the Risorgimento. A few came of their own volition, among others Piero Maroncelli (1795–1846) and Count Federico Confalonieri (1785–1846), both well known to American liberal literary circles because they both featured in Silvio Pellico's widely read *Le mie prigioni* (1833), the autobiographical account of his imprisonment in the infamous Austrian dungeon of Spielberg. Several, however, were deported to the United States. The most prominent group of these deportees landed in New York in 1836 on the Austrian brig *Ussero*. Most, like E. Felice Foresti (1793–1858) and Gaetano de Castillia (1794–1870), had been arrested in 1821 for membership in the anti-Austrian secret society Carboneria, and spent several years in Spielberg. Others, like Giovanni Albinola (c. 1809–1883) and Luigi Tinelli (1799–1872), had been convicted following a series of unsuccessful revolutions in the Papal States in 1831. All had been given the alternative of either protracted incarceration or exile to the United States, which the Austrian Empire considered sufficiently far from Italy to neutralize their subversive potential.

Contrary to these expectations, however, the Italian exiles organized strong forms of diaspora nationalism. Foresti adhered to Giovane Italia, the secret society founded by republican Giuseppe Mazzini (1805–1872), and established a very active cell in New York in 1841, which backed the cause of Italian nationalism by gathering funds and especially by influencing American public opinion in its favor. Giovanni Francesco Secchi De Casali (1819–1885), who advocated a monarchical solution to Italian nationalism, started a newspaper, *L'eco d'Italia*, to keep the exile community informed about political developments in Italy. Transatlantic events prompted several exiles to travel back to Italy. Foresti returned to Italy in 1848 with the intention of joining the republic established in Rome by Mazzini, but abandoned the plan because of the French intervention in support of the pope. Giuseppe Avezzana (1797–1879), who had sought refuge in the United States in 1834 to escape a sentence of death in absentia, also returned in 1848 to become minister of war of the short-lived Roman Republic.

The failure of the revolutions of 1848 to 1849 brought yet another wave of Italian political refugees to the United States. Foresti and Avezzana both went back to New York, where they were followed in 1850 by the most famous of the Italian exiles, Giuseppe Garibaldi (1807–1882), who had directed the defense of the Roman Republic during the French siege. Garibaldi's American exile lasted only one year, but he returned to New York in 1853, this time to affect a reconciliation between the monarchists and republicans as it became clear that the only hope for Italian unification and independence lay with the Piedmontese House of Savoy.

It was to King Victor Emmanuel II (1820–1878) that Garibaldi relinquished control of the southern Kingdom of the Two Sicilies, which he had successfully invaded with a group of only one thousand followers in 1860. The proclamation of the Kingdom of Italy in 1861 eliminated the reason for Italian political immigration to the United States. Several of the exiles, in fact, returned to Italy to become members of the parliament of the newly established independent nation.

At the same time, however, the unification of Italy under a northern dynasty created a climate of discontent that spurred immigration. The new government failed to grant the promised land reforms. Instead, common lands, which had existed in every southern village, were enclosed and appropriated. New duties and new tributes were imposed, namely, a seven-year-long compulsory military service and a tax on the milling of grains, the staple of the diet of the poor. When southern peasants evaded the draft and attacked tax collectors, the state imprisoned them, which eventually gave post-unitary Italy the highest proportion of incarcerated population in Europe. The government interpreted southern unrest as the criminal acts of an inferior, primitive race, and responded with massive military occupation, at one point involving 120,000 soldiers, or half of the national army. The south reacted with brigandage first and with a veritable exodus later. In the fifty years following unification, one-third of the population left the country. Between 1880 and 1920, 4 million went to the United States.

SEE ALSO *1848 Revolutions; Immigration*

BIBLIOGRAPHY

Gabaccia, Donna R. *Italy's Many Diasporas*. Seattle: University of Washington Press, 2000.

Mangione, Jerry, and Ben Morreale. *La Storia: Five Centuries of the Italian American Experience*. New York: HarperCollins, 1992.

Pellegrino, Joanne. "An Effective School of Patriotism." In *Studies in Italian American Social History: Essays in Honor of Leonard Covello*, edited by Francesco Cordasco, 84–104. Totowa, NJ: Rowman and Littlefield, 1975.

Paola Gemme
Professor of English
Arkansas Tech University

ROBBER BARONS

In the latter half of the nineteenth century, the United States underwent a broad industrial transformation. Railroads helped provide cheap, reliable transportation for an ever-increasing stream of manufactured goods and agricultural products, and railroads themselves became huge consumers of materials, especially wood, coal, and iron (later steel). Railroads also helped create a financial industry, so-called Wall Street, to provide necessary capital for expansion. Millions of migrants—immigrants from Europe and East Asia, along with Americans from the countryside—flooded cities, providing cheap labor to power this industrial revolution. As a consequence, there arose a tremendous disparity between the leaders of this transformation and the workers who helped create it.

The term *robber baron* dates back to the 1870s, when it was used to describe business tycoons who amassed considerable wealth using questionable tactics. In the 1930s, American author Matthew Josephson wrote about extremely wealthy industrial giants, such as John D. Rockefeller (1839–1937, oil), Cornelius Vanderbilt (1794–1877, railroads), Andrew Carnegie (1835–1919, steel), and J. P. Morgan (1837–1913, international finance), whom he dubbed "robber barons." These men created huge industrial concerns, amassed vast fortunes, and lived exceedingly privileged lives. By way of contrast, many at the bottom of the social ladder lived in poverty, exposed to disease, with shortened life expectancies and little hope of improvement.

By the 1950s, the view of these industrial leaders had changed. Historians Alfred Chandler, Allan Nevins, and Glenn D. Porter described them as "captains of industry," and focused more on the challenges they faced and the management revolution they led as they created and directed huge industrial concerns, rather than on the great disparities of wealth they fostered. Porter argued, for example, that technology predated the Industrial Revolution, and business leaders mastered the arts of transportation, strategic planning, finance, and the like. Scholars also began drawing attention to the charitable works of these industrial leaders, reflecting the idea of the "gospel of wealth" of that era.

Ray Ginger (1965) called the period from 1877 to 1914 an "age of excess," and that helps explain a new era of American engagement abroad. According to Ginger, American industry could produce far more goods than US businesses and consumers needed. This led to a search for markets abroad, as well as an era of consolidation to end ruinous competition within industrial sectors. Jerry Israel and Thomas J. McCormick (1967) wrote about the drive for markets in China. Naval theorist Alfred Thayer Mahan, having studied the rise of the British Empire, believed that nations needed a large oceangoing navy that could protect commerce. This called for a battleship-centered fleet, coaling stations across the great oceans, and ports for trade.

All this fit together. In 1899 and 1900, Secretary of State John Hay (1838–1905) circulated the so-called Open Door Notes, by which the US government sought to protect Chinese territorial integrity by preventing the European powers and Japan from carving China into colonial empires, thus retaining opportunities for American business expansion abroad. Michael Hunt has studied the impact of the notes on the difficult geopolitical situation in Manchuria from the 1890s to the 1930s.

American diplomats also worked with industrialists to help reduce British and German influence in Latin America. President Theodore Roosevelt's (1858–1919) expansion of the 1823 Monroe Doctrine, the 1904 Roosevelt Corollary, sought to formalize this expanding

American empire within the Western Hemisphere. The goal was to facilitate American penetration of the China market while protecting the Western Hemisphere for American economic exploitation, all to help industry sell the excess production Americans could not consume.

America's great industrial leaders were committed to this economic expansion. Morgan began as an American agent for British financial interests when Britain had surplus capital and sought investment opportunities abroad. With the help of Morgan and others, British funds helped finance American railroads and even the great cattle drives that took place before railroads reached down to the cattle herds in Texas. Rockefeller's Standard Oil Trust operated from the Mideast to the Dutch East Indies. Railroad developer E. H. Harriman (1848–1909) dreamed of building a "round the globe" railroad, but competing colonial interests doomed this endeavor. Inventor Cyrus McCormick (1809–1884) provided reapers, threshers, and combines.

Indeed, this American drive for economic empire was boosted by the great expenses the warring powers incurred during World War I (1914–1918), turning the United States from a net debtor nation into a net creditor nation and leading to the British system of imperial preferences to protect the empire as a closed system that could absorb British industrial production. The various World War II (1939–1945) agreements on the postwar economic world, including Bretton Woods and Dumbarton Oaks, exchanged reduced tariffs and increased worldwide trade for an end to such imperials trade arrangements, presumably to spur global economic recovery and American economic domination.

SEE ALSO *Carnegie Endowment for International Peace; Morgan, J. P.; Rockefeller Foundation*

BIBLIOGRAPHY

Brands, H. W. *American Colossus: The Triumph of Capitalism, 1865–1900.* New York: Doubleday, 2010.

Ginger, Ray. *Age of Excess: The United States from 1877 to 1914.* New York: Macmillan, 1965.

Josephson, Matthew. *The Robber Barons: The Great American Capitalists.* New York: Harcourt, Brace, 1962. First published in 1934.

McCormick, Thomas J. *China Market: America's Quest for Informal Empire, 1893–1901.* Chicago: Quadrangle, 1967.

Morris, Charles R. *The Tycoons: How Andrew Carnegie, John D. Rockefeller, Jay Gould, and J. P. Morgan Invented the American Supereconomy.* New York: Holt, 2005.

Charles M. Dobbs
Professor Emeritus
Iowa State University

ROBESON, PAUL LEROY
1898–1976

Paul Robeson was an African American singer, actor, and activist whose advocacy for labor and civil rights and whose articulation of the linkages between American foreign policy and the violence of racism and capitalism made him the target of US government persecution, Federal Bureau of Investigation (FBI) surveillance, House Un-American Activities Committee hearings, racist attacks, and ultimately the revocation of his passport. Within a matter of years, Robeson went from being among the most popular and well-paid African Americans in the nation to one of the most persecuted figures of the Red scare.

Born in Princeton, New Jersey, the son of an escaped slave turned preacher, Robeson achieved incomparable success in his early life. After graduating as the valedictorian of Rutgers College in 1919, he went on to play for the National Football League while completing his law degree at Columbia Law School. When racism prevented Robeson from working in law offices in New York City, he pursued an acting and singing career, where he found immediate success performing in the musical review *Shuffle Along*; the Eugene O'Neill plays *All God's Chillun Got Wings*, *The Hairy Ape*, and *The Emperor Jones*; the musical *Show Boat*; and in the title role of *Othello*, still the longest-running Shakespeare production to play on Broadway. Robeson also achieved major acclaim for his innovative renditions of Negro spirituals and work songs.

While beginning a study of African languages and culture at the School of Oriental and African Studies in London in 1934, Robeson began a lifelong commitment to celebrating African cultures and fighting the perpetuation of colonialism around the world. Upon his return to the United States, Robeson's singing career took off, as he traveled extensively on major concert tours. Robeson's increasing advocacy for civil rights and international workers' rights, his sympathy for socialism, his 1939 performance of Earl Robinson's patriotic song "Ballad for Americans" on CBS radio and his stumping for the 1948 presidential campaign of the Progressive Party candidate Henry A. Wallace made him an icon for the ascendant Left of the Popular Front culture of the 1930s.

Following the end of World War II (1939–1945), Robeson's political activism made him a target for anticommunists and segregationists alike. In a 1949 speech at the World Congress of Advocates of Peace in Paris, Robeson infamously declared that it would be "unthinkable" for African Americans to fight in a war against the Soviet Union, given the United States' deplorable record in defending the rights of blacks in America. Upon his return to the United States, Robeson was depicted as a traitor in the mainstream press.

With his American career in distress from an effective blacklisting, the US State Department seized Robeson's passport in 1951. Despite numerous appeals, the US government prohibited Robeson's international travel, citing his promotion of anticolonial movements while abroad. Meanwhile, in December 1951 Robeson joined members of the Civil Rights Congress and other activists in submitting the petition *We Charge Genocide* to the United Nations (UN), asserting that by failing to protect African Americans from lynching that the United States was in violation of the 1948 UN Genocide Convention.

Despite his physical confinement to the United States, Robeson's international popularity continued. Refused passage to sing for Canadian union members in Vancouver, Robeson gave annual concerts from 1952 to 1955 at the Peace Arch on the US/Canada border, where he sang from the US side to the audience in Canada. He was awarded the Stalin Peace Prize in absentia in Moscow in 1952, sent recorded and written missives to the 1955 Bandung Conference of Asian and African countries, had a mountain named after him in the Soviet Union and was supported by the "Let Robeson Sing" movement in Great Britain. In 1957, unable to accept an invitation to travel to sing for Welsh miners, Robeson gave a concert to them over the newly laid transatlantic telephone line.

At a subpoenaed appearance before the House Un-American Activities Committee in 1956, Robeson not only refused to answer the infamous "$64,000 question" ("Are you now or have you ever been a member of the Communist Party?") and to name names, but also used the occasion of his hearing to lay bare the connections of race, colonialism, and global capitalism that constituted America's economy and foreign policy. Cited for contempt of Congress for refusing to answer questions, based on his Fifth Amendment right, Robeson was once again pilloried in the mainstream press.

In 1958, Robeson's passport was restored without his having to sign a noncommunist affidavit. Robeson immediately set off on a surge of concert tours around the world, antinuclear rallies and a reprisal of *Othello* in Stratford-upon-Avon, UK. After a failed suicide attempt under suspicious circumstances in Moscow, Robeson recuperated in London and East Germany. Upon returning to the United States in 1962, Robeson made only a few more public appearances and statements before retiring from public life. It was only after six years of continuous hospital care that, in 1974, the FBI ended its investigation of Robeson. Robeson died in Philadelphia in 1976.

SEE ALSO *Cold War; Cold War: Race and the Cold War; Hollywood; Human Rights; McCarthyism*

BIBLIOGRAPHY

Duberman, Martin. *Paul Robeson: A Biography*. New York: New Press, 1989.

Perucci, Tony. *Paul Robeson and the Cold War Performance Complex: Race, Madness, Activism*. Ann Arbor: University of Michigan Press, 2012.

Robeson, Paul. *Here I Stand*. Boston: Beacon Press, 1958.

Robeson, Paul. *Paul Robeson Speaks: Writing, Speeches, Interviews, 1918–1974*. Edited by Philip S. Foner. Secaucus, NJ: Citadel, 1978.

Tony Perucci
Associate Professor
University of North Carolina at Chapel Hill

ROCK 'N' ROLL

Rock 'n' roll was a controversial yet fashionable genre of popular music that emerged in the early 1950s. Its evolution was tied to the rising popularity, particularly among middle-class white adolescents, of black rhythm and blues. Although often viewed as a synonym for all youth-oriented popular music that followed in its wake (it did influence nearly every subsequent worldwide popular musical style from the mid-1950s onward, including rock *and* roll, rock, and its various derivations), by 1963 and the explosive arrival of the Beatles, rock 'n' roll had concluded its course.

ORIGINS AND CONTEMPORARY RECEPTION

Like jazz of a previous era, rock 'n' roll became an international phenomenon. The two musical genres shared similar characteristics. They both originated within underclass African American urban communities, and each could point to a strong southern provenance. Both stressed improvisation, and each contained a rhythmic impulse that encouraged liberation, particularly through bodily movement and dance. The expression of such freedom generally provoked condemnation, especially among defenders of middle-class morality and decorum. Unlike jazz, however, rock 'n' roll never completely eluded its early detractors. While jazz, in its ensuing years toward maturation, was able to establish a reputable pedigree, particularly attaining esteem within intellectual circles, rock 'n' roll and those who initially produced and consumed it remained virtually invisible to those in academe (perhaps because most rock 'n' roll performers, unlike their fellow jazz musicians, often could not read music). They were, for all intents and purposes, banished to the academic hinterlands.

Puzzled and dismayed by the popularity of a musical commodity (and its makers) it considered inferior, the

Teenagers at a rock 'n' roll dance in the 1950s. *Rock 'n' roll underwent an explosive transition from regional—having first gained notice in the American South—to national and international sensation. As a biracial working-class phenomenon, rock 'n' roll blurred many societal boundaries.* **MICHAEL OCHS ARCHIVES/GETTY IMAGES**

intelligentsia and its cohorts in the 1950s concluded that rock 'n' roll represented something less than authentic. Tracing its origins to socially marginalized groups, critics noted that the music entered mainstream consciousness just as the post–World War II teenage consumer market reached fruition. Undoubtedly, rock 'n' roll arose outside of a contemporary intellectual environment that distrusted mass culture and marketing techniques that appeared to promote style over substance. Belonging to a generation that recently had witnessed the Nazi use of technology to disseminate successfully anti-Semitic and nationalistic propaganda, the era's cultural guardians believed that trends in popular music likewise stemmed from the calculating machinations of an entertainment industry manipulating passive audiences. Consequently, although

rock 'n' roll displayed a social significance and depth that belied contemporary and generic criticisms of mass culture, it garnered little favor among potential patrons who were influential and well placed. Unfortunately, for many, rock 'n' roll continues to be remembered nostalgically through the frame that such gatekeepers constructed: a lighthearted, lightweight, innocuous musical fad that served as the sound track for a supposedly simple and carefree *Happy Days* sitcom-like time and place.

This is unfortunate. As at least one contemporary predicted, no history of the twentieth century would be able to ignore rock 'n' roll; it was that important. And much of this importance involved its explosive transition from regional to national and international sensation, a circumstance that certainly resulted at least in part from intense marketing campaigns. Its significance, however, went deeper than simply arriving unexpectedly on the larger scene and taking the world by storm. A biracial working-class phenomenon, rock 'n' roll blurred many of the boundaries that its society worked so hard to keep distinct. In matters regarding race, class, gender, sex, youth, and work and leisure, not to mention music, rock 'n' roll defied existing practices and conventions. That such an unruly form of expression emerged at the height of the Cold War and bureaucratic conformity certainly caused alarm; that it materialized in tandem with formal and organized challenges to the racial status quo inexorably ratcheted up the tension. This "rebelliousness" imparted exceptional meaning in the land where it evolved and first gained notice, the American South. Indeed, besieged segregationists of the period loudly and stridently shouted that rock 'n' roll was subversive, impetuously conflating their feelings about the music with fears of communist infiltration or influence and anxieties about racial integration.

That reactionary southerners believed rock 'n' roll supplied or embodied a leftist-inspired cultural component of the black freedom struggle, of course, did not necessarily make it so. Popular music's relationship to social change, after all, is complicated business. Yet rock 'n' roll and its associated rituals, vehicles, and progressions (including the very instrumental rise of postwar black radio programming, the influence of personality disc jockeys, the popularization of rhythm and blues, and the pursuit of African American urban style as deployed through fashion, speech, and overall bodily deportment) did provide a novel lens and means through which adherents viewed and experienced the world around them. That southern white working-class teenagers living in a racially segregated Dixie were attracted to black rhythm and blues is significant. Not only did their attachment to rhythm and blues help expand the African American genre's appeal (astute popular music industry insiders eventually coined a new term, *rock 'n' roll*, as a marketing ploy to broaden the audience), it also signified the music's racially inclusive nature. It does not seem to be a coincidence that it was a southern white working-class teenage fan of rhythm and blues, Elvis Presley (1935–1977), who contributed so greatly to rock 'n' roll's global popularization.

REGIONAL, CLASS, AND GENERATIONAL CHARACTERISTICS

The regional quality of rock 'n' roll is evident in the demographic composition of its artists and the historical function of their music. Vernacular music in the South traditionally consisted of a mixed West African and British ancestry that flowed from working-class sources. Music had customarily provided a means for the region's powerless to create a space for themselves that indulged

self-expression, psychological release, creative sustenance, and personal satisfaction. Although they may not have enjoyed status, political prerogative, or affluence, the South's working classes, both black and white, traditionally relied on music to get through the day. The generation of rock 'n' roll performers who came of age in the late 1940s and early 1950s were well-versed in this tradition; figures such as Presley, Chuck Berry, Little Richard, Jerry Lee Lewis, Fats Domino, Buddy Holly, LaVern Baker, Gene Vincent, Ruth Brown, Sam Cooke, Carl Perkins, and Clyde McPhatter all shared a common regional, class, and generational background. Before establishing themselves as successful entertainers, all had labored in occupations that promised little save work, alienation, and continued powerlessness. They understood well what it meant to be a truck or tractor driver, a dishwasher, a tenant farmer or sharecropper, a domestic servant, or an attendant of some sort. Significantly, all emerged from the same audiences they later entertained.

While rock 'n' roll certainly was not restricted to the South (or to Presley, for that matter), most artists who performed in the genre hailed from below the Mason-Dixon Line or were the children of southern natives who had migrated to northern and western cities. The music would represent a response to urbanization that retained a distinctive regional character. With a foot planted both in a rural past and an urban present, socially invisible and angst-ridden southern teenage migrants, black and white, sought novel ways to craft requisite identities. Their often-uncertain endeavors within an unfamiliar modern environment included a turn to popular culture and music.

Although never perfect or comprehensive in their course or scope, the negotiations undertaken through rock 'n' roll demonstrated that the attitudes of younger southerners during the postwar period were neither monolithic nor uncomplicated. They were under construction. White youngsters, in particular, throughout the region were struggling to reconcile segregationist dogma with an integrationist agenda provided by popular music and culture. Obviously, some struggled less than others, as video footage from the period makes evident. The imagery of adolescent white mobs throwing bricks and spitting epithets at African American students attempting to desegregate public schools certainly should caution against a rudimentary reading of rock 'n' roll's larger ramifications. Yet as additional contemporary evidence reveals, many of Dixie's musically oriented teenagers frequently deviated from the stock and stereotypical discriminatory behavior long associated with the American South.

GLOBAL LEGACY

By the early 1960s, rock 'n' roll as a musical and cultural force was spent, at least in the United States. Its original audience was now facing its third decade, many of its members now raising children of their own. The performers most associated with the music had also matured. Almost all had abandoned rock 'n' roll for other musical genres or entertainment vehicles. In emphasizing almost exclusively its youthful character, the industry increasingly had shorn rock 'n' roll of its racial, class, and regional characteristics. In the end, all that was left was its legacy, one that continually would influence new generations of popular music artists and audiences.

Interestingly, rock 'n' roll, even as it declined in popularity within the United States, served as the vanguard for modernity around the globe. It was a modernity associated with Americanization, a freshness that emphasized consumption, leisure, and generational division. In the Cold War era, there was no better propaganda that could be used to demonstrate the superiority of capitalism and democracy: adolescents in the United States, no matter what their class origins, seemed to be free, lively, and having fun. For the young living in countries "closed" to the West, rock 'n' roll encouraged an alternative version of youth culture. Like their American counterparts, teenagers throughout Europe (and Asia) consequently embraced the music and its related rituals as a means to establish adolescent style. They often were met by government opposition to such Americanization from below. Nevertheless, a perceived authenticity associated with working-class and racial musical forms from faraway places like Mississippi, Memphis, and Chicago proved particularly fascinating; ironically, it also, at least momentarily or superficially, displaced local aspects of teen life. Youngsters emulating rock 'n' roll records, for instance, tried to sound like their vinyl and celluloid heroes, at least when performing. John Lennon, Paul McCartney, George Harrison, Mick Jagger, and Keith Richards, to name only a few, referenced, both in their music and in their public statements, the influence of the rock 'n' roll generation.

As literal works in progress, southern teenagers who came of age in the late 1940s and early 1950s were impressionable and conflicted. They had a foot in two worlds, uncertain of the path before them. A few became recording artists, with some even attaining stardom, however fleeting it may have been. The majority, however, remained as an audience. In a sense rarely captured by television sitcoms or nostalgic movies and stage plays, rock 'n' roll did serve as their soundtrack. It was a compilation to which modern youth everywhere could relate, articulating realistically the joys, anxieties, and especially the possibilities of youth. Above all, as a historical artifact, it possesses the power to complicate what often has been assumed to be uncomplicated.

SEE ALSO *Dylan, Bob; Hollywood; Jazz; Levi Strauss & Co.; Presley, Elvis Aaron; Television; USA for Africa ("We Are the World"); Voice of America*

BIBLIOGRAPHY

Altschuler, Glenn C. *All Shook Up: How Rock 'n' Roll Changed America.* New York: Oxford University Press, 2003.

Bertrand, Michael T. *Race, Rock, and Elvis.* Urbana: University of Illinois Press, 2000.

Daniel, Pete. *Lost Revolutions: The South in the 1950s.* Chapel Hill: University of North Carolina Press, 2000.

Fenemore, Mark. *Sex, Thugs, and Rock 'n' Roll: Teenage Rebels in Cold War East Germany.* New York: Berghahn, 2007.

Lipsitz, George. *Rainbow at Midnight: Labor and Culture in the 1940s.* Urbana: University of Illinois Press, 1994.

Malone, Bill C., and David Stricklin. *Southern Music/American Music.* Rev. ed. Lexington: University Press of Kentucky, 2003.

Marcus, Greil. *Mystery Train: Images of America in Rock 'n' Roll Music.* New York: Dutton, 1975. 6th ed., New York: Plume, 2015.

Poiger, Uta G. *Jazz, Rock, and Rebels: Cold War Politics and American Culture in a Divided Germany.* Berkeley: University of California Press, 2000.

Wagnleitner, Reinhold. *Coca-Colonization and the Cold War: The Cultural Mission of the United States in Austria after the Second World War.* Translated by Diana M. Wolf. Chapel Hill: University of North Carolina Press, 1994.

Ward, Brian. *Just My Soul Responding: Rhythm and Blues, Black Consciousness, and Race Relations.* Berkeley: University of California Press, 1998.

Werner, Craig. *A Change Is Gonna Come: Music, Race, and the Soul of America.* Rev. ed. Ann Arbor: University of Michigan Press, 2006.

Yoffe, Mark, and Andrea Collins, eds. *Rock 'n' Roll and Nationalism: A Multinational Perspective.* Newcastle, UK: Cambridge Scholars, 2005.

Michael T. Bertrand
Associate Professor of History
Tennessee State University

ROCKEFELLER, JOHN D.

SEE *Robber Barons; Rockefeller Foundation.*

ROCKEFELLER FOUNDATION

The Rockefeller Foundation, established in 1913, was one of the first American philanthropic organizations to become active internationally. Its founder, John D. Rockefeller Sr. (1839–1937), the owner of Standard Oil, donated the first $100 million in the first two years of the foundation's existence. His son, John D. Rockefeller Jr. (1874–1960), became the foundation's president. In its early years, the foundation focused on medical research and public health, especially in the field of infectious diseases such as hookworm disease, malaria, and yellow fever. Having eradicated hookworm disease in the American South, the foundation's Sanitary Commission in the late 1910s and in the 1920s took its experience abroad and fought the disease in Egypt, Brazil, and Mexico, among others. The transnational transfer of knowledge rested on the assumption that science was universally valid, and that the expertise developed by Rockefeller Foundation scientists could help "to promote the well-being of humanity around the world," the foundation's motto.

The foundation's global aspirations and its internationalist outlook became pronounced in the interwar years. For one, the Rockefeller Foundation supported medical research and public health work in China, India, Japan, and Latin America. Furthermore, the foundation contributed large sums to the League of Nations' Health Organization and set up schools of public health in central-eastern and southeastern Europe. Second, Rockefeller Foundation staff promoted the academic study of international relations in the United States and Western Europe. The foundation's motive was to produce the expertise considered necessary to solve the political problems of the interwar period, and thereby to help secure peace. Relatedly, the Rockefeller Foundation funded American-type social scientific research in Europe, thus acting as a transatlantic cultural broker. Similarly, by supporting the League of Nations, the Rockefeller Foundation in part replaced the United States, which had not joined the league, and tried to strengthen internationalist and prodemocratic circles in interwar Europe. When the National Socialists came to power in Germany in 1933, the Rockefeller Foundation brought European refugee scholars to the United States, especially to the New School of Social Research in New York.

World War II (1939–1945) interrupted some of the Rockefeller Foundation's international work in Europe, yet it remained active in the fields of health and nutrition, as hunger gained a new meaning in the context of the war. To make more food available, Rockefeller Foundation experts promoted agricultural extension approaches, some of which had been tried out in the United States and in China earlier. In the early 1940s the foundation encouraged the mechanization of agriculture and the use of hybrid varieties, a combination that resulted in what became known as the Green Revolution. In the 1950s and early 1960s, the Rockefeller Foundation used its Mexican experiences to increase agricultural yields in Asia and to replicate the Green Revolution there.

Closely connected to solving the food problem was the foundation's effort to reduce population growth in the so-called developing countries. Toward that goal, John D. Rockefeller III (1906–1978) established the Population Council in 1952. The council, which also received support from the Ford Foundation, funded research on reproduction and birth control, as well as family planning programs. The Rockefeller Foundation's work in the fields of food and population was, at least in part, driven by the neo-Malthusian fear that lack of food together with high birthrates would cause political unrest and violence in the so-called developing world. In the context of the Cold War, many Western observers believed that the Soviet Union might use this situation to expand its sphere of influence. In this situation, the Rockefeller Foundation's international experience and its ability to produce applicable scientific knowledge appeared extremely valuable and added to the organization's international prestige.

The foundation's reputation for being a nonpolitical actor helped it to become one of the most respected American organizations in the field of international development in the post-1945 years. By the 1960s, the foundation was spending about $10 million annually on overseas programs, especially on the establishment of research institutions, universities, and education centers in Asia, Africa, and Latin America, sometimes in cooperation with the Ford Foundation and the Carnegie Corporation. Meanwhile, in continuing and expanding its work of the interwar period, the Rockefeller Foundation funded social scientific research and area studies at universities in the United States and abroad, thereby helping to produce the expertise needed by politicians to deal with increasingly complex national and international demands in many fields of social life.

In the 1970s the Rockefeller Foundation experienced a generational transformation that coincided with a widespread loss of confidence in the power and universal quality of science, which had been the basis of much of the foundation's work in the previous decades. Thus, the organization revised its structure and outlook in the 1970s and 1980s, shifting away from large-scale projects conducted in cooperation with governments toward smaller ones following bottom-up approaches and conducted in cooperation with nongovernmental organizations. Today, the Rockefeller Foundation's focus areas are health, ecosystems, livelihoods, and cities. Although competition in the field of international philanthropy has increased notably since the 1990s, the Rockefeller Foundation's status as an influential American player in the world remains unchanged.

SEE ALSO *Borlaug, Norman; Ford Foundation; Green Revolution; Nongovernmental Organizations (NGOs); United States Agency for International Development (USAID)*

BIBLIOGRAPHY

Hess, Gary R. "Waging the Cold War in the Third World: The Foundations and the Challenges of Development." In *Charity, Philanthropy, and Civility in American History*, edited by Lawrence J. Friedman and Mark D. McGarvie, 319–39. New York: Cambridge University Press, 2003.

100 Years: The Rockefeller Foundation. http://rockefeller100.org/

Parmar, Inderjeet. *Foundations of the American Century: The Ford, Carnegie, and Rockefeller Foundations in the Rise of American Power*. New York: Columbia University Press, 2012.

Rosenberg, Emily S. "Missions to the World: Philanthropy Abroad." In *Charity, Philanthropy, and Civility in American History*, edited by Lawrence J. Friedman and Mark D. McGarvie, 241–57. New York: Cambridge University Press, 2003.

Sealander, Judith. "Curing Evils at Their Source: The Arrival of Scientific Giving." In *Charity, Philanthropy, and Civility in American History*, edited by Lawrence J. Friedman and Mark D. McGarvie, 217–39. New York: Cambridge University Press, 2003.

Zunz, Oliver. *Philanthropy in America: A History*. Princeton, NJ: Princeton University Press, 2012.

Corinna R. Unger
Associate Professor of Modern European History
Jacobs University Bremen

ROGERS ACT OF 1924

SEE *Foreign Service, US.*

ROOSEVELT, ELEANOR

1884–1962

Eleanor Roosevelt was born into an influential New York family. Her uncle, Theodore Roosevelt (1858–1919), was to become the twenty-sixth president of the United States, and she was to marry the thirty-second president, Franklin Delano Roosevelt (1882–1945), a distant relative. After her primary education by private tutors, Eleanor Roosevelt left the United States at the age of fifteen to attend Allenswood, a finishing school in London, where she became fluent in French. After her return to the United States in 1902, she taught calisthenics and dance classes at a settlement house in New York City and was influenced by the pacifist and internationalist thinking of the US settlement house movement and its leader, Jane Addams (1860–1935).

PACIFISM AND ANTIFASCISM EFFORTS

In January 1919 Eleanor Roosevelt accompanied her husband—then assistant secretary of the navy—to France where he oversaw the liquidation and distribution of US naval installations. The devastation she witnessed on the former battlefields made her a firm internationalist and, the following year, she advocated for the participation of the United States in the League of Nations during her husband's campaign for the vice presidency. She later helped organize and publicize the American Peace Award, supported the US entry into the World Court, and campaigned for the outlawing of war. Unlike her husband, Eleanor Roosevelt identified with the peace movement in the 1920s and 1930s, defining herself as a "realistic pacifist." She opposed unilateral disarmament but participated in antiwar rallies, attended conventions, spoke on peace broadcasts, and publicized the activities of groups like the American Friends Service Committee, the Fellowship of Reconciliation, the War Resisters' League, and the National Committee on the Cause and Cure of War.

In the face of fascist expansion in Europe and Japanese imperialism in Asia, Roosevelt increasingly advocated preparedness and modified her position on neutrality legislation. In her newspaper columns, she publicized the fight of the Spanish Republicans against General Francisco Franco (1892–1975), and she defended the Abraham Lincoln Brigade during the Spanish Civil War (1936–1939). To her, fascism threatened the future of civilization. In Germany and Italy, the public was well aware of Roosevelt's antifascist publications and advised her to stay out of diplomatic affairs. Her inability to achieve changes to US immigration laws that would have allowed Jewish children from Germany into the country greatly distressed her. If Roosevelt ever harbored any sympathy for the Soviet Union, it disappeared with the Hitler-Stalin pact of 1939.

WORLD WAR II

During World War II (1939–1945), Roosevelt played a significant role in promoting relations between Great Britain and the United States. She vigorously defended the Lend-Lease program, and a private meeting with King George VI (1895–1952) and his wife Elizabeth in 1939 did much to change public opinion about Anglo-American relations. In October 1942 Roosevelt went to Great Britain to visit US troops and to study the British home-front efforts, especially women's war work. Her visit boosted the morale of both the troops and the British population. Chalmers Roberts (1910–2005) of the Office of War Information wrote that "Mrs. Roosevelt has done more to bring real understanding of the spirit of the United States to the people of Great Britain than any other single American who has ever visited these islands" (Lash 1971, 669). In August and September 1943 she traveled more than 25,000 miles in the South Pacific as a Red Cross delegate, visited about 400,000 servicemen, and met with representatives of women's groups. In Australia, her appearances drew large crowds and received extensive press coverage.

UN AMBASSADORSHIP

After 1945 Roosevelt joined those who advocated a New Deal for the world, supporting democracies abroad and combating racism at home. In December 1945, President Harry Truman (1884–1972) appointed her the US delegate to the United Nations (UN), a position she was initially reluctant to accept because she felt she lacked diplomatic experience. Prominent critics of the former First Lady included John Foster Dulles (1888–1959), who thought she was too liberal, and William Fulbright (1905–1995), who thought she was too inexperienced.

At the first meeting of the UN General Assembly in London in 1946, Roosevelt was assigned to Committee Three, which dealt with humanitarian, social, and cultural issues, including the fate of over a million displaced East Europeans in Western detention camps. While the Russian delegates favored forcible repatriation, Roosevelt successfully argued the Allied position for voluntary repatriation and defended the right to political and religious asylum. When the General Assembly adjourned, she embarked on a whirlwind trip to Germany, where she visited two displaced persons camps, held press conferences (one with female German journalists), met with UN Relief and Rehabilitation Administration personnel, and visited with US occupation troops.

After her return to the United States, Roosevelt advocated assistance for rebuilding Europe, pointing out that Russia would take the lead if the United States did not and emphasizing the economic potential of a recovery program. Her 1946 publications and speeches presented a positive view of the Soviet Union, because she feared that anti-Soviet sentiment in the United States would undermine the work of the UN. Roosevelt did not regard communism as the primary problem in the postwar world, but rather poverty, ignorance, discrimination, and the denial of civil liberties. One of the leading anti-Stalinist liberals in the United States, Roosevelt moved closer to the foreign policy of the Truman administration by the end of 1947, although she was ambivalent about the implications of the Truman Doctrine. She supported the Marshall Plan because of its emphasis on both economic and humanitarian assistance.

Roosevelt returned to the United Nations in January 1947 to chair the UN Human Rights Commission, which was to frame a UN Declaration of Human Rights. She sensed that a detailed and binding covenant would be difficult to enforce and might not produce the intended effect. After the preparation of four lengthy drafts, in June 1948 Roosevelt proposed the preparation of a shorter text "which would be readily understood by all peoples" (Berger 1981, 69) and include the American Bill of Rights and the French Declaration of Human Rights. The Communist delegates to the United Nations staunchly opposed this and wanted to confine the charter to social and economic rights. Soviet conduct at the United Nations often infuriated Roosevelt because she felt that the Soviet delegates would never compromise. Shortly before a comprehensive human rights bill went to the General Assembly in the fall of 1948, Roosevelt gave her famous human rights speech at the Sorbonne in Paris, defending her version of the declaration. Speaking in French and at the height of the Berlin blockade, she accused the Communist delegates of tampering with the definitions of *democracy, freedom*, and *human rights*, "making these words synonymous with suppression and dictatorship" (Berger 1981, 72). The declaration was ratified by the General Assembly on December 10, 1948; the Communist bloc abstained from the vote. Most non-Communist observers recognized Roosevelt as the personification of unselfishness who did not represent a faction, whereas the Soviet newspapers called her a "hypocritical servant of capitalism" and a "schoolmistress."

Although Roosevelt initially thought that the North American Treaty Organization (NATO) pact violated the spirit of the UN, she soon endorsed the alliance, arguing that Europe needed collective military strength. She also supported US involvement in Korea, evoking Europe's failed appeasement policies of the 1930s and arguing that failure to support South Korea would undermine the work of the UN. In 1952, she broadcast for the Voice of America from Paris during the tenth session of the General Assembly, creating more "goodwill for the U.S. in western Europe than any other American" (Cook 1984, 119).

Afterward, Roosevelt embarked on what she called her "round-the-world trip home." The trip began in Lebanon, where she visited refugee camps of Palestinian Arabs. Overall, she received a cool reception in Lebanon, Syria, and Transjordan because of her unwavering support for Israel—she had lobbied Truman for immediate US diplomatic recognition in 1948. In Israel, she met with Prime Minister David Ben-Gurion (1886–1973) and

Statue of First Lady Eleanor Roosevelt at the Franklin Delano Roosevelt Memorial, Washington, DC. *Even though her initial idealism was often frustrated during her years of official and unofficial diplomatic service, Roosevelt continued her international work until her death. She is best remembered for her work with the UN Human Rights Commission and in support of the Universal Declaration of Human Rights, as well as her tireless efforts on behalf of refugees.* **PHOTOGRAPHS IN THE CAROL M. HIGHSMITH ARCHIVE, LIBRARY OF CONGRESS, PRINTS AND PHOTOGRAPHS DIVISION**

Golda Meir (1898–1978) and visited a kibbutz. She remained infatuated with the young nation and would return in 1954. Traveling on to Pakistan, she visited another refugee camp and met with women's groups. In India, she was especially interested in the effects of Point Four aid money and hoped to increase American support for this program. She also addressed a special session of the Indian parliament. On her way home, she made brief stops in Singapore, Indonesia, Thailand, the Philippines, Guam, and Hawai'i. According to Dean Acheson (1893–1971), Roosevelt's trip "served the public interest exceedingly well," and "she appears to have done much to increase understanding of United States foreign policy objectives," especially in India and Pakistan (Lash 1972, 204).

OFFICIAL AND UNOFFICIAL DIPLOMATIC AND HUMAN RIGHTS WORK

After Dwight Eisenhower (1890–1969) became president in 1953, Roosevelt resigned from her UN post. She immediately began working for the American Association for the United Nations, speaking frequently to defend the organization against neo-isolationism. She embarked on a five-week trip to Japan in the summer of 1953 to study the progress of democracy. Although Roosevelt inadvertently joined the controversy on rearmament when she advocated preparedness, she was generally received with a friendliness that surprised her. Once more, she proved to be an unrivaled goodwill ambassador. Before returning home, she visited Hong Kong, Bangkok, Rangoon, New

Delhi, and Istanbul on her way to Greece, went to Yugoslavia from there, and then to Vienna and London. The main purpose of this long trip home was to meet and interview Tito (Josip Broz, 1892–1980), the leader of Yugoslavia. Although Roosevelt had long supported US relations with, as well as food aid for, Yugoslavia, Tito failed to convince her that he was democratic, and the trip left her disheartened. After her return, she concluded that McCarthyism had harmed American prestige in Asia and Europe.

Although Roosevelt remained deeply suspicious of the Soviet Union, she traveled there as a journalist in 1957 and interviewed Soviet premier Nikita Khrushchev (1894–1971). They discussed, among other things, disarmament and the recent Middle East crisis, and Roosevelt made appeals on behalf of Russian Jews. They agreed on nuclear disarmament, but could not agree on inspections.

Even though her initial idealism was often frustrated during her years of official and unofficial diplomatic service, Roosevelt continued her international work until her death. In 1961, President John F. Kennedy (1917–1963) reappointed her to the United NationsN, and she eagerly served on the National Advisory Committee of the Peace Corps. Internationally, Roosevelt is best remembered for her work with the UN Human Rights Commission and in support of the Universal Declaration of Human Rights, as well as her tireless efforts to help refugees around the world. In 1954 she became the first recipient of the Nansen Refugee Award, established by the United Nations to recognize service on behalf of refugees. In 1968, the "First Lady of the World" was honored posthumously with the UN Prize for Outstanding Achievement in Human Rights.

SEE ALSO *Human Rights; Roosevelt, Franklin D.; United Nations; Universal Declaration of Human Rights; World War II*

BIBLIOGRAPHY

Beasley, Maurine H., Henry R. Beasley, and Holly C. Shulman, eds. *The Eleanor Roosevelt Encyclopedia.* Westport, CT: Greenwood Press, 2001.

Berger, Jason. *A New Deal for the World: Eleanor Roosevelt and American Foreign Policy.* New York: Columbia University Press, 1981.

Cook, Blanche Wiesen. "'Turn toward Peace': ER and Foreign Affairs." In *Without Precedent: The Life and Career of Eleanor Roosevelt,* edited by Joan Hoff-Wilson and Marjorie Lightman, 108–121. Bloomington: Indiana University Press, 1984.

Glendon, Mary Ann. *A World Made New: Eleanor Roosevelt and the Universal Declaration of Human Rights.* New York: Random House, 2001.

Lash, Joseph P. *Eleanor and Franklin: The Story of Their Relationship, Based on Eleanor Roosevelt's Private Papers.* New York: Norton, 1971.

Lash, Joseph P. *Eleanor: The Years Alone.* New York: Norton, 1972.

Roosevelt, Eleanor. *The Autobiography of Eleanor Roosevelt.* New York: Harper, 1961.

Anja Schüler
Research Associate
Heidelberg Center for American Studies at the
University of Heidelberg

ROOSEVELT, FRANKLIN D.
1882–1945

Franklin Delano Roosevelt's family, education, and early political career propelled him to think of the United States in a world context. Above all, the circumstances of his presidency from 1933 to 1945 required Roosevelt to adapt to and seek remedies for world crises—the Great Depression and World War II—that threatened the stability and security of the United States. While he improvised solutions and built political and international coalitions, his powerful rhetoric resonated abroad, offering people throughout the world greater hope for political rights and economic security. Roosevelt's influence outlasted him and extended outside and beyond his own specific concerns and solutions. Under his guidance, the United States became a leader in world affairs.

ROOSEVELT'S COSMOPOLITAN YOUTH

Roosevelt's patrician parents taught him about his Dutch and Belgian Huguenot ancestors. For the Roosevelt family, the Protestants, challenging the Catholic Church and absolutist monarchs, were the heroes of Enlightenment Europe. The family traveled to Britain, France, and Germany eight times, and young Franklin received instruction in French and German from tutors and governesses there. He also attended a German school during the summer of 1891. His European stays undoubtedly gave him a sense of Europe's importance, as well as a more cosmopolitan background than most previous presidents.

Anchored by self-confidence and a sense of American virtue, the young Roosevelt was hardly overawed by the Old World. He later claimed to have been struck by German intolerance and militarism while he was in Germany. As a college student, he was one of the organizers of the Boer Relief Fund, formed to assist Boer women and children in British concentration camps during the Boer War (1899–1902). It was one of a number of ways in which he showed an early social conscience that carried over into later politics (Ward 1985; Breitman and Lichtman 2013, 1–11).

ROOSEVELT'S INTERNATIONALISM AND COMMITMENT TO MULTILATERAL COOPERATION

In 1910, Roosevelt won election to the New York State Senate, where he quickly demonstrated his ambition, political skills, and courage by leading independent, progressive Democrats who were challenging the corrupt New York City Democratic machine. In 1912 the *New York Times* lauded Roosevelt as one of a handful of young Americans "unknown four years ago who have jumped into fame and become factors in national affairs" (Breitman and Lichtman 2013, 12–13).

In 1913, another progressive Democrat, newly elected president Woodrow Wilson (1856–1924), tapped Roosevelt as assistant secretary of the US Navy—the post that his cousin, Theodore Roosevelt (1858–1919), had used to vault himself toward the presidency. Franklin Roosevelt pushed for American involvement in World War I (1914–1918) and became one of Washington's most important wartime administrators. Although turned down for a combat role in the war, in mid-1918 he toured the war zone in Europe—an experience he would later exaggerate in White House conversations. As the Democratic nominee for vice president in 1920, he sidestepped blame for Wilson's failure in negotiating a peace settlement and getting the Senate to confirm the treaties, but he supported American entrance into the League of Nations. The young Roosevelt believed in Wilson's selectively idealistic principles backed by military strength (Smith 2007, 99–186).

During the 1920s, Roosevelt followed dominant liberal currents toward internationalism and pacifism. He particularly favored greater political and economic cooperation with Japan. A Japanese push toward rearmament and the 1931 Japanese invasion of Manchuria made improvement of ties difficult, if not impossible, but early in his presidency Roosevelt was careful not to provoke Japan. Even before his election as president, Roosevelt had also backed the establishment of a Jewish homeland in Palestine, a commitment that he maintained throughout his presidency (Dallek 1995, 16–17, 76; Breitman and Lichtman 2013, 25–38).

Latin America was another region where Roosevelt wanted a new course. Although he had once championed US intervention in Haiti, he perceived that commitment to multilateral cooperation would reduce anti-US sentiments in the Western Hemisphere. His Good Neighbor Policy, announced in his inaugural address in March 1933 and later formalized in diplomatic agreements, renounced the unilateral use of force in Latin America and pushed for hemispheric consultation on issues of common interest. The policy was never fully realized, but it did shift emphasis and win over many Latin American states. Shortly before and during World War II (1939–1945), the Good Neighbor Policy, combined with the Monroe Doctrine (1823), allowed the president to swing much of Latin America behind the idea of hemispheric defense against potential German incursion (Dallek 1995, 38–39, 176–177, 233).

FOREIGN POLICY DURING THE 1930s

During the Great Depression, which brought unemployment to about a quarter of the American workforce and massive capital withdrawals from Europe, outgoing president Herbert Hoover (1874–1964) tried to bind Roosevelt to international efforts to mitigate the economic downturn. However, the newly elected president refused to tie his hands and showed an inclination to experiment at home, whatever the consequences internationally. Initially, the "economic nationalist" Roosevelt had far greater impact on the world than the internationalist one.

In his inaugural address on March 4, 1933, President Roosevelt asked Congress to act decisively or to give him unprecedented executive authority, because the economic emergency was as dire as if a foreign foe had invaded the country. The passage of fifteen major new laws in the first one hundred days of the Roosevelt administration included authorization for the administration to reset the price of gold and to spend billions of dollars on public works, abandoning the notion that austerity and deflation would cure the economy by themselves—or that international cooperation was paramount. Roosevelt's New Deal suggested to foreign observers that capitalism and democracy might still coexist. Roosevelt later tried to bolster confidence across the world in democratic government (Smith 2007, 278–332).

Many of Roosevelt's Republican opponents at home—and not a few Democrats—convinced that the New Deal had illegitimately expanded the power of the federal government and the president, struck back in foreign affairs. The first-term Roosevelt could do little to convince Congress and the American public that the threats to peace arising in Europe and Asia posed a problem for the United States. American military budgets actually declined, while Nazi Germany went from a country itself vulnerable to invasion to the strongest military power on the continent (by 1936) and a threat to its eastern neighbors. By invading Ethiopia in October 1935, Italy defied halfhearted sanctions imposed by the League of Nations and took over the one independent

African state. During the dispute between Italy and Ethiopia, Congress quickly passed a Neutrality Act designed to prevent America from arming any belligerent in a conflict. Revisions in 1936 and another Neutrality Act in 1937 only added new restrictions. It seemed that the idea of collective security had faded or expired, while the United States watched. Even in October 1937, after winning reelection decisively, when Roosevelt vaguely suggested quarantining aggressors, critics forced him to back off from initiating any positive measures (Schmitz 2007, 17–53).

Responding in 1938 to the German annexation of Austria and later acts of aggression and Nazi persecution, Roosevelt pursued a quixotic and underpowered campaign to bring about the emigration of millions of Jews and other persecuted peoples from Europe. For the first time in his presidency, the United States filled its immigration quota from Germany. Still, with Congress more inclined to reduce immigration quotas than to expand them, the administration could at best stretch them slightly, which meant a greater burden would fall to other countries (or their colonies).

An American-led intergovernmental committee failed to negotiate an orderly emigration of Jews from Germany because of resistance from Nazi authorities and unavailability of any single site for mass immigration. US efforts to persuade other countries to take in substantial numbers of Jews met with far more resistance than expected, but did not collapse. Under pressure from the United States, Latin American nations received more Jews in the years preceding the Holocaust than the British allowed into Palestine.

THE WARTIME TRANSFORMATION OF AMERICA'S ROLE IN WORLD AFFAIRS

As the prospect of war increased, Roosevelt's priorities shifted toward getting Congress to loosen the restrictions of the Neutrality Acts—which he achieved with difficulty only after war broke out—and devising means for aiding Britain and France short of American entrance into the war. The dynamics of mobilizing resistance to Nazi Germany required postponement of major refugee resettlement efforts. By 1940, fears of Nazi subversion and sabotage created suspicion of foreigners, whether or not they were victims of Nazi persecution. Roosevelt retained his vision of up to 20 million Europeans leaving for homes in other parts of the world, but it was of little practical value for targets of Nazi persecution and murder during most of the war (Breitman and Lichtman 2013, 98–183).

During his "fireside chat" with the American people in late December 1940, Roosevelt called the United States the "arsenal of democracy." In his annual message to Congress the next month, he spoke of pursuing four

essential freedoms worldwide: freedom of speech, freedom of religion, freedom from want, and freedom from fear. Roosevelt thus provided a rationale for the United States to emerge from its isolationist shell and help preserve democracy and freedom worldwide. The president articulated a broad internationalist vision of human freedom, including not only America's constitutional protections of free speech and religion but also economic security and protection from the violence of war. The Four Freedoms speech coincided with the introduction of Roosevelt's Lend-Lease program that would turn America into the "Arsenal of Democracy," by providing military aid to nations battling Nazi aggression. It anticipated America's postwar participation in the United Nations and its efforts to rebuild war-torn Europe and promote economic development in less affluent nations.

Roosevelt's next step in articulating a world vision, the Atlantic Charter, was an Anglo-American enterprise. Given domestic opposition, Roosevelt could not commit to allying the United States with Britain, but he could offer a shared statement of principles to the world. The Atlantic Charter called for a peace "which will afford assurance that all the men in all the lands may live out their lives in freedom from fear and freedom from want." Ironically, British prime minister Winston Churchill (1874–1965) suggested the phrase "all the men in all the lands," yet Britain had to qualify such expansive language, seemingly endorsing universal political rights and economic justice. Churchill had to explain later to the House of Commons that the Atlantic Charter was primarily aimed at areas under the Nazi yoke (Borgwardt 2005, 4, 28–30; Kimball 1997, 63–87).

Isolationists complained that Roosevelt was recklessly pushing America into the war in Europe. Yet interventionists argued that he was too timid in seeking an end to US neutrality and providing support for the Allies. Again, Roosevelt's intent was to oppose international aggression and fascism within the limits of public opinion and the American system of government.

After the Pearl Harbor attack on December 7, 1941, US involvement in the war required the greatest mobilization of manpower and resources in history. It not only brought about economic recovery; it brought about economic prosperity. The war allowed Roosevelt to win one more election and continue the transformation of America's role in world affairs.

Roosevelt oversaw the creation of the modern military-industrial complex as his government turned private production to military purposes. Given nearly universal public support for the war effort, the US government did not engage in the censorship or opinion manipulation that had marked World War I. The government did incarcerate numerous German and Italian

Americans, as well as more than 100,000 Japanese Americans, for the duration of the war. Forty years later, a committee established by Congress would conclude that "race prejudice, war hysteria and a failure of political leadership" had led to a "grave injustice" against Japanese Americans (Robinson 2001, 250–251).

Roosevelt strongly influenced wartime strategy and postwar objectives. Early in 1942 Roosevelt and Churchill decided to concentrate on defeating Germany first, then Japan. At the Casablanca Conference in January 1943, they announced the strategic bombing and their demands for the unconditional surrender of the enemy. Unlike World War I, there would be no armistice. Postwar politics brought Roosevelt, Churchill, and Joseph Stalin (1879–1953) together for the first time in November 1943. In a decisive rejection of prewar American isolationism, Roosevelt described his idea of a postwar international organization in which the great powers would act as "guarantors" of the peace. The "Big Three" also agreed on an invasion of France the following year. At the Yalta Conference in February 1945, the Big Three agreed to a postwar international organization (the United Nations); the division of Germany; the payment of reparations by Germany; the entry of the Soviet Union into the war against Japan; and vague promises for free elections in Eastern Europe. Conservatives would later harshly criticize Roosevelt for giving too much away to Stalin at Yalta. But Roosevelt's primary purpose at the time was to hold the fragile Allied coalition together and win Soviet agreement to enter the war against Japan. The Soviets already had a dominant military position in Eastern Europe, and the atom bomb was not yet ready for use against Japan (Kimball 1997; Burns 1970; Dallek 1995, 506–525).

POSTWAR LEGACY

Although Roosevelt did not live to see the end of World War II, under his leadership the United States made a decisive break from prewar isolationism. America took the lead in forming the United Nations and in negotiating at the July 1944 Bretton Woods conference in New Hampshire new international economic agreements that, in effect, pegged the world economy to the dollar. Unique among nations, the United States could, if necessary, pay for imported goods, the economic recovery of war-torn nations, the arming of anticommunist governments, and the launching of an American military presence abroad by printing more dollars—what French president Charles de Gaulle (1890–1970) called the "exorbitant privilege."

Within the framework of Bretton Woods, America supplied the lion's share of funding for an International Monetary Fund designed to maintain currency stability in the world economy and a World Bank to finance infrastructure projects—roads, bridges, railways, dams—

initially in Europe and then in less-developed nations. The United States also strengthened the Export-Import Bank to provide overseas loans for purchasing American goods. The World Bank, the Export-Import Bank, and the American-financed United Nations Relief and Rehabilitation Administration helped reconstruct postwar Europe. Roosevelt and his advisers believed that the international depression had led to the outbreak of war and that the preservation of peace required active measures to avoid another worldwide economic meltdown (Borgwardt 2005; Dallek 1995).

News of Roosevelt's death of a massive cerebral hemorrhage on April 12, 1945, saddened people across the globe who had looked to the American president for leadership and inspiration. Adolf A. Berle (1895–1971), the American ambassador in Rio de Janeiro, Brazil, watched in amazement as a steady stream of Brazilians, some humble laborers without shoes, came to the American embassy to offer their condolences. Berle wrote in his diary that Roosevelt had been a friend of nations and of peoples. His foreign policy had included friendship with various classes, especially "the large humbler classes who do not usually find expression in their governments." Roosevelt's policies, therefore, brought into consideration "problems which normally do not find the place to which they are entitled in foreign relations" (Berle 1973, 527).

SEE ALSO *Cold War; Dollar Diplomacy; Four Freedoms; Good Neighbor Policy; League of Nations; Missionary Diplomacy; Nazism; Roosevelt, Theodore; Wilson, Woodrow; World War II*

BIBLIOGRAPHY

Atlantic Charter. August 14, 1941. http://avalon.law.yale.edu/wwii/atlantic.asp

Berle, Adolf A., Jr. *Navigating the Rapids, 1918–1971: From the Papers of Adolf A. Berle.* Edited by Beatrice Bishop Berle and Travis Beal Jacobs. New York: Harcourt Brace Jovanovich, 1973.

Borgwardt, Elizabeth. *A New Deal for the World: America's Vision for Human Rights.* Cambridge, MA: Belknap Press of Harvard University Press, 2005.

Breitman, Richard, and Allan J. Lichtman. *FDR and the Jews.* Cambridge, MA: Belknap Press of Harvard University Press, 2013.

Burns, James MacGregor. *Roosevelt: The Soldier of Freedom.* New York: Harcourt Brace Jovanovich, 1970.

Casey, Steven. *Cautious Crusade: Franklin D. Roosevelt, American Public Opinion, and the War against Nazi Germany.* New York: Oxford University Press, 2001.

Dallek, Robert. *Franklin D. Roosevelt and American Foreign Policy, 1932–1945.* New York: Oxford University Press, 1995. First published in 1979.

Kimball, Warren F. *Forged in War: Roosevelt, Churchill, and the Second World War.* New York: Morrow, 1997.

Robinson, Greg. *By Order of the President: FDR and the Internment of Japanese Americans.* Cambridge, MA: Harvard University Press, 2001.

Schmitz, David F. *The Triumph of Internationalism: Franklin D. Roosevelt and a World in Crisis, 1933–1941.* Washington, DC: Potomac, 2007.

Smith, Jean Edward. *FDR.* New York: Random House, 2007.

Ward, Geoffrey C. *Before the Trumpet: Young Franklin Roosevelt, 1882–1905.* New York: Harper and Row, 1985.

Richard Breitman
Distinguished Professor of History, Emeritus
American University

Allan J. Lichtman
Distinguished Professor of History
American University

ROOSEVELT, THEODORE
1858–1919

Theodore Roosevelt became the youngest president in US history at the age of forty-two when he assumed office in 1901 after William McKinley's assassination. Roosevelt's ascendancy coincided with the United States assuming a new international role. Its population and wealth had expanded considerably in the late nineteenth century. After war with Spain in 1898, it also expanded territorially with the acquisition of new colonies in the Caribbean and Pacific. At the outset of the twentieth century, the United States was a rising world power.

PREPAREDNESS

Roosevelt played his own part in this expansion. From the late 1880s onward, he had taken a passionate interest in global affairs. Drawing on his voracious reading, Roosevelt wrote prolifically on international subjects and corresponded with leading scholars and practitioners on both sides of the Atlantic. An intellectual and cosmopolitan, Roosevelt was also an avowed nationalist and urged his countrymen to approach global affairs with a patriotic outlook. Roosevelt was adamant that the United States must adopt an active global role, forcefully defending its national interests while also responsibly discharging its international duties. Most critically, Roosevelt believed that the United States should ensure that it was prepared to defend itself and its interests against any opponent, by force if necessary. This was a lesson that he had taken from his reading of history. It underpinned his first book, a study of *The Naval War of 1812* (1882), and remained an obsession throughout his career.

Roosevelt's preparedness creed was reinforced by the writings of Alfred Thayer Mahan (1840–1914). The two became regular correspondents and together worked for the development of the US Navy. However, Roosevelt was unprepared to lobby for American expansion from the sidelines. Rather, he was determined to take an active role in establishing the United States as an international power. Whenever the United States was involved in an international dispute, Roosevelt harbored visions of participating in any potential struggle. An outspoken champion of the Monroe Doctrine (1823), Roosevelt wished to prevent European powers from establishing new dependencies in the Western Hemisphere and was ultimately committed to removing any trace of European colonialism from the Americas. Concerned that Americans were becoming overly materialistic and enfeebled, Roosevelt was convinced that the United States needed to test itself in battle.

ROLE IN THE SPANISH-AMERICAN WAR

Conflict would occur with Spain in 1898. Roosevelt was appalled by Spanish colonial conduct in Cuba. In addition, he believed war with Spain would warn other European powers against expanding in the Americas and enable the acquisition of US naval bases. Roosevelt left his position as assistant secretary of the navy, assembled his own volunteer regiment of "Rough Riders," and helped wrest Spain from Cuba. The assault that Roosevelt led on Kettle Hill in July 1898 was widely publicized in accounts of the war, not least Roosevelt's own, and ensured that he was celebrated as a war hero back home. His subsequent rapid rise to the presidency, via the governorship of New York and the vice presidency, led Lewis Einstein (1877–1967), a diplomat and Roosevelt biographer, to claim that it was "a charge which began in the jungle and ended in the White House" (Einstein 1930, 69).

ROOSEVELTIAN DIPLOMACY

Roosevelt embraced the public profile of the presidency, determined to use it as a "bully pulpit" to educate Americans in their global responsibilities. He possessed a sophisticated appreciation of international power relations, but he was not a practitioner of Bismarckian-style realpolitik. His foreign policy philosophy was shaped by an "ideology of civilization," based on a Lamarckian racial framework, a commitment to averting wars between the most advanced nations, and a conviction that colonial expansion by "civilized" powers advanced global order.

Central to Roosevelt's diplomatic outlook was the conviction that the United States and the British Empire had common interests and a shared civilizing mission in the world. This did not mean that he was willing to compromise his nationalism, and he was unyielding in disputes with Britain over US control of an interoceanic canal and Alaska's boundary with Britain's Canadian Dominion. However, after Britain accepted settlements favorable to the United States and decided against challenging US hegemony in the Americas, Roosevelt sought to strengthen the rapprochement between the two nations. As a result of American popular animosity to its former colonial ruler, and, in particular, the strong resentment felt by Irish Americans to Britain's control of their homeland, Roosevelt sought to cement the entente through informal and largely unpublicized acts. Roosevelt practiced a personalized diplomacy, establishing close relations with ambassadors in Washington, such as the French representative Jean-Jules Jusserand (1855–1932) and the German diplomat Hermann Speck von Sternburg (1852–1908); utilizing his network of intimate international friends, such as the British diplomat Cecil Spring Rice (1859–1918) and his compatriot, the soldier-statesman Arthur Lee (1868–1947); and corresponding directly with heads of state, such as Kaiser Wilhelm II (1859–1941) and King Edward VII (1841–1910).

The Panama Canal. Roosevelt's principal foreign policy preoccupation during his first term in office was the construction of an interoceanic canal connecting the Atlantic and Pacific Oceans. This ambition preceded Roosevelt's administration. His resolute determination that the canal must be US controlled helped lead to the signing of Hay-Pauncefote Treaty with Britain in November 1901. Having decided that the Isthmus of Panama was more suitable than Nicaragua as a site, Roosevelt entered into negotiations with Colombia, which held sovereign rights to the territory. When the Colombian congress rejected the agreement in an attempt to extract a higher price, Roosevelt was furious and encouraged a Panamanian uprising. Aided by Roosevelt's dispatch of US ships to the region, the revolution succeeded. The State Department quickly signed a treaty that granted the United States control over a zone within the new republic. Democrats accused the president of acting illegally, but the acquisition of the canal zone proved extremely popular with the American public. In his autobiography, Roosevelt proudly declared, "I took the canal zone and let Congress debate; and while the debate goes on, the Canal does also" (quoted in Morris 2010, 134).

The Roosevelt Corollary. The procurement of the Panama Canal strengthened Roosevelt's determination to prevent European intervention in the Western Hemisphere. When Venezuela reneged on its debt repayment to its European creditors in 1901, Roosevelt was initially prepared to allow the powers to "spank it," as he informed von Sternburg, as long as they did not annex any territory. However, Roosevelt was alarmed by an Anglo-German-Italian blockade of Venezuela. In 1904,

when the failure of the Dominican Republic to pay its international debts risked another intervention, Roosevelt announced his corollary to the Monroe Doctrine, as a means to prevent European interference in the Americas and to sanction US interventions in the region, like that in Panama. Roosevelt's critics in the United States and Europe viewed the Roosevelt Corollary as naked imperialism. However, when Roosevelt felt compelled to temporarily take over Dominican customs houses, he was adamant that he had "the same desire to annex [the territory] as a gorged boa constrictor might have to swallow a porcupine wrong-end-to" (Roosevelt 1904). Another intervention in Cuba to prevent revolution in 1906 was followed by a swift withdrawal of US troops, although the sovereignty of both islands remained heavily compromised.

The Philippines and Japan. Roosevelt's resistance to formal colonialism in the Americas was influenced by US experience in the Pacific. Roosevelt had embraced the expansion that followed the war with Spain and was a prominent advocate of annexing the Philippines. As president, he maintained the campaign to establish American rule over the archipelago. Although Roosevelt proclaimed a general amnesty and declared the Philippine-American conflict over in July 1902, Filipino fighters would continue to wage a guerrilla campaign against US forces. Roosevelt believed that US colonial rule should be accompanied by economic benefits for its subjects and that proper provisions must be put in place to defend the islands. However, having failed to convince Congress or the American public to support his colonial policies, Roosevelt privately admitted to his chosen successor, William Howard Taft (1857–1930), in 1907 that the Philippines would soon have to be granted independence as the islands were a security hazard, terming them "our heel of Achilles."

The principal threat to the Philippines came from Japan. Roosevelt initially welcomed Japan's rise to great power status, admiring its constitutional system of government. Furthermore, he perceived Japan as a counter in East Asia to Russia, which threatened the US Open Door Policy in China and whose government's persecution of its Jewish subjects led Roosevelt to protest diplomatically after the Kishinev pogrom in 1903. Therefore, when Japan launched a devastating preemptive attack on the Russian fleet at Port Arthur in 1904, Roosevelt privately welcomed Japan's early success in the conflict.

As Japan grew increasingly war weary and Russia descended into revolution, Roosevelt worked behind the scenes to bring the combatants to a peace conference in Portsmouth, New Hampshire. Roosevelt's interventions helped prevent the talks from collapsing, and the final treaty confirmed Japan's victories but ensured Russia was not completely wiped out as an East Asian power. For his role in ending the conflict, Roosevelt in 1906 became the first American to win the Nobel Peace Prize.

While Roosevelt believed his peacemaking had also served American interests, he was increasingly concerned about growing Japanese nationalism. When peace terms were presented, popular Japanese perceptions that the United States had prevented Japan from securing their war spoils led to riots in Tokyo. During the conflict, Roosevelt had accepted Japan's occupation of Korea, regarding Japanese dominance as preferable to Russian control and aware that, in any case, the United States did not have the resources or the will to prevent it. However, Japan's regional ambitions now posed a threat to the American position in the Philippines.

As tensions rose after California attempted to segregate Japanese children in its public schools, Roosevelt negotiated the "Gentlemen's Agreement" with Japan in 1907 to restrict the number of Japanese immigrants. While determined to avoid giving Japan cause for offense, Roosevelt also ensured that the United States built up its naval strength. In his final years in office, Roosevelt sent the US Navy battle fleet, dubbed the Great White Fleet, around the world. Demonstrating that the United States was now a major naval power, the fleet completed its successful voyage in February 1909, just two weeks before Roosevelt left the White House.

The Balance of Power in Europe. Under Roosevelt, the United States also adopted a more active diplomatic role in Europe, the main arena of power politics in this era. Tensions between Germany and France over Morocco led, in 1906, to an international conference at Algeciras, Spain, to which Roosevelt sent US representatives. Concerned at the prospect of a European conflict, the president nudged the two sides to the conference table. Roosevelt maneuvered clandestinely to help secure a settlement favorable to France, judging it a more responsible colonial power and in favor of its entente with Britain. Roosevelt's opponents in Congress protested that his intervention in European affairs violated the traditional US stance of noninvolvement on the Continent, and the administration was forced to emphasize that the United States had no obligation to enforce the treaty.

ROOSEVELT AND WORLD WAR I

Roosevelt's fellow countrymen did not share his growing concerns about Germany's threat to the European balance of power. The limited involvement in Europe during Roosevelt's presidency did not continue under Taft. When a second Moroccan crisis occurred in 1911, Taft made clear that the United States had no interests in the squabble. When war broke out in Europe in 1914, Taft's successor, Woodrow Wilson (1856–1924), maintained the convention of noninvolvement in his declaration of US neutrality. Although initially unwilling to publicly condemn Germany's violation of Belgian sovereignty, Roosevelt was sympathetic to the Allied cause and soon became the most prominent critic of Wilson's foreign policy. Roosevelt's long-standing conviction that the United States should be militarily prepared to defend itself ensured that he was a leading advocate of strengthening the nation's armed forces in response to the war. Roosevelt recognized that Wilson's neutrality policy commanded broad support among the American public. However, he continued to rail against the administration and accused Wilson of cowardice in his response to the German sinking of the *Lusitania* in May 1915.

Although Roosevelt tempered his public criticism of the White House after Wilson declared war on Germany in April 1917, he returned to the offensive after the administration rejected his request to organize a voluntary cavalry to fight Germany. Roosevelt assailed the administration for its handling of the war effort and demanded "100 percent Americanism" from US citizens in their attitude to the conflict. Although Roosevelt was an early advocate of a league of nations, he was an outspoken opponent of Wilson's "Fourteen Points" and was convinced that postwar order was dependent on continued US cooperation with the Allies. Roosevelt was proud that his four sons saw active wartime service but was devastated by the death of his youngest son, Quentin, in July 1918.

Many Americans believed US entry into the war vindicated Roosevelt, and he was widely regarded as the front-runner for the Republican presidential nomination in 1920. However, his health deteriorated following Quentin's death. Theodore Roosevelt's death in January 1919 robbed his party of its leading foreign policy spokesman and deprived his country of the figure most likely to convince Republicans to support postwar international commitments.

SEE ALSO *Dollar Diplomacy; League of Nations; Missionary Diplomacy; Panama Canal; Paris Peace Conference (1919); Philippines; Roosevelt Corollary (1904); Spanish-American War; Taft, William Howard; Wilson, Woodrow; World War I*

BIBLIOGRAPHY

Beale, Howard K. *Theodore Roosevelt and the Rise of America to World Power.* Baltimore, MD: Johns Hopkins University Press, 1956.

Dyer, Thomas. *Theodore Roosevelt and the Idea of Race.* Baton Rouge: Louisiana State University Press, 1980.

Einstein, Lewis. *Roosevelt: His Mind in Action.* London: Murray, 1930.

Harbaugh, William H. *Power and Responsibility: The Life and Times of Theodore Roosevelt.* New York: Farrar, Straus and Cudahy, 1961.

Holmes, James R. *Theodore Roosevelt and World Order: Police Power in International Relations.* Washington, DC: Potomac, 2006.

Marks, Frederick W., III. *Velvet on Iron: The Diplomacy of Theodore Roosevelt.* Lincoln: University of Nebraska Press, 1979.

Morris, Edmund. *Colonel Roosevelt.* New York: Random House, 2010.

Ninkovich, Frank. "Theodore Roosevelt: Civilization as Ideology." *Diplomatic History* 10, 3 (1986): 221–245.

O'Toole, Patricia. *When Trumpets Call: Theodore Roosevelt after the White House.* New York: Simon and Schuster, 2005.

Ricard, Serge. "Theodore Roosevelt and the Diplomacy of Righteousness." *Theodore Roosevelt Association Journal* 12, 1 (1986): 14–17.

Roosevelt, Theodore. "Letter from Theodore Roosevelt to Joseph Bucklin Bishop." February 23, 1904. Theodore Roosevelt Collection, bMS Am 1514 (72). Harvard College Library. http://www.theodorerooseveltcenter.org/en/Research/Digital-Library/Record.aspx?libID=o281261 Theodore Roosevelt Digital Library, Theodore Roosevelt Center, Dickinson State University.

Tilchin, William N. *Theodore Roosevelt and the British Empire: A Study in Presidential Statecraft.* New York: St. Martin's Press, 1997.

Widenor, William C. "Theodorus Pacificus." In *Henry Cabot Lodge and the Search for an American Foreign Policy*, chap. 4. Berkeley: University of California Press, 1980.

Charles Laderman
Research Fellow, Peterhouse
University of Cambridge

ROOSEVELT COROLLARY (1904)

On December 6, 1904, US president Theodore Roosevelt (1858–1919) delivered his annual message to the US Congress, in which he outlined his corollary to the 1823 Monroe Doctrine. Roosevelt's famous corollary declared that if "chronic wrongdoing" or "impotence" caused breakdowns in "the ties of civilized society" in the Western Hemisphere, then it would require intercession by "some civilized nation." Under the Monroe Doctrine, the United States, "however reluctantly, in flagrant cases" would be required to assume the obligation of carrying out "the exercise of an international police power."

The announcement of Roosevelt's corollary was sparked by the threat of European intervention in the Western Hemisphere against Latin American states, most notably Venezuela and the Dominican Republic, to collect unpaid international debts. Its longer-term origins derived from a statement made by the British prime minister, Lord Salisbury (1830–1903), at the time of the Venezuela boundary dispute in 1895. Salisbury reproached President Grover Cleveland (1837–1908)

and his secretary of state, Richard Olney (1835–1917), for declaring that "the Monroe Doctrine [was] a universal proposition" and claiming that the interests of the United States were connected to the welfare of all the republics in the Western Hemisphere while assuming "no responsibility" for their conduct. While Roosevelt was far more concerned by German, than British, threats to the Monroe Doctrine, he recognized that Salisbury's warning still applied. Roosevelt accepted that if the United States wished to "perpetually assert the Monroe Doctrine on behalf of all American republics," then it would need to take "some responsibility in connection there-with." The 1904 annual message was intended to develop Cleveland and Olney's response to the Venezuela dispute into a more explicitly interventionist tool.

In addition, the announcement of the corollary was intended to defend interventions that the United States had already engaged in—most significantly, the protectorate over Cuba that it had assumed since the 1898 war with Spain and its acquisition of the territory surrounding the American-controlled Panama Canal. Virtually all historians of Roosevelt's diplomacy regard the corollary as explicitly transforming the Monroe Doctrine into a more interventionist instrument of US policy in the Western Hemisphere than it had been during the nineteenth century. Roosevelt's corollary was motivated by a dislike for disorder, a belief that America's newly acquired power brought with it fresh responsibilities and a commitment to spreading "civilization," of which he considered the United States to be the principal agent. It was described as being in America's "own interest as well as in the interest of humanity at large" and ranked the United States alongside the great European states as "civilized" powers policing the Caribbean, as Europe did Africa and Asia.

The British government, in particular, welcomed the Roosevelt Corollary. Before the Monroe Doctrine was announced in 1823, British foreign secretary George Canning (1770–1827) had hoped Britain and the United States would make a joint declaration denying any nation from further colonizing territory in the Western Hemisphere, but US secretary of state John Quincy Adams (1767–1848) had persuaded his cabinet colleagues to issue the Monroe Doctrine unilaterally. Nevertheless, due to the weakness of the US fleet, responsibility for upholding the Monroe Doctrine had in fact devolved to the British navy, which shared American concerns for the maintenance of open markets and free trade in the hemisphere. As American power grew in the 1890s and British policy makers began to sense that their country was becoming overburdened with imperial commitments, statesmen in London looked to Washington to relieve Britain's responsibility for maintaining the doctrine. Roosevelt's 1904 message was regarded as confirmation that the United States was now prepared to assume that burden. Soon after its announcement, Britain's naval strategists withdrew its major vessels from its Atlantic stations. The announcement of the Roosevelt Corollary served as an important step in the establishment of the "Great Rapprochement" between the British Empire and the United States.

Soon after announcing the corollary, Roosevelt asked the Senate to ratify an agreement that he had reached with the Dominican Republic to take control of its customs houses. When the Senate demurred, Roosevelt authorized the intervention by issuing an executive order and invited private American financiers to administer the Dominican debt. Nevertheless, while personally committed to ensuring US hegemony in the Caribbean, Roosevelt was determined to ensure that the intervention remained limited in scope. He noted that he had "about the same desire to annex ["the territory"] as a gorged boa constrictor might have to swallow a porcupine wrong-end-to" (Roosevelt 1904a). Roosevelt's recognition that most Americans were reluctant to engage in overseas interventions led him to act with restraint for the rest of his presidency.

However, Roosevelt's successors felt themselves less constrained in the face of new regional crises and used the Roosevelt Corollary to justify their interventions in the Caribbean and Central America. It was under Woodrow Wilson's (1856–1924) administration that the most hemispheric interventions occurred during this era, including another intercession in the Dominican Republic in 1916. Franklin Delano Roosevelt's (1882–1945) announcement of his Good Neighbor Policy in 1934 was intended to signal a departure from the interventionist creed proclaimed by his distant cousin's corollary. Nevertheless, the United States continued to exercise a hegemonic role in the hemisphere under Franklin Roosevelt and his successors. As tensions between the United States and the Soviet Union escalated during the Cold War, US presidents would invoke the Monroe Doctrine and, less explicitly, the right of intervention proclaimed by the Roosevelt Corollary to justify their hemispheric interventions.

SEE ALSO *Internationalism; Interventionism; Isolationism; Monroe Doctrine (1823); Roosevelt, Theodore; Taft, William Howard; Wilson, Woodrow; World War I*

BIBLIOGRAPHY

Gilderhus, Mark T. "The Monroe Doctrine: Meanings and Implications." *Presidential Studies Quarterly* 36, 1 (2006): 5–16.

Mitchell, Nancy. *The Danger of Dreams: German and American Imperialism in Latin America*. Chapel Hill: University of North Carolina Press, 1999.

Detailed critique of the significance of the perceived German threat in Roosevelt's thought.

Ricard, Serge. "The Roosevelt Corollary." *Presidential Studies Quarterly* 36, 1 (2006): 17–26.

Roosevelt, Theodore. "Letter from Theodore Roosevelt to Joseph Bucklin Bishop." February 23, 1904a. Theodore Roosevelt Collection, bMS Am 1514 (72), Harvard College Library. http://www.theodorerooseveltcenter.org/en/Research/Digital-Library/Record.aspx?libID=o281261 Theodore Roosevelt Digital Library, Theodore Roosevelt Center, Dickinson State University.

Roosevelt, Theodore. "Theodore Roosevelt's Corollary to the Monroe Doctrine." Excerpted from Roosevelt's annual message to the US Congress, December 6, 1904b. http://www.ourdocuments.gov/doc.php?flash=true&doc=56

Sexton, Jay. *The Monroe Doctrine: Empire and Nation in Nineteenth-Century America*. New York: Hill and Wang, 2011. See pages 199–241.

Veeser, Cyrus. *A World Safe for Capitalism: Dollar, Diplomacy, and America's Rise to Global Power*. New York: Columbia University Press, 2002.

ROOSEVELT'S DIPLOMACY IN THE CARIBBEAN AND CENTRAL AMERICA, CONTRASTING INTERPRETATIONS

Collin, Richard H. *Theodore Roosevelt's Caribbean: The Panama Canal, the Monroe Doctrine, and the Latin American Context*. Baton Rouge: Louisiana State University Press, 1990.

Schoonover, Thomas D. *The United States in Central America, 1860–1911: Episodes of Social Imperialism and Imperial Rivalry in the World System*. Durham, NC: Duke University Press, 1991.

SIGNIFICANCE OF THE ROOSEVELT COROLLARY IN THE CONTEXT OF ANGLO-AMERICAN RELATIONS

Adams, Iestyn. *Brothers across the Ocean: British Foreign Policy and the Origins of the Anglo-American Special Relationship, 1900–1905*. London: Tauris, 2005.

Perkins, Bradford. *The Great Rapprochement: England and the United States, 1894–1914*. New York: Atheneum, 1968.

Charles Laderman
Research Fellow, Peterhouse
University of Cambridge

ROSENBERG, ETHEL AND JULIAN

SEE *Spies and Espionage.*

ROSIE THE RIVETER

The *We Can Do It!* poster, known widely as the *Rosie the Riveter* poster, is a powerful and affirming image of the female worker during World War II (1939–1945). In recent decades, it has become a feminist image, representing the idea that women can accomplish whatever they want.

In 1942, freelance artist J. Howard Miller of Pittsburgh produced the *We Can Do It!* poster for Westinghouse Electric and Manufacturing Company, which displayed it in factories in February 1943. The poster featured a brunette with a polka-dot headband, a work shirt with rolled-up sleeves, toned arms posed, and a determined facial expression. The renaming from *We Can Do It!* to *Rosie the Riveter* stemmed from a 1942 hit song titled "Rosie the Riveter," written by Redd Evans and John Jacob Loeb. The lyrics, "She's making history, working for victory," paid homage to the many competent and strong women defense workers of the era. Because the song was about women who took on men's roles during World War II, it became associated with images that depicted the impact of the war on the roles and status of women, challenging ideas of what it meant to be a woman. The name *Rosie the Riveter* also became prominent after Norman Rockwell painted a picture of a wartime woman worker.

Though the most famous example of Rosie the Riveter now is the original Westinghouse poster by Miller, it was not as well known at the time. The more popular image during the war was the cover that Rockwell created for the May 29, 1943, *Saturday Evening Post* Memorial Day issue. Rockwell's version featured a plumped-up interpretation of a petite nineteen-year-old phone operator from Vermont. In the Rockwell painting, she is holding a sandwich that likely came from the lunchbox with the name "Rosie" on it that sits on her lap.

Not long after the *Saturday Evening Post* issue featuring Rosie appeared on newsstands, media began to tell the story of a woman named Rose Hickey, who worked in a Tarrytown, New York, assembly plant, and another named Rose Monroe, a riveter from Michigan who made a film to sell war bonds and a commercial movie called *Rosie the Riveter*. As a result of the song, the name on the lunchbox on Rockwell's magazine cover, and the media's coverage of working women named Rose, Rosie the Riveter became synonymous with women who worked during World War II.

The female worker became prominent during World War II when the need for workers exceeded the number of men available to fill the jobs, and women and minorities stepped into the open positions as welders, riveters, assemblers, and inspectors. Some women expected to return to their domestic lives once the war was over. Others who found their domestic lives uninspiring were excited about the chance to contribute to society in a bigger way. Still other women were already working and saw it as an opportunity to move into jobs with higher pay and union membership.

Rosie the Riveter poster, 1942. *Rosie the Riveter is an affirming image of the female worker during World War II. This icon of the wartime American woman combined an original image from a Westinghouse poster that was displayed in factories with lyrics to the song "Rosie the Riveter," which paid homage to women "working for victory."* **WORLD HISTORY ARCHIVE/ALAMY**

America's success in mobilizing women as workers gave the United States an advantage over Germany, where hostile views about new roles for women inhibited the government's ability to produce war materials. As the war continued, however, women were encouraged to assist in the effort in countries throughout the world, including Germany, Australia, Canada, Britain, Finland, Italy, Poland, Romania, the Soviet Union, and Yugoslavia, where women worked as mechanics, shipbuilders, plumbers, and engineers. The most common job for women during the war was that of searchlight operator.

Today, Miller's image of Rosie the Riveter is easily the most famous and recognizable. Miller's image gained wider circulation than Rockwell's because the Rockwell picture carried copyright restrictions and Miller's did not.

Miller's Westinghouse poster has become one of the most popular images from the World War II era. It can be found on coffee mugs, lunchboxes, facial tissue wrappers, mouse pads, aprons, refrigerator magnets, earrings, and many other products. Rosie the Riveter is also a popular Halloween costume, and the faces of contemporary female political figures are often superimposed onto the image to suggest that they can get elected and do the job.

At the time of its release, the Rosie the Riveter image challenged the public to reconsider its perception of what it means to be a woman, and it has since taken on a life of its own as a cultural depiction of women's empowerment. The image and its ongoing reinterpretation live on in American minds and in American culture.

SEE ALSO *LIFE (Magazine); World War II*

BIBLIOGRAPHY

Anderson, Karen. "Teaching about Rosie the Riveter: The Role of Women during World War II." Special issue, "Women's History and History of the 1970s," *OAH Magazine of History* 3, 3–4 (1988): 35–37.

Campbell, D'Ann. "Women in Combat: The World War II Experience in the United States, Great Britain, Germany, and the Soviet Union." *Journal of Military History* 57, 2 (1993): 301–323.

Davenport, Sue. "The Life and Times of Rosie the Riveter, Invisible Working Women." *Jump Cut: A Review of Contemporary Media* 28 (April 1983): 42–43.

De Groot, Gerard J. "I Love the Scent of Cordite in Your Hair: Gender Dynamics in Mixed Anti-aircraft Batteries during the Second World War." *History* 82, 265 (1997): 73–92.

Harvey, Sheridan. "Rosie the Riveter: Real Women Workers in World War II." Library of Congress. 2006. http://www.loc .gov/rr/program/journey/rosie.html

Rupp, Leila J. *Mobilizing Women for War: German and American Propaganda, 1939–1945.* Princeton, NJ: Princeton University Press, 1978.

Nichola D. Gutgold
Professor of Communication Arts and Sciences
Associate Dean for Academics, Schreyer Honors College
The Pennsylvania State University

ROSTOW, WALT W.
1916–2003

Born in Brooklyn, New York, Walt Whitman Rostow rose from humble beginnings to embody the contradictions of US foreign policy during the 1960s. A brilliant scholar of British economic history, Rostow was recognized for his lucid prose and a persuasive presentation that endeared him to US policy makers for three decades. Seeking to replicate nineteenth-century British modernization in the twentieth-century Third World through US economic and military engagement, Rostow ultimately became the chief intellectual architect of US involvement in the Vietnam War.

Graduating from Yale at the age of nineteen, Rostow was awarded a Rhodes scholarship to study at Oxford in 1936, the first of many sojourns in the United Kingdom. He returned to Yale in 1938 to pursue a PhD, which he completed in two years. While teaching economic history at Columbia University in the early 1940s, Rostow coauthored a two-volume treatise on nineteenth-century Britain with Queen's College professor Arthur David Gayer (1903–1951) and Anna Jacobson Schwartz (1915–2012) of the National Bureau of Economic Research. Published by Oxford's Clarendon Press after the war, *The Growth and Fluctuation of the British Economy, 1790–1850* (1953), cemented Rostow's reputation as a preeminent scholar of Britain's modernization.

During the war, Rostow picked bombing targets for the Office of Strategic Services, followed by a brief appointment to the State Department economics office in 1945. The following year, Rostow returned to Oxford as Harmsworth Professor of American History, where he published (also under Oxford's Clarendon imprint) his first sole-authored book of essays, *British Economy in the Nineteenth Century* (1948). Having advocated for US aid to postwar Europe, in 1947 Rostow turned down a Harvard post to serve as adviser to the Marshall Plan in Geneva, where he contributed to Central Intelligence Agency (CIA) operations, such as Radio Free Europe (Stern 2012, 19–20). Rostow took leave of government service once again in 1949 to assume Cambridge University's one-year Pitt Professorship in American History and Institutions, where he published on the developmental impact of terms of trade.

Having spent the first decade of his career alternating between government and elite academia, Rostow was poised to become one of the nation's foremost policy intellectuals with an appointment at the Massachusetts Institute of Technology in 1950. Working with his former Yale classmate Max Millikan (1913–1969), Rostow participated in Project Troy, a CIA-sponsored program that culminated in 1952 with the establishment of the Center for International Studies (CENIS) (Gilman 2003, 158). CENIS brought Rostow together with other developmentalists who sought to provide policy makers with Third World applications of a nebulous set of ideas that eventually coalesced into "modernization theory."

As a CENIS associate, Rostow parlayed his scholarship on nineteenth-century Britain into policy-friendly theories of Third World development. As a member the Eisenhower administration's Operations Coordinating Board on covert operations in 1954 (Stern 2012, 50), Rostow became a strong advocate for utilizing US aid to guide uncommitted nations toward noncommunist modernization. These proposals were first articulated in a 1956 article, "The Take-Off into Self-Sustaining Growth," and further developed during a Carnegie-funded sabbatical at Cambridge in 1959, resulting in his widely read *The Stages of Economic Growth: A Non-Communist Manifesto* (1960).

Rostow was invited to advise the presidential campaign of John F. Kennedy (1917–1963), who appointed Rostow deputy national security adviser in January 1961 before shifting him to director of the State Department Policy Planning Council in November. As Rostow evolved from scholarship to policy prescriptions for the contemporary Third World, he betrayed a militaristic affinity for employing counterinsurgent operations throughout the world. This culminated in October 1961 with Rostow becoming the first civilian to advocate for US troop deployment and strategic bombing in Vietnam (Milne 2008, 98–102). Under President Lyndon Johnson (1908–1973), Rostow's sharp intellect and supreme confidence ensconced him as the administration's principal scholarly voice, particularly after Johnson appointed him national security adviser in 1966.

In the wake of divisions over Vietnam, some critics blamed Rostow and modernization theory for the war. After resigning his post in 1969, Rostow was spurned by the elite universities that had courted him since 1930. The beleaguered Anglophile spent the remainder of his life as the Rex G. Baker Professor of Political Economy at the University of Texas, where he published a flurry of tomes defending modernization theory and expressing concern for global demographic shifts.

SEE ALSO *Cold War; Johnson, Lyndon Baines; Kennedy, John Fitzgerald; Modernization Theory; Third World; United States Agency for International Development (USAID)*

BIBLIOGRAPHY

Armstrong, David Grossman. "The True Believer." PhD diss., University of Texas, Austin, 2000.

Gayer, Arthur David, Walt Whitman Rostow, and Anna Jacobson Schwartz. *The Growth and Fluctuation of the British Economy, 1790–1850.* Oxford, UK: Clarendon Press, 1953.

Gilman, Nils. *Mandarins of the Future: Modernization Theory in Cold War America.* Baltimore, MD: Johns Hopkins University Press, 2003.

Latham, Michael. *Modernization as Ideology: American Social Science and "Nation Building" in the Kennedy Era.* Chapel Hill: University of North Carolina Press, 2000.

Milne, David. *America's Rasputin: Walt Rostow and the Vietnam War.* New York: Hill and Wang, 2008.

Rostow, Walt Whitman. *The American Diplomatic Revolution.* Oxford, UK: Clarendon Press, 1946.

Rostow, Walt Whitman. *British Economy of the Nineteenth Century.* Oxford, UK: Clarendon Press, 1948.

Rostow, Walt Whitman. "The Historical Analysis of the Terms of Trade." *Economic History Review* 4, 1 (1951): 53–76.

Rostow, Walt Whitman. "The Take-Off into Self-Sustaining Growth." *Economic Journal* 66, 261 (1956): 25–48.

Rostow, Walt Whitman. *The Stages of Economic Growth: A Non-Communist Manifesto.* Cambridge: Cambridge University Press, 1960.

Rostow, Walt Whitman. "Population in the Twenty-First Century: The Limited Horizon of Public Policy." *Technological Forecasting and Social Change* 67, 1 (2001): 19–34.

Stern, John Allen. *C. D. Jackson: Cold War Propagandist for Democracy and Globalism.* Lanham, MD: University Press of America, 2012.

Thomas C. Field Jr.
Assistant Professor, College of Security and Intelligence
Embry-Riddle Aeronautical University

ROTARY CLUB

Four business associates looking to improve both their social life and their business prospects met on February 23, 1905, in Chicago to form the first Rotary club. Paul Harris (1868–1947), a lawyer seeking to re-create the camaraderie of small-town America in the hectic, impersonal world of Chicago, proposed a new kind of fraternal club comprised solely of business and professional peers committed to making new friends, as well as boosting each member's business. The new club took its name from the habit of rotating meetings among each member's place of business in order to learn about the nature of their work and how best to promote it within the fast-growing ranks of the club. To maintain harmony within the club, membership was defined according to the "classification principle," wherein each member stood as representative of his specific line of business or profession. As a result, to join the Rotary club was to gain immediate access to new business prospects and social contacts throughout the city of Chicago—without any direct competition within one's own specific line of business.

At the height of the Progressive Era, however, such naked "backscratching" attracted public scrutiny, even ridicule. So the Chicago Rotary club began to take on matters of public interest and charitable endeavors, first on an ad hoc basis and then in more formal ways. By 1910, the Rotary club had established regular forms of philanthropy and public service as a means of cultural legitimacy and civic uplift. Within its first five years, the Rotary club thus came to define its primary mission as service to the community and to the city of Chicago. From the second national convention in 1911 emerged the principle "Service, not Self," which eventually evolved into Rotary International's official motto since 1950: "Service above Self."

Rotary's organizational model and service ideology soon proved a compelling and translatable formula for businessmen in other cities, who then helped forge a national organization. Contrary to the nostalgia for Main Street and later stereotypes of Babbittry, in fact, the first Rotary clubs appeared in the largest cities of the West Coast and then throughout the United States, Canada, and the British Isles between 1910 and the outbreak of war in Europe in 1914. Rotary clubs only began branching into smaller US cities and towns as the war effort mounted (Liberty Loan drives were a common project) and later in reaction to the rapid growth of Kiwanis (1915) and Lions Clubs (1917).

Rebranded as Rotary International (RI) in 1922, the nongovernmental organization (NGO) expanded quickly into East Asia, Latin America, and continental Europe during the interwar period through informal networks of trade associations, chambers of commerce, US diplomatic channels, and other NGOs like the YMCA and missionary societies. Although US Rotarians often spoke of RI's international growth in quasi-religious terms like "spreading the gospel of American business," RI touted a secular vision of a "world fellowship of business and professional men" driven by high ethical standards and united in a common purpose: "the advancement of international understanding, goodwill, and peace" (Rotary's Fourth Object on international service; Constitution of Rotary International, Art. 4). In the end, Rotarians saw themselves as salesmen of the "American way of life," as much as missionaries of American business culture.

But RI's vision of civic internationalism—so centered on a US model of civil society—inevitably ran into significant resistance abroad. Germany closed down all Rotary clubs soon after the Nazis took power, followed by Italy, Japan, and many other nations. Fascist states ultimately would not tolerate Rotary clubs any more than Communist ones. After World War II, however, Rotary clubs sprang up again in occupied nations as RI entered a second major phase of international expansion, this time linked proudly with key international institutions like the United Nations and United Nations Educational, Scientific and Cultural Organization. Moreover, the death of Harris in 1947 brought new energy and financial resources to the Rotary Foundation, resulting in Ambassadorial Scholarships for thousands of students seeking an education abroad, countless group exchange and cross-border volunteer programs, and, in 1985, the Polio Plus program. As a partner with the World Health Organization, United Nations Children's Fund, and the Centers for Disease Control and Prevention (CDC) in the Global Polio Eradication Initiative since 1988 (and the Gates Foundation more recently), RI has contributed over $1.2 billion toward the cause while urging governments to donate another $9 billion. Instrumental in bringing immunizations to millions of people, Rotary clubs worldwide helped reduce annual polio cases from 350,000 per year in more than 120 countries in 1985 to fewer than 250 per year in just three countries in 2014.

RI's growth has tapered off in recent decades, even after the US Supreme Court ruled in 1987 that women should be able to join its ranks. While RI encompasses about 1.22 million members today (with the majority outside the United States since the 1970s), Lions Clubs International counts 1.35 million members worldwide. Kiwanis International trails both with about 600,000 members. Operating both as salespeople and missionaries of American business culture and civic values, these three NGOs have also served, in aggregate, as a nexus for international exchange and humanitarian activities during the past century, and it seems likely they will continue to do so well into the future. It was the Rotary club, however, that paved the way.

SEE ALSO *Europe; Nongovernmental Organizations (NGOs)*

BIBLIOGRAPHY

Arnold, Oren. *The Golden Strand: An Informal History of the Rotary Club of Chicago*. Chicago: Quadrangle, 1966.

Board of Directors, Rotary International v. Rotary Club of Duarte, 481 US 537 (1987).

Charles, Jeffrey A. *Service Clubs in American Society: Rotary, Kiwanis, and Lions*. Urbana: University of Illinois Press, 1993.

de Grazia, Victoria. *Irresistible Empire: America's Advance through Twentieth-Century Europe*. Cambridge, MA: Harvard University Press, 2005.

Forward, David C. *A Century of Service: The Story of Rotary International*. Evanston, IL: Rotary International, 2003.

Goff, Brendan. "The Heartland Abroad: The Rotary Club's Mission of Civic Internationalism." PhD diss., University of Michigan, 2008.

Rotary International. Constitution of Rotary International. https://www.rotary.org/myrotary/en/learning-reference/policies-procedures/governance-documents

Rotary International. "Rotary and Polio Fact Sheet." https://www.rotary.org/myrotary/en/document/rotary-and-polio

Brendan Goff
Assistant Professor, American History
New College of Florida

ROUGH RIDERS

The Rough Riders is the nickname of the First US Volunteer Cavalry, a regiment of the US Army that fought in the Spanish-American War (1898). Although technically a cavalry, the regiment's horses never made it to Cuba, and the men ended up fighting as infantry. Initially led by Colonel Leonard Wood (1860–1927), the regiment was subsequently led by its second-in-command, Lieutenant-Colonel Theodore Roosevelt (1858–1919), after Wood was promoted during the war. Roosevelt, who had been assistant secretary of the navy, resigned his post after the United States declared war on Spain in April 1898. He successfully petitioned Secretary of War Russell Alger (1836–1907) for permission to form a volunteer cavalry regiment. Although Alger allowed three volunteer cavalry regiments to organize, only the Rough Riders saw action. After vetting more than twenty-three thousand applications, Roosevelt and Wood selected the men for the new regiment and began training in San Antonio, Texas. Since the 1880s, cavalry regiments were organized into twelve companies, each of which contained approximately one hundred men.

Most of the recruits were cowboys, college athletes, hunters, and Indians from Western states. Their unique uniform consisted of a blue flannel shirt, brown pants, leggings, boots, a wide-brimmed slouch hat with chin strap, and a handkerchief smartly tied about the neck. American newspapers promptly dubbed these dashing cowboys the "Rough Riders." Due to lack of space on transport vessels, only eight of the regiment's twelve companies, and virtually none of the horses and mules, departed from Tampa, Florida, for Cuba in June. The Rough Riders participated in two major battles in Cuba: the Battle of Las Guasimas on June 24, and the Battle of Kettle Hill on July 1. Roosevelt, who had taken command of the regiment just prior to the Battle of Kettle Hill, led a

A poster advertising a theatrical show portraying Theodore Roosevelt and the Rough Riders, 1899. The Rough Riders, a volunteer regiment that fought in the Spanish-American War under the leadership of Theodore Roosevelt, became heroes to the American public, who saw the dashing cowboys, often portrayed in traveling shows, as the epitome of American manhood. © EVERETT HISTORICAL/ SHUTTERSTOCK.COM

series of charges up the hill on his horse, Texas. The Rough Riders returned to the United States in August and disbanded in September.

Roosevelt and the Rough Riders became heroes to the American public. Although many of the Rough Riders wanted Roosevelt to receive the Medal of Honor, Secretary of War Alger, still miffed that Roosevelt had written a critical report during the war demanding the immediate return to the United States of soldiers suffering from disease, refused to support the recommendation. Nevertheless, Roosevelt emerged as a major national figure. He capitalized on that image to become governor of New York, vice president, and then president when William McKinley (1843–1901) was assassinated in 1901.

Roosevelt spent his life trying to live up to his astonishingly demanding definitions of true American manhood and to impose that vision of manhood on the American nation. His beliefs had an impact on many of those with whom he had personal contact, especially the Rough Riders. Roosevelt became the embodiment of the Rough Riders. Roosevelt and the Rough Riders were popularized in William Frederick "Buffalo Bill" Cody's (1846–1917) *Buffalo Bill's Wild West and Congress of Rough Riders of the World* show. Cody helped to create and preserve the image of the Rough Riders for subsequent generations. Viewed by most Americans as a manly man of action at home, in the eyes of many Europeans Roosevelt (and the Rough Riders) came to occupy the pivotal role as America's most important cultural emblem of American masculinity, at once embodying the ideal and the contemporary reality.

SEE ALSO *Americanization; Buffalo Bill's Wild West; Exceptionalism; Roosevelt, Theodore; Spanish-American War; Whiteness*

BIBLIOGRAPHY

Cosmas, Graham A. *An Army for Empire: The United States Army in the Spanish-American War.* College Station: Texas A&M University Press, 1984. First published by the University of Missouri Press in 1971.

Roosevelt, Theodore. *The Rough Riders.* New York: Random House, 1999. First published by Scribner's in 1899.

Walker, Dale L. *The Boys of '98: Theodore Roosevelt and the Rough Riders.* New York: Forge, 1998.

Watts, Sarah. *Rough Rider in the White House: Theodore Roosevelt and the Politics of Desire.* Chicago: University of Chicago Press, 2003.

Michael R. Hall
Professor of History
Armstrong State University

RUSK, DEAN
1909–1994

David Dean Rusk served as secretary of state from 1961 to 1969 under Presidents John F. Kennedy (1917–1963) and Lyndon Johnson (1908–1973). A Rhodes scholar who witnessed Nazism firsthand, Rusk joined the War Department during World War II. During the early Cold War, he moved to the State Department, becoming a deputy undersecretary in 1949. Rusk devoted his life to projecting American values in the international arena and contesting aggression, as he (and the Cold War consensus) saw it. He also became famous for his unerring loyalty to superiors, especially President Johnson. After heading the Rockefeller Foundation and turning its focus even more than before to what was then called the Third World, and specifically agriculture and food (and less toward health issues), Rusk—a lifelong liberal, supporter of civil rights, internationalist, and cold warrior—accepted Kennedy's invitation to be secretary of state.

Rusk did not fit the snappy image of the Kennedy team, but he was a reliable, devoted adviser who eagerly put into practice both the internationalist crusades and the tough-minded anticommunist stances of the president. Having a daughter who married an African American, Rusk especially opposed racism and embraced the anticolonial tide then sweeping over Africa and Asia. A believer in the ideals of the United Nations, he advocated nationhood for former colonies and those struggling for independence, as he met hundreds of delegates from the Third World in Washington, DC, and abroad.

Yet he staunchly believed that the Soviet Union and People's Republic of China threatened international security. As a realist, Rusk pushed for defending the "free world" against communism. In Europe, he supported America's traditional stance of bolstering the North Atlantic Treaty Organization and refusing to back out of Berlin. In Africa, he hoped the United Nations could quell a civil war in the Congo, but he bowed to an anticommunist government and Belgian economic interests against a leftist rebel. Rusk opposed the introduction of nuclear weapons by Israel in the Middle East, but after the Six-Day War in 1967, like most Americans, he backed this recalcitrant ally as a bulwark against Arab overtures to Soviet influence in the region. He sympathized with Latin America voices of liberation, but Rusk's worries about socialism in Cuba turned to alarm once Fidel Castro accepted Soviet missiles in 1962. During the missile crisis, the reticent Rusk noted that the superpowers stood "eyeball to eyeball," but his calm advocacy for diplomacy over war won the day when a deal to trade US for Soviet missiles ended the standoff.

In retirement, Rusk admitted that his hard-line stance against the "Red" Chinese was unimaginative and boxed the Johnson administration into a corner of irreconcilability toward communism, but the secretary of state stood his ground during the 1960s on the cardinal foreign policy issue of the day: the Vietnam War. Rusk never apologized for his unbending stance in favor of a military response in South Vietnam—a seeming contradiction to his usual diplomatic approach on other matters—because he believed in the American mission of defending small nations from aggression.

The erroneous belief that conflict in Vietnam stemmed from an international communist conspiracy, rather than a homegrown rebellion, tragically veered Rusk away from liberal internationalist principles. He had advised Kennedy not to neutralize Vietnam (as he had agreed to do in Laos), and he agreed with Johnson on slow escalation of American ground forces, coupled with bombing. But Vietnam was no Munich, or even Korea, to which to apply a blanket of containment. The means of military force that expended lives undermined the very objective of winning the hearts and minds of the Vietnamese to the anticommunist cause, and Rusk, to his great frustration, knew it. But he loyally defended Johnson's war to the end, and justified his staunch support for the intervention by arguing that history showed aggression must be met by determined resistance. Vietnam, he held, was a pawn in the larger strategic battle against China and the Soviet Union (USSR). Protesters, including some of his own friends in Congress, focused their wrath on him; Rusk became the symbol for war opponents of a pointlessly destructive war that questioned American values and undermined the country's image abroad.

Vietnam led to Rusk's departure from Washington under a cloud of recrimination that forever tarnished his liberal reputation. To his credit, Rusk intensified diplomatic efforts to end the war, and he flexibly modified American demands for peace by 1967. But he could convince neither the enemy nor his own president to change course, and he could not balance interests of stalwart anticommunism with the ideals of Wilsonian internationalism. Rusk quietly took up a law professorship at the University of Georgia. He never abandoned his principles, but he acknowledged his mistakes.

SEE ALSO *Cold War; Decolonization; Johnson, Lyndon Baines; Kennedy, John Fitzgerald; Rockefeller Foundation; Vietnam War*

BIBLIOGRAPHY

Cohen, Warren I. *Dean Rusk*. Totowa, NJ: Cooper Square, 1980.

Papp, Daniel S., ed. *As I Saw It*. New York: Norton, 1990.

Schoenbaum, Thomas J. *Waging Peace and War: Dean Rusk in the Truman, Kennedy, and Johnson Years*. New York: Simon and Schuster, 1988.

Zeiler, Thomas W. *Dean Rusk: Defending the American Mission Abroad*. Wilmington, DE: Scholarly Resources, 2000.

Thomas W. Zeiler
Professor of History
University of Colorado Boulder

RUSSIA

Relations between the United States and Russia existed even before the 1783 Treaty of Paris recognized the thirteen former British colonies in North America as an independent and sovereign nation. However, attempts to involve the supposedly liberal Russian monarch Catherine the Great (1729–1796) directly on behalf of the American revolutionaries did not materialize. The American envoy, Francis Dana (1743–1811), was not well chosen because he spoke neither French—the diplomats' lingua franca of that period—nor Russian. During his time in Russia, he was not even received by the empress or any Russian official. Although the Americans were desperate for support in their drive for independence, their struggle was of little concern for the Russian Empire, which remained neutral but nonetheless continued to trade with the rebellious colonies.

RELATIONS WITH RUSSIA DURING AMERICA'S FIRST CENTURY

The ill treatment of the American envoy may have soured the American attitude toward Russia. Still, at the beginning of the nineteenth century, an American consul general was appointed to St. Petersburg, and before the end of the decade ambassadors had been exchanged. John Quincy Adams (1767–1848), later to become James Monroe's (1758–1831) secretary of state and the sixth president of the United States, represented the United States at the Russian court from 1809 to 1814. The United States was eager to find new trade opportunities after the Non-Intercourse Act of 1809 had curtailed trade with Great Britain and France, its major customers. Although the exchange of goods increased, commercial opportunities could not make up US losses. After the War of 1812 ended and trade with America's traditional partners resumed, interest in commercial relations with Russia remained but was vulnerable to internal economic crises, as well as wars in which either nation was involved.

In the next decade, US-Russian relations revolved around territorial questions in the Western Hemisphere. With North America's territorial boundaries not yet fixed, the Monroe Doctrine (1823) was, in part, a response to the establishment of the Russian colony of Fort Ross just north of San Francisco Bay and to Russia's claim in 1821 to exclusive shipping, fishing, and fur-trading rights along the coast of North America north of what is now the northernmost part of Vancouver Island. The first formal treaty between the two nations, the Russo-American Treaty of 1824, handed claims to territory south of the 54°40′ parallel to the United States. A similar treaty in 1825 with Great Britain, defining the border between Russian and British interests, settled the issue between those two nations at the same latitude without an impact on the conflicting British and American claims on the Oregon Territory. With the Oregon Treaty of 1846, these land titles were settled. A few years later, the Mexican-American War (1846–1848) extended US territory at the Pacific Coast as far north as the forty-ninth parallel. These developments provided the basis for American economic predominance and for trade opportunities with the Russian territory of Alaska.

Trade increased between the two nations during the antebellum period, leading to mutual political and cultural interest, as well as American interest in railroad building in Russia beginning in the 1840s and humanitarian support during the Crimean War (1853–1856). The beginning of the American Civil War in 1861 coincided with the freeing of the serfs in Russia, and Russian sympathy during that US conflict was with the North. Nonetheless, Russia suggested mediation between the Union and the Confederacy, which would have entailed diplomatic recognition of the Confederate States of America, something that President Abraham Lincoln (1809–1865) very much tried to avoid. His Emancipation Proclamation (1863) then made it impossible for Russia, as well as the other dominant European powers, Great Britain and France, to side with the Confederacy.

THE SALE OF ALASKA

In the meantime, Russia had realized that the expense of maintaining a foothold on the North American continent was greater than the gain, particularly because American shipping dominated trade along the Pacific Coast, and Russian settlements were dependent on US traders. With an increasing British and American population in British Columbia augmented by the Fraser gold rush in 1858, Russian politicians reasoned that Alaska might soon fall into the hands of either the British or the Americans. They had contemplated selling the vast territory to the Americans as early as 1856, and, after the American Civil War, Russia responded to overtures to negotiate such a sale to eager Americans, while cunningly raising the price well above the $5 million they expected to receive. In the end, Alaska changed hands for $7.2 million, a bargain in hindsight but not perceived as such at the time.

CONFLICT IN NORTHEAST ASIA

Although Russian literature, infrastructure, and political and social issues attracted attention in the United States

before the turn of the century, anti-Jewish pogroms and Russia's rejection of the Open Door Policy were not received favorably by Americans. When Russia declined to leave Chinese soil after the Boxer Rebellion had been put down by European and American expeditionary forces in 1900 and attempted to annex Manchuria, Japan—which had similar interest in that area—attacked the Russian navy at Port Arthur (Lǐshùn). During the subsequent Russo-Japanese War (1904–1905), President Theodore Roosevelt (1858–1919) was asked to broker a peace settlement. At the peace conference held in Portsmouth, New Hampshire, in the summer of 1905, Roosevelt successfully mediated the differences, establishing Japan as the dominant power in the Far East. This earned him the Nobel Peace Prize the following year.

THE BOLSHEVIK REVOLUTION AND THE TWO WORLD WARS

Russia entered World War I (1914–1918) immediately on the side of Great Britain and France against Germany and the Central powers. The United States remained neutral until April 1917, but did provide the Allies, including Russia, with supplies. The czarist regime had been toppled one month earlier, and the United States became the first nation to recognize the Russian Provisional Government led by Aleksandr Fyodorovich Kerensky (1881–1970). The Bolsheviks' October Revolution (1917), brought about by war weariness and increased German pressure on the battlefield, as well as Communist rhetoric proclaiming a world revolution in which the workers were to rise up against their bourgeois oppressors, did not go down well in the United States. Although the American ambassador did remain in Soviet Russia until November 1918, the new government under Vladimir Lenin (1870–1924) was never recognized.

US-Russian relations became more difficult after Soviet Russia signed the Treaty of Brest-Litovsk, ending the war with Germany for Russia in early March 1918. American forces remained on Soviet soil to safeguard Allied stores at Murmansk, Archangel, and Vladivostok, and to support the so-called Czech legion in their translocation from Russia to the western front. Allied forces continued operating in northern Russia even after the end of World War I, hoping to reverse the Bolsheviks' revolution, and it was not until June 1919 that the last American soldiers left Russia. The mutual hostility this situation created had repercussions in the United States, culminating in the anticommunism of the Red scare and the Palmer raids of the 1920s.

Russia did not take part in the 1919 peace conference in Versailles, and although most nations recognized the Soviet Union after the signing of the Treaty of Rapallo (1922) between Germany and Russia, none of the

American interwar administrations was willing to establish diplomatic relations. Nonetheless, US-Soviet trade increased and diplomatic tensions did not stop the American Relief Administration, led by Secretary of Commerce Herbert C. Hoover (1874–1964), from providing aid during the Russian famine in the early 1920s. President Franklin D. Roosevelt (1882–1945) realized shortly after taking office that the nonrecognition policy had achieved nothing. Faced with international political challenges along with massive economic problems within the United States, Roosevelt invited the USSR to establish official ties in 1933. William C. Bullitt (1891–1967) became the first US ambassador to the Soviet Union, but decreasing trade and increasing friction did not bode well for friendly relations. The Roosevelt administration nevertheless tried to improve the US-Soviet relationship, despite the Stalinist purges of 1934 to 1938, the 1939 Molotov-Ribbentrop Pact between the Soviet Union and Nazi Germany, the Soviet attack on Finland in 1939, the seizure of the Baltic states in July 1940, and the conclusion of the Russo-Japanese Neutrality Pact in April 1941.

When Germany launched Operation Barbarossa and invaded the Soviet Union on June 22, 1941, public and official support for Russia in the United States was immediate. The United States offered assistance, first through "cash and carry" and then "lend-lease," resulting in $9.5 billion in US aid to Russia by the end of World War II (1939–1945). After Japan attacked Pearl Harbor on December 7, 1941, and Germany and Italy declared war on the United States four days later, Russia and the United States became allies. Soviet distrust of the Western powers grew the following year when the Western Allies failed to open a second front in France to ease the German military pressure on the eastern front, while Allied forces landed in northern Africa and Italy. This distrust had been restrained until then by the fight against the common enemy, but the invasion of Normandy on June 6, 1944, finally opened a second theater of war, providing the hoped-for military support.

Wartime conferences—beginning with meetings in Tehran (November to December 1943) and Yalta (February 1945)—shaped the Allies' war and peace aims. Roosevelt, Soviet leader Joseph Stalin (1879–1953), and British premier Winston Churchill (1874–1965) demanded the unconditional surrender of the Axis powers, the division of Germany into zones of occupation, and the creation of a United Nations organization. During the Potsdam Conference (July 17–August 2, 1945), Harry S. Truman (1884–1972)—who became president after Roosevelt died on April 12, 1945—learned about the successful test of the atomic bomb that the Americans and the British had built in secret, without informing their Soviet ally. To end the war in the Far East

while avoiding heavy American and Allied losses, Truman ordered atomic bombs to be dropped on Nagasaki and Hiroshima in August 1945, forcing Japan to surrender. The two bombs may also have been intended as a show of power directed at the USSR, which seemed unwilling to come to a settlement over the controversial question of reparations to be paid by Germany.

THE COLD WAR

The wartime conferences did not lead to long-term cooperation after the anti-Hitler coalition fell apart in 1945, having achieved its goal of defeating Nazi Germany and Imperial Japan. Obstructive Soviet policy toward a joint administration of occupied Germany alienated the Western nations, as did the Soviets' anticapitalist propaganda and proclamation of world revolution. The ensuing Cold War was marked by an increasing estrangement. Soviet leaders became convinced that the Western Allies were trying to encircle the Soviet Union to eliminate the Soviet system. Russia was soon perceived in the United States as not unlike Nazi Germany, a nation where a ruling minority forcefully denied its population inalienable civil rights and was set on world domination and conquest.

To counter the perceived threat of a monolithic communist bloc controlled from Moscow, the United States increased military spending and shaped a policy of political containment known as the Truman Doctrine. This policy was implemented in 1947 through support for the Turkish and Greek governments in their fight against communist insurgents, and in the Marshall Plan that aided European recovery beginning in 1948. The anti-Soviet attitude in the United States was fostered by such developments as the 1948 communist coup in Czechoslovakia and the 1948–1949 Berlin crisis. The 1950 invasion of South Korea by North Korean troops supported by the Soviet Union was perceived as a possible precursor to a Soviet attack on Western Europe. After the establishment of the North Atlantic Treaty Organization (NATO) in 1949 and the signing of the Warsaw Pact in 1955, military alliances faced one another over what Winston Churchill termed an Iron Curtain. The antagonism between the United States and the Soviet Union increased after the first successful explosion of a Russian nuclear device in September 1949, creating the foundation for the anticommunist witch hunt led by Senator Joseph R. McCarthy (1908–1957).

Stalin's death in 1953 led to a short-lived conciliatory period. In 1959, Vice President Richard M. Nixon (1913–1994) traveled to Moscow and Soviet leader Nikita Sergeyevich Khrushchev (1894–1971) visited the United States. By that time, a space race had begun with the Soviets' launching of the first human-made satellite, *Sputnik*, on October 5, 1957. After a series of Soviet

Soviet leader Mikhail Gorbachev and US president Ronald Reagan sign a nuclear forces agreement in the East Room of the White House, December 1987. When Gorbachev rose to power, he was ready to improve relations with the United States and to initiate reforms in the Soviet Union. Although these democratic reforms, termed glasnost, *did not begin before 1988, Reagan, a staunch anticommunist, saw an opportunity to initiate a process of mutual reassurance and accommodation.* **HISTORICAL/CORBIS**

successes in space, Americans began to fear that the United States had fallen behind technologically and was vulnerable to a Soviet attack from space. When an American U-2 spy plane was shot down over Soviet territory in May 1960, the conciliatory period ended.

The Bay of Pigs disaster, in which Central Intelligence Agency–trained Cuban refugees tried to invade Cuba on April 17, 1961, and the building of the Berlin Wall in August 1961 revealed even more sharply the political and ideological differences. Both sides had accepted a military stalemate and avoided direct military confrontation, which provided little room for the détente favored by both John F. Kennedy (1917–1963) and Khrushchev. The deployment of long-range Soviet missiles on Cuba in October 1962 curtailed any attempts at rapprochement, bringing the world to the brink of a third world war. The crisis was resolved when the Soviet Union agreed to withdraw its missiles from Cuba, and the United States, in turn, promised to honor Cuba's sovereignty. In the aftermath, the United States and the

Soviet Union agreed to establish a line of direct communications to help avoid future dangerous conflicts.

Kennedy had already pushed the United States military into the Vietnam conflict by sending so-called advisers to the South Vietnamese regime, in addition to the financial support previously extended by the Dwight D. Eisenhower (1890–1969) administration. Kennedy's successor, Lyndon B. Johnson (1908–1973), fully engaged the United States in the escalating conflict by sending ground troops to help South Vietnamese forces fighting the Soviet-supported Vietcong.

Partially as a result of the outcome of the Cuban missile crisis, Khrushchev was deposed in October 1964, and his successors, Leonid Ilyich Brezhnev (1906–1982) and Alexei Nikolayevich Kosygin (1904–1980), tried to attain nuclear parity with the United States. Despite these efforts, negotiations with the United States resulted in a process of de-escalation, leading to a treaty on peaceful uses of outer space in 1967 and the Nuclear Non-Proliferation Treaty in July 1968. Even the Soviet invasion in Czechoslovakia in 1968, which deposed the reform government of Alexander Dubček (1921–1992), did not challenge coexistence. President Nixon traveled to Moscow in May 1972 and signed a number of treaties, including the Strategic Arms Limitation Treaty (SALT I) and the Anti-Ballistic Missile (ABM) Treaty, with Brezhnev, who visited the United States the following year.

Soviet involvement in internal struggles in African, Southeast Asian, Latin American, and Caribbean nations, as well as the establishment of diplomatic relations between the United States and the People's Republic of China, again led to a deterioration of relations. The Soviet invasion of Afghanistan in December 1979 resulted in strong responses by the Jimmy Carter administration, including deferral of economic relations, a boycott of the 1980 Summer Olympics in Moscow, suspension of grain exports to the USSR, and restrictions on exports of high-tech products.

Carter's successor, Ronald Reagan (1911–2004), was swept into office on a strongly enunciated anticommunist platform. Reagan denounced détente as a one-way street and, in a speech on March 8, 1983, referred to the Soviet Union as an "evil empire." On March 23, 1983, Reagan announced that the United States would research the possibility of shielding itself from attacks by nuclear missiles, a program known as the Strategic Defense Initiative. This proposal was sharply criticized by the USSR as a possible breach of the ABM and other treaties. US-Soviet relations became further strained when the Soviet air force shot down Korean Air Lines Flight 007, which had strayed into Soviet airspace, on September 1, 1983, and by the Soviets' retaliatory boycott of the Los Angeles Olympic Games in 1984.

This reinvigorated Cold War abated somewhat when Mikhail Sergeyevich Gorbachev became general secretary of the Communist Party in 1985. Gorbachev was willing to reestablish friendly relations with the United States and to initiate reform processes in the USSR to restructure the socialist planned economy. New Year's greetings by Reagan and Gorbachev to the peoples of the United States and the Soviet Union were televised in January 1986. Although democratic reforms, termed *glasnost*, were not initiated in the Soviet Union before 1988, Reagan saw an opportunity at a meeting in Reykjavik on October 11 and 12, 1986, to initiate a process of mutual reassurance and accommodation.

INCREASED COOPERATION AFTER THE DISSOLUTION OF THE SOVIET UNION

George H. W. Bush (in office 1989–1993), Reagan's successor, continued this policy of reconciliation, while political changes in Eastern Europe (particularly in Bulgaria, Czechoslovakia, Romania, and the German Democratic Republic), the unification of Germany, and the disintegration of the power of the Soviet Communist Party weakened the Soviets' global influence. The Soviet Union broke apart after a failed attempt to remove Gorbachev from power in 1991. The United States subsequently recognized the Baltic states, and, in December 1991, Boris Nikolayevich Yeltsin (1931–2007), the chairman of the Russian Supreme Soviet since 1990, conferring with the leaders of the Soviet republics, agreed to dissolve the Soviet Union and to form a Commonwealth of Independent States consisting of eleven former Soviet republics, including the Russian Federation. When Gorbachev resigned as president on December 25, the USSR ceased to exist and Russia was officially recognized, headed by its president, Yeltsin.

The United States feared for the safety of the nuclear arsenal now in the domain of the Russian Federation, and relations between the two countries again became strained, until Russia agreed to continue the process of reducing nuclear warheads in exchange for a multibillion economic aid package. Ratification of the Strategic Arms Reduction Treaty (START) II by the US Senate in January 1996, as well as joint space missions and the building of the International Space Station beginning in 1998, seemed to indicate almost cordial relations. During the presidency of Bill Clinton (in office 1993–2001), even a closer integration of Russia with the West through membership in organizations such as Partnership for Peace and the Euro-Atlantic Partnership Council led by NATO as well as by inviting Russia to join the G7 meetings after 1998 was attempted.

The administration of George W. Bush (in office 2001–2009) was initially less favorable to amiable relations with Russia. However, the terrorist attacks of September 11, 2001, fostered increased cooperation, particularly in matters of intelligence. The United States and Russia signed an additional arms reduction treaty in Moscow on May 24, 2002, and Bush and President Vladimir Vladimirovich Putin agreed to a NATO–Russia Council that would focus on nonproliferation, international terrorism, military cooperation, and civil emergencies. In July 2006, the United States and Russia announced a global initiative to combat nuclear terrorism.

SHIFTING RELATIONS IN THE EARLY TWENTY-FIRST CENTURY

Tensions mounted during Bush's second term. Relations had already become strained after the United States withdrew from the ABM Treaty so as to continue pursuing the missile-defense program that Reagan had proposed. The expansion of NATO into the former Eastern bloc and the invasion of Iraq in 2003, which

Russia opposed, also damaged US relations with Russia. American plans for building missile-defense installations in Poland and the Czech Republic in 2007, clashes over the Georgian invasion of South Ossetia and the subsequent Russian intervention on behalf of Ossetian separatists in 2008, and joint Russian-Venezuelan naval exercises that same year further indicated that festering fundamental differences had not been resolved.

President Barack H. Obama favored reconciliation, and he and Russian president Dmitry Anatolyevich Medvedev promised a "fresh start" in American-Russia relations in a joint statement at the G20 summit in London in 2009. In 2010, an additional nuclear arms reduction treaty, known as New START, further reduced long-range nuclear weapons, and joint antihijacking exercises indicated that US-Russian cooperation was indeed again based on friendly relations and mutual interest.

Tensions have increased since 2012, however, in part because Russian military operations were geared toward pressuring the United States to resolve the still-lingering conflict over missile-defense installations in Poland. Russia's granting of temporary asylum and later a residency permit to National Security Agency whistle-blower and activist Edward Snowden led to the cancellation of a one-on-one meeting between Putin and Obama scheduled for September 2013 in Moscow. Russian support for separatists in Ukraine, the 2014 annexation of the Crimean Peninsula in gross violation of Ukrainian sovereignty and international law, and Russia's support of separatists in the Donbass area of eastern Ukraine resulted in executive orders by President Obama that put severe restrictions on Russian interests in the United States.

Meanwhile, the United States and Russia continued to cooperate in other areas, such as the building of a new space station. In April 2015, Russia and the United States, with the other permanent members of the United Nations Security Council and Germany, brokered an agreement with the Islamic Republic of Iran on curtailment and supervision of its nuclear program.

Frictions between Russia and the United States since Putin's reelection as president in 2012 are the product of clashing interests driving their respective foreign policies. While the United States favors and tries to foster democratization processes and stability, Russia—depending on internal economic development and playing to Russian nationalist sentiment—is foremost interested in being recognized as a world power that has a right to advance its own particular aims. Mutual distrust exists, yet both nations nonetheless cooperate on issues of secondary political importance. The increasing trade between them despite economic sanctions imposed since 2014 is another indication that lines remain open for more constructive political relations in the future.

SEE ALSO *Central Intelligence Agency (CIA); China; Cold War; Eisenhower, Dwight D.; Internationalism; Interventionism; Isolationism; Manchuria; Marshall Plan; Marx, Karl; North Atlantic Treaty Organization (NATO); Open Door Policy; Reagan, Ronald Wilson; Red Scare; Roosevelt, Theodore; Strategic Defense Initiative (Star Wars); Taft, William Howard; Truman, Harry S.; Truman Doctrine; United Nations; Wilson, Woodrow; World War I; World War II; Yalta Conference (1945)*

BIBLIOGRAPHY

Bolkhovitinov, Nikolai N. *The Beginnings of Russian-American Relations, 1775–1815*. Translated by Elena Levin. Cambridge, MA: Harvard University Press, 1975.

Boyle, Peter G. *American-Soviet Relations: From the Russian Revolution to the Fall of Communism*. New York: Routledge, 1993.

Chang, Gordon H. *Friends and Enemies: The United States, China, and the Soviet Union, 1948–1972*. Stanford, CA: Stanford University Press, 1990.

Gaddis, John Lewis. *We Now Know: Rethinking Cold War History*. New York: Oxford University Press, 1997.

Isaac, Joel, and Duncan Bell, eds. *Uncertain Empire: American History and the Idea of the Cold War*. New York: Oxford University Press, 2012.

Jensen, Oliver, ed. *America and Russia: A Century and a Half of Dramatic Encounters*. New York: Simon and Schuster, 1962.

LaFeber, Walter. *America, Russia, and the Cold War, 1945–1992*. New York: Wiley, 1993.

Laserson, Max M. *The American Impact on Russia: Diplomatic and Ideological, 1784–1917*. New York: Macmillan, 1950.

Leffler, Melvyn. *For the Soul of Mankind: The United States, the Soviet Union, and the Cold War*. New York: Hill and Wang, 2007.

Loth, Wilfried. *Overcoming the Cold War: A History of Détente, 1950–1991*. Translated by Robert F. Hogg. New York: Palgrave, 2002.

Paterson, Thomas G. *Meeting the Communist Threat: Truman to Reagan*. New York: Oxford University Press, 1988.

Stent, Angela E. *The Limits of Partnership: U.S.-Russian Relations in the Twenty-First Century*. Princeton, NJ: Princeton University Press, 2014.

Michael Wala
Professor of North American History
Ruhr–Universität Bochum

S

SACCO, NICOLA

SEE *Anarchism.*

SAGE AIR DEFENSE SYSTEM

SEE *International Business Machines Corporation (IBM);
Military-Industrial Complex.*

SAID, EDWARD

1935–2003

Edward Wadie Said was a Palestinian American literary critic and public intellectual. He was among the most important American critics of his generation and one of the major literary scholars of the last half century. Said was famous (and controversial) in the Anglophone academy for his willingness to transgress disciplinary and professional boundaries, and for his often brilliant practice of a historicist criticism that sought to locate the canonical texts of modern Western literature within the context of empire. Even more controversially, both within and beyond the academy, Said was the foremost intellectual advocate in the West of the cause of Palestine, the place of his birth and patrimony.

Said was born in Jerusalem in Mandate Palestine to a wealthy Palestinian family. He spent his childhood in Jerusalem, Dhour el-Shweir in Lebanon, and Cairo in Egypt. His family left Palestine for the last time in 1947. He attended schools in Jerusalem and Cairo, and then was sent to boarding school in Massachusetts—his father being an American citizen. Said took his BA degree at Princeton University and his PhD at Harvard University, where he wrote a thesis on the Polish-English writer Joseph Conrad (1857–1924).

Said began teaching at Columbia University in New York City in 1963, and spent the rest of his career there, attaining the position of university professor. He also held visiting positions at several other universities and research institutions. Said wrote a number of major books on literature, criticism, and theory. He was one of the earliest and most important American critics to respond to the new and radical French and continental literary and cultural theory of the 1960s. His second book, *Beginnings* (1975), was a landmark in the American appropriation of the work of thinkers such as Michel Foucault (1926–1984), Jacques Derrida (1930–2004), and Gilles Deleuze (1925–1995).

It was Said's third book, *Orientalism* (1978), that made his career. In this volume, Said took as his purview not only the learned discipline of the study of Oriental languages, culture, and politics, but he discussed in the same context other European and American writings, focusing particularly on the Arab and Muslim Middle East. Said traced a lineage of Western visions of the Orient, stretching from classical times to the late twentieth century, which stressed the putative decadence, primitivism, femininity, and irrationality of that region and its denizens. Furthermore, Said argued that the production of knowledge of the Orient by Westerners had been and still was irreducibly related to and served the purposes of imperial dominance. Orientalism was for Said a form of "power/knowledge," and he argued that this tendency encompassed writings in linguistics, history, literature, travel writing, anthropology, political science, and area studies.

Orientalism was a huge success. It helped to inaugurate modern postcolonial studies, a field Said himself further contributed to with his major volume *Culture and Imperialism* (1993), and it decisively engendered a radical current in American Middle East studies. But Said's activism and writing in regard to Palestine also by now had raised his public profile to make him one of the most recognized and admired (and reviled) public intellectuals in the world. Said was a nonaligned member of the Palestine National Council, the Palestinian parliament-in-exile from 1977 to 1991. He was an early advocate of the "two-state solution," though he eventually was a vocal critic of the Oslo peace process in the 1990s and of the emergent Palestinian Authority.

Said was an accomplished pianist, and in 2000 he founded the West-Eastern Divan Orchestra with the Israeli conductor Daniel Barenboim—an orchestra composed of young Arab and Israeli musicians. Said was awarded numerous honorary degrees. In addition, he was the inaugural recipient of the Spinoza Lens Prize in 1999, received a Lannan Literary Award in 2001, and in 2002 became the first American citizen to win the Sultan Owais Prize.

Said died of lymphatic leukemia, which had been diagnosed in 1991, in September 2003. He was buried in Lebanon.

SEE ALSO *Middle East; Orientalism*

BIBLIOGRAPHY

Ashcroft, Bill, and Pal Ahluwalia. *Edward Said*. Rev. 2nd ed. London: Routledge, 2008.

Hart, William D. *Edward Said and the Religious Effects of Culture*. Cambridge: Cambridge University Press, 2000.

Hussein, Abdirahman. *Edward Said: Criticism and Society*. London: Verso, 2002.

McCarthy, Conor. *The Cambridge Introduction to Edward Said*. Cambridge: Cambridge University Press, 2010.

Conor D. McCarthy
Department of English
Maynooth University, Ireland

ST. PATRICK BATTALION

The St. Patrick Battalion was a company of mostly Irish-born American deserters from the US Army who fought for Mexico during the Mexican-American War (1846–1848). The seventy-two-man cohort, which carried a battle flag bearing an image of St. Patrick with the words

"Erin go Bragh" and "San Patricio," exacerbated American nativist criticism and distrust of Irish immigrants, even though there were native-born Americans and German immigrants in the battalion as well.

The Mexican-American War occurred during a high point of anti-Catholic activity and nativist violence in the United States. Due to increased Irish immigration, this anti-Catholic nativism often was indistinguishable from anti-Irish sentiment. At the same time, Americans by the 1840s had come to believe that their "manifest destiny" as a dynamic and Protestant Anglo-Saxon people was to spread their population and republican government throughout North America. Consequently, even before the San Patricio defection, many Americans doubted whether Catholics could be loyal in a war against a Catholic nation like Mexico. In response, many American Catholics displayed their enthusiasm for the war overtly.

The American army in the Mexican-American War included regular soldiers, as well as volunteers. In the nativist climate of the 1840s, foreign-born men were rarely welcome in these volunteer companies. Although in some large cities Irish Americans formed their own, ethnic-based companies, foreign-born Americans tended to join the regular army. Approximately 20 percent of regular US soldiers were foreign born when war broke out between the United States and Mexico. Yet even in the regular army, foreign-born Catholic soldiers faced unequal discipline and religious oppression at the hands of nativist officers.

As anti-Catholic and Anglo-Saxonist rhetoric ramped up in the early weeks of the war, some Irish soldiers began to wonder why they were supporting the conquest of a Catholic country by a triumphalist Protestant nation. The captains of volunteer companies even used the possibility of looting Mexican Catholic churches as a recruitment tool. Such sentiment reminded the immigrant Irish of England's oppression of Ireland and the Anglo-Saxonist rationale that underlay it. John Riley, a Clifden-born Irishman, was among those who deserted once he deemed the US Army to be just another Anglo-Saxon force bent on subjugating non-Anglo-Saxons. He then organized and led what became the St. Patrick Battalion, which joined with Mexico to fight the US Army in several battles.

Most deserters, of course, did not join the Mexican Army. More than 110,000 Americans went to Mexico as part of the US Army. Of this, nine thousand deserted (Miller 1989, 23). Nativists claimed these deserters were foreign-born men who lacked love for their new country, while Catholics tried to refute this.

Nativist abuse within the army, ethnic identity, and the American climate of religious bigotry only partially explain the defection. Crucial to the story is that the

Mexican Army systematically solicited Irish American soldiers with offers of free farmland for men who would desert and join the Mexican Army. This propaganda drew upon the 1844 anti-Catholic riots in Philadelphia, as well as the desire of immigrant Irish, who had come from a starving land of tenant farms, to own their own property. The evidence suggests that, in the name of General Antonio López de Santa Anna (1794–1876), Riley authored these broadsides (Pinheiro 2014, 103). But abuse in the army, much more than religious or any other affinity with Mexicans, inspired these men to fight for Mexico.

After several battles, the St. Patrick Battalion met defeat at Churubusco on August 20, 1847. The surviving members were captured by American forces and put on trial for treason and desertion. All told, twenty-seven were hanged. Journalists present at the hanging of the San Patricios claimed that Irish American soldiers rejoiced the loudest, for they knew that these few deserters had tarnished their entire ethnic group. Moreover, they now feared even harsher abuse in the army by nativists.

While religion certainly played a role in the San Patricio affair, Mexico and American nativists emphasized religion much more than did the members of the St. Patrick Battalion. So, too, did American soldiers, who felt sure their comrades had fought for Mexico solely on account of religion. The Irish, according to these Americans, could not leave their Old World religious attachments behind.

The San Patricios who had deserted the army prior to the outbreak of hostilities were not hanged. Instead, the US Army branded each on the face with a *D* for *deserter*. Among these was Riley, although he seems lost to history after this fact. Monuments to the St. Patrick Battalion still stand in Mexico City, as well as in Clifden, Ireland.

SEE ALSO *Immigration; Mexican-American War; Polk, James K.; Santa Anna, Antonio López de*

BIBLIOGRAPHY

Miller, Robert Ryal. *Shamrock and Sword: The Saint Patrick Battalion in the U.S.-Mexican War.* Norman: University of Oklahoma Press, 1989.

Pinheiro, John C. *Missionaries of Republicanism: A Religious History of the Mexican-American War.* New York: Oxford University Press, 2014.

Stevens, Peter F. *The Rogue's March: John Riley and the St. Patrick's Battalion, 1846–48.* Washington, DC: Potomac, 1999.

John C. Pinheiro
Professor of History
Aquinas College, Michigan

SALVATION ARMY

In 1880, when a Salvation Army delegation disembarked in lower Manhattan, the small team of seven women and one man were unlikely agents of the British Empire. Yet their first act on American soil was to plant their flag outside the immigration reception center and claim America for God. Subsequent activities—parading through city streets, "invading" brothels and saloons, and praying with society matrons alongside down-and-outers—further conveyed the surety that their overseas evangelistic army was far superior to anything local.

The Salvation Army emerged from the transatlantic revivalist movements that spanned the nineteenth century, bringing a steady stream of Americans to the British Isles and Brits back to America. But General William Booth (1829–1912), despite his own debts to American religious leaders Charles Finney (1792–1875) and Phoebe Palmer (1807–1874), had no doubt that his very British

Salvation Army poster, 1918. The Salvation Army sent "lassies" to the French front during World War I, instructing the girls to "mother" the troops—offering coffee and doughnuts, sewing on buttons, and writing letters home. American soldiers praised the lassies' goodness and generosity. BUYENLARGE/ARCHIVE PHOTOS/ GETTY IMAGES

organization was better equipped than any other religious group to spread the gospel worldwide. Booth established the Salvation Army in London in 1878, building on his earlier attempts to create a viable missionary movement. When he seized upon the idea of a Christian army, he consciously modeled it on Britain's respected and revered imperial forces. The Salvation Army adopted uniforms, military ranks, and a martial vocabulary. Paraphrasing a slogan used to describe the British Empire, the *War Cry*, the Salvationist newspaper, proclaimed that "the sun never sets on the Salvation Army."

Though few in number, the Salvationists sent to the United States were determined to win souls and assemble an American army. Within several years, they had grown beyond beachheads in New York and Philadelphia to rally troops from California to Connecticut. American Salvationists faced similar challenges to those their British coreligionists encountered. While young people were attracted to the Salvation Army's crusading spirit and opportunities for adventure, older people, especially churchgoers, were appalled by its tactics. Salvationists used brass bands, female preachers, and hymns set to barroom tunes to attract crowds. These practices, as well as the army's openness to racially mixed worship, elicited rebukes from the pulpit, censure from the newspapers, and antagonism on the streets.

Yet the Salvation Army's decision to provide social services, such as shelters for homeless men and women, food kitchens, and outreach to unwed mothers and prostitutes, began to change public opinion. By the early twentieth century, its work among the poor won praise both in Britain and the United States. At the same time, Booth was sending soldiers to conquer the Continent and spread his army into Asia and Africa. By the time he died in 1912, Salvationists spanned the globe.

The American contingent, however, had proved more independent than the general desired. In 1886, Booth placed his son Ballington (1857–1940) and daughter-in-law Maud (1865–1948) at the head of his US troops. Booth, whose first international trip had been to America, was initially pleased by Maud and Ballington's success at cultivating wealthy patrons while growing army ranks and expanding social services. But his approval turned into disapprobation when he decided that the "Americanization" of his forces had gone too far.

In most foreign countries, the Salvation Army tried to soften its Britishness and fidelity to London International Headquarters by integrating elements from the local culture into its routines. But the Ballington Booths' wholesale promotion of American officers and their adoption of American symbols angered General Booth. He decided to transfer his son and daughter-in-law to another foreign post, but the young couple refused to leave. When a full-scale rebellion broke out, threatening to divide the army between British and American supporters, the general sent his daughter Evangeline (1865–1950) to restore order. Initially outflanked, Evangeline's oratorical power eventually won over skeptics in the ranks and among the army's wealthy supporters. After resigning, the Ballington Booths launched the Volunteers of America, a new organization, which borrowed tactics and techniques from the Salvation Army.

After the Ballington Booths' aborted coup, their successors—another Booth daughter and her husband—maintained close ties to London. But when Evangeline took over in 1904, she was determined to grow the American army's strength and prestige, even challenging her elder brother Bramwell's (1856–1929) leadership of the international army. Evangeline won over even America's hardest hearts when she sent Salvationist "lassies" to the French front during World War I (1914–1918). She instructed her girls to "mother" the troops—offering coffee and doughnuts, sewing on buttons, and writing letters home. American doughboys (the nickname for soldiers in the American Expeditionary Force) lionized the lassies' goodness and generosity, and after the war ended, the Salvation Army was deemed as American as apple pie. Its days as a renegade group long past, the army began raising millions of dollars for its social service programs.

Evangeline succeeded in mainstreaming the Salvation Army because she downplayed its evangelistic mission and emphasized its humanitarian outreach. Americans across the religious spectrum supported the army because of its good works. This strategy proved remunerative; by the end of the twentieth century, the Salvation Army was one of the country's most successful charitable fundraisers and one of its largest private social service providers. But many Americans were unaware of the army's evangelical identity and its primary commitment to soul-winning.

The American army is the wealthiest among the Salvation Army's international outposts. Yet its identity as a social service provider is singular. In other nations, the Salvation Army is seen first and foremost as a church and its social work is a secondary feature. The high public profile that the army enjoys in the United States, a result not only of its wide array of social services but also its work in disaster relief, is unique. The Salvation Army uniform and its red shield are recognizable worldwide, but only in the United States are the emblems equated more with humanitarian service than with evangelical Christianity.

SEE ALSO *Americanization; Britain; Imperialism; Protestantism; Red Cross; Secularization; Transatlantic Reform; World War I; World War II*

BIBLIOGRAPHY

Eason, Andrew M. *Women in God's Army: Gender and Equality in the Early Salvation Army.* Waterloo, ON: Wilfrid Laurier University Press, 2003.

Hattersley, Roy. *Blood and Fire: William and Catherine Booth and Their Salvation Army.* New York: Doubleday, 2000.

McKinley, Edward H. *Marching to Glory: The History of the Salvation Army in the United States, 1880–1992.* 2nd ed. Grand Rapids, MI: Eerdmans, 1995.

Walker, Pamela J. *Pulling the Devil's Kingdom Down: The Salvation Army in Victorian Britain.* Berkeley: University of California Press, 2001.

Winston, Diane. *Red-Hot and Righteous: The Urban Religion of the Salvation Army.* Cambridge, MA: Harvard University Press, 2000.

Diane Winston
Knight Chair in Media and Religion
Annenberg School for Communication and Journalism
University of Southern California

SAMOA

SEE *Pacific Islands.*

SANDINISTAS

SEE *Freedom Fighters.*

SANTA ANNA, ANTONIO LÓPEZ DE

1794–1876

Antonio López de Santa Anna had a long and turbulent career in Mexican politics. He rose to prominence when Mexico was still a Spanish colony and, although slow to embrace the move toward independence, Santa Anna subsequently played a significant role in ejecting royalist factions from his home province of Veracruz. As Will Fowler notes, Santa Anna "also acquired fame, albeit not entirely justified, as the author of Agustín I's downfall and the founder of the Republic of Mexico," a reputation augmented by Santa Anna's involvement in the repulsion of a Spanish force intent on reconquest in 1829 and his role in the Pastry War (1838–1839), during which he was injured fighting against the French and had much of his left leg amputated (Fowler 2007, xxii). Such successes, however, were countered by failures that led to the loss of half of the national territory of Mexico.

It is for these defeats that Santa Anna is now remembered. He is also notable for his conduct at the Alamo (February 23–March 6, 1836) during the Texan Revolution, where his force of 1,400 Mexicans gave no quarter to the 183 men who rejected his offer of surrender. One of these was the prominent frontiersman David Crockett (1786–1836), and there is some debate as to whether Crockett died fighting or was later executed on Santa Anna's orders (Lind 1998; Crisp 1998, 2005; Groneman 1998; Connelly 1960). The decisive battle of the revolution was not at the Alamo but at San Jacinto, where Santa Anna was routed by a smaller force under the command of Sam Houston (1793–1863). Santa Anna was asleep when the battle began; without his watchful command, the sentries had lowered their guard and Houston seized the moment, allowing his numerically inferior force to triumph. The majority of popular accounts, however, incorrectly cite the technical superiority of the Mexican forces, who were exhausted and, as Santa Anna stressed, also included many raw recruits who froze in battle.

Despite this major defeat, Santa Anna was able to rebuild his career and retain high office until 1845, when he was overthrown, tried, convicted of a range of offences, and went into exile in Cuba. This was not the end of Santa Anna, though. After the annexation of Texas by the United States in 1845, war between Mexico and the United States looked increasingly likely as border disputes erupted. Even from Cuba, Santa Anna played a part: he was visited by emissaries from President James K. Polk (1795–1849) in an attempt to negotiate a peaceful settlement. When war began, Santa Anna returned to Mexico, broke all promises made to the Americans, and was warmly welcomed by his compatriots. He then set about organizing the Mexican army to resist the Americans. His forces were never properly resourced, though, and Mexico was also subject to internal unrest. As a result, and due to the errors of Santa Anna and others, the war went badly. Santa Anna failed to break General Zachary Taylor's (1784–1850) troops at the Battle of Angostura–Buena Vista (February 22–23, 1847), losing thousands of his own men to death, desertion, or disability. A string of defeats followed. By September 1847, Mexican forces had abandoned Mexico City and withdrawn to Guadalupe Hidalgo.

Santa Anna resigned as president, was stripped of all military command by the new government, and then suffered the further indignity of the capture of his prosthetic leg by American troops, as well as the destruction and theft of his luggage. The new government agreed to terms with the United States and, despite Santa Anna's absence, blame for the defeat was set on his shoulders by many, then and now. Critics highlighted his acceptance of American money as an indication of traitorous intentions, but as Wilfrid Hardy Callcott concludes, "no one can doubt the sincerity of his effort who reads the accounts of the northern campaign" (1964, 243).

Santa Anna again went into exile, though he was able to return to Mexico in 1853, when he was installed as president and then sold more territory to the United States through the Gadsden Purchase (1853). By 1855, he had lost power and fled into exile again, only returning to Mexico in 1874 when an amnesty was proclaimed. On his death two years later, "over eight thousand people paid their last respects … and a procession of over forty carriages accompanied him on his last journey" (Fowler 2007, 346). It is in his divisive life and legacy, his departure into and briefly triumphant returns from exile, that Santa Anna most lives up to his nickname of the "Napoleon of the West."

SEE ALSO *Mexican-American War*

BIBLIOGRAPHY

Callcott, Wilfrid Hardy. *Santa Anna: The Story of an Enigma Who Once Was Mexico.* Hamden, CT: Archon, 1964.

Connelly, Thomas Lawrence. "Did David Crockett Surrender at the Alamo? A Contemporary Letter." *Journal of Southern History* 26, 3 (1960): 368–376.

Crisp, James E. "Crockett Controversy Continues." *Wilson Quarterly* 22, 2 (1998): 7–8.

Crisp, James E. *Sleuthing the Alamo: Davy Crockett's Last Stand and Other Mysteries of the Texas Revolution.* Oxford: Oxford University Press, 2005.

Fowler, Will. *Santa Anna of Mexico.* Lincoln: University of Nebraska Press, 2007.

Groneman, William. "Crockett Controversy Continues." *Wilson Quarterly* 22, 2 (1998): 8–9.

Lind, Michael. "The Death of David Crockett." *Wilson Quarterly* 22, 1 (1998): 50–57.

Moore, Stephen L. *Eighteen Minutes: The Battle of San Jacinto and the Texas Independence Campaign.* Lanham, MD: Rowman and Littlefield, 2004.

Vázquez, Josefina Zoraida. "The Texas Question in Mexican Politics, 1836–1845." *Southwestern Historical Quarterly* 89, 3 (1986): 309–344.

Michael Goodrum
Senior Lecturer, Department of History & American Studies
Canterbury Christ Church University

SCIENTIFIC RACISM

SEE *Race.*

SECESSIONISM

SEE *The Civil War.*

SECULARIZATION

For much of the twentieth century, leading intellectuals in Europe and the United States posited that religion would decline, or even disappear, as societies modernized. Industrialization and urbanization, the rise of science to a position of unchallenged legitimacy in intellectual life, and the emergence of rationalized bureaucracies across government, corporations, and education would all lead, in the words of the famed German sociologist Max Weber (1864–1920), to "disenchantment." This fundamental theory of modernization, usually called *secularization theory*, provided a powerful framework to explain the trajectory of change in the modern world.

But secularization theory came under increasing scrutiny in the 1970s and 1980s, and has been a subject of intense debate ever since. Its fate has seesawed in recent decades in sync with political and religious developments. The 1979 Islamic Revolution in Iran, the rise of the Religious Right in the United States, the spread of Pentecostalism in Africa and Latin America, and the fall of communism in Eastern Europe all called secularization into question, as religion reasserted itself across the globe. The persistence of religious belief and practice in the United States, and its apparently growing political clout, proved especially challenging to secularization theory in these years. The United States, after all, represented a society in the vanguard of modernity—with an advanced economy, high technology, world-class research universities, a diverse population, and a highly differentiated social structure—yet it remained resolutely religious. "Secular Europe" and "religious America" became the paradigm that scholars scrambled to understand.

The realities of the late twentieth and twenty-first centuries, however, have complicated secularization theory once again. Religious disaffiliation has soared in the United States since the 1990s, reaching by 2015 more the 20 percent of the total population and fully one in three Americans under age thirty—a powerful trend that challenges the previous understanding of US religiosity as the great contrast to European secularity. Meanwhile, the rapidly growing Muslim populations in Britain, France, and elsewhere in Europe have resisted the longstanding social and political arrangements that regulated the dominant secularism of public life. These tensions have been especially acute in France, where the regime of *laïcité*—meaning the official secularism of public institutions, including schools, established by law in 1905—has conflicted with Islamic norms, most particularly regarding the wearing of the hijab or veil.

DEFINITIONS AND MODELS

Much of the challenge of assessing secularization comes with defining the term, a problem bound up with the problem of defining religion. The word *secular* derives from a Latin word meaning "worldly" or "temporal," and from this usage the term *secularization* first meant the transfer of church property to the state or to private ownership, such as in sixteenth-century England or revolutionary France. Another related usage indicated the release of clergy from monastic vows. The most widespread understanding of *secularization* in contemporary usage, however, is as a process of broad social and political change under the conditions of modernity. This usage of *secularization* typically comes in two forms: secularization as the decline or disappearance of religious belief and practice, and secularization as the privatization of religion.

Secularization in the first sense, as decline or disappearance, raises with particular acuity the importance of clearly defining what is meant by religion. Most discussions of religious decline in North America, Europe, and elsewhere around the world focus on the fate of historically dominant religious groups. These analyses of decline, therefore, rely on what scholars call a substantive definition of religion—meaning an understanding that religion is defined by certain set characteristics, such as belief in God or participation in customary ritual practices. For these reasons, substantive understandings of religion generally conform to common understandings of the term, meaning most often the great, historic traditions, such as Christianity, Islam, Judaism, Buddhism, and Hinduism. Religion in this sense declines or disappears if large numbers of people in a given society no longer hold widely acknowledged "religious" beliefs or participate in "religious" communities or activities. Northern and western Europe, parts of Canada, Australia, and New Zealand, and increasingly the United States with the rise of the so-called religious "nones" (meaning those who respond "none" when asked about religious affiliation by pollsters) serve as examples of this kind of secularization.

Functional understandings of religion, in contrast, see religion as any cultural phenomenon that meets fundamental human needs for community, meaning, and transcendence. This notion of religion draws attention to religious mutation and evolution rather than extinction under the conditions of modernity, and presents more significant challenges to secularization theory. Psychological and group therapies, allegiance to sports teams, nationalism, and participation in the arts, yoga, and meditation are all seen, according to functionalists, as potential forms of religion, even or perhaps especially prevalent among those who claim no traditional religious affiliation. Even though each of these practices may be understood to incorporate many of the functional aspects of religion, and can be studied fruitfully with the tools of religious studies scholarship, functional models of religion do not lend themselves to analysis according to

secularization theory. If religion is a mutating but persistent response to universal human needs, secularization as a theory of broad social change loses much of its analytical force. For these reasons, debates about secularization generally assume, at least implicitly, a substantive definition of religion, typically through reference to one of the historically dominant religious traditions.

SECULARIZATION AS THE PRIVATIZATION OF RELIGION

Secularization as the disappearance of religion fits commonsense understandings of "the secular" as the absence of "religion," and matches the lived experience of many of the European societies where early theorists of secularization resided. Nevertheless, many contemporary scholars of secularization rely on the second, subtler understanding of secularization—secularization as privatization. This notion of secularization describes the process by which religion (substantively understood) declines in significance or disappears altogether from public life, even if it persists at the level of communities, families, and individuals. The landmark Supreme Court cases of the 1960s in the United States—*Engel v. Vitale* (1962), which prohibited state-sponsored prayers in public schools, and *Abington School District v. Schempp* (1963), which prohibited compulsory, devotional Bible reading—represent this second form of secularization. The Court compelled the secularization of the public schools, relegating religious practice to the private sphere of family life and individual conscience, where it often continued to thrive.

The legal history of religion in the United States, in fact, demonstrates most clearly the process of secularization as privatization, even as much of Europe most clearly demonstrates secularization as substantive decline. The public life of colonial British North America was thoroughly suffused with Christianity. Puritan New England stands out for its fully theocratic character, but Christianity marked public affairs across the colonies. Execution sermons, fast days, required religious oaths, and blasphemy laws enforced and reinforced the Christian character of American society and governance. Limited as religious diversity was according to twenty-first-century standards, however, the American colonies contained a wide array of Protestant groups, as well as small numbers of Jews and Catholics, and eventually this diverse social environment combined with the emerging values of the Enlightenment in the eighteenth century to bring about a revolutionary transformation in the place of religion in American life.

In short, the American Revolution (1775–1783) secularized the United States, even as the American people remained deeply religious. The great American child of the Enlightenment, Thomas Jefferson (1743–1826), collaborated with Virginia Baptists, a marginalized and often persecuted sect before the Revolution, to promote and ultimately pass into law in 1786 the Virginia Statute for Religious Freedom, which became the model for the First Amendment's guarantee of religious free exercise and prohibition on government religious establishment. The Virginia Statute famously begins with Jefferson's statement of conscience, "Whereas, Almighty God hath created the mind free," a testimony to the newfound valuation of the individual in liberal political philosophy and a landmark moment in the history of secularization as privatization. Ever since, religion in the United State has been understood by law to exist first and foremost in the conscience of the individual.

This privatized notion of religion, however, took some time to become normative, and has never been fully realized. Even as states quickly dropped their formal religious establishments in the wake of the Revolution— Massachusetts was the last to do so, in 1833—a de facto "moral establishment" took hold, in the words of historian David Sehat (2011). Laws banning the delivery of the mail on Sundays, for example, enforced Christian norms, while the public schools across the country provided Protestant indoctrination in subtle and overt ways. The 1878 Supreme Court case *Reynolds v. United States* upheld the federal legal ban on polygamy, and more importantly refused to recognize the argument of the defendant, a member of the Church of Jesus Christ of Latter-day Saints, that plural marriage was protected by the free exercise clause of the First Amendment. This case enshrined into law the critical distinction between belief and practice; whereas the mind might "be free" to believe as it chooses, the state could nevertheless regulate the actions of the body, often in accord with the dictates of the religious majority.

The *Reynolds* case reveals the limits of religious liberty in the United States, and the reality that religious practice can never be fully privatized, free of public concern or implications. Nevertheless, the history of religion in the twentieth-century United States shows how powerfully the combination of religious disestablishment, political liberalism, and consumer capitalism drives religion into the private sphere, where it becomes a matter of voluntary association and private conscience. At the social level, the denomination emerged in the United States as the quintessential religious formation early in the nineteenth century, while at the same moment both evangelical Christianity and transcendentalist spirituality placed unprecedented emphasis on religion as the free choice of free individuals. The Harvard psychologist and philosopher William James (1842–1910) best captured this quintessentially American form of religious individualism in his famous (or infamous) early twentieth-century

definition of religion as "the feelings, acts, and experiences of individual men in their solitude, so far as they apprehend themselves to stand in relation to whatever they may consider the divine" ([1902] 1929, 31–32).

THE US PARADOX

This focus on secularization as privatization helps explain one of the central paradoxes in the comparative study of secularization around the world. The United States, after all, is at once one of the most secular and one of the most religious societies on earth, and each of these realities is critical to the country's self-understanding and international reputation. From presidential speeches to country music, religious language and imagery pervades American culture. Along and often in tandem with the global reach of American corporations, the US military, and the latest spectacle from Hollywood, American religiosity profoundly shapes the ways Americans interact with the rest of the world. The most significant new religions of the nineteenth and twentieth centuries, including Mormonism and Pentecostalism, have been American exports, and American evangelical missionaries have reached nearly every society on earth. And yet the United States is the oldest officially secular nation on earth. The Constitution enshrined into fundamental law the radical Enlightenment notion that a free society could exist without legally established religion as the basis of cohesion and order.

Some scholars have argued, in fact, that the official secularism of American law has created the conditions that have allowed religion in the private sphere to flourish. With no monopoly religion, all manner of religious entrepreneurship has blossomed in the United States. In contrast, the state-established religions in Britain and the Scandinavian countries led to religious apathy, especially in the decades after the Second World War (1939–1945) as the welfare state assumed many of the social functions once performed by the churches.

THE FRENCH MODEL OF SECULARISM

The case of France, however, provides perhaps the most instructive contrast to the United States. Whereas the Anglo-American Enlightenment foregrounded liberty as a defining virtue, and therefore emphasized freedom *of* religion, the Enlightenment in revolutionary France foregrounded reason, which combined with a powerful reaction against the dominant Catholic Church to create a political culture that emphasized freedom *from* religion. The 1905 law on the Separation of the Churches and the State codified these revolutionary principles, as it ceased state funding of religion and declared all church properties to be properties of the state (typically leased back to the religious communities free of charge for worship purposes). More broadly, the norms of French *laïcité* mean that politicians refrain from using religious speech, unlike their American counterparts, and the conspicuous display of religious affiliation, especially through clothing, is generally discouraged, and even prohibited by law in some instances.

The French model of secularism, sometimes called negative *laïcité*, has served as an important model for other countries and regions, especially Turkey, Quebec, and Mexico, and has become especially influential in debates about the role of the state in promoting gender equality. The effort to ban the burqa in France (according to legislation first voted on in 2010), an act that would be clearly unconstitutional in the United States, has become the latest flashpoint in these ongoing struggles over the nature of French secularism. Nevertheless, each of these societies in recent years has considered reforms that would move in the direction of an American-style, positive or religion-affirming secularism, even as controversies in the United States over marriage equality and contraception have once again raised questions about the limits of religious liberty in a diverse and formally secular nation. If history serves as any guide, the course of secularization will continue to be uneven, divisive, and thoroughly unpredictable in the years ahead.

SEE ALSO *American Revolution; Americanization; Buddhism; Catholicism; The Civil War; Clash of Civilizations (Samuel Huntington); Cold War; Exceptionalism; Federal Council of Churches; Foreign Mission Movement; Hinduism; Internationalism; Interventionism; Islam; Isolationism; Jewish Welfare Board; Judaism; Knights of Columbus; Moorish Science Temple; Nation of Islam; Protestantism; Rastafari; Shinto; Spanish-American War; Vietnam War; World War I; World War II; World's Fairs; World's Parliament of Religions (1893); World's YWCA/ YMCA*

BIBLIOGRAPHY

Asad, Talal. *Formations of the Secular: Christianity, Islam, Modernity.* Stanford, CA: Stanford University Press, 2003.

Berger, Peter, Gracie Davie, and Effie Fokas. *Religious America, Secular Europe? A Theme and Variations.* Aldershot, UK: Ashgate, 2008.

Bruce, Steve, ed. *Religion and Modernization: Sociologists and Historians Debate the Secularization Thesis.* Oxford: Oxford University Press, 1992.

Calhoun, Craig, Mark Juergensmeyer, and Jonathan VanAntwerpen, eds. *Rethinking Secularism.* New York: Oxford University Press, 2011.

Casanova, José. *Public Religions in the Modern World.* Chicago: University of Chicago Press, 1994.

Fernando, Mayanthi L. *The Republic Unsettled: Muslim French and the Contradictions of Secularism.* Durham, NC: Duke University Press, 2014.

Jakobsen, Janet R., and Ann Pellegrini, eds. *Secularisms.* Durham, NC: Duke University Press, 2008.

James, William. *The Varieties of Religious Experience: A Study in Human Nature, Being the Gifford Lectures on Natural Religion Delivered at Edinburgh in 1901–1902.* New York: Modern Library, 1929. First published 1902 by Longmans, Green.

Scott, Joan Wallach. *The Politics of the Veil.* Princeton, NJ: Princeton University Press, 2007.

Sehat, David. *The Myth of American Religious Freedom.* New York: Oxford University Press, 2011.

Sullivan, Winnifred Fallers. *The Impossibility of Religious Freedom.* Princeton, NJ: Princeton University Press, 2005.

Taylor, Charles. *A Secular Age.* Cambridge, MA: Harvard University Press, 2007.

Warner, Michael, Jonathan VanAntwerpen, and Craig Calhoun, eds. *Varieties of Secularism in a Secular Age.* Cambridge, MA: Harvard University Press, 2010.

Matthew S. Hedstrom
Associate Professor of Religious Studies and American Studies
University of Virginia

SECURITY COUNCIL, UN

The United Nations Security Council has been a source of controversy for the United States almost since its inception in 1945. Domestic critics of the United Nations claim that other countries use the Security Council to constrain the United States. By contrast, many outside observers, especially in the non-Western world, believe the United States wields excessive influence over Security Council decisions.

STRUCTURE AND AUTHORITY

The Security Council consists of five permanent members (the P5) with veto powers over substantive decisions (China, France, Russia, the United Kingdom, and the United States) and ten nonpermanent members who hold seats for two years, in rotation with other UN member states. The number of nonpermanent members was expanded from six to ten in 1965 to reflect the growing number of UN member states following decolonization. However, the P5 have always dominated Security Council diplomacy. Britain, France, and the United States (the P3) drive most policy initiatives, although they have split over some issues, such as the 2003 invasion of Iraq.

Under the UN Charter, the Security Council has the legal power to authorize the use of force to maintain international peace and security. It has used this power only in rare cases, including the Korean War (1950), the liberation of Kuwait (1991), and the international interventions in Somalia (1993) and Libya (2011) (Jones 2011). The Council also oversees the United Nations' peacekeeping operations and sanctions regimes. Since 2002, the Council has also had the right to refer countries to the International Criminal Court (ICC). Although neither the United States nor Russia and China are members of the ICC, Washington has backed the court's engagement in some cases, including those related to Sudan and Libya.

RELEVANCE DURING THE COLD WAR

The Security Council's relevance has fluctuated in line with the overall state of international affairs. During the Second World War (1939–1945), President Franklin Roosevelt hoped that the United Nations would sustain close postwar cooperation among the Allies who fought Germany and Japan, including the USSR. With the advent of the Cold War, however, Soviet diplomats used their veto power regularly to block Western initiatives. Nonetheless, the United States was able to use the Security Council to its advantage. In 1950, it secured Security Council Resolution 84, authorizing UN military action in Korea (Russia was boycotting the Council at the time, so could not use its veto). During the 1962 Cuban missile crisis, the US ambassador to the United Nations, Adlai Stevenson (1900–1965), gained international attention with a presentation to the Security Council demonstrating the presence of Soviet nuclear forces on Cuba. In a more cooperative spirit, the United States and the Soviet Union also used the Council to arrange the cessation of hostilities following the 1967 and 1973 Arab-Israeli wars.

The Security Council became increasingly sidelined during the later Cold War. From 1970 onward, the USSR and developing countries aimed to embarrass the United States by tabling resolutions on issues such as the Israeli-Palestinian conflict and Israel's military operations in Lebanon that Washington was bound to veto. As of August 2015, members of the P5 have cast 275 vetoes since the Security Council's creation. Although the USSR/Russia cast the most vetoes (132), the United States has used the veto 83 times. 42 of the US vetoes dealt with resolutions criticizing Israel (Security Council 2013).

NEW OPPORTUNITIES AND TENSIONS AFTER THE COLD WAR

Nonetheless, the end of the Cold War created new opportunities for cooperation in the Security Council. President George H. W. Bush signaled the change of mood by gaining Council authorization for the international military response to Iraq's 1990 invasion of Kuwait. Bush talked of a "new world order" with the United Nations at its center. But the Bill Clinton administration became increasingly frustrated with the Council in the 1990s, especially over the Balkan wars. Britain and France insisted on trying to manage the collapse of Yugoslavia through the Security Council, but UN peacekeepers were unable to stop the massacre of eight thousand men and boys in the UN-designated "safe area" of Srebrenica. However, the Clinton administration's own record at the United Nations was also damaged by its refusal to act decisively in response to the 1994 Rwandan genocide.

America's impatience with the Security Council came to a head in 1999, when the Clinton administration and its NATO allies intervened in Kosovo without UN authorization after Russia threatened to veto any action. Although President Clinton attempted to rebuild bridges at the United Nations after Kosovo, President George W. Bush adopted an instinctively skeptical approach to the organization. The United States succeeded in winning UN support for a series of resolutions on counterterrorism after the terrorist attacks of September 11, 2001, and attempted to get Security Council authorization for the invasion of Iraq in 2003. The Bush administration's eventual decision to invade without UN support did lasting damage to America's reputation at the United Nations.

The Barack Obama administration made restoring the US position at the United Nations an early priority, and the president underlined this by requesting Security Council backing for the Libyan intervention in 2011. The Obama administration also put UN sanctions at the center of its approach to the Iranian nuclear program. However, President Obama's investment in the Council had a heavy cost, as Russia and China repeatedly blocked resolutions aimed at resolving the Syrian civil war by increasing pressure on the regime in Damascus.

The Syrian crisis that began in 2011 provided fresh ammunition for those who believe that the United States weakens itself by (in the words of President George W. Bush) asking for a "permission slip" from the United Nations before acting (Bush 2004). Foreign critics of US policy argue that the United States is as tough as Russia, or more so, in defending its interests and allies—most notably Israel—at the United Nations. China and Russia argue that the United States, Britain, and France have used their leverage in the Security Council to infringe on the sovereignty of smaller states, especially by imposing sanctions, and should show more restraint.

Despite these rhetorical arguments, the Security Council has continued to function surprisingly well. While it agreed to 646 resolutions before 1990, it has passed nearly 1,600 since then. This level of cooperation has allowed a huge expansion in United Nations' peacemaking and peacekeeping efforts, especially in

Africa, which has been largely unaffected by arguments like those over Iraq and Syria. As of mid-2015, the United Nations had more than one hundred thousand peacekeepers at work around the world. While the Security Council often fails to serve US interests in the most acute geopolitical crises, its ability to manage less-prominent conflicts in such countries as Liberia and the Democratic Republic of Congo has both saved lives and reduced pressure on the United States to act directly in these cases.

SEE ALSO *Central Intelligence Agency (CIA); Cold War; Department of Defense, US; Department of Homeland Security; Department of State; National Security Agency (NSA); World War II*

BIBLIOGRAPHY

Bosco, David L. *Five to Rule Them All: The UN Security Council and the Making of the Modern World.* Oxford: Oxford University Press, 2009.

Bush, George W. "State of the Union Address." January 20, 2004. http://georgewbush-whitehouse.archives.gov/news/releases/2004/01/20040120-7.html

Einsiedel, Sebastian von, David M. Malone, and Bruno Stagno Ugarte. *The UN Security Council in the 21st Century.* Boulder, CO: Rienner, 2015.

Jones, Bruce D. "Libya and the Responsibilities of Power." *Survival* 3, 3 (2011): 51–60.

Jones, Bruce D., Shepard Forman, and Richard Gowan. *Cooperating for Peace and Security: Evolving Institutions and Arrangements in a Context of Changing US Security Policy.* Cambridge: Cambridge University Press, 2010.

Patrick, Stewart. *The Best Laid Plans: The Origins of American Multilateralism and the Dawn of the Cold War.* Lanham, MD: Rowman and Littlefield, 2008.

Security Council Report. "In Hindsight: The Veto." *November 2013 Monthly Forecast.* October 31, 2013. http://www.securitycouncilreport.org/monthly-forecast/2013-11/in_hindsight_the_veto.php

Richard Gowan
Adjunct Associate Professor
Columbia School of International and Public Affairs

SELF-DETERMINATION

As the First World War (1914–1918) drew to a close and the victorious powers gathered for peace talks in Paris, a small group of Vietnamese activists petitioned US president Woodrow Wilson (1856–1924) to lend his support for their campaign against French rule in Indochina. The petition, signed by Nguyen Ai Quoc (1890–1969)—later known to the world as Ho Chi Minh—noted that "the subject peoples" of the world were "waiting for the principle of national self-determination to

pass from ideal to reality" (Engel, Lawrence, and Preston 2014, 91).

THE POST–WORLD WAR I ERA

Wilson had raised the hopes of anticolonial activists with a series of widely disseminated speeches suggesting that the subject peoples of Europe had the right to self-determination. During the spring and summer of 1919, however, the president ignored the petition and hundreds like it from anticolonial activists who hoped to use the postwar moment to lend legitimacy to their movements. Many went on to adopt more radical discourses—such as communism—when Wilson failed to extend this endorsement to the colonial world.

Self-determination occupies a central place in the history and ideology of US foreign relations, although the idea was not an American one, having already been deployed by British prime minister Lloyd George (1863–1945), Soviet leader Vladimir Lenin (1870–1924), and others. Twentieth-century US presidents have invoked the idea as rooted in the country's anticolonial heritage and democratic politics. Successive US administrations after 1941, however, have expressed deep ambivalence toward expansive self-determination claims, fearing that they could produce secessionist movements, superpower conflict, and an unraveling of the international order.

The dramatic expansion of self-determination claims and movements during the twentieth century prompted fierce debates among American diplomats and social scientists over what constitutes a "people" or "nation," what form self-determination could take, and what its rightful limits should be. US officials have rarely produced clear answers to these questions, and over the twentieth century they advocated a host of contradictory positions that often seemed to mock the role they claimed for self-determination as a foundation of US foreign policy.

Following the territorial settlements of the First World War, US officials largely abandoned talk of self-determination, adopting an ambivalent stance toward the continuation of European colonialism during the interwar period and embracing the League of Nations mandate system. A wide range of Americans, however, continued to circulate self-determination discourses, including supporters of Marcus Garvey (1887–1940) and black nationalists calling for "black self-determination" and the creation of an independent state in the US South (Slate 2012).

THE WORLD WAR II ERA (1939–1945)

The outbreak of war in Europe and Asia in the late 1930s and the temporary collapse of European empires galvanized anticolonial activists everywhere, many of whom again loudly demanded self-rule. The need to articulate a set of Allied war aims that would motivate British and US citizens, and perhaps dampen these anticolonial calls, prompted Winston Churchill (1874–1965) and Franklin D. Roosevelt (1882–1945) in August 1941 to jointly proclaim the Atlantic Charter. The charter pledged the Allied powers to "respect the right of all peoples to choose the form of government under which they will live" and "to see sovereign rights and self-government restored to those who have been forcibly deprived of them."

Anticolonial activists, as they had during the World War I period, seized upon the charter's promises of self-rule to describe and lend legitimacy to their struggles against European colonialism. They and their socialist allies offered a radical vision of self-determination encompassing economic as well as political sovereignty and embracing national liberation as a means to achieve it. Their vision was predicated on full and rapid decolonization of European empires.

Following US entry into the war, officials sought to embrace self-determination as a basic principle of an American-led global order. But they also shied away from the expansive vision of anticolonial activists, advancing a limited vision of self-determination as popular self-rule. State Department officials routinely acknowledged self-determination as a basic principle of US foreign policy, but they were reluctant to concede it as a right and worked to downplay its role in plans for a postwar international organization.

THE POSTWAR ERA

US planners sought to balance the need to support European allies during World War II, acknowledge anticolonial nationalism, and defend US global interests—now including hundreds of overseas military bases, many located in non-self-governing territories. Although self-determination appeared in the UN charter as one of the world body's primary goals, Washington fought efforts to include the principle in the Universal Declaration of Human Rights. In 1952, US officials voted against a landmark General Assembly resolution claiming self-determination as a human right, and they bitterly resisted requirements that colonial powers report on the progress of non-self-governing territories toward self-government.

Despite US efforts to the contrary, in 1960 African and Asian states secured passage of the landmark Declaration on the Granting of Independence to Colonial Countries and Peoples. The declaration established self-determination as "the legal foundation for the establishment of the sovereign state from the colonial territory" (Quataert 2009, 72). Six years later the United Nations

General Assembly adopted the International Covenant on Economic, Social and Cultural Rights, which declared that "all peoples have the right of self-determination. By virtue of that right they freely determine their political status and freely pursue their economic, social and cultural development."

Through the 1960s US administrations sought to encourage gradual decolonization efforts while resisting efforts to legitimize armed struggle in the name of self-determination. The UN General Assembly, however, its ranks now dominated by newly independent states, repeatedly urged member states to recognize and support national liberation movements. US administrations vigorously opposed such measures, as they opposed armed liberation movements in Palestine, southern Africa, and elsewhere.

THE COLD WAR

The Kennedy, Johnson, and Nixon administrations had little to gain in publicly opposing a right to self-determination. Each sought to limit it through their response to specific claims and movements. Like their predecessors, they opposed secessionist self-determination movements in the Congo, Biafra, and Bangladesh, although they backed separatist movements elsewhere when doing so suited broader Cold War agendas. Other places, such as Goa, Portuguese Timor, and the Pacific and Caribbean dependencies, they argued, were too primitive to merit self-rule, although they might have the legal right.

The Soviet Union's embrace of these more expansive visions made self-determination a Cold War issue. The deeply held belief of US officials that self-determination and communism were incompatible was cited to justify numerous interventions in the decolonizing and developing world, from Iran to Guatemala to Vietnam. Thus, after ousting Guatemalan president Jacobo Árbenz (1913–1971) in 1954, the administration of Dwight D. Eisenhower (1890–1969) claimed that "the people of Guatemala in a magnificent effort have liberated themselves from the shackles of international communist direction and reclaimed their right of self-determination" (Gleijeses 1992, 369).

The mere fact that US officials referred to support for self-determination as a rationale for intervention does not make it a more satisfactory explanation for US policy than geopolitical considerations, anticommunism, or political economy. But the remarkable persistence with which officials insisted on it as a motivation for their actions served—then as now—as an important marker of national identity, one seemingly immune from challenge regardless of how wide the gap was between rhetoric and practice.

Perhaps most significantly, US officials fought to prevent recognition of a right to "economic self-determination." The issue was of course central to the hopes of newly independent (and some long independent) states for equitable and autonomous development. The United States and other great powers, however, rejected the notion that self-determination implied the right to control natural resources, nationalize foreign firms, or otherwise opt out of the Bretton Woods system.

Unsurprisingly, US and other Western officials, business leaders, and social scientists viewed assertions of a "right to economic self-determination," resource sovereignty, or nationalization as threats to the framework of foreign trade and investment underpinning the world economy. They argued that there was no such thing as economic self-determination and that acknowledging such a right would lead to expropriation and capital flight from so-called developing countries, imperiling their economic futures.

The growing legitimacy of expansive definitions of self-determination at the United Nations, and its association with the twin projects of human rights and national liberation struggles, eventually produced a partisan backlash. By the mid-1970s, some conservatives began to critique the idea of self-determination for the so-called Third World as a challenge to America's Cold War interests, although they supported the idea for the peoples of Soviet-controlled Eastern Europe. President Ronald Reagan (1911–2004) helped to rehabilitate the idea of self-determination for conservatives, littering his speeches with references to America's unending quest to secure self-determination and liberty for the world's peoples. His vision of self-determination, however, was deployed almost solely against communist or leftist governments and used to justify the 1983 US invasion of Grenada, support for mujahedeen forces in Afghanistan, and other interventions.

NATIONAL AND TRANSNATIONAL MOVEMENTS

While US officials and others sought to contain self-determination claims and discourses globally within narrow bounds, they proved unable to do so. Just as significantly, they proved unable to prevent a wide range of groups and movements in the United States—including African Americans, Puerto Ricans, and Native Americans—from deploying self-determination claims in ways that both connected with and transcended the transnational movements from which they often drew inspiration.

During the long black freedom struggle of the 1950s and 1960s, many civil rights activists drew on the language of self-determination, human rights, and anticolonialism to frame their struggle and place it in a global context. Native American nations and organizations also embraced self-determination as a way of framing their collective struggles for political, economic, and cultural autonomy. They joined a global stream of indigenous sovereignty movements that "cannot be understood apart from the larger politics of modernization and decolonization or the turbulent contests over race, poverty and war at home" (Cobb 2010, 4).

The indigenous movements for self-determination grew out of but transcended the Cold War and the era of decolonization. Indigenous activists were in many ways simply reimporting ideas that had long circulated abroad and refashioning them for use in the advanced industrial democracies. Their efforts demonstrate that the idea of self-determination, far from exhausting itself as European empires collapsed, had instead become a global vernacular for articulating sovereignty and rights claims, even inside the United States.

Other domestic forces made self-determination claims in the 1970s, including the Chicano rights movement and feminist groups. These movements nestle uneasily in narratives that frame self-determination merely as an outgrowth of the Cold War or decolonization, although they intersected with each in important ways. The indigenous movement for self-determination, in particular, represented a distinctly postcolonial, post–Cold War form of politics that transcended East-West or North-South divisions. Collectively, however, they suggested that even as the era of formal colonialism was drawing to a close, the appeal of self-determination as a way of framing collective rights and sovereignty claims, even in the United States, was far from exhausted.

From the early twentieth century to the present, Americans have viewed self-determination as a source of both promise and peril. They have simultaneously sought to embrace and contain it, demand it for others while decrying the expansive claims made on its behalf and the excesses committed in its name. The American identification with self-determination as a way of explaining the US role in the world *was* distinctive, forming a core component of US identity. Debates over the scope and meaning of self-determination have shaped and been shaped by US foreign policy, the timing and breadth of decolonization, the boundaries of economic and political sovereignty in the international system, and basic features of the federal government's relationship to its own citizens.

These ideas continue to resonate with US presidents and the wider public. After coming into office, President Barack Obama (b. 1961) repeatedly stated that the United States stood "not for empire but for self-determination," a principle he believed has universal application. Following Russia's 2014 annexation of Crimea and its intervention in Ukraine, for example, Obama publicly warned that the actions of Russian president Vladimir Putin (b. 1952) violated the rights of people there to freedom and self-determination. As a principle and guide to the way Americans think about foreign policy and their role in the world, self-determination will continue to carry substantial weight.

SEE ALSO *Anti-imperialism; Atlantic Charter (1941); Black Power Movement; Imperialism; Internationalism; Interventionism; Isolationism; League of Nations; Paris Peace Conference (1919); Preparedness; Roosevelt, Franklin D.; Treaty of Versailles; United Nations; Universal Negro Improvement Association (UNIA); Wilson, Woodrow; World War I*

BIBLIOGRAPHY

Avalon Project, Yale Law School. Atlantic Charter, August 14, 1941. http://avalon.law.yale.edu/wwii/atlantic.asp

Cobb, Daniel M. *Native Activism in Cold War America: The Struggle for Sovereignty.* Lawrence: University Press of Kansas, 2010.

Engel, Jeffrey A., Mark Atwood Lawrence, and Andrew Preston, eds. *America in the World: A History in Documents from the War with Spain to the War on Terror.* Princeton, NJ: Princeton University Press, 2014.

Gleijeses, Piero. *Shattered Hope: The Guatemalan Revolution and the United States, 1944–1954.* Princeton, NJ: Princeton University Press, 1992.

Manela, Erez. *The Wilsonian Moment: Self-Determination and the International Origins of Anticolonial Nationalism.* New York: Oxford University Press, 2009.

Obama, Barack. Address to the Nation on the Drawdown of U.S. Military Personnel in Afghanistan, June 22, 2011. American Presidency Project. http://www.presidency.ucsb.edu/ws/index.php?pid=90556

Quataert, Jean H. *Advocating Dignity: Human Rights Mobilizations in Global Politics.* Philadelphia: University of Pennsylvania Press, 2009.

Slate, Nico, *Colored Cosmopolitanism: The Shared Struggle for Freedom in the United States and India.* Cambridge, MA: Harvard University Press, 2012.

United Nations. Declaration on the Granting of Independence to Colonial Countries and Peoples, December 14, 1960. http://www.un.org/en/decolonization/declaration.shtml

United Nations, Office of the High Commissioner of Human Rights. International Covenant on Economic, Social and Cultural Rights, December 16, 1966. http://www.ohchr.org/EN/ProfessionalInterest/Pages/CESCR.aspx

Bradley Simpson
Associate Professor of History and Asian Studies
University of Connecticut

SENATE FOREIGN RELATIONS COMMITTEE

The US Senate shares some unique foreign policy responsibilities with the executive branch. Article II, Section 2 of the Constitution of the United States provides that the president "shall have Power, by and with the Advice and Consent of the Senate, to make Treaties, provided that two thirds of the Senators present concur; and he shall nominate, and by and with the Advice and Consent of the Senate, shall appoint Ambassadors, other public Ministers and Consuls." Beginning with the first Congress in 1789, the Senate fulfilled these responsibilities by referring treaties and nominations to ad hoc, select, committees. The War of 1812 prompted the Senate to formalize the committee process by establishing eleven permanent standing committees in 1816, including the Committee on Foreign Relations.

With institutional jurisdiction over treaties, diplomatic nominations, and foreign policy legislation, including trade, the Committee on Foreign Relations plays a pivotal role in shaping international perceptions of the United States around the world, as well as in formulating and supporting strategies to protect and serve the national interest. Though the majority of its work is collaborative or advisory in nature, the committee has generally refused to provide a "rubber stamp" for executive branch policies. At times, the committee has been criticized as overly combative, or partisan, as during the debates over the Treaty of Versailles in 1919 and during the divisive Vietnam War era in the second half of the twentieth century. Despite these challenges, the Committee on Foreign Relations has attracted some of the institution's most capable members, more than twenty of whom have gone on to serve as secretaries of state or US presidents.

The committee supported the Monroe Doctrine and the concept of manifest destiny throughout the nineteenth century, approving for ratification a series of treaties that vastly expanded US territory. One notable exception was the committee's rejection in 1844 of the treaty to annex Texas, prompting the administration of President James K. Polk (1795–1849) to submit a compromise joint resolution in 1845 that required a bare majority approval. During the Civil War, the committee served as an advisor to President Abraham Lincoln (1809–1865) on trade-related issues, and generally supported his efforts to maintain the Union. It approved for ratification the Lyons-Seward Treaty of 1862, pledging cooperation with Great Britain to end the Atlantic slave trade. Committee chairman Charles Sumner (1811–1874) joined Secretary of State William Seward (1801–1872) to negotiate a treaty providing for the purchase of Alaskan territory; the Senate approved the treaty for ratification in 1867. In the late nineteenth century, the committee approved treaties to expand US influence in Asia and the Pacific, including Hawaii, Guam, and the Philippines.

As US global influence grew, the committee's role in foreign policy increased proportionately. Disagreements over terms of the treaty to end World War I, brokered by President Woodrow Wilson (1856–1924), led to a public confrontation between members of the committee—led by its chairman Henry Cabot Lodge (1850–1924), a Republican from Massachusetts—and the president. Wilson's refusal to compromise with the committee on key provisions of the treaty, especially US membership in a newly formed League of Nations, led the Senate to reject the Treaty of Versailles in 1919 and 1920. Consequently, the United States never ratified the treaty, and the United States never joined the League of Nations.

So-called isolationists dominated the committee during the interwar years, approving a series of Neutrality Acts designed to prevent the executive branch from taking the nation to war. After the attack at Pearl Harbor in December 1941, the committee supported the war effort, handling, among other issues, immigration petitions. Following World War II, committee members played a critical role in developing international and regional institutions to structure the new world order. Committee member Arthur Vandenberg (1884–1951), a Republican from Michigan and chairman of the committee from 1947 to 1948, joined a delegation to the UN Conference in 1945 and served as a delegate to the General Assembly in 1946.

Since World War II, the committee has been instrumental in supporting programs that improve perceptions of the United States abroad. One of the most well-known examples is the Fulbright Exchange Program, named after Senator J. William Fulbright (1905–1995), a Democrat from Arkansas and chairman of the committee from 1959 to 1974, who proposed the bill in 1945. The program's popularity abroad led to its expansion during the Cold War, supporting the exchange of scholars as well as students. Over the decades, this program has "graduated" hundreds of thousands of participants. These informal ambassadors have educated people around the world to better understand and appreciate the role of the United States in the world.

During the 1960s and 1970s, the committee advised administrations on military-base treaty renegotiations and arms control and disarmament issues, and considered bills related to the sale of weapons (on some of these issues, the committee shares jurisdiction with the Senate Armed Services Committee). Following the reported attacks on US and allies' ships in the Gulf of Tonkin in 1964, the committee swiftly approved the Southeast Asia Resolution (also known as the Gulf of Tonkin Resolution), which, upon congressional approval, provided the legislative authority to pursue a war in Southeast Asia.

Under Chairman Fulbright's leadership, the committee became the locus of opposition to the war in Vietnam by the late 1960s, holding public hearings to challenge administration policy and privately entreating President Lyndon Johnson (1908–1973) and his top advisors to seek a political solution and bring the troops home. The committee's disapproval of US foreign policy in Southeast Asia led to a series of confrontations between members of the committee and the White House. The committee proposed and Congress approved a resolution rescinding the Gulf of Tonkin Resolution and built a bipartisan coalition to support the War Powers Resolution in 1973. The resolution provided a legal basis for Congress to reassert its constitutional prerogatives on issues of foreign policy and national security.

The committee has played an evolving role in shaping the US image abroad by funding exchanges, approving and rejecting treaties, and approving for nomination diplomatic personnel to represent US interests and implement US policy abroad. The committee continues to serve as an advisory body to the executive branch, at times making, or enhancing and revising, proposals to achieve US foreign policy goals.

SEE ALSO *Department of Defense, US; Department of Homeland Security; Department of State; National Security Agency (NSA); Security Council, UN*

BIBLIOGRAPHY

Byrd, Robert C. *The Senate, 1789–1989.* Washington, DC: GPO, 1989.

Congressional Quarterly. *Guide to Congress.* 5th ed. Washington, DC: CQ Press, 2000.

Senate Committee on Foreign Relations. *United States Senate: 1816–2000.* Millennium ed. Washington, DC: GPO, 2000.

Stennis, John, and J. William Fulbright. *The Role of Congress in Foreign Policy.* Washington, DC: American Enterprise Institute for Public Policy Research, 1971.

Woods, Randall Bennett. *Fulbright: A Biography.* New York: Cambridge University Press, 1995.

Katherine A. Scott
Assistant Historian
US Senate Historical Office

SEPTEMBER 11, 2001

It was a beautiful Tuesday morning, September 11, 2001, when Mohamed Atta and Abdul Azis al-Omari boarded a flight from Portland, Maine, to Boston's Logan International Airport. Once in Boston, Atta and Omari joined Satam al-Suqami, Wail al-Shehri, and Waleed al-Shehri on American Airlines Flight 11, bound for Los Angeles. In another part of Logan, five others—Marwan al-Shehhi, Fayez Banihammad, Mohand al-Shehri, Ahmed al-Ghamdi, and Hamza al-Ghamdi—boarded United Airlines Flight 175, also bound for Los Angeles. All ten had passed through metal detectors and answered security questions at the departure gate. None of them aroused suspicion at the airport.

Down the eastern corridor, in Washington, DC, five more men tried to board a domestic flight, American Airlines Flight 77, to Los Angeles. At Dulles International Airport's main terminal, Khalid al-Mihdhar and Majed Moqed set off the metal detectors with their carry-on baggage. Mihdhar was sent through a second metal detector, and this time no alarm sounded. He was waived through to the departure gate. Moqed set off the second alarm too, but was given a personal wand inspection and was allowed to proceed to the gate. Mihdhar and Moqed waited patiently at their departure gate for three more members of their group, Hani Hanjour, Nawaf al-Hazmi,

and his brother, Salem al-Hazmi. Hanjour and Salem al-Hazmi cleared the first security checkpoint with no problem. Nawaf al-Hazmi set off the alarms at both the first and second metal detectors, but again airport security conducted a personal wand inspection and cleared him for entry to the departure area. In Newark, New Jersey, four more men, Saeed al-Ghamdi, Ahmed al-Nami, Ahmad al-Haznawi, and Ziad Jarrah boarded United Airlines Flight 93, going to Los Angeles, without incident.

THE ATTACKS

By 8:00 A.M. on the morning of September 11, nineteen men, most of them in their early twenties, had boarded four transcontinental flights at three different international airports, avoiding detection despite setting off security alarms and paying for their first-class or business-class tickets with cash. Fifteen of the nineteen were from Saudi Arabia, one was from Lebanon, one from Egypt, and two were from the United Arab Emirates (UAE). None were from Iraq. The men aboard American Airlines Flight 11

A newspaper vendor outside the London stock exchange following the 9/11 terrorist attacks on the United States. In response to the 9/11 attacks, President George W. Bush vowed to prevent sponsors of terrorism from threatening America or its allies with weapons of mass destruction. Britain soon joined the United States, along with Afghani resistance fighters, in launching air raids and ground assaults against the Taliban and al-Qaeda in Afghanistan. **NICOLAS ASFOURI/AFP/GETTY IMAGES**

from Boston moved into action first, stabbing several passengers and gaining access to the cockpit. The flight crew called airline headquarters to warn that the plane had been hijacked and was now flying erratically. At 8:46 A.M., approximately thirty minutes after United Airlines Flight 175 left Boston, American Airlines Flight 11 smashed into the North Tower of the World Trade Center in Manhattan, killing all on board instantly and causing severe damage on impact. United Airlines Flight 175 was hijacked at about this same time. Shortly thereafter, at 9:03 A.M., the plane hit the South Tower of the World Trade Center, setting off a series of events that would lead to the ultimate collapse of both towers.

In Washington, American Airlines Flight 77 prepared for departure. Unaware that two planes had just hit the towers in New York, air traffic control at Dulles International Airport cleared the pilots for takeoff. At 9:37 A.M., the plane hit the Pentagon, home to the US Defense Department, at over 530 miles (850 kilometers) per hour, killing hundreds instantly. By this time, airline management knew something was wrong and accordingly ordered all American Airline flights on the East Coast suspended.

The last plane, United Airlines Flight 93 from Newark to San Francisco, had already departed by the time the other three planes had hit their targets. Passengers were now aware of what had happened in New York and Washington and determined that they were not going to allow a similar fate to befall Flight 93. Passengers rushed the cockpit, but were stymied when one of the hijackers flew the plane violently to disrupt the passengers' forward momentum. It now seems clear that the passengers saved the plane from hitting the US Capitol or the White House. Instead, at 10:02 A.M. on September 11, Flight 93 crash-landed in a field near Shanksville, Pennsylvania. All passengers were killed instantly upon impact.

THE US GOVERNMENT'S RESPONSE

At the time of the attacks, President George W. Bush was in Sarasota, Florida, visiting an elementary school to promote his new administration's education policy. Told first that a twin-engine plane had hit the North Tower in New York, the president assumed pilot error had created the disaster. At 9:05 A.M., Andrew Card, the chief of staff, whispered to the president that a second plane had hit the second tower in New York. Bush concluded that the United States was under attack. The Secret Service rushed the president to the airport, not sure if it was safe for him to return to Washington. President Bush took calls from Vice President Richard Cheney, New York governor George Pataki, and FBI director Robert Mueller to gain a better sense of what was happening.

In the late afternoon of September 11, Bush met with his national security team through a secure video teleconference. During this conversation, all agreed that al-Qaeda, a terrorist organization with cells around the globe, was most likely responsible for the attacks. Al-Qaeda had been behind the 1993 terrorist attacks against the North Tower of the World Trade Center that had killed six people and injured more than a thousand. The terrorists had planted a truck bomb in the parking garage, hoping to kill several hundred people and to disrupt life in the center of New York's financial district. At the time, the Bill Clinton administration created a counterterrorism task force designed to gauge al-Qaeda's strength and track its activities. Al-Qaeda attacks against other US assets, particularly the terrorist bombing of the US embassy in Kenya in 1998 and the October 2000 attack against the *USS Cole* in Yemen, convinced Clinton to devote more resources to combating international terrorism.

The Bush administration continued to monitor terrorist activities, and in the days before the September 11 attacks, there was significant intelligence to suggest something big was about to happen. The Bush team would later claim that it was very difficult to pinpoint specific threats amid all of the reports warning of potential attacks. On the evening of September 11, the president announced that the United States would hunt down the killers, making "no distinction between the terrorists who committed these acts and those who harbor them." In his January 2002 State of the Union address, Bush told the nation and the world that the terrorists who attacked the United States on September 11 were like "ticking time bombs" set to go off without warning and fully supported by "outlaw regimes." The primary foreign policy objective of the United States in the post–September 11 world was clear, the president warned: "to prevent regimes that sponsor terror from threatening America or our friends and allies with weapons of mass destruction."

Indeed, within weeks of the September 11 attacks, the United States, Britain, and the Northern Alliance (Afghani resistance fighters) launched air raids and ground assaults against the Taliban and al-Qaeda in Afghanistan. The Bush administration correctly surmised that the Taliban leadership in Kabul had supported al-Qaeda, allowing the terrorist group to use Afghanistan as a training base and sanctuary. The military response was swift, focused, and deadly. Within two months, the Taliban had been driven from power and had taken refuge with al-Qaeda leaders in the mountainous border region with Pakistan. The American public overwhelmingly supported the attacks, as did the US Congress. By mid-2002, several senior Bush administration officials believed that the war had been won in Afghanistan and that it was now time to focus on other terrorist threats, most notably Iraq.

THE BROADER WAR AGAINST TERRORISM

At the time of the September 11 attacks, few could have predicted a renewed American war in Iraq, but from those early days following the attacks until the March 2003 invasion, the Bush administration made a strong connection between the hated Iraqi leader Saddam Hussein and the terrorists. Secretary of Defense Donald Rumsfeld argued that the United States should not limit its reprisal attacks to just the al-Qaeda terrorist network. Rumsfeld believed that the United States should put pressure on all states that supported and harbored terrorists, including Iraq, Afghanistan, Libya, Sudan, and Iran. The Bush administration also believed that the United States possessed transformative power, and that it could shape the political outlook in Iraq and inside other states in the region. Furthermore, the Bush administration argued that the quick removal of Saddam Hussein from power coupled with rapid liberalization would create conditions for stable and lasting peace. The ultimate goal was to align Iraq and Afghanistan with other states in a region-wide diplomatic and economic framework that downplayed sectarianism and terrorism, and increased membership in a regional order. This long war against the terrorists was difficult to manage, costly, and controversial. But it did fundamentally alter US foreign policy following the September 11 attacks.

SEE ALSO *Bush, George W.; War on Terror*

BIBLIOGRAPHY

Brigham, Robert K. *The United States and Iraq since 1990*. Malden, MA: Wiley, 2014.

Bush, George W. "State of the Union Address." January 29, 2002. http://georgewbush-whitehouse.archives.gov/news/releases/2002/01/20020129-11.html

Bush, George W. "Statement by the President in His Address to the Nation." September 11, 2001. http://georgewbush-whitehouse.archives.gov/news/releases/2001/09/20010911-16.html

Gardner, Lloyd. *The Long Road to Baghdad: A History of U.S. Foreign Policy from the 1970s to the Present*. New York: New Press, 2008.

Haass, Richard N. *War of Necessity, War of Choice*. New York: Simon and Schuster, 2009.

Hahn, Peter L. *Missions Accomplished? The United States and Iraq since World War I*. New York: Oxford University Press, 2012.

May, Ernest R., ed. *The 9/11 Commission Report, with Related Documents*. Abridged ed. Boston: Bedford/St. Martin's, 2007.

Robert K. Brigham
Shirley Ecker Boskey Professor
of History and International Relations
Vassar College

SETTLEMENT HOUSE MOVEMENT

The United States settlement house movement is arguably the most important nondenominational US social movement whose origins are directly traceable to an international influence. Conversely, between 1890 and 1914, the settlement house movement represented American reform ideas to America-watchers and wandering intellectuals in Europe. Though preceded and inspired by the British social settlements, the US movement grew to be the largest in the world, and by the 1920s American settlements joined British houses in modeling public health, recreation, arts, and youth programs to social workers and volunteers in other European and Asian countries.

THE BRITISH MODEL

From 1885, US settlement house founders eagerly adapted the liberal Protestant ideas of revamped and humbled *noblesse oblige* that they discovered in British Christian Socialist tracts and in the settlement houses, signally Toynbee Hall of London, that embodied those ideas. US reformers were saturated in the Victorian literature excoriating the economic practices that had generated urban industrial poverty. Charles Dickens, Thomas Carlyle, John Ruskin, and the lesser lights Arnold Toynbee, Thomas Arnold, and F. D. Maurice, as well as the passionate novelist Mary Arnold (Mrs. Humphry) Ward, were variously familiar to those socially concerned American youngsters who tended to bookishness. The guiding ideas of the movement, articulated by Jane Addams (1860–1935), Graham Taylor (1851–1938), Lillian Wald (1867–1940), and Robert Woods (1865–1925), envisioned an organic urban community in which middle-class Americans would meet urban settlers on the newcomers' terms and offer whatever aid was useful in integrating immigrants into new neighborhoods and a new society. While settlement founders rejected the condescension of the Charity Organization idea, they found it hard to abandon all assumptions of class and cultural superiority. After all, many had been steeped not only in social concern, but also in privilege. Addams and Woods, for example, had traveled abroad for study or recreation, and found immediate inspiration with the people and institutions they would emulate.

The settlements reflected Anglo-American traditions of women taking the lead in voluntary social amelioration and comfort. Both British and American women entered early and enthusiastically into settlement work, in single-sex settlements as well as houses staffed by both women and men. More American than British women were attending college in 1900. It was these college women in both societies who found the settlements a refreshing and stimulating escape from what Jane Addams would soon call "the snare of preparation": young women's pursuit of educational and cultural refinement that ultimately had no outlet or social purpose.

IMPACT ON SOCIAL WELFARE PRACTICES

Offering services and relationships to largely immigrant urban populations through bold program development, US settlements had an outsized impact on social welfare practices in the United States. Depending solely on private funding and volunteer staffing, the settlement houses became the most important social service gateway for European immigrants—with the exception of the urban political machines, Jewish and Catholic charities, and, for some families, the public schools. The settlements became proving grounds and laboratories for sociology and social work students and faculty in urban universities in Chicago, New York, and Boston. These activities and connections, as well as the stimulating and ever-changing daily life of the settlements, were magnets to European visitors, from British Fabian socialists to Russian revolutionary leaders. At the same time, the very size and success of the leading settlements moved them toward hierarchy and routine. By the 1920s, the settlement houses had developed "group work" as a social work specialty and had helped create career paths for youth workers, public health nurses, and nonprofit organization administrators.

TIES TO PEACE WORK

Before the US entry into the Great War, Jane Addams, Emily Greene Balch (1867–1961), and other US settlement workers helped found an international network of women pacifists who eventually became the Women's International League for Peace and Freedom (WILPF). Their ties to the settlement movement tainted the houses with the fictive brush of sedition, but for European liberals and feminists, the American peace workers kept the settlements on the map as American institutions of note. Despite the short-term price they paid for these peace activities, both Addams and Balch eventually won the Nobel Peace Prize.

THE DEPRESSION AND WORLD WARS

Besides inspiring several of its prominent leaders to peace work, World War I (1914–1918) pushed the US settlements into intensified neighborhood and family work as immigrant men were called up by their own or their new countries, and then US mobilization further disrupted life at home. In the 1930s, settlements tried to mitigate the devastating effects of the Depression, while a few settlements helped Jewish refugees connect with family and friends after the rise of Adolf Hitler. World War II (1939–1945) presented the US settlements with intensified family needs for day care and relief as men enlisted and women entered the workforce. Thanks to the service of Lillie M. Peck (1888–1957) as president of the National Federation of Settlements from 1934 to 1949, the impetus toward international cooperation in the 1920s was not entirely lost in the pressing economic needs and political crises of the 1930s. Peck then served as president of the International Federation of Settlements (IFS) from 1949 to 1951.

RACIAL ISSUES

White settlement leaders failed in one large area: their implicit belief that black Americans could not be integrated into the United States body politic, nor into "mainstream" (white) settlement houses. Black volunteers created African American settlement houses, which served black neighborhoods in many of the same ways that "mainstream" settlements served white immigrant neighborhoods, and the National Urban League became the *de facto* coordinator of the black settlements until the 1960s. The mainstream movement finally focused on racial discrimination and race-based poverty during the 1960s, under the leadership of Margaret Berry (1915–2002) and then the National Federation of Settlements' first nonwhite leader, Walter Smart. Thus, in the 1960s and 1970s, the US settlement movement returned to the social justice and social research thrust of the Progressive Era. Simultaneously, settlement and neighborhood-center work was reinvigorated in many places in the world, particularly in response to initiatives against poverty and racism and the coordination of public and private welfare programs.

SINCE 1980

Since 1980, settlement and neighborhood-center workers around the world have expanded their international cooperation while facing chilling reductions in public funding for social services, along with intensified structural inequalities. The end of the Cold War in the late 1980s opened communication between eastern and western European social agencies. The IFS multiplied its contacts and cooperation with United Nations offices, such as UNICEF, and US settlements extended a hand, somewhat belatedly, to Central and South American social agencies.

SEE ALSO *Addams, Jane; Federal Council of Churches; Immigration; Immigration Quotas; Nativism; Protestantism; Secularization; Transatlantic Reform; Whiteness; World's YWCA/YMCA*

BIBLIOGRAPHY

Carson, Mina. *Settlement Folk: Social Thought and the American Settlement Movement, 1885–1930.* Chicago: University of Chicago Press, 1990.

Garcia, Maricela. "Migrant Rights in an Era of Globalization." *Journal of Poverty* 15, 4 (2011): 475–480.

Gilchrist, Ruth, and Tony Jeffs, eds. *Settlements, Social Change and Community Action, Good Neighbours.* London: Jessica Kingsley, 2001.

Hansan, John E., et al. "The Social Welfare History Project." http://www.socialwelfarehistory.com

Lasch-Quinn, Elisabeth. *Black Neighbors: Race and the Limits of Reform in the American Settlement House Movement, 1890–1945.* Chapel Hill: University of North Carolina Press, 1993.

Mina Carson
Associate Professor, College of Liberal Arts
Oregon State University

SEWARD, WILLIAM H.
1801–1872

William Henry Seward served as US secretary of state from 1861 to 1869 in the successive administrations of Abraham Lincoln (1809–1865) and Andrew Johnson (1808–1875). A New Yorker by birth, Seward committed himself to the Whig Party in the early 1830s before moving into the Republican coalition in late 1855. Seward's Whig politics shaped his understanding of the United States' foreign relations, and he maintained his early commitment to the cultivation of American commerce and industry, internal improvements, and the orderly settlement of western lands throughout his career. Despite his later reputation as an exuberant proponent of American expansion, Seward's antislavery politics led him to oppose the two great expansionist questions of his lifetime: the annexation of Texas (1845) and the Mexican-American War (1846–1848).

THE CIVIL WAR YEARS

Naturally, the Civil War (1861–1865) and its associated foreign policy dilemmas dominated Seward's time as Lincoln's secretary of state. He worked assiduously to prevent both foreign intervention and mediation in the conflict. His dispatches to US ministers mostly demonstrated him to be an intelligent and shrewd diplomat and a relentless propagandist of the Union war effort. Stable Anglo-American relations were, of course, of crucial importance to the Union cause. Seward's antebellum career had earned him a reputation as an Anglophobe; during the Civil War he occasionally cultivated this reputation—largely with a domestic audience in mind—though simultaneously he worked to sustain good relations with British ministers who served in Washington during and after the war. Despite his early bombast—he warned of war if the British government recognized the

Confederacy—he proved a pragmatist in dealing with the greatest challenge to peaceful Anglo-American relations, the *Trent* affair of late 1861. The detention of two Confederate diplomats on board the *Trent*, a British merchant ship, threatened to provoke war. Seward pursued a conciliatory course, persuading the rest of Lincoln's cabinet that the diplomats' release was both politic and consonant with long-held American principles regarding neutrality in wartime.

Elsewhere, Anglo-American relations were smoother and even, in East Asia, where the two governments had a common interest in developing commercial interests, collaborative. Seward's minister to China, Anson Burlingame (1820–1870), explicitly developed a "cooperative policy" with the resident British minister, and the idea for his celebrated mission to Europe on behalf of the Chinese imperial government was developed and encouraged by Robert Hart (1835–1911), the British inspector-general of the Chinese customs service. Collaboration was also in evidence in the context of the suppression of the slave

William H. Seward, secretary of state (1861–1869) under Presidents Lincoln and Johnson. *Seward deserves credit for his work to prevent the Civil War from becoming an international conflict. After the war, his negotiations for the purchase of Alaska from Russia, though initially mocked, turned out to be a foreign policy success.* © EVERETT HISTORICAL/SHUTTERSTOCK.COM

trade when, in April 1862, Seward and the British minister, Lord Lyons (1817–1887), signed a treaty that granted each country the right to seize vessels believed to be implicated in the trade. Just as secession was a necessary precondition for a US commitment to act against the slave trade, so it allowed the formal recognition of the Republic of Haiti, which took place in June 1862.

The likelihood of European—especially British—intervention in the Civil War is an issue that has attracted much historiographical attention. Mediation was seriously considered by both British and French statesmen, though in neither instance did it come to pass. A more concrete New World manifestation of European geopolitics was French intervention in Mexico, beginning as part of a multilateral enterprise in late 1861. Seward's low-level opposition to Louis Napoléon's (1808–1873) dream of reestablishing French influence in the Americas was quiet, firm and, ultimately, successful, though it disappointed those in the United States who sought a more vigorous assertion of the Monroe Doctrine.

THE POSTWAR YEARS

In March 1867, Seward negotiated the purchase of Alaska from Russia for $7.2 million. Russia's willingness to sell was prompted by a reassessment of its own geopolitical interests; American interest in Alaska was long-standing, dating back to the 1850s. The process of securing ratification in the United States was dogged by allegations of corruption but, despite later characterizations as "Seward's folly," the purchase was accepted relatively easily by the US Congress. It proved to be a rare postwar foreign policy success for the secretary of state, who, due to his proximity to President Andrew Johnson (1808–1875) on questions of Reconstruction and civil rights, found himself increasingly isolated from his former allies in the Republican Party. Seward likely saw the Alaska purchase as part of broader program of expansion, including the long-term lease of Santo Domingo's Samaná Bay and the purchase of territory in the Danish West Indies, though neither scheme came to fruition.

Seward's time at the State Department defies easy categorization. His most important achievement was undoubtedly in preventing the realization of the great fear of antebellum statesmen: that American disunion would serve as prelude to foreign intervention and, ultimately, to the reestablishment of Old World balance-of-power politics in the Western hemisphere. He, like many of his contemporaries, understood the cause of the Union as being of fundamental significance to the future of self-government around the world, and his use of threats, conciliation, and public diplomacy was instrumental in limiting the scope of the conflict.

Elsewhere he was rather less successful. His attempts to secure a US naval base in the Caribbean failed. Projects to fund and build two intercontinental telegraph lines were also unsuccessful. In the closing months of his secretaryship, he worked hard to put together a syndicate that would fund a transisthmian canal, but it fell apart shortly after he left office. The official counterpart to this—a proposed treaty with the Colombian government securing American control over a 20-mile (32-kilometer) strip of land across the isthmus—was ultimately rejected by both the Colombians and the US Senate. For all his antebellum talk about the inevitability of Canada one day becoming part of the American Union, he made little headway in persuading either the British government or Canadians themselves that the future of British North America lay with its southern neighbor.

HISTORICAL ASSESSMENT

Historians have generally described Seward as a farsighted statesman who established the blueprint for the later projection of American power, though they have sometimes been too quick to draw a straight line between his own preoccupations—overseas markets, a transisthmian canal, and a focus on East Asia as a site of economic and imperial rivalry—and the imperial ventures of later generations. His time as secretary of state was not an unqualified success, but he deserves great credit for his work to prevent the Civil War becoming an international conflict, which in turn was essential to the Union's ultimate success.

SEE ALSO *The Civil War; Lincoln, Abraham; Manifest Destiny*

BIBLIOGRAPHY

Hendrickson, David C. "Seward and the New Imperialism." In *Union, Nation, or Empire: The American Debate over International Relations, 1789–1941*, 285–289. Lawrence: University Press of Kansas, 2009.

Jones, Howard. *Blue and Gray Diplomacy: A History of Union and Confederate Foreign Relations.* Chapel Hill: University of North Carolina Press, 2010.

Myers, Phillip E. *Caution and Cooperation: The American Civil War in British-American Relations.* Kent, OH: Kent State University Press, 2008.

Sexton, Jay. "William Seward in the World." *Journal of the Civil War Era* 4, 3 (2013): 398–430.

Stahr, Walter. *Seward: Lincoln's Indispensable Man.* New York: Simon and Schuster, 2012.

Van Deusen, Glyndon G. *William Henry Seward.* New York: Oxford University Press, 1967.

David Sim
Lecturer in US History
University College London

SHINTO

Shinto today is an umbrella term that covers a number of different religious practices and popular traditions in contemporary Japan: a residue of imperial cults, very little known by the majority of the public; rituals related to the seasonal cycle and life stages of individuals; aspects of folk religiosity; and the beliefs and practices of new religious organizations dating from the mid-nineteenth century. It is important to emphasize that many people, perhaps a majority in Japan today, do not participate in any Shinto rituals, and when they do, they do so in a sporadic, agnostic fashion. Only a tiny fraction (less than 10 percent) of the Japanese consider themselves "Shintoists"; indeed, most Japanese do not consider Shinto as a "religion" but rather as a set of ideas and practices that constitute a part of Japan's traditional culture.

At the same time, Shinto is normally defined as Japan's indigenous religious tradition, something dating back to the beginning of Japanese culture in prehistoric times. This definition came to be widely accepted only in the late nineteenth century as part of Japan's moderniza-tion process, in which the elimination of traditional forms of religiosity was associated with the invention and the imposition of new traditions, including a revisionist image of Shinto as the primordial and unchanging core of Japanese culture and spirituality. During the premodern period there was no unified tradition called "Shinto"; even the very concept of a Japanese indigenous form of spirituality, different from imported religions and philos-ophies such as Buddhism and Confucianism, was missing. What we now consider part of the Shinto tradition is in fact a multifarious set of discourses that developed in direct engagement with Buddhism, Confucianism, Daoism, and Western thought and religion.

The modern understanding of Shinto as the immutable essence of Japanese spirituality, actively promoted by the Japanese state, was explicitly related to Japanese nationalism and militarism and underpinned Japan's war efforts between 1895 (the Sino-Japanese War) and 1945 (World War II).

Following Japanese immigration to the United States, especially Hawai'i and California, in the early twentieth century, several Shinto shrines were established to carry out communal rituals for immigrants (proselytism among non-Japanese on US soil was not among their goals). During World War II, these shrines, considered to be potential centers of anti-American (pro-Japanese) propa-ganda, were closed, removed, or strictly controlled.

America, together with many other countries during that period, was particularly receptive to this association of Shinto with Japanese nationalism, militarism, and imperialism. Several influential authors in the first part of the twentieth century thought that Shinto was the spiritual root of Japanese militarism, an ideological "enemy" that needed to be defeated in order to keep Japan under control. This understanding of Shinto spread beyond discourses related to US strategic and geopolitical interests. The mass media, in particular, used Shinto to evoke images of collectivism, militarism, and irrational imperial cults that were associated with Japan, and America came to define itself against these images as a democratic country of free, individual citizens. Of course, this was a gross simplification—both of the complex nature of Shinto in Japan and of America's society—but it continued to play a role after the end of World War II, especially in anti-Japanese discourses of the 1980s.

The understanding of Shinto as forming the core of Japanese nationalism and militarism motivated America's contribution to Shinto identity, especially during the occupation after the end of World War II. In December 1945, a few months after Japan's surrender, the American-led General Headquarters (GHQ) occupation government issued the so-called Shinto Directive, with the aim to put an end to "the perversion of Shinto theory and beliefs into militaristic and ultranationalistic propaganda, designed to delude the Japanese people and lead them into wars of aggression" (Breen and Teeuwen 2010, 13). The directive prohibited all forms of official "sponsorship, support, perpetuation, control, and dissemination" (13) of Shinto rites or ideas, as well as all financial contribution to Shinto shrines from public funds. At the same time, all Japanese were freed from "any compulsion to believe or to profess to believe in Shinto" (13). Public education and all official propaganda were purged of all Shinto-inspired national-ism. The content of this directive was later expanded to sanction the complete separation of the Japanese state from any religious organization, a principle codified in the new Japanese constitution promulgated in 1947.

In this way, American intervention eliminated from public discourse the understanding of Shinto as closely related to the state and its authoritarian and military policies, in favor of a redefinition of Shinto as a set of innocuous cultural traditions; Shinto shrines were also allowed to reconfigure themselves as private religious organizations, independent of state control.

An interesting new phenomenon that has emerged since around the 1980s is the presence of themes that are more or less related to aspects of Shinto in Japanese mass-culture products (novels, movies, and above all *manga,* anime, and computer games). Such themes include animistic ideas, supernatural forces, Shinto-derived narra-tives, figures of gods (*kami*), and rituals. Many of these mass-culture products have become popular in America as well. Given the absence of a unified, normative discourse about Shinto in contemporary Japan, and the lack of formal religious education about Shinto in the public schools and in many private schools as well, mass-culture texts constitute, for many young people, the primary source of information on Shinto, in Japan as well as in the United States.

SEE ALSO *Japan; World War I; World War II; World's Parliament of Religions (1893)*

BIBLIOGRAPHY

Ballou, Robert O. *Shinto, the Unconquered Enemy: Japan's Doctrine of Racial Superiority and World Conquest.* New York: Viking, 1945.

Breen, John, and Mark J. Teeuwen. *A New History of Shinto.* Chichester, UK, and Malden, MA: Wiley-Blackwell, 2010.

Hardacre, Helen. *Shintō and the State, 1868–1988.* Princeton, NJ: Princeton University Press, 1989.

Holtom, Daniel Clarence. *Modern Japan and Shinto Nationalism: A Study of Present-Day Trends in Japanese Religions.* Chicago: University of Chicago Press, 1943.

Josephson, Jason Ananda. *Invention of Religion in Japan.* Chicago: University of Chicago Press, 2012.

Fabio Rambelli
*Professor of Japanese Religions and Cultural History and ISF Endowed Chair of Shinto Studies
Department of East Asian Languages and Cultural Studies and Department of Religious Studies
University of California, Santa Barbara*

SILENT SPRING (RACHEL CARSON, 1962)

Rachel Carson's 1962 *Silent Spring* is one of the most famous books of the twentieth century and one of the most politically and culturally influential in American history. *Silent Spring* was an exposé of the serious consequences of the widespread overuse of synthetic chemical pesticides. It contributed to a new cultural understanding of the human place in the natural world and is often credited with ushering in modern environmentalism.

There are several reasons for the outsized impact of the book. First, it synthesized existing research on the environmental and health effects of pesticides in accessible language. Rachel Carson (1907–1964), trained as a scientist, already had three best-selling science books to her credit. She used poetic language to elicit wonderment at nature and shock at its desecration, for instance describing "Earth's Green Mantle," despoiled by pesticides or "Elixirs of Death." A second reason for the great impact of *Silent Spring* was its carefully structured argument, first discussing environmental degradation by various pesticides, and culminating in the dire effects on human health, including cancer. Third, Carson made it

clear that she was not repudiating modern industrial agriculture or calling for a ban on all pesticides; instead, her call to cease "indiscriminate" use was a moderate recommendation that won widespread support. Another reason for the far-reaching impact of the book was that press stories had recently publicized problems with ambitious government pesticide programs, as well as episodes of food contaminated with pesticide residues. Thus, by 1962, the reading public was already skeptical about the use of agricultural chemicals.

The passionate response to *Silent Spring* was reflected in reviews and articles in the mainstream press, reactions from industry spokesmen, and actions from government officials. The overwhelming number of press articles about the book were positive, even if some were more enthusiastic and some more cautious. Both supporters and critics addressed the question of Rachel Carson's qualifications. Those who celebrated her analysis called her "a realist," a "trained biologist," and "thoroughly scientific." Meanwhile, critics, especially those from the chemical industry, challenged Carson's qualifications, as well as her objectivity. Carson was painted as an "alarmist," "hysterical," and emotional, especially because she was a woman.

Carson, in her own defense, charged that it was those who were wedded to the overuse of pesticides that had a "fanatic zeal" to create an insect-free world and an unrealistic understanding of nature: "The illusion that salvation … lies at the end of a spray nozzle is a dangerous will-o'-the-wisp" (Carson [1962] 2002, 114). Carson indicated that the desire to control nature was based on dangerous hubris: "The 'control of nature' is a phrase conceived in arrogance, born of the Neanderthal age of biology and philosophy, when it was supposed that nature exists for the convenience of man" (297).

Silent Spring quickly led to concrete government action. In the wake of the book's publication, President John Kennedy (1917–1963) formed a Scientific Advisory Commission to report on dangers from the misuse of pesticides. A number of congressional committees also held hearings into pesticides, and proposed legislation to regulate them. Rachel Carson's testimony before Congress was an opportunity to focus on particular themes in *Silent Spring* and to make recommendations for government action, especially the strict control of aerial spraying and the eventual elimination of *persistent* pesticides.

Although actual legislative accomplishments were initially modest, passage of narrowly focused laws began a decade of debate about pesticide regulation, which would culminate at the federal level in the creation of the Environmental Protection Agency, the banning of numerous persistent chemicals, and far-reaching laws that succeeded in curbing some abuses of the environment.

Meanwhile, numerous state legislatures also introduced their own regulations of pesticides.

The legacy of *Silent Spring* goes far beyond the state and federal laws passed in the United States. The book is most significant for reframing how people throughout the world understood the relationship between humans and the environment. Almost immediately, there was international attention to the book, which was on best-seller lists in other countries and was translated into all the languages of the industrialized world. *Silent Spring* helped to create modern environmentalism by convincing people that they were part of a "balance of nature" and were stewards of the natural world, not just its exploiters. The book was successful in inaugurating a new consciousness about the environment, but it was unsuccessful in curbing the continued reliance on pesticides or in convincing many people in the industrialized world that protection of the environment should remain a top priority.

SEE ALSO *Earth Day; Earthrise (Bill Anders, 1968); Greenpeace*

BIBLIOGRAPHY

Carson, Rachel. *Silent Spring.* 40th anniversary ed. Boston: Houghton Mifflin, 2002. First published 1962.

Hazlett, Maril. "Voices from the *Spring: Silent Spring* and the Ecological Turn in American Health." In *Seeing Nature through Gender*, edited by Virginia J. Scharff, 103–128. Lawrence: University Press of Kansas, 2003.

Hynes, H. Patricia. *The Recurring Silent Spring.* New York: Pergamon Press, 1989.

Lear, Linda. *Rachel Carson: Witness for Nature.* New York: Holt, 1997.

Lytle, Mark Hamilton. *The Gentle Subversive: Rachel Carson, Silent Spring, and the Rise of the Environmental Movement.* New York: Oxford University Press, 2007.

Murphy, Priscilla Coit. *What a Book Can Do: The Publication and Reception of Silent Spring.* Amherst: University of Massachusetts Press, 2005.

Sideris, Lisa H., and Kathleen Dean Moore, eds. *Rachel Carson: Legacy and Challenge.* Albany: State University of New York Press, 2008.

Michelle Mart
Associate Professor of History
Penn State University, Berks Campus

SIMCOE, JOHN GRAVES
1752–1806

For John Graves Simcoe, a British veteran of the American Revolution, the outcome of that conflict was regrettable. In his eyes the British constitution was the best government, ordered and led by the wisdom of the monarch and aristocracy balanced with limited popular government (Fryer and Dracott 1998). Experiments in republican government were dangerous, a sentiment seemingly confirmed by the excesses of the French Revolution.

Simcoe's disdain for the United States provided a foundation for his vision of the place of Upper Canada (largely the present province of Ontario) within the British Empire. As the United States faltered under the Articles of Confederation, Simcoe envisioned a British presence, not unlike that of the French prior to the Seven Years' War, arcing through the heart of North America from eastern Canada to the Great Lakes, down the Mississippi to the Gulf of Mexico. But where scattered fur-trading forts typified the French presence, Simcoe envisioned a peaceable, vibrant commercial colonial empire flowing along the extensive waterways. Colonial prosperity would result as emigrants from Europe and the United States naturally gravitated to the better government and protection that Britain would provide.

In his mind's eye, Vermont would be a pivotal testing ground. The northward flow of the Lake Champlain watershed through the Richelieu River to the St. Lawrence River made it a natural extension of Canada (Fryer and Dracott 1998). In 1791 Parliament partitioned Canada into the new province of Upper Canada and Lower Canada, the latter consisting of the older French colony. Simcoe's appointment as the first lieutenant governor of Upper Canada seemed an opportunity to advance the British cause, even if his initial goals remained modest. Vermont's admission to the United States in 1791, however, just prior to his departure from Britain, did not augur well for Simcoe's empire-building project.

Upon his arrival in North America, Simcoe found his influence on British policy severely limited. He sparred with a local population that, though eschewing the republican government of the United States, enjoyed popular government and the absence of a meaningful aristocratic estate. His request for British Regulars to defend the territory was denied; Simcoe's superior, Commander in Chief and Governor General of Canada Guy Carleton, Lord Dorchester (1724–1808), routinely recalled the district's Queen's Rangers—trained units— whenever the United States struck a threatening pose. British bureaucratic organization of the Indian Department officially removed Simcoe as an authority in Indian affairs, and when he did exercise some influence, he occasionally found his efforts undermined by Dorchester.

Despite these limitations, Simcoe successfully led the initial development of the western Canadian colonial economy. Among the early actions he took was to open up lands for settlement. Aggressively seeking to draw population away from the United States, which he believed still teemed with Loyalists, he offered American émigrés generous land grants and pledged to exempt them from taxes. Some four thousand applications followed, with many petitioners hailing from New Jersey and Pennsylvania (Taylor 2010). He established a new seat of provincial government at York (present-day Toronto). He pursued an expansionist agenda, negotiating with Indians to consolidate imperial land holdings on the Ontario peninsula. Moving away from fur trading, he encouraged agriculture and animal husbandry, deploying the Queen's Rangers to build roads, open waterways, construct buildings, and develop infrastructure designed to link distant settlements and foster commerce. By the middle of the 1790s, Upper Canada became an exporter of pork, wheat, and other products to Lower Canada, the United States, and England (Bergmann 2012). To improve defense, he expanded the militia service. And despite having limited authority over Indian affairs, Simcoe leveraged his position to influence Indian superintendents and agents, at times working directly with Indian leaders to build alliances and convince them to maintain the Ohio River as an absolute boundary with the United States (Wise 1953).

When Anthony Wayne (1745–1796) launched his expedition into the Ohio country in 1794—the third for the United States in four years—his troops lacked the resources and political will for an invasion of Upper Canada. Yet Simcoe interpreted Wayne's decision not to engage British troops as an indicator of his success in creating a defensible and economically successful territory for the British Empire, despite his failure to certify a buffer Indian territory between American and Canadian settlement zones. By the middle of the 1790s, events in Europe swept away whatever little potential existed for Simcoe's ambitious imagined arc of empire. Jay's Treaty (1794) confirmed Britain's pivot from North American concerns. Simcoe departed Upper Canada for Britain in 1796—the same year Britain shifted local authority over Indian affairs to the lieutenant governor—and resigned his position in 1798. He never returned, despite an active career until his death in 1806.

SEE ALSO *American Revolution; Canada; Loyalists; War of 1812*

BIBLIOGRAPHY

Bergmann, William H. *The American National State and the Early West.* Cambridge and New York: Cambridge University Press, 2012.

Cruikshank, E.A., ed. *The Correspondence of Lieutenant-Governor John Graves Simcoe, with Allied Documents Relating to His Administration of the Government of Upper Canada.* 4 vols. Toronto: Ontario Historical Society, 1932–1935.

Fryer, Mary Beacock, and Christopher Dracott. *John Graves Simcoe, 1752–1806: A Biography.* Toronto and Tonawanda, NY: Dundurn Press, 1998.

Taylor, Alan. *The Civil War of 1812: American Citizens, British Subjects, Irish Rebels, and Indian Allies.* New York: Knopf, 2010.

Wise, S. F. "The Indian Diplomacy of John Graves Simcoe." *Report of the Annual Meeting of the Canadian Historical Association* 32, 1 (1953): 36–44.

William H. Bergmann
Assistant Professor, Department of History
Slippery Rock University

SINGER MANUFACTURING COMPANY

The Singer Manufacturing Company was one of America's first truly international businesses. Founded in 1851 in New York as I. M. Singer & Co., it quickly became the largest seller of domestic sewing machines in the world. As it pioneered retail strategies and spread American consumer goods around the world, the Singer brand became synonymous with global capitalism (Bissell 2010).

The Singer Manufacturing Company had its origins in a patent pool that allowed founders Isaac Merritt Singer

Advertisement for the Singer automatic sewing machine, 1897. Founded in 1851, the Singer company quickly became the largest seller of domestic sewing machines worldwide. As it pioneered retail strategies and spread American consumer goods around the world, the Singer brand became synonymous with global capitalism. **JAY PAULL/ARCHIVE PHOTOS/GETTY IMAGES**

(1811–1875) and Edward Clark (1811–1882) to control some of the most important inventions essential for the manufacture of the domestic sewing machine. The sewing machine had been around since the eighteenth century, but Singer, an American inventor and actor, improved its suitability for household use. His changes helped make the sewing machine a popular technology in homes in the United States and overseas. Two of his machines were displayed at the Crystal Palace in London in the early 1850s, and the Singer Manufacturing Company soon became the first American firm to market extensively in Europe. Singer took out patents in France and England, and in 1855 began licensing to a Parisian manufacturer (Davies 1969, 303). Singer's first forays into European markets yielded lackluster sales, but the company persisted, devoting significant resources to hiring international selling agents and opening sales rooms overseas (Godley 2006, 270).

SINGER'S MARKETING INNOVATIONS AND INTERNATIONAL SUCCESS

By 1864, 40 percent of the company's sales were exports (Gordon 2008, 671). Renamed the Singer Manufacturing Company in 1865, it opened its first overseas factories two years later in Scotland. This expansion abroad coincided with the end of the American Civil War (1861–1865) and the appreciation of the US dollar, which caused most US companies to withdraw from foreign markets. Singer, conversely, ramped up its global efforts, pioneering marketing techniques that would eventually be adopted by other American companies (Davies 1969, 300). These marketing techniques were largely responsible for Singer's success outside the United States.

In Britain, Singer launched a canvassing system, in which company agents went door to door to demonstrate the sewing machine and take individual orders (Godley 2006, 281). It also advertised in women's magazines and implemented a monthly payment plan that made it easier for middle-class consumers to purchase its machines (Kupferschmidt 2004, 197). While Singer was largely successful at convincing foreign consumers of the superiority of its machines, it often had to overcome market challenges, such as Germany's protectionist policies and "buy domestic" movement (Davies 1969, 321–322). Additionally, the company struggled in China,

Singer Manufacturing Co. advertisement card showing six people from Zululand (South Africa) and a sewing machine, distributed at World's Columbian Exposition, Chicago, 1893. *At the World's Columbian Exposition in Chicago in 1893, the domestic sewing-machine display garnered more attention than any other, and the Singer sewing machine, in particular, was admired for its mechanical perfection.* **LIBRARY OF CONGRESS PRINTS AND PHOTOGRAPHS DIVISION [LC-USZC4-2763]**

where reservations about machine-stitching prevented widespread adoption of the American sewing machine (Kupferschmidt 2004, 200; Davies 1969, 323). In general, however, Singer enjoyed robust global sales. It moved into the Middle East in the 1880s and, overtaking English, French, and German brands, secured 80 percent of all sales in the region (Kupferschmidt, 2004, 202). Russia became Singer's biggest market around the turn of the twentieth century, and within twenty years Singer was successful in Japan, the Philippines, and South Africa as well (Godley 2006, 275; Gordon 2008, 683).

A SYMBOL OF AMERICAN INDUSTRIALIZATION

In addition to its status as a popular household item, the Singer sewing machine served as a symbol of American industrialization. Showcased at world's fairs throughout the second half of the nineteenth century, the machine represented American ingenuity and innovation on an international stage. At the World's Columbian Exposition in Chicago in 1893, in fact, the domestic sewing-machine display garnered more attention than any other, and the Singer sewing machine, which had improved significantly since the 1876 Centennial International Exhibition in Philadelphia, was admired for its mechanical perfection (World's Columbian Commission, Committee on Awards 1901, 1409–1413). Although Singer employed hand craftsmanship through the last decades of the nineteenth century, its mass production capabilities made Singer sewing machines the antecedents of many twentieth-century industrial consumer goods, such as the motor car and the television (Hounshell 1985, 6; Godley 2006, 296).

OPPOSITION AND CHALLENGES ABROAD

Despite, or perhaps because of, its success, Singer ran up against opposition to both its products and its labor management. Internationally, sewing machines sparked anxiety about gender and the division of labor and consumption, especially in the Middle East (Coffin 1994; Kupferschmidt 2004, 197). To overcome many cultures' assumptions that women and machines were incompatible, Singer published pamphlets that portrayed sewing machines as safe for women. Conversely, the company also distributed literature aimed at appealing to male "machine operators," rather than "seamstresses," by minimizing their acknowledgment of women's expertise in clothing production (Durack 1998, 185, 193). Additionally, Singer's standardized retail system was not universally accepted. The company equated its sales techniques with progress and civilization, but this often proved insulting to employees and consumers in other countries (Gordon 2008, 685). In Japan, for example, Singer employees protested the company's "American"

style of capitalism in the 1920s and 1930s, particularly its wage cuts and layoffs (Gordon 2008, 688). Although the company had occasionally acquiesced to labor demands in Japan and elsewhere earlier in the century, it did not do so in the 1930s, and lost much of its market share as a result (Gordon 2008, 693).

In general, the decades following World War I (1914–1918) were difficult for Singer. Its global sales peaked in 1913 and never recovered from wartime disruptions (Gordon 2008, 698). The company shifted much of its production to munitions during both world wars, and by the 1950s its sewing-machine sales had declined sharply. Singer no longer had a competitive advantage in supplying sewing machines on credit (Godley 2006, 297). Additionally, the sewing machine had been losing its global prominence since the beginning of the twentieth century. First, the ready-made garment industry made it more fashionable to purchase clothing than to make it at home, meaning that sewing machines became "invisible" in households (Connolly 1999, 31, 48). And as the pride in owning a sewing machine declined, so too did the general demand for them, especially among European and American women. Although the private market for sewing machines remained strong in the Middle East, Singer had to close some of its biggest factories in Scotland, and in Hong Kong underwent a takeover by outside entrepreneurs (Kupferschmidt 2004, 213).

As a result of these changes, the company diversified in the 1960s. It began producing a variety of electronic devices, including calculators, simulators, and typesetting machines. While it continued to manufacture electronic sewing machines, Singer was absorbed into SVP Worldwide. In the first decades of the twenty-first century, Singer was no longer a global retail giant, but its brand lives on as the company that brought American consumer durables into millions of people's homes all over the world.

SEE ALSO *Industrialization; World's Fairs*

BIBLIOGRAPHY

Bissell, Don. *The First Conglomerate: 145 Years of the Singer Sewing Machine Company.* Grantsville, UT: Harvest Lane Press, 2010.

Coffin, Judith G. "Credit, Consumption, and Images of Women's Desires: Selling the Sewing Machine in Late Nineteenth-Century France." *French Historical Studies* 18, 3 (1994): 749–783.

Connolly, Marguerite. "The Disappearance of the Domestic Sewing Machine, 1890–1925." *Winterthur Portfolio* 34, 1 (1999): 31–48.

Davies, Robert Bruce. "'Peacefully Working to Conquer the World:' The Singer Manufacturing Company in Foreign

Markets, 1854–1889." *Business History Review* 43, 3 (1969): 299–325.

Davies, Robert Bruce. *Peacefully Working to Conquer the World: Singer Sewing Machines in Foreign Markets, 1854–1920.* New York: Arno Press, 1976.

Durack, Katherine T. "Authority and Audience-Centered Writing Strategies: Sexism in 19th-Century Sewing Machine Manuals." *Technical Communication* 45, 2 (May 1998): 180–196.

Godley, Andrew. "Selling the Sewing Machine around the World: Singer's International Marketing Strategies, 1850–1920." *Enterprise and Society* 7, 2 (2006): 266–314.

Gordon, Andrew. "Selling the American Way: The Singer Sales System in Japan, 1900–1938." Special issue on salesmanship, *Business History Review*, 82, 4 (2008): 671–699.

Hounshell, David. *From the American System to Mass Production, 1800–1932: The Development of Manufacturing Technology in the United States.* Baltimore, MD: John Hopkins University Press, 1985.

Kupferschmidt, Uri M. "The Social History of the Sewing Machine in the Middle East." *Die Welt des Islams*, New Series 44, 2 (2004): 195–213.

World's Columbian Commission, Committee on Awards. *World's Columbian Exposition, Chicago, Ill., 1893.* Vol. 2. Washington, DC: US Government Printing Office, 1901.

Lindsay Schakenbach Regele
Assistant Professor
Miami University

SLAVE REGIMES

Observers in 1776 could not have anticipated with surety that the US South would emerge from the eighteenth century a full-blown slave society ruled by an increasingly consolidated planter class. Many presumed that slavery, a system they blamed on British tyranny, would expire in the new nation. Others, notably slave-owning residents of the Lower South colonies of Georgia and the Carolinas, deemed slavery fundamental to their economic survival. Compromises between those who desired slavery's end and those who required its continuance assured the institution's survival in the new nation. Yet US slavery still might have faded were it not for the 1790s "cotton revolution" (Berlin 2000, 360). More than any other crop, cotton undergirded the growth and power of an American slave regime.

THE RISE OF KING COTTON

Several technological and economic changes drove King Cotton to the fore. Mid-eighteenth-century British industrialists fed raw cotton into newly developed steam-powered machines, a process that "sharply lowered the cost of spinning cotton into yarn and weaving that yarn into fabric" (Kolchin 2003, 95). British steam-driven machinery generated cheap calicoes and muslins that transatlantic consumers increasingly demanded.

North American cotton producers contributed relatively little raw fiber to the British by midcentury. US growers were hampered by the long-staple cotton that flourished only in the South Carolina Sea Islands. The seeds of short-staple cotton, which throve in inland areas, "clung far more tenaciously to the cotton" fibers than did the seeds of the long-staple variety, making it difficult and expensive to process (Kolchin 2003, 95). The 1793 mechanical gin reinvigorated US cotton production. The gin dramatically sped the process of separating seeds from fiber, making short-staple cotton a practical and lucrative commercial crop. In 1790, US planters recorded three thousand cotton bales and exported one-eighth of their crop to England in 1791 (Johnson 2013, 255; Rothman 2005, 46). By 1810, growers reported 178,000 cotton bales. Through the antebellum period, three-quarters of US cotton was transported to Britain, while the remaining one-quarter nourished northern industrial growth and textile production (Kolchin 2003, 95).

From the start, slaveholders strongly influenced American government and cotton's proliferation strengthened their hand. The wealthy held office, and slave owners were prosperous. Rice, and later, sugar planters commanded the greatest fortunes, but cotton topped antebellum US exports. In fact, cotton "exceeded in dollar value all other exports combined" (Kolchin 2003, 95; Rothman 2005, 4–5). Cotton, and thus slavery, were linked to the national economy. Supported by northern industrialists and slave traders, planters bolstered the "plantation regime" (Berlin 2000, 346) in several ways. They insisted slavery be regulated by each individual state, not the federal government, as one way of ensuring control over the expanding institution. During the antebellum period, state legislatures passed laws meant to control slaves' movement and assembly and to limit manumission of slaves (Kolchin 2003, 127–128).

The federal government also assisted the slave regime's spread. The government negotiated treaties, purchased new lands, and removed Indians as planters spilled into new territories, including six new states established between 1790 and 1821: Kentucky, Tennessee, Louisiana, Mississippi, Alabama, and Missouri. Slaveholders, who dominated the Louisiana territorial government, halted the Spanish *coartación*, a contract between slave and slave owner and the government through which slaves arranged to purchase their freedom. Slave owners also harnessed the state's power in other ways. For example, sugar planters advocated and won government tariffs on sugar imports. These tariffs kept them in business, as without such protection, the cheaper, foreign-produced sugar would have put Louisiana planters out of business (Rothman 2005, 178, 171).

THE GROWTH OF THE US SLAVE POPULATION

Congress banned the African slave trade in 1808, a move widely supported by slave and nonslave owners alike. Prior to this legislation, most individual states had at least temporarily halted African slaves' entry. Georgia, for example, banned commercial importation of slaves between 1817 and 1853 (Kolchin 2003, 129; Rothman 2005, 19).

The African slave trade's close did not lessen planters' demand for slaves. They simply found other ways to acquire enslaved laborers. Southern planters' desire for enslaved workers coincided with economic shifts in the Upper South. Chesapeake planters cultivated more wheat in their tobacco-drained soil, and they needed fewer workers to tend wheat than either tobacco or cotton. Thus, Virginia planters possessed a surfeit of enslaved individuals. In fact, Virginia counted more slaves among its population than any other state at the American Revolution's end in 1783. Propelled by a growing international demand for their crops, cotton and rice planters purchased the "surplus of the slaves" to their north (Deyle 2009, 834). The domestic or internal slave trade relocated "more than 1 million African American slaves from the Upper South to the Lower South" between 1790 and 1860 (Deyle 2009, 839).

The US slave population increased after the African slave trade ended. In Cuba, Jamaica, Brazil, and most New World regions, enslaved populations expanded only by continued importation. But in the United States, alone among New World slaveries, slave numbers swelled through natural increase (Genovese 1976, 57). This antebellum growth was remarkable, particularly when one considers that only 6 percent of African slaves shipped to the New World were delivered to the North American mainland. By 1860, the United States contained four million slaves, making it one of the largest slave societies in the Western Hemisphere. Prior to 1790, Brazil commanded the largest slave society in the Americas. But by the nineteenth century, the US South claimed this distinction (Klein 1986, 114).

The burgeoning slave population was gradually confined to the South. Starting in the 1780s, several northern states approved gradual emancipation acts that slowly freed their already small enslaved populations. Some sold their human property south before they could be freed. Southern slave numbers grew steadily between the internal slave trade and natural increase. Mississippi's enslaved population grew fourfold in the early nineteenth century (Rothman 2005, 511). And slave prices rose steadily through the century. A prime male field hand sold for $500 in 1800 New Orleans, but by 1860, that same prime field hand would cost $1,800. Indeed, human chattel became the "most valuable form" of southern property (Deyle 2009, 8).

OTHER NEW WORLD SLAVE REGIMES

US planters' commitment to cotton affected other slave regimes. Brazilian growers supplied 30 percent of British raw cotton in the 1790s, but their product was supplanted by ginned, and therefore cheaper, American cotton (Klein 1986, 78). Yet Brazilians did not lessen their reliance on enslaved laborers, though importation, not natural increase, swelled their numbers. In Brazil, slaves increasingly toiled over sugar or coffee rather than cotton.

In the eighteenth century, French Saint-Domingue (Haiti) dominated the world sugar market. Sugar production stopped there after the successful slave insurrection. After the Haitian Revolution (1791–1804), planters in Brazil, Jamaica, several French-owned islands, and Cuba turned to sugar and coffee cultivation. Like US planters, Brazilian slaveholders moved into new regions and shifted slaves to these new areas, where coffee and sugar would be produced. By 1805, Brazil provided 15 percent of the world's sugar (Klein 1986, 115).

Sugar exacted a terrible price from enslaved laborers. Sugar required crushing, often round-the-clock labor, which proved lethal to the enslaved. Further, sugar growers often preferred male slaves and purchased few females. The grueling work and unhealthy environments in which sugar grew exacted a high death rate, while the lack of female slaves—particularly well-fed ones who were not overworked—meant these slave populations did not increase, but decreased. Sugar growing required a constant influx of slaves. Between 1826 and 1850, one million slaves were imported into Brazil (Dunn 2014, 141). The continual addition of bondspeople from Africa meant that Brazil's nineteenth-century slave population was more heterogeneous and embraced African traditions longer than those in the United States.

Some sugar was cultivated in the United States by the early 1800s. Sugar estates necessitated a large capital outlay for equipment, substantial property, multiple buildings, and numerous enslaved laborers, constantly needing to be replaced. The tropical plant matured only in southeastern Louisiana, where wealthy planters, some of them émigrés from Saint-Domingue, moved from indigo and tobacco to sugar production in the early 1800s. Encouraged by federal protection, high demand, and high returns on investment, US sugar plantations doubled in number between the 1820s and 1830s (Follett 2005, 21).

Slaves' lives transformed under the nineteenth-century "second slavery" (Kaye 2009, 627). New commercial crops like cotton, sugar, and indigo were cultivated by enslaved laborers. In the United States, three-fourths of slaves toiled in fields, usually in gangs, while the remainder worked in cities, iron manufacturing, boating, and other work. Enslaved women and children were not exempt from the plantation regime: they harvested most US cotton, for instance (Rothman 2005, 52).

Influenced by rising slave populations and slave resistance, particularly the Haitian Revolution, planters exerted tighter control over slaves in all New World slave regimes (Klein 1986, 90). In Brazil, Cuba, and other sugar-growing areas, planters purchased "more enslaved men and women, worked them harder, and policed their movements more closely" (Schmidt-Nowara 2011, 125–126). Sugar and rice planters confronted a black majority, whereas US slaves rarely exceeded one-third of the population. In Cuba and Brazil, the black majority included many Africans, who were considered more likely to revolt than native-born slaves.

RESISTANCE AND REBELLION

In the United States, most cotton planters owned fewer than ten slaves and lived year-round on their property, often working alongside their slaves. Sugar and rice planters possessed far more slaves and tended to be absentee owners; that is, they hired overseers for their estates while they resided in London, Charleston, or other cities. American masters' close proximity to their slaves, along with rising antislavery sentiment and growing humanitarian concerns, aroused a paternalistic creed in nineteenth-century America. Paternalistic planters at least said that they considered slaves "their people," and believed that they bore the responsibility to care for and guide, often through punishment, these wards. On one hand, paternalism motivated US planters to supply improved housing, food, and medical care to their slaves. On the other hand, paternalism inspired planters to interfere in virtually all aspects of their slaves' lives. Planters exerted more control over slaves' diet by curtailing slaves' provision grounds, on which slaves raised much of their food. Instead of provision grounds, which were the norm in Jamaica and other islands, US planters doled out slaves' food. In addition, antebellum masters oversaw slaves' religious instruction in ways they did not in the eighteenth century. Nineteenth-century masters desired Christian slaves, who, they believed, were more docile and, owners argued, offered proof that slavery exerted a civilizing influence on slaves.

Planters sought control of their human chattel and feared rebellion, not without cause, as slaves actively demonstrated their desire to be free. Their resistance took many forms: slaves feigned illness and ignorance, slowed work, and temporarily or permanently ran away from their owners. Slaves found marronage more challenging as slave regimes commanded more and more territory, leaving fewer frontier areas in which maroon communities could hide. As a result, marronage declined everywhere in the nineteenth century. Maroon communities persisted in isolated regions like the Amazon, but these communities were challenged by slave patrols and state-initiated efforts to destroy them (Klein 1986, 199–200). Of course, marronage had always been relatively infrequent in the United States, where a white majority carefully policed the enslaved minority.

Slaves also mounted revolts and outright rebellions. Like marronage, slave revolts were attempted less in the United States than in Latin America and the West Indies. Slaves openly revolted less in the United States due, at least in part, to demographic reality. From the mid-eighteenth century, blacks outnumbered whites in Jamaica ten to one, and most blacks were African born. Similar slave demographics existed on other Caribbean islands. In the United States, however, slaves in most regions made up only one-third of the population, and, unlike Cuba and Brazil, where Africans continued to be imported, most US slaves were American-born, particularly after 1808 (Dunn 2014, 4; Kolchin 1987, 238).

The heavily armed white majority in the United States posed an essentially insurmountable tactical conundrum for the dispersed, native-born, and unarmed enslaved minority. Between 1807 and 1835, slaves in Bahia, Brazil, mounted more than twenty armed rebellions (Graden 1996, 255). American slaves coordinated perhaps four rebellions during roughly the same years. Gabriel Prosser's 1800 Virginia plan and Denmark Vesey's 1822 South Carolina attempts were thwarted before they began. Two other revolts were launched, one an 1811 German Coast rebellion in the Louisiana sugar parishes, and the other Nat Turner's 1831 Virginian revolt. Given the odds against open, armed revolt in the United States, this comparative paucity makes sense. One historian, in fact, noted that "organized rebellion" by US slaves was "virtually suicidal" (Kolchin 1987, 253–354). Wherever slave revolts were rumored or happened, whites exacted harsh retribution. In the wake of such events, new laws restricted manumission and curtailed the activities of enslaved, as well as free, African Americans.

THE RISE OF THE ANTISLAVERY MOVEMENT

For a variety of reasons, antislavery sentiments emerged and gained wider acceptance throughout the eighteenth-century Western world. Antislavery prodded the British and US legislatures to terminate importation of Africans in 1807 and 1808, respectively. Cotton and sugar strengthened and reinvigorated planters' commitment to slavery. In the early 1800s, then, New World planters, particularly in the United States, worked to protect their institution, ensure slavery's spread to new territories and states, and guarantee the return of fugitive property, even if recovered in slave-free regions.

Antislavery sentiments gained greater traction and coalesced into a more vocal abolitionism in the first part of the nineteenth century. US slaveholders were confronted with a well-organized abolition movement by the 1830s. Southerners contended that slavery was supported by the Bible and that slavery was a "positive good" that civilized, Christianized, and controlled a savage race. In addition, they insisted that slavery was superior to wage labor because they cared for their workers, whereas industrialists paid subpar wages and left their workers to suffer.

Slaveholders everywhere vocally supported slavery, but southerners reacted with an unusually ardent defense. Southerners faced a largely free Western world. Only Cuba, Brazil, and Puerto Rico permitted slavery. Abolitionists were outsiders, not southerners, which encouraged southern defensiveness. More importantly, slavery was so closely interwoven with southern life that "defense of slavery became tantamount to defense of the South." Further, southerners had much to defend: in 1860, the South contained more slaves than Cuba, Brazil, and Puerto Rico combined (Kolchin 1987, 189).

In most countries, legislators slowly put an end to slavery. Governments first cut off the African slave trade: Britain in 1807, the United States in 1808, and most Latin American countries by the 1820s. Next, regions instituted gradual emancipation, as in the northern US states in the late eighteenth century and several Spanish colonies, such as Columbia, Peru, Venezuela, and Argentina, as they declared independence in the 1820s (Schmidt-Nowara 2011, 112–113). Vermont freed bondspeople in 1777, Massachusetts not long after, and Chile in 1823 (Klein 1986, 252). The British terminated slavery in Britain with the 1833 Abolition Act. In 1834, British West Indian bondspeople were transformed into forced indentured laborers, but they were categorically freed in 1838.

Only in the US South did slavery's end involve a civil war. Still, congressional action officially ended slavery with the 1865 Thirteenth Amendment, leaving Puerto Rico, Cuba, and Brazil the only remaining Western slave regimes. In all three, slavery ended fitfully. In 1870, the Spanish Moret Decree, which applied to Cuba and Puerto Rico, ruled that those born after 1870 were free but leashed those born previously to apprenticeships until they were twenty-two years old. The Spanish Cortes abolished slavery in Puerto Rico in 1873 and in Cuba in 1886 (Klein 1986, 254).

After four hundred years of Atlantic slavery in the New World, the institution was confined to Brazil. As in Cuba and Puerto Rico, emancipation in Brazil went through long, even torturous steps until the Golden Law of 1888 finally destroyed the last American slave regime.

SEE ALSO *Act Prohibiting Importation of Slaves (1807); Africa Squadron; Amistad; Antislavery; Atlantic Slave Trade; Emancipation Day; Haitian Revolution; Race*

BIBLIOGRAPHY

Berlin, Ira. *Many Thousands Gone: The First Two Centuries of Slavery in North America*. Cambridge, MA: Harvard University Press, 2000.

Deyle, Stephen. "An 'Abominable' New Trade: The Closing of the African Slave Trade and Changing Patterns of U.S. Political Power, 1808–1860." *William and Mary Quarterly* 66, 4 (2009): 833–850.

Dunn, Richard. *A Tale of Two Plantations: Slave Life and Labor in Jamaica and Virginia*. Cambridge, MA: Harvard University Press, 2014.

Follett, Richard. *The Sugar Masters: Planters and Slaves in Louisiana's Cane World, 1820–1860*. Baton Rouge: Louisiana State University Press, 2005.

Genovese, Eugene. *Roll Jordan Roll: The World the Slaves Made*. New York: Vintage, 1976.

Graden, Dale T. "An Act 'Even of Public Security': Slave Resistance, Social Tension, and the End of the International Slave Trade to Brazil, 1835–1856." *Hispanic American Historical Review* 76, 2 (1996): 249–282.

Johnson, Walter. *River of Dark Dreams: Slavery and Empire in the Cotton Kingdom*. Cambridge, MA: Harvard University Press, 2013.

Kaye, Anthony E. "Modernity in the Nineteenth-Century South and the Atlantic World." *Journal of Southern History* 75, 3 (2009): 627–650.

Klein, Herbert S. *African Slavery in Latin America and the Caribbean*. New York: Oxford University Press, 1986.

Kolchin, Peter. *Unfree Labor: American Slavery and Russian Serfdom*. Cambridge, MA: Harvard University Press, 1987.

Kolchin, Peter. *American Slavery, 1619–1877*. Rev ed. New York: Hill and Wang, 2003.

Rothman, Adam. *Slave Country: American Expansion and the Origins of the Deep South*. Cambridge, MA: Harvard University Press, 2005.

Schmidt-Nowara, Christopher. *Slavery, Freedom, and Abolition in Latin America and the Atlantic World*. Albuquerque: University of New Mexico, 2011.

Christine E. Sears
Associate Professor of History
University of Alabama in Huntsville

SMALLPOX ERADICATION

The World Health Organization's 1948 constitution stipulates that the organization will "work to eradicate epidemic, endemic and other diseases," a lofty goal first achieved in 1980 with the eradication of smallpox. Caused by the *variola* virus, smallpox killed an estimated three hundred million people in the twentieth century and was at the time of the WHO's founding still endemic in seventy-five countries, mostly in Africa, Asia, and South America, despite the existence of an effective and inexpensive vaccine in use since the early nineteenth century. Although the WHO's director general, Brock Chisholm (1896–1971), proposed smallpox eradication in 1953, the World Health Assembly (WHA, the representative decision-making body of the WHO) did not back such an effort until 1958, when the Soviet Union advocated a global smallpox-eradication program. The WHA enthusiastically endorsed the USSR proposal but offered little material support, providing a paltry $100,000 in annual funding. In part, this ambivalence reflected the reluctance of the United States to fund a program that might compete with the WHO's Malaria Eradication Program, which began in 1955 and relied heavily on American support. Nor did smallpox present a clear danger for the United States, where the disease had not been endemic since 1949, although occasional importations of smallpox caused outbreaks and panics, most notably in New York City in 1947.

American ambivalence about smallpox eradication turned to enthusiasm in 1965, when President Lyndon B. Johnson's administration (1963–1969) not only backed the WHO's languishing eradication effort, but also approved a bilateral eradication program in eighteen (later expanded to nineteen) countries in West and Central Africa. Funded by the United States Agency for International Development (USAID) and directed by the Communicable Disease Center (CDC, later the Centers for Disease Control and Prevention), the Smallpox Eradication and Measles Control Program represented an effort to improve global health and exercise influence in so-called "less-developed countries," where US interests seemed vulnerable in a postindependence and Cold War era. The CDC's program was also a response to the demands of health professionals in less-developed countries, such as Dr. Paul Lambin, the minister of health in Upper Volta (now Burkina Faso), who pressured the United States to initiate a smallpox-eradication program in combination with an ongoing measles-control campaign.

Under the leadership of the CDC's Dr. J. Donald Millar, enthusiastic CDC staff and their local African counterparts adopted a variety of vaccination tools (such as the Ped-O-Jet vaccination gun and, later, the bifurcated

needle) and strategies, in particular "surveillance-containment," in which mobile teams isolated cases of smallpox and vaccinated all suspected contacts, thereby preventing further spread of the disease. Although the CDC's program failed to control measles—much to the frustration of participants in the program—smallpox was eradicated in the nineteen countries of the program in 1970.

The CDC's success in West and Central Africa energized the WHO's ongoing Smallpox Eradication Program (SEP), which "intensified" in 1967 with an annual budget of $2.4 million supplemented by voluntary contributions that eventually totaled nearly $65 million. The WHO's program also intensified under the leadership of an American doctor, D. A. Henderson, who helped plan the CDC's program in West and Central Africa. Other Americans soon joined the WHO effort, and the United States contributed more than $7.5 million in cash and material to the SEP. Far more than an "American" program, though, the SEP was a truly international endeavor, with a staff made up of forty-three nationalities and nearly $40 million in contributions from forty-one countries, including, especially, the Soviet Union, which initially proposed the SEP and contributed more than 1.4 billion doses of vaccine over the course of the eradication program. Through perseverance, adaptation, and, occasionally, coercion, participants in the SEP chased smallpox throughout the endemic world, isolating the last naturally occurring case of the disease in Somalia in 1977. Although a tragic laboratory accident with smallpox virus samples led to three fatalities in 1978, the WHO officially certified the eradication of smallpox in 1980.

In the following decades, proposals to eliminate all known specimens of the smallpox virus met increasing opposition, spurred by hope for future scientific discoveries and fear that the disease might return, unleashed by a bioterrorist or accidentally released from forgotten virus samples, such as those discovered in 2014 in a National Institutes of Health storage facility in Maryland. Despite the continued existence of the virus, smallpox the disease has not existed since 1978—a remarkable achievement for both global health and American efforts to engage a globalizing world.

SEE ALSO *United States Agency for International Development (USAID); World Health Organization*

BIBLIOGRAPHY

Fenner, Frank, D. A. Henderson, Isao Arita, Zdenek Ježek, and Ivan D. Ladnyi. *Smallpox and Its Eradication.* Geneva, Switzerland: WHO, 1988.

Foege, William H. *House on Fire: The Fight to Eradicate Smallpox.* Berkeley: University of California Press, 2011.

Henderson, D. A. *Smallpox: The Death of a Disease.* Amherst, NY: Prometheus, 2009.

Hopkins, Donald R. *The Greatest Killer: Smallpox in History.* Chicago: University of Chicago Press, 2002.

Bob H. Reinhardt
Executive Director
Willamette Heritage Center

SMITH, ADAM

SEE *The Wealth of Nations (Adam Smith, 1776).*

SMITH–MUNDT ACT (US INFORMATION AND EDUCATIONAL EXCHANGE ACT OF 1948)

The Smith-Mundt Act, formally known as the US Information and Educational Exchange Act of 1948 (Public Law 80-402), authorizes the US government to communicate with foreign audiences through radio broadcasts, films, educational and scientific exchanges, printed materials, and other public diplomacy initiatives.

On March 21, 1947, Karl Mundt (1900–1974), a Republican congressman from South Dakota, introduced legislation (H.R. 3342) authorizing peacetime US international information and exchange activities. On June 24, 1947, the US House passed H.R. 3342 by a 273-to-97 margin. H. Alexander Smith (1880–1966), a Republican from New Jersey, cosponsored the bill in the Senate.

In the fall of 1947, a team of senators evaluated twenty-two US Information Service (USIS) outposts in Western and Eastern Europe. The investigators described contemporary Europe as "a vast battlefield of ideologies in which words have to a large extent replaced armaments as the active elements of attack and defense." They concluded that US officials were "woefully inadequate" in combating the "misrepresentation, falsification, division, chaos, compromise, despair and ultimate absorption" fostered by communist propaganda. They declared "a strong and effective information and educational exchange program" essential to US national security (US House Committee on Foreign Affairs 1947, 1–23).

In January 1948, having amended the original H.R. 3342 more than one hundred times, Congress hammered out final compromises that ensured passage of the Smith-Mundt bill. In deference to those wary of government bureaucracy, the law directed the State Department "to utilize, to the maximum extent practicable, the services and facilities of private agencies, including existing American press, publishing, radio, motion picture, and other agencies." To appease those who feared communist infiltration, the Smith-Mundt bill required all information officials to undergo FBI loyalty investigations and mandated the deportation of exchange participants found to be engaging in subversive political activities. Finally, to ensure that no individual, party, or agency used government propaganda to influence the American people, the Smith-Mundt legislation prohibited the dissemination of US information materials to the general public. While representatives of the press and members of Congress could request transcripts of government programming, private US citizens could not.

Satisfied with these compromises and recognizing the imperative need to explain American foreign policy and political culture to the rest of the world, the Senate unanimously passed the Smith-Mundt bill on January 16, 1948. Designed "to promote a better understanding of the United States in other countries," the measure established an information service and an educational exchange division of the US State Department. Separate advisory committees supervised each and were required to report to Congress twice a year on expenditures, activities, and effectiveness. President Harry S. Truman (1884–1972) signed the bill into law eleven days later.

In 1972 and again in 1985, the law was amended to strengthen prohibitions on domestic access to propaganda materials created for foreign audiences. The Smith-Mundt Modernization Act of 2012 amended the US Information and Educational Exchange Act of 1948 to allow people in the United States access to newscasts produced by the State Department and the Broadcasting Board of Governors, including Voice of America, the Middle East Broadcasting Networks, and Radio Free Asia.

SEE ALSO *Cold War; Marshall Plan; Voice of America*

BIBLIOGRAPHY

Hart, Justin. *Empire of Ideas: The Origins of Public Diplomacy and the Transformation of U.S. Foreign Policy.* New York: Oxford University Press, 2013.

Krugler, David F. "'If Peace Is to Prevail:' Karl E. Mundt and America's International Information and Education Programs, 1943–1953." *South Dakota History* 31 (Spring 2001): 53–75.

Ninkovich, Frank A. *The Diplomacy of Ideas: U.S. Foreign Policy and Cultural Relations, 1938–1950.* New York: Cambridge University Press, 1981.

US House Committee on Foreign Affairs. *The United States Information Service in Europe,* 80th Cong., 2d sess., 1947, Committee Print, 1–23.

Laura Belmonte
Professor of History
Oklahoma State University

SOCIAL DARWINISM
SEE *Whiteness.*

SOCIALISM

The socialist movement in America never threatened state power, nor did it redirect American political culture. Yet it did on occasion achieve a certain success, even if its overall experience proved to be, at best, bittersweet.

As European socialist émigrés arrived in America in the 1850s, following the failure of European revolutions, they found a sharply different political culture. White males generally possessed the individual right to vote, and the prevailing political culture extolled social mobility, individualism, and the preeminence of American democracy. While not all Americans held these beliefs with equal fervor, they nonetheless formed, as Alexis de Tocqueville (1805–1859) noted, the foundation of American political consciousness. As these immigrant socialists experienced the appeal of America's promise to working people, some were incredulous. Friedrich Sorge (1828–1906), Karl Marx's (1818–1883) representative in America from the early 1850s, dismissed these political beliefs as a "delusion [that] transforms itself into a sort of creed." Writing to Marx two decades later, Sorge reported that, despite the evident industrial development that Marx held would create class consciousness, American "workingmen in general ... are quite unconscious of their own position toward capital" and thus "slow to show battle against their oppressors" (Sorge 1910, 361). While not Marxists, American workers did engage in sustained strikes and formed (often short-lived) independent political movements to protest the arbitrary power of capital over their lives. The small socialist movement, as it adjusted to American conditions, gained more adherents and, in 1901, formed the Socialist Party of America (SPA). Its leader was deeply attuned to the possibilities of American democratic ideals.

Eugene Victor Debs (1855–1926) led the SPA's varied constituencies: new immigrants, native-born workers, intellectuals, and reformers. Between 1900 and 1920, Debs was his party's candidate for president five times, and in 1912 he received 6 percent of the national vote. In 1920, as a federal prisoner jailed for his opposition to American entry into World War I (1914–1918), Debs nonetheless received almost one million votes. Debs presented socialism as the fulfillment of American democratic ideals in an era of industrial capitalism. That system, he repeated throughout his career, consistently violated America's democratic promise. To democratize industrial capitalism, through shared decision making in the plant and equitable distribution of that work's profits, was his central goal.

The decades after 1920 were difficult for the SPA. Its new leader, Norman Thomas (1884–1968), a socialist, pacifist, and ordained Presbyterian minister, lacked Debs's popular appeal. Between 1928 and 1948, although Thomas ran for president six times, factional fighting weakened the SPA internally, while the impact of the Great Depression, the momentary appeal of communism, and the deep hopes attached to President Franklin D. Roosevelt's (1882–1945) New Deal programs further reduced the SPA's political presence. Neither Thomas nor other socialists could convince most working people that Roosevelt's policies were reformist, no threat to industrial capitalism, and thus inadequate.

A. Philip Randolph (1889–1979), journalist, socialist, trade unionist, and black activist for equality, never led the SPA, but his efforts greatly influenced American social policy. As leader of the Brotherhood of Sleeping Car Porters, he worked to integrate the American labor movement, to establish fair employment practices for all during World War II (1939–1945), and to transform America's vision of racial equality through demonstrations, negotiations, and consistent support for civil rights over seven decades. This agitation created few socialists, but it expanded the sense of the possible for many, black and white.

By the 1950s, the socialist movement was a mere shadow of itself. It possessed few areas of institutional strength, and was increasingly hard-pressed to distinguish itself from New Deal liberalism. But not all followed that path. Michael Harrington (1928–1989), a midwesterner grounded in the Catholic social justice tradition, emerged as a creative Marxist thinker and activist. His approach to socialism reflected a Debsian sensibility, while his intellectual ability surpassed most previous socialists. His book, *The Other America* (1962), startled the nation with its analysis of American poverty and was the catalyst for President John F. Kennedy (1917–1963) to raise that issue. In later books, Harrington's critical, intelligent analysis raised core questions about American political culture, the economic crisis of the 1970s, and the potential he yet saw in the democratic socialist approach. Harrington's perspective on socialism and American culture clearly differentiated itself from the Norman Thomas era; in turn, many of the New Left activists of the 1960s and 1970s dismissed his approach as not revolutionary enough.

When Harrington and others formed the Democratic Socialists of America (DSA) in 1982, they aligned their socialist perspective with the progressive wing of the Democratic Party. But events beyond anyone's control, deeply embedded in American political culture, undermined American socialism's future. The rise of modern conservatism, the 1980 election of Ronald Reagan

(1911–2004) with significant working-class support, and the simultaneous decline of trade union strength into the next century created enormous obstacles for socialist expectations. Nor did the alliance with progressive Democrats bear fruit. The conservative ascendency changed liberalism itself, as it became more centrist and turned away from critiques of global corporate capitalism's practices and policies. In 1989, with the destruction of the Berlin Wall signifying the collapse of communism, socialism too went into eclipse. Always a minor note in American politics, it all but disappeared as an institutional presence by the end of the twentieth century.

SEE ALSO *Americanization; Anarchism; Bolshevism; China; Cold War; Debs, Eugene V.; Eisenhower, Dwight D.; Exceptionalism; Great Depression; Internationalism; Isolationism; Marx, Karl; Reagan, Ronald Wilson; Red Scare; Roosevelt, Franklin D.; Russia; Truman, Harry S.; Vietnam War; Wilson, Woodrow; World War I; World War II*

BIBLIOGRAPHY

Buhle, Mari Jo. *Women and American Socialism, 1870–1920.* Urbana: University of Illinois Press, 1981.

Harrington, Michael. *The Other America: Poverty in the United States.* Baltimore, MD: Penguin, 1962.

Harris, William H. *Keeping the Faith: A. Philip Randolph, Milton P. Webster, and the Brotherhood of Sleeping Car Porters, 1925–37.* Urbana: University of Illinois Press, 1977.

Howe, Irving. *Socialism and America.* San Diego, CA: Harcourt, Brace, Jovanovich, 1985.

Isserman, Maurice. *The Other American: The Life of Michael Harrington.* New York: PublicAffairs, 2000.

Noyes, John Humphrey. *History of American Socialisms.* New York: Hillary House, 1961. First published 1870 by Lippincott.

Pfeffer, Paula E. *A. Philip Randolph: Pioneer of the Civil Rights Movement.* Baton Rouge: Louisiana State University Press, 1990.

Salvatore, Nick. *Eugene V. Debs: Citizen and Socialist.* Urbana: University of Illinois Press, 1982.

Sorge, Friedrich. "To the General Council...." In *A Documentary History of American Industrial Society*, Vol. 9: *Labor Movements, 1860–1880*, edited by John R. Commons, Ulrich B. Phillips, Eugene A. Gilmore, Helen L. Sumner, and John B. Andrews. Cleveland, OH: Clark, 1910.

Swanberg, W. A. *Norman Thomas: The Last Idealist.* New York: Scribner's, 1976.

Nick Salvatore
*Maurice and Hinda Neufeld Founders Professor
of Industrial and Labor Relations
Cornell University*

SOUTH AMERICA

The United States has been involved in South America since its founding. Commerce formed the basis of this relationship, but over time the two regions developed close political and cultural ties as well. These ties were not always amicable, and despite common colonial and revolutionary origins, the United States and South America have experienced ups and downs in their diplomatic and commercial interactions over the past two centuries.

THE SPANISH AND PORTUGUESE COLONIAL ERA

At the time of its founding, the United States' relationship with South America was mediated by Spain and Portugal, which had colonized the majority of the continent. Spain had long maintained royal monopolies by granting favorable commercial contracts to Spanish merchant houses and levying onerous duties and restrictions on foreign vessels. Except for foodstuffs and lumber, Spain enforced a Crown-protected trade between European and American Spaniards, which operated to the detriment of US traders seeking outlets for European and Asian goods, as well as for North American produce like tobacco (Ramírez and Ortiz de la Tabla 1979). Monopolies were especially burdensome for merchants seeking silver, which was one of the most valuable commodities of the early modern world. By 1800, Spanish silver constituted 80 percent of legal tender in the United States, yet merchants could not legally acquire it directly from South American mines because of imperial trade policy (Fichter 2010). The only sector in which Spain permitted free trade was slave trading. US merchants participated in this until the Napoleonic Wars broke out in 1803 and British naval power cut off the Spanish dominions from the African sources of supply (Marichal and Souto Mantecón 1994). Royal monopolies ended once the independence wars began in 1808.

The South American independence wars brought the United States and its southern neighbors closer together. South American revolutionaries, such as Francisco Miranda (1750–1816) and Simón Bolívar (1783–1830), visited the United States to drum up support for their independence movements, and American men joined filibustering and privateering expeditions against Spain. Popular support for Latin American independence ran high in the United States, and both US citizens and South American patriots spoke of a sisterhood between the regions. The United States began appointing consular agents to various port cities to serve the merchants and seamen who lived in and traveled throughout the region and to improve commerce between the Americas. US citizens and politicians in general, though, knew little about their neighbors to the south.

In 1817, the Monroe administration sent a commission to southern South America to ascertain whether to formally recognize independence from Spain. The commissioners traveled throughout Chile, Argentina, and Brazil to collect political, cultural, and geographical information, which was publicized in American newspapers and pamphlets. Despite popular support for independence, the US government waited until the 1820s to officially recognize national sovereignty throughout South America.

THE MONROE DOCTRINE

Following South America's independence from Spain and Portugal, the relationship between South America and the United States changed. In an 1823 presidential address that became known as the Monroe Doctrine, President James Monroe (1758–1831) made pretenses to being the dominant interest in the region. The United States appointed ministers plenipotentiary and, by the 1840s, entered into several favorable treaties of amity and commerce with South American nations. As the United States industrialized, it came to depend on Latin America for raw goods, like minerals, hides, and dyewoods, which it imported in exchange for manufactured goods and agricultural produce. In the 1840s and 1850s, the United States claimed land belonging to Peru and Chile from which to extract guano and sodium nitrate for fertilizer production (Leonard 1999). Throughout most of the nineteenth century, though, the United States had closer ties with other areas of Latin America, notably Mexico and Cuba, than with South America. Its influence was greatest around the Caribbean Basin, while Great Britain, France, and Germany dominated trade, investment, and political influence in southern South America (Smith 1994, 28).

Relations between the two regions became strained in the second half of the nineteenth century, as military conflicts on both continents created tension between the United States and South America. The United States increasingly began to assert the rhetoric of the Monroe Doctrine. The Mexican-American War (1846–1848) revealed US willingness to use military force to achieve territorial aims and the US Civil War (1861–1865) sparked diplomatic tension, as some South American nations granted belligerent trading rights to the Confederate States of America (Smith 2005, 38).

The United States did not intervene when Argentina, Brazil, and Uruguay invaded Paraguay in the War of Triple Alliance (1865–1870), but it deployed naval power during regime changes in Chile and Brazil in the 1890s in order to protect US commercial interests (Smith 2005). The United States also intervened in territorial disputes between Britain and Venezuela as a means not only of protecting Venezuela, but also of asserting its status as the sole power in the Western Hemisphere (Smith 2005, 58). Actions such as these contradicted the goals of the First International Conference of American States, which sought to establish peace and cooperation throughout the hemisphere. Held in Washington, DC, in 1890, the conference was the brainchild of US secretary of state James G. Blaine (1830–1893), who wanted to prevent war in South America and improve commercial relations. The Commercial Bureau of the American Republics was created to adopt laws to protect patents and copyrights and provide for international arbitration. While it represented eighteen American governments, it fell under the direction of the US secretary of state and had little practical impact, beyond some bilateral reciprocity treaties (Smith 1994, 32).

THE TWENTIETH CENTURY

By the twentieth century, the United States had successfully demonstrated to Europe that it would be the dominant foreign influence in South America. It emerged victorious in the Spanish-American War in Cuba in 1898, and from 1904 to 1914 constructed a canal across Central America. The United States purchased the land for the canal from France in 1902, but failed to gain permission for construction from Colombia, which still controlled Panama. In what became known as "gunboat diplomacy," the United States assisted Panama in an independence movement against Colombia in exchange for canal rights. The United States controlled the Canal until 1999, when it handed over complete rights to Panama.

During World War I (1914–1918), European trade with Latin America sharply declined and the United States assumed a bigger economic presence, opening branch banks throughout the region and assuming the debt of various countries. Yet "dollar diplomacy" yielded more than economic exchange. Between 1898 and 1934, the United States intervened more than thirty times, as US–South American relations oscillated between political conflict and Pan-American unity (Smith 1994, 52). When the United States intervened during the Mexican Revolution, Argentina, Brazil, and Chile stepped in to prevent full-on war between Mexico and the United States (Smith 2005, 75). Recognizing that these sorts of interventions generated mistrust and hostility in the region, US president Herbert Hoover (1874–1964) took a goodwill tour of South America in 1928 and pledged that the United States would be more cooperative and less imperialistic in its dealings with its southern neighbors (Smith 1994, 64).

The administration of Franklin Delano Roosevelt (1882–1945) continued these pretensions to benevolence when Roosevelt proclaimed the "Good Neighbor" policy and withdrew military troops from the region. Roosevelt promised to treat Latin American nations as sovereign entities rather than subordinates (Smith 1994, 65). Although the United States' discriminatory trade duties in the early 1930s created resentment across South America, the decade as a whole is considered a "golden era" in US–South American relations.

During World War II (1939–1945), the United States maintained its nonmilitaristic approach toward South America as it became more interventionist in the rest of the world, but worked to strengthen cultural ties in the region. In 1940, President Roosevelt created the Office of Inter-American Affairs as one of the first government agencies to specifically establish cultural diplomacy. It distributed American news and films throughout South America to counter Axis propaganda during World War II and published classroom guides to educate US students about their southern neighbors (Sadlier 2012, 10). Meanwhile, South American popular culture gained a mainstream presence in the United States as Hollywood films began to center on South American characters and settings, and Brazilian performer Carmen Miranda (1909–1955) became a sensation. Caribbean influences transformed American jazz, and Brazilian sambas, Colombian salsas, and Argentinian and Uruguayan tangos and milongas became popular forms of music and dance (Rivera 2007, 85). Advertisements in the United States played up the exoticism of South American products like coffee and bananas, which served to link exports with their countries of origin in US consumer culture (Bandeira 2006).

Popular cultural exchange continued after the war, alongside an increase in US political and military involvement. As Cold War tensions between the United States and the Soviet Union increased, the United States sought to combat any communist threats in the region. President John F. Kennedy (1917–1963) launched the Alliance for Progress, a set of government policies that attempted to cultivate political and economic cooperation between the United States and Latin America through investment, health programs, and education initiatives. The program continued under the administration of President Lyndon Johnson (1908–1973), which contributed public aid for farm loans and rural electrical cooperatives and for the construction of hospitals, schools, roads, and sewage and irrigation systems (Allcock 2014). In addition to undertaking development projects in the region, the United States supported South American governments that would serve as US allies—including those that violated human rights. It supported a Venezuelan dictator in the 1950s, employed military force to assist coups d'état in Brazil in 1964 and Chile in 1973, and partnered with Argentina's right-wing

government in an effort to counter socialist movements in Central America in the 1980s.

Increased military contact in the decades following World War II was not at first accompanied by an increase in trade. Balance-of-payment crises throughout South America, combined with resentment over US military intervention, led to nationalist moves to decrease reliance on imports and develop domestic industry. As a result, US manufactured exports decreased (Georgiou and Thoumi 1989). In 1975, however, the Commission on US–Latin American Relations, which was comprised of business and academic leaders, issued a report that advocated an end to military intervention in the interest of commercial exchange. The commission recommended that the US government respect the sovereignty of other nations and use its resources to offer foreign aid to the region's impoverished populations rather than for military action (Smith 1994, 140).

In addition, debt crises prompted many Latin American nations to abandon the import-substitution policies that dominated South America from the 1950s to the 1980s in favor of free-trade initiatives, especially as many of their economists were trained in the "Chicago school" of neoclassical economics. During the 1990s and 2000s, South American nations advocated a free-trade zone in the Western Hemisphere, which met resistance from protectionist factions within the United States, despite President George W. Bush's (b. 1946) support of the proposed Free Trade Area of the Americas (FTAA) (Feinberg 2002). Additionally, opposition from Venezuela, Bolivia, and Ecuador hindered the passage of the FTAA (Weintraub 1997, 62). Regardless of barriers to free trade, US exports to Latin America have grown at 20 percent per year since 1987 (Christian 1997, 72).

THE EARLY TWENTY-FIRST CENTURY

Throughout the last decades of the twentieth century and the beginning of the twenty-first century, immigration to the United States from South America has also increased. Historically, South Americans have comprised a minuscule percentage of US immigrants, but South Americans' share of the overall immigrant population in the United States has been growing steadily for the past fifty years, from less than 1 percent in 1960 to almost 7 percent in 2011 (Stoney, Batalova, and Russell 2013). Colombia, Peru, Ecuador, and Brazil send more immigrants than any other South American country, and immigrants from these four nations, as well as from Uruguay, enjoy dual-nationality status, which helps maintain links between countries (Jones-Correa 2001, 998). Additionally, immigrant businesses and restaurants foster greater cultural connectivity.

Despite cultural connectivity, in the first decades of the twenty-first century, tensions between the United

States and leftist governments in South America have increased. While the United States has cooperated with Colombian governments over such issues as business development and drug trafficking, it has actively opposed President Hugo Chávez (1954–2013) in Venezuela and stationed military troops in allied countries, such as Paraguay, to protect US interests in the region. It has also opposed leftist governments in Argentina, Brazil, and Ecuador, and did little to prevent the 2012 overthrow of Paraguay's president, who had begun to question the US military presence in the nation. The United States has continued to view the continent through a national security lens and, in the second decade of the twenty-first century, has begun to fear Islamic influence in the region.

Yet even as the United States has attempted to impose its political interests, it has been kept in check by the Organization of American States (OAS), which was created in 1948 to foster solidarity and hemispheric security (Shaw 2003). This organizational body, which is comprised of the thirty-five independent nations of the Americas, prevents the United States from acting unilaterally in the region. Despite differing interests throughout the Americas, the OAS works toward peace, democracy, and stability. The United States and South America have a long history of balancing nationalist agendas with Pan-American interests, and, as the twenty-first century progresses, it seems likely that both conflict and cooperation will continue.

SEE ALSO *Bolívar, Simón; Mexican-American War; Monroe Doctrine (1823); Pan-Americanism*

BIBLIOGRAPHY

Adelman, Jeremy. *Sovereignty and Revolution in the Iberian Atlantic*. Princeton, NJ: Princeton University Press, 2006.

Allcock, Thomas Tunstall. "Becoming 'Mr. Latin America': Thomas C. Mann Reconsidered." *Diplomatic History* 38, 5 (2014): 1017–1045.

Bandeira, Luiz Alberto Moniz. "Brazil as a Regional Power and Its Relations with the United States." Special issue, "Brazilian Workers as National and International Actors," *Latin American Perspectives* 33, 3 (2006): 12–27.

Christian, Shirley. "Latin American Trade Relations." Special issue, "US–Latin American Relations," *Journal of Interamerican Studies and World Affairs* 39, 1 (1997): 71–83.

de la Balze, Felipe A. M. "Finding Allies in the Back Yard: NAFTA and the Southern Cone." *Foreign Affairs* 80, 4 (2001): 7–12.

Feinberg, Richard E. "Regionalism and Domestic Politics: U.S.–Latin American Trade Policy in the Bush Era." *Latin American Politics and Society* 44, 4 (2002): 127–151.

Fichter, James R. *So Great a Proffit: How the East Indies Trade Transformed Anglo-American Capitalism*. Cambridge, MA: Harvard University Press, 2010.

Fisher, John. "Imperial 'Free Trade' and the Hispanic Economy, 1778–1796." *Journal of Latin American Studies* 13, 1 (1981): 21–56.

Georgiou, George C., and Francisco E. Thoumi. "U.S.–Latin American Trade Flows: 1967–1985." *Journal of International Economic Integration* 4, 2 (1989): 70–84.

Jones-Correa, Michael. "Under Two Flags: Dual Nationality in Latin America and Its Consequences for Naturalization in the United States." *International Migration Review* 35, 4 (2001): 997–1029.

Langley, Lester D. *The Americas in the Age of Revolution, 1750–1850*. New Haven, CT: Yale University Press, 1996.

LaRosa, Michael J., and Frank O. Mora, eds. *Neighborly Adversaries: Readings in US–Latin American Relations*. 2nd ed. Lanham, MD: Rowman and Littlefield, 2007.

Leonard, Thomas M. *United States–Latin American Relations, 1850–1903*. Tuscaloosa: University of Alabama Press, 1999.

Lewis, James E., Jr. *The American Union and the Problem of Neighborhood: The United States and the Collapse of the Spanish Empire, 1783–1829*. Chapel Hill: University of North Carolina Press, 1998.

Liss, Peggy K. *Atlantic Empires: The Network of Trade and Revolution, 1713–1826*. Baltimore, MD: Johns Hopkins University Press, 1983.

Lynch, John. *The Spanish American Revolutions, 1808–1826*. New York: Norton, 1986.

Marichal, Carlos, and Matilde Souto Mantecón. "Silver and *Situados*: New Spain and the Financing of the Spanish Empire in the Caribbean in the Eighteenth Century." *Hispanic American Historical Review* 74, 4 (1994): 587–613.

Racine, Karen. *Francisco de Miranda: A Transatlantic Life in the Age of Revolution*. Wilmington, DE: Scholarly Resources, 2003.

Ramírez, Bibiano Torres, and Javier Ortiz de la Tabla, eds. *Reglamento para el comercio libre, 1778*. Seville, Spain: Escuela de Estudios Hispano-Americanos, 1979.

Rivera, Ángel G. Quintero. "Migration, Ethnicity, and Interactions between the United States and Hispanic Caribbean Popular Culture." *Latin American Perspectives* 34, 1 (2007): 83–93.

Sadlier, Darlene J. *Americans All: Good Neighbor Cultural Diplomacy in World War II*. Austin: University of Texas Press, 2012.

Schulz, Donald E. *The United States and Latin America: Shaping an Elusive Future*. Carlisle, PA: US Army War College, 2000.

Sexton, Jay. *The Monroe Doctrine: Empire and Nation in Nineteenth-Century America*. New York: Hill and Wang, 2011.

Shavit, David. *The United States in Latin America: A Historical Dictionary*. New York: Greenwood Press, 1992.

Shaw, Carolyn M. "Limits to Hegemonic Influence in the Organization of American States." *Latin American Politics and Society* 45, 3 (2003): 59–92.

Smith, Gaddis. *The Last Years of the Monroe Doctrine, 1945–1993*. New York: Hill and Wang, 1994.

Smith, Joseph. *The United States and Latin America: A History of American Diplomacy, 1776–2000*. New York: Routledge, 2005.

Smith, Peter H. *Talons of the Eagle: Dynamics of US-Latin American Relations.* New York: Oxford University Press, 2008.

Stoney, Sierra, Jeanne Batalova, and Joseph Russell. "South American Immigrants in the United States." Migration Policy Institute, 2013. http://www.migrationpolicy.org/article/south-american-immigrants-united-states

Weintraub, Sidney. "U.S.–Latin American Economic Relations." Special issue, "US–Latin American Relations," *Journal of Interamerican Studies and World Affairs* 39, 1, (1997): 59–69.

Lindsay Schakenbach Regele
Assistant Professor
Miami University

SOUTH KOREA

Before Americans first arrived on the shores of the Korean peninsula in the nineteenth-century, it had been host to a series of international conflicts that left mixed legacies. Ancient kingdoms in Korea fought with Chinese dynasties, and the Koreans fought back against a sixteenth-century Japanese invasion. Since the end of World War II (1939–1945), and the political division of Korea, the relationship between the United States and South Korea has emerged as one of the most significant in the East Asian–Pacific region.

THE HISTORY OF US-KOREAN INTERACTION

Nineteenth-century Protestant missionaries were the first Americans to interact with Koreans. American missionaries built numerous religious and educational institutions in Korea. Yonsei University, one of the most prominent universities in South Korea, was founded by American missionaries in 1885. A landmark moment for US-Korean political relations came in 1905, when American president Theodore Roosevelt (1858–1919) initiated peace talks and crafted the Treaty of Portsmouth to end the Russo-Japanese War (1904–1905), which was fought as Russia and Japan sought to expand their influence in Korea. The treaty helped elevate Japan into a regional power in Northeast Asia, a status further solidified by Japan's annexation of Korea five years later.

Thereafter, Korea rarely factored in US foreign policy until the end of World War II. As the war was bringing a violent end to Japan's empire, the Soviet Union invaded Manchuria, placing the Soviets in a prime position to become the first of the victorious allies to enter Korean territory. In addition to this geographic advantage, the Soviets enjoyed a slight political advantage, having supported Korean rebels waging guerrilla warfare against the Japanese Empire beginning in the 1930s (Olsen 2005, 61). In contrast, there was no American military presence in South Korea until 1945. Scrambling to ensure that the Soviets did not take all of Japan's former colonies, American military figures Dean Rusk (1909–1994) and Charles Bonesteel (1909–1977) quickly devised a plan to divide Korea into two zones at the thirty-eighth parallel, with the North managed by the Soviet Union and the United States overseeing the South. The Soviets agreed to the plan, which became known as General Order No. 1. The United States favored Syngman Rhee (1875–1965), a Korean who was educated at Princeton University and had spent two decades campaigning for Korean independence, to be the first leader of the new Korean state.

By June of 1950, the relationship between the Soviet-backed regime in Pyongyang and the American-backed regime in Seoul had deteriorated. The North Korean army crossed the thirty-eighth parallel and quickly overran most of South Korea. Timely intervention by the United States and other countries resulted in the three-year-long Korean War (1950–1953). Though the war was costly and did not result in a complete victory for either side, the United States and its allies in the United Nations saved the Seoul government. Immediately after the war, the two countries signed a Mutual Defense Treaty that lasts to this day.

With the preservation of a democratic South Korean state under Rhee, American policy makers realized that maintaining a high profile in Northeast Asia would be crucial. The United States quickly sought to solidify alliances with South Korea and former adversary Japan in order to counter the communist leadership in Moscow and Beijing. As a result, South Korean political leaders, though unpopular at home, would reap the benefits of American military and financial backing.

The Vietnam War (1954–1975) was the first major event that demonstrated the strengthening US–South Korean ties after the Korean War. Under President Park Chung-Hee (1917–1979), a military strongman, South Korea deployed more than three hundred thousand ground troops to Vietnam in alliance with American interests (Lee 2010, 37). The contribution of the South Korean military in Vietnam greatly solidified relations between the United States and South Korea (Lee 2010, 41).

SOURCES OF TENSION IN THE US–SOUTH KOREAN RELATIONSHIP

Although the United States supported Park for his unwavering anticommunist stance, his regime notoriously imprisoned and silenced political dissidents. Park remained president of South Korea for thirteen years, bypassing laws that would have restricted his time in office (Kim 2003, 228–229). The human rights abuses and political corruption under Park's presidency put strains on his relationship with American leaders, particularly

President Jimmy Carter. The government of Park's successor, another military strongman named Chun Doo-Hwan (b. 1931), killed civilians in the South Korean city of Gwangju in 1980, when what began as a peaceful protest in Gwangju for greater democratic reforms in the aftermath of Park's abuses of power escalated into violence as police fired into the crowd, killing an estimated 600 people. Chun also declared martial law and imprisoned several pro-democracy activists. Although the South Korean government's actions in Gwangju outraged many South Koreans and Americans, the US government was unwilling to discredit an important US ally during the Cold War and did not intervene (Kim 2003, 232). The American failure to prevent the massacre in Gwangju has consequences today, as citizens of Gwangju hold a more negative view of the United States than do South Koreans living elsewhere (Shin and Chang 2006, 55).

The controversy over the Gwangju massacre is not the only source of tension between the two allies. Anti-American sentiments flared up during the presidencies of Kim Dae-Jung (1925–2009) and Roh Moo-Hyun (1946–2009), in response to several incidents involving Americans. In 2002, a US Army tank accidentally hit and killed two South Korean girls in Yangju. Further tensions arose among the Korean people after the United States refused to allow the South Korean government to prosecute the American soldiers who were involved. A few years later, fears over mad cow disease in US cattle led South Koreans to protest a new trade deal with the United States. A rise in nationalism among South Koreans and a more favorable attitude toward reconciliation with North Korea contributed to further cracks in the US–South Korean relationship (Shin and Chang 2006, 56).

SOURCES OF STRENGTH IN THE US–SOUTH KOREAN RELATIONSHIP

North Korean belligerence has helped sustain the US–South Korean alliance. US president Barack Obama and his first secretary of defense, Robert Gates, both publically reaffirmed American support for South Korea (Bumiller and McDonald 2011; *Economist* 2012). Militarily, the United States still maintains a presence in South Korea, although there is a greater degree of bilateralism than in the past.

Economically, the two countries are dependable partners. Hyundai and Kia, South Korea's largest automobile companies, maintain a noticeable presence in the United States. The rise of mobile technology has boosted the profiles of South Korean companies Samsung and LG in the US market. Likewise, American corporate giants, such as Starbucks and McDonald's, have franchises scattered throughout Seoul and other major South Korean cities.

Higher education constitutes one of the most important forms of direct interaction between the United States and South Korea. In an effort to counter North Korean ideology, the United States instituted student-exchange programs in the 1960s (Brazinsky 2007, 190–191). In addition, the Council on International Educational Exchange, the Critical Language Scholarship Program, and the Fulbright Program, among others, operate in South Korea, and major South Korean universities sponsor exchange programs both to and from the United States.

TWENTY-FIRST-CENTURY CHALLENGES

Tensions related to the United States' tricky efforts to balance its alliances with South Korea and Japan will likely continue in the twenty-first century. Unresolved historical conflicts between Japan and South Korea will pose constant challenges to American foreign policy makers as they endeavor to build a three-country alliance (see Dudden 2008). In addition, the increasing influence of China, the resurgence of Russia, and the continuing threat of North Korea will continue to test the friendship between South Korea and the United States. Despite all this, the United States and South Korea enjoy an amiable working relationship that will remain, at the very least, relevant for the foreseeable future.

SEE ALSO *China; Cold War; Kennan, George F.; Korean War; Russia; United Nations*

BIBLIOGRAPHY

Bumiller, Elisabeth, and Mark McDonald. "In Seoul, Gates Reaffirms American Support for South Korea." *New York Times International*, January 14, 2011. http://www.nytimes.com/2011/01/15/world/asia/15military.html

Brazinsky, Gregg. *Nation Building in South Korea: Koreans, Americans, and the Making of a Democracy.* Chapel Hill: University of North Carolina Press, 2007.

Cumings, Bruce. *The Origins of the Korean War*, Vol. 1: *Liberation and the Emergence of Separate Regimes, 1945–1947.* Princeton, NJ: Princeton University Press, 1981.

Dudden, Alexis. *Troubled Apologies among Japan, Korea, and the United States.* New York: Columbia University Press, 2008.

Economist. "Obama's Most Improved Bilateral Alliance." March 31, 2012.

Kim, Yong Cheol. "The Shadow of the Gwangju Uprising in the Democratization of Korean Politics." *New Political Science* 25, 2 (2003): 225–240.

Lee, Jin-Kyung. *Service Economies: Militarism, Sex Work, and Migrant Labor in South Korea.* Minneapolis: University of Minnesota Press, 2010.

Moon, Katharine. "US–South Korean Relations." In *The Future of US-Korean Relations: The Imbalance of Power*, edited by John Feffer, 29–44. London and New York: Routledge, 2006.

Nakamura, David. "In Speech to South Korean Students, Obama Describes a North Korea Their Social Networks Can't Reach." *Washington Post*, March 26, 2012. http://www.washington-post.com/pb/politics/in-speech-to-south-korean-students-obama-describes-a-north-korea-their-social-networks-cant-reach/2012/03/26/gIQAnkFQbS_story.html

Olsen, Edward A. *Korea: The Divided Nation*. Westport, CT: Praeger Security International, 2005.

Shin, Gi-Wook, and Paul Y. Chang. "The Politics of Nationalism in US-Korean Relations." In *The Future of US-Korean Relations: The Imbalance of Power*, edited by John Feffer, 45–63. London and New York: Routledge, 2006.

Yonsei University. "About Yonsei: Overview." http://www.yonsei.ac.kr/eng/about/overview/

Dennis Choi
Madison, Wisconsin

SPANISH FLU

SEE *Flu Epidemic, 1918-1919.*

SPANISH-AMERICAN WAR

Described by Secretary of State John Hay (1838–1905) as a "splendid little war," the Spanish-American War (1898) is now more properly, if less elegantly, referred to as the Spanish-American-Cuban-Filipino War. The change in title goes some way toward providing an insight into the international forces that shaped the war and its perception. This was not just a war fought between two nations; it was a war in which Cuba and the Philippines sought to secure their independence, while the United States pursued its own political ends in bringing an end to the Spanish Empire.

BACKGROUND

The origins of the war can be traced back to a number of sources, but it is perhaps best to begin in 1891. In the US Census Bureau Bulletin No. 12 of April 1891, the frontier that had long defined American identity was declared closed. In 1893, Frederick Jackson Turner (1861–1932) catapulted himself into the first rank of American historians with his *frontier thesis*, introduced in an essay that claimed it was constant contact with the frontier that had produced the uniquely American character and its associated dynamism and prosperity. With the frontier gone, and further internal expansion impossible, some Americans began to consider the expansion of American borders overseas. Captain Alfred Thayer Mahan (1840–1914) of the US Navy had also made this case in 1890. Turner, however, delivered his thesis at the Chicago World's Columbian Exposition, which celebrated Europe's discovery of the Americas some four hundred years earlier, providing him with a far more prominent platform. The imperial drive behind Christopher Columbus's (1451–1506) voyage would soon seep into the nation founded on an anti-imperial platform.

American naval preparedness had been increasing throughout the 1890s. There had been the first significant naval appropriation by Congress since the Civil War (1861–1865) in 1888, and in 1889 a storm sank three obsolete wooden American ships, providing a further stimulus to naval building projects. An external factor would also prompt acceleration when, in 1891, the United States had a war scare with Chile. Further difficulties emerged in January 1893 when the Hawaiian monarch, Queen Lili'uokalani (1838–1917), was overthrown by American businessmen to protect their interests in the islands. President Benjamin Harrison (1833–1901), in his final months in office, tried to force through the annexation of Hawai'i but before it could be completed, Grover Cleveland (1837–1908) took office and withdrew the treaty.

The year 1893 also saw the United States pitched into a global depression, marking the 1890s as a distinctly problematic time. And it just got worse. In 1895, the United States got involved in a border dispute between Venezuela and British Guiana that escalated into a substantial diplomatic crisis. Swathes of the American public had called for war against Chile in 1891; many of them now called for war against Great Britain. The crisis revolved around President Cleveland's broad interpretation of the Monroe Doctrine (1823) as giving the United States a say in any territorial matter in its hemisphere. The problem was not resolved until 1899. Although the US government effectively lost the point in question, the United States improved relations with South America by standing up to the British, while also improving relations with the British through the measured tone of the negotiations.

If things were looking up in South America, they looked bad in Cuba which, in 1895, descended into civil war with the result being the destruction of much of Cuba's main cash crops, tobacco and sugar. This was not only bad for Cuba, it was bad for the Americans who had money invested there. By 1897, both sides in the war in Cuba spent a great deal of time involved in scorched earth policies, throwing Cuba and Spain, its imperial master, into confusion. By early 1898, the "yellow press"—sensationalized reporting with little basis in fact perpetuated by William Randolph Hearst's *New York Journal* and Joseph Pulitzer's *New York World*—was agitating for war against Spain, representing riots in Cuba as acts against American citizens there and inflaming domestic public opinion.

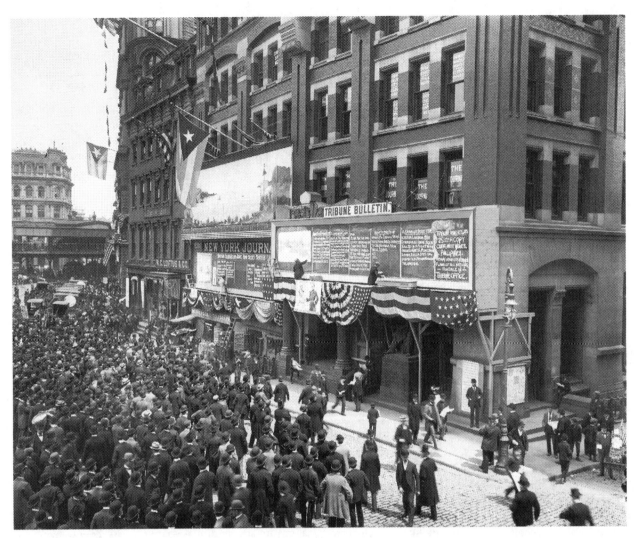

A crowd watches as news announcements are posted at the New York Tribune building on Newspaper Row during the Spanish-American War, 1898. By early 1898, the "yellow press"—sensationalized reporting with little basis in fact as appeared in the New York Journal *and the* New York World—*was agitating for war against Spain, representing riots in Cuba as acts against American citizens there and inflaming domestic public opinion.* **BETTMANN/CORBIS**

THE USS *MAINE* AND THE SLIDE TOWARD WAR

To keep an eye on things and provide a safe haven for any US citizens on the island, the USS *Maine* anchored in Havana Harbor. On February 15, 1898, the *Maine* exploded: 266 of its crew of 354 were killed. President McKinley ordered an investigation the next day, and a fortnight later Congress appropriated $50 million to prepare for war against Spain. President McKinley, elected in 1896, was insufficiently strong to retain control of the national debate over the war. Opinion split between interventionists and conservative isolationists, some of whom feared the impact of war on business interests (the markets tended to drop whenever war looked likely). That businessmen were opposed to the war runs contrary to some contemporary interpretations, even those running

into the 1950s, which speculated that it had been brought about almost entirely by US financial imperialism (Sklar 1959). Other elements in the United States saw the war as a positive move for the economy: war led to inflation, and this would help to push the campaign to introduce paper money backed by silver rather than gold, something that William Jennings Bryan (1860–1925) had advocated since 1895.

Preparations for war were definitely ongoing in both countries though, as demonstrated by the congressional appropriation and Spain's decision in mid-March to dispatch torpedo boats to its imperial possessions in the area. Theodore Roosevelt (1858–1919), then assistant secretary of the Navy, saw this as hostile mobilization by Spain and urged McKinley to accelerate the inquiry into the cause of the explosion. Meanwhile, McKinley sought to separate the issues of the ongoing struggle in Cuba and the destruction of the *Maine*, a task in which he was singularly unsuccessful. The results of the *Maine* inquiry did not help McKinley. Both the United States and Spain conducted inquiries into the explosion and reached very different conclusions. The Spanish found that it had been an internal explosion, while the Americans came to the conclusion that the explosion had an external source, and was therefore an attack on the ship (Musicant 1998, 147–152). The results of the American inquiry chimed with Roosevelt's assessment of the incident: "the *Maine* was sunk by an act of dirty treachery on the part of the Spaniards" (Roosevelt [February 16, 1898] 1951–1954, 1:775; cited in Pérez 1989, 294).

The *Maine*'s demise, however, was not solely responsible for the drift to war. Much of the historiography has argued that it was the "attack" on this ship that roused public opinion to such a height that war became inevitable, which is always a problematic principle. (A commission in the 1970s decided that the *Maine* had most likely been destroyed by an internal explosion, hence the need to treat the idea of it as an "attack" with care). There was also significant opposition to the war outside elite circles (Freidel 1969). However, a great deal of prowar groundwork was accomplished through the publication, a week before the *Maine* incident, of a letter from the Spanish ambassador to the United States, Enrique Dupuy de Lôme (1851–1904), which described President McKinley as a "low politician" who was "weak and catering to the rabble" (Barrón 1979, 51).

It is perhaps unsurprising then that the chant "Remember the *Maine*! To hell with Spain!" echoed throughout the United States during the buildup to the war. Cultural preparation was underway as early as 1896 when John Philip Sousa's operetta, *El Capitan*, premiered and portrayed the Spanish Empire as "little more than a farce." Its march, "El Capitan," was subsequently used at state occasions related to the Spanish-American-Cuban-Filipino War (Hess 1998, 2). In addition to this, Lyman Abbott (1835–1922), a prominent figure in the liberal Protestant community, stated that "America is permitted to fight God's battles for him," positioning the United States as a divinely appointed bringer of justice and an example to the world (Wetzel 2012, 410). Kristin L. Hoganson (1998), however, has persuasively argued that jingoism based on chivalric masculine codes was also a contributing factor to the onset of war, with virile masculinity creating a framework through which empire looked like a way to save the nation's men from degenerating into effeminacy. Conversely, Thomas Schoonover (2003) overlooks much of the American aspect of the war and positions it as part of a longer struggle between the great powers for access to Pacific markets. Several factors, over several years, were therefore at play in the slide toward war between the United States and Spain.

TENSION IN THE PHILIPPINES

Events were also picking up speed in Spain's other imperial outposts. The Philippines had been ruled by Spain for nearly four hundred years and had entered into periodic bouts of revolt throughout that time. Spanish rule was harsh, and in the 1890s the Filipino doctor José Rizal (1861–1896) began to campaign for the improvement of the islands and their people. The Spanish treated this as treason, and Rizal was executed in 1896. The Philippines descended into open war, with a brief pause in 1897 when a truce was struck but not completely honored.

When war broke out between the United States and Spain, both the United States and the Filipino rebels saw the potential of the other to help their cause. Emilio Aguinaldo (1869–1964), leader of the Filipino provisional government, undertook negotiations with the United States, whose representatives seemed to suggest that the Philippines would be treated like Cuba and granted independence—at least that is Aguinaldo's version of events. The Americans, however, did not take the Filipinos seriously as prospective soldiers or leaders of a nation. Initially, the military element did not seem to matter: the US Asiatic Squadron made short work of the Spanish Pacific Squadron in the Battle of Manila Bay on May 1, 1898, and US Marines were landed on May 2. The Americans finished destroying what was left of the Spanish ships and effectively ended Spain's control over the islands, which was tenuous at best given the armistice signed with Filipino forces at Biak-na-Bato even before the destruction of the fleet.

The Filipinos took full advantage of the situation. Under Aguinaldo, the provisional government began increasing its control. Meanwhile, the Americans consolidated their position around Manila, the capital. Interactions between the two developing states were often tense, and domestic racial politics informed American approaches to the islanders. A black soldier fighting for the United States remarked that the subsequent war between the United States and the Philippines would not have occurred "if the army of occupation would have treated [Filipinos] as people" rather than as degenerate savages (Gatewood 1971, 279; cited in Kramer 2006, 174).

THE WAR IN CUBA

The Americans joined the war in Cuba when, on June 10, US forces landed in Guantánamo Bay. Reinforcements were subsequently landed at Santiago on June 22 and 24. The fighting was short and intense, culminating in the Battle of San Juan Hill on July 1, where Theodore

Roosevelt's Rough Riders earned their greatest fame, though much of the Rough Riders' success was dependent on the skill and courage of the Twenty-Fourth Infantry and Tenth Cavalry, both regiments of African American soldiers, who prevented the Rough Riders from being wiped out. A force of Americans and Cubans overpowered the Spanish defenders of the city of Santiago, and when the Spanish attempted to break through the naval blockade surrounding the city, the Spanish Caribbean squadron was destroyed. A truce was called on August 12, and the war officially ended with the Treaty of Paris in December.

THE TERMS OF PEACE

In the terms of the treaty, Spain ceded Guam and Puerto Rico to the United States, Cuba earned its independence, and the Philippines was sold to the United States for $20 million. The United States also installed a permanent naval base at Guantánamo Bay, formalized in the Cuban-American Treaty of 1903. An indirect outcome was that the war encouraged McKinley to think more favorably of the annexation of Hawai'i as a base for US business and military operations in the Pacific; it was incorporated as a territory on August 12, the day of the truce.

ASSESSMENT AND LONG-TERM IMPACT

The war had a prominent impact on three imperial powers: it brought the United States closer to Great Britain, still the world's greatest imperial power, ended Spain's status as one, and made the United States into one. The Spanish-American-Cuban-Filipino War occurred during a period known as the Great Rapprochement, a coming together of the interests of the United States and Great Britain. Britain had pursued a policy of pro-American neutrality during the war, sabotaging attempts by the European great powers to present a united front in a quest to keep the peace between Spain and the United States and making little secret of their support for the Americans (Einstein 1964; Neale 1965; Seed 1958).

The Americans would return the favor in the Boer War (1899–1901), with elite politicians such as Theodore Roosevelt, then governor of New York, arguing against those who felt the United States should be supporting those seeking to throw off the imperial yoke. British affinity for US empire is best summed up by Rudyard Kipling's 1899 poem "The White Man's Burden: The United States and the Philippine Islands," which urged Americans to take it upon themselves to "improve" "your new-caught sullen peoples, half-devil and half-child." If this suggests clarity in the racial politics of the war, of order being enforced by white English-speaking peoples (another sentiment in vogue at the time), the heroic involvement of black soldiers complicates this: in the

Philippines, attitudes informed by domestic racism were directed toward the Filipinos, even as black soldiers were helping the United States to victory; and in Cuba, "buffalo soldiers" had saved the Rough Riders, a mixture of western cowboys and wealthy eastern playboys.

Although a short war, lasting less than one hundred days, the Spanish-American-Cuban-Filipino War fundamentally altered the way the United States operated in the world of international politics through its acquisition of formal colonies and its arrival as a great power.

SEE ALSO *Empire, US; Great Depression; League of Nations; Paris Peace Conference (1919); Roosevelt, Theodore; Rough Riders; Treaty of Versailles*

BIBLIOGRAPHY

Barrón, Carlos García. "Enrique Dupuy de Lôme and the Spanish American War." *The Americas* 36, 1 (1979): 39–58.

Einstein, Lewis. "British Diplomacy in the Spanish-American War." *Proceedings of the Massachusetts Historical Society*, 3rd Series, no. 76 (1964): 30–54.

Freidel, Frank. "Dissent in the Spanish-American War and the Philippine Insurrection." *Proceedings of the Massachusetts Historical Society*, 3rd Series, no. 81 (1969): 167–184.

Gatewood, Willard B., Jr., comp. *"Smoked Yankees" and the Struggle for Empire: Letters from Negro Soldiers, 1898–1902.* Urbana: University of Illinois Press, 1971.

Hess, Carol A. "John Philip Sousa's *El Capitan*: Political Appropriation and the Spanish-American War." *American Music* 16, 1 (1998): 1–24.

Hoganson, Kristin L. *Fighting for American Manhood: How Gender Politics Provoked the Spanish-American and Philippine-American Wars.* New Haven, CT: Yale University Press, 1998.

Kramer, Paul A. "Race-Making and Colonial Violence in the U.S. Empire: The Philippine-American War as Race War." *Diplomatic History* 30, 2 (2006): 160–210.

Musicant, Ivan. *Empire by Default: The Spanish-American War and the Dawn of the American Century.* New York: Holt, 1998.

Neale, R. G. *Britain and American Imperialism, 1898–1900.* Brisbane: University of Queensland Press, 1965.

Pérez, Louis A., Jr. "The Meaning of the *Maine*: Causation and the Historiography of the Spanish-American War." *Pacific Historical Review* 58, 3 (1989): 293–322.

Roosevelt, Theodore. "To Benjamin Harrison Diblee, Feb. 16, 1898." In *The Letters of Theodore Roosevelt*, edited by Elting E. Morison, Vol. 1: *The Years of Preparation, 1868–1898*, 775. 8 vols. Cambridge, MA: Harvard University Press, 1951–1954.

Schoonover, Thomas. *Uncle Sam's War of 1898 and the Origins of Globalization.* Lexington: University Press of Kentucky, 2003.

Seed, Geoffrey. "British Reactions to American Imperialism Reflected in Journals of Opinion, 1898–1900." *Political Science Quarterly* 73, 2 (1958): 254–272.

Sklar, Martin J. "The N.A.M. and Foreign Markets on the eve of the Spanish-American War." *Science and Society* 23, 2 (1959): 133–162.

Wetzel, Benjamin J. "Onward Christian Soldiers: Lyman Abbott's Justification of the Spanish-American War." *Journal of Church and State* 54, 3 (2012): 406–425.

Michael Goodrum
Senior Lecturer, Department of History and American Studies
Canterbury Christ Church University

SPEAKEASY

SEE *Temperance Movement.*

SPIES AND ESPIONAGE

Spying is often called the world's second-oldest profession. It has been part of societal behavior since Judas betrayed Jesus at Gethsemane. It has also played an important part in American history.

EIGHTEENTH AND NINETEENTH CENTURIES

General George Washington (1732–1799) was an active employer of spies during the war for American independence. For example, the Continental Congress established a fund for special correspondence that General Washington used to pay spies keeping track of British sympathizers in New York City, and the fund continued after the new nation was formed. Presidents Thomas Jefferson (1743–1826) and James Madison (1751–1836) used the fund to pay spies in Florida who were keeping an eye on Spanish activities there in the early days of the republic.

Nonetheless, no separate civilian department of intelligence was ever formed within the US government at this time, although the US Army and Navy established intelligence gathering entities in the late nineteenth century. President Abraham Lincoln (1809–1865) was frequently pictured during the American Civil War with his eyes and ears attuned to a telegraphed communication from the front. He also employed the detective Allan Pinkerton (1819–1884) to provide intelligence relating to the president's safety in moving about the battlefield.

WORLD WARS I AND II

It was not until World War I (1914–1918) that the US State Department provided President Woodrow Wilson (1856–1924) with the intercepted Zimmermann telegram (probably provided by the British) that indicated Germany was willing to help Mexico reclaim the territories then in the United States that had been taken or purchased from the Mexicans during the nineteenth century if the Mexican government would join the Germans in fighting the United States. During the war, the United States itself even developed a capability to intercept foreign telegrams through the State Department (the Black Chamber) and maintained this capacity until 1929 when the then secretary of state discontinued the funding, reportedly stating that "Gentlemen do not read other Gentlemen's mail."

Thus, it was not until just prior to World War II that President Franklin D. Roosevelt (1882–1945) and Prime Minister Winston Churchill (1874–1965) of the United Kingdom began to discuss the formation of an intelligence organization on the US side of the Atlantic to keep up with Adolf Hitler's (1889–1945) movements in Europe. The British had successfully stolen the German portable field coding machine so that it could read Nazi military traffic (the "enigma machine") throughout the war. In response, the United States sent some of its brightest mathematicians and code-breakers to Bletchley Park in the United Kingdom to expand the reach of the "enigma" interceptions. In order to match the allied intelligence capability, President Roosevelt established the Office of Strategic Services (OSS), which began to join its British counterpart in landing spies on European shores to link up with local resistance movements and monitor the Nazi armies. After the war, although President Harry S. Truman (1884–1972) was not certain he wanted to maintain a permanent foreign intelligence capability, the rising hostility of relations between the USSR and the United States convinced him otherwise.

THE COLD WAR AND VIETNAM

Hence, in 1947 was born the Central Intelligence Agency (CIA), with responsibility for keeping the president and his foreign policy advisers abreast of efforts worldwide to undermine the peace and spread communism. The United States suffered some embarrassing intelligence losses in those early years after World War II. The USSR stole the United States' atomic secrets and built an atomic bomb long before they would have been able to do so without the help of Soviet spies, such as Klaus Fuchs (1911–1988) and Kim Philby (1912–1988). By the same token, the Soviets moved relentlessly in Europe to undermine US and Western influence in Greece and elsewhere in Western Europe.

President Dwight D. Eisenhower (1890–1969) fought back by mounting so-called "covert operations," which were political operations where the role of the United States was intended to be deniable, such as in Iran in 1953, Guatemala in 1954, and disastrously in Cuba in 1961. Although these were more than classical espionage operations designed to steal opposition secrets, they were thought to be inexpensive ways of advancing US interests without overtly committing troops, as had been done in Korea in 1950.

In October 1962, President John F. Kennedy (1917–1963) presided over the most significant intelligence success of the Cold War. U-2 spy craft took pictures of Soviet troops installing medium- and intermediate-range ballistic missiles in Cuba that were aimed at the United States. This information was corroborated by pictures and verbal descriptions from US spies on the ground. In the event, President Kennedy decided not to mount an airborne surprise attack on the emplacements, but rather a blockade to quarantine further deliveries from Russia, because, among other things, he was persuaded by the United States' top spy in the USSR, Oleg Penkovsky (1919–1963), that Premier Khrushchev (1894–1971) might back down from his impulsive action, since it was opposed by his own top advisers.

Beginning fatefully in 1961, the United States had decided to answer the call for help from France and South Vietnam to prevent South Vietnam from being swallowed up by North Vietnam and by China. In many ways, the war in Vietnam was a colossal intelligence failure. There were certainly outside elements at play in South Vietnam, but in the end it was more a national struggle to reunite the country and gain independence than a Chinese or Russian power-play to extend their influence. The war in Vietnam dragged on for over ten years, engulfing the Lyndon B. Johnson (1908–1973) and Richard Nixon (1913–1994) administrations. American intelligence coped in every way possible, recruiting human sources and marshaling local bands of fighters to contest Vietcong dominance in the provinces, but the war continued until it was terminated under President Nixon in 1973.

President Jimmy Carter sought to revive US efforts at détente with the USSR, but he was deceived by Soviet efforts to undermine its neighbors in Africa and the Middle East. Carter decided to contest the USSR's foray into Afghanistan by covert action. These efforts were continued and enhanced by President Ronald Reagan (1911–2004), who believed strongly that the United States had let its guard down, and that the intelligence services had been permitted to atrophy in their anticommunist capabilities. Reagan beefed up US clandestine support to the Mujahideen in Afghanistan, finally driving the Soviets out of the country under his successor, George H. W. Bush. This was the beginning of the end of the Soviet regime, and while this took place in 1992, the diminution of US intelligence accompanied it.

THE WAR ON TERRORISM

The decade of the 1990s saw many experienced intelligence officers retire or depart for the private sector with inadequate replacements. It has only been since the terrorist attacks of 9/11 that the US intelligence community, civilian and uniformed, has worked itself back to strength, but it is still underequipped in critical language skills and area knowledge to cope successfully with al-Qaeda and other jihadists in the region. The essential problem has been one of access. The United States has been unable to build personal relationships with Arab and Middle Eastern jihadist elements that are determined to rebuild their own countries, peacefully or more often with guns or bombs. The United States maintains a dominating signals and satellite reconnaissance presence in the region, but it is challenged in its efforts to recruit and run human spies.

SEE ALSO *Cold War; Nuclear Weapons*

BIBLIOGRAPHY

Andrew, Christopher. *For the President's Eyes Only: Secret Intelligence and the American Presidency from Washington to Bush.* New York: Harper Collins, 1995.

Johnson, Lock K., and James J. Wirtz, eds. *Intelligence: The Secret World of Spies, an Anthology.* 4th ed. Oxford: Oxford University Press, 2014.

Weiner, Tim. *Legacy of Ashes: The History of the CIA.* New York: Doubleday, 2007.

Frederick P. Hitz
Senior Lecturer in Public Policy
Frank Batten School of Leadership and Public Affairs
University of Virginia
Former Inspector General, Central Intelligence Agency (1990–1998)

SPUTNIK

The Soviet Union launched *Sputnik-1*, the first artificial earth satellite, on October 4, 1957. *Sputnik*, meaning "fellow traveler" in Russian, was a polished metal sphere, 23 inches (58 centimeters) in diameter. Its four external antennas broadcast short radio pulses that could easily be heard by amateur radio operators. The satellite was placed in an elliptical orbit of 139 miles (223 kilometers) by 590 miles (950 kilometers) above the earth's surface. The orbit was inclined 65 degrees to the equator, so the satellite passed over most of the planet's land masses. The satellite's batteries lasted for twenty-two days, after which it fell silent. It reentered the earth's atmosphere on January 4, 1958. Orbiting along with the satellite was the 85-foot-long (26-meter) core stage of its launch vehicle. It was that rocket upper stage, rather than the small and faint satellite itself, that was visible to observers on the ground as a bright object transiting the night sky.

Sputnik-1 was explicitly designed so that the Soviet Union could be the first country to launch a satellite. When development of a complex scientific satellite fell behind schedule, the Soviets' chief space engineer, Sergei Korolev (1906–1966), received Kremlin permission to

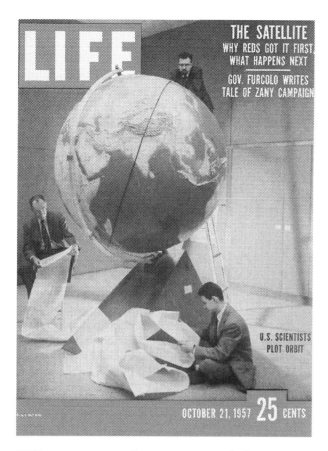

LIFE *magazine cover showing scientists calculating* Sputnik's *orbit, October 21, 1957. Many nations, and much of the American media and public, interpreted the success of* Sputnik *as symbolizing a much higher level of Soviet technological capability than had been previously supposed. There were also worries that the Soviet Union was capable of sending a nuclear warhead over intercontinental distances.* DMITRI KESSEL/LIFE MAGAZINE, COPYRIGHT TIME INC./TIME LIFE PICTURES/THE LIFE PREMIUM COLLECTION/GETTY IMAGES

construct a much simpler vehicle so that the Soviet Union could launch a satellite before the United States could do so. That "elementary satellite" became *Sputnik-1*.

After a successful test of the Soviet R-7 international continental ballistic missile on August 21, 1957, Korolev got approval to modify the missile for use as a satellite launcher. The US satellite program, Vanguard, was not scheduled for an initial orbital test launch until late 1957 or early 1958, and the administration of President Dwight D. Eisenhower (1890–1969) did not emphasize beating the Soviet Union into orbit. This lack of urgency, combined with Korolev's competitiveness, gave the Soviet Union the opportunity to score the first victory in what soon came to be called the "space race."

While *Sputnik-1* may have been modest in technical complexity and scientific payoff, it had profound security and political impacts. Soviet leader Nikita Khrushchev (1894–1971) and his associates claimed that the achievement was an indication of the superiority of the communist form of social and political organization. This was a direct challenge to the assumption on which the Eisenhower administration based its national security policy: that the United States was the unsurpassed world leader in military, economic, and technological power. The Soviet space success was interpreted by US allies, uncommitted nations, and much of the American media and public as symbolizing a much higher level of Soviet technological capability than had been previously supposed. The "beep, beep" of *Sputnik-1* passing overhead and the visibility of its orbiting booster stage also demonstrated to the world that the Soviet Union now had the capability of sending a nuclear warhead over intercontinental distances. By not requesting permission for its satellite to orbit over other countries, the Soviet Union gave first support to the legal principle that orbital space was not subject to national sovereignty.

President Eisenhower indicated that he did not judge the Soviet satellite to be a significant achievement; at a press conference on October 9, he told reporters that it did not "raise my apprehensions, not one iota" (Eisenhower 1958, 730). But he was not successful in limiting Americans' distress at the Soviets' success. The almost hysterical media treatment of *Sputnik-1* reinforced public concerns. Democratic politicians, led by Senate Majority Leader Lyndon B. Johnson (1908–1973), claimed that the satellite launch was clear evidence of the failure of the Eisenhower administration to adequately provide for the nation's security. The "space and missile gap" became a major theme in the 1960 presidential election. Rather than interpret the satellite as a Soviet success, many saw it as an indication of the failure of the US educational and industrial systems. This concern prompted Congress to pass the 1958 National Defense Education Act to provide increased funding for scientific and engineering education.

President Eisenhower also gave scientists an unprecedented degree of access to the top levels of the White House, creating the position of presidential science advisor and establishing an elite Presidential Science Advisory Committee. On the advice of this committee and others, Eisenhower proposed the creation of a new civilian space agency, the National Aeronautics and Space Administration (NASA), to manage the US response to *Sputnik-1* and its successors, while at the same time accelerating American military and intelligence satellite efforts as well as the US ballistic missile program.

The Soviet Union launched two more satellites called *Sputnik. Sputnik-2*, launched on November 2, 1957, carried a small dog, Laika, which died from excessive heat a few hours after takeoff. *Sputnik-3*, launched on May 3,

1958, was the original Soviet scientific satellite. It carried a variety of instruments for geophysical research.

SEE ALSO *Apollo Program; Intercontinental Ballistic Missiles; National Aeronautics and Space Administration (NASA); Nuclear Weapons; Strategic Defense Initiative (Star Wars)*

BIBLIOGRAPHY

Bulkeley, Rip. *The Sputniks Crisis and Early United States Space Policy: A Critique of the Historiography of Space.* Bloomington: Indiana University Press, 1991.

Dickson, Paul L. *Sputnik: The Shock of the Century.* New York: Walker, 2001.

Divine, Robert A. *The Sputnik Challenge: Eisenhower's Response to the Soviet Satellite.* New York: Oxford University Press, 1993.

Eisenhower, Dwight D. "The President's News Conference of October 9, 1957." *Public Papers of the Presidents of the United States: Dwight D. Eisenhower, 1957,* 710–732. Washington, DC: GPO, 1958.

Launius, Roger D., John M. Logsdon, and Robert W. Smith, eds. *Reconsidering Sputnik: Forty Years since the Soviet Satellite.* Amsterdam, Netherlands: Harwood Academic, 2000.

McDougall, Walter A. *The Heavens and the Earth: A Political History of the Space Age.* Baltimore, MD: Johns Hopkins University Press, 1997.

Mieczkowski, Yanek. *Eisenhower's Sputnik Moment: The Race for Space and World Prestige.* Ithaca, NY: Cornell University Press, 2013.

Siddiqi, Asif A. *Sputnik and the Soviet Space Challenge.* Gainesville: University Press of Florida, 2003.

John M. Logsdon
Professor Emeritus, Space Policy Institute
Elliott School of International Affairs, The George Washington University

STEAMSHIP

The steamship, which came into widespread use in the last quarter of the nineteenth century, was among the most important innovations in a transportation revolution that connected America and Europe in ways that could not have been previously imagined. Faster and more reliable transatlantic passage led to growing European-American connections along a number of dimensions: commercial ties, immigration and tourism, and information flows. These developments were among the most important catalysts that ushered in the era of modern globalization.

STEAMSHIP TECHNOLOGY

Steamships depended on a reliable steam engine, which originated with Thomas Newcomen's (1664–1729) early eighteenth-century design. Practically all the early attempts at steam engines were based on his original design, even though the Newcomen engine itself was not easily adapted to marine propulsion (it was originally designed to pump water out of mining shafts). Jonathan Hulls (1699–1758) was the first to think of mounting a Newcomen engine on a ship. Hulls's pioneering efforts at early steam navigation were important enough that the Cunard Company would later hang his portrait in a stateroom aboard the *Queen Mary* (Rowland 1970).

James Watt (1736–1819) made critical improvements to the steam engine in 1763. Watt designed a separate condenser that condensed steam without cooling the cylinder. The result was an impressive increase in the efficiency of the engine, since less steam would be required to do the same work (Rowland 1970).

The innovations in steam engines and applications to marine vessels soon migrated to America. Indeed, in 1819 an American vessel was the first steamship to cross the Atlantic, although most of that trip was actually made under sail since the steam engines were designed to supplement wind power. The first British-built steamboat to make a long-duration voyage on the open ocean was the *Rising Star*, which sailed from England to Chile in 1821 (Rowland 1970). Perhaps the most noticeable advance in steamship technology came with the first truly oceangoing steam vessel in Britain, the *Great Western*, which completed its maiden voyage in 1838. This vessel had berths for 120 first-class passengers and twenty second-class passengers and, with a crew of sixty, the ship could accommodate a total of three hundred people (Rowland 1970). While the *Great Western* was a remarkable improvement over sailing vessels, halving the time of the average sailing ship, this time itself would be cut in half over the next fifty years (Tyler 1972).

THE SHIFT FROM SAIL TO STEAM POWER: IMPACTS ON TRAVEL TIME AND FARES

The shift from sail- to steam-powered vessels occurred gradually, first with mail transportation in the 1840s and then finally to passenger and freight traffic during the 1870s and 1880s. By the time Mark Twain (1835–1910) published *Innocents Abroad*, his 1867 chronicle of the vagaries of travel aboard a sailing vessel to Europe, transatlantic shipping had already largely begun to rely on steam-powered vessels. Steamships provided regular, predictable service and eventually undercut fares offered by sailing vessels, although they initially competed primarily by improving quality: more spacious and comfortable accommodations and better food, for example.

The North Atlantic passenger shipping lines offered different classes of travel: first and second class, as well as steerage class, sometimes known as emigrant class or third class. Fares varied according to the size, vintage, and quality of ships within each shipping line, season, and even day of the week. While fares fluctuated from year to year, the average cost of travel declined through the 1880s, but rose again at the turn of the century. By the 1870s, steamships had taken over the previous passenger traffic on sailing ships due to improvements in speed, safety, and cost (Dupont, Keeling, and Weiss 2012, 13). Whatever impact the transition from sail to steam power may have had on passenger fares, it certainly resulted in shorter and more predictable crossings, which brought considerable benefits. Perhaps the most important benefit was time-saving and the corresponding reduction in the overall cost of passage. While the direct costs of passage for the typical European migrant in the late nineteenth century should not be overstated—the average thirty dollar steerage fare on steamships between Europe and the United States in the period from 1900 to 1914 would have required roughly three weeks of work for a low-skilled worker—the reduction in opportunity costs compared to a lengthy voyage by sailing vessel was considerable.

GROWING COMMERCIAL TIES

Trade between Europe and America had been occurring ever since the British settlement at Jamestown in 1607; however, the high costs of transportation were an obvious impediment. These costs fell as the reliability and duration of the voyage improved in the nineteenth century. To provide just one measure of the cost of the North Atlantic voyage, consider that the length of an average trip by sailing vessel ranged anywhere from four to eight weeks, depending on the speed and direction of the wind (Keeling 2012, 9). The reliable power provided by steam engines lowered the costs of transportation and helped to more fully integrate the North Atlantic economy. These changes led to stronger commercial ties that were beneficial to both the United States and its European trading partners. By 1900, the business of transatlantic migration generated $20 million in revenues (Keeling 2012, 1), but the broader impact on commerce was much more substantial.

IMMIGRATION AND TOURISM

One of the transportation sector's most pivotal roles in world history was to facilitate the massive North Atlantic migration of the nineteenth century. Between 1870 and 1914, twenty-two million Europeans migrated to the United States, nearly all of them travelling via steamship and entering at one of four American ports. It was also during the late nineteenth century that leisure travel began in earnest. While only a small fraction of Americans actually made the trip to Europe, there was a steady increase in the number of people who did so. According to Brandon Dupont, Alka Gandhi, and Thomas Weiss, "overseas travel by Americans rose at an average annual

rate of around 5 percent per year from 1820 to 2000, a rate that exceeded the growth of population or GDP by a noticeable amount" (2012, 145). They point out, however, that prior to World War II (1939–1945), most of that increase reflected population growth and that the share of the American population going overseas never exceeded 0.5 percent (for some perspective, the share was only 8.9 percent in 2000). Nevertheless, by the late nineteenth century, most of those who did make the trip travelled aboard a steamship. Indeed, even as late as the 1950s, the vast majority of Americans who travelled to Europe still did so aboard a steamship.

SEE ALSO *Atlantic Ocean; Grand Tour*

BIBLIOGRAPHY

Dupont, Brandon, Alka Gandhi, and Thomas Weiss. "The Long-Term Rise in Overseas Travel by Americans, 1820–2000." *Economic History Review* 65, 1 (2012): 144–167.

Dupont, Brandon, Drew Keeling, and Thomas Weiss. "Passenger Fares for Overseas Travel in the 19th and 20th Centuries." Working paper prepared for the Annual Meeting of the Economic History Association, Vancouver, BC, Canada, September 21–23, 2012.

Feys, Torsten. "The Battle for Migrants: The Evolution from Port to Company Competition, 1840–1914." In *Maritime Transport and Migration: The Connections between Maritime and Migration Networks*, edited by Torsten Feys, Lewis R. Fischer, Stéphane Hoste, and Stephan Vanfraechem, 27–47. St. John's, NL: International Maritime Economic History Association, 2007.

Keeling, Drew. *The Business of Transatlantic Migration between Europe and the United States, 1900–1914.* Zurich, Switzerland: Chronos, 2012.

Kennedy, John. *The History of Steam Navigation.* London: Birchall, 1903.

Rowland, K. T. *Steam at Sea: A History of Steam Navigation.* Newton Abbot, UK: David and Charles, 1970.

Tyler, David B. *Steam Conquers the Atlantic.* New York: Arno Press, 1972.

Brandon Dupont
Associate Professor of Economics
Western Washington University

STEIN, GERTRUDE

SEE *Lost Generation.*

STONEWALL RIOTS

The Stonewall riots were a series of demonstrations that erupted in June 1969 in protest of police raids on a Greenwich Village gay bar. The riots marked a major turning point in the movement for lesbian, gay, bisexual, and transgender (LGBT) equality in the United States and abroad.

After a period of relative freedom during World War II (1939–1945), LGBT Americans faced intensifying oppression in the early Cold War era. The medical profession defined homosexuality as a mental illness. Convinced that gays were mentally unstable and easily targeted for blackmail, the US government declared them "security risks," and thousands of gay men and women were forced out of civil service jobs and the armed forces. Police raids on parks, bars, clubs, and other spaces frequented by homosexuals were commonplace.

To escape such persecution, many LGBT Americans flocked to urban enclaves like New York's Greenwich Village. Long a bastion for artists, writers, activists, and the unconventional, the Village was home to many gay bars, most of which were run by organized crime. Although the clubs were often grungy and served overpriced, watered-down drinks, they offered gays a place to congregate.

Located at 51-53 Christopher Street, the Stonewall Inn was one of the most popular of such establishments. Converted to a gay bar by the Genovese family in 1966, it had poor lighting, no running water, and no fire exits. But it was the only gay bar in New York that allowed dancing, and it drew a racially mixed crowd that included drag queens and homeless gay youth. Because the bar did not have a liquor license, its mobster owners secretly paid off the police. Although raids were frequent, police usually tipped off the owners and came early in the evening on weeknights when crowds were small. Usually as soon as the police showed up, the lights were turned on to alert patrons. People then produced identification and were let go or scattered in all directions to avoid being arrested.

An early morning raid on the Stonewall on June 28, 1969, met dramatically different results. Many patrons refused to cooperate and stood their ground rather than flee. After police decided to take people in and called for paddy wagons, an angry crowd gathered outside the bar and began throwing pennies, beer bottles, rocks, and other items. As police barricaded themselves in the bar, some rioters threw trash cans through the windows, used an uprooted parking meter as a battering ram, and set things on fire. Others taunted police with campy songs and chorus line dances. After years of being persecuted, punished, and treated as criminals, gays had finally united and struck back. With the situation outside escalating, the police inside the bar began to destroy everything inside the Stonewall. When members of the riot control unit arrived, they fought with demonstrators for several hours.

The next day, the exhausted rioters mobilized once more, and activists produced five thousand leaflets that attacked the relationship among the mafia, the bars, and the NYPD. The Stonewall Inn reopened that evening in a silent protest against the police's brutality the night before, and people made it clear that they were not afraid. Several more clashes erupted between police and demonstrators over the next six days, and the events received wide media coverage.

The Stonewall riots had a profound and enduring impact. No longer cowed by the threat of exposure and inspired by the civil rights and antiwar movements of the era, gays soon formed activist groups and launched LGBT newspapers across the United States, Great Britain, Holland, France, Belgium, West Germany, Argentina, Canada, New Zealand, and Australia. In many places, these organizing efforts resulted in the passage of nondiscrimination protections, the repeal of sodomy laws, and the end of police harassment. In 1973, the American Psychiatric Association removed homosexuality from its list of mental illnesses.

On June 28, 1970, gay rights marches marking the anniversary of the Stonewall protests were held in New York, Los Angeles, and Chicago. Within two years, Boston, Dallas, Milwaukee, Paris, West Berlin, and Stockholm also organized annual gay pride events. Such celebrations are now held all over the world in communities both large and small. In 1994, 1.1 million people from dozens of nations participated in the Stonewall 25 march in front of the headquarters of the United Nations in New York. Five years later, the US Department of the Interior made the site of the Stonewall Inn a National Historic Landmark, the first such designation marking an event of major significance in LGBT history.

SEE ALSO *Human Rights*

BIBLIOGRAPHY

Carter, David. *Stonewall: The Riots That Sparked the Gay Revolution*. New York: St. Martin's Press, 2004.

Duberman, Martin B. *Stonewall*. New York: Dutton, 1993.

Laura Belmonte
Professor of History
Oklahoma State University

STRATEGIC AIR COMMAND

SEE *Air Force, US.*

STRATEGIC ARMS LIMITATION TALKS (SALT I AND SALT II)

More than an agreement on the reduction of arms and a step toward nuclear disarmament, the Strategic Arms Limitation Talks (SALT) I and II were aimed at curbing the Soviet-American arms race, and more significantly, at maintaining the strategic balance between the two superpowers. The talks took place between 1969 and 1979, and resulted in one agreement (SALT I), signed in May 1972, followed by SALT II, negotiated from 1972 to 1979, ending in a treaty that was never ratified.

BACKGROUND TO THE TALKS

The incentive for SALT was the development of antiballistic missiles (ABMs) by the Soviet Union and the United States during the 1960s. The Lyndon B. Johnson (1908–1973) administration, and mainly Secretary of Defense Robert McNamara (1916–2009), doubted the value of the ABM system, arguing that it would not be able to intercept incoming ballistic nuclear missiles in a way that would significantly reduce the damage caused by such missiles. The Soviets gradually came to the same conclusion, and they reached out to the United States with an offer to discuss an agreement to mutually ban or limit the deployment of ABM systems. The talks were scheduled to commence in the summer of 1968, but they were derailed by the Soviet Union's invasion of Czechoslovakia in August. Negotiations resumed after President Richard Nixon (1913–1994) assumed office in 1969.

Under the slogan "negotiations, not confrontation," Nixon, a hard-core cold warrior, sought to improve relations with the Soviet Union, a policy that became known as *détente*. The negotiations to limit strategic arms were part of this policy. For the Americans, the dominant aspect of the talks was the United States' loss of strategic superiority over the Soviet Union, a result of decisions by previous administrations, mainly Johnson's, to stop building intercontinental ballistic missiles (ICBMs). The Soviets, meanwhile, had launched a massive arms-buildup project that brought them to strategic parity with the United States.

Nixon and his national security adviser, Henry Kissinger, concluded that SALT would be the best way to stop the Soviet buildup of strategic arms. Thus, they insisted that SALT be about not only ABMs, as the Soviets wanted, but also offensive strategic arms. The Soviets agreed, especially after Nixon won congressional approval for the American ABM system, known as Safeguard. Nixon needed the Safeguard program as a bargaining chip. He asked Congress to appropriate funds for the buildup of antiballistic defense missiles, so as to pressure the Soviet Union to negotiate an agreement limiting antiballistic and offensive ballistic systems. After a bitter struggle in Congress, the Safeguard program was approved by one vote.

SALT I

The SALT I negotiations took place on two tracks. The official talks began in November 1969 and were conducted by American and Soviet delegations meeting in Vienna and Helsinki. However, the delegations' talks were secondary. The primary negotiations took place clandestinely through a secret backchannel established between Anatoly Dobrynin (1919–2010), the Soviet ambassador to the United States, and Henry Kissinger (b. 1923), national security advisor to the Nixon administration and later secretary of state. It was through this backchannel that the critical issues and arguments were resolved.

Negotiations over the ABM systems evolved over two issues: the number of permitted systems and their locations. The major issue concerning offensive ballistic missiles was the Soviet demand to include in the agreement American forward bases in Europe, which the Soviets considered equivalent to their offensive ballistic missiles. After nearly three years of negotiations, Nixon and Soviet leader Leonid Brezhnev (1906–1982) signed the agreement, SALT I, in May 1972 in Moscow.

SALT I comprised two elements. The first was a formal agreement to limit the deployment of ABMs to two sites in either country, one around the national command authority (NCA), which meant the national capitols, and another around an ICBM site. The United States had already deployed ABM systems around ICBM sites, while the Soviets deployed ABM systems around Moscow. That meant that each country was permitted to add one ABM system. Both countries gave up those additions during the negotiations on SALT II.

The second element was an interim agreement that would be in force for five years. It froze the construction of ICBMs for deployment on both land and sea platforms. Documents that were not disclosed to the public contained exact numbers of launch vehicles that would be permitted. The United States could have no more than 710 submarine-launched ballistic missiles (SLBMs) on forty-four submarines, while the Soviet Union was permitted no more than 950 SLBMs on sixty-two submarines. The agreements would be monitored and verified, with each side committed to not interfering with the other's means of verification.

Only the agreement limiting ABMs was a formal treaty, requiring Senate ratification. Because the interim agreement was not a formal treaty, the president was only required to notify Congress about it.

SALT II

While the process of ratification was underway, the Soviet Union and the United States continued to discuss limits for offensive strategic weapons. The format of the negotiations remained the same as SALT I: official American and Soviet delegations discussed the treaty in

Geneva, while Kissinger and Dobrynin ran the real negotiations in Washington, DC.

Kissinger, who negotiated under the heavy cloud of the Watergate scandal, had to reconcile the demands of opponents of SALT I who wanted an agreement that would give both sides an equal number of strategic ballistic missiles. SALT I gave a quantitative advantage to the Soviets as compensation for the Americans' forward base system in Europe.

Another matter of controversy, both within the administration and between the Soviet Union and the United States, concerned multiple independently targetable reentry vehicles (MIRVs), a new type of ballistic missile system with multiple warheads, each capable of being directed toward a specific target. The United States had an advantage in technology and number of MIRVs, and it wished to prevent the Soviet Union from building up its supply of MIRVs. Lengthy negotiations over this issue concluded with the Vladivostok agreement, signed by Brezhnev and Nixon's successor, President Gerald Ford (1913–2006), in November 1974. The two agreed that the basis for SALT II would be 2,400 ICBMs for each side by 1985, and 1,320 MIRV missiles for each side.

At this point, all that remained was sorting out the technical details, but two major problems emerged, which stalled negotiations for years. The first was US development of guided cruise missiles. The Soviets wanted to include such missiles within the agreement along with ballistic missiles, while the Pentagon strongly objected. The second problem was the development of a new Soviet bomber, known as Backfire. The Pentagon argued that the new bomber had intercontinental capabilities, and thus should be included in the agreement, while the Soviets denied that it had such capabilities and refused to include it. The result was a stalemate that continued after the election of President Jimmy Carter in 1976.

A breakthrough occurred in 1978 when Secretary of State Cyrus Vance (1917–2002) and his Russian counterpart, Andrey Gromyko (1909–1989), settled on an agreement that would be based on the earlier Vladivostok agreement. The Backfire bomber would not be part of the agreement, with the Soviets committing in writing to not equip the bomber with intercontinental capabilities. The United States, however, agreed to include limits on cruise missiles.

Brezhnev and Carter signed the SALT II Treaty in Vienna on June 18, 1979. It included a three-year protocol to defer discussions over certain strategic arms, such as mobile ICBMs, until the next round of talks, as part of a statement of principles outlining the topics to be discussed in SALT III. Shortly after the signing ceremony, Carter sent the treaty to the Senate for ratification. The ratification process moved forward slowly, until it was

ended abruptly with the Soviet invasion of Afghanistan in December 1979. A month later, President Carter asked the Senate to terminate the ratification process. With that, the process that started in the late 1960s came to an end. Negotiations aimed at curbing the strategic arms race between the United States and the Soviet Union would continue several years later, but under a different name and different concept.

SEE ALSO *Cold War; Détente; Deterrence; Intercontinental Ballistic Missiles; Mutual Assured Destruction (MAD); Nuclear Weapons*

BIBLIOGRAPHY

Brzezinski, Zbigniew. *Power and Principle: Memoirs of the National Security Adviser, 1977–1981.* New York: Farrar, Straus, Giroux, 1983.

Carter, Jimmy. *Keeping Faith: Memoirs of a President.* New York: Bantam, 1982.

Dallek, Robert. *Nixon and Kissinger: Partners in Power.* New York: Harper Collins, 2007.

Dobrynin, Anatoly. *In Confidence: Moscow's Ambassador to America's Six Cold War Presidents (1962–1986).* New York: Random House, 1995.

Ford, Gerald R. *A Time to Heal: The Autobiography of Gerald R. Ford.* New York: Harper and Row, 1979.

Garthoff, Raymond L. *Détente and Confrontation: American-Soviet Relations from Nixon to Reagan.* Rev. ed. Washington, DC: Brookings Institute, 1994.

Geyer, David C., and Douglas E. Selvage, eds. *Soviet-American Relations: The Détente Years, 1969–1972.* Washington, DC: GPO, 2007.

Haldeman, H. R. *The Haldeman Diaries: Inside the Nixon White House.* The Complete Multimedia Edition. Santa Monica, CA: Sony Electronic, 1994.

Johnson, U. Alexis, with Jeff O. McAllister. *The Right Hand of Power.* Englewood Cliffs, NJ: Prentice-Hall, 1984.

Kissinger, Henry. *White House Years.* Boston: Little, Brown, 1979.

Kissinger, Henry. *Years of Upheaval.* Boston: Little, Brown, 1982.

Murray, Lori E. "SALT I and Congress: Building Consensus for Nuclear Arms Control." PhD diss., John Hopkins University, 1990.

Nixon, Richard. *RN: The memoirs of Richard Nixon.* New York: Grosset and Dunlap, 1978.

Rumsfeld, Donald. *Known and Unknown: A Memoir.* New York: Sentinel, 2011.

Savel'yev, Alexkadr' G., and Nikolay N. Detinov. *The Big Five: Arms Control Decision-Making in the Soviet Union.* Translated by Dmitriy Trenin. Westport, CT: Praeger, 1995.

Smith, Gerard C. *Doubletalk: The Story of the First Strategic Arms Limitation Talks.* Garden City, NY: Doubleday, 1980.

Tal, David. "Negotiations and Confrontation: The Making of US SALT Policy, 1969–1979." Manuscript, 2015.

Vance, Cyrus. *Hard Choices.* New York: Simon and Schuster, 1983.

Zubok, Vladislav M. *A Failed Empire: The Soviet Union in the Cold War from Stalin to Gorbachev.* Chapel Hill: University of North Carolina Press, 2007.

David Tal
Yossi Harel Chair in Israel Studies, Department of History
University of Sussex

STRATEGIC DEFENSE INITIATIVE (STAR WARS)

On the evening of March 23, 1983, twenty-five minutes into a nationwide radio and television address on defense and national security, President Ronald Reagan (1911–2004) offered a new vision of strategic defense for the United States:

> Let me share with you a vision of the future which offers hope. It is that we embark on a program to counter the awesome Soviet missile threat with measures that are defensive. Let us turn to the very strengths in technology that spawned our great industrial base and that have given us the quality of life we enjoy today. What if free people could live secure in the knowledge that their security did not rest upon the threat of instant U.S. retaliation to deter a Soviet attack, that we could intercept and destroy strategic ballistic missiles before they reached our own soil and that of our allies?

Although only a short section of the wider address, Reagan's announcement of what would subsequently be termed the *Strategic Defense Initiative* (SDI) profoundly recast the terms of the Cold War nuclear standoff. It was a vision that, if fulfilled, he claimed, would not only radically alter America's relations with the Soviet Union, but which also held "the promise of changing the course of human history."

Reagan's own characterization of SDI explained the rationale with breathless simplicity. For too long, he argued, US engagement with the Soviet Union had rested upon a perilous balance of terror and a logic of deterrence predicated on the US and Soviet capacity to assure annihilation of their opponent in the event of a nuclear first strike, a strategy known as *mutual assured destruction*. The unveiling of SDI came amidst increasing domestic concerns over levels of US defense spending and the rise of the "Nuclear Freeze" campaign, a mass movement of peace groups and other civil society organizations that argued that the only way to reduce the risk of US-Soviet nuclear conflict was to stop testing, production, and deployment of nuclear weapons. Reagan rejected both these lines of criticism (Bjork 1992, 14–15). Instead, he

argued in his 1983 address that America had both the investment capacity and the technological capabilities to "break out of a future that relies solely on offensive retaliation."

The initiative envisaged that such technological capabilities would include outer-space and ground-based laser weapons that would be used to shoot down incoming intercontinental ballistic missiles (ICBMs) midflight, as well as electromagnetic rail guns and intercept missiles launched from the ground. The idea of lasers in space almost immediately led to SDI being labeled "Star Wars" (in reference to George Lucas's 1977 space opera) in the media and popular imagination.

The concept of technological systems that could intercept and destroy nuclear weapons before they reached the United States was not in itself novel, even if it achieved an unprecedented level of prominence and technological ambition during the Reagan era (Reiss 1992, 21–41; Peoples 2010, 78–80). From the advent of nuclear weapons, the United States had experimented with various technologies of this kind, as had the Soviet Union. But both states, under the Anti-Ballistic Missile (ABM) Treaty, signed in 1972, had agreed to strictly limit their pursuit and deployment of such systems. The logic behind such restraint was that such systems would undermine the basic principle of nuclear deterrence: if one side could not be entirely confident of completely destroying the other with its offensive nuclear capabilities, then the calculus of nuclear planning would be radically destabilized.

For that reason, the Soviet Union, in particular, expressed grave concern about the SDI proposal, and it became a major issue of contention between the two superpowers. This was particularly evident at the 1986 Reykjavík summit (see FitzGerald 2000, 347–365), where President Reagan characterized SDI as "America's security guarantee," to be preserved even if both sides agreed to cuts in their offensive nuclear forces. Soviet general secretary Mikhail Gorbachev replied that, to the contrary, "SDI has become an obstacle to ending the arms race" (1986, 65). Ultimately, the ambitious nature and scale of the SDI vision became victim to budget cuts later in the 1980s, and the revolutionary suite of technologies never materialized (Reiss 1992, 179). The vision of strategic defense—of technologies capable of intercepting ICBMs—has, however, continued to persist in the post–Cold War era in programs such as "National Missile Defense" in the 1990s and "Ballistic Missile Defense" in the 2000s (see Peoples 2010).

SEE ALSO *Cold War; Intercontinental Ballistic Missiles; Nuclear Weapons; Reagan, Ronald Wilson*

BIBLIOGRAPHY

Bjork, Rebecca S. *The Strategic Defense Initiative: Symbolic Containment of the Nuclear Threat.* Albany: State University of New York Press, 1992.

FitzGerald, Frances. *Way Out There in the Blue: Reagan, Star Wars, and the End of the Cold War.* New York: Simon and Schuster, 2000.

Gorbachev, Mikhail S. *Speeches and Writings.* Oxford, UK: Pergamon, 1986.

Peoples, Columba. *Justifying Ballistic Missile Defence: Technology, Security, and Culture.* Cambridge: Cambridge University Press, 2010.

Reagan, Ronald. Address to the Nation on Defense and National Security. March 23, 1983. In *Public Papers of the Presidents, Ronald Reagan, 1983.* Washington, DC: US Government Printing Office, 1984. http://www.reagan.utexas.edu/archives/speeches/1983/32383d.htm

Reagan, Ronald. Address to the Nation on the Meetings with Soviet General Secretary Gorbachev in Iceland. October 13, 1986. In *Public Papers of the Presidents, Ronald Reagan, 1986.* Washington, DC: US Government Printing Office, 1989. http://www.reagan.utexas.edu/archives/speeches/1986/101386a.htm

Reiss, Edward. *The Strategic Defense Initiative.* Cambridge: Cambridge University Press, 1992.

Columba Peoples
Senior Lecturer in International Relations
School of Sociology, Politics, and International Studies
University of Bristol, United Kingdom

STUDENT NONVIOLENT COORDINATING COMMITTEE (SNCC)

The Student Nonviolent Coordinating Committee (SNCC) was founded April 16–18, 1960, during the Southwide Student Leadership Conference on Nonviolent Resistance to Segregation at Shaw University in Raleigh, North Carolina. Ella Baker (1903–1986), a longtime activist who cut her teeth with the National Association for the Advancement of Colored People (NAACP) and the Southern Christian Leadership Conference (SCLC), organized the gathering in an effort to bring southern youth leaders together to create an autonomous student-led organization to support indigenous black organizing efforts to overturn Jim Crow segregation and political disenfranchisement.

SNCC quickly became the most ubiquitous student organization working to secure voting rights and desegregate public space in the US South. In addition to its local efforts, SNCC took a concerted interest in international affairs, particularly as they pertained to anticolonial and nationalist movements on the African continent. From its inception, SNCC supported the "African struggle" and worked closely with continental African students attending US colleges and universities to develop bonds of solidarity and cultivate mutual understanding.

SNCC organizers came of age in the 1950s when the black press featured regular articles on anticolonial struggles in Africa and Asia. Just three weeks before its founding, SNCC members witnessed the Sharpeville massacre in South Africa, in which more than two hundred Africans were killed or wounded for their participation in the Defiance Campaigns. This event, along with others, spurred SNCC to adopt the African National Congress's organizing slogan, "One Man, One Vote," as its own.

In 1964, singer, actor, and longtime black freedom movement activist Harry Belafonte (b. 1927) organized a trip to Guinea, West Africa, for some of SNCC's core leadership. Guinean president Ahmed Sékou Touré (1922–1984) treated the SNCC group like foreign dignitaries and exposed them to an African country at the forefront of postcolonial nation-building. Following the Guinea trip, several members went on to Liberia, Ghana, Zambia, and Egypt. This trip put SNCC activists in direct conversation with African American expatriates and national liberation movements fighting imperialism and colonialism. Africa proved to be a transformative experience for SNCC members because it provided a glimpse into the complex geopolitical terrain of the continent and the Third World in general.

By 1965, SNCC became firmly ensconced within the New Left, "an amorphous body of young activists seeking new ideological alternatives to conventional liberalism" (Carson 1981, 175). SNCC's organizing efforts inspired the Black Panther Party for Self-Defense (BPP), the Berkeley Free Speech Movement, and the Students for a Democratic Society (SDS), among others. Individually, many SNCC activists were opposed to the Vietnam War (1954–1975); however, the organization did not make opposition to the war official policy until January 1966, following the death of Sammy Younge (1944–1966). Younge, a navy veteran, worked on SNCC initiatives in Mississippi and Alabama and was shot at a gas station while attempting to use a segregated bathroom. Outraged by the irony and hypocrisy of a military veteran losing his life to segregation, SNCC's Executive Committee drafted an antiwar policy that opposed the war and outlined the inextricable linkages between militarism and the socioeconomic challenges facing the larger Third World.

As its opposition to the Vietnam War intensified, SNCC increasingly began to search for political and ideological alternatives in the Third World. By 1966, SNCC led the call for Black Power, and though its leadership began to splinter ideologically, the organization took positions against apartheid in South Africa and drafted a statement in support of Palestinians during the Arab-Israeli conflict in 1967. Moreover, in the same year, SNCC leader Stokely Carmichael (1941–1998) embarked on an unsanctioned international speaking tour to Europe, Latin America, Africa, and Asia. In London, he attended the Congress on the Dialectics of Liberation. He then went on to Havana, Cuba, where he toured the Sierra Maestres with Fidel Castro (b. 1926) to the chagrin of the US State Department. Carmichael would stay on in Havana and attend the Organization of Latin American Solidarity (OLAS), along with official SNCC delegates invited to the meeting.

Drawing inspiration from Che Guevara's (1928–1967) charge to create "many Vietnams," Carmichael called for the internationalization of the black freedom movement and insisted that the world recognize that "Detroit and New York [were] also Vietnam" (*New York Times* 1967, 10). Carmichael's rhetorical genius made him an iconic international political figure almost overnight. His global celebrity carried him to Conakry, Guinea, where he met President Ahmed Sékou Touré and the deposed Ghanaian president Kwame Nkrumah (1909–1972), two avid proponents of Pan-Africanism.

SNCC would go on to develop fledgling political alliances with the Black Panther Party for Self-Defense and other groups. As SNCC drifted from its early roots in local organizing, some of its members began a variety of initiatives that placed greater emphasis on international solidarity and Pan-Africanism. SNCC leader James Forman (1928–2005) intensified antiapartheid initiatives at the United Nations, while Irving Davis (1937–1981) created the Pan-African Skills Project to send skilled African Americans to postcolonial African nations to assist in national development. SNCC organizers in Washington, DC, went on to create the Center for Black Education and the Drum and Spear Press and to spearhead the organization of the Sixth Pan-African Congress in 1974.

SEE ALSO *Black Power Movement; Cold War: Race and the Cold War; Human Rights; King, Martin Luther, Jr.; Malcolm X; New Left; Pan-Africanism*

BIBLIOGRAPHY

Carmichael, Stokely, with Ekwueme Michael Thelwell. *Ready for Revolution: The Life and Struggles of Stokely Carmichael (Kwame Ture).* New York: Scribner, 2003.

Carson, Clayborne. *In Struggle: SNCC and the Black Awakening of the 1960s.* Cambridge, MA: Harvard University Press, 1981.

"Carmichael Urges a 'Vietnam' in U.S." *New York Times* (July 28, 1967): 10.

Joseph, Peniel E. *Waiting 'til the Midnight Hour: A Narrative History of Black Power in America.* New York: Holt, 2006.

Lewis, John, with Michael D'Orso. *Walking with the Wind: A Memoir of the Movement.* New York: Simon and Schuster, 1998.

Ransby, Barbara. *Ella Baker and the Black Freedom Movement: A Radical Democratic Vision.* Chapel Hill: University of North Carolina Press, 2003.

Wilkins, Fanon Che. "The Making of Black Internationalists: SNCC and Africa before the Launching of Black Power, 1960–1965." *Journal of African American History* 92, 4 (2007): 468–490.

Wilkins, Fanon Che, "'A Line of Steel': The Organization of the Sixth Pan-African Congress and the Struggle for International Black Power, 1969–1974." In *The Hidden 1970s: Histories of Radicalism,* edited by Dan Berger, 97–114. New Brunswick, NJ: Rutgers University Press, 2010.

Fanon Che Wilkins
Associate Professor of African American History and Culture Graduate School of Global Studies, Doshisha University

STUDENT VOLUNTEER MOVEMENT FOR FOREIGN MISSIONS

From the 1890s through the mid-1930s, the Student Volunteer Movement for Foreign Missions (SVM) was the primary missionary recruiting organization for the mainline Protestant denominations in the United States. In 1890, there were only 934 American Protestant missionaries in the world. Due to the efforts of the SVM and the general heightening of interest in Protestant missions in this period, the number of missionaries rose to about five thousand by 1900, nine thousand by 1915, and fourteen thousand by 1930.

ORIGINS OF THE SVM

The SVM emerged at a conference for college students held in the summer of 1886 at the Mount Hermon School for Boys in western Massachusetts. The school was founded by Dwight L. Moody (1837–1899), the most famous Protestant evangelist of the era. Moody, who presided over the meetings, allowed a number of mission speakers to address the 251 students who came from eighty-nine colleges and universities. When one hundred conferees pledged to become foreign missionaries, the "Mount Hermon One Hundred" became the inspiration for the movement. Present at the conference was the Reverend Dr. Arthur T. Pierson (1837–1911), who probably coined the expression that would become the "watchword" of the movement: "The evangelization of the world in this generation."

The Mount Hermon conference had been organized by Luther D. Wishard (1854–1925) and Charles Kellogg Ober (1856–1948), secretaries of the intercollegiate Young Men's Christian Association (YMCA), which had associations in 225 American colleges, universities, and seminaries. Two of the Mount Hermon One Hundred, Robert P. Wilder (1863–1938) and John N. Forman (1863–1917), visited 162 of the collegiate YMCAs during the 1886–1887 academic year and succeeded in persuading 2,106 to join the movement and pledge to serve as foreign missionaries. YMCA leaders officially launched the SVM on December 6, 1888, appointing an executive committee to oversee the work that was chaired by John R. Mott (1865–1955). A recent graduate of Cornell University and one of the original Mount Hermon One Hundred, Mott would lead the SVM until 1920.

The SVM promoted missions among college students in a variety of ways. Most importantly, it appointed traveling secretaries to visit institutions of higher learning to urge students to sign the SVM missionary pledge card and form SVM bands. Beginning in 1891, the SVM held the first of its quadrennial conventions, large student gatherings where mission speakers made their appeals to interested listeners. And the SVM published journals, tracts, and a small library of books that student volunteers could study in preparation for missionary careers. By 1920, 33,726 young people had volunteered, about a quarter of whom became missionaries.

THE LEADERSHIP OF JOHN R. MOTT

During the SVM's first three decades, Mott not only chaired the Executive Committee but presided over all the quadrennial conventions and was the organization's leading spokesman. He wrote a number of books on mission, including *The Evangelization of the World in This Generation* (1901), the definitive defense of the organization's watchword. Mott believed that Western prestige and technological advances had made it possible for the gospel to be taken to all the nations in the world in a single generation, a providential opportunity that no previous generation had enjoyed. Because it was possible, he argued, it therefore was a Christian responsibility. Sidestepping possible theological or biblical pitfalls—such as the postmillennial-premillennial debate then raging in Protestant America—the watchword was a simple statement of the possible, a bold declaration of purpose, and a dramatic summons to duty.

Following the establishment of the World Student Christian Federation (WSCF) in 1895 at Vadstena, Sweden, Mott began a twenty-month world tour to enlist the various Christian collegiate organizations to join the federation, believing that these student organizations could become "strategic points" for world evangelization. On this tour, he visited twenty-two countries. Beginning in France, he traveled east through the Middle East, South Asia, Australasia, and East Asia, ending in Japan. He succeeded in incorporating into the WSCF twelve national Christian student organizations, most of whom had their own SVMs. As the leading missionary statesman of his generation, Mott organized and presided over the World Missionary Conference of Edinburgh 1910, which promoted greater cooperation among mission organizations. Later, he would become a leader in the ecumenical movement and, in 1946, receive the Nobel Peace Prize for his work in helping to found the World Council of Churches.

THE SVM AND THE SOCIAL GOSPEL

Once recruited by the SVM, the student volunteers were to enlist as missionaries under the auspices of denominational mission organizations or independent missions. Though their success as evangelists and church planters can be seen in the existence today of churches throughout the Global South, their work as missionaries was not limited to this. Wanting to give physical manifestation to the idea of the kingdom of God, they also sought to transform societies through the introduction of economic development plans, new agricultural techniques, modern medical care, and—above all—education. They established primary and secondary schools as well as colleges as a way of improving low literacy rates and introducing Western values, science, and technology. Such institutions often taught the first generation of national leaders who led their countries in the postcolonial era.

One of the SVM's major recruiting arguments was the opportunity missionaries would have to challenge the "social evils" present in non-Christian lands. The objects of their reforming zeal included the continuance of slavery in Africa and the Middle East, cannibalism in places such as Australia and the Pacific Islands, and human sacrifices in the West Indies, Guinea, and Africa. Often highlighted were outrages against women: female infanticide in China, the *sati* (widow-burning) in India, female slavery and concubinage in Japan, plural marriages and the harem in Muslim lands, and the chattel-like treatment of women among many African ethnic groups. Although missionaries are sometimes accused of being the religious arm of colonialism because they benefited from the protection offered by Western colonial governments, they also often opposed the oppression and exploitation of nationals, using their access to authorities and media outlets to call attention to abuses.

INFLUENCE WITHIN THE UNITED STATES

While the influence of missionaries abroad is well recorded, their influence within the United States is less certain since opinion polls did not yet exist to assess it. What is certain is that, during their furloughs home, missionaries were the honored guests of their supporting churches. In an age when international travel was still difficult and often dangerous, returning missionaries traveled from church to church telling the story of their adventures abroad, displaying cultural artifacts, and giving magic lantern presentations. No doubt much of what they said confirmed popular stereotypes of benighted peoples abroad, but their presentations would also have provided factual information, broadened some cultural horizons, and occasionally pricked consciences about Western excesses abroad. Mott believed that missionaries played a mediating role in these years between East and West and constituted "the greatest force for the promotion of friendship, good-will, and brotherhood between races" (Parker 2008, 101). Returning missionaries may also have helped to wean American citizens from their reflexive isolationism to an acceptance of a more active role for the United States in international affairs.

In the SVM's heyday, the 1890s through mid-1920s, it was a crucial organization in the launching and sustaining of modern Protestant missions in the United States. Its watchword inspired a generation of Protestant Americans and those from other nations as well. WSCF reports indicate that by 1920 SVM organizations in colleges around the world had recruited 11,079 missionaries. Of these, 8,140 were North American, 2,322 British, 181 Australasian, 161 South African, and 275 continental European. This does not include home missionaries or those who were inspired by the SVM but never became members.

A REFLECTION OF ITS TIME

The SVM, as a student organization, readily reflected the shifting cultural themes of its time. In the 1890s and early 1900s, it exuded the Victorian optimism, belief in progress, and pietism of the era. Later in the 1900s and 1910s, it took on the hues of the social gospel movement. In the post–World War I period, it suffered its first serious check as American culture, in the Jazz Age, became less demonstratively Protestant and more pluralistic and secular in perspective. The SVM reached the apogee of its success as a missionary recruiting organization in 1921 when 637 student volunteers reached the mission field. Over the course of the decade, however, the number of new SVM members dropped precipitously. With the Great Depression, which began in 1929, the churches' financial ability to support missionaries rapidly declined, and the SVM soon became moribund. Nevertheless, it soldiered on, reinventing itself through various merger and consolidation schemes, until it finally closed down in 1969.

SEE ALSO *Foreign Mission Movement*

BIBLIOGRAPHY

Hopkins, C. Howard. *John R. Mott, 1865–1955: A Biography.* Grand Rapids, MI: Eerdman's, 1979.

Mott, John R. *Strategic Points in the World's Conquest.* New York: Revell, 1897.

Mott, John R. *The Evangelization of the Word in This Generation.* New York: Student Volunteer Movement, 1900.

Mott, John R. *The Decisive Hour of Christian Missions.* New York: Student Volunteer Movement, 1910.

Parker, Michael. *The Kingdom of Character: The Student Volunteer Movement for Foreign Missions, 1886–1926.* Pasadena, CA: William Carey Library, 2008.

Michael Parker
Professor of Church History and Director of Graduate Studies
Evangelical Theological Seminary in Cairo

STUDENTS FOR A DEMOCRATIC SOCIETY (SDS)

Students for a Democratic Society (SDS) was the major organization of the left-wing student movement during the 1960s. It played a significant role in the broader New Left and was closely connected to other social movements of the era such as the Black Freedom Struggle and the anti–Vietnam War movement. It bore a more complicated relationship to the resurgent liberalism of the time, drawing from and contributing to it but also sharply criticizing it.

SDS was founded out of an earlier student socialist organization, Student League for Industrial Democracy, at a 1960 meeting at the University of Michigan. The organization sought to escape the sectarianism of the Old Left of the 1930s and 1940s and transcend debates over Communist Party politics that had split leftists of an older generation. In 1962, SDS met at Port Huron, Michigan, to draft an organizational manifesto. Twenty-two-year-old Tom Hayden (b. 1939) wrote the initial text. The result, the Port Huron Statement, was a classic statement of political idealism. The Port Huron Statement applauded the civil rights movement and criticized Cold War policies and the military-industrial complex. But its signature emphasis was on using politics to achieve richer and more meaningful lives. It viewed humans as "infinitely precious and possessed of unfulfilled capacities for reason, freedom, and love" (Flacks and Lichtenstein 2015, 241). The statement was also optimistic about the political impact that its members—students at elite universities—could have. Criticizing the lack of citizen input into government decisions, the statement called for a "participatory democracy" in which all individuals contributed to the decisions that affected their lives.

The Port Huron Statement was widely distributed and helped the fledgling SDS spread to many universities across the country. But it was the organization's early opposition to the Vietnam War that made it a truly mass organization. SDS organized the first national protest march against the war in Washington, DC, in March 1965. Addressing the audience, SDS president Paul Potter (1939–1984) famously asked, "What kind of system is it that justifies the United States … seizing the destinies of the Vietnamese people and using them callously for its own purposes?" (Miller 1987, 232). Potter and SDS members saw the war as symptomatic of an unjust political system that, instead of embracing its stated democratic values, projected American power abroad in the name of anticommunism and tolerated poverty and racism at home.

SDS's loose organizational structure meant that its membership and activities varied considerably from branch to branch. Its reach was far from universal. In fact, there was no SDS branch at the most famous site of 1960s student activism, the University of California at Berkeley (despite the presence of a character from the Berkeley SDS in the 1994 film *Forrest Gump*). Nevertheless, in the mid-1960s, the organization spread widely throughout the nation to a broad range of universities.

SDS was riven by internal conflict by the end of the 1960s. Many SDS activists came to support increasingly radical tactics in response to the slow pace of domestic change and the continuance of the Vietnam War. Their militancy, as reflected in the 1968 Columbia student sit-in organized by SDS and the 1968 Democratic Party Convention protests in Chicago, was met with increasingly violent and repressive responses by the state, which in turn fed radicalization. In 1969, SDS split into three factions, the most famous being the Weather Underground, named after a line from a Bob Dylan song. Though small in numbers, the Weathermen won attention with their call to organize violent resistance to the US government. The Weathermen were quite tame by the standards of European groups such as the Red Army Faction; the only people they ever harmed were themselves when three Weathermen died after a bomb they were constructing unexpectedly exploded. Nevertheless, that the Weathermen descended from an organization designed to promote "participatory democracy" was an irony observed by many contemporaries.

For a time, it seemed that the implosion of SDS hardly mattered. Left-wing activism in much the spirit as the original SDS flourished at university campuses in the late 1960s and early 1970s. But when activism sharply declined in the mid-1970s, the absence of SDS created an institutional lack of continuity with 1960s activism for future generations of left-leaning student activists.

SEE ALSO *Human Rights; New Left; Vietnam War*

BIBLIOGRAPHY

Flacks, Richard, and Nelson Lichtenstein, eds. *The Port Huron Statement: Sources and Legacies of the New Left's Founding Manifesto.* Philadelphia: University of Pennsylvania Press, 2015.

Miller, James. *Democracy Is in the Streets: From Port Huron to the Siege of Chicago.* New York: Simon and Schuster, 1987.

Rossinow, Douglas C. *The Politics of Authenticity: Liberalism, Christianity, and the New Left in America.* New York: Columbia University Press, 1998.

Daniel Geary
Mark Pigott Assistant Professor of US History
Trinity College Dublin

SUFFRAGE

As the first established democratic republic among the world's nations, the United States was also a pioneer in the development of women's rights activism and ideas. Yet there was no mention of women in the 1789 Constitution. Those into whose hands the future of the young republic were to be placed were expected to be rational, educated, and independent of outside forces controlling their political choices. Women were, by definition, the essence of dependency.

EARLY WOMEN'S RIGHTS ACTIVISM

The first declaration in the English language that was explicitly devoted to women's rights appeared in *A Vindication of the Rights of Woman* (1792) by the English feminist Mary Wollstonecraft (1759–1797). Wollstonecraft insisted on women's equal capacity for rationality and education, but she did not yet address political rights. Nonetheless, her ideas were a crucial first step toward political empowerment. Forward-thinking American women read Wollstonecraft's *Vindication*. Philadelphia Quaker Elizabeth Drinker (1735–1807), for example, thought that the revolutionary Wollstonecraft "speaks my mind" (Kelley 2006, 163). Another Quaker, Lucretia Mott (1793–1880), shared her knowledge of Wollstonecraft with younger women under her tutelage, notably Elizabeth Cady Stanton (1815–1902).

Despite these early stirrings, women's rights ideas, demands, and activism only began to thrive in the 1830s and 1840s in the context of popular democratic impulses in both the United States and Europe. By 1840, property restrictions on voting in the United States were almost everywhere abolished. Although this dramatic expansion of America's enfranchised population went far beyond that of any other nation, women, free blacks, native people, and slaves continued to be excluded.

Chattel slavery especially remained the most egregious blot on the democratic reputation of the United States. Abolitionist activism in Great Britain, which concentrated on the transatlantic slave trade, eventually spread to the United States, where the institution of slavery flourished. In the 1830s, a small group of activists, white and black, male and female, demanded immediate rather than gradual abolition, with no compensation for slave holders and no deportation for former slaves. US abolitionism laid the basis for the birth of a genuine American women's rights movement by raising the issue of universal human equality, and by drawing women into public action on profound political and moral issues.

By the 1840s, the American abolitionist movement had shifted from moral invocations to political engagement, which greatly affected the prospects for women rights. In 1848, Cady Stanton joined with veteran abolitionist Mott to call a reform meeting dedicated exclusively to women's rights in Seneca Falls, New York, the first such meeting in the United States. The meeting passed a Declaration of Sentiments, which listed a wide range of grievances and demanded changes in women's condition, most controversially for women to enjoy "the sacred right of franchise." The 1848 women's rights convention in Seneca Falls coincided with related developments in Europe and was noted by sister activists in Great Britain, France, Germany, and elsewhere. A small international group of women's rights proponents, linked closely across national borders, carried the movement for the next two decades.

POST–CIVIL WAR FOCUS ON EQUAL FRANCHISE RIGHTS

In the 1860s, in the wake of the Civil War (1861–1865), the US women's rights movement moved decisively forward as it became newly focused on equal franchise rights enacted at the national level. After the ratification of the Fourteenth Amendment in 1868, any person born in the United States and under its jurisdiction was deemed to be a citizen, possessed of equal rights and privileges with all others. During the presidential election of 1872, numerous women, most famously Susan B. Anthony (1820–1906), cast votes on the grounds that the Fourteenth Amendment had made them national citizens. In 1874, the US Supreme Court ruled against this argument, contending that voting was a privilege bestowed from on high rather than a right claimed from below.

From this point on, white suffrage leaders made the case for women's voting rights in explicitly gendered rather than broadly universalist terms, arguing that the right to vote should not be denied to someone because she was a woman, rather than arguing that voting was a right held by all citizens. Meanwhile, as the white South ramped up its attacks on black people's freedoms, African American women began to claim and defend political rights for their people and for themselves. In the post–Civil War decades, the US woman suffrage movement developed along these segregated lines.

GROWTH IN WOMAN'S PARTICIPATION IN PUBLIC LIFE

Through the late nineteenth century, public life grew steadily and with it support for women's political rights. More women were able to receive a full college education. Women also became involved in—and leaders of—nationwide voluntary organizations. Finally, growth in female wage labor was of great significance. By 1890, the United States was the fastest-growing industrial power in the world. Twenty percent of the workers in the nation's factories were young women. They were already living lives in the public realm, and were affected by labor law.

By comparison in Great Britain, higher education for women was stirring, but more slowly. The first women's college was established in 1869, but Oxford and Cambridge Universities resisted awarding college degrees to women until well into the twentieth century. On the other hand, Great Britain was well ahead of the United States in industrial labor, class consciousness, and union organization. The British Women's Trade Union League was formed in 1874 to encourage trade unions to organize women workers, especially in the textile mills and garment industries. In 1903, a US version was founded, which played a major role in advocating for wage-earning women and also in diversifying the class basis of the US woman suffrage movement.

Two of the most important American women to cultivate these new female publics were Florence Kelley (1859–1932) and Jane Addams (1860–1935). Both were college graduates who discovered their sense of public vocation outside of the United States. Kelley became associated with socialists in Germany and returned to the United States to press for labor reform laws. In London, Addams learned of a group of college-educated young men working and living among urban and immigrant populations and brought the idea of "settlement houses" back to America. The role of such publicly minded, professionally skilled, politically adept women predated the national enfranchisement of women, but their political contributions helped to bring the issue of woman suffrage into mainstream American politics.

THE INTERNATIONAL CONTEXT FOR WOMAN SUFFRAGE IN THE UNITED STATES

As the national suffrage movement regrouped and grew, American activists were once again being influenced by events outside the United States. The first nations to

The suffragist Emmeline Pankhurst (left), with her daughters Christabel and Sylvia in London, before setting off for a lecture tour of the United States and Canada, October 1911. American suffragists took great inspiration from their British counterparts, such as the militant Pankhurst family. The Pankhursts worked through dedicated groups of cadres, cultivating publicity, mounting public actions, and pressuring politicians. **MUSEUM OF LONDON/HERITAGE IMAGES/HULTON ARCHIVE/GETTY IMAGES**

enfranchise women were New Zealand (1893) and Australia (1903), English-speaking populations on the world periphery. Similarly, western American states, with less hidebound political cultures and standards for female propriety, produced the first victories for enfranchisement in the United States. From the 1890s through the early 1910s, woman suffrage advocates won full voting rights via changes in state constitutions, beginning in South Dakota (1896) and Colorado (1893). By 1915, sixteen states, all in the West, had revised their constitutions to enfranchise women, but it was becoming clear that although enfranchising women state by state would strengthen the "women's vote" in national politics, it would never enfranchise women in all the states of the Union.

American suffragists continued to note national enfranchisements abroad, by the 1910s including Finland

and Norway. Contingents of immigrants from these countries marched proudly under their national flags on behalf of woman suffrage in the United States. When short-lived provincial governments in revolutionary China enfranchised women in 1911, a sign in the New York City suffrage parade read "Even China," a message meant to shame Americans who were proud of their democratic heritage.

However, developments in England had the greatest influence on the US movement. British suffrage militants, led by women of the Pankhurst family, embraced the disparaging epithet "suffragette" as a badge of pride. British suffragettes were so disruptive to parliamentary politics that the government began to arrest them. The suffragettes undertook hunger strikes, to which the government responded by force-feeding them. Boldly challenging the government at the heart of the world's most powerful empire brought the British suffragettes international attention.

These developments in Great Britain both energized the American suffrage movement and created significant disagreements within it. The National American Woman Suffrage Association, a moderate group insisting that American politics did not require such confrontational methods, concentrated on assembling large numbers of supporters to use conventional pressure politics to gain support from the major parties. A smaller and more militant group, initially called the Congressional Union and later the Woman's Party, took great inspiration from the British. The woman who would go on to lead this group, Alice Paul (1885–1977), traveled to London in 1908 to serve an apprenticeship with the Pankhursts. The militants, who proudly accepted the epithet "suffragette," worked through dedicated groups of cadres, cultivated publicity, mounted spectacular public actions, and sought to pressure politicians from the outside.

In the end, it was world war that was the most important international context for woman suffrage in the United States. When President Woodrow Wilson (1856–1924) ran in 1916 for a second term, he did so by promising to keep the United States out of the war already raging in Europe. Within weeks of his second inauguration, he reversed course and brought the United States into the war. Women moderates energetically offered their experience, organization, and energies to the war effort, hoping that votes for women would be their reward for serving their country. By contrast, militants accused the president of hypocrisy in going to war abroad to defend the principle of democracy while refusing it to American women. They mounted the first demonstration ever held at the White House. In Britain, the suffragette contingent itself split, even the women of the Pankhurst family dividing over whether to submerge their demands in British war needs.

ADOPTION OF THE NINETEENTH AMENDMENT

American suffragettes accelerated their public demonstrations after the United States declared war in April 1917, drawing angry accusations of disloyalty. Police arrested them for disturbing the peace. Following the British suffragette playbook, the arrested activists undertook a hunger strike, which generated public outrage at their treatment. Finally, in late November, the government released the protestors, and the US House of Representatives summoned the necessary two-thirds vote to pass the Nineteenth Amendment on to the Senate.

One year later, the war ended. Across Europe, nations emerging from the collapse of the Russian and Austro-Hungarian empires enfranchised women in their new constitutions. In the United States, President Wilson, recognizing he would need support from women voters for his plans for international peace, reversed course and announced that he supported a federal suffrage amendment. In June 1919, the Senate finally passed the amendment. All that remained now was ratification by three-quarters of the forty-eight state legislatures. Fourteen months after Senate passage, the final enactment of the amendment was accomplished by the actions of the Tennessee state legislature.

Securing constitutional recognition of women's right to vote, after more than a half century of steady political effort, was a great achievement, but it was not the end. In 1921, the US Supreme Court ruled that the Nineteenth Amendment did not extend to women in US colonies, forcing Puerto Rican and Filipino women to organize separately to win the right to vote. In Puerto Rico, local activists organized throughout the 1920s, ultimately forcing the US government to grant woman suffrage in the colony. In the Philippines, organized women secured the vote in 1944 on the eve of national independence. Back at home, there was also unfinished business. African American women, especially in the South, were prohibited by discriminatory practices from making full use of their franchise rights until the civil rights movement of the 1950s and 1960s.

Nonetheless, securing woman suffrage, which had stood for five decades as the ultimate demand of American women's rights activists, cleared the way for new legal frontiers. On the heels of ratification of the Nineteenth Amendment, suffrage veterans championed an Equal Rights Amendment to insure full legal equality. Reproductive rights, beginning with the legal right to obtain and use contraception, also began to grow in the immediate wake of women's enfranchisement. Both issues would help give birth to a new women's rights movement decades later.

SEE ALSO *Gender; Transatlantic Reform*

BIBLIOGRAPHY

Baker, Jean H., ed. *Votes for Women: The Struggle for Suffrage Revisited*. New York: Oxford University Press, 2002.

DuBois, Ellen. *Harriot Stanton Blatch and the Winning of Woman Suffrage*. New Haven, CT: Yale University Press, 1997.

Flexner, Eleanor. *Century of Struggle: The Woman's Rights Movement in the United States*. Cambridge, MA: Belknap Press, 1959.

Kelley, Mary. *Learning to Stand and Speak: Women, Education, and Public Life in America's Republic*. Chapel Hill: University of North Carolina, 2006.

Rowbotham, Sheila. *Women in Movement: Feminism and Social Action*. New York: Routledge, 1992.

Terborg-Penn, Rosalyn. *African American Women in the Struggle for the Vote, 1850–1920.* Bloomington: Indiana University Press, 1998.

Ellen DuBois
Distinguished Professor of History and Gender Studies
University of California, Los Angeles

SUPERMAN

From his first appearance in 1938, Superman has reflected a complex set of relationships between the United States and the world. Created by writer Jerry Siegel (1914–1996) and artist Joe Shuster (1914–1992), both second-generation Jewish American "outsiders" who wanted very much to celebrate and share in the "American dream," the Man of Steel's story has been read as an allegory of immigration and assimilation that allowed his creators to stake a claim to their own inclusion in the mainstream society. Superman's "ethnic" origins, however, also point to how the immigrant experience often pitted newcomers to the United States against different ethnic groups that had arrived earlier in a struggle for social mobility and economic success. Thus, from the start, Superman has reflected both positive and negative interactions between Americans and the world, even as he has been celebrated as representative of "truth, justice, and the American Way."

EARLY POPULARITY

After initial struggles to publish Superman, Siegel and Shuster got their big break when DC Comics offered their hero a chance to star in a new series, *Action Comics.* Superman was an instant hit, and the hero quickly helped his owners at DC build an impressive media empire. The company added a title for Superman himself, the first such solo comic title, but executives understood that money-making possibilities existed outside of comic books too. They sold a Superman newspaper strip through the McClure Syndicate, which, by 1941, had placed the Man of Steel into hundreds of newspapers with an estimated twenty million or more readers. The publishers also cut a deal with the Fleischer Studio to produce a cartoon version of Superman. Constantly worried about critical attacks concerning the influence of comic books on children, DC executives hoped all of these venues would demonstrate the patriotic and virtuous nature of Superman and the company's other superheroes (as Batman, Wonder Woman, and others quickly arrived), and the onset of World War II further boosted the profits generated by comic books, read now by both kids and, according to the *New York Times*, a substantial number of servicemen as well.

WORLD WAR II AND THE VILIFICATION OF THE JAPANESE AND JAPANESE AMERICANS

As the United States entered World War II (1939–1945), Superman engaged the global conflict only tentatively, although his wartime service would help cement his reputation as a leading symbol of the United States. While the covers of his comic books promoted war bonds and national pride, Superman rarely fought the war in his stories. (If he did so, such battles usually came with a comic twist—for example, saving Santa Claus from the Axis dictators; after being freed, Santa delivered an empty box to Adolf Hitler.) Superman did go to war more actively in his cartoon, confronting evil, subhuman Japanese soldiers in *The Eleventh Hour* and battling a Japanese American fifth column in *Japoteurs.*

The latter cartoon worked in combination with Superman's newspaper strip to explain and endorse the US government's decision to exile and incarcerate all Japanese Americans living on the West Coast. The strip, which saw the hero go undercover to root out Japanese American subversion in a US-run concentration camp and society at large, went to great lengths to portray the government-run camps as "democratic" undertakings. It also worked hand-in-hand with *Japoteurs* to paint a racist picture of the Japanese and Japanese American enemies—conflated by the term "Japs"—that made government policies seem all too sensible.

In this way, Superman's adventures in newspapers and on the silver screen argued for incarceration, accurately reflecting, in many ways, broader social attitudes about Japanese Americans and the war. Superman's adventures depicted mass incarceration of Japanese Americans as a "necessary" measure given the assumed disloyalty of some portion of that group. While the comic strip ended with the hero conceding that "most Japanese Americans are loyal citizens," the almost two months of material that preceded this admission showcased Superman facing down dehumanized "Japs" uniformly identified by their stereotypical buck teeth, thick glasses, and ominous mustaches. As presented in the Man of Steel's adventures, the Japanese proclivity for violence—tied to an assumed tendency toward subversion and treachery—made exile and incarceration the only logical solution during war.

This vilification of Japanese and Japanese Americans also served to rehabilitate Chinese Americans while simultaneously celebrating white Americans. The comic strip, for example, highlighted loyal Chinese Americans—long the target of American racism—who, while not fully assimilated, were allowed to demonstrate their loyalty (if always in ways that marked them as not quite equal to Clark Kent and Lois Lane). The despicable nature of the

Japanese also led readers to assume Superman's (and thus Americans') virtue. This assumption, in turn, allowed Superman to dole out violent retribution to the racialized enemy.

COLD WAR ESCAPISM

As the Cold War set in after 1945 and superheroes faced attacks from the psychiatrist Frederic Wertham (1895–1981) and others, Superman's adventures quickly took on largely childish qualities, diving into an escapism meant to insulate the Man of Steel from the vicissitudes of postwar politics. While such print stories from time to time revealed a racism against nonwhite people, Superman's television and radio shows in the late 1940s and 1950s occasionally presented a more liberal view of race (although the results here were mixed, at best).

Try as he might to avoid Cold War issues, Superman had to deal with the atomic bomb on occasion, and his powers quickly ramped up to match the growing lethality of modern nuclear weapons (as he could survive an atomic blast) and to battle villains such as Atom Man, perhaps providing some small comfort to readers living in an age of atomic anxiety. Still, when the film *Superman IV: The Quest for Peace* bombed at the box office in 1987, actor Christopher Reeve (1952–2004) captured a reality for the postwar career of Superman when he noted, "It is probably best, in retrospect, not to have Superman politicized in any way" (Daniels 1998, 146).

A DEPOLITICIZED SYMBOL OF THE AMERICAN WAY

Superman continued in his role as a depoliticized symbol of "truth, justice, and the American Way" in the aftermath of the Cold War. Indeed, when creators crossed into "real" issues, controversy often followed, most recently in 2011, when writer David S. Goyer used a short story in *Action Comics* #900 to have Superman renounce his American

citizenship. While Superman did not directly reject American values—his decision reflected instead his desire to apply them more broadly—controversy ensued, and DC executives never followed up on this story, letting it quietly die, thus allowing Superman to continue to serve in his important, if necessarily vague, role as representative of America to the rest of the world.

SEE ALSO *Cold War; Hollywood; Television*

BIBLIOGRAPHY

Austin, Allan W. "Superman Goes to War: Teaching Japanese American Exile and Incarceration with Film." *Journal of American Ethnic History* 30, 4 (2011): 51–56.

Chang, Gordon H. "'Superman Is about to Visit the Relocation Centers' and the Limits of Wartime Liberalism." *Amerasia Journal* 19, 1 (1993): 37–60.

Cronin, Brian. *Was Superman A Spy? and Other Comic Book Legends Revealed!* New York: Penguin, 2009.

Daniels, Les. *DC Comics: Sixty Years of the World's Favorite Comic Book Heroes.* Boston: Bullfinch Press, 1995.

Daniels, Les. *Superman: The Complete History.* San Francisco: Chronicle, 1998.

Hajdu, David. *The Ten-Cent Plague: The Great Comic-Book Scare and How It Changed America.* New York: Farrar, Straus, and Giroux, 2008.

Jones, Gerard. *Men of Tomorrow: Geeks, Gangsters, and the Birth of the Comic Book.* New York: Basic Books, 2004.

Jones, Gerard, and Will Jacobs. *The Comic Book Heroes.* Rocklin, CA: Prima Press, 1997.

Savage, William W. *Comic Books and America, 1945–1954.* Norman: University of Oklahoma Press, 1990.

Wright, Bradford. *Comic Book Nation: The Transformation of Youth Culture in America.* Baltimore, MD: Johns Hopkins University Press, 2001.

Allan W. Austin
Professor of History
Misericordia University

T

TAFT, WILLIAM HOWARD
1857–1930

William Howard Taft, who served as president of the United States from 1909 to 1913, became an element in American relations with the world in 1900 when he accepted the offer of President William McKinley (1843–1901) to head the Philippine Commission that sought to establish civilian rule over the United States' new overseas possession. Before then, Taft, a lawyer, had been solicitor general and a federal appeals court judge. In his new post, Taft was charged with overseeing the transition from a military to a civilian government. From 1900 to 1904, Taft performed in a capable manner as a colonial governor. He treated individual Filipinos without the racial prejudice that many Americans displayed, and he was broadly popular with his charges. When President Theodore Roosevelt (1858–1919) sought to have him join the US Supreme Court in 1902, prominent Filipinos urged Taft to stay at his post, and the president reluctantly agreed.

DIPLOMATIC SERVICE IN THE FAR EAST

Taft's years in the Philippines, as well as his subsequent service under Theodore Roosevelt as secretary of war (1904–1908), introduced him to the challenges that faced American foreign policy in the Far East. Having occupied the Philippines in the 1898 Spanish-American War, could the United States defend the islands from a possible attack from Japan, also an expansionist power in the region? If the American military could not defend the Philippines against invasion, should Washington seek an accommodation with Tokyo and recognize that nation's

preeminence in Korea in exchange for Japan's acceptance of the American presence in the Philippines? That point of view was embodied in the so-called Taft-Katsura agreement of 1905. Taft was traveling back to the Philippines as secretary of war and stopped off in Tokyo to meet with Japanese officials. In what was essentially a restatement of where the two nations stood on the issues between them, Taft accepted that the Japanese would dominate Korea, while Tokyo did the same for the American presence in the Philippines.

In 1906, Taft had to deal with the tangled affairs of the island of Cuba as a diplomatic troubleshooter for Roosevelt. By that time, he was emerging as the president's designated successor and likely candidate for the Republican presidential nomination in 1908. Taft made another visit to Asia in 1907 as part of a round-the-world tour for Roosevelt.

DOLLAR DIPLOMACY

During his travels and as his presidential candidacy developed, Taft reached different conclusions about American foreign policy and Asia than President Roosevelt had articulated. The secretary of war had doubts about the wisdom of appeasing Japan to protect the Philippines, which he thought was not in the interest of China. He felt that American investment in Asia would be a positive good for China. In these conclusions lay the origins of what would become "dollar diplomacy" during the Taft presidency. Once he had defeated William Jennings Bryan (1860–1925) and secured the presidency in 1908, Taft named Philander Knox (1853–1921), a Pennsylvania senator and conservative Republican, as his

President William H. Taft in the Oval Office, c. 1910. *The major thrust of Taft's foreign policy was dubbed "dollar diplomacy" by his Democratic opponents. Rather than military intervention overseas, the White House would encourage American businesses to expand their commitments in Latin America and Asia, thus helping to promote American ascendancy in those regions. As an attorney, Taft also believed that arbitration of disagreements between contending nations by a legal tribunal was preferable to a reliance on diplomatic negotiations or military might.* © **EVERETT HISTORICAL/SHUTTERSTOCK.COM**

secretary of state. Knox was not an especially hardworking cabinet member. As a result, one of Knox's subordinates, Francis M. Huntington Wilson (1875–1946), played a large role in the overall formulation of diplomatic strategies under Taft.

Dollar diplomacy, as Democratic politicians dubbed the policy, became the major thrust of Taft's foreign policy. Rather than military intervention overseas, the White House would encourage American businesses to expand their commitments in Latin America and Asia. In that manner, American ascendancy in the region would be assured with less need for the threat of actual force. In Latin America, for example, a network of treaties with countries that behaved rationally, as the Taft

administration defined such behavior, would reward nations that fulfilled their obligations and encourage economic development. The United States, for example, sought to enlist Mexico in a kind of alliance that would limit the power of such countries as Nicaragua, under its dictator, Jose Santos Zelaya (1853–1919), to obstruct American influence in the region. The Mexicans did not agree with that initiative, and the United States broke diplomatic relations with Nicaragua in December 1909. After Zelaya was ousted, the United States negotiated the Knox-Castrillo Convention (1911), which gave the United States control over Nicaraguan state finances. In Nicaragua, Honduras, and Chile, dollar diplomacy, as it was applied south of the border, had as many critics as supporters and led to only a few treaties. Political opposition from Democrats derided the Taft policy, and the administration had little to show for its primary diplomatic effort by 1910.

Dollar diplomacy also focused on Asia, where Knox and Taft hoped to strengthen the territorial integrity of China against inroads from Russia and China. The favored method was to gain concessions for railroads that American capitalists would finance, but that strategy encountered resistance from both Tokyo and St. Petersburg. In the end, Washington actually drove Russia and Japan closer together against the American effort. The Taft administration had little to show for its major diplomatic effort in Asia after a year in office.

TRADE WITH CANADA

In North America, Taft spent much of his political capital in pursuit of better trade relations with Canada through a series of agreements that became known under the general heading of "Canadian Reciprocity." The agreements involved mutual reductions on the tariff rates in the Payne-Aldrich Tariff of 1909, and included lower tariffs on Canadian products, such as lumber and wood pulp, coming into the United States in return for greater access for American industrial products across the northern border. The thrust of the policy alienated proponents of the protective tariff in the United States, and Taft faced major opposition to his initiative within the Republican contingent in Congress.

Another blow to Taft's hopes came in the congressional elections of 1910, when the Democrats, riding a wave of popular unhappiness with inflation, regained control of the House of Representatives for the first time since 1894. Failing to get the needed legislation through the lame-duck Republican Congress in 1910 to 1911, Taft summoned the lawmakers back into special session in the spring and summer of 1911 and eventually achieved passage of Canadian Reciprocity. Taft's political triumph was brief. Responding to demagogic attacks on the arrangement, Canadian voters defeated Reciprocity in September 1911, and the deal was dead. Despite the defeat, the Reciprocity campaign attested to Taft's belief in tariff reduction and better trade between the two North American nations. In that sense, he anticipated the future trade liberalization policies of the United States.

ADVOCACY OF INTERNATIONAL ARBITRATION

A third major policy initiative in the international sphere reflected Taft's deepest convictions but brought him into conflict with Theodore Roosevelt, Henry Cabot Lodge (1850–1924), and other senior Republican figures. As an attorney, Taft believed in the legal system as the best means of resolving conflicts. Applying that principle to

international disputes, the president was convinced that arbitration of disagreements between contending nations by a legal tribunal was preferable to a reliance on diplomatic negotiations. In 1910, the president made it clear that he favored a large program of international arbitration treaties to which most disputes would be submitted for settlement. In the years before the outbreak of the First World War in 1914, Taft believed that nations could settle their differences through peaceful procedures akin to the American legal system.

Such an optimistic view of the world, which paralleled growing military alignments in Europe, seemed naive and misguided to Theodore Roosevelt and others within the Republican Party who believed diplomacy and arbitration were limited in their usefulness to international disputes. They were ready to accept arbitration on minor issues with a friendly power such as Great Britain, but opposed the process, and preferred armed defense, when the vital interests of the United States might be at stake. Taft was willing to live with a decision adverse to American interest where the case might be weak, as any good lawyer would, but Roosevelt would not accept such an outcome. When arbitration pacts were signed with Great Britain and France in early August 1911, Taft hailed the treaties as a step toward peace. Roosevelt blasted them as a betrayal of the national interest. Their battle over arbitration further worsened personal relations between the one-time friends and political allies, contributing to a myriad of issues that led Roosevelt to eventually split with the Republican Party in 1912. The Senate watered down the arbitration treaties that Taft did negotiate with friendly powers, but, on the whole, the policy did not produce significant results. Nevertheless, Taft remained committed to arbitration as a worthy international principle.

In other areas of foreign policy, Taft refused to intervene in Mexico, where a revolution had begun in 1911, without the approval of Congress, which he knew would not occur. Under pressure from Jewish leaders, Taft abrogated the 1832 treaty with Russia over that country's treatment of Jews within its borders. On the whole, Taft was a cautious, prudent chief executive whose signal foreign-policy initiative, dollar diplomacy, had more noise than substance. He left office in March 1913 with the nation at peace.

LATER INFLUENCE IN INTERNATIONAL AFFAIRS

As a former president, Taft taught law at Yale College and pursued an active career as a lecturer on public issues, one of which was international arbitration. Until war broke out in Europe in August 1914, Taft believed that legal procedures and international courts were a preferable technique to balance-of-power diplomacy. Once the fighting began, however, Taft was as dismayed as most Americans at the irrational slaughter he saw erupting across the Atlantic. Although he retained his general faith in legal procedures as the answer to international quarrels, he joined with other Americans in the League to Enforce Peace. That body contemplated an association of nations dedicated to using force if necessary to bring to heel those countries that violated international norms. In time, Taft became president of the league and a major advocate in the United States for such an association.

Taft's identification with the League to Enforce Peace further complicated his ambivalent relationship with President Woodrow Wilson (1856–1924). Despite being rivals in the 1912 presidential election, the two men had a cordial public relationship. At key points during the period of American neutrality, such as the crisis arising over the sinking of the *Lusitania* in May 1915, Taft urged the public to support the Democratic president in his conduct of foreign affairs. In private, however, Taft regarded Wilson as a tricky politician whose word could not be trusted. As a Republican who hoped the next Republican president might appoint him as chief justice of the US Supreme Court, Taft had to move carefully between his innate Republican partisanship and the need to keep Wilson, who controlled American foreign policy, friendly to the goals of the League to Enforce Peace.

In the spring of 1916, Wilson addressed the League to Enforce Peace and spoke about his vision of an association of nations along the lines of what Taft seemed to endorse. It represented a high point in the relations between the former president and Wilson. In the presidential election of 1916, however, Taft worked to defeat the Democrat by writing articles attacking Wilson's candidacy. For Wilson, these actions strengthened his resolve not to give Taft any kind of serious part in the making of postwar policy in diplomacy. The former president did strongly support the American war effort after April 1917, but he also hoped to have a substantive role in framing the peace.

Taft defended Wilson's right to attend the Paris Peace Conference in person over the objections of some fellow Republicans. He would have liked to have been a member of the American delegation that accompanied Wilson to Paris, but the president had such a low opinion of Taft's judgment that his participation was never seriously considered. In the spring of 1919, as Wilson struggled with opposition to his idea of the League of Nations at home and abroad, Taft sent the president some proposals that, if adopted, might diminish Republican opposition to Wilson's brainchild. Among other things, Taft suggested that language recognizing the Monroe Doctrine as an American policy be included in the proposed treaty, along with wording allowing the United

States to withdraw after giving sufficient notice. Taft was out of touch with Republican enemies of the League of Nations, and these concessions, even though Wilson adopted some of them, were far from enough to placate Wilson's Republican critics. Most Republican senators, filled with hatred for the president, wanted to defeat the treaty, not find a way of getting it through the Senate.

Taft had maintained throughout the fight over the League of Nations that the Treaty of Versailles should achieve Senate approval without any crippling reservations. That too was the position of the League to Enforce Peace. Then, during the summer of 1919, Taft declared a public shift in his position. Believing that the treaty was doomed if it did not include reservations acceptable to Republican senators, Taft wrote what he hoped would be a confidential letter to the chairman of the Republican National Committee outlining what he deemed necessary reservations. As Taft should have expected, the letter was political dynamite, and its contents were quickly leaked to the press. The most prominent Republican proponent of the treaty was now saying that reservations were imperative. Taft's new position undercut the White House and President Wilson. Taft also undermined the position of the League to Enforce Peace, causing the organization to lose most of its clout. Though he remained committed to the Treaty of Versailles and its approval in the Senate with reservations, Taft was not a serious factor in the debate after July 1919. His ability to influence foreign policy ended twenty years after he arrived in the Philippines.

By maintaining his Republican credentials, Taft did achieve his lifelong ambition when President Warren G. Harding (1865–1923) nominated him as chief justice of the US Supreme Court during the summer of 1921. Until his death in 1930, Taft dealt most often with domestic legal issues, and his foreign-policy views were confined to letters to friends. For more than a decade and a half of his public life, however, Taft played a significant role in the making and implementation of American foreign policy. His advocacy of dollar diplomacy, though not successful in either Latin America or Asia, added an enduring term to the language of diplomacy. In his support of arbitration and the League of Nations, Taft embodied the internationalist strain of American foreign relations.

SEE ALSO *Dollar Diplomacy; League of Nations*

BIBLIOGRAPHY

Bartlett, Ruhl J. *The League to Enforce Peace*. Chapel Hill: University of North Carolina Press, 1944.

Escalante, Rene R. *The Bearer of Pax Americana: The Philippine Career of William Howard Taft, 1900–1903*. Quezon City, Philippines: New Day, 2007.

Gould, Lewis L. *The William Howard Taft Presidency*. Lawrence: University Press of Kansas, 2009.

Gould, Lewis L. *Chief Executive to Chief Justice: Taft betwixt the White House and Supreme Court.* Lawrence: University Press of Kansas, 2014.

Minger, Ralph Eldin. *William Howard Taft and United States Foreign Policy: The Apprenticeship Years, 1900–1908.* Urbana: University of Illinois Press, 1975.

Pringle, Henry F. *The Life and Times of William Howard Taft: A Biography.* 2 vols. New York: Farrar and Rinehart, 1939.

Lewis L. Gould
Professor Emeritus
University of Texas

TARIFF

Tariffs are taxes on imports and exports whose primary purpose is to generate public revenue. They can take the form of ad valorem taxes, which are calculated as a percentage of the value of the product, or non–ad valorem taxes, which are levied according to a good's quantity, weight, or size. Tariffs have a secondary purpose, however, as tools of economic development and foreign relations. As such, they have generated a significant amount of controversy, both domestically and overseas, over the past two-plus centuries.

THE EARLY REPUBLIC TO THE CIVIL WAR

Following independence, the United States struggled to trade on equal terms with Britain. The central government under the Articles of Confederation was not strong enough to pass national commercial legislation, and so it was left to the individual states to levy tariffs on foreign goods. Once the US Constitution was ratified in 1788, federal legislation and foreign relations became much easier. One of the first acts of the First Congress was the passage of a tariff that aimed to repay war debts and protect nascent American manufacturing from foreign imports. Although some policy makers had hoped to use the tariff to discriminate against Britain, the final law placed French and British commerce on equal footing.

This first tariff by no means solved the United States' economic or diplomatic woes. Its markets were still glutted with British manufactures, and Americans debated whether England or France should be the nation's primary trading partner. This issue was partly decided by Jay's Treaty, which was signed in 1794 and gave Britain most-favored-nation status. Although the 1790 and 1792 tariffs raised duties slightly, the United States could no longer levy excessively burdensome duties on British imports (McCoy 1980, 175). No major tariff legislation would be passed again until 1816.

Tariffs became an especially contentious issue in the antebellum period. The United States attempted to wage commercial warfare against Britain in the early 1800s with a trade embargo, but after the War of 1812 (1812–1815), American markets were once again flooded with British manufactures. For many merchants and consumers, especially in the South, this was a good thing. For aspiring manufacturers, however, foreign goods posed stiff competition. Policy makers had to balance the interests of northern manufacturers with southern cotton producers, who sold raw cotton to Britain and did not want to diminish the sales of their British consumers (Irwin and Temin 2001, 779). The 1816 tariff was the first explicitly protective tariff, and rates continued to increase throughout the 1820s, as manufacturers petitioned for greater levels of protection (Peart 2013). Ad valorem tariffs on manufactured goods would range anywhere from 20 to 50 percent throughout the 1820s and 1830s as legislators battled sectional interests (Irwin and Temin 2001, 779). During these decades, the United States also began exporting manufactured goods to Latin America, Africa, and eventually Asia. US diplomats took advantage of their increasing diplomatic and economic power to push for more favorable tariff rates for American exports. This was especially the case in Latin America, where many newly independent nations levied high tariffs to stimulate domestic manufacturing and generate revenue in the wake of their independence wars (Coatsworth and Williamson 2004).

In the 1840s, international trade policy began to shift toward greater liberalization. Much of Western Europe implemented free trade laws, and China, which had hitherto maintained prohibitive trade policies, opened five ports to Western trade. Once Britain repealed its Corn Laws—high protectionist tariffs on imported grains—the United States reciprocated by drastically lowering its tariffs with the Walker Tariff of 1846 (Taussig 1915, 114). Reduced tariff rates led to growth in foreign trade, including an increase in textile imports from China and India (Irwin and Temin 2001, 792). Tariff rates were reduced further in 1857, and the United States engaged in reciprocal free trade with Canada from 1854 to 1866, which led to an expanded volume of trade between the two neighbors (Marvin 1929, 469).

The American Civil War (1861–1865) changed tariff policies once again. The costs of waging war prompted the federal government to steadily increase duties throughout the conflict (Taussig 1915, 160). Higher rates remained in place following the war, even as much of Western Europe practiced free trade and pressured Asian and Latin American governments to remove protectionist tariffs. Although tariffs hurt the agricultural export sector more than they helped import-competing manufacturers, they contributed to the United States' rise as one of the world's leading industrial powers (Irwin 2007, 596, 605).

THE TWENTIETH AND TWENTY-FIRST CENTURIES

In the twentieth century, the federal government used tariffs less as a measure of industrial protection or as a source of revenue and more as a tool of diplomacy and commercial reciprocity. President William Howard Taft (1857–1930) advocated minimal tariffs, especially because negotiations with France and Germany had led to reductions in duties for American goods. Even Canada, which after 1866 refused to enter a reciprocal agreement with the United States, made slight concessions in its tariff rates (Taussig 1915, 404). The interwar years saw a return to protectionist tariffs, which had a detrimental effect on international economic cooperation. The Smoot-Hawley Tariff of 1930 was the most controversial, sparking boycotts and tariff retaliation from foreign governments (Maier et al. 2006, 740). It was especially detrimental to Latin American economies (LaRosa and Mora 2007, 104). The United States changed course several years later with the implementation of reciprocal trade agreements, and in 1947 signed the General Agreement on Tariffs and Trade (GATT) with twenty-three other countries (Pahre 1998, 488).

During the Cold War (1947–1991), the United States promoted low tariffs and free trade among capitalist countries. It also reversed course on its protective agricultural policies, which had included high tariffs and surplus exports, in order to promote food security in war-torn and developing countries (McGlade 2009, 85). These policies were intended to contain the spread of communism. Although the second half of the twentieth century was, in general, a period of liberalized trade, the United States implemented a retaliatory tariff against West Germany in the 1960s. Also, during the following decade, US autoworkers lobbied for protection from Asian imports; the result was import quotas rather than higher tariff rates. With the end of the Cold War came an increased commitment to low tariffs. The United States entered into a free trade agreement with Canada in 1987 and Mexico in 1994 (North American Free Trade Agreement, or NAFTA). In the early 2000s, the United States and a host of Pacific nations began discussing the possibility of an international agreement called the Trans-Pacific Partnership (TPP), which would reduce barriers to trade, including tariff rates. As has been the case with tariffs and trade policies throughout history, TPP has met resistance in the United States and overseas for its negative implications for labor and ethical business arrangements.

Because of their impact on consumers and producers worldwide, and on international relations, tariffs will no doubt continue to cause controversy. They can be used as tools of economic prosperity or retaliation, of friendship or animosity, and of international cooperation or commercial warfare. Indeed, tariffs have helped shape the United States' interactions with other nations and have carved out its place in the global economy.

SEE ALSO *Economics; Exports, Exportation; North American Free Trade Agreement (NAFTA)*

BIBLIOGRAPHY

Akyüz, Yilmaz. "WTO Negotiations on Industrial Tariffs: What Is at Stake for Developing Countries?" *Economic and Political Weekly* 40, 46 (2005): 4827–4836.

Bergsten, Fred C. "The United States and the World Economy." Special issue, "The Internationalization of the American Economy." *Annals of the American Academy of Political and Social Science* 460 (1982): 11–20.

Coatsworth, John H., and Jeffrey G. Williamson. "Always Protectionist? Latin American Tariffs from Independence to Great Depression." *Journal of Latin American Studies* 36, 2 (2004): 205–232.

Irwin, Douglas A. "Tariff Incidence in America's Gilded Age." *Journal of Economic History* 67, 3 (2007): 582–607.

Irwin, Douglas A., and Peter Temin. "The Antebellum Tariff on Cotton Textiles Revisited." *Journal of Economic History* 61, 3 (2001): 777–798.

LaRosa, Michael J., and Frank O. Mora, eds. *Neighborly Adversaries: Readings in US-Latin American Relations*. Lanham, MD: Rowman and Littlefield, 2007.

Maier, Pauline, Merritt Roe Smith, Alexander Keyssar, and Daniel J. Kevles. *Inventing America: A History of the United States*, Vol. 2: *From 1865*. 2nd ed. New York: Norton, 2006.

Marvin, Donald M. "The Tariff Relationship of the United States and Canada." Special issue, "Tariff Problems of the United States." *Annals of the American Academy of Political and Social Science* 141 (1929): 227–233.

McCoy, Drew R. *The Elusive Republic: Political Economy in Jeffersonian America*. Chapel Hill: University of North Carolina Press, 1980.

McGlade, Jacqueline. "More a Plowshare than a Sword: The Legacy of US Cold War Agricultural Diplomacy." *Agricultural History* 83, 1 (2009): 79–102.

Pahre, Robert. "Reactions and Reciprocity: Tariffs and Trade Liberalization from 1815 to 1914." *Journal of Conflict Resolution* 42, 4 (1998): 467–492.

Peart, Daniel. "Looking Beyond Parties and Elections: The Making of United States Tariff Policy during the Early 1820s." *Journal of the Early Republic* 33, 1 (2013): 87–108.

Peskin, Lawrence A., "From Protection to Encouragement: Manufacturing and Mercantilism in New York City's Public Sphere, 1783–1795." *Journal of the Early Republic* 18, 4 (1998): 589–615.

Taussig, Frank William. *Some Aspects of the Tariff Question: An Examination of the Development of American Industries under Protection.* Cambridge, MA: Harvard University Press, 1915.

Lindsay Schakenbach Regele
Assistant Professor
Miami University

TAYLOR, ZACHARY

SEE *Mexican-American War.*

TELEGRAPH

International telegraphy broke through the isolationist inclinations of the United States in the late nineteenth century by furnishing the public with a flood of news from abroad. From the Spanish-American War through the Cold War, government officials managed to keep pace with new technology and complex codes to deal with crises in both war and peace.

THE INTRODUCTION OF TELEGRAPHY

The movement of electrical current through copper cables requires a set of signals in order to transmit information. Samuel Morse (1791–1872), an artist with a talent for mechanical experimentation, developed a code made up of dots and dashes representing the letters of the alphabet. This simple code gained widespread use in the middle of the nineteenth century in competition with other codes. Morse received international recognition, thus making him one of the founding fathers of telegraphy. Morse's status was unusual because leadership in international telegraphy came from British companies that connected London with India, Australia, China, and the Americas. New York businessman James Scrymser (1839–1918) challenged the British in South America. He organized two cable companies—the Mexican Telegraph Company and the Central and South American Telegraph Company—that transmitted telegrams between Lima, Peru, and Galveston, Texas, where the messages entered Western Union's lines. Scrymser became a full-fledged competitor with British companies in South America. A little-known upstart in the cable business established a presence for the United States in international communications.

THE USE OF TELEGRAPHY DURING THE SPANISH-AMERICAN WAR

The Spanish-American War (1898) brought public attention to submarine cables and the information they carried. Before the war began, Assistant Secretary of the Navy

Theodore Roosevelt (1858–1919) cabled the US squadron in the western Pacific to prepare to attack the Spanish in the Philippines. The same cables carried the news of the victory to the United States in early May 1898. President William McKinley (1843–1901) established a war room in the White House with maps, charts, and a steady flow of information via telegraphy. The United States gained a major advantage through an intercepted telegram. Admiral Pascual Cervera's (1839–1909) squadron departed the Cape Verde Islands for Cuba on April 29, 1898. The US Navy was unable to locate these warships for nearly three weeks. Cervera's force slipped into Santiago harbor undetected on May 19. Cervera telegraphed his arrival to officials in Havana, but a well-placed spy saw the telegram and quickly notified Washington. Within weeks, the US Navy destroyed Cervera's vessels, and the US Army forced the surrender of the Spanish. Although the story of the intercepted telegram remained unpublicized, newspapers, fed by cabled reports from Cuba, filled their front pages with details of US victories.

The international cables that linked with newspapers, newsmagazines, and wire services such as the Associated Press formed an information system that provided the US public with unprecedented coverage of events from foreign lands. The world's submarine cable system expanded rapidly from 1892 to 1908. Cable mileage nearly doubled from 153,000 to 294,000. Although US companies operated only 19.5 percent of this total in 1908, foreign news reporting became prominent in the US press. The Spanish-American War dramatized these connections, and subsequent international crises entered the routine flow of information.

THE RISE OF FOREIGN CORRESPONDENTS AND NEWS AGENCIES

Foreign correspondents became well-known figures. Richard Harding Davis (1864–1916) was the prototype, with reportage from Central America in the 1890s to Europe in 1914. Floyd Gibbons (1887–1939) covered the battlefields of World War I (1914–1918). Several reporters tracked the controversial path of the Communist regime in the Soviet Union after 1917 and the twists and turns of the Mexican Revolution from 1910 to the 1930s. Carleton Beals (1893–1979) interviewed Nicaraguan rebel leader Augusto Sandino (1895–1934) in 1927, while US Marines campaigned against him. Dorothy Thompson (1893–1961) and William Shirer (1904–1993) discussed the rise of Adolf Hitler (1889–1945) in Germany. African American editor Robert Vann (1879–1940) of the *Pittsburgh Courier* covered the 1936 Berlin Olympics and the Italian fascist invasion of Ethiopia. Jack Belden (1910–1989) reported the Japanese invasion of China in 1937. Belden and a host of journalists brought World War II (1939–1945) to the newspaper readers at home.

The Associated Press and other wire services in the United States were concerned about European preeminence in the submarine cable network that carried international news. A powerful news organization or cartel made up of the Reuters agency headquartered in London, Havas of Paris, and the Wolff organization in Berlin dominated the selection and content of news from around the globe from the 1870s until 1914. World War I broke up this cartel, and the US government and news agencies campaigned for the open movement of news through the worldwide cable and radio telegraph system. In spite of the dedication of Kent Cooper (1880–1965) of the Associated Press and other advocates, this campaign was unsuccessful in the 1920s and 1930s but came to symbolize an international version of the US ideal of a free press.

DIPLOMATIC AND MILITARY USE OF TELEGRAPHY

While submerged cables and inexpensive newspapers exposed the US public to international events, military leaders and diplomats devised clandestine operations and secret codes to exploit electronic means of communication. German foreign minister Arthur Zimmermann (1864–1940) sent a presumed secret telegram to Mexico City to persuade Mexico to ally with Germany against the United States in World War I. Mexico rejected the plan, but British agents intercepted the cable and released it in the United States, where press coverage of the German enticement of Mexico caused a furor and contributed to the US entry into the war.

In subsequent decades, military communications often used radio telegraphy, which meant messages were broadcast and therefore available to radio receivers. The use of secret codes became a necessity. In response, intelligence agencies placed a priority on deciphering these telegraphic signals. The United States could read Japanese coded messages before the attack on Pearl Harbor in December 1941. These interceptions, however, did not specify the point of attack in time to give US commanders sufficient warning. US codebreakers did succeed in pinpointing the location and date of Japan's attack on Midway Island. The Japanese intended to destroy the remainder of the US Pacific fleet, but the cryptanalysts working in a basement office in Pearl Harbor gave Admiral Chester Nimitz (1885–1966) a translation of the Japanese plan. US forces destroyed four Japanese aircraft carriers on June 6–8, 1942, and the task force abandoned its plan. Nimitz called Midway a victory made possible by communications intelligence.

International telegraphy also played a vital role in the Cold War. On February 22, 1946, George Kennan (1904–2005), a US State Department specialist in Moscow, sent his secret but soon-to-be-famous "Long Telegram" to Washington, in which he warned of the Soviet Union's

aggressive intentions. He used the impact of this lengthy electronic message to emphasize the need for a long-term policy of containment. Kennan's hopes for peaceful containment nearly failed in the Cuban missile crisis of October 1962, which carried the United States and the Soviet Union dangerously close to nuclear war. The two superpowers negotiated their dispute regarding the placement of Soviet missiles in Cuba by telegraphic communications. Contrary to the popular image on film and television, there was no "hotline" by telephone. Instead President John Kennedy (1917–1963) and Premier Nikita Khrushchev (1894–1971) avoided verbal conversation through translators by sending messages via teletype machines—updated versions of the telegraph equipment of earlier years. For two decades, teletype machines continued to serve at both ends of the so-called hotline. By the late twentieth century, fiber optic cables and the Internet dominated international communications.

SEE ALSO *Airplanes; Americanization; Automobiles; Exceptionalism; Industrialization; Internationalism; Isolationism; Trains; World's Fairs*

BIBLIOGRAPHY

Britton, John A. *Cables, Crises, and the Press: The Geopolitics of the New International Information System in the Americas, 1866–1903*. Albuquerque: University of New Mexico Press, 2013.

Hamilton, John Maxwell. *Journalism's Roving Eye: A History of American Foreign Reporting*. Baton Rouge: Louisiana State University Press, 2009.

Headrick, Daniel. *The Invisible Weapon: Telecommunications and International Politics, 1851–1945*. New York: Oxford University Press, 1991.

Kahn, David. *The Codebreakers: The Comprehensive History of Secret Communications from Ancient Times to the Internet*. Rev. ed. New York: Scribner's, 1996.

Nickles, David Paull. *Under the Wire: How the Telegraph Changed Diplomacy*. Cambridge, MA: Harvard University Press, 2003.

Winseck, Dwayne R., and Robert M. Pike. *Communication and Empire: Media, Markets, and Globalization, 1860–1930*. Durham, NC: Duke University Press, 2007.

John A. Britton
Professor Emeritus
Francis Marion University

TELEVISION

Over the course of the twentieth and twenty-first centuries, television has made significant contributions in bringing America to the world and the world to America. According to some industry insiders, television is quintessentially American: "America is to television what Switzerland is to clocks and banking, what Holland is to tulips, and what France is to wine" (Aldridge, 1999). In the 1920s and 1930s, television was introduced as an experimental technology in Europe, Asia, the former Soviet Union, and North and South America. Following World War II (1939–1945), television quickly became an accepted form of mass communication around the world, albeit under different national regulatory arrangements. For example, France and China adopted it as a state-controlled medium (1945 and 1956, respectively), England as a subsidized public service (1946), the United States and Brazil as a commercial medium (1948 and 1950, respectively), Canada as a national system (1952), Japan as a dual public and commercial network (1953), and Australia as a free and governmentally regulated broadcast service (1956) (see Bielby and Harrington 2015, 80). Television was rapidly adopted as an important source of news, information, and entertainment worldwide and contributed to growing interdependencies among countries; however, its long-term business cycle—innovation and diffusion as a novel technology, establishment and system growth as a communications industry, maturation and popularity, and specialization and diversification—took decades to unfold (Cunningham 2000), and did so differently in different contexts.

THE EXPORT OF AMERICAN PROGRAMMING

The international market for the export of American television programming was launched in the mid-1950s by the big three domestic broadcast networks—first CBS in 1954, followed by NBC and ABC. With airtime on newly established networks abroad needing to be filled, the market for the screening of "telefilms" (as the filmed series were called) outside the United States was thus realized (Bielby and Harrington 2008, 22). A now-classic UNESCO report (Nordenstreng and Varis 1974) represents one of the earliest attempts to systematically document the global market for television programming. The report uncovered a one-way flow of television from the United States, Britain, France, and the Federal Republic of Germany to the rest of the world. The United States led the way with an estimated 150,000 hours of programming exported each year (compared to about 20,000 hours each for Britain and France), and entertainment programming comprised a greater portion of exported content than did other genres, such as news or sports (Bielby and Harrington 2008, 38).

While follow-up studies (Varis 1984) showed that other countries were also major producers of programming for international distribution within regional markets (for example, Mexico distributed throughout Latin America), the clear dominance of the United States

in the international market led to scholarly concerns that America was asserting "cultural imperialism" through its television programming (Schiller 1976). Cultural imperialism refers to both economic and ideological forms of domination, or "the domination of one country's system of symbolically producing and reproducing constructed realities over another's production and re-production of self-identity" (de la Garde 1993, 27). As America continues to be a major player in the global television marketplace, its ability to attract or co-opt as a means of cultural persuasion—its use of "soft power" (Nye 2004) in foreign relations—remains widely debated.

America (along with the rest of the world) has exported all kinds of television content—including telefilms, sitcoms, sports, lifestyle programming, news, and cop shows—but as noted earlier, entertainment programming dominates the global market. Why? Mainly due to the reason exports were successful to begin with: emergent networks around the world found it easier and cheaper to import programming (at least initially) than develop and produce their own. This was true in the 1950s and proved true during the rapid expansion of satellite and cable in the 1980s and 1990s, an era when global demand for all TV programming skyrocketed. We do know, however, that imported programs tend to be replaced by local programming as soon as local markets mature. One of the first instances of this was in Latin America, where US soap operas were routinely imported in early years but were then marginalized once Latin American telenovelas became widely available. Still today, television viewers worldwide prefer domestic programming over imported programming, and if imported, they prefer it to be from the same region of the world (e.g., the Latin American market) (Hoskins and Mirus 1988).

THE INTERNATIONAL APPEAL OF AMERICAN TELEVISION

Over the course of the twentieth century, American soap operas (both daytime and prime time) were particularly successful as export products to other countries. For example, the daytime soap *Santa Barbara* (NBC) was the first TV program from the United States to air in Russia after the collapse of the Soviet Union (Matelski 1999, 45–46), the 1980s prime-time soaps *Dallas* (CBS) and *Dynasty* (ABC) were among the first international programming broadcast on Chinese television (Gu 2002), and by the early 1990s *The Bold and the Beautiful* (CBS) was the most-watched daily series in the world.

Why the international appeal of American soaps? Historically, US daytime soaps were important in opening new commercial markets because they allowed very large blocks of airtime to be filled at relatively low cost. Other countries could import years or even decades of a program that could be aired either daily or in hefty blocks, thus providing a major source of scheduling content. In addition, the soap opera form—with its "cliffhanger" episodes and "what will happen next?" storytelling—has a unique ability to generate habitual viewing patterns and allow a network to build a loyal audience. Both daytime and prime-time soaps also share universally appealing themes; their focus on love, romance, and family conflict has proven durably appealing all over the world.

American soaps continue to be popular on the world market, though in the late 1990s and 2000s other genres of programming were favored more, as niche marketing (aiming for specific segments of the viewing audience) supplanted mass marketing in the industry. For example, from 2000 to 2005, reality shows such as *Survivor* (CBS) and *Queer Eye for the Straight Guy* (Bravo) dominated the international market; in 2006 and 2007, the appeal was serialized drama thrillers, such as FOX's *24* and *Prison Break*; and in 2015, the emphasis was on "rule-breaking" cable dramas, such as *The Walking Dead* (AMC) and *Game of Thrones* (HBO) (Harrington and Bielby 2008; Roxborough 2015).

BRINGING THE WORLD TO AMERICA THROUGH TELEVISION

Perhaps surprisingly, Americans' exposure to the rest of the world through imported entertainment content took time to unfold. Certainly throughout the history of US television, genres such as news, sports, and documentaries visually revealed the world and its inhabitants in unprecedented ways. For example, legendary CBS newscaster Walter Cronkite (1916–2009) was called "the most trusted man in America" for his reportage of world events to a then-mass television audience. The anthology program *Wide World of Sports* (ABC) launched in 1961 and showcased nearly forty years of national and international sport events and athletes, while the *National Geographic* series (also launched in 1961) introduced decades of American viewers to human-nature dynamics in a wide range of cultural and historical contexts. But entertainment programming from other countries— sitcoms and dramas, game shows, and lifestyle shows— was informally closed to American viewers for decades. Why? From an industry perspective, with a "huge domestic television production infrastructure, the world's richest market to absorb high production costs, and program suppliers able to offer programming to the networks for less than their actual cost of production … there was no incentive to seek alternative, off-shore sources of programming" (Allen 1995, 16). The public service channel PBS occasionally showed programming from overseas (e.g., dramas from the United Kingdom), but in general the networks believed that "since there was

no tradition of watching programs dubbed or subtitled, or even programs with different English accents on network television, [American] audiences would not tolerate such programming" (Allen 1995, 16).

The 1980s/1990s shift from mass audience programming (in the era of only three or four broadcast networks) to niche market programming (in the current era of hundreds of shows available via cable, satellite, and online), combined with the gradual affordability of cable, satellite, and Internet to American viewers, allowed for the emergence of unprecedented heterogeneity in US television. The continued enjoyment of British-made dramas, such as *Downton Abbey* on PBS, is now accompanied by the easy availability of Latin American telenovelas, Japanese game shows, Scandinavian reality shows, and Australian nature shows. Moreover, the recent shift in the global TV market from the buying and selling of finished programs to the buying and selling of locally adaptable formats, along with the shift toward coproduction business models (wherein two or more companies in different parts of the world collaborate on creating a show), has internationalized American television content even more.

We are clearly moving away from understanding and experiencing television as "the box in the corner," and scholars have begun to debate the global implications of a postnetwork, postbroadcast, and perhaps even post-TV era. Considering that "video snacks," "binge watching," and "event series" are the current (somewhat contradictory) rage among American TV viewers, that big global markets such as India and China continue to develop, that online and mobile platforms are rapidly expanding viewing contexts, that the recent economic recession has reduced US industry investment on program development and acquisition, the future of global television for America and American viewers remains an open question.

SEE ALSO *Hollywood; Musicals*

BIBLIOGRAPHY

Aldridge, Ron. "How We Do It: A U.S. Television Market Primer." Videotaped remarks from NATPE Educational Foundation Conference, New Orleans, 1999.

Allen, Robert C. "Introduction." In *To Be Continued … : Soap Operas around the World*, edited by Robert C. Allen, 1–26. London and New York: Routledge, 1995.

Bielby, Denise D., and C. Lee Harrington. *Global TV: Exporting Television in the World Market*. New York: New York University Press, 2008.

Bielby, Denise D., and C. Lee Harrington. "Video Cultures: Television." In *International Encyclopedia of the Social & Behavioral Sciences*, 2nd ed., edited by James D. Wright, Volume 25, 80–86. Oxford, UK: Elsevier, 2015.

Cunningham, Stuart. "History, Context, Politics, Policy." In *The Australian TV Book*, edited by Graeme Turner and Stuart Cunningham, 13–32. St. Leonards, NSW, Australia: Allen and Unwin, 2000.

de la Garde, Roger. "Dare We Compare?" In *Small Nations, Big Neighbour: Denmark and Quebec/Canada Compare Notes on American Popular Culture*, edited by Roger de la Garde, William Gilsdorf, and Ilja Wechselmann, with Jorgen Lerce-Nielsen, 25–64. London: Libbey, 1993.

Gu, Linn. "Latino Soaps Enthrall Chinese." *Hollywood Reporter*, July 3, 2002, 8.

Hoskins, Colin, and Rolf Mirus. "Reasons for the U.S. Dominance of the International Trade in Television Programmes." *Media, Culture, and Society* 10 (1988): 499–515.

Matelski, Marilyn J. *Soap Operas Worldwide: Cultural and Social Realities.* Jefferson, NC: McFarland, 1999.

Nordenstreng, Kaarle, and Tapio Varis. *Television Traffic—A One-Way Street?* Reports and Papers on Mass Communication, No. 70. Paris: UNESCO, 1974.

Nye, Joseph S. *Soft Power: The Means to Success in World Politics.* New York: Public Affairs, 2004.

Roxborough, Scott. "Why the Global TV Business Is Betting on Risky Drama." *Hollywood Reporter*, March 16, 2015.

Schiller, Herbert I. *Communication and Cultural Domination.* White Plains, NY: International Arts and Sciences Press, 1976.

Varis, Tapio. "The International Flow of Television Programs." *Journal of Communication* 34, 1 (1984): 143–152.

C. Lee Harrington
Professor of Sociology
Miami University

Denise D. Bielby
Professor of Sociology
University of California–Santa Barbara

TELLER, EDWARD

SEE *Nuclear Weapons.*

TEMPERANCE MOVEMENT

During the late eighteenth and early nineteenth centuries, concern about excessive drinking emerged in Great Britain and America. Clergymen, physicians, and public officials on both sides of the Atlantic worried that intemperance among the lower classes would produce poverty, crime, and social disorder. The first local societies dedicated solely to battling intemperance arose in the United States: historians generally recognize a temperance society established in 1808 in Saratoga, New York, as the first such group.

THE SPREAD OF THE ALCOHOL REFORM MOVEMENT

Interest in alcohol reform spread rapidly by the 1820s both in the United States and Great Britain. During this early period, American temperance advocates relied heavily on the opinions and writings of British alcohol reformers. Medical publications by prominent British and Scottish physicians, such as George Cheyne (1671–1743), Thomas Garnett (1766–1802), Thomas Trotter (1760–1832), and Robert Macnish (1802–1837), lent scientific authority to the American temperance movement's condemnation of alcohol. This sharing of information did not flow in only one direction, however. British medical thinking on temperance certainly influenced Dr. Benjamin Rush (1746–1813), whose pamphlet, *An Enquiry into the Effects of Spirituous Liquors on the Human Body* (1784), inspired American reformers. In turn, Rush's pamphlet, which went through many editions on both sides of the Atlantic, informed British efforts to curb intemperance.

After the formation of the American Temperance Society in 1826, US temperance reformers' efforts to spread their message, at home and abroad, accelerated. In 1827, the Society commissioned Nathaniel Hewitt (1788–1867), a Presbyterian minister from Connecticut, to travel around the United States for five months. Hewitt's dynamic, impassioned preaching against intemperance won many converts to the cause. This success at home led wealthy temperance supporter John Tappan (1781–1871) to finance a trip for Hewitt to Great Britain and the Continent, so that he could spread the antiliquor message abroad. Hewitt reached London in 1831 and soon aided British temperance supporters in establishing the British and Foreign Temperance Society. He also preached in France, but found the French less receptive to his temperance doctrine.

Other Anglo-American ties also spread the temperance message from the United States to Great Britain during this period. Transatlantic correspondence between reformers, trade relationships among temperance-minded merchants, and personal interaction promoted the formation of American-style temperance societies in Scotland and Ireland by 1829. For their part, British temperance reformers radicalized the Americans' message. By 1833, Joseph Livesey (1794–1884), a Preston merchant, had established a working-class temperance society based on teetotalism, or total abstinence from all alcoholic beverages, distilled or fermented. Total abstinence made its way back across the Atlantic, as the Washingtonians, a workers' temperance movement founded in Baltimore in 1841, adopted a pledge of total abstinence as the defining condition of membership. In 1842, English immigrant and drunkard John B. Gough (1817–1886) took the

Washingtonian total abstinence pledge and became the most celebrated temperance orator in the Anglo-American world, lecturing widely in United States and Britain over the next four decades. Communication, cooperation, and the interchange of ideas would characterize Anglo-American temperance reform throughout the nineteenth century.

MID-NINETEENTH-CENTURY APPROACHES TO REFORM

Events in Europe shaped the American approach to temperance reform in the mid-nineteenth century as well. During the early part of the century, waves of German and Irish immigrants arrived in the United States, bringing with them patterns of alcohol consumption deeply imbedded in their culture and traditions. The majority of native-born Americans, of British and Protestant heritage, resented the newcomers' alien language (many Irish immigrants spoke Gaelic, not English), Catholic religion, and fondness for alcohol. They feared that hordes of intemperate immigrants would increase poverty, crime, and immorality in the United States. Moreover, they felt unable to reform the newcomers, as mutual distrust, combined with linguistic, religious, and cultural differences, made German and Irish immigrants unreceptive to the moral suasion that American temperance reformers used successfully with the native-born population. For this reason, Protestant alcohol reformers put aside their distrust of Catholic clergy to welcome Father Theobald Mathew (1790–1856), a Capuchin friar and Irish temperance leader, to the United States in 1849. During the 1840s, Father Mathew gained fame in Ireland and abroad for administering the total abstinence pledge to three million Irish by 1844. Father Mathew traveled widely in the United States, administering the total abstinence pledge to tens of thousands of Irish Americans and establishing a number of Catholic temperance societies.

During the 1840s, the flow of European immigrants to the United States increased, as political radicals from the German states fled persecution after a series of failed democratic revolutions across Europe in 1848 and starving farmers and laborers sought to escape the Irish potato famine (1845–1849). This influx of German and Irish immigrants may have influenced American temperance reformers in the early 1850s to abandon moral suasion in favor of legal coercion as their primary tactic in the battle against intemperance. The product of this change in approach, the Maine Law, which became a generic term for prohibition legislation, gained renown after the state of Maine adopted a law prohibiting the sale of alcoholic spirits in 1851. Thirteen US states and territories adopted their own version of prohibition, and

the Maine Law sparked interest among temperance reformers in Europe. In Britain, the Maine Law inspired Nathaniel Card (1805–1856), a Manchester cotton manufacturer, to establish in 1853 the United Kingdom Alliance, an organization dedicated to the prohibition of the British liquor trade.

THE RISE OF TEMPERANCE ORGANIZATIONS

The growth of temperance societies, organizations, and institutions in the United States during the last half of the nineteenth century spread the American approach to alcohol reform across Europe and beyond. In 1852, temperance advocates in Syracuse, New York, established the Independent Order of Good Templars (IOGT). The

Postcard of a temperance movement organization, c. 1900. In 1835 a group of British temperance advocates founded the Independent Order of Rechabites, a teetotal organization that also provided the benefits of a "friendly" society, such as funeral and medical benefits. American temperance supporters soon established a rival order. **CULTURE CLUB/HULTON ARCHIVE/GETTY IMAGES**

Good Templars spread rapidly throughout the United States and into the Canadian province of Ontario. In 1868, Joseph Malins (1844–1926), an English immigrant to the United States, joined the Good Templars in Philadelphia. Upon returning to England, Malins established a Good Templars lodge in Birmingham, the first IOGT lodge outside of North America. By 1874, the British branch of the IOGT boasted more than two hundred thousand members. During the same decade, the New England–based Blue Ribbon movement, a total abstinence offshoot of the larger Gospel Temperance movement, spread throughout the United States. By the end of the 1870s, the Blue Ribbon movement expanded into Canada and Great Britain.

British temperance efforts also shaped the US temperance landscape. In 1835, a group of Salford temperance advocates founded the Independent Order of Rechabites (IOR), a teetotal organization that also provided the benefits of a "friendly" society: funeral and sickness benefits, and later, medical benefits. Perhaps in response to American temperance supporters' establishment of a rival Rechabite order in 1842, the British IOR chartered Rechabite "tents" of its own in the United States.

Another British temperance export to the United States was the Salvation Army, a Christian mission organization founded by a Methodist couple, William Booth (1829–1912) and Catherine Booth (1829–1890). When Catherine heard John B. Gough speak on temperance in 1853, she became convinced of the necessity of reclaiming drunkards as part of the Booths' religious ministry. In 1878, the couple established the Salvation Army, a group with a strong commitment to temperance. Beginning in the 1880s, the Booths founded Salvation Army posts in many parts of the United States, as well as other countries.

The Woman's Christian Temperance Union (WCTU), by far the most influential international temperance organization, originated in the United States in 1874. Under the leadership of its second president, Frances Willard (1839–1898), the WCTU undertook a wide range of reforms—Willard's "Do Everything" policy—that linked advocacy of temperance and national prohibition to other causes, such as women's suffrage. Willard also expanded the WCTU's reach beyond the United States by establishing branches in countries around the world. By the late 1870s, WCTU representatives had helped to establish the British Women's Temperance Association (BWTA), which later affiliated with the WCTU and organized chapters in much of the British Empire, including Canada, South Africa, India, and Australia. In 1884, Willard launched the World's Woman's Christian Temperance Union to facilitate further international expansion.

PROHIBITION

By the first decade of the twentieth century, support for national alcohol reform increased in the United States, culminating in the ratification of the Eighteenth Amendment in 1919 and the enactment of Prohibition in 1920. Enthusiasm for prohibition emerged in other parts of the world during this period as well, motivated in part by US influence, along with the political, economic, and social crises produced by World War I (1914–1918). Finland, the first Western nation to adopt prohibition, enacted an alcohol ban in June 1919, six months before the start of US Prohibition. Some Canadian provinces, though not the government in Ottawa, adopted prohibition during World War I. Norway, though neutral in the war, enacted partial prohibition in 1916, extending the ban to all spirits in 1919. American temperance agitation in India, often allied to similar British efforts, promoted limited prohibition in various parts of the country, and led to the inclusion of prohibition in the Indian constitution adopted upon independence from Great Britain in 1947.

Not all European nations embraced American-style prohibition. England and France, both with entrenched traditions and national identities related to drinking, demurred, despite US recommendations and the pressures of World War I. Sweden instituted alcohol rationing during the war, but narrowly rejected prohibition in 1922. Sweden's neighbor, Denmark, which had never demonstrated much interest in American temperance or prohibition, never came close to a total ban on alcohol. New Zealanders expressed more interest in prohibition than their English counterparts, but failed by a small margin to vote in prohibition in 1911 and 1919. Even in nations that adopted prohibition, support for the alcohol ban waned rapidly, just as it did in the United States. By the mid-1930s, Europe, like the United States, had abandoned efforts to proscribe alcoholic beverages.

SEE ALSO *Transatlantic Reform*

BIBLIOGRAPHY

Blocker, Jack S., Jr. *American Temperance Movements: Cycles of Reform.* Boston: Twayne, 1989.

Hames, Gina. *Alcohol in World History.* New York: Routledge, 2012.

Harrison, Brian. *Drink and the Victorians: The Temperance Question in England, 1815–1872.* London: Faber and Faber, 1971.

Quinn, John F. *Father Mathew's Crusade: Temperance in Nineteenth-Century Ireland and Irish America.* Boston: University of Massachusetts Press, 2002.

Tyrrell, Ian R. *Woman's World/Woman's Empire: The Woman's Christian Temperance Union in International Perspective, 1880–1930*. Chapel Hill: University of North Carolina Press, 1991.

Scott C. Martin
Professor of History and American Culture Studies
Bowling Green State University

TET OFFENSIVE

SEE *Vietnam War.*

TEXAS REPUBLIC

Perhaps the earliest impact of Texas felt by the United States came in the form of the hundreds of horses and thousands of cattle shipped east by the Spanish to equip and feed their troops fighting the British on the Gulf Coast after Spain had joined the rebellious American colonies in their war against England. Between 1779 and 1781, Spanish troops captured Natchez, Baton Rouge, Mobile, and Pensacola—opening a third front in North America and contributing to the ultimate British defeat (Thonhoff 1995, 514–515).

EARLY AMERICAN PENETRATION OF MEXICAN TEXAS

The independent United States, especially after the vague boundaries of the 1803 Louisiana Purchase gave President Thomas Jefferson (1743–1826) a pretext to claim that his bargain included Texas, discreetly conspired with a number of filibustering adventurers who hoped to wrest not only Texas but all of Mexico from Spanish hands. Some of these efforts, involving both native Mexicans and Anglo-Americans, produced ephemeral declarations of Texan independence, but Spain managed to crush each one before Mexico itself achieved independence in 1821 (Kennedy 2013, 219, 250–251).

Mexico inherited from Spain the boundary line separating Texas from the United States that was established by the Transcontinental (or Adams-Onís) Treaty of 1819, but Anglo-Americans had found previous Spanish boundaries no serious obstacle when, between 1795 and 1819, the very cities of Natchez, Baton Rouge, Mobile, and Pensacola had all been acquired by the United States in separate legal and quasi-legal transactions.

The most serious American penetration of Texas, however, was effected by a naturalized Mexican citizen—Stephen Fuller Austin (1793–1836)—who arrived in Mexico in 1821 just as it slipped from Spain's grasp. He came to make good on a contract that his late father,

Moses Austin (1761–1821), had arranged with the Spanish to bring three hundred families from the United States to settle in central Texas as Spanish subjects. After spending a year in Mexico City, Austin persuaded the government of the newly independent country to follow through on the colonization project. Under its terms, Austin and his colonists thus became not Spanish subjects, but Mexican citizens. Subsequent Mexican contracts with Austin and other land *empresarios* brought in thousands of settlers from the United States (Cantrell 1999, 84–91).

The bet made by Spain and accepted by Mexico—that taking in land-hungry Americans would protect Texas from American hunger for land—was a desperate attempt to prevent Texas from sharing the fate of Florida and the rest of the Spanish holdings on the Gulf Coast, where sparse Spanish populations and an underfunded military were unable either to control local Indians or to keep out the *norteamericanos*. Perhaps offering Americans generous legal landholdings could turn them into loyal Mexicans.

Mexico also sought new settlers for Texas beyond the United States. Two settlements of Irish Catholics were established in South Texas, at San Patricio and Refugio; nearby, a native Mexican *empresario*, Martín De León (1765–1833), had founded a predominantly Hispanic colony headquartered at Victoria. Despite legal conflicts over land-grant boundaries, during the late 1820s and early 1830s the Irish and Mexican Catholics of these contiguous areas began to blend their cultures through both intermarriage and mutual assimilation (Crimm 2003, 106–107). However, while these non-Anglo colonies attracted hundreds of settlers, the Anglo-American colonies of Austin and other *empresarios* from the United States were attracting settlers (and their slaves) in the thousands.

THE TEXAS REVOLUTION AND INDEPENDENCE FROM MEXICO

Nevertheless, it seemed at first that the risky Mexican immigration policies might be working. Austin sincerely, albeit naively, attempted to have his Anglo settlers provide the leaven to raise all of Mexico to their own particular standards of democracy and economic development. However, Mexico's political instability, and its bipolar tendency to either neglect or dictate to the populations of its frontier regions, produced rebellions all across its northern arc. The civil war in Mexico between supporters and opponents of the central government developed by 1836 into a full-blown secession movement in Texas that was supported by many influential *tejanos* (Hispanic Texans), as well as most of the settler population (Weber 1982, 242–255).

Such a development had been prophesied in 1833 by Samuel Houston (1793–1863), a former governor of

Tennessee who had been sent to Mexican Texas in 1832 by President Andrew Jackson (1767–1845), whose administration had earlier tried to persuade Mexico to sell Texas to the United States. Houston saw the potential for a revolt in Texas, and vowed to Jackson that he would himself settle there and do everything in his power to bring his new home into the American Union (Haley 2001, 95–96).

Neither Austin nor Houston was eager for an armed revolt to begin in 1835, in their view prematurely, but when President Antonio López de Santa Anna (1794–1876) threatened to forcibly bring all of Mexico under his centralist dictatorship, both the formerly loyal citizen Austin and the Jacksonian expansionist Houston took leading roles in the Texas Revolution. After a brief stint as the rebels' military commander, Austin turned to diplomacy in the United States, where he found no direct help from the American government, but considerable popular support for Texan independence. Texas received critical assistance in the form of ships, weapons, supplies, and volunteer soldiers, especially from merchants and land speculators in New Orleans eager for access to a Texas free of restrictive Mexican land laws and tariffs (Miller 2004, 4–5; Jordan 2006, 37–41).

In March 1836, the same convention that declared independence from Mexico gave Sam Houston the command of all Texan ground forces. The rebels were joined by a considerable number of native Mexicans. Juan Nepomuceno Seguín (1806–1890) was one of the first Texan officials to call for an armed revolt against Santa Anna; he commanded a company of *tejano* cavalrymen during the revolution and later became a senator in the Texan Congress and mayor of San Antonio. The declaration of independence was signed by San Antonio representatives José Antonio Navarro (1795–1871) and José Francisco Ruíz (1783–1840). Another signer, Lorenzo de Zavala (1788–1836), was a prominent Mexican statesman and a native of Yucatán who became the first vice president of the Republic of Texas (de la Teja 2002, 23–34, 40–41; McDonald 2010, 129–131).

THE SLAVERY QUESTION

Thanks to Houston's skill and luck as the commander of the Texan army, the overconfident Santa Anna was decisively defeated at the Battle of San Jacinto on April 21, 1836, producing an independent republic whose population (perhaps 90 percent English-speaking by this time) overwhelmingly favored immediate annexation to the United States. However, the growth of antislavery sentiment in the United States made the acquisition of Texas too controversial even for President Jackson to attempt. Both Austin and his Mexican allies in Texas, including Navarro, had believed that large-scale cotton production (and thus a reliance on slaves) was necessary for the economic progress of the underpopulated region, and they had colluded to evade Mexican antislavery laws to bring in thousands of so-called indentured servants who remained, in reality, slaves (Torget 2013, 122–123; Campbell 1989, 23–24).

The slavery issue, while by no means the chief cause of the Texas Revolution, nevertheless deeply colored Americans' disparate reactions to that conflict, and the question of slavery's expansion and survival also lay behind some of the fiercest political battles within the Texas Republic. Houston, the new nation's first elected president and ardent supporter of annexation, was followed in office in 1838 by a proslavery Texan nationalist, Mirabeau Buonaparte Lamar (1798–1859), who saw an independent Texas as a bulwark against growing abolitionism in the United States (Narrett 1997, 281–283).

Slavery, cotton, and abolition were, moreover, major considerations in the foreign relations of the Texas Republic. Both Britain and France were eager to gain untrammeled access to Texan cotton for their cloth manufacturers, but British policy was fraught with ambivalence. England had close ties and large investments with Mexico, and was reluctant to see that nation damaged by a war over Texas. Once Texas became independent, Britain's desire for both Texan cotton and slavery's ultimate demise not only complicated its diplomacy but caused many Americans and Texans to fear the establishment of an antislavery British protectorate in the place of a weak Texan Republic (Haynes 2010, 231, 238–39, 258).

France, with fewer scruples concerning slavery and fewer inhibitions with regard to Mexico, was in 1840 the first European nation to establish diplomatic ties with Texas. The French had earlier done a vulnerable Texas Republic the great service of sweeping the Gulf clear of Mexican warships during their short-lived "Pastry War" with Mexico from 1838 to 1839 (Jordan 2005, 115–117).

However, President Lamar's imperial adventures, including a controversial naval alliance with Yucatán and a botched expedition to New Mexico, had virtually bankrupted his ambitious young republic by the time he left office in 1841. Even more serious Texan weaknesses were soon manifest, as two Mexican invasions in 1842 (each resulting in the brief occupation of San Antonio) resulted in further economic stagnation, a decline in immigration to Texas, and the souring of once-promising relations between the republic's Anglo and Hispanic citizens (Crisp 1995, 44–48). Even Seguín, the revolutionary hero, was forced into a lengthy exile in Mexico (de la Teja 2002, 43–51).

ANNEXATION BY THE UNITED STATES

Interestingly, the population of the Texas Republic began to swell once more by the mid-1840s, this time by settlers from Europe, as well as from the United States. A few English arrivals successfully established themselves in the Peters Colony in North Texas in an *empresario* grant authorized by the Texas Republic in 1841, but most of the new arrivals were French and German speakers (Connor 2005, 21, 107). Many of these were Alsatians brought to Texas by Henri Castro (1786–1865), a French citizen of Portuguese Jewish ancestry who was awarded an *empresario* grant by the Republic in 1842. In 1844, he founded the community of Castroville, a village southwest of San Antonio that still retains its European flavor in the twenty-first century (Weaver 1985, 13–16, 50–54). Even more successful in the long run was the Adelsverein, a society founded in Mainz in 1842 by German nobles who sponsored thousands of settlers in Texas from the depressed rural areas of west-central Germany. These settlers, with their sponsors, founded the successful towns of New Braunfels and Fredericksburg (Jordan 1966, 41–43).

Houston, in his second term as president from 1841 to 1844, sought to stimulate renewed American interest in acquiring Texas by ostentatiously courting the British government and its representatives, and even his rival Lamar had by 1844 turned to annexation by the United States as the best means of saving Texas from British-supported abolitionism (Narrett 1997, 295–296). A treaty of annexation negotiated with the American secretary of state John C. Calhoun (1782–1850), however, went down to defeat in the US Senate in June 1844 after Calhoun, in response to an inquiry from Britain, foolishly proclaimed that the annexation of Texas was necessary for the benefit of slavery in the United States (Haynes 2010, 243–244).

The calculus of annexation was altered the following November, when James Knox Polk (1795–1849) was elected president of the United States on an unabashedly expansionist platform calling for American ownership of both Texas and Oregon. His predecessor in the White House, John Tyler (1790–1862), immediately moved to secure a joint resolution of Congress to offer Texas statehood in the American Union. The Texas Resolution was narrowly passed in February, and Tyler signed it into law on March 1, 1845, three days before leaving office (Crapol 2006, 220).

A special Texas convention convened in the city of Austin on the Fourth of July to accept the American offer and to write a constitution for the state of Texas. Navarro, who had only recently escaped from prison in Mexico (for his participation in President Lamar's ill-fated Santa Fe expedition), was the only native Texan (and the only *tejano*) delegate (Crisp 2010, 156). On December 29, 1845, the US Congress made Texas the twenty-eighth state, and in a formal ceremony in Austin on February 19, 1846, the national flag of the Republic of Texas was lowered for the last time (Kerr 2013, 215).

SEE ALSO *Borderlands; Mexican-American War; North America*

BIBLIOGRAPHY

Campbell, Randolph B. *An Empire for Slavery: The Peculiar Institution in Texas, 1821–1865*. Baton Rouge: Louisiana State University Press, 1989.

Cantrell, Gregg. *Stephen F. Austin: Empresario of Texas*. New Haven, CT: Yale University Press, 1999.

Connor, Seymour V. *The Peters Colony of Texas: A History and Biographical Sketches of the Early Settlers*. Austin: Texas State Historical Association, 1959. Reprint, McKinney, TX: Collin County Historical Society, 2005.

Crapol, Edward P. *John Tyler: The Accidental President*. Chapel Hill: University of North Carolina Press, 2006.

Crimm, Ana Carolina Castillo. *De León: A Tejano Family History*. Austin: University of Texas Press, 2003.

Crisp, James E. "Race, Revolution, and the Texas Republic: Toward a Reinterpretation." In *The Texas Military Experience: From the Texas Revolution through World War II*, edited by Joseph G. Dawson III, 32–48, 200–210. College Station: Texas A&M University Press, 1995.

Crisp, James E. "José Antonio Navarro: The Problem of Tejano Powerlessness." In *Tejano Leadership in Mexican and Revolutionary Texas*, edited by Jesús F. de la Teja, 146–168. College Station: Texas A&M University Press, 2010.

de la Teja, Jesús F., ed. *A Revolution Remembered: The Memoirs and Selected Correspondence of Juan N. Seguín*. Austin: Texas State Historical Association, 2002.

Haley, James L. *Sam Houston*. Norman: University of Oklahoma Press, 2001.

Haynes, Sam W. *Unfinished Revolution: The Early American Republic in a British World*. Charlottesville: University of Virginia Press, 2010.

Jordan, Jonathan W. *Lone Star Navy: Texas, the Fight for the Gulf of Mexico, and the Shaping of the American West*. Washington, DC: Potomac, 2005.

Jordan, Terry G. *German Seed in Texas Soil: Immigrant Farmers in Nineteenth-Century Texas*. Austin: University of Texas Press, 1966.

Kennedy, Roger G. *Cotton and Conquest: How the Plantation System Acquired Texas*. Norman: University of Oklahoma Press, 2013.

Kerr, Jeffrey Stuart. *Seat of Empire: The Embattled Birth of Austin, Texas*. Lubbock: Texas Tech University Press, 2013.

McDonald, David. *José Antonio Navarro: In Search of the American Dream in Nineteenth-Century Texas*. Denton: Texas State Historical Association, 2010.

Miller, Edward L. *New Orleans and the Texas Revolution*. College Station: Texas A&M University Press, 2004.

Narrett, David E. "A Choice of Destiny: Immigration Policy, Slavery, and the Annexation of Texas." *Southwestern Historical Quarterly* 100, 3 (1997): 271–303.

Thonhoff, Robert H. "Texas and the American Revolution." *Southwestern Historical Quarterly* 98, 4 (1995): 511–517.

Torget, Andrew J. "Stephen F. Austin's Views on Slavery in Early Texas." In *This Corner of Canaan: Essays on Texas in Honor of Randolph B. Campbell*, edited by Richard B. McAslin, Donald E. Chipman, and Andrew J. Torget, 107–128. Denton: University of North Texas Press, 2013.

Weaver, Bobby D. *Castro's Colony: Empresario Development in Texas, 1842–1865*. College Station: Texas A&M University Press, 1985.

Weber, David J. *The Mexican Frontier, 1821–1846: The American Southwest under Mexico*. Albuquerque: University of New Mexico Press, 1982.

James E. Crisp
Professor of History
North Carolina State University

THINK TANKS

Home to over 1,800 think tanks, the United States boasts the largest and most visible population of policy research institutes in the world. When the term *think tank* was coined in the United States during World War II (1939–1945), it simply meant a secure room or environment in which military planners and policy makers met to discuss wartime strategy. In contemporary discourse, *think tank* generally refers to a nonprofit, tax-exempt, nonpartisan (not to be confused with nonideological) institution engaged in research and analysis on one or more issues related to domestic or foreign policy.

THE RISE OF AMERICAN FOREIGN-POLICY THINK TANKS

The first half of the twentieth century proved to be a formative period for think-tank growth in the United States. From 1910 to 1921, four of the most distinguished think tanks with expertise in foreign policy were created: the Carnegie Endowment for International Peace (1910); the Institute for Government Research (1916), which merged with two other organizations to form the Brookings Institution in 1927; the Hoover Institution on War, Revolution, and Peace (1919); and the Council on Foreign Relations (1921). In the ensuing years, the desire on the part of policy entrepreneurs to establish think tanks became even greater. In 1943, the American Enterprise Institute for Public Policy Research (AEI) was formed, and although initially it did not concentrate on foreign policy, this field of research has become one of its trademarks. Five years later, the Rand Corporation, with the financial support of the US Department of Defense, was chartered in Santa Monica, California, to "further and promote scientific, educational, and charitable purposes, all for the public welfare and security of the United States of America." Rand's star-studded lineup of scientists, including Herman Kahn (1922–1983), Bernard Brodie (1910–1978), and Thomas Schelling (b. 1921), were, along with their colleagues, entrusted with helping the United States develop its nuclear strategy. Using systems analysis, game theory, and various simulation exercises, Rand scientists devoted themselves in the immediate postwar years to serving the needs of the US Air Force.

In the years following Rand's founding, several more foreign-affairs think tanks joined the fray. Among the many organizations that soon populated the think-tank community were the Foreign Policy Research Institute (1955), the Hudson Institute (1961), the Center for Strategic and International Studies (1962), the Institute for Policy Studies (1963), the Center for Defense Information (1972), the Heritage Foundation (1973), the Worldwatch Institute (1974), the Carter Center (1982), the Nixon Center for Peace and Freedom (1994, now known as the Center for the National Interest), the Project for the New American Century (1997, replaced by the Foreign Policy Initiative), the Center for Security Policy (1998), the Center for a New American Security (2007), and the Foreign Policy Initiative (2009).

INFLUENCE ON DEFENSE POLICY

Recently, scholars have begun to delve more deeply into the domestic sources of US foreign and defense policy, and have identified fingerprints left by a select group of think tanks on several policy initiatives. When Ronald Reagan (1911–2004) toured the North American Aerospace Defense Command (NORAD) on July 31, 1979, he internalized how vulnerable the United States was to a nuclear attack, and began to consider other options to shelter the American people. One such option was presented by General Daniel O. Graham (1925–1995), the former head of the Defense Intelligence Agency, who briefed Reagan on the concept of a missile shield that, in theory, would protect the United States from incoming ballistic missiles. His idea was to construct a multilayered ground-based and space-based defense system that could track, intercept, and destroy missiles. In September 1981, Graham founded High Frontier, a Virginia-based think tank, with the intention of continuing research on this and related programs. With the assistance of the Heritage Foundation, which provided space for the nascent think tank to conduct research, High Frontier published a report that examined in greater detail how the system would function. When President Reagan unveiled the Strategic Defense Initiative (SDI) during a televised address on March 23, 1983, it was clear that Graham and High Frontier had made an impression. Indeed, on several occasions during his presidency, Reagan paid homage to High Frontier and its founder for advancing a new strategic vision for the United States.

Every president since Reagan has pursued missile defense, and several think tanks have offered their support along the way. Few think tanks have invested more resources in keeping this initiative alive than the Center for Security Policy (CSP). Headed by Frank Gaffney (b. 1953), a former official in the Pentagon, the CSP has developed an extensive network of current and former policy makers, academics, journalists, and representatives from the private sector to extol the virtues of missile defense. Since its inception in 1988, CSP has generated an impressive body of research on missile defense and related technology. Following the events of 9/11, the CSP and other think tanks reminded the American people why the government should make an even greater investment in missile defense. Think tanks also joined the chorus of voices calling for the United States to take military action against states that harbored terrorists.

INVOLVEMENT IN SHAPING MIDDLE EAST POLICY

Founded in 1997, the Project for a New American Century (PNAC) was a small think tank with powerful ties to the George W. Bush (b. 1946) administration. Several of its members, including Donald Rumsfeld (b. 1932), Richard Armitage (b. 1945), Paul Wolfowitz (b. 1943), and Richard B. "Dick" Cheney (b. 1941), had assumed key positions in Bush's inner circle and understood what steps the United States had to take to reduce its vulnerability. In several of its reports, the PNAC urged the US military to prepare for simultaneous wars in multiple theaters. It also urged both the Clinton and the Bush administrations to remove Saddam Hussein (1937–2006) from power. When President Bush issued an executive order to invade Iraq, journalists on both sides of the Atlantic seem convinced that his foreign policy had largely been influenced by the PNAC. Only later did the veteran *Washington Post* reporter Bob Woodward (2006) discover that the AEI also had a hand in urging the president to topple the Iraqi dictator. At the request of Wolfowitz, Chris DeMuth (b. 1946), a former president of the AEI, organized a small policy task force that included some of America's leading experts on the Middle East. Among other things, the task force produced a report titled *Delta of Terrorism* (2001) that recommended that the Iraqi people be liberated from their dictatorial leader. The report was circulated to top foreign policy officials in Bush's inner circle, the so-called "vulcans," who, according to Woodward's account, found the report

very persuasive. But the involvement of think tanks in shaping US foreign policy toward the Middle East did not end there.

In December 2006, two AEI scholars, the retired general Jack Keane (b. 1943), a former vice chief of staff of the US Army and a member of the advisory Defense Policy Review Board, and Fred Kagan (b. 1970), a military historian, met with Vice President Cheney to discuss their plans for a so-called surge in Iraq. After presenting the results of months of work that they had conducted at the AEI, Keane and Kagan found an ally in Cheney and in Senator John McCain (b. 1936), who played a key role in selling the idea to President Bush. Though the PNAC should be credited with bringing scholars and policy makers together to reconsider how to pursue US defense- and foreign-policy interests in the twenty-first century, it would be an exaggeration to suggest that this organization alone was responsible for laying the foundation for US foreign policy during the Bush years.

SOURCES OF FUNDING

As long as there are policy entrepreneurs and philanthropists in the United States who believe in the power of ideas, there will be think tanks willing to propose policy recommendations to policy makers and to the public. However, as historians, political scientists, and, more recently, a group of investigative reporters remind us, ideas can and often do have profound consequences. This is why it is important to pay close attention to the individuals, philanthropic foundations, corporations, and governments (both domestic and foreign) that finance these institutions. In response to a 2014 exposé in the *New York Times* that, among other things, documented the large contributions made by several foreign governments to top-tier think tanks, including the Brookings Institution, the Atlantic Council, and the Center for Strategic and International Studies, the US Congress considered a new rule that would require think-tank scholars testifying before congressional committees to disclose their sources of funding (Lipton, Williams, and Confessore 2014). This new rule, described in H. Res. 5, 114th Congress 1st Session, was approved on January 5, 2015.

Both the US Congress and the Internal Revenue Service have expressed concern that some think tanks may have violated their charitable status by engaging in various lobbying activities, an issue the new legislation is intended to help address. Additional pressure for think tanks to be more transparent with respect to sources of funding is being applied by Transparify, an organization established by two European academics to encourage think tanks around the globe to provide this and related information about their donors on their website. In an annual report, Transparify assigns a rating from one to five (five being the highest) to think tanks based on their willingness to comply. As think tanks come to occupy an even stronger presence on the political landscape, and as their ties to affluent donors become more pronounced, students of US foreign policy may want to pay closer attention to the various factors that motivate policy institutes to influence decisions that have and may very well shape American and world history.

SEE ALSO *Carnegie Endowment for International Peace; Rand Corporation*

BIBLIOGRAPHY

Abelson, Donald E. *American Think-Tanks and Their Role in U.S. Foreign Policy.* London: Macmillan; New York: St. Martin's Press, 1996.

Abelson, Donald E. *A Capitol Idea: Think Tanks and U.S. Foreign Policy.* Montreal, QC: McGill-Queen's University Press, 2006.

Abelson, Donald E. *Do Think Tanks Matter? Assessing the Impact of Public Policy Institutes.* 2nd ed. Montreal, QC: McGill-Queen's University Press, 2009.

Higgott, Richard, and Diane Stone. "The Limits of Influence: Foreign Policy Think Tanks in Britain and the USA." *Review of International Studies* 20, 1 (1994): 15–34.

Lipton, Eric, Brooke Williams, and Nicholas Confessore. "Foreign Powers Buy Influence at Think Tanks." *New York Times,* September 7, 2014.

McGann, James G., and R. Kent Weaver, eds. *Think Tanks and Civil Societies: Catalysts for Ideas and Action.* New Brunswick, NJ: Transaction, 2000.

Parmar, Inderjeet. *Think Tanks and Power in Foreign Policy: A Comparative Study of the Role and Influence of the Council on Foreign Relations and the Royal Institute of International Affairs, 1939–1945.* New York: Palgrave Macmillan, 2004.

Rich, Andrew. *Think Tanks, Public Policy, and the Politics of Expertise.* New York: Cambridge University Press, 2004.

Smith, James Allen. *The Idea Brokers: Think Tanks and the Rise of the New Policy Elite.* New York: Free Press, 1991.

Woodward, Bob. *State of Denial: Bush at War, Part III.* New York: Simon and Schuster, 2006.

Donald E. Abelson
Professor, Department of Political Science
The University of Western Ontario

THIRD WORLD

The idea of the "Third World" has had a storied career in world politics, and has been contested and destabilized by American and European political and economic elites as well as revolutionaries and nationalists throughout the world for as long as the term has been used.

Most scholars agree that the term was the invention of French demographer Alfred Sauvy (1898–1990). A liberal academic and public intellectual whose influence in his home country dated back to the 1930s, Sauvy had spent the years after the Second World War representing France at the United Nations, where he became deeply engaged with the humanitarian problems surrounding decolonization. In the summer of 1952, then, as Cold War tensions between the Soviet Union and the United States ran high, simmering conflicts far removed from Washington and Moscow captured Sauvy's attention. As many of his fellow Frenchmen labored to keep a lid on anticolonial movements in Tunisia and Vietnam and as the American military remained bogged down on the Korean Peninsula, Sauvy penned an article for Paris's leftist weekly, *L'Observateur,* entitled "Trois Monde, Une Planète." In the article, Sauvy compared the yearnings and desires of the millions of people who were struggling to cast off the yoke of empire in Asia, Africa, Latin America, and the Middle East to those of the members of the Third Estate during the French Revolution. He argued that the needs of the inhabitants of these regions posed a much greater challenge to the world than the bipolar rivalry between the West and the East. "We speak willingly of two worlds ... of their possible war and their possible coexistence ... but we too often forget that there exists a third world" (Sauvy 1952, 14). Paraphrasing the famous eighteenth-century pamphlet by Father Emmanuel Joseph Sieyès (1748–1836) titled "What is the Third Estate," Sauvy (1952) wrote: "In the end, this Third World, ignored, exploited, and despised, wants also to become something" (14).

"Third World" quickly took on a life of its own in the United States. Throughout the 1950s, many in the United States interpreted it to mean a "Third Force" in global politics, one that was aligned with neither the Soviets nor the Americans but that was equal in importance to both and could tip the scales in the global Cold War. In 1955, the Non-Aligned Movement (NAM) gave meaning to this definition of the term. Spearheaded by nationalist leaders in India, Indonesia, and Egypt, the Bandung Conference brought twenty-nine independent countries together to discuss the importance of neutrality in the increasingly dangerous confrontation between the Soviets and Americans. American policy makers were concerned about this rising tide of what many saw as anti-Americanism. By the 1960s, however, the NAM had faltered under the pressure of Cold War power politics and *Third World* had become a term more often used by American development economists than Asian, African, or Latin American nationalists. In this era, the term took on a hierarchical cast, denoting economic and political backwardness. American policy makers, enchanted by modernization theory, equated the Third World with poverty, rurality, and "underdevelopment." That poverty proved a vexing problem for the US government, which sought to stem the perceived expansion of communism to the Western Hemisphere and other parts of the resource-rich periphery but often ran afoul of nationalist movements seeking autonomy rather than alliances with a superpower. The 1970s witnessed a revival of Sauvy's notion of the Third World as a force in world politics. As the failures of modernization theory and of American development efforts became clear and as new theories about Third World poverty—generated by economists and political leaders from the Third World itself—began to circulate, many African, Asian, and Latin American countries mobilized this collective identifier to demand international economic reform. The Group of 77 countries that self-identified as "developing" joined forces at the United Nations to promote the New International Economic Order, which would be more conducive to development and political autonomy.

Because of changes in the global economy and in the Cold War conflict, the scales of world power tipped back toward the United States in the 1980s, dealing a blow to the nascent "Third World solidarity" of the 1970s. The end of the Cold War made a Third Force insignificant. The term then returned to its 1960s definition as a signifier of poverty, backwardness, and inferiority, a term deployed by elites in the developed world to explain the problems of the underdeveloped one. The term lost salience as a way to explain the interconnectedness of developing countries, too, when patterns of development changed quite drastically in the context of the globalization of the late 1980s and early 1990s. The term has since fallen out of favor in development discourse. It has been replaced by a variety of terms—*developing countries, less-developed countries,* and *Global South* most common among them—each imbued with its own political and economic meaning and each subject to debates no less fulsome than those that surrounded the term *Third World.*

SEE ALSO *Bandung Conference (1955); Cold War; Decolonization; Global South; Modernization Theory; Non-Aligned Movement*

BIBLIOGRAPHY

Kolko, Gabriel. *Confronting the Third World: United States Foreign Policy, 1945–1980.* New York: Pantheon, 1988.

Painter, Davis S. "Explaining U.S. Relations with the Third World." *Diplomatic History* 19, 3 (July 1995): 525–548.

Sauvy, Alfred. "Trois Mondes, Une Planète." *L'Observateur,* August 14, 1952, 14.

Tomlinson, B. R. "What Was the Third World?" *Journal of Contemporary History* 38, 2 (April 2003): 307–321.

Wolf-Phillips, Leslie. "Why the 'Third World'? Origin, Definition, and Usage." *Third World Quarterly* 9, 4 (October 1987): 1311–1327.

Worsley, Peter. *The Three Worlds: Culture and World Development.* Chicago: University of Chicago Press, 1984.

Sheyda F. A. Jahanbani
Assistant Professor of History
University of Kansas

THOMPSON, GEORGE

SEE *Transatlantic Reform.*

THOMPSON-URRUTIA TREATY (1921)

SEE *Colombia.*

TOUSSAINT LOUVERTURE
1743–1803

Toussaint Louverture was the leader of the Haitian Revolution (1791–1804) in the French colony of Saint-Domingue (later known as Haiti). He was born into slavery on a plantation in northern Saint-Domingue. When the enslaved Africans took up arms in 1791, Louverture had been a free man for roughly two decades. News of enslaved people rebelling against an imperial power horrified most Americans. Many Americans condemned the Dominguan fighters as "wild tigers" who pillaged and massacred to destroy a profitable slave-plantation system. President George Washington (1732–1799) intervened in the Haitian Revolution with funding, arms, and munitions in an effort to thwart the black revolutionaries' stride toward freedom.

Louverture rose through the ranks of the revolutionary army. He led armies that defeated successively the French, Spanish, and British militaries. Louverture became the colony's top military commander in 1797. He led a military force that conjured palpable fear within white Americans from Maryland to Georgia. By then, however, Louverture had earned a reputation across the United States for his honest treatment of Americans and Europeans. Americans skeptical of the Haitian Revolution began to warm to Louverture's leadership.

In 1798, Louverture approached President John Adams (1735–1826) as a fellow Atlantic leader with an offer of bilateral relations and trade. He sent an emissary to the United States who understood the business interests of northern merchants and calmed the fears of slave rebellions in southern slaveholders. Louverture pledged to "do everything in my power to protect Americans who will frequent the ports of this Colony" (Johnson 2014, 41). The backing of the offer, and the foundation of Dominguan-American diplomacy, was the security of Louverture's word. Secretary of State Timothy Pickering (1745–1829) assessed the Dominguan leader as prudent and judicious. US politicians opposed to Dominguan-American relations acknowledged that Louverture "had behaved well to Americans" (Johnson 2014, 37). American officials treated Louverture as a de facto head of state. The United States forged a diplomatic alliance with revolutionary Saint-Domingue as northern merchants and proslavery southerners came to see Louverture as a man to be trusted.

US engagement with Saint-Domingue underscored stark differences in policy and worldview between Presidents Adams and Washington. The Adams administration engaged the Louverturian government fully aware that US involvement could lead to the Atlantic world's first independent nation-state of black people. Adams dispatched a minister-level diplomat to Louverture and ordered the US Navy to take up station off the Saint-Domingue coast in a show of support. Consul General Edward Stevens (1754–1834) expressed esteem for Louverture's leadership: "He is a man of great humanity, good sense, and integrity" (Johnson 2014, 103). Louverture and Stevens concluded an important commercial treaty and cultivated an intimate partnership. Commodore Silas Talbot (1751–1813) executed joint military operations with the Dominguan army and engaged an American warship in the US Navy's first military action on behalf of a foreign ally. Through military prowess, Louverture commanded the political respect and diplomatic engagement of the Atlantic world's most powerful leaders. According to one contemporary writer, "There has never been a man of his color to reach such an eminent position of power" (Johnson 2014, 176).

The governments of the United States and Saint-Domingue entered the nineteenth century in a partnership that illustrated the human capacity to circumvent racial conventions. The Adams-Louverture alliance inspired white Americans and Dominguans of color to employ extraordinary measures to accomplish bilateral objectives. The cross-cultural collaboration empowered white Americans to engage men of color in ways that they had never done before—and would never do again. People of color in the United States gained inspiration from Louverture's leadership of the Haitian Revolution. However, most prominent black figures, with the notable exception of Prince Hall (1735–1807) in Boston, remained silent throughout the 1790s on Saint-Domingue's sociopolitical transformations.

Through transracial diplomacy, the United States and Saint-Domingue jointly possessed the potential to shape subsequent independence movements and racial conflicts across the western Atlantic world. In 1801, Louverture took over the neighboring colony of Santo Domingo and emancipated the remaining enslaved peoples there. Louverture governed all of Hispaniola, and the United States became the island's closest ally and largest trading partner. Later that year, President Thomas Jefferson (1743–1826), who had defeated Adams in the last election, recalled the US emissary and the Navy from Saint-Domingue. A year later, a French expeditionary force sent by Emperor Napoléon (1769–1821) to put down the revolution arrested Louverture and deported him. In 1803, Louverture died unceremoniously in France's Fort de Joux prison, prompting American diarist Elizabeth Drinker (1734–1807) to record, "My heart is heavy; as the saying is—star light—'Toussaint Louverture, the celebrated African Chief, is dead'" (Johnson 2014, 181).

In that same year, British poet William Wordsworth (1770–1850) penned "To Toussaint L'Ouverture," an elegy that predicted, "Thou hast left behind Powers that will work for thee" (Wordsworth 1889, 89). Louverture's Atlantic world legacy, indeed, lived on. The military Louverture maintained with American collaboration defeated the French army. In 1804, the victorious revolutionaries established Haiti as the first nation-state to originate from a slave revolt. The historic moment of black liberation and independence offered hope for freedom and equality to disenfranchised and enslaved people of color in the United States. African Americans embraced and identified with Louverture as a transatlantic hero.

In the United States, the memory of Louverture became embroiled in the battle over slavery through the Civil War (1861–1865). Abolitionists insisted that enslaved peoples, "American Toussaints," would rise up and fight for their freedom. Proslavery factions stoked white American fears of slave rebellions to assert that a civil war would provoke a US-version of the Haitian Revolution. Frederick Douglass (c. 1817/8–1895) and prominent people of color employed the memory of the Haitian Revolution to establish the famed Fifty-Fourth Massachusetts Regiment, arguing that by copying Louverture black soldiers would open the door to freedom and equality. Following the Civil War and the abolition of American slavery, African Americans named their children after Haiti's revolutionary leader. Louverture's achievements remained a powerful symbol of resilience for African Americans during the nadir of American race relations and well into the twentieth century.

SEE ALSO *Adams, John; Caribbean; French Revolution; Haitian Revolution; Jefferson, Thomas; Washington, George*

BIBLIOGRAPHY

Clavin, Matthew J. *Toussaint Louverture and the American Civil War: The Promise and Peril of a Second Haitian Revolution.* Philadelphia: University of Pennsylvania Press, 2010.

de Cauna, Jacques, ed. *Toussaint Louverture et l'indépendance d'Haïti: Témoignages pour un bicentenaire.* Paris: Karthala, 2004.

Johnson, Ronald Angelo. *Diplomacy in Black and White: John Adams, Toussaint Louverture, and Their Atlantic World Alliance.* Athens: University of Georgia Press, 2014.

Wordsworth, William. *Select Poems of William Wordsworth.* Edited by William J. Rolfe. New York: Harper, 1889.

Ronald Angelo Johnson
Assistant Professor of History
Texas Sate University

TRAINS

Railways emerged in the early nineteenth century in England as a result of a series of inventions that led to, first, the development of steam power, and then engines that could be mounted on wheels to provide mobility. This process, which took decades and was replete with false starts and failed inventions, culminated in the construction of two pioneering railways. The Stockton and Darlington, which started operating in 1825, was a rather crude affair but important in being the first railway open to both passengers and freight, and powered, at least partly, by steam locomotives. More significantly, five years later, the Liverpool and Manchester Railway, which was much more recognizable as a modern railway in that it was double tracked throughout, linked two major towns, and operated solely by steam engines, was opened amid great fanfare and celebrations.

THE INFLUENCE OF BRITISH PREDECESSORS ON EARLY AMERICAN RAILROADS

These events were keenly observed by railway pioneers from the United States, and consequently the early American railroads were greatly influenced by their British predecessors. At the time, America was a couple of decades behind the United Kingdom in terms of industrial development, and it was to be the new nation's enthusiastic adoption of the iron road that would provide the spur to catching up with its former colonial master and then rapidly overtaking it.

In the United States, various projects for railway construction had been mooted since the mid-1810s but none had come to fruition. A few short lines, either horse-powered or using standing engines, were built in the 1820s to serve mines or wharves, but these were modest affairs that did not carry passengers. Horatio Allen (1802–1889), the engineer of the line built at Carbondale, Pennsylvania, by the Delaware and Hudson Railway Company, visited the United Kingdom in the late 1820s to look at locomotive technology and was so impressed that he arranged to import a British locomotive, the *Stourbridge Lion*, named after the town in the Midlands where it was built. It arrived in kit form and had to be rebuilt by Allen, but nevertheless attracted considerable public interest when in August 1829 it became the first locomotive to be operated on railway tracks in the United States. That test run along the existing line, however, was the only time the locomotive was in steam because the rails were insufficiently robust to bear its weight safely and groaned ominously when the locomotive passed over them. The engine consequently ended up ignominiously dismantled for spare parts for its successors.

The first fully fledged American railway, the Baltimore and Ohio, or B&O, was also built strongly on British engineering. The eastern seaboard cities were each vying to become the gateway to the interior of the nation, and transport was clearly the key. However, the people of Baltimore were more adventurous than their rivals in considering a railroad, rather than a canal, as the best mode of transport. The origins of the railway lay in the formation of the awkwardly named Pennsylvania Society for Promotion of Internal Improvements, which sent William Strickland (1788–1854) across the Atlantic to view the progress of Britain's burgeoning railways. His subsequent glowing report on the Stockton and Darlington, presented to the society in 1826, convinced the townspeople that the future lay in railways rather than canals. Two other prominent and farsighted Baltimore residents, Philip E. Thomas (1776–1861) and George Brown (1787–1859), were also sent that year to the United Kingdom and returned to try to raise money for the new railway, which was intended to stretch all the way from Baltimore to Wheeling, Virginia (now West Virginia), on the Ohio River. At 380 miles (612 kilometers), it would be some thirty times longer than the Stockton and Darlington.

THE RAPID SPREAD OF RAILROADS IN THE UNITED STATES

Construction began on Independence Day in 1828 with a suitably newsworthy event. Charles Carroll (1737–1832), the last surviving signatory of the Declaration of Independence, turned the first sod and observed: "I consider what I have just now done to be among the most important acts of my life, second only to my signing the Declaration of Independence, if indeed, it be even second to that" (Wolmar 2012, 1). It was a prescient remark given the importance of the railways in American history. In fact, while a section of the B&O opened in

1830, at the same time as the Liverpool and Manchester in England, it would not reach its original planned destination, Wheeling, until 1852.

Meanwhile, Horatio Allen had not retired from the fray. He moved south, where he helped developed what became, for a time, the world's longest railway using American technology based on the experience gleaned from studying British engines. This was the Charleston and Hamburg, where, in December 1830, the first US-built engine, the quaintly named *Best Friend of Charleston*, pulled its first train on a well-publicized inaugural run. Soon, locomotive-hauled trains were running regularly on the first six miles (9.7 kilometers) of track. Indeed, most histories focus on the B&O, a company that survived until after the Second World War (1939–1945) as the key pioneering railway. However, the Charleston and Hamburg railroad, which completed its 136-mile (219-kilometer) line by 1833 and used only steam power—unlike the B&O, which flirted with horses—has claim to being the most significant development. But the Charleston and Hamburg has largely been forgotten because it was soon absorbed by a rival, the South Carolina Railroad Company.

The men who built these lines and the other early railway pioneers all had visions of railways as being a key transport development, but perhaps none could have envisaged just how fast the technology would spread and how important the railways would become as the catalyst in the economic growth of the United States. The technology would soon become distinctly American, partly dictated by the geography of the United States and the availability of resources. The length of the lines, far greater than in the smaller countries of Europe, meant that the railways had to be built relatively cheaply, given the shortage of capital and the sparsely populated areas through which the lines would travel, which meant usage was unlikely to be heavy. Therefore, the tracks were often routed round hills and rivers, rather than through or over them, in order to save costs, although following the contours of the countryside inevitably meant lines were longer. Engines had to be more powerful to cope with the greater inclines and the long distances, and they were soon all fitted with the distinctive smokestacks in order to minimize sparks from the wood that was mostly used as fuel in the early days. Cowcatchers—which in effect are cow killers—a slanting V-shaped frame mounted to the front of a locomotive, became necessary because, unlike many European railways, the tracks were left unfenced to save costs and consequently were vulnerable to animal intruders. Even the name was changed, as *railroads*, a term used for some of the earliest horse- or human-powered lines, became prominent in the United States.

The spread of the railroads in the United States was remarkable and rapid. By 1835, just seven years after

Carroll's prescient speech, there were nearly 1,000 miles (1,610 kilometers) of railway on thirty-nine different lines across the United States. The growth soon accelerated and reached a peak of more than 250,000 miles (402,336 kilometers) of line just before the First World War. In other words, the United States built about 3,000 miles (4,828 kilometers) of railroad every year during that period, which works out to a remarkable eight miles (12.9 kilometers) per day.

SEE ALSO *Airplanes; Americanization; Automobiles; Cold War; Exceptionalism; Exports, Exportation; Industrialization; Internationalism; Isolationism; World War I; World War II; World's Fairs*

BIBLIOGRAPHY

Grant, H. Roger. *The Railroad: The Life Story of a Technology.* Westport, CT: Greenwood Press, 2005.

Holbrook, Stewart H. *The Story of American Railroads.* New York: Crown, 1947.

Martin, Albro. *Railroads Triumphant: The Growth, Rejection, and Rebirth of a Vital American Force.* Oxford: Oxford University Press, 1992.

Taylor, George Rogers. *The Transportation Revolution, 1815–1860.* New York: Holt, Rinehart, and Winston, 1951.

Wolmar, Christian. *The Great Railroad Revolution: The History of Trains in America.* New York: PublicAffairs, 2012.

Christian Wolmar
London, United Kingdom

TRANSATLANTIC REFORM

In the eighteenth century a new perception of the capacity and moral responsibility of individuals to effect events far away and in the future, combined with heightened sympathy for the suffering of strangers, gave rise to humanitarianism. A transnational "empire of humanity" developed: a network of philanthropists who transmitted ideas and institutions and fostered a new sense of cosmopolitanism. This was in large part a secular endeavor in which men of the medical profession played an important part, and it overlapped significantly with the Republic of Letters. As reformers cherished ever greater ambitions, such as the global eradication of smallpox or the slave trade, their projects were necessarily based increasingly on cooperation on a global scale. But these growing ambitions were also supported by infrastructural innovations: In particular, the success of voluntary organizations for philanthropic purposes in the decades between 1780 and 1820 had instilled in many people in Europe and the United States the sense that any charitable and reform project was possible now they knew how to organize it. Throughout the century, women participated in these projects, networks, and organizations, crafting a new public role for themselves that, when contested, led to the articulation of demands for women's rights.

RELIGIOUS AND SECULAR REFORM

British reform was a model to aspire to for friends of humanity around the world. However, as a result of the revolutionary era the nature of transatlantic reform changed. Cosmopolitanism could partly bridge the new divide between the United States and Great Britain, but the fear of the effects of the French Revolution led many philanthropists to downplay their international ties and stress instead the Anglo-American Protestant civilizing mission, both at home and abroad. Somewhat paradoxically, at the beginning of the century the new American nation wanted to prove its independence by emulating the British example, as the origins of missionary, bible, and religious tract societies indicate. Seeking partnership with Britain made sense: The shared history and language, but above all the similar effects of evangelical revivalism on considerable parts of the middle classes, produced a shared rhetoric of religious reform and a deeply felt desire to enlist in the global struggle against Satan. Still, it is important to note that this culture was shaped by the older philanthropic tradition that was rooted in the European Enlightenment, which formed the intellectual and infrastructural background for "philanthropic tourism" to institutions and reformers all over the world.

Prison reform offers a case in point: The notion that criminals could be reformed was shared by large groups of reformers in the eighteenth and nineteenth century, not all of whom were touched by evangelicalism. The most famous example is Alexis de Tocqueville (1805–1859), who was sent to the United States in 1831 by the French government to study prison reform. Whereas new ideas on penitentiary reform had been developed mainly by British and Continental reformers, they were not widely recognized or applied in Europe until a new generation of European reformers had witnessed the American experiments with penitentiary reform. The United States may have adopted foreign reform initiatives more often than it contributed initiatives of its own making (with the temperance movement as an important exception), but the country was undeniably an experimental zone for the transnational reform community to profit from. Recent literature has convincingly argued that it was mainly in the period from 1870 to 1940 that the United States was open to social policy exchange with other countries. However, prison reform, educational reform, and smallpox vaccination are examples of earlier issues on which a transnational network of reformers and government officials cooperated.

INTERNATIONAL CONNECTIONS

Revolutionary events in Europe and South America increased reformers' sense of momentum in the 1830s and 1840s. In response to the post-Napoleonic Restoration from the 1820s, a globalization of revolutionary ideology and practices took place. Networks of political exiles developed into a "liberal international" that was built on notions of international solidarity and the interconnectedness of all movements for emancipation worldwide. Americans participated in this network, fascinated by the freedom struggle of which their country's revolution was often cited as an example. The Greek freedom struggle, and later those of the Italians and Hungarians, were closely followed; the heroes of the struggle for freedom received a warm welcome when they traveled to the United States, among them Giuseppe Mazzini (1805–1872), Lajos Kossuth (1802–1894), and Giuseppe Garibaldi (1807–1882). Refugees and immigrants brought European utopian and socialist ideas across the Atlantic but never gained massive support. Growing numbers of Irish immigrants supported the Irish independence movement back home. Its leader, Daniel O'Connell (1775–1847), was hailed in the United States as a champion of freedom, not just for the Irish but also for slaves.

Nationalist struggles worldwide fostered a romantic notion of being part of a global struggle for freedom and of a transnational community of reformers, which motivated ambitious young men like William Lloyd Garrison (1805–1879) to fight American slavery. Black abolitionists likewise felt empowered by these struggles and by the support of British public opinion, which inspired them to become more vocal (and more militant) as a result. Together with British and American white abolitionists they chastised their nation for still harboring slavery and for supporting colonization of black Americans as a solution. Here the tensions between cosmopolitanism and nationalism came to the fore. While abolitionists believed mobilizing "patriotic shame" was a pure expression of love for their country, their criticism was interpreted as unpatriotic. Especially when radical British abolitionists started touring the United States, this was seen as a British conspiracy to destroy the Union, incite slave insurrections, and ruin the American economy.

Personal contacts among reformers, both in visits and correspondence, were the most powerful means of communication in forging ties. Transatlantic correspondence among reformers was so common that in 1840 educational reformer Horace Mann (1796–1859) wrote to another American reformer: "If we were on opposite sides of the Atlantic, I think we might hear from each other oftener than at present" (Komline 2014, 34). In the course of the century, steamships shortened the trip across the Atlantic considerably. In addition to these personal contacts, the use of print media, cheaper now than ever before because of technological innovations, was crucial in creating a global reach and spreading reform ideas to large groups of people. As a result, during the second quarter of the nineteenth century the expectations of transnational reform collaboration grew to new heights. Especially within evangelical reform networks, communication intensified: Periodicals and pamphlets were distributed and reprinted, innovative reform methods were discussed at great length, and numerous personal correspondences and friendships emerged across the Atlantic. From 1833, temperance advocates throughout the world organized yearly "simultaneous meetings" to symbolize the international dimension of the reform community. The imagined transnational community eventually manifested itself in large-scale gatherings when this optimistic transnational reform impulse culminated in the international congress movement, which was launched by the World Anti-Slavery Conventions of 1840 and 1843; the Universal Peace Congresses of 1843 and 1848–1853; the International Penitentiary Congress of 1846 and 1847; and the World Temperance Convention of 1846. To the disappointment of many reformers, it often turned out that the imagined community of global reformers was far more harmonious than the real one. Both the peace movement and the antislavery movement disintegrated as a result of the conventions. And when establishing a world temperance union was debated in 1846, the idea was discarded as reformers began to realize that there was "a difference betwixt the word union—and the thing union" (Boggs 1846, 45).

"MODERN" DEVELOPMENTS

The international congress movement formed the basis of a newly emerging and increasingly important reform network that discussed social reform based on the new method of statistical analysis. World exhibitions, such as were held regularly from 1851, strengthened a sense of a shared experience of modernity, both in social problems and in solutions. Reform organizations as well as independent reformers, most notably representatives of the new social sciences, focused less on moral reform and more on social policies. In many European countries the state took over some of the functions that philanthropists and reformers had taken upon themselves in the eighteenth and nineteenth centuries, including poor relief, social security arrangements, and factory, prison, and educational reform, whereas in the United States similar developments can be witnessed only in the decades after the end of the Civil War, and then in limited form.

It is undeniable, however, that from 1870 to 1940 America participated fully in the new transnational network

of reform. Here as elsewhere, the effects of urbanization and industrialization led a broad public, including government officials, to accept that industrialized nations shared similar problems and that scientifically developed solutions in one city or country could be successfully transferred to another. Evangelically based reform movements lost their dominance, as the new wave of reform that characterized the Progressive Era was inspired less by religion and more by social science. "Reformers" now often referred to politicians and government officials. This is not to say that transnational reform organizations lost significance. Rather, because of the relative openness to reform initiatives, they could be more successful in influencing government policy. Now calls for humanitarian intervention by the American government, which had been issued from the 1820s, were incidentally taken up, for instance, in Cuba (1898) and the Philippines (1899), as they dovetailed with growing imperial ambitions. Meanwhile, the influence of the World's Woman's Christian Temperance Union (1884) and the growth of the mission movement in the late nineteenth century testify to the ongoing importance of evangelical Protestantism for American participation in transatlantic, and increasingly transnational, networks of reform.

SEE ALSO *American Board of Commissioners for Foreign Missions; American Colonization Society; American Peace Society; Antislavery; Communitarian Socialism; Dickens, Charles; Foreign Mission Movement; Student Volunteer Movement for Foreign Missions; Suffrage; Temperance Movement*

BIBLIOGRAPHY

Bender, Thomas. *A Nation among Nations: America's Place in World History.* New York: Hill and Wang, 2006.

Boggs, Thomas, ed. *The Proceedings of the World's Temperance Convention.* London: C. Gilpin, 1846.

Conroy-Krutz, Emily. "Dissenters from the Mainstream: The National and International Dimensions of Moral Reform." In *World of the Revolutionary American Republic: Land, Labor, and the Conflict for a Continent*, edited by Andrew Shankman, 370–390. New York: Routledge, 2014.

Davies, Thomas. *NGOs: A New History of Transnational Civil Society.* Oxford: Oxford University Press, 2014.

Isabella, Maurizio. *Risorgimento in Exile: Italian Émigrés and the Liberal International in the Post-Napoleonic Era.* Oxford: Oxford University Press, 2009.

Komline, David. "An American *Sonderzeit?* Reconsidering Rodgers in Light of Antebellum Educational Reform." In *Transatlantic Social Politics: 1800–Present*, edited by Daniel Scroop and Andrew Heath, 19–41. Basingstoke, UK: Palgrave Macmillan, 2014.

McDaniel, W. Caleb. *The Problem of Democracy in the Age of Slavery: Garrisonian Abolitionists and Transatlantic Reform.* Baton Rouge: Louisiana State University Press, 2013.

Moniz, Amanda Bowie. "'Labours in the Cause of Humanity in Every Part of the Globe': Transatlantic Philanthropic Collaboration and the Cosmopolitan Ideal, 1760–1815." PhD diss., University of Michigan, 2008.

Rodgers, Daniel T. *Atlantic Crossings: Social Politics in a Progressive Age.* Cambridge, MA: Harvard University Press, 1998.

Rodogno, Davide, Bernhard Struck, and Jakob Vogel, eds. *Shaping the Transnational Sphere: Experts, Networks and Issues from the 1840s to the 1930s.* New York: Berghahn Books, 2015.

Russo, David J. *American History from a Global Perspective: An Interpretation.* Westport, CT: Praeger, 2000.

Scroop, Daniel, and Andrew Heath, eds. Introduction to *Transatlantic Social Politics: 1800–Present.* Basingstoke, UK: Palgrave Macmillan, 2014.

Thistlethwaite, Frank. *The Anglo-American Connection in the Early Nineteenth Century.* Philadelphia: University of Pennsylvania Press, 1959.

Tyrrell, Ian. *Transnational Nation: United States History in Global Perspective since 1789.* Basingstoke, UK: Palgrave Macmillan, 2007.

Tyrrell, Ian. *Reforming the World: The Creation of America's Moral Empire.* Princeton, NJ: Princeton University Press, 2010.

Wilson, Ann Marie. "Taking Liberties Abroad: Americans and International Humanitarian Advocacy, 1821–1914." PhD diss., Harvard University, 2010.

Wright, Conrad Edick. *The Transformation of Charity in Postrevolutionary New England.* Boston: Northeastern University Press, 1992.

Maartje Janse
Lecturer
Institute of History, Leiden University

TRANS-SIBERIAN RAILWAY

The Trans-Siberian Railway in Russia owes its origins partly to events in North America. The first transcontinental rail line across the United States opened in 1869 and was soon followed by several others, demonstrating that such long railroads were technically feasible and were important in pulling together large nations and encouraging settlement in remote regions. It was the completion of the first Canadian transcontinental railway, the Canadian Pacific, in 1885 that helped spur the Russians into building what would be the world's longest railway. The Canadian Pacific shortened the journey between England and Japan from fifty-two to thirty-seven days, which was seen by the Russians as posing a military threat to its control of Siberia.

The idea for a Trans-Siberian Railway had been discussed in Russian government circles for many years, but the advent of the Canadian Pacific helped its supporters finally persuade the czar, an absolute monarch, to sanction the scheme. Not only would it cement the vast and distant region of Siberia into Mother Russia and allow the immigration of vast numbers of peasants from western Russia, but it would ensure that any military challenge to the area could be met by a rapid deployment of troops.

In what must rank as one of the greatest engineering feats in world history, the Trans-Siberian, which stretches 5,750 miles (9,254 kilometers) from Moscow to Vladivostok, was constructed in a mere ten years, starting in 1891, in a nation that had only just emerged from the feudal serf system and lagged far behind both Europe and North America in terms of industrial development. The technology used to build the line was mostly primitive, with one exception: the bridges that spanned both the vast rivers of Siberia and the many smaller tributaries. The steel bridges over the larger rivers were based on designs that Russian engineers had copied on trips to the United States, where many had traveled to learn bridge engineering skills. Some of these bridges were actually purchased in kit form from American designers and simply fitted together at the site, which meant that at the peak of construction, in the mid 1890s, thousands of Americans were employed in factories supplying the line.

Several early travelers on the line who wrote accounts of their journeys were American. One of them, Francis Clark (1851–1927), a New England Congregational pastor, recounted how he endured both the best and worst of travel on the Trans-Siberian in 1900. Traveling on hard benches in third class, Clark described some of his fellow travelers, in a manner somewhat bereft of Christian charity, as "unmentionable parasites" giving out "odours indescribably offensive" (Wolmar 2014, 108). He later enjoyed traveling in the first-class section, where he was offered a bath and where the small compartments were, he noted, preferable to the open-plan Pullman cars in the United States. But, while he could enjoy reading books from an onboard library, he commented on the lack of English-language books.

The railway, like the American transcontinentals, proved to be a success in attracting immigrants and stimulating the development of the region through which it passed. The Trans-Siberian played a major role in the civil war between the Bolsheviks and the White Russian forces that followed Russia's withdrawal from the First World War (1914–1918) and which had the side effect of bringing American troops onto Russian soil for the only time in history. In the summer of 1918, seventy thousand Czech soldiers who had been fighting alongside the Austrians and Germans found themselves stranded in Siberia. They sought to leave the country via the Trans-Siberian Railway after opting not to continue fighting the Russians, but they feared they would be massacred if they tried to reach their homeland through the Eastern Front.

A dispute with the Reds' leadership, however, led to the Czechs taking control of the railway.

As a result, in August 1918, President Woodrow Wilson (1856–1924) reluctantly sent 8,500 American troops to protect the Czechs during their evacuation. Some bullish politicians in both Europe and the United States saw this as an opportunity to reclaim Russia from the Communists, but the Allies were far too war weary after four long years to launch another conflict, and the Americans were eventually recalled, having lost a few troops in various skirmishes with local warlords.

The Trans-Siberian railway would play a significant role in the Second World War (1939–1945) too, as it enabled the Russians, then allies of the Americans, to move large parts of their industry to relative safety away from German invaders. During the Cold War, however, the railway was turned against its former American allies when it was used to site missile launchers targeted at the United States. The advantage over silo-based systems was mobility. The trains could travel up to 620 miles (998 kilometers) every day, and the launchers looked like ordinary railway stock from the air, except that they were so heavy they required three locomotives to haul them. After resolving various technical problems, the rail launchers were deployed in 1987. They could dispatch SS-24 missiles with a payload equivalent to more than half a million tons of TNT. At their peak, there were thirty-five launchers, each with three missiles and a range of 6,000 miles (6,956 kilometers), which meant they could reach parts of the western United States. After the thaw in relations following the collapse of communism in the early 1990s, the rail launchers were withdrawn and finally scrapped in 2003.

Today, the railway, which is electrified and double track throughout, is very heavily used mostly by freight but with considerable passenger traffic as well. In Siberia, with limited internal flights and roads which are not reliable, the railway remains the key method of moving around, and its intensive use has led to the construction of parallel routes to reduce congestion.

SEE ALSO *China; Manchuria; Orientalism; Russia; Trains; World War II*

BIBLIOGRAPHY

Marks, Steven G. *Road to Power: The Trans-Siberian Railroad and the Colonization of Asian Russia, 1850–1917*. Ithaca, NY: Cornell University Press, 1991.

Richard, Carl J. *When the United States Invaded Russia: Woodrow Wilson's Siberian Disaster*. Lanham, MD: Rowman and Littlefield, 2013.

Tupper, Harmon. *To the Great Ocean: Siberia and the Trans-Siberian Railway*. Boston: Little, Brown, 1965.

von Laue, Theodore. *Sergei Witte and the Industrialization of Russia*. New York: Columbia University Press, 1963.

Wolmar, Christian. *To the Edge of the World: The Story of the Trans-Siberian Express, the World's Greatest Railroad*. New York: PublicAffairs, 2014.

Christian Wolmar
London, United Kingdom

TREATY OF ALLIANCE (1778)

SEE *American Revolution.*

TREATY OF GHENT (1814)

SEE *War of 1812.*

TREATY OF MEDICINE LODGE (1867)

SEE *Frontier Wars.*

TREATY OF PARIS (1783)

SEE *American Revolution.*

TREATY OF PARIS (1898)

SEE *Spanish-American War.*

TREATY OF TIANJIN (1858)

SEE *China.*

TREATY OF VERSAILLES

The Treaty of Versailles was signed on June 28, 1919, and entered into force on January 10, 1920. The treaty ended the First World War between Germany and the Allied and Associated Powers, principally France, Italy, Japan, the United Kingdom, and the United States, together with twenty-five other states. The treaty's 440 articles defined Germany's new frontiers, stripped it of its colonies, limited its armed forces, and demanded restitution for damage caused to Allied civilian populations. In a development of international law, Germany undertook to surrender, for trial by an international tribunal, not only persons accused of operational war crimes but those held responsible for the outbreak and conduct of the war. Singularly unsuccessful at the time, this became an important precedent for the Nuremberg and Tokyo war crimes trials after 1945 and the establishment of the International Criminal Court in 2002. The treaty also contained aspirational clauses dealing with gender equality and labor relations.

THE TERRITORIAL AND MILITARY TERMS FOR GERMANY

Under the treaty, France regained Alsace-Lorraine, lost in 1871; Belgium gained Eupen and Malmédy; Denmark regained the northern part of Schleswig, lost in 1864; and Poland was awarded former German territory and a "corridor" to the Baltic, dividing East Prussia from the remainder of Germany. Germany lost 13 percent of its prewar territory and 10 percent of its population. Its armed forces were reduced to a long-service volunteer army and navy of 100,000 and 15,000 men respectively. Germany was forbidden to have an air force, heavy artillery, tanks, poison gas, submarines, dreadnought battleships, and a general staff.

PRESIDENT WILSON'S ASPIRATION FOR GLOBAL PEACE AND STABILITY

US representatives played a major role in these decisions. Principal among them was the twenty-eighth president, Woodrow Wilson (1856–1924), who was absent from America from December 4, 1918, until July 8, 1919,

President Woodrow Wilson (hat in hand) leading a procession that followed the signing of the Treaty of Versailles, June 1919. *Wilson, who played a major role in establishing the terms of the treaty, advocated for the rights of peoples to choose their allegiance and governments, and promised a "new world order" to replace the failed security mechanisms of 1914.* **BETTMANN/CORBIS**

briefly returning in late February to early March. Wilson arrived in Europe with a messianic aura. His iconic 1918 speeches, of which the Fourteen Points address of January 8 was the most famous, had a huge impact across the belligerent lines. Wilson advocated a peace of justice, based upon the rights of peoples to choose their allegiance and governments, and he promised a "new world order" to replace the failed security mechanisms of 1914. In October 1918, Germany appealed to Wilson for an armistice, requesting that the eventual treaty should reflect the values of those speeches, a condition conceded with reluctance in the pre-armistice agreement of November 5, 1918, by Wilson's major European partners, the British and French premiers, David Lloyd George (1863–1945) and Georges Clemenceau (1841–1929). En route to Europe, Wilson feared that failure to deliver the huge worldwide expectations he had raised could mean that the conference's outcome might be "a tragedy of disappointment."

Wilson's first priority was to establish the League of Nations to facilitate peaceful resolution of international disputes. In theory, collective security depended on the immediate application of sanctions against any league member that resorted to hostilities before exhausting the league's procedures, but neither Wilson's advisers nor his allies would accept such an infringement of national sovereignty. Although Article 10 of the League of Nations Covenant promised to guarantee the territorial integrity and independence of its members, Article 16 allowed individual states to determine their response to unprovoked aggression, rendering support for any victim conditional rather than automatic. Unsurprisingly, states were reluctant to stake their national security on this, but the league did play a major role in dealings with refugees, minority populations left on the wrong side of new frontiers, slavery, and international health. The League of Nations was also responsible for overseeing the mandates system, under which the German and Ottoman empires were redistributed, substituting, in principle, international trusteeship for colonialism.

CHALLENGES

In Paris, Wilson struggled to reconcile his belief in national self-determination with the complexities of European ethnography, the aims and objectives of his fellow peacemakers, and the need to create viable states. He refused to allow France to detach the Rhineland from Germany or to annex the Saar, but he did offer, in partnership with Lloyd George, Anglo-American guarantees against further German aggression, though both proved abortive. The left bank of the Rhine and a 50-kilometer (31-mile) strip parallel to the right bank were permanently demilitarized. A fifteen-year Allied occupation of the left bank and three Rhine bridgeheads would

be withdrawn, provided Germany fulfilled its treaty obligations, in three five-year stages. Sovereignty of the Saar was transferred to the League of Nations for fifteen years to allow France to exploit its coal mines in restitution for the damage done to French mines. A plebiscite would then determine its future.

Wilson conceded, with reluctance, some of the territory promised to Italy in the 1915 Treaty of London, notably the South Tyrol, giving Italy a frontier on the Brenner Pass. He was adamant, however, that Fiume (Rijeka) must go to Yugoslavia. This bitter dispute with the Italian premier, Vittorio Orlando (1860–1952), precipitated an Italian walkout in April 1919. Fearing the loss of another major power from the conference, Wilson accepted, against his better judgment, Japan's demand for Germany's former concession in Shandong, China. Wilson and his advisers were more sympathetic to the ambitions of the revived state of Poland. Here it was Lloyd George who was anxious to limit losses of German population and territory, notably seeking revisions in Germany's favor in the Polish Corridor and gaining a plebiscite to determine the fate of Upper Silesia, reminding Wilson that this was merely the application of his own principles.

Wilson opposed Anglo-French demands for an indemnity to recover their complete war costs from Germany because the pre-armistice agreement had specified that the victors would require only compensation for damage to civilians and their property. This dispute, which threatened to break the conference, was "solved" by two compromises. John Foster Dulles (1888–1959), a young American lawyer, suggested wording that declared Germany (and its allies) morally responsible for all the damage caused by their aggression (the basis of Article 231 of the treaty, the so-called "war guilt" clause) but under which Allied demands were limited to civilian damage (Art. 232). Admitting its illogicality, Wilson acquiesced in the British definition that civilian damage encompassed payments of pensions and allowances to wounded soldiers and their dependents because servicemen were only civilians in uniform. He did so to facilitate a fairer distribution of what he believed would be a fixed sum accepted from Germany to cover all its liabilities. The conference could not agree on a figure, instead creating a Reparation Commission, which decided in May 1921 that Germany should pay $32 billion, financed by three bond issues. This figure included a great deal of "phony money" designed to satisfy Allied public opinion. No one expected the $20 billion of "C" bonds to be paid. Germany's debt under the "A" and "B" bonds was thus $12 billion, within Anglo-American estimates of its capacity to pay, but reparations became a major problem of treaty enforcement when Germany resisted payment.

Wilson insisted that the League of Nations Covenant be the first twenty-six articles of each of the treaties, with the former Central powers (Germany, Austria, Bulgaria, Hungary, and the Ottoman Empire) hoping thereby to outmaneuver opposition to the league in the Senate. He failed. On November 19, 1919, and finally on March 19, 1920, the Senate refused the two-thirds majority necessary for the treaty's approval. America's reneging upon a settlement that its representatives had heavily influenced left Britain and France to squabble over the execution of a treaty that neither would have negotiated without American involvement and as the reluctant guardians of Wilson's orphaned league.

On August 25, 1921, America signed the Treaty of Berlin, a separate peace with Germany. This reflected an apparent American reversion to "isolationism" and a reluctance to participate in international politics, particularly in Europe. America took no part in the League of Nations, rapidly withdrew its occupation force from Germany, and ended its involvement in the various commissions to execute the treaty. The United States did, however, make two attempts in the 1924 Dawes Plan and 1929 Young Plan to solve the problems associated with reparations, and it continued to invest heavily in Europe in the 1920s.

THE HISTORICAL VERDICT

The Economic Consequences of the Peace (1919), a best-selling book by the British economist John Maynard Keynes (1883–1946), expressed the deep disappointment of many Anglo-American participants, a sentiment reinforced by the memoirs of Robert Lansing (1864–1928) and Stephen Bonsal (1865–1951). Keynes's castigation of the "Big Four" (Clemenceau, Lloyd George, Orlando, and Wilson) for creating a vindictive, "Carthaginian" treaty has profoundly influenced historical verdicts on the settlement. North American scholars, using archives opened by most major states since the 1960s, have been prominent in attempting to produce more nuanced judgments, stressing that international politics is the art of the possible. The work of Erik Goldstein, William Keylor, Margaret MacMillan, Sally Marks, Stephen Schuker, Zara Steiner, and Marc Trachtenberg (see bibliography below, under "Collections" subhead) has produced a detailed analysis of the negotiations and emphasized the enormous pressure under which the peacemakers struggled as they sought to rebuild a shattered world and create order in Eastern Europe before a perceived threat from Bolshevism materialized. A developing consensus among scholars that the peace was probably the best that could have been achieved at the time, with positive as well as negative aspects, has not yet changed popular perceptions of the treaty as a failure that bears responsibility for the outbreak of a second major conflict in 1939.

SEE ALSO *Internationalism; Isolationism; League of Nations; Paris Peace Conference (1919); Senate Foreign Relations Committee; Wilson, Woodrow; World War I*

BIBLIOGRAPHY

COLLECTIONS: THE EDITED PAPERS OF TWO INTERNATIONAL CONFERENCES TO WHICH MANY OF THE SCHOLARS MENTIONED IN THE ENTRY CONTRIBUTED.

Boemeke, Manfred F., Gerald D. Feldman, and Elisabeth Glaser, eds. *The Treaty of Versailles: A Reassessment after 75 Years.* Cambridge: Cambridge University Press, 1998.

Dockrill, Michael, and John Fisher, eds. *The Paris Peace Conference, 1919: Peace without Victory?* New York: Palgrave Macmillan, 2001.

GENERAL

Bonsal, Stephen. *Unfinished Business.* Garden City, NY: Doubleday, 1944.

Cohrs, Patrick O. *The Unfinished Peace after World War I: America, Britain, and the Stabilisation of Europe, 1919–1932.* Cambridge: Cambridge University Press, 2006.

Keynes, John Maynard. *The Economic Consequences of the Peace.* London: Macmillan, 1919.

Lansing, Robert. *The Peace Negotiations: A Personal Narrative.* Boston: Houghton Mifflin, 1921.

MacMillan, Margaret. *Peacemakers: The Paris Peace Conference of 1919 and Its Attempt to End War.* London: Murray, 2001.

Sharp, Alan. *The Versailles Settlement: Peacemaking after the First World War, 1919–1923.* 2nd ed. New York: Palgrave Macmillan, 2008.

Steiner, Zara. *The Lights That Failed: European International History, 1919–1933.* New York: Oxford University Press, 2005.

Trachtenberg, Marc. *Reparation in World Politics: France and European Economic Diplomacy, 1916–1923.* New York: Columbia University Press, 1980.

US Department of State. *The Treaty of Versailles and After: Annotations of the Text of the Treaty.* Washington, DC: GPO, 1947. Annotations by Denys P. Myers. Reprint, New York: Greenwood Press, 1968.

Alan Sharp
Emeritus Professor of International History
University of Ulster

TREATY OF WANGHIA (WANGXIA; 1844)

SEE *China.*

TRIPLE ENTENTE

The Triple Entente was the alignment of Russia, France, and the United Kingdom that evolved during the two decades prior to the outbreak of the Great War (World War I, 1914–1918). The Entente formed the foundation of the Allies during the war. The Triple Entente grew out of two parallel relationships that merged in response to the perceived threat of Germany and the Triple Alliance (initially consisting of Germany, Austria-Hungary, and Italy). Originally, France was the catalyst for the Entente, insofar as its desire for security led to the creation of a formal military alliance with Russia and to the Entente Cordiale and closer military ties with Great Britain. The French eventually helped arrange a nonaggression pact between the British and Russians, which led to the creation of the Triple Entente. The American relationship with the individual members of the Entente superseded the American relationship with the Entente itself prior to the outbreak of World War I.

ORIGINS OF THE TRIPLE ENTENTE

The Triple Entente originated in the decline of Russo-German relations after German Kaiser Wilhelm II (1859–1941) dismissed Chancellor Otto von Bismarck (1815–1898). The French quickly sought to formalize an arrangement with the Russians to counter the Germans, culminating in a Franco-Russian treaty of alliance in 1894. At the same time, the French sought improved relations with the United Kingdom, seeking both to further isolate Germany and reduce colonial conflict. The resultant Entente Cordiale, signed in 1904, signaled an end to Britain's "splendid isolation" and led to increased coordination between the military staffs of the two countries.

The First Moroccan Crisis of 1905, triggered by the inclusion in the Entente Cordiale of the recognition of British control of Egypt and France's control of Morocco, further worsened relations between the Germans and French. When Kaiser Wilhelm traveled to the Moroccan capital of Tangier on March 31, 1905, and announced his support for Moroccan independence, he hoped to undermine the Franco-British agreement and assert German claims to be included or compensated elsewhere. Instead, his announcement helped reinvigorate the Franco-Russian Alliance and strengthened the Entente Cordiale in light of the apparent threat from Germany. American interaction with the Entente (and later the Allies) was generally cordial with an undercurrent of imperial rivalry. Indeed, the Americans' mediation of the First Moroccan Crisis at the Algeciras Conference in Spain in January 1906 directly contributed to the Entente's formation. In response to the growing hostilities and potential for military action, President Theodore Roosevelt (1858–1919) offered American mediation for a peace conference to be held in Algeciras. The kaiser's attempts to convince the Americans and/or the British to support his position failed; instead, the Americans worked with the French, Spanish, and Italians to craft a settlement, accepted by all sides in April, whereby the French and Spanish maintained oversight of the Moroccan government and military. The German saber rattling and subsequent increase in naval appropriations further facilitated French attempts to bring the British and Russians together. With French encouragement, the British and Russians ended a half century of hostility through the Anglo-Russian Entente of 1907. With this agreement, the Triple Entente was formally brought into existence.

OUTBREAK OF WAR

Over the next seven years, the Entente survived and grew closer amid a series of war scares in Morocco, the Balkans, and the Middle East. Ultimately the assassination of the heir to the Austro-Hungarian throne, Archduke Franz Ferdinand (1863–1914), by a Serbian nationalist set in motion the chain of events that brought the Entente into military conflict with the Triple Alliance (Central Powers). The Russian decision to partially mobilize against the Austro-Hungarians in support of Serbia led to the German decision to implement the Schlieffen Plan, the invasion of France through neutral Belgium. With the outbreak of hostilities, the Triple Entente evolved into a formal military alliance that subsequently included Belgium and Italy (and later Japan and China). The Allies, as they were known, quickly found themselves bogged down in trench warfare that lasted most of the next three years.

The Americans declared neutrality in the conflict, a position complicated by the nation's sizable foreign-born population (roughly 30 percent), the empathy felt by much of the American government for the British, and the American economy. In response to the British blockade of the Continent, American businesses and farmers, taking the path of least resistance, traded primarily with the Allies. Over the course of the next three years, the massive disparity in trade and loans to the Allies made the American economy increasingly dependent on an Allied military victory. Hence, the Americans were considerably more tolerant of the Allies' naval blockade than they were of German U-boat activity. Indeed, American president Woodrow Wilson's (1856–1924) decision to protest the Germans' violation of human rights rather than the Allies' violation of property rights in the aftermath of the sinking of the *Lusitania* on May 7, 1915, grew in part out of this economic reality.

The Allies also signed a series of secret protocols for the future division of German, Austro-Hungarian, and

Ottoman territories and colonies upon successful completion of the war. It was this complex set of secret territorial agreements that caused President Wilson to bring the United States into the war on April 4, 1917, as an associated power rather than as an ally. By maintaining this formal distance from the Allies' acquisitive agreements, Wilson sought to maintain the moral high ground for the United States and put himself in a stronger position to influence, if not write, the peace treaty at war's end. Wilson pressured the Allies to make significant changes to their command structure before allowing American troops to integrate with Allied forces.

The prewar Triple Entente formally ended with the Bolshevik seizure of power in November 1917. Lenin and the Bolsheviks withdrew Russia from the war and negotiated a separate peace with the Germans, the Treaty of Brest-Litovsk (1918). Additionally, to foment the workers' revolution that the Bolsheviks believed and hoped was imminent, they published the secret treaties to undermine the morale of Allied soldiers. In response to this, Wilson created and published the Fourteen Points in January 1918, formally laying out a set of idealistic goals for the Americans and the Allies. Two key goals elucidated by the Fourteen Points were self-determination for the peoples of central and eastern Europe and the creation of an international organization to prevent future wars through collective security.

Wilson's commitment to creating the League of Nations to embody the call for keeping the peace via collective security and his call for self-determination as the organizing principle for boundary adjustments in Europe were both implicit criticisms of the Triple Entente's (and Triple Alliance's) inability to keep the peace through their mutually hostile alliance systems. The two decades of war scares culminating in the most destructive war to that point in history seemed to demonstrate conclusively the failings of the Triple Entente. Article X of the League of Nations charter, which empowered the League Council to call on member nations to defend fellow members against aggression, represented for Wilson both a moral commitment to collective security and a rejection of the Triple Entente (and Triple Alliance) form of security through military alliances. Unfortunately for Wilson and the cause of peace, the League of Nations failed to fulfill his hoped-for creation of collective security; the two decades between its formation and the outbreak of World War II paralleled the two decades between the origin of the Triple Entente and the outbreak of World War I.

SEE ALSO *Britain; Cold War; Empire, US; Exceptionalism; France; Internationalism; Interventionism; Isolationism; League of Nations; Ottoman Empire; Paris Peace Conference (1919); Russia; Treaty of Versailles; World War I; World War II*

BIBLIOGRAPHY

Gildea, Robert. *Barricades and Borders: Europe 1800–1914.* 3rd ed. New York: Oxford University Press, 2003.

McCullough, Edward E. *How the First World War Began: The Triple Entente and the Coming of the Great War of 1914–1918.* Montreal, QC: Black Rose Books, 1999.

Rich, Norman. *Great Power Diplomacy 1814–1914.* New York: McGraw-Hill, 1992.

Richard M. Filipink
Associate Professor
Western Illinois University

TRUMAN, HARRY S.
1884–1972

On January 15, 1953, Harry Truman delivered a farewell address to the American people in which he said:

> I suppose that history will remember my term in office as the years when the "cold war" began to overshadow our lives. I have had hardly a day in office that has not been dominated by this all-embracing struggle—this conflict between those who love freedom and those who would lead the world back into slavery and darkness. And always in the background there has been the atomic bomb.

The president then outlined the containment strategy his administration embarked on in order to "win" the Cold War. It was a strategy that reflected Truman's moralistic view of the world where democracy and freedom were on one side and the "menace of communism" and "communist tyranny" were on the other. The containment policy the Truman administration developed laid the foundation for how the United States engaged with the world during the Cold War and included working with the United Nations, formulating a foreign policy that provided economic aid to other countries, developing policies for the control of nuclear weapons, fostering international collective security alliances, and crafting a national security state.

POSTWAR US-SOVIET RELATIONS

Truman became president on April 12, 1945, after Franklin Roosevelt (1882–1945) died, and he stepped onto the world's stage at Potsdam, Germany, where he pushed Soviet leader Joseph Stalin (1879–1953) to hold free elections in Poland. Stalin remained noncommittal, and American and British distrust of the Soviet Union began to grow. This distrust blossomed after the end of World War II when the Soviet army occupied Eastern Europe and showed no intention of withdrawing. The

Soviets maintained a four-million-person army even after suffering devastating losses during the war and, consequently, posed a significant military challenge.

The Soviets not only refused to remove troops from Eastern Europe; they also would not honor an agreement to remove troops from Iran in 1945 and 1946 despite a plea from the United States to respect the sovereignty of Iran. It was during the Iranian crisis that Stalin announced on February 9 that capitalism and communism were not compatible. In February 1946 American diplomat George Kennan (1904–2005) drafted the Long Telegram, which argued that the Soviets intended to spread communism but that the United States might be able to stop it through forceful response. Former British prime minister Winston Churchill (1874–1965) traveled to Fulton, Missouri, and delivered the famous "Iron Curtain" speech at Westminster College on March 5, 1946. The Soviets withdrew from Iran in May 1946.

The Iranian crisis, coupled with the Soviet occupation of most of Eastern Europe and the advice of advisers like Kennan, convinced Truman that the Soviets intended to spread communism. Furthermore, Truman viewed the actions of the Soviet Union within the context of the genesis of World War II and Hitler's effort to expand his authority by annexing neighboring countries. The theme of an expansionist Soviet Union emerged again in early 1947 when the British informed the United States that it could no longer afford to support its troops stationed in Greece and Turkey.

On March 12, 1947, Truman announced the Truman Doctrine: "It must be the policy of the United States to support free peoples who are resisting attempted subjugation by armed minorities or by outside pressures." The Truman Doctrine became one of the most important components of the containment policy and also committed the United States to an unprecedented involvement in world affairs.

THE MARSHALL PLAN AND THE POINT FOUR PROGRAM

In June 1947 Secretary of State George Marshall (1880–1959) outlined the Marshall Plan, which provided economic aid to rebuild Europe after the war. The idea of the United States providing economic aid to other countries was new and faced significant political opposition. It required the president to draw a clear distinction between democratic free peoples and what he referred to as a tyrannical Soviet Union. In addition to the Marshall Plan, the United States, under the direction of Douglas MacArthur (1880–1964), who served as the supreme commander for the Allied powers, oversaw the reconstruction of Japan during the American occupation from 1945 to 1952.

In 1949 Truman announced in his inaugural address that the United States would share its scientific and technical knowledge with developing countries in order not only to improve the standard of living in those countries but also to ensure they would be free and not predisposed to embracing communism. This announcement, which became known as the Point Four Program, fused Truman's moral crusade against communism with his strong belief that modernization could also play an important role in stopping communism. More than thirty countries participated in the program, and some of the money they contributed supported the United Nations Educational, Scientific, and Cultural Organization (UNESCO).

NUCLEAR WEAPONS AND COLLECTIVE SECURITY

Truman attempted to include the global management of nuclear weapons as part of his containment strategy; however, the Baruch Plan, drafted by Bernard Baruch (1870–1965), which called for the UN's Atomic Energy Commission to oversee how countries developed nuclear weapons, was rejected by the Soviet Union because the Soviets believed the plan would allow the United States to gain a monopoly in nuclear weapons development. At home, Truman supported the Atomic Energy Act of 1946. The law created an Atomic Energy Commission, which effectively established civilian control of the nation's atomic energy program and utilized the nation's universities to provide military, industrial, and medical applications of nuclear technology.

Truman's containment policy also featured a peacetime commitment to create a worldwide collective security network to thwart an expansionist Soviet Union. In the summer of 1947 Truman traveled to Rio de Janeiro, Brazil, to negotiate the Inter-American Treaty of Reciprocal Assistance—better known as the Rio Pact—which continued Franklin Roosevelt's Good Neighbor Policy and established a collective defense pact for Latin America. The creation of the Organization of American States at the Inter-American Conference in Bogotá, Columbia, in April 1948 expanded the collective defense for Latin America. These peacetime collective security treaties paved the way for the North Atlantic Treaty of 1949, which resulted in the creation of the North Atlantic Treaty Organization (NATO) in January 1950. NATO provided for the collective security of the United States, Canada, and ten Western European countries.

THE NATIONAL SECURITY STATE

The establishment of a national security state was another important component of Truman's containment strategy. The National Security Act of July 1947 created the National Security Council and the Central Intelligence

Agency. In 1949 China became a communist country under the leadership of Mao Zedong (1893–1976), and the Soviet Union successfully detonated its first atomic weapon. The National Security Council assessed American foreign policy in light of these significant events and in April 1950 released an influential report that came to be known as National Security Council Paper 68 (NSC-68). The report called for the United States to meet the growing Soviet threat with increased expenditures for both conventional and nuclear weapons, including the hydrogen bomb, which Truman authorized the development of in January 1950. While NSC-68 met with some opposition, Truman used the Korean War, which began in June 1950, as justification for tripling the size of the defense budget.

The test of Truman's containment strategy came with the Berlin Crisis of 1948–1949, but especially with the Korean War, which Truman regarded as the most challenging situation he faced as president. In June 1950 Secretary of State Dean Acheson (1893–1971) informed the president that North Korea had invaded South Korea. Truman decided that the response to the invasion should directly involve the United Nations and that if the international body did not act, then it would become irrelevant, much like the League of Nations had when it refused to act on the eve of World War II. Truman successfully obtained UN support to commit troops to push the North Korean army out of the South, selected General Douglas MacArthur to lead the UN forces, and tried to sell the war to the American people.

Initially, Truman and his advisers wanted to push the advancing North Korean army back to the 38th parallel (the established dividing line between North and South Korea after the end of World War II). In the wake of the success of MacArthur's daring raid at Inchon, Truman decided to pursue the North Korean army above the 38th parallel, prompting the Chinese to enter the war. After Truman and MacArthur squabbled over war strategy, Truman relieved him from his command. The war stalemated, and despite Truman's public insistence on the necessity of the war to stop the spread of communism, his approval rating fell significantly and he decided not to seek reelection in 1952.

In his January 1953 farewell speech Truman indicated that he firmly believed the containment strategy that he followed in Korea would allow a democratic "free society" to eventually prevail over "a system [communism] that has respect for neither God nor man." He also returned to the faith in modernization that could be found in his Point Four Program and the United Nations when he noted: "If we can get peace and safety in the world under the United Nations, the developments will come so fast we will not recognize the world." Truman's containment policy and the moral tone that undergirded

it, along with his commitment to modernization, charted a new course for the United States and its role in the world—a role that is still debated today.

SEE ALSO *Atomic Bomb; Central Intelligence Agency (CIA); Cold War; Department of Defense, US; Domino Theory; Korean War; Marshall Plan; NSC-68; Nuclear Weapons; Point Four; Potsdam Conference (1945); Roosevelt, Franklin D.; World War II*

BIBLIOGRAPHY

Donoghue, Michael. "Harry S. Truman's Latin American Policy." In *A Companion to Harry S. Truman,* edited by Daniel S. Margolies, 389–409. Chichester, UK: Wiley-Blackwell, 2012.

Ekbladh, David. *The Great American Mission: Modernization and the Construction of an American World Order.* Princeton, NJ: Princeton University Press, 2010.

Ferrell, Robert H. *Harry S. Truman: A Life.* Columbia: University of Missouri Press, 1994.

Hamby, Alonzo L. *Man of the People: A Life of Harry S. Truman.* New York: Oxford University Press, 1995.

Hogan, Michael J. *A Cross of Iron: Harry S. Truman and the Origins of the National Security State, 1945–1954.* Cambridge and New York: Cambridge University Press, 1998.

Holloway, David. *Stalin and the Bomb: The Soviet Union and Atomic Energy 1939–1956.* New Haven, CT: Yale University Press, 1994.

Inboden, William. *Religion and American Foreign Policy, 1945–1960: The Soul of Containment.* Cambridge and New York: Cambridge University Press, 2008.

Leffler, Melvyn P. *A Preponderance of Power: National Security, the Truman Administration, and the Cold War.* Stanford, CA: Stanford University Press, 1992.

Truman, Harry S. "The President's Farewell Address to the American People, January 15, 1953." Public Papers of the Presidents: Harry S. Truman. Harry S. Truman Library, Independence, MO.

Shannon, Kelly J. "Truman in the Middle East." In *A Companion to Harry S. Truman*, edited by Daniel S. Margolies, 362–388. Chichester, UK: Wiley-Blackwell, 2012.

Spaulding, Elizabeth Edwards. *The First Cold Warrior: Harry Truman, Containment, and the Remaking of Liberal Internationalism.* Lexington: University Press of Kentucky, 2006.

Jon E. Taylor
Associate Professor of History
University of Central Missouri

TRUMAN DOCTRINE

The Truman Doctrine, originating in a presidential statement to Congress delivered by President Harry S. Truman (1884–1972) on March 12, 1947, refers to a US foreign policy intended to curtail the expanding influence of the Soviet Union and Communism. Unlike the

Western Hemisphere focus of the Monroe Doctrine of 1823 or its Roosevelt Corollary of 1904, the Truman Doctrine was worldwide in scope; however, as a policy of containment, it represented a *via media* between rollback and appeasement. The doctrine was the first in a series of early-Cold-War US containment policies; others included the 1948 Marshall Plan, which aided Western Europe through economic assistance, and the 1949 North Atlantic Treaty Organization (NATO), which instituted a military alliance for the collective defense of Western Europe.

BACKGROUND

The Truman Doctrine arose in the wake of World War II (1939–1945). After hostilities ceased, the Soviet Union expanded its influence in Eastern Europe, delayed its withdrawal from Iran, and became less cooperative with its wartime allies. By early 1947, the geopolitical situation beyond the Western Hemisphere seemed dire. US and Soviet troops in Korea faced each other at the thirty-eighth parallel; China was disintegrating despite US policy; the economic mission to Germany and Austria of former president Herbert Hoover (1874–1964) had assessed the acute food crisis in Europe and had sharply critiqued aspects of US economic and occupation policy; and the United Kingdom, under the stress of near-bankruptcy and shortages, was winding down commitments in India, Egypt, and the Near East. Against this backdrop, in February of 1947, the United Kingdom informed the United States that Great Britain was no longer in a position to give aid to Turkey and Greece.

Turkey and Greece were at critical junctures. The Soviet Union coveted Turkey's control of the Dardanelles, the straits connecting the Black and Mediterranean seas, so as to have warm-water, continuously accessible ports. When negotiations between the states failed to satisfy the Soviet Union, Soviet troops were sent to the Turkish border, and Turkey appealed for US help. Greece, meanwhile, was in the midst of a civil war, the first stages of which arose in the wake of the 1942–1944 German occupation of Greece during World War II. The leftist National Liberation Front (EAM) and its military branch, the Greek People's Liberation Army (ELAS), which were effectively controlled by the Greek Communist Party (KKE), were suppressed with British assistance, for the United Kingdom considered a stable Greece to be crucial to continued British access to the Middle East. However, postwar Greek governmental corruption prompted a KKE boycott of the national elections in March of 1946 and led to civil war by the fall of that same year. The neighboring Communist states of Albania, Yugoslavia, and Bulgaria supported the Greek Communists, especially those operating in the north of the country. Thus, Communist rule seemed poised to expand

into both Turkey and Greece. If Turkey and Greece became Communist, all of southeastern Europe would then be Communist, and the Soviet Union would have unimpeded access to the Mediterranean Sea. Egypt and the Suez Canal would lie just across the waters.

IDEATIONAL FOUNDATION

In addition to the setting of the above events, the Truman Doctrine must be understood in light of an important ideational foundation, the "Long Telegram" that US diplomat George F. Kennan (1904–2005) wrote in February of 1946. Kennan saw Soviet Communist ideology as layered upon a substratum of historical Russian insecurity that was desirous of excluding, and even destroying, the foreign world. Moreover, the Soviet leadership was fearful of the effect that Western conceptions of capitalism and freedom could have on the Soviet people. Thus, there could be "no permanent peaceful coexistence" in the long run (Kennan 1946). Although Kennan saw the Soviet Union as committed to opportunistic international conflict (including subversion), he believed that the Soviet Union could be defeated without recourse to war both because the West was stronger than the Soviet Union and because the internal soundness of the Soviet system was questionable. Faced with Soviet expansion, Kennan proposed that a policy of containment be employed, for Kennan believed that, when challenged, the Soviet Union would back down before a determined show of Western economic, political, and ideological strength. Hence, the United States should provide fledgling postwar democracies with aid to assure their democratic and capitalist development. Kennan's proposal thus married Wilsonian idealism and power politics.

THE US RESPONSE TO THE TURKISH AND GREEK CRISES

If Kennan's "Long Telegram" was the theory, then the handling of the Turkish and Greek crises was the practice. Truman feared that both Turkey and Greece would fall to Communism unless they received US aid. Although Truman never doubted the need for aid, he was concerned that congressional support might not be forthcoming, for Republicans controlled both houses of Congress, and isolationist sentiment, such as that of Senator Robert A. Taft (1889–1953), could not be ignored. As a result, Truman invited a congressional delegation, including Republican Senator Arthur Vandenberg (1884–1951), chair of the Senate Foreign Relations Committee, to meet with him on February 27, 1947, six days after the British indicated that they could no longer support Turkey and Greece. When the legislators seemed unmoved by the problems of the two countries, Undersecretary of State Dean Acheson (1893–1971) explained how, over the previous eighteen months, Communist activity raised the question "of whether two-thirds of the area of the world and three-fourths of the world's territory" would be ruled by Communists (quoted in Merrill 2006, 32). The lawmakers, taken aback, agreed to endorse the White House program provided that Truman work out a specific aid program and that he address Congress and the American people about the severity of the crisis.

As writers drafted a single speech for both Congress and radio listeners, it was agreed that Truman should stress the threat to core American values rather than the strategic importance of Turkey and Greece. Furthermore, Acheson advised that the speech should treat the spread of Communism in general rather than accuse the Soviet Union in particular. When it was realized that the speech made no reference to the newly formed United Nations, remarks were added to indicate that the unilateral US action was faithful to the spirit of the United Nations. (The desire to maintain control over US funds, and the threat of a Soviet veto in the UN Security Council, yielded a consensus that such unilateral action was necessary.)

Interestingly, Kennan had reservations. Kennan identified himself as a realist, and he saw public opinion as something that could interfere with the politics of balancing power. Indeed, Kennan believed that the United States had erred by basing its World War I and post–World War I statecraft on values. Kennan wanted to avoid such mistakes in the future. Therefore, although he favored aiding Turkey and Greece, Kennan opposed recourse to the mass politics of ideological appeals. His point of view did not prevail, so Kennan's articulation of a restrained approach to containment was superseded by the Truman Doctrine's more confrontational tenor.

Truman asked that Congress provide $400 million to Turkey and Greece and that Congress authorize the sending of American civilian and military personnel to Turkey and Greece to assist in reconstruction and to supervise financial and material assistance. The bill to aid Turkey and Greece was signed into law on May 22, 1947.

In addition to financial aid, Turkey received modern weapons. In Greece, Americans who administered aid were able to restructure Greek tax and budgetary policies. The American embassy prevented conservative Greek politicians from removing centrists from government by threatening to halt aid. US military advisors trained the Greek army and crafted counterinsurgency plans. The doctrine seemed successful: the Soviet Union never tested US resolve over the Dardanelles, and the Greek civil war ended by 1949.

CONTEMPORARY RECEPTION AND LONG-TERM LEGACY

In terms of the reception of Truman's speech, *Life* magazine stated, "Like a bolt of lightning the speech cut through the confused international atmosphere. But, like lightning, it left turbulence in its wake" (March 24, 1947, 40). Domestically, Congress generally supported the president, although members of Congress objected to aspects of Truman's program: Senator Taft, for one, opposed military support for Greece. In the United Kingdom, editorial reaction was favorable, although the bluntness of Truman's speech evoked some surprise. Moscow's reaction was less favorable.

The Truman Doctrine also left a lasting legacy in terms of how it was received in American popular culture. In contrast to Franklin Roosevelt (1882–1945), who reassured the American people that they had nothing to fear "but fear itself," the Truman Doctrine ingrained in the American imagination the idea that the world is fraught with potential dangers. By emphasizing the insecurity of the postwar world, the Truman Doctrine struck a note of vulnerability, a note that has found echoes in subsequent presidential doctrines, not only those of the Cold War but also those of the war on terror.

The Truman Doctrine, although of strategic import, is nevertheless principally an American statement about US culture, identity, and global purpose. If strategy implies taking into full account the reasoning of another with whom one interacts, and if the Truman Doctrine lacks a truly strategic vision in this sense, then it is unsurprising that the doctrine was most effective in parts of the world that hold historical and cultural traditions in common with the United States (e.g., Europe) or that enjoy economic and technological levels comparable with the United States (e.g., Japan). The doctrine was used only selectively to intervene outside of Europe: compared to Greece, for example, US involvement in China's civil war was limited. However, as the Cold War began to heat up, the logic of containment was applied to the Korean conflict in 1950. Indeed, involvement in Korea in some ways foreshadowed later US involvement in Vietnam, and it should be noted that the Truman administration extended financial and military assistance to the French in 1950 as they dealt with a Communist anticolonial uprising in Indochina. Another example of the collision between the Truman Doctrine and anticolonial nationalism can be seen in the Truman administration's support for Saudi Arabia in order to contain both Communism and Arab nationalism.

Overall, the Truman Doctrine treated the world as a whole, shaped the development of US postwar internationalism, engaged the United States both in Europe and in the decolonizing world, broke the mold of previous regional presidential doctrines, set the pattern of subsequent presidential doctrines, and shaped the US public's attitude toward national and international security.

SEE ALSO *Internationalism; Interventionism; Isolationism; Monroe Doctrine (1823); Roosevelt Corollary (1904);*

Roosevelt, Franklin D.; Roosevelt, Theodore; Taft, William Howard; Wilson, Woodrow; World War I; World War II

BIBLIOGRAPHY

Belair, Felix, Jr. "Tuman Acts to Save Nations from Red Rule; Asks 400 Million to Aid Greece and Turkey; Congress Fight Likely but Approval Is Seen." *New York Times*, March 13, 1947, A1.

Kennan, George F. Telegram, George Kennan to George Marshall ("Long Telegram"), February 22, 1946. Harry S. Truman Administration File, Elsey Papers. Harry S. Truman Library and Museum, Independence, MO. http://www.trumanlibrary .org/whistlestop/study_collections/coldwar/documents/pdf/6-6.pdf

Merrill, Dennis. "The Truman Doctrine: Containing Communism and Modernity." *Presidential Studies Quarterly* 36, 1 (2006): 27–37.

"The President's Speech: Congress Gives Grave Attention to His Plan for Meeting World Crisis." *Life* 22, 12 (March 24, 1947): 40.

Truman, Harry S. "Address of the President of the United States: Delivered before a Joint Session of the Senate and the House of Representatives, Recommending Assistance to Greece and Turkey." March 12, 1947. Harry S. Truman Library and Museum, Independence, MO. http://www.trumanlibrary.org/ whistlestop/study_collections/doctrine/large/documents/pdfs/ 5-9.pdf

"U.S. Faces Up to a Diplomatic Crisis." *Life* 22, 11 (March 17, 1947): 31–37.

Wiecek, William M. "America in the Post-War Years: Transition and Transformation." *Syracuse Law Review* 50 (2000): 1203–1221.

Brian K. Muzas
Assistant Professor
School of Diplomacy and International Relations
Seton Hall University

TURNER, FREDERICK JACKSON
1861–1932

Although historian Frederick Jackson Turner is often portrayed as a quintessentially American figure, a careful reading reveals his transnational legacy. For generations, historians equated Turner with founding a school of US exceptionalism that focused only on the continental United States. Such an interpretation was largely obscured by a tendency to conflate Turner with a few of the more dramatic passages from his famed frontier thesis. Something of a reputational reversal has occurred in recent years, however, as scholars of global history have awakened to Turner's internationalist sensitivities.

Historian Ian Tyrrell (1999) observed that context, rather than content, led to Turner being remembered as a primarily national and nationalistic scholar.

EDUCATION AND INTERNATIONAL INHERITANCE

Turner was born in the small town of Portage, Wisconsin, in 1861. He enrolled at the University of Wisconsin, where he studied history and learned to recognize the importance of economic and social forces in shaping nations and their place in the world. Intent on becoming a college professor, in 1888 Turner entered a PhD program at Johns Hopkins University. The curriculum, modeled after the German seminar style of graduate education, provided a cosmopolitan and European-centered foundation. Turner was less versed in American literature, and many of his key influences—including G. W. F. Hegel, Johann Gottlieb von Herder, David Hume, and Thomas Babington Macaulay—were imported from across the Atlantic. The net result was an acquired international inheritance when Turner received his PhD in 1890, qualifying him for long teaching careers at the University of Wisconsin at Madison and then Harvard University.

Of particular note, the Italian political economist Achille Loria (1857–1943) played a leading role in Turner's early development. Subscribing to the Hegelian notion that history unfolded in a series of stages, Loria argued that the availability of free lands determined social evolution. Turner appropriated both this framework and emphasis, further agreeing with Loria that the exhaustion of free land marked the end of an era of freedom and the start of a new industrial age. Although Turner applied his reading of Loria to the American frontier, he drew another broad lesson. Quoting the Italian approvingly in his frontier thesis, Turner commended Loria's *Analisi della proprietá capitalista* (Analysis of Capitalist Property, 1889) for its pursuit of "universal history," which he understood as synthesis on the grand level (Turner [1893] 1998, 38). Instead of focusing on a region or nation at the exclusion of others, Turner sought connections between a diversity of geographies over time and space.

A pair of essays reflects these sensitivities. The first, "The Significance of History" (1891), stands as Turner's youthful rumination on the craft of history, as well as a treatise striving to articulate a global imperative. "We cannot select a stretch of land and say we will limit our study to this land," he insisted, "for local history can only be understood in the light of the history of the world." In short, the forces of history surpassed the boundaries of nation-states, since all countries were "inextricably connected." For Turner, the key to unlocking the past lay in tracing this mosaic of connections (Turner [1891] 1998, 22). A second essay, "Since the Foundation of

Clark University" (1924), attests to Turner's continued transnationalism as he matured. Somewhat chastened by the First World War (1914–1918), Turner nevertheless remained convinced of the need to "comprehend the mighty changes that have come upon this planet," a nexus of connections that isolationists ignored at their peril (Turner [1924] 1932, 218–219).

FRONTIER THESIS

Of course, it is for his frontier thesis that Turner is most known. Delivered as a conference paper in 1893, "The Significance of the Frontier in American History" launched his career. Its most remembered pronouncements suggested that American history could be explained by the regeneration stimulated by the frontier, which fostered individualism and an especially American democratic equalitarianism. That such a sweeping argument contributed to a mythos of American exceptionalism is undeniable. On the other hand, Turner paired his reductionist thesis with some strikingly sophisticated analysis informed by his transnational background. As a result, regardless of the uneven final product, Turner's work is more complex than typically allowed. It challenged as much as it seemingly affirmed American uniqueness, comparing the frontier territories—as sites inspiring discovery and civilizational growth—to the Mediterranean Sea of ancient Greece. Further, Turner contested as much as he aided the notion of a singular American West, likening the frontier settlements, marked by "a wide mixture of nationalities," to "reflections of the map of Europe in their variety" (Turner 1893, 51). Turner's thesis treated the borderlands as sites of transferences. His frontier relied upon "cross-fertilization of ideas and institutions," a "mediating" fusion that wrought "death to localism" and "reached back from the frontier and affected profoundly the Atlantic coast and even the Old World" (Turner 1893, 53). These international exchanges ensured "the promotion of democracy here and in Europe."

Turner's global credentials can be overdramatized. Certain passages from the frontier thesis deserve the criticism they receive for casting a nationalistic interpretation, namely Turner's insistence that the wilderness transformed peoples, especially immigrants, into quintessential Americans (Turner [1893] 1998, 34). Perhaps such contradictory Turnerian impulses are a result of latent insularity. Turner occasionally exhibited a proudly provincial streak, displayed in regular retreats into a rugged sportsman's lifestyle. His mastery of languages was poor: he flailed through French- and German-language exams at Johns Hopkins, required a graduate student to translate Loria, and rarely bothered to improve his fluency. Nor did Turner much travel abroad. The exception was a family tour through Switzerland and Italy in 1900 to 1901. Though Turner marveled at Europe's diversity, he avoided universities, did not lecture or research, and formed no intellectual contacts (Bogue 1998, 161).

TRANSNATIONAL LEGACY

Turner's work traveled considerably better than he did. By the middle of the twentieth century, translated editions of Turner's collected essays appeared in French, German, Italian, Spanish, and other languages. Moreover, as Francois Weil (2002) has argued, Turner attained wide international circulation because of his firm commitment to grand narratives instead of specialization. Then too, in contrast to many other practitioners of the much-maligned grand narrative tradition, Turner resisted making his "universal" synthesis an exclusively American story. The surprisingly nuanced transnational character of his writing belies the oft-caricatured perception of a rank nationalist. His pioneering efforts in early global historiography ultimately give Turner modern relevance, even where his efforts in the history of pioneers are outmoded.

SEE ALSO *Buffalo Bill's Wild West; Manifest Destiny; Northwest Ordinance (1787)*

BIBLIOGRAPHY

Bender, Thomas. "Historians, the Nation, and the Plentitude of Narratives." In *Rethinking American History in a Global Age*, edited by Thomas Bender, 1–21. Berkeley: University of California Press, 2002.

Benson, Lee. *Turner and Beard: American Historical Writing Reconsidered*. New York: Free Press, 1960.

Billington, Ray Allen. *Frederick Jackson Turner: Historian, Scholar, Teacher*. New York: Oxford University Press, 1973.

Bogue, Allan G. *Frederick Jackson Turner: Strange Roads Going Down*. Norman: University of Oklahoma Press, 1998.

Brown, David S. *Beyond the Frontier: The Midwestern Voice in American Historical Writing*. Chicago: University of Chicago Press, 2009.

Hofstadter, Richard. *The Progressive Historians: Turner, Beard, Parrington*. New York: Knopf, 1968.

Jacobs, Wilbur R. *The Historical World of Frederick Jackson Turner*. New Haven, CT: Yale University Press, 1968.

Turner, Frederick Jackson. *The Significance of Sections in American History*. New York: Holt, 1932.

Turner, Frederick Jackson. "The Significance of History" (1891). In *Rereading Frederick Jackson Turner: "The Significance of the Frontier in American History" and Other Essays*, edited by John Mack Faragher, 11–30. New Haven, CT: Yale University Press, 1998.

Turner, Frederick Jackson. "The Significance of the Frontier in American History" (1893). In *Rereading Frederick Jackson Turner: "The Significance of the Frontier in American History" and Other Essays*, edited by John Mack Faragher, 31–60. New Haven, CT: Yale University Press, 1998.

Turner, Frederick Jackson. "Since the Foundation of Clark University" (1924). In *The Significance of Sections in American History*. New York: Holt, 1932.

Tyrrell, Ian. "Making Nations/Making States: American Historians in the Context of Empire." *Journal of American History* 86, 3 (1999): 1015–1044.

Weil, Francois. "Do American Historical Narratives Travel?" In *Rethinking American History in a Global Age*, edited by Thomas Bender, 317–342. Berkeley: University of California Press, 2002.

Jeff Ludwig
Director of Education
William Seward House Museum

TWAIN, MARK
1835–1910

In 1982, when he was eighty-three and nearly blind, the Argentinian writer Jorge Luis Borges (1899–1986) made a pilgrimage to Hannibal, Missouri. He wanted to put his hand in the Mississippi River as it flowed past Mark Twain's home town. Borges's reverence reflects the power of the midwestern geography Twain (born Samuel Langhorne Clemens) etched onto the literary landscape in works like *Tom Sawyer* (1876), *Huckleberry Finn* (1884), and *Old Times on the Mississippi* (1876). With this, the spirit of boyhood and the racial hierarchies that Twain inscribed on that landscape has rendered lasting impressions on generations of readers.

In 1910, the year of Twain's death, Danish writer Johannes V. Jensen (1873–1950) opined that "the description Mark Twain gives us of the Mississippi … is imperishable in its Herodotian sense of the place and the people that inspired the memory" (Fishkin 2010, 120), and Russian poet Marina Tsvetaeva (1892–1941) recorded the "golden names" Huck Finn and Tom Sawyer into her homage to childhood reading (Fishkin 2010, 116). More recently, American writer Toni Morrison (b. 1931) noted that in *Huck Finn*, Jim provides the catalyst whereby "unmanageable terror gives way to a pastoral, idyllic, intimate timelessness minus the hierarchy of age, status, or adult control" (Fishkin 2010, 412). Over time, Twain's Mississippi Valley came to represent America's geographic, racial, and moral landscapes. Even today, Chinese and Indian schoolchildren study his work, one sign of his continuing power to shape the world's vision of the United States.

TWAIN'S BATTLE FOR INTERNATIONAL COPYRIGHT PROTECTION

As Twain's reputation blossomed, his publications became vulnerable to international piracy. Careful readers may notice that the quintessentially American novel *Adventures of Huckleberry Finn* was published in the United States in 1885, several months after its 1884 English edition. The publication sequencing was a deliberate strategy to prevent the book from being pirated by British publishers, as had been *Tom Sawyer* and other recent works. Flattering as it was to have his works filched, Twain needed cash to keep his household afloat, and pirated editions pay no royalties. As a result, he routinely visited Canada to secure British copyrights before his books appeared in the United States.

In 1887, Twain took his complaints to court; however, the case, *Clemens v. Belford*, was decided for the publisher. Twain then engaged in long-term battles to convince Congress to pass international copyright laws safeguarding American authors from foreign piracy, with reciprocal rights for foreign authors in the United States. Twain testified before Congress in 1886 and in 1906, and to the British House of Lords in 1900, pleading both for piracy protection and for extension of copyright. His efforts eventually bore fruit: in 1891, Congress passed the Chace Act, granting international copyright protection, and, in 1909, a major revision of the copyright laws extended copyright to twenty-eight years past the date of publication, renewable once for a total of fifty-six years. In 1957, the American Bar Association passed a special resolution that "recognized the efforts of Mark Twain, who was so greatly responsible for the laws relating to copyrights which have meant so much to all free peoples throughout the world" (Evina 2004).

SOCIAL AND POLITICAL COMMENTARY

Copyright protection abroad did not spell protection from prior censorship at home. In 1959, the Soviet writer Yan Bereznitsky (1922–2005) suggested that a tacit conspiracy of American editors and critics had prevented Twain's political writings from reaching the American public. He was right. Although Twain's political writings had long been accessible in the Soviet Union, China, and Latin America, in the United States they did not circulate freely until the 1990s. As a result, few Americans know that Mark Twain engaged passionately in debates about both domestic and foreign policies. Whereas readers abroad have long seen Twain as a fearless critic of US internal and external practices, Americans are still discovering that their beloved humorist inveighed against American political systems, world imperialism, and the very concept of "patriotism."

Twain's social and political commentary is rooted in the iconoclastic spirit that grounds his sensibility and lifts his writings from the local to the global. In his early writings, his carefully honed aphorisms transformed the native skepticism of the American West into a high verbal art that he deployed in ever-expanding arenas. Although his satiric bent had already been evident to Americans in his early tales and sketches, it hit the international stage with his first travelogue, *The Innocents Abroad* (1869), which mocked Americans' uncritical reverence for European culture, questioned the intrinsic value of famous works of art, and exposed the hypocrisies of Christian pilgrims in the Holy Land.

Twain's critical skepticism continued to evolve across the spectrum of his writing, especially the political and anti-imperialist essays of his last two decades. "The United States of Lyncherdom," written in 1901 but not published until 1923, wedded his general distrust of missionaries abroad to his outrage at the rising tide of lynchings in the United States. The essay suggests that Americans, not the heathens, are the people who really need "Christianizing." A number of essays argue that "patriotism" is only a cowardly response to peer pressure generated by jingoistic media. And his commentary on Congress continues to reverberate; his three lines "Suppose you were an idiot. And suppose you were a member of Congress. But I repeat myself," describes a political profile few Americans would not recognize (Paine 1912, 724).

OPPOSITION TO COLONIALISM

Twain did not restrict his political commentary to the domestic United States. An acute observer of the contemporary scene and an earnest student of history, he increasingly lashed out at the West's habit of justifying imperialist land grabs as altruistic interventions into backward cultures. His interest in international affairs emerged early: in 1868, he published a critical analysis of the recently signed Burlingame Treaty with China, and he continued to follow US/Chinese relations throughout his life, earning him the lasting respect of the Chinese.

In 1895 and 1896, Twain lectured throughout the British Empire, a journey that gave him a crash course in patterns of colonialism in Australia, New Zealand, India, and South Africa. By journey's end, he understood the inexorability of Europe's bid for global domination. It was inevitable, he realized, that the world was to be divided up among the Great Powers. If so, he resignedly believed, better the British than the other powers.

However Twain's recognition of the limits of any colonial rule led him to fiercely oppose the United States' decision to annex the Philippines in 1899. His most famous anti-imperialist essay, "To the Peoples Sitting in Darkness," was published in the *North American Review* in 1901. In it, he weaves the Philippine-American War (1899–1902), the vicious suppression of the Boxer Rebellion (1900) in China by the Great Powers, and the Anglo-Boer War (1899–1902) into a pattern of Western rapacity thinly disguised as Christian benevolence. Five years later, he privately denounced President Theodore Roosevelt's affirmation that the US Army's 1906 massacre of six hundred Moro men, women, and children in the Philippines was a "brilliant feat of arms" that "upheld the honor of the American flag" (Zwick 1992, 173–173). Roosevelt, Twain fumed, "knew perfectly well that our uniformed assassins had not upheld the honor of the American flag … [but] had dishonored it." In 1960, Chinese writer Lao She (1899–1966), who saw Twain as an "exposer of imperialist aggression and the hypocritical civilization of U.S. capitalism," noted that Twain's "reprimand of the imperialist aggressive powers and sympathy for the anticolonialist Asian and African people are especially significant for us" (Fishkin 2010, 283–284). Lao's comments aptly summarize the profile of Mark Twain as seen from abroad: engaged, informed, and outspoken about the failure of the United States to live up to its principles.

SEE ALSO *Anti-imperialist League; Melville, Herman*

BIBLIOGRAPHY

Baggett, J. Mark. "Copyright." In *The Mark Twain Encyclopedia*, edited by J. R. LeMaster and James D. Wilson. New York: Garland, 1993.

Evina, Frank. "Copyright Lore." *Copyright Notices*. May 2004. US Copyright Office, Historical Documents. http://copyright .gov/history/lore/2004/may04-lore.pdf

Fishkin, Shelley Fisher, ed. *The Mark Twain Anthology: Great Writers on His Life and Works*. New York: Library of America, 2010.

Paine, Albert Bigelow. *Mark Twain, a Biography: The Personal and Literary Life of Samuel Langhorne Clemens*. 2 vols. New York: Harper and Brothers, 1912.

Twain, Mark. *Mark Twain: Collected Tales, Sketches, Speeches, and Essays, 1891–1910*, edited by Louis J. Budd. New York: Library of America, 1992.

Zwick, Jim, ed. *Mark Twain's Weapons of Satire: Anti-Imperialist writings on the Philippine-American War*. Syracuse, NY: Syracuse University Press, 1992.

Susan K. Harris
Hall Distinguished Professor of American Literature and Culture
University of Kansas

U

UNCLE TOM'S CABIN (HARRIET BEECHER STOWE, 1852)

Uncle Tom's Cabin; or, Life among the Lowly (1852), a landmark antislavery novel by Harriet Beecher Stowe (1811–1896), relates to the world scene in Stowe's treatment of transatlantic themes and in the revolutionary impact that the novel has had abroad. Stowe's best-selling novel is widely associated in the public mind with its title character, whose name has come to signify docile kowtowing. This popular stereotype, which evolved in the racist plays that proliferated during the Jim Crow era, is distant from the character Uncle Tom as he actually appears in the novel, where he is compassionate but also principled and strong. In Stowe's novel, Uncle Tom is despised by the slaveholder Simon Legree precisely because of his stubborn refusal to obey a command to betray fellow slaves. And the novel itself is in no way soft or syrupy. To the contrary, it makes an impassioned call for radical social change, a call that has been closely heeded by revolutionaries around the world.

ENDORSEMENT OF LIBERIAN COLONIZATION

Many readers of *Uncle Tom's Cabin* are struck by a chapter toward the end of the novel where Stowe endorses colonization: that is, the shipment of black Americans to Liberia, on the western coast of Africa. In the novel, Stowe has George Harris, who has escaped from slavery in Kentucky and has fled with his wife and son to Canada, announce his plan to move to Liberia. At first glance, George's proposal seems to be a reactionary idea of the kind opposed by abolitionists like William Lloyd Garrison (1805–1879) and Wendell Phillips (1811–1884), who

denounced conservative colonizationists such as Henry Clay (1777–1852) and James Monroe (1758–1831). But the way George Harris expresses his plan puts him closer in spirit to black colonizationists like Martin R. Delany (1812–1885), Henry Highland Garnet (1815–1882), and, later, Marcus Garvey (1887–1940) than to the earlier figures. George Harris explains that his dream of the integration of blacks into American society can be most effectively pursued if he goes to Liberia and helps to make it a strong nation that will become a voice to be heeded by the world's major powers. George believes that the advance of black people, both in America and elsewhere, will result from the spread of Christianity and other "civilizing" influences in Liberia. In the future, he predicts, African representatives will meet at "a council of free nations" with Europeans to devise solutions to the problems of slavery and racial prejudice. George says,

> Then, in the great congress of nations, we will make our appeal, and present the cause of our enslaved and suffering race; and it cannot be that free, enlightened America will not then desire to wipe from her escutcheon that bar sinister which disgraces her among nations, and is as truly a curse to her as to the enslaved. (Stowe 1852, 2:302)

George's views are not distant from those of Henry Highland Garnet, who argued that black Americans should prepare the way for world liberation by spreading "civilization" and Christianity in Africa, or Martin R. Delany, who advocated colonization and black nationalism in his 1852 book *The Condition, Elevation, Emigration, and Destiny of the Colored People of the United States.*

Illustration by E. F. Skinner of a scene from* Uncle Tom's Cabin, *in which Tom is taken away in fetters after being sold at auction. *Within a decade of its publication in 1852, the landmark antislavery novel had been translated into 20 languages. By 1893, the World's Columbia Exposition in Chicago displayed it in 42 translations.* **CULTURE CLUB/HULTON ARCHIVE/GETTY IMAGES**

However, Stowe did not repose in the expectation that colonization would work. The American Colonization Society, founded in 1816, had had little success in transporting black Americans to Africa. Also, Liberia, established in 1821, had not fulfilled its initial promise. By the early 1850s, it was marked by the same kind of social stratification and oppression that characterized America. George Harris concedes that "Liberia [has] subserved all sorts of purposes, by being played off, in the hands of our oppressors, against us" (Stowe 1852, 2:301). The main solutions to the degradation of blacks, Stowe proffers in *Uncle Tom's Cabin*, are the education of black Americans and a proposed change of heart on the part of whites. If African Americans receive proper schooling, she maintains, they will develop the capacity to become respected, productive members of society. Whites, for their part, must learn to "*feel right*" (Stowe 1852, 2:317), in her words; that is, they must develop a recognition of the humanity of blacks and the injustice of slavery.

REVOLUTIONARY IMPACT AROUND THE WORLD

Stowe saw that these goals were far from being achieved at the time she wrote *Uncle Tom's Cabin*, and so in the novel she warns that violent uprisings by enslaved blacks and other oppressed peoples could be forthcoming. Two years before *Uncle Tom's Cabin* was published, the Philadelphia labor reformer George Lippard (1822–1854) had written "that there are only two nations in the world—the oppressed and the oppressors" (Lippard 1986, 213). This view was close in spirit to that of Lippard's and Stowe's German contemporary, Karl Marx (1818–1883), who averred that society was divided between "freeman and slave, patrician and plebeian, lord and serf, … in a word, oppressor and oppressed" (Marx 1994, 159). Both Lippard and Marx foresaw a future working-class revolution. Stowe, who later became a strong supporter of the insurrectionist John Brown (1800–1859), gave fresh visibility to this Marxian idea in *Uncle Tom's Cabin* through her portrayal of Augustine St. Clare, the bitterly meditative New Orleans slave-owner who questions slavery and foretells a cataclysmic revolt by the masses. St. Clare says,

> One thing is certain,—that there is a mustering among the masses, the world over; and there is a *dies irae* coming on, sooner or later. The same thing is working in Europe, in England, and in this country.... If there is anything that is revealed with the strength of a divine law in our times, it is that the masses are to rise, and the under class become the upper one. (Stowe 1852, 2:25)

St. Clare's statement was prescient. Revolutions across the world did occur, and *Uncle Tom's Cabin* played a significant role in some of them.

Within a decade of its publication, the novel had been translated into twenty languages: not just major languages like French, German, and Spanish, but also Wallachian, Wendish, Magyar, and Welsh. By 1893, the number of foreign translations had more than doubled. At the World's Columbia Exposition in Chicago that year, *Uncle Tom's Cabin* was given a prime place in the Women's Building, where forty-two foreign versions were displayed. In Russia, the novel was promoted by writers like Nikolai Turgenev (1789–1871), Aleksandr Herzen (1812–1870), and Nikolai Chernyshevsky (1828–1889), progressives who spearheaded the 1861 emancipation of the nation's twenty-two million serfs. Sixty-seven separate editions of Stowe's novel were published in Russia between 1857 and 1917, adding fuel to proletarian unrest there. Chernyshevsky drew upon it for his 1863 novel *What Is to Be Done?*, a major inspiration behind the Russian Revolution. For V. I. Lenin (1870–1924), the leader of the October Revolution of 1917, *Uncle Tom's Cabin* was his favorite book in childhood, and he declared that it provided "a charge to last a lifetime" (quoted in Garrard and Garrard 1990, 20; see also Service 2000, 43). A Russian-born Harvard professor, Leo Wiener (1862–1939), an expert on the origins of the Russian Revolution, wrote in 1917, "It may be asserted that *Uncle Tom's Cabin* was ... the prime cause for the progressive ideas in both countries" (i.e., the United States and Russia) (Wiener 1917, 9–10).

Spanish translations of the novel reverberated in Brazil and Cuba, where antislavery activists counted it as a catalyst for the overthrow of slavery in those countries. The black Cuban champion of freedom, José Martí (1853–1895), who led that nation's separation from Spain, considered Stowe's work the basic text of liberation for the Western Hemisphere (Reynolds 2011, 176). In 1901, *Uncle Tom's Cabin* became the first American novel to be translated into Chinese when it appeared under the title *The Black Slave Appeals to Heaven*. Its translators, Lin Shu and Wei Yi, said they issued the book "to cry out for the sake of our people because the prospect of

enslavement is threatening our race" (quoted in Yu 2009, 1), a foretaste of the populist passion behind the 1911–1912 Chinese Revolution.

SEE ALSO *Antislavery; Colonization Movement; Liberia*

BIBLIOGRAPHY

Garrard, John Gordon, and Carol Garrard. *Inside the Soviet Writers' Union.* New York: Free Press, 1990.

Lippard, George. "Speech Delivered on 4 March 1850 before a Philadelphia Mass Meeting in Support of Philadelphia Tailoresses." In *George Lippard, Prophet of Protest: Writings of an American Radical, 1822–1854*, edited by David S. Reynolds. New York: Lang, 1986.

Marx, Karl. *The Communist Manifesto* (1848). In *Marx: Selected Writings*, edited by Lawrence H. Simon. Indianapolis: Hackett, 1994.

Reynolds, David S. *Mightier than the Sword:* Uncle Tom's Cabin *and the Battle for America.* New York: Norton, 2011.

Service, Robert. *Lenin: A Biography.* Cambridge, MA: Harvard University Press, 2000.

Stowe, Harriet Beecher. *Uncle Tom's Cabin; or, Life among the Lowly.* 2 vols. Boston: Jewett, 1852.

Wiener, Leo. "Russian-American Intellectual Alliance." *Russian Review* 3, 3 (1917): 9–12.

Yu Shiao-ling, introduction and trans. "*Cry to Heaven*: A Play to Celebrate One Hundred Years of Chinese Spoken Drama, by Nick Rongjun Yu." *Asian Theatre Journal* 26, 1 (2009): 1–53.

David S. Reynolds
Distinguished Professor
The Graduate Center of the City University of New York

UNITED FRUIT COMPANY

Gunrunning, a CIA-assisted coup d'état, and bribes: From its founding in 1899, through its demise as a publicly traded corporation in 2015, the United Fruit Company was notorious in Central America for its willingness to go beyond the law in pursuit of power. Nevertheless, the company's business success resulted primarily from a strategy of vertical integration that produced enormous profits and a near-monopoly over the banana trade during the first half of the twentieth century. United Fruit acquired vast tracts of land, built infrastructure (including ports, railroads, and company towns), assembled migrant labor forces, and maintained an international distribution network. In the process, the company was a catalyst in transforming cultures, economies, and environments in the Americas and beyond. In Latin America, the powerful reach of United Fruit—known as "El Pulpo," or "the Octopus"—stirred the imaginations of such literary giants as Gabriel García Márquez (1927–2014), Pablo Neruda

(1904–1973), and Miguel Ángel Asturias (1899–1974). However, the company's legendary power did not enable it to control the political, social, and ecological dynamics that it helped to create.

UNITED FRUIT'S "CIVILIZING MISSION" AND ITS DISCONTENTS

United Fruit was built not only on the labor of tropical people but also on an appropriation of their knowledge, a relationship often obscured by invocations of "banana republics" as backward, tropical states in need of "civilizing." For example, the company made most of its money on a banana variety—the Gros Michel—nurtured in the garden plots of slaves and the rural poor in the nineteenth-century Caribbean. The company's early growth and profitability resulted from innovations not in agriculture per se but rather in the transportation and distribution of a highly perishable, delicate fruit. Initially, the company purchased fruit from independent growers in the Greater Caribbean (including Cuba, Jamaica, and Caribbean Central America). Seeking greater control over the supply chain, United Fruit began securing land suitable for large banana farms in the 1910s. In Central America, the company gained control over land and water resources in exchange for building railroads. Coffee planters in Costa Rica and Guatemala backed these infrastructure projects. Throughout Central America, the company's expansion was linked to a "civilizing mission" akin to that undertaken by the US government in the Panama Canal Zone: railroads, electricity, ice factories, hospitals, schools, and malaria control became symbols of modernity not only for elites but also for migrant workers drawn to banana zones by the lure of relatively high paying jobs.

United Fruit's version of civilization was not limited to Yankee dollars and techno-science. Migrant workers drawn from Caribbean islands and highland Central America inhabited company towns and work camps segregated by race, class, and nationality. Social hierarchies largely determined the nature of work and sociability in banana zones; United Fruit managers tried to exploit racial and ethnic fault lines to keep workers divided. These tactics did not entirely quell workers' collective action; major strikes took place in United Fruit's tropical divisions in Colombia (1928), Costa Rica (1934 and 1959), Guatemala (1944–1954), Honduras (1932 and 1954), and Panama (1960 and 1974). However, the image of a "vanguard" proletariat challenging capital captured only part of the reality. For many men and women, working for United Fruit was combined with other livelihoods including small-scale farming, ranching, domestic service, laundering, or vending. In Ecuador, worker-peasants successfully challenged United Fruit by squatting on land and invoking nationalism when presenting legal challenges before government officials. Elsewhere, communities pressed United Fruit to relinquish abandoned lands and maintain infrastructure.

THE FALL OF AN EMPIRE

Following World War II, democratic movements in Central America pressed for land reform and increased rates of taxation on companies such as United Fruit. In Guatemala, elected president Jacobo Arbenz (1913–1971) expropriated fallow lands held by United Fruit in 1952, prompting the company to contact its well-placed friends in the US State Department. The administration of President Dwight Eisenhower (1890–1969) subsequently authorized the Central Intelligence Agency to orchestrate a covert overthrow of Arbenz. However, declassified records indicate that the State Department's main complaint with Arbenz was his cozying up to communists and not United Fruit's loss of land. Nevertheless, the Guatemalan coup of 1954 cemented United Fruit's reputation for doing business with dictators.

Arbenz was not United Fruit's biggest problem in the 1950s; a plant pathogen known as Panama disease reached epidemic proportions throughout Central America and Ecuador, driving up production costs. The soil fungus, identified as early as 1910, followed in the ecological wake of large-scale monocultures, which, along with the circulation of people, plants, and goods via United Fruit's transportation networks, enabled the disease to spread quickly. Unable to eradicate the pathogen from the soil and loath to replace Gros Michel bananas in US markets, United Fruit tried to outrun the disease by abandoning infected farms and eventually entire divisions in favor of uncultivated (often forested) lands. From 1910 to 1960, United Fruit relied on access to land in order to sustain large-scale shifting agriculture. This strategy increased rates of lowland tropical deforestation and destabilized local livelihoods and economies.

Facing plummeting profit margins and stock values for the first time, United Fruit underwent a major transformation in the early 1960s, adopting Cavendish bananas, a variety which was resistant to Panama disease but whose delicate peels required on-farm packing in boxes. The Cavendish era was marked by an intensification of production: Yields soared due to greater planting densities and a big increase in the use of fertilizers, irrigation, and pesticides. The company's workforce shrank due to the outsourcing and mechanization of labor-intensive tasks. The heavy use of pesticides (United Fruit began using them intensively as early as the 1930s) created new health hazards for fieldworkers and packers. One pesticide used by the company, DBCP, became linked to serious chronic health problems including cancer and sterility. Litigation over the use of DBCP continued into the early twenty-first century in both Central America and the United States.

The history of United Fruit is a story of the rise and fall of an economic empire. The term "empire" is appropriate given the combination of economic and ideological motivations that drove the company's tropical operations and in light of the challenges to its power. Ultimately, the very social and ecological dynamics catalyzed by El Pulpo would squeeze company profit margins, sully its reputation, and compel it to diversify into areas beyond tropical agriculture. By no means unique, the history of United Fruit remains important for understanding contemporary food systems and agribusiness, even as Brazilian citrus firms swallow up the remains of a potent symbol of US power in Latin America.

SEE ALSO *Banana Republics; Guatemala*

BIBLIOGRAPHY

Bohme, Susanna Rankin. *Toxic Injustice: A Transnational History of Exposure and Struggle*. Berkeley: University of California Press, 2014.

Bucheli, Mario, and Ian Read. "Banana Boats and Baby Food: The Banana in U.S. History." In *From Silver to Cocaine: Latin American Commodity Chains and the Building of the World Economy, 1500–2000*, edited by Steve Topik, Carlos Marichal, and Zephyr Frank, 204–227. Durham, NC: Duke University Press, 2006.

Gleijeses, Piero. *Shattered Hope: The Guatemalan Revolution and the United States, 1944–1954*. Princeton, NJ: Princeton University Press, 1991.

Marquardt, Steve. "'Green Havoc': Panama Disease, Environmental Change, and Labor Process in the Central American Banana Industry." *American Historical Review* 106, 1 (February 2001): 49–80.

Putnam, Lara. *The Company They Kept: Migrants and the Politics of Gender in Caribbean Costa Rica, 1870–1960*. Chapel Hill: University of North Carolina Press, 2002.

Soluri, John. *Banana Cultures: Agriculture, Consumption and Environmental Change in Honduras and the United States*. Austin: University of Texas Press, 2006.

Striffler, Steve, and Mark Moberg. *Banana Wars: Power, Production and History in the Americas*. Durham, NC: Duke University Press, 2003.

John Soluri
Associate Professor
Carnegie Mellon University

UNITED NATIONS

The United States played a key role in the founding of the United Nations (UN) and has continued to loom large in its operations. The Charter of the United Nations was signed on June 26, 1945, at a meeting of the fifty founding members in San Francisco; Poland was acknowledged later as the fifty-first founding member despite its absence at the actual meeting. The official implementation of the charter took place on October 24, 1945, and the United Nations set up its headquarters in the Turtle Bay area of Manhattan in New York City, where it remains to this day. Not surprisingly, although the United States was among the leading advocates of the UN, relations between the United States and the United Nations have been uneven. US political commentators and politicians have both damned and praised the organization. Despite this ambivalence, and despite the growth in UN membership to 193 nation-states, Washington plays a dominant role in many UN activities.

THE UNITED STATES AND THE EMERGENCE AND EXPANSION OF THE UNITED NATIONS DURING THE COLD WAR

There is considerable debate about both the diverse origins of the United Nations in general and the motives of the United States for the establishment of the United Nations in particular. Some commentators emphasize that the administration of President Franklin Delano Roosevelt (1882–1945, president, 1933–1945) viewed the United Nations as a potential pillar of a wider effort to construct a post–Second World War international order. This perspective focuses on efforts to enable US manufacturers and investors to continue benefitting economically when the guns fell silent in 1945, producing economic stability and, therefore, international order. This latter concern relied upon the liberal idealism (Wilsonianism) that informed some of those involved in the foundation of the UN as an effort to move beyond, or at least better mediate, the great power rivalry of the pre-1945 era. Before his death, Roosevelt along with other observers viewed the UN as a potential vehicle for bringing the Soviet Union into a more cooperative and less confrontational international order. In this context, the UN was a way of maintaining and even broadening the alliance after 1945 between the victorious powers in the Second World War.

The organization that was set up in 1945 has survived for over seventy years and has undeniably prospered in some of its endeavors despite its shortcomings and continuous debate among critics, reformers, and exponents. While the United Nations is unlikely to grow significantly in the twenty-first century, it is not for want of aspiring members. According to one count (Roeder 2007), if every group that viewed itself as a "nation" was successful in its goal to have its own "state," the membership of the United Nations would grow to as many as five thousand sovereign nation-states. Commitment to a secessionist cause, however, does not confer nation-state status. Likewise, intragroup identification as a "nation" does not make a group a part of the United Nations.

Through the Security Council, the United Nations provided an explicit forum where the great powers could, in theory, mediate and/or act on a range of international issues. Despite emphasis on the equality of all member nation-states, it is clear that the Security Council possesses special rights and obligations in relation to the wider international order. This configuration harkened back to an idea central to the earlier League of Nations, even though some of its members sought to challenge that idea. Security Council membership was grounded by the presence of five permanent members, each of which possessed the right to veto any decision made by the council. The five members, with one change, have remained the same since the UN was founded: they are the United States; the Union of Soviet Socialist Republics (USSR; later the Russian Federation); the United Kingdom of Great Britain; France; and the Republic of China (located exclusively on Taiwan until 1949; now the People's Republic of China, or PRC). Although the Chinese position was initially held by Taiwan, a shift in US foreign policy in the early 1970s included a rapprochement with the PRC spearheaded by US president Richard Nixon (1913–1994) and his National Security advisor, Henry Kissinger (b. 1923).

In this context the overall US strategy in the 1970s had two key elements that impacted on the UN generally and on the Security Council more specifically. One was the rapprochement with the People's Republic of China. The second one was détente with the USSR, which was manifested in US engagement in ongoing and wide-ranging talks with the USSR over limiting nuclear missiles. These were known as Strategic Arms Limitation Talks (SALT). SALT I was signed on May 26, 1972, and specifically sought to put a cap on the number of antiballistic missiles the two main protagonists of the Cold War (and the most important members of the UN Security Council) possessed. In the 1970s what became known as SALT II involved significant diplomatic efforts between Washington and Moscow. Although SALT II amplified SALT I and was finalized in 1979, as soon as incoming US president Ronald Reagan (1911–2004, president, 1981–1989) could, he blocked its implementation as a response to the Soviet invasion of Afghanistan in late 1979. The Reagan administration revitalized the Cold War, thus ensuring that the Security Council remained marginalized throughout the 1980s. With the end of the Cold War there has been ongoing nuclear arms reduction treaty making, including the Strategic Arms Reduction Treaty (START I), which was signed by Moscow and Washington on July 31, 1991. After it expired, it was renegotiated and officially adopted on January 26, 2011, as the "New START" Treaty. While the Security Council was gridlocked during the Cold War, its two most important members did work toward the reduction of nuclear missiles and have continued to do so into the post–Cold War era.

Interaction between the great powers grounded the US approach to the United Nations as a forum and/or actor in international relations. Cold War geopolitics permeated the UN. The Security Council, for example, served as yet another demonstration of America's global influence. In fact, if it had not been for the United States, the Republic of China under Chiang Kai-shek (1887–1975) would never have been on the Security Council. In theory, China under Chiang (with pressure from the United States and with the encouragement of the Soviet Union) entered into a World War II alliance with the Chinese Communist Party (CCP). Neither side trusted the other and on numerous occasions fought against each other rather than against the Japanese Imperial Army. The CCP's particularly corrupt leadership and its dubious ability to govern China added to its ineffectiveness in fighting Japan. It came as no great surprise that with the end of the war in 1945 the CCP rapidly assumed control of the entire mainland, forcing the Kuomintang, or KMT, to retreat to Taiwan, officially inaugurating the People's Republic of China in October 1949. Yet through US efforts the PRC replaced Taiwan as a permanent member of the Security Council. Meanwhile, despite this shift, the Security Council the PRC joined in the early 1970s had been and would continue to be paralyzed by the Cold War. As noted earlier, all members of the Security Council have the right of veto, ensuring that in the context of the Cold War and the animosity between some of the permanent members, the Security Council was noticeably unsuccessful at passing any significant motions from the late 1940s to the early 1990s.

In general, and in relation to the United States in particular, the Security Council is thus probably the most significant branch of the UN. It continues to be primarily responsible for war and peace across the nation-state system. However, the International Monetary Fund (IMF) and the International Bank for Reconstruction and Development (World Bank), established as subordinate branches of the UN, have grown so much in scale and scope that their connection to the UN has become profoundly attenuated. The United States and its key allies have exercised a very high level of influence over these two organizations, both of which are headquartered in Washington, DC. The General Assembly (which is the main forum for all member nation-states to meet), on the other hand, was put in charge of social and economic issues, and by the twenty-first century there were nineteen different branches of various UN agencies dealing with poverty and development and its social implications. The UN also established the World Health Organization

(WHO), which is both important and remains beholden to the UN; the United Nations Educational, Scientific and Cultural Organization (UNESCO); and the Food and Agriculture Organization (FAO). Also of significance are the United Nations Conference on Trade and Development (UNCTAD) and the United Nations Development Programme (UNDP).

THE UNITED STATES, THE UNITED NATIONS, AND THE RISE OF THE THIRD WORLD DURING THE COLD WAR

The Korean War (1950–1953) was a turning point for the UN, and even more specifically for US Cold War policy. In September 1947 the United States had placed the Korean question before the General Assembly. This was done in an effort to roll back the US commitment to the Korean peninsula. Subsequently the General Assembly formally called for the unification of what was at that point a Korea divided between a northern government allied to the Soviet Union (and later the PRC) and a southern government allied to the United States. Following the outbreak of war between the north and the south on June 25, 1950, the Security Council quickly began organizing a UN military force, under US leadership, to intervene in Korea.

This was made possible by the fact that Moscow had been boycotting the Security Council since the start of 1950. The Soviet Union was protesting the fact that China's permanent seat on the Security Council continued to be held by the KMT government. It was also unhappy with the choice of the UN secretary-general. In Korea it quickly became clear that the United States (and its UN allies) were entering a major war. The resolutions of the General Assembly on Korean unification were soon being used to justify a full-scale military effort against the North Korean regime. The initial aim of US/UN intervention to achieve the limited goal of ending northern aggression was quickly transformed into a wider set of aims, centered on the reunification of the peninsula under a pro-US/UN government. The ensuing conflict eventually brought the PRC directly into the war. It was initially thought that US/UN intervention in Korea indicated that the UN had overcome the paralysis that had afflicted the League of Nations in any conflict where the interests of great powers were involved. But once the Soviet Union resumed its seat on the Security Council in August 1950, Moscow challenged the validity of the Security Council resolutions that underpinned UN operations in Korea. Moscow also discovered that boycotting the Security Council weakened its power at the UN vis-à-vis the United States and its allies in particular.

There were major constraints on US influence at the United Nations that were not just a result of Security Council gridlock. Washington's weight at the United Nations was also diminished as the process of decolonization increasingly altered the balance of power in the General Assembly. By the 1970s the emergence of a growing number of new nation-states in Africa and Asia over the preceding decades had clearly altered the balance in the UN in favor of the so-called Third World. This shift was readily apparent in April 1974 when the Sixth Special Session of the General Assembly of the United Nations passed the Declaration and Programme of Action for the Establishment of a New Economic Order. This represented a formal call for a New International Economic Order (NIEO) in an effort to improve the terms on which the countries of the Third World participated in the global economy. In the late 1970s the UN also established the Independent Commission on International Development (the Brandt Commission), presided over by former West German chancellor Willy Brandt (1913–1992). However, by the start of the 1980s, calls at the UN and elsewhere to address the north-south question were increasingly rebuffed, particularly with the debt crisis and the subsequent spread of neoliberal economic policies and practices. With the support of the administration of Ronald Reagan in the United States and Margaret Thatcher's government in Britain (1979–1990), the International Monetary Fund and the World Bank increasingly encouraged Third World governments to liberalize trade, privatize their public sectors, and deregulate their financial sectors. The end of the Cold War strengthened this trend, by which time virtually all branches of the United Nations had become sites for the promotion of economic liberalism and what has come to be known as globalization.

THE UNITED STATES AND THE UNITED NATIONS AFTER THE COLD WAR

The Cold War had undermined the expectation, prevalent in the late 1940s and early 1950s, that the United Nations would provide an overall framework for international security after 1945. With the end of the Cold War, however, the UN was presented with an opportunity to revive the major peacekeeping and security activities that many of its early proponents had anticipated. For example, while the UN dispatched a total of ten thousand peacekeepers to five operations (with an annual budget of about $233 million in US dollars) in 1987, the total number of troops acting as peacekeepers under UN auspices by 1995 was seventy-two thousand. They were operating in eighteen different countries, and the total cost of these operations was over $3 billion. Early post–Cold War initiatives were thought to augur well for the UN's new role. The major civil war in El Salvador, which had been fueled by the Cold War, came to a negotiated end in 1992 under the auspices of the United Nations. Apart from El Salvador, the countries in which the UN has provided peacekeepers and election monitors include Angola, Bosnia-Herzegovina, Cambodia, Croatia, East Timor, Macedonia, Mozambique, Rwanda, Somalia, and the Western Sahara. While Cambodia and East Timor, for example, are seen as UN success stories thus far, the failure of the United Nations in Angola and Somalia highlights the constraints on the UN's role in the post–Cold War era (and the constraints in turn on US influence). In the case of Somalia, the United States left precipitously in 1992 after a major Somali warlord took down a US helicopter and killed a number of US soldiers, a move that had more to do with US domestic politics than the situation on the ground.

The UN's new post–Cold War initiative in relation to peacekeeping was linked to the appointment of Boutros Boutros-Ghali (b. 1922) as secretary-general at the beginning of 1992. Shortly after taking up the post, Boutros-Ghali presented the Security Council with "An Agenda for Peace," which laid out a range of major reforms to facilitate a greatly expanded peacekeeping role. Boutros-Ghali wanted member states to provide permanently designated military units that could be deployed quickly and overcome the UN's well-known inability to act quickly in a time of crisis. As a result of concerted US opposition, Boutros-Ghali was not reappointed as secretary-general for a second term, further dampening the momentum toward a more assertive United Nations in the post–Cold War era. His replacement, Kofi Annan (b. 1938), who was awarded the Nobel Peace Prize in 2001, was a much more cautious and conciliatory secretary-general, as has been his successor, Ban Ki-moon (b. 1944), who took over from Annan in 2007.

The United States played a role in ousting Boutros-Ghali, while the end of the Cold War more generally has meant that the United States has been able to influence both the Security Council specifically and the organization more generally in ways that were not possible during the Cold War. At the same time, the United States has also demonstrated its own ability to ignore the United Nations if it does not get what it wants. This was exemplified by Washington's attempt to get UN support of Operation Iraqi Freedom (OIF) in March 2003. The US secretary of state, Colin Powell (b. 1937), spoke to the UN in an open session, arguing that, based on what proved to be dubious evidence that Saddam Hussein (1937–2006) possessed "weapons of mass destruction," the United Nations should sanction a US-led invasion and occupation of Iraq. The United States failed to get UN support and formed its own ragtag "coalition of the willing." However, once Saddam Hussein had been overthrown and democracy and stability had failed to spontaneously appear, as had been promised by key US

officials and their supporters, the United Nations found itself drawn into the ensuing chaos. OIF had been preceded by Operation Enduring Freedom (OEF) in late 2001, which involved the United States overthrowing the Taliban in Afghanistan and trying to track down al-Qaeda's leadership, who were based in the more remote parts of the country. Both conflicts increasingly made it clear that "regime change" did not lead to democracy or even political stability. In the United States and at the UN there was an increased concern regarding both failed states and "nation-building," the latter term sidelined in the wake of the end of the Vietnam War in 1975.

As in an earlier era, both the United States and the UN continue to view postcolonial boundaries in the twenty-first century as the context in which failing or failed states could be rehabilitated as stable pieces of the overall international order. No matter how contested existing borders are, they continue to ground much of ascendant theory and practice of nation-building. A good example of this is found in the influential book *Nation-Building: Beyond Afghanistan and Iraq* (2006), edited by Francis Fukuyama, in which he and his contributors continue to take existing national boundaries for granted and generate broad technocratic prescriptions for nation-building, or "postconflict reconstruction" and "capacity building," to use some of the other terms that have emerged as less loaded synonyms for "nation-building." Despite this acceptance, like many other observers Fukuyama emphasizes at the start and finish of the book that "the relatively weak degree of institutional learning on the part of the U.S. government concerning approaches to nation-building" is central to the problem. Significantly he also argues that while the UN "may have done a bit better in preserving institutional knowledge," it has also repeatedly demonstrated a "short memory and disorganization at the start of each new effort" at postconflict reconstruction and nation-building (231–232). Other observers have been even less optimistic. In the case of Afghanistan one informed observer was arguing by 2008 (by which time the US was trying to extricate itself from Afghanistan) that not only was the job not being finished in Afghanistan, but that Afghanistan and Pakistan and the region more generally had begun a "descent into a chaos" (Rashid 2009). Meanwhile, James F. Dobbins (a key US participant observer, who had briefly been director of the US liaison office in Kabul with the fall of the Taliban in late 2001 until the US embassy was reopened in 2002) makes a similar point about the limits on nation-building, albeit in more diplomatic language, in *After the Taliban: Nation-Building in Afghanistan* (2008). He went on to be US special representative for Afghanistan and Pakistan from May 2013 to July 2014.

THE UNITED NATIONS IN THE TWENTY-FIRST CENTURY

Despite its problems, there are and will continue to be many observers and participants who view the United Nations as effective even as efforts to strengthen it move forward. For example, in his book *The Parliament of Man: The Past, Present, and Future of the United Nations* (2007), Paul Kennedy stakes out a middle path between shelving the UN and radically transforming it in favor of "a United Nations organization, duly modified from the world of 1945, but still recognizable to its founding fathers, and still dedicated to their lofty purposes" (xvii). He emphasizes the dramatic changes in power politics and the pressing array of global environmental problems as crucial parts of the context in which the UN needs to be reformed to keep pace with twenty-first-century issues. To this end Kennedy not only prescribes changes to the makeup and character of the Security Council, he also links security to development. He emphasizes that there has been much consternation in the General Assembly and beyond that international development is given short shrift. This is a problem that is clearly reflected in the low priority that the UN's Economic and Social Council has in relation to the Security Council, an imbalance that Kennedy and like-minded observers seek to change.

Throughout its existence, the United Nations and its member governments have presented the nation-state as a constitutive and universal element of freedom and self-determination uniting citizens and leading them toward development and modernity. This view continues to have considerable purchase. However, in an era of renewed geopolitical competition alongside a large number of weak or failed nation-states, it is hard to see how the United Nations can sustain this ideological basis for its organizational structure. Its influence in geopolitical terms remains constrained by geopolitical actors that are not traditional nation-states. The long-term success of the UN is also compromised by US attitudes concerning this international body. Even as nonstate actors become increasingly influential in the UN, Americans continue to be ambivalent toward the UN because of their commitment to US nationalism.

SEE ALSO *Internationalism; Interventionism; Isolationism; Paris Peace Conference (1919); Roosevelt, Eleanor; Roosevelt, Franklin D.; Roosevelt, Theodore; Taft, William Howard; Treaty of Versailles; Universal Declaration of Human Rights; Wilson, Woodrow; World War II*

BIBLIOGRAPHY

Coyne, Christopher J. *After War: The Political Economy of Exporting Democracy.* Stanford, CA: Stanford University Press, 2008.

Dobbins, James F. *After the Taliban: Nation-Building in Afghanistan.* Washington, DC: Potomac Books, 2008.

Fukuyama, Francis, ed. *Nation-Building: Beyond Afghanistan and Iraq.* Baltimore, MD: Johns Hopkins University Press, 2006.

Hilderbrand, Robert C. *Dumbarton Oaks: The Origins of the United Nations and the Search for Postwar Security.* Chapel Hill: University of North Carolina Press, 1990.

Kennedy, Paul. *The Parliament of Man: The Past, Present, and Future of the United Nations.* New York: Vintage, 2007.

Mazower, Mark. *No Enchanted Palace: The End of Empire and the Ideological Origins of the United Nations.* Princeton, NJ: Princeton University Press, 2009.

Meisler, Stanley. *United Nations: The First Fifty Years.* New York: Atlantic Monthly Press, 1997.

Rashid, Ahmed. *Descent into Chaos: The U.S. and the Disaster in Pakistan, Afghanistan, and Central Asia.* Rev. ed. New York: Penguin Books, 2008.

Roeder, Philip G. *Where Nation-States Come From: Institutional Change in the Age of Nationalism.* Princeton, NJ: Princeton University Press, 2007.

Mark T. Berger
*Adjunct Professor, Department of Defense Analysis
Naval Postgraduate School*

UNITED STATES AGENCY FOR INTERNATIONAL DEVELOPMENT (USAID)

Established in 1961, the United States Agency for International Development (USAID) became the wing of the US government responsible for economic development programs in poor nations around the world during and after the Cold War. At its establishment, it represented a reorganization, expansion, and intensification of US efforts at economic development in former colonies in Asia, Africa, and Latin America known at the time as the "Third World." For historians, USAID and development more broadly provide a way to expand the definition of foreign relations during the second half of the twentieth century by moving the focus of attention away from Europe and military matters and toward the developing world, economics, and technological change.

EARLY US INTERNATIONAL AID

USAID was not the first American foreign-aid program. The United States administered public health, infrastructure, education, and agriculture programs in the Philippines and Cuba during the early twentieth century, as well as programs in Latin America during World War II (1939–1945). In 1949 President Harry S. Truman (1884–1972) expanded US aid programs around the world with the Point Four Program, named after the fourth point of his inaugural address that year. The programs also drew from government-sponsored natural resource planning on an increasingly broad scale during the 1930s and 1940s, as with the Tennessee Valley Authority and the Manhattan Project.

Shifts in the Cold War but also the wave of decolonization in the postwar decades helped spur the establishment of USAID in 1961. During the late 1950s, as the Cold War in Europe, especially tensions over Berlin and Germany, moved toward a nuclear stalemate, the so-called Third World became an increasingly important site of competition between the Western capitalist democracies and the Communist bloc. The Third World included Latin American nations as well as the impoverished former colonial areas that won their independence after World War II: India, Pakistan, Burma, Korea, and Indonesia in the late 1940s; Vietnam, Laos, and Cambodia in 1954; and forty more countries, mostly in Africa, in the late 1950s and 1960s. For Americans, the overlap of the new Cold War with this wave of decolonization brought to the fore such issues as imperialism, racial discrimination, nationalism, and especially poverty. Many of these nations also possessed great supplies of strategic minerals and other resources needed by the Western economies and militaries: Southeast Asia had tin and rubber, India had manganese, the Middle East had oil, Africa had uranium, industrial diamonds, and cobalt, Latin America had aluminum, oil, and copper. Many countries also held productive lands and forests.

THE FIGHT AGAINST INTERNATIONAL POVERTY

Perhaps no American politician emphasized fighting international poverty more than President John F. Kennedy (1917–1963), who saw great opportunities for economic development to promote humanitarian values but also score victories against international communism. More so than perhaps anything except the space program, Kennedy's international development programs helped define his "New Frontier" agenda. "Man," Kennedy announced in his inaugural address, "holds in his mortal hands the power to abolish all forms of human poverty" (Kennedy 1961). A 1961 White House task force called for less military and more economic aid. A 1962 National Security Council report reiterated the threat posed by the Soviet economic offensive. Kennedy responded with a host of programs aimed at winning friends in the Third World through economic assistance, including the Peace Corps, the Alliance for Progress (programs for Latin America), and the reorganization of US aid efforts under USAID.

To develop Third World economies, Kennedy turned to advisers who promoted "modernization" programs.

Modernizers such as Walt Rostow (1916–2003), an economist and Kennedy administration official, built their programs on three tenets. They attributed poverty to cultural deficiencies, not fixed racial characteristics; they saw progress as possible; and they believed that Western nations could accelerate the evolution from tradition to modernity with an injection of advanced technology. "The central fact about the traditional society," Rostow wrote in *The Stages of Economic Growth: A Non-Communist Manifesto* in 1960, "was that a ceiling existed … [because] the potentialities which flow from modern science and technology were either not available or not regularly and systematically applied" (4). The emphasis on culture as opposed to race helped modernizers distinguish themselves, at least in their minds, from the old imperial powers of Europe, which often saw poverty as a function of the racial inferiority of colonial peoples.

USAID worked in scores of nations around the globe. It built roads in Bolivia, pushed for land reform in Colombia, developed tourism programs in Brazil, conducted herding-improvement programs in Morocco, fought malaria in Nepal, and designed hydroelectric dams in Thailand. From 1951 to 1971, in Asia alone, the United States gave $20 billion in economic aid and $80 billion in food aid. USAID played a particularly large role in Afghanistan's Helmand Valley, in Iran under the shah, and in Vietnam before and during the American war there.

During these years, the Soviets, Chinese, several Western European nations, the United Nations, and the World Bank also ran international development programs, often with clear political agendas, as with American programs. The economic Cold War spanned the globe. Interestingly, despite slight variations, all the various donors tended toward large, centrally planned, state-centric, technology-based resource extraction programs.

A SHIFT IN EMPHASIS

Over the decades, the emphasis of USAID shifted. In the 1970s, USAID began to move away from technical and capital assistance programs and toward a "basic human needs" approach focusing on food and nutrition, health, population planning, and education. During the 1980s, after the election of conservative Republican Ronald Reagan (1911–2004), US development assistance began stressing free-market approaches designed to restructure the policies and institutions of developing nations. In the 1990s, in the wake of the end of the Cold War and the election of President Bill Clinton (b. 1946), USAID put more focus on social, economic, and environmental sustainability, as well as strengthening democratic foundations. During the 2000s, USAID played an important but not always successful role in helping Afghanistan and Iraq construct governmental capacity, infrastructure, and civil society. In the second decade of the twenty-first century, USAID works in more than a hundred countries around the world.

The programs can be analyzed from many different angles: Did they advance US strategic and economic interests? What effect did they have on the recipient countries? Did they promote inclusive democratic practices or corruption and authoritarianism? How did the economically impoverished people in whose name they were created understand and shape these programs? Did their quality of life improve or did they find options curtailed? What unintended consequences resulted, such as environmental change? Historians are only beginning to address these questions, and much archival and ethnographic research and analysis remains to be done.

Ultimately, the impact of American Cold War international development programs must be understood as mixed. Geopolitical competition brought new attention and resources to impoverished peoples around the world, but American programs often created as many problems as they solved. Projects often fell into the hands of elites, who captured the best benefits or pocketed funds meant for the poor. Big projects, especially grand infrastructure projects such as dams, often devastated ecosystems and sometimes tore apart the social fabric of communities. Today, many peoples around the world still live with these mixed results.

SEE ALSO *Alliance for Progress; Decolonization; Department of Agriculture, US; Green Revolution; Kennedy, John Fitzgerald; Modernization Theory; Peace Corps; Point Four*

BIBLIOGRAPHY

Adas, Michael. *Dominance by Design: Technological Imperatives and America's Civilizing Mission.* Cambridge, MA: Harvard University Press, 2006.

Biggs, David A. *Quagmire: Nation-Building and Nature in the Mekong Delta.* Seattle: University of Washington Press, 2012.

Cullather, Nick. "Development? It's History." *Diplomatic History* 24, 4 (2000): 641–653.

Cullather, Nick. *The Hungry World: America's Cold War Battle against Poverty in Asia.* Cambridge, MA: Harvard University Press, 2010.

Kennedy, John F. Inaugural Address, January 20, 1961. John F. Kennedy Presidential Library and Museum. http://www .jfklibrary.org/Asset-Viewer/BqXIEM9F4024ntFl7SVAjA.aspx

Latham, Michael E. *The Right Kind of Revolution: Modernization, Development, and U.S. Foreign Policy from the Cold War to the Present.* Ithaca, NY: Cornell University Press, 2011.

Rostow, Walt W. *The Stages of Economic Growth: A Non-Communist Manifesto.* Cambridge: Cambridge University Press, 1960.

Tucker, Richard. "Containing Communism by Impounding Rivers: American Strategic Interests and the Global Spread of High Dams in the Early Cold War." In *Environmental Histories of the Cold War,* edited by John R. McNeill and Corinna R. Unger, 139–163. New York: Cambridge University Press, 2010.

Tom Robertson
Associate Professor of History
Worcester Polytechnic Institute

UNIVERSAL DECLARATION OF HUMAN RIGHTS

The Universal Declaration of Human Rights (UDHR) was adopted and proclaimed by the United Nations General Assembly in Resolution 217(III) just before midnight in the Palais de Chaillot in Paris on December 10, 1948. Unlike the Convention on the Prevention and Punishment of the Crime of Genocide, which was adopted the day before, on December 9, the UDHR was not a legally binding document. However, it is precisely because of this that many scholars believe it has achieved the status in international human rights law that it has. It is undisputedly the founding document of international human rights and provided the grounds upon which to build human rights law, paving the way for the Covenant on Civil and Political Rights (1966), the Covenant on Economic, Social, and Cultural Rights (1966), and numerous other treaties and conventions.

ROOTS IN THE UN CHARTER AND ROOSEVELT'S FOUR FREEDOMS

The UDHR is closely related to the UN Charter. When the UN Charter was drafted at the Dumbarton Oaks Conference (August–October 1944) and the San Francisco Conference (April–June 1945), the proposals for human rights provisions were diluted and weakened. Many had pushed for stronger human rights protections, but the resulting language of the Charter was quite general. The Charter does reference human rights—specifically, nondiscrimination in Articles 1.3 and 13.1, and self-determination of peoples in Article 1.2—but it did not make them legally binding, carried no provisions for enforcement, and offered no system to monitor abuses and violations of rights; they were merely proclaimed as a general goal for members.

In addition to the UN Charter, the UDHR had roots in US president Franklin D. Roosevelt's (1882–1945) Four Freedoms (of speech and expression, of worship, from fear, and from want), outlined in his State of the Union Address in January 1941. That August, Roosevelt and UK prime minister Winston Churchill (1874–1965) concluded the Atlantic Charter, which established principles of future foreign policy and a new international legal order that took direction and inspiration from Roosevelt's Four Freedoms "for a better future for the world."

DRAFTING THE DECLARATION

The UN established the Commission on Human Rights in 1946 by Resolution 9(II) and tasked it with drafting an "international bill of rights." The commission was made up of eighteen governmental representatives from Australia, Belgium, Byelorussia, Chile, China, Egypt, France, India, Iran, Lebanon, Panama, the Philippine Republic, the Ukraine, the United Kingdom, the United States, the Soviet Union, Uruguay, and Yugoslavia. The United

States sent a delegation headed by Eleanor Roosevelt (1884–1962), known for her previous advocacy of human rights. She was elected chairperson of the drafting committee, guiding it through three consecutive sessions. The most influential representatives in the drafting process were Roosevelt, John Humphrey (Canada, 1905–1995), Charles Malik (Lebanon, 1906–1987), René Cassin (France, 1887–1976), Peng Chun Chang (China, 1893–1957), Hernán Santa Cruz (Chile, 1906–1999), General Carlos P. Romulo (Philippines, 1898–1985), Hansa Mehta (India, 1887–1995), and Alexander Bogomolov (1900–1969), followed by Alexei Pavlov (Soviet Union). Roosevelt's contributions and leadership proved crucial to the committee's success, despite her efforts being occasionally undermined by the US State Department.

First Lady Eleanor Roosevelt holds up a copy of the Universal Declaration of Human Rights, c. 1947. In 1946 the UN established a commission of eighteen government representatives to draft an "international bill of rights." Eleanor Roosevelt, who was known for her previous advocacy of human rights, led the US delegation and became the drafting committee chair. **FOTOSEARCH/ ARCHIVE PHOTOS/GETTY IMAGES**

The resolution did not give details on the form or status of the text to be prepared. Australia, India, and the United Kingdom favored a binding declaration, while China, the USSR, the United States, and Yugoslavia did not. In the end, the commission took a third approach favored by Chile, Egypt, France, Uruguay, and others of adopting a nonbinding declaration that would be immediately followed by a binding convention that UN members would ratify.

The UDHR consists of a Preamble and thirty articles designed to be a "common standard of achievement for all peoples and nations." It differs from the Nuremberg principles and Genocide Convention in that it assumes the goal of prevention, not punishment. The Preamble of the UN Charter had already highlighted the importance of securing rights, especially in light of World War II (1939–1945): "to save succeeding generations from the scourge of war, which twice in our lifetime has brought untold sorrow to mankind, and to reaffirm faith in fundamental human rights, in the dignity and worth of the human person, in the equal rights of men and women and of nations large and small." The UDHR's Preamble begins on a similar note, claiming that "disregard and contempt for human rights have resulted in barbarous acts which have outraged the conscience of mankind," yet it also asserts the need for rights as establishing "friendly relations between nations" in addition to improving "standards of life." It holds that rights are basic requirements for peace and social progress, and declares that securing such rights helps peace and stability.

The horrors of World War II were not yet a distant memory, and every article enumerates the very rights and freedoms which the Nazis denied to their victims. In brief, the UDHR includes basic rights of security; economic, cultural, and social rights; legal rights; freedom of speech and religion; education and marriage rights; and even the right to leisure. While there was much wrangling and debate over many of the rights listed and the language used to delineate them, one of the most arduous obstacles was Article 1, which dealt with the foundations of human rights. It reads: "All human beings are born free and equal in dignity and rights. They are endowed with reason and conscience and should act towards one another in a spirit of brotherhood." The Brazilian delegation proposed a reference to a "deity" who endowed humans with rights that would have grounded rights in religion. Others proposed language of "by their Creator," while some went even further, suggesting the declaration say that all humans were "created in the image and likeness of God." Some favored the phrase "by nature."

All of those proposals were rejected in favor of leaving the foundation of human rights unspecified. Instead, according to the UDHR, people have rights simply by being born human. Due to their exchanges over Article 1, the drafters believed that omitting any specific reference to the foundation of human rights enabled people from all over the world to have their own reasons for the existence of such rights. They believed that this omission paved the way for a kind of overlapping of justifications in that not all justifications would be the same, but they would agree on the rights therein. This way, people of many different religions and ideologies could find consensus.

THE PHILOSOPHER'S COMMITTEE

A separate philosopher's committee, working at the request of the United Nations Educational, Scientific, and Cultural Organization (UNESCO) at approximately the same time as the drafting committee, had independently arrived at a similar conclusion. The committee, chaired by political historian E. H. Carr (1892–1982), sent a questionnaire soliciting responses from Americans, Europeans, and socialists, as well as Chinese, Islamic, Hindu, and customary law perspectives. They received responses from such notable figures as Mohandas Gandhi (1869–1948), Pierre Teilhard de Chardin (1881–1955), and Aldous Huxley (1894–1963), among others. The philosopher's committee found that the principles upon which human rights rested were present in many different cultures and traditions, but they were not always expressed in the language of rights. On the list of basic rights, however, there was remarkable similarity. The French Catholic philosopher Jacques Maritain (1882–1973) famously said that they all believed in rights so long as no one asked them why.

ADOPTION

After nearly two years of work, the UDHR was put to a vote. Forty-eight UN member nations voted in favor, with none against; eight nations abstained. The abstentions came from socialist states (Soviet Union, Byelorussia, Ukraine, Poland, Czechoslovakia, and Yugoslavia), South Africa, and Saudi Arabia. Saudi Arabia rejected the idea that freedom of religion meant freedom to change one's religion, while South Africa did not agree with the inclusion of economic and social rights. The Soviet Union and the other socialist states claimed that the declaration did not detail any attending duties or obligations by which to secure the rights specified. However, some have speculated that Saudi Arabia's main reason for abstaining revolved around equality of the sexes and that South Africa took issue with racial equality. Although the United States and the United Kingdom voted to approve the declaration, they aimed to keep the language general and the document unenforceable, since America countenanced systematic racial inequality and the United Kingdom still owned colonies.

IMPACT

The UDHR, because it only had moral and political force as a declaration, was essentially just a recommendation. Yet in the sixty years since its adoption, many believe that something akin to a Copernican revolution has taken place, in that the world, which once revolved around state sovereignty, now revolves around the individual as viewed through the lens of rights. Of course, states are still sovereign, but they are seen as having the responsibility and task of securing their peoples' rights. In addition, monitoring by numerous nongovernmental bodies functions as a check on state power, and the language of rights is now the default setting of international political rhetoric, even for those states that do no more than pay it lip service.

The two covenants of 1966 made binding rules out of the UDHR's provisions. They also bolster and further specify what is already included in the UDHR. More treaties and declarations on human rights followed on the heels of these covenants: the American Convention on Human Rights (1969); the African Charter on Human and Peoples' Rights (1981); and conventions on genocide (1948), racial discrimination (1965), discrimination against women (1979), torture (1984), rights of the child (1989), migrant workers (1990), and those dealing with child soldiers and child sex trafficking (2000). Watchdogs and observing bodies were also set up to monitor rights abuses and violations. The UDHR has been invoked by the International Court of Justice, the International Criminal Court, various regional and domestic courts, and national constitutions, as well as human rights court cases. It has been influential in or served as a model for some ninety constitutions, including those drafted by countries whose independence came after 1948, many of which were former colonies. But perhaps the most important development is that the UDHR, according to many international lawyers, has come to assume the status of customary international law.

CRITICISM AND DEFENSE

There are two main lines of criticism against the UDHR, both of which doubt the document's universality: that non-Western countries were underrepresented during the drafting process, and that the initial draft by Humphrey drew from European and North and South American documents. Proponents of this view claim that colonialism prohibited more Asian and African countries from participating and that the main drafters were Europeans, Westerners, and non-Westerners who were only nominally so. Chang and Malik had received Western educations, Chang at Clark College and at Columbia, where he completed doctoral work under John Dewey, and Malik at Harvard, where he subsequently taught.

Those who defend the UDHR's universality point out that the Third Drafting Committee had six members from Asia (China, India, Pakistan, Burma, Philippines, and Siam), nine representatives from Islamic countries (Afghanistan, Egypt, Iran, Iraq, Pakistan, Saudi Arabia, Syria, Turkey, and Yemen), four from African countries (Egypt, South Africa, Ethiopia, and Liberia), six Europeans from the Communist bloc, and numerous Latin American members. They also argue that Chang and Malik had significant experience with other religions, languages, and peoples, and were intellectually equipped to reflect on their Western education. Finally, they point to three main contributions by smaller states: the rights of women (due in large part to Mehta), the antidiscrimination clause, and the condition that those living in "dependent" states (i.e., colonies) were subject to the UDHR (despite the fierce opposition of colonial powers).

On the sixtieth anniversary of the UDHR, former UN high commissioner for human rights Louise Arbour (b. 1947) noted that "it is difficult to imagine today just what a fundamental shift the Universal Declaration of Human Rights represented when it was adopted 60 years ago" (Baderin and Ssenvonjo 2010, 4). There had been prior attempts after World War I (1914–1918) to include specific human rights provisions in the Covenant of the League of Nations, but nothing had succeeded on the scale of the UDHR. Between January 1947 and December 1948, the committee worked tirelessly to incorporate diverse views and settle on a specific list of rights. Roosevelt's leadership was crucially important for the group's speed and success. Time was of the essence—World War II was fading from memory as fears of the Cold War began to grow and calls rang out for self-determination and the end of colonialism. In claiming that human beings had rights purely by virtue of being human, the committee members spoke normatively in a moral register. For them, the universality of human rights reflected in the title of the UDHR is not a mirror image of the world as it was at the time (or currently is), but rather a vision for how the world should be.

SEE ALSO *Armenian Genocide; Contemporary Genocides and US Policy; Ethnic Cleansing; Genocide; Holocaust; Roosevelt, Eleanor; Roosevelt, Franklin D.; Truman, Harry S.; United Nations*

BIBLIOGRAPHY

Alfredsson, Gudmundur, and Asbjørn Eide, eds. *The Universal Declaration of Human Rights: A Common Standard of Achievement*. Boston: Martinus Nijhoff, 1999.

Atlantic Charter. August 14, 1941. http://avalon.law.yale.edu/wwii/atlantic.asp

Baderin, Mashood A., and Manisuli Ssenyonjo, eds. *International Human Rights Law: Six Decades After the UDHR and Beyond.* Burlington, VT: Ashgate, 2010.

Bucar, Elizabeth M., and Barbra Barnett, eds. *Does Human Rights Need God?* Grand Rapids, MI: Eerdmans, 2005.

Cassese, Antonio. *International Law.* 2nd ed. New York: Oxford University Press, 2005.

Danieli, Yael, Elsa Stamatopoulou, and Clarence J. Dias. *The Universal Declaration of Human Rights: Fifty Years and Beyond.* Amityville, NY: Baywood, 1999.

Donnelly, Jack. *Universal Human Rights in Theory and Practice.* 2nd ed. Ithaca, NY: Cornell University Press, 2003.

Glendon, Mary Ann. *A World Made New: Eleanor Roosevelt and the Universal Declaration of Human Rights.* New York: Random House, 2002.

Henkin, Louis. *The Age of Rights.* New York: Columbia University Press, 1990.

Hoffman, Stefan-Ludwig, ed. *Human Rights in the Twentieth Century.* New York: Cambridge University Press, 2011.

James, Stephen. *Universal Human Rights: Origins and Development.* New York: LFB, 2007.

Kelsay, John, and Sumner B. Twiss, eds. *Religion and Human Rights.* New York: Project on Religion and Human Rights, 1994.

Moyn, Samuel. *The Last Utopia: Human Rights in History.* Cambridge, MA: Belknap Press, 2010.

Nickel, James W. *Making Sense of Human Rights.* 2nd ed. Malden, MA: Blackwell, 2007.

Posner, Eric A. *The Twilight of Human Rights Law.* New York: Oxford University Press, 2014.

Robertson, Geoffrey. *Crimes against Humanity: The Struggle for Global Justice.* 3rd ed. New York: New Press, 2006.

Tierney, Brian. *The Idea of Natural Rights: Studies on Natural Rights, Natural Law, and Church Law, 1150–1625.* Grand Rapids, MI: Eerdmans, 2001. First published 1997 by Scholar's Press.

Universal Declaration of Human Rights. 1948. http://www.un .org/en/documents/udhr/

Jeff Gottlieb
PhD Candidate in Religion, Ethics, and Philosophy
Florida State University

UNIVERSAL NEGRO IMPROVEMENT ASSOCIATION (UNIA)

The Universal Negro Improvement Association (UNIA) was a product of the Pan-African tradition, which emerged out of the evangelical revivals of the eighteenth century and was carried across the Atlantic world in the years following the American Revolution. The organization's founder, Jamaican-born Marcus Garvey (1887–1940), lived a restless early life, engaging in peripatetic travels through Central America and Europe, and imbibing the wisdom of great Pan-African heroes past and present, including Paul Bogle, George William Gordon, J. Robert Love, Edward Wilmot Blyden, J. Casely Hayford, and Booker T. Washington. Arriving in the United States in 1916, Garvey thrust himself into Harlem's burgeoning "New Negro" movement and its ascendant antiracist, antiwar, and anti-imperial ferment. He translated Pan-Africanism's vague prophecy of racial deliverance—"Princes shall come out of Egypt, Ethiopia shall soon stretch forth her hands unto God" (Psalms 68:31)—into a doctrine of immediate liberation, demanding the return of Africa to the Africans and the mobilization of Africans the world over to bring this about. Catalyzing the ferment generated by the Great War, Garvey built a mass movement that quickly spread to nearly every American state and to nearly every corner of the globe.

Garvey's followers, known as Garveyites, found their most fertile ground for organizing in the United States, where the UNIA established hundreds of divisions. The Harlem-based parent body hosted four spectacular international conventions between 1920 and 1924, drawing delegates from around the world to debate the affairs of the race. Garvey positioned his organization as a government in exile, and Garveyites set about crafting a charter, a declaration of rights, a flag, a national anthem, and a nurses' and officers' corps. Garvey was elected provisional president of Africa. The UNIA's message of race pride, unity, and economic and political self-sufficiency resonated with—and bound together—a diverse collection of black women and men, including West Indian and southern migrant workers in northern urban centers, lawyers and doctors in Los Angeles, cane cutters in Louisiana, dockworkers in coastal Virginia, and cotton farmers in the Mississippi-Yazoo Delta. Garveyism both built on and gave new energy to political and religious traditions dating back to the years of slavery. It invited African Americans to imagine their activism as part of a grand global project.

The call to consider the black American experience as part of a larger diasporic drama was far more than simple rhetoric. The organization established information networks and utilized migrant labor streams in a manner that connected American Garveyites to UNIA supporters across the Western Hemisphere and throughout sub-Saharan Africa. News of the UNIA's Black Star Line Steamship Company was carried with breathless excitement throughout the Caribbean basin and into the West African hinterland. The organization's official organ, *The Negro World*, was carried around the world by black sailors and smuggled into African colonies, hidden inside mattresses or folded inside other papers. During the radical postwar period, UNIA organizing and propaganda work played a significant role in sparking labor rebellions in Belize, Trinidad, and the Panama Canal Zone. In Africa, news of the "Negro Moses" and his fleet of ships sparked millennial rumors throughout much of the continent. In Kenya, Kikuyu activist Harry Thuku (1895–1970) built a threatening anticolonial movement that was inspired by the confluence of local conditions and the twin intellectual streams of Gandhiism and Garveyism.

The radical moment that propelled the rise of the UNIA did not last. The organization's grand projects—particularly its Black Star Line and its efforts to establish a settlement in Liberia—came crashing down amidst government repression, poor business management, and a generally unfavorable climate for black capitalist and diplomatic enterprise. It was during this reactionary era, however, that Garveyites left their greatest legacy. In the British Caribbean, UNIA activists helped craft a reformist model of labor politics that framed cautious worker organizing within a grander narrative of racial redemption. In Cuba and Central America, UNIA divisions proliferated as social and cultural centers for both West Indian migrants and Afro-Latinos. Throughout Africa, a class of mission-educated men adopted the tenets of Garveyism, established lines of communication with American Garveyites, and founded reform organizations and independent churches that translated the movement to suit local conditions and opportunities. Throughout the 1920s, the UNIA instructed Garveyites to engage in the unglamorous work of institution building. It framed those efforts within a global narrative in which the mounting efforts of nonwhite peoples in Africa, Asia, and the Americas were signs of the inevitable end of global white supremacy.

The success of Garveyites in sustaining these containers of organization and activism bore fruit after World War II. In Africa, the nationalist struggles were spearheaded by men like Kwame Nkrumah (1909–1972), Nnamdi Azikiwe (1904–1996), and Jomo Kenyatta (c. 1894–1978), who had grown up in—or been inspired by—the Garvey movement of the previous decades. So too with the labor leaders who emerged in the Caribbean in the late 1930s, or the disciples of the Rastafarian movement, who viewed Garvey as a John the Baptist figure. Rastafarian icon Bob Marley (1945–1981), as well as several other reggae stars, have celebrated Garveyism in their music. After the decline of the UNIA in the United States, Garveyites brought their experience to the labor, civil rights, and black nationalist movements that would propel a new era of struggle. Garveyism was lionized by the Black Power

advocates of the 1960s, like Malcolm X (1925–1965) and Walter Rodney (1942–1980), who sought to revivify Garvey's dream of Pan-African unity amidst the emergence of new, black-led nation-states and persistent American and European global hegemony.

SEE ALSO *Ali, Muhammad; Black Power Movement; Harlem Renaissance/New Negro Movement; Islam; Malcolm X; Moorish Science Temple; Nation of Islam; Rastafari*

BIBLIOGRAPHY

Ewing, Adam. *The Age of Garvey: How a Jamaican Activist Created a Mass Movement and Changed Global Black Politics*. Princeton, NJ: Princeton University Press, 2014.

Grant, Colin. *Negro with a Hat: The Rise and Fall of Marcus Garvey*. Oxford: Oxford University Press, 2008.

Martin, Tony. *Race First: The Ideological and Organizational Struggles of Marcus Garvey and the Universal Negro Improvement Association*. Westport, CT: Greenwood Press, 1976.

Rolinson, Mary G. *Grassroots Garveyism: The Universal Negro Improvement Association in the Rural South, 1920–1927*. Chapel Hill: University of North Carolina Press, 2007.

Vinson, Robert Trent. *The Americans Are Coming!: Dreams of African American Liberation in Segregationist South Africa*. Athens: Ohio University Press, 2012.

Adam Ewing
Assistant Professor
Virginia Commonwealth University

UNIVERSITIES

Universities have long played a role in teaching Americans about the world and presenting America's history, culture, and values to international audiences. These activities have taken different forms over the past two hundred years, often changing as a result of new initiatives by various students, scholars, foundations, and elected officials, as well as in response to political changes on the world stage. Today, this legacy has made international education and exchange an inextricable part of the American higher education sector.

EARLY INTERNATIONAL EXCHANGES

American universities were, from their origins, host to many scholars who had been born or trained abroad. In almost all academic fields it was common for intellectuals to have spent time in Europe and to have international connections through which they advanced their scholarship. With the founding of the Republic, many scholars took pride in their new country and endeavored to represent its virtues internationally. There also developed a sense among the new nation's leaders that, to exert the country's independence from Britain, students should be discouraged from studying in Europe. Time spent abroad was a mark of prestige in elite circles, however, and graduate study or other European touring remained common among the upper classes throughout much of the nineteenth century.

This began to change with the founding of the first graduate schools in the century's closing decades (beginning with Johns Hopkins in 1876). The need for students to pursue graduate study in Europe was reduced, and with the ease of travel in the country's interior, many universities began to take on a more national, rather than local, identity. In many places, the study of foreign languages such as Sanskrit and Hebrew expanded, but this was due to the particular efforts of individual scholars at their universities rather than a coordinated, national effort. Similarly, the 1880s saw Indiana University offer a series of "summer tramps" for students to study language and culture while traveling in Europe, forming one of the antecedents to modern study abroad as it would develop later. Meanwhile, foreign students, particularly from Japan, China, and Europe, began to appear, although they remained rather small in numbers, estimated at only twenty-seven hundred in 1904 (Hoffa 2007, 293).

THE TURN OF THE TWENTIETH CENTURY

The turn of the century brought growing awareness of the wider world and America's role in it. On many campuses this was reflected in the foreign mission movement, which galvanized young students to travel to many countries to evangelize and otherwise aid in their development. Perhaps the most famous example occurred in 1898 at Princeton, where students raised funds for the YMCA in China and began sending students there to volunteer. The program developed over time into "Princeton in Asia," which has sent students to build international understanding with China for more than a century. Although isolationism remained a strong sentiment in the United States during this time, the close of the First World War was followed by increased efforts to formally organize international education and exchange. The Institute of International Education (IIE) was founded in 1919 with the explicit purpose of helping to facilitate these goals. That year also saw the founding of the American University in Cairo, which, along with the American University in Beirut (founded in 1862), aimed to help these regions develop as well as improve their relations with the United States.

This growth in international activity carried over into the 1920s. With damage done to some of Europe's universities during the First World War, more foreign students began seeking degrees in the United States. The Rockefeller Foundation gave grants to set up international houses in Philadelphia, New York City, Berkeley, and Chicago. Along with the Carnegie Corporation of New York, they also offered scholarships to foreign academics to spend time at US universities. Teaching and research concerning foreign languages and world areas also began to expand on various campuses, with increasing coverage of the Middle East and East Asia. Meanwhile, numerous experiments with international education began to appear. A handful of universities developed junior year abroad (JYA) programs, designed for foreign language majors, including the University of Delaware, Marymount College, and Smith College. Women predominantly attended these programs, which provided an opportunity for cultural immersion in Europe. In 1926, the University Travel Association operated its first "World University Cruise," where more than five hundred students and thirty-three faculty members sailed to thirty-five countries in a span of seven and half months. The onset of the Great Depression affected the viability of this "floating university" though, which had been designed to develop students' worldly thinking and spread international goodwill. It ended after its seventh cruise in 1936 because too few students were able to afford it.

WORLD WAR II AND THE POSTWAR ERA

Increasing political turmoil in Europe and the onset of the Second World War (1939–1945) then began to affect American universities. The Rockefeller Foundation and IIE were instrumental in providing refuge for scholars from Nazi Germany, many of whom were given posts at The New School for Social Research in New York City. In 1942, the War Department created the Army Specialized Training Program (ASTP), which was set up on various university campuses as a program to train military servicemen in the foreign languages and cultures of the world where the army was engaged. Meanwhile, Latin America emerged as an important ideological battleground with Germany and Italy, so the State Department commissioned IIE to administer a program to bring a thousand students from this region to study in the United States from 1941 to 1943.

Victory in 1945 ushered in a wave of attention to international exchange by the federal government, viewed as a means of enhancing national security and promoting world peace. In 1946 Congress supported the legislation of Senator J. William Fulbright (1905–1995) to create a program that would sponsor scholarly exchange between the United States and other countries. Over the next seven decades, the eponymous Fulbright Program became a flagship of the US government, sending more than 120,000 American scholars abroad and welcoming more than 200,000 scholars to US campuses. This was followed in 1948 by the passage of the United States Information and Educational Exchange Act (known as the Smith-Mundt Act), which authorized the federal government to engage in public diplomacy with foreign audiences. The range of international exchanges sponsored since have formed a significant mechanism for bringing international students and scholars to learn about the United States, as well as sending Americans abroad.

The year 1948 also saw the founding of NAFSA (the National Association of Foreign Student Advisers) to help university professionals who were working with the growing population of foreign students, which now totaled over twenty-five thousand. Campus populations also swelled in the postwar years as the GI Bill (the Servicemen's Readjustment Act of 1944) gave support to veterans pursuing higher education. Many of these new students had spent time abroad during the war and brought those experiences into mainstream student life on campus. The American Council on Education (ACE) meanwhile began actively sponsoring symposia and conferences for university leaders and faculty designed to advance the ways that universities were serving world affairs and educating students for international understanding.

The deepening of the Cold War in the 1950s provided ongoing impetus for efforts in this area. In response to the Soviet launch of the satellite *Sputnik* in 1957, Congress passed the National Defense Education Act (NDEA) in 1958. Title VI of the act authorized federal support for university-based area studies centers to develop experts in the world's foreign regions, languages, and cultures. With an influx of financial support from the federal government, as well as from private foundations such as Rockefeller, Ford, and Carnegie, many universities developed these centers, each focused on a different region of the world. Foreign Language and Area Studies (FLAS) fellowships were also introduced to send students abroad for advanced foreign language training, favoring "critical" languages that were seen as important to national security, such as Russian and Arabic. Meanwhile, study abroad programs were likewise becoming more organized with the expansion of JYA programs and the development of various study abroad consortia. In one of the more unique developments at the time, Stanford University opened overseas campuses in various European countries in the late 1950s and 1960s to better facilitate their students' experiences abroad. Various study abroad and exchange programs expanded sporadically into the 1960s and 1970s, and there was also growth in formal attention to teaching and researching in world areas such as Africa and Latin America.

THE END OF THE COLD WAR AND A NEW WAVE OF INTERNATIONALIZATION

In the late 1980s and 1990s, a new wave of interest in higher education internationalization gained significant momentum. Such organizations as NAFSA, IIE, and ACE all became deeply entwined with efforts to recruit more international students, send more students abroad, and introduce more global perspectives into university curricula. Universities began to appoint high-level senior international officers (SIOs) with the responsibility for coordinating and overseeing their international activities. The passage of the National Security Education Act (NSEA) by Congress in 1991 complemented these efforts, introducing a new tier of federal scholarships such as the Boren Fellowships. From the mid-1980s, IIE also became more active in counting the international students coming to the United States, as well as American students going abroad, in their biennial, and then annual, *Open Doors* reports.

The twenty-first century has seen internationalization intensify, with many universities opening campuses and research centers overseas, engaging in new international partnerships, recruiting students and scholars worldwide, sending students abroad, and adopting a mission to produce "global citizens." Academic programs and institutes with some kind of global orientation continue to proliferate in both disciplinary and professional fields (e.g., global health). With more than 880,000 foreign students coming to the United States (in academic year 2013–2014), and 289,000 American students studying abroad (in 2012–2013), international mobility is at an all-time high (Institute of International Education 2014). Study abroad options have also diversified, with the popularization of short-term trips, faculty-led trips, voluntary service opportunities, and professional internships. International branch campuses that export American liberal arts education as well as expertise in STEM fields (science, technology, engineering, and mathematics) have also gained in popularity. Although these were historic draws for international students to come to the United States, this expansion promises to bring America's academic traditions to greater numbers of students around the world.

International partnership and collaboration in American universities is thus today at a premium; but so is knowledge of the world's peoples, cultures, and history. Programs such as Fulbright, area studies centers, and exchanges sponsored by the State Department remain in operation, and they have been buttressed by a new imperative to internationalize the experience of all students. There is every reason to expect that universities will continue as key arbiters of international education and exchange in the years to come.

SEE ALSO *Americanization; Exceptionalism; Foreign Mission Movement; Industrialization; Internationalism;*

Isolationism; Qutb, Sayyid; Religions; Secularization; Smith–Mundt Act (US Information and Educational Exchange Act of 1948); World's Fairs

BIBLIOGRAPHY

Bayles, Martha. *Through a Screen Darkly: Popular Culture, Public Diplomacy, and America's Image Abroad.* New Haven, CT: Yale University Press, 2014.

de Wit, Hans. *Internationalization of Higher Education in the United States of America and Europe: A Historical, Comparative, and Conceptual Analysis.* Westport, CT: Greenwood Press, 2002.

Education and World Affairs. *The University Looks Abroad: Approaches to World Affairs at Six American Universities, a Report.* New York: Walker, 1965.

Engerman, David C. *Know Your Enemy: The Rise and Fall of America's Soviet Experts.* Oxford: Oxford University Press, 2009.

Hoffa, William W. *A History of Study Abroad: Beginnings to 1965.* Carlisle, PA: Forum on Education Abroad, 2007. Special issue of *Frontiers: The Interdisciplinary Journal of Study Abroad,* 2007.

Institute of International Exchange. *Open Doors 2014: Report on International Educational Exchange.* New York: Institute of International Education, 2014.

Loss, Christopher P. *Between Citizens and the State: The Politics of American Higher Education in the 20th Century.* Princeton, NJ: Princeton University Press, 2012.

McCaughey, Robert A. *International Studies and Academic Enterprise: A Chapter in the Enclosure of American Learning.* New York: Columbia University Press, 1984.

Merkx, G. W. "The Two Waves of Internationalization in U.S. Higher Education." *International Educator* 12, 1 (Winter 2003): 6–12.

Nelson, Adam R. "The Emergence of the American University: An International Perspective." *History of Education Quarterly* 45, 3 (September 2005): 427–437.

Nelson, Adam R. "Citizens or Cosmopolitans? Nationalism, Internationalism, and Academic Identity in the Early American Republic." *Asia Pacific Education Review* 14, 1 (2013): 93–101.

Jonathan Z. Friedman
Adjunct Professor
New York University

US ARMY SCHOOL OF THE AMERICAS (WESTERN HEMISPHERE INSTITUTE FOR SECURITY COOPERATION)

The School of the Americas (SOA) is a US Army training center for Latin American militaries that was established in the Panama Canal Zone in 1946 to instruct soldiers in combat-related skills and counterinsurgency doctrine. Originally known as the Latin American Ground School, it was reorganized in 1949 and renamed the US Caribbean School, which was again restructured following the Cuban Revolution (1953–1959) to reemerge as the School of the Americas in 1963. During the Cold War, the SOA trained the militaries of the Americas to fight communists and integrated them into a hemispheric security apparatus under the tutelage of the United States. Counterinsurgency doctrine legitimated state violence as a way to manage both peaceful dissent and armed insurgency, as authoritarian governments criminalized nonviolent protesters and labeled critics of the status quo communists, justifying the use of lethal violence against them. It promoted the formation of clandestine paramilitary forces, elite special forces, and centralized intelligence agencies.

After the Cuban Revolution, the school experienced a 42-percent increase in the number of trainees. Changing geopolitical circumstances amid an escalating Cold War shaped the size and composition of the student body. Bolivian recruits surged into the school in 1967, when Che Guevara (1928–1967) initiated his guerrilla campaign in the eastern lowlands. Chilean soldiers predominated in the early 1970s, a period that coincided with the 1970 election of Latin America's first socialist president, Salvador Allende (1908–1973), and his death in a 1973 US-backed military coup. In the 1980s, with civil wars raging in Central America and newly powerful guerrilla insurgencies in Colombia, Salvadoran, Honduran, Colombian, and Mexican students filled the institution. The presence of the Mexican and Honduran armies expanded because US policy makers saw Mexico and Honduras as buffers against the conflicts in Central America and as transshipment points for Colombian drugs flowing northward. Following the Cold War, the "war on drugs" provided new justification for US intervention in Latin America and for the maintenance of the SOA, as the United State turned away from fighting communism and targeted "narcoguerrillas."

For much of the school's history, Latin American military personnel circulated between the SOA and a number of different training centers, including US-based service schools, the military schools of US allies, clandestine CIA-sponsored training camps, and courses taught by US instructors in Latin America. A declassified list of SOA graduates released in 1993 revealed that many alumni had perpetrated heinous human rights crimes. Salvadoran death squad organizer Roberto D'Aubuisson (1944–1992), who ordered the execution of Archbishop óscar Romero (1917–1980), and Honduran general Gustavo Álvarez (1937–1989), who established a death squad known as Battalion 3-16, were among a substantial list of SOA graduates linked to human rights violations. In addition, several SOA alumni participated in the 1981 massacre of nearly a thousand people in the Salvadoran village of El Mozote, and approximately half of 247 Colombian officers cited for human rights violations in 1992 trained at the school. Following the disclosure of SOA graduates' names, a 1996 *Washington Post* article revealed the use of training manuals at the SOA that appeared to advocate torture. Together with the list of alumni, the so-called torture manuals opened the door to thinking about the United States as a perpetrator of terrorism and fueled a social movement that pressured the US government to abolish the institution.

Led by a Maryknoll priest, Father Roy Bourgeois, the movement grew to include thousands of progressive Christians, students, antiwar veterans, and trade unionists who converged on Fort Benning in Georgia every year for a vigil to commemorate the victims of SOA violence. Under pressure from activists, the House of Representatives cut funding for the school in 1999. Although the Senate failed to take similar action, the SOA officially closed on December 31, 2000, but was rechristened the next day in the same building as the Western Hemisphere Institute for Security Cooperation. The name change did not convince critics of the school that it had reformed, and demonstrations continued, peaking after the 2003 invasion of Iraq and the Abu Ghraib prison-torture scandal.

As the United States turns to new missions in the Middle East in the current "war on terror," the institution stands as a symbol of anticommunist zealotry and US interventionism on the sidelines of a larger, global network of diverse military training initiatives. It does so even as democratized Latin American governments have closed Cold War torture and detention centers and convened truth commissions to clarify the violent past.

SEE ALSO *Cold War; Department of Defense, US*

BIBLIOGRAPHY

Gill, Lesley. *The School of the Americas: Military Training and Political Violence in the Americas.* Durham, NC: Duke University Press, 2004.

Grandin, Greg. *Empire's Workshop: Latin America, the United States, and the Rise of the New Imperialism.* New York: Metropolitan, 2006.

McSherry, J. Patrice. *Predatory States: Operation Condor and Covert War in Latin America.* Lanham, MD: Rowan and Littlefield, 2005.

SOA Watch. www.SOAWatch.org.

Lesley Gill
Professor
Vanderbilt University

USA FOR AFRICA ("WE ARE THE WORLD")

United Support of Artists (USA) for Africa was a temporary nongovernmental organization (NGO) founded in 1985 by American celebrities concerned for famine sufferers in the Horn of Africa. Best known for the hit song "We Are the World," the charity raised millions for famine relief in 1985.

USA for Africa took its lead from Band Aid, a British charity formed in October 1984 by Irish singer-songwriter Bob Geldof, who had become outraged by images of refugee camps he saw on the BBC news. In response to the BBC report, as well as a public outcry, Geldof assembled a group of friends and fellow artists to record "Do They Know It's Christmas" in an attempt to raise money and awareness for famine relief. Released in November 1984, the single featured numerous popular

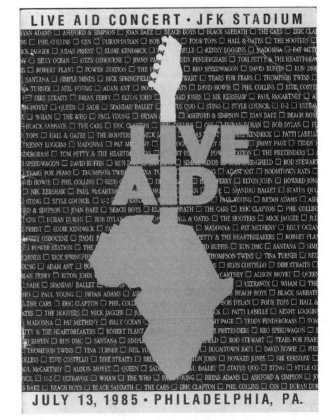

Front cover of the program from the Live Aid concert in Philadelphia, July 13, 1985. The largest benefit concert ever held, Live Aid was a 16-hour-long concert performed simultaneously in London's Wembley Stadium (attendance 70,000) and Philadelphia's Kennedy Stadium (92,000). The concert was broadcast live to an estimated 1 million viewers in 150 countries and raised over $70 million. **BLANK ARCHIVES/ HULTON ARCHIVE/GETTY IMAGES**

British artists and became the fastest-selling single to hit the UK charts, selling three million records and holding the Christmas number one position on the charts for five weeks. "Do They Know It's Christmas" raised over ten million British pounds.

Following Geldof's lead, on March 5, 1985, Harry Belafonte gathered forty-five recording artists in Burbank, California, to produce the soon-to-be hit single "We Are the World." Composed by Lionel Ritchie and Michael Jackson, the song immediately rose to the number one spot on the charts, where it remained for four weeks in the United States and for two weeks in the United Kingdom. Selling over seven and a half million copies in the United States alone, "We Are the World"—along with related USA for Africa merchandise—is estimated to have grossed over fifty million dollars (Shuker 2001, 237). "We Are the World" received four Grammy Awards in 1986, including Song of the Year and Best Music Video. Both the UK and US singles were international hits. In addition, they inspired similar singles for famine relief, such as Germany's "Nackt Im Wind," Canada's "Tears Are Not Enough," and South Africa's "Operation Hunger."

Encouraged by the success of the Ethiopia singles, Band Aid and USA for Africa joined forces to produce Live Aid, the largest benefit concert ever held. Touted as a global extravaganza, the sixteen-hour-long concert was performed simultaneously on July 13, 1985, on two continents. Attended by seventy thousand at Wembley Stadium in London and ninety-two thousand at Kennedy Stadium in Philadelphia, the concert was broadcast live to an estimated one million viewers in 150 countries. Over the course of one weekend, Live Aid raised over seventy million dollars (Shuker 2001, 237).

Despite great success in raising funds for famine relief, the Band Aid and USA for Africa charities, along with the Live Aid concert, have been criticized for redirecting attention away from famine sufferers toward celebrities (Straw, Rijven, and Greil 1985; Rijven and Straw 1989) and for promoting one-world sentiment (Davis 2010). Although the concert was heralded by the press as a feat of "technological wizardry," a "global jukebox," and a charity rock triumph, Live Aid has also been condemned as a gratuitous spectacle that enabled celebrity and corporate profiteering (Straw, Rijven, and Greil 1985; Rijven and Straw 1989). For example, Lionel Ritchie earned $5 million for a Pepsi commercial that aired throughout the United States at various points during the concert (Shales 1985). Meanwhile, Pepsi (along with the three other concert sponsors: AT&T, Chevrolet, and Eastman-Kodak) gained "the catch phrase of its advertising campaign sung for free by Ray Charles,

Stevie Wonder, Bruce Springsteen, and all the rest" (Greil, quoted in Garofalo 1992, 29).

In January 2010, US celebrities resurrected "We Are the World," rerecording the song in response to the Haitian earthquake. Although USA for Africa no longer existed, the song was packaged and sold as marking the twenty-fifth anniversary of the original hit single. Revised to reference the Haitian earthquake, with an ending sung in Haitian Creole by Haitian singer and activist Wyclef Jean, the new version immediately rose to number two on the US charts, and stayed on the charts for five weeks. The song only rose to number fifty in the United Kingdom, staying there for one week only. As with the original single, the remake raised a considerable amount of money for those suffering as a result of the disaster. Although the exact amount raised by the single itself has never been released by the song's producers, the celebrity-driven Hope for Haiti Now telethon to which the single was connected raised over $66 million (Preston 2010).

Since 1985, several parodies of "We Are the World" have been produced, some by professional comedians and musicians, others by amateurs either participating in karaoke-style performances or in music videos intended to raise awareness of the ethnocentric undertones of celebrity charity movements in general. Whether considered to be a successful tool of charity or yet another example of the narcissistic tendencies of celebrities in the Global North, the song certainly has had an impact on more than one generation.

SEE ALSO *Human Rights; Rock 'n' Roll*

BIBLIOGRAPHY

Davis, H. Louise. "Feeding the World a Line?: Celebrity Activism and Ethical Consumer Practices from Live Aid to Product Red." *Journal for Nordic Studies in English* 9, 3 (2010): 89–118.

Garofalo, Reebee, ed. *Rockin' the Boat: Mass Music and Mass Movements.* Boston: South End Press, 1992.

Preston, Caroline. "Haiti Telethon Organizers Award $35-Million in Relief Grants." *Chronicle of Philanthropy*, February 5, 2010. https://philanthropy.com/article/Haiti-Telethon-Organizers/161611

Rijven, Stan, and Will Straw. "Rock for Ethiopia." In *World Music, Politics, and Social Change: Papers from the International Association for the Study of Popular Music*, edited by Simon Frith. Manchester, UK: Manchester University Press, 1989.

Shales, Tom. "After the Music, The Memories; On TV—Hype, Hoopla and the Whole World." *Washington Post*, July 15, 1985.

Shuker, Roy. *Understanding Popular Music.* 2nd ed. New York: Routledge, 2001.

Straw, Will, Stan Rijven, and Marcus Greil. "Rock for Ethiopia." Third International Conference on Popular Music Studies, Montreal, Canada, July 1985.

H. Louise Davis
Chair of Integrative Studies, Associate Professor of American Studies
Miami University

USDA

SEE *Department of Agriculture, US.*

UTOPIANISM

SEE *Communitarian Socialism.*

V

VANZETTI, BARTHOLOMEO

SEE *Anarchism.*

VIETNAM WAR

The Vietnam War (1954–1975), also known as the Second Indochina War, ranks among the longest and bloodiest wars of the twentieth century. The war was a major international conflict in which the United States, China, the Soviet Union, and other foreign nations intervened. Yet it was also an intra-Vietnamese civil war in which multiple Vietnamese groups, parties, and governments fought to shape their country's postcolonial destiny. In the United States and around the world, the war provoked widespread protest and controversy. Disputes over the history and memory of the conflict continue to shape American politics, culture, and society even today.

COLONIAL ORIGINS

The origins of the Vietnam War lay in the earlier First Indochina War (1945–1954) and in France's efforts to preserve its colonial dominion over Vietnam, Laos, and Cambodia. The resistance was led by Ho Chi Minh (1890–1969), the founder of the Vietnamese Communist Party and the head of the Viet Minh, a pro-independence front organization. In 1945, Ho and the Viet Minh rode a wave of popular support to power and proclaimed the formation of an independent state, the Democratic Republic of Vietnam (DRV). After negotiations with the French failed, Ho and the Viet Minh retreated to the countryside to fight an insurgency modelled on Mao Zedong's (1893–1976) theory of "people's war." While the French controlled most of Indochina's cities and towns, the Viet Minh successfully mobilized large segments of the rural population, especially in northern and central Vietnam.

Because of Ho's affinity for communism, US officials ignored his pleas for recognition and support in 1945 and 1946. Yet American leaders were also initially reluctant to back France's war against a nationalist movement with a broad popular following. It was only in 1950, after the "loss" of China to communism, that US leaders agreed to dispatch military and economic aid to French forces in Indochina. But this aid was matched by Chinese and Soviet support for the Viet Minh. The resulting military stalemate lasted until 1954, when Viet Minh forces besieged and captured a French base at Dien Bien Phu in northern Vietnam. During the siege, US President Dwight Eisenhower (1890–1969) briefly considered a French request for an American airstrike to save the garrison, but backed away when Congress and British leaders expressed opposition.

At an international conference in Geneva in mid-1954, French and DRV officials agreed to a compromise deal under which Vietnam would be temporarily divided at the seventeenth parallel. Ho's DRV state took control of the northern zone, including Hanoi; the South was administered by a French- and US-backed anticommunist state based in Saigon. DRV officials accepted this arrangement on the condition that the two states would hold national elections in July 1956 to choose a single Vietnamese government. Because of the Viet Minh's nationalist reputation, almost all observers—including

Eisenhower—expected that the elections would produce a communist victory. Washington therefore refused to endorse the Geneva Accords, promising only that it would "refrain from the threat or use of force to disturb" them.

THE TWO VIETNAMS

The 1956 elections were never held. This was due largely to the efforts of Ngo Dinh Diem (1901–1963), the newly appointed leader of the Saigon government. A staunch anticommunist and devout Catholic, Diem consolidated his power via intrigue and military force. In mid-1955, he announced that South Vietnam (as the southern state was now called) would not participate in the Geneva-mandated elections—a position supported by Washington. Diem then used a rigged referendum to establish a new state known as the Republic of Vietnam (RVN), with himself as president. From this platform, Diem embarked on an ambitious program of nation building, including rural-development initiatives, the creation of a National Assembly, and the drafting of a constitution. These measures were coupled with harsh internal security practices to root out the stay-behind communist operatives who had remained in the South after Geneva. By the late 1950s, RVN police and military units had virtually wiped out the "Viet Cong" (as Diem and his officials disparagingly called them) in many parts of South Vietnam.

Diem's apparent success in South Vietnam was celebrated by the Eisenhower administration, which showered his regime with military and economic aid. The American media hailed Diem as "the miracle man of Southeast Asia." Diem's achievements seemed to present a stark contrast to the situation in communist North Vietnam. In late 1956, party leaders in Hanoi suspended a land-reform campaign due to "errors" that had led to the imprisonment and execution of thousands, including many former Viet Minh supporters.

Diem's triumph, however, was more transient than it first appeared. During the late 1950s, some of the stay-behind communist cadres in the South began to carry out assassinations and small-scale attacks against government targets. In January 1959, senior leaders in Hanoi belatedly authorized a shift toward armed struggle in the South, and also made plans to ship weapons and supplies to the insurgents. The following year, party operatives in the Mekong Delta organized a series of "concerted uprisings." In December 1960, Radio Hanoi announced the formation of the National Liberation Front (NLF), an anti-Diem organization dedicated to establishing a neutralist government in the South. Ostensibly independent and noncommunist, the NLF was in fact created and controlled from the outset by senior communist officials.

In 1961, newly elected US president John Kennedy (1917–1963) sought some means to halt the expanding

US Army helicopters and US and South Vietnamese soldiers in the Mekong Delta, southwest of Saigon, August, 1967. The Vietnam War was a major international conflict in which the United States, China, the Soviet Union, and other foreign nations intervened. Yet it was also an intra-Vietnamese civil war in which multiple Vietnamese groups, parties, and governments fought to shape their country's postcolonial destiny. **AP IMAGES/DANG VAN PHUOC**

insurgency and shore up the Diem government's flagging support. After making a deal with the Soviet Union to neutralize Laos, Kennedy felt pressure to show that he could be tough on communism in South Vietnam. His advisors proposed that the US-RVN relationship be upgraded to a "limited partnership," in which the United States would provide increased military and economic aid and advice. In exchange, Washington wanted Diem to implement reforms and allow Americans to play a larger role in the war against the NLF. Diem accepted the aid and a sharp increase in the number of US military advisors, but rejected the reform demands.

Despite Diem's intransigence on the reform issue, the new arrangements initially seemed to work. During 1962, units of the Army of the Republic of Vietnam (ARVN) used US-supplied helicopters and armored vehicles to inflict heavy losses on NLF units. Diem also launched the Strategic Hamlet Program, a new counterinsurgency scheme that aimed to isolate the insurgents from the rural population by fortifying every hamlet in South Vietnam. By early 1963, Diem and many senior US officials had become strongly optimistic about the war. This official optimism persisted even after the January 1963 Battle of Ap Bac, in which NLF forces shot down several helicopters and inflicted heavy casualties on a much larger ARVN force. Based on the positive reports he received, Kennedy eventually approved a Pentagon plan to begin a phased withdrawal of US advisors from South Vietnam in late 1963.

Diem correctly predicted that the year 1963 would be a turning point in the war—though the turn was not in the direction he expected. In May, the killing of eight demonstrators by RVN security forces in the city of Hue touched off an urban antigovernment protest movement led by Buddhist monks. The protestors accused Diem of religious discrimination and persecution. When one monk was photographed burning himself to death on a Saigon street, the movement garnered worldwide attention and sympathy. Although US officials warned Diem not to use force against the protestors, he allowed his younger brother, Ngo Dinh Nhu (1910–1963), to crush the movement with nighttime raids and mass arrests. In response, Kennedy authorized the US embassy to encourage a group of ARVN generals to overthrow the government. The coup took place on November 1. Diem and Nhu were detained and killed the next day—just three weeks before Kennedy's own assassination in Dallas.

ESCALATION

In the wake of Diem's overthrow, both North Vietnamese and US leaders took steps to escalate the war. In Hanoi, a senior communist party official named Le Duan (1907–1986) argued successfully in late 1963 for a go-for-broke strategy. After infiltrating the South with large numbers of North Vietnamese army troops via the "Ho Chi Minh trail" through Laos and Cambodia, Le Duan planned to use conventional operations to destroy the ARVN and bring down the South Vietnamese regime. Given the political infighting and chaos that had prevailed in Saigon since Diem's ouster, this seemed like a feasible goal.

But Lyndon Johnson (1908–1973), the new president in Washington, had escalation plans of his own. In August 1964, an American destroyer reported that it had been attacked twice by North Vietnamese naval forces in international waters in the Gulf of Tonkin. Although the report of the second attack turned out to be false, Johnson used the incident to secure a congressional resolution

authorizing him to take "all necessary measures" to prevent "further aggression." A few months later, after winning a landslide victory in the 1964 US presidential election, Johnson launched Operation Rolling Thunder, a strategic bombing campaign designed to force North Vietnam to end its support for the insurgency in the South. The following month, he ordered the first US ground combat units to deploy to South Vietnam. By late 1965, the number of US military personnel in South Vietnam exceeded 180,000, with more on the way.

As designed by US Army General William Westmoreland (1914–2005), American military strategy during the "big war" of 1965 to 1968 was designed to use US advantages in firepower and mobility to kill maximum numbers of enemy fighters and destroy the communists' will to fight. For example, the bombing of North Vietnam was intended to push Hanoi to its "breaking point." Meanwhile, a CIA-sponsored "secret war" in Laos and US Navy operations in the South China Sea aimed to disrupt North Vietnam's ability to send supplies and soldiers to the South. Inside South Vietnam, Westmoreland sought to wage a war of attrition; his plans included both counterinsurgency operations against the "Viet Cong infrastructure" in villages and conventional operations against the "main force units" of the NLF and North Vietnamese Army.

Under Westmoreland's direction, US forces inflicted widespread damage in North Vietnam, severely disrupted Hanoi's efforts to send supplies and reinforcements to the South, and killed significant numbers of enemy fighters. But the communists' "breaking point" remained elusive. Meanwhile, critics at home and around the world charged that the US war effort was strategically flawed, if not downright immoral. The bombing of North Vietnam appeared to be a massively disproportionate use of force against a poor and underdeveloped country. In South Vietnam, critics deplored the American reliance on tactics that were likely to cause massive civilian casualties; these tactics included unobserved artillery fire, tactical bombing, large-unit sweep operations, the deliberate destruction of farmers' homes and property, and the infamous practice of "body counts," in which dead noncombatants were invariably counted as enemy fighters. The routine use of napalm (jellied petroleum that burns at 1,500 degrees Fahrenheit [815.6 degrees Celsius]) and Agent Orange (one of several toxic defoliants used to destroy crops and forest cover) also raised troubling ethical questions. Most troubling of all were reports that US military personnel routinely committed war crimes, including the torture, rape, and murder of Vietnamese civilians. Although commanders denied that atrocities by American forces were common, those denials were undermined by revelations about the My Lai massacre, a 1968 episode in which a US Army company slaughtered hundreds of defenseless villagers.

TET '68

American doubts about the wisdom and morality of the US involvement in Vietnam were powerfully reinforced by the communists' Tet Offensive of 1968. As conceived by Le Duan, the plan envisioned a "General Offensive, General Uprising"—an all-out military and political attack on South Vietnam's large towns and cities, with the goal of triggering a popular rebellion against the RVN state. By Le Duan's own criteria, the offensive was a failure. Neither the initial wave of assaults in January and February nor a series of follow-up attacks in May and August produced the hoped-for uprising. In virtually every case, the attackers were thrown back with heavy losses, often within hours or a few days. By some estimates, as many as 15 percent of all of the NLF and North Vietnamese combat fighters in South Vietnam died in the first month of the offensive.

But if Tet '68 was not a victory for the revolutionaries, neither was it a clear-cut triumph for the United States or for Lyndon Johnson. While US and RVN forces killed far more enemy fighters than they lost, American casualty rates during Tet were still the highest of the entire war, with more than 2,100 US military personnel killed during May 1968 alone. Americans were also disturbed by the media coverage of the offensive, especially by a horrifying photograph of the chief of the RVN National Police shooting a bound "Viet Cong" prisoner to death. The offensive raised doubts about Johnson's ability to continue to finance the war through deficit spending, as investors rushed to exchange dollars for gold. In March, Johnson nearly lost the New Hampshire presidential primary to peace candidate Eugene McCarthy (1916–2005). Three weeks later, Johnson suspended bombing operations over most of North Vietnam and called for peace talks. He then shocked the nation by withdrawing from the 1968 presidential race.

NIXON'S WAR

The unravelling of Johnson's presidency provided a political opening to Republican candidate Richard Nixon (1913–1994), who promised to end the war. Nixon was a shrewd politician who recognized that military victory in Vietnam was infeasible. But he was also paranoid and vindictive, and determined to deflect blame for defeat. He described his objective as "peace with honor"—a purposely vague slogan that suggested he would extricate the US from the war without actually losing. During his first term, Nixon's strategy was a mix of seemingly contradictory policies. In 1969, he began a unilateral withdrawal of US troops from South Vietnam, coupled with a "Vietnamization" program to strengthen the South

Vietnamese armed forces. He also ordered National Security Advisor Henry Kissinger (b. 1923) to open secret bilateral negotiations with North Vietnam in the hopes of getting the "honorable" peace settlement he craved. At the same time, the president selectively expanded the war with a covert bombing campaign in eastern Cambodia in 1969, followed by ground invasions of both Cambodia and Laos in 1970 and 1971.

In formulating his policies on Vietnam, Nixon had to take account of a broad and diffuse antiwar movement within the United States. The movement began in the mid-1960s as a loose coalition of civil rights activists, antinuclear advocates, and leftist student groups. Its tactics borrowed heavily from the black freedom struggle, and included marches, demonstrations, and "teach-ins" on college campuses. As the war intensified in the late 1960s, many politically moderate Americans embraced the antiwar cause. The new supporters included a significant number of military veterans who had turned against the war while serving in Vietnam.

Yet the antiwar movement never gained majority support, despite the growing unpopularity of the war. In the minds of many Americans, the protestors were associated with hippies, drugs, draft dodging, and other controversial aspects of the 1960s counterculture. Media coverage of the movement focused disproportionately on its most radical participants, especially on the small minority of activists who advocated violence. When National Guardsmen killed four students during a protest at Kent State University in Ohio in May 1970, opinion polls showed that a majority of Americans blamed the students. The movement was also weakened by a white backlash against African American civil rights demands, and by bloody clashes between police and the black residents of northern US cities. Nixon's implementation of a lottery system for the US military draft in December 1969 effectively reduced the number of young American men who were likely to be inducted, and thus undercut one of the key drivers of antiwar sentiment.

Nixon eventually succeeded in negotiating a peace deal of sorts with Hanoi. In March 1972, North Vietnamese forces made a new bid to win the war with a conventional offensive that nearly shattered South Vietnam's defenses. But the ARVN eventually stalled the enemy advance, thanks largely to large-scale deployments of US airpower. As the communist offensive wound down, Kissinger and North Vietnamese negotiators finally came to terms: in exchange for a ceasefire in the South and the return of all American prisoners of war, Nixon withdrew all remaining US combat forces from Vietnam. Nixon, who deliberately put off the finalization of the deal until after his November 1972 reelection victory, declared that "peace with honor" had been achieved. But South

Vietnamese president Nguyen Van Thieu (1923–2001) considered the accords an American betrayal, because the text made no mention of the hundreds of thousands of North Vietnamese troops who remained in the South. It took extensive cajoling by Nixon, including one last round of bombing of the North in December 1972, to make Thieu acquiesce.

ENDINGS AND LEGACIES

The ceasefire in South Vietnam broke down almost immediately, as both North and South Vietnamese forces scrambled for advantage in the wake of the US withdrawal. Although the South initially seemed capable of holding its own, North Vietnamese commanders discerned in late 1974 that ARVN defenses in the Central Highlands had become dangerously weak. In March 1975, Hanoi launched yet another offensive, one that communist strategists expected would take two years. It lasted just fifty-five days. By early April, communist forces had overrun South Vietnam's northern half and were advancing toward Saigon. US officials in Saigon, fearful of triggering panic in the city, delayed the implementation of evacuation plans. While more than one hundred thousand South Vietnamese escaped during the final weeks of the war, thousands of others were left behind when the last American helicopter lifted off the roof of the US embassy early on the morning of April 30, 1975. A few hours later, North Vietnamese forces captured Independence Palace, the seat of the RVN government.

For Vietnamese communist leaders, the fall of Saigon marked the glorious conclusion of the party's long struggle for national liberation. But the fruits of victory were not what the party expected. Post-1975 attempts to impose socialist economic policies on the South were disastrous; by the early 1980s, reunified Vietnam ranked among the poorest countries in the world. At the same time, Hanoi found itself embroiled in the Third Indochina War, which pitted Vietnam against two of its former allies, China and the Cambodian communist regime of Pol Pot (1925–1998). Conditions inside Vietnam improved only in the late 1980s, following the death of Le Duan and rise of a party-led "renovation" movement that advocated market liberalization. The 1990s were marked by the return of peace and by rapid economic growth, as well as the normalization of Hanoi's diplomatic relations with Washington. Amid these changes, the communist party assiduously maintained its official narrative about the "War of Resistance against America." Still, Vietnamese writers, filmmakers, and others found ways to challenge the party's triumphalism, as expressed in Bao Ninh's novel *The Sorrow of War* (1991). Even the death rituals performed by the family members of deceased soldiers could provide alternative modes of commemoration.

In the United States, post-1975 memories of the Vietnam War were as diverse and contentious as the debates that had split the country during the war years. While some Americans professed a desire simply to forget the conflict, this impulse was soon overwhelmed by an explosion of Vietnam memory-making practices. Beginning in the late 1970s, Americans examined the war via novels, memoirs, oral histories, films, and television shows. Debates over the "lessons" of Vietnam unfolded in museum exhibits, college classrooms, and even political campaigns. In 1980, Ronald Reagan (1911–2004) described the war as a "noble cause." In contrast, the journalist Neil Sheehan lamented American leaders' inability to admit that the war had been "unwinnable" for the United States (*A Bright Shining Lie*, 1988, 8).

At first, American collective memories of the war revolved mostly around the battlefield experiences of American combat soldiers. This focus was apparent in Hollywood portrayals, such as *Platoon* (1986, dir. Oliver Stone), and in Maya Lin's design for the Vietnam Veterans Memorial (1982) in Washington, DC, which emphasized the more than fifty-eight thousand Americans who died in the war. Yet the legacies of Vietnam were also apparent in the high incidence of posttraumatic stress disorder (PTSD) and Agent Orange–linked illnesses among veterans. At the same time, the war and its aftermath gave rise to thriving communities of Vietnamese-Americans, who numbered more than two million by 2010. In the early twenty-first century, the Vietnam War was frequently invoked in discussions of the American wars in Afghanistan and Iraq. Like the US Civil War that preceded it by a century, the Vietnam War had become a defining feature of American collective memory, even as Americans remained deeply divided on how to interpret its significance and consequences.

SEE ALSO *Agent Orange; Gulf of Tonkin Resolution; Ho Chi Minh; Johnson, Lyndon Baines; Kennedy, John Fitzgerald; Kissinger, Henry; McNamara, Robert S.; Nguyễn Ngọc Loan executing Nguyễn Văn Lém (Eddie Adams, 1968); Nixon, Richard Milhous; Phan Thị Kim Phúc (Nick Ut, 1972); The Quiet American (Graham Greene, 1955)*

BIBLIOGRAPHY

Berman, Larry. *No Peace, No Honor: Nixon, Kissinger, and Betrayal in Vietnam.* New York: Free Press, 2001.

Brocheux, Pierre. *Ho Chi Minh: A Biography.* New York: Cambridge University Press, 2007.

Caputo, Philip. *A Rumor of War.* New York: Holt, Rinehart, and Winston, 1977.

Daddis, Gregory A. *Westmoreland's War: Reassessing American Strategy in Vietnam.* New York: Oxford University Press, 2014.

Elliott, David. *The Vietnamese War: Revolution and Social Change in the Mekong Delta, 1930–1975*. Concise ed. Armonk, NY: Sharpe, 2006.

Elliott, Duong Van Mai. *The Sacred Willow: Four Generations in the Life of a Vietnamese Family*. New York: Oxford University Press, 1999.

Herring, George C. *America's Longest War: The United States and Vietnam, 1950–1975*. 4th ed. Boston: McGraw-Hill, 2002.

Hess, Gary R. *Vietnam: Explaining America's Lost War*. Malden, MA, and Oxford: Blackwell, 2009.

Hughes, Ken. *Fatal Politics: The Nixon Tapes, the Vietnam War, and the Casualties of Re-election*. Charlottesville: University of Virginia Press, 2015.

Jamieson, Neil L. *Understanding Vietnam*. Berkeley: University of California Press, 1993.

Lair, Meredith H. *Armed with Abundance: Consumerism and Soldiering in the Vietnam War*. Chapel Hill: University of North Carolina Press, 2011.

Logevall, Fredrik. *Choosing War: The Lost Chance for Peace and the Escalation of War in Vietnam*. Berkeley: University of California Press, 1999.

Logevall, Fredrik. *Embers of War: The Fall of an Empire and the Making of America's Vietnam*. New York: Random House, 2012.

Longley, Kyle. *Grunts: The American Combat Soldier in Vietnam*. Armonk, NY: Sharpe, 2008.

Miller, Edward. *Misalliance: Ngo Dinh Diem, the United States, and the Fate of South Vietnam*. Cambridge, MA: Harvard University Press, 2013.

Nguyen, Lien-Hang T. *Hanoi's War: An International History of the War for Peace in Vietnam*. Chapel Hill: University of North Carolina Press, 2012.

Phillips, Rufus P. *Why Vietnam Matters: An Eyewitness Account of Lessons Not Learned*. Annapolis, MD: Naval Institute Press, 2008.

Pribbenow, Merle L. "General Vo Nguyen Giap and the Mysterious Evolution of the Plan for the 1968 Tet Offensive." *Journal of Vietnamese Studies* 3, 2 (2008): 1–33.

Sheehan, Neil. *A Bright Shining Lie: John Paul Vann and America in Vietnam*. New York: Random House, 1988.

Edward Miller
Associate Professor of History
Dartmouth College

VIRGIN ISLANDS

SEE *Caribbean.*

VIVEKANANDA, SWAMI
1863–1902

Swami Vivekananda arrived in the United States in the summer of 1893, a few weeks before the World's Parliament of Religions was scheduled to convene on September 11. Attempting to escape the artificially inflated prices for food and lodging that racked Chicago during the World's Columbian Exhibition, he travelled to Boston in the company of Kate Sanborn (1839–1917), a writer with personal connections to Massachusetts' intellectual and cultural elite. At Sanborn's home in Metcalf, Massachusetts, Vivekananda met John H. Wright (1852–1908), a classics professor at Harvard University who, along with his wife Mary, was stunned by the depth and clarity of Vivekananda's intellectual and spiritual vision. Sanborn and the Wrights were just the kind of educated, cosmopolitan Americans who were fascinated by Vivekananda during his two years in the United States. Determined to give this extraordinary visitor from India an audience in America, the Wrights arranged for him to give the first of what would become a highly successful series of lectures in their Unitarian church in Annisquam, Massachusetts. The support from these friends in Massachusetts meant that by the time Vivekananda reached the Parliament of Religions, he had already honed his public persona before friendly American audiences.

Swami Vivekananda was an influential presence throughout the World's Parliament of Religions, but it was his opening address that received the most attention. Greeting the audience and his fellow delegates as "Brothers and Sisters of America," he received enthusiastic and sustained applause for so poignantly enunciating the theme of equality among religions as the theme of the gathering. He went on to call for an appreciation of the unity of all religions, insisting that differences in culture, theology, or ritual practices should not obscure the deeper reality that "in the heart of everything the same truth reigns" (Vivekananda 1893, 2:977). While many of the liberal American Protestants in the audience were ready for such affirmations, they were less prepared for Vivekananda's spirited and philosophically sophisticated defense of the Hindu tradition and his sharp critique of the ways in which European and American missionaries caricatured the faith traditions of South Asia without understanding them. American missionaries had long insisted that India's social problems were the result of a corrupt and false religion, but Vivekananda rejected such notions as self-interested distortions. If Western missionaries wanted to help the people of India, he insisted, they should provide food, clothing, and medical care rather than using colonial power to compel conversions to another religion. The discomfort that such statements generated among the more conventional Christians, combined with Vivekananda's truly charismatic stage presence, generated substantial media attention, a fact that helped pave the way for an extended lecture and fund-raising tour of the United States.

Vivekananda's two-year stay in the United States focused on two distinct, but related goals. First, in numerous public appearances across the Midwest and the

East Coast, he continued to defend both the legitimacy of the Hindu tradition and his own critique of Christian missionary activity in India. Liberal, reform-minded Protestants, especially those influenced by the most recent trends in science, biblical criticism, and comparative religion, responded extremely well to his speeches. But to conservative Christians, who were disturbed by these developments and concerned with any threat to Christianity's status as a unique and final revelation of divine truth, Vivekananda's forthright defense of concepts such as karma and reincarnation were deeply troubling. In this way, Vivekananda's lecture tour revealed growing divisions in American religious life that would deepen considerably over the next several decades.

Vivekananda's second objective for his American tour was to teach the principles of yoga to small but devoted groups of American disciples. Convinced that America's emphasis on work, efficiency, and materialism had produced a culture that was both distracted and spiritually hollow, he taught a form of yoga that emphasized breath meditation as a path to sustained concentration and spiritual insight. Vivekananda was extremely gifted in his ability to make Hinduism understandable and relevant to sympathetic American audiences, and he emphasized that the practice of yoga did not require metaphysical beliefs and was therefore fully compatible with a scientific worldview. As historian Diana Eck (2001) has observed, this combination of spirituality and science attracted both liberal Christians and secular-minded inquirers to the practice of yoga. The effectiveness of Vivekananda's teaching resulted in the establishment of the American Vedanta societies, the first of which was founded in New York in 1894, with later chapters on the West Coast established during Vivekananda's second and briefer visit to the United States in 1899.

Swami Vivekananda's visit to the United States represents a pivotal moment in the religious and cultural history of the United States. For many thousands of Americans, he was the first Hindu they had or would ever encounter in person, and his defense of South Asian traditions marked a sharp contrast with the long, anti-Hindu monologue of Western missionaries. The extensive press coverage of Vivekananda's visit meant that thousands more heard his message even without seeing him face to face. The creation of the Vedanta societies remains an important legacy of his visit and has introduced the practice of yoga to generations of Americans.

SEE ALSO *Hinduism; World's Fairs; World's Parliament of Religions (1893)*

BIBLIOGRAPHY

Burke, Mary Louise. *Swami Vivekananda in America: New Discoveries.* Calcutta: Advaita Ashrama, 1958.

Eck, Diana. *A New Religious America: How a "Christian Country" Has Become the World's Most Religiously Diverse Nation.* New York: Harper Collins, 2001.

Jackson, Carl T. *Vedanta for the West: The Ramakrishna Movement in the United States.* Bloomington: Indiana University Press, 1994.

Vivekananda. "Hinduism." In *The World's Parliament of Religions: An Illustrated and Popular Story of the World's First Parliament of Religions, Held in Chicago in Connection with the Columbian Exposition of 1893,* edited by John Henry Barrows, Vol. 2, 968–978. Chicago: Parliament Publishing Company, 1893.

Paul E. Teed
Professor of History
Saginaw Valley State University

V-J DAY IN TIMES SQUARE (ALFRED EISENSTAEDT, 1945)

V-J Day in Times Square is an iconic picture taken by Alfred Eisenstaedt (1898–1995) shortly after the news that Japan had surrendered on August 14, 1945, ending World War II. It portrays an American sailor kissing a woman in a white dress and was published in the August 27, 1945, issue of *LIFE* magazine in a twelve-page section titled "Victory Celebrations," accompanied by fourteen photographs titled "The Men of War Kiss from Coast to Coast." Eisenstaedt's image was given a full-page display opposite three other kissing couples celebrating in Washington, DC, Kansas City, and Miami. Unlike those posed photographs, Eisenstaedt's was taken spontaneously. He was looking for a picture that epitomized the American victory. The black-and-white composition required a woman in a white dress, and he focused his Leica on one, hoping that a soldier would come along and kiss her. Eisenstaedt captured an image with "classical symmetries, sharp contrasts of light and shadow … and the romantic swoon ritualized in classic ballet" (Hariman and Lucaites 2007, 124). US Navy photojournalist Victor Jorgensen (1913–1994) took another version of the same scene, which was published in the *New York Times* the following day under the title *Kissing the War Goodbye.*

Eisenstaedt's photo instantly became a cultural icon. Like many iconic images of the twentieth century, it comes from the century's leading art form—photojournalism. Possibly, it was the most famous photo in Eisenstaedt's distinguished career. In 1999, it became the cover image of *LIFE, Decades of the Twentieth Century: The Way We Were.* It is telling that one of the most popular pictures of World War II was taken on the home front. The photo symbolizes the excitement and relief over the end of World War II that manifested itself all over the country in spontaneous parades, dancing in the street, and uninhibited

V-J Day in Times Square. *A jubilant American sailor plants a kiss on a woman in Times Square as crowds celebrate the victory over Japan. Photo by Alfred Eisenstaedt, August 14, 1945.* An instant cultural icon when it appeared on a full page in LIFE *magazine, the photo captured the excitement and relief over the end of World War II that manifested itself all over the country in parades, dancing in the street, and hugs and kisses. It also celebrated the ordinary Americans who won the war.* ALFRED EISENSTAEDT/PIX INC./TIME & LIFE PICTURES/MASTERS/GETTY IMAGES

hugs and kisses. It also celebrated the nation and the ordinary people that won the war, in this case a soldier and a dental assistant (mistaken for a nurse) in their uniforms.

While Eisenstaedt's photograph has become the epitome for spontaneity and surprise, it is probably more accurate to say that it depicts the soldier's spontaneity and the woman's surprise. The identity of the couple in the photograph has not been established unequivocally, which is also due to the fact that we cannot see the face of the sailor or the nurse. This speaks for the ubiquity of the situation: a number of sailors kissed nurses in the Times Square vicinity on that day. While George Galdorisi and Lawrence Verria (2012) claim to have identified the couple through forensic analysis and photographic interpretation, they admit that there are probably four or five legitimate candidates for the sailor and about three for the woman, including Edith Shain, who attended the reenactment of the scene in 2005.

The two most likely candidates, George Mendonsa and Greta Zimmer Friedman, were perfect strangers on that day in Times Square. They did not see the photograph until 1980 and the 1960s, respectively, and did not meet again until 1980. Their experience on that day reflects the euphoria the photograph evokes. Mendonsa was a first-class sailor in the Navy, one of the almost one hundred thousand servicemen and women circling through New York City every week. He was on a date at Radio City Music Hall when he heard the news. The show was stopped, and the couple went to a nearby bar to celebrate. Back on the street, Mendonsa went up to a number of women to kiss them. Friedman, a dental aid on her lunch break who had come to Times Square to read the *New York Times* news ticker, recalled distinctly that "It wasn't my choice to be kissed. The guy just came over and grabbed!" In her memory, the kiss was not "a romantic event … It was just somebody celebrating. It was just an event of 'thank god the war is over'" (Redmond 2005). While Mendonsa's action would not have been acceptable in ordinary circumstances in 1940s America, on August 14, 1945, it clearly was, even to his later-to-be wife, who was present at the scene.

V-J Day in Times Square is also a window on the often painful realities of the first half of the twentieth century. German-born Eisenstaedt had served in World War I (1914–1918) as a soldier and was nearly killed at Flanders. He went on to become one of the most renowned photojournalists of the twentieth century, emigrated to the United States in 1935, and was one of the original four photographers LIFE hired in 1936. Greta Zimmer was an Austrian Jew who had emigrated before World War II; her parents perished in the Holocaust. Mendonsa was on his last day of leave from the Pacific theater. Their encounter on Forty-Fourth Street and Broadway, highly unlikely in the first place, would have never happened without the Japanese surrender.

On the last day of World War II, Eisenstaedt created a picture that symbolizes the end of a traumatic era and the promise of something new for millions of Americans. For seven decades, it has invited its viewers to experience and reenact the exultation of this moment, including many lesbian and gay couples in the military who reenacted the scene with public kisses and embraces after the US military repealed its "don't ask, don't tell" policy in 2011. The picture's global popularity attests to the fact that this experience is shared around the world when war ends and loved ones return home.

SEE ALSO *LIFE (magazine); World War II*

BIBLIOGRAPHY

Eisenstaedt, Alfred, as told to Arthur Goldsmith. *The Eye of Eisenstaedt.* New York: Viking, 1969.

Galdorisi, George, and Lawrence Verria. *The Kissing Sailor: The Mystery behind the Photo That Ended World War II.* Annapolis, MD: Naval Institute Press, 2012.

Hariman, Robert, and John Louis Lucaites: "The Times Square Kiss: Iconic Photography and Civic Renewal in U.S. Public Culture." *Journal of American History* 94, 1 (2007): 122–131.

Jordan, Killian, ed. *LIFE, Decades of the Twentieth Century: The Way We Were.* New York: Life Books, 1999.

Redmond, Patricia. "Interview with George Mendonsa." Veterans History Project, Library of Congress, American Folklife Center. http://lcweb2.loc.gov/diglib/vhp/story/loc.natlib.afc2001001.42868/

Redmond, Patricia. "Interview with Greta Friedman (8/23/2005)." Veterans History Project, Library of Congress, American Folklife Center. 2005. http://lcweb2.loc.gov/diglib/vhp/story/loc.natlib.afc2001001.42863/transcript?ID=sr0001

Anja Schüler
Research Associate
Heidelberg Center for American Studies
at the University of Heidelberg

VODOU

Vodou, or Voodoo as it is often written in the English-speaking world, is a syncretized religion developed in Haiti during the eighteenth century at the height of the Atlantic slave trade. Enslaved peoples from West Africa, who came from several different ethnic groups, provided labor for France's lucrative sugar-producing colony in the Caribbean. Facing high mortality rates and an exceptionally brutal version of slavery in the New World, the relatively unassimilated slaves forged a new spirituality that blended West African beliefs—such as reverence for deceased ancestors; the use of song, dance, and drumming in religious rituals; and possession by spirits—with Roman Catholicism. At the same time, these slaves also developed a syncretized linguistic system known as *Kreyól*, which is frequently called *Creole* by English speakers. Currently, Vodou and Kreyól, rather than Roman Catholicism and French (the dominant colonial religious and linguistic constructs), are the most prevalent religious and linguistic systems in Haiti. Since virtually all Vodou spirits (*loas*) are associated with Christian saints, most Haitians see nothing incongruent with practicing both Vodou and Roman Catholicism. Many anthropologists argue that more than 90 percent of the Haitian population (both at home and abroad) adheres to the basic Vodou belief system.

The term *Vodou* is derived from a term meaning *spirit* in the Fon language of Dahomey. A complex set of beliefs that emphasizes Dahomean *vodou*, Congolese *simbi*, and Yoruba *orisha*, the Haitian version of Vodou stresses a very close relationship between the spirit world and one's ancestors. A key aspect of the faith is the healing of people from various forms of physical and mental illness. The priesthood of Vodou includes both male (*houngans*) and female (*mambos*) priests. Although there is no strict religious hierarchy in the religion, *houngans* and *mambos* perform religious ceremonies to pacify the spirits, initiate new priests, create protection devices, cast spells, and interpret dreams. Spirits often take possession of a participant's body during the services.

Some *houngans* and *mambos* are also sorcerers, known as *bokors* and *caplatas*, respectively. In addition to the ability to practice the benevolent acts of *houngans* and *mambos*, these sorcerers, who are a minority among the Vodou clergy, can also practice black magic, such as the creation of zombies. Within the belief system, it is argued that dead people whose souls have not been taken to the afterlife can be revived and placed under the control of a sorcerer. Even among *bokors* and *caplatas*, who perform their activities in secret and sell their skills to the highest bidder, these dark magic services are infrequent. Nevertheless, partially as a result of ethnocentric Hollywood films that popularized the misconception that Vodou priests spent much of their time creating zombies to attack (and often devour) mankind, many Americans, especially fundamentalist Protestants, have accused Vodou adherents of devil worship and cannibalism.

Until the 1960s, Haitian Vodou was confined mostly to the island nation. Vodou played a key role in Haiti's independence from France. The Haitian Revolution (1791–1804) was initiated during a Vodou ceremony presided over by a *houngan* who led a community of runaway slaves united by their syncretized belief system. After independence, Vodou remained widely popular among the black masses. By 1964, the Roman Catholic Church, which had tried to suppress Vodou, decided to adopt a more conciliatory approach and incorporated Vodou music, dance, and drumming into the Catholic liturgy. At the same time, brutal dictator François Duvalier (1907–1971) co-opted the black magic side of the religion as a form of social control.

Following the overthrow of the Duvalier dictatorship in 1986, hundreds of thousands of Haitians began to flee their homeland. As a result of the Haitian diaspora, Vodou has spread to other parts of the world, especially the United States, the Dominican Republic, Canada, and France. Over one million Haitians (and their descendants) live in the United States, with large concentrations in New York City and Miami. Haitian and Haitian American Vodou adherents are organized into neighborhood communities of practitioners (known as a *société*) that meets in a structure (known as a *hounfour*) presided over by a *houngan* or *mambo*. This has facilitated the retention of the cultural heritage of many Haitians in the United States. As such, the number of people practicing Vodou in the United States has increased dramatically.

Haitian Vodou should not be confused with Louisiana Voodoo, a highly commercialized African-infused religion found in Louisiana that also has its roots in the Atlantic slave trade. Whereas the African roots of Haitian Vodou can be found in Dahomey, Louisiana Voodoo's roots can be traced to the Senegambia region and northern Ghana. This can be observed in Louisiana Voodoo's use of *gris-gris* (talismans), an Islamic cultural practice from northern Ghana that is not found in Haitian Vodou. In addition, the divergent development of the two religious paths was conditioned by the excessively brutal version of slavery implemented in Haiti during the eighteenth century. During the 1930s, New Orleans became a popular tourist destination and Louisiana Voodoo underwent a commercialization process whereby the cultural phenomena became more of a business venture than a belief system. Significantly, Louisiana Voodoo does not permeate Louisiana culture the way that Haitian Vodou permeates Haitian culture.

SEE ALSO *Africa; Atlantic Slave Trade; Caribbean*

BIBLIOGRAPHY

Bellegarde-Smith, Patrick, and Claudine Michel, eds. *Vodou in Haitian Life and Culture: Invisible Powers*. London: Palgrave Macmillan, 2006.

Galembo, Phyllis. *Vodou: Visions and Voices of Haiti*. Berkeley, CA: Ten Speed Press, 2005.

Hall, Gwendolyn Midlo. *Africans in Colonial Louisiana: The Development of Afro-Creole Culture in the Eighteenth Century*. Baton Rouge: Louisiana State University Press, 1992.

McAlister, Elizabeth. *Rara! Vodou, Power, and Performance in Haiti and Its Diaspora*. Berkeley: University of California Press, 2002.

Pierre-Louis, François, Jr. *Haitians in New York City: Transnationalism and Hometown Associations*. Gainesville: University Press of Florida, 2006.

Michael R. Hall
Professor of History
Armstrong State University

VOICE OF AMERICA

The Voice of America (VOA), the United States' largest and only publically funded global broadcaster, began transmission on February 1, 1942. Born during World War II (1939–1945) amid concerns over Nazi propaganda, the VOA was conceived as a "response to the need of peoples in closed and war-torn societies for reliable news"

(Inside VOA, "Fast Facts"). First broadcast via short-wave radio, the VOA was—and in many ways remains—America's official voice, delivering to its audience an American perspective on the events of the day. A "full-service" broadcasting model separates the VOA from other US public international broadcasters, like the "surrogates" Radio Free Europe (RFE) and Radio Liberty (RL, founded as Radio Liberation), which narrate events for a target audience in a specific society (Price 2002, 202).

During World War II, the VOA broadcast to Europe twenty-four hours a day, with a message that shifted from agitation to news reportage (Shulman 1990). By 1944, the VOA's reach had grown to more than forty languages (Inside VOA, "The Beginning"). Wartime VOA was generally regarded as less propagandistic than Nazi radio, but it did not achieve the perception of credibility enjoyed by the British Broadcasting Corporation (BBC).

The first of several peacetime crises of legitimacy occurred after World War II, when American disquiet over the use of propaganda led the US Congress to cut VOA funding. With the onset of the Cold War, however, the VOA again found its footing. The 1948 Smith-Mundt

Russian-born American broadcaster Victor Franzusoff speaking to the Soviet Union from the Voice of America studios, New York, March, 1948. With the onset of the Cold War, the Congress guaranteed funding to VOA, whose programs were broadcast 24 hours a day in Europe in an effort to counter the Soviet communist message. **FPG/HULTON ARCHIVE/GETTY IMAGES**

Act guaranteed funding, and in 1950 the VOA began one of its best-known missions in support of President Harry S. Truman's (1884–1972) "Campaign of Truth," which aimed to counter the communist message and the Soviet appropriation of the rhetoric of peace. By 1953, as the VOA moved under the auspices of the newly created US Information Agency (USIA), the broadcaster's unambiguous anticommunist tone reflected America's recommitment to propaganda in the service of the Cold War (Hale 1975).

In the 1960s, the VOA sought a role in fostering the "peaceful evolution" of socialist countries (Price 2002, 202). US international broadcasting, led by the VOA, was increasingly acknowledged as a crucial weapon in the Cold War. When the Soviets and Cubans "jammed" the VOA and other Western broadcasters, claiming the transmissions were a violation of state sovereignty, the Western rejoinder was that blocking ostensibly neutral communication was a breach of international law (Price 2002). The degree to which international broadcasting facilitated the collapse of the Soviet Union is disputed, but the Cold War era is generally considered the golden age of the VOA, of other Western international broadcasters, and of Western public diplomacy generally.

In the post-Soviet era, the VOA's mission moved closer to that of RFE and RL: to encourage media freedom; to aid in transforming authoritarian societies; to garner appreciation for US values; to enhance educational opportunities; and to bolster US tourism, culture, and trade (Price 2002). But the geopolitics of that era, coupled with technological advances like satellite television, spelled the nadir of the VOA's public and congressional support. Streamlining and consolidation were the order of the day. All US international broadcasting was eventually placed under the Broadcasting Board of Governors (BBG) within the USIA. The latter was merged into the Department of State in 1999, while the BBG became an independent and autonomous agency. The BBG continues to oversee the VOA, along with all congressionally funded international broadcasting entities.

The terrorist attacks on September 11, 2001, and the global fight against terror have refocused attention on the VOA and other instruments of American public diplomacy. The post-9/11 era has also called into question the VOA's ability to adhere to its guiding charter, drafted in 1960 and signed into law by President Gerald Ford (1913–2006) in 1976, which mandates that VOA news be "accurate, objective, and comprehensive" (Inside VOA, "Fast Facts"). The terror war is an ideological battle, and commentators and politicians alike have asserted that America's chief taxpayer-funded broadcaster should remain true to the official US perspective (Price 2002).

Some have lauded the VOA's journalistic integrity and its ability to break news over the decades (Heil 2003). Others charge that the VOA has been myopic in its US-centrism and frequently dull in its coverage (Hale 1975). Several twenty-first-century challenges confront the VOA: how to maintain relevance in an age of information abundance, as global citizens increasingly have access to sources that may be perceived as more credible; how best to adapt to the proliferation of digital platforms, when technology-based US public diplomacy has historically been risk averse (Cull 2013); and how to adjust to a multipolar world, in which the old war logics of the VOA's heyday are but a memory.

From its headquarters in Washington, DC, the VOA broadcasts in forty-five languages. Its television, radio, and Internet programs are delivered globally via FM, satellite and cable, short-wave and medium-wave, and streaming audio and video. The VOA claims to reach more than 164 million people every week, fully 80 percent of the total publicly funded US international media audience (Inside VOA, "Fast Facts").

SEE ALSO *Cold War; Smith–Mundt Act (US Information and Educational Exchange Act of 1948)*

BIBLIOGRAPHY

Broadcasting Board of Governors (BBG). "Voice of America." http://www.bbg.gov/broadcasters/voa/

Cull, Nicholas J. "The Long Road to Public Diplomacy 2.0: The Internet in U.S. Public Diplomacy." *International Studies Review* 15, 1 (2013): 123–139.

Hale, Julian. *Radio Power: Propaganda and International Broadcasting.* Philadelphia: Temple University Press, 1975.

Heil, Alan L., Jr. *Voice of America: A History.* New York: Columbia University Press, 2003.

Price, Monroe E. *Media and Sovereignty: The Global Information Revolution and Its Challenge to State Power.* Cambridge, MA: MIT Press, 2002.

Shulman, Holly Cowan. *The Voice of America: Propaganda and Democracy, 1941–1945.* Madison: University of Wisconsin Press, 1990.

Voice of America: Inside VOA. "The Beginning: An American Voice Greets the World." 2007. http://www.insidevoa.com/content/a-13-34-beginning-of-an-american-voice-111602684/177526.html

Voice of America: Inside VOA. "About VOA." http://www.insidevoa.com/info/about_us/1673.html

Voice of America: Inside VOA. "Fast Facts." http://www.insidevoa.com/info/voa-faqs/2317.html

B. Theo Mazumdar
Annenberg School for Communication
University of Southern California

W

WAR HAWKS

The term *war hawks* designates those congressmen who urged war with Great Britain in 1812, a war that the United States entered politically deeply divided and for which it was militarily unprepared. Most of the war hawks were young and many were serving their first term in Congress. All were Jeffersonian Republicans. But, by 1809, it was clear that Thomas Jefferson's embargo, a costly experiment in commercial coercion designed to force Britain to respect American sovereignty in international waters, had failed. The war hawks demanded more aggressive measures.

Their acknowledged leader was Henry Clay of Kentucky (1777–1852). "I prefer the troubled ocean of war, demanded by the honor and independence of the country … to the tranquil, putrescent pool of ignominious peace," he told the Senate in February 1810 (Clay 1959, 449). In 1811, frustrated by the Senate's inertia, Clay moved to the House, was elected speaker, and packed the Committee on Foreign Relations with likeminded members. The list of influential war hawks included John C. Calhoun (1782–1850), Langdon Cheves (1776–1857), and William Lowndes (1782–1822) of South Carolina; Richard M. Johnson (1780–1850) and Joseph Desha (1768–1842) of Kentucky; Felix Grundy (1775–1840) of Tennessee; Peter B. Porter (1773–1844) of New York; and John A. Harper (1779–1816) of New Hampshire.

The war hawks came predominantly from the South and West or from northern districts close to the western frontier. Except for South Carolina, which had a major international port, most of the states and regions represented by war hawks had little direct stake in the maritime trade whose harassment by Great Britain formed the central justification for war; indeed, the maritime states of the Northeast were strongly opposed to war. But the constituencies represented by war hawks displayed an acute sense of offended national honor in the face of British seizure of American merchant ships and impressment of American seamen. The regions represented by war hawks were also those most tempted by the prospect of annexing Florida (which at that time belonged to Britain's ally Spain), and most committed to westward expansion into territories inhabited by American Indians. British officials in Canada had formed an uneasy alliance with Indians against the United States. Clay argued that by conquering Canada the United States could "extinguish the torch that lights up savage warfare" (Clay 1959, 450).

Some have alleged that the war hawks pushed President James Madison into a war he would otherwise have opposed. In fact, Madison had decided by early 1812 that war with Britain was necessary because all peaceful measures had been exhausted and the only alternatives were war or complete submission to British control of American commerce.

But in coming belatedly to the same conclusion as the war hawks, Madison's outlook remained distinguishable from theirs in important respects. Madison would not himself call for a declaration of war but left this decision to Congress. It was John C. Calhoun of South Carolina, a war hawk critical of Madison's faith in commercial sanctions, who made the public case for war. Calhoun wrote the Foreign Relations Committee's June 3, 1812, *Report on the Causes and Reasons for War*, which opened by arguing that "the United States must support their character and station among the Nations of the Earth, or submit to the most shameful degradation," and closed by calling for "an immediate appeal to Arms" (Hickey 2013, 11, 22).

The war hawks displayed little of Jefferson's and Madison's anguish about resorting to war. In early 1810, Clay argued that war would reproduce "a martial spirit among us," invoked the "glory and renown" of the Revolutionary generation, and called for "a new race of heroes to supply their place" (Clay 1959, 450). Calhoun in 1811 argued that "true courage regards only the cause, that it is just and necessary" and "despises the pain and danger of war" (Calhoun 1959, 80). The war hawks were confident of victory despite Britain's enormous military superiority, especially on the sea. The key was to invade Canada, which appeared weakly defended; Clay quipped that the Kentucky militia alone could conquer it (Clay 1959, 450). The Madison administration "always denied that it intended to annex Canada"; the goal of the ultimately disastrous invasion of Canada was to "pressure the British to make peace" (Wood 2009, 676). Clay however, along with many other war hawks, called for a United States "embracing ... the entire country east of the Mississippi, including East Florida, and some of the territories to the north of us also" (Pratt 1925, 41).

The war hawks were more effective in securing a declaration of war than in persuading Americans to pay for it. Republican ideology had traditionally emphasized the threat to liberty posed by military establishments. The same congressional majority who voted to declare war refused to fund the armies and navies essential to the war effort, and even cut military expenditures as war threatened. Clay and Calhoun consistently supported military preparations and the taxes to fund them. But Clay's prediction that Americans would "spend their last cent ... in the preservation of our neutral privileges," and Calhoun's faith that "if taxes should become necessary ... the people will pay cheerfully," proved unfounded (Clay 1959, 449; Calhoun 1959, 78–79).

Some war hawks went on to enjoy long careers in national politics; others faded from view. Clay and Calhoun stayed at the center of national politics for the rest of their lives. Both appear to have been chastened by their early experience of rushing into war. In 1846, when a new generation of war hawks pushed an expansionist war with Mexico, Clay and Calhoun opposed it, fearing accurately that it would worsen sectional conflicts over slavery.

SEE ALSO *Manifest Destiny; War of 1812*

BIBLIOGRAPHY

Bickham, Troy O. *The Weight of Vengeance: The United States, the British Empire, and the War of 1812.* New York: Oxford University Press, 2012.

Brown, Roger Hamilton. *The Republic in Peril: 1812.* New York: Norton, 1971. First published 1964 by Columbia University Press.

Calhoun, John C. *The Papers of John C. Calhoun.* Vol. 1. Edited by Robert L. Meriwether. Columbia: University of South Carolina Press, 1959.

Clay, Henry. *The Papers of Henry Clay.* Vol. 1. Edited by James F. Hopkins and Mary W. M. Hargreaves. Lexington: University of Kentucky Press, 1959.

Hickey, Donald R., ed. *The War of 1812: Writings from America's Second War of Independence.* New York: Library of America, 2013.

Horsman, Reginald. *The Causes of the War of 1812.* Philadelphia: University of Pennsylvania Press, 1962.

Mayo, Bernard. *Henry Clay: Spokesman of the New West.* Boston: Houghton Mifflin, 1937.

Niven, John. *John C. Calhoun and the Price of Union: A Biography.* Baton Rouge: Louisiana State University Press, 1988.

Pratt, Julius W. *Expansionists of 1812.* New York: Macmillan, 1925.

Remini, Robert V. *Henry Clay: Statesman for the Union.* New York: Norton, 1991.

Stagg, J. C. A. *The War of 1812: Conflict for a Continent.* New York: Cambridge University Press, 2012.

Taylor, Alan. *The Civil War of 1812: American Citizens, British Subjects, Irish Rebels, and Indian Allies.* New York: Knopf, 2010.

Wood, Gordon S. *Empire of Liberty: A History of the Early Republic, 1789–1815.* New York: Oxford University Press, 2009.

James H. Read
Professor of Political Science
College of St. Benedict and St. John's University

WAR OF 1812

The War of 1812 developed as an extension of the French Revolutionary and Napoleonic Wars and was a response to the Anglo-French economic conflict initiated by Napoléon's Continental System. The United States declared war on Great Britain in 1812 to assert its rights as a neutral power at sea and to counter presumably British-sponsored Native American raids on the frontier. Following two and a half years of conflict, the war ended in *status quo ante bellum* between the United States and Great Britain, yet it helped forge both American and Canadian national identities. It also represented the last strong effort of Native American resistance in the Ohio Valley and enabled the American acquisition of Florida and the Gulf coast from Spain.

THE ROLE OF NAPOLÉON

Starting in 1792, the French Revolutionary Wars pitted a shifting coalition of European states against France, which also suffered from political turbulence until Napoléon Bonaparte (1769–1821) seized power in 1799. Although Napoléon's most frequent foes on the battlefield were Austria, Prussia, or Russia, he recognized that British subsidies continued to fund those armies in their wars against France. Napoléon therefore considered plans for an invasion of the island nation as early as 1802. However, the destruction of the French navy at the Battle of Trafalgar, along with continuing conflict on the Continent, prevented any serious plans for a direct assault on Britain after 1805. Instead, Napoléon turned his efforts toward the British treasury, which was sustained by global trade and preserved by the Royal Navy. His attempts to weaken the British economy while strengthening the United States as a maritime rival had begun prior to Trafalgar, with the Louisiana Purchase in 1803. He expected that the purchase would encourage American friendship with France while leading to divisions between the United States and Britain.

The war between France and England began to affect America more directly when Napoléon formalized his Continental System with the Berlin Decree in November 1806, closing the ports of Europe to British trade. London responded with several Orders in Council, placing Napoleonic Europe in a state of blockade. Back and forth measures intensified throughout 1807, with both sides determined to cripple the other's economy. Enforcement from both sides required searches and seizures of merchant vessels in the waters throughout the Atlantic and Mediterranean. Such a system forced neutral states to choose sides or remain vulnerable to the navies of both.

THE AMERICAN RESPONSE

Feeling pressure from both sides of the Franco-British conflict, Congress passed an Embargo Act in December 1807 outlawing all American exports. The embargo was a complete failure, harming American merchants far more than it did European markets. It was followed in March 1809 with the Non-Intercourse Act, which targeted only Britain and France, and finally in May 1810 by Macon's Bill No. 2, which offered to resume trade with whichever of the two European powers removed its anti-American regulations first. Napoléon agreed, and American policy became unilateral against Britain. The United States and Britain had already come close to war in June 1807 when the HMS *Leopard* opened fire on the USS *Chesapeake,* killing three Americans and wounding eighteen more before boarding the ship and seizing as deserters four crewmen, three of whom were American citizens.

For Britain, American measures remained little more than a nuisance, and few in the government paid much attention to them or to protestations about the rights of neutrals. For Americans, though, perceptions of continued British tyranny at sea encouraged discussion of war. Although the nascent US Navy had fought both the French in the Quasi-War and Tripoli in the First Barbary War, 1812 was the first time the nation voted for war. President James Madison (1751–1836) addressed Congress on June 1, 1812, enumerating four grievances against Britain: impressment of thousands of American sailors, an illegal blockade of American ports, offensive Orders in Council, and support for Native American attacks on the American frontier. Citing those grievances, Madison argued that a state of war already existed. Congress agreed, but by a slim margin. The vote remains the most contentious and closest declaration of war in American history, passing the House of Representatives 79 to 49 and the Senate by a mere six votes, 19 to 13. At one point in the debate, a Senate proposal to add France to the same declaration of war failed by only two votes, 17 to 15.

Divisions in Congress reflected those in the nation at large. Coastal states in the Northeast opposed war. Although they suffered the most from British impressment and seizures, many merchants were willing to assume the risk or to play by Britain's rules to maintain a profitable trade. Southerners and frontier states, with populations pushing further west, generally supported war. Additionally, many Americans welcomed war as a means to acquire Canadian territory along the Great Lakes. Politically, the nation fell between Federalists, whose strong relations with Britain discouraged war, and Democratic-Republicans. Among the Republicans, Henry Clay (1777–1852), John C. Calhoun (1782–1850), and about a dozen other congressmen came to be known as War Hawks for their strident calls for war.

THE BRITISH RESPONSE

The declaration, ratified on June 18, came late. British prime minister Spencer Perceval (1762–1812) had been assassinated in May, and his successor, Robert Jenkinson, the Earl of Liverpool (1770–1828), repealed the Orders in Council on June 23, before word of the declaration reached London. The declaration also came late for the French, who might have welcomed the war in 1807 or 1808. In June 1812, however, the French army was in its fifth year of Napoléon's Spanish "ulcer" in the Iberian Peninsula, with the allied army of Sir Arthur Wellesley, the Duke of Wellington (1769–1852) in the midst of its successful Salamanca offensive. Additionally, on June 24, less than a week after the American declaration of war, Napoléon led his *Grande Armée* of 600,000 men into his greatest debacle in Russia. Among the half million casualties of that campaign was Joel Barlow (1754–1812), American minister plenipotentiary to Napoléon's court, who died of pneumonia in Poland while seeking an audience with the emperor. Chief on his agenda was the American declaration of war against Britain. Alliance with France had been the key element of victory in the American Revolution, but in 1812, the fledgling United States faced Britain alone, and with no army or navy to speak of.

HOSTILITIES

With British efforts prioritized against France, Sir George Prevost (1767–1816), governor and commander in chief of British North America, adopted a defensive strategy in Canada at the outset of the war. American strategy involved seizing Canadian territory to force Britain to negotiate, yet opposition in New England made direct attacks on Québec unlikely. Therefore, the Great Lakes became the most active theater. The nation was wholly unprepared for war and the first two campaigns of 1812 ended in complete failure on Lake Erie in August and Lake Ontario in October. British forces meanwhile captured both Detroit and present-day Chicago.

Despite an overwhelming disparity of naval forces, the young US Navy fared much better than the army in the early stages of the war, amassing several shocking victories in ship-on-ship action at sea. Bold young captains, sailing a new class of American frigates like the USS *Constitution,* frequently defeated their British counterparts and captured merchant prizes in the Atlantic, the Caribbean, and even into the Pacific throughout 1812 and 1813. In September 1813, Oliver Hazard Perry (1785–1819) gained control of Lake Erie when he defeated the British flotilla there, opening up the possibility for another land campaign in the region. Kentucky volunteers under William Henry Harrison (1773–1841) took advantage of that opportunity, winning a victory on Canada's Thames River that regained Detroit in October. Shawnee leader Tecumseh (1768–1813) was killed during the battle, destroying the alliance of his Native American confederacy with the British. Meanwhile, however, American designs on Canada were thwarted again when operations around Lake Ontario ended inconclusively and an American attack toward Montréal failed in November.

In 1813, a conflict among Creek Indians along the Gulf Coast was absorbed into the war, as were territorial disputes in Florida and the Gulf Coast between the United States and Spain. Using a liberal interpretation of the terms of the Louisiana Purchase, the United States had claimed since 1804 that Spanish West Florida, including Mobile and Pensacola, had been included in

the territory. American militia occupied parts of Mobile in 1810 and had taken parts of East Florida prior to 1812 as well. In 1811, Tecumseh encouraged Creeks to join his movement to thwart the encroachment of white settlers on Native American lands. Some chose to join Tecumseh while others preferred peace. The internal dispute triggered a Creek civil war in 1813 that Americans took advantage of by attacking Creek settlements along the Gulf. In March 1814, Andrew Jackson (1767–1845) destroyed Creek resistance at Horseshoe Bend, Alabama, forcing them to cede West Florida to the United States. With few troops in the area, Spain was powerless to respond.

Although American troops won a series of victories in 1814 in the Great Lakes theater, most notably at Chippewa, it was insufficient to force a decision in Canada. Defeated by a coalition of enemies on all sides, Napoléon abdicated his imperial throne in April 1814 and was exiled to the Mediterranean island of Elba, allowing Britain to reinforce the American theater. More than sixteen thousand British troops arrived in 1814, bringing Prevost's strength in North America to forty-eight thousand. Even the previously victorious American navy remained bottled up in port as the British blockade tightened. In addition to occupying Maine, Britain launched three broadly separated campaigns in 1814. The first targeted Maryland and Washington, DC, and succeeded in destroying and burning several government facilities, including the Washington Navy Yard, the Capitol, and the White House before being repulsed at Baltimore and Fort McHenry, Maryland. The second campaign, and main effort for Britain, was intended to seize Plattsburgh, New York, on Lake Champlain. However, American sailors under Thomas Macdonough (1783–1825) defeated Prevost's squadron on the lake, dooming his land campaign as well. Following his failure at Plattsburgh, Prevost was recalled, and Liverpool recommended command of the American war effort to Wellington. Wellington did not refuse the command, but he did not believe he could succeed because of American control of the Great Lakes. Wellington never departed for North America. Although British reinforcements continued to cross the Atlantic, the defeat of the French left no reason to continue the policies that had led to the American declaration of war in the first place. By November 1814, Wellington advised Liverpool to end the war. Liverpool agreed and focused his efforts on securing a satisfying peace through negotiation. Meanwhile, the final British campaign launched in 1814 sailed into the Gulf of Mexico under the command of Wellington's capable brother-in-law, Sir Edward Packenham (1778–1815). When it landed outside New Orleans in January 1815, Andrew Jackson annihilated it.

The Signing of the Treaty of Ghent, Christmas Eve, 1814, *oil on canvas by Sir Amédée Forestier, 1914. Smithsonian American Art Museum. Although Andrew Jackson's tremendous victory in the Battle of New Orleans propelled him to fame and later into the White House, it had no part in ending the War of 1812. Nine days before the battle, talks in Ghent, Belgium, with John Quincy Adams as the chief US negotiator, had resulted in a treaty concluding the war.* **DEA PICTURE LIBRARY/GETTY IMAGES**

THE WAR'S CONCLUSION AND AFTERMATH

Although Jackson's tremendous victory propelled him to fame and later into the White House, it had no part in ending the war. Nine days prior to the Battle of New Orleans, Parliament had ratified the Treaty of Ghent concluding the war. Czar Alexander I of Russia (1777–1825) had previously extended an offer to host peace negotiations in March 1813, but London rejected it. After the fall of Napoléon, though, Britain agreed to open bilateral talks in Ghent, Belgium. Madison's chief negotiator, John Quincy Adams (1767–1848), had *status quo ante bellum* as his primary objective, while the British sought *uti possidetis,* allowing each side to retain any territory taken.

The negotiations began in August 1814, coinciding with the British descent on Washington. After the British failure at Baltimore, British negotiators consented to *status quo ante bellum,* and the two sides agreed on preliminary terms on Christmas Eve 1814. The United States agreed to restore Indian possessions, but those terms were

unenforceable and never fulfilled. Additionally, the United States held on to the area seized from the Creek, and through continued pressure on Spain, purchased the rest of Florida in 1819.

For Britain, the conclusion of the war was timely, as Napoléon escaped his exile and returned to France in March 1815. War resumed immediately, concluding with final French defeat at the Battle of Waterloo in June 1815. For the United States, regional and political divisions continued even as peace negotiations progressed, most notably when a group of New England Federalists met in Hartford, Connecticut, from December 1814 through January 1815. Although calls for secession from more radical delegates to the Hartford Convention were defeated, Massachusetts governor Caleb Strong (1745–1819) sent a secret delegation to Britain to discuss the possibility of a separate peace with New England. Following the Hartford Convention, a smaller delegation went to Washington to negotiate grievances. However, news of Andrew Jackson's astounding victory at New

Orleans and the signing of the Treaty of Ghent arrived just ahead of them and discredited their work, leading also to the collapse of the Federalist Party.

Although Britain largely dismissed the War of 1812 as a sideshow of the Napoleonic Wars, it yielded several important consequences. Canada ended the war with a feeling of success, having defeated multiple American invasions. Pride in the accomplishment helped start the process of creating a national identity distinct from, yet loyal to, Great Britain. With the loss of Florida, Spanish influence in North America dwindled, and the United States spent the next four decades fighting the Seminole Wars in the new territory. The United States emerged from the war with a sense of victory that discredited Federalist opposition, reshaped the American political landscape, and strengthened American national identity. The navy also proved its importance to the nation's economy and prestige. In the years to come, it would help defeat piracy along the North African coast and spread the influence of America around the globe.

SEE ALSO *Britain; Embargo Act (1807); Impressment; Napoleon Bonaparte; Neutrality Act of 1794; Non-Intercourse Act (1809); Simcoe, John Graves; War Hawks*

BIBLIOGRAPHY

Black, Jeremy. *The War of 1812 in the Age of Napoleon.* Norman: University of Oklahoma Press, 2009.

Bowes, John P. "Transformation and Transition: American Indians and the War of 1812 in the Lower Great Lakes." *Journal of Military History* 76, 4 (October 2012): 1129–1146.

Cusick, James G. *The Other War of 1812: The Patriot War and the American Invasion of Spanish East Florida.* Gainesville: University Press of Florida, 2003.

Hickey, Donald. *The War of 1812: A Forgotten Conflict.* Rev. ed. Urbana: University of Illinois Press, 2012.

McCranie, Kevin D. *Utmost Gallantry: The U.S. and Royal Navies at Sea in the War of 1812.* Annapolis, MD: Naval Institute Press, 2011.

Owsley, Frank L. *Struggle for the Gulf Borderlands: The Creek War and the Battle of New Orleans, 1812–1815.* Tuscaloosa: University of Alabama Press, 2000.

Stagg, J. C. A. *Mr. Madison's War: Politics, Diplomacy and Warfare in the Early American Republic, 1783–1830.* Princeton, NJ: Princeton University Press, 1983.

Stagg, J. C. A. *The War of 1812: Conflict for a Continent.* Cambridge and New York: Cambridge University Press, 2012.

Taylor, Alan. *The Civil War of 1812: American Citizens, British Subjects, Irish Rebels, and Indian Allies.* New York: Alfred A. Knopf, 2010.

Jason R. Musteen
United States Military Academy

WAR OF 1967

SEE *Arab-Israeli Conflict.*

WAR ON DRUGS

Government regulation of common drugs of abuse (e.g., opiates, marijuana, coca products, certain prescription drugs) is largely a twentieth-century phenomenon. Prior to this period, some psychoactive substances (e.g., cannabis, the coca leaf, tobacco, coffee) had been stigmatized in some cultures—Mexicans, for instance, believed marijuana triggered madness and violence in its users—and historical evidence suggests morphine addiction became a cause for concern in the United States following the Civil War (1861–1865). Formal controls over these addictive substances, however, were slow to develop. The modern era of drug control only emerged in the latter half of the nineteenth century, alongside developments in industrial production, professionalized medicine, and global connectivity.

The early twentieth century saw the United States and other Western countries control the use of addictive drugs through taxation. The Harrison Narcotics Tax Act of 1914 and the Marijuana Tax Act of 1937 exemplify contemporary US drug-control policies. The Federal Bureau of Narcotics (FBN), established under the Department of Treasury in 1930, assumed the primary role of drug enforcement. With an increasing US footprint abroad and a spike in the use of addictive drugs following World War II (1939–1945), drug control became an important function of the US government. During the 1950s, drug-control efforts were limited to specific efforts and initiatives. FBN agents began working missions overseas to control the drug supply, but these efforts were uncoordinated, incomprehensive, and under-funded compared to the missions undertaken later by the Drug Enforcement Administration (DEA). Nevertheless, throughout the 1960s, US policy makers continued to debate the extent to which addictive narcotics threatened US society, ways to limit the public's access to them, and alternatives to criminalized drug-control policies.

The war on drugs, the US-led antidrug campaign inaugurated under President Richard Nixon (1913–1994) in 1971, represents the official triumph of the punitive and prohibitive drug-enforcement mentality at home and abroad. At its essence, the antidrug campaign is characterized by a significant escalation of US authority, power, and resources to reduce US drug demand and to control supply. On the domestic front, policy makers privileged criminalized drug laws over prevention and treatment methods. On the international front, the United States established myriad arrangements and relationships to target drug supply. However, a relentless US focus on controlling the use, transit, and sale of addictive narcotics in the years that followed had unforeseen consequences, and would ultimately complicate the US antidrug campaign over time. Domestically, prison populations reached never-before-seen levels. Internationally, the US antidrug campaign facilitated violence and instability in supply and transit countries, often at the same time US drug-control efforts became entangled with larger US geopolitical objectives.

DRUG DEMAND AND THE DOMESTIC FRONT

Nixon's immediate objective when declaring the war on drugs in June 1971 was to use more aggressive measures to reduce domestic drug use. By inaugurating a more comprehensive drug-control campaign, Nixon responded to an increase in US drug use, associated with 1960s countercultural movements across the globe and large-scale opposition to US involvement in Vietnam, which threatened authority figures. A rise in the use of heroin, psychedelic drugs, marijuana, and other prescription drugs (e.g., amphetamines, barbiturates), as well as an escalation in violent crime, demanded a government response. "Public enemy number one in the United States is drug abuse," Nixon told the American people in 1971. "In order to fight and defeat this enemy, it is necessary to wage a new, all-out offensive." While it is important to note that Nixon also directed government funds to treatment initiatives in this period, these efforts would ultimately be overshadowed by the more aggressive efforts of the antidrug campaign.

The US governmental bureaucracy adjusted so as to accommodate this stance toward drug control. Soon after coming into office, Nixon ordered the southern border closed in an operation known as Intercept to cut off the flow of Mexican marijuana into the United States. But when the complete shutdown of border commerce debilitated the Mexican economy, it was clear that Intercept was also intended to force Mexico into complying with newly established US drug policies. In 1970, the Controlled Substances Act consolidated previous domestic legislation against users and sellers of narcotics, and established schedules to group psychoactive substances based on their potential for addiction. The placement of marijuana in the most addictive schedule of substances is a decision that remains controversial today. Nixon administration officials decided to replace the Bureau of Narcotics and Dangerous Drugs (BNDD) with the DEA in 1973, under the Department of Justice. In the years that followed, the DEA and other US agencies played a prominent role in responding to the shifting geographic loci of the drug trade.

SUPPLY CONTROL AND THE INTERNATIONAL FRONT

US authority, power, and resources to control the drug supply abroad became significantly more pronounced with Nixon's 1971 declaration. While much of the supply, especially of opiates (e.g., heroin), came from Eastern Europe, Asia Minor, and parts of East Asia in the 1960s, by the early 1970s, due in part to US supply-control efforts, the cultivation and trafficking of drugs shifted to Latin American countries, especially to the Andes region and Mexico. In 1976, with US assistance, the Mexican government began a large-scale drug-crop destruction program using harmful herbicides to degrade marijuana and opium cultivation. By the late 1970s and early 1980s, the US antidrug campaign focused on suppressing cocaine trafficking throughout the Caribbean.

That drug control was often subordinated to higher geopolitical priorities complicated the US antidrug campaign as a whole. Notwithstanding, levels of US power and resources directed toward supply control were higher than ever. With the shift in control efforts to Latin America and the Caribbean, the United States waged its drug war in an area traditionally known as America's backyard. This notion helped legitimize US intervention as a tool in drug control. In doing so, the US government, under the administrations of Ronald Reagan (1911–2004) and his successor George H. W. Bush (b. 1924), remained committed to the punitive and prohibitive drug-enforcement mentality at the same time they practiced increasingly militarized approaches to drug control.

Indeed, whenever it was necessary, US policy makers prioritized aggressive supply control behind geopolitical priorities. The Reagan administration's involvement in the Iran-Contra affair—a scandal involving an attempt to secure the release of US hostages in Iran and also to fund the ongoing efforts of Nicaragua's anticommunist Contras—was allegedly supported by drug money and dealings with Latin American dictators who participated in the drug trade. George H. W. Bush's administration was not any less aggressive against the threat of drugs. For years, Bush had tried to tame Panama's dictator, General Manuel Noriega (b. 1934), previously an ally of the United States and a willing conspirator during the Iran-Contra affair years before. By the end of 1989, Bush would use Noriega's participation in the drug trade as one rationale among others for sending twenty-five thousand US troops into Panama to topple the dictator.

THE DRUG WAR IN THE 1990s AND BEYOND

A relentless American focus on controlling the use, transit, and sale of addictive narcotics in the years that followed would have a number of unforeseen consequences domestically and abroad. One important contribution of the Reagan administration's domestic drug war, which remains in effect today, was harsher mandatory sentencing laws for drug offenses. As increasing numbers of first-time marijuana users were thrown in jail throughout the 1980s and 1990s, one important outcome of the policy was that the United States' prison population would grow to be the largest in the world. Because a disproportionate number of the inmates are black males, some scholars draw attention to the racialized nature of the US drug-control regime. The administrations of Bill Clinton (1993–2001), George W. Bush (2001–2009), and Barack Obama (2009–) have done little to bring about change to the impacts of US antidrug policies at home.

Internationally, the US antidrug campaign is still predicated on using US power and resources to facilitate supply control. However, policies influenced by the US drug war have caused violence and instability in supply and transit countries, spurring widespread debate about their overall efficacy. The promulgation of the North American Free Trade Agreement (NAFTA), established in 1994, which opened the US-Mexico border for free trade, highlighted the correlation between the drug trade and local instability. As cheap US agricultural goods flooded Mexican markets, the Mexican farming industry was severely hit, prompting the cultivation of drugs. In due time, the increased flow of north-south commerce also included illegal substances from Mexico and other parts of the Americas. At the same time, the US government's strict targeting of the drug supply over air and water in the Caribbean created a balloon effect, which shifted the geographic locus of the drug trade to Mexico, empowering Mexican cartels and facilitating their control of land routes in the early 2000s.

Thus aid packages and drug-control measures of the 1990s not only targeted drug-supply reduction, but also the effects—violence, instability, security issues, and so forth—of US drug policies themselves. Clinton and his Colombian counterpart, President Andrés Pastrana Arango (b. 1954), for example, established Plan Colombia in 1999, which provided assistance to counter the Andean cocaine trade. Plan Colombia was also intended to promote stability and disempower armed insurgent groups. The results of much of this aid have been mixed.

Mexico's drug violence in recent years exemplifies the export of the US supply-control impetus to another society, and the violent consequences of doing so. Between 2006 and 2012, with US assistance, Mexican president Felipe Calderón (b. 1962) presided over an unparalleled mobilization of Mexican resources to fight off drug cartels, with a resulting death toll of more than seventy thousand. Calderón's counterpart in the United States, George W. Bush, responded to additional calls for

aid by establishing the Mérida Initiative in 2008. A security cooperation agreement between the United States, Mexico, and Central American countries, the Mérida Initiative was intended to combat drug trafficking and crime.

Since 1971, the US drug war has taken on a number of dimensions, but throughout, it has been premised on the use of US authority, power, and resources to reduce US drug demand and control drug supply at home and abroad, even as the policies themselves have produced unforeseen consequences. In recent years, the question of whether or not the US war on drugs has been effectively retired has been a contentious item debated by American politicians and the public, especially considering the legalization of marijuana in some US states and foreign countries. While rhetorically US politicians have distanced themselves from the language of militarized drug control that permeated US thinking throughout the 1970s, 1980s, and 1990s, billions of dollars continue to be funneled to the US global antidrug campaign each year.

SEE ALSO *Bush, George H. W.; Central Intelligence Agency (CIA); Covert Wars; Reagan, Ronald Wilson*

BIBLIOGRAPHY

Alexander, Michelle. *The New Jim Crow: Mass Incarceration in the Age of Colorblindness.* New York: New Press, 2010.

Bertram, Eva, Morris Blachman, Kenneth Sharpe, and Peter Andreas. *Drug War Politics: The Price of Denial.* Berkeley: University of California Press, 1996.

Campos, Isaac. *Homegrown: Marijuana and the Origins of Mexico's War on Drugs.* Chapel Hill: University of North Carolina Press, 2012.

Frydl, Kathleen J. *The Drug Wars in America, 1940–1973.* New York: Cambridge University Press, 2013.

McAllister, William B. *Drug Diplomacy in the Twentieth Century: An International History.* New York: Routledge, 2000.

Musto, David F. *The American Disease: Origins of Narcotic Control.* 3rd ed. New York: Oxford University Press, 1999.

Nixon, Richard. "Remarks about an Intensified Program for Drug Abuse Prevention and Control." June 17, 1971. American Presidency Project, edited by Gerhard Peters and John T. Woolley. http://www.presidency.ucsb.edu/ws/?pid=3047

Walker, William O., III. *Drug Control in the Americas.* Rev. ed. Albuquerque: University of New Mexico Press, 1989.

Weimer, Daniel. *Seeing Drugs: Modernization, Counterinsurgency, and U.S. Narcotics Control in the Third World, 1969–1976.* Kent, OH: Kent State University Press, 2011.

Aileen Teague
PhD Candidate (History)
Vanderbilt University

WAR ON TERROR

The American war on terror (WOT) can be traced back to the terrorist attacks of September 11, 2001; the phrase was first used inadvertently by President George W. Bush (b. 1946) on September 16 during impromptu remarks to the press: "This crusade—this war on terrorism—is going to take a while" ("Remarks by the President upon Arrival"). Then on September 20, Bush told a joint session of Congress that the "war on terror begins with al Qaeda, but it does not end there. It will not end until every terrorist group of global reach has been found, stopped and defeated" ("Address to a Joint Session of Congress and the American People").

The war on terror began as an international campaign to eliminate al-Qaeda and other militant nonstate actors. The Bush administration used the term to refer to a global military, political, legal, and conceptual struggle against terrorist organizations and their state sponsors. Although the administration of President Barack Obama (b. 1961) stopped using the term, it continued to be used by media and scholarly sources.

LAUNCHING THE WAR ON TERROR

On September 11, 2001, al-Qaeda operatives used planes to attack the World Trade Center and the Pentagon in what was the worst terrorist attack on American soil in history, killing over three thousand people. Despite condemnations from Muslim countries around the world, anti-Islamic sentiment rose steadily in the United States and Europe. Following the attack, on September 14, the Authorization for Use of Military Force against Terrorists, a Senate joint resolution, targeted those terrorists responsible for the attack. As a result, the United States engaged in a war with Afghanistan's Taliban government, which was harboring al-Qaeda and its leader, Osama bin Laden (1957–2011). The war in Afghanistan launched the first stage in the global WOT, but the objectives of the war on terror were yet to be defined.

In February 2003, the Bush administration released a report titled *National Strategy for Combating Terrorism*. It built upon Bush's 2002 State of the Union address, which declared the existence of an axis of evil, including Iraq, Iran, and North Korea. The phrase *axis of evil* was used to describe governments that the administration accused of supporting terrorism and seeking weapons of mass destruction (WMD). Most significantly, the administration expressed serious concerns about the potential coupling of terrorism and WMD. Moreover, the notion of an axis of evil was used to rally the country around the war on terror and against specific enemies, in this way overcoming the ambiguity of terrorism as a concept.

National Strategy for Combating Terrorism enshrined and expanded upon the ideas in Bush's axis of evil speech and defined the objectives of the war on terror. First and foremost, the administration explained that its strategy was designed to defeat and demolish terrorists and terrorist organizations, including Osama bin Laden and al-Qaeda. This entailed identifying, locating, and attacking these terrorists and their organizations. However, the strategy went beyond terrorists and terrorist organizations, aiming to deny sponsorship, support, and sanctuary to terrorists. Specifically, the administration emphasized ending state sponsorship of terrorism by maintaining an international standard of accountability for combating terrorism, strengthening and sustaining the international effort to combat terrorism, employing a coalition of willing and able states in combating terrorism, and abolishing terrorist sanctuaries and havens. The strategy also called for diminishing the underlying conditions that terrorists sought to exploit, including the strengthening of weak states and "winning the war of ideas." The strategy's ultimate aim was to defend American interests at home and abroad, an effort that included the creation of the Office of Homeland Security.

OPERATION ENDURING FREEDOM AND BEYOND

While the WOT began in Afghanistan, it was universal in character. Operation Active Endeavor began in October 2001 and consisted of a North Atlantic Treaty Organization (NATO) naval operation in the Mediterranean designed to prevent the movement of WMD and terrorists in shipping lanes in the region. The main focus of the WOT, however, was Afghanistan. Operation Enduring Freedom was launched on October 7, 2001; Kabul, Afghanistan's capital, fell in mid-November. The remaining al-Qaeda and Taliban remnants, including Osama bin Laden, retreated to Tora Bora in eastern Afghanistan. Coalition forces launched Operation Anaconda in March 2002 with the goal of destroying the remaining al-Qaeda and Taliban elements. It is believed that Osama bin Laden escaped into Pakistan during this time. The Taliban regrouped in western Afghanistan, unleashing insurgent attacks that continued for nearly a decade. In February 2010, coalition forces launched Operation Moshtarak in an attempt to destroy the Taliban once and for all; meanwhile, peace talks between the Taliban and coalition forces were ongoing. American troops began their withdrawal from Afghanistan at the end of 2014, with all remaining forces scheduled to be removed by 2016.

Operation Enduring Freedom went well beyond Afghanistan, globalizing the WOT. In the Philippines, the United States advised and assisted the government in its battle with Islamist groups. The operation focused on removing the Abu Sayyaf and Jemaah Islamiyah terror groups from the Philippine island of Basilan. Also, in the

AL-QAEDA

Al-Qaeda is a multinational terrorist organization founded by Osama bin Laden (1957–2011) in Afghanistan in 1988. Bin Laden studied Islam under Muhammad Qutb (1919–2014), the brother of Sayyid Qutb (1906–1966), a leading member of the Muslim Brotherhood of Egypt who is often seen as the father of modern political Islam, at King Abdul Azziz University in Jeddah, Saudi Arabia. Bin Laden also studied under Dr. Abdullah Azzam (1941–1989), a key figure in the Muslim Brotherhood in Jordan, who is often identified as the intellectual architect of the jihad against the Soviet invasion of Afghanistan, and ultimately al-Qaeda. In 1979, bin Laden joined Azzam in Afghanistan. Both men cast the Soviet invasion as an attempted conquest by a non-Muslim power on sacred Muslim territory and people. Bin Laden allegedly provided funds for recruitment and volunteers throughout the conflict.

By 1984, Azzam and bin Laden managed to create a structural network of fund-raising offices located throughout the Arab world, Europe, and the United States. This network, the Maktab al-Khidamat (services office), is generally considered the organizational precursor to al-Qaeda. In 1988, as the war in Afghanistan was winding down, bin Laden and Azzam contemplated how to utilize the network they had cultivated. While Azzam wanted this al-Qaeda (Arabic for "the base") to be an Islamic rapid-reaction force capable of intervening to deal with perceived threats to Islam, bin Laden saw an opportunity to use the network to topple secular, pro-Western Arab leaders, such as Hosni Mubarak (b. 1928) in Egypt and the Saudi royal family. In November 1989, Azzam was assassinated, giving bin Laden control of the organization.

The American response to the August 2, 1990, Iraqi invasion of Kuwait transformed bin Laden from a nominal American ally against the Soviet Union in Afghanistan to an enemy of the United States. Having returned home to Saudi Arabia, bin Laden had lobbied Saudi officials not to host American troops in Saudi Arabia, which housed the holiest places in Islam, instead arguing for a mujahideen army to oust Iraq from Kuwait. He then relocated to Sudan in 1991, where he trained al-Qaeda militants. Bin Laden transformed al-Qaeda into an organization aimed at ousting secular powers in the region and, most significantly, the influence of the perceived supporter of those powers, the United States. During the 1990s, al-Qaeda became a national security threat to American interests and was linked to a variety of terrorist attacks throughout the world, including the 1992 bombing of a hotel in Yemen, the 1993 bombing of the World Trade Center in New York City, the 1998 bombing of American embassies in Kenya and Tanzania, and the 2000 attack on the USS *Cole* in Yemen.

On September 11, 2001, al-Qaeda attacked the World Trade Center and Pentagon. Following these attacks, the United States launched a war in Afghanistan against al-Qaeda and the Taliban government, its major sponsor. The September 11 attacks instilled great urgency in the United States, which launched a general war on terror aimed at significantly reducing the threat from al-Qaeda and other terrorist groups.

BIBLIOGRAPHY

Bergen, Peter L. *Holy War, Inc.: Inside the Secret World of Osama Bin Laden.* New York: Free Press, 2001.

Gunaratna, Rohan. *Inside Al Qaeda: Global Network of Terror.* New York: Columbia University Press, 2002.

National Commission on Terrorist Attacks upon the United States. *The 9/11 Commission Report: The Final Report of the National Commission on Terrorist Attacks upon the United States.* Chaired by Thomas H. Kean and Lee H. Hamilton. Washington, DC: GPO, 2004. http://www.9-11commission.gov/report/911Report.pdf

Wright, Lawrence. *The Looming Tower: Al Qaeda and the Road to 9/11.* New York: Vintage, 2006.

Michael F. Cairo
Professor of Political Science
Transylvania University

Horn of Africa, the United States focused efforts on detecting and disrupting militant activities, including piracy, and working with governments to prevent the emergence of militant activities in the region. Much of the focus of this operation was on Somalia, where a United Nations–backed Transitional Federal Government took control in 2006. In the trans-Sahara, the United States engaged in counterterrorism efforts, which consisted mainly of policing the movement of arms and drug trafficking across central Africa.

THE WAR IN IRAQ

The WOT expanded significantly with the Bush administration's engagement with Iraq. Iraq had been a central part of American foreign policy since the Iran-Iraq War in the 1980s. Following that war, in August 1990, Iraq's president, Saddam Hussein (1937–2006), invaded Kuwait. An American-led and United Nations–backed coalition of forces successfully evicted Iraq from Kuwait, which led to Iraq's placement on the US State Department's list of state sponsors of terrorism and to UN-backed military, economic, and political sanctions. Iraq had been on the list of state sponsors of terrorism from 1979 to 1982, but it was removed during the Iran-Iraq War so that the United States could provide Iraq with material support. However, Iraq had been a diplomatic problem because of its use of chemical weapons against Iran and Iraqi Kurds in the late 1980s.

In the 1990s, the United States and its allies instituted no-fly zones in Iraq to protect Iraq's Kurdish and Shia populations in the north and south, respectively. At the same time, the United Nations was engaged in weapons inspections aimed at eliminating Iraqi WMD capabilities. Throughout the 1990s, Iraq failed to meet US demands for unconditional cooperation, leading to air strikes against Iraq known as Operation Desert Fox. Iraq responded by announcing that it would no longer respect the no-fly zones and attempted to shoot down American and coalition aircraft.

When the George W. Bush administration entered office, it was clear that Iraq was a primary concern. In the administration's first National Security Council meeting, Iraq dominated the agenda. The administration was determined to deal with the problem of Saddam and Iraq; September 11 provided that opportunity and increased concerns among the administration that terrorists would eventually use WMD. Following Operation Enduring Freedom in Afghanistan, the administration began its campaign to remove Hussein and his regime from Iraq. The axis of evil speech was the first step in attempting to build an international coalition against Saddam and Iraq.

The administration, however, faced significant domestic and international opposition to a war with Iraq. In an attempt to build support for the invasion, Bush relied on UN Security Council Resolution 1441 (2002), which declared Iraq in "material breach of its obligations" under the UN sanctions and warned Iraq that it would face "serious consequences" if it failed to comply. However, other members of the Security Council, particularly France, Russia, and China, came to different conclusions about the intent of the resolution, arguing that the resolution required further Security Council deliberation before any military action could be taken.

Bush, along with Prime Minister Tony Blair (b. 1953) of the United Kingdom, drafted another Security Council resolution, which would have authorized the use of force against Iraq. Seeing that the resolution would fail in the Security Council, however, the Bush administration did not pursue it further. As a result, the administration continued to move forward in its plans with a "coalition of the willing." In March 2003, Operation Iraqi Freedom began with air strikes immediately followed by a ground invasion. By April 2003, Baghdad was under the control of American forces and Saddam's government quickly dissolved. An insurgency, which included al-Qaeda-affiliated militants and former members of Saddam's Baathist regime, arose against the American-led coalition and post-Saddam Iraqi government. In December 2003, American forces captured Saddam, and he was subsequently executed by the Iraqi regime in 2006.

In 2004, the insurgents grew stronger. By 2007, it was necessary for the Bush administration to pursue a new strategy for dealing with the insurgency. In January 2007, Bush announced a strategy known as the troop surge. Developed by General David Petraeus (b. 1952), the surge was a part of a "new way forward." It also involved American support of Sunni groups the administration had previously sought to defeat. The "new way forward" proved effective in reducing the violence significantly ("President's Address to the Nation" and "Fact Sheet: The New Way Forward in Iraq").

With the 2008 election of President Barack Obama, the war entered a new phase, and on December 18, 2011, the last American troops exited Iraq. However, the situation in Iraq intensified when al-Qaeda in Iraq invaded Syria and began participating in the Syrian civil war. As a result, al-Qaeda in Iraq gained enough support and strength to reenter Iraq's western provinces, declare itself the Islamic state in Iraq and the Levant, take over a large portion of the country, and expand the Syrian conflict by combining it with the Iraqi insurgency. As a result, the Obama administration reengaged in Iraq with air strikes that began on August 10, 2014.

OTHER TARGETS

While the WOT was reigniting in Iraq, the Obama administration was faced with continuing challenges in South Asia. After the fall of the Taliban regime in Afghanistan, many members of the Taliban resistance fled to the Afghanistan-Pakistan border region where the Pakistani army had little control. With military support from the United States, the Pakistani military captured or killed numerous al-Qaeda operatives and Taliban insurgents. Under the Obama administration, the United States expanded a drone campaign begun by the Bush administration on targets within Pakistan. On May 2, 2011, during a raid conducted by American Special Operations Forces in Abbottabad, Pakistan, Osama bin Laden was killed.

The United States also conducted numerous operations against al-Qaeda militants in Yemen. Yemen's weak central government and largely lawless tribal areas led to a strong al-Qaeda presence. In 2009, the United States increased its military aid to Yemen, providing over $70 million, and also provided development assistance in the hope that al-Qaeda in the Arabian Peninsula could be diminished.

RESPONSE TO THE WAR ON TERROR

A highly controversial aspect of the WOT was the use of enhanced interrogation techniques, which many observers regard as torture, in gathering information on militants and terrorist organizations. Also controversial was the practice of rendition, or the extrajudicial transfer of captured terrorists to countries known to practice torture. The initial human-rights abuses emerged at the Abu Ghraib prison in Iraq, which was under the control of American military forces; the incidents received widespread condemnation both within the United States and abroad. Additional abuses occurred at Guantánamo Bay, Cuba, an American military prison established in January 2002 to detain, interrogate, and prosecute detainees suspected of terrorism and war crimes. Controversial interrogation techniques were used despite denials by the Bush administration; documents known as the torture memos, prepared before the invasion of Iraq, later confirmed that the Bush administration had authorized certain enhanced interrogation techniques. While the Bush administration argued that international legal conventions, mainly the Geneva Conventions, did not apply to American interrogators overseas, the US Supreme Court ruled in *Hamdan v. Rumsfeld* (2006) that the Geneva Conventions did apply. While Obama claimed during his candidacy for president that he would close the Guantánamo Bay detention center if elected, it remained open as of early 2015.

Additional criticism of the WOT focused on morality, economics, and even the phrase itself. First, as of 2014 the WOT had cost nearly ten thousand military and civilian American lives, and over fifty-six thousand Americans were wounded or injured. Also, as of 2011, a congressional report estimated the war's cost at $1.2 trillion; spending through 2021 was estimated to add an additional $1.8 trillion. Moreover, the notion of a war on terror proved contentious, with critics charging that the concept of "terrorism" was exploited by participating governments to pursue military objectives, reduce civil liberties, and infringe upon human rights. Others suggested that the WOT only increased the resentment that led to terrorist threats and attacks against the West.

SEE ALSO *Abu Ghraib; Afghanistan; Bush, George W.; Central Intelligence Agency (CIA); Cheney, Dick;* *Department of Defense, US; Guantánamo Bay; Iran; Iraq; Islam; Middle East; Obama, Barack Hussein; Powell, Colin; Think Tanks*

BIBLIOGRAPHY

"Address to a Joint Session of Congress and the American People." The White House: President George W. Bush, September 20, 2001. http://georgewbush-whitehouse.archives.gov/news/releases/2001/09/20010920-8.html

Authorization for the Use of Military Force. S.J. Res. 23. 107th Congress (2001). http://news.findlaw.com/hdocs/docs/terrorism/sjres23.enr.html

Bergen, Peter L. *The Longest War: The Enduring Conflict between America and Al-Qaeda.* New York: Free Press, 2011.

Cairo, Michael F. *The Gulf: The Bush Presidencies and the Middle East.* Lexington: The University Press of Kentucky, 2012.

Clarke, Richard A. *Against All Enemies: Inside America's War on Terror.* New York: Free Press, 2004.

"Fact Sheet: The New Way Forward in Iraq." The White House: President George W. Bush, January 10, 2007. http://georgewbush-whitehouse.archives.gov/news/releases/2007/01/20070110-3.html

Final Report of the Guantanamo Review Task Force. Department of Justice, January 22, 2010. http://www.justice.gov/sites/default/files/ag/legacy/2010/06/02/guantanamo-review-final-report.pdf

Hamdan v. Rumsfeld, 548 U.S. 557 (2006). http://www.oyez.org/cases/2000-2009/2005/2005_05_184

Kean, Thomas H., and Lee H. Hamilton. *The 9/11 Report: The National Commission on Terrorist Attacks upon the United States.* New York: St. Martin's Press, 2004.

Mayer, Jane. *The Dark Side: The Inside Story of How the War on Terror Turned into a War on American Ideals.* New York: Anchor Books, 2009.

National Security Archive, George Washington University. The Torture Archive. http://nsarchive.gwu.edu/torture_archive/

National Strategy for Combating Terrorism, February 2003. https://www.cia.gov/news-information/cia-the-war-on-terrorism/Counter_Terrorism_Strategy.pdf

"President Delivers State of the Union Address." The White House: President George W. Bush, January 29, 2002. http://georgewbush-whitehouse.archives.gov/news/releases/2002/01/20020129-11.html

"President's Address to the Nation." The White House: President George W. Bush, January 10, 2007. http://georgewbush-whitehouse.archives.gov/news/releases/2007/01/20070110-7.html

"Remarks by the President upon Arrival." The White House: President George W. Bush, September 16, 2001. http://georgewbush-whitehouse.archives.gov/news/releases/2001/09/20010916-2.html

United Nations Security Council Resolution 1441 (2002). http://www.un.org/depts/unmovic/documents/1441.pdf

Michael F. Cairo
Professor of Political Science
Transylvania University

WASHINGTON, BOOKER T.
1856–1915

During his famous Atlanta Compromise speech of 1895, Booker Taliaferro Washington urged Americans black and white to "cast down your bucket where you are" in the American South (Harlan 1974, 584). Yet Washington's ideas and their proponents would exhibit a global mobility in the decades that followed: Tenets of his philosophy were promoted to social theorists in Britain, France, and Germany; solicited by capitalists in Cuba, South America, and the North Pacific; emulated by African intellectuals in the Gold Coast, Southern Rhodesia, Nyasaland, and South Africa; and formally implemented in a series of cotton and forestry schools run by Tuskegee personnel in Togo, the Anglo-Egyptian Sudan, Nigeria, Liberia, and the Belgian Congo, inspiring similar ambitions for eastern Prussia and among colonial authorities for German East Africa and Morocco. The broad appeal of Washington's program across continents and classes derived from its capacity to embody multiple and sometimes contradictory ideals of social control during an era of considerable flux.

THE TUSKEGEE MODEL

For the governing regimes of Western nations and their colonies, the example set by Washington's Tuskegee Institute provided several ways to underwrite labor hierarchy after the abolition of slavery and serfdom. Under Washington's principalship, Tuskegee had grown rapidly since 1881, from a small Alabama school training black teachers in the former Confederate states to a world-renowned institution propounding a model for the education and employment of former slaves and their descendants. Central to the model was industrial training: Washington did not innovate this priority, for Edward Wilmot Blyden (1832–1912) and Alexander Crummell (1819–1898) had extolled its virtues long before him, but Washington did go further than his predecessors in minimizing the relative importance of the literary education offered by religious missions. Tuskegee's industrial program was then combined with a theory of race: In his rhetoric to white American audiences, Washington had constructed "the Negro" as a figure predisposed to rurality, manual labor, and even specifically to cotton cultivation—a sociological interpretation of race that could be exported to Africa or adapted to states and colonies elsewhere in the world that sought to rationalize the subordination of agriculturalists. During his collaboration with the German government in the first decade of the twentieth century, Washington also came increasingly to promote share contracts over autonomous farms and cash-cropping over subsistence; both policies proved amenable to colonial statism and its export monoculture. The appeal of Washington's program to European colonial administrators was therefore paradoxical: Book-erites and their ideas became transnationally mobile precisely because they could be used to restrict the geographic and social mobility of labor.

This global replication of the New South elicited various justifications from many Africans, African Americans, and other diasporans. It was founded upon a creed of exceptionalism: According to Washington's autobiography, the "school of American slavery" had equipped African Americans to play the lead role in international race relations by modeling habits of industry and bourgeois values for the developing world (Washington 1900, 16). Rather than advocating a permanent hierarchy, Washington argued that Africans who successfully absorbed American or European tutelage must be granted adequate pay, suffrage, and fair treatment under the law. The failure of colonial systems to pursue or achieve these objectives was viewed by Washington and his supporters as a violation of the "civilizing mission" rather than as grounds for its broader indictment. Even those like Marcus Garvey (1887–1940) who were more critical of the colonial project could nevertheless interpret Washington's support of racial segregation as a form of black national separatism and economic independence in the tradition of Martin Delany (1812–1885). For South Africa specifically, Washington's promotion of land tenancy and the purported rurality of his "Negro" archetype were marshaled by Davidson D. T. Jabavu (1885–1959) in his critique of the 1913 Natives Land Act, which barred black Africans from the most productive agricultural land and compelled their unequal integration as migrant wage laborers in areas zoned for white settlement (Davis 2003). The Tuskegee agenda could thus be construed as both support and reform of colonial rule.

THE EVOLUTION OF WASHINGTON'S VIEWS

A search for ideological consistency across Washington's international work risks overlooking its evolution. Among the early seeds of his cosmopolitanism toward the end of the nineteenth century were visits to the United States by the English missionary Joseph Booth (1851–1932) and the Zulu educator John Dube (1871–1946), both of whom proposed the export of Tuskegee's industrial curriculum to Africa. These encounters were immediately followed by the return of African American soldiers from the Spanish-American War, servicemen whose participation in overseas conquest signified to Washington the emergence of "a New Negro for a new century" (Washington et al. 1900). The Booker T. Washington who traveled to Europe in 1899 was a man intrigued by the possibility of African American stewardship in the movement for black global solidarity, but he was only just beginning to formulate the policy implications of this goal: During his visit to London, Washington praised the Haitian revolutionary Toussaint Louverture (1743–1803) and described the approaching Pan-African Conference as an opportunity to alleviate "the widespread ignorance which is prevalent in England about the treatment of native races under European and American rule" (Hooker 1974, 20). The next year, a Tuskegee representative joined with W. E. B. Du Bois (1868–1963) at the Paris Exposition to present the New South as an example of racial coexistence. The foreign policies of the Tuskegee Institute and Du Bois's Niagara Movement diverged only years later, as leaders reacted differently to the growing record of European imperialism.

Washington's own reaction developed across the complex histories of his many international projects, but the causes and effects of that development are revealed most clearly in a sequence of three African examples: Togo, the Congo Free State, and Liberia. Between 1901 and 1908, Washington's vision of black progress coevolved alongside the priorities of his German collaborators in Togo, so that independent farming, crop diversification, and local manufacture were subordinated to the external demand for industrial-grade cotton; even the Tuskegee curriculum in America was modified in the process to reduce literary education and instead mirror the school's industrial reputation among European colonial authorities. Just as Tuskegee was shaped by German interests, Max Weber's (1864–1920) famous theorization of the "Protestant work ethic" was reciprocally informed by his sojourn at Tuskegee in 1904 (Zimmerman 2010). Washington's subsequent criticism of colonial abuse would be consistently tempered by his own Togolese commitment: His reproach of King Leopold II (1835–1909) simultaneously positioned German rule as a humane alternative. In 1907, Liberian insolvency counterposed the interests of European creditors, Americo-Liberian debtors, and African taxpayers; Washington responded by leveraging African American votes to induce a US protectorate that would pay Liberia's debts in return for control of customs and border defense. Washington himself never set foot on Liberian soil—or indeed on any part of the African continent.

BOOKER T. WASHINGTON'S GLOBAL LEGACY

After Washington's death in 1915, the explicit invocation of Tuskegee's program as panacea would be gradually undermined by a combination of factors on both sides of the Atlantic. Previously imagined as a model of administrative efficiency and racial amity, Germany's colonial experiment in Togo was recast after World War I as the work of an imperial oppressor. At the same time, the supposed rurality of Washington's "Negro" was contradicted by America's Great Migration and by many Africans' eschewal of the plow in favor of the pen and their departure from the countryside to the metropole. In South Africa, the apartheid election of 1948 marginalized liberal politics and its support for black schools of any kind. Yet the frequent disavowal of Washington's methods and ideology that resulted from these factors across the latter half of the twentieth century belies a deeper structural legacy: By replicating abroad practices from America's New South, Tuskegee and its proponents forged a Global South that would persist into the twenty-first century as an economically vulnerable exporter of raw materials to international markets.

SEE ALSO *Global South; Pan-Africanism*

BIBLIOGRAPHY

Davis, Hunt. "*Up from Slavery* for South Africans: Booker T. Washington's Classic Autobiography Abridged." In *Booker T. Washington and Black Progress*: Up from Slavery *100 Years Later*, edited by W. Fitzhugh Brundage, 193–219. Gainesville: University Press of Florida, 2003.

Harlan, Louis R. "Booker T. Washington and the White Man's Burden." *American Historical Review* 71, 2 (January 1966): 441–467.

Harlan, Louis R., ed. *The Booker T. Washington Papers*, Vol. 3: *1889–95*. Assistant editors Stuart B. Kaufman and Raymond W. Smock. Urbana: University of Illinois Press, 1974.

Hooker, J. R. "The Pan-African Conference 1900." *Transition* 46 (1974): 20–24.

Marable, W. Manning. "Booker T. Washington and African Nationalism." *Phylon* 35, 4 (1974): 398–406.

Spivey, Donald. "The African Crusade for Black Industrial Schooling." *Journal of Negro History* 63, 1 (January 1978): 1–17.

Washington, Booker T. "The American Negro and His Economic Value." *International Monthly* 2 (1900): 672–686.

Washington, Booker T. *Up from Slavery: An Autobiography*. New York: Doubleday, Page & Company, 1900.

Washington, Booker T., John E. MacBrady, Norman Barton Wood, and Fannie Barrier Williams. *A New Negro for a New Century: An Accurate and Up-to-Date Record of the Upward Struggles of the Negro Race*. Chicago: American Publishing House, 1900.

West, Michael O. "The Tuskegee Model of Development in Africa: Another Dimension of the African/African American Connection." *Diplomatic History* 16, 3 (July 1992): 371–387.

Zimmerman, Andrew. *Alabama in Africa: Booker T. Washington, the German Empire, and the Globalization of the New South*. Princeton, NJ: Princeton University Press, 2010.

Jeremy W. Pope
Assistant Professor of History
The College of William and Mary

WASHINGTON, GEORGE
1732–1799

In 1789, George Washington entered the American presidency as one of the most famous people in the Western world. Already admired for securing American independence by leading his country's forces to victory over Britain, Washington cemented his reputation by then resigning his commission at the end of the war. Even British king George III (1738–1820) recognized the significance of Washington's act, predicting that if the American had truly retired to his farm, "he will be the greatest man in the world" (Wood 2006, 42). Washington returned to public life a few years later, first as president of the Constitutional Convention and then as the first president of the United States, out of concern that the young American Republic was crumbling into disparate parts. His foreign policy as president extended from his primary domestic objective: secure the stability and authority of the new US government under the Constitution.

RECEPTION OF FOREIGN GUESTS

The Constitution granted the president significant power in directing foreign relations. Washington appointed the talented Thomas Jefferson (1743–1826) as the nation's first secretary of state, but viewed himself as an expert in foreign affairs, having coordinated strategy and business with foreign diplomats and military leaders during the American Revolutionary War (1775–1783). The president sought to reinforce America's standing in all matters, down to how the government would receive foreign guests. For foreigners traveling on state business, Washington would "let them come to me through the Secretary of State." For prominent foreigners with private business, the president insisted on receiving them at one of his weekly formal levees. "Etiquette of this sort is essential with all foreigners to give respect to the Chief Magistrate and the dignity of the Government," Washington explained, "which would be lessened if every person who could procure a letter of introduction should be presented otherwise than at Levee hours in a formal manner" (Rasmussen and Tilton 1999, 219–220).

RELATIONS WITH FRANCE

In his first term, Washington's state-building agenda benefitted from relative peace in the Atlantic world. Yet the threat of discord loomed. Just a few months after Washington's inauguration in April 1789, the fall of the Bastille in Paris signaled the beginning of the French Revolution. The president, like most Americans, initially viewed events in France with pride for their apparent similarities to the American Revolution. In October

1789, Washington wrote to his European envoy, Gouverneur Morris (1752–1816): "The Revolution, which has been effected in France is of so wonderful a nature that the mind can hardly realize the fact" (Sears 1960, 56). The feelings were mutual. In March 1790, the Marquis de Lafayette (1757–1834), one of Washington's most trusted officers during the American Revolution, sent him a key to the Bastille with the dedication: "It is a tribute which I owe as a son to my adopted father, as an aide-de-camp to my general, as a missionary of liberty to its patriarch" (Reuter 1983, 140). Washington displayed the key in his presidential houses in New York and Philadelphia before placing it in the main front passage of his home, Mount Vernon, where it remains to

Washington taking leave of his officers in New York after US independence was secured, December 4, 1783. Print by Edmund Ollier, c. 1880. *Already admired for securing American independence by leading his country's forces to victory over Britain, Washington cemented his reputation by then resigning his commission at the end of the war. He returned to public life a few years later out of concern that the young American republic was crumbling into disparate parts.* **PRINT COLLECTOR/HULTON ARCHIVE/GETTY IMAGES**

this day. In August 1792, the National Assembly of France honored Washington and a handful of other Atlantic luminaries for their commitment to liberty by granting them honorary French citizenship.

By then, however, the French Revolution had begun its radical turn. In fall 1792, Washington learned of Lafayette's exile from France for his moderate views and imprisonment for treason in Austria. The following spring, a month after the president's second inauguration in March 1793, Americans received word that the French king, Louis XVI (1754–1793), had been guillotined and that France had declared war on Britain and the Netherlands. Maintaining America's neutrality and sovereignty amidst the European war signified the main challenge of Washington's second term.

America's Treaty of Alliance with France, completed in 1778, complicated Washington's efforts to keep the United States out of the French Revolutionary Wars. In April 1793, he issued a statement that became known as the Proclamation of Neutrality, although the word "neutrality" did not appear in it for fear of offending the French. The president declared it was "the duty and interest of the United States ... that they should with sincerity and good faith adopt and pursue a conduct friendly and impartial toward the belligerent powers" (Malanson 2012, 516). The principle of favoring neutrality and commerce over foreign entanglement, as expressed in the proclamation, became the centerpiece of Washington's foreign policy. When the new French minister to the United States, Edmond Charles Genet (1763–1834), challenged American neutrality by appealing directly to the American people to support France militarily in the spring and summer of 1793, Washington's administration requested the minister's recall.

RELATIONS WITH BRITAIN

Thereafter, Britain most threatened Washington's policy of neutrality. Beginning in the summer of 1793, the British Royal Navy detained dozens of American ships, most carrying foodstuffs, bound for France and the French West Indies. The British navy also captured and impressed (forced into service) American sailors suspected of being British deserters. The British depredations at sea added to a list of outstanding issues between Britain and America from the American Revolution, including the British refusal to evacuate military posts in America's Northwest Territory, their failure to compensate American slaveholders for slaves freed during the war, and the unwillingness of American merchants to pay off debts that predated American independence.

In 1794, the United States came closer to war with Britain than at any time between the Revolution and the War of 1812. But Washington favored peace and dispatched the Supreme Court chief justice, John Jay (1745–1829), to London to negotiate a treaty. The resulting agreement, completed in November 1794 and known informally as the Jay Treaty (or Jay's Treaty), appeared to many Americans, particularly in the Democratic-Republican Party, to have sold out the nation's interests. By the terms of the treaty, the British agreed to leave their posts in the Northwest (which was already precipitated by the US victory over British-backed Native Americans at the Battle of Fallen Timbers in August 1794) and to increase American trade access to British ports in the West Indies. On all other issues, most importantly free trading rights and impressment, the treaty failed to achieve American objectives. Moreover, in granting Britain favored-nation status, the agreement formally ended America's Treaty of Alliance with France.

Washington responded to the Jay Treaty with disappointment but reasoned that it was the best agreement possible given the weak position of the United States. The president withstood public criticism—the most extensive of his charmed political career—to support the ratification of the treaty in the Senate before ultimately signing it in August 1795. Public opinion soon turned in favor of the treaty when America experienced the economic benefits of relaxed tensions and increased trade with Britain. In October 1795, Pinckney's Treaty with Spain further advanced American economic interests by securing use of the Mississippi River and the port of New Orleans, thereby providing western farmers with an attractive new option for shipping their products to global markets.

WASHINGTON'S FAREWELL ADDRESS

Washington's Farewell Address provided an elegant summary of his foreign policy, particularly American neutrality. Composed with the help of Washington's close political ally and first Treasury secretary, Alexander Hamilton (1757–1804), the address first appeared in Philadelphia's *American Daily Advertiser* newspaper on September 19, 1796. Washington warned his countrymen against the perils of both domestic political factions and foreign political alliances. Yet he did not, as is often mistaken, advocate American isolation from the world. Rather, Washington expressed a preference for economic over political engagement with other countries. "The Great rule of conduct for us," he stated, "in regard to foreign Nations is in extending our commercial relations to have with them as little *political* connection as possible" (Spalding and Garrity 1996, 186). Washington's Farewell Address helped to guide American foreign policy for more than a century and is still read aloud annually in the US Senate chamber.

SEE ALSO *Adams, John; American Revolution; Franklin, Benjamin; Jay, John; Jay Treaty (1795); Jefferson, Thomas; Lafayette, Marquis de*

BIBLIOGRAPHY

Ammon, Harry. *The Genet Mission.* New York: Norton, 1973.

Combs, Jerald A. *The Jay Treaty: Political Battleground of the Founding Fathers.* Berkeley: University of California Press, 1970.

DeConde, Alexander. *Entangling Alliance: Politics and Diplomacy under George Washington.* Durham, NC: Duke University Press, 1958.

Elkins, Stanley, and Eric McKitrick. *The Age of Federalism: The Early American Republic, 1788–1800.* New York: Oxford University Press, 1993.

Estes, Todd. *The Jay Treaty Debate, Public Opinion, and the Evolution of Early American Political Culture.* Amherst: University of Massachusetts Press, 2006.

Gilbert, Felix. *To the Farewell Address: Ideas of Early American Foreign Policy.* Princeton, NJ: Princeton University Press, 1961.

Malanson, Jeffrey J. "Foreign Policy in the Presidential Era." In *A Companion to George Washington*, edited by Edward G. Lengel, 506–523. Malden, MA: Wiley-Blackwell, 2012.

Malanson, Jeffrey J. *Addressing America: George Washington's Farewell and the Making of National Culture, Politics, and Diplomacy, 1796-1852.* Kent, OH: Kent State University Press, 2015.

Rasmussen, William M. S., and Robert S. Tilton. *George Washington: The Man behind the Myths.* Charlottesville: University of Virginia Press, 1999.

Reuter, Frank T. *Trials and Triumphs: George Washington's Foreign Policy.* Fort Worth: Texas Christian University Press, 1983.

Sears, Louis Martin. *George Washington and the French Revolution.* Detroit, MI: Wayne State University Press, 1960.

Spalding, Matthew, and Patrick J. Garrity. *A Sacred Union of Citizens: George Washington's Farewell Address and the American Character.* Lanham, MD: Roman and Littlefield, 1996.

Wood, Gordon S. *Revolutionary Characters: What Made the Founders Different.* New York: Penguin, 2006.

Denver Brunsman
Associate Professor of History
George Washington University

THE WEALTH OF NATIONS (ADAM SMITH, 1776)

Adam Smith (1723–1790), a Scottish professor of moral philosophy, became the "father of modern economic science" with the publication of his seminal *An Inquiry into the Nature and Causes of the Wealth of Nations* in London in 1776. This book provided great insight into the functioning of a free-market system for maximizing and sustaining national wealth (which he called "opulence"). Though praised as a theoretical work of scholarship, it was, nonetheless, ignored by the British government and the opulent landed gentry; neither was at all interested in freeing up British markets.

But to the colonies in America that declared independence from Britain in that seminal year, *The Wealth of Nations* was a gift of enormous importance. Most of America's founders, thirsty for all new ideas about the governance of nations, read and studied Smith much more extensively than their British counterparts.

The new American nation, albeit one of spirited immigrants who had defeated the mighty British, had much to learn about transforming itself into a country that could prosper and endure. There had to be organizing principles of government, law, and economics that could survive the many tests that new nations faced. Indeed, the absence of these principles might have brought an early end to American independence. As it was, the new country got off to a very poor start; political, legal, and economic disorder was so great during the Confederation period (1776–1788) that an unexpected consensus arose for a new federal republic to be established under a Constitution for the governance of the (finally) United States.

The Constitution provided for the political institutions of the United States, but not its economic institutions. These were important—if they were poorly designed or failed in operation, the country could become too weak to survive and be lost to counterrevolution, invasion, or dictatorship. These new economic institutions had to be created *de novo*, by persons with no knowledge of government other than what they could ingest from the powerful discourses of the Enlightenment then occurring in Europe.

The enlightened expert the American founders turned to was Adam Smith, who advanced the basic, but new, idea that opulence would flourish best in an environment of competitive markets that were free of interference or favor by governments or by privileged classes. Free markets, driven by individuals and groups seeking to improve their "self interest," would be guided by an "invisible hand" to balance supply and demand, and establish a "just equilibrium" of wages sufficient to support a family. Anything else would require rules that needed enforcement at a cost that would make most such rules inefficient and, in a voting republic, threaten political opposition. Smith also described the critical importance of sound national finances based on a solid banking system, a central bank, and taxation and spending policies that enabled the currency to remain stable.

Alexander Hamilton (1757–1804), the country's first treasury secretary to whom the task of erecting the important economic institutions was given, was familiar with everything Smith had written, and he copied almost everything he thought could be applied to the fledgling nation. He established the dollar as the national currency, and persuaded a reluctant Congress to approve a central bank, the Bank of the United States, to support and expand a national system of money and credit. Hamilton also arranged for the federal government to take over and manage all of the debts of the states, fortified the new national debt with sinking funds, and established a mechanism for collecting customs duties, which would be the primary revenue source for servicing the debt. He vigorously encouraged the granting of banking and corporate charters in the private sector (where almost none had existed in colonial days) to collect savings and promote free markets for new entrepreneurial activity and commerce.

By the time of Hamilton's death in 1804 during Thomas Jefferson's first term as president, the United States had established a prime credit rating, its debt securities traded in markets at premium rates, the currency was sound, and business was flourishing. Even though he was Hamilton's main ideological rival, Jefferson changed very little of Hamilton's highly functional Smithian financial system, which had already hardened into place.

America's political experiment succeeded, not because it was a republic—there had been many of those that had not succeeded—but because the economic system based on Adam Smith's ideas succeeded. With success came opulence and a lasting commitment to entrepreneurship. For the next hundred years, America attracted investment capital from Britain, France, and Germany, along with millions of immigrants seeking jobs and the classless opportunities for self-improvement that were inherent in the American system. Through America's well-studied economic success, Adam Smith's ideas spread throughout the world.

SEE ALSO *Economics*

BIBLIOGRAPHY

Smith, Roy C. *Adam Smith and the Origins of American Enterprise.* New York: St. Martin's Press, 2002.

Roy C. Smith
Kenneth Langone Professor of Finance and Entrepreneurship
Stern School of Business, New York University

WEAPONRY

The United States is by far the largest armaments manufacturer and distributor in the world. In 2011, the United States led the world with 77.7 percent of all arms agreements to other nations, with a total value of $66.3 billion. By contrast, Russia, the second largest arms distributor, concluded 5.6 percent of worldwide arms agreements with a value of $4.8 billion.

During World War II (1939–1945), the United States distributed arms to its allies through the Lend-Lease program, and by the end of the war the United States was a major arms manufacturer. After the war ended, the United States continued to provide arms to allies and other friendly states, enabling US allies to protect themselves from possible Soviet aggression. Since the end of the Cold War, economic factors have become more important, with weapons sales sometimes counteracting the goals of US foreign policy.

Weapons have been used since prehistoric times to project power beyond the strength of the human body. Ancient and medieval warriors fought with handheld weapons or projectiles powered by human strength, gravity, or tension. The discovery of gunpowder as an explosive enabled the development of a variety of new projectile systems such as artillery and handheld firearms. Today, more powerful chemicals have replaced black gunpowder as a propellant, but the concept of moving a projectile at high velocity remains the basis for most weapons systems.

FIREARMS

The earliest gunpowder firearms were smoothbore (smooth barrel interior), muzzle-loading muskets firing solid spherical shot. They were inaccurate beyond forty yards but could be fired at the rate of three rounds per minute. Rifled muskets, with spiral grooves cut into the inside of the barrel, were more accurate but difficult to load, and the rifling became clogged with gunpowder residue.

In the 1840s, the French invention of a bullet known as the Minié ball made rifles easier to load, and by the Civil War, rifles were in common use by both sides. In 1865 Springfield made its first breech-loading rifle, and the "Trapdoor Springfield," so called because of its hinged breech, was used by the US Army until the Spanish-American War. The Springfield Model 1903 was used by the US Army from World War I until the 1930s, when it was replaced by the M1 semiautomatic rifle. In 1957, the army began issuing the M14 automatic rifle, which fired 7.62 NATO rounds and had full automatic capability. (A NATO round is one that can be fired from the corresponding weapon of any member of NATO.) In 1970 the M14 was replaced by the M16 rifle, which fires a smaller 5.56 NATO round but is lighter and produces less recoil. The standard-issue M16 fires in three-round bursts, but some versions are capable of automatic fire. The M16 and its variants are used by the military forces of more than eighty nations, and the rifle has been used in virtually all significant conflicts since the Vietnam War. It is the most common rifle of its type in the world; over eight million have been produced since 1962.

ARTILLERY

Artillery includes larger-caliber weapons with ranges beyond those of typical firearms and is used against massed troops, fortifications, ships, and enemy artillery. Different types of artillery, or cannon, have specific characteristics, although definitions are not clear-cut. Guns have long barrels, high velocity, and long range, but they have a flat firing trajectory. Howitzers have shorter barrels, lower velocity, and a shorter range, but they can be used for high- or low-angle fire. Mortars have very short barrels, low velocity, short range, and a high firing arc. They are used only for high-angle fire.

In American military usage, "howitzer" is often used to indicate indirect-fire artillery, where there is no direct line of sight from the gunner to the target. Indirect fire requires calculations, observation, and adjustment for accuracy.

In the nineteenth century, smaller field artillery pieces were pulled to the battlefield by horses or mules. By the mid-twentieth century motorized vehicles replaced animals. Towed artillery is inexpensive to build and maintain, and it can be deployed on many types of terrain. Self-propelled artillery (SP artillery) is mounted on tracked vehicles resembling tanks. SP vehicles are lightly armored to protect the crew from shrapnel, and they can move around the battlefield quickly in a maneuver known as "shoot and scoot."

The projectiles launched from firearms and artillery have changed greatly since the Minié ball made rifling the norm in firearms. Traditionally, cannon fired solid shot, but artillery could also fire exploding shells such as the "bombs bursting in air" mentioned in "The Star-Spangled Banner." Shrapnel shells, invented by a British officer in 1784, were filled with shot and explosive and were designed to detonate close to the target.

In the twentieth century, various chemical compounds known as "smokeless powder" replaced black gunpowder as the propellant in artillery and firearms. Smokeless powder was more powerful than black gunpowder, and it did not create the clouds of black smoke that reduced visibility on the battlefield. However, it was somewhat unstable, and by the early twentieth century, trinitrotoluene (TNT) became the standard explosive in high-explosive (HE) shells. Percussion fuzes enabled shells to detonate on a timer or on impact, increasing the explosive power of the shell. Modern conventional weapons like the GBU-57 A/B Massive Ordnance Penetrator "bunker buster" can weigh up to thirty thousand pounds and deliver over two tons of HE material.

In the 1920s, American and European scientists began to develop rockets, or self-propelled unguided munitions. Rocket fuel, usually solid but sometimes liquid, is burned or goes through a chemical reaction to drive the rocket forward. Rockets usually include fins or subsidiary engines to stabilize their trajectory.

A missile is a rocket with a guidance system to direct it toward the target. During World War II, Nazi Germany developed "V-1" and "V-2" missiles, and after the war, US missile development was based on German designs. Modern missiles use guidance systems based on heat or radio waves the target is emitting; radar systems or satellite guidance embedded in the missile itself; or guidance systems controlled from the launch platform or the ground.

A ballistic missile uses rocket power at the beginning of its flight, then depends on gravity for most of its flight before its reentry or descent phase. Missiles can carry conventional or nuclear payloads.

Nuclear weapons, using fission or fusion reactions to unleash energy, were developed by the United States toward the end of World War II. The amount of energy a modern nuclear bomb will release if detonated can equal hundreds of thousands or millions of tons of TNT. Nuclear weapons can be tactical or strategic. Tactical nuclear weapons include missiles, artillery shells, torpedoes, and other projectiles designed for use on the battlefield. Although they are usually smaller than strategic weapons, they have the power of dozens or hundreds of tons of TNT. Strategic weapons are designed for use against enemy cities or military installations, and are extremely powerful. Intercontinental ballistic missiles (ICBMs) contain multiple warheads and have ranges of thousands of miles. Nuclear weapons are deployed on sea, land, and air platforms.

NAVAL WEAPONS

Naval vessels are for the most part platforms for weapons. In the era of sail, guns lined the sides of vessels, and range and accuracy determined the course of battle. In the late nineteenth century, the battleship became the capital ship of the US Navy and other major naval forces. Early battleships carried a variety of different caliber guns, but in 1906, the British launched the first "dreadnought," an all-large-gun battleship. In the decade before World War I, the United States and other nations developed dreadnought-class fleets. Battleships made it possible for the US Navy to compete for supremacy on the seas.

The Washington Naval Treaty of 1922 limited the number of battleships that signatory nations could build, but, driven by advances in aircraft technology, some battleships were converted to aircraft carriers, from whose decks specially designed aircraft could be launched. In

World War II the aircraft carrier replaced the battleship as the most important naval ship, and the United States used aircraft carriers in pivotal battles against the Japanese. Since the end of World War II, aircraft carriers have gotten larger; in 1960 the United States launched the USS *Enterprise,* the world's first nuclear-powered carrier. Today, the United States has a fleet of ten supercarriers (displacing more than seventy thousand tons), more than any other nation. Some have argued that aircraft carriers are obsolete because they are vulnerable to powerful missiles. However, they have effectively projected US power in unstable regions such as the Persian Gulf.

Another naval weapons platform is the submarine. Submarines were used in both world wars, and today they are central to naval warfare. Nuclear-powered attack submarines armed with Tomahawk cruise missiles are used against other submarines and ships. Guided-missile submarines are armed with cruise missiles to attack land targets. Ballistic-missile submarines carry submarine-launched ballistic missiles (SLBMs) with nuclear warheads. These are deployed as a deterrent and have special acoustic quieting systems that allow them to operate in virtual silence.

Submarines are themselves targets of enemy weapons systems, and the United States deploys antisubmarine warfare (ASW) systems. ASW includes using sonar, radar, and other systems for detection, and mines, torpedoes, and depth charges to destroy enemy submarines.

LAND WEAPONS

In addition to infantry and artillery, the main weapons platform for land warfare in the twentieth century was the tank. A tank is a tracked, armored fighting vehicle with a large-caliber cannon mounted on a turret. Tanks were first used in World War I (1914–1918) by the British and the French, and the United States sent the US Tank Corps, commanded by George Patton (1885–1945), to operate French and British tanks. After the war the Tank Corps was disbanded, and US Army theorists insisted that tanks should be developed only for infantry support. However, forward-looking cavalry officers realized that the age of the horse was over, and they developed "Combat Cars," similar to tanks, to be deployed independently. As army chief of staff from 1930 to 1935, General Douglas MacArthur (1880–1964) directed the mechanization and motorization of the army, and increased efforts were put into tank research. Tanks were eventually assigned to the cavalry as a separate arms branch.

In early tank technology, size and maneuverability were mutually exclusive. Tanks were developed for different purposes and classified by size: light tanks weighed less than ten tons, medium tanks weighed ten to twenty-five tons, and heavy tanks weighed more than twenty-five tons. In 1940–1941, the Lend-Lease program sent large numbers of M3/M5 Stuart light tanks to Great Britain and the Soviet Union, but these tanks were underarmored and underarmed, with a small 37-millimeter gun. The M24 Chaffee and the M3 medium tank, equipped with the more powerful 75-millimeter gun, saw service in Europe, but the M4 Sherman tank, with a 75-millimeter (later 76-millimeter) main gun, is most associated with World War II tank warfare.

Toward the end of World War II, the heavy M26 Pershing, with a 90-millimeter gun, was deployed in limited numbers. It was replaced after the war by the M46 and M48 Patton tank. The M48 was used by many US allies and saw extensive service in the 1960s and 1970s.

In the 1960s, the US Army began to replace its variously sized tank fleet with the main battle tank (MBT), a multirole tank. The M60 Patton, a widely used MBT, carried a 105-millimeter main gun and was sold to many US allies. Its replacement, the M1 Abrams, carried a 105-millimeter rifled gun, while a later version, the M1A1, had a 120-millimeter smoothbore gun. Some versions of the M1A1 have depleted uranium armor. The Abrams tank was deployed in Europe during the Cold War and saw service in the Gulf War of 1991. The Abrams is used by several nations in the Middle East and by other US allies.

At the beginning of World War II, tank destroyers—lightly armored tracked vehicles with 76- or 90-millimeter guns—were deployed against tanks, but as tank-against-tank battles established the tank as an independent arms branch, the tank destroyer was phased out. Today antitank weapons such as bazookas and rocket-propelled grenade (RPG) launchers are armed with armor-penetrating high-explosive anti-tank (HEAT) rounds.

AIRCRAFT

From the first flights of the early twentieth century, American military leaders envisioned the use of aircraft in reconnaissance, and in World War I, pilots fought individual dogfights over the trenches. In the 1930s, proponents of aircraft technology developed the doctrine of strategic bombing, with advocates like General Billy Mitchell (1879–1936) arguing that wars could be won from the air without involving ground forces. Bombers, fixed-wing aircraft carrying large payloads of bombs to drop on military or civilian targets, never eliminated the importance of ground forces, but they were used extensively in World War II and after. Modern bombers like the B-52 Stratofortress carry up to seventy thousand pounds of bombs and can be armed with a variety of air-to-ground missiles (AGMs), both nuclear and conventional.

Bombers are large and relatively slow, and they are often protected by fighter aircraft. Fighters are fast, maneuverable aircraft capable of attacking other aircraft. The US Air Force deploys fighters such as the F-22 Raptor, the F-18 Fighting Falcon, and the F-15 Eagle; the US Navy also deploys fighters on aircraft carriers. Fighters are often armed with the short-range AIM-9 Sidewinder or the medium-range AIM-7 Sparrow missiles.

Attack aircraft are used to attack targets on the ground. The A-10 Thunderbolt, armed with a 30-millimeter GAU-8/A Avenger Gatling-style gun firing armor-piercing rounds, is designed for close air support of ground troops. Other fixed-wing aircraft used for ground support include the F/A-18 Hornet, which has both fighter and attack capabilities.

Helicopters such as the AH-1 Cobra and the AH-64 Apache provide close air support as well. The Apache carries a 30-millimeter gun and also AGM-114 Hellfire missiles, which are used against tanks and other armored vehicles. Aircraft are among the most common and most valuable armaments sold by the United States to other nations. The AH-64, for example, has been sold to at least a dozen nations since the 1980s. Most recently, the RQ-1 Predator unmanned aerial vehicle (UAV) has been armed with Hellfire missiles and has provided close air support in Central Asia and the Middle East.

Antiaircraft weapons include not only the air-to-air missiles launched from fighters but also weapons launched from the ground, or surface-to-air missiles (SAMs). Air Defense Artillery (ADA) systems the Nike-Ajax, the Nike-Hercules, the MIM-23 Hawk, and the MIM-104 Patriot were deployed during and after the Cold War. The Patriot is not only an antiaircraft system but also a tactical antiballistic missile (ABM) system, and it is used by fifteen nations in addition to the United States.

WEAPONS OF MASS DESTRUCTION

Along with nuclear weapons, chemical and biological agents and radiological dispersion devices are known as weapons of mass destruction (WMD). They are regulated by treaties between nations, although there is ongoing concern about their potential use by terrorist groups.

Chemical weapons include nonliving substances that are toxic to humans. Although outlawed in two peace conferences at the turn of the twentieth century, chlorine, mustard, and phosgene gas were used in World War I. In 1928 the Geneva Convention repeated prohibitions against chemical weapons, and they were not widely used in World War II. The United States and other nations hold stockpiles of chemical weapons, including nerve agents, blood agents, blistering agents, choking agents, and others.

Biological weapons include living organisms that cause illness. Major biological weapons include anthrax, smallpox, plague, and other diseases.

Radiological weapons are bombs or other devices that spread radioactive material, which is harmful or lethal to organisms exposed to it. "Dirty bombs," as these are sometimes called, are not nuclear weapons, but an explosive agent is used to spread radioactive material.

ARMS CONTROL AND ARMS PROLIFERATION

The United States has participated in many arms-control efforts, some leading to treaties. Throughout the late 1960s and 1970s, the United States and the Soviet Union negotiated limitations on ballistic missiles and strategic nuclear weapons, culminating in the SALT I and SALT II treaties (Strategic Arms Limitation Talks [SALT]). In 1987 the INF Treaty (Intermediate-Range Nuclear Forces [INF]) banned intermediate-range nuclear weapons. In 1991, the United States and the Soviet Union agreed to the Strategic Arms Reduction Treaty (START), which limited the number of nuclear warheads held by the two nations.

The United States did not start its history as a military power or a major arms producer. In fact, most nineteenth-century innovations in weaponry came from European designers and were adopted by the United States. The Cold War, however, spurred the United States to pursue weapons development more vigorously. In 1958, President Dwight Eisenhower (1890–1969) authorized the creation of the Advanced Research Projects Agency (ARPA, later DARPA), a Department of Defense (DoD) agency charged with developing technologies for military and civilian use. DARPA, the individual armed services, and the DoD work with civilian corporations to develop and produce weapons systems. The largest arms manufacturers in the United States include Lockheed Martin, Boeing, BAE Systems, Raytheon, Northrop Grumman, General Dynamics, and United Technologies Corporation. The defense industry employs over six million people in the United States, not including uniformed personnel.

Many critics have noted that, in spite of its declarations of peaceful intentions, the United States is the world's largest exporter of arms. Of particular concern is the increase in the number of weapons systems being sold to developing nations in unstable regions of the world. In 2011, the value of US arms agreements with the developing world, over $56 billion, was more than that of its top ten competitors combined. Most US sales are to buyers in the Middle East and Asia. Saudi Arabia is the top purchaser of US weapons, with India in second place. The United States also sells systems to India's rival, Pakistan. Other major Middle Eastern buyers include the UAE and Oman, nations intent on stopping Iran's growing strength in the region. In recent years the United States has also directed arms sales to Asian nations near China as a bulwark against potential Chinese aggression. Arms sales have always been an important foreign policy tool for the United States, with sales agreements used to cement alliances and compel friendly behavior from buyers. However, since the end of the Cold War, arms sales have become increasingly lucrative for defense contractors and the government, and economic gain has become more important.

Since the 1950s, the sale and deployment of US weapons have sparked protests in many regions, particularly in Europe, where US basing has been especially heavy. In the 1950s the Easter March movement in West Germany opposed nuclear weapons, and the movement continued through the 1980s, when huge protests in Europe arose in opposition to the deployment of Pershing II nuclear weapons. In the Middle East, opposition to US military interventions has turned deadly. Al-Qaeda was originally formed in large part to oppose the US military presence in Saudi Arabia. Although Americans often perceive US armaments and military strength to be deployed in the cause of peace, many around the world remain suspicious of the overwhelming superiority of US weapons technology.

SEE ALSO *Airplanes; Atomic Bomb; Automobiles; Bikini Atoll; Cold War; Einstein, Albert; Ford, Henry; Manhattan Project; Trains; Truman, Harry S.; World War I; World War II*

BIBLIOGRAPHY

Bernstein, Jeremy. *Nuclear Weapons: What You Need to Know.* Cambridge: Cambridge University Press, 2008.

Cameron, Robert S. *Mobility, Shock, and Firepower: The Emergence of the U.S. Army's Armor Branch, 1917–1945.* Washington, DC: Center of Military History United States Army, 2008.

Defense Department. *U.S. Army Weapon Systems 2013.* Washington, DC: Defense Department, 2013.

Foss, Christopher, and Will Fowler. *The Encyclopedia of Tanks and Armored Fighting Vehicles.* London: Amber Books, 2002.

Fredriksen, John C. *Warbirds: An Illustrated Guide to U.S. Military Aircraft, 1915–2000.* Santa Barbara, CA: ABC-CLIO, 1999.

Grimmett, Richard F., and Paul K. Kerr. "Conventional Arms Transfers to Developing Nations, 2004–2011." Congressional Research Service, August 24, 2012. http://www.fas.org/sgp/crs/weapons/R42678.pdf

Haskew, Michael. *Postwar Artillery: 1945–Present.* London: Amber Books, 2011.

Langford, R. Everett. *Introduction to Weapons of Mass Destruction: Radiological, Chemical, and Biological.* Hoboken, NJ: Wiley-Interscience, 2004.

Millett, Allan R., and Peter Maslowski. *For the Common Defense: A Military History of the United States of America.* Rev. ed. New York: Free Press, 1994.

Williamson, Murray. *War, Strategy and Military Effectiveness.* New York: Cambridge University Press, 2011.

Anni Baker
Associate Professor, Department of History
Wheaton College, Norton, Massachusetts

WEBSTER, DANIEL
1782–1852

Daniel Webster served as US secretary of state from March 1841 to May 1843 and from July 1850 until his death in October 1852. In a career that spanned forty years in public life, Webster made lasting contributions to American diplomacy and is remembered as one of America's great secretaries of state.

CONGRESSIONAL CAREER

Webster entered politics as a Federalist congressman from New Hampshire during the War of 1812. As a member of the House Foreign Affairs Committee, he introduced a series of resolutions in June 1813 calling on President James Madison (1751–1836) to explain when he had become aware that Napoléon Bonaparte (1769–1821) intended to rescind the Berlin and Milan Decrees. Federalists suspected that the administration had remained silent about it since 1811, fearing Britain would repeal its Orders-in-Council, and thus remove a cause for war. The resolutions passed the House, and Webster and John Rhea (1753–1832) of Tennessee were chosen to deliver them to Madison in person. Webster also opposed legislation for war measures, including embargos, military enlistments and conscription, and invasions of Canada.

Webster left Congress after the war, but returned to the House in 1823, this time as a representative from Massachusetts, where he took up Greek independence as a special cause. The Greek rebellion against Ottoman rule in 1821 stirred the public imagination in both Europe and America. The Monroe Doctrine provided the occasion for Webster's support for the Greeks. In his December 1823 annual message, the president had declared that the United States would not interfere in the affairs of Europe, and the Old World should not interfere with the new nations of the Western Hemisphere. Webster delivered a stirring speech on Greece on January 19, 1824, recounting mankind's debt to ancient Greece for the idea of democracy and comparing that ancient ideal with the modern conflict between absolutism and liberty. The speech criticized the absolutism of the Holy Alliance of Russia, Prussia, and Austria, which had asserted that constitutional rights were granted to the people by their rulers and that their governments had the right to intervene in the affairs of other nations. The Greeks, Webster said, were cruelly oppressed by the Turks, but their struggle had been opposed simply because it was a revolution. Webster avowed that, in accordance with Monroe's dictum, the United States would not go to war over Greece, but America could lend its moral support and sympathy. Congress took no action on Webster's proposal, but the speech gained him national attention and the sobriquet the "Demosthenes of America." Thereafter his political career advanced steadily. He was elected to the US Senate in 1827 and became a serious candidate for the presidency, a position that he coveted, in 1836 and 1840.

FIRST TERM AS SECRETARY OF STATE

Webster served as secretary of state in William Henry Harrison's (1773–1841) brief presidency in 1841, and after Harrison's death, in the John Tyler (1790–1862) administration from 1841 to 1843. Of major concern during this period was the critical state of Anglo-American relations. Ever since the 1783 peace treaty ending the American Revolution, the two nations had quarreled about the precise boundary between the United States and Canada. The determination of both countries to exploit timber resources in Maine's Aroostook region was made more volatile due to the presence of combative lumbermen and contentious local officials on both sides, resulting in clashes known as the Aroostook War (1838–1839).

The participation of American filibusters in the 1837–1838 Canadian Rebellions also roiled diplomatic relations. In December 1837, Canadian volunteers crossed the Niagara River near the falls and burned the American steamboat *Caroline*, which had been supporting Canadian rebels, and killed an American. When Alexander McLeod (1796–1871), a Canadian deputy sheriff, was arrested in New York for his alleged role in the affair, Britain demanded his release on the grounds that the raid was an act of state. The conflict over the *Caroline* and McLeod affairs led Britain and the United States to the brink of war, and British antislavery added to the friction. In November 1841, slaves on board the brig *Creole*, bound from Hampton Roads, Virginia, to New Orleans, rose up, killed some crew members, and sailed to the Bahamas, where British authorities freed them. The United States demanded their extradition as mutineers, but Britain refused, holding that they became free once they came into British jurisdiction.

In 1842, the United States accepted a British proposal for comprehensive negotiations in Washington.

Over a period of months, Webster and British representative Lord Ashburton (Alexander Baring, 1774–1848) compromised on the *Caroline* and McLeod affairs, as well as the *Creole*, and agreed upon the Canadian-American boundary from Maine to the Great Lakes. The resulting Webster-Ashburton Treaty had severe critics on both sides of the Atlantic but resolved nearly all outstanding conflicts between the countries.

OPPOSITION TO THE ANNEXATION OF TEXAS AND THE WAR WITH MEXICO

Conclusion of the treaty meant the end of Webster's tenure in the Tyler administration. When the president proposed the annexation of Texas to Webster as a new goal, the Massachusetts statesman felt he had to resign, which he did on May 8, 1843. Returning to the Senate in 1845, Webster opposed the annexation of Texas as a slave state by joint resolution of Congress, which he considered unconstitutional. He supported James Polk's (1795–1849) Oregon boundary treaty as a peaceful settlement, but disapproved of the War with Mexico (1846–1848) as unwarranted aggression that would aggravate the slavery question in the United States. As many had predicted, territorial acquisitions from Mexico led to a political crisis that threatened the Union. Webster supported the Compromise of 1850, and when President Zachary Taylor (1784–1850) died in July, Millard Fillmore (1800–1874) appointed Webster secretary of state, making him the only person to serve in that capacity for three different presidents.

SECOND TERM AS SECRETARY OF STATE

This time, Webster was less statesmanlike. When the Austrian chargé to the United States, Johann Georg Hülsemann (d. 1864), criticized the United States for expressions of support toward the Hungarian Revolution, Webster replied that compared to the United States, the "possessions of the House of Hapsburg, are but as a patch on the earth's surface," and he praised Hungarian nationalist Lajos Kossuth (1802–1894) "for his part in the great struggle for Hungarian national independence" (Shewmaker 1987, Vol. 2, 53, 97). Webster later said that he wished to encourage national feeling in the midst of the 1850 political crisis, but his actions severely damaged relations with Austria and sullied the principle of nonintervention in European affairs. Webster also was less than adept in defending US fishing rights off the coast of Canada, granted by Britain decades earlier, and he adopted an unjustifiably bellicose tone in a dispute with Peru over American claims to guano deposits in the Lobos Islands off South America.

Despite such missteps, Webster had many accomplishments in the realm of foreign affairs. In addition to the Webster-Ashburton Treaty, he was responsible for the Tyler Doctrine, which supported the territorial integrity of the Hawaiian Kingdom against European encroachment, and he initiated American contact with China in 1844. As Millard Fillmore's secretary of state, he played an important role in putting in motion Commodore Matthew Perry's (1794–1858) mission to Japan (1852–1853).

Webster's health was in serious decline by 1852. On October 24, 1852, still serving as secretary of state, he died in Marshfield, Massachusetts.

SEE ALSO *Britain; Greek Revolution; Kossuth, Louis; Monroe Doctrine (1823)*

BIBLIOGRAPHY

Jones, Howard. *To the Webster-Ashburton Treaty: A Study in Anglo-American Relations, 1783–1843*. Chapel Hill: University of North Carolina Press, 1977.

Merk, Frederick, with Lois Bannister Merk. *Fruits of Propaganda in the Tyler Administration*. Cambridge, MA: Harvard University Press, 1971.

Shewmaker, Kenneth E. "Daniel Webster and the Politics of Foreign Policy, 1850–1852." *Journal of American History* 63, 2 (1976): 303–315.

Shewmaker, Kenneth E., et al. *The Papers of Daniel Webster: Diplomatic Papers*, Vol. 1: *1841–1843*; Vol. 2: *1850–1852*. Hanover, NH: University Press of New England, 1983, 1987.

Stevens, Kenneth R. *Border Diplomacy: The Caroline and McLeod Affairs in Anglo-American-Canadian Relations, 1837–1842*. Tuscaloosa: University of Alabama Press, 1989.

Kenneth Stevens
Professor of History
Texas Christian University

WEBSTER-ASHBURTON TREATY (1842)

SEE *Manifest Destiny.*

WELLS-BARNETT, IDA B.
1862–1931

On April 5, 1893, Ida Bell Wells-Barnett sailed for England, her first ocean voyage, to begin a speaking tour in London and Scotland in support of her antilynching campaign. This opportunity marked a transition for Wells, not only as a journalist and social activist but generally as a rhetor in her becoming a writer and speaker of considerable consequence in reform discourses—

nationally and internationally. With the publication in Memphis of her editorial in the *Free Speech* (May 21, 1892) and her subsequent speaking engagements in the Northeast about her imposed exile from Memphis, Wells had evolved from being an up-and-coming owner and editor of a relatively small paper in the South, especially among African American readers and journalists, to an outspoken nationally recognized leader and courageous crusader.

RISE TO GLOBAL PROMINENCE

In 1893, however, the story was about to change exponentially with the combination of an international speaking tour, a strategic move to reach international visitors attending the Chicago World's Fair, and a second international tour in the following year. With this trifecta, Wells transitioned from a recognizable but relatively modest presence in civil rights activism in the United States to a much larger space in the narrative of human rights activism in global sociopolitical reform. Her enhanced presence as a crusading journalist on this larger stage catapulted the complexities of lynching into the global public sphere. The strategic advantage for Wells was that, while lynching gained more resonance in international discourses, such attention brought to her campaign a brighter spotlight for making lynching an inescapable issue on the US geopolitical radar as well.

WELLS'S FIRST BRITISH LECTURE TOUR

Wells was presented the opportunity for an international lecture tour by Catherine Impey (1847–1923), a British Quaker, anti-imperialist, and dedicated member of the British social reform community. Impey was also the writer, publisher, and editor of the journal *Anti-Caste*, published from 1888 to 1895. The journal's mission was to be a platform against racist oppression in the United States and imperialist oppression across the British Empire. It had a solid distribution within the Quaker community and a much larger monthly circulation through freely distributed copies among British and American reform communities. In 1893, while visiting relatives and friends in Philadelphia and gathering information about conditions in the United States, Impey heard a lecture delivered by Wells and then called on her at the home of Wells's host, abolitionist leader and political activist William Still (1821–1902). Impey was impressed. Wells continued to speak in cities in the northeastern United States, but by the time she reached Washington DC, where she was hosted by Frederick Douglass (c. 1817/8–1895), she received and accepted an invitation from Impey to lecture in Britain. Wells considered this opportunity to be just the invigoration that her campaign needed. As she stated, "It seemed like an open door in a stone wall" (Wells-Barnett 1970, 86).

From April through May 1893, Wells was invited to speak in several venues connected with the British reform community. She was well received by the audiences and by the British press, which was in stark contrast to the lack of engagement by the white press in the United States. Unfortunately, the tour was disrupted by a rift between Impey and her Scottish counterpart, Isabella Fyvie Mayo (1843–1914), a poet, novelist, fellow anti-imperialist, and the person who was arranging many of the speaking venues. With the split, Wells faced a decline in speaking engagements and decided not to place herself in the middle of this intense internal situation. She ended her tour and returned to the United States.

THE CHICAGO WORLD'S FAIR CAMPAIGN

At that point, Wells moved from New York, where she had been living since her exile from Memphis, to Chicago, the site of the 1893 World's Columbian Exposition, where she had already joined forces with her future husband, Ferdinand L. Barnett (1852–1936), a lawyer and journalist; Frederick Douglass, who was serving during the exposition as the representative for the nation of Haiti; I. Garland Penn (1867–1930), author and journalist; and Albion W. Tourgée (1838–1905), lawyer, author, judge, and social reformer. This group had determined that with an international spotlight on Chicago, it was to the great advantage of their cause to produce a publication, *Why the Colored American Is Not in the World's Columbian Exposition*, which Wells would edit. In anticipation of a huge number of international visitors to the exposition, they managed to produce the volume with the inclusion of a preface in English, French, and German (rather than their preferred strategy of fully rendered versions in each of the three languages). Wells and Douglass raised the funds to distribute ten thousand copies from the Haitian Pavilion during the final days of the exposition. Wells reported in her autobiography that the Haitian building, as presided over by Douglass, was a popular venue for international visitors and that the distribution of the volume was very successful, with responses coming to her subsequently from Germany, France, Russia, India, and other distant places (Wells-Barnett 1970, 115–117).

WELLS'S SECOND BRITISH LECTURE TOUR

With the basic success of these first two events, Wells accepted an invitation to return to Britain from the Society for the Recognition of the Universal Brotherhood of Man (SRUBM), one of two organizations that had been founded during Wells's first lecture tour. SRUBM had been organized by Impey and Mayo, whose disagreements had not ceased in the intervening months since Wells's first tour. These tensions continued to be a source of concern for Wells, but the rift did not dampen her desire to journey forth a second time. The second organization was the British Anti-Lynching Committee. The leadership of this group was made up of members of the British Parliament, prominent clergy, and top journalists, including Peter William Clayden (1827–1902), editor of the London *Daily News*, who served as Wells's London host. Notably, the British Anti-Lynching Committee sparked the formation of a few similar organizations in the northern United States—for example, the Massachusetts Anti-Lynching League. In other words, within the British reform community, Wells's first lecture tour had created significant waves of activism among the diversely defined anti-imperial, antilynching, and human rights–focused causes that were in motion in Great Britain. In contrast, the rebound effect in the United States from the first tour generated only modest attention, with very little to none coming from the white press, and it was only with the strategic advantages of the second tour that arguments began to take better hold.

Wells left for her second British tour in March 1894. Despite a rough start with the logistics of her arrangements, she ultimately spent six months there, instead of the three that she had planned, and delivered more than one hundred speeches in various settings, including churches, clubs, civic gatherings, and board rooms. As with the first tour, she was well received by both audiences and the British press, as evidenced by the fifteen hundred people who attended her first presentation in Liverpool at Pembroke Chapel at the invitation of Charles Frederic Aked (1864–1926), a renowned Baptist minister. This pace for audience attendance was sustained throughout her tour, as were the levels of attention to her message in the British press.

In contrast to the consistently positive aspects of the tour, there were also challenges related primarily to the controversy that continued to rise between Wells and another American, Women's Temperance Movement leader Frances Willard (1839–1898), over the lack of attention to lynching by the religious community in the United States. Occasionally, Wells was pressured to respond to difficult questions about their differences in perspective. As was her habit, when asked to respond, Wells did not mince words, and the rising feud generated a backlash among Willard's allies.

Despite this lingering controversy, Wells had a value added in terms of impact in the United States in the second tour that she did not have in the first. She had been hired as a correspondent during her tour by the Chicago *Daily Inter-Ocean* (published from 1872 to 1914). The *Inter-Ocean* was one of the few white-owned newspapers in the United States that took the position that the nation needed to be held accountable for the outrages that were happening across the South and the lack of active opposition to these outrages in the North. Throughout the tour, Wells sent back to the *Inter-Ocean* dispatches about her activities under the byline "Ida B. Wells Abroad."

With this three-part combination, Wells was able to garner the public attention among the white community that she had desired since leaving Memphis. The press (and others) were no longer "dumb," but the backlash against Wells was substantial, including attacks against her personal integrity, the integrity of African American women in general, and what Wells had presented as the "truth" of lynching. Hearing about the vitriolic nature of the attacks through their transatlantic social networks, African American clubwomen rose quickly to affirm their knowledge of lynching horrors, with Florida Ruffin Ridley (1861–1943) from the Woman's Era Club in Boston taking the lead in sending an open letter to London during Wells's tour that was broadly distributed. Wells's success on the tour continued.

LASTING IMPACT

Upon returning to Chicago, Wells continued to be active with the African American women's clubs and their agenda for sociopolitical activism and national organization. Until the end of her life, she continued documenting the horrors of lynching as acts of lawlessness and terrorism, especially since the United States did not succeed in passing antilynching legislation, either during Wells's era or now. In 1895, with her marriage to Barnett, her circles of engagement became more local in nature and impact. From a contemporary perspective, however, the importance of her international campaign was critical. Wells succeeded in: (1) establishing herself as a national and international public figure; (2) focusing the British reform community on the failures of the United States to live up to its own principles, as well as the principles of human rights; and most of all (3) placing lynching far more boldly and specifically on the American public agenda, which enabled the shift in public sentiment that, at the end of the day, was indeed Wells's driving passion as a crusader for justice.

SEE ALSO *Global South; Lynching; Pan-Africanism; Paris Peace Conference (1919); World War I*

BIBLIOGRAPHY

Bressey, Caroline. *Empire, Race, and the Politics of Anti-Caste.* New York: Bloomsbury Academic, 2013.

Duster, Michelle, ed. *Ida from Abroad: The Timeless Writings of Ida B Wells from England in 1894.* Chicago: Benjamin Williams, 2010.

Giddings, Paula J. *Ida: A Sword among Lions: Ida B. Wells and the Campaign against Lynching.* New York: Amistad, 2008.

McMurry, Linda O. *To Keep the Waters Troubled: The Life of Ida B. Wells.* New York: Oxford University Press, 1998.

McPherson, James M. *The Abolitionist Legacy: From Reconstruction to the NAACP.* Princeton, NJ: Princeton University Press, 1975.

Royster, Jacqueline Jones, ed. *Southern Horrors and Other Writings: The Anti-Lynching Campaign of Ida B. Wells, 1892–1900.* Boston: Bedford, 1997.

Schechter, Patricia A. *Ida B. Wells-Barnett and American Reform, 1880–1930.* Chapel Hill: University of North Carolina Press, 2001.

Silkey, Sarah L. *Black Woman Reformer: Ida B. Wells, Lynching, and Transatlantic Activism.* Athens: University of Georgia Press, 2015.

Wells-Barnett, Ida B. *Crusade for Justice: The Autobiography of Ida B. Wells.* Edited by Alfreda M. Duster. Chicago: University of Chicago Press, 1970.

Wells-Barnett, Ida B. *The Light of Truth: Writings of an Anti-Lynching Crusader.* Edited by Mia Bay. New York: Penguin, 2014.

Jacqueline Jones Royster
Dean, Ivan Allen College of Liberal Arts
Georgia Institute of Technology

WEST, BENJAMIN
1738–1820

Benjamin West was the first American artist to achieve an international reputation. His seminal painting *The Death of General Wolfe* (1770, National Gallery of Canada, Ottawa) established a new genre of painting known as contemporary history painting and paved his path to becoming one of the most important history painters during the eighteenth century in the English-speaking world. The contemporary history paintings of West and fellow American John Singleton Copley (1738–1815) found success and popularity by tapping into pressing topical issues in the Atlantic world.

STUDIES ABROAD

Born in Pennsylvania in 1738, West began his career modestly as a colonial portraitist. In 1760, he left his home country to broaden his horizons and develop his career as a history painter in the Old World, spending three years in Italy. He was the first American artist to take a Grand Tour of Europe. History painting, with subjects drawn from classical history, the Bible, literature, and modern history, was considered the most elite category of painting, but it did not have an audience in the colonies. While in Italy, West spent his time assiduously studying antique and old master examples, elevating his own artistic skills.

The Artist and His Family, *by Benjamin West. Oil on canvas, c. 1772, Yale Center for British Art, New Haven, CT. West (standing), who began his career rather modestly as a colonial portraitist, traveled to Europe to broaden his horizons. He established a new genre known as contemporary history painting, sealing his path to becoming one of the most important history painters of the English-speaking world in the eighteenth century.* **PAINTING/ALAMY**

En route home, West stopped in London, where he was lured to remain by his American patrons and British artist Sir Joshua Reynolds (1723–1792), who saw great potential in the young history painter. With no major schools or collections in the North American colonies, London, as the cultural center of the English-speaking world, was *the* major destination for artists. West was enticed by the capital city and its vibrant art scene. He stayed and never returned to America. This transatlantic journey from the colonies to Italy to England had a profound effect on his career.

WEST AND HIS STUDENTS

When West arrived in London in 1763, his reputation for being an exceptional colonial American artist preceded him. Shortly after his arrival, the press bestowed the moniker "American Raphael," which spoke to his colonial roots and his history paintings, which were already identified as being entrenched in the old master traditions he learned in Italy. West established himself in London, setting up a studio and sending for his fiancé, Elizabeth Shewell, back in Pennsylvania. Less than two years after his arrival, he began welcoming to his studio American students who traveled to London in hopes of elevating their own careers. *The American School* (1765, Metropolitan Museum of Art) by Matthew Pratt (1734–1805) depicts a group of colonial artists in West's London studio during the early years. West trained and mentored dozens of students who would go on to become the founding artists in American art of the late eighteenth and early nineteenth centuries, including Charles Willson Peale (1741–1827), Gilbert Stuart (1755–1828), and John Trumbull (1756–1843). For his role as a generous teacher and advocate, West is often referred to as the "Father of American Art."

ARTISTIC INNOVATIONS

In his early history paintings, such as *Agrippina Landing at Brundisium with the Ashes of Germanicus* (1768, The Yale University Art Gallery) and *The Departure of Regulus* (1769, Royal Collection), West astutely advertised his artistic lineage and debt to the old masters to gain the confidence of his new London audience. Once established as a force in the London art world, West began painting images of contemporary events in the Atlantic world and highlighting, in particular, his North American background and knowledge, which differentiated him from his native-born contemporaries. In *The Death of General Wolfe*, West depicted a Native American, a reference to their importance in the North American campaigns. West used Native American artifacts from his personal collection as props in the picture, such as the pouch over the ranger's shoulder, which added a sense of place and authenticity to the scene. He also looked to paintings and prints by old masters, such as Guido Reni (1575–1642) and Anthony Van Dyck (1599–1641), to imbue the pose of the fallen hero with references to Christ in scenes of the deposition.

These contemporary and old master references and juxtapositions made West an innovator in the field of history painting during the period. With great business acumen, West also capitalized on the print market by partnering with engravers and publishers to produce prints of his history paintings. West's partnership with engraver William Woollett (1735–1785) and publisher John Boydell (1720–1804) in 1776 to produce a print after *The Death of General Wolfe* elicited the most financially successful and famous engraving of the period. West's reputation in Britain, America, and the Continent was in large part due to the success and wide dissemination of prints after his most famous paintings.

OFFICIAL POSITIONS AND POLITICAL NEUTRALITY

Unlike many of his contemporaries, West enjoyed royal patronage for much of his career, and was made official history painter to the king in 1772. In 1779, King George III (1738–1820) commissioned West to paint the so-called Chapel of Revealed Religion at Windsor Castle, one of the most ambitious history painting projects in the eighteenth century. Though never installed, it was considered by West to be the greatest work of his career, consuming him for over twenty years.

Following the death of Reynolds in 1792, West was elected as the second president of the Royal Academy. The roles of Royal Academy president and history painter

to the king were exceptionally sought after, and West's achievement was all the more remarkable considering he was American and held these posts during a period marked by British and American conflict. At the end of the century, West's position with the king became unsteady due to the king's failing health and questions about West's own democratic sympathies, and the patronage halted around 1801. West also faced challenges at the Royal Academy, largely brought on by John Singleton Copley, which caused West to temporarily step down as president in 1805.

Throughout his career in London, West generally maintained a neutral stance politically and shied away from painting images of the American Revolution. The only history painting relating to the subject that he painted, but did not complete, was *American Commissioners of the Preliminary Peace Negotiations with Great Britain* (1783, Winterthur Museum). West maintained close ties with the American community abroad, entertaining fellow expatriates, including artists and diplomats, such as Benjamin Franklin (1706–1790) and John Adams (1735–1826). West's large home at 14 Newman Street in Marylebone became a destination for many Americans living in or visiting the metropolis. West and his wife entertained Americans frequently, and Mrs. West's menus often included American cuisine. The house was filled with West's great history paintings, as well as his extensive art collection. Fourteen Newman Street became a primary exhibition space for his paintings, including his late works *Death on the Pale Horse* (1817, Pennsylvania Academy of Fine Arts) and *The Death of Lord Nelson* (1806, Walker Art Gallery, Liverpool), in addition to the annual exhibitions at the Royal Academy until his death in 1820.

Benjamin West's more than sixty-year career was marked by great achievements as well as some disastrous failures, but his position as one of the greatest history painters of his age on either side of the Atlantic has endured.

SEE ALSO *American Revolution; Copley, John Singleton; Expatriate Artists; Franklin, Benjamin; Grand Tour; Loyalists*

BIBLIOGRAPHY

Abrams, Ann Uhry. *The Valiant Hero: Benjamin West and Grand-Style History Painting.* Washington, DC: Smithsonian Institution Press, 1985.

Alberts, Robert. *Benjamin West: A Biography.* Boston: Houghton Mifflin, 1978.

Dillenberger, John. *Benjamin West: The Context of His Life's Work.* San Antonio, TX: Trinity University Press, 1977.

Evans, Dorinda. *Benjamin West and His American Students.* Washington, DC: National Portrait Gallery and Smithsonian Institution Press, 1980.

Galt, John. *The Life, Studies, and Works of Benjamin West, Esq., President of the Royal Academy of London, Composed from Materials Furnished by Himself.* 2 vols. London: Cadell and Davies, 1820.

King, Jonathan C. H. "Woodland Artifacts from the Studio of Benjamin West, 1738–1820." *American Indian Art Magazine* 17, 1 (1991): 34–47.

Kraemer, Ruth. *Drawings by Benjamin West and His Son, Raphael Lamar West.* Boston: Godine; New York: Pierpont Morgan Library, 1975.

Marks, Arthur. "Benjamin West and the American Revolution." *American Art Journal* 6, 4 (1974): 15–35.

Meyer, Jerry. "Benjamin West's Chapel of Revealed Religion: A Study of Eighteenth-Century Protestant Religious Art." *Art Bulletin* 57, 2 (1975): 247–265.

Mitchell, Charles. "Benjamin West's *Death of General Wolfe* and the Popular History Piece." *Journal of the Warburg and Courtauld Institutes* 7 (1944): 20–33.

Monks, Sarah. "The Wolfe Man: Benjamin West's Anglo-American Accent." *Art History* 34, 4 (2011): 653–673.

Montagna, Dennis. "Benjamin West's *The Death of General Wolfe*: A Nationalist Narrative." *American Art Journal* 13, 3 (1981): 72–88.

Muller, Kevin. "Pelts and Power, Mohawks and Myth: Benjamin West's Portrait of Guy Johnson." *Winterthur Portfolio* 40, 1 (2005): 47–76.

Neff, Emily, and Kaylin Weber. *American Adversaries: Benjamin West and John Singleton Copley in a Transatlantic World.* Houston, TX: Museum of Fine Arts, Houston; New Haven, CT: Yale University Press, 2013.

Pressly, Nancy. *Revealed Religion: Benjamin West's Commissions for Windsor Castle and Fonthill Abbey.* San Antonio, TX: San Antonio Museum of Art, 1983.

Prown, Jules David. "Benjamin West and the Use of Antiquity." *American Art* 10, 2 (1996): 29–49.

Rather, Susan. "Benjamin West, John Galt, and the Biography of 1816." *Art Bulletin* 86, 2 (2004): 324–345.

Richardson, E. P. "West's Voyage to Italy, 1760, and William Allen." *Pennsylvania Magazine of History and Biography* 102, 1 (1978): 3–26.

Staley, Allen. *Benjamin West: American Painter at the English Court.* Baltimore, MD: Baltimore Museum of Art, 1989.

Trumble, Angus, and Mark Aronson. *Benjamin West and the Venetian Secret.* New Haven, CT: Yale Center for British Art, 2008.

von Erffa, Helmut. "Benjamin West at the Height of his Career." *American Art Journal* 1, 1 (1969): 19–33.

von Erffa, Helmut. "Benjamin West: The Early Years in London." *American Art Journal* 5, 2 (1973): 5–14.

von Erffa, Helmut, and Allen Staley. *The Paintings of Benjamin West.* New Haven, CT: Yale University Press, 1986.

Wind, Edgar. "The Revolution of History Painting." *Journal of the Warburg and Courtauld Institutes* 2, 2 (1938): 116–127.

Kaylin Haverstock Weber
Assistant Curator, American Painting and Sculpture
The Museum of Fine Arts, Houston

WESTERN HEMISPHERE INSTITUTE FOR SECURITY COOPERATION

SEE *US Army School of the Americas (Western Hemisphere Institute for Security Cooperation).*

"THE WHITE MAN'S BURDEN" (RUDYARD KIPLING, 1899)

A poem written by Rudyard Kipling (1865–1935), "The White Man's Burden" has typically been read as a call to empire and an important statement of Anglo-American affinity. It was printed in the United States in *McClure's* magazine in February 1899, while the United States debated its policy toward the Philippines following the Spanish American War. With the signing of the Treaty of Paris, Spain had ceded the Philippines and other American and Pacific colonial possessions to the United States, but Americans were divided about the prospect of administering them. Kipling, who sent an advance copy of the poem to Theodore Roosevelt (1858–1919), intended the poem as advice and encouragement for the United State to join European imperial powers in the project of colonial administration.

The poem depicts this project as an honorable, altruistic endeavor, but one that is likely to have great costs and be little appreciated by the colonized. Despite these hardships, the poem suggests that this burden must be borne for the United States to mature, leaving behind its national "childhood" and joining the European powers as an equal. The final stanza advises that the United States be no longer satisfied with "easy, ungrudged praise" from these European peers, who are now searching the "manhood" of the United States through the test of empire building.

The poem was extensively reprinted around the country through *McClure's* newspaper syndicate. According to one estimate, it appeared in at least six hundred thousand copies of newspapers and magazines and reached more than one million American readers. Reception in the United States was highly varied; while imperialists, including Roosevelt, praised the poem's sentiment, anti-imperialists saw the catchy rhyme and meter of the ubiquitous poem as ripe for satire and parody. For example, one 1899 parody mimicked the poem's emphatic rhyme and meter while pointing out its self-serving rationale for exerting power: "Take up the sword and rifle, / Still keep your conscience whole— / So soon is found an unction / To sooth a guilty soul" (Shadwell 1899, 714). Kipling's poem was also printed in the February 4, 1899 issue of the London *Times* and was met favorably by the British press. The *Spectator*, the *Economist*, and the *Daily Mail* praised the poem and expanded on its implication that Great Britain should serve as a mentor to its former colony, a relationship that would manage this new potential rival for world power.

Despite the poem's immense popularity, its actual influence on US foreign policy is difficult to gauge. While it did appear in a few syndicate newspapers (including the *New York Sun*) on February 5, the day before the Senate decided by a margin of one vote to ratify the Treaty of Paris, it is doubtful that the poem swayed the decision. Indeed, South Carolina senator "Pitchfork" Ben Tillman (1847–1918) read passages from the poem aloud on the Senate floor during the debate to support his argument that US imperialism would be damaging to the United States, highlighting all the difficulties and hardships that the poem details. For Tillman, one of the southern Democrats who objected to US empire on the grounds that administering the Philippines would compound the nation's race problem, the poem was a warning, not an encouragement. Thus if Tillman's arguments persuaded any senators, the poem may have had an effect opposite to what Kipling intended.

Tillman's seeming misreading of the poem exemplifies a broader trend in American responses to the poem that questioned its racial meaning in the American context. If Kipling's "white man" stood for the racially Euro-American or Anglo Saxon imperialist, the poem's equation of American foreign policy with whiteness raised problems for readers who recognized the distinctive multiracial nature of the United States. Unlike most of the European powers, the US metropole was racially heterogeneous, and unlike most polyglot settler nations, the United States was becoming an imperial power. Kipling's poem became an occasion to comment on this particularity through parodies that pointed out the hypocrisy of "helping" Filipinos while African Americans suffered disenfranchisement and terror in the Jim Crow South, or through pointing out the irony of African American soldiers carrying the "white man's burden" in the Philippines.

Beyond the immediate historical context of the debate about the Philippines, Kipling's title has become a synonym for nineteenth-century imperialism and for later forms of Western political interventionism, usually carrying a negative connotation and used by those who criticize such policies. The phrase can now broadly signify US and British expansion or global influence as a set of policy choices, a popular mood, or a political ideology.

SEE ALSO *Colonialism; Race; Spanish-American War*

BIBLIOGRAPHY

Foster, John Bellamy, Harry Magdoff, and Robert W. McChesney. "Kipling, 'The White Man's Burden,' and U.S. Imperialism." In *Pox Americana: Exposing the American Empire*, edited by John Bellamy Foster and Robert W. McChesney, 12–21. New York: Monthly Review Press, 2004.

Harris, Susan K. "Kipling's 'White Man's Burden' and the British Newspaper Context." *Comparative American Literature* 5, 3 (2007): 243–263.

Murphy, Gretchen. *Shadowing the White Man's Burden: US Imperialism and the Problem of the Color Line.* New York: New York University Press, 2010.

Shadwell, Bertrand. "The Gospel of Force." In *Republic or Empire: The Philippine Question*, edited by William Jennings Bryan, 713–715. Chicago: Independence Press, 1899.

Gretchen Murphy
University of Texas–Austin

WHITENESS

The analytical category of "whiteness" is useful for probing numerous facets of American culture and politics as they intersect with transnational and global concerns, from historical and contemporary interactions among different communities within the United States, to political engagement between the United States and other nations. As an ideologically laden category that has defined the limits of citizenship and national belonging, attention to ideas about and performances of whiteness helps to explain the complicated ways in which American subjectivity is inextricably tied to racial formation. Important concepts within American nationalistic discourse—including democracy, modernity, and freedom—have developed in tandem with ideas about whiteness and racial difference. Seemingly straightforward, the term nonetheless has multifarious connotations, its definition further complicated by the way its meaning has changed over time. The historical development of American culture and society has led to shifts in the meaning of whiteness from the founding of the United States through the present day. Since the beginning of the twenty-first century, ideas about whiteness have continued to change, demonstrating its capacity to conform to and redefine new ideas about identity, belonging, and difference at both the local and global levels.

TERMINOLOGY AND DEFINITIONS

Whiteness, at its surface, seems to be a term that describes a particular skin tone, racial identity, or ethnicity. In common usage and on official documents and forms seeking demographic information, the term *white* is used as a category to denote one's light skin tone, "Caucasian" race or ethnicity, or European heritage. The US Census Bureau, for example, in accordance with 1997 Office of Management and Budget regulations, defines someone who is "white" as "having origins in any of the original peoples of Europe, the Middle East, or North Africa." Thus, the term seems to primarily symbolize one's physical appearance, biological characteristics, or ancestry.

However, scholars engaged in the study of race and whiteness argue that there is no biological basis for whiteness or any other racial category. Rather than a neutral descriptor referring to a particular group of people, whiteness is instead an unstable conceptual container that bears numerous implications regarding the physical and nonphysical characteristics of individuals and groups. As with other racial terms, *whiteness* links seemingly physical, tangible attributes, such as phenotype, biology, and heritage, to a variety of intangible features, including intelligence, psychology, cultural practices, propensity to work, and spiritual capacity. Like the broader concept of "race," whiteness is mutable, multifaceted, constructed, and enacted; it is at once an ideology, a discourse, and a performance. Subjects shape notions of whiteness in different spheres—in public and in private, during day-to-day interactions, through the creation of cultural artifacts, and via official government policy.

Significantly, whiteness is a relative term, one that developed in a way that has served to sort individuals into different groups with unequal access to resources and power. More so than other racial categories, whiteness is tied to supremacy; the category of whiteness has historically afforded privilege to those who claim it. As with other racial categories, the fact that whiteness is a social construct does not mean that it is insignificant for understanding culture, history, and politics. Likewise, although whiteness itself is technically immaterial, effects of the ideology of whiteness are quite tangible as they have played out in political, social, and cultural spheres. Whiteness is thus also a form of capital, power, and domination. Actors may both draw on or perform whiteness in order to access resources and deny it—and the privileges it affords—to others (Lipsitz 1998).

THE CHANGING MEANING OF WHITENESS IN AMERICAN HISTORY

The concept of "whiteness" is salient for understanding a number of points in the history of the United States, from European exploration and settlement in the Americas to the birth and expansion of the country, and from the increase of immigration in the nineteenth century to the rise of the United States as a global power in the twentieth century. During each of these eras, the meaning of whiteness developed upon and beyond previous understandings. As a complex and contentious category, the origin of the concept of whiteness is itself subject to discussion; indeed, scholars have debated the provenance of the broader concept of "race." Some suggest that the concept of race only arose in the nineteenth century, with

the advent of scientific or biological racism. Throughout the nineteenth century, white European and American anthropologists constructed a hierarchy of races and world cultures, drawing on accepted scientific theories of the day (Horsman 1991). Researchers rendered people of European descent as ideal human specimens, racially neutral and representing the highest stage of physical development. Furthermore, they tied the idea of whiteness as a supposedly pure or ideal biological form, heritage, or race to theories of cultural development. Scientists theorized that all human groups progressed along a scale of cultural evolution; they presented Euro-American culture as superior to that of other world cultures. Other branches of human sciences, from linguistics to the study of art, also drew on these theories of cultural development. In these ways, scholars constructed hierarchical notions of "white" language, culture, art, and biology and presented each as exemplary.

Some scholars have cautioned against using the more recent terms *race* and *whiteness* to describe interactions among different communities in earlier eras. Historical particularities are certainly important for understanding the development of racial terms; however, despite the more recent development of the term *race*, scholars indicate that a longer history of notions about essential differences formed a foundation for the development of a modern racial imaginary in Europe and the Americas. Before the modern era, notions of religious difference did play a role in notions of essential difference. For example, scholars have identified discourse on essential, inherited differences by early writers in the ancient Mediterranean world who articulated differences between Greeks and Persians and between Christians and Jews. From this early era, thinkers have identified physical characteristics and ancestry as markers of difference (Eliav-Feldon, Isaac, and Ziegler 2009).

Furthermore, interactions between empires and nations in and beyond Europe, including the periods of war between competing Christian and Muslim groups, shaped Europeans' interactions in the Americas. The motivations behind the Crusades, the *Reconquista*, and the Inquisition in part drew on ideas about essential differences. Theories about the purity of blood, which Spanish inquisitors put to test in the courts of the Inquisition, pointed to notions of essential, inherited difference that separated Christians, Muslims, Jews, and, when the Inquisition spread to the Americas, Indigenous Americans (Silverblatt 2004). These theories of difference influenced European interactions with Indigenous and African communities in the Americas. Thus, earlier ideas about essential differences—religious, cultural, and social—served as an important backdrop for the development of the notion of whiteness in the Americas and remerged at different points in American history (Kidd 2006; Boyarin

2009). Ideas about racial difference in the Americas emerged during historical moments marked by Europeans' genocide of Indigenous populations in the Americas and by the racialized system of European enslavement and subjugation of African people. Particular ideas about whiteness thus developed in the Americas, in part, due to a specific social and economic system legitimated by social and, eventually, scientific ideologies.

THE DEVELOPMENT OF WHITENESS STUDIES

Even as anthropologists sought to uphold whiteness in the nineteenth century, others noted and challenged assumptions about white biological and cultural supremacy. The development of the field of critical whiteness studies occurred over successive periods, as individuals occupying a variety of positions relative to whiteness commented on its nature and questioned its naturalness. African American and Native American thinkers—including abolitionist David Walker (1796–1830), scholar W. E. B. Du Bois (1868–1963), and Indigenous activists Sarah Winnemucca (1844–1891) and Gertrude Bonnin (1876–1938)—engaged in critiques of whiteness during periods in which mainstream American growth, progress, and optimism privileged white citizens at the same time that racist laws and social practices targeted members of other communities. Throughout the twentieth century, writers such as James Baldwin (1924–1987) and Frantz Fanon (1925–1961) further developed this line of inquiry, offering critiques of a mainstream white citizenry and European and American imperialism that rendered nonwhite individuals as incapable of self-rule.

In the 1990s, the academic field of whiteness studies emerged within and alongside the broader fields of American and ethnic studies. Scholars have since explored the intersection of white racial politics with numerous other facets of identity, including gender, sexuality, ability, and class. David Roediger's *Wages of Whiteness* (1991) discussed the development of a white working class that positioned itself in opposition to freed African American slaves, launching a line of inquiry into the relationship between race and class. Scholars of gender and race, including Ruth Frankenberg (1993) and Gail Bederman (1995), have articulated the significance of gender and sexuality in the development of white identity. These thinkers note the co-constitution of race and other facets of individual subjectivity. Propelled by scholars such as Toni Morrison (1992), a conversation about whiteness and racial categories in literature and the arts has examined how white authors and artists have developed white and nonwhite characters in a way that has furthered distinctions between each.

In addition to discussing whiteness as it relates to other identity-related categories and outlining its cultivation through cultural forms, scholars of whiteness have examined its broader role in the modern American democratic project. The process of modernity, as imagined by philosophers such as Immanuel Kant (1724–1804), G. W. F. Hegel (1770–1831), and Jürgen Habermas (b. 1929), has been a racial project. These thinkers' analyses of concepts such as liberty, freedom, democracy, and equality have privileged whiteness, describing it in opposition to other racial categories (Hesse 2007). The racial category of "whiteness" thus developed in tandem with notions about civilization, citizenship, and modernity. A particular racial economy placed more value on "whiteness" than other racial forms, constructed as its opposites. Whiteness was used to represent something normative, and held European culture, identity, and civilization as the highest level of culture and a model for other forms of culture. The United States has played a particular role in this process of shaping racialized notions of modernity via specific violent racialized projects that played an important role in the country's formation and expansion; these projects have included the extermination of Indigenous populations and the exploitation of African American, Asian, and Hispanic laborers (Limerick 1987). The notions of freedom and democracy, which many Americans see as central tenets of the country's national identity, have excluded these and other individuals and communities. Some argue that the violent targeting of particular nonwhite ethnic groups is not tangential to but a constitutive feature of democracy (Mann 2005).

THE BUREAUCRATIC CONSTRUCTION OF WHITENESS

While literature and the arts have been important arenas for the development of ideas about whiteness, historians have also sought to describe its construction via bureaucratic methods. A primary way in which the US government has shaped official ideas about whiteness has been through immigration regulations. Passed in 1790, the United States' first naturalization act restricted the granting of citizenship to "free white persons," language that was also present in the Constitution. A longer 1795 immigration act included the same wording of "free white persons"; in addition, the act described further characteristics necessary for naturalization. To be granted citizenship, an individual needed to be a "man of a good moral character, attached to the principles of the constitution of the United States, and well disposed to the good order and happiness of the same." These requirements linked physical characteristics with a predilection for order and compliance, suggesting that white individuals were superior democratic citizens. Through the process of lawmaking with regard to immigration, the early federal government defined "white" identity of European immigrants in distinction to African-descended slaves and Native Americans, groups that white citizens saw as threats to the order of the early Republic (Jacobson 1998).

Although early immigration acts included the language of "whiteness," in this era the term did not include all individuals with European heritage, some of whom arrived on US soil as indentured servants. Scholars have noted that the general association of European ancestry with whiteness did not fully develop until the twentieth century. In earlier eras, whiteness was often tied to "Anglo-Saxon" identity, which according to the *Oxford American Dictionary*, specifically describes the "Germanic inhabitants of England from their arrival in the 5th century." More broadly, Anglo-Saxon describes those of English descent; throughout the nineteenth and early twentieth centuries, Protestants of northwestern European descent were primarily considered white. Immigrants from other places, such as Italy, Ireland, and Eastern Europe, and with different religious heritages, such as Catholics and Jews, were set apart from the Anglo-Saxon majority culture (Ignatiev 1995; Guglielmo 2003; Goldstein 2006). National organizations, including the Know-Nothing party and proponents of the racist nativist movement, viewed these communities as threats to society and engaged in organized violence against them. Yet, by the mid-twentieth century, the notion of a broader "Caucasian" race, which included those with European heritage, had emerged, grouping into one category individuals with diverse European ethnic heritage that had previously been considered distinct racial communities (Painter 2010).

The gradual development of a "Caucasian" identity occurred even as other immigration policies sought to restrict workers from other parts of the world. As immigration increased after the Civil War (1861–1865), individual states began to set rules on immigration and naturalization. Many US industries in the North and South welcomed the immigration of laborers from different parts of the world. At this point, the US Supreme Court determined that the federal government would standardize these regulations and requirements. After this decision, the first immigration laws that were passed restricted the immigration of individuals from areas outside of Europe. The Chinese Exclusion Act of 1882 limited the immigration of individuals from Asian countries. The Alien Labor Contract laws of 1885 and 1887 also targeted immigrants from Asia in restricting companies from helping to bring laborers from this region into the United States.

Throughout the early to mid-twentieth century, US immigration laws continued to impose racialized restrictions on immigration. These laws changed in the mid-twentieth century; from the 1950s onward, the United States saw an increase in immigrants from throughout the world. At this point, politicians and the mainstream public began to increasingly express concerns over "illegal aliens," which in popular usage often referred to immigrants from Latin American countries. Scholars have noted that the phrase "illegal alien" is generally racialized and serves to deny personhood to immigrants (Ngai 2004; Molina 2014). Despite the burgeoning discourse about diversity and multiculturalism within the United States, some contemporary visions still tie American identity to whiteness, in ways similar to the earlier nativist ideologies.

THE ROLE OF WHITENESS IN US FOREIGN POLICY

In addition to historical interactions between immigrants from different regions of the world that moved to the United States, the concept of whiteness has played a role in American foreign relations, including imperial expansion and war. In the late nineteenth century, the United States sought to expand its land base and influence, primarily targeting regions where inhabitants were not considered "white." The civilizing mission that propelled US empire, including interventions in Central and South America, was in part cultivated domestically as the federal government sought to reform and assimilate Native Americans and manage other nonwhite groups. Paragovernmental religious groups, such as the American Board of Commissioners for Foreign Missions, also played a role in this worldwide civilizing mission (Reynolds 2009).

The persistence of inequality during the mid-twentieth century raised questions about the commitment of the United States to social progress as the nation justified foreign interventions based on its role as a democratic nation that sought to spread freedom. During World War II (1939–1945), for example, black soldiers were segregated from white soldiers, and were frequently assigned to menial roles. Black soldiers demonstrated their commitment to the American armed services, and the participation of black soldiers abroad during the war years was significant for the development of civil rights in the United States. Even so, racialized systems of inequality persisted when soldiers returned after the war. Those who implemented the GI Bill, meant to help returning soldiers gain education and transition back into civilian life, discriminated against black soldiers, preventing them from fully benefitting from educational, financial, and job-related benefits (Self 2005).

After World War II, one can observe a connection between race relations in the United States and US foreign policy and interventions abroad (Borstelmann 2001).

During the Cold War, two primary opposing developments were at play regarding racial discrimination. On one hand, anticommunist fears cast suspicion on radical movements by people of color who sought to challenge racism. At the same time, global movements for independence brought heightened attention to the persistence of racism and white supremacy in the United States. In Africa, Asia, and the Middle East, citizens sought to overthrow colonial rule, challenge racist state practices, and reclaim sovereignty. Allies and opponents of the United States critiqued race relations within America (Dudziak 2000).

TWENTY-FIRST-CENTURY DEVELOPMENTS

Notions of whiteness have continued to change in the twenty-first century. One of the most recent ways in which the idea of whiteness has developed has been the reassertion of religious difference and racial difference since September 11, 2001. In the wake of the attacks on the World Trade Center, popular discourse has developed in the United States suggesting that Islam is an un-American religion. Despite the ethnic diversity of American Muslims, many non-Muslims assume Muslims are predominantly from the Middle East; according to the US census definition, those with Middle-Eastern heritage are considered "white." Yet popular and media discourse present American Muslims as racially "other" (Jamal and Naber 1998). These contemporary, popular conversations both collapse and obscure difference, further demonstrating the extent to which the category of whiteness is mutable, serves to define difference, upholds social hierarchies, and plays a role in determining the limits of American identity.

SEE ALSO *Anti-imperialism; Black Power Movement; Catholicism; Chinese Exclusion Act (1882); Decolonization; Ethnic Cleansing; Exceptionalism; Genocide; Harlem Renaissance/New Negro Movement; Immigration; Immigration Quotas; Imperialism; Judaism; Lynching; Middle East; Miscegenation; Moorish Science Temple; Nation of Islam; Nativism; Orientalism; Pan-Africanism; Pogrom; Protestantism; Religions; Said, Edward; United Nations; Universal Declaration of Human Rights; Universal Negro Improvement Association (UNIA); "The White Man's Burden" (Rudyard Kipling, 1899)*

BIBLIOGRAPHY

Bederman, Gail. *Manliness and Civilization: A Cultural History of Gender and Race in the United States, 1880–1917.* Chicago: University of Chicago Press, 1995.

Borstelmann, Thomas. *The Cold War and the Color Line: American Race Relations in the Global Arena.* Cambridge, MA: Harvard University Press, 2001.

Boyarin, Jonathan. *The Unconverted Self: Jews, Indians, and the Identity of Christian Europe.* Chicago: University of Chicago Press, 2009.

Dudziak, Mary L. *Cold War Civil Rights: Race and the Image of American Democracy.* Princeton, NJ: Princeton University Press, 2000.

Eliav-Feldon, Miriam, Benjamin Isaac, and Joseph Ziegler, eds. *The Origins of Racism in the West.* Cambridge: Cambridge University Press, 2009.

Fanon, Frantz. *Black Skin, White Masks.* New York: Grove Press, 1952.

Frankenberg, Ruth. *White Women, Race Matters: The Social Construction of Whiteness.* Minneapolis: University of Minnesota Press, 1993.

Goldstein, Eric L. *The Price of Whiteness: Jews, Race, and American Identity.* Princeton, NJ: Princeton University Press, 2006.

Guglielmo, Thomas. *White on Arrival: Italians, Race, Color, and Power in Chicago, 1890–1945.* Oxford: Oxford University Press, 2003.

Hesse, Barnor. "Racialized Modernity: An Analytics of White Mythologies." *Ethnic and Racial Studies* 30, 4 (2007): 643–663.

Horsman, Reginald. *Race and Manifest Destiny: The Origins of American Racial Anglo-Saxonism.* Cambridge, MA: Harvard University Press, 1991.

Ignatiev, Noel. *How the Irish Became White.* London: Routledge, 1995.

Jacobson, Matthew Frye. *Whiteness of a Different Color: European Immigrants and the Alchemy of Race.* Cambridge, MA: Harvard University Press, 1998.

Jacobson, Matthew Frye. *Roots Too: White Ethnic Revival in Post–Civil Rights America.* Cambridge, MA: Harvard University Press, 2006.

Jamal, Amaney, and Nadine Naber, eds. *Race and Arab Americans Before and After 9/11: From Invisible Citizens to Visible Subjects.* Syracuse, NY: Syracuse University Press, 1998.

Kidd, Colin. *The Forging of Races: Race and Scripture in the Protestant Atlantic World, 1600–2000.* Oxford: Oxford University Press, 2006.

Limerick, Patricia Nelson. *The Legacy of Conquest: The Unbroken Past of the American West.* New York: Norton, 1987.

Lipsitz, George. *The Possessive Investment in Whiteness: How White People Benefit from Identity Politics.* Philadelphia: Temple University Press, 1998. Rev. ed., 2006.

Mann, Michael. *The Dark Side of Democracy: Explaining Ethnic Cleansing.* Cambridge, MA: Cambridge University Press, 2005.

Molina, Natalia. *How Race Is Made in America: Immigration, Citizenship, and the Historical Power of Racial Scripts.* Berkeley: University of California Press, 2014.

Morrison, Toni. *Playing in the Dark: Whiteness and the Literary Imagination.* Cambridge, MA: Harvard University Press, 1992.

Ngai, Mai M. *Impossible Subjects: Illegal Aliens and the Making of Modern America.* Princeton, NJ: Princeton University Press, 2004.

Painter, Nell Irvin. *The History of White People.* New York: Norton, 2010.

Reynolds, David. *Empire of Liberty: A New History of the United States.* New York: Basic Books, 2009.

Roediger, David. *The Wages of Whiteness: Race and the Making of the American Working Class.* New York: Verso, 1991. Rev. ed., 2007.

Self, Robert O. *American Babylon: Race and the Struggle for Postwar Oakland.* Princeton, NJ: Princeton University Press, 2003.

Silverblatt, Irene. *Modern Inquisitions: Peru and the Colonial Origins of the Civilized World.* Durham, NC: Duke University Press, 2004.

US Census Bureau. "Race: About." 2013. http://www.census.gov/topics/population/race/about.html

Winant, Howard. *The World Is a Ghetto: Race and Democracy since World War II.* New York: Basic Books, 2001.

Wynn, Neil A. *The African American Experience during World War II.* Lanham, MD: Rowman and Littlefield, 2010.

Sarah Dees
Lecturer
University of Tennessee

WILSON, JOHN LEIGHTON

SEE *Liberia.*

WILSON, WOODROW

1856–1924

Thomas Woodrow Wilson, the twenty-eighth president of the United Sates, was born in Staunton, Virginia, on December 28, 1856. His childhood and early adolescence spanned the Civil War (1861–1865), and this childhood experience of war, along with his intensely religious family, would influence his outlook on the world. Wilson was also heavily influenced by the British political theorist Edmund Burke (1729–1797), an advocate of pragmatic, conservative change. Over time, Wilson's political thought evolved to become what many have viewed as idealistic rather than pragmatic. The term *Wilsonian idealism* is commonly used to describe idealism in foreign policy. Wilson's political influences, however, are complex, and his approach to foreign policy challenges the simple idealist/realist divide.

HOW WILSON'S IDEALISM PLAYED OUT IN US HISTORY

When he became president in 1913, Wilson lacked experience or specific proposals that he could bring to American international relations. But he had a deeply held set of beliefs and a comprehensive philosophy regarding *how* America should relate to other nations, derived from his scholarship, personal history, and religion. He had confidence in what his role should be as leader of the nation in regard to doing good in the world. Wilson had developed a comprehensive *way* of thinking, of balancing contradiction in his mind. He rooted his method of thought in a religious understanding of the world and a certain kind of progressive millennial view dominant in some wings of the American Protestant church. As a result, he could imagine the possibility of a world remade into a peaceful community of democracies.

Wilson was interested in how to create a government that would facilitate the most orderly kind of reform. He fused the need for a representative body with his desire for a representative leader, an idea he developed in his 1879 article "Cabinet Government in the United States." It is in this context that Wilson praised Burke and defended him against critics who accused him of inconsistency for opposing the French Revolution. Burke was, according to Wilson, consistent but holding out for reform, as opposed to the Reign of Terror. Wilson held Burke's view that politics was a matter of barter and compromise. Though not always consistent in his practice, these were Wilson's views upon entering office; World War I (1914–1918) gave him the opportunity to rethink this.

Wilson took his speeches seriously and was prone to quibble over specific words. This frustrated his contemporaries, who saw this as a weakness. The British economist John Maynard Keynes (1883–1946), present in Paris at the postwar Versailles negotiations in 1919, commented on this tendency in Wilson's personality: "his theological or Presbyterian temperament became dangerous.... Although compromises were now necessary he remained a man of principle and the Fourteen Points a contract absolutely binding upon him.... they became a document for gloss and interpretation ... the intellectual apparatus of self deception" (Keynes 1920, 46). Wilson thought of words, be they treaty or scripture, as substance. The Fourteen Points, which Wilson proposed in 1918 as the basis for the postwar peace, can be understood this way.

The result of Wilson's approach to foreign policy has left the term *Wilsonian* in the vocabulary of international politics. The term itself is contested and has great variation of meaning. Nevertheless, at its core it refers to a kind of grand vision presumed to be idealistic regarding the promotion of democracy around the world. Wilson's views themselves were more complex than the term *Wilsonian* would imply. Indeed, Wilsonianism can be argued to have preceded Wilson. Both Wilson and Wilsonianism fell out of favor in the United States between the two world wars. During that time, many Americans came to believe that the idealistic reasons for entering World War I had been a mistake, and they wished to return to traditional isolation.

INTERNATIONAL INFLUENCE

Despite Wilson's profound influence on American domestic policy, including the creation of the modern Federal Reserve and the implementation of the income tax and many other domestic programs that helped create the modern United States, he is best known for his venture into international politics. Because of his theological frame of mind, Wilson tended to personalize his views of international relations. An obscure theological idea called *federal headship*, according to which a representative could stand in for a whole group of people, such as a nation or its government, encouraged Wilson's tendency to personalize nations in the form of their leaders. It also made him feel more responsible when a representative of the US government became involved in another country.

Britain. Wilson was an anglophile who identified deeply with Britain. In his *History of the American People* (1902), he argued that President James Madison (1751–1836) had blundered into an unnecessary war with Britain while trying to avoid a war with France. According to Wilson, Napoléon Bonaparte (1769–1821) was the real danger, but Madison fixated on the legal issues surrounding the conflict over impressment. It can be argued that in trying to avoid Madison's error, Wilson blundered into a war with Germany. In his discussions and writings, he held British prime minister William Gladstone (1809–1898) in high regard, and his admiration for the British leader translated into an admiration for Britain.

France. When it came to France, Wilson was influenced both by Burke's criticism of the French Revolution and his own Protestant prejudice against the Catholic Church. Wilson considered the French to be constantly rushing to extremes. In his essay "Self Government in France" (1879), he expressed a negative view toward governments and organization when they existed as ends in themselves. While Wilson complimented the noble aims of the French Revolution, he argued that its original leaders and the subsequent leaders of France had thwarted those aims, and they would continue to do so until the French could rid themselves of their tendency toward centralized government. Wilson argued that France careened between despotism and disorder because the individuals who made up French society were incapable of moderate constitutional action: "The French mind seems to run at right angles to the law, and parallel with every dangerous extreme" (Wilson 1966–1994, 1:515–539).

In a set of lecture notes, dated September 4, 1879, Wilson argued that the failure of the French government was due to a flaw in the mind of the *individual* French citizen to comprehend that the state is the servant of the individual. "Thus were even the imaginations of the most hopeful reformers enslaved by a pernicious idea of the functions of the state. To recognize in a government only the agent or instrument of the governed would have been to them as impossible as to efface all the past history of France. To them the state *was* the nation." Displaying his Presbyterian prejudice, Wilson argued that a large part of the social problem in France was due to the Catholic Church, which had conditioned the French to place the organization in too high a regard, with too low a regard for the individual. This failure to keep the proper priority between organization and individual produced a society that vacillated between violent revolution and passivity in the face of tyranny (Wilson 1966–1994, 1:515–539).

Germany. Wilson had an early bias against Germany that was more complex than that which he held toward France. He decried "German theology" and accused the Germans of building a powder keg and lighting the match that started World War I. He referred to Otto von Bismarck (1815–1898), the Prussian leader, as a divine hedge around German kaiser Wilhelm II (1859–1941). The kaiser's dismissal of the chancellor removed that hedge, and thus the kaiser, as the representative, implicated the German people in his militarism.

INTERNATIONAL PHILOSOPHY IN WORLD

Wilson believed that because he had been given the power to do good, he had a responsibility to do good. He often approached international situations with this goal in mind, rather than purely addressing what was in the US national interest.

Mexico. Despite his evolving belief in national self-determination, Wilson was prone to intervening in other nations. Among the many interventions designed, as Wilson himself once said, "to teach the South American republics to elect good men," was Mexico (apparently forgetting that Mexico was actually in North America). In 1913, during the Mexican civil war (1910–1920), Wilson ordered the occupation of the port city of Veracruz after a minor incident when an American shore patrol, in search of supplies, was arrested and then immediately released by the Mexican authorities. Veracruz was occupied by US forces from April 21, 1913, until November 23, 1914, when the US withdrew its forces. In the initial fighting nineteen Americans were killed and seventy-two wounded. Mexican forces defending their city lost between 150 and 175, with perhaps as many as 250 wounded. The intervention generated resentment and suspicion between the United States and all the parties involved in the

Mexican civil war. The United States was ultimately unable to influence the outcome of the war in any substantial way.

Neutrality during World War I. Although conspiracy theories abounded after the US entry into World War I in April 1917—for example, that the president intended to go to war all along but hid that fact from the American people in order to be reelected—the evidence indicates that Wilson truly did wish to remain neutral. Even when the United States entered the war, it did so as an "associated power," not an ally of the Europeans. Wilson did this in part to honor Washington's famous advice to avoid entangling alliances, but also to maintain a free hand for the United States as it conducted the war on its own terms. The president felt that America was somehow above the fray. He believed that the United States would ultimately mediate the peace and oversee the creation of a new world order.

MAJOR CONTRIBUTIONS TO INTERNATIONAL HISTORY

Wilson's major contribution to the world was the introduction of a new approach, a new synthesis of ideas, to the practice of international politics. This could be called a new synthesis in that, while the elements of his policy embodied in such initiatives as the Fourteen Points proposal and Wilson's support for the League of Nations already existed in some form, Wilson synthesized these ideas in new combinations and was willing to put the weight of the United States behind them. Even though these initiatives largely failed in the short term, they became the foundation for larger changes in the international system, such as decolonization and the United Nations organization following World War II (1939–1945).

The initial reception to Wilson's proposals embodied in the Fourteen Points address was enthusiastic among many of the educated populations around the world. V. I. Lenin (1870–1924) and Léon Trotsky (1879–1940) had copies of the Fourteen Points address translated into Russian, printed, and distributed to the masses, despite paper being scarce at that moment in Bolshevik Russia.

IDEALISM IN FOREIGN POLICY

One of the more telling and farsighted speeches that highlight Wilson's idealism was his "Peace without Victory" speech, delivered to the US Senate on January 22, 1917. Wilson recognized that the European system was flawed and that, to a large extent, all the participants in the war were to blame. Moreover, he wanted to find a way to keep the winners from provoking such animosity that it would breed another war. Peace without victory

was the only way he could see this working. Even after Germany had signed the armistice and there was a clear victor, he continued to speak of "peace without victory."

Fourteen Points. Wilson's Fourteen Points plan, given in a speech to the US Congress on January 8, 1918, was the most complete expression of his international idealism. The speech stated clearly his idea that the peace that would follow the cataclysmic war would need to result in a world that was substantially different. He was firmly convinced that there would need to be significant changes, based upon the nineteenth-century liberal creed, freedom of the seas, free trade, national self-determination, reduction of arms, slow steady liberation of colonies, as well as an international body that could administrate or at least encourage these changes. Wilson was convinced that such changes were inevitable.

The Fourteen Points address was the clearest embodiment of the "Wilsonian creed" (Preston 2012). In this speech, many of the liberal international ideals that had preceded Wilson were interwoven into one proposal. The key to such ideals as the right of nations to self-determination, freedom of the seas, free trade, reduced armaments, and collective security was the League of Nations. In his final political battle, Wilson fought to include the proposals outlined in the Fourteen Points speech as part of the final peace treaty.

Versailles. The ultimate failure of the Wilsonian vision was, as Herbert Hoover (1874–1964) wrote in *The Ordeal of Woodrow Wilson* (1958), a failure on the scale of a Greek tragedy. Hoover, who considered Wilson to be a mentor, saw Wilson's failure to have ultimately been a detriment to the history of the world. Despite Wilson's insistence that the Fourteen Points be part of the peace plan, and despite his goal of a peace without victory and the avoidance of a punitive peace, the final treaty negotiated in Paris obliterated the president's idealistic proposals. Wilson's only real victory was the inclusion of the League of Nations in articles 1 through 30 of the final treaty. This institution, Wilson believed, would be able to fix the problems caused by the flawed treaty. The US Senate's ultimate rejection of the treaty was not just an emotional tragedy for Wilson; the treaty fight also worsened his declining health, leading to his stroke in 1919 and likely hastening his death in 1924.

LEGACY

Leaving the White House in January 1921, Wilson lived long enough to witness what looked like the complete repudiation of his international vision. At the time of his death, he truly believed he had failed. Despite Warren Harding's "return to normalcy" during the 1920s and the repudiation of Wilson's idealistic international policies, Wilson's vision was vindicated after World War II, and today his legacy remains important. The United Nations, the Cold War, and all the many alliance systems that were born after the war give credence to what Wilson attempted to do more than two decades earlier. The foreign policies of all subsequent presidents have been compared to Wilson's. They become Wilsonian when they pursue goals that are humanitarian or not in the immediate national interest of the United States. The recurring goal in US foreign policy of spreading democracy around the world, no matter how imperfect, is one of the greatest legacies of the Wilson administration. In the long run of history, particularly the history of American involvement with the rest of the world, Wilson can be considered one of the most significant theorists of American foreign policy.

SEE ALSO *Dollar Diplomacy; Haiti; League of Nations; Mexico; Missionary Diplomacy; Panama Canal; Paris Peace Conference (1919); Philippines; Roosevelt Corollary (1904); Roosevelt, Theodore; Spanish-American War; Taft, William Howard; Treaty of Versailles; World War I*

BIBLIOGRAPHY

Ambrosius, Lloyd E. *Woodrow Wilson and the American Diplomatic Tradition: The Treaty Fight in Perspective.* Cambridge: Cambridge University Press, 1987.

Benbow, Mark E. *Leading Them to the Promised Land*: *Woodrow Wilson, Covenant Theology, and the Mexican Revolution, 1913–1915.* Kent, OH: Kent State University Press, 2010.

Bragdon, Henry W. *Woodrow Wilson: The Academic Years.* Cambridge, MA: Belknap Press, 1967.

Burke, Edmund. "Speech of Edmund Burke, Esq., on Moving His Resolutions for Conciliation with the Colonies" (1775). In *Burke: Select Works*, edited by E. J. Payne, Vol. 1: *Thoughts on the Present Discontents; The Two Speeches on America.* Oxford: Clarendon Press, 1892.

Hoffman, Elizabeth Cobbs. *American Umpire.* Cambridge, MA: Harvard University Press, 2013.

House, Edward M. Edward Mandell House Papers. New Haven, CT: Yale University Library: Manuscripts and Archives.

Keynes, John Maynard. *The Economic Consequences of the Peace.* London: Macmillan, 1920.

Magee, Malcolm D. *What the World Should Be: Woodrow Wilson and the Crafting of a Faith-Based Foreign Policy.* Waco, TX: Baylor University Press, 2008.

Manela, Erez. *The Wilsonian Moment: Self-Determination and the International Origins of Anticolonial Nationalism.* Oxford: Oxford University Press, 2007.

Preston, Andrew. *Sword of the Spirit, Shield of Faith: Religion in American War and Diplomacy.* New York: Knopf, 2012.

Wilson, Woodrow. *A History of the American People.* New York: Harper, 1901.

Wilson, Woodrow. *The Papers of Woodrow Wilson*, edited by Arthur S. Link. 69 vols. Princeton. NJ: Princeton University Press, 1966–1994.

Malcolm Magee
Associate Professor, Department of History
Michigan State University

WINDTALKERS
SEE *Code Talkers.*

WINFREY, OPRAH
1954–

Born January 29, 1954, in Kosciusko, Mississippi, Oprah Gail Winfrey had an uneven childhood. Initially raised by her grandmother, at age six Winfrey was sent to live with her mother in Milwaukee, where she was sexually abused by several male relatives. Winfrey acted out in response, and as a result she was shuttled between her parents for several years. After giving birth at age fourteen to a child who did not survive, Winfrey vowed to turn her life around. She became a model student, won the title of Miss Black Tennessee, and earned a full scholarship to Tennessee State University. While in university she began working in local media, first anchoring a news program at age nineteen.

After a brief period in Baltimore coanchoring the news, in 1984 Winfrey moved to Chicago to host a morning talk show, soon to be renamed *The Oprah Winfrey Show*. In 1986 the show went national, becoming the highest rated daytime talk show. Winfrey, however, eventually tired of the show's sensationalism, so she remade the program to focus on uplifting stories and featured such initiatives as a book club, the Angel Network, lifestyle experts, and inspirational stories. A magazine and website soon followed, bolstering the message as well as Winfrey's brand. Winfrey's viewers cite her frequent disclosures about her own mistakes, her struggles with weight, and her ability to poke fun at herself as the source of her relatability (Harris and Watson 2007). At its peak, the show garnered over thirty million viewers a week in the United States alone and was syndicated in 149 additional countries, from Abu Dhabi to Zimbabwe ("*The Oprah Winfrey Show* Global Distribution List" 2011). Her media endeavors made Winfrey a millionaire in her thirties; according to *Forbes*, her net worth as of early 2015 was estimated at $3 billion.

Winfrey's childhood shaped her commitments. She was a driving force behind the passage of the National Childhood Protection Act, testifying before Congress in 1991. The "Oprah bill" as it came to be known,

Winfrey and students at the Oprah Winfrey Leadership Academy graduation ceremony in Johannesburg, South Africa, December, 2012. A strong advocate for education, Winfrey founded the Oprah Winfrey Leadership Academy to train underprivileged girls to be future leaders, providing university scholarships to the first graduating class. By 2013, Winfrey had invested over $100 million in the academy and its students. **NERISSA D'ALTON/GALLO IMAGES/ALAMY**

mandated a national database of convicted child abusers that child-care centers could consult when hiring. She has also been a strong advocate for education, donating to schools, universities, and museums. A ten-day stay with Nelson Mandela (1918–2013) in 2000 led to the founding of the Oprah Winfrey Leadership Academy, a school in South Africa that educates underprivileged girls to be future leaders. All members of the first graduating class received university scholarships to study in the United States or South Africa. By 2013, Winfrey had invested over $100 million in the academy and its students, and, advised by Mandela, donated additional resources to over fifty thousand other South African schoolchildren (Winfrey 2006). Oprah's Angel Network further funded the building of fifty-nine schools in twelve other countries ("Free the Children's Global Schools").

In May 2011, after twenty-five years and seven Emmys (before removing herself from consideration), Winfrey ended her show, although it continues to be shown internationally and in syndication. Winfrey, who had cofounded the Oxygen network in 1998 and a

channel for XM Satellite Radio in 2006, turned her attention to her own cable channel, the Oprah Winfrey Network (OWN), a partnership between Discovery Communications and her company Harpo Productions. OWN launched in January 2011 in the United States and slowly expanded to other markets in various forms, including the United Kingdom, eastern Europe, and South Africa. A South African edition of *O, The Oprah Magazine,* was published from 2002 to 2014.

Winfrey also returned to acting, appearing in *Lee Daniels' The Butler* (2013) and *Selma* (2014). Her acting career was spotty, reflecting her multiple commitments. She was nominated for an Academy Award and a Golden Globe for her debut in *The Color Purple* (1985), but subsequent roles in television movies were less acclaimed, as was her turn as the lead in *Beloved* (1998). Regardless, Winfrey has established herself as a noted producer of her own work and that of others, including the films *Precious* (2009) and *Selma* and a Broadway adaptation of *The Color Purple.*

Winfrey has appeared open about her personal life, but little is known about her family, including two siblings (now deceased) and a third recently discovered sister. Her relationship with longtime fiancé Stedman Graham (b. 1951) has also been maintained out of the spotlight.

SEE ALSO *Globalization; Television*

BIBLIOGRAPHY

Bryson, Donna. "Oprah Winfrey Opens Up on Academy Graduates." *Huffington Post,* January 13, 2012. http://www.huffingtonpost.com/2012/01/13/oprah-winfrey-oprah-winfrey-leadership-academy—graduates_n_1204501.html

"Free the Children's Global Schools." Oprah.com. 2015. http://www.oprah.com/angelnetwork/Oprahs-Angel-Network-and-Free-The-Children-Global-Schools-Video#!

Harris, Jennifer, and Elwood Watson. *The Oprah Phenomenon.* Lexington: University of Kentucky Press, 2007.

O'Connor, Clare. "How Nelson Mandela Inspired Oprah Winfrey to Change the Lives of South African Girls." *Forbes,* December 5, 2013. http://www.forbes.com/sites/clareoconnor/2013/12/05/how-nelson-mandela-inspired-oprah-winfrey-to-change-the-lives-of-south-african-girls/

"Oprah Winfrey." *Forbes,* March 1, 2015. http://www.forbes.com/profile/oprah-winfrey/

"*The Oprah Winfrey Show* Global Distribution List." Last updated March 2011. Oprah.com. http://www.oprah.com/pressroom/Global-Distribution-List-of-The-Oprah-Winfrey-Show

Oprah Winfrey, statement. *National Child Protection Act of 1993: Hearing before the Subcommittee on Civil and Constitutional Rights of the Committee on the Judiciary.* House of Representatives, 103rd Congress. July 16, 1993.

Winfrey, Oprah. "My Story." In *Me to We: Finding Meaning in a Material World,* edited by Craig Kielburger and Marc Kielburger, 134–136. New York: Fireside, 2006.

Jennifer Harris
Associate Professor
University of Waterloo

WISE, ISAAC

SEE *Judaism.*

WISE, STEPHEN

SEE *Zionism.*

WOLLSTONECRAFT, MARY
1759–1797

Joseph Johnson (1738–1809) published Mary Wollstonecraft's *A Vindication of the Rights of Woman* [*A Vindication* of the Rights of Woman: with structures on political and moral subjects*] in London in 1792. The book was a response to Charles Maurice de Talleyrand-Périgord's (1754–1838) contention in *Rapport sur l'instruction publique* [*Report on Public Education*] (1791) that daughters did not require public education to become wives and mothers. Although many read *A Vindication of the Rights of Woman* as a companion to *A Vindication of the Rights of Men* (1790), which Wollstonecraft had written in response to Edmund Burke's (1729–1797) *Reflections on the Revolution in France* (1790), the larger significance of *A Vindication of the Rights of Woman* lay in its very existence as a model of female authority, as well as in its content. Like other women writers in Great Britain, Ireland, and the United States at the end of the eighteenth century, Wollstonecraft successfully engaged men in print on equal terms.

The widespread availability of *A Vindication of the Rights of Woman* beyond London made it a touchstone of radical social reform. Within months, *Vindication* appeared in Dublin, in translation in Paris and Germany, and in Philadelphia and Boston. Demand was high enough in Philadelphia to justify another edition, which appeared in 1794. *Vindication's* publishing history was not unusual. Irish and American publishers had reprinted London titles for decades, in large part because they published few new books and because it was cheap and easy to add a new title page to an English edition.

As in Europe, the initial reaction to Wollstonecraft's book in the United States was positive, part of a larger transatlantic conversation about the possibilities of humanitarian reform in everything from the slave trade to prisons. Well-educated young women and men in northeastern cities and villages engaged with Wollstonecraft's demand that women be taken seriously as human beings and her assertion that gender equality required education for men as well as women. Wollstonecraft and her work were cited in commencement addresses and mentioned in diaries. Among her readers were Abigail Adams (1744–1818), Aaron Burr (1756–1836), Judith Sargent Murray (1751–1820), and Charles Brockden Brown (1771–1810).

Reaction to *Vindication* changed after Wollstonecraft's death following the birth of her second daughter, Mary, in September 1797. In 1798, her husband, William Godwin (1756–1836), the renowned author of *Enquiry concerning Political Justice* (1793), which celebrated the human capacity for self-government and denounced government and marriage as forms of tyranny, published a *Memoir of the Life of the Author of A Vindication of the Rights of Woman.* Godwin neglected Wollstonecraft's writing in favor of her private life, including her infatuation with the married painter Henry Fuseli

(1741–1825); her affair with the American adventurer Gilbert Imlay (1754–1828), which produced a daughter, Fanny (1794–1816); and her unconventional marriage to Godwin himself.

Critics in Britain and America pounced on these details to mock Wollstonecraft and Godwin as embodiments of the anarchic tendencies of a society unmoored from institutions such as marriage, the state, and churches. Protestant ministers, among others, tied the personal tribulations of the author of *Vindication* to the fates of revolutionary France and Haiti. Her posthumous notoriety facilitated equations of the rights of woman with antisocial desire: young women who read Wollstonecraft would forsake their roles as wives and mothers to enjoy an independence and sexual freedom that would ultimately ruin them at the hands of irresponsible men such as Imlay.

Despite these denunciations, American women and some men continued to read *A Vindication of the Rights of Woman* for inspiration as well as edification. Readers, writers, and reformers who paid attention to Wollstonecraft included Hannah Mather Crocker (1752–1829), Martha Meredith Read (177?–18??), Lucretia Mott (1793–1880), and Sarah Grimké (1792–1873). In 1868, Elizabeth Cady Stanton (1815–1902) and Susan B. Anthony (1820–1906) hung Wollstonecraft's portrait in the office of *The Revolution*, the newspaper they founded in support of female suffrage. Although almost no one dared to broach the subject of female sexuality, a few heralded Wollstonecraft as an example of female authority and an advocate of egalitarian marriage. Margaret Fuller (1810–1850), in *Woman in the Nineteenth Century* (1845), termed Wollstonecraft and Godwin's marriage a model of "intellectual companionship." Americans also read about Wollstonecraft in the work of popular English authors, such as her daughter Mary Shelley (1797–1851), George Eliot (1819–1880), and Virginia Woolf (1882–1941).

In these and other ways, Wollstonecraft remained central to the transatlantic conversation about the rights of woman. By the last third of the twentieth century, when scholars in Britain and America wrote about her career and her ideas, *Vindication* took its deserved place as a foundational text in the development of modern feminism.

SEE ALSO *French Revolution; Gender; Transatlantic Reform*

BIBLIOGRAPHY

Botting, Eileen Hunt, and Christine Carey. "Wollstonecraft's Philosophical Impact on Nineteenth-Century American Women's Rights Advocates." *American Journal of Political Science* 48, 4 (2004): 707–722.

Cayton, Andrew. *Love in the Time of Revolution: Transatlantic Literary Radicalism and Historical Change, 1793–1818.* Chapel Hill: University of North Carolina Press for the Omohundro Institute of Early American History and Culture, 2013.

Andrew Cayton
University Distinguished Professor of History
Miami University

WOMEN'S MOVEMENT
SEE *Feminism, Women's Rights.*

WOMEN'S SUFFRAGE
SEE *Feminism, Women's Rights; Suffrage.*

WOMEN'S UNION MISSIONARY SOCIETY
SEE *Foreign Mission Movement.*

WORCESTER V. GEORGIA (1832)

On March 3, 1832, the US Supreme Court found for the plaintiff in *Worcester v. Georgia*, issuing a writ of error against the Superior Court of Georgia. Chief Justice John Marshall (1755–1835) wrote the majority opinion in the case, which ostensibly concerned the unlawful imprisonment of missionaries in the Cherokee Nation. In this landmark decision, the Supreme Court recognized the Cherokee Nation's sovereignty. "The Cherokee nation is a distinct community occupying its own territory," Marshall declared. "The whole intercourse between the United States and this [Cherokee] nation is, by our constitution and laws, vested in the government of the United States," and not within individual states.

In their efforts to remove the Cherokees from land claimed by Georgia, the state's leaders recognized that the American citizens who were missionaries in the Cherokee Nation were impeding removal interests. Consequently, the state legislature passed a law requiring all Americans residing within the Cherokee Nation to sign a document acknowledging the sovereignty of Georgia. Two missionaries, Rev. Samuel Austin Worcester (1798–1859) and Dr. Elizur Butler (1794–1857), refused to sign, and the Superior Court of Georgia condemned them to four years of hard labor in the Georgia Penitentiary.

The American public was outraged over the arrest of the missionaries, and enough Supreme Court justices were sufficiently nudged toward their six-to-one decision. Writing the majority opinion for *Worcester* v. *Georgia* (1832), Marshall announced that Georgia's laws "have no force to divest the plaintiff [Samuel Worcester] in error of his property or liberty." Further, the state's laws were "repugnant to the Constitution of the United States and the treaties and laws made under it." Georgia did not have the right to remove the missionaries from the Cherokee lands; the state's actions were void and unconstitutional.

The principal source of the *Worcester* opinion came from an attorney, Jeremiah Evarts (1781–1831). He was secretary for the American Board of Commissioners for Foreign Missions (ABCFM), a predominantly northeastern reform agency that sponsored the missionaries. From August to December 1829, Evarts published a series of newspaper articles, known as the "William Penn" essays, which defended the Cherokee Nation's sovereignty in their remaining southeastern homelands. Evarts apologized for his lengthy and detailed arguments, but he wanted to "enable every dispassionate and disinterested man to determine where the right of the case is" (Evarts 1981, 8). To establish the credibility of his account, Evarts collected his materials from federal treaty law and the congressional reports of past presidents, including George Washington (1732–1799), Thomas Jefferson (1743–1826), James Madison (1751–1836), and James Monroe (1758–1831). Congressional supporters of the Cherokee Nation and Marshall himself relied heavily on Evarts's presentation.

The William Penn essays and *Worcester* compare in the following ways: Evarts and Marshall discussed the same treaties and congressional acts, such as the Treaties of Hopewell (1785) and Holston (1791–1792) and the Indian Civilization Act of 1819. They expressed similar ideas about the federal government's intentions toward the Indians through these acts. They reviewed the characteristics of Cherokee dependency upon federal protection and the nature of Cherokee sovereignty as understood by past presidents. Both Evarts and Marshall acknowledged Georgia's actions toward the Cherokees as a states' rights issue, but concluded that Georgia ultimately needed to support national interests. They also considered the significance of presidential precedent. At times, Marshall expressed alternative views to Evarts's rationale. Yet whether or not the chief justice agreed with Evarts, a textual comparison reveals that Marshall used the rhetorical order of the William Penn essays.

The greatest difference between Evarts's and Marshall's sovereignty arguments was their position on natural and positive law. A common view in Evarts's day, natural law is premised on self-evident rights that are inherent to living in a civilized nation. To Evarts, the Cherokees were the first owners of their land; therefore, they had first

rights to it. Marshall respected natural law. "The law of nature," Marshall acknowledged in *Worcester*, "which is paramount to all other laws, gives the right to every nation, to the enjoyment of a reasonable extent of country, so as to derive the means of subsistence from the soil." However, the chief justice preferred to delineate natural law's principles through positive law, or explicit delineations of societal rights and responsibilities. Thus, Marshall defined Cherokee sovereignty rights in specific positive law terminology involving discovery, conquest, and peace through the mutual benefits of trade. In this way, Marshall aligned with Evarts's natural law conclusions without utilizing them. "By the constitution," Marshall explained, "the regulation of commerce among the Indian tribes is given to Congress."

Marshall had likely read the William Penn essays when Evarts published them in 1829, two years before the *Cherokee Nation v. Georgia* (1831) decision. The historian Jill Norgren, who has written extensively on the Cherokee cases, recognizes Evarts's influence on the debates over Cherokee sovereignty. Norgren argues that Marshall's opinion differed between the two cases. In *Cherokee Nation*, Marshall appeared mentally exhausted by the case, and had abandoned the Cherokee cause. The next year, with *Worcester*, Marshall provided the "clearest, most pro-Indian doctrine of the time" (Norgren 2004, 118).

Evarts's earlier writings from 1829 indicate that Marshall had Cherokee sovereignty in mind when he wrote both *Cherokee Nation* (1831) and *Worcester* (1832). Marshall intentionally combined Emer de Vattel's (1714–1767) doctrine-of-discovery treatise in *The Law of Nations* (1758) with his support for Indian sovereignty. Using Evarts's reasoning, Marshall outlined his justifications to restrain the most blatant imperial acts. He suggested that the Cherokee Nation should remain protected, as long as the Cherokees recognized who protected them. While the doctrine's display of military and political power was certainly unfair, Marshall's work with the doctrine could also be viewed as realistic. He provided legal guidance for powerless sovereignties to negotiate effectively with greater military powers. Toward a goal of national stability, Marshall adopted and altered the doctrine of discovery to encourage imperial nations to channel individual interests through a larger frame of honor-bound rights and responsibilities across differences in power.

SEE ALSO *Cherokee Nation v. Georgia (1831); Civilization Fund; Foreign Mission Movement; Indian Removal Act (1830); Reservation*

BIBLIOGRAPHY

Burke, Joseph C. "The Cherokee Cases: A Study in Law, Politics, and Morality." *Stanford Law Review* 21, 3 (1969): 500–531.

Cherokee Nation v. Georgia, 30 U.S. 5 Pet. 1 (1831).

de Vattel, Emer. *The Law of Nations; Or, Principles of the Law of Nature, Applied to the Conduct and Affairs of Nations and Sovereigns*. Edited by Bela Kapossy and Richard Whatmore; translated by Thomas Nugent. Indianapolis, IN: Liberty Fund, 2008. First published 1758 in French.

Evarts, Jeremiah. *Cherokee Removal: The "William Penn" Essays and Other Writings*. Edited by Francis Paul Prucha. Knoxville: University of Tennessee Press, 1981.

Morgan, Nancy. "Jeremiah Evarts: The Cherokees' Forgotten Counsel." In *"Our Cause Will Ultimately Triumph": Profiles from the American Indian Sovereignty Movement*, edited by Tim Alan Garrison, 27–38. Durham, NC: Carolina Academic Press, 2014.

Newmyer, R. Kent. *John Marshall and the Heroic Age of the Supreme Court*. Baton Rouge: Louisiana State University Press, 2001.

Norgren, Jill. *The Cherokee Cases: Two Landmark Federal Decisions in the Fight for Sovereignty*. Norman: University of Oklahoma Press, 2004.

Worcester v. Georgia, 31 U.S. 6 Pet. 579–580 (1832).

Nancy Morgan
Instructor, School of Historical, Philosophical & Religious Studies
Arizona State University

WORLD BANK

Created at the Bretton Woods Conference in 1944, the World Bank is a financial institution based in Washington, DC. Officially named the International Bank for Reconstruction and Development, its mission has changed over the decades since its creation. Established conjointly with the International Monetary Fund (IMF), the World Bank originally sought to help finance development projects with the purpose of rebuilding Europe after World War II (1939–1945). It is a specialized agency of the United Nations.

CREATION AND INITIAL MISSION

Political differences at Bretton Woods led to the World Bank and the IMF being created together, which further led to confusion over each institution's role and mission. Referring to this dilemma, the architect of the Bretton Woods system, John Maynard Keynes (1883–1946), quipped "the Bank is a fund, and the Fund is a bank." Originally, both institutions were underfunded, leading the World Bank to operate mostly by guaranteeing private loans—an inauspicious debut. Operations began in 1946, and bank membership was open to all IMF member states.

At that point, it was unclear whether the World Bank would be a temporary solution to the postwar reconstruction of Europe or a more permanent effort. In any case,

the World Bank proved so anemic at its designated task that the majority of the aid needed to rebuild Europe was disbursed via the Marshall Plan. With the rebuilding of Europe thereby financed and successful in the decade after the war, the original mission of the World Bank came to an end, and the organization had to adapt to the world as it was in the 1960s, when the Cold War constrained politics and the world faced the decolonization of what were then called "third world" nations.

EVOLVING MISSION

A turning point occurred in 1960 when the World Bank established a new component, the International Development Agency (IDA). At this point, the bank began to function more as a development agency and less as a public-sector lender. The transition was slow until Robert McNamara (1916–2009) took over the presidency of the bank in 1968. McNamara's term was characterized by an emphasis on development research and projects. During the decade after his departure in 1981, the bank focused on problems of debt. The post–Cold War period of the 1990s saw issues of emerging markets, "submerged" markets, currency valuation, and equity, which also began to fall under the bank's purview. Over the decades since its creation, the World Bank's mission has therefore evolved significantly, in concert with a changing global environment.

Although the World Bank was not originally designed to directly address poverty, the result of the historical ebb and flow of the bank's mission was an institution more focused on economic development in lesser-developed nations. Today, the bank's development mission has at least five components. One, the World Bank provides funds to government-sponsored programs in middle-income or poorer member nations. Two, the bank encourages the development of productive facilities and resources in poorer nations. Three, the bank provides funding when private capital is not available. Four, the bank promotes international trade and development by encouraging international investment. Five, the bank helps member states increase productivity and improve standards of living and labor conditions. Thus the bank's mission has expanded far beyond its original purpose. In addition to the above, the bank also sometimes addresses issues of population, education, health, social security, environment, and poverty alleviation, as well as cultural and human rights issues, such as gender inequality and discrimination against women.

By the 1970s, many developing nations struggled with debt owed to private banks or the World Bank. John Williamson, an IMF adviser, composed a ten-point plan to help lift nations out of debt. This plan, which became known as the Washington Consensus, informed not just the IMF but also the World Bank. This Washington Consensus assumed that neoliberal economics provided the best model for development, such that democracy, a robust private-sector economy, free markets, and open or "free" international trade would lead to the greatest development results. Any policy that "liberalized" the economy of a debtor nation would lead to growth and thus the ability to pay off debt, and debtor nations were pushed into these agendas, even though in many cases their debts arose from corruption, such as in Zaire during the presidency of Mobutu Sese Seko (1930–1997). The Washington Consensus led to widely criticized "structural adjustment programs" (SAPs) in the IMF, which coerced debtor nations into neoliberal policies, often to the detriment of their public sectors and infrastructure.

CRITICISM OF THE BANK

Normally, the World Bank is 51-percent funded by the United States, and typically the president of the bank is appointed by the president of the United States. Technically, the bank president is chosen by a board within the bank, but the board usually votes to approve the appointment after the fact. This practice was challenged after US president George W. Bush appointed Paul Wolfowitz as World Bank president in 2005. The bank's board forced Wolfowitz out of office after a number of controversies surfaced. Critics assert that this structure makes the World Bank effectively a US policy tool, and they question the motives and impact of the bank's operations, especially since the 1980s. For example, the World Bank's own literature at one point promised $1.30 in revenues for American contractors for every $1 lent to a developing nation.

While the World Bank claims to operate benevolently as an international development organization, many critics, including a former bank president, Joseph Stiglitz, argue that the bank acts in the interests of developed countries because they have the most influence in its structure and funding. Stiglitz also noted that the World Bank (and IMF) provide for "global governance without global government" (2002, 21), indicating that developing nations did not have enough say in the World Bank's policies.

The World Bank has sponsored a number of dubious projects in the neoliberal era. In Zambia in 2004, for example, the bank funded school-building projects, but the repayment scheme was such that Zambia had no money left to hire teachers, and the new schools were left empty. In Uganda under World Bank direction from 2000 to 2004, the government sold off four-fifths of its enterprises, thus liberalizing its economy, but the end result was an increase in poverty. Perhaps the most notable failure was Argentina, which liberalized its economy according to World Bank norms during the 1990s, and yet its GDP fell by 11 percent, leading to higher unemployment and nationwide protests in 2001 and 2002. The World Bank nevertheless advised Argentina to adopt further liberalization.

SEE ALSO *Bretton Woods; International Monetary Fund; United Nations; World Trade Organization*

BIBLIOGRAPHY

Gilbert, Christopher L., and David Vines, eds. *The World Bank: Structure and Policies.* Cambridge: Cambridge University Press, 2000. See pages 10–38, 87–107, and 159–195.

Marshall, Katherine. *The World Bank: From Reconstruction to Development to Equity.* New York: Routledge, 2008. See pages 10–92 and 136–151.

Schaeffer, Robert K. *Understanding Globalization: Social Consequences of Political, Economic, and Environmental Change.* 4th ed. Lanham, MD: Rowman and Littlefield, 2009. See pages 80–98.

Steger, Manfred. *Globalization: A Very Short Introduction.* New York: Oxford University Press, 2009. 3rd ed., 2013. See pages 54–55.

Stiglitz, Joseph E. *Globalization and Its Discontents.* New York: Norton, 2002. See pages 13–24 and 257–258.

van Meerhaeghe, M. A. *International Economic Institutions.* 6th ed. Dordrecht, The Netherlands: Springer Science & Business Media, 2013.

Peter A. McCord
Professor of History
State University of New York, Fredonia

WORLD HEALTH ORGANIZATION

The World Health Organization (WHO) is a specialized intergovernmental agency created under the auspices of the United Nations with the objective of attaining the highest possible level of health by all peoples. The United States played an integral role in the creation of WHO; indeed, the present structure and operations of WHO cannot be understood without reference to the historical context in which it was created, and the role of the United States in this process.

AMERICAN INFLUENCE ON THE CREATION OF WHO

The United States was a prominent player in the field of international health before the formation of a single global health agency. The International Sanitary Bureau, later renamed the Pan American Sanitary Bureau (PASB), was established in 1902 by the International Union of American States at the behest of the United States, which sought to expand its trade with Latin America but faced significant transactional barriers in the form of varying quarantine and inspection regulations. PASB, which was largely staffed by members of the US Public Health Service, implemented a uniform sanitary code across the Americas by 1936 (Fee and Brown 2002, 1888), facilitating trade across the region and improving health through targeted activities designed to reduce the burden of disease.

In the wake of World War II (1939–1945), calls for improved global governance to avert further international warfare ultimately led to the formation in 1945 of the United Nations, which replaced its predecessor, the beleaguered League of Nations. At the international Dumbarton Oaks Conference (1944), where the decision was made to create the United Nations, attendees also voted on a proposal by Brazil and China to establish a specialized global health agency: the World Health Organization. WHO came into existence in 1948, when the first World Health Assembly (WHA) ratified the constitution of the organization in Geneva, Switzerland.

Although the United States was broadly supportive of the creation of WHO, it played a contradictory role in the organization's establishment process. The United States generally stood behind the goals of the United Nations and was directly involved in the founding of WHO through Thomas Parran (1892–1968), the sixth surgeon general of the United States and an influential member of the commission created to plan the new organization. The United States was also one of the first major contributors to the WHO budget. However, throughout negotiations, the United States maintained the right to unilateral intervention in the Americas on the basis of national security, causing consternation (Brown, Cueto, and Fee 2006, 64). Moreover, incorporation of PASB, by then a well-established, independent regional body, into WHO's structure presented a significant challenge to those seeking to create the new, unified organization.

PASB was adamant that its independence from WHO should be maintained in the event that it join the organization. At the Twelfth Pan American Sanitary Conference in 1947, the members of PASB voted to create the Pan American Sanitary Organization (PASO), incorporating the PASB as headquarters and secretariat of this new organization. PASO's Directing Council later decided that its Executive Committee could negotiate to join WHO, but only on the condition that PASO continue to function as "an independent entity for the solution of problems of continental character" (Howard-Jones 1981, 18).

In 1949, the American director of PASO, Dr. Fred Soper (1893–1977), concluded an agreement with the WHO director general by which PASO became the WHO regional organization for the Western Hemisphere. This agreement confirmed that PASO would remain independent from WHO—that is, PASO could carry out and finance its own programs, provided they were compatible with the policy and programs of WHO. This negotiation process is one of the key reasons that the distinctive decentralized structure of WHO exists today.

STRUCTURE OF WHO

WHO was composed of 194 member states as of 2015; members direct the WHO agenda through the World Health Assembly (WHA), with the organization's operations carried out by the Executive Board and its Secretariat (WHO 1946). The Executive Board is responsible for implementation of policy directives, and also elects members of the Secretariat, who are the technical and administrative stakeholders of WHO.

WHO has six regional offices, which are responsible for regional policy formulation and the monitoring of regional activities. One of these offices is the Pan American Health Organization (PAHO), the successor to PASO, which represents the Americas within WHO. This decentralized structure remains unique among UN agencies. The head of each regional office—the regional director—can only be appointed by the Executive Board in agreement with the relevant regional committee. Similarly, the staff of the regional office are appointed in a manner agreed upon by the director general and relevant regional director (WHO 1946), resulting in significant power being wielded by the WHO regional offices. Indeed, PAHO has been described as an international health organization "second in scope, usefulness, influence and prestige, only to WHO, of which it is functionally, if not legally, an integral part" (Howard-Jones 1981, 20).

Over the decades since WHO's creation, the relative power of both WHO and PAHO have declined in the context of the rapidly changing global health landscape—in part, due to the United States' own direct activities in the global health arena. However, American involvement in WHO has been, and remains, significant.

AMERICAN INVOLVEMENT IN WHO

Since the 1960s, the United States has exerted an extraordinary influence on WHO's operations. One important mechanism of the United States' control has been financial. WHO has two major funding sources: regular budget funds (assessed contributions) and extrabudgetary funds (voluntary contributions) (Lee 2009, 38). Assessed contributions are received only from UN member states based on the United Nations' scale of assessments, which takes into account such factors as gross national income (UN Committee on Contributions). Voluntary contributions can be made to WHO by individuals, groups, and foundations, along with member states, and can be given to the organization conditionally (Lee 2009, 39). Assessed contributions are primarily used to fund the core activities of WHO and constitute around 25 percent of its income, while voluntary contributions are often designated for specific projects, making up the remainder of WHO's funding. In totality, 80 percent of WHO's budget is funded by governments (Feig 2011).

To prevent dependency on any one member, no member state can contribute more than one-third of WHO's assessed contributions. The United States has been the largest voluntary contributor to WHO, contributing more than one-quarter of the organization's total regular budget funds in 2012.

US influence on WHO has primarily been leveraged by its large financial contribution to the organization, but the aims of the United States in wielding this influence have varied. The United States has, at times, acted as a champion and supporter of various WHO initiatives. In other cases, the United States has obstructed the implementation of new public health initiatives and the involvement of actors perceived as less desirable from a US foreign policy perspective.

The Soviet Union exited from the United Nations and WHO in 1949 in the midst of the Cold War and partly due to pressure from the United States and its allies. Accordingly, until the Soviet Union's return in 1956, the United States was able to exert a dominating influence on WHO without significant opposition. During that time, WHO was closely allied with US interests (Brown, Cueto, and Fee 2006).

The United States was one of the nations that drove WHO's efforts in the 1950s and 1960s to eradicate malaria throughout the world. The United States contributed over 85 percent of the total funds to the WHO Malaria Special Account, established in 1955 to fund the Global Malaria Eradication Program (Nájera, González-Silva, and Alonso 2011). The United States had eradicated malaria within its own borders in 1951, and with the widespread use of novel agents such as DDT, it was hoped that worldwide malaria eradication would represent WHO's first major global health victory, simultaneously bringing significant economic and political benefits to the United States. Although these efforts resulted in a significant reduction in the burden of malaria throughout the world, the program was not sustained, leading to a resurgence in the incidence of the disease in many countries. The program was scaled back significantly in 1969, with a new focus on control rather than eradication (Mendis et al. 2009, 803), representing a significant blow to the young organization and its largest supporters.

The Soviet Union then led the drive to eliminate smallpox, beginning in the 1950s. The United States initially demonstrated less of an appetite for these efforts, given the relative failure of WHO's malaria eradication campaign. However, by 1965, President Lyndon Johnson had instructed the US delegation to the WHA to support the program. In 1967, with the support of the United States, the WHO Intensified Smallpox Eradication Program was established. The program was led by the American epidemiologist Donald A. Henderson, who coordinated efforts that culminated in the eradication of smallpox by 1980 (Brown, Cueto, and Fee 2006, 65–66; WHO 2015).

Since then, the United States has contributed to many other WHO initiatives, including programs on measles eradication, H1N1 influenza, and primary healthcare advocacy. The United States has also participated in and initiated programs to reduce the global incidence of tuberculosis and infection from the human immunodeficiency virus (HIV).

However, the United States' contributions to WHO have not been entirely positive. In the 1970s, the United States came into conflict with WHO director general Halfdan Mahler, who espoused a view of universal healthcare that angered multinational companies. In the 1980s, the United States was the only country to oppose an international code on breast-milk substitutes, on the grounds that WHO was interfering with global trade, the implication being that the United States was representing the interests of Nestlé, a multinational with large holdings in America. The United States subsequently withheld its regular contributions to WHO's budget, partly due to WHO's Essential Drug Program, which was opposed by the pharmaceutical industry. At the time, eleven of the eighteen largest drug companies in the world were based in the United States (Godlee 1994, 1492). The Palestinian Liberation Organization was also indefinitely denied membership to WHO in 1989 due to strong opposition from the United States, Israel, and other members of the European community (Lee 2009, 24).

Since the mid-1980s, the influence of WHO has gradually waned in the context of a rapidly changing global political environment and as a result of internal challenges at WHO. By the 1990s, the World Bank had begun to dominate the field of global health, while WHO suffered under the controversial leadership of its director general, Dr. Hiroshi Nakajima (1928–2013), whose appointment in 1988 the United States and many other countries did not support (Brown, Cueto, and Fee 2006, 68). The relevance of the organization diminished significantly during Nakajima's tenure, a development vividly demonstrated by the actions of the prominent American physician Jonathan Mann (1947–

1998), who resigned from his position as director of WHO's Global Program on AIDS in 1990 to protest WHO's lack of response to the global HIV/AIDS epidemic (Hilts 1990, 1).

In the absence of clear health-systems delivery capacity from WHO in relation to the HIV/AIDS epidemic, as well as resistance to the strengthening of UN institutions during the administration of US president George W. Bush, various organizations were created to combat the epidemic. These included the Global Fund—to which the United States pledged $1.7 billion in 2014, the largest contribution by an individual country (IHME 2014, 18)—and the President's Emergency Plan for AIDS Relief, established by Bush in 2003, which has been estimated to have reduced the burden of HIV/AIDS in some sub-Saharan African countries by 10.5 percent (Walensky and Kuritzkes 2010, 273).

The organization subsequently recovered its credibility through the strong leadership of Gro Harlem Brundtland, who was elected director general in 1998. Brundtland arranged partnerships with external organizations, such as the US-based Bill and Melinda Gates Foundation, and appointed prominent American experts on various issues to chair committees and programs, including economist Jeffrey Sachs, who headed up WHO's Commission on Macroeconomics and Health (Brown, Cueto, and Fee 2006, 70). Although US support for WHO has persisted since this time, much of the US expenditure and effort in global health occurs separately from the organization.

TWENTY-FIRST-CENTURY INTERACTIONS BETWEEN WHO AND THE UNITED STATES

Although the United States has increasingly dominated the field of global health, its relative power with respect to WHO has altered significantly. In 2013, the United States was the largest single donor to global health efforts worldwide, contributing a total of US $7.4 billion in development assistance for health through its bilateral development agencies (IHME 2014, 10). By way of contrast, WHO's entire programme budget for the 2012-2013 biennium was $4.42 billion (WHO 2014, 3) and WHO's total expenditure on development aid for health for 2013 was $2.15 billion, and PAHO's total expenditure for 2013 was US $414 million (IHME 2014, 75). This situation has afforded the United States an extraordinary amount of leverage in the field of global health, allowing it to operate almost without reference to WHO in many respects.

This changing dynamic is well illustrated by the United States' evolving contribution to global efforts to combat malaria. The United States remains one of the world's largest donors to malaria control and eradication efforts. In the 1950s, the US contribution to malaria control was largely conducted through WHO, along with the Centers for Disease Control (CDC) and former iterations of what is now USAID. Now, most such activities occur independently through the President's Malaria Initiative, established in 2005, and through donations to such bodies as the Global Fund, to which the United States has contributed over US $8.7 billion for malaria programs (Kaiser Foundation 2015). The CDC still operates as a WHO Collaborating Center for prevention and control of malaria, but the vast majority of US fiscal support for malaria programs is not routed through WHO.

Concerns also persist in relation to the impact of WHO policies on the US trade agenda. In 2005, the United States refused to support WHO's groundbreaking Framework Convention on Tobacco Control (FCTC), which establishes binding legal obligations on states to take measures to reduce tobacco use. Due to concerns for its thriving tobacco industry, the US strongly resisted implementation of the FCTC, claiming that it interfered with private markets. The United States is one of only a small number of countries that have not ratified the FCTC. Of the 180 states that have ratified the treaty, 80 percent have strengthened existing tobacco laws or introduced new legislation designed to reduce tobacco use (Nikogosian and da Costa e Silva 2015).

CONCLUSION

The United States has had a profound influence on WHO's history, successes, failures, and core strategy since its inception. Through its technical expertise, political power, and financial contributions, the United States has shaped many of WHO's programs and initiatives, and will continue to do so as the sphere of global health evolves and WHO seeks to shore up its position as the preeminent global health organization in a rapidly changing political arena.

SEE ALSO *Acquired Immunodeficiency Syndrome (AIDS); Americanization; Cold War; Exceptionalism; Flu Epidemic, 1918-1919; Industrialization; United Nations; World War I; World War II*

BIBLIOGRAPHY

Brown, Theodore M., Marcos Cueto, and Elizabeth Fee. "The World Health Organization and the Transition from 'International' to 'Global' Public Health." *American Journal of Public Health* 96, 1 (2006): 62–72.

Fee, Elizabeth, and Theodore M. Brown. "100 Years of the Pan American Health Organization." *American Journal of Public Health* 92, 12 (2002): 1888–1889.

Feig, Christy. "Setting the Record Straight on WHO Funding." *Foreign Affairs*, November 18, 2011.

Godlee, Fiona. "WHO in Retreat: Is It Losing Its Influence?" *British Medical Journal* 309 (1994): 1491–1495.

Henry J. Kaiser Family Foundation. *The U.S. Government and Global Malaria.* Menlo Park, CA: Kaiser Family Foundation, 2015. http://kff.org/global-health-policy/fact-sheet/the-u-s-government-and-global-malaria/

Hilts, Philip J. "Leader in U.N.'s Battle on AIDS Resigns in Dispute Over Strategy." *New York Times*, March 17, 1990.

Howard-Jones, Norman. *The Pan American Health Organization: Origins and Evolution.* Geneva, Switzerland: WHO, 1981.

Institute for Health Metrics and Evaluation (IHME). *Financing Global Health 2013: Transition in an Age of Austerity.* Seattle: University of Washington, 2014. http://www.healthdata.org/policy-report/financing-global-health-2013-transition-age-austerity

Lee, Kelley. *The World Health Organization (WHO).* London: Routledge, 2009.

Mendis, Kamini, Aafje Rietveld, Marian Warsame, Andrea Bosman, Brian Greenwood, and Walter H. Wernsdorfer. "From Malaria Control to Eradication: The WHO Perspective." *Tropical Medicine and International Health* 14, 7 (2009): 802–809.

Nájera, José A., Matiana González-Silva, and Pedro L. Alonso. "Some Lessons for the Future from the Global Malaria Eradication Programme (1955–1969)." *PLoS Medicine* 8, 1 (2011): e1000412–e1000419.

Nikogosian, Haik, and Vera Luiza da Costa e Silva. "WHO's First Global Health Treaty: 10 Years in Force." *Bulletin of the World Health Organization* 93, 4 (2015): 211. http://www.who.int/bulletin/volumes/93/4/15-154823/en/

United Nations, Committee on Contributions. http://www.un.org/en/ga/contributions/

Walensky, Rochelle P., and Daniel R. Kuritzkes. "The Impact of the President's Emergency Plan for AIDS Relief (PEPfAR) beyond HIV and Why It Remains Essential." *Clinical Infectious Diseases* 50, 2 (2010): 272–275.

World Health Organization (WHO). Constitution of the World Health Organization. Adopted in 1946; entered into force in 1948. http://www.who.int/governance/eb/who_constitution_en.pdf

World Health Organization (WHO). Global Alert and Response (GAR). Pandemic and Epidemic Diseases: Smallpox. 2015. http://www.who.int/csr/disease/smallpox/en/

World Health Organization. Financial Report and Audited Financial Statements for the year ended 31 December 2013. A67/43, Sixty-Seventh World Health Assembly, Provisional agenda item 20.2, 17 April 2014. http://apps.who.int/gb/ebwha/pdf_files/WHA67/A67_43-en.pdf

Matthew Basilico
Department of Economics, Harvard University
Harvard Medical School

Kiran Bhai
Partners In Health

Fiona Lander
Harvard T. H. Chan School of Public Health

THE WORLD IS FLAT (THOMAS L. FRIEDMAN, 2005)

The World Is Flat: A Brief History of the Twenty-First Century (2005) is a best-selling book by the *New York Times* columnist Thomas L. Friedman (b. 1953), an optimist who represents one extreme of the debate over globalization. Friedman sees the free market and meteoric advances in technology as a great boon, as well as an irreversible phenomenon. A cheerleader for corporate globalization, Friedman believes that beginning in the 1990s, the world had entered a period of unity (unlike the divisive years of the Cold War) that rewarded flexibility, high technology, and individualism. In this book, he explains the next phase of globalization, in which a world of hypertechnology has provided unprecedented opportunities for equality by flattening the economic playing field. Technology-induced globalization has empowered individuals to engage faster, more cheaply, and more profoundly than ever before, to the extent that anyone—from India to America—can prosper by engaging in the world economy.

The metaphor of a flat world is a colorful way of describing how the process of globalization has changed the world and has given a huge advantage to those, particularly large multinational corporations, who master technology and the global integration of communications and transport systems. Friedman's core argument, based on anecdotal observations he recorded as he traveled the world, centers on the ten forces that supposedly flattened the world. These include the end of the Cold War, which brought down barriers to creativity; the flourishing of global Internet connectivity, which allowed citizens to share in new ideas and practices; integrated software that allowed more people to collaborate in the exchange of business data; a community-based, bottom-up sharing of goods and ideas (like *Wikipedia*), rather than reliance on traditional hierarchies of state- or corporate-driven dissemination; outsourcing elements of the production or service process to the most efficient manufacturers overseas; offshoring the entire factory process to places with cheaper costs; horizontal integration through the building of global supply chains (Walmart has perfected this); managing parts of the supply chain in collaborative ways (UPS provides mailing labels and shipping for products bought on eBay and paid for by PayPal); making knowledge widely available by accessible search engines, such as Google; and enhancing all of the aforementioned processes through digitization, performed anywhere in the world and by any individual. Thus, through technology, global citizens can take advantage of this flat world.

That is a bold, spritely vision—one full of metaphors so imaginative that at times Friedman appears either as a naïve Pangloss or an analyst neglectful of the dark side of globalization. When globalization does not work for everyone—terrorists, religious fundamentalists, protectionists, and so on—they are merely standing in the way of inevitable and healthy technocapitalism. There are only dangers, not alternatives, to a flattened world, and these threats are to be contested. The United States stands to gain tremendously, shoring up and expanding its global economic power if its citizens adopt this view. Individuals need only become flat-world "strategic optimists" who seize on Friedman's ten forces, and flourish. His view meshes with neoliberal voices who applaud free-market capitalism, and who, above all, blame participants rather than the system or ideology for poverty, slack mobility, and lack of competitiveness.

That is an argument in much dispute and with implications for the United States. Critics assail Friedman for engaging in wishful thinking, at the least, and distortion in the main. Outsourcing, insourcing, open sources, supply chains, and the like have worked for some companies and sectors, but by no means have swept the field in the world economy. His book, like his early work on globalization, are viewed as dot-com boosterism. It is also an ahistorical and inaccurate analysis of how the world economy works. Neither terrorism nor nationalism fit into his triumphal approach to techno-globalization, but no matter; they are to be somehow ignored or treated as obstacles to his part reality, part vision of how the world should work. But for many across the planet, the counterview is just as real as the supposed flattening of the world. In India, for example, critics note that Friedman presents the perspective of the top 0.1 percent—from the golf courses and CEO corner offices—and brushes aside the masses living in squalor who have no idea of the existence of this profitably dynamic flattened world. In a similar vein, those living in capitalist-imposed austerity in Spain, Greece, and Argentina, and those millions who have gone on strike in South Africa, Argentina, Nigeria, and South Korea, do not buy into the neoliberal paradigm. In fact, many observers counter that the world is still, very much, round.

SEE ALSO *Globalization; Neoliberalism; World Trade Organization*

BIBLIOGRAPHY

Appelbaum, Richard, and Nelson Lichtenstein. "A New World of Retail Supremacy: Supply Chains and Workers' Chains in the Age of Wal-Mart." *International Labor and Working-Class History* 70, 1 (2006): 106–125.

Bhagwati, Jagdish. *In Defense of Globalization.* New York: Oxford University Press, 2004.

Friedman, Thomas L. *The World Is Flat: A Brief History of the Twenty-First Century.* New York: Farrar, Straus, and Giroux, 2005.

Friedman, Thomas L. *The Lexus and the Olive Tree.* Rev. ed. New York: Picador, 2012. First published 1999 by Farrar, Straus, and Giroux.

Ghemawat, Pankaj. "Why the World Isn't Flat." *Foreign Policy* 159 (March–April, 2007): 54–60. http://www.foreignpolicy.com/articles/2007/02/14/why_the_world_isnt_flat

Stiglitz, Joseph E. *Globalization and Its Discontents.* New York: Norton, 2002.

Zachary, G. Pascal. *The Global Me: New Cosmopolitans and the Competitive Edge: Picking Globalism's Winners and Losers.* New York: PublicAffairs, 2000.

Thomas W. Zeiler
Professor of History
University of Colorado Boulder

WORLD TRADE ORGANIZATION

The World Trade Organization (WTO) is a global multilateral institution that negotiates, sets, and enforces rules of international trade among nations, with the aim of reducing barriers to the exchange of goods and services. Established in 1995, it is administered by a Secretariat of six hundred staff based in Geneva, Switzerland. Decision-making power rests in a biannual Ministerial Conference, but when this is not in session, a General Council of ambassadors and politicians governs the WTO. To implement and monitor trade agreements, the General Council provides a legal framework for reviewing the consistency of national trade policies with the WTO's multilateral goals and for settling disputes among its 160 members, who account for nearly all of world trade. The bulk of these nations are developing and poor countries, which gives the WTO a charge of offering technical assistance and training programs in the field of trade policy. These nations have challenged the WTO to reform the trade system. Thus, the WTO has been a powerful—and controversial—force in the world economy and development politics. Developing nations are especially critical of the WTO for embracing the so-called neoliberal "Washington Consensus" that became the driver of globalization.

ORIGINS IN THE GATT

The precursor to the WTO was the General Agreement on Tariffs and Trade (GATT), which improbably lasted for nearly a half century after it came into force in 1948 as the chief multilateral negotiating forum to reduce trade barriers among its member states. The GATT was originally conceived as a bargaining forum for a more comprehensive trade body, the International Trade Organization, which never came into being. By the

1980s, the forum's historic role pointed to the need for extending the GATT system into more economic arenas than before. The system required the formalization of rules and enforcement mechanisms, under a world trade organization.

The WTO also emerged during the deepening of the market capitalist ethic and practices that blossomed in the wake of the Cold War. Alongside the International Monetary Fund (IMF) and World Bank, both of which guided the Washington Consensus in the global financial, monetary, and development realms, the WTO became a symbol of America's neoliberal push behind the process of globalization. Like these financial institutions, the WTO prompted internal reforms by nations with struggling economies and political systems that appeared to stymie market-based trade and money policies. That integrative process fed into the WTO's purpose of liberalizing trade and dealing with trade disputes on a global basis, meshing with the Washington Consensus under President Bill Clinton in the 1990s. In response to the competitive potential of regional trade arrangements, the United States, Mexico, and Canada established the North American Free Trade Area (NAFTA) in 1992 to promote trade and investment. Opponents saw NAFTA as a threat to jobs, safety, and the environment. The WTO was even worse, for it seemingly tossed aside national regulations in favor of neoliberal market practices, and did so on a massive global scale. Clinton won congressional approval of NAFTA, but the effort proved that the protesters were strong.

The supporters of the WTO, however, were just as worried. They were concerned that the multilateral system developed under GATT would splinter into preferential regional trade blocs, thereby undermining the Washington Consensus through exclusive arrangements that distorted trade. A world umpire to guide all of the regional groupings along the road of multilateral trade liberalization was in order. The European Union and seventy-five GATT members incorporated the GATT into the WTO in 1995 after the conclusion of the Uruguay Round of negotiations. The remaining fifty-two GATT members joined within two years. The WTO had actually not been part of the original negotiating mandate but ultimately incorporated all of the Uruguay agreements, as well as the provisions of GATT.

The idea for the WTO had bounced around until Canada formally proposed a permanent trade organization, in April 1990, and the European Community endorsed it. Negotiations among the so-called "Quad" nations (Japan, the European Union, Canada, and the United States) got underway on the shape and purpose of the organization. The Americans were lukewarm to the idea, cognizant that Congress opposed losing its constitutional sovereignty over trade and worried that institutional reform would supplant the drive for trade liberalization.

ISSUES OF CONTENTION

The key issues of contention were decision making, dispute settlement and procedures, and whether participants would adhere to all provisions of the GATT. America got its way on decisions made by consensus. This was the old GATT procedure, but failing that, voting would follow the "one-nation, one vote" principle (the United Nations method) preferred by many others, especially the developing nations who sought more clout. Dispute procedures were greatly strengthened, and the WTO instituted tighter discipline over the veto power. In addition, all provisions of the Uruguay Round and of GATT itself would be brought into a "single undertaking" under WTO supervision.

This political wrangling resulted in a compromise between developing countries who wanted a strong multilateral organization so they could have more influence, and the industrialized nations who wanted every participant, the developing countries in particular, to adhere to the Uruguay Round commitments as the price for WTO membership. In addition, the US Congress balked at joining the WTO out of a fear that American law would be supplanted by rulings of an unelected international bureaucracy, but Congress approved of the Uruguay Round, which included the WTO, by large majorities.

By 2009, the WTO had 153 members, but it was troubled from the very start. For example, who would be appointed the first WTO director-general in 1995? Competing Italian, Mexican, and South Korean candidates failed to win approval. In addition, the European Union sought a one-nation, one vote scheme, for it had seventeen member-state votes, as well as numerous African associated-nation votes. An Italian, Renato Ruggiero (1930–2013), emerged as the winner because of the EU bloc, but the WTO got off on the wrong foot. Still, dozens of elements—from tariff reductions to tariff conversion in agriculture, to phasing out import quotas on textiles to frameworks for services, intellectual property rights, investments, dumping, countervailing duties and export subsidies, and government procurement—now existed in the new WTO agreement.

Essentially policing national trade policies to ensure their compatibility with liberal trade rules, the powerful WTO had a myriad of functions that quickly drew attention from critics and supporters. In its first two decades, the WTO rose to become a global trade organization that included nearly all of the world's trading nations. Its strengthened dispute-settlement procedures were largely successful in liberalizing trade. But its decision-making process, which enforced a rules-based system, moved the organization toward a UN-type grouping of nations, in which the developing countries coalesced against the industrial powerhouses. That reality actually slowed liberalization, by giving more decision-making power to the developing nations—the very countries the WTO aimed to help through freer trade.

THE DOHA TALKS AND THE UNDERMINING OF THE WTO

Because of its high profile and sweeping responsibilities, the WTO became a lightning rod for grievances against the inequities in the trade regime, the power of corporations, globalization, and the hegemony of the North. The dichotomy of the developing-developed world became the most detrimental issue for the WTO over its first two decades. The advanced nations pressed the developing countries for greater obligations in freeing trade and lowering barriers to investment, but during the Doha Development Agenda talks—the WTO's first round of trade negotiations—the Third World members jettisoned this firmer obligation for a much weaker one. They purposively created a categorical dichotomy of advanced versus developing nations. Coupled with the urge of many nations to move away from multilateral trade liberalization and toward bilateral or regional free-trade agreements, this dichotomy threatened the WTO's (and America's) position as trade regime leader.

The seven-year Doha trade talks became a contest of wills between the North and a large contingent of angry traders from the South. The talks began at the WTO's Fourth Ministerial Conference in Doha, Qatar, in November 2001. In 2003, a new bloc called the G-20, led by Brazil, China, India, and South Africa, prevented resolution of four so-called "Singapore issues" (trade and investment, competition, government procurement, and customs issues) that had arisen from WTO meetings the year before. The developing and developed worlds were also at loggerheads over nearly every trade item, the most prominent being agriculture, and more specifically export subsidies, which allowed an edge for European and US farmers by an artificially priced world market. By mid-2006, the Doha talks were in trouble, and the crisis deepened when the US Congress renewed farm subsidies for another five years. The Doha Round collapsed in July 2008. Recrimination erupted, and the WTO foundered in the ensuing global financial meltdown of 2008.

The Doha Round also revealed that, especially for rising, industrializing Asian nations like South Korea, Singapore, and Malaysia, separate free-trade agreements—outside the framework of the WTO—were more beneficial than relying on the complicated WTO multilateral

negotiating process that had been commandeered by poor countries focused on agriculture. The idea for lumping bilateral or regional free-trade arrangements into a plurilateral agreement under the WTO surfaced, but there was obvious competition between the two tracks of trade negotiations—WTO multilateralism versus the regional/bilateral approach. This furthered the North-South division as well, and the WTO itself witnessed a decline of its role as the dominant center of the multilateral world trade system.

Part of the undermining of the WTO reflected political and constitutional controversy within the United States over the course of trade liberalization. For instance, such nongovernmental organizations as the Sierra Club and World Wildlife Federation demanded a seat at the WTO table to shape global economic policies that would protect the environment. On the other side, however, were nations arrayed against US regulatory policies that were dominated by interest groups; in a reversal of roles, several Asian nations won their appeal in the WTO in 1998 against a US ban on imported shrimp from nations that did not protect sea turtles from dying in fishing nets. Saying otherwise could set a precedent that might gut the goal of curbing discrimination in an open-door system by allowing nations any excuse to restrict trade. This was a victory for the Third World, but it gave protesters in the United States leverage against the WTO. Conservative (and some liberal) groups found the organization to be undemocratic because unelected bureaucrats dictated rules to which national governments had to adhere. Undeniably, the WTO pushed nations toward embracing the ideal of "one world," in which goods, money, and services were exchanged across borders regardless of national origins, and with consequences both good and bad for the integrative process.

That the trade system made both American domestic observers and the developing nations unhappy boded ill for the WTO. The Doha round came on the heels of antiglobalization protests and the terrorist attacks on the United States on September 11, 2001, both of which wrought changes in the global economy. The multilateral negotiations were slated to open in Seattle under the name Millennial Round in 1999, but the developing nations balked when the United States and the European Union excluded them from talks on agricultural trade barriers. They walked out of the forum, and the Seattle talks collapsed. Massive street demonstrations erupted simultaneously, led by an unlikely coalition of organized labor, environmentalists, anarchists, students, religious groups, consumer advocates, and political activists who all, in general, lobbied against globalization by protesting the symbol of the WTO.

That the WTO's first round of trade talks stalled did not signify the end of liberalization efforts and a crimping of globalization. Analysts lauded the WTO, which ensured greater inclusiveness, prioritized development, and provided a rule-based system well beyond the efforts of GATT. But the problems could not be ignored, and the deadlock at Doha showed that the WTO needed to coordinate trade with other policies to ensure equality and growth, consider broadening its mandate (without overstretching its capabilities) to include issues such as climate change, and continue the policy of inclusiveness and transparency without bogging down in political deals. The WTO was clearly an historic achievement, but the challenges it faced also spoke to the need for continued reform.

SEE ALSO *Clinton, William Jefferson; Globalization; Group of Five and its Successors (G5, G7, G8, G20); International Monetary Fund; Neoliberalism; North American Free Trade Agreement (NAFTA); World Bank*

BIBLIOGRAPHY

Barton, John H., Judith L. Goldstein, Timothy E. Josling, and Richard H. Steinberg. *The Evolution of the Trade Regime: Politics, Law, and Economics of the GATT and the WTO.* Princeton, NJ: Princeton University Press, 2006.

Jackson, John. *Restructuring the GATT System.* London: Royal Institute of International Affairs, 1990.

Narlikar, Amrita. *The World Trade Organization: A Very Short Introduction.* Oxford: Oxford University Press, 2005.

Narlikar, Amrita, Martin Daunton, and Robert M. Stern, eds. *The Oxford Handbook on the World Trade Organization.* Oxford: Oxford University Press, 2012.

VanGrasstek, Craig. *The History and Future of the World Trade Organization.* Geneva: WTO, 2013. http://www.wto.org/english/res_e/booksp_e/historywto_e.pdf

Thomas W. Zeiler
Professor of History
University of Colorado Boulder

WORLD WAR I

World War I (1914–1918) was called the "war to end all wars" by many who survived or observed the four years of carnage. And so it seemed, as accounts, accusations, explanations, and justifications began to appear in print a century ago—a process that continues unabated to the present. In retrospect, of course, we understand that no war can ever be the one that would "end all wars." And indeed, the human costs of World War II (1939–1945) and conflicts thereafter—replete with fire bombings, death camps, and nuclear warfare—have equaled if not exceeded those of the earlier conflict, which ended barely twenty years before its sequel started in 1939. Nevertheless, those who first wrote about World War I sensed that in certain ways it was unlike any prior human struggle that had occurred in modern history. In this, they were correct.

In time of peace, according to an old maxim, prepare for war. By 1910, the four major powers in Western Europe—Austria-Hungary, France, Germany, Great Britain—and Russia had followed this injunction to extremes. They prepared to defend themselves from external attacks not only by maintaining vast military divisions in reserve, but also by reaping the benefits of the industrial era—producing prodigious amounts of modern weaponry and, in the case of Great Britain, the largest navy with the largest battleships afloat. All these measures were intended to contribute toward crushing assaults against the attacker, hopefully before any counteraction might occur. In such a scenario, however, the major European powers would not act alone.

By the second decade of the twentieth century, a network of alliances and agreements had evolved, which obligated one country to come to the assistance of the other, if attacked. Thus, Germany was closely linked to Austria-Hungary, while France and Russia enjoyed a cordial understanding, a dual entente as it were. At the same time, Russia also supported the Balkan state of Serbia. Great Britain claimed to have joined no entangling alliances, yet it had indicated its strong mutuality of interests with France. Both powers were pledged to protect and preserve the neutrality of Belgium. In addition to these diplomatic agreements, the Romanovs in Russia, the House of Saxe-Coburg-Gotha (after 1917, the House of Windsor) in Great Britain, the Hapsburgs in Austria-Hungary, and the Hohenzollerns in Prussia all had additional bonds of matrimonial kinship. The ruling dynasties of Western Europe, some of which had been established for more than two centuries, contributed to an atmosphere of mutual diplomacy, as well as suspicion and distrust.

In retrospect, one wonders if the diplomats of that day had ever considered Sir Isaac Newton's famous law that for every action there is an equal and opposite reaction. If all the major powers prepared for a war by striving to become the most powerful country in Europe, any forthcoming attack could only conclude in stalemate, because no one of them would be strong enough to launch a massive, overwhelming strike against the other. Their quest for stability through multilateral strength ultimately nurtured the possibility of total war. Such a result is precisely what took place. In this bloodiest of conflicts of the twentieth century, territorial gains were often measured in yards or a few miles as the war ground on for four years. And when it was all over in November

1918, or so it seemed, three of the four dynasties mentioned above were gone, along with approximately nine million military casualties. While the benefits of this war are not easy to assess, its legacy in terms of the costs—human, financial, and political—became obvious upon its conclusion.

BACKGROUND

As is true of many great historical events, there is no one single, underlying incident to which historians can point as the cause of World War I. There were, however, a number of developments in late nineteenth-century European history that made such a conflict probable. First was the legacy of the Franco-Prussian War (1870–1871), which resulted in the humiliating defeat of France and the unification of Germany under the leadership of Prussia, as well as German annexation of the French territories Alsace and Lorraine. The ill-concealed French desire for what came to be known as "*le grand revanche*" (the great revenge) dates from 1871. Second was the unmistakable drift toward alliances, already mentioned, that obligated signatories to come to each other's aid, as seen in the understandings between Russia and France, later supported by Great Britain, and the dual alliance between Austria-Hungary and Germany. Well before 1914, Western Europe was thus defined by two large power blocs that viewed each other's existence as justification for their mutual suspicions. Third was the ongoing quest for colonial dominance and military supremacy, sometimes seen as a substitute for effective diplomacy, best characterized by the race between Great Britain and Germany for the largest and most powerful navy afloat. Although by 1910 Great Britain could not point to a date when war would break out, there was little doubt it would involve Germany. Fourth, there was the growing disconnection between military and political leadership evident to some extent in much of Europe, in particular Russia, Germany, Austria-Hungary, and Serbia. Finally, strong currents of ethnic unrest were evident in these countries.

By 1912, these European powers all accepted a general assumption, that regional—if not global—power was measured by expansions to empire through territorial acquisition. Such expansion could occur at the expense of another nation, or its ethnicity and culture. Thus tensions between Austria-Hungary and neighboring Serbia had worsened to a great extent due to Austria's unilateral annexation of two provinces, Bosnia and Herzegovina, four years earlier. Formerly part of the Ottoman Empire and containing a heavy mixture of Slavs, Serbs, and Muslims, these two provinces were a polyglot amalgam of bitter, ethnic antagonisms and home to numerous dissidents who looked to both Russia and Serbia in their determination to eliminate control by Austria-Hungary. Serbia, in particular, viewed Russia as a champion of an expanding pan-Slav-Serbian sphere of influence. Such a development could only occur at the expense of Austria-Hungary, which in turn looked to Germany as its key source of support. It was in this context that the heir to the Hapsburg throne, Franz Ferdinand (1863–1914), insisted on making a state visit to Bosnia. On June 28, 1914, when visiting the town of Sarajevo, both he and his wife were assassinated by a young Bosnian patriot and Serbian nationalist, nineteen-year-old Gavrilo Princip (1894–1918). While the underlying causes of the war can be found among the points just noted, there is no doubt as to the immediate cause, which triggered the outbreak of war exactly one month later. Determined to move against its hostile neighbor, Austria-Hungary delivered an ultimatum to Serbia on July 23, and five days later declared war.

PREPARATIONS AND PLANS

Unlike modern warfare with its push-button mentality, plans for war in 1914 were conceived as a sort of ritualistic formula within the context of tradition. Thus every major European participant in what was to come (Russia, Austria-Hungary, France, Germany, and even Great Britain) had well-developed war plans. The advantage of prewar planning meant that one might anticipate and establish in advance various timetables, as well as identifying needed sources of weaponry and manpower. The two great disadvantages rested, first, in the fact that mobilization—once it had been ordered—was impossible to halt, for the process was so logistically complex that with such a step in effect, a formal declaration of war became inevitable, making any annulment of the war plans impossible. Second, the more military leaders became locked into their preconceived strategic goals, the less flexibility for compromise or maneuvering they gave their diplomats. While true to some extent during the four years of actual war, this assertion has even greater validity for July and August 1914.

Upon receiving word that his nephew had been murdered, Franz Joseph I (1830–1916) wrote a personal appeal to Kaiser Wilhelm II (1859–1941). The aged Hapsburg emperor described Serbia as "this hotbed of criminal agitation in Belgrade." Only when such a state had been "neutralized as a power factor in the Balkans," might the decrepit Hapsburg Empire be secure (Clark 2012, 401). Although his letter avoided specifics, it left no doubt that Austria intended to take severe action against Belgrade. For its part, the German government made it clear that, as the Austrian ambassador to Germany noted, "we could be confident that Germany as our ally and a friend of the Monarchy would stand behind us" (Clark

2012, 414). Two days after the assassinations, the kaiser had written "it was high time [that] a clean sweep was made of the Serbs" (Clark 2012, 412).

Thus there can be no doubt that Germany supported and encouraged Austria to move against Serbia with some rapidity. This conclusion, however, does not mean that Germany pressured Austria into any sort of premature attack, even though Germany was well aware that such was precisely what Austria intended. On the other hand, the Germans did nothing to discourage Austria from taking such action. Moreover, both the kaiser and his chancellor, Theobald von Bethmann-Hollweg (1856–1921), were fully cognizant of Serbia's close relationship to Russia. They assumed (as will be seen, wrongly) that the czar would not condone such an incident of regicide by supporting Serbia, all the more as his Romanov family represented one of the oldest ruling houses in Europe, and some of its members had themselves been assassinated. Further, they were assured by the German military leadership that its armed forces were fully prepared for any eventuality, even if it included a Russian military response against Austria. Feeling confident in its ability to cope with a future war in Europe of admittedly unknown dimension, Germany awaited the next step, which was the delivery of an Austrian ultimatum to Serbia on July 23, 1914.

Apparently crafted in such a way as to invite Serbian rejection, it contained some ten demands, of which at least two seemed utterly incompatible with state sovereignty. One required that Serbia accept within its borders the involvement of Austrian officials in suppressing subversion against the Dual Monarchy of Austria-Hungary, while the other reiterated a demand for similar involvement concerning investigation of accessories to the assassinations. Serbia was given forty-eight hours to respond with an unconditional acceptance. As word of the ultimatum spread through European diplomatic channels, reactions were prompt. Winston Churchill (1874–1965) called it "the most insolent document of its kind ever devised" (Clark 2012, 456). More important was the comment of the Russian foreign minister who stated that "no state could accept such demands without committing suicide" (Clark 2012, 462).

The Serbian officials working to draft a response based it on the assumption that as the leading figure of a pan-Slav movement, Russia simply would not tolerate an attack on Serbia from Austria-Hungary, all the more as behind the bellicosity of the Dual Monarchy, Russian diplomats saw the massive image of Germany. Confident that Russian support would materialize, as indeed it did, Serbia ordered general mobilization even before the official response had been delivered. Similarly, assuming that Serbia would not accept the ultimatum as a whole,

the Austrian minister had prepared in advance a notice that he and his staff would be leaving Belgrade. Thus, within half an hour of receiving Serbia's reply, the Austrian legation entrained for Vienna. Three days later, the Dual Monarchy declared war on Serbia.

If Germany had encouraged Austria to be firm (and prompt) in its actions concerning Serbia, so France had urged similar firmness on the part of Russia toward Austria. Russia appears to have needed little such encouragement. Chancellor Bethmann-Hollweg had warned, however, that continued Russian moves toward mobilization could only produce a similar response from Berlin. On July 29, while preparing to order mobilization, an urgent appeal from Kaiser Wilhelm to his cousin, Czar Nicholas II (1868–1918), prompted the czar to order a partial mobilization instead. But this distinction, flying in the face of the complicated logistics required for any sort of mobilization, was meaningless, and one day later, Nicholas reversed himself. Russia ordered general mobilization. If not yet well traveled, the road to total war was now clearly marked.

The German response to Russia's move was predictable. On July 31, Wilhelm proclaimed a state of "*der drohenden kriegsgefahr*" (imminent danger of war). It was the penultimate step before general mobilization, and when Russia refused to cancel its own mobilization, Germany declared war on Russia one day later. Thus, by August 1, 1914, Serbia and Austria were at war. Russia and Germany declared war on each other, and it had been barely one week since Austria had delivered its ultimatum to Serbia. France, in accord with the "*entente cordiale*," determined to support Russia, and while the French prime minister insisted that mobilization was not the same thing as war, in 1914 this was a distinction without a difference. The French mobilized even as Germany declared war on Russia. French military leaders had long been aware that the German war plans called for a swift march through Belgium into French territory on the way to the main objective, attacking Russia.

Assuming that possible British intervention was not significant militarily, and faced with Russian and French mobilization, on August 2, Germany presented an ultimatum to Belgium in order to defend itself against a potential French attack. Germany claimed it was forced to go through Belgium. In return for its cooperation (some described it as complicity), Belgian territory and possessions would be guaranteed, Germany would evacuate the country upon completion of its military goals, and all Belgian costs and damages would be paid by a German cash indemnity. Belgium was given twelve hours to respond. In retrospect, German actions concerning Belgium were unfortunate, as they cast Berlin in the role of a brutal, lawless invader—an image that was not only to endure but also gain intensity as the war continued. Further, whether deserved or not, Germany's actions gave the entente powers an aura of moral superiority. German foreign policy found itself chained to an inflexible military timetable concerning Belgium. One day later, the Belgians rejected the ultimatum out of hand and appealed to England for support.

Great Britain had observed the events of the previous ten days with a mixture of disdain, disinterest, and shock. Divided over its initial response to the European crisis, the British government found itself pushed by the German assaults in Belgium toward intervention in support of France and Russia, all the more as England had been one of the guarantors of perpetual Belgian neutrality since 1839. Now, the British foreign secretary, Sir Edward Grey (1862–1933), described to Parliament the military violation of Belgian neutrality and asked "could this country stand by and watch the direst crime that ever stained the face of history, and thus become participators in the sin?" (Hastings 2013, 92–93). On August 4 2014, Great Britain issued an ultimatum of its own to Germany, demanding withdrawal from Belgium by midnight. Germany did not even bother to reply. After little more than a month, the major powers at war could all claim that "theirs was a war of defence, that their countries had been attacked or provoked by a determined enemy, and that their respective governments had made every effort to preserve the peace" (Clark 2012, 552). By the middle of August, with each belligerent nation feeling under attack and claiming to seek peace, Europe was at war. Unaware at first of its probable contagion, the American ambassador to England, Walter Hines Page (1855–1918), observed that "again and ever I thank Heaven for the Atlantic ocean" (Cooper 2009, 163).

AMERICAN REACTIONS AND RESPONSES

Coping with the death of his wife even as Europe went to war, President Woodrow Wilson (1856–1924), in his initial response, issued a message on the absolute necessity for American neutrality. His statement had several themes, which barely hinted at the difficulties such a course would encounter during the next two years. He did not refer to any specific belligerent. Rather, he pointed to the American need, as the one great nation at peace, to hold "itself ready to play a part of impartial mediation and speak the counsels of peace and accommodation, not as a partisan, but as a friend" (Wilson, 1914). In order to attain such a goal, "the United States must be neutral in fact as well as in name during these days that are to try men's souls." But more was required. "We must be impartial in thought as well as in action, must put a curb upon our sentiments as well as upon every transaction that might be construed as a preference of one party to the

struggle before another." Such impartiality was all the more essential because the American people "are drawn from many nations, and chiefly from the nations now at war." Thus, "the utmost variety of sympathy and desire among them" would arise. It was all the more essential, therefore, to maintain a determined, genuine, and lasting neutrality.

In August 1914, Wilson could not know that the war would drag on for more than four years, rapidly becoming a war of attrition. But he well understood the pressures that would ultimately make adherence to the pronouncements in his message impossible. For the next two and a half years, the president genuinely tried to maintain the neutrality he had called for, despite his love for British literature, his sympathy for their cause, and his lifelong commitment toward Great Britain's parliamentary system of government. He confronted a difficult challenge because American attitudes toward the European conflict were as varied as the backgrounds of those who constituted the American people. Yet if groups differed as to whom they supported, once the war broke out, they were united in their opposition to any American involvement. Such consistency made it easier, at first, for Wilsonian neutralism to be persuasive.

Thus, strident criticism of Germany as brutal and militaristic, or bitter condemnation of British conduct toward Ireland, invariably stopped short of calls for any kind of American involvement. Further, the more Americans observed the growing applications of force in Europe as trenches were constructed and the opposing armies settled in to a grinding routine of attrition, the more determined they were not only to oppose the use of force, but also any appearance or preparation for it. Reflecting the same sentiment, Wilson had tapped into a deep vein of national awareness.

There can be little doubt that, late in 1914, a strong American sentiment favored an Allied victory, especially for France and England, whose ties to American history and culture ran deep. Such support did not extend to Russia, already regarded as the weaker link in the alliance. Further, while many Americans considered Germany as an aggressive, if not arrogant, power, with war now an actuality they accepted the fact that its origins and causes were complex and could not be ascribed to one single country. Even as ardent an anglophile as Theodore Roosevelt (1858–1919) at first conceded that the German invasion of Belgium "was precisely the kind of deed that all great powers, including the United States, had done when they believed that their vital interests" required such a step (Link 1960, 15). Within a few months, however, and in concert with public opinion, Roosevelt adopted a much more critical posture concerning German ruthlessness.

As war broke out, the desire for American neutrality was genuine, but there were multiple dimensions to the term. Military assistance was out of the question in 1914, yet possible financial support represented a very different question. Lending money to warring powers might be of significant financial benefit to American interests, but did it compromise real neutrality? Secretary of State William Jennings Bryan (1860–1925) had no doubts that it did. "Money is the worst of all contrabands because it commands everything else" (Cooper 2009, 264).

Thus Bryan stated publicly that loans by American bankers to any foreign belligerent are "inconsistent with the true spirit of neutrality." The realities of war indicated otherwise, and Bryan soon modified his proposed ban. He altered his stance by insisting that a loan (in this instance to France) be labeled as "commercial credit" and agreed to without any publicity. By 1915, American banking houses were routinely issuing multimillion-dollar loan packages to the European powers at war, creating an "ever tightening financial entanglement" with the world conflict (Cooper 2009, 264–265). Apparently, neutrality was not violated as long as all belligerents were willing to pay the financial costs associated with such loans.

While there may have been a larger element of American support for the British and French cause, in 1914 it was not as vocal or probably as effective when compared with German American partisans who were united in support of their "fatherland" to a remarkable extent. Active on the political front, on the pulpit, and in the press, German sympathizers raised millions of dollars in revenue bonds and distributed more than "one million propaganda pamphlets just in the first year of war alone" (Link 1960, 21). Besides these two largest groups, Irish, Jewish, and Swedish Americans responded to the war, with the Irish and Jewish Americans strongly opposed to the Allies. While aware that Russia, England, and France were loosely linked in alliance, Jewish Americans recalled Russian history, replete with pogroms, anti-Semitism, and czarist absolutism. Thus, between 1914 and 1917, conflicting opinions concerning the world war were widely available for public consumption. While it remains unclear to what extent they actually shaped American diplomatic responses, they served as a key indicator of how far Wilson could go in foreign policy as he reacted to ongoing events.

In theory, the assumption in American foreign policy was that because the United States was a neutral nation that treated all parties to the war alike, its commerce and trade would remain unhindered and unhampered. Such a perspective, if not naive, was unrealistic, and flew in the face of two practices, one implemented by England and the other by Germany shortly after hostilities commenced. The British imposed an increasingly harsh and effective blockade against Germany, while Germany, unable to challenge the supremacy of the British navy in terms of numbers, resorted to a newly improved weapon at sea, the submarine. A blockade on the one hand, and submarine attacks on the other, could only affect American neutral interests, all the more as both Great Britain and Germany considered these actions absolutely essential to their war efforts. Americans found both of them unacceptable and—especially in the case of Germany—offensive.

It made little difference to American objections that England reminded Washington of its conduct during the American Civil War (1861–1865), when, with only a few ships available, Abraham Lincoln (1809–1865) had proclaimed a blockade of the southern East Coast. England had accepted its dubious legitimacy, and now, in 1914, asked merely that the United States return the favor, as it were. But when push came to shove, England fully recognized that without American support and assistance, victory over Germany was uncertain, if not impossible. British officials were unprepared and unwilling to antagonize the United States to such an extent; although in theory it might insist on the blockade, in fact England tried to mitigate the resulting negative effects on American trade and commerce. Thus, for example, when shipments of southern cotton were caught up in the blockade, the English authorities quietly made sure that the cotton was purchased by British interests at an appropriate price.

To many Americans, submarine warfare represented an unpleasant synthesis of German brutality and technology, foreign to those values which, supposedly, had been traditional to both sides at the onset of the war. Submarine attacks turned conventional theory concerning battle on the high seas upside down. Unseen and undetected until the emergence of sonar and radar, they struck without warning—although in broad daylight, an observant passenger might be able to spot the telltale wake of a torpedo, streaking toward its target. By the spring of 1915, Germany had determined that aggressive use of submarines was its only effective weapon against a British blockade intended to deny war materials, as well as foodstuffs. Already, at least one American had been killed when a U-boat sunk the British steamship *Falaba* on March 28, resulting in numerous public expressions of outrage but minimal demands for retaliation. On the other hand, the legal destruction of property was very different from any legality to destroy life. Sinking of cargo ships was not the same as wanton destruction of a passenger liner, or so it seemed.

On May 7, a German U-boat sunk the *Lusitania*, the largest and fastest Cunard passenger liner in service. The ship went down in less than twenty minutes, with 1,198 deaths, including, women, children, and 124 American citizens (Link 1960, 372). If the assassinations on June 28, 1914, had marked the start of actual descent into a European war, the destruction of the *Lusitania* triggered the start of an unmistakable American movement toward war with Germany. Within two years, pro-Allied partisanship was transformed into demands for active intervention. In 1915, however, calls for war were rare.

By May, the war had been in progress for almost ten months, and the American public was well aware of its horrific aspects. Already poison gas had been introduced, soon to be followed by machine guns, airplanes, barbed-wire trenches, and tanks. Many thousands of casualties had already been counted, and there were few illusions remaining about the peculiar horrors of this particular war (Cooper 2009, 285). The United States finally entered the war in April 1917, a step made easier by German diplomatic missteps concerning Mexico and an incorrect assumption that unrestricted submarine warfare was

Military parade down New York's Fifth Avenue on the eve of US entry into World War I, 1917. *Although American military participation in World War I was relatively brief, the war had lasting effects on American society. For the first time, the United States found its security endangered by the conduct of an autocratic European power, and thus the Great War dispelled the long-held assumption that America was not vulnerable to the repercussions of conflicts overseas in Europe.* **PHOTO 12/UIG/GETTY IMAGES**

worth the risk of American intervention. Wilson did not exaggerate when he asked that America now join in "the most terrible and disastrous of all wars, civilization itself seeming to be in the balance." But American military intervention would last only until November 1918.

SIGNIFICANCE AND CONSEQUENCES

Although American military participation in World War I was relatively brief, the war had lasting effects on American society. In the first place, and for the first time, the United States found its security endangered by the conduct of an autocratic European power, a condition that would repeat itself as the twentieth century progressed. The Great War dispelled the long-lasting assumption that America was invulnerable to European developments, although occasionally during the next twenty years, shadows of this old sentiment would reappear. They were facilitated by the collapse of Wilson's efforts to gain Senate ratification of the peace treaty, a process that his declining health and rigidity of outlook exacerbated. Further, early in 1919, conservative interests supporting prohibition achieved ratification of the Eighteenth Amendment, and while Wilson vetoed the enforcement legislation enacted by Congress, that body promptly overrode him. Similarly, Wilson found immigration restriction inimical to American values and had vetoed such a measure in 1917, only to see Congress disregard his veto.

But while Wilson realized all too well that leading a country into war would also unleash forces for repression and enforced conformity, with one exception he consistently refused to prevent such actions from taking place. German Americans suffered more in this regard than other ethnic groups. Some states forbade the teaching of the German language and barred musicians from performing German classical music. Further, Congress enacted the Espionage Act in June 1917, shortly after the declaration of war, followed by the Sedition Act. Both enabled the federal authorities not only to prohibit certain materials from being printed and distributed, but also to freely use its provisions banning delivery through the mail of any publications deemed disloyal. Thus the federal authorities effectively "hobbled dissent and criticism in print" (Cooper 2009, 398). Yet Wilson consistently declined to protect in wartime the quality of open debate that he had so freely endorsed prior to 1917.

The one exception turned out to be women's suffrage. As president, Wilson had consistently declined to endorse the suffrage amendment, earning the bitter resentment of the National Woman's Party, a militant women's group who labeled him "Kaiser Wilson" and employed such tactics as chaining themselves to the White House fence. This behavior only stiffened Wilson's resistance, a fact recognized by the more conservative National American Woman Suffrage Association. Their leadership suggested that suffrage could be seen as a war measure, reflecting not only the expansion of democracy but women's support for the war itself. By January 1918, Wilson had accepted the principle of the suffrage amendment. Indeed, after this date, his support for it never wavered, although the measure did not receive final congressional approval until June 1919. Despite his arduous work at the 1919 Paris Peace Conference and the stroke he suffered in October, he pushed for ratification, which finally was proclaimed in August 1920. John Cooper notes that, among men, "Woodrow Wilson deserved more approbation than anyone else" for such an accomplishment (Cooper 2009, 414).

Thus the legacy of American involvement in World War I was mixed, although some 126,000 American soldiers were killed in battle. This figure is small when compared to the horrific casualties of the original combatants, yet it remains the third deadliest war in US history, even though it was the shortest in duration. Antiradical and anti-German opposition in the guise of a strident and hysterical patriotism was unfortunate for German Americans, all the more as Wilson's consistent rhetoric concerning freedom, morality, and democracy seemed to fly in the face of reality as the war drew to a close. His "peace without victory" and his "Fourteen Points" (French prime minister Georges Clemenceau [1841–1929] liked to observe that the Lord had only ten) as the proposed basis for peace negotiations similarly raised high expectations that the harsh and brutal conditions of the four-year conflict made unattainable. The sad conclusion of his presidency is well known, and though it be tragic, Wilson himself must bear major responsibility for this fact.

Exhausted after attending the Peace Conference in Paris, where stringent peace terms against Germany were drafted, Wilson returned home to present what became known as the Treaty of Versailles to the Senate for ratification. Wilson had been absent from the United States for more than six months—longer than any American president before or since. Already in an intransigent mood, he showed no willingness to compromise with the Senate. Instead, early in September, he set forth on a cross-country speaking tour intended to mobilize public support not only for the treaty but also for the newly established League of Nations, in which Wilson had pledged American membership. For more than three weeks, amid intense heat and without a microphone, he gave speech after speech, only to collapse on September 25. After a hasty return to Washington, he suffered a stroke from which he never fully recovered. His rigid refusal to discuss or negotiate, exacerbated by his poor health, resulted in Senate rejection of the League of Nations. After 1919, many wondered what the United States—and indeed the other major participants as well—had gained from the Great War.

In fact, what delegates had attained in Paris was a twenty-year armistice in the face of casualties so extensive that they still inspire shock: 1,390,000 French soldiers killed, at least twenty-one million soldiers wounded, more than 400,000 from the British Empire dead, resting in unknown graves. If the war's aim had been to prevent Germany from controlling Western Europe, then the resulting peace treaty did not succeed in such a quest. Rather, it set the stage for the emergence of German National Socialism (Nazism) and the dictatorship of Adolf Hitler (1889–1945).

LEGACY

Debate over what such bloodletting accomplished endures to this day. Was the "horrendous death toll" truly necessary to block German aggression, or was the war in fact "an unmitigated catastrophe" and "a spasm of brutal carnage that in every conceivable way remade the world for the worse?" (Hochschild 2011, 371–372)

Whichever answer is selected, the effects of this war linger, more than a century after it began. At least half a million tons of war materials are still gathered each year from fields in Belgium and France, where there are "more than 2,000 British cemeteries alone" cared for "by almost 500 gardeners" (Hochschild 2011, 375) in what Winston Churchill described as "a crippled, broken world." But these are tangible legacies. More important and subtle results can also be identified.

Distinctions between military and civilians now mean much less than was true in 1914. The torpedoing of ships was matched by British efforts to starve Germany into negotiations. Further, future developments flowed almost in a linear pattern from the war. Poison gas became napalm and Agent Orange in Vietnam. The crude detention centers for forced labor by French and Belgium refugees became the concentration camps of another war. The makeshift zeppelin bombings of London became the horrendous destruction by fire of London, Dresden, Hamburg, and Tokyo, with increased and indiscriminate bombing of urban centers. The genocide of Armenians became the Nazi death camps of Auschwitz and Dachau, while the terrible climax was the advent of nuclear warfare, sought by Hitler but attained by the United States and demonstrated for all to see over Hiroshima and Nagasaki in 1945. War had "irrevocably unleashed the prostitution of science for purposes of pure destruction." What Adam Hochschild describes as "the most toxic legacy" of World War I "and its misbegotten peace settlement lies in the hardly imaginable horrors" that were yet to come (Hochschild 2011, 373).

Coupled with these grim realities must be some positive and lasting results of World War I for US history. The war gave an impetus, albeit tardy, to the expansion of civil rights not just for women but for returning veterans, who would be treated much better in 1945 than were their counterparts in 1919. It forced the federal government toward modernization, and made issues of social justice more immediate. Yet the war overshadows US foreign policy aspirations as much in the present as in 1917 to 1919. How different is "making the world safe for democracy" from keeping American citizens free from terror? For better or for worse, foreign developments will continue to embroil the United States as they did in World War I, and while the lessons and legacy of the Great War remain visible, their possible impact on the future should always be kept in mind.

SEE ALSO *Great Depression; League of Nations; Missionary Diplomacy; Paris Peace Conference (1919); Treaty of Versailles; United Nations; Wilson, Woodrow*

BIBLIOGRAPHY

Clark, Christopher. *The Sleepwalkers: How Europe Went to War in 1914.* New York: Harper Collins, 2012.

Cooper, John Milton, Jr. *Woodrow Wilson: A Biography.* New York: Knopf, 2009.

Englund, Peter. *The Beauty and the Sorrow: An Intimate History of the First World War.* Translated by Peter Graves. New York: Vintage, 2011.

Fussell, Paul. *The Great War and Modern Memory.* New York: Oxford University Press, 1975.

Hastings, Max. *Catastrophe 1914: Europe Goes to War.* New York: Knopf, 2013.

Hochschild, Adam. *To End All Wars: A Story of Loyalty and Rebellion, 1914–1918.* Boston: Houghton Mifflin Harcourt, 2011.

Link, Arthur. *Wilson: The Struggle for Neutrality.* Princeton, NJ: Princeton University Press, 1960.

Wilson, Woodrow. "Message on Neutrality." August 20, 1914. http://millercenter.org/president/wilson/speeches/speech-3791

Wilson, Woodrow. "Joint Address to Congress Leading to a Declaration of War against Germany." April 2, 1917. http://www.ourdocuments.gov/doc.php?flash=true&doc=61

Jonathan Lurie
Professor of History, Emeritus
Rutgers University

WORLD WAR II

World War II is best understood as started by Germany's invasion of Poland on September 1, 1939, but the United States only became fully involved in December 1941.

This timing is related to the decision of American voters in the 1918 and 1920 elections to entrust the country to Republican leaders who opposed formal international connections. The US Senate did not ratify the 1919 peace treaty ending World War I (1914–1918), and the treaty of guarantee for France that had persuaded France not to detach the Rhineland from Germany was also not ratified. The US Army was shrunk drastically, warships were scrapped rather than built, and there was practically no air force. The United States also did not enter the League of Nations, and while international trade continued, tariffs were raised and very drastic restrictions were imposed on immigration. In the 1930s, the Great Depression made it extremely difficult to reverse these policies in the face of Japanese and German aggression. Rearmament would be extremely expensive, and during the Depression, most Americans did not favor an influx of Jewish immigrants whose assets had been stolen by Germany and who might compete for scarce jobs.

BACKGROUND

In the 1930s, as more Americans came to believe that the United States' entrance into World War I had been a mistake, the US Congress passed a series of "neutrality laws" that restricted US assistance for victims of German or Japanese aggression. These laws discouraged Britain and France from confronting Germany, while encouraging the German government as it moved aggressively in Europe and, in 1937, began developing the airplanes and warships it believed it needed to defeat the United States after it achieved victories over the Western powers and the Soviet Union.

As Japan repudiated naval limitation treaties it had signed, the United States began to build warships again, and, after the 1938 crisis over Czechoslovakia, President Franklin D. Roosevelt (1882–1945) initiated a major air force buildup. After German victories in the spring and summer of 1940 Congress was persuaded in July 1940 to finance what was called a "two ocean navy" and to enact in October 1940 a military draft to create a substantial army, but came within one vote of ending the draft in October 1941.

President Roosevelt had carefully followed developments in Europe, but he could see little opportunity for the United States to play any substantial role in view of the weak economy and Americans' predominantly isolationist sentiments. He similarly observed Japanese expansionism and, in minimal ways, assisted the Chinese Nationalist government after the outbreak of war between Japan and China in July 1937.

In the summer of 1939, as war in Europe looked likely, Roosevelt took two steps designed to discourage Germany from striking. He encouraged Soviet dictator

Joseph Stalin (1878/9–1953) to sign an agreement with Britain and France lest a Germany victorious in Western Europe strike at the Soviet Union and the United States. Stalin, however, used his public negotiations with the Western powers to further secret Soviet negotiations with Germany, which led to the German-Soviet Nonaggression Pact of August 23, 1939. Roosevelt was equally unsuccessful in trying to persuade Congress to amend neutrality legislation to allow belligerents to purchase weapons and other military supplies. This "cash and carry" concept would enable the British and French, who were expected to control the North Atlantic, to take advantage of the provision while Germany could not. Until Germany invaded Poland, the majority in Congress was still confident that there would be no war. Thereafter, the change was made, leading to massive Allied orders for supplies, which played a major role in the growth of the American war industry.

THE WAR AND THE UNITED STATES

German victories in April, May, and June 1940 not only convinced the United States to build up the American navy but also had two further effects: one immediate and one quickly following. Roosevelt decided to run for an unprecedented third term and to create an equally unprecedented coalition government. He asked the Republican Party's most recent presidential candidate, Alf Landon (1887–1987), to join his cabinet. When Landon refused, Roosevelt brought in the defeated candidate for vice president, Frank Knox (1874–1944), who became secretary of the navy. Another prominent Republican, former secretary of state Henry Stimson (1867–1950), joined the cabinet as secretary of war. Both Knox and Stimson appointed additional Republicans to high office, while Roosevelt made still another Republican, William Donovan (1883–1959), the head of a new agency that became the Office of Strategic Services (OSS) and later the Central Intelligence Agency (CIA).

The immediate effect was an increase in public support for aid to Great Britain, which continued the struggle after the fall of France, a trend enhanced by radio and newspaper reports on German bombing of London and other cities. More Americans worried about the danger Germany might pose, and responded to the president's efforts to alert them. The other side of Britain's refusal to surrender was a dual change in German policy.

Adolf Hitler (1889–1945) originally intended to invade the Soviet Union in the fall of 1940, but practical problems in the redistribution of German forces, supplies, and communication systems led to his end-of-July decision to postpone the invasion until 1941. With the French defeated and the British obliged to concentrate on defense of the home islands against a likely German invasion, Hitler urged Japan to strike for Singapore, and thereby help force a British surrender. The Japanese explained that they expected to seize the French, Dutch, and British possessions in South and Southeast Asia in 1946. Realizing that 1946 was chosen because in that year the United States expected to give up bases in the Philippines that were to become independent in 1944, Hitler and his associates understood Japan's concern about the Americans on the flank of any strike south. Germany was planning to crush the United States, but had not completed the intercontinental bombers or battle fleet that it would need for that purpose. The obvious alternative was to secure an ally with the needed fleet. German leaders accordingly promised the Japanese that Germany would join them in a war against the United States the moment Japan struck, and Germany repeated this promise ever more urgently thereafter.

As war in Europe and North Africa continued in the winter of 1940 to 1941, the United States exchanged World War I–era destroyers that the British needed in the battle for the Atlantic for bases on British colonies in the Western Hemisphere. At the same time, the advantage for the British of being able to purchase military equipment from American industry and of taking over contracts France had made for similar purchases also had the effect of exhausting Britain's foreign-exchange reserves. Prime Minister Winston Churchill (1874–1965) appealed to Roosevelt in December 1940 for assistance on the financial aspect of aid to Britain, which led to the president's proposal of what became the Lend-Lease program. Passed by Congress in March 1941, Lend-Lease allowed the president to designate countries important for the defense of the United States to receive American products against promises instead of payments. The president so designated Great Britain, and it was under this law that American aid was sent to Great Britain and its dominions.

The German invasion of the Soviet Union in June 1941 confronted Roosevelt with the question of whether to make the latter eligible for Lend-Lease. This was difficult because of the US public's disapproval of the Soviet regime, a level of disapproval that had led to American military intervention against the Soviet Union and delayed formal recognition and diplomatic relations until Roosevelt arranged them in 1933. Over a period of months in 1941, the president moved in the direction of aid to the Soviet Union, supported both by Churchill's immediate decision to help the Soviets and by the American public's recognition of the increasingly successful resistance of the Red Army against the German invasion.

Incidents in the Atlantic as ships carrying supplies to Britain were attacked by German submarines drew much attention but did not lead the United States into war as in

1917. There was restraint on both sides. Hitler rebuffed the head of the German navy, Admiral Erich Raeder (1876–1960), who pushed for open war on American shipping, and thus war with the United States, beginning in October 1939. It is no coincidence that Hitler instructed the German navy to sink American ships and those of eight other countries in the Western Hemisphere the moment he got word of Japan's December 1941 attack on Pearl Harbor; he would not let the war with the United States wait for the three or four additional days needed to assemble Germany's parliament and carry out the appropriate diplomatic steps.

On the other side, although the US government was able to intercept and decode Germany's radio traffic with its submarines, Roosevelt did not use this information to assure daily incidents in the Atlantic. Rather, the intercepts allowed the United States to systematically route convoys and individual ships around German submarine packs. The incidents that did occur were used to raise the alarm level of the American public, but the general policy was to avoid incidents as much as possible. When Hitler asked the German navy whether it would be possible to send submarines into American harbors and sink the bulk of the US Navy—a sort of underwater Pearl Harbor attack—the answer was no, which likely reinforced Hitler's effort to urge Japan to strike.

The Japanese explained to the Germans that they expected to strike south in 1946 but would consider moving up the timetable if Germany promised to join them in war against the United States. The Japanese worried, however, about the continuing war with China, in which they had turned down German mediation in early 1938. Believing that foreign aid was keeping China at war, Japan built on the German victories in Western Europe in 1940 to occupy northern French Indochina in the fall of 1940, thus closing the Haiphong-Hanoi railway to China and simultaneously obliging Britain to close the Burma Road, which was used to carry supplies to China. Since these steps clearly related to Japan's campaign in China, the American response was mild. But when Japan reacted to the German invasion of the Soviet Union by deciding not to join the war against the Soviet Union but to initiate the move south toward an anticipated war against Britain, the Dutch, and the United States by occupying southern French Indochina in July 1941, the American reaction was quite different.

This step obviously pointed away from fighting in China and toward war with the United States and its potential allies. The US president, who had warned Stalin about German plans to attack his country and had been ignored, did not want to follow the Soviet leader's policy of providing Germany with oil and other critical materials until Germany invaded. Earlier controls and embargoes

on various materials were now enhanced by a refusal to sell oil to Japan, a measure joined by the British and Dutch. Roosevelt invested an enormous amount of time into negotiations with Japan in 1941 in the hope of delaying any Japanese attack on the United States until Japanese authorities could see that Germany was not certain to win the war in Europe. He had much of the US fleet moved from the West Coast to Hawai'i, and many of the new B-17 Flying Fortresses were sent to the Philippines in the hope of deterring Japan.

While Hitler worried about Japan possibly not striking, in the final talks between Tokyo and Washington the idea was raised that if the Japanese evacuated southern Indochina, the United States would sell them all the oil they wanted. Japanese diplomats in Washington were immediately instructed not to discuss this proposal, since Tokyo had decided on war. When the United States decoded this instruction, along with other communications in which Germany and Italy confirmed their promise to join Japan in its war with the United States, US leaders sent a message to Pearl Harbor and other locations warning of an imminent Japanese attack, but the commanders at Pearl Harbor failed to take this warning sufficiently seriously.

In the same week in October that the US House of Representatives nearly ended the draft, Japan's naval staff yielded to Admiral Yamamoto Isoroku's (1884–1943) threat to resign as commander of the Combined Fleet unless they accepted his plan for an attack on American warships in Pearl Harbor, using aircraft flown from carriers, in lieu of their prior plan for a fleet engagement in the Pacific when the American fleet moved to relieve the Philippines. Japan's attack on Pearl Harbor on December 7, 1941, was successful in its immediate aim of immobilizing the United States fleet while Japan initiated its move south. It was, however, both a major strategic defeat for Japan's hopes in the war and had significant tactical advantages for the Americans.

THE US FORCED INTO THE CONFLICT

The strategic aspect belongs to the context of Japanese hopes for a negotiated settlement after a short war, a settlement in which Japan could keep substantial portions of what it had seized in the conflict's initial phase. The attack on Pearl Harbor in peacetime on a Sunday so enraged Americans that there was not the slightest chance of a compromise settlement. The Japanese belief that the American people would never pay the price in blood and treasure to retake places they had never heard of so that these could be returned to colonial masters of whom they disapproved was made false by the December 7 attack. Americans, who had sent aid to Japan after the great Kanto earthquake in the 1920s, had increasingly turned against Japan as they learned of Japanese atrocities in China from newspapers and in reports from American missionaries. The level of anger against Japan remained extremely high until Japan surrendered in 1945.

The tactical advantages for the Americans were, first, that all but two of the battleships hit in the attack sank into the mud of the shallow waters of the harbor and could be raised, repaired, and returned to duty. This process, as well as the general revival of American naval power by new construction, was greatly assisted by a second aspect of the attack: in spite of the high casualties on the battleships *Arizona* and *Oklahoma*, the overwhelming majority of the trained crew members of the attacked ships survived to serve in the war thereafter.

The US Congress, with one House member dissenting, responded by declaring war on Japan. Likewise, when Germany and Italy declared war on the United States, Congress reciprocated. When Hungary, Romania, and Bulgaria followed Germany in declaring war, President Roosevelt tried by diplomatic means to convince them to withdraw their declarations. German and Italian submarines could strike US ships, but what could Hungary, Romania, and Bulgaria do to the United States, and why? The negotiations in Ankara, neutral Turkey's capital, were unsuccessful. In June 1942, Roosevelt gave up and notified Congress that since these states insisted on war, Congress should accommodate them, which it promptly did.

In earlier discussions with the British, American leaders had agreed that if the United States became involved in a war with Germany and Japan, the strategic emphasis would place the defeat of Germany and its Italian ally first, both because Britain and the Soviet Union had no choice and because Germany was the more dangerous enemy. Right after the Japanese attack on Pearl Harbor, Churchill traveled to Washington to make sure that American anger at Japan did not produce a reversal of the "Europe First" strategy. Roosevelt and Churchill had met at the Atlantic Conference in August 1941, and their military leaders had become acquainted with each other in the process. The former chief of the Imperial General Staff, Field Marshall Sir John Dill (1881–1944), who had gotten along very well with the US Army chief of staff, General George C. Marshall (1880–1959), became the head of the British military mission in Washington. He was a central figure in US-British military relations until his death in November 1944, a role marked by his being entrusted with American operational secrets while alive and his burial in Arlington National Cemetery. The "Europe First" strategy was reaffirmed at the December 1941 conference, but in practice the rapid Japanese advance obliged the United States to send the majority of newly mobilized forces to the Pacific in 1942 and the first months of 1943.

Although the policy was not formally announced until January 1943 at the Casablanca meeting of Roosevelt and Churchill, when the British cabinet vetoed Churchill's suggestion that Italy might be exempted, the concept of unconditional surrender was President Roosevelt's position from December 1941 on. He had held that view when he served as assistant secretary of the navy in 1918, but, as a loyal member of the administration of President Woodrow Wilson (1856–1924), he had kept quiet. This time, no one was going to pretend that they had not been defeated at the front, and American soldiers would not have to fight Germany a third or Japan a second time.

In the months following the December 1941 attack, a carefully planned and coordinated Japanese advance destroyed numerically superior British forces in Malaya preliminary to conquering the Dutch East Indies and Burma. Simultaneously, but more slowly, the Japanese defeated American and Filipino forces in the Philippines and moved on to conquer Allied-held islands in the South Pacific. Japanese forces were finally checked in May 1942 in a battle primarily between aircraft carriers in the Coral Sea, where the Japanese were forced to abandon their plan to capture Port Moresby on the south coast of New Guinea, which they planned to use as a base for invading Australia.

A successful Japanese naval strike into the Indian Ocean did not lead anywhere after the British landed at the northern end of the island of Madagascar to secure the sea supply route to the Middle East and to the Soviet Union. At Yamamoto's insistence, the Japanese navy moved toward occupying Hawai'i by first taking Midway Island while diverting American forces with landings on Attu and Kiska in the Aleutians. American intelligence officers in Hawai'i had discovered the Japanese plan, and acting on that information, the new commander of the American fleet there, Admiral Chester Nimitz (1885–1966), sent out his carriers. In the Battle of Midway in early June 1942, the Japanese lost four carriers, while one of the three American carriers was damaged and subsequently sunk by a Japanese submarine. At this point, the war in the Pacific turned. A significant result of the reality that primarily US forces had halted the Japanese advance and thereby shielded Australia and New Zealand was that these British dominions came to look to America as their protector.

After the Coral Sea battle in May 1942, the Japanese hoped to seize Port Moresby by an overland route, but they were halted by Australian forces. President Roosevelt had ordered General Douglas MacArthur (1880–1964) to leave the Philippines for Australia, and he now became commander of Allied forces in the Southwest Pacific theater. MacArthur was a great showman who built up a reputation within the United States while the soldiers under his command generally despised him.

To maintain control of the route to Australia, American marines landed on Guadalcanal and nearby Tulagi in the Solomons in early August 1942. The Japanese adopted the same policy that circumstances imposed on the United States, dribbling in additional men, planes, and warships, resulting in a six-month battle of attrition that Americans won.

US PLANS FOR VICTORY IN THE PACIFIC

Looking toward the defeat of Japan, America adopted a two-thrust strategy, hopefully assisted by two more. The US Navy, supported by marine and army units, would strike across the central Pacific from island to island until ready to assault the Japanese home islands if these could not be throttled by blockade and bombardment. The Southwest Pacific theater forces would move along the northern shore of New Guinea and nearby islands toward the Philippines and then the Japanese home islands.

These two thrusts were to be assisted by one from China and one from the Soviet Union. The interest in both was based on the hope that the large Japanese forces in China would remain there, instead of meeting the American thrusts. Furthermore, it would be easier to bomb Japan from China and perhaps invade it from there. Because of these expectations, the United States argued for a campaign in northern Burma to reopen a land route to China and developed an air-supply route over the Himalayas from India's Assam Province, called "The Hump."

The British were skeptical, but the Americans pushed the two projects in 1942 to 1944 both to help keep China fighting and as a possible base for air raids and an invasion of Japan. After some Allied success in clearing northern Burma and basing American bombers, and not only fighters, in China, Japan reacted in June 1944 by launching the "Ichigo" offensive. This operation—also designed to assure a railway connection to resources Japan had conquered in Southeast Asia that were increasingly difficult to ship to Japan after American submarines obtained torpedoes that worked in 1943—was successful. Japanese forces seized most of the airfields from which the bombing of Japan had been launched and also demolished the Chinese Nationalist army. The immediate effects were the transfer of bombers to bases the Americans had seized in the Marianas and the abandonment of any idea of invading Japan from China. The long-term effect was defeat of the Nationalists by the Communists in the civil war that followed Japan's 1945 surrender.

US hopes that the Soviet Union would attack Japan reinforced the pressure to send as much aid to the Soviets as possible, a policy General MacArthur pushed in 1945

by reminding Washington of the need for Soviet intervention when he was appointed to lead the invasion of the home islands. At the first meeting of Roosevelt, Churchill, and Stalin at Teheran at the end of November 1943, Stalin promised to join the war against Japan after the defeat of Germany, a promise he reiterated to President Harry Truman (1884–1972) at their meeting in Potsdam in July 1945.

THE US HOME FRONT

While the fighting in the Pacific drew most of the attention among Americans for much of 1942, the home front was being mobilized. The roles of women and of African Americans began to change, as the need for labor in rapidly growing war industries drew both into jobs previously generally closed to them. The armed forces remained segregated, but the large number of African Americans serving and some agitation by civil rights advocates at home initiated an impetus toward further changes after the war. The effort to avoid a recurrence of the problems associated with returning veterans after World War I became codified in the GI Bill of Rights of July 1944. It provided loans for the purchase of homes, a kind of unemployment insurance, and educational benefits that transformed the country socially after the war as many veterans became the first in their family to attend college. Eligibility for benefits was calculated on length of service without regard to race or gender.

At the same time, there were restrictions on those designated as "enemy aliens" and a program of interning Japanese Americans from two whole states (California and Nevada) and parts of three western states (Oregon, Washington, and Arizona) to conceal breaks into Japan's codes that showed considerable risks of disloyalty by some of them. Because Roosevelt, Secretary of State Cordell Hull (1871–1955), and many others had held high office at the end of World War I when the peace settlement had been repudiated, the president worked hard to preclude any repetition. Several major international organizations, including the United Nations Relief and Rehabilitation Administration, the World Bank, and the World Refugee Organization, were created during the war. Roosevelt pushed in this direction. His administration held the preliminary meeting to form a United Nations organization at Dumbarton Oaks in Washington, DC, in 1944, and scheduled the UN organizing conference for San Francisco, rather than Geneva, because he wanted its physical location to be in the United States. Although he died in 1945 before the latter event took place, he had involved both Republican and Democratic Party leaders in the process to secure broad support.

The president had sent Admiral William D. Leahy (1875–1959), a former chief of naval operations, to Vichy in 1941 as part of an effort to keep the regime of French Marshal Philippe Pétain (1856–1951) from aiding Germany as much as Pétain was inclined to do. Roosevelt recalled Leahy in the summer of 1942 to serve as his immediate military advisor and to chair the Joint Chiefs of Staff, in which he joined General Marshall, Admiral Ernest J. King (1878–1956), and Army Air Force general Henry H. "Hap" Arnold (1886–1950). Since the British refused to make any cross-channel attempt in 1942 when Roosevelt wanted to take serious action against Germany, he and Churchill agreed on an Allied landing in French northwest Africa. Roosevelt had earlier taken steps to assist Britain in the Middle East. In April 1941, after the British crushed Italian forces in northeast Africa, he had opened the Red Sea route for American ships to supply the British in Egypt. This supplemented the air route from Takoradi on Africa's Atlantic coast. When it seemed in the summer of 1942 that the Germans under Erwin Rommel (1891–1944) might occupy Egypt, Roosevelt stripped an armored division of tanks to send to Egypt and had the American air force being developed in the China-Burma-India theater moved to the Middle East.

WAR IN THE MEDITERRANEAN AND ALLIED CONFERENCES

Allied forces landing in Algeria and Morocco in early November 1942 could not seize the Tunisian ports because German and Italian troops halted them. As a result, a cross-channel invasion had to be postponed until 1944, while further operations in the Mediterranean followed the Axis surrender in Tunisia in May 1943. In January 1943, Roosevelt and Churchill had met in Casablanca to coordinate plans for the next military steps. They also tried to resolve problems between French leaders Charles de Gaulle (1890–1970) and Henri Giraud (1879–1949), and publicly announced the unconditional surrender policy. A personnel decision Roosevelt had made on Marshall's recommendation was to appoint General Dwight D. Eisenhower (1890–1969) commander of the northwest Africa operation. Eisenhower's success in coordinating the efforts of the American, British, and some French units there encouraged the president to appoint him to higher command in spite of an American setback at Tunisia's Kasserine Pass in February 1943.

The higher command grew out of conferences with the British and Chinese at Cairo and with Stalin and Churchill at Teheran at the end of November 1943. In the interim, the Western powers had invaded Sicily and then landed in mainland Italy, fighting their way up the peninsula and tying down two German armies as Italy surrendered in September 1943. Stalin reminded Churchill that a continued advance in Italy would run into very high mountains. Like the Americans, Stalin wanted a

landing on the channel coast, a subject of endless arguments between American and British military and civilian leaders. Although Churchill harbored reservations until May 1944, there came to be agreement that the invasion, code-named Overlord, would occur on May 1, 1944, though it was postponed for one month to assure adequate assault shipping. Since the majority of the forces involved after the initial phase would be American, there was to be an American commander. Roosevelt picked Eisenhower because he had coordinated operations well in the Mediterranean. Roosevelt wanted to keep Marshall in Washington, and Marshall was the only possible candidate to command a second invasion in the west if the first effort failed.

The Cairo Conference also brought agreement that China would regain what it had lost to Japan both in the prior and the current war with the Japanese. Roosevelt and Churchill further agreed that the Soviet Union would regain what it had lost to Japan in the 1904–1905 war. At Teheran, there was considerable discussion of what to do with Germany after it had been defeated. Earlier, in October, the foreign ministers of the three countries had met in Moscow and, in addition to reviewing current issues, publicized the Allies' determination to try war criminals after victory, with those whose actions were concentrated in a specific area being returned to that area for trial, and with those whose actions had wider scope being tried by a method still to be devised. This agreement led to the extradition of many Germans accused of war crimes to the countries where they had operated. The Nuremberg trials also had their origins in these discussions, since the United States insisted on trials in opposition to the British proposal of publishing lists of war criminals and executing them when caught.

The meeting of the foreign ministers in Moscow called for the creation of a new international organization, a critical point because the Soviet Union had been thrown out of the League of Nations in 1939. It was agreed that Austria would regain independence within its former borders. The decision was also made to establish a European Advisory Commission to meet in London and take part in planning the occupation of Germany. One important issue before this commission was that of occupation zones in Germany. There was agreement that Berlin would be jointly ruled by the Allies, a circle to which France was added. There was, however, fundamental disagreement between the American and British plans for occupation zones. Roosevelt wanted the Western zones to meet the Soviet zone at Berlin. Churchill was terrified that the Soviets might stop on reaching their 1941 border and leave the Western powers to finish the job. He therefore had a proposal presented to the commission that placed Berlin deep inside the Soviet zone. The Soviets immediately accepted this plan, though it took until the fall of 1944 for the United States to agree. Ironically, in 1945, as British and American forces drove into what was to become the Soviet zone, Churchill had second thoughts. President Truman adhered to the original agreement, because he believed governments should stick to agreements they had signed and he very much wanted the Soviets to adhere to their agreements, especially the one to join the war against Japan that was heating up as the European war was winding down.

Two further aspects of the zonal issue needed to be resolved. Roosevelt wanted the American zone to be in northwest Germany, not in the interior south, as the British proposed. This difference was resolved when the British yielded a port in northwest Germany and a railway connection to the American zone. The other question involved the role of France. There came to be agreement on a French zone of occupation in southwest Germany carved out of the British and American zones. General planning for occupied Germany was tough; the Germans were to get a rough deal, while the Japanese would get a new deal. Many Germans were obliged to watch burials or movies depicting the horrors of German concentration camps, while nothing of the sort occurred in Japan. In the US occupation zone in Germany, American soldiers carried arms, but not in Japan. In Japan, the administration was purged but remained in charge, while in Germany there were no German central authorities at all for several years. The last occupation forces left Japan in 1952 and Germany in 1994, and Germany's last head of state, Admiral Karl Dönitz (1891–1980), was arrested, tried at Nuremberg, and sentenced to jail, although he considered himself the legal head of Germany until his death. Meanwhile, Japan's emperor, Hirohito (1901–1989), was neither arrested nor tried and remained emperor until his death.

OVERLORD: THE INVASIONS IN THE WEST

The decision for Overlord was reaffirmed at several American-British conferences, but one aspect remained controversial. An invasion of the Mediterranean coast of France was part of the concept but was vehemently opposed by the British. American insistence was based on several considerations. First, the ports of Toulon and Marseille would be needed to supply the advancing Allied forces, a belief events completely justified. A Mediterranean invasion also became a way for French forces to play a significant role in liberating their country when French units fighting in Italy formed the French First Army in the mid-August 1944 landing. This proved a real success. Some friction between the Americans and Free French continued as the Americans planned for the French corps destined for the Pacific to be utilized in the follow-up to the second invasion of the Japanese home islands instead

of retaking French Indochina as de Gaulle preferred. There was also a bitter dispute when Truman thwarted de Gaulle's plan to annex a piece of northwest Italy. Basic American policy, however, continued its pro-French tradition, a policy symbolized by having the only French division in Overlord sent first into Paris in August 1944.

By the time of the liberation of Paris, American forces in the Pacific had moved forward in the two thrusts. MacArthur's push along the north coast of New Guinea, which included some Australian units, pushed further toward the Philippines, while Nimitz's forces assaulted a series of islands, culminating in the invasion of the Marianas in June 1944. The attendant naval battles were won by the Americans, and that was also the case when American troops landed in the Philippines in October. The fighting there was lengthy and on some islands continued until Japan surrendered, but bases for an assault into Japan's inner defenses were now available.

The Allied offensive in Western Europe was launched on June 6, 1944. The offensive stalled in the fall, but there had been two major shifts in the conflict. In the summer of 1943, the United States, Britain, and Canada had defeated German submarines in the North Atlantic, and all German efforts to reverse the tide failed. On the other hand, the bombing offensive against Germany, with the Americans trying to hit specific targets in daytime and the British area-bombing German cities at night, was in trouble in the fall of 1943. But the Allies succeeded in gaining control of the air over Western Europe in the first months of 1944. Hoping to defeat the Americans and drive them out of the war, thereby forcing Britain to surrender and making a massive transfer of German forces to the eastern front possible, the Germans launched a major December offensive in the Ardennes, which came to be called the Battle of the Bulge. It was halted after initial local success, and in February 1945, American, British, Canadian, and French armies resumed offensives into Germany to meet the Red Army, which had launched its offensive in January.

CONFERENCES

At the same time, American and British military leaders met in Malta on their way to Stalin's Yalta meeting with Roosevelt and Churchill. At Malta, the final strategy for the war with Germany was agreed upon and plans were made to defeat Japan. It was anticipated that this could be accomplished in 1947, although there remained concern that Japanese soldiers outside the home islands might continue to fight after the occupation of Japan. By the time the three Allied leaders met in early February, the Red Army had occupied all of Poland, so that the subject that took the largest share of conference time, the broadening of the Soviet-created Provisional Government

Soldiers of Pennsylvania's 28th Infantry Division march along the Champs Elysées four days after the liberation of Paris, August, 1944. *In keeping with the pro-French tradition of American policy, the first division sent in to liberate Paris from German occupation was French. After the war, a large portion of the American public saw themselves and their country as playing a major role in world affairs and supported the country's leaders in the policy of containment and aid to Western Europe in the early years of the Cold War.* AP IMAGES/PETER J. CARROLL

of Poland that Roosevelt and Churchill wanted, was effectively precluded by Stalin's preference for total Communist domination.

The issue of Poland's boundaries was discussed at length. Roosevelt and Churchill agreed to an eastern boundary for Poland that left areas inhabited primarily by Ukrainians and Belorussians to the Soviet Union, but they preferred that Poland retain more of its prewar lands than Stalin planned. Stalin did leave the Bialystok area to Poland, but would not yield on L'viv. Stalin's insistence on a Polish western border on the Oder-Neisse line precluded the concept the two Western leaders preferred, which had been suggested by Treasury Secretary Henry Morgenthau (1856–1946). It called for Germany to have a high standard of living like Denmark and Holland but without heavy industry—as Churchill put it, "fat but

impotent." This would have required that Germany keep much of its eastern agricultural land, something Stalin's border prevented. The other border issue reflected a change in Stalin's own prior view. All three had thought it best to turn over East Prussia to Poland, but because of Roosevelt's refusal to recognize Soviet annexation of the Baltic states and his pressure on Churchill preventing the latter from recognizing it, Stalin demanded the northern half of East Prussia as a staple holding the Baltic states in the Soviet Union. This meant Poland would not obtain Königsberg, now Kaliningrad, but would be compensated with the German city of Stettin on the west bank of the Oder River.

The question about the veto procedure in the United Nations, left over from Dumbarton Oaks, was resolved. The Soviets had insisted on great-power veto over procedural as well as substantive issues, against American and British preference. Declassified documents show both American and British leaders prepared to yield on this point if essential for Soviet participation, but Stalin's concession on it greatly relieved Roosevelt and Churchill. Stalin's insistence on separate membership for Ukraine and Belarus in the United Nations was agreed to by Churchill, who wanted India admitted, and most reluctantly by Roosevelt.

The three leaders agreed to return prisoners held by the Germans to their home countries. Roosevelt's and Churchill's agreement to what became forced repatriation of former Red Army soldiers and slave laborers arose in the context of their eagerness to bring home American and British POWs, whom the Germans had mostly moved eastward, where they were expected to be liberated by the Soviets.

Stalin reiterated his intent to join the war against Japan for a return of prior Russian concessions in Manchuria, while recognizing and supporting the Chinese Nationalist government. Since Roosevelt disliked the deal on zones of influence in the Balkans that Churchill had made in Moscow in October 1944, there was a declaration that the liberated countries of Europe would have free choice in their regimes, but in practice the Soviets imposed Communist regimes on Romania, Hungary, and Bulgaria, and later on Czechoslovakia.

THE END OF THE WAR

On April 30, 1945, when Allied forces had occupied most of Germany and the Red Army was in the streets of Berlin, Hitler committed suicide and appointed Dönitz to succeed as head of state. The latter authorized unconditional surrender on May 8. By that time, American forces had conquered Iwo Jima in the Bonin Islands, and on April 1 landed on Okinawa. During the lengthy fighting there, Roosevelt died and was succeeded by Truman. The latter attended the Allied conference at Potsdam in July, at which there was much debate about the future of Europe and a declaration was issued calling on Japan to surrender. With the prior approval of Britain and the Soviets, Truman had up to two atomic bombs diverted from support of Olympic, the invasion of the Japanese island of Kyushu, planned for November as preliminary to Coronet, the landing on Tokyo Bay scheduled for March 1946. The two bombs, dropped on Hiroshima and Nagasaki, produced a split in the Tokyo leadership that was resolved by the emperor's decision for surrender. By then, the Soviets had entered the Pacific war, and the surrender call was heeded by Japanese troops everywhere. Japan was not divided into occupation zones, but retained its government under the Allied supreme commander, General MacArthur, with American and British Commonwealth troops occupying the country.

During the course of the war, the role of the United States in the world changed dramatically from isolation to one of military and economic leadership. Even as its domestic situation changed as a result of mobilization and social upheaval, it became the leader of the West in the Cold War that developed in response to Soviet actions and threats in Europe and the Middle East.

Unlike after World War I, a very large portion of the American public after World War II saw themselves and their country as playing a major role in world affairs and accordingly supported the country's leaders in the policy of containment and aid to Western Europe in the early years of the Cold War. At the same time, people elsewhere on the globe increasingly looked to the United States either for help in crisis situations or as difficult and meddling folk who stuck their noses into places and matters that did not concern them. In varying and alternating strengths, both attitudes have persisted ever since World War II.

SEE ALSO *Atomic Bomb; Great Depression; League of Nations; Manhattan Project; Paris Peace Conference (1919); Roosevelt, Franklin D.; Rosie the Riveter; Treaty of Versailles; Truman, Harry S.; United Nations*

BIBLIOGRAPHY

Bennett, Edward M. *Franklin D. Roosevelt and the Search for Victory: American-Soviet Relations, 1939–1945.* Wilmington, DE: Scholarly Resources, 1990.

Bercuson, David, and Holger Herwig. *One Christmas in Washington: The Secret Meeting between Roosevelt and Churchill That Changed the World.* New York: Overlook Press, 2005.

Campbell, D'Ann. *Women at War with America: Private Lives in a Patriotic Era.* Cambridge, MA: Harvard University Press, 1984.

Dear, I. C. B., ed. *The Oxford Companion to the Second World War.* Oxford and New York: Oxford University Press, 1995.

Divine, Robert A. *Second Chance: The Triumph of Internationalism in America during World War II.* New York: Atheneum, 1971.

Frank, Richard B. *Downfall: The End of the Imperial Japanese Empire.* New York: Random House, 1999.

Herring, George C., Jr. *Aid to Russia, 1941–1946: Strategy, Diplomacy, the Origins of the Cold War.* New York: Columbia University Press, 1973.

Jeffries, John W. *Wartime America: The World War II Home Front.* Chicago: Ivan R. Dee, 1996.

Kimball, Warren F. *Forged in War: Roosevelt, Churchill, and the Second World War.* New York: William Morrow, 1997.

Kochavi, Arieh J. *Prelude to Nuremberg: Allied War Crimes Policy and the Question of Punishment.* Chapel Hill: University of North Carolina Press, 1998.

Lowman, David D. *Magic: The Untold Story of U.S. Intelligence and the Evacuation of Japanese Residents from the West Coast during World War II.* Provo, UT: Athena Press, 2001.

McNeill, William Hardy. *America, Britain, and Russia: Their Cooperation and Conflict, 1941–1946.* New York: Johnson, 1970.

O'Connor, Raymond G. *Diplomacy for Victory: FDR and Unconditional Surrender.* New York: Norton, 1971.

Plokhy, S. M. *Yalta: The Price of Peace.* New York: Viking, 2010.

Reynolds, David. *Summits: Six Meetings That Shaped the Twentieth Century.* New York: Basic Books, 2007.

Stoler, Mark A. *Allies and Adversaries: The Joint Chiefs of Staff, the Grand Alliance, and U.S. Strategy in World War II.* Chapel Hill: University of North Carolina Press, 2000.

Weinberg, Gerhard L. *A World at Arms: A Global History of World War II.* New York: Cambridge University Press, 2005. Note the bibliographic essay, pages 921–944.

Weinberg, Gerhard L., and Mark R. Peattie, primary consultants. *World War II Chronicle.* Lincolnwood, IL: Legacy, 2007.

Zimm, Alan D. *Attack on Pearl Harbor: Strategy, Combat, Myths, Deceptions.* Philadelphia: Casemate, 2011.

Gerhard L. Weinberg
William Rand Kenan, Jr., Professor of History Emeritus
University of North Carolina at Chapel Hill

WORLD'S FAIRS

In pondering US perceptions of the rest of the world, and the rest of the world's perceptions of the United States, especially before the Second World War (1939–1945), few institutions have mattered as much as world's fairs (variously called universal expositions, international exhibitions, and, most recently, world expos). Between 1851, when London's Crystal Palace Exhibition kicked off the world's fair movement, and 1940, the final year of the two-year New York World's Fair, about one billion people attended the hundreds of world's fairs held primarily in Europe, Australia, and the United States, but also in French and British colonies across Asia and to some extent in northern and southern Africa. During the Cold War, major world's fairs, especially the 1958 Brussels Universal Exposition, became sites of cultural and political confrontation between the Soviet Union and the United States. Since the end of the Cold War, major world expos have been held around the globe, with the 2010 Shanghai exposition attracting some seventy million visitors. Although the US government withdrew in 2001 from the international convention that governs international expositions and no longer provides public funds for American pavilions at overseas world's fairs, the United States is still represented in official US pavilions that are now privately funded. In the twenty-first century, world's fairs have become less important for Americans for their understanding of the world, but they remain an important medium through which the rest of the world gains insights into American culture and its influence overseas (Greenhalgh 2011).

VICTORIAN-ERA WORLD'S FAIRS

The starting point for understanding the role played by world's fairs in shaping popular opinion is London's 1851 spectacle. With negligible support from the US government, American industrialists and agriculturalists determined to develop exhibits that would promote American inventiveness to English and European audiences. The results exceeded expectations. Exhibits of Samuel Colt's firearms and Cyrus McCormick's reapers knocked the British public back on its heels and alerted the British government to America's rapid deployment of technology to advance economic growth. At the same time, responses to exhibits of America's arts, centering on Hiram Powers's sculpture *The Greek Slave*, suggested that America's fine arts were still derivative and reflective of European styles and fashions—a conundrum that would plague the perception of American arts both in the United States and abroad for several generations (Rydell, Findling, and Pelle 2000).

US exhibits at the Paris universal expositions that followed the Crystal Palace Exhibition excited both attention and alarm. French writer Charles Baudelaire, contemplating the displays at the 1855 Paris exposition, which included exhibits of Singer sewing machines, coined the word *Americanize* to warn Europeans of the damaging effects of American democratic and commercial values for European "Culture" and "Civilization." The 1889 Paris Universal Exposition, which featured Gustave Eiffel's famous tower and Buffalo Bill's Wild West Show, added grist to the mills of intellectuals who likened modernization to Americanization and expressed equal measure of scorn and envy about America's exhibits. In 1889, Thomas Edison received a hero's welcome in Paris, where the fair's Palace of Electricity highlighted Edison's inventions. Similarly, the 1900 Paris Universal Exposition, which attracted some fifty million visitors, put on exhibit electrical dynamos that elicited both praise and agony. The Otis Elevator Company's display of its escalator excited less alarm than delight as many French newspapers carried stories extolling American ingenuity (Rydell and Kroes 2005).

The success of European and British fairs in promoting the nation-states that hosted these spectacles inspired American political and business leaders to follow suit. A small-scale Crystal Palace was erected in New York City in 1853, but the world's fair medium failed to take hold in the United States until after the Civil War (1861–1865), when the 1876 Philadelphia Centennial Exhibition inspired a nationwide world's fair movement as part of the effort to reconstruct the nation after its devastating

A giant electric lamp, representing the inventions of Thomas Edison, at the Paris Exposition Universelle of 1889. US exhibits at the Paris universal expositions elicited both praise and alarm, with some scornful Europeans concerned about the damaging effects of modernization and Americanization. Nevertheless, at the 1889 Paris exposition Thomas Edison received a hero's welcome. **TARKER/FINE ART/CORBIS**

War between the States. By the time of America's entry into the First World War (1914–1918), world's fairs had been held in New Orleans (1884–1885) Chicago (1893), Atlanta (1895), Omaha (1898), Buffalo (1901), St. Louis (1904), Portland (1905), Seattle (1909), and San Francisco and San Diego (1915–1916). Smaller-scale international exhibitions also took place in Nashville

(1897) and Jamestown (1907). All of the fairs provided forums for national displays in the arts and technology and featured technological innovations that could send shivers across international political landscapes. For instance, Germany's Krupp armaments exhibits at the 1893 Chicago World's Columbian Exposition alerted the US military to its own technological backwardness when it came to military preparation (Rydell 1984).

Exactly why technology and military preparedness mattered was clear from another aspect of European and American fairs—their colonial exhibits. The French and British governments embedded large colonial exhibits into most of their fairs and organized specialized expositions specifically dedicated to advancing their national imperial agendas. The United States followed suit. At the 1904 St. Louisiana Purchase Exposition, the US government showed its willingness to respond to Rudyard Kipling's admonition that the United States "take up the white man's burden" by organizing a 47-acre exhibit of 1,200 Filipinos to underscore America's capacity to control the destiny of its "outlying possessions" acquired through the 1898 war with Spain. Most American fairs also featured exhibits of Native Americans who were often juxtaposed to people from Asia, Africa, and the Middle East. Often, these exhibits, featured as part of the commercial entertainment zones at fairs, were promoted as authentic anthropological exhibits and received favorable notice from leading anthropologists eager to disseminate ideas about racial hierarchies (Breitbart 1997).

Colonial exhibits reinforced prevailing imperial and racist presuppositions. But the fairs could also spark human capacities for creativity and resistance. Indigenous people were not simply exhibited at fairs; they performed at these festivals of progress. Their music inspired fellow artists. For instance, the Dahomeyan Village at the 1893 Chicago fair featured performers playing instruments brought from West Africa. Their syncopated rhythms gained the attention of American musicians like Scott Joplin who would incorporate their sound into his own emergent ragtime compositions. At the 1900 Paris Universal Exposition, African American sociologist W. E. B. Du Bois, who organized the so-called Negro Department at the fair, seized the opportunity provided by that exposition to interact with anti-imperialists from European colonies who, in turn, increased his own interest in Pan-Africanism (Lewis and Willis 2003).

FAIRS OF THE INTERWAR PERIOD

As important as these festivals of imperial progress proved to be between 1851 and the First World War, the world's fairs that blossomed across Europe's and America's cultural landscapes during the interwar period proved just as vital for informing the cultural politics and public diplomacy of the era. At the 1933 Century of Progress Exposition, a squadron of Benito Mussolini's air force landed in Chicago. At the 1937 dedication ceremonies for the Golden Gate International Exposition held on Treasure Island in San Francisco Bay, representatives from Imperial Japan and Nazi Germany stood side-by-side with European and US representatives in what, in retrospect, seemed like a tipping point in international relations. In New York, when the Soviet Union decided not to continue into 1940 its participation in the New York World's Fair, its pavilion was torn down and replaced by an American Common, hinting at the tensions between the two nations that would explode once the Second World War ended in 1945. Intended to function as a blueprint for building "the world of tomorrow" from the rubble of the Great Depression, the New York World's Fair, which included a Palestine Pavilion, suggested that the map of the world was already changing and that Americans would need to leave behind the isolationism of the previous two decades (Rydell 1993).

Between the world wars, international expositions continued to promote internationalism and transnational political alliances. They also fostered controversies about modern art. For instance, when Secretary of Commerce Herbert Hoover refused to allow an official representation of American modern art at the 1925 Paris Decorative Arts Exposition because he believed American artists had rejected "modernist" trends, American artists and industrial designers responded by doubling down on their efforts to show their engagement with modernism by shaping the form and content of American fairs held in Chicago (1933–1934), Dallas, San Diego, Cleveland, New York, and San Francisco. All of these fairs featured more streamlined buildings and innovative uses of building materials like asbestos and plywood, and replaced uniform coloring schemes with pavilions painted in bright, sometimes clashing colors. By showing American audiences how European ideas about modernist aesthetics could be applied to products like toasters and luggage, the fairs of the 1930s helped Americans overcome some of their earlier resistance to European modernist influences on design (Rydell and Schiavo 2010).

POSTWAR FAIRS

Following the Second World War, the medium of the world's fair became central for rebuilding the world—and its faith in science-based technology as the primary agent of progress. Beginning in 1955 and 1956 with small displays at exhibitions in India and Afghanistan and continuing with its massive pavilion at the Brussels fair in 1958, the US government turned international exhibitions into bulwarks against the spread of both Soviet and Chinese communism by promoting American consumer goods, especially television, and American business models associated with free enterprise. The results were mixed. Many Europeans, while welcoming American economic aid to rebuild their nations after the war, responded warily to what they perceived as even more intensive and extensive efforts to Americanize Europe.

No less important than the Brussels fair was the 1970 exposition in Osaka, Japan—a vital component of the US government's effort to cement its Cold War political and economic alliance with Japan. The Osaka exposition marked the largest world's fair held to date in Asia and along the Pacific Rim. Followed by smaller expositions in Okinawa (1974) and Tsukuba (1985), the fairs in Japan are perhaps best viewed as efforts to promote investments by US corporations in Asia and to draw Asian tourists to the United States. These fairs also provided Americans the opportunity to appreciate the growing economic and political power of Asian nations (Rydell, Findling, and Pelle 2000).

At the same time that the exposition medium was making inroads in Asia, the US government, after two economically unsuccessful world's fairs in Knoxville (1982) and New Orleans (1984) and a failed effort to hold another world's fair in Chicago in 1992, was beginning to rethink the value of supporting world's fairs in the United States. Beginning in the 1990s, Congress passed legislation making it difficult to use federal dollars to fund world's fairs held in US cities. Then, in 2001, the United States withdrew its membership from the Bureau of International Expositions, the international organization that oversees the frequency and content of international expositions, thus making it virtually impossible to hold another internationally sanctioned world's fair in the United States. Nevertheless, the US State Department continued to sponsor privately funded US pavilions at foreign expositions. These exhibits have made an impression on other nations, especially at the 2010 Shanghai Expo, where, with its large movie screens describing American life, the US Pavilion served notice that the United States is perhaps best understood in the twenty-first century not so much in terms of its political values associated with its founding political documents than as the world's leading center of entertainment.

For about 125 years, world's fairs accompanied and hastened America's rise to becoming a global superpower. US pavilions at foreign expositions focused attention on American economic and cultural exports and, especially at the 1958 Brussels exposition, highlighted American political values in opposition to the values of other nations, especially the Soviet Union. Since the end of the Cold War, US pavilions at foreign fairs have highlighted American technology, science, and mass entertainment.

Since no world's fair has been held in the United States since 1984 and since US media coverage of foreign fairs has been negligible, the American public in recent years has learned little about the rest of the world through world expos. Whether the United States holds another world's fair remains in doubt, and US participation in foreign expositions is never certain. What is certain is that questions about US engagement with the rest of the world through world's fairs are as old as the medium itself.

SEE ALSO *World's Parliament of Religions (1893)*

BIBLIOGRAPHY

Breitbart, Eric. *A World on Display: Photographs from the St. Louis World's Fair, 1904.* Albuquerque: University of New Mexico Press, 1997.

Findling, John E., and Kimberly D. Pelle, eds. *Encyclopedia of World's Fairs and Expositions.* Jefferson, NC: McFarland, 2008.

Greenhalgh, Paul. *Fair World: A History of World's Fairs and Expositions from London to Shanghai, 1851–2010.* London: Papadakis, 2011.

Lewis, David Levering, and Deborah Willis. *A Small Nation of People: W. E. B. Du Bois and African American Portraits of Progress.* Washington, DC: Library of Congress, 2003.

Masey, Jack, and Conway Lloyd Morgan. *Cold War Confrontations: US Exhibitions and Their Role in the Cultural Cold War.* Baden, Switzerland: Lars Muller, 2008.

Rydell, Robert W. *All the World's a Fair: Visions of Empire at American International Expositions, 1876–1916.* Chicago: University of Chicago Press, 1984.

Rydell, Robert W. *World of Fairs: The Century of Progress Expositions.* Chicago: University of Chicago Press, 1993.

Rydell, Robert W., John E. Findling, and Kimberly D. Pelle. *Fair America: World's Fairs in the United States.* Washington, DC: Smithsonian Institution Press, 2000.

Rydell, Robert W., and Rob Kroes. *Buffalo Bill in Bologna: The Americanization of the World, 1869–1922.* Chicago: University of Chicago Press, 2005.

Rydell, Robert W., and Laura Schiavo. *Designing Tomorrow: America's World's Fairs of the 1930s.* New Haven, CT: Yale University Press, 2010.

Robert W. Rydell
Professor of History
Montana State University

WORLD'S PARLIAMENT OF RELIGIONS (1893)

At the most historically important of the world's fairs held in the United States—the 1893 Columbian Exposition in Chicago—the organizers featured what they called "intellectual congresses" to showcase the current state of knowledge in every field at a time when the professional research university and specialized academic disciplines were just beginning to consolidate. The historian Frederick Jackson Turner (1861–1932) delivered his famous paper on "The Significance of the Frontier in American History" at the Expo, but his historical congress was far eclipsed by the seventeen-day World's Parliament of Religions, the biggest headliner, biggest draw, and arguably the biggest success of the entire event. At least that is what its sponsors, especially the Presbyterian minister John Henry Barrows (1847–1902), believed, and indeed the World's Parliament of Religions became a model for peaceable, cross-cultural, interreligious dialogue around the world. Barrows's edited proceedings of the congress ran to two volumes and 1,500 pages, selling one hundred thousand copies in the first year of publication, while countless forms of commentary on the parliament spun around America and the world. The stunning success of Swami Vivekananda (1863–1902) at the podium began the westward evangelism of Hinduism. At the nexus of religion and science, the German immigrant Paul Carus (1852–1919) dedicated the rest of his life to "the parliament idea" and ultimately brought D. T. Suzuki (1870–1966) and Zen Buddhism to America. The historic ecumenical conference also became a global touchstone for diverse religious advocates of "unity and brotherhood"—the keywords of the parliament—across the twentieth century.

INCLUSIVE APPROACH TOWARD RELIGIOUS AND ETHNIC DIVERSITY

The "unity of religion" and "the fatherhood of God and brotherhood of man" are the stock phrases Barrows used in his invitations and promotional material before the parliament, which he proposed would "unite religion against irreligion" and outshine the modernization and glorification of consumerism so visible elsewhere in the Expo. Barrows did not anticipate that a unified form of religion would be anything other than Protestant Christianity, which he and other liberal Protestants considered to be the only universal religion, the only complete religion, because it was the only whole truth and the only church open to all. Barrows invited representatives of the so-called "ethnic religions" to participate in a conversation about what such great religions had in common, and especially how their religious ethics supported social justice, confident that the full glory of the Protestant form of this grand truth would prevail at the congress.

Using channels of communication through social reform at home and the growing missions of evangelical Protestant Christianity abroad, Barrows invited representatives not only of Hinduism and Buddhism, Confucianism, Jainism, Shintoism, and Islam, but also—just as historically—Eastern Orthodoxy, Roman Catholicism, and Judaism. Since Catholics and Jews were rapidly growing populations in the United States in the 1890s, their inclusion both honored a new demographic reality and gave their representatives an important opportunity to legitimate their faith traditions within a dominant Anglo-Protestant mainstream. All of these groups easily co-opted the language of unity and brotherhood to claim ownership of the idea that religion should advance social welfare, rooting this idea within the texts and traditions of their own commitments and claiming a universalism far wider than evangelical Protestantism.

Chicago in the 1890s in some ways epitomized modern American life. It was the "Hog Butcher for the World," in the words of Carl Sandburg (1878–1967), but also a center of progressive reform, social science, the social gospel, and the new working class, with an ethnic diversity comparable to that of New York City. Thus the World's Parliament of Religions not only reflects the growing engagement of liberal Protestants with non-Christian religions, it also represents an inclusive approach toward ethnic and religious diversity that differed from the hierarchical depiction of peoples in the wider Expo. The grand neoclassical halls of the Expo's "White City," the buildings named after industries, the bridges and waterways, and the wide promenades encompassed the inventions, artwork, mounded produce, and civilized achievements of culture.

The Expo largely excluded African Americans and denigrated their culture as well as African civilization. On "Colored Day," local newspapers ran mocking cartoons of minstrels eating watermelon. The memorial book *The Dream City* described a replica of the African *bimba* as "surely the worst boat at the World's Fair." The situation was so bad that Frederick Douglass (c. 1817/8–1895) and Ida B. Wells (1862–1931) produced a pamphlet, *The Reason Why the Colored American Is Not in the World's Columbian Exposition*, in which the barbarism of lynching was detailed in telling contrast to the many achievements of African Americans since emancipation. There was an intellectual congress devoted to Africa, but other than that and the World's Parliament of Religions, non-Anglo cultures were contained in the world's first midway, the section of the Expo featuring rides—including the first Ferris Wheel—thrills, and spectacles of exotic others. Aunt Jemima and her pancake mix debuted there, as did many dancing girls, the donkey boys of Cairo, and an entire Dahomeyan village.

LINKING THE IDEALS OF RELIGIOUS UNITY AND SOCIAL PROGRESS

Against this backdrop, the delegates of the World's Parliament of Religions believed they were fighting against injustice. The 1882 Chinese Exclusion Act had just been renewed in Congress, and the speakers and audiences of the parliament thundered against it. Fannie Barrier Williams (1855–1944) and Bishop Benjamin W. Arnett (1838–1906) pitted the social gospel against racial prejudice. Vivekananda argued against British colonialism, as did the Sri Lankan Anagarika Dharmapala (1864–1933). Soyen Shaku (1860–1919) and Hirai Kinzo protested Western ideas of superiority over Japanese culture. Archbishop James Cardinal Gibbons (1834–1921), Bishop John Keane (1839–1918), and Archbishop John Ireland (1838–1918) linked their Catholic faith with social service to "all races and nations and peoples and tongues" (Kittelstrom 2009, 257). Rabbis Emil G. Hirsch (1851–1923), Kaufmann Kohler (1843–1926), Henry Berkowitz (1857–1924), and Isaac Mayer Wise (1818–1900) represented the modern Reform Jewish faith as the original social religion.

The Protestants at the parliament—the most numerically superior yet not the most prominent group there—were overwhelmingly represented by social activists in the growing Progressive reform movement: Frances Willard (1839–1898) of the Women's Christian Temperance Union, Jane Addams (1860–1935) of Hull House, the economist Richard T. Ely (1854–1943), the sociologist Albion Small (1854–1926), and the ministers and theologians George Dana Boardman (1801–1831), Theodore Munger (1830–1910), Washington Gladden (1836–1918), Jenkin Lloyd Jones (1843–1918), and Shailer Mathews (1863–1941). The World's Parliament of Religions linked the ideal of religious unity with the hope of social progress.

SEE ALSO *Buddhism; Hinduism; Islam; Judaism; Vivekananda, Swami; World's Fairs*

BIBLIOGRAPHY

Burris, John P. *Exhibiting Religion: Colonialism and Spectacle at International Expositions, 1851–1893.* Charlottesville: University of Virginia Press, 2002.

Kittelstrom, Amy. "An International Social Turn: Unity and Brotherhood at the World's Parliament of Religions, Chicago, 1893." *Religion and American Culture: A Journal of Interpretation* 19, 2 (2009): 243–274.

Seager, Richard Hughes. *The World's Parliament of Religions: The East/West Encounter, Chicago, 1893.* Bloomington: Indiana University Press, 1995.

Snodgrass, Judith. *Presenting Japanese Buddhism to the West: Orientalism, Occidentalism, and the Columbian Exposition.* Chapel Hill: University of North Carolina Press, 2003.

Wacker, Grant. "A Plural World: The Protestant Awakening to World Religions." In *Between the Times: The Travail of the Protestant Establishment in America, 1900–1960*, edited by William R. Hutchison, 253–277. New York: Cambridge University Press, 1989.

Ziolkowski, Eric J., ed. *A Museum of Faiths: Histories and Legacies of the 1893 World's Parliament of Religions.* Atlanta, GA: Scholars Press, 1993.

Amy Kittelstrom
Associate Professor of History
Sonoma State University

WORLD'S WOMAN'S CHRISTIAN TEMPERANCE UNION

SEE *Temperance Movement.*

WORLD'S YWCA/YMCA

The Young Women's Christian Association (YWCA) and Young Men's Christian Association (YMCA) were founded in London in the 1840s and 1850s, and quickly spread to the United States. Their original objective was to help young men and women moving to cities, and included spiritual work as well as a broad range of services, such as residence halls, job training, and cafeterias. For much of the history of both organizations, they maintained divisions focused on work abroad (the "International Division" for the YMCA, and the "Foreign Division" for the YWCA). Both groups made a conscious effort to form ties between people of different nations through publications, programming, and personnel.

Unlike missionaries, YM/YWCA secretaries did not tend to be permanently stationed abroad, and their service both within and outside the United States formed direct ties between YM/YWCAs in the United States and those around the world. Both the YMCA and YWCA have global organizations—the World Alliance of YMCAs and the World's YWCA—located today in Geneva, Switzerland. These worldwide groups serve as

ONE OF THE THOUSAND Y.M.C.A. GIRLS IN FRANCE

United War Work Campaign Nov. 11th to 18th

Poster for the United War Work Campaign, November 1918. In World War I, the YMCA ran military canteens in Europe, and the YWCA ran "Hostess Houses" that attempted to replicate a type of domesticity abroad for male soldiers. The YWCA also ran recreation facilities for women who were involved in the war effort in such roles as nurses and telephone operators. **UNIVERSAL HISTORY ARCHIVE/ UIG/GETTY IMAGES**

liaisons between the various national YMCAs and YWCAs, and as fundraisers for global and regional programs. While many people conflate the two organizations, they are separate and maintained sex-segregated facilities for much of their history.

In the late 1800s, YM/YWCAs were spread abroad partly through the missionary movement and the military. In the United States, they had a strong presence on college campuses, where the Student Volunteer Movement (a group that recruited college students for missionary careers) flourished, and the work of evangelists Dwight L. Moody and John Mott was influential. College graduates who became either missionaries or "foreign secretaries" for the YM/YWCA took the idea of youth programming with them abroad. Of particular note is the connection between Yale graduates who went on to be YMCA workers, or members of the YMCA, in China. YMCA secretaries also traveled with the US military and formed organizations where troops were deployed. For example, during the Spanish-American War (1898), US soldiers in Manila founded the first YMCA in the Philippines, which was originally geared toward recreation and sports programs for enlisted men. The YM/YWCAs around the world had similar programs and functions to those within the United States, including Bible study, cafeterias, hostels, job training, and recreation facilities.

During World War I and World War II, the YM/YWCAs were a large part of the support structure for American military personnel. In World War I, the YMCA ran military canteens in Europe, and the YWCA ran "Hostess Houses" that attempted to replicate a type of domesticity abroad for male soldiers. In addition to these, the YWCA ran recreation facilities for women who were involved in the war effort in such roles as nurses and telephone operators. After the war, Hostess Houses were placed at US national cemeteries abroad for Americans visiting the graves of loved ones. During World War II, the YM/YWCAs were part of a coalition of groups that formed the United Service Organization (USO) and worked with refugees and prisoners of war. Both groups supported relief efforts within Europe. For example, in the mid-1940s, the YWCA began a "Round-the-World YWCA Reconstruction Fund" that raised over two million dollars to aid YWCA personnel in war-torn areas.

Both the YMCA and YWCA attempted to foster international cooperation and peace between people of different nations, as well as class and racial equality. For example, former YWCA secretary Mary Dingman helped found the Women's International League for Peace and Freedom in 1915. In 1925, the YMCA in Honolulu launched the Institute of Pacific Relations to bring Christian leaders together and foster ongoing dialogue about Pacific nation concerns. Maud Russell, who was a

Christian Socialist, was active in the Chinese Revolution, and Max Yergan, an African American YMCA secretary, was very involved in African—particularly South African—affairs. Both groups had members who were also part of international religious organizations for young people, such as the World Student Christian Federation.

The Great Depression hit both groups hard, particularly the work of their International/Foreign Divisions. After World War II, there was an increased effort within the YWCA to transition to local staff who were supported by their resident communities abroad, as funds within the United States continued to contract (this trend continued throughout the 1960s and 1970s). In the late 1950s and early 1960s, the YMCA maintained a strong presence abroad, and in 1958 the US and Canadian YMCA conducted a "Buildings for Brotherhood" fundraising campaign, which raised over sixty million dollars for renovation or construction of YMCAs in thirty-two countries. In the 1970s, however, many YMCAs abroad were closed, and the secretaries returned home because of anti-US sentiment or lack of interest. In 1970, the YWCA's focus within the United States shifted to eliminating racism, and the organization would use this to call for an end to apartheid in South Africa in the 1980s.

SEE ALSO *Student Volunteer Movement for Foreign Missions; Transatlantic Reform*

BIBLIOGRAPHY

Anthony, David Henry, III. *Max Yergan: Race Man, Internationalist, Cold Warrior.* New York: New York University Press, 2006.

Boyd, Nancy. *Emissaries: The Overseas Work of the American YWCA, 1895–1970.* New York: Woman's Press, 1986.

Garner, Karen. *Precious Fire: Maud Russell and the Chinese Revolution.* Amherst: University of Massachusetts Press, 2003.

LaTourette, Kenneth. *World Service: A History of the Foreign Work and World Service of the Young Men's Christian Associations of the United States and Canada.* New York: Association Press, 1957.

Miller, Matthew Lee. *The American YMCA and Russian Culture: The Preservation and Expansion of Orthodox Christianity, 1900–1940.* Lanham, MD: Lexington, 2013.

Phoenix, Karen. "A Social Gospel for India." *Journal of the Gilded Age and Progressive Era* 13, 2 (2014): 200–222.

Karen Phoenix
Instructor
Washington State University

WOUNDED KNEE (1890 AND 1973)

Wounded Knee, a town on the Oglala Lakota (Sioux) reservation in South Dakota, was the site of a massacre of Indians by US Army troops in 1890 and of a seventy-one-day armed standoff that pitted members of the American Indian Movement (AIM) against US law enforcement personnel in 1973. The incidents revealed the strength, and limitations, of the United States as a colonial power. The 1890 massacre, "the last major armed encounter between Indians and whites in North America," completed the process of westward expansion, subdued Indian resistance, and accelerated the assimilationist policies of the government in Washington (Utley 1984, 257). But the 1973 showdown, which occurred at the height of Red Power activism, had the opposite effect, of helping to loosen the federal government's control over Indian reservations under President Richard Nixon's policy of "self-determination without termination" (Kotlowski 2001, 220).

THE 1890 MASSACRE

The Wounded Knee massacre of 1890 had its roots in the military subjugation of the Indian peoples. Having defeated the western tribes, the US government tried to pacify them by eradicating their traditional culture and forcing their assimilation into the United States as settled, Christian farmers. By 1890, Indian tribes were no longer independent nations; major elements of the reservation system had taken root; and US government agents oversaw tribes. These agents recruited and commanded police from the Indian populace, while missionaries founded schools and churches to educate and convert Indians to non-Indian ways. Such practices resembled European imperialism in Asia and Africa. In some respects, the Dawes Act of 1887, designed to encourage Indians to forsake reservation life for a new existence as citizen-farmers, paralleled the racist assumptions and devastating effects (on indigenous life and culture) of French colonial policy, under which West Africans received instruction in French language and culture along with the promise of French citizenship.

By 1890, the Sioux had reached a state of desperation in South Dakota. The tribe "gave up military resistance to the U.S. expansion" in 1877, and thereafter fell under the authority of the government in Washington (Ostler 2004, 2). In the years that followed, deer and buffalo, the principal source of the Sioux's livelihood, diminished in number, as non-Indians slaughtered these animals. Moreover, agricultural yields had proven small; the Sioux relied on US agents for food; and attacks on their culture continued. "Reservation life for the Sioux had brought degradation rather than the revitalization that its promoters envisaged," the historian Francis Paul Prucha averred (1986, 726).

The promise of salvation came via a messianic religion derived from the teachings of Wovoka (Paiute, c. 1856–1932), a shaman from Nevada, who predicted the demise of the white man following a succession of natural disasters. As part of this religion, Wovoka promoted a ceremonial dance, the Ghost Dance, which involved "scenes of intense excitement, spasmodic action, and physical exhaustion" (Washburn 1975, 221). Sioux leaders, including Sitting Bull (c. 1831–1890), adapted the Ghost Dance faith into means of opposition to white rule. Dancers believed that wearing a ghost shirt would enable them to see visions and become impervious to bullets—a preview of the supernatural sensibility of China's Boxers, who resisted European imperialism and insisted that rigorous training would make them invulnerable to ammunition. "The dance came to represent the last vestige of Lakota [Sioux] sovereignty and national identity," historian Gary Anderson explained (1996, 159). As members of the tribe left churches and agency schools, US officials acted to stop the Ghost Dance by, among other things, summoning the army and arresting Sitting Bull, who was killed by Indian police following a scuffle that left a dozen Indians dead. Cold, hungry, and facing a large military force, Sitting Bull's remaining followers surrendered to the US Army.

What followed was, in the words of one army colonel, "the most damnable outrage ever committed by United States troops" (Anderson 1996, 173). Major Samuel Whiteside (1839–1904) escorted 106 Sioux warriors, in addition to women and children, to Wounded Knee Creek, near the Pine Ridge Agency, where Colonel James Forsyth (1835–1906) had nearly five hundred troops. On December 29, 1890, as Forsyth's men disarmed the Indians, a shot rang out and the soldiers opened fire. "In the first seconds of violence," the historian Dee Brown noted, "the firing of the carbines was deafening" (1970, 444). "We tried to run," an Indian survivor recalled, "but they shot us like we were a buffalo" (Brown 1970, 444). In the end, 153 Indians were massacred, including forty-four women and eighteen children, although others later died of wounds. The army also suffered losses, including twenty-five soldiers killed. Surviving Sioux surrendered a couple of weeks later, and the US government awarded twenty soldiers the Medal of Honor for their part in the campaign—awards that the National Congress of American Indians later condemned.

Scholarly reaction to Wounded Knee ranges from Dee Brown's hauntingly evocative account, replete with a photograph of a slain Indian sprawled in the December snow, to Robert M. Utley's nuanced characterization of "a regrettable, tragic accident of war that neither side intended" (Prucha 1986, 729). The massacre, as Utley observed, marked "the passing of the Indian frontier" (1984, 257). And it had "a chilling effect on all the Dakota reservations" where "the residue of people [were] anxious to become Christians" (Anderson 1996, 173). US assimilationist policies continued until the 1930s and then

Oscar Running Bear, a member of the American Indian Movement (AIM), poses during an armed standoff at Wounded Knee, South Dakota, February 1973. Wounded Knee, a town on the Oglala Lakota (Sioux) reservation in South Dakota, was the site of a massacre of Indians by US Army troops in 1890. In 1973 AIM occupied the site at gunpoint, proclaimed an independent Sioux nation, and appealed to the United Nations for recognition. **BETTMANN/CORBIS**

revived in a different form following World War II (1939–1945). Meanwhile, the wistful phrase "Bury My Heart at Wounded Knee" gained currency, in the closing line of Stephen Vincent Benet's poem "American Names" (1927), and in the title of Dee Brown's 1970 Indian history of the West.

THE 1973 STANDOFF

Wounded Knee became identified with the American Indian Movement (AIM) after that organization occupied the South Dakota site. In February 1973, two hundred members of AIM went to the Pine Ridge Reservation in an effort to replace the elected tribal government, headed by the autocratic Richard Wilson (1936–1990), with a hereditary one run by traditional Sioux leaders. AIM leaders also demanded revision of the Oglala Sioux's 1868 treaty with the US government. To achieve their goals, AIM occupied the town of Wounded Knee at gunpoint, proclaimed an independent Sioux nation, and appealed to the United Nations for

recognition—an excellent example of the international dimension of domestic political protest. After Wilson threatened to eject the outsiders by force, US marshals, Federal Bureau of Investigation (FBI) agents, and Bureau of Indian Affairs (BIA) police surrounded Wounded Knee. AIM members and their allies thereupon took up arms and dug defensive positions. Over the next three months, the two sides traded gunfire. Two Indians lost their lives.

The standoff at Wounded Knee derived from many considerations. Young Indian radicals sought to undermine established tribal leaders, such as Wilson, who seemed tied to the US government, especially the BIA. They also wanted to generate press attention and steal thunder from the Nixon White House, which was implementing, however slowly and rhetorically, a policy of Indian self-determination (greater tribal control over federal programs). At Wounded Knee, AIM achieved its minimum objective, of reminding people at home and abroad of the mistreatment of American Indians. Fuming

1138

over the occupation, Nixon aide Bradley H. Patterson Jr. conceded its historical significance: "The whole thing [was] symbolism, marvelous symbolism. When those guys picked Wounded Knee—what a place!" (Kotlowski 2001, 215). Except for beefed-up surveillance of AIM, which the FBI regarded almost as a terrorist organization, the Nixon administration handled the crisis calmly, for it wished no repeat of the butchery of 1890. Nixon never ordered the Department of Defense to dispatch troops to South Dakota, and the occupiers surrendered their arms on May 6, 1973, in exchange for an investigation of Wilson's leadership of the Pine Ridge Reservation.

Following the "Second Battle of Wounded Knee," federal officials reaffirmed their commitment to tribal self-determination. The White House resubmitted its Indian proposals to Congress, which then passed several reforms, such as the Indian Financing Act of 1974, a measure to lend tribes money, and the Indian Self-Determination and Education Assistance Act, which allowed federal agencies to contract out services to tribes. The head of the Association on American Indian Affairs lauded the Ninety-Third Congress (1973–1975) as "perhaps the most constructive Congress in the field of Indian affairs in our history" (Kotlowski 2003, 217). The enactment of such laws enabled federal Indian policy to come full circle since the First Battle of Wounded Knee. Writing in 1988, the historian Lawrence C. Kelly observed that Indian policy had evolved over a century from "virtual denial of tribal sovereignty to almost full recognition" (Kotlowski 2001, 220).

SEE ALSO *Frontier Wars; General Allotment Act (Dawes Severalty Act, 1877); Reservation*

BIBLIOGRAPHY

Anderson, Gary C. *Sitting Bull and the Paradox of Lakota Nationhood.* New York: HarperCollins, 1996.

Brown, Dee. *Bury My Heart at Wounded Knee: An Indian History of the American West.* New York: Holt, Rinehart, and Winston, 1970.

Kotlowski, Dean J. *Nixon's Civil Rights: Politics, Principle, and Policy.* Cambridge, MA: Harvard University Press, 2001.

Kotlowski, Dean J. "Alcatraz, Wounded Knee, and Beyond: The Nixon and Ford Administrations Respond to Native American Protest." *Pacific Historical Review* 72, 2 (2003): 201–227.

Ostler, Jeffrey. *The Plains Sioux and U.S. Colonialism from Lewis and Clark to Wounded Knee.* New York: Cambridge University Press, 2004.

Prucha, Francis Paul. *The Great Father: The United States Government and the American Indian*, Vol. 2. Abridged ed. Lincoln: University of Nebraska Press, 1986.

Utley, Robert M. *The Indian Frontier of the American West, 1846–1890.* Albuquerque: University of New Mexico Press, 1984.

Washburn, Wilcomb E. *The Indian in America.* New York: Harper and Row, 1975.

Dean J. Kotlowski
Professor of History
Salisbury University

WRIGHT, WILBUR

SEE *Airplanes.*

X–Z

XYZ AFFAIR

The XYZ Affair of 1797 to 1798 proved to be an important early test of American standing in European affairs. When President John Adams (1735–1826) sent three American diplomats to France to negotiate a treaty, the officials were met by hostility and demands for bribes and coerced loans for France. Refusing such pressure, the Americans sent back a report to the United States, producing widespread outrage, military preparation, and ultimately the undeclared but very real Quasi War with France. The passion of the XYZ Affair derived at least partially from the distance between how Americans believed the world should view them and how France had actually treated them.

BACKGROUND

The background to the conflict lay in the ongoing war between the French Directory and Great Britain. While Britain and France battled, America insisted on its right to neutral status and free passage on the seas. Both sides had claimed the right to stop American ships sailing to trade with the opposing country. American tensions with Great Britain had diminished due to the Jay Treaty (1795), but problems remained with the French, who saw in that treaty a repudiation of the Franco-American Alliance of 1778. The Americans had also stopped loan repayments to the French Republic on the grounds that the loans had been due to the French monarchy, not the current republic. In 1796, the French Directory authorized the seizure of American merchant ships, and it issued the decree in such a way as to catch Americans by surprise. Through 1797, French privateers increased their depredations, and, when the American government appointed Charles Cotesworth Pinckney (1746–1825) of South Carolina as minister to France, the Directory refused to recognize him.

THE AFFAIR

With this backdrop, President Adams determined to act to preserve America's neutral status. Adams, against the wishes of the more Anglophile wing of his own Federalist Party, aimed to settle the conflict peacefully. He decided to send a delegation to France in the hope that they would produce a settlement along the lines of John Jay's (1745–1829) accomplishment with Great Britain. Adams's representatives were the recently rebuffed Pinckney, John Marshall (1755–1835) of Virginia, and Elbridge Gerry (1744–1814) of Massachusetts. Pinckney and Marshall were Federalists, and although Gerry was a Democratic-Republican, Adams believed he was personally trustworthy. The three had arrived in Paris by October 1797.

Once in Paris, they had to deal with the French foreign minister, Charles-Maurice de Talleyrand-Périgord (1754–1838), or simply Talleyrand. Talleyrand, who before the French Revolution had been a Roman Catholic bishop, was a political animal and, significantly, a survivor who always managed to better his position. Yet, in this regard, he miscalculated. Talleyrand, who had previously spent time in the United States, considered the American situation as low on his priorities and easily delayed. From the European perspective, he evaluated the American Republic as weak and insignificant. This attitude explains his next move, which was to treat the American ministers as akin to representatives of small, conquered European principalities, like Geneva or Genoa, which the French Republic had previously preyed upon. Rather than open negotiations between equals, Talleyrand decided to demand a substantial forced loan of thirty-two million Dutch florins, as well as a bribe of fifty thousand pounds sterling for Talleyrand and the French directors. Talleyrand privately sent several individuals in succession to the American delegation to communicate these demands. In dispatches made public back in the United States, these intermediaries were identified only as X, Y, and Z. Historians have determined that these three Frenchmen were Jean-Conrad Hottinguer (X), Pierre Bellamy (Y), and Lucien Hauteval (Z). Other intermediaries were Nicholas Hubbard and Pierre Beaumarchais. Only after the funds were promised and only after the ministers had publicly repudiated speeches made by President Adams would the Directory (through Talleyrand) consider whether they would deal with the Americans and on what terms.

The Americans repeatedly rebuffed these demands. Pinckney, shocked at the suggestion, replied, "No! No! Not a sixpence!" Marshall, who had been documenting affairs, quickly sent dispatches back to America reporting on the attempted coerced loan. These documents, which President Adams had edited to identify the agents only as X, Y, and Z, became the first public reports of French relations going amiss. As time passed, the French became more audacious and began to threaten an invasion of the United States. Talleyrand also worked to split the American delegation, as he believed Gerry was the one most disposed to cooperate with French goals, and so he considered ejecting Pinckney and Marshall and allowing only Gerry to stay in Paris. It became apparent that without some payments, the Americans would not be received, even though Talleyrand made a last-minute, private counteroffer. With this resistance, Marshall and Pinckney would soon return to America, while Gerry remained in Europe, open to new initiatives from the French.

DOMESTIC RESPONSE

When word of the XYZ Affair reached the United States, the popular reaction was dramatic, and became more so when Marshall and Pinckney arrived and confirmed the contents of the dispatches. Popular passion roiled the country, as an American honor culture collided with European realpolitik. Newspaper articles, public meetings, and voluntary militia activities all expressed American outrage. Americans believed that the French were failing to treat the United States as an equal state. The French demands had belittled American standing, seeing the United States as a weak, dependent territory. They had also revealed the French Directory as predatory and piratical, no better than the Barbary pirates that prowled

the Mediterranean. It was in this context that Robert Goodloe Harper (1765–1825) provided a rallying cry—"Millions for defense but not one cent for tribute!"

The diplomatic realities of the XYZ Affair and the popular passions it aroused resulted in significant military action. Congress officially broke off diplomatic relations with France—a precursor to war. With this step, the United States and France entered into a conflict known as the Quasi War. War was never declared, but that did not prevent actual naval conflicts from breaking out, especially in the Caribbean. In particular, American merchant ships armed themselves to repel any French attempts to seize crew and cargo. Meanwhile, expecting a French declaration of war and a subsequent invasion of the United States, President Adams commissioned the formation of a new, standing army that could meet wartime demands. Adams saw this as a prudential step for defense, but that did not stop others, such as Alexander Hamilton (1755–1804), from fantasizing about how such an army might be used to suppress domestic opposition or to expand American territory.

These military encounters also produced subsequent domestic political conflict. Concerns over French power and subversion were expressed during events on the National Fast Day in May 1798 (called for by President Adams) and that year's July 4th celebrations. During this time, prominent ministers, such as Jedidiah Morse (1761–1826) and Timothy Dwight (1752–1817), called for a religiously motivated resistance to the French. Morse even speculated that behind the French threat to America was a conspiracy orchestrated by a shadowy group known as the Illuminati.

Fear of foreign influence and interference also found expression in the 1798 passage by the Federalist-dominated Congress of the Alien and Sedition Acts. Adams reluctantly signed them into law—a definite political mistake on his part. The Alien Act made naturalization and citizenship a much longer and more difficult process, forcing immigrants to work much harder to qualify as integrated into America's political community. Meanwhile, the Sedition Act was intended to protect the administration from criticism during wartime. Adams's Democratic-Republican opponents felt—not entirely wrongly—that both were aimed against them. This was demonstrated as those prosecuted under the Sedition Act were exclusively Democratic newspaper printers critical of the Adams administration. In response, Democrats organized more strenuously for the 1800 election, and Vice President Thomas Jefferson (1743–1826) and James Madison (1751–1836) penned the Virginia and Kentucky Resolutions in protest.

Although war fever had cooled by 1800, the disputes of 1798 to 1799 remained a part of the presidential campaign, during which Democrats accused Adams of being a monarchist willing to destroy American liberties. The conflict with France continued to simmer, until it was resolved with the Treaty of Mortefontaine (the Convention of 1800). This treaty had been negotiated by three new commissioners—Oliver Ellsworth (1745–1807), William R. Davie (1756–1820), and William Vans Murray (1760–1803). They had been appointed after Gerry returned later in 1798, carrying a message that Talleyrand and the French were willing to talk and resolve differences. The convention was helped along by Napoléon Bonaparte's rise to power and his desire to pacify American relations. The convention abrogated the 1778 Franco-American Alliance and replaced it with an agreement more similar to the 1776 Model Treaty. This treaty, however, did not help President Adams, because it arrived after votes had been cast for the election of 1800. Adams was defeated by Jefferson, despite Adams's attempt to follow a disciplined, moderate course designed to preserve American neutrality.

SEE ALSO *Adams, John; France; French Revolution*

BIBLIOGRAPHY

DeConde, Alexander. *The Quasi-War: The Politics and Diplomacy of the Undeclared War with France, 1797–1801.* New York: Scribner's, 1966.

Den Hartog, Jonathan. *Patriotism and Piety: Federalist Politics and Religious Struggle in the New American Nation.* Charlottesville: University of Virginia Press, 2015.

Elkins, Stanley, and Eric McKitrick. *The Age of Federalism: The Early American Republic, 1788–1800.* New York: Oxford University Press, 1993.

Ray, Thomas M. "'Not One Cent for Tribute': The Public Addresses and American Popular Reaction to the XYZ Affair, 1798–1799." *Journal of the Early Republic* 3, 4 (1983): 389–412.

Stinchcombe, William. *The XYZ Affair.* Westport, CT: Greenwood Press, 1980.

Ziesche, Philipp. *Cosmopolitan Patriots: Americans in Paris in the Age of Revolution.* Charlottesville: University of Virginia Press, 2010.

Jonathan Den Hartog
Associate Professor of History
University of Northwestern–St. Paul, Minnesota

YALTA CONFERENCE (1945)

By January 1945, it was clear that the Allies would soon defeat Nazi Germany. The German Battle of the Bulge offensive had failed, and the western Allies were moving to the Rhine, the last natural defense boundary on Germany's west. Meanwhile, the Soviet Red Army was about to begin a winter offensive that would carry it from Warsaw to the Oder River and threaten to take Berlin, Adolf Hitler's last redoubt.

BACKGROUND

The favorable course of the war did not imply warm relations among the wartime Allies. US president Franklin Roosevelt (1858–1919) had begun an unprecedented fourth term, but his health was failing rapidly. He believed he had the political ability to befriend Soviet leader Joseph Stalin (1878/9–1953) to create a kind of American-Soviet-dominated postwar world to replace the former colonial empires of Europe. In contrast, British prime minister Winston Churchill (1874–1965) had stated that he had not become his majesty's prime minister to preside over the dismemberment of the British Empire. Though Churchill was well aware of Britain's perilous financial situation, he sought to retain Britain's influence in the world and contain the danger that he saw in Stalin and Soviet Russia. Stalin, for his part, had justifiable security concerns after the third major invasion of the Russian heartland from Europe (Napoléon in 1812, the Germans in the First World War, and Hitler after June 1941). He wanted spoils to compensate for the horrendous losses the Soviet people had suffered during the war (estimates range from a low of twenty million dead to forty million and more) and the concomitant destruction of cities, factories, and transportation systems. Stalin realized that the millions of Red Army soldiers flooding into Central Europe gave him a powerful hand in negotiations about postwar Europe.

Thus the stage was set for a meeting of the Big Three leaders and their civilian and military advisors. Yalta, a city on the Crimean peninsula, was selected after Stalin claimed that he could not leave Russia because the conflict on the eastern front was at a crucial stage; he also said his doctors warned him not to travel far. The proposed meeting would be the second of three meetings between the wartime allies. The first took place in Teheran in November 1943 and focused on Roosevelt's interest in a postwar United Nations and Stalin's demand for a second front in Europe (the fighting in Italy simply did not drain enough German troops from the eastern front to satisfy the Soviet leader). The three governments agreed to punt other issues—the fate of postwar Poland and Germany, for example—to a future conference. The leaders decided to meet at Yalta in early February 1945. The third and final meeting would take place in July 1945 at Potsdam, a suburb of Berlin.

KEY AGREEMENTS AND CONCESSIONS

The meeting at Yalta lasted from February 4 to 11. Each party left claiming to have achieved key goals. Roosevelt gained Stalin's promise to enter the Pacific war at some

Soviet leader Joseph Stalin, US President Franklin D. Roosevelt, and UK Prime Minister Winston Churchill at the final dinner held at the Yalta conference, February 11, 1945. *Given the military realities of the winter of 1945, there were probably no reasonable alternatives to the Yalta agreement, which Roosevelt's American critics felt was a sellout to Stalin. Churchill, with the British people drained by war and seeking a domestic-focused government, had the weakest hand and achieved the fewest goals.* AP IMAGES

point after the fighting in Europe ended. Fighting at Peleliu in fall 1944 (the so-called horror in the Pacific) had followed the pattern of battles at Guadalcanal, Tarawa, Kwajalein, and the Marianas, where Japanese soldiers fought to the death and caused about as many American casualties as Japanese deaths. American military experts predicted perhaps one-half million American deaths if the United States were forced to invade the Japanese home islands and face bitter Japanese resistance. Soviet help liberating Northeast Asia and Japan's northernmost main island, Hokkaido, would ease the task the American military faced. In turn, Roosevelt promised Stalin that the Americans would reverse Japan's gains from the Russo-Japanese War (1904–1905), giving southern Sakhalin Island and the Kuriles to Russia, as well as the warm water ports of Port Arthur and Dairen in Manchuria.

Equally important, Stalin agreed to support Roosevelt's cherished United Nations proposal. Roosevelt envisioned a general assembly where all nations of the world could discuss issues without resorting to fighting, with a security council dominated by the great powers— the United States, the Soviet Union, China, Great Britain, and France—each of which would have a veto over proceedings and decisions. Stalin agreed, although he asked and Roosevelt agreed to allow the USSR to have three members in the general assembly: the Soviet Union, Ukraine, and Byelorussia.

Roosevelt believed that he extracted as much as he could from Stalin on the fate of Eastern European governments. Stalin promised to establish separate Allied Control Councils and to seek out leaders untarnished by wartime collaboration with Nazi Germany. Unless Roosevelt envisioned sending the US Army eastward

1144

against the Red Army, what else could he demand and reasonably receive?

The western Allies accepted Stalin's establishing of Eastern European regimes favorable to the USSR. The Soviet definition of *democratic* differed significantly from that of the Americans and the British, and Stalin selected local leaders whose loyalty to Moscow was unquestioned. He also secured a zonal division of Germany (including Austria, which the Nazis seized in the *Anschluss* of March 1938), a promise of reparations, and a commitment to keep Germany weak so no power in Central Europe could rise up to threaten Moscow's control over Eastern Europe. To help further Soviet control, Stalin also gained approval for a redrawing of Eastern European borders, including moving the German border further west to the Oder-Neisse, dividing East Prussia between Poland and the Soviet Union, moving the border of Poland further west, assigning the eastern tip of Czechoslovakia to the USSR, and returning Moldova to Soviet control.

Churchill had the weakest hand and achieved the fewest goals. He understood the reality of the Red Army liberating eastern and southeastern Europe from Nazi control. He also understood that both the American people and the people of the British Commonwealth looked forward to an end to the fighting. He had no "hammer" with which to threaten Stalin. And he could not have failed to notice Roosevelt's poor health and would have had concerns about the untested vice president, Harry Truman (1884–1972). Churchill did secure a French zone of occupation in Germany (including Berlin) and Austria (including Vienna), as if France remained the great power it once was. Stalin also agreed to include members of the Polish government-in-exile in London in a future Polish government, but it was all show. The so-called Lublin Poles dominated the government the Red Army established.

ASSESSMENT

Regardless of what was possible to achieve at Yalta, Republicans subsequently charged a US "sellout" to Stalin, that Roosevelt and his State Department were soft on communism, and that many Polish Americans would believe that Roosevelt had failed them.

Were there any reasonable alternatives? Given the military realities of the winter of 1945, the answer is no. The Red Army had defeated the Wehrmacht, and the Russian people had suffered grievously in victory. It would have been unrealistic to expect that Stalin or any Soviet leader would permit the establishment of unfriendly regimes on Russia's sensitive borders. Churchill's determination to preserve British influence could not overcome the British people's desire for a more domestic-focused government that would work to improve and expand

housing, the social services network, and other measures designed to improve living conditions for the people. Two world wars had drained Britain, while Japan's initial and easy victories over the European colonial empires in East and Southeast Asia had doomed them.

Finally, perhaps Roosevelt followed the best course in befriending Stalin and attempting to maintain the wartime relationship because, short of another war, there were few viable alternatives. However, Roosevelt's policy of friendship faded as the Cold War extended from Truman's presidency through the administrations of Dwight Eisenhower, John F. Kennedy, Lyndon Johnson, and Richard Nixon, up to perhaps even George H. W. Bush and the collapse in the early 1990s of the Soviet Union and the Eastern European empire that Stalin had created in the aftermath of the Second World War.

SEE ALSO *Britain; Germany; Potsdam Conference (1945); Roosevelt, Franklin D.; Russia; Truman, Harry S.; United Nations; World War II*

BIBLIOGRAPHY

Clemens, Diane Shaver. *Yalta*. New York: Oxford University Press, 1970.

Harbutt, Fraser J. *Yalta 1945: Europe and America at the Crossroads*. Cambridge: Cambridge University Press, 2010.

Laloy, Jean. *Yalta: Yesterday, Today, Tomorrow*. Translated by William R. Tyler. New York: Harper and Row, 1990.

Wettig, Gerhard. *Stalin and the Cold War in Europe: The Emergence and Development of East-West Conflict, 1939–1953*. Lanham, MD: Rowman and Littlefield, 2008.

Charles M. Dobbs
Professor Emeritus
Iowa State University

YELLOW JOURNALISM

Yellow journalism is a pejorative term. It is often invoked casually as an accusation of sensational reporting that may also imply inaccurate and even deliberately false reporting, stunts, and other self-serving activities sometimes designed to increase a medium's notoriety and circulation.

Yellow journalism existed before the term was coined in the late nineteenth century, and it continues to this day. In fact, sensationalism is a basic, perhaps essential, element of journalism that has long been a part of American reporting. It was "yellow journalism" when Thomas Jefferson was accused of sleeping with his slave, and it was "yellow journalism" when a newspaper in 1828 published a pamphlet saying that Andrew Jackson had fought a man, chased him away, and stolen his wife.

Nineteenth-century newspaper stories about political scandals, crimes, hoaxes, stunts, and disasters regularly were handled in a sensational manner, often crossing the line into "yellow journalism."

DEFINITIONS

Webster's Encyclopedic Unabridged Dictionary of the English Language offers both a primary and a secondary definition. *Yellow journalism* is "(a.) sensational, especially morbidly or offensively so: *That yellow rag carried all the gory details.* (b.) dishonest in editorial comment and the presentation of news, especially in sacrificing truth for sensationalism" (1654).

The term *yellow journalism* was probably first used in 1897 by Ervin Wardman, the editor of the *New York Press,* as an epithet aimed at both William Randolph Hearst's (1863–1951) *New York Journal* and Joseph Pulitzer's (1847–1911) *New York World,* which were then engaged in a press war that was building the circulations of both newspapers. Earlier, Wardman had attacked the newspapers as "fake mongers, chambers of horrors, cesspools, sloths, purveyors of mendacity," but the phrase "yellow journalism" was the one that stuck and provided a

name for the Hearst-Pulitzer era, from 1895 to roughly 1910 (Campbell 2001, 5, 31).

Hearst had bought the *Journal* in 1895 and transformed it into what he believed was the most entertaining newspaper in town. "It is the *Journal's* policy to engage brains as well as to get the news, for the public is even more fond of entertainment than it is of information," wrote Hearst in 1896 after luring away a number of *World* writers and editors, including Richard F. Outcault (1863–1928), the creator of the *Yellow Kid* cartoon (Campbell, "A Timeline of Yellow Journalism"). Hearst became so associated with the term *yellow journalism* that in 1906 *The Times* of London called him "the 'yellow' candidate" (Weekly ed., November 9).

YELLOW JOURNALISM AND THE WAR WITH SPAIN

The Hearst-Pulitzer press war was often fought over the Spanish occupation of Cuba. Both newspapers favored the Cuban rebellion, presenting vivid feature stories and accusations of Spanish cruelty against Cuban noncombatants. When the battleship USS *Maine* exploded in

Caricature of President William McKinley trying to hush the yellow journalist whose war talk is disturbing the goose that laid the golden egg of prosperity. When the battleship USS Maine *exploded in Havana Harbor in 1898, the Hearst- and Pulitzer-owned newspapers, which favored the Cuban rebellion, jumped on the story to such a degree that the antiwar New York Evening Post blamed the "yellow press" for inciting the Spanish-American War.* **UNIVERSAL HISTORY ARCHIVE/UNIVERSAL IMAGES GROUP EDITORIAL/GETTY IMAGES**

Havana Harbor in 1898, the newspapers jumped on the story to such a degree that the antiwar *New York Evening Post* blamed the "yellow press" for inciting the Spanish-American War, a dubious accusation that has been repeated ever since (Campbell, "A Timeline of Yellow Journalism").

The Oxford English Dictionary (OED) provides two 1898 quotations. From the *Daily News*: "The yellow press is for a war with Spain, at all costs." And from author Elizabeth L. Banks (1872–1938): "All American journalism is not 'yellow,' though all strictly 'up-to-date' yellow journalism is American!" For the OED, yellow newspapers or yellow writers of newspaper articles were "of a recklessly or unscrupulously sensational character" (*Compact Edition* 1971, 3855).

Yellow journalism in the Hearst-Pulitzer era included the use of bold headlines, illustrations (including competing *Yellow Kid* cartoons), and public crusades (which would later be called muckraking) (Campbell 2001, 7–8). But unlike muckraking, which began as an insult and is now a compliment, "yellow journalism" has remained a term of unvarnished contempt despite the fact that many of the elements of yellow journalism have now been incorporated into mainstream journalism.

RECENT EXAMPLES

The term is still so unclearly defined and political in nature, however, that one person's sensationalism can be another's Pulitzer Prize, as in the case of Eddie Adams's (1933–2004) extraordinarily graphic Vietnam War photo of a street execution that, in fact, won a Pulitzer in 1969 (see Banwell, "Saigon Execution").

Coverage of ISIS (the Islamist terrorist organization) in 2014 included videos of journalists just before they were beheaded, and the *CBS Evening News* broadcast of October 28, 2014, featured a report from correspondent Holly Williams in which she introduced and then voiced over an ISIS Internet video of "a young Syrian woman… accused of adultery." Williams reported: "This ISIS Internet video appears to show the moments before she is stoned to death." She added: "The video shows the stones battering the young woman but not the woman's death" (Williams 2014).

These 2014 videos of the journalists and the woman being stoned exemplify the essence of yellow journalism. They are morbidly and even offensively sensational. The videos were the carefully staged products of ISIS public relations, and yet, despite their source, they were eagerly displayed by mass media around the world. But who is to say just what was too offensive in 2014? And who is to say that these ISIS videos were not news and should not have been broadcast at all?

ETHICAL ISSUES SURROUNDING YELLOW JOURNALISM

In today's world, the mainstream mass media attempt to walk a fine line between what they feel is acceptable and what they might call "yellow journalism"—between pictures of a woman being stoned and pictures of a woman being stoned to death, between pictures of a journalist about to be executed and pictures of a journalist being beheaded. And some images are almost never shown, such as the bodies of the victims of airplane crashes and even traffic accidents.

Journalists who are faced with morbid, offensive, sensational stories and pictures are under great pressure to go with the stories. The news medium that reports such stories first has a "scoop," and the accusations of yellow journalism that are raised often come from the families of the bereaved or members of the groups being vilified.

Sensationalism is so pervasive in modern journalism—in the coverage of murders and mass murders and the on-the-ground coverage of war—that it is the norm. "If it bleeds, it leads" could be the motto of local television news. And all too often, the thin, unclear line between sensationalism and yellow journalism is crossed.

This has not always been the case. There have been eras in American journalism when certain topics (such as adultery and realistic images of war) were considered inappropriate subjects for the news. But in the twenty-first century, few hot stories are held back for the sake of either privacy or decency. Thus, some have expanded the definition of yellow journalism to include anything the reader feels is reprehensible. For example, in a *New York Times* op-ed piece titled "The Sony Hack and the Yellow Press" (December 15, 2014), screenwriter Aaron Sorkin (b. 1961), whose e-mails were among those stolen from Sony Pictures Entertainment and then widely published by journalists, argued that the news outlets that published the stolen information were "morally treasonous and spectacularly dishonorable" and perhaps even worse than the hackers themselves. "As demented and criminal as it is, at least the hackers are doing it for a cause. The press is doing it for a nickel," he said.

While it is arguable that Hearst and Pulitzer were unjustly attacked as yellow journalists for a style of journalism that would soon become commonplace, and it is equally arguable that sensationalism is a necessary and essential part of modern journalism, the term *yellow journalism* has remained a pejorative for more than a hundred years, and this epithet could accurately be applied to many reports in today's mass media.

SEE ALSO *Advertising and Marketing; Americanization; Cuba; Exceptionalism; Haiti; Industrialization; Internationalism; Isolationism; LIFE (magazine);*

Lippmann, Walter; The New Republic (Magazine); Philippines; Roosevelt, Theodore; Rough Riders; Spanish-American War; World War I

BIBLIOGRAPHY

Adams, Eddie. "Saigon Execution," February 1, 1968. *Rare Historical Photos and the Story behind Them.* http://rarehistoricalphotos.com/saigon-execution-murder-vietcong-saigon-1968/

Banwell, Rory. "'Saigon Execution': The Consequences of Eddie Adams Pulitzer Prize Winning Photograph." Photo taken February 1, 1968, published by the Associated Press in *New York Times.* http://rbp2013.wordpress.com/2013/09/19/saigon-execution-the-consequences-of-eddie-adams-pulitzer-prize-winning-photograph/comment-page-1/

Campbell, W. Joseph. *Yellow Journalism: Puncturing the Myths, Defining the Legacies.* Westport, CT: Praeger, 2001.

Campbell, W. Joseph. *The Year That Defined American Journalism: 1897 and the Clash of Paradigms.* New York: Routledge, 2006.

Campbell, W. Joseph. *Getting It Wrong: Ten of the Greatest Misreported Stories in American Journalism.* Berkeley: University of California Press, 2010.

Campbell, W. Joseph. "A Timeline of Yellow Journalism." American University. http://academic2.american.edu/~wjc/yellowjo/timeline.html

Cohen, Daniel. *Yellow Journalism: Scandal, Sensationalism, and Gossip in the Media.* Brookfield, CT: Twenty-First Century Books, 2000.

The Compact Edition of the Oxford English Dictionary. Oxford: Oxford University Press, 1971.

Ember, Steve. "The Making of a Nation: Andrew Jackson Overcomes Accusations to Win the 1828 Election." *Learning English,* February 20, 2014. http://learningenglish.voanews.com/content/andrew-jackson-rachel-1828-election-john-quincy-adams/1742793.html

Skog, Jason. *Yellow Journalism.* Minneapolis, MN: Compass Point Books, 2007.

Smythe, Ted Curtis. *The Gilded Age Press, 1865–1900.* Westport, CT: Praeger, 2003.

Sorkin, Aaron. "The Sony Hack and the Yellow Press." *New York Times,* New York ed., December 15, 2014, A23.

Spencer, David R. *The Yellow Journalism: The Press and America's Emergence as a World Power.* Evanston, IL: Northwestern University Press, 2007.

"Thomas Jefferson and Sally Hemings: A Brief Account," Monticello.org. http://www.monticello.org/site/plantation-and-slavery/thomas-jefferson-and-sally-hemings-brief-account

The Times, Weekly ed., November 9, 1906. In *The Compact Edition of the Oxford English Dictionary.* Oxford: Oxford University Press, 1971, 3855.

Webster's Encyclopedic Unabridged Dictionary of the English Language. New York: Portland House, 1989.

Williams, Holly. "ISIS Wields a Particular Brand of Cruelty Toward Women." *CBS Evening News,* October 28, 2014.

David B. Sachsman
George R. West, Jr., Chair of Excellence in Communication and Public Affairs and Professor of Communication University of Tennessee at Chattanooga

YOM KIPPUR WAR

SEE *Arab-Israeli Conflict.*

YUGOSLAV WARS

The 1991 breakup of the Yugoslav federation played a key role in redefining US foreign policy during the post–Cold War era. Immediately prior to the breakup, there was uncertainty about the overall purpose of US hegemony, especially with the impending collapse of the familiar Soviet adversary. There was also uncertainty about the utility of the North Atlantic Treaty Organization (NATO), which was an expression of US power in Europe. During the 1990s, the United States and NATO directed a series of diplomatic and military interventions in the various Balkan wars that followed Yugoslavia's breakup. These interventions established a new sense of purpose for the Atlantic Alliance and for the overarching project of US hegemony.

THE EARLY US AND EUROPEAN RESPONSE TO THE DISSOLUTION OF YUGOSLAVIA

The dissolution of Yugoslavia began with the secessions of the Slovenian and Croatian republics—events that caused the collapse of the multiethnic central government and the beginning of a complex series of wars. At first, the European Community (EC) was the leading external influence in the Balkans, while the United States played a secondary role. Taking their lead from Germany, the EC states sought an orderly dissolution of Yugoslavia, which would allow for the secession and eventual recognition of the various Yugoslav republics. The Europeans also sought to orchestrate international condemnation of military actions by the Yugoslav National Army and (somewhat later) by various Serb-led militias against several of the new states that emerged from Yugoslavia.

Through the first six months of the Balkan crisis, President George H. W. Bush was distracted by the momentous events of 1991, which had begun with the First Gulf War against Iraq—the largest use of US military force since Vietnam—and ended with the breakup of the

Soviet Union. In this context, US officials acquiesced to the European lead in the Balkans, assuming that the conflict was of second-tier significance. The resulting lack of US leadership in this case was soon recognized as an embarrassment, which cast doubt on the US global role after the Cold War. In light of this concern, the Bush administration shifted to a more assertive stance, beginning with US support for the Republic of Bosnia and Herzegovina, which declared its independence in April 1992.

THE BOSNIAN CIVIL WAR

The new Bosnian state was immediately beset by a destructive civil war, involving fighting among three main ethnic groups—the Bosnian Muslims, the Croats, and the Serbs. The new state was officially led by a predominantly Muslim government under President Alija Izetbegović (1925–2003); throughout most of the war, the Muslims aligned with the Croat ethnic group. Opposed to this Muslim-Croat alliance were the ethnic Serbs of Bosnia, who constituted approximately one-third of the population. Being the best armed of the three groups, and with backing from the Republic of Serbia and its unsavory president, Slobodan Milošević (1941–2006), the Bosnian Serbs quickly established control over most of the country's territory, combined with forced expulsions of hundreds of thousands of non-Serbs. While all three ethnic groups engaged in significant atrocities, the Serbs undoubtedly perpetrated the worst atrocities. Serb massacres in the town of Srebrenica in 1995 were later determined by an international court to be a case of genocide (though that determination has been contested by many legal authorities, who fear the concept of genocide has been unreasonably broadened).

During the three and a half years of the Bosnian war (1992–1995), the United States became the principal backer of the Izetbegović government while it opposed the Serbs, a policy that was followed by both Republican president Bush and his Democratic successor, Bill Clinton. In addition, US officials worked to undermine European- and UN-directed mediation efforts, which aimed at achieving a compromise among the three ethnic groups and a settlement of the conflict. Officials in both the Bush and Clinton administrations derided international mediation activities as constituting appeasement of Serb aggression. The chief European negotiator during most of this period, David Owen (1995), would later describe how US officials repeatedly undercut his efforts to shorten the war.

The Bosnian war presented a dilemma for US policy makers: On the one hand, the United States had publicly committed its prestige to resolving the war, and policy makers sought to do so without any European- or UN-sponsored peace agreements. On the other hand, both Bush and Clinton were reluctant to intervene with military force, since intervention raised the possibility of US combat causalities and public disapproval. In addition, the US military was divided on the Balkan issue, with the Air Force favoring some degree of intervention, and the Army opposing it. There thus was no immediate military intervention, and US involvement in Bosnia was confined to diplomatic maneuvering.

In April 1994, President Clinton undertook a policy shift and began arranging international arms shipments for both Croatia and the Muslim-led government in Bosnia, to be directed against Serb militias in both republics. In addition, the State Department licensed American military contractors to train the Croatian military for planned offensives against the Serbs, to be undertaken in cooperation with the Bosnian government forces. During the summer of 1995, the Croat/Bosnian offensives were launched, with US support. In addition, the United States unleashed a series of air strikes—as part of a larger NATO operation—also against the Serbs. These combined air and ground operations eroded Serb power throughout the region. Following Serb military defeats, the Clinton administration organized peace talks in Dayton, Ohio, which in December 1995 reestablished Bosnia as a multiethnic federation. Implementation of the agreement was to be supervised by a NATO-directed peacekeeping force.

THE RELEVANCE OF NATO

The US intervention in Bosnia produced a mixed legacy. On the one hand, the intervention ended the Bosnian war (though the resulting peace settlement was remarkably similar to European and UN peace plans that US officials had repeatedly opposed). On the other hand, the US-supported offensives generated mass ethnic cleansing and other atrocities against Serb civilians in both Croatia and Bosnia. From the standpoint of US power, the interventions were a clear benefit: the perceived Western victory in Bosnia conferred a new prestige on NATO, which had officially directed the air strikes.

NATO's supposed value was demonstrated once again in 1999, when the alliance orchestrated renewed air strikes against Serb forces, this time to alleviate the suffering of ethnic Albanians in the Kosovo region. The new US-led intervention again defeated the Serbs, which generated another round of ethnic cleansing against Serbs who had lived in Kosovo. The Kosovo war was nevertheless considered a major accomplishment for US policy, as well as a personal triumph for President Clinton and his secretary of state, Madeleine Albright, who had long advocated military action in the Balkans.

The war also helped to reinvigorate the NATO alliance, along with US power in Europe, which was closely associated with NATO. An editorial in the *Financial Times* summed up the matter this way:

> The Kosovo crisis has confirmed the relevance of NATO—just as criminals confirm the relevance of policemen. Ten years ago, when the Berlin wall came down, it seemed destined to join its Warsaw Pact adversary in the dustbin of history. But the [Kosovo] crisis and Mr. Milošević's brutal ethnic cleansing of Albanians, have helped to confirm the continuing relevance of an international military force. (Buchan and Fidler 1999)

Western interventions in the Balkans thus established a post–Cold War relevance for both the Atlantic Alliance and US hegemony more generally, while the new language of human rights and genocide prevention—closely associated with the Yugoslav wars—helped legitimate later interventions in Afghanistan, Iraq, and Libya.

SEE ALSO *Albright, Madeleine; Clinton, William Jefferson; Genocide; Human Rights; North Atlantic Treaty Organization (NATO)*

BIBLIOGRAPHY

Buchan, David, and Stephen Fidler. "An Uneasy Anniversary." *Financial Times*, April 23, 1999.

Burg, Steven L., and Paul S. Shoup. *The War in Bosnia-Herzegovina: Ethnic Conflict and International Intervention.* Armonk, NY: Sharp, 1999.

Gibbs, David N. *First Do No Harm: Humanitarian Intervention and the Destruction of Yugoslavia.* Nashville, TN: Vanderbilt University Press, 2009.

Layne, Christopher. *The Peace of Illusions: American Grand Strategy from 1940 to the Present.* Ithaca, NY: Cornell University Press, 2006.

Owen, David. *Balkan Odyssey: An Uncompromising Personal Account of the International Peace Efforts Following the Breakup of the Former Yugoslavia.* Orlando, FL: Harcourt, Brace, 1995.

Posen, Barry R. "The War for Kosovo: Serbia's Political-Military Strategy." *International Security* 24, 4 (2000): 39–84.

Woodward, Susan L. *Balkan Tragedy: Chaos and Dissolution after the Cold War.* Washington, DC: Brookings Institution, 1995.

David N. Gibbs
Professor of History
University of Arizona

ZIONISM

Zionism is Jewish nationalism, the aspiration for a Jewish collective. Zionism emerged in the nineteenth century in conversation with the many other nationalist movements. Though it is rightfully seen as a precursor to the establishment of the State of Israel in 1948, not all Zionists hoped for a Jewish state, nor was Zionism exclusively tied to the land of Palestine. Several proto-Zionist movements for Jewish peoplehood appeared in the mid-nineteenth century, such as Hibbat Zion in eastern Europe. Theodor Herzl (1860–1904), an Austro-Hungarian journalist, is the traditional founder of political Zionism. In the wake of the Alfred Dreyfus trial (1894) in France and rising antisemitism across Europe, Herzl published *The Jewish State* (1896). He argued that assimilation was neither possible nor desirable and that the creation of a Jewish state would be a solution to the twin problems of assimilation and antisemitism. Herzl did not consider initially that such a state needed to be in Palestine, and briefly pursued possibilities such as in Uganda. However, the powerful symbolism of the land of Palestine in the views of many of his supporters convinced him to concentrate on it.

In contrast to Herzl's belief in the power of a political entity, Ahad Ha'am (1856–1927, the pen name of Asher Ginsberg, meaning "one of the people" [Gen. 26:10]) argued that a slow cultural revival needed to precede the ability of Jews to flourish in any political entity. And where Herzl had hoped that the majority of Jews would relocate to the Jewish state, Ahad Ha'am envisioned a Jewish homeland as a center that would radiate outward to the Diaspora. European Zionist ideas were influential in the United States, though they were transformed in America. Ahad Ha'am's vision for the connection between a Jewish homeland and the Diaspora proved especially compelling, although Americans placed more confidence in a two-way exchange rather than a unidirectional influence from the national center outward. Israel Friedländer (1876–1920), who came to the United States to teach at the Jewish Theological Seminary in 1904, translated Ahad Ha'am's works for an American audience. Friedländer presented Ahad Ha'am as authorizing an ideology of "Zionism plus Diaspora, Palestine plus America." This opened up Zionism to focus on activities in the United States, even as they related to an imagined future in Palestine.

ZIONISM IN AMERICAN THOUGHT, PHILOSOPHY, AND POLITICS

While in Europe Zionism largely developed as an alternative to religious Judaism, for the most part Zionist Americans have argued that Jewish religion and nationalism are complements. Louis Brandeis (1856–1941) and Horace Kallen (1882–1974) argued that multiple loyalties are problematic only if they are inconsistent, but the various forms of Jewish life are perfectly compatible with American democracy. For Kallen and Brandeis—who largely set a pattern for other Zionist Americans—the mechanism for harmonizing Jewish interests in Zionism with broader American patriotism is cultural pluralism. Martin Buber (1878–1965)—a Zionist who was born in Austria and immigrated to Israel—argued that Jews would not have needed a state if they had been emancipated in Europe as a group instead of as individuals. However, Zionist Americans believed there was still space for Jews to gain rights in America as a community—and that such rights would have important ramifications for non-Jewish Americans as well, allowing a fuller democracy to come into being during the twentieth century.

Horace Kallen argued that human experience could not be reduced to conformity to a single way: various groups had to be able to fulfill their own cultures and experiences without justifying themselves to a single universalist model. This idea, plus Kallen's sense that religion was human-made and not revealed, led him to argue that one only gained identity through group life, so the best political model would allow this group life to flourish. He saw the possibility for this in cultural pluralism. Kallen argued that secular cultural pluralism was the appropriate model for America and Israel. Louis Brandeis developed Kallen's argument for cultural pluralism as a response to the criticism of Jewish "dual allegiance," the idea that if Jews were loyal to Israel they could not be loyal citizens of other nations. He argued that multiple loyalties were only problematic if they were inconsistent, yet he believed most Americans already managed multiple loyalties—not only to nation, but state, city, family, trade, college, and so on. He fit Zionism into this model and suggested that, although he was already fully American and fully Jewish, striving to assist international Jews would allow the Jewish American community to further develop the best aspects of Jewishness and thereby benefit the entire American community by giving it the best the Jewish group could offer.

Religious Zionists tended to emphasize and expand similar importance of group rights along with an inextricable link between religion and Jewish nationalism, whereas Zionist nationalism served as religion or its alternative for many secularists. The Conservative Jewish leader Solomon Schechter (1847–1915)—who predated Kallen and Brandeis on the American scene—argued that Zionism would guard against Jewish assimilation, although assimilation and acculturation were not the same thing for Schechter. While nineteenth-century American Reform Jews had eschewed Zionism, believing it to undermine their security in America, Schechter offered a different model for Jewish religion in America. He believed that maintaining Jewish identity even while adapting to American values (acculturation) was essential, and for him Zionism awoke this Jewish consciousness. He believed Zionism had already accomplished great things for Diaspora Jews—an argument Judah Magnes (1877–1948) continued. Magnes believed that peoplehood, Torah, and Israel constituted Jewish life. Although he did not believe the first two needed the third, like Schechter, Magnes argued that Israel could revivify Jewish peoplehood and Torah, as, for example, he believed that the revival of Hebrew had already accomplished.

These forms of American religious Zionism drew heavily on Ahad Ha'am's cultural Zionism rather than Herzl's political Zionism, though Zionist Americans transformed Ahad Ha'am as well. While Ahad Ha'am believed that Palestine would have to serve as a cultural center to the Jews of the Diaspora because most Jews would never be able to immigrate to Palestine, he also thought negatively of Jewish life in the Diaspora as culturally bankrupt. Yet Schechter and Magnes saw the Diaspora holding substantially more power for mutual benefit between Israel and the Diaspora, and encouraged the prospect for Jews to choose to remain in the Diaspora. Brandeis thought similarly—he believed Jews would establish their loyalty to America most clearly when they could choose to live there, and without a Jewish home state, their life in America was less clearly a choice. Combining cultural and religious renaissance with a greater sense of political freedom, Zionists argued that their commitment to Israel in no way undermined their loyalty to America but actually heightened it by cultivating their group's (and thus each individual Jew's) best qualities.

This framework for Jewish American identity represented an optimism that antisemitism was not incurable, an optimism shared with non-Zionists and anti-Zionists, indicating a larger theme of Jewish American identity beyond the group of early twentieth-century Zionists. Indeed, the founder of Reconstructionism, Mordecai Kaplan (1881–1983), argued that a culture built on despair would be traumatic as an educational paradigm for younger generations of Jews, and that Jewish identity could not be maintained by pointing to antisemitism. For Kaplan, the sense that Jewishness was a total civilization or way of life meant that Israel could help cultivate positive identity markers and practices. In Israel, he believed this civilization could flourish completely, but he initiated the synagogue center as a means for creating possibilities in America for all of Jewish life to take place within the Jewish community, rather than merely theology or religious worship.

RESPONSES TO JEWISH ZIONISM

In addition to the many vectors of Jewish Zionism, Christian Zionism has also been a strong current in America. Specific readings of the Hebrew Bible that emerged during and after the Protestant Reformation led some Protestants to expect Jews to play an important role in the end of the current era on Earth and have contributed to the formation of Christian Zionism. Christian Zionism links expectations about roles for Jews, the land of Palestine-Israel, and messianic anticipation of a Second Coming of Christ. As a result, Christian Zionists have supported and at times even spearheaded contemporary political movements to bring Jews to the Holy Land. In the late nineteenth century, the American Christian Zionist William E. Blackstone (1841–1935), a premillennial dispensationalist, interpreted new settlements in Israel as the beginning of the end times. Blackstone urged politicians to support actions to restore Jews to Palestine, setting a lasting pattern for the role of Christian Zionism in the United States, and influencing much later figures, organizations, lobbies, and presidents, such as Jimmy Carter, Ronald Reagan, George H. W. Bush, and George W. Bush. Viewing themselves as a kind of contemporary Cyrus permitting Jews to reestablish a national religious home in Jerusalem, American Christian Zionists have supported political events from the 1917 Balfour Declaration (which the US government formally accepted in 1926) to the establishment of the State of Israel. Christian support for the State of Israel has expanded since the creation of the state and especially after the Six-Day War in 1967. Jewish and Christian Zionists have generally been aware of each other's differing motives, producing occasional ambivalence, but nevertheless they have often forged pragmatic cooperation.

Not all Jewish Americans considered Zionism a fulfillment of their understanding of the essence of Judaism or even compatible with either Judaism or American values. Taking the 1885 Pittsburgh Platform as representative of early Reform Judaism, many Reform Jews, especially rabbis, critiqued Zionism as inherently pessimistic about antisemitism or the idea that Jews were rightful citizens of the United States or other nations around the world. Reform Jews and other Jewish anti-Zionists typically supported Jewish rights to live as citizens in Palestine, but within a liberal democratic state rather than an ethnically Jewish state. As a movement, Reform Judaism remained aloof from Zionism until the 1930s. By then, many more American Reform Jews had begun to support some measure of Zionism, and the 1937 Columbus Platform created room for Zionism in Reform without explicitly endorsing Zionism. However, a minority of Reform rabbis formed the American Council for Judaism to argue against incorporating conceptions of a separate Jewish nation-state into Reform ideology.

Many Haredi Jews have also rejected Zionism as a Jewish political framework. Prior to the nineteenth century, most Jews expected that the Messiah would come to Earth to reestablish the Jewish kingdom and nation in the land of Israel. Early secular Zionists argued that Jews need not wait for the Messiah to create a Jewish nation-state. Though many Jews in the United States and throughout the world have understood the new State of Israel in diverse connections to their range of religious positions, some Haredim—especially those from the Bobov and Satmar communities—have considered Zionism and the creation of a Jewish political state prior to the coming of the Messiah problematic and even contrary to the covenant with God. Some Satmar Hasidism so radically oppose the state that they hold anti-Israel rallies. These positions do not describe all Haredim and Hasidim, however, and Haredim constitute an increasing number of the residents of the contemporary State of Israel, though they have not always subscribed to all Zionist ideas or participated in the operation of the state, such as through military service.

Arab and Palestinian anti-Zionism should also be distinguished from Jewish anti-Zionism. Most Jewish anti-Zionists have opposed the creation of a Jewish state, though they have nevertheless advocated the right of Jews to settle in the land of Palestine/Israel under some other political framework. Jewish anti-Zionism has not necessarily been connected to any alternative activism for Arab or Palestinian rights in the region. Arabs, Palestinians, and others have participated in movements for various models of government since the nineteenth century from monarchism to Pan-Arabism to Palestinian nationalism to Pan-Islamism, only partially in reaction to Zionism. Many have rejected Zionism as a political framework and the existence or operations of the State of Israel. While some movements have sought to accommodate Jewish settlement in the region, some have seen Jewish settlement or land ownership as stifling the possibilities for Arab or Palestinian political rights and self-determination.

ZIONISM IN AMERICAN PRACTICE

Focusing on the institutions, programs, and spaces designed in America by Zionists, such as the synagogue center, is central to understanding the significance of Zionism to Jewish American identity and practice. Because Americans argued that Zionism came out of their investment in life in America, it is important to see the ways the Americanization of Zionism meant an

Americanization of Israel. Jewish American politics, economics, gender norms, literature, and fund-raising left imprints on the development of the prestate settlement of Palestine and later the State of Israel. At the same time, Zionism deeply influenced America. The strength of American Zionism was neither solely nor centrally fund-raising abilities or political support for Israel, but in the programs it was able to create in America, which cultivated a sense of kinship among Jews in America, as well as a sense of responsibility for the international Jewish population, especially those in the land of Israel. Youth programs, education, and summer camps cultivated a sense of Jewishness among Jewish Americans. Zionism thus became an important influence or aspect of the practice of Judaism for many, and for some, Zionism was their practice of Judaism. Additionally, Zionist literature in America offered images of Jews compatible with American values of democracy, social justice, and gender norms. Images of muscular, healthy Jews working the land and tied to nature reinforced the sense that Jewish values and American values were completely compatible.

The measure of the success or strength of American Zionism must be gauged based on the tie between Zionism and other issues of Jewish concern in organizations and activities on American soil for Jewish Americans. Therefore, making *aliyah* (moving permanent residence to Israel) cannot be understood as the ultimate value of American Zionism. This measure comes out of the values of methodological European Zionism, but it should not be imposed on understandings of Zionism in America. Additionally, politics are not the only way to measure American commitment to creating a Jewish homeland in Palestine, nor should they be valued as necessarily having been the best way to achieve that goal. A substantial number of Jewish Americans invested in creating a Jewish presence in Palestine chose not to participate in American politics. Some, such as Stephen Wise (1874–1949) and Abba Hillel Silver (1893–1963), became rabbis and entered politics out of their understanding of the structures of power in America and their understanding of the link between the religious and political realms influenced by the Social Gospel and American progressivism.

ZIONIST-AMERICAN ORGANIZATIONS

In 1898, the Federation of American Zionists (FAZ) was founded in New York as an affiliation of an unknown number of individual Zionist societies. Yet, in total, the organization was small, representing a minority of Jewish Americans. Prior to World War I (1914–1918), though these affiliated societies joined the federation, they would not consent to complete centralization of authority in the FAZ. Louis Brandeis came to the front of the organization's leadership in 1914. His administration united Zionists with eastern and western European heritage, as well as eastern (New York) and midwestern (Chicago) Zionists. In addition to this reconciliation, Brandeis brought progressive followers who were attracted to the democratic principles of the FAZ. Under Brandeis, in 1918, the FAZ was reorganized as the Zionist Organization of America (ZOA), when leadership was centralized.

The ZOA was the largest men's Zionist American organization; however, many women's organizations, such as Hadassah, the National Council of Jewish Women (NCJW), the women's auxiliary to the Workmen's Circle, and Pioneer Women, believed they gained a certain amount of power by remaining outside of politics and the Jewish men's organizations that declared political commitments to parties or platforms in America and Israel. By refusing to take such political stances, women maintained leadership over their own organizations; they were able to reach larger audiences and accommodate a wider range of ideological commitments, allowing them to grow in larger proportions than men's organizations; they were able to start programs on the ground, such as hospitals, schools, and wellness/nutrition programs in Palestine, without first having to resolve political debates, thereby creating a foundation for Jewish life in Palestine regardless of statehood; and finally, they avoided violating gender norms that suggested women did not belong in politics. Women believed their programs were more pragmatic than the efforts of men, which became bogged down in the political process and required that Jewish politics be subject to the opinions of non-Jews to a greater extent. Women's organizations—especially, for example, the NCJW, which chose to join the American League of Women Voters rather than the Women's International Zionist Organization (as Hadassah did)—were certainly pulled by their commitment to upholding American values. But this commitment to broader American values may not have exerted the same level of pressure or authority on the NCJW's ultimate right to define their organization's goals for themselves.

While Revisionist Zionists in America were more tied to political commitments in prestate Palestine and openly declared their commitment not only to establishing a Jewish state but also a strong Jewish military presence in that state, some Revisionists, such as Peter Bergson (1915–2001, the pseudonym of Hillel Kook), felt more freedom in America by remaining aloof to American politics. While Silver and especially Wise had to tailor their demands and ideology to political programs of the non-Jewish American political figures they were lobbying, Bergson more easily declared radical commitment to

Jewish plans for statehood—a commitment largely shared with Wise and Silver. Further, Bergson could use more creative means to garner American Jewish support for both the Jewish state—such as public relations campaigns drawing on the celebrity power of members of Hollywood and arts circles, like Ben Hecht (1894–1964)—and attempts to rescue Jewish Holocaust victims, including the illegal transfer of munitions.

On the one hand, the history of American Zionism is a history of arguing the compatibility and even fusion of American and Jewish politics. On the other, it is also a history of how these two realms have at times been understood to be separate. Groups such as the NCJW argued a conjunction of American-Jewish-Palestine interests that suited their understandings of themselves as middle-class Jewish American women, but which grew problematic when they encountered lower-class, Yiddish-speaking immigrants with commitments to labor concerns. Such Yiddish-speaking women were rejected by the NCJW and therefore joined Pioneer Women. While Pioneer Women attempted to hold the same parlor meetings and fund-raising parties that the NCJW held, these were typically overshadowed by their labor concerns and slogans, such as "Let's hear it for women workers!" While members of the NCJW could theoretically tolerate Yiddish-speaking, lower-class immigrants' presence in Palestine, the presence of such immigrants in America actually undermined many middle-class women's understandings of Jewish American identity.

Men's political conflicts might be understood within a similar paradigm. Jewish Americans displayed a tension or ambivalence between their desire to see themselves as completely American and their understanding of important distinctions between Jews and non-Jews in America, and they experienced conflict when their ideological identities did not conform to their practical experiences in America. Jewish group interactions illuminate these narratives and show how these groups' power and powerlessness arose out of the forms of Jewish American Zionism they constructed.

SEE ALSO *Balfour Declaration (1917); Holocaust; Judaism; Protestantism; United Nations; World War I; World War II*

BIBLIOGRAPHY

Ariel, Yaakov. "An Unexpected Alliance: Christian Zionism and its Historical Significance." *Modern Judaism* 26, 1 (2006): 74–100.

Bernstein, Deborah S., ed. *Pioneers and Homemakers: Jewish Women in Pre-State Israel.* Albany: State University of New York Press, 1992.

Brinner, William, and Moses Rischin, eds. *Like All the Nations? The Life and Legacy of Judah L. Magnes.* Albany: State University of New York Press, 1987.

Cohen, Naomi. *The Americanization of Zionism, 1897–1948.* Hanover, NH: Brandeis University Press, 2003.

Davidson, Lawrence. *America's Palestine: Popular and Official Perceptions from Balfour to Israeli Statehood.* Gainesville: University Press of Florida, 2001.

Dawisha, Adeed. *Arab Nationalism in the Twentieth Century: From Triumph to Despair.* Princeton, NJ: Princeton University Press, 2003.

Dawson, Nelson L., ed. *Brandeis and America.* Lexington: University Press of Kentucky, 1989.

Eisenberg, Robert. *Boychiks in the Hood: Travels in the Hasidic Underground.* New York: Harper Collins, 1995.

Friesel, Evyatar. "Ahad Ha-amism in American Zionist Thought." In *At the Crossroads: Essays on Ahad Ha-am,* edited by Jacques Kornberg, 133–141. Albany: State University of New York Press, 1983.

Greenstein, Howard R. *Turning Point: Zionism and Reform Judaism.* Chico, CA: Scholars Press, 1981.

Gurock, Jeffrey S., ed. *American Zionism: Missions and Politics.* London: Routledge, 1998.

Halpern, Ben. *A Clash of Heroes—Brandeis, Weizmann, and American Zionism.* New York: Oxford University Press, 1987.

Heilman, Samuel. *Sliding to the Right: The Contest for the Future of American Jewish Orthodoxy.* Berkeley: University of California Press, 2006.

Hertzberg, Arthur, ed. *The Zionist Idea: A Historical Analysis and Reader.* Philadelphia: Jewish Publication Society, 1997.

Hyman, Paula. *Gender and Assimilation in Modern Jewish History: The Roles and Presentations of Women.* Seattle: University of Washington Press, 1995.

Kaplan, Dana Evan, ed. *The Cambridge Companion to American Judaism.* Cambridge: Cambridge University Press, 2005.

Kaufman, Menachem. *An Ambiguous Partnership: Non-Zionists and Zionists in America, 1939–1948.* Jerusalem: Magnes Press, 1991.

Kolsky, Thomas. *Jews against Zionism: The American Council for Judaism, 1942–1948.* Philadelphia: Temple University Press, 1990.

McCune, Mary. "Social Workers in the *Muskeljudentum*: 'Hadassah Ladies,' 'Manly Men,' and the Significance of Gender in the American Zionist Movement, 1912–1928." *American Jewish History* 86, 2 (1998): 135–165.

McCune, Mary. *"The Whole Wide World, without Limits": International Relief, Gender Politics, and American Jewish Women, 1893–1930.* Detroit, MI: Wayne State University Press, 2005.

Medoff, Rafael. *Militant Zionism in America: The Rise and Impact of the Jabotinsky Movement in the United States, 1926–1948.* Tuscaloosa: University of Alabama Press, 2002.

Merkley, Paul. *The Politics of Christian Zionism, 1891–1948.* London: Frank Cass, 1998.

Meyer, Michael. *Response to Modernity: A History of the Reform Movement in Judaism.* Detroit, MI: Wayne State University Press, 1995.

Raider, Mark A. *The Emergence of American Zionism.* New York: New York University Press, 1998.

Raider, Mark A., Jonathan D. Sarna, and Ronald W. Zweig, eds. *Abba Hillel Silver and American Zionism.* London: Frank Cass, 1997.

Raphael, Marc Lee. *Abba Hillel Silver: Profile in American Judaism.* New York: Holmes and Meier, 1989.

Reinharz, Shulamit, and Mark Raider, eds. *American Jewish Women and the Zionist Enterprise.* Waltham, MA: Brandeis University Press, 2004.

Shapiro, Yonathan. *Leadership of the American Zionist Organization, 1897–1930.* Urbana: University of Illinois Press, 1971.

Shenhav, Yehuda. *The Arab Jews: A Postcolonial Reading of Nationalism, Religion, and Ethnicity.* Stanford, CA: Stanford University Press, 2006.

Urofsky, Melvin. *A Voice That Spoke for Justice: The Life and Times of Stephen S. Wise.* Albany: State University of New York Press, 1982.

Jessica Carr
Assistant Professor in Religious Studies
Lafayette College

Index

France, 1:379
Hollywood, 1:458
immigrants, 1:474
Immigration Restriction League, 1:483
North America, 2:762
Panama Canal, 2:818
rock 'n' roll, 2:899
Zionism, 2:1152–1153
See also Cultural imperialism
The Americanization of the World (Stead), 1:52
American-Ottoman Company, 2:798
America's Forgotten Pandemic (Crosby), 1:362
Americo-Liberians, 1:613–614
Amistad, 1:**56–57**
Amnesty International
　Dylan, Bob, 1:303
　human rights, 1:470, 471
　United Nations, 2:760
Amundsen-Scott South Pole Station, 1:70
Amusement parks. *See* Theme parks
Anaconda Plan, 2:741
Anarchism, 1:**63–65**, 452–453, 2:878
Anarchist Exclusion Act of 1903, 1:64
Ancient Greece, 1:429
Anders, Bill, 1:306–307
Anderson, Bonnie, 1:353
Anderson, Eugenie, 1:376
Anderson, Rufus, 1:371
Andrews, Julie, 2:711
Angel Island, 1:**65–66**, 481
Angel Network, 2:1100, 1101
Angell, James, 1:205
Angelou, 1:113
Anglo-American Expedition of 1978, 1:130
Anglo-French Wars, 1:489
Anglo-Iranian Oil Company, 2:679, 703
Anglo-Persian Agreement of 1919, 2:703
Anglophobia, 1:**67–68**
"Anglo-Saxon" identity, 2:1095
Angola, 1:21–22, 252, 253
The Animal Kingdom (Cuvier), 1:60
Animal rights, 1:433
Anna and the King of Siam (Landon), 2:709
Annan, Kofi, 2:1036
Antarctic Treaty System, 1:69–70
Antarctica/Arctic, 1:**68–70**
Anthony, Susan B., 1:353, 2:983, 1103

Anthropology, 2:1093
Antiaircraft weapons, 2:1083
Anti-Americanism
　The Quiet American (Greene), 2:865
　South Korea, 2:964
　Third World, 2:1007
Anti-Asian sentiment, 1:99, 552
Anti-Ballistic Missile Treaty
　nuclear weapons history, 2:773
　Russian-US relations, 2:923
　Strategic Defense Initiative, 2:977
Antiballistic missiles, 2:975
Anti-British sentiment. *See* Anglophobia
Anti-Caste (journal), 2:1086
Anticolonialism
　Bandung Conference, 1:116–117
　Black Power movement, 1:135–136
　Bolívar, Simón, 1:141
　human rights, 1:470
　King, Martin Luther, Jr., 1:590
　Malcolm X, 2:640–641
　Monroe Doctrine, 2:698
　multiculturalism, 2:706
　National Association for the Advancement of Colored People, 2:721
　Pan-Africanism, 2:815
　Qutb, Sayyid, 2:866
　Robeson, Paul, 2:896
　Rusk, Dean, 2:918
　self-determination, 2:935–936, 937
　Student Nonviolent Coordinating Committee, 2:978
　Third World, 2:1007
　Truman Doctrine, 2:1024
　Twain, Mark, 2:1028
　Universal Negro Improvement Association, 2:1044
　whiteness, 2:1096
　See also Decolonization; Independence movements; Self-determination
Anticommunism
　Caribbean, 1:180–181
　Catholicism, 1:191
　Central American military regimes, 1:234
　Cold War, 1:224
　Department of State, 1:283
　Disney, Walt, 1:290
　Einstein, Albert, 1:314
　The Feminine Mystique (Friedan), 1:352
　freedom fighters, 1:383–384
　Graham, Billy, 1:422
　human rights, 1:470

Knights of Columbus, 1:595
Luce, Henry, 1:630–631
McCarthyism, 2:660–662
modernization theory, 2:694, 695
Oppenheimer, J. Robert, investigation of, 2:645
Organization of American States, 2:787
race and the Cold War, 1:229
Reagan, Ronald, 2:874, 875–876, 877
Red scares, 2:883–886
Robeson, Paul, targeting of, 2:895–896
Rusk, Dean, 2:918–919
South Africa, 1:80
US Army School of the Americas, 2:1047–1048
Voice of America, 2:1061
white Christian conservatism, 2:889
Anti-Coolie bill, 1:244
Antidrug campaign, 2:1068–1070
Antiestablishment politics, 1:55
Anti-French sentiment, 1:380
Anti-immigrant sentiment. *See* Nativism
Anti-imperialism, 1:**70–75**
　Fuerzas Armadas de Liberación Nacional, 1:391
　India, 1:491
　King, Martin Luther, Jr., 1:590
　Melville, Herman, 2:671
　Middle East-US relations, 2:680
　Schurz, Carl, 1:485
　Twain, Mark, 2:1027–1028
　Wilson, Woodrow, 2:690
Anti-Imperialist League, 1:72, **75–77**
Anti-Irish sentiment, 1:428–429, 2:715–716
Anti-Japanese sentiment, 1:552
Antinuclear activism, 1:432–433
Anti-preparedness coalition, 2:848–850
Antisemitism
　Ford, Henry, 1:366
　Jewish Welfare Board, 1:566
　Judaism, 1:576, 577
　melting pot, 2:670
　Morgan, J. P., 2:702
　nativism, 2:731
　Nazism, 2:737
　pogroms, 2:839
　Zionism, 2:1150, 1152
Antislavery, 1:**77–79**
　American Revolution, 1:50
　Amistad, 1:57
　back-to-Africa movement, 1:111
　Black Atlantic, 1:134–135